1996

WRITTEN IN BLOOD

The Story of the Haitian People
1492-1995

D1453452

Robert Debs Heinl, Jr.
Nancy Gordon Heinl

Revised and Expanded
by

Michael Heinl

University Press of America, Inc.
Lanham • New York • London

Copyright © 1996 by
University Press of America,® Inc.
4720 Boston Way
Lanham, Maryland 20706

3 Henrietta Street
London, WC2E 8LU England

Originally published by Houghton Mifflin Co.,
Boston, Mass.

Library of Congress Cataloging-in-Publication Data

Heinl, Robert Debs, 1916-1979
Written in blood : the story of the Haitian people, 1492-1995 / Robert
Debs Heinl, Jr., Nancy Gordon Heinl.--(2nd ed.) rev. and expanded /
by Michael Heinl.
        p.   cm.
    Includes bibliographical references and index.
1. Haiti--History. I. Heinl, Nancy Gordon. II. Michael. III. Title.
    F1921.H44   1996   972.94--dc20   95-42547 CIP

ISBN 0-7618-0229-0 (cloth: alk. ppr.)
ISBN 0-7618-0230-4 (pbk: alk. ppr.)

⊖™The paper used in this publication meets the minimum
requirements of American National Standard for information
Sciences—Permanence of Paper for Printed Library Materials,
ANSI Z39.48—1984

In Memory of Robert Debs Heinl
Soldier, Writer, Husband, Father
Touched Deeply, as were we all, by Haiti

*Il y avait une fois une île où les esclaves voulurent
être libres; ils se levérent tous ensembles et ils le furent. Cette
île s'appellait autrefois St. Domingue; elle s'appelle à cette
heure Haïti . . .*

Alexandre Dumas, *Georges, 1843*

Contents

Illustrations

Maps

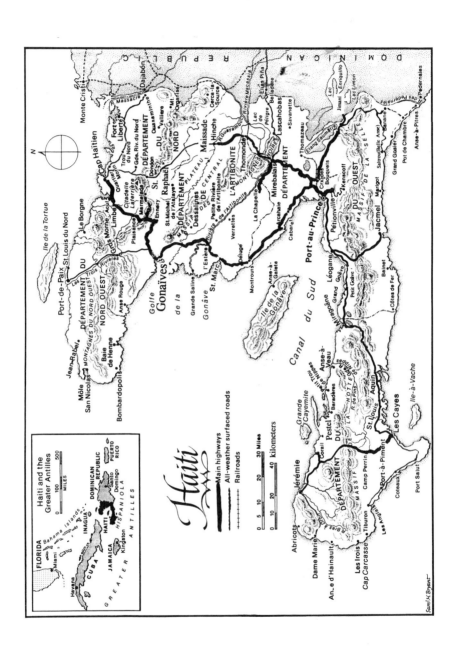

Preface to the Second Edition

Robert Debs Heinl outlived Papa Doc by eight years. Most of his time (and my mother's) in those eight years was spent researching and writing the first edition of *Written in Blood*. It was one of his greatest wishes to return to Haiti after he was declared *persona non grata* by Papa Doc in 1963. He tried, in his second career as syndicated newpaper columnist, to get into Haiti to cover Papa Doc's funeral and was sent out on the next flight. Escorting him to the plane, an army officer whispered, "You come too soon Colonel. Wait a month." He was never, despite that army officer's prediction, to be vouchsafed his wish, because, against all odds, the Duvalier regime lasted long after the death of its creator and many of its opponents.

Since the publication of the first edition seventeen years ago, much has changed in Haiti. And nothing. Some sixty years after Marines ended an American Occupation of nineteen years by withdrawing from the Cap, they hit the beach there again. Again a Washington-backed President sits in the National Palace to opposition from a small but powerful group of his countrymen. One observer, returning to Haiti after thirty years for a second tour of duty, was asked whether he was startled by the changes he found. He replied that the changes were changes largely of degree - more people, more erosion, more violence.

Haiti has continued to be the subject of vast amounts of impressionistic writing and analysis. Many interesting books were written in the eighties and nineties on various aspects of Haitian life. To mention just a few, Ian Thomson's *Bonjour Blanc*, Elizabeth Abbott's *The Duvaliers and Their Legacy*, Amy Wilentz's *The Rainy Season*, Herb Gold's *Best Nightmare on Earth* and Wade Davis's *The Serpent and the Rainbow* all contribute much to the body of writing about Haiti. Within Haiti, Roger Gaillard remains a prolific and thought-provoking author. Editions Karthala in Paris has published a number of interesting books such as Kern Delince's *Quelle Armée pour Haiti?* Tiny Haiti, once covered almost as an afterthought by reporters assigned to a Latin American beat, now merits its own specialists. The reportage of Howard French for the *New York Times* and Douglas Farah for *Washington Post* has been very good indeed. And yet, with seven thousand foreign troops on the ground, no complete English language history of the country is today in print. Hence a second edition of this book.

Many are due thanks for the encouragement and assistance given with this edition. Bruce Cronander's long friendship has been my bedrock constant for more than a decade. Sylvia Lacy-Crow and Jim O'Kane helped me become computer-literate. Bob Corbett presides with humor over the Haiti site on the internet, enabling the free, if somewhat forceful at times, exchange of ideas. Tony Ennis enabled my manumission from corporate servitude. John Davis with his "Don't get it right, get it written" spurred me on. Gerry O'Donoghue, Irish Navy, and Lynn Sladsky, AP, proved worthy debating companions as the lights flickered on and off in the Roi Christophe. Herb Gold warned me at the outset about the difficulty of publishing things on Haiti. He was right. Wagnès Matthieu provided geographical advice. John Burdick opened Gros Morne to me and reminded me once again that Haiti is the hardest country in the world to help. Michelle Harris and Helen Hudson at U.P.A. believed enough in this book to see the project through.

Tony Venbrux gave unstinting support to my increasing immersion in a project about a country he has never been to. Ruby Parrett drummed into me the necessity of "meeting one's public". Finally, my mother, Nancy Gordon Heinl, trusted me to leave intact the spirit of a work of which she is justifiably proud.

Michael Heinl
Washington, Fall 1995

E-Mail : 74301.1466@compuserve.com

CITY MAP OF PORT-AU-PRINCE

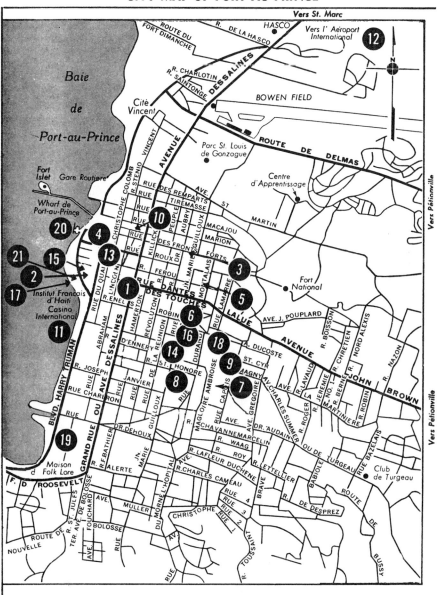

1. Air France Office
2. American Embassy
3. Old Cathedral
4. Post Office
5. Cathedral Ste. Trinite
6. Police Department
7. National Department of Education
8. University of Port-au-Prince
9. Haitian-American Institute
10. Iron Market
11. Casino Internationale
12. International Airport
13. Office of Tourism
14. Palace of Justice
15. Legislative Palace
16. National Palace
17. Pan American Office
18. Square of the Heroes of the Independence
19. Theatre de Verdure Folkloric Theater
20. Christopher Columbus Wharf
21. Chamber of Commerce

Written in Blood

The Story of the Haitian People

1492-1995

Introducing Haiti

J'habite l'île d'émeraude
Ou règne un eternel printemps
Où le coeur a toujours vingt ans
Et, près de lui, l'amour qui rôde.

- Dominique Hyppolite

In Haiti I believe nothing I hear, and only half of what I see.

- Gerald A. Drew

How does one explain Haiti? What *is* Haiti? Haiti is the eldest daughter of France and Africa.

It is a place of beauty, romance, mystery, kindness, humor, selfishness, betrayal, cruelty, bloodshed, hunger, and poverty. It is a closed and withdrawn society whose apart-ness, unlike any other in the New World, rejects its European roots.

Haiti is roosters crowing at dawn, drums in the night, coffee plucked wild from mountainsides, rum from ancient iron kettles. Haiti is green or, too often, brown, denuded mountains, headlong valleys, burning canefields, dark sea, bright flowers, vast ruins and gingerbread houses.

Haiti's romance comes in the throbbing, hypnotic beat of a *compas*, the call of the *lambi* (conch) the swirl of white-robed voodoo priestesses dancing for the gods of Africa.

Yet romance and mystery, Haiti's like any other, lie in the eye of the beholder. In that gaze the real Haiti has for nearly two centuries been obscured by distance, prejudice, illusion, misunderstanding, and accumulated misinformation. Much that is obscured, moreover, is neither beautiful nor romantic. Venality and selfishness are everywhere; so are faithlessness, revenge, and misery.

Above all Haiti is poor, primitive, proud, and hungry.

Haiti's only ties with its hemisphere are latitude and longitude. Think rather of Haiti as a fragment of black Africa, a fragment dislodged from the mother continent that drifted across the Atlantic and grounded in the Antilles.

The dominant institutions of Latin America, originating in Iberia, are Christian and Hispanic. The institutions of Haiti are Jacobin and Voodoo, watered in blood under the Tree of Liberty, and go back not to the gardens of Spain but to the Coast of Slaves.

When a Haitian dies, people say, "He has gone to Guinée." Setting Haiti beside West Africa, Jean Price-Mars, Haiti's distinguished anthropologist, observed,

> the same skill as agricultural workers; the same techniques of hoe and knife; the same social habits, with the male dominating a polygamous family; identical patriarchal habits and subordination of the wife; the same custom of going barefoot and carrying burdens on the head; the same animistic beliefs and the same piety towards divinity, along with a fantastic capability for religious assimilation and conciliation of beliefs; the same political organization with the sacrifice of the individual to the advantage of the state, embodied in the person of an all-powerful ruler.

More subjectively, historian-anthropologist J.-C. Dorsainvil simply declared, "I am an African displaced by historic accident from my original homeland."

Haiti is the second free nation of the Western hemisphere and the world's first black republic. Yet in 1991 - almost two centuries' freedom notwithstanding - Haiti remained more underdeveloped than much of Africa from which it emerged. Haiti is not merely the poorest country in the hemisphere but one of the poorest anywhere. In 1994 her annual per capita income amounted to $270. Haiti is also one of the few countries in the latter twentieth century whose gross national product has stagnated or declined more years than it has advanced.

In the first half of 1995 Haiti exported $65 million, a figure that, 202 years

later, falls far short, when adjusted for inflation, of the $41 million in exports
of St. Domingue (French colonial Haiti) in 1788. During the same period, its
imports amounted to $265 million, or *four times* its exports. Haiti has to import
all petroleum products, machinery, processed goods, and the bulk of even the
simplest consumer goods. In only four years of the last fifty did Haiti enjoy a
favorable balance of trade.

Haiti is hungry. Few countries of Africa have less to eat. Haiti is dependent
on the outside world for more of its food than any other country in the world
but one. The country whose sugar exports financed the building of Châteaux in
the Loire and town houses in France's great cities and which, in 1789, produced
three-quarters of the *world's* sugar must now import it.

By the guess of census-takers, whose figures often owe more to art than
accuracy, the 1995 population numbers 7 million souls. Their life expectancy at
birth, the lowest in the New World, is fifty-six years. In 1863 there were 1
million Haitians; in 1920, 2 million; in 1960, 4 million; and in 1994 there were
some 6.8 million. In 2004, two hundred years after seizing its place in the
family of nations, Haiti's population will number 9 million people. One in four
Haitians now live outside Haiti.

With nearly 5 million mouths to feed, Haiti - the size of Rhode Island and
Massachusetts combined - subsists upon the leached, scrabble-poor, least arable
third of Hispaniola. The neighboring Dominican Republic, with whom Haiti
shares a 135-mile frontier, lives in comparative ease with the same population
on the remaining two thirds of the island.

Few countries have regressed so far or been so misused by man. In 1789 a
flourishing Haiti, France's richest colony, ran its mills and ground its grains by
water power. In 1995 - an anthropolpogical regression measurable in centuries -
the water wheel and flume were largely forgotten, and the Biblical ox and beam
prevailed.

Only 13 percent of Haiti's 7 million acres are worth cultivating. Four fifths
of the people (to whom the plow remains unknown) till their plots with hoes,
machetes, or sharp sticks. The whole of Haiti, acre by acre, bursts with an
average of 500 persons per square mile, going above 1000 where the land is
good - a density unequaled save in Java or the Nile Valley. Paradoxically, this
teeming population often lives in relative isolation from its own cities and towns
and even its neighbors. Interior regions of Haiti are very inaccessible. Peasants
can live their lives without seeing the main towns. Citizens of Port-au-Prince
know little of Haiti's back country. Most villages of the interior can be reached
only on foot, by donkey, or, under the most favorable conditions, by jeep.

The country is serrated by rugged mountains, isolated hidden valleys, and
irregular pockets of plain clinging to the coasts. These steep ranges, over 3000
feet straight up in places, make roads hard to build and harder to maintain and
impose immovable barriers to overland communications. The story goes that in

1801, when Napoleon was planning his attempt to reconquer Haiti, he asked about the terrain. An intelligence officer crumpled a sheet of foolscap and let it fall. "That, Sire," he said, "is the terrain."

Not since the eighteenth century (except during the interlude of American occupation and as a result of a spurt of international aid following Papa Doc Duvalier's death) has Haiti enjoyed roads worth the name. When the Americans left in 1934, Haiti had 1200 miles of well-constructed all-weather highways. By 1994, the French, then American, then International efforts were yet again decaying. One Duvalierist attributed this to the "fact" that "foreigners don't know how to build roads for Haiti."

Besides having too many people, too little land, and few roads, Haiti - except for some bauxite and traces of copper - has practically no natural resources. Its once magnificent forests, whose mahogany was prized above any by cabinetmakers of the eighteenth and nineteenth centuries, have been stripped away. Peasants in 1995 hack down even coffee bushes in an increasingly vain search for fuel for cooking - and every year millions of tons of irreplaceable topsoil wash down denuded hillsides into the sea.

Though Haiti measures 183 miles by 114 (but with 850 miles of coast), its land area is only 10,714 square miles. (Hispaniola, roughly the size of Ireland, comprises 30,528 square miles.) In this country, which is three-quarters mountains, the highest peak is Morne la Selle, 8793 feet. The climate is sublime. The cycle consists of a May to December "wet" season (not inconveniently wet) and a crisp dry season from January to April. September is the rainiest month (though the May rains, called *"les Toussaints,"* can be heavy). August to October bring hurricanes whose track runs across the Southern peninsula and thence to the sea. Throughout the year, northeast trades water the northern mountainsides, leaving Southern slopes perpetually parched.

The main regions of Haiti are spoken of as "the North," "the Northwest," "the Artibonite" (taking its name from the central valley of that title), "the Center," "the West," and "the South." It is an oddity of Haitian geography and history that the region known as the West - generally made up of Port-au-Prince and the Cul-de-Sac lies *East* of the North, the Northwest, and the South. The reason for this contrary usage is that the West indeed comprises the deeply indented principal Western shore of Hispaniola, excluding, of course, the two long fingerlike peninsulas, North and South, that reach many miles farther West than the West. More logically, Santo Domingo is still sometimes called *"l'Est"* (the East).

Haitian society can be visualized in terms of a simple (though nothing connected with Haiti is simple) bar graph with a cutoff line 15 percent down from the top, leaving 85 to 90 percent below that line.

- About 90 percent of all Haitians *(noirs)* are pure ebony black. The remaining

10 percent have varying traces of Caucasian blood and are known as "*jaunes*" or "*mulâtres.*" This racial division - Haitians call it exactly that and speak of "the two races" - is the most important fact of life in Haiti. It dominates the country's whole existence. It is also, in the words of one of Haiti's ablest thinkers, Alcius Charmant, ". . . the supreme evil of our Republic, the virus that ravages it, and the road to its ruin."

- Roughly 65% of all Haitians are illiterate. The other 35% - among whom a superbly educated elite boasts degrees from the world's greatest universities - can read and write. Haiti has the highest rate of illiteracy in the Western hemisphere and one of the highest in the world.

Haiti speaks two languages. French, the official administrative tongue, is understood by 15 percent at most of the people. Créole, a pungent blend of seventeenth-century provincial French and West African dialects, is Haiti's true national language and sole tongue of 85 percent of the country. But Créole is only newly viable as a written language, so Haiti is still largely administered in French. To communicate with the other 85 percent of their fellows, the Francophone minority must resort to a second language. And the fact that Haiti has a private language, imperfectly understood if at all by outsiders, contributes further to the defensive impenetrability of an already closed society.

- Haiti is overwhelmingly rural. Seventy percent of all Haitians live on the land. The remaining thirty percent are townsmen.

- It is an old saying that Haiti is 80 percent Catholic and 100 percent Voodoo. This may not be the literal truth, but it is doubtful whether more than 15 percent of Haiti - including a small but vigorous Protestant community - practices Christianity exclusively. For the humble masses, no incompatability estranges *houngan* and priest.

Voodoo has sunk its roots deep into Haitian soil; it is an amalgam of the animist cults of West Africa infused with Catholic ritual. Voodoo plays so central a role in the life and history of Haiti that to disregard it (as the Americans did during their occupation) is to foreclose serious understanding of its people. Voodoo is discussed at length in the Appendix.

- "Nowhere else in the Western World," writes James G. Leyburn in *The Haitian People,* "has there been so little marriage in proportion to population as in Haiti." A century and a half earlier, Moreau de Saint-Méry, that most meticulous observer of colonial times, said nearly the same thing: "All the Africans in St. Domingue are polygamous and," he added, "jealous." Statistics, ephemeral in Haiti where not Aesopian, cannot be marshaled to support either Moreau or Leyburn, but common knowledge and observation do so absolutely.

Haiti then consists of two separate but interlocking worlds:

10-35 PERCENT	65-90 PERCENT
Mulâtre	*Noir*
Literate	Illiterate
French-speaking	Créole-speaking
Townspeople	Rural peasants
Christian or agnostic	Voodoo
Monogamous	Polygamous
Prosperous	Desperately poor
Proud	Apathetic
Elite	Non-elite

Naturally, none of the above correlates absolutely or, in many cases, more than approximately. Not all the tens and nineties cross-match. Haiti boasts literate, highly cultivated *noir* statesmen and intellectuals, such as the great Salomon and Price-Mars. It also has poor, non-elite *mulâtres* (although one Haitian leader long ago said, "A poor *mulâtre* is a *noir*. A rich *noir* is a *mulâtre.")*
But the correlations are there to see.

Then there is the mysterious something foreigners are always being told they can never fathom: *"la psychologie Haïtienne..."*
Deep in the psyche of Haiti - in certain respects one of the most peaceable countries in the world - lies a violence that goes beyond violence. That this is so is demonstrated by more than five centuries of history dominated at every turn by death and terror.
Robert Rotberg, whose *Haiti, The Politics of Power* was written with the collaboration of a psychiatrist deeply versed in Haitian studies, speaks also of "the unusual extent to which paranoia - well-systematized delusions of persecution and/or grandeur, the elaborations of which are logically constructed on false premises - seems to afflict peasants and elite alike."
There is paranoia in Haiti, no doubt about it.
Moreover there are deep feelings of insecurity and inferiority, rarely acknowledged, that typically appear in the people's reluctance if not inability to recognize, let alone accept, the Haitian situation as it really exists. They rarely acknowledge Haiti's national incompetence or the fact that this poor black country, no matter why, in almost two centuries of freedom has little to show but uninterrupted failure.
Foreigners long in the country sometimes say, "Haiti is the land of the four

'Pas' - *Pas ginyin* (I don't have it) . . . *Pas connais* (I don't know) . . . *Pas capab'* (I can't do it) . . . *Pas faute moin* (It's not my fault)."
This is all true, *pas faute moin* especially.
It is indeed not Haiti's fault. Haiti is imprisoned by its past.

Despite a story that is dramatic, eventful, tragic, ironic, and bizarre, the world's first black republic, born of the only successful slave insurrection in history, can claim no complete history in print today in any language.

Not that Haiti has gone unnoticed: it has been the object of more impressionistic writing (much of it passing for history) than any other country in Latin America. John Candler, a visiting Englishman, wrote in 1842 that, "The history of Hayti has yet to be written."

In the nineteenth century, Haiti had two histories. That by her Thucydides, Thomas Madiou, ends with 1847. The other is the long and tendentious chronicle of Beaubrun Ardouin, going up to 1860. A third, the highly argumentative work of Jacques-Nicolas Léger, appeared in 1906. Since then, aside from school texts, only Dantès Bellegarde, who brought the story to 1950, and Roger Gaillard, who may be said to have inherited Bellegarde's mantle with his prolific output, have sought to chronicle the history of their country.

None of the aforementioned histories is more than at best occasionally documented. The aim of the first edition of this work was to recount for the first time the true, complete, and verifiable story of Haiti (including its French predecessor, St. Domingue) from arrival of Columbus in 1492 until the death of François Duvalier in 1971. The aim of the current edition is to bring that chronicle forward to its latest milestone, the return of U.S. Occupation forces in 1994 together with Jean-Bertrand Aristide, overthrown in 1991. There is a lush jungle of myth, *histoire reçue,* and invention that envelops Haiti. Recited here is only that which can be verified, from credible sources and materials.

The foregoing sounds simple enough, but nothing, unfortunately, connected with Haiti is simple or straightforward.

The rebel slaves who founded Haiti were largely illiterate or semiliterate. They kept no records. The few public documents of the time, together with donations of books intended for a national library, were allowed to be destroyed or dispersed during the 1820's under the Boyer régime; and the upheavals and conflagrations of a country with nearly 200 subsequent revolutions, coups, insurrections, and civil wars, aside from the ravages of the tropics, of theft and of neglect, did for the rest.

To cite only a few examples, the entire records of the Haitian government were destroyed when the National Palace exploded in 1869; ten years later, the Foreign Ministry had to ask the U.S. State Department for copies of previous treaties and agreements and related diplomatic correspondence because the ministry's files had been wiped out by fire; within four more years, in 1883, the events of the *Semaine Sanglante* consumed not only the national archives but virtually every government bureau and its files in Port-au-Prince. In 1888 the reconstituted archives perished when the building burned to the ground. And in 1912, when the National Palace again blew up, the explosion took with it the government's records.

Where fire and strife failed to complete the job, fragmentary remaining materials in the Archives Générales have been further (and extensively) depleted by pilferage and sale to private collectors, mainly during the past four decades; for example, the *Acte d'Indépendance*, Haiti's 1804 declaration of independence, is said to be in the hands of a foreign collector. The New York Public Library was able to purchase in the 1970's, from a long-time foreign resident in Haiti, what in scope and bulk constituted, prima facie, a major cross-section of the country's surviving archives, ranging from early times to twentieth-century exchanges between Franklin D. Roosevelt and a president of Haiti.

For all the above reasons documentation of Haitian history in the conventional way, from internal primary sources and national archives, is an impossibility. The way out of this dilemma - which in the long run has opened a wholly new body of material, yielded lodes of unsuspected information, and dispelled many hoary legends - has led through the diplomatic archives of the great powers.

The steady year-in, year-out flow of diplomatic and consular reports from Haiti, found in the National Archives in Washington, the Public Records Office in London, and the Quai d'Orsay in Paris, provides a matchless record of events by skilled observers on the scene, protected in their reporting by confidentiality, and trained to seek out and analyze developments and personalities. These reports, extending from the country's earliest years into the middle of this century, strikingly illuminate personalities, life, and times, like those of the Venetian ambassadors to Elizabethan England. They form the backbone of much of this work. Halted, at the thirty-year barrier behind which archives become current and closed, we have gleaned the extensive, attentive, and often accurate Haitian reportage of leading American and foreign journals. We have also gone through the entire French and English published literature, books and periodicals, dealing with Haiti, St. Domingue, and the people, who after all are the building blocks of history.

As we ourselves entered the Haitian scene in the late 1950's, we did not hesitate to rely on firsthand observations and impressions and personal records. In the words of Virgil, "These things I saw, and a part of them, I was." And it is fair to add that few foreigners and, surprisingly, few Haitians, are as likely to have seen the remote places of Haiti, end to end, as we have.

This paradoxic place, as we have already seen, presents the historian with the special complication of a nation with two languages, one of which, Créole, is vexed by conflicting orthographics. So irreconcilable are the different written versions of Créole that we have simply taken them as they come in particular sources and pass them on to the reader. To anticipate a related question: readers will find a glossary at the end of this book, translating Créole or idiomatic French words or phrases whose use has seemed necessary to convey the color or savor of some particular happening.

Foreigners, may find redundancy and repetition in the details of political intrigue and of successive insurrections, struggles, and plots; yet these are warp and woof of Haitian life and dominate the past that has produced Haiti today. No Haitian reader could regard a history as serious or complete or even fair without such information.

And so we come now to Haiti, "that true paradise on earth," wrote Edgar La Selve, "which has been the theater of such horrible scenes and frightful dramas, whose soil has drunk more blood than sweat." Yet, for those who have known and loved it, this small, poor land of powerful feelings and brilliant contrasts remains above all, in the words of an old favorite song, *"Haïti Chérie!"*

FOOTNOTES - INTRODUCTION

(1) *Haïti-Observateur* (17 June 1977) maintained that the Duvalier family approved and in fact organized the sale abroad of historical artifacts (for example, Emperor Soulouque's gold sword) from the National Museum, as well as bulk documents from government archives. This article cites as an example the New York Public Library's document acquisition, said to exceed more than 8000 historical documents, mentioned here.

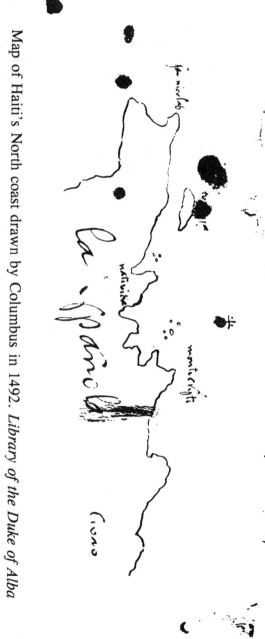

Map of Haiti's North coast drawn by Columbus in 1492. *Library of the Duke of Alba*

CHAPTER I

A Very Great Island

1492-1788

Where the banana grows, man is sensual and cruel.

- Ralph Waldo Emerson

THE FIRST SKETCH Columbus made of the New World depicts the north coast of Haiti. Visitors can see it in the library of the Dukes of Alba in Madrid. The ink is rusty, the parchment faded, but the outline is clear, the strokes and lettering neat and firm, and the place names that he gave, San Nicolas and Tortuga, survive to this day.

On the afternoon of Wednesday, 5 December 1492, from the high poopdeck of *Santa María,* Columbus made out "a very great island." Approaching the harbor, "which was like the Bay of Cadiz," he sent in a boat to sound while *Santa María* lay off for the night.(1)

Next day at the hour of vespers, 2:00 P.M., Columbus wrote in his journal:

He entered the said harbor and gave it the name of Puerto de San Nicolao, because it was the feast of St. Nicholas, for his honor; and at the entrance thereof he marveled at its beauty and graciousness . . . The whole harbor is very breezy and uninhabited, clear of trees. All this island seemed to him more rocky than any other he had found hitherto . . . The land is very high . . . with very good air.

Then as now, Môle St. Nicolas was a lonely place. The admiral contented himself with sounding up into Carénage, where, he noted, a ship could "put her gunwales alongside the grass." He landed briefly on a fine beach but found no inhabitants: Haiti's original natives, the Taino Indians, had taken to the hills at the sight of European ships. Columbus got underway next morning and, with a brisk Southwest wind, weathered Cap St. Nicolas and sailed East along the mountainous coast.

La Tortue's rounded regular silhouette reminded him of a tortoise and so he named the island: Tortuga. Coasting along the ironbound shore that well merits its later name, Côtes de Fer, *Santa María* and *Niña,* the tiny consort, sailed past and noted the deep valley where in 1743 the town of Jean-Rabel would rise.

After midday, as the weather worsened, Columbus put into "a very wide and deep harbor." That day was the Feast of the Immaculate Conception so this bay was named Puerto de la Concepcíon; more realistically, when he charted the place in 1599, Samuel de Champlain gave it the name it bears today, Port au Moustiques.

Mosquitoes or not, the harbor is a pretty one, and here, weathered in by rain and contrary winds, Columbus spent a week. Ashore, he found the country "the most beautiful in the world . . . almost like the lands of Castile; rather, these are better."

For such an island there could be no name more fitting than "Ysla Espanola" (Spanish Island). Peter Martyr, the first man to write a history of the New World, simply latinized it into Hispaniola.

The Indians called their island Quisqueya, Bohio, or Babeque (all meaning "vast country"), or Hayti (mountainous), the name that finally stuck.

During their time at Moustiques the Spaniards "raised a great cross." They also captured a young and comely Indian woman clothed only in a tiny clout and wearing a nose plug of gold. "The Admiral," recounts Columbus's journal, "had her clothed and gave her glass beads and hawk's bells and brass rings; and he sent her ashore very honorably."

By this bit of psychology Columbus sought to reassure the Indians and find the source of that nose plug. And so, within twenty-four hours, "a great mass of people" who had fled the shore returned to greet and wonder at the Spaniards. "They are lovable," he wrote, "tractable, peaceable, gentle, decorous. They bear no arms and are so completely defenseless and of no skill in arms, and very cowardly, so that a thousand would not face three; and so they are fit to be ordered about and made to work, to sew and do all else that may be needed."

So be it. The Spaniard would be master; the native, his slave; Hispaniola, an island of slaves.

The Rape of Quisqueya

On Christmas Eve, 1492, with every man of the ship's company, off watch or on, fast asleep save for an apprentice at the helm, *Santa María* drove hard aground on a coral reef in Limonade Pass, five or six miles East of Cap Haïtien.

There was no getting her off. Even with guns and ballast jettisoned and mainmast cut away, *Santa María* was done for. The local Indian *cacique* and his subjects helped the Spaniards land their stores "without losing a lace point." Timbers from the hulk were salvaged to build a fort and quarters on the beach, and forty volunteers, mostly *Santa María's* crew, commenced the first colony in the New World while Columbus sailed home.

They were never seen again.

When Columbus returned in 1493 he found, wrote Abbé Raynal, "nothing but ruins and carcasses where he had left fortifications and Spaniards."

The quarreling, gold-crazed settlers had been fallen upon, slain, and probably eaten by nearby Indians whose women they had raped.

Nothing remains of this settlement (christened "Navidad" by Columbus) but a mound near the beach at Limonade Bord-de-Mer. Close to this site, while digging a ditch in 1784, slaves found an ancient anchor, which is generally thought to be that of *Santa María,* as well as twenty-five human skeletons, very likely those of the murdered Spaniards.

Columbus resettled Hispaniola, but the Spaniards had come not to found colonies but to find gold. Parceling out the Arawak Tainos among themselves according to rank, the Spanish might just as well have set out to exterminate them. Spanish brutality combined with smallpox, soon exported from Europe, laid low the "lovable" Indians. (But the debt was repaid when syphilis soon afterward reached Europe.)

Probably exaggerating, Bishop Bartolomé de las Casas put the Indian population at 3 million when Columbus came. By 1508 a Spanish census could tally but 60,000 of Queen Isabella's "dearly beloved Indian subjects." Six years later 14,000 survived; by 1533 the count had fallen to 600. In 1550 only 150 Caribs could be found. Genocide, a word often used loosely in the twentieth century, is the only name for what the Spaniards did.

Sugar came to Hispaniola from the Canary Islands in 1506. At about the same time, already concerned over his dwindling labor force, Nicolás de Ovando, the cruel royal governor, imported 40,000 Indians from the Bahamas. Ovando recruited his victims by offering to transport them to a delightful region inhabited by the souls of their ancestors and departed friends.

Even this outrage did not suffice to work the canefields and mines. The Indians perished under the rod of Spain. All the labors of good Bishop de las Casas (Queen Isabella's "Protector of the Indians") could not halt the sickening hecatomb. Ironically - and he later reproached himself for it - it was Las Casas who, in hopes of sparing the Indians, pled with Carlos V to bring Africans to the Indies.

African slavery was not new to Spain. The fifteenth-century Portuguese navigators had brought slaves to Iberia. Columbus himself may well have carried the first blacks to the New World, for when Ovando came in 1502, some were already there. Père Charlevoix, the eighteenth-century chronicler, says they first arrived in 1500 and goes on to explain their superiority over Indians: "Besides the fact that a black can do more work than six Indians, he accustoms himself readily to slavery, for which he seems to have been created; he is uncomplaining, contents himself with little to eat, and, even on bad food, stays strong and robust. He has a bit of natural pride, but, in order to tame him, a few lashes will suffice to remind him that he has a Master."

By 1503, according to Juan Manuel de Ayala, African slaves were not only numerous but had already begun to seek freedom in what would later be known as *"marronage"*: "They run away from their owners in gangs through the country into the mountains to the Indians and they steal from them what they have in their houses."

In 1510, King Ferdinand sent the first official shipment of Africans to Hispaniola - a contingent to work the Cibao mines in what is now Santo Domingo, but soon the canefields as well. As the Indians melted away, blacks replaced them. Within eight years, by *asiento* (royal license) Carlos V granted a slaving monopoly to two Flemish favorites, Ciguer and Sailler. This they in turn sold for 25,000 ducats to Genoese slavers. Under the royal patent the annual limit was to be 4000 slaves. Later the *asiento* passed to Portuguese traders, whose captives mostly came from "forts" or settlements along the coasts of Dahomey and Guinea.

In the decades after 1492, colonial enterprise and activity shifted to central and Eastern Hispaniola. Here, as early as 1496, Columbus's brother, Don Diego, had founded the city of Santo Domingo. Gonzalo de Oviedo, in his *Historia General y Natural de las Indias Occidentales,* described it in 1528 as "not inferior to any in Spain, the houses mostly built of stone like those of Barcelona, but the streets much better, being large and plain, crossing each other at right angles . . . The houses are fit to receive any nobleman of Spain with his suite, and the grandeur of Don Diego's palace was beyond conception, and every way fitting to receive the king, his master."

But the gold of the Cibao had petered out; Hispaniola was already a burden. By midcentury Cortez had conquered Mexico; and Pizarro, Peru. By contrast, all Hispaniola could offer was sugar, tobacco, and cotton.

And the sun of Spain was setting. In 1586, with twenty-eight ships out of Plymouth and Bideford, Francis Drake pillaged Ciudad Santo Domingo. Two years later, in home waters, Drake led Queen Elizabeth's ships to sea past Plymouth Hoe and smashed Philip II's Armada and his "Enterprize of England."

These events had their echo in Hispaniola. In the words of Captain Marcus Rainsford, the lively British historian and adventurer in St. Domingue, "Their mines were deserted, agriculture was neglected, and their cattle ran wild in the plains. They employed themselves . . . not only in illicit foreign trade but in piracies against the property of their own country."

Flouting Spain, British and French ships entered the ports of Hispaniola, underselling Spanish merchants and bypassing the Casa de Contratación, through which legal imports arrived under Spain's monopoly.

To obstruct this contraband, Spain resorted to a harsh and rigorous embargo. By royal edict all ports save Ciudad Santo Domingo were closed and dismantled. But Champlain, who navigated the North coast in 1599, counted thirteen English, French, and Flemish armed merchantmen, embargo-runners all, at Môle St. Nicolas. In his journal he noted: "Foreigners aren't permitted to trade in these waters and those who do run the risk of having their ships confiscated and being themselves hanged or sent to the galleys. Further, the King of Spain has given a standing promise to free any Negro who gives information to the general or governor leading to the discovery of a foreign vessel."

The effects of the embargo were disastrous. Colonists who failed to return to the mother country lived in poverty and idleness, cohabiting with slave women. Abbé Raynal described them as "demi-savages, plunged in the extremes of sloth, living upon fruits and roots, in cottages without furniture, and, most of them, without clothes. Their slaves had little more to do than to swing them in their hammocks."

The Boucaniers of Tortuga

While Spain continued to assert sovereignty over the entire New World, the King of Spain's writ did not run unchallenged. France was the first to protest a Hispano-Portuguese monopoly of the New World, and England soon seconded the move. British, French, and Dutch seamen, like those observed by Champlain, boldly entered the Spanish Main and traded with the colonists. At first intermittent and surreptitious, this trade gradually assumed regular proportions. Its centers were Curaçao, Jamaica, and Hispaniola.

In 1623 a company of Englishmen and Frenchmen occupied St. Christopher (St. Kitts) in the Leeward Islands. Their leaders were Thomas Warner and Pierre Belain, Sieur d'Esnambuc, who would later colonize Martinique for France. Their object was to establish a base where they could provision and from which they could harry Spanish *guarda costas* attempting to maintain the embargo.

Galled by Dutch trading posts in Brazil and by the presumptuous English and French of St. Kitts, Philip III sent one of his boldest admirals, Don Federico Toledo Osorio, to the New World with orders to harry them out of the Spanish Main. Reaching St. Kitts in September 1629, the *almirante* quickly overpowered the colonists and crowded them aboard captured small craft with the warning that if, on his return from Brazil, he found any French or English on the island, they would be put to the sword. Don Federico then sailed away and, as best they could, so did the pirate-settlers.

After circling about various possible new nests such as Antigua, the smoked-out hornets came to rest on Tortuga, that beautiful island "eight leagues long and two broad, in a fine air," which Columbus himself had named.

At this time, French hunters, Norman in origin, had begun to range the North and West of Hispaniola, curing meat to sell to passing ships, and drying the skins of wild cattle. Conceivably, the French of St. Kitts knew of Tortuga from them. Joining forces with the hunters of the mainland and with Dutch refugees from Santa Cruz, also expelled by the Spaniards, they in turn fell upon a small Spanish garrison and established their new colony. In the words of James Burney, their early historian: "They elected no chief, erected no fortifications, set up no authorities, nor fettered themselves by an engagement. All was voluntary; and they were negligently contented at having done so much toward their security."

The Tortuga settlement enriched the English language with three nouns: "buccaneer," "barbecue," and "filibuster." Each arose from the life of the settlers, which, Burney remarked, was "one of amphibious character," for the men who had seized Tortuga were interchangeably hunters and seamen. As hunters they pursued, killed, and salted wild cattle and hogs. As seamen they harried the commerce of Spain.

"Buccaneer," which we now associate with piracy, came from the shoregoing pursuits of the Tortugans and is the Anglicized version of *boucanier,* a French word derived from *boucan,* a Gallicization of the Indian word *boucacoui,* a process for smoking meat. A buccaneer, or *boucanier,* was described by the early Antillean historian, Père du Tertre, in 1667 as one who cured meat ". . . after a manner learnt from the Caribbe Indians, which was as follows: the meat was laid to be dried upon a wooden grate or hurdle which the Indians called *barbecu,* placed at a good distance over a slow fire. The meat when cured was called *boucan* and the same name given to the place of their cookery."

"Filibusterer," now associated with one who commits crimes ashore, comes from the French *flibustier,* meaning pirate or freebooter. "The Brethren of the Coast," as the men of Tortuga called themselves, did not think of themselves as pirates, but the Spanish did.

Abbé Raynal has a classic description of the *flibustiers* and their life:

The dress of these barbarians consisted of a shirt dipped in the blood of the animals they killed in hunting; a pair of drawers dirtier than the shirt, and made in the shape of a brewer's apron; a girdle made of leather, on which a very short sabre was hung, and some knives; a hat without any rim, except a flap before, in order to take hold of it; and shoes without stockings. The buccaneers spent their life hunting the wild bulls, of which there were great numbers in the island, since the Spaniards had brought them. The best parts of these animals, when seasoned with pimento and orange juice, were the most common food of their destroyers, who had forgotten the use of bread.(3)

From 1630 until 1659 the Tortugan settlement repeatedly changed hands among English, Dutch, and French, and was as repeatedly raided or occupied by Spaniards from the main island. In 1638, one Spanish expedition laid waste all Tortuga, slaughtered men, women, and children without exception, and left the gibbeted bodies as a monition to survivors who had hidden in La Tortue's caves.

Finally, in 1659, bearing the commission of Louis XIV as royal governor, Seigneur Jérémie Deschamps brought the Fleur-de-Lys to Tortuga and, resisting British and Spanish counterattacks, also assumed governance over the small Huguenot settlements that had sprung up on the mainland across the channel.

La Tortue was finally French. "That mere clod of earth and rocks," wrote Père Labat, "which has given such pain to the Spaniards, which has been repeatedly taken and retaken, and which, despite its tiny size and scant value, must be regarded as the mother of the flourishing colonies we hold at the Cap, Port-de-Paix, Léogane, Petit-Gôave, Ile-à-Vache, and elsewhere . . ."

From this moment in 1659 began 130 years of French domain over Western Hispaniola or, as it began to be known, St. Domingue.

I Have Given a Hand to Everyone

As Louis XIV's first minister (and father of the French navy), Jean-Baptiste Colbert originated the colonial and maritime policies that exalted France under the sun king. Colbert's masterly handiwork included the French West India Company, chartered in March 1664 to consolidate the trade and holdings of predecessor companies and of individual French subjects (such as the *boucaniers)* throughout the West Indies.

The man Colbert chose to govern La Partie Française de St. Domingue was already an old West Indies hand. Bertrand d'Ogeron de la Bouère, of Anjou, had first come to the New World in 1665 as an officer in one of the French regiments of Marines. Subsequently, he traded and colonized in Martinique and Jamaica, and, after reverses, set up as a *boucanier* on La Tortue. It was to this *boucanier,* because of his native resourcefulness, known integrity, and gift for handling men, that Colbert turned.

Ogeron's task was not easy. Unfettered freedom - freedom, especially, to trade with all comers, as opposed to Spanish monopolism had been the earliest tie that joined the Brethren of the Coast. Now one of their own number was sent among them to be governor and as Versailles saw it, to extend monopoly - that of France and the West India Company - over St. Domingue.

In February 1665 Ogeron reached La Tortue and, soon after, the new mainland settlement, Port-de-Paix.

Cheers greeted Ogeron when he published his royal warrant, but there were no illusions as to the difficulties he faced in governing pirate subjects to whom force had been the sole argument. Quite bluntly the *boucaniers* assured him that, while they would be loyal subjects to the king's representative, they would never submit to the company, and most particularly, would never give up their trade with the Dutch, who, as Charlevoix said, "had never let them lack for anything at a time when the presence of French at Tortuga and St. Domingue was unknown in France."

Ogeron concentrated on aiding settlers. Those who chose to build and plant got loans, some from Ogeron's own pocket, at low or no interest. During spells of fitful peace between France and Spain, Ogeron contrived to obtain Portuguese letters of marque so that his men, acting as privateers, could at least avoid outright piracy while still keeping their arms bright. This last was important: he had no garrison.

Women were needed. Combing French jails for whores and pickpockets, breveted "female orphans," Ogeron obtained a hundred woman settlers. First pick among this shopworn cargo went to men who could raise bond to liquidate expenses of the transaction. Couples were then united when the husband vowed: "I take thee without knowing, or caring to know, who thou art . . . Give me only thy word for the future. I acquit thee of what is past." Then, striking his musket butt, he added, "If thou shouldst prove false, this will certainly be true to my aim."

Ogeron thus increased the number of planters from 400 on his arrival to 1500 in 1669. For these planters he introduced a new money crop -cocoa, or cacao, first discovered by Cortez in Mexico 150 years earlier.

The next and most difficult step for the governor was to bring the commerce of the colony - trade, much tobacco, some sugar, buccaneering, and filibustering - under the West India Company. Alas, Ogeron's fair dealing and gradualism came to nothing. In 1670 the company exploited its monopoly by raising all prices by two-thirds. Dutch trading vessels were thereupon received with cheers in the ports of St. Domingue. By June 1670 the colony was in revolt. Aided by the redoubtable Admiral Gabaret (who since the first of the year had had a three-ship detachment of the French navy in the West Indies), Ogeron put down the rebels and then immediately urged Colbert to grant general amnesty and, more important, to bring down prices. Colbert acceded.

Ogeron next obtained two ships, ostensibly for his own ventures, but in reality to enable settlers to ship their crops to France at reasonable charges and import manufactured goods for sale in the colony at prime cost.

With pardonable pride Ogeron could write Colbert: "I have given a hand to everyone . . . I have made loans to captains, soldiers, and colonists . . . I have anticipated every need. I have had to govern fierce people who have never known any yoke and I have governed them so readily that they have attempted only two small seditions."

Ogeron spoke truth, and so did Père le Pers when he wrote that Ogeron must be considered the true father of French St. Domingue. The record was impressive: between 1665 and 1674, his last year in St. Domingue, Ogeron, frequently at his own expense or aboard his own ships, lured some 2500 emigrants to the island. Exports of tobacco (then, as in the case of Virginia, the colony's prime crop and virtual local currency) went from 1.2 million pounds in 1669 to 3 million pounds five years later.

Ogeron made his last trip home, in 1675, to try to convince Versailles that all Hispaniola was to be had for the plucking. But before he could get to see Colbert, he was, wrote a contemporary, "seized with a flux" and died, 31 January 1676, in Paris, in a house on Rue Maçons. A tablet, to be seen today on the ancient Left Bank church of St. Sévérin, bears his epitaph:

> Bertrand Ogeron
> Sieur de la Bouère-en-Jallais
> Qui MDCLXIV a MDCLXXVI

> Jeta les fondemans d'une Société Civile et réligieuse au milieu des Flibustiers et des boucaniers des Isles de la Tortue et de St Domingue.
> Il prépara ainsi par les voies mystérieuses de la Providence, les destinés de la République d'Haïti (4)

La Partie Française de St. Domingue

Under Ogeron and his successor, Jacques Nepveu, Seigneur de Pouancey, the French settlements multiplied, and planters outnumbered *boucaniers* and *flibustiers*. Cayonne (or Cayona), the buccaneers' nest on La Tortue, once reputed the richest and most dissolute town in the West Indies, was abandoned. When de Pouancey came, La Tortue was deserted save for passing freebooters.

The decline of La Tortue fattened Port-de-Paix. Here, commanding the channel, de Pouancey raised a fort on whose foundations today stands the local garrison's caserne.

Not far from the bay where the coral-crusted bones of *Santa María* lay forgotten, flibustiers in 1670 began a new settlement. Giving refuge to Calvinists driven from France, Ogeron sent them to the *flibustier* site and named it Cap François.(5)

French settlements began to take root in the South and Southwest as well as the North. By the end of the seventeenth century, the "Partie Française" was divided into three provinces: the North, centering on Cap François and Port-de-Paix; the West, which comprised the central part of the colony; and the South.

By 1671, the Cul-de-Sac - that fertile plain which, running Westward to the sea, adjoins Port-au-Prince - already had 1300 inhabitants, virtually all planters. Land was also good along the North shore of the long Southern peninsula. Besides having good soil for cane and indigo (another crop Ogeron brought to St. Domingue), the coves and sounds of this coast were made for *flibustiers*. (6)

Petit-Goâve, long a pirate rendezvous, and Léogane were settled by the French in 1663. Originally an Arawak village, Léogane was one of the ports built and then closed by the Spaniards. Like Petit-Gôave fifteen miles West, it was to serve briefly as the colonial capital.

Up to this time there were no permanent garrisons (and, until 1684, not even a judiciary). An indication of the rough-cut simplicity of life comes through in a request by de Pouancey in 1681 for a handful of soldiers to maintain law and order: "It is pretty hard on the Governor to have personally to arrest a thief, a troublemaker, or a drunk . . . Besides, we don't even have a jail . . . and the Governor has to be policeman, turnkey, and sentinel."

The *flibustiers* still terrorized the Spanish Main, but they contributed even less to the defense of the settlements and nothing whatever to colonial order and stability. Moreover, they continually drew Spanish attention to the French presence on what was still nominally a Spanish Hispaniola.

But de Pouancey had other problems, not least of which was St. Domingue's first slave insurrection. Unlike the Spanish, the early French had little use for slaves. But some blacks, mostly runaways, had settled in the Northwest between Port-de-Paix and St. Louis du Nord. In 1679, aroused by grievances no longer known, Padrejean, formerly a Spanish slave, led an uprising against the French colonists and their governor.

Padrejean massacred white settlers and burned plantations around Port-Margot, Le Borgne, and St. Louis du Nord. De Pouancey's revenge was to hire buccaneers to storm Padrejean's mountain stronghold inland of St. Louis. The black outlaws were killed. Their memory survived.

In 1682, just back from France, de Pouancey sickened and died, and his deputy, de Franquesnay, governed in his stead. De Pouancey had completed the work of Ogeron. Freebooters and lawless hunters had become planters. In the year before de Pouancey's death a census of St. Domingue listed 6658 planters, wives, children, indentured servants and slaves, as well as eight priests serving thirteen churches and chapels.

De Pouancey was succeeded in 1683 by Pierre-Paul Tarin de Cussy. De Cussy's problems were familiar: How to restrain and domesticate the *flibustiers*? How to accommodate free-trading contraband ways of the settlements with monopolist French concessions and chartered companies? How to encourage peaceful colonization and plantations of cotton, indigo, sugar, and cocoa?

At last recognizing these problems, the ministry wrote de Cussy in 1684, "His Majesty esteems nothing more important than to render these vagabonds good inhabitants of St. Domingue." While thus exhorting de Cussy to reform the lifestyle of his colonists, the government's only practical contribution was, in 1686, to send him as emigrants 150 convicted galley slaves flushed out of the hulks of Toulon and Brest.

As for the neighboring Spaniards, war or no war, in 1687 they fell upon Petit-Gôave, captured its fort, and laid waste the neighborhood. But the nearby planters rose in arms, pushed the invaders back inside the fort, carried it, and hanged the Spanish leaders.

By 1689 Louis XIV was at war with Europe, personified at first by the League of Augsburg, soon enlarged to the Grand Alliance, and notably including England and Spain. For the *flibustiers,* now said to number 3000, there was work to do. In January 1689, de Cussy received secret instructions to prepare to conquer the Spanish in the East. Within six months, after the spring rains, at the head of 450 infantry, 400 horse, and a supply train of 150 slaves, de Cussy marched East on Santiago, took and sacked the town, and retired on St. Domingue. This was an invitation for the Spaniards to invade the North, which they promptly did.

Sixteen ninety-one was only a fortnight old when 3000 Spaniards crossed the border. One column marched across what would later be called Rivière Massacre; the other descended by sea at Caracol near the site of Columbus's ill-fated fort, Navidad. With a scant thousand men raised from settlements in the North, de Cussy rashly chose to meet the invaders in the open rather than fall back on the ramparts of Cap François. On 21 January 1691, the French formed on the plain of Limonade, their right on a small knoll near the village, their left on the mangrove swamps and the sea. Despite a deep ravine across their front, they were no match for Spanish assaults.

Soon [recorded Père Charlevoix] the two wings were separated and routed, and there remained only a forlorn hope around de Cussy and de Franquesnay, who performed prodigies of valor. The Governor..... already wounded in the body, found himself hemmed in by six lancers..... He killed two before they could close with him, he blew off the head of a third with his pistol, then, transfixed by lances, he fell dead amid his brave men among whom already lay Franquesnay.

A relief column from Port-de-Paix, arriving after the Spanish had pillaged the Cap and the Plaine du Nord, found the corpses of the two leaders and nearly 500 other dead.

To rule the leaderless, ravaged colony, Louis XIV named a naval officer with a distinguished record in the Royal Company of Senegal. Jean-Baptiste du

Casse, a fiery Béarnais, brought to his task, like Ogeron before him, energy, military skill, and colonial experience. Amid the ruins, his talents were needed.

Luckily for the French, the Spaniards seemed to tire of the game. There were no further attacks and du Casse got the breather he needed.

In June 1694, du Casse launched a powerful raid on Jamaica. French *flibustiers* and soldiers laid waste a hundred sugar estates, looted them of machinery and distilleries, carried off 3000 slaves for the plantations of St. Domingue, and took £60,000 booty.(7)

Almost exactly a year later, leagued with Spaniards from Santo Domingo, the English struck back. A British squadron landed troops at Mancenille Bay in the North, and Spaniards again marched overland. On 30 May 1695, with scarcely a shot fired, the British took Cap François. Then, while the fleet coasted offshore, British and Spanish columns advanced on Port-de-Paix.

Beleaguered by land and sea, Port-de-Paix held out for a fortnight. Then, on the night of 13 July, the defenders (270 French musketeers and sailors and 100 armed blacks) spiked their guns, drenched the remaining powder, and cut their way out. Content with what the British commander, Colonel Luke Lillington, reported as "a vaft Plunder," including 107 great guns, the invaders departed, taking with them the wife and two daughters of de Graff, the renowned chief *flibustier.*(8)

Once again the North and the Northwest lay in ruins. Cap François and Port-de-Paix had been sacked and burned. The latter was so demolished that, despairing of slaves, du Casse transferred the governor's seat to Léogane, where he concentrated his forces while de Graff vainly tried to hold the North. Thus in 1695 Léogane became the colonial capital, from which, for the second time in five years, du Casse set about reconstruction.

By early 1697 he had done so well that St. Domingue fielded, under his command, a quarter of the troops for the expedition that took and sacked Cartagena in the spring of that year. Du Casse's contingent included 170 soldiers, 110 colonist volunteers, 650 buccaneers, and the first record we have found of New World blacks serving in an organized military capacity - 180 blacks acting as pioneers. The loot of Cartagena was staggering: 7,646,948 francs' worth of bullion, 1051 pounds of cut emeralds, 71 amethysts, a huge coffer of sacramental vessels and other ecclesiastic silver, and a solid silver Madonna garbed in a robe of precious stones. In addition to this treasure the French brought away 82 guns and 32 huge church bells.

But the tide of war was ebbing. In May 1697, even as the French were sacking Cartagena, the ambassadors of France, the Netherlands, Britain, and Spain met in the Dutch town of Ryswick to come to terms.

The Peace of Ryswick, concluded 20 September 1697, gave formal recognition to French sovereignty over Western Hispaniola. The agreed frontier traced its way from the North along the Rivière Massacre, dipped far West down the Artibonite Valley (with lands North of the river still under Spain), then swung East again to include most of the Cul-de-Sac, and thence ran South over the pine forests and peaks of Morne la Selle to the sea.

To confirm and stabilize what Versailles had gained, du Casse in 1698 obtained the king's warrant for a chartered company, the Compagnie de St. Louis, to colonize the Southern peninsula from Cape Tiburon and lle-à-Vache to the Spanish outposts at Neyba. The company would bring 1500 French emigrants and 2500 blacks into the South, would receive land and capital, and join what remaining *flibustiers* du Casse could seduce to planting.

The Compagnie de St.Louis never succeeded commercially but it colonized well. Plantations of tobacco, sugar, and indigo sprang up, and, among them, the towns of the South coast: St. Louis du Sud (1702), Aquin (1711), Bainet (1718), and Cavaillon (1720). Besides these there were already the two towns of Cayes, originally found by Ogeron in 1667, and Jacmel, on whose pretty bay houses had stood since 1680.

Important as were the new settlements, du Casse, future admiral, still saw St. Domingue, flanking the Windward Passage, in strategic terms. To the Minister of Colonies, he wrote on 13 January 1699, "I do not see St. Domingue in terms of sugar, indigo, tobacco, or other commodities of America, but as a strategic position *[une place d'armes]* to gain for France the keys to Mexico, Peru, and the kingdom of Santa Fe."

Settling the South was du Casse's final contribution to St. Domingue. While retaining title as governor until 1703, when promoted admiral and returned to sea, he was absent after 1700. Like Ogeron, he left his mark and can worthily be ranked with Gallieni and Lyautey in France's long line of soldier-colonizers.

Pour les Ancêtres

In Haiti today, "*un authentique*"(a "true" Haitian) is a *noir* of undiluted African antecedents, descended only from the slaves the French brought to the island. Yet a paradox of Haiti's history was forcibly expressed by a *mûlatre* taxed, one day, by a *noir* acquaintance for his lack of "authenticity": "*Après tout, mon cher,*" he rejoined, "*it was my ancestors who brought yours to Haiti.*"(9) Nonetheless, when Haiti's stirring national anthem, "*La Dessalinienne,*" invokes "*les ancêtres,*" that invocation is directed exclusively to African forebears.

As the first French settlers in St. Domingue were not planters, neither were they slave-owners. During the seventeenth century, slaving in Hispaniola was conducted largely under the *asiento* of Madrid, and the slaves were brought to the Spanish end of the island. The few blacks in Western Hispaniola were runaways from Santo Domingo. Most of these became slaves of early French planters, but a few remained at large. When planting replaced freebooting, slaves quickly became an economic necessity.

The first French slaving into St. Domingue was authorized by Louis XIII, in June 1633, because, it was piously argued, this would rescue the blacks from idolatry and gain souls for Christ. The trade was only a trickle until 1664, when the *Compagnie des Indes Occidentales* began carrying slaves to all the French West Indies.

The census of May 1681 numbered more than 10,000. In 1720 the annual importation was 4000; by 1764 it had jumped to 10,000. In 1786 alone, 27,000 slaves were shipped to St. Domingue, and in 1787 -on the eve of catastrophe - although the slave population had attained at least 450,000, 40,000 more were imported. The census of 1791 gives a final figure of 500,000, but Thomas Madiou, in his 1847 history, points out that this total was based on numbers submitted for the annual capitation tax, and makes a persuasive case that slaves not shown on tax rolls brought the actual population to over 700,000.

According to Moreau de Saint-Méry, a careful man, in 1789 60 percent of all French slaves in the Americas were on St. Domingue and, of these, two-thirds were African-born. In that same year, slaving for the French Antilles alone required 105 ships. (From beginning to end, according to one estimated census, it has been conjectured that some 10 million blacks were carried to the New World from Africa.)

The slaves of St. Domingue came of several races. Bantus, from the Congo and Angola, formed the majority. Guineans of the Gold Coast and Coast of Slaves were also numerous. Least common and most prized were the tall, proud, warlike Senegalese, whose lineage traced back to the Sudanese and Tuareg of the desert. Almost equally prized were Aradas of Dahomey, whom King Christophe was to import as his royal police, or Dahomets.

The slaves brought with them an African culture and, most important, an African religion. As early as 1722 Père Labat, scandalized, recorded, "The *noirs* do without scruple that which did the Philistines: they worship Dagon beside Jehovah and secretly commingle the superstitions of their old idolatry with the liturgy of Christ."

Père Labat's sharp eyes did not mislead him. What he reported is the first precise account of the beginnings of Voodoo: a commingling of African "idolatry" with Christian liturgy, an accommodation of the slaves to new gods while holding fast to the old.

To regularize slavery in his island possessions, Louis XIV in March 1685 issued the celebrated *Edit Touchant la Police des Isles de l'Amérique Française*. This royal order, which quickly came to be known as the "*code noir*," can be summarized as follows:

. It accorded certain human rights to slaves: the right to marry (with the master's consent);the right to formal trial (in effect of due process) when accused of serious offenses; the integrity of the family, which, once established, could not be put asunder. Under priests designated as "slave-chaplains," slaves were also to be baptized, given religious instruction, and sent to mass on Sundays and feast days.

. It established special limitations and sanctions. Slaves might not carry arms, conduct commerce (except in special cases where authorized), hold meetings, testify against their masters, or of course leave their plantations. The most serious offenses - theft, assault, and escape - were specially provided for with rigorous penalties.

. It accorded certain powers and responsibilities to the master. The latter must feed, clothe, and provide for the general well-being of the slave. The master could inflict corporal punishment but could not punish a slave with torture, mutilation, or death.

. It provided an avenue to freedom, or *affranchissement*. Masters could liberate slaves, and, once liberated, the freedman - styled an *affranchi* - was to enjoy "the same rights, privileges and immunities of persons born free."

The *code noir* made no provision for slave education, and this was no oversight. "The security of the whites," wrote an early planter, "demands that we keep the Negroes in profound ignorance."

Although the *code noir* prohibited sexual relations between Europeans and slaves, it could not stop white planters from wenching with African maids, and in due course there came into being a new class, or, in later usage, *mulâtres*. This class benefited most often from *affranchissement*, so, as years passed, an intermediate stratum of mixed-blood *affranchis* developed between the French colonists and their African slaves. The grievances of the *affranchis*, who hated their fathers and despised their mothers, and the abuse of their rights by the whites, were to fuel the conflagration that was to come.

Had the *code noir* been administered by angels rather than by greedy, insensitive planters, it would, within the moral and legal context of the times, have provided a relatively endurable situation for the slave. Unfortunately, not in observance but more often in breach, the code sanctioned atrocities whose horrors equaled or exceeded those of the slave ship and the Middle Passage.(10)

In a memorable passage written years later, Vastey, Henry Christophe's secretary and privy counselor, who had lived half his life as a slave, was to cry out the crimes perpetrated against the slaves of St. Domingue by French masters:

Have they not hung up men with heads downward, drowned them in sacks, crucified them on planks, buried them alive, crushed them in mortars? Have they not forced them to eat shit? And, after having flayed them with the lash, have they not cast them alive to be devoured by worms, or onto anthills, or lashed them to stakes in the swamp to be devoured by mosquitoes? Have they not thrown them into boiling caldrons of cane syrup? Have they not put men and women inside barrels studded with spikes and rolled them down mountainsides into the abyss? Have they not consigned these miserable blacks to man-eating dogs until the latter, sated by human flesh, left the mangled victims to be finished off with bayonet and poniard?

Besides the atrocities cited in Vastey's outcry, colonial archives tell of tin masks hung on slaves to keep them from gnawing cane; of cinders, aloes, salt, pepper, and citron rubbed into flesh raw from the lash; of red-hot irons laid across buttocks; of boiling wax poured into ears; of gunpowder exploded inside a slave's rectum.

The slave's recourse was narrow indeed. He could revolt; he could run away; or he could kill himself.

Uprisings were no novelty. The first recorded outbreak against the Spaniards took place in 1522, only twelve years after Ferdinand sent Africans to replace the Indians in the mines of Cibao. Before the end of the century there were at least three more - in 1533, 1537, and 1548. Padrejean's insurrection at Port-de-Paix in 1679 was the first black rising against French colonists, who then still had few slaves. In 1691 two slaves, Janot Marin and Georges Dollot (sometimes called "Pierrot"), were, with a white indentured servant, convicted of plotting a general massacre of every white man, woman, and child in and about Port-de-Paix. In May 1697 some 300 slaves of Quartier Morin and Petite-Anse raised a general insurrection, which, after customary savageries on both sides, was put down. In 1704, during the War of the Spanish Succession, Spanish agents were accused of suborning the slaves at the Cap to rise in the night and cut their masters' throats.

There was no Spanish subornation, however, in the Cul-de-Sac revolt by Michel in 1719. Leading his followers into the pine-covered mountains of Bahoruco in the Southwest, overlooking the frontier to the East and the sea to the South, Michel was the first but by no means the last fighter for freedom to find sanctuary in these fastnesses. Fifteen years later, Polydor, Noël, Isaac, Pyrrhus Candide, and Télémaque Canga sacked and harried the sugar plantations and refineries of the Northeast around Trou du Nord and Fort Dauphin.

But the greatest early rebel was François Macandal, a one-armed slave on the Plantation Normand de Mézy, near Limbé, where, before many years, a certain midnight ceremony would drench St. Domingue in blood. Macandal, originally from Guinea, must have been a sorcerer, or *bocor*. By contemporary accounts he had Arab blood, spoke some Arabic, and professed Islam. He predicted the future, practiced clairvoyance and held himself to be invulnerable, and immortal.

For six years, commencing about 1751, when he fled into the mountains of the North, Macandal was the scourge of the French. Beyond the usual deeds of slave revolt - pillage of isolated plantations, cattle and sheep rustling, and burning of refineries - Macandal preached a fanatic vision: death to all *blancs*, after which the slaves would be masters of St. Domingue. In a report dated 1758, the year of his final capture, Macandal was said to have killed some 6000 persons, white and black.

Before Macandal met death at the stake in Cap Français in January 1758, he said he would be reincarnated as a deadly *maringuioin* (mosquito). As the fagots flamed, Macandal writhed in a fearful last convulsion and the stake snapped. From the watching blacks a great shout arose: *"Macandal sauvé!"* Now his soul had escaped and Macandal was free.

In French, the word *marron* means a domesticated animal run wild; runaway slaves who sought freedom in the mountains of St. Domingue were called *marrons* and *marronage* was the name used by the planters for their condition.

The first blacks in St. Domingue were Spanish runaways. It was not until the end of the seventeenth century reflecting the same conditions that caused initial slave revolts - that *marronage* became a problem for the French.

But by March 1705 the Council of Léogane had to note,

> some *[marrons]* run in packs in the forests and exist free of their masters and with no leaders save of their own choosing; others, taking cover by day in canefields, lie in wait at night to rob passersby, and go from plantation to plantation, stealing livestock for food, or hide among friendly slaves who are usually accomplices, knowing what is going on and tipping off the *marrons* so that the latter can operate without being caught.

Marronage was thus not mere reversion to Rousseau's natural state of man. By necessity it involved brigandage and, by extension under such natural leaders as Michel and Macandal, it became what the twentieth century would call guerrilla war.

Like their guerrilla successors, the *marrons* established sanctuary areas in the mountains and forests. Here, said one 1783 report, they built entrenched camps with palisades, ditches as much as fifteen feet deep and ten feet wide, and obstacles of sharpened stakes. In one Bahoruco stronghold, French forces found a well forty feet deep, obviously dug by hand. Some bands were said to number 1500 to 2000 men with accompanying dependents. These figures can be believed. As early as 1720, 1000 runaways were officially reported, and by 1751 the number had tripled. In 1785 Moreau de Saint-Méry wrote of *marrons* fifty and sixty years old, born of runaway families, who had never known slavery.

The great and undefeated example of *marronage* was the eighty-three year insurgency of Bahoruco. As early as March 1702, *marron* brigandage in and around Bahoruco forced the French to send columns into the mountains, but with little success. When, in 1719, Michel based his band in these cave-riddled mountains and forests, the region was already out of French control. Despite pacification efforts mounted from both the Cul-de-Sac and Jacmel during the half century from 1728 to 1781, runaways continued to swell *marron* ranks. Under leaders such as Kebinda and Santiago, the latter a Spanish runaway, the *marrons* not only maintained their freedom and conducted severe depredations, but inflicted appreciable casualties on pursuers. In the best guerrilla tradition they skillfully exploited the ill-defined Spanish frontier, behind which, when hotly pressed, they would retire.

In 1782, Saint-Larry, a French officer, persuaded the authorities to propose a political settlement. In concert with the Spanish over the border, Saint-Larry negotiated an agreement, finally ratified in 1786 by all parties - French, Spanish, *Marrons* - that conceded personal freedom to the *marrons,* gave them a territory of their own, and bound them to cease depredations and to accept the authority of the king. To the credit of all parties, these undertakings were faithfully kept.

Back in 1685 de Cussy had already noted, "In the Negroes, we have redoubtable domestic enemies." Echoing this fear after the execution of Macandal in 1758, the council of Cap Français enacted repressive measures against the slaves. These included prohibitions against sorcery and profanation of religious places or objects, and thus of Voodoo; the banning of the preparation and distribution of remedies by slaves (an antipoisoning measure); rules forbidding funeral assemblies; and the tightening of existing regulations governing commerce, carrying of arms, and nocturnal meetings by slaves. In the words of historian C. L. R. James, "The only privilege the whites allowed them was the privilege of lending white men money."

This interaction of *marronage,* the slowly but surely rising tempo of slave resistance, and the corresponding heightened repression held deep bearing and importance on events to come. *Marronage* gave the slaves attainable hope of escape from bondage. It also kept alive African traditions and practices. And in such liberation wars as those of Bahoruco, the slaves maintained a warrior tradition and gained proficiency in arms that would later well serve such *noir* leaders as Toussaint, Christophe, and Dessalines.

Rich as a Créole

Almost imperceptibly, St. Domingue was beginning to rank as France's greatest colony. *Flibustiers* had given way to *habitants:* from 1709 on, colonial governors could not muster enough *flibustiers* to keep British frigates from using Môle St. Nicolas as their base to control the Windward Passage.

A reaction to the eighteenth-century wars in Europe was the establishment of regular garrisons in the colony besides the independent companies of Marines that had been St. Domingue's only regulars. In April 1705, by royal ordinance, the *milice*, a home-guard militia made up of every freeman entitled to bear arms, was organized into regiments of infantry and cavalry. The *milice* was a white-only local force. In contrast, there was also formed the Corps de Maréchaussée, a constabulary recruited among the *affranchis*, whose missions were to run down fugitive slaves, suppress *marronage,* and maintain internal security against the *noirs*. The unrewarding duties of the *maréchauseé* and the highhanded way it was maintained by forced levies on the *affranchis*, were to become festering grievances of that class and, at the same time, their school in arms.

Because of the vulnerability of coastal shipping, the eighteenth-century governors began to integrate the colony's interior communications. In 1702, following the opening of a highway from the Cap to Léogane (with a ferry at the Artibonite), regular stagecoaches - ancestors of later *camionnettes* and *tap-taps* (the small buses and vans that are the backbone of modern Haiti's transportation system) ran that route and soon went as far as Les Cayes. Four years later, the parallel interior route was opened from Dondon in the North to Mirebalais (still only a cluster of houses for herdsmen and hunters) and then down over the mountain wall into the Cul-de-Sac.

Even with these and other improvements, ruling the colony was little easier than it had been. To the old seventeenth-century rallying cry of "*Vive le Roi! Point de Compagnie!*" there was another revolt in 1722 against burdensome taxes and unfair devaluation of the peso gordo, the colonial money. As France's colonial historian Pierre de Vaissière wrote, insolence and mutiny were everywhere. Nor was this surprising. considering that the population, as described in 1700 by the king's lieutenant at Léogane, consisted "mainly of indentured servants, bankrupts, burglars *[gens de sac et de corde],* escaped or transported convicts, and people bereft of honor and virtue."

To uplift and minister to such disreputable colonists, there was a growing religious establishment, which included an almost submerged cadre of slave-chaplains for the *noirs*. (11)

Towns were growing and flourishing. St. Marc was founded in 1716 and within six years was principal port for the Artibonite. Bainet, the miniature Jacmel, was already established, as was Cavaillon, and Jérémie, birthplace of General Thomas Alexandre Dumas, dates from 1765. In the North, Limbé and Terrier Rouge existed in 1722.

When the ship *Prince* anchored in 1706 at the foot of Morne l'Hôpital (a former *flibustier* nest overlooking the Cul-de-Sac) her captain christened the broad bay "Port-au-Prince." In 1738, renaming it "Port Royal," the governor, de Fayet, selected the site as the new colonial capital. A 12-gun battery built in

1743 on l'Ilet du Prince offshore (henceforth known as Fort Ilet) defended the harbor, and here, in 1749, the new town was proclaimed capital of St. Domingue.

De Fayet described Port-au-Prince in 1738: "The air is pure, the harbor safe, and the water supply is healthy." But in 1805 the English Captain Rainsford took a quite different tack: "It must have been one of the unaccountable caprices that sometimes direct the settlement of towns, that could have obtained for this place, indefensible at all points, the distinction it received. It was neither healthy nor inviting . . . The water is of a brackish and otherwise disagreeable taste . . . The town extending along the seashore, is damp, and cheerless, except from the hurry of business."

The final division of Hispaniola had not yet taken shape. Throughout the eighteenth century the Spanish-held central plateau, arid and mostly fit for grazing, still projected deep into St. Domingue with St. Michel de l'Atalaye as the frontier post.

The conventional view of eighteenth-century St. Domingue is one of wealth, splendor, luxury, elegance, and gaiety. Accounts are many of splendid roads, magnificent plantations, beautiful gardens, opulent and easy living in a dazzling and brilliant society. Without being deceived as to underlying realities, Moreau de Saint-Méry wrote:

> In St. Domingue everything takes on an air of opulence that dazzles Europeans. That throng of slaves who await the orders and even the lifted finger of a lone individual, confers grandeur on him who commands them. To have four times as many servants as one needs marks the grandiloquence of a wealthy man. As for the ladies, their main talent is to surround themselves with a useless cohort of maidservants . . . Since the supreme happiness for a European is to be waited on, he even rents slaves until able to possess them in his own right.

Amid this suffocating materialism education was feeble. The colony had hardly any schools. (France, to be sure, was little better off: originated by the First Republic, the *lycée* was yet to be born.) But St. Domingue, in contrast with Peru, Argentina, New Spain, and even sleepy Santo Domingo, had no university.

Superficially - and so much of St. Domingue was superficiality - the cultural stirrings of the Age of Enlightenment seemed well enough represented. Not only the Cap, but Port-au-Prince, St. Marc, Léogane, Les Cayes (where James Audubon would be born in 1785), and Jérémie, had repertory theaters: between 1764 and 1791 some 3000 theatrical productions were recorded. In 1764 came the first newspaper, the *Gazette de St. Domingue*. Within a few years, fifty journals or reviews were appearing in the colony.

By the middle of the eighteenth century the enterprising French planters of St. Domingue had driven the British from the sugar markets of Europe. St. Domingue thus supplied not only France but much of Europe with sugar, coffee, and cocoa. As early as 1742, more sugar went to France from St. Domingue than the combined output of all the British West Indies. By 1783 the commerce of St. Domingue amounted to more than a third of the foreign trade of France.

Since Haiti consists mainly of great mountain ranges, the productive areas of St. Domingue were the rich alluvial Plaine du Nord, the Artibonite Valley, the Cul-de-Sac, and the Plaine de Léogane. In 1791 there were 792 sugar plantations, 2180 of coffee, 705 of cotton, 3097 of indigo, 69 of cocoa, and 623 raising subsistence crops. Haiti's exports to France alone that year totaled approximately $41 million. The net worth of the colony was put at $300 million. "Rich as a Créole"(12) had become a common saying in France.

"Every part," reported Rainsford, "teemed with population and smiled with industry."

Yet this veneer of prosperity and productivity was thin and brittle. Absentee landlordism had become rife. By 1752, of thirty-nine sugar plantations on the Plaine de Léogane, only ten were administered by resident owners; the rest were run by stewards for proprietors in France whose Loire châteaux and Paris town houses had been built on chocolate, indigo, coffee, and cotton. Planters in St. Domingue almost universally looked to the day when they could return to France and live off their wealth.

Amid its supposed glitter, colonial life could be stifling: in the words of a foreign visitor, Baron de Wimpffen, "Nothing resembles a state of wretchedness so much as their opulence."

At the pinnacle of an immense pyramid of misery and bondage some 30,000 whites looked down on 25,000 *affranchis* and more than 700,000 slaves whose services were in reality uneconomic. A slave in prime condition cost 2000 livres.(13) He was allocated land for a truck garden and two days a month to work it. His rations and allowances amounted to an ounce of salt fish or meat and a bottle of lemonade a day; a bottle of taffia (crude rum) a month; eighteen pounds of salt per year, together with a hat, a wool shirt, and four yards of cloth. Most of these were imported, and all cost money. Yet the planter had no alternative for the labor of his slaves.

For planter and slave alike, such an existence was dehumanizing.

"Have pity on us [wrote the daughter of a planter] for an existence cut off from the world. We are five whites, my father, my mother, my two brothers and me, surrounded by over 200 slaves, the domestics alone amounting to 10. From morning to night their faces stare at us . . . and they are involved in the least details of our intimate existence. Our talk is taken up with the health of the slaves, the care they require, their schemes for revolt, and all our lives are bound up with these wretched beings."

The whites were deeply divided, often corrupt, and frequently seedy. In de Vaissière's words, one could see "a kinsman of the de Vaudreuils, a Châteauneuf or Boucicaut, last descendant of the renowned marshal of France, passing his life between a bowl of rum punch and a concubine *négresse.*"

The regular officers of the royal regiments of infantry and artillery scorned the civilians, who returned the sentiment with interest. Townsmen were at odds with planters. Rich *habitants* looked down their noses at *petits blancs,* or poor whites. Créoles, whose lives were truly committed to St. Domingue, resented absent proprietors or get rich quick planters eager to return to France. Government officeholders grafted, exploited, and despised all but the rich and powerful, who alone had any voice in the administration of the colony. Aristocratic, imperious soldier-governors squabbled with quill-driving, functionary civilian intendants.

Even to eyes and noses conditioned to the kennels of eighteenth century Paris, the towns seemed noisome and fetid. Amid the clear air and natural beauty of Haiti, Moreau de Saint-Méry could write, "The streets of Cap Français are nothing but common sewers. "As for Port-au-Prince," wrote Paul Dubuisson in 1780, "if it rains the night before, you can't walk in the streets, which resemble huge avenues of mud that sticks to your feet and makes movement impossible."

Baron de Wimpffen, arriving in 1788, was anything but impressed:

> When one has been acquainted in France with colonials, and above all, Créole colonials, he cannot approach Port-au-Prince . . . capital of the richest country on the face of the globe! the most fertile in delights! the throne of luxury! the center of voluptuousness! without experiencing that secret shiver, that pleasant and vague anxiety which precedes admiration and prepares the soul for enthusiasm -To be brief, I entered upon two rows of huts, jolting along a dusty track called a street, and searching in vain for Persepolis amongst a chaotic mass of wooden barracks! The comparison that most forcibly strikes one is that of a Tartar camp.

In such conditions natural disaster may have served certain purposes.

On 20 September 1734, Cap Français burned to the ground. Three years later, St. Louis de Sud was leveled by a hurricane. In 1748 and 1749, measles decimated the slaves; pest and blight and animal epidemics ravaged the Cul-de-Sac the year following. In the wake of these plagues came heavy earthquakes in the fall of 1751, but these were but a foretaste. At seven in the evening of 3 June 1770, Port-au-Prince was riven by a fearful earthquake that opened the ground, leveled every public building, and left over 200 dead in the streets.

Who can wonder that the atmosphere of St. Domingue must, save to all but the most insensitive, have seemed charged with presentiments of calamity? These at any rate were the feelings of a Jérémie planter and captain of *milice* in 1773: "The colony is weaker than it has ever been . . . Every day I curse the hour I got the idea of coming to this country and being shut up here all my life. I tremble for us, I tell you . . . I read people's hearts and see written there the ill fortunes that loom ahead!"

Loaded Barrels of Gunpowder

During the eighteenth century the *affranchis* - now being mostly referred to as *"gens de couleur"* or *"hommes de couleur"* - multiplied. In 1790, opposed to 40,000 white colonists, St. Domingue had 28,000 *affranchis*; seventy-five years earlier there had been but 1500. Many had not known slavery in their families for three or, four generations, and most had land and slaves. About a quarter of the land and slaves of the colony belonged to *hommes de couleur;* in the West and South, the proportion was higher. The parish (14) of Jérémie, for example, was almost entirely owned, populated, and run by *gens de couleur.*

Hommes de couleur who did well associated with the *grands blancs.* Like these powerful whites, they sent their children to France to be educated; and certain among them "crossed over" by prudent marriages and purchase of letters-patent certifying they were white. Among the latter, certain acted out their insecurities by maltreating slaves and by contemptuous snobbism toward darker-skinned *mulâtres* (15) and dangerously - toward less prosperous and often worse educated *petits blancs.*

These developments begot rancor and ill will from the *petits blancs,* who felt most immediately challenged, and mounting apprehension on the part of government. In consequence, despite liberal provisions in the *code noir,* the eighteenth century saw *affranchis* progressively reduced to second-class citizens at best and, at worst, subjected to discrimination and repression different only in degree from slavery.

After 1734, with heavy penalties against any *blanc* involved, *affranchis* and Europeans could no longer marry. (Officers, for example, were cashiered for marrying *mulâtresses.)* Increasing numbers of obstacles were interposed against *affranchissage,* and social and public pressure was applied against planters who persisted in conferring freedom on favorite slaves (or, frequently, favorite mistresses and *mulâtre* offspring). Nonetheless, a 1774 census showed that, out of 7000 female *affranchies* in the colony, 5000 were recorded as mistresses of white men. The *Conseil Supérieur* (the island's governing body) in 1758 barred *hommes de couleur* from carrying side arms. Within nine years this restriction had been extended to all firearms and even the purchase of ammunition except by special license.

Culminating in 1771 with Louis XV's "Instructions to Administrators," a series of decrees had created what amounted to a separate code of restrictions, repressions, special disabilities - and therefore humiliations - applying to the *homme de couleur*. On maturity he had to serve three years in the *maréchaussée*. Subsequently, without pay, he was liable to further service in the militia, under white officers. The *corvée* (forced labor levied by French feudal law for upkeep of highways) fell upon the *affranchi* but bypassed the *petit blanc*. The *homme de couleur* could not hold public office or even pursue the professions: he was excluded from law, the priesthood, medicine, pharmacy, (16) and schoolteaching. He had to be off the streets by 9:00 P.M. and, in theater or church, could occupy only segregated seats.

An *homme de couleur* could not eat at table with a white, nor could he dance in the evening. He was debarred from bearing a European name (but the rule requiring African names for slaves and new *affranchis* alike was often annulled by the plantation practice of giving slaves classical names, such as Scylla, Scipio, Pompey, Télémaque). The *affranchi* was forbidden to wear clothes of normal European fashion and material; men or women of color would have clothes stripped off their backs in the streets if some drunken planter thought the cut or cloth too near his own. In the courts no white man lost to an *affranchi*. If the latter struck a *blanc*, his hand would be struck off. If a white hit an *homme de couleur*, he was liable only for a fine.

Thus far, in less than a century, had the *code noir*'s "same rights, privileges and immunities as persons born free" been perverted.

Neither the authorities nor the white population generally seems to have perceived the inconsistency of rules that, on the one hand, virtually disarmed the *gens de couleur* and, on the other, enforced their training and service in *maréchaussée* and *milice*. This tradition in arms was reinforced (and the *hommes de couleur* exposed to revolution under the standard of liberty) when, in 1779, France sent a West Indian expeditionary force, led by Comte d'Estaing, to aid the hard-pressed American Continentals defending Georgia and the Carolinas against the British.

D'Estaing's 1750-man force included detachments from Guadeloupe, Martinique, and the smaller French islands. The contingent from St. Domingue, commanded by the Vicomte de Fontanges, numbered 1550 -a grenadier battalion of whites and the *Chasseurs Volontaires de Couleur*, officered by whites and led by a veteran French soldier, the Marquis du Rouvray. Among the chasseurs were names Haiti would have cause to remember: André Rigaud, Jean-Baptiste Chavannes, Laurent Férou, Louis-Jacques Bauvais, and Henry Christophe.

Savannah, held in force by the British, was d'Estaing's objective. Landing unopposed on 8 September 1779, and joining 4000 American troops under Major General Benjamin Lincoln, the French surrounded the town. Fighting of mounting intensity culminated on 9 October. With the troops of St. Domingue in the van, d'Estaing attacked three times, and three times was repulsed. In what George Washington would afterward gloomily call "the disaster of Savannah," the British won. At the head of his troops, d'Estaing was wounded twice; among other wounded was young Henry Christophe.

As the eighteenth century drew to a close, St. Domingue, for all its opulence, was a sick society at war with itself. The slaves mutely endured hideous grievances; the *affranchis* were systematically denied basic rights and freedoms theirs in law; and the white *colons* bickered selfishly, or blindly devoted themselves to the pursuit of wealth and pleasure.

"This colony of slaves,"wrote the Marquis du Rouvray in 1783, "is like a city under the imminence of attack; we are treading on loaded barrels of gunpowder."

Du Rouvray was right. The long fuze had burned very short.

FOOTNOTES - CHAPTER 1

1. Ironically, despite most histories, it was not Columbus who first sighted Hispaniola nor was the date of that first landfall the schoolboys' 5 December 1492. Five days earlier, Martín Alonso Pinzón, captain of *Pinta*, separated from Columbus off the North coast of Cuba, raised Cap San Nicolas, and thereby qualifies as the discoverer of Haiti. But Pinzón, greedy for gold, sailed past San Nicolas and made directly for Montecristi in what was to become Santo Domingo, a region said by Cuban Indians to be rich in the yellow metal.

2. For simplicity and consistency we shall use French or Haitian names of places as they are now known, rather than Columbus's Spanish names for the same localities.

3. Soldiers who have passed to leeward of the blood-soaked clothing or stretchers outside a battlefield aid station may be pardoned for doubting that even the *boucaniers* dyed their clothing with blood.

4. "Bertrand Ogeron, Lord of la Bouère-en-Jallais, who from 1664 to 1676 laid the foundations of a civil and religious society amid the flibustiers and boucaniers of the Islands of La Tortue and St. Domingue. Thus, through the mysterious ways of Providence, he assured the destinies of the Republic of Haiti."

5. In the old French of the early settlers, it was "Cap François" until the mid-eighteenth century, when the name was modernized to "Cap Français."

6. As late as 1962 the Haitian Coast Guard was trying to suppress what the twentieth century called "hijacking" by coastal marauders based at Cayemites and Baradères.

7. Twenty years later, Père le Pers would write: "The descents of the *flibustiers* on Jamaica to carry off blacks were so frequent that the latter island became known in St. Domingue as 'Petite Guinée (Little Guinea).'" To this day, a section of Cap Haïtien bears

the same name.

8. Mme. de Graff, wrote W. J. Gardner in his *History of Jamaica,* "was treated with respect by her captors, and knew how to obtain it." Well she might. A spirited daughter of Normandy, Marie-Anne de Graff was from her first marriage widow of one of the earliest colonists of La Tortue. Years later, in 1708, again a widow, in a dispute over a debt he owed her, she took her broom to Chevalier Donon de Gallifet, a former governor of the colony, and chased him down the street.

9. While the Haitian color differentiations, *noir* and *mulâtre,* translate literally into English, their nuances and significance among Haitians transcend the English "black" and "mulatto." Thus we shall generally employ *noir* and *mulâtre* (or *jaune*) when speaking of the two races.

10. The worst infractions of the *code noir* and mounting maltreatment of the *affranchis* did not commence until after royal expulsion of the Jesuits from St. Domingue in 1764. Here, as in Brazil, the Jesuits angered planters by standing up for the slaves while also striving to socialize them.

11. The first priest in the colony was Father Marc, a Capuchin shipwrecked in 1665. In his footsteps (licensed by Louis XIV to ensure loyalty to Versailles) came other Capuchins, who established missions in the North. In 1704, Jesuits relieved the Capuchins, only to be expelled by the Crown in 1764. Meanwhile, Dominicans had come to the Cul-de-Sac and, by the end of the century, to the South as du Casse settled it. Among these soldiers and servants of Christ were students and historians without whose work the early history of St. Domingue would be a closed book: the Dominican Labat; Le Pers, who lies buried in Dondon; and, above all, his fellow Jesuit, Charlevoix.

12. Créole, as used here, carries no connotation of race or color. A Créole was simply a person born in the West Indies as distinct from metropolitan France. In a wholly different definition, the same word, Créole, also denotes the language commonly spoken today by most Haitians.

13. Two thousand livres was a good average price, but from the papers of Lefranc de Saint-Haulde, the Norman architect-engineer of the Cul-de-Sac during the eighteenth century, we find him paying 3000 livres for a stonemason, 4000 for a pastry cook, and in 1775 - for a lot comprising a *mulâtre,* a woman of Carib Indian blood, two Negresses from the Congo, and one child - 10,900 livres (an average of 2180 livres apiece). But a *"vielle négresse"* went for only 400 livres.

14. The "parish" in St. Domingue was (as it remains in Louisiana) a civil administrative division corresponding to the American county.

15. With typical thoroughness Moreau de Saint-Méry works out 170 basic classifications of racial coloration, recognized in St. Domingue, that might result from the mating of whites, *noirs, mulâtres,* or those with Carib Indian strains.

16. In a tradition that persists even in twentieth-century Haiti, the blacks were thought to be adept at poisoning, and the literature of St. Domingue abounds in accounts of supposed poisonings, poison conspiracies (including one attributed to Macandal), and the use by slaves of secret potions.

CHAPTER 2

Bois Cayman and Carmagnole

1788-1794

Périssent les colonies, plûtot qu'un Principe!

- Robespierre, 1791

So now, in the Autumn of 1791, looking from the sky-windows of Cap Français, thick clouds of smoke girdle our horizon, smoke in the day, in the night, fire, preceded by fugitive shrieking of white women, by Terror and Rumor. St. Domingue is shaken. Writhing in horrid death-throes, it is Black without remedy; and remains as African Haiti, a monition to the world.

- Carlyle, *The French Revolution*

IN Louis XVI, the French of St. Domingue had the king they deserved. Inert, indolent, corpulent - *"Le Gros garçon, mal élevé,"* du Barry called him - the King of France never realized, until the lava choked him, that he had been enthroned on a volcano.

With poverty and royal profligacy as outriders, famine and fierce winter scourged France in 1788. In this bitter time, tugged this way and that by his nobility, by the clergy, and by others who sought an end to the intolerable privileges of both, Louis XVI was induced to convene the States-General of France, dormant 150 years, to meet at Versailles, 1 May 1789.

Of the distant grievances of France at this time, St. Domingue had no part. As they had been since the days of Ogeron, the complaints of the colony were against French monopoly and French entrepreneurs. The objects of these discontents were not the men at Versailles but the merchants of Marseilles, Bordeaux, Nantes, and Dieppe.

To press such claims and, more to the purpose, to win economic emancipation for St. Domingue, some planters, styling themselves "Commissioners of St. Domingue," had formed a commission that, when the States-General met in 1788, demanded and was granted representation. Even as the Commissioners of St. Domingue were drafting remonstrances for the States-General, a more profound grievance was coming to a head: to men of feeling in both France and England, the notion of African slavery had become revolting.

Led in England by Thomas Clarkson and William Wilberforce, those in favor of abolition of the slave trade brought the matter before the Privy Council in 1788, and to debate in the House of Commons in March 1789. In France, also in 1788, there was formed a *Société des Amis des Noirs* (Society of the Friends of Blacks). These *Amis des Noirs* (most of whom had never seen a *noir*) were led by men of intellect and influence. Among many distinguished names, membership rolls listed Condorcet, Abbé Gregoire, Mirabeau, and La Fayette. What the Amis demanded was not merely the end of slaving but of slavery itself.

Among those who influenced the *Amis des Noirs* were free *mulâtres* from St. Domingue, whose immediate interest lay in reclaiming the human and political rights originally theirs under the *code noir*. The leaders included Vincent Ogé, born in Dondon; Jean-Baptiste Chavannes, veteran of Savannah; and Julien Raymond, a lawyer who busied himself in advocacy of the *mulâtres'* cause. Bitterly opposing the *Amis des Noirs* was a very different kind of party, composed of former colonists and absentee proprietors of St. Domingue, whose economic existence the *Amis* challenged head-on. This group, convened in 1789, was entitled *Société Correspondante des Colons Français*, but quickly came to be known as the "Club Massiac," taking its name from the Marquis de Massiac, a St. Marc sugar proprietor in whose town house the members met.

Ten days before the Bastille fell, in July 1789, the French National Assembly, as the States-General now called itself, voted to seat six delegates from St. Domingue. In debate, Mirabeau demanded to know why a slate of white *colons* should speak for free, taxpaying, property-owning *hommes de couleur* who had been denied participation in selection of the island representatives. Mirabeau also suggested that were the *gens de couleur* to be excluded from the delegation of St. Domingue, then the size of the latter should be reduced proportionally by the number of *mulâtres* disenfranchised.

Meanwhile, events had overtaken political process.

On 14 July the Bastille fell to the Paris mob. When Louis XVI sputtered, "Why, this is a revolt," La Rochefoucauld-Liancourt corrected the king: "No, Sire it is a revolution."

In less than three months, already sequestered in the Tuileries, Louis XVI, on 5 October, gave royal assent to a manifesto composed by La Fayette and passed by the National Assembly. This "Declaration of the Rights of Man and of the Citizen" dealt a mortal blow to the white planters of St. Domingue. Its first article proclaimed, "All men are born and live free and equal in their rights."

To make the matter abundantly clear, on 22 October the Assembly accepted a petition of rights presented by "free citizens of color" from St. Domingue. In seating this *mulâtre* delegation, the president of the Assembly pronounced, "Never shall any citizen ask in vain for his rights from this Assembly."

To bypass the French Assembly and its liberalism, the colons now proceeded, with the assent of the Ministry of Marine, to organize a colonial assembly directly answerable to the Crown. Remarkably, considering what the colonists were up to, the National Assembly approved. Then - having conferred "states' rights" on the colonists, the French National Assembly, on 28 March, granted the franchise in St. Domingue to "all persons aged twenty-five, owning property, or failing property ownership, to taxpayers of ten years standing." Since "all persons" clearly included *hommes de couleur* suitable qualifications, the stage was set for inevitable collision between white *habitants* and free *mulâtres*.

Already, at home, there had been clashes between *gens de couleur* demanding their rights and colonists adamant on denying them. In April 1790, while the Colonial Assembly was sitting at St. Marc, blood had been shed at Fond-Parisien in the Cul-de-Sac; over the mountains in the Artibonite and in Jacmel *mulâtres* were also in arms.

To Vincent Ogé and even the more cautious Chavannes, time seemed ripe to enforce the National Assembly's grant of franchise and, behind it, the heady implications of the Declaration of the Rights of Man.

Going first to London - here he got money from Clarkson - Ogé sailed for Charleston, bought arms and landed, on 12 October 1790, on the North coast of St. Domingue. (Although Ogé and Chavannes had met contemptuous rebuff in Paris when the *mulâtres* tried to reach a compromise with the Massiac faction, the element in St. Domingue most hostile to the *hommes de couleur* - was not the high-born *grands blancs* but the lower-class *petits blancs*. It mattered not what the Assembly decreed; the *petits blancs* would never concede that *gens de couleur* were persons and equals because, if they were, so were the slaves. This was the reason why Ogé's object - to secure promulgation and implementation of the Assembly's March decree - however just and lawful, was doomed to fail.)

Ogé's first step was to petition the royal governor, the Comte de Peynier. The logic of Peynier's reply was understandable: to accede to any such demands was simply impracticable in colonial St. Domingue. Ogé's reaction was to incite the *gens de couleur* of the North, a step that determined local planters to arrest him forthwith. After a band of white vigilantes failed to take the young leader at Grande Rivière, Ogé, at the head of 300 *mulâtres*, disarmed every white in the parish. Shots were exchanged, a planter was killed, and Ogé became a rebel.

Refusing to arm or inflame the wondering slaves - which would have horrified the *mulâtres* - Ogé and Chavannes marched on the Cap. Their first collision with the white soldiery went well: attacking briskly, they drove in their opponents' pickets and pushed on. But 1500 white militia and black volunteers (including a *noir* gunner, Henry Christophe) were waiting. The outnumbered *mulâtres* were overwhelmed. Ogé and Chavannes made their escape across the frontier near Ouanaminthe, but the Spaniards, no more enchanted with *mulâtres* insurrection than the French, quickly returned them to their pursuers.

The Provincial Assembly (1) wasted no mercy on the rebels. Twenty-two, including Ogé's brother and a French priest who had joined the band, were hanged. Thirteen lesser offenders received life sentences in the galleys. For Ogé and Chavannes, a supreme punishment was reserved:

> They are to be taken to the Place d'Armes, and to the opposite side from that set for the execution of white criminals, to have their arms, legs and ribs broken, while alive, upon a scaffold erected for the purpose, and placed by the executioner upon wheel;, with their faces turned toward Heaven, there to remain as long as it shall please God to let them live; after this, their heads to be severed from their bodies and exposed on stakes.

On 9 March 1791, the two young *hommes de couleur* paid this awful penalty. Chavannes died with lips sealed. Ogé broke. Hoping for reprieve or commutation, he gave an extensive confession, which included details of *mulâtre* plots for a general uprising, slaves included. For reasons today unaccountable, the confession was suppressed and - incredibly - ignored.

The *blancs* had won the first battle, but the rack on the Place d'Armes had sundered not merely the bodies of Ogé and Chavannes; even more irrevocably, it had broken any last hope for union, based on common interest, between white planters and *gens de couleur.*

Bois Cayman

While 70,000 whites and *mulâtres* intrigued and contested, 700,000 slaves watched with seeming impassivity.

They had nothing to lose save misery. Because of the enormous increase in slaving to St. Domingue during the late eighteenth century, these captive *noirs* were preponderantly new from Africa. They were barely broken to the yoke. They were savage, sullen, surely resentful of the oppression and tribulation that fell to their lot in St. Domingue. In 1764, a planter at Les Cayes, Brueys d'Aigailiers, wrote a friend in France: "The harshness of their servitude is revolting to human nature. Everyone says they are lazy, untruthful, full of malice; these defects, common enough among white men, can only be worsened by their captivity . . . exposed to the unjust caprice of absolute masters who on the whim of anger are capable of inflicting the ultimate excesses of cruelty."

After the sun had set on certain days known to devotees and priests of the *loa,* drums could be heard from the slaves' quarters, beating out different rhythms from those played during the day's work. There was a dance called *"cabitida";* there would be choruses and chants, the words half African, half French:

> We come from Guinée,
> We have no mother,
> We have no father,
> Marassa Eyo!
> Papa Damballah,
> Show us,
> Show us Dahomey again . . .

These were mysteries that could not be spoken, let alone revealed, to any white or *mulâtre.* Amid them, from slave to slave, from plantation to plantation along the beaten footpaths beside the canefields or over the ridge lines, dawned certain realizations and from those realizations a sense that the slaves' hour had come.

On the Plantation Normand de Mézy, that same plantation near Limbé in the North where thirty-four years earlier Macandal had raised the blacks against their masters, there was a slave named Boukman. By all accounts Boukman was an overseer, or *commandeur,* who supervised other slaves and laid on the lash when ordered; in short, a *gros nègre* possessed of power and authority.

At Le Normand de Mézy, in the shadow of Morne Rouge, Boukman convoked nocturnal meetings in the summer of 1791. These meetings were attended by slave representatives from other plantations on the Plaine du Cap. Haitian traditions say, but have never fully established, that Toussaint Bréda, as he was then named, the intelligent, taciturn coachman-veterinarian of the Comte de Bréda's plantation at the Haut-du-Cap, took part under the nickname of "Fatras Bâton" (Broomstick, owing to his skinniness). Others known to have conspired with Boukman that hot June and July included Jean-François Papillon, Georges Biassou, and Jeannot. These men were also *commandeurs.*

On 11 August, overeager slaves at Habitations Chabaud and La Gossette misconstrued the plan and set fire to the great houses. The *maréchaussée* promptly put down these risings, and slaves who survived were as promptly hanged.

At ten o'clock on the night of the 14th, Boukman held his final meeting at Le

Normand. In a remote wood, Bois Cayman (Alligator Woods), following certain forms of Voodoo (2), Boukman, himself a *houngan,* assisted by a *mambo,* slit the throat of a pig and commanded all to drink. Then Boukman pronounced an invocation:

> Good Lord who made the sun that shines upon us, that riseth from the sea, Who maketh the storm to roar; and governeth the thunders, The Lord is hidden in the heavens, And there He watcheth over us. The Lord seeth what the *blancs* have done. Their god commandeth crimes, Ours giveth blessings upon us. The Good Lord hath ordained vengeance. He will give strength to our arms and courage to our hearts. He shall sustain us. Cast down the image of the god of the *blancs,* Because he maketh the tears to flow from our eyes. Hearken unto Liberty That speaketh now in all our hearts.(3)

Still on their knees, warm blood sticky on their lips, the slaves swore a fearful oath of obedience to their leaders and death to all *blancs.* As they did, a thunderstorm burst from the heavens, drenching the bonfire, and all dispersed to await the sign that Boukman promised would be given after nightfall on 22 August.

Soon after ten on the appointed night, the drums changed their beat, and the sky reddened over Acul and Limbé. At Noé, Climent, Flaville, Gallifet, and of course Le Normand, the slaves, armed with pruning hooks, machetes, and torches, surrounded the houses, slaughtered the men, drank the rum, raped the women, and fired the estates and canefields.

As dawn broke, roads leading toward the Cap were choked with refugees, some carrying a few valuables, most possessing only the clothes they could throw on. The horizon behind them, wrote one, was

> ...a wall of fire from which continually arose thick vortices of smoke whose huge black volumes could be likened only to those frightful storm clouds which roll onwards charged with thunder and lightning. The rifts in those clouds revealed flames equally great which rose darting and flashing to the very sky . . . The most striking feature of this terrible spectacle was a rain of fire composed of burning cane-straw which whirled thick before the blast like snow and which the wind whipped, now toward the harbor and ships, now over the houses of the town.

Survivors who reached the fragile security of the Cap, where the population numbered 3000 white men and 15,000 blacks, were the lucky ones.

An officer of the hated *maréchauseé* was nailed alive to a gate and then dismembered by axmen, who chopped off his limbs. The carpenter at Flaville was lashed between two of his planks and sawed in two. Women were thrown across the warm bodies of murdered husbands, father, or brothers, and raped by gangs of slaves. M. Odeluc, steward of the great Gallifet plantation, who had been spending the night in town, led a patrol of soldiers toward the estate. As they approached, they were overwhelmed by furious slaves whose standard was the body of a white baby impaled on a pike.

Leading a relief column of troops and Créole militia, Colonel de Touzard, a veteran who had lost an arm in the American Revolution, encountered 4000 armed slaves at the Latour plantation near Dondon. While the disciplined volleys of the French knocked them down, the slaves' casualties, reported Touzard, seemed to be replaced a hundred for one. When his ammunition ran low, Touzard had to retire.

Amid these horrors occurred repeated instances of slaves who warned and saved former masters whose kindnesses they remembered. The Baillon family, on a coffee plantation in the mountains behind Port-Margot, were hidden, fed, and guided to safety by one of their slaves, who was himself a leader of mutineers. Toussaint, the wizened coachman at Bréda, restrained the whole slave force until mid-September in order to assure safe evacuation of Bayon de Libertat, the plantation steward who had befriended him and taught him to read and write. Only when Bayon and his wife were safe at the Cap with their possessions did Toussaint raise the standard of revolt.

As the inexorable wall of fire rolled past Limonade and Quartier Morin, du Rouvray, the old soldier who had foreseen the wrath to come, was put in charge of the defense of Cap Français. He had some 1200 regulars, assorted militia, and a *mulâtre maréchausée* of dubious allegiance. His first measures were to put every able-bodied man (including several thousand loyal slaves) to work on palisades and like obstacles around the town. At the ferry landing on the road to Fort Dauphin (where today the airport road bridge stands) he emplaced a battery. Ships in port were forbidden to sail and were ordered to be ready to receive refugees, women, and children. Seamen were landed to reinforce the soldiery.

The Plaine du Nord, populated by prowling bands of slaves, was ringed in flame. The Cap was besieged. Dragging up cannon captured from smaller coastal towns, the slaves tried to bombard Cap Français. Fortunately for du Rouvray and the town, they had no knowledge of artillery. Powder charges were rammed home forward of the ball; the relationship of range to elevation was unknown. Confident that *Ogun*, god of war, made them invulnerable, the slaves would charge the muzzles of French muskets or, triumphantly shouting *"Moin trapé li!"* (I've got him now!), shove their arms up the bores of guns to hold back cannonballs. In the mountains that wall the plain, planters and militia (now beginning, after the fashion of Paris, to style themselves "national guards") tried to control their own districts and maintain a *cordon sanitaire* around the seething plain. Avenues leading to plantations were festooned with gibbeted bodies of hanged slaves, and rebel nests grinned with the skulls of murdered Frenchmen.

At the headquarters of the *noir* leader Biassou (who had an entire general staff of *bocors*) skulls were not the only objects to be found. As described by Thomas Madiou: "[Biassou's] tent was filled with kittens of all shades, with snakes, with dead men's bones, and other African fetiches. At night, huge campfires were lit with naked women dancing horrible dances around them, chanting words understood only on the shores of Africa. When the excitement reached its climax, Biassou would appear amid his *bocors* to proclaim in the name of God that every slave killed in battle would re-awaken in the homeland of Africa."

The cordons established by du Rouvray were intended to confine the revolt to its initial limits.

Following one fight near the Gallifet plantation (outside Grande Rivière du Nord), du Rouvray cut down some 600 slaves. A Créole in the column wrote, "One could not find a living black within a circle of two-and-a-half miles, and the roads were strewn with their bloody remains." In another fight at Limonade, du Rouvray killed 150 slaves in an afternoon and captured a renegade white leader who paid for his disaffection by being broiled over a charcoal fire.

Cap Français, too, was a place of death. "The City," wrote a British army officer in 1791, "presents a terrible spectacle; surrounded by ditches and palisades, the streets blocked by barricades, and the squares occupied by scaffolds on which captured negroes are tortured the whole forming a depressing picture of devastation and carnage.

On the Place de Clugny stood five gallows and two wheels reserved for direst retribution. Looking out his window on 28 September, Bryan Edwards, the British historian of the West Indies, saw two slave leaders broken by the executioner.

> One of them expired on receiving the third stroke on his stomach, each of his legs and arms having been first broken in two places . . . The other had a harder fate. When the executioner lifted up the instrument to give the finishing stroke on the breast . . . the mob, with the ferociousness of cannibals, called out *"arretez"* and compelled him to leave his work unfinished. In that condition the miserable wretch, with his broken limbs doubled up, was put on a cart-wheel, which was placed horizontally, one end of the axle-tree being driven into the earth. At the end of some forty minutes, some English seamen, who were spectators of the tragedy, strangled him in mercy.

Edwards estimated that 10,000 slaves were killed in the merciless fighting, together with many hundreds as mercilessly executed. Two thousand French, he said, had been massacred; and, within two months after Bois Cayman, 180 sugar plantations and 900 of coffee, cotton, and indigo had been sacked and burned.

On the plain, war of Goya-esque disasters and proportions raged between slaves and Frenchmen. Early in this confused struggle Boukman was taken. The

French beheaded him on the Place d'Armes at the Cap, where, after his body had been burned, his head, impaled on a pike, glared sightlessly at the hated *blancs*.

Jeannot, most ferocious among the slaves, succeeded Boukman. Describing Jeannot's army, a young Frenchman wrote home:

> His troop numbered about 6000, some naked, some in tatters, and some grotesquely draped in rich apparel taken from our wardrobes. They were armed with guns, knives, sticks, and all the sharp utensils of kitchen and farm. As artillery they had 15 cannon taken from our villages where they had served as alarm guns, and mounted them on carts as improvised gun carriages. Their musicians made a hideous din beating caldrons - all this as accompaniment to the accustomed shrieks of African warriors.

Jeannot was the ex-slave of a brutal planter named Bullet, and his sadism toward white prisoners was legendary. Procureur Gros, a French notary captured by the slaves; described the fate of Berchais, his commander taken at the same time: "Jeannot first chopped off one hand, and then triced him to a ladder, where he received two hundred lashes; afterward, they hauled him to Grande Rivière, where he was hung up to a stake by a hook through his chest. He lasted thirty-six hours and when Jeannot finally finished him off, he was still gasping."

Jeannot's savageries sickened Jean-François and Biassou, his fellow leaders. One night in October, Jean-François surrounded his camp, took Jeannot prisoner, and, after a "trial" at Dondon, tied him to a tree and shot him. Then, in Jeannot's own fashion, they hung the corpse up by a meat hook and vanished into the darkness.

But the rebels were not all slave nor all *noirs*. In the East at Ouanaminthe, *hommes de couleur* led by one of their own, Candy (who plucked out his victims' eyes with a corkscrew) armed themselves from Ogé's caches. Overrunning St. Suzanne and nearby Trou du Nord by late September, Candy suborned the *maréchaussée,* who turned coat and murdered their French officers. Two months' hopeless resistance ensued as, one by one, planters saw their estates pillaged. The day belonged to the French, but night was the slaves'. "Night and day," wrote a young planter, "we pursued an enemy who never awaited our approach save to harm us, was never found sleeping. Each tree, each hole, each piece of rock hid from our unseeing eyes a cowardly assassin who, if undiscovered, would emerge to pierce our breasts; but who fled or begged for mercy when we caught him face to face."

By November it was over, and the whites of Trou du Nord abandoned the remains of their coffee plantations and fell back toward the sea. The only Frenchman allowed to stay unmolested was the priest, Père Sulpice, Capuchin *Curé* of Trou.

Why was Père Sulpice permitted to remain? What was the role of the Church, if any, in the slave risings of 1791?

We know that at least five, and almost certainly several more, priests stayed at their posts and remained in the slaves' lines and acted in effect as chaplains, a role not different from their former one as *curés des noirs.* It has been speculated - the evidence is dim, even in Church annals - that certain priests hoped to maintain a Catholic, royalist presence among the slaves whom they saw in rebellion against a Jacobin, regicide regime in Paris. We also know that sympathy for oppressed slaves was one reason the Jesuits had been expelled from the colony in 1763.

There were other whites, mostly *petits blancs,* who stayed or were forced to stay among the slaves. These provided some military skills but mainly served as letter-writers in later negotiations between slaves and French. Gros, the notary, who wrote the only account of life in the rebel camps, came through unharmed.

France Must Renounce All Hope

Compounded by the political divisions of revolutionary France, the heaped-up racial and social divisions of St. Domingue had brought about indescribable confusion. While the vitals of the colony were being clawed apart by slave rebellion in the North, uprisings by *hommes de couleur* flamed in the West and South. To understand these events we must return to Paris and the National Assembly.

The Assembly's Declaration of the Rights of Man put the notion of white supremacy on collision course with that of racial equality. Although, when faced with the practicalities of abolishing the color line, the Assembly wavered, the men of 1789 were adamant. Thus, when word reached Paris in 1791 that the white colonists had revenged themselves so terribly on Ogé and Chavannes (both well known to the *Amis des Noirs*), the shock resembled that in Washington, 170 years later, brought about by atrocities perpetrated on civil rights workers in Mississippi and Alabama.

Impassioned by the martyrdom of Ogé and Chavannes, the National Assembly decreed, on 15 May 1791, that *gens de couleur* born to free parents were to be admitted to Colonial or Parish assemblies. The next day the colonial delegates from St. Domingue stalked out of the Chamber. As soon as this news reached St. Domingue, the colonists replied by electing their all-white Colonial Assembly, which convened at Léogane on 9 August 1791.

Intent on holding the color line and defying revolution in France, the delegates could not realize that a fortnight would see the North in flames and the South and West on the brink of civil war.

Yet grim logic trapped the white supremacists of St. Domingue. De Wimpffen had written a French friend in 1789, "Your colonies cannot exist without slavery." Less than two years later, the man who knew St. Domingue better than any other Frenchman, Moreau de Saint-Méry, was even more explicit: "If our slaves once suspect there is power other than their masters which holds the final disposition of their fate; if they once see that the *mulâtres* have successfully invoked this power and by its aid have become our equals - then France must renounce all hope of preserving her colonies."

Moreau spoke only what was on every white tongue. The Provincial Assembly at the Cap had a year before bluntly memorialized the National Assembly: "St. Domingue will never sacrifice her indispensable prejudice regarding the *mulâtres* . . . As for the *noirs,* the colony will never suffer this sort of property, which it holds by law, to be called into question."

Thus did the planters defend their "particular institution" and, come what might, hewed to this line until white St. Domingue crashed down about their heads.

Between the upper millstone of the French Revolution and the nether millstone of slave insurrection, the colonists had lost sight of the necessity to present a united front. In the West, even before the May decree and the revolt of the *noirs,* the whites were virtually at war. The royal governor and planters supported the Crown and the *ancien regime.* The *petits blancs,* like their cousins in Paris, rallied to the National Assembly, the red cap of liberty, and the rights of man.

In August 1790, regular troops led by a resolute royalist, Chevalier Mauduit, had marched up the highway from Port-au-Prince to St. Marc and unseated the Colonial Assembly. At the point of Mauduit's bayonets a rump of St. Marc delegates had been packed aboard the frigate *Léopard,* riding in the bay, and sent to France to seek redress from the National Assembly.

The Assembly's rejoinder - not to the grievances of St. Marc as much as in general concern over the mounting disturbance of St. Domingue - had been to send more troops to the colony. A battalion each of the Regiments of Artois and Normandy had reached Port-au-Prince on 3 March 1791. Within forty-eight hours, already infected with revolution in France, these units had mutinied and brought over Mauduit's people to their side. Mauduit, recounts Bryan Edwards, "offered his bosom to their swords - it was pierced with a hundred wounds." Then the French troops hacked off their colonel's genitals and delivered them in a box to the high-born lady who had been his dearest friend.

Thus it happened that during that summer of 1791 the whites of the West and Cul-de-Sac had become a microcosm of revolutionary France. The capital, Port-au-Prince, had fallen to the mob, while the plantation countryside, like the Vendée and Gironde in France, stood for the Crown and property - which in St. Domingue also meant slavery and the color line.

At this moment, property and slavery were quite as important to the rich *mulâtre* planters as to their white neighbors, and, following the revolt of the *noirs* in the North, an alliance, known as "the concordat," was forged between white and *mulâtre* landowners of the Cul-de-Sac against the white revolutionary canaille of Port-au-Prince. The mainspring of the concordat was white acceptance - nominal though it might be - of the May decree admitting *mulâtres* to the franchise. Aside from mutual self-interest, what precipitated the concordat was the evident determination of the *gens de couleur* to enforce their rights.

On 7 August, at the same time as Boukman and the *noirs* of the North were plotting, Pierre Pinchinat, of St. Marc, was chosen leader of the *mulâtres* in a meeting at Mirebalais.

Two weeks later, on 20 August at Nerette (just below where Pétionville is today), an armed clash occurred between *hommes de couleur,* who had assembled at Habitation Diègue, and white planters going down the road to Port-au-Prince. The *mulâtres* thereupon pulled back across the Cul-de-Sac to Trou Cayman, at the foot of the road leading down from Mirebalais. When another French column sortied from Port-au-Prince, the *gens de couleur,* led by Louis-Jacques Bauvais and a talented young officer named Alexandre Pétion,(5) advanced to meet them at Pernier (two miles East of what was, until 1994, the Académie Militaire), where the French were again thrown back.

These developments, not solicitude for *mulâtre* political rights, prompted the French to work out the concordat and, for the moment, to restore peace.

But the marriage of convenience was annulled by another inconsistent, impulsive decision in Paris. On 24 September 1791, alarmed by continuing bad news from the colony - of slave revolt, civil conflict, of rebellion against France itself - the National Assembly again reversed itself and revoked the 15 May decree, which had granted political rights to the *mulâtres.*

Now in their turn the *gens de couleur* were as outraged as the white planters and the Club Massiac had been in May.

Think This Over

The explosion of the *hommes de couleur* in the West and Candy's insurrection in the North ought not to have taken the *colons* unaware.

In October 1791 du Rouvray and Touzard, the two experienced soldiers who had assumed command of the campaign to put down the slaves, warned the Colonial Assembly of the facts of life:

What is the white population (asked du Rouvray) compared to the hordes of slaves in revolt? Don't we have enough of the latter for enemies without also provoking the *gens de couleur?* But, you will say, do we have to give way before the threats of an inferior caste and grant them full civil rights, as blackmail for the trouble they can make? Yes, gentlemen. Expediency is going to have to stifle resentment because you are not going to bring France around . . . But even if matters were entirely in your hands and France had no misgivings, I don't hesitate to say that whatever they might send would be insufficient. Six thousand troops won't restore peace. In three months out here, the climate would kill the majority. Don't overlook history . . . In 1756 the English wanted to take Cuba . . . 18,000 troops debarked; six months later they had barely 1800. . . Think this over. It is not very hard to apply the same lesson here.

Rising to second du Rouvray, Touzard hammered home each point with the stump of the arm he had lost in America:

For three months the campaign against the slaves has gone on. In spite of all successes we are farther behind than on the opening day . . . We are up against an enemy whose principal, I would even say only, resource is the ability to keep ahead of us. Only in snapping at their heels with flying columns that threaten them every minute and run them down everywhere, can you hope to subdue them. Where is the army that can do this? Where are you going to find fight cavalry for such a campaign? Troops properly acclimated, hardened against fatigue, immune to the insalubrities of the air and climate - soldiers you can garrison, feed, equip, without difficulty and without special gear - *are any other such available except mulâtres?* No. All right then, why do you reject the help they can provide? Do you want them among our enemies or would you rather have them in the ranks of our defenders?

Had these two practical men - each a landowner as well as soldier -been listened to, history in St. Domingue might have taken a different course.

Kill, Sack, Burn

When, in November 1791, word of the National Assembly's turnabout reached St. Domingue, it was the West's turn to explode. On 22 November, under Bauvais, *mulâtre* troops on Bel Air hill attacked the white townsmen of Port-au-Prince. By sunrise next day the city was in flames. Driven from town after fierce street fighting, the soldiers began to put the torch to buildings on their line of retreat. In the heart of the city the mob pillaged, plundered, burned, and killed. Around the outskirts, reinforced from Jacmel, Léogane, and all the Cul-de-Sac, furious *hommes de couleur* laid siege to the wasted town, cutting off its water supply and all food - the townsmen, reported a merchant captain on return to France, "living on salt meat and putrid water."

These were terrible events in Port-au-Prince, but those elsewhere in the West were worse. Everywhere, enraged *hommes de couleur* turned on former white allies, rightly judging them to support the 24 September decree. As in the North, hideous atrocities were the order of the day. White ears were sliced off and worn as cockades; live infants were thrown as food to hogs; and the bellies of pregnant women were ripped open.(6)

At Jacmel, as in Port-au-Prince, bitter fighting left the town in ruins. Battles took place at Bainet and Saltrou. André Rigaud, who had learned his trade as an infantryman at Savannah, blockaded the Bizoton approaches of Port-au-Prince with *mulâtres* from the South. Even the remote Southern peninsula flamed up. Here *hommes de couleur*, like Boukman's *noirs* in the North, scourged planters from the countryside into Les Cayes and surrounded the town. In December, St. Louis du Sud fell while slave-owners, *mulâtre* and white alike, armed slaves to fight each other. So reinforced, French planters of the Grande-Anse put down the *hommes de couleur* in fighting replete with atrocities such as this described by Edwards: "In the neighborhood of Jérémie a body of *[mulâtres]* attacked the house of M. Sejourné, and secured the persons both of him and his wife. This unfortunate woman (my hand trembles while I write!) was far advanced in her pregnancy. The monsters, whose prisoner she was, having first murdered her husband in her presence, ripped her up alive and threw the infant to the hogs - They then (how shall I relate it!) sewed up the head of the murdered husband in - !!!"

While *gens de couleur* fought whites, and armed slaves fought both, *marron* bands began to creep away into the hills. In the mountains behind Léogane, for example, Romaine, a Spanish *mulâtre*, heard the voice of God amid the tumults, consecrated himself to the Virgin as "Romaine-la-Prophetesse," and gathered together a congregation of *marrons*, who hacked, sacked, and slew in the name of the saints.

Ruins, Solitude, and Scattered Bones

As 1792 dawned, the situation was as follows: In the North, where slaves and some *mulâtres* (Candy and his band) were fighting whites, an uneasy stalemate held along the cordons established by du Rouvray. In the West, *hommes de couleur*, after initially siding with whites of the Cul-de-Sac against the town *canaille*, were now attacking all whites impartially but still held down their slaves. In the South, whites were leading armed slaves against *mulâtres*, and more and more *noirs* were splintering away into *marronage* in the hills.

To cool this seething furnace, there had arrived from France, on 29 November 1791, three commissioners sent by the National Assembly: Frédéric-Ignace de Mirbeck, Philippe-Rose Roume, and Edmond de Saint-Léger. These men, in no way whatever prepared for the convulsion that awaited them at the

Cap, were stunned.

Because the commissioners had first set foot in the North, which was (or had been) the most prosperous region of the colony, their first efforts were directed in this area. Hardly had they arrived when an opportunity arose that may well have been the last hope for French St. Domingue: Boukman's successors, Jean-François and Biassou, proposed a deal to end the slave insurrection in the North. Evincing a readiness to betray followers that students of Haitian politics would come to recognize, the two chieftains (no doubt in language drafted by Gros or one of the priests) described the slaves as "a host of *noirs* from the African coast who for the most part do not know two words of French yet who have been warriors in their homeland." Then, continued the letter, if the commissioners would simply grant freedom to a few hundred *gros nègres,* themselves included, they would guarantee to deliver the slaves back into bondage, and the revolt would be over.

Shaken by the situation they had found, the commissioners were overjoyed. On 21 December, through the offices of Touzard, a parley between the commissioners and Jean-François was arranged at Habitation St. Michel, outside the Cap near Petite-Anse. As an earnest of good faith, Jean-François brought in and returned a group of French prisoners, but the meeting did not go well. Bullet, former master of the late Jeannot, lashed out in anger with a horsewhip at Jean-François; the latter, though armed with a pistol, flinched in submission. The habits of servitude were still strong. Yet the parley ended on a better note. The slaves would send envoys to Cap Français to negotiate a general pacification.

When the slave leaders entered, the bar of the assembly was decked in black, signifying mourning, and scarlet, for vengeance. The atmosphere was one of hauteur and contempt, which left no room for negotiation, and the assembly's treatment of the commissioners, who were aghast at the proceedings, was hardly better. Their prestige with the slaves thus demolished, they were now informed that the assembly deemed them mere "intercessors," without authority. Saint-Léger and Mirbeck thereupon went home in April 1792, while Roume, who had involved himself in the politics of the Cap, decided to stay on.

The slaves' response was a new burst of fury. In a fierce night attack on January 22d, Biassou burst into the Cap itself to rescue his mother, a slave in the hospital of the Holy Fathers. Then he killed the patients in their beds, cut his way out, and returned in triumph to the hills. And there was worse news: the Northwest peninsula, until now undisturbed, erupted in revolt, and the flames of burning habitations reddened the sky as far as Môle St. Nicolas.

An unforeseen by-product of collapse of the negotiations and armistice was that Candy (". . . the horrible Candy -what a face! what eyes!" wrote a Frenchman), was induced to change sides and, with his people, fought well. At Jacquézy, near Terrier Rouge, with 600 *affranchis,* Candy gave Jean-François one of the latter's few serious beatings. In treating with Candy while scorning Jean-François and Biassou, it is hard not to surmise, the Colonial Assembly seemed willing to accord *gens de couleur* terms and consideration it refused to *noirs* whose offenses had been no different.

Mirbeck and Saint-Léger, their mission a failure, were still at sea, en route home, when another - and this time final - change of mind overcame the National Assembly in Paris. On 4 April 1792, less than a year from the guillotine, Louis XVI gave royal assent to a Jacobin decree that unequivocally granted full and equal political rights to all *gens de couleur* and free *noirs* in St. Domingue. Three new commissioners and 6000 soldiers were to be sent to the colony to enforce the decree. The troops, under a young and energetic general, Etienne Maynard Laveaux, were hand-picked for political reliability, not only to restore order but to deal with the royalist formations that still garrisoned the North. There, under Colonel de Cambefort, the veteran regiment "Le Cap," reinforced by two Irish battalions (perennial foreign legion of the Kings of France), were stoutly loyal to the ancien regime.

Word of the decree reached St. Domingue in May. Within four months, on 18 September, the Jacobin commissioners and their army landed at Cap Français.

The commissioners were Etienne Polverel; Léger-Felicité Sonthonax; and an aged colleague, Ailhaud, a person of no importance who soon returned to France. Polverel, though a fiery Jacobin, was a mature man of principle and honesty, which could be not said for Sonthonax. The latter, a twenty-nine-year-old Girondin lawyer and one of the most ferocious *"enragés"* of the French Revolution, was prepared to lie, betray, consign to the Terror and the guillotine, and line his own pockets in the process. All these things he did in St. Domingue. But Sonthonax had one principle he would never betray: he was devoted to the abolition of slavery. It was not for nothing that in 1791 he had written, "The lands of St. Domingue should belong to the blacks. They have earned them with the sweat of their brow."

This was the state of affairs that confronted these latest commissioners. After thirteen months of slave insurrection in the North, the countryside around the Cap was a devastated no man's land - "ruins, solitude, and scattered bones," recorded a Créole who traversed it. Toward the East, Ouanaminthe, Fort Dauphin, Terrier Rouge, and Trou du Nord were again, thanks to Candy, under French control.

The West - with the exception of Port-au-Prince - was largely royalist and more or less stabilized. Jacmel and Léogane had both known fire and violence but were relatively calm. Back in the mountains the *marrons* of Bahoruco, led by one Hyacinthe, had been augmented by runaways from all quarters and were again ravaging the Cul-de-Sac. Hyacinthe's targets were plantations owned by *gens de couleur* to whom - as members of the old *maréchaussée* - the black *marrons* owed many a score. (Like Biassou and other *noir* chieftains, Hyacinthe relied heavily on magic, especially a bull's tail that he always carried: its property was to turn aside French bullets and change cannonballs into dust.)

The hommes de couleur of the South had raised *noir* slaves against white planters, who had armed their slaves, too. Since August 1792, several thousand *noirs* had occupied Les Platons, a formidable escarpment fifteen miles Northwest of Cayes, and were laying waste the fertile plain below. When Blanchelande, the governor, personally took the field against them, his three columns were successively ambushed, defeated in detail, and pushed back into Cayes. (For Blanchelande the worst was yet to come: soon afterward he was recalled to Paris and was guillotined in 1793).

The planters in the South were nevertheless winning their fight. But the cost was heavy; the Gôaves and the Plaine des Cayes were laid waste. St. Domingue was near anarchy. White planters defied the decree of 4 April; the *petits blancs* of the Cap and Port-au-Prince hated the planters. *Hommes de couleur* hated all whites but wanted *noir* slaves kept down. The slaves hated all, biding their time in some localities, mindlessly slaying in others.

The *gens de couleur* ("Citizens of April Fourth," Sonthonax called them) were the natural allies of the Jacobin commissioners. With their aid and with the fresh regiments from France, Sonthonax vigorously attacked Jean-François and Biassou and advanced the cordons higher into the mountains. In the West, Polverel beat down the royalists of the Cul-de-Sac, established control over Port-au-Prince, and, with Sonthonax, once and for all split the *mulâtre* planters away from the royalist whites.

Polverel and Sonthonax had subjugated the North and West, but the planters of the South still defied the decree of 4 April. The South, wrote Polverel to Paris on 22 January 1793, was "a sterile land where the seed of Revolution will not grow." To implant that seed, Polverel chose André Rigaud. With the French Republic's commission as general, Rigaud took command of the Legion d'Egalité, armed slaves who would earn freedom by a year of war against their former masters. Nothing more illuminates the intentions of the Jacobins than the creation of the legion.

The hard-fighting levies of the Grande-Anse proved too strong. At the fortified Habitation Desrivaux, near Pestel, on 19 June 1793, they fell upon Rigaud and cut his column to pieces. Leaving 300 dead, Rigaud abandoned the field. After the long retreat from Les Cayes, he somberly reported to the commissioners: "If you want any peace, you must deport half the white population of St. Domingue."

C'est la Fin du Monde

Sonthonax would never have left the Cap for Port-au-Prince in March 1793 had he not felt safe in doing so. Yet the preceding months had been unsettling. In January, mounting the scaffold to the roll of drums, Citizen Capet lost his head and St. Domingue its last French king. Ten days later, proclaiming "war of all peoples against all kings," France declared war on England and Holland. As the not surprising result of British diplomacy and coalition warfare, France soon found herself confronting Austria, Prussia, Portugal, and Spain.

If the commissioners were to set France's house in order in St. Domingue, time was short, and they had much to do. Sonthonax was not long absent before bad news began to reach him from the Cap. Despite General Laveaux's taut control, the situation seemed uneasy. On 29 March the general wrote: "Lose not an instant in returning . . . We fear a violent explosion."

Laveaux's fears had already found an echo in Paris. Only too well aware that St. Domingue lay between the jaws of British Jamaica and Spanish Santo Domingo, the National Assembly had decided that the colony needed a well-qualified senior soldier on the scene. Their choice, a cool-headed regular, Thomas-François Galbaud, a gunner with no interest in politics, had been born in Port-au-Prince and, on his mother's death in 1792, had come into properties at Léogane and Dame Marie. Galbaud pwas appointed governor and was told to defend St. Domingue and leave politics to the commissioners.

Like many simple instructions from distant authority, Galbaud's proved, on the spot, anything but simple to execute. Arriving at the Cap from France on 7 May, he found Laveaux sick and the North in chaos. Government depots were empty, the treasury drained dry by the commissioners, troops unpaid and recalcitrant.

The proceedings that seemed so necessary to Galbaud during the next four weeks had two effects. They won unanimous support from the propertied, conservative (and therefore royalist) elements of the Cap; and, for that reason, aroused first the disapproval, then the fear and anger, of Sonthonax and Polverel. Occupied though they were with subjugating Port-au-Prince and the Cul-de-Sac, and organizing Rigaud's expedition into the Grande-Anse, the commissioners nonetheless marched North with 200 French infantry, 400 *hommes de couleur,* and a mounted support of Orleans Dragoons. Their colonel was a resolute *mulâtre,* Antoine Chanlatte, who had fought well under Polverel in the West.

On 10 June, as Citizens of April Fourth cheered and French colonists peered silently from their windows, the commissioners and their soldiers entered the Cap. Boucher, their man in the North, had already told the commissioners of

Galbaud's doings. Galbaud, said Boucher, had aligned himself with the *anciens colons,* had raised the money he needed by illegal transactions with American merchants, and had demonstrated open contempt for the authority of the commissioners. At Government House, Sonthonax and Polverel confronted the general. Characteristically, Sonthonax demanded to know the basis of the new governor's authority. Galbaud produced his commission, an imposing brevet drafted, Sonthonax broke out, "in the high old style of Louis Fourteenth or Ferdinand the Catholic", and signed in Paris for the convention by no less an authority than Clavière, its president.

With disdain Sonthonax handed back the parchment. His lawyer's eye had caught a fatal flaw: that very decree of 4 April that Sonthonax knew so well also disqualified any colonial proprietor in the Americas from governance in St. Domingue. Coldly the commissioners reminded Galbaud of his new inheritance at Léogane and Dame Marie.

The general might have saved his remonstrances; the Jacobins had already made up their minds. Galbaud's commission was void; his actions illegal. Three days later, in a scathing proclamation drafted by Sonthonax, the commissioners formally annulled all Galbaud had done: "We are constrained without regret to accede to [Galbaud's] wish to return to France. We have had no occasion to pass judgment on his military talent or his Republicanism. We know nothing of him save his instructions formally countermanding our orders, his perfidious schemes to raise a faction in the North against the Republic . . . his inimical and absurd measures, which were bound to produce famine and deplete the public credit . . ."

This having been said, the commissioners placed Galbaud under arrest and, with his brother and adjutant general, César Galbaud, sent him under guard on board, the transport *La Normandie* for return to France.

The French squadron in the bay was a powerful one. Once afloat, Galbaud took his commission to the two admirals (Cambis and Gersey) and, with their assent, to the sailors. On the 19th, proclaimed governor commandant of the land and naval forces, the general was rowed through the fleet while seamen manned the yards and cheered, *"Vive la République! Vive Galbaud!"*

Next day, as the afternoon heat of June began to beat down on Cap Français, a blue flag was hoisted to the forepeak of *Jupiter,* and a signal gun boomed from the flagship. From every ship, boats went into the water and armed men clambered down the sides. Galbaud was returning ashore at the head of 1200 sailors reinforced by 800 loyalist deportees Sonthonax had clapped aboard ship as well as 200 young cavaliers from the town. One unit was commanded by Gauvain, a royalist leader at the Cap, the other by the general's brother.

In the narrow streets leading to Government House (where Sonthonax had effaced the Fleur-de-Lys and crown), Gauvain's column collided with

Chanlatte's *mulâtres* and the commissioners' *Garde Nationale.* A furious fight ensued. Grapeshot from the commissioners' bronze cannon scythed down the attackers. Meanwhile, in house-to-house fighting, César Galbaud's people flanked the defenders and threatened Government House until the sailors stumbled on a wine cellar and the attack disintegrated. As fighting became general, Citizens of April Fourth rose to defend the commissioners, white royalists rallied to Galbaud, and masterless slaves pillaged. César Galbaud fell into the hands of the commissioners. Polverel's son was taken by a band of cutlass-swinging sailors. When Galbaud proposed an exchange, Polverel replied that the boy knew his duty and was ready to die if need be.

At dawn on the 21st, Galbaud landed his reserve from afloat, and secured the royal arsenal and harbor forts, whose French artillerists joined the counter-revolutionaries. By noon the commissioners and their troops were in retreat to Bréda plantation on the Haut du Cap, where Laveaux's republicans still manned the cordon.

But the royalist victory was short. During the night the Jacobins had managed to communicate with the slave leaders beyond the cordons. Their message was simple: any *noir* who takes up arms for the republic will be free. Biassou and Jean-François suspected a trap and held back. A third leader, Macaya, accepted, bringing with him 3000 slaves armed with machetes, scythes, bows, fowling pieces, and pikes. On Macaya's heels came Pierrot, with thousands more. How many slaves swarmed down from the hills, no one will ever know. Some accounts go as high as 10,000.

As Macaya and Pierrot burst into the Cap, the slaves of the town joined the slaves of the hills. The city was theirs. Fires broke out; pillage was universal. To escape slaughter, torture, and rape, the townspeople fled with what they could carry to the quays, where Galbaud's troops, unable to stem the *noir* onrush, could at least protect the landings. Gazing down from the cordons on the heights, republican soldiers and the remaining planters saw the columns of smoke and flame rising from the city and realized, to their horror, that Cap Français at last belonged to the slaves.

The most Galbaud could do was to spike the guns of the forts and dump the remaining ammunition in the harbor. Then, after some 10,000 emigres had been crammed on board the warships and merchantmen in the bay, he sadly re-embarked aboard *Jupiter,* and, on the 23d, while flames still rolled through the corpse-ridden town, the ships weighed anchor, not for France but for the capes of the Chesapeake and exile.

As for Sonthonax and Polverel, they stayed aloof at Bréda while, for five days, Macaya and Pierrot had a free hand in the ruins. Only on 26 June did they move to restore order, to burn the dead by heaps in the public squares, and group the newly freed slaves into battalions designated *Liberté, Egalité,* and (looking over their shoulders toward Paris) *Convention Nationale.* As the new units *("régénéres,"* Sonthonax called them) were given muskets, Sonthonax thundered: "These are your liberty! If you want to keep it, make good use of these weapons on the day when the white leaders tell you to turn them in. Such demands will infallibly portend your return to slavery."

When news of the holocaust reached the du Rouvrays in New York, where they had been living in exile since January, the marquise wrote her daughter (herself a fugitive in Dusseldorf from the Terror), *"C'est la fin du monde, mon enfant . . . "*(7)

The Evangel of France

The flames that consumed Cap Français signaled the end of white supremacy and slavery in St. Domingue. Sonthonax *("le tigre Sonthonax, "* wrote an emigre in Philadelphia), whom France had sent to enforce the convention's decree of 4 April 1792, had in effect substituted the Assembly's Declaration of the Rights of Man.

Literally this is what he did. On 29 August 1793, when the ruins of the Cap were barely cool, Sonthonax decreed that the Declaration be proclaimed in the shadow of the revolution's scarlet liberty cap on a pike, in every town and camp of St. Domingue:(8)

> Behold, Citizens, the Evangel of France! . . .The slave-drivers and cannibals are no more. Those whites who remain are friends of the law and the principles of France. The Republic desires liberty and equality among all men regardless of color: kings are content only amid slaves. The Republic adopts you among its children.

Then, having taken a step he knew to be irreversible, Sonthonax told the convention what he had done and superfluously asked its approval.

In law, the decree of 29 August applied only to the North. Polverel in the West (who had not been consulted) knew better. Angry though he was, and dubious as to practical consequences, he had no option but to concur, and at Port-au-Prince on 22 September he proclaimed liberty for the slaves of the South and West.

Sonthonax's decree reverberated like thunder.

On 15 Pluviose (3 February 1794) there arrived in Paris a symbolic delegation from St. Domingue, whose election Sonthonax had arranged. One member, Dufay, was a white Jacobin; the second, Mills, was an *homme de couleur;* and the third, a *noir,* was Jean-Baptiste Belley-Mars, who, as one of Sonthonax's officers, had fought Galbaud at the Cap, and was to be the progenitor of Haiti's most distinguished anthropologist.

At the bar of the National Convention the three delegates received the fraternal embrace of the president and were seated amid tumultuous applause. Next day, as recorded in *Le Moniteur Officiel,* the following took place:

> LEVASSEUR (of Sarthe). I demand that the Convention . . . decree from this moment that slavery is abolished throughout the territory of the Republic. I demand that all men be free without distinction as to color . . .
> The Assembly rises by acclamation.
> The President pronounces the abolition of slavery to the plaudits and thousandfold cries of *Vive la République! Vive la Convention!* . . .
> The two colored deputies mount the tribune and embrace. (Applause) Lacroix conducts them to the President, who gives them the kiss of brotherhood. They are successively embraced by every deputy.

Amid this tableau "a citizeness of color" faints with joy. On motion of Cambon, a member of the convention, she is revived and conducted to a seat of honor on the left of Vadier, the president, where, *Le Moniteur* records, she dries the tears produced by the affecting scene.

FOOTNOTES - CHAPTER 2

1. The Provincial Assembly at the Cap, not to be confused with the Colonial Assembly first at St. Marc and then Léogane, was a rump body that, in contradistinction to the latter, recognized the French National Assembly as the source of final authority. The latter answered only to the Crown.
2. Some question remains to this day whether the *Cérémonie Bois Cayman* can properly be called a Voodoo service. Unquestionably, Voodoo forms were followed, some say to bind the oaths and underscore the solemnity of the enterprise, others saying that the Voodoo masked the congregation of conspirators. Conceivably, very likely in fact, both speculations are true.
3. No scribe wrote this down as Boukman pronounced it. There are numerous versions in Créole, handed down traditionally, of which this is a synthesis.
4. Priests with the slaves included Père Bienvenu, curé of Marmelade (who gave Jeannot the last rites before execution); Abbé Boucher of Terrier Rouge; Abbé Osmond of Ouanaminthe; Père Sulpice of Trou; and Abbé de la Haye of Dondon. All were bitterly traduced by the white *colons* and shown no mercy when caught: the unnamed *curé* of Limbé was said to have been hanged by Touzard, who, when he retook the town, rescued eighty women and children who denounced the priest as their betrayer. (But might he not have been their preserver? Priests in many instances restrained the slaves.) Haitians remember de la Haye as devoted and saintly, but French records say he was taken in 1793, accompanied by a mistress, and jailed at the Cap. One account says he was drowned by the French in 1803; another, that he lies buried near his old church, beside Père le Pers and Clervaux, in Dondon.

5. Alexandre Sabès Pétion was born in Port-au-Prince on 2 April 1770, son of a free *mulâtresse* and a Frenchman (who withheld his name because the child was too dark). The name Pétion came from the French-patois nickname *"Pichoun"* (my little one), bestowed by a foster mother. Although he learned the trade of goldsmith, the boy was fascinated by the soldiers of the garrison and enlisted in the militia at the age of eighteen.

6. With considerable documentation, American historian Lothrop Stoddard asserts that these assaults against pregnant women amounted almost to a practice during the revolts in the West and South.

7. The Marquis du Rouvray had fallen on evil times. In the same letter, the marquise confided that he was keeping an English mistress *"qui lui avait donné une très vilaine maladie."*

8. Sonthonax also chose this moment, propitious, he thought, to introduce the guillotine to St. Domingue. Setting one up in Port-au-Prince, he executed an unfortunate royalist named Pélou. The sight so unnerved those watching that they pulled it down like a goal post, and the guillotine was never employed again.

Slaves revolt, massacre owners, and sack plantations of the North. *Library of Congress*

French Revolution playing-card depicts armed slave of St. Domingue. *Yale University* RIGHT: Toussaint Louverture, who led the world's only successful slave revolt. *Library of Congress*

CHAPTER 3

I Am Toussaint Louverture

1794-1801

Cet homme fût une Nation . . .
- Lamartine

IN 1794, as the Terror in France subsided into the Directory, St. Domingue presented a tempting prize to the enemies of France. What those who so clearly recognized the vulnerability of France's richest colony could not perceive was that forces were stirring that in the end would place St. Domingue beyond the rule of France and outside the grasp of any white man - governor, king, or consul - then alive or to be born.

Britain and Spain Intervene

When the Revolution proclaimed war against all kings, the latter were not slow to reciprocate.

Ever since 1791 the British government had been entertaining feelers from royalist emigres who sought to bring St. Domingue under the Union Jack. As in most emigre causes the going was uphill: what was of passionate, obsessive concern to exiled planters of St. Domingue held only the slightest interest for England so long as peace obtained.

But the war was less than a month old before the British cabinet remembered St. Domingue and, within four months, General Adam Williamson, governor general of Jamaica, was authorized to accept submission to the Crown of districts that might so propose. To ensure that submissions would be forthcoming, Vernault de Charmilly, a Grande-Anse emigre, was smuggled from Jamaica into Jérémie. Meanwhile, General Williamson prepared plans and forces for an expedition.

Spain had been fishing in the French colony's troubled waters ever since Boukman's rising in the North.(1) Even before, the Spaniards had established a *cordon sanitaire* from Montecristi to Lascahobas with the dual purpose of containing rebellion on the French side of the border and of according support to aggrieved royalist subjects of His Most Catholic Majesty's cousin in the

Tuileries. In line with the latter purpose the captain general of Santo Domingo, Don Joaquin García y Moreno, sent arms and ammunition to Biassou (who, after all, was fighting a republican France) and, for the same reason, to Hyacinthe and the *marrons* of Bahoruco.

The events of 1793 therefore merely focused a Spanish policy toward French St. Domingue that was in fact mainly limited by Spain's military disarray along the frontier. Nonetheless, in the same month that the cabinet in London was giving General Williamson a free hand in St. Domingue, Don Joaquin presented Jean-François and Biassou fancy dress gold-lace uniforms, received their submission, and breveted them, respectively, "General and Admiral of the Reunited Troops" and "Generalissimo of the Conquered Territories."

Having at that moment been opportunely assured that, among all kings of the world arrayed against the French Republic, the "King of the Congo" had duly taken his place, the two *noir* chieftains warmly pledged allegiance to Madrid. In July, gorged with the plunder of Cap Français, Macaya yielded to the same arguments and joined his fellows under the banner of Castille. When Polverel attempted to woo him back, Macaya replied, "I am the subject of three kings: of the King of the Congo, master of all *noirs;* of the King of France, who represents my father: of the King of Spain, who represents my mother. These three Kings are the descendants of those who, led by a star, came to adore God made Man."

Rather more shortly, Jean-François and Biassou dismissed Sonthonax's overtures on similar grounds: "Since the beginning of the world we have obeyed the will of a king. We have lost the King of France but we are dear to him of Spain, who constantly shows us reward and assistance. We therefore cannot recognize you until you have enthroned a king."

Another *noir* leader whose star was rising was Toussaint, the coachman-veterinarian of Bréda (now coming to be known as "Louverture"(2). In February 1793 he, too, adhered to Spain. His reason was probably the realistic consideration drily stated by Père Cabon, Haiti's priestly historian: Toussaint felt that the propositions of kings were somewhat more solid than those of the Republic.

Thus Spanish policy seemed ready-made for the fall of the North in 1793. By early July more than a thousand French regulars and white national guards had deserted to Spain. The Cordon of the West had gone with them, and so had most of the Eastern cordon. The entire French naval station at the Cap - ships, shore establishment, and crews - had sailed for America.

On 17 July the Spaniards occupied Dondon; on the 28th, Ouanaminthe went over. Nine days later, Toussaint led his already well disciplined bands into Marmelade. Fort Liberté (formerly Fort Dauphin; Port-au-Prince had, by a similar change, become Port Républicain) was invested by land. But Candy, whom Sonthonax had charged with its defense, showed no signs of surrender.

Despairing of the North, the Jacobin Sonthonax on 8 October departed to join Polverel in the West. Behind, he left Laveaux with a provisional appointment as governor. Laveaux, however, was ordered to withdraw from the charnel house of the Cap and concentrate his wrecked European battalions at Port-de-Paix. Cap Français would remain in the hands of Commandant Villatte, a *mulâtre* officer with an aggregation of "free companies," made up of former slaves from the Battalions of Liberty and Equality. The final orders Sonthonax gave Laveaux were to burn towns and plantations if forced to yield them and, all else failing, to take to the highest mountains ("the boulevards of Liberty," Sonthonax called them) and wage guerrilla war against Spanish, English, and loyalists alike.

Only ominous and imperative events could have compelled Sonthonax to abandon the North at a time when the Spaniards and their *noir* adherents were overrunning the province. On 20 September 1793, following signature of an agreement with the Grande-Anse planters in the far South, a British expeditionary force from Jamaica had occupied Jérémie to the peal of church bells and the roar of a royal salute to George III. The redcoats, reported Captain John Ford, R.N., the British commodore, "were received by the inhabitants with every demonstration of joy and fidelity." Forty-eight hours later, landing his troops, Ford received Môle St. Nicolas, with 200 guns and fortifications intact, from Major O'Farrell and the remaining 150 "Wild Geese" of the Dillon Irish Regiment, who since January no longer had a French king to serve and asked only to be put ashore in America.

It was to contain the British within the arid Northwest that Sonthonax ordered Laveaux to concentrate at Port-de-Paix, while he himself hastened to rally the South and West.

The British Advance

The understanding between Britain and Spain was that Spain was to have a free hand in the North, the Upper Artibonite, and hinterlands of the West, while the British would take the South, the Northwest, and the Western shore of Haiti's great gulf. The political arrangements were simple: laws of France under the *ancien régime* would be observed in full force except as regarded slavery, concerning which the British and Spanish, who still retained it, would substitute their own existing variations. Precise delineation of boundaries and other such matters would be left for the peace conference. As Fall wore on in 1793 the Spanish had all but accomplished their objectives while the British and their new French subjects were rapidly moving to attain theirs.

Save for a setback in October, when Rigaud's *mulâtres* stood them off in an attempt to take Tiburon, the British, swiftly closed in from the extremities toward Port-au-Prince in the center. Place after place submitted without a shot:

Jean Rabel, St. Marc, Arcahaie, and Léogane. But there was a cloud, and already it was larger, not smaller. than a man's hand. "That never-failing attendant on military expeditions in the West Indies," wrote Bryan Edwards, "the yellow or pestilential fever, raged with dreadful virulence, and so many, both of the seamen and soldiers, perished daily, that the survivors were stricken with astonishment and horror."

So General Williamson (who had assured London he could bring off the campaign with 877 troops on hand - at a time when, however disarrayed, the commissioners could muster nearly 20,000) put in his first request for replacements, and the first fatal piecemeal driblet was sent forward.

Meanwhile, Toussaint was heard from again. Driving a wedge between Laveaux and Villatte in December, he swept through the North, carrying Terre-Neuve, Acul, Limbé, Port-Margot, and even remote Le Borgne, one of the few parishes where slaves still toiled and plantations flourished. Then he swung South to Gonaïves, which received him with open arms, whereupon he reconcentrated on Marmelade and established headquarters under the flag of Spain.

On 2 February of the new year the British had better luck. After a brisk landing at Tiburon under hostile fire, they took the fort by storm. Tiburon and Môle St. Nicolas thus gave them control not only of the entire Gulf of Gonâve but, even more important, of the Windward Passage and the approaches to Jamaica.

The next fort to fall, on 19 February 1794, was l'Acul de Léogane, a position that commanded the roads to the South and to Jacmel. Here also a sharp fight took place: when the redcoats finally gained the ramparts the republican commander calmly sent an unfortunate *noir* down into the magazine with a flaming fagot and blew the place up in the attackers' faces.

Bombardopolis, a colony of Germans living, wrote Edwards, "in unambitious poverty" amid the rocky ledges South of the Môle,(3) would not accept the authority of Sonthonax but neither would it yield to Britain. With heavy losses (40 killed and wounded out of a 200-man column) the British tried and failed to take Bombarde and had to fall back on the Môle.

St. Domingue seemed lost to France.

In early January the Spaniards had taken Mirebalais from Bauvais. Petite Rivière de l'Artibonite had also fallen. On 28 January, surrounded by land and by sea, Candy was finally forced to yield Fort Liberté. No sooner was the Tricolor down than the Spaniards had Candy in chains and on his way to the mines of Mexico.(4)

Port Républicain (Port-au-Prince) still held out, but the British were secure on one side in Arcahaie and on the other at Léogane. And, as May 1794 dawned, a new British squadron and landing force were en route to St. Domingue to take the capital.

I Am Bent on Vengeance

The day Sonthonax proclaimed the liberation of the slaves, a shorter but equally historic proclamation was heard:

29 August 1793

Brothers and Friends,
I am Toussaint Louverture. My name has perhaps become known to you. I am bent on vengeance. I desire the establishment of Liberty and Equality in St. Domingue. I strive to bring them into being. Unite with us, brothers, and fight with us in the common cause. Your most obedient and humble servant,
TOUSSAINT LOUVERTURE

Toussaint was forty-seven years old. In the description by Dantès Bellegarde, as in likenesses that survive, he was "small, frail, very ugly." He had already come a long way from the stables at Bréda.

In the early days of the revolt in the North, Toussaint the veterinarian was all the surgeon Boukman, Jean-François, and Biassou had. Soon, however, by shrewdness, literacy, above all by insight into the ways and minds of the *blancs,* Toussaint had become military secretary to Biassou. They were an ill-assorted pair - the ascetic, inward-looking little coachman beside the lascivious *taffia*-drinking hulk of black ferocity - yet Toussaint was stronger.

In 1793, already leader of 600 *noirs,* Toussaint, with Biassou, had declared for Spain. Yet if we take his proclamation at true value, he had more profoundly declared for Haiti. When the cordons crumbled after the terrible days at the Cap, Toussaint had engaged French deserters to teach his *"congos"* the rudiments of tactics, drill, weapons, and discipline. Still under the Spanish flag, he himself selected and trained lieutenants whose names would be remembered: Maurepas, Dessalines, Clervaux, and Moyse. In the process he expanded his band to a trained regiment of 4000; no longer now a mere *chef de bande,* Toussaint became a colonel. Moreover, commander in his own right, he was receiving orders directly from the Spanish authorities rather than from Jean-François or Biassou. His headquarters were at Marmelade.(5)

By May 1794 the cause of the Republic seemed desperate. Villatte was blockaded at the Cap. His troops subsisted on oranges, sugar cane, and mangos. At Port-de-Paix, Laveaux's men would have starved but for provisions smuggled across the channel from La Tortue. Under siege in Les Cayes, Rigaud was living on potatoes and plantains. Laveaux reported: "We have been reduced to six ounces of bread a day . . . If we had powder we would rest easier. We have no shoes, shirts, clothes, soap or tobacco. Our soldiers mount guard barefooted. We have not even a flint to issue. "

At this moment of despair, on 6 May 1794, to be exact, having communicated secretly with Laveaux, Toussaint repaired to Marmelade. There, at the side of the Spanish commandant, he heard early mass. These devotions concluded, he mounted his horse, drew sword, unfurled the Tricolor of France and, at the head of his regiment and like-minded *noirs,* cut the throats of the Spanish garrison. Before the Spaniards had finished matins, Toussaint had restored to France Limbé, Acul, Dondon, Gros Morne, and Plaisance. When word of Toussaint's *volte-face* reached Paris, men remembered Danton's exultant prophecy of 1793: "The Englishman is dead!"

Toussaint's motives can only be guessed at; he has left no record. He must have opposed British and Spanish restoration of slavery just as he must have discountenanced Jean-François's practice of selling his own trouble makers into Spanish slavery. Moreover, the British had come to St. Domingue as allies of the white *colons* and *mulâtres.* Toussaint was a *noir.* Ambition, too, must have entered in: Toussaint could never hope to equal, let alone surpass, Jean-François or Biassou in the ranks of Spain. Laveaux had secretly promised that Toussaint, like Jean-François and Biassou, would be a general, too.

A consideration speaks for itself. That is the resolution, self-confidence, and sense of timing with which Toussaint acted (not to mention his secrecy, which detractors have called duplicity). All these qualities would appear and reappear.

Leaving covering forces at Marmelade and Plaisance, Toussaint marched across the mountains into the Artibonite. In a series of blows that would have done credit to Stonewall Jackson, he swooped on Biassou at Ennery, scattering Spanish units on the way, then veered toward the sea to capture Gonaïves, heaped high with supplies. When Jean-François pursued, Toussaint struck back like a coiled spring, capturing his opponent's headquarters intact: "He saved his shirt and breeches, nothing more," Toussaint told Laveaux. The Artibonite was his.

While Toussaint was reconquering the Artibonite for France, the British campaign reached high-water mark. On 4 June 1794, the English took Port-au-Prince.

The British first bombarded the fort at Bizoton, then put ashore 800 men at Lamentin. On the afternoon of 31 May in a deluge of rain, 60 Welsh grenadiers burst into the fort defended by the *mulâtre* Montbrun with 450 of the Legion of the West. In a flash of bayonets the grenadiers swept out the defenders and cleared the way to the city. The British took twenty-two merchant ships in the bay and got over £400,000 in prize money. Their first action was to erect a fort on a commanding hill behind the barnlike wooden cathedral of 1770. As Fort National it stands today.

Five days later, crossing South over the mountain ever after to bear the title "Morne des Commissaires," Sonthonax and Polverel fled to Jacmel. Sonthonax and Polverel had little opportunity to enjoy the clear air of Jacmel. Three days after their arrival, the corvette *L'Espérance* dropped anchor, bearing Robespierre's warrant for the commissioners' arrest and return to Paris to account for their stewardship. Before embarking, Polverel found time to write Rigaud. "It is no longer the *Commissaire* who writes you: Sonthonax and I have been recalled. You are the only man left in the colony who can frustrate these perfidious plots and assure the triumph of Liberty and restore the authority of the French people."

Polverel also mentioned Toussaint, though evidently without full knowledge of the little coachman's victories. Yet as *L'Espérance* dropped the hills of St. Domingue, Polverel must have understood that the country was finally in the hands of those who alone could truly save it: two Haitians, Toussaint, the *noir;* Rigaud, the *mulâtre.*

After God, Laveaux

Hardly was the Union Jack run up over Port-au-Prince than the noon of victory was overshadowed by the sickness that destroyeth in the noonday. Within sixty days after the city capitulated, General Whyte's returns showed 40 officers and 600 other ranks dead of the Yellow Jack. Of a replacement draft embarked from Guadeloupe 560 strong; on arrival at Port-au-Prince, 8 June, only 300 were alive to debark, and most of these died in the lazarettos ashore.

While Whyte was burying his dead and beginning to wonder what St. Domingue might cost in the end, the unconquered remainder of the colony was split three ways. *Mulâtre* generals, Rigaud in the South and Villatte at the Cap, held the extremities; Toussaint the *noir* had an iron grip on the center. Laveaux, nominally governor, was at Port-de-Paix but exercised scant control over Villatte, whose behavior was ever more independent. Laveaux and Villatte, whose enclaves Toussaint had reunited, roughly held the North and Northwest from Jean Rabel to Fort Liberté.

At this point everyone was fighting everyone else.

Hard hit though they were by sickness, the British remained strong. In September 1794 they repulsed Toussaint when he tried to take St. Marc. On 5 December, Fort Bizoton withstood three fierce attacks by Rigaud. Toussaint had by now immobilized the Spanish, and in September Rigaud had expelled the royalist French from Léogane.

At the start of 1795, Europe was resounding with the victories of republican France. Although the tired Spaniards in Santo Domingo did not yet know it, French columns were on the Ebro, and, with Robespierre headless on his own guillotine, the diplomats, gravely taking snuff at Basel, were discussing how the war might be ended. On 22 July 1794, arrangements between His Most Catholic Majesty and the Directory of the Republic were concluded: France was no longer at war with all kings, at least not Spain's; the French would return to their side of the Pyrenees, and Santo Domingo would be ceded to France as soon as the Republic could take possession. Meanwhile the Spaniards would hold the colony in fee for France.

Peace with Spain was advantageous to Toussaint. The armies of Biassou and Jean-François disbanded and many of their *congos* rallied to his standard. Biassou went to Spanish Florida, where he died in a brawl. Jean-François - who had made a good thing of campaigning - retired with his gold lace and jeweled court sword to Cadiz, where he enjoyed the willing favors of a succession of ladies.

Thus the campaign of 1795 and 1796 was against England alone. The British forces had declined to a sorry state. On the last day of 1795, of 1490 on the rolls at Port-au-Prince, St. Marc, the Môle, Jérémie, and Tiburon, the newest British commander, Brigadier General Hornbeck, could muster but 752 effectives. General Williamson, who now held title as royal governor of British St. Domingue, bluntly told Whitehall, "At St. Marc [we] cannot mount a sergeant's guard from the great sickness and mortality."

In this hour of opportunity Toussaint (who in late 1794 had, on Laveaux's nomination, been commissioned *général de brigade)* was immobilized for want of supplies, and was trading coffee and rum to American blockade-runners for barrels of powder (6). Typically, he made a virtue out of enforced inactivity by raising and training four new regiments.

But the British, too, were committing new regiments. Despite mounting disputes with French planter allies, the British government had determined to make an all-out effort to win the colonial prize that seemed to glitter so. Between April 1795 and the same month in 1796, 4930 British replacements arrived. To fight the pestilence, the War Office tried transferring the 82d Foot directly from another tropical station, Gibraltar. Momentarily Sir Adam Williamson thought their good state on arrival was due to their having subsisted on Spanish wine rather than spirits. Promptly he advised London, "Some very good Teneriffe wines might be contracted for at a very reasonable rate - The loss of hundreds, nay thousands, of valuable men might be saved."

Sir Adam's letter had hardly reached Whitehall (where, in the fashion of distant defense ministries, no attention was paid to it) than, wine or no wine, the 82d sickened like the rest. Within ten weeks 630 of the men from Gibraltar were dead. By September 1796, according to Bryan Edwards, another replacement regiment, the 96th Foot, had perished to a man. As the redcoats were dying, still more units were embarking for St. Domingue: regiments of British infantry;

Dutch, Hanoverian, and French emigre cavalry; and Dutch artillerymen. By June 1796 these totaled 7900 more. To support these Europeans, Williamson was raising slave regiments purchased from obliging royalist planters at 2000 livres a head (with liberty promised after five years' service - but Sir Adam cynically observed, "At the expiration of that period, probably very few of these individuals will be alive to partake of the terms now offered"). Known among the *colons* as "Royal Goudrons" (tarpots), slave auxiliaries more often than not found themselves back at work on their original plantations.

While the English reeled under the beating sun, malaria, and, worst of all, the Yellow Jack (7), the French (in this case including Villatte and Toussaint) were contending for the North. Unable to take the field against the British, they could still intrigue against each other.

After the enclaves around Port-de-Paix and the Cap had merged, Laveaux returned to the Cap but got no warm welcome from Villatte. During the latter's occupancy, the Cap, at first defended by black *régénerés,* had gradually been repopulated and to some extent rebuilt by *mulâtres* and *noirs* of the old *affranchi* class, whose interests were, after all, identical.

Like Rigaud in the South, Villatte in the North was working to establish *mulâtre* hegemony. Laveaux was hardly back before, in January 1796, he reported: "An abominable jealousy exists here among the *gens de couleur* against the whites and blacks . . .the *gens de couleur* are in despair at seeing Toussaint Louverture, a *noir,* become brigadier general . . . All the *gens de couleur* and black *affranchis* are the enemies of emancipation and equality. They cannot even conceive that a former black slave can be the equal of a white man, a *mulâtre,* or a black *affranchi.* "

To support the intrigues of Villatte, Rigaud sent one of his most trusted agents, Pierre Pinchinat, originally of St. Marc, who had led *mulâtre* uprisings at Mirebalais in 1791.

On the 30 Ventose (20 March), Villatte and Pinchinat felt strong enough to move against Laveaux. As the latter subsequently described it:

> At ten that morning I was seated in my bedroom conferring with the Chief Engineer. Some seven or eight people entered through the door on the left, and about a hundred through the salon, all *gens de couleur,* not a single *noir,* not a single white . . .
>
> I asked them, What do you want, citizens? Immediately the ringleader threw a punch at my head. I dodged, jumped on him and knocked him down. I said to the others, Assassins, I am unarmed! At the same time, a dozen jumped me, saying, In the name of the people we will drag him to jail. I asked: Where is the Municipal Council?
>
> You don't need it - move, rascal, they replied. No, I said, you are not the

people. There are neither black citizens nor white citizens here, you are assassins.
At this they deluged me with blows. I fought back furiously and for a moment threw
them off. I called my aide-de-camp, who came running. They hit him with sticks
and he could not get to me. I then seized one and threw him down. He was carrying
pistols and daggers . . . Finally, barefooted and bareheaded, I was dragged out by
my hair and my arms and taken to jail.

After being hauled through the streets, Laveaux was locked in a cell and there
he stayed for the next three days. While the governor was sweating in the
malodorous prison of the Cap, word of his predicament made its way to
Toussaint at Gonaïves, and from that headquarters very rapidly back again to the
noir commander at the Haut du Cap, Colonel Pierre Michel. Michel wasted no
time. Sending his most forceful officer, Major Henry Christophe, Michel
ordered the immediate release of Laveaux and promised that if harm came to the
Frenchman he would march into town and "sacrifice everything alive."

There could be no mistaking such a message nor any doubt as to its real
originator. The Municipal Council repaired in a body to the jail, released
Laveaux, and conveyed him in civic state to the Hotel de Ville, where, to the
applause of those who had dragged him the other way three days before, he
resumed office.

A week later, at the head of a squadron of cavalry and two battalions of
infantry, Toussaint marched into the Cap and received from a grateful Laveaux
the appointment as lieutenant governor of St. Domingue. "After God, Laveaux!"
replied Toussaint. Then, making sure that Villatte and Pinchinat had dispersed
their partisans and left town, Toussaint returned to Gonaïves with authority from
Laveaux to recruit a personal bodyguard, two more regiments of horse, and
three of infantry. Michel was promoted *général de brigade* and Henry
Christophe to colonel. The latter's new command included the Habitation
Portelance, where, as a lad, Christophe had been a cook. While these
momentous events were transpiring, the War Office in London had come to the
conclusion that Sir Adam Williamson had played out his string. Word had
perhaps not yet reached the Horse Guards of a diminutive Corsican general who
in Italy this very month, March 1796, was launching 30,000 soldiers, "starving
and all but naked . . . into the most fertile plains in the world" - but the war
was going as badly in Europe as in St. Domingue. To conquer St. Domingue,
which Sir Adam had promised to do with 877 soldiers, had already cost the
Treasury near £3 million, not to mention ten men dead of pestilence for each of
the original 877. So Sir Adam was called home with a pension and a promotion,
to be replaced by a General Forbes, who lasted out the year in desultory
campaigning, until, in March 1797, he too was recalled.

Toussaint Consolidates

At the Cap, Laveaux had acclaimed Toussaint as "that black Spartacus foreseen by Raynal, whose destiny is to avenge the outrages on his race." Toussaint had become the most powerful man in St. Domingue, and this the French Directory would soon learn.

On 1 May 1796, with instructions to re-establish the authority of the Republic, a third set of commissioners arrived from France. The new commissioners - five, this time - were no strangers to the island. Sonthonax, politically unsinkable despite a long and at times ridiculous trial, was at their head. To balance this outspoken friend of the *noirs,* Raymond, the *mulâtre* lawyer, was included. And to prepare for the transition from Spain to France, Roume, another earlier commissioner, was assigned as French Resident in Santo Domingo. Besides these old hands, there were two specialists: Leblanc, who would try to rebuild commercial relations with America; and Giraud, a financial adviser. With the commissioners came powder, 30,000 muskets, a fat war chest, a naval squadron that eluded the British, and 900 troops under General Donatien-Marie-Joseph de Vimeur Rochambeau (not to be confused with his better-known father, one of George Washington's generals), who had commanded a regiment in the American Revolution and had served in St. Domingue.

Like all those who come from abroad to solve the problems of Haiti, the commissioners were received with effervescent acclaim which soon dissipated. Within a fortnight they faced their first crisis in the person of Villatte, who had concentrated his *mulâtres* at Martellière, near Fort Liberté. St. Domingue was hardly big enough to hold Laveaux and Villatte, or to contain a *mulâtre* army in the North as long as Toussaint was lieutenant governor. Villatte was called before the commissioners at the Cap. As he entered the city the *gens de couleur* and the whites, who recalled him as preserver and rebuilder of the Cap, hailed him in triumph - another black mark in Sonthonax's ledger.

The proceedings, like many such since the fall of the Bastille, were short and arbitrary; on 23 June, Villatte found himself aboard *Wattigny,* with eight subordinates, bound for France and, events finally disclosed, for the dungeons of Rochefort.

Rochambeau was next to go. Without sufficient troops, he and his headquarters lay idle at the Cap. On 20 July, Rochambeau too found himself relieved and on his way home aboard the first ship.

Leblanc and Giraud soon followed. The former died amid rumors, typical of Haiti, that he had been poisoned; the latter broke physically and was invalided home. Taking care to keep quiet and out of the way, Raymond stayed on.

In September, under the French Constitution of the Year III, elections were held to send delegates from St. Domingue to the *Corps Législatif* (no longer the National Assembly) in Paris. In voting evidently influenced by Toussaint, both Laveaux and Sonthonax were among those chosen. One of the few French officers ever to depart from St. Domingue with reputation intact, Laveaux left immediately, aboard the same ship as Giraud. Sonthonax opted to stay.

Now the only Frenchman of consequence left in St. Domingue, Sonthonax stood square in the path of Toussaint. When and how the inevitable reckoning would take place was deferred by three pressing problems. Fomented by the British, guerrilla war had broken out in the North and Northwest. In the South, Rigaud ("ever rebellious to authority," wrote Sonthonax) had spurned the commissioners. Throughout the country, economic distress, occasioned by collapse of the plantations, urgently dictated reconstruction. But how could St. Domingue be reconstructed without slaves?

In the old mountain territories of Jean-François, the British, working through French royalist auxiliaries, had supplied money and arms to bands in the North. Bidding for their allegiance, the commissioners had imprudently done the same. On 10 July 1796, the dissident *noirs* launched attacks from Ouanaminthe to Grande Rivière, supported soon after by mutiny at Fort Liberté. Toussaint had to fall back from Gonaïves, where he was containing the British, and launch a pacification campaign into the mountains, which Sonthonax now described as "the Vendée of St. Domingue." Led by Christophe, Moyse, Leveille, and Michel, Toussaint's columns swept the hills and restored uneasy peace, only to be challenged from the Northwest, where, in September, a general *noir* uprising had exploded against whites and *gens de couleur.*

Port-de-Paix was invested and once again had to depend on La Tortue for food. Planters were slaughtered and habitations burned. Again the hand of the English was suspected. Riding tirelessly, Christophe reached the mountains behind Port-de-Paix, sought out the rebel leaders, and, by sheer moral force, quelled the revolt.

Soon after Toussaint's intervention, however, the French commander at Port-de-Paix, General Pageot, and the remaining French garrison were quietly withdrawn and relieved by Toussaint's troops.

At the same time (late August), Sonthonax was engaged in an effort to bring Rigaud under control. In the South, cut off by the British in the west from the rest of St. Domingue and supplied independently by American traders, Rigaud had carved out an autonomous domain where *gens de couleur* ruled, remaining whites functioned as little more than technicians and advisers, and *noirs* were re-enslaved.

To bring Rigaud to heel, Sonthonax sent a mission, headed by General Kerverseau. "We are come hither," Kerverseau indiscreetly proclaimed, "to end the tyranny of the *mulâtres.*" This was more than enough for Rigaud, who promptly spread word among the *noirs* that Kerverseau's object was to restore slavery. On 27 August the *noirs* rose, not against Rigaud or the *gens de couleur*, but against the whites and Kerverseau and his fellow emissaries, who were lucky enough merely to be thrown into the jail at Les Cayes. After a suitable interval, Rigaud released his visitors, sent them packing, and promptly turned off the insurrection. Like Toussaint in the North, he was now absolute master of the South. Which would become master of St. Domingue remained to be seen.

Unlike most of their contemporaries, Toussaint and Rigaud held one view in common: neither regarded warfare as an end in itself. Each realized the economic distress of St. Domingue and the need to remedy it. Rigaud's solution amounted to restoration of slavery. Toussaint was still too occupied with politics and battles to give his whole attention to reconstruction, but one of his principal subordinates, Henry Christophe, had already conceived a system of serfdom (though not slavery) called *"fermage"*, which would eventually shape the rural life of Haiti.

Once 1797 arrived, Toussaint bore Laveaux's old title, *Général-en-Chef des Armées de Saint-Domingue*. Lieutenant governor as well, he had received another promotion from the Directory *(général de division),* together with a dress sword and brace of handsomely chased pistols made for him by the national arsenal at Versailles. A few months earlier, he had sent his two boys, Isaac and Placide, to France to be educated: evidently he trusted the Directory, and it relied on him.

Now, at last, the time had come to deal with Sonthonax. The relationship between the commissioner and Toussaint had come under increasing strain. Sonthonax had infiltrated agents into Toussaint's regiments (a process of which the latter had characteristically kept himself well informed). Sonthonax proclaimed the authority of metropolitan France; Toussaint personified the aspirations of what would soon become the free nation of Haiti. Bent on reconstruction, Toussaint willingly collaborated with former planters, emigres, and royalists so long as they furthered his goals. Sonthonax, still the Terrorist of 1793, ruthlessly proscribed the enemies of the Revolution. (Bayon de Libertat, now an old man of seventy and back at Toussaint's invitation, was clapped into prison by Sonthonax as an emigre (8).

On 20 August 1797, Toussaint marched on the Cap at the head of two regiments. The message he delivered was brief: a year had elapsed since the election of Sonthonax to the *Corps Législatif* in France; his seat in that body awaited him. Frustrated and furious, Sonthonax boarded ship and, for the last time, saw the green mountains drop below the horizon. Ironically, neither he nor Toussaint could realize that this epilogue was superfluous. A ship from France was already at sea, bringing word that, again arraigned, Sonthonax was again recalled.

A Brigand Island

The Directory still had hopes for St. Domingue. To replace Sonthonax, came one final commissioner. Gabriel-Théodore-Joseph Hédouville, a forty-three-year-old splinter of the *ancien régime*, had escaped the guillotine during the Terror and risen to eminence in the pacification of the Vendée. Aside from these professional credentials, Hédouville's brother had been a classmate at Brienne of the Directory's ablest general, young Napoleon Bonaparte.

Hédouville was sent to St. Domingue not to conquer but to pacify. Unlike previous commissioners, he had few troops: a mere headquarters detachment of 200 men.

Hédouville's instructions were to regain effective control over both Rigaud and Toussaint and support them against the English; to reestablish the laws of the Republic and its administrative machinery; to favor Rigaud (whose republican zeal and love of France were undimmed); and to dampen Toussaint's suspected ambitions for independence.

Hédouville reached the island in April 1798. Scarcely three weeks before, a British general landed at Môle St. Nicolas bearing secret instructions more important (because they were fulfilled) than those of Hédouville (who failed).

Brigadier General the Honorable Thomas Maitland, son of an earl, commissioned in the British army at birth, was an ambitious and opinionated political soldier. Besides the obvious qualification of previous service in St. Domingue, he was a favorite of his fellow Scot Henry Dundas, Secretary of War, and he was acutely aware that the dragging campaign of St. Domingue was unpopular at home.

Maitland's instructions were simple. Regardless of what military retrenchment might be required, operating costs in St. Domingue must be cut to £25,000 a month. The only position he must hold was the Môle, and possibly Jérémie, which Lord Balcarres, governor of Jamaica, was keen to retain "as an outpost" for covering that island.

The first report Maitland sent to Dundas was a gloomy one: "Our situation here is worse than even I, who was never sanguine respecting it, could have possibly imagined."

Maitland had reason to be pessimistic. Toussaint, confronting him in the West and Northwest, had 20,000 troops (including 700 Frenchmen, sole survivors of the 12,000 France had sent to St. Domingue since 1791). Rigaud had 12,000 more. Besides these regular formations, the country swarmed with the black guerrilla bands known as *congos,* and the coastal waters were menaced by pirate barges. Including loyalist French, Maitland could muster only 2500 European bayonets plus a few thousand Royal Goudrons of dubious effectiveness.

While Toussaint began to encircle Port-au-Prince, Rigaud was advancing over the mountains toward Jérémie, where Brigadier General Spencer had a thousand troops, "the remains of the British here," glumly noted Maitland.

Twelve days after reaching St. Domingue, Maitland sent Toussaint a proposal. The British would evacuate the West and pull out of Port-au-Prince if allowed to do so peacefully and if Toussaint would suspend operations against the Môle and Grande-Anse during a truce to be arranged.

Toussaint quickly agreed. By 6 May, the British had embarked their equipment and the people (mainly royalist French) who, despite Toussaint's assurances, preferred the protection of the Union Jack. Two days later, at eight in the morning, the redcoats formed fours, shouldered firelocks, and, to the defiant shrill of fifes, marched stiffly out the road to Bizoton, where Commodore Ford's cutters were waiting to put them aboard ship. Now the West belonged to Toussaint.

If Maitland found things worse than could have been anticipated, Hédouville might have rendered the same report. Reaching the Cap overland from Santo Domingo (British cruisers had the Windward Passage under blockade), he found not a sou in the treasury, troops unpaid, government accounts in disorder - and, in charge, a prosperous Julien Raymond, who had bought a large number of habitations and was doing not badly. For more than a year, not a single official communication had gotten through from France.

Yet, as in the case of Raymond, there was private prosperity. With Sonthonax gone, planters had begun to slip back from the United States, and both town and plain were being renewed. But for the British blockade, times might have been good. As it was, however, sugar, which a year earlier had gone for ten gourdes (9) a hundred pounds, now brought only half as much. Coffee was even worse.

For the moment, at least, Toussaint and Rigaud both made punctilious submissions; Hédouville studied the situation and watched both.

Hédouville's conclusion was that, unless checked by Rigaud, Toussaint intended to make himself master of St. Domingue. From this moment, Hédouville therefore determined to fan the rivalry between the two. In July, he brought both to the Cap. Toussaint, artful as ever, joined Rigaud when the latter's carriage reached Gonaïves and suggested they concert forces in dealing with Hédouville. Rigaud agreed reluctantly. At the Cap, Hédouville stage-managed an outburst against Toussaint by Rigaud. The two parted icily - Rigaud for his stronghold at Les Cayes, Toussaint for the cordon he had already thrown around Môle St. Nicolas.

As Toussaint's campfires flickered on the heights behind the Môle, Maitland concluded that, however important it might be as a naval base, the place was indefensible, at least with the small British force in hand. The Grande-Anse, on the other tip of the island, was, he thought, better for covering Jamaica against France and Spain; and so did Lord Balcarres in Jamaica, with whom Maitland kept close touch.

As long as Rigaud held Tiburon, the Grande-Anse was no good either. Under General Spencer, two thin brigades assembled at Les Irois and, on 11 June, embarked aboard five warships for Britain's last offensive, a land-sea attempt to capture Tiburon. But no sooner was the force at sea than a fierce Southeast blow came up. Boating was impossible, and the British troops never got ashore to join forces with the royalist French, under Colonel Dessource, who attacked by land and were easily repulsed.

Rigaud was not slow to strike back. At the head of Legion of the West, a battalion from Jacmel, and veterans of the old Légion d'Egalité, the *mulâtre* general marched on Jérémie.

His hopes lost for the Grande-Anse, with Jérémie surrounded by Rigaud, and the Môle encircled by Toussaint, Maitland took the final step. "I shall," he wrote Dundas on 31 July, "with all convenient speed evacuate the whole of the Island." In the Grande-Anse the game was already up. Rigaud, hoping to match Toussaint in the West, called on Spencer to capitulate. Spencer refused but, on the night of 20 August, marched Eastward out of town, unopposed. Ships were waiting at Corail, and the British embarked. Meanwhile, at Les Irois, frigates picked up the troops of Spencer's Western cordon, which had been covering Tiburon. On 23 August, the squadron sailed. The South belonged wholly to Rigaud, and only the Môle remained to England.

But the same day Spencer was issuing orders for abandonment of Jérémie, Toussaint and Maitland were conferring secretly at the Môle. The resulting agreement paralleled that for the capitulation of Port-au-Prince. On 30 August, Idlinger, Toussaint's skilled French adjutant general, crossed the lines and entered the fortress to effect detailed arrangements.

During the next month the British demobilized their Haitian regiments. But, as units disbanded, except for some picked men re-enlisted in the British West India Regiment, they moved intact into Toussaint's ranks. And so, on 2 October 1798, in the evening, the Union Jack came down for the last time over Haitian soil, and Admiral William Bligh (he of the *Bounty)* embarked the British survivors of the long campaign and a shipload of loyalist French planters for exile in America. "St. Domingue," wrote Balcarres, "can only be henceforward considered as a Brigand Island."

The cost to Britain of what Bryan Edwards called "this disastrous enterprise" has been put as high as £20 million, but this seems inflated; £5 million might be closer. The direct loss of lives of British troops and European mercenary levies (greater than at Waterloo) exceeded 14,000 men, not counting many hundreds of seamen dead of the Yellow Jack. But Sir John Fortescue, in his magisterial history of the British army, goes far higher: "The West Indian campaigns . . . which were the essence of Pitt's military policy, cost England in Army and Navy little fewer than one hundred thousand men, about one-half of them dead, the remainder permanently unfit for service."

Summing up the melancholy lesson, Edmund Burke had the last word: "It is not an enemy we have to vanquish, but a cemetery to acquire. The hostile sword is merciful: the country itself is the dreadful enemy."

Hédouville Fails

During all this, where was Hédouville? The answer, according to Maitland's final report to Dundas, was that the commissioner had become "a kind of State Prisoner at the Cape, completely in the power of Toussaint . . . against, whom all his schemes evidently pointed. But neither the nominal power of Hédouville or the cunning and talents of Rigaud were sufficient to enable them to cope with Toussaint."

With some understatement Maitland added that he had thrown "every impediment in Hédouville's way." Just as, from differing assumptions, Hédouville had concluded that his own tactic should be to fan the rivalries of Rigaud and Toussaint, Maitland had played the same game between Toussaint and Hédouville.

On 31 July Maitland had written Dundas of his intention to evacuate. Exactly a month later he reinsured his decision by a secret agreement with Toussaint. Britain would not again land troops or attack any part of St. Domingue under Toussaint's control, or "meddle in any way" with Toussaint's internal political arrangements. For his part, Toussaint engaged to keep hands off Jamaica (where British slaves were with less success waging their "Brigands'" or "Maroons' War."(10) The Royal Navy would lift its blockade against Toussaint's ports to allow British (and, though not stated, American) ships to supply and trade with Toussaint.

When arrangements for evacuation were complete, Maitland received Toussaint as an honored visitor at the Môle; paraded a guard of honor; dined him sumptuously; and suggested that he proclaim himself, under British protection, King of Haiti. Toussaint's ambitions, like those of Washington, were never quite regal - he preferred the substance to the shadow of power - but he never forgot his treatment by the British. "The Republic never rendered me such honors," he later said, "as the King of England."

Having learned well how to deal with French commissioners, Toussaint now turned his attention to Hédouville. Unwisely, the latter had attempted to demobilize and disarm some black regiments in the North, diverting the troops to work in the fields. Word soon began to spread that Hédouville, representing France, was about to restore slavery. Revolt flamed across the Plaine du Nord. As the tide surged higher, Hédouville implored Toussaint for help. Marching from Gonaïves with a picked regiment, Toussaint encountered furious bands burning habitations and killing whites as if it were 1791.

Hédouville threw in his hand. On 22 October, less than three weeks after Maitland's departure, the unlucky agent of the Directory embarked 1800 refugees aboard three frigates and, himself aboard *Bravoure,* sailed for France.

As suddenly as it had exploded, the insurrection quieted. Toussaint made a state entrance into the Cap and was received with a Te Deum. In the streets, the *Capois* cried, *"Après Dieu, c'est lui!"* If Toussaint's thoughts turned back to Laveaux, he gave no sign. The blacks went peacefully back to the land.

But Hédouville fired a parting shot. Leaving St. Domingue, he promoted Rigaud to equal rank with Toussaint, and, in the name of France, declared Rigaud independent commander of the South. He also left behind a proclamation calling on the country to beware of Toussaint, whom he did not name, and ordering Rigaud to act independently. In his report, Hédouville warned the Directory, "The sole hope of checking Toussaint Louverture even for the moment lies in sedulously fostering the hate between the *mulâtres* and *noirs*, and by opposing Rigaud to Toussaint."

Civil War

With Hédouville out of the way, only two obstacles stood between Toussaint and his goals of absolute power and independence. Rigaud, unconquered in the South, of course remained to be subdued. And far to the East, in Ciudad Santo Domingo, Roume still represented the Republic.

Toussaint reacted characteristically. Hédouville's final act having been to arm Rigaud against Toussaint with the authority of France, Toussaint, in the name of that same authority, now invited Roume to come to mediate between himself and Rigaud.

Roume accepted. Moreover, as Toussaint had anticipated, Roume quickly chose sides. Toussaint, he reported to Paris in February 1799, was supported by 90 percent of the population, Rigaud by 10. "Toussaint Louverture," wrote Roume, "and the other black generals are truly the saviors of St. Domingue and the benefactors of France." If, he continued, Toussaint was lenient toward the emigres, this was because St. Domingue had become an island of universal fraternity: color no longer mattered, all men were brothers.

In this euphoric frame of mind, having ratified Toussaint's conduct toward Hédouville, Roume proceeded to adjudicate his difference with Rigaud. The agent's decision infuriated the *mulâtres:* the Gôaves, Jacmel, and Léogane were detached from Rigaud's South and rejoined to Toussaint's West. On 12 February 1799, in one of his towering rages, Rigaud stormed out of Port-au-Prince.

Toussaint, too, left Port-au-Prince. Before he departed, he called together the *mulâtre* population in the cathedral.

Gens de couleur [Toussaint warned from the pulpit] who since the beginning of the revolution have betrayed the *noirs*, what are you up to today? Everyone knows that you are seeking mastery over the colony, that you wish to exterminate the whites and enslave the *noirs* . . . *Mulâtres*, I see to the bottom of your souls. You are ready to rise against me. But even though my troops are being pulled out, I leave here my eye and my arm: my eye to watch, my arm to strike.

Then he went to the foot of the altar, knelt for a moment, and left the cathedral. Outside, his troops' bayonets sparkled in the sun. Swinging quickly into the saddle, he led his black regiments into the field.

While Toussaint concentrated at Gonaïves, a final flurry of politics set the stage for civil war. In an exchange of pamphlets and broadsides, Toussaint declared Rigaud a traitor, Rigaud proclaimed Hédouville's final instructions; and Roume, openly flouted by Rigaud, denounced the *mulâtre* as a rebel against France.

On 18 June 1799, fighting commenced. Rigaud's troops crossed the bridge at Miragoâne, ancient boundary between South and West, and marched on Petit-Gôave. They overran Fort Garit, fell upon a garrison under Laplume (who escaped), sacked the town, and slaughtered the white planters Toussaint had re-established there.

As the troops of the South advanced into Grand-Gôave, disaffected *mulâtres* rose behind Toussaint's lines at the Môle, the Cap, in the Artibonite, and in Léogane, where Alexandre Pétion and Jean-Pierre Boyer, *mulâtre* officers until then loyal to Toussaint, rallied to Rigaud.

Toussaint's response would have done credit to Napoleon. Riding, as he could and often did, 65 or 70 miles a day, he thundered South into Port-au-Prince, then along the shore road to the canefields of Léogane. With him came his most terrible lieutenants, Moyse and Dessalines. Laplume he relieved immediately. To Moyse he entrusted overall command. Dessalines he posted at Léogane. Then he wheeled about and galloped back toward the West and North.

To Christophe at the Cap he wrote, "I count on your unwavering severity. Let nothing escape your vigilance." Christophe needed no urging: his squads marched from house to house and thence outside town to the dread Savanne de la Fossette, traditional place of execution, where the firing squads awaited. The rising at the Cap was quelled before the end of August.

Toussaint swung Northwest toward Gros Morne, Port-de-Paix, and the Môle.

En route, crossing the Pont de l'Estère, through the salt marshes where the Artibonite reaches the sea, Toussaint rode into a night ambush, "having," reported a U.S. naval officer a few days later, "his Doctor & Aide de Camp killed and two balls passed through his hat - It is the general opinion of the people of this Island that should any accident happen to him, this place would be once more drenched in blood."

But the bath of blood had already commenced; Michel, Toussaint's once-trusted subordinate who had rescued Laveaux at the Cap, was summarily executed. *Hommes de couleur* and all shades of *affranchis* were massacred or impressed into the ranks, where for many death became preferable. Leaders of the disaffected *mulâtres* were blown from the muzzles of guns loaded with grapeshot - a mode of punishment Maitland had introduced the year before. At Port-au-Prince, reported Hugh Cathcart, British vice consul, *600 hommes de couleur* were lashed back to back, towed to sea aboard barges, bayoneted, and flung overboard to the waiting shark and barracuda.

On 25 July, Toussaint broke the siege at Port-de-Paix, where Maurepas had resisted stoutly. After recapturing Jean Rabel and marching across the rockbound spine of mountains and thorn, Bombardopolis, he again entered the Cap. But, instead of further bloodletting, he had the surviving *mulâtre* prisoners, some nearly naked, all in chains, brought before him in the cathedral, where, again mounting the pulpit, Toussaint preached a sermon of forgiveness and had their fetters struck off.

The Northwest pacified, battle could be joined in the South. In numbers, the armies were unequal. Rigaud initially had some 2500 men(11) under arms in four regular regiments: Toussaint had 30,000. But Rigaud's army, seasoned by hard fighting against the English in the Grande-Anse, well equipped and valiantly led, was an elite corps. Rigaud also had the support of the *marrons,* who, through all the turmoil of the decade, had maintained freedom in their mountains.

Toussaint's formations included thousands of slave militia, but he also had good troops. Captain Rainsford, the British agent, had observed one of Henry Christophe's demibrigades in early 1798: "At a whistle a whole brigade ran three or four hundred yards and then, separating, threw themselves flat on the ground . . . and all the time keeping up a strong fire . . . This movement is executed with such facility and precision as totally to prevent cavalry from charging them in bushy and hilly countries."

Pamphile de Lacroix (later historian of the revolution in St. Domingue), another highly qualified soldier who, as their opponent, was perhaps the best judge of Toussaint's units, spared no praise:

Officers commanded, pistol in hand, and had power of life and death over their subordinates. It was remarkable to see these Africans with bare torsos and equipped only with cartridge pouch, sword and musket, give an example of perfect self-control . . . When quartered in a town, they would not touch any provisions displayed in the markets or brought in by the cultivators. They trembled before their officers and were respected by the people. To have succeeded in disciplining these barbarians was Toussaint's supreme triumph.

Besides the strengths of the opposing armies, a new factor had to be weighed. Writing from Philadelphia on 16 January 1799, Benjamin Stoddert, the American Secretary of the Navy, had instructed Commodore Thomas Truxtun, U.S.N.. "General Toussaint has a great desire to see some of our Ships of War at Cape François - and the President has a desire that he should be gratified."

With the connivance of Britain, using Maitland as a go-between, President John Adams had been in touch with Toussaint. Britain was still at war with the Directory; in a state of undeclared war, American frigates throughout the Atlantic and West Indies were taking or sinking every Frenchman they could catch. Hungry for the sugar, molasses, rum, and coffee of St. Domingue, American merchants wanted to export salt fish, meat, breadstuffs, horses, and the consumer goods of the day. (A typical American cargo for the Cap in 1798 included lumber, pipe staves, hoops, shingles, gunpowder, musket balls, livestock, and tobacco).(12)

Now that the British were gone, Toussaint wasted no time in establishing relations with the United States. In November 1798, Toussaint's French treasurer, Joseph Bunel - "a man of no parts and of mean character," wrote British minister Robert Liston - was sent to Philadelphia to open negotiations with the Americans. Five months later, in March 1799, Dr. Edward Stevens, staunch Federalist and kinsman of Alexander Hamilton (and, like Hamilton, born in the West Indies) reached the Cap as American consul general. Hamilton could hardly have chosen better: Stevens had previously been in business at Cap Français, spoke French, and was well known to and trusted by Toussaint.

The entente between John Adams and Toussaint was simple. The latter would halt French privateering from St. Domingue against American ships, and open Port-au-Prince and the Cap to U.S. and British merchantmen. In return, U.S. or British cruisers would honor Toussaint's *laissez-passer* granted to any French ship. There would, Hamilton wrote in 1799, be "no guaranty, no formal treaty - nothing that can rise up in judgment. It will be enough to let Toussaint be assured verbally, but explicitly . . ."

Stevens was accredited to Toussaint, not Roume, or, least of all, Rigaud. Against the last, as civil war flamed, a strict American embargo was applied. U.S. warships were ordered, in September 1799, "to scour the South side of the Island."

Within ten days, Stephen Higginson, navy agent in Boston, was coordinating with Secretary of State Timothy Pickering a shipment to Toussaint of ammunition and flints and 2680 muskets aboard an American vessel ballasted with lead, which was to be melted into musket balls.

Like Spain and France and Britain before her, America had entered the ring.

War in the South

Toussaint now had to advance into the South, but Jacmel flanked his line of communications and covered the narrow neck held by Rigaud.

For two months (November 1799 to January 1800), supported by the divisions of Laplume and Christophe, Dessalines tightened his grip on Jacmel, but to no avail. Toussaint himself assumed command: on 6 January of the new year the besiegers carried two positions, Grand Fort and Talavigne, where Toussaint sited mortars to bombard the ruined town, day and night. Pétion, whom Rigaud had sent in with a handful of grenadiers on the night of the 19th by sea to take command, found the garrison reduced to a diet of horses, dogs, cats, rats, and lizards, and loading their cannon with rocks.

Offshore, the U.S. Navy maintained its blockade. On 4 February Rigaud tried to run in reinforcements and food from Les Cayes, but *U.S.S. Experiment* sank one blockade-runner and captured the other. At the end of the month, the frigate *General Greene* hammered Pétion's seaward forts.(13)

Five days later, with nearly 4000 soldiers and townsmen dead from hunger or battle, Pétion tried to send out the women and children, many of whom perished at the hands of Dessalines (and, some accounts say, of Christophe as well).

On 11 March, as night fell, the end came. Pétion, sword in hand, led the remaining 1400 defenders in a forlorn hope through Christophe's lines into the mountains toward Grand-Gôave. Next morning, Jacmel was occupied by the black regiments of the North. Dessalines and his soldiery indiscriminately massacred stragglers, old men, and the few women and children who were left.

The fall of Jacmel broke the back of the South. As soon as he could organize offensive operations in April, Dessalines, reported Consul Stevens, "took two strong camps of Rigaud's in the neighborhood of Benet[sic]", then, according to Consul Ritchie at Port-au-Prince, he "performed a rapid march across the country, and, by his sudden appearance and the judicious positions that detachments were placed in, caused an immediate evacuation of Grand and Petit Gôave by the troops of Rigaud."

As Rigaud retired, he left the Gôaves in flames, burned the canefields and habitations, and interposed scorched earth between the South and Dessalines. To no avail: torrential rains deluged the South and West in April and May. Besides frustrating Rigaud's defense, they overwhelmed the irrigation works of the Cul-de-Sac and the Artibonite, never again to be restored.

At Petit-Gôave, Dessalines received replacements, raised in the North by Toussaint's *levée-en-masse*. He also picked up several guns earlier taken from three American merchantmen by Rigaud's cutthroat bargemen, whose piracies forced the U.S. Navy to send a frigate into the Bight of Léogane.

Dessalines marched the main body inland of Lake Miragoâne, bypassing Pétion and taking the last position between Toussaint and the South.

Along the winding road across the mountains, Dessalines overran point after point: St. Michel, then Fond des Nègres - never without a fight; but Dessalines could afford casualties and Rigaud could not.(14)

At this moment, just as the Army of the North was about to burst into the South, politics intervened. Once again, and for the last time, France sent a troika of commissioners to try to take hold of St. Domingue. But there was one difference: the new commissioners (Michel, a general; Vincent, a colonel who was known and trusted by Toussaint; and, not so new, the *mulâtre* Raymond) no longer represented the Directory. On 18 Brumaire (9 November 1799), Napoleon Bonaparte had become First Consul of the Republic.

What was in Toussaint's mind while these commissioners were preparing to sail for St. Domingue was reported by Consul Stevens in a carefully enciphered dispatch to Secretary Pickering: "While I was uncertain of the real Intentions of Toussaint, I was loth to say any Thing to you about them . . . He is taking his measures slowly but securely. All connection with France will soon be broken off . . . As soon as France interferes with this colony he will throw off the mask, and declare it independent."

Like Hédouville before them, the commissioners landed at Santo Domingo. When they reached the frontier, Toussaint promptly had Moyse arrest both Michel and Vincent while he inspected their baggage and papers. Then (it was all a mistake, he said) he had them released. Michel took the hint and promptly returned to France. Raymond busied himself with his extensive interests, and Vincent, a colonel of engineers, again made himself useful to Toussaint. The latter suppressed the conciliatory proclamation Napoleon had sent ("Brave blacks, remember that France alone recognizes your freedom and the equality of your rights...") and once again (but, if one read Napoleon's new Constitution of the Year VIII, perhaps not unfounded) rumors stirred abroad that slavery was to be restored.

Momentarily, while he dealt with the commissioners, Toussaint returned to the Cap, offering as he did, on 19 June ("like the father of the Prodigal Son," he proclaimed) general amnesty to the South, and halting the advance of Dessalines. But this gesture was spurned by Rigaud and on 7 July war resumed.

At the Vieux Bourg d'Aquin, where the road debouches onto the South coast, Rigaud himself ranged 1800 men against Dessalines's thousands. There was a fierce fight: Rigaud, his horse shot from under him, his hat and uniform pierced with bullet holes, barely escaped; the *mulâtre* army once again retreated, this time to St. Louis du Sud. Again, Toussaint sought to negotiate. But Rigaud would have none of it.

On 25 July, the final advance resumed. St. Louis du Sud gave way; then Cavaillon. Rigaud put tarpots in the public buildings and ordered Cayes burned, but nobody obeyed. A week later, with his family and the bulk of the régime's funds, he took ship from Tiburon for Guadeloupe and, after many vicissitudes, France. Pétion (who, as a defeated defector, had good reason to fear Toussaint) and other senior officers (Geffrard, Bellegarde, Dupont, Birot, and Boyer) also sailed into exile. Seven hundred of Rigaud's *mulâtre* troops took refuge in Cuba.

Toussaint entered Les Cayes in triumph on 1 August. As bells pealed and gun salutes resounded, he went directly to the cathedral. There, after his customary Te Deum, he mounted the pulpit and with sacerdotal mien pronounced yet another sermon of forgiveness and proclaimed general amnesty.

Then, designating Dessalines governor of the South, Toussaint returned first to Léogane, where, on his orders, 300 prisoners of war were shot and bayoneted.

Leaving their bodies unburied in the August sun, he proceeded to Port-au-Prince. Here he promoted Dessalines to *général de division*, Christophe to brigadier, and ordered the execution of 50 captured Rigaudin officers. The site where they met their death is known to this day as Croix-des-Martyrs. At St. Marc, 600 more rebels awaited Toussaint's vengeance; it took three days to kill them off in batches on the blood-drenched sandy beach. At Gonaïves, 72 prisoners were shot, and 8 of their leaders blown from gun muzzles.

As for the conquered South, Dessalines - in Lacroix's words, "one of the most ferocious beings ever born" - had Toussaint's mandate to purge it of Rigaud sympathizers. Surrounded by a corps of executioners and torturers, Dessalines complied. Burying victims alive; impaling them, upright, on bayonets (his own specialty, which came simply to be known as "*La Baïonnette*"); sawing them between planks; or shooting or cutting the throats of the more fortunate; Dessalines is said to have slaughtered anywhere from 5000 to 10,000 - predominantly *gens de couleur* - persons over twelve years of age.

When it was over and the South pacified, Toussaint reproached his bloodthirsty lieutenant with characteristic mildness: "I told him to prune the tree, not uproot it."

Then on 22 November, Toussaint came home to the Cap. Under an archway inscribed *TOUSSAINT PACIFICATEUR DU SUD*, he received a crown of laurels, a triumphal ode, and an ecstatic welcome from Mme. Allier, one of the most beautiful Frenchwomen in the North. In the welcoming addresses he heard himself compared to Hercules, Alexander the Great, Napoleon Bonaparte, and Bacchus. On the streets the crowds roared their own verses to the "Marseillaise":

Les Anglais ces foudres de guerre,
Ont éprouvé nos bataillons;
Leur sang a rougi la poussière
Leurs corps ont comblé nos sillons
Armé d'un courage intrépide,
Toussaint partout guidait nos pas,
Et dans l'action de nos combats
Son panache était notre guide.
Terrible aux ennemis,
Humain pour ses amis,
Toussaint, Toussaint, reçois nos voeux,
Par toi, tout est heureux!

("The English, those thunderbolts of war,/Put our battalions to the test;/Their blood has reddened the dust/Their corpses heaped our fields./Armed with intrepid courage,/ Toussaint guided our steps everywhere,/And in the shock of our battles/His plume was our fanion./Terrible to his enemies,/Humane to his own,/Toussaint, Toussaint, receive our acclaim,/Through thee all is good fortune!")

Santo Domingo Occupied

Toussaint entered the Cap in triumph. Three days later, Roume and his family were under arrest. Toussaint well knew that he had gained his successes at the cost of defiance to France and worse, defiance of the First Consul. If he was to consolidate his position as master of the island, two steps remained. One was to rid St. Domingue of the last vestige of the authority of metropolitan France; the other was to assume control over Santo Domingo. Neither end could be attained while Roume remained.

As early as December 1799, when the mutinies in the North and the Artibonite had barely been quelled and Dessalines was still breaking his teeth against Jacmel, Toussaint first suggested to the agent that the hour had come to invoke the Treaty of Basel and bring Santo Domingo under the Tricolor.

Ordinarily pliant, the seventy-four-year-old Roume balked. Within four months, Toussaint had changed the old man's mind. Toussaint's methods of persuasion were described by Consul Stevens: "All the adherents of the Agent [Roume] have been seized, imprisoned, & the seals put on their Effects & Papers . . . The Agent and his Secretary are kept close Prisoners to the Government House: nor are Papers, Money or any Kind of Effects suffer'd to be carried out. All this is by order of general Toussaint." On 27 April 1800, Toussaint laid the necessary decree before Roume and said, "Sign this, or all the whites in the colony are done for, and I'll march into La Partie Espagnole with fire and sword."

Roume capitulated. Early in May, Toussaint sent his French chief of staff, General Agé, to Ciudad Santo Domingo by sea, with an escort of sixty soldiers, to take possession from Spain. The Spaniards, who had been viewing events in St. Domingue with horror, would have no part of unification. Antoine Chanlatte, who had succeeded Roume as French resident, refused to honor the decree, and Agé and his detachment had to be escorted to the frontier by Spanish dragoons to protect them against angry Dominicans. Roume thereupon revoked his decree.

Toussaint waited only until Rigaud had been defeated and Dessalines had finished his work in the South. With Roume in custody in Dondon, Toussaint massed troops on the frontier and sent a dispatch to Don Joaquín García, the Spanish governor, announcing his intent to enter Santo Domingo.

There were two Haitian columns: 3000 men at Ouanaminthe in the North under Moyse, and 4500 at Mirebalais under Paul Louverture, the general's brother. Toussaint himself would accompany the latter.

Toussaint's dispatch reached Don Joaquín on the night of 6 January 1801, when the society of Ciudad Santo Domingo was enjoying a grand ball in honor of the Feast of the Three Kings. Amid a general exodus of all who had means to fly, Don Joaquín mustered 1500 men, who, under Chanlatte and Nuñez, a Spanish brigadier, marched to oppose Toussaint.

After a week's brisk fighting, Toussaint advanced. Meanwhile Moyse swept virtually unopposed into Santiago, from there moving on Vega and Cotuy.

Don Joaquín surrendered on 21 January; next day, Chanlatte took ship for Venezuela, and, on the 26th, Toussaint received the keys to Ciudad Santo Domingo. Slavery, he proclaimed, was henceforth abolished. Three hundred years had elapsed since the first black slave had been brought to Santo Domingo by the Spaniards. Now, one of his descendants had returned to the city as conqueror and liberator.

A month later, Don Joaquín and the bulk of the Spanish garrison sailed for Cuba. Toussaint divided Santo Domingo into two departments - the Engaño in the South, under Clervaux; Samaná in the North, under Paul Louverture. Four thousand troops, held to strict discipline, made up the Haitian occupation force.

Before returning to St. Domingue in March, Toussaint inspected his new provinces (population: 50,000 whites, 60,000 *mulâtres* or black *affranchis,* and 15,000 slaves nominally free but still in fact attached to the land). His decrees focused mainly on economic reconstruction. Ports, long closed by Spain, were opened to American and British ships; free trade was established between the two parts of the island; rehabilitation of ruined highways and plantations was commenced; and import taxes reduced.

Now that he had conquered all Hispaniola, Toussaint was determined to set the island in order. As he may have realized, not much time remained.

Toussaint Reigns

If Santo Domingo was in decay, St. Domingue was in ruins. As early as 1796, Bryan Edwards calculated that 300,000 persons of all colors had perished. Two years later, Becker, one of Hédouville's staff officers, reported that the white population of the colony had diminished by at least two thirds, the *mulâtres* by one quarter, and the *noirs* by over a third.

Insurrection, disorganization, and neglect had wrecked the plantations and the irrigation works on which they depended. Many if not most of the former slaves had abandoned the *ateliers* and were living in vagabondage or *marronage*. Ever since Sonthonax, former slaves refused to work: *"Moin pas esclave, moin pas travayé"* (I'm not a slave, I don't have to work). In 1800, a French officer wrote the Minister of Marine, "The towns are deserted and men are fleeing a country in which they can no longer exist."

Secure in his island for the time being, Toussaint now had a nation to build. Plantations and roads and sugar mills and irrigation systems had to be reconstructed. Altered patterns of production and trade had to be taken into account. The remaining population - primitive *congos,* resentful *hommes de couleur,* and whites, whether greedy and intriguing or loyal - had to be forged into a people.

These challenges, Toussaint knew, were not simply those of peace and reconstruction but of survival. As early as 30 September 1800, the United States had mended its quarrel with France in the Agreement of Mortfontaine, ending the naval war that had blanketed Haitian waters with friendly American warships, and ending also Toussaint's special relationship with the United States. Peace between France and England would lift the British blockade and give Napoleon a free hand in the West Indies. Time was running short.

Toussaint's central problem was that intensive agricultural production had to be restarted in order for the people to earn money so that he could tax them and thus pay his generals and buy the imports, including arms, that St. Domingue required. But how to restore prosperity without restoring slavery? That was the dilemma.

The colony no longer had an administrative cadre. Trained people who knew how to govern and who possessed the technical skills to rebuild had long since fled. All Toussaint had to work with were his generals and his military staff. The latter, survivors of the foreign regiments that had poured into St. Domingue since 1791, were predominantly European. Agé, his chief of staff, was French; so was Pageot. Idlinger and d'Hébécourt, the two adjutants general, were European.

Among the generals, Clervaux, now commanding occupied Santo Domingo, alone was a *mulâtre;* before the revolution he had been an *affranchi*. The rest were *noirs*. Jean-Jacques Dessalines, born not on the Ivory Coast, as some say, but at Habitation Cormiers, outside Grande Rivière du Nord, had been a fieldhand owned by a black *affranchi* whose vicious floggings brutalized him. Charles Belair, aged twenty-three in 1801, was a youthful kinsman of Toussaint; he was a man of intelligence and was also from the North. Moyse, one-eyed and almost as fierce as Dessalines, though reputed to be Toussaint's nephew, was not. From the same plantation as his "uncle," Moyse had been savaged by slavery and was fond of saying, "I will never love the whites until they give me back the eye they have taken from me." Paul Louverture and easy-going, popular Laplume had both been slaves. Henry Christophe, ablest and most far-seeing of the generals, had come as a lad from British Grenada. Next to Christophe, Jacques Maurepas, staunch and resolute in battle, born free in an old free family, was a man of brains and vision. Like Clervaux, Maurepas had been well educated and was the only one of the generals who had never known slavery. These men represented all the administrative resources Toussaint had. Through them he set out to govern and reconstruct as best he could.

Dividing the island into three districts, he assigned them as follows: the East to Clervaux, Paul Louverture, and Pageot; the North to Moyse, Christophe, and Maurepas; and the West and South to Dessalines, Laplume, and Belair. Besides military responsibilities for defense and internal security, these commanders had an even more pressing task: to restore the ruined plantations of cane, coffee, cotton, and indigo.

Before a start could be made, the ex-slaves had to be returned to the land. Little they cared for development and reconstruction: freedom and subsistence were all they wanted. In late 1800, before Dessalines had even finished with the South, Toussaint's flying columns were already scouring the countryside for vagabond *noirs* who were needed in the fields. To run down these ex-slaves and keep them at work, Toussaint established 55-man gendarmerie companies - little different from the old *maréchaussées* - one in each parish.

The system Toussaint decreed was *fermage,* the innovation conceived in 1798 by Christophe and his French friend and collaborator, Vincent. It had already regenerated much of the North, and Toussaint quickly recognized it as the substitute for slavery that the situation demanded. Under *fermage*, the state took over the abandoned habitations and the remaining estates and leased them out, usually to senior army officers or deserving public officials. These, in turn, had to pay out a quarter of their revenue to the workers and provide quarters, subsistence, and medical care. The tenant took a fixed share and the government the rest. Laborers worked under military supervision, but with fixed hours and working conditions. Like a medieval serf, the ex-slave (in all but name, now a slave of the state) was fixed to the land; he could not change plantations or drift into town or the mountains. *Fermage* was a direct descendant of the old *code noir*, as it was the inspiration for successive future Codes Rurals.

It was up to the generals to make *fermage* work. Above them was Toussaint, riding his superb stallions a hundred miles from dawn to sundown, appearing everywhere, always unexpected. Dessalines, who, as Stoddard said, ranged his region "like a King of Dahomey," would, as the lightest punishment, order shirkers or, for that matter, incompetent overseers to be stripped and run through a gauntlet of soldiers. More serious delinquents were shot or hanged or sawn between planks or simply buried alive. Agriculture in the South and West improved by leaps and bounds. As Pamphile de Lacroix remarked, ten of the new, so-called free citizens, faced with an inspection by Dessalines, did more work and farmed more land than thirty slaves in the old days.

But neither the prodigious efforts of Toussaint and Christophe nor the ferocities of Dessalines could restore the ravages of a decade. In 1801 St. Domingue's export of raw sugar was only 19 percent of that in 1789; of finished sugar, it was but 8 tons, compared with over 35,000 tons in 1791. Coffee, already challenging sugar for first place, was down 45 percent from 1789. The indigo export amounted to 804 pounds; in 1789 it had exceeded 375 tons. Cotton was down nearly two thirds from 1789. And so on.

Nor were other conditions yet ideal. A French agent reported to the Minister of Marine in Paris:

> There is no law left in St. Domingue. The will of Toussaint and the other generals' arbitrary whims are the basis for all that is done . . . Toussaint, hypocritical, sly, playing the religious devotee, orders crimes and covers up the abuses and dilapidations of his underlings, whom he disavows according to circumstances and on whom he throws the blame for his own Machiavellian conduct. Dessalines, a ferocious and barbarous *congo,* swears he will drink the blood of the whites.

To get white planters back had been one of Toussaint's concerns. Even those who had collaborated with the British were welcomed by the general-in-chief if not by Moyse and Dessalines. A new planter society began to take shape.

Toussaint's administration was also setting precedents that would endure for more than a century. Military government of the countryside, the recognized right of high officials to enrich themselves, (15) the sequestration of part of the budget into accounts known and controlled only by the chief of state, the derisory pay of the army, and the caprice and corruption of the courts, were among the less attractive features of the régime. The chief of state was all powerful. "Remember," he said, "there is but one Toussaint Louverture in St. Domingue, and at his name, all must tremble."

All Trembled...

All trembled indeed. Toussaint reigned as well as ruled. Restoring the etiquette of the governors of France, the general-in-chief had his velvet-draped priedieu in the cathedral chancel and received white *colons* and Haitian officials at state levees and receptions usually set aside for the planters and their ladies. When approached by an importunate office-seeker, Toussaint would brush him aside with mumbo-jumbo Latin recollected from his days as a choir boy in the slaves' chapel: *"Dominus tecum, salve Domine, tibi gratia* . . . You want to be a judge and can't speak Latin? *Vade retro!"* And the abashed petitioner would retreat in confusion. Displeased with a ministerial report, *"Ministre* . . . " he would sniff, *"valet!"*

But Toussaint would labor all night with his secretaries until the cool of the morning. In a series of decrees he established tariffs, levied taxes, suppressed smuggling, stabilized the currency, organized a budget (33 million francs for 1801), created administrative subdivisions, set up courts, opened schools, built roads (reactivating the French *corvée*), reopened the theater at Cap Français, restored the Gregorian calendar, and returned the clergy to their ancient place and offices. The new coinage of St. Domingue, though still carrying the superscription of France, bore the image of Toussaint. And he addressed a letter to Napoleon inscribed, *"Le premier des noirs au premier des blancs."* The First Consul did not reply.

There followed a still more incautious step. In the spring of 1801, Toussaint convened a hand-picked "Central Assembly" - Bernard Borgella, Lacour, Viard, the pliant Raymond, Collet, Nogéré, and four Dominicans, Roxas, Munoz, Monceibo, and Morillas. Seven were white, three were *hommes de couleur,* and not one was a *noir.* They met on 22 March. Their task: to frame, in Toussaint's words, "a constitution for the island of St. Domingue, according to its interests, which are different from those of France."

On 9 May 1801, the assembly presented to Toussaint the island's first constitution. The general-in-chief was named *gouverneur-general-à-vie* (governor general for life), with power to choose his successor. All was centralized: Toussaint would propose and promulgate the laws; make all appointments, civil, military, and ecclesiastic; control the finances; and command the armies. Distinctions of color were abolished, and so was slavery. (Curiously, however, "cultivators" could not be brought from Africa into the colony.) The Catholic Church was expressly reestablished. Pursuant to the constitution and forthwith, the island was divided into six new departments: North, West, South, "Louverture" (ultimately the Artibonite and the Center), and the Ozama and Cibao (formerly Engano and Samaná).

Promulgated to the boom of cannon and the clangor of church bells at the Cap on 8 July 1801, Toussaint's constitution was authoritarian and centralizing, if not despotic, in every provision, and thus set the model for nearly every Haitian constitution among the many to come. When Christophe read it, his thoughts turned immediately to Napoleon. To Vincent, Henry somberly observed, "This constitution has been drawn up by our most dangerous enemies."

Vincent alone had the courage to face Toussaint. The constitution, he said, should go to the First Consul in draft form for approval, rather than printed and promulgated. Toussaint cut him off: "If there is anything they disapprove, they will send commissaries to treat with me."

Among the cultivators, rumor spread word that Toussaint was pondering restoration of slavery. Throughout the North and Northwest the *ateliers* stirred uneasily.

Just after midnight on 22 October 1801, Limbé and Acul, then Dondon and Marmelade, exploded as fiercely as they had ten years before. Swarming into the plain with firebrands, machetes, bill hooks and Sonthonax's muskets, the cultivators set fire again to the habitations and cut the throats of 300 whites before dawn. At the Cap a nocturnal coup de main was averted only by the vigilance of Henry Christophe, who had the town under control by sunrise and was on the march for Limbé with two infantry battalions and a squadron of dragoons. From his old headquarters at Fort Liberté, Moyse sent out messengers and awaited results.

Reports were not slow in coming. Christophe had crushed the insurrections at Limbé and Port-Margot. Dessalines, whom Moyse had counted on, would not betray Toussaint and was marching North. Toussaint had shifted headquarters from Gonaïves to the d'Héricourt plantation on the Plaine du Nord near Limonade.

Moyse tried to pretend it had all been fomented by Joseph Flaville, the commandant at Limbé whom Christophe had already clapped in chains. To test his loyalty, Toussaint told Moyse to take a body of troops and put down the rising at Port-de-Paix. Moyse gladly marched West, but when he reached Port-de-Paix, all was quiet. Under the muskets of the garrison, Maurepas, whom Toussaint had told what to do, thereupon put Moyse in irons and locked him in a dark cell beneath the old French fort. Moyse had exactly a month to live.

Toussaint and Dessalines had already taken their own measures. According to the estimate of Thomas Madiou, fully one fourth of the cultivators in disaffected districts were cut down by Dessalines. Entering the Cap on 4 November, Toussaint formed his troops in the three sided hollow square of execution and addressed the trembling townsmen: "Here is the man Moyse represented as a traitor! here is the assassin of his brothers! here is the man who tried to re-establish slavery!" Next, he called forward several suspected officers from the ranks. "Shoot yourselves," he ordered. Each blew out his brains with his own pistol. Then, as cannoneers held smoking port fires above the touchholes of three guns, forty trussed rebels, Flaville among them, were herded under the gun muzzles. At Toussaint's command the slow matches descended. As the cannon roared and bounded in recoil, a blast of grape disemboweled the prisoners, and the crowd took to its heels in terror.

Next day Toussaint repeated the scene at Fort Liberté, then again at Trou du Nord, where at the foot of an ancient cayemite tree fully a thousand cultivators were shot or bayoneted. On 29 November, Moyse bravely faced a firing squad while Clervaux and Maurepas watched. Afterward, in a mood of dark foreboding, Toussaint returned to Gonaïves and Port-au-Prince.

To Vincent had fallen the luckless task of delivering Toussaint's constitution to the First Consul. His reward came quickly: he was relieved from duty and ordered to Elba. (16) On 1 October 1802, just thirteen days before Vincent reached Paris, an armistice had been concluded with England. Meeting in London, plenipotentiaries of Napoleon and Pitt had signed the preliminaries to what was to become, next March, the Peace of Amiens.

Napoleon was at length free to deal with St. Domingue.

FOOTNOTES - CHAPTER 3

1. On 16 June 1793, the Marquis du Rouvray wrote a friend, "The Spanish are taking advantage of us. They are providing powder and arms to our brigands. Their priests never cease telling them we are a nation of incendiaries, assassins and regicides."

2. The origin of Toussaint's soubriquet, "Louverture," is obscure. Most authorities, including Dantès Bellegarde, one of Haiti's great historians, say it came from the fact that wherever he went, Toussaint always forced an opening. But Thomas Madiou, an earlier but equally respected historian, wrote in 1847 that the nickname "L'Ouverture" was often applied in both North and West to slaves who, like Toussaint, had missing front teeth.

3. About a thousand Germans, remnants of an unsuccessful colony at Cayenne, came to Bombardopolis in the middle of the eighteenth century and eked out a living growing coffee. After the War of independence, the survivors, like Poles elsewhere in the country, received Haitian citizenship and gradually mingled.

4. Unquenchable as ever, Candy survived three years in the mines, made his escape, and returned to St. Domingue, only to be deported by an implacable Sonthonax, who had come to fear and despise all *hommes de couleur*.

5. The Haitian place names Marmelade and Limonade, underscored by Henry Christophe's creation of a Duc de Marmelade and Comte de Limonade, have long evoked foreign snickers. Both places, however, were settled and named by Frenchmen long before the revolution and, in any case (as Henry once remarked) are no more ridiculous than the high-born French titles of the Prince de Poix or Duc de Bouillon.

6. The infant United States was already playing a role in St. Domingue. In March 1791, a U.S. consul was sent to Cap Français, but the French refused to recognize him. Later, after Bois Cayman, the latter changed their tune and sent agents to Philadelphia to buy up desperately needed arms to resist the slaves. The American government furnished the money but charged it off against the U.S. war debt to France. By 1793, taking his

characteristic long view, Thomas Jefferson wrote Monroe: "I become daily more & more convinced that all the West India islands will remain in the hands of the people of colour & a total expulsion of the whites sooner or later take place..."

7. At home, Britain was beginning to reel under the costs. In 1796, according to Fortescue, historian of the British army, the appropriation for St. Domingue was £2 million, while in January 1797 alone, costs of £700,000 were incurred.

8. But Toussaint had the final word. On 23 July 1798, Sir Thomas Maitland, the British general, wrote that he had "sent him back his old master, a prisoner with us, whom he immediately reinstated to his property."

9. The eighteen-century peso gordo (sometimes called "piastre gordo") had now been Gallicized into "piastre gourde" or, with increasing frequency, just "gourde."

10.Lord Balcarres was acutely sensitive to the fact that, as he put it on 4 July 1798, "Jamaica, being under the lee of [St. Domingue], lies open to her arms, and - what is ten times worse - her opinions. The successes of the Brigands there, holds forth such an example to our Negroes here, as to place Jamaica in a new point of view..."

11. Ultimately, Rigaud's strength reached 9000.

12. As early as 1790, tiny St. Domingue ranked second only to Great Britain in the foreign trade of the United States.

13. Toussaint was not ungrateful. On 21 March he wrote Stevens,"It is with the aid of one of your fregates that Jacmel has surrendered; I shall never forget such a great favor." To the captain and crew of *General Greene,* he presented 10,000 pounds of Jacmel's incomparable coffee.

14. Even so, the 30,000 men with whom Dessalines had first laid siege to Jacmel were now reduced by sickness and battle to 14,000.

15. By 1801, Dessalines had become proprietor of 33 sugar plantations, which brought him well over 300,000 francs a year. In 1799, Cathcart, the British consul, reported that Christophe was already worth more than $250,000.

16. Thirteen years later, when Napoleon arrived at Elba after his abdication, Vincent was on hand to greet him.

Jean-Jacques Dessalines, first emperor of Haiti.
Columbus Library Right: Victor-Emmanuel
Leclerc, Napoleon's brother-in-law, died of
yellow fever while striving to keep St. Domingue
French. *Columbus Library*

CHAPTER 4

The Death of St. Domingue

1801-1803

Damn sugar! Damn coffee! Damn colonies!

- Napoleon Bonaparte, 1803

FOR MANY MONTHS the First Consul had been preparing for the day when he could deal with the "gilded Africans" of St. Domingue. But gilded Africans, however exasperating, were not the only reason St. Domingue was in Bonaparte's mind. Naturally he sought to regain and restore France's once-richest colony, but there was more to it than that. His grand object was to re-establish colonial France in North America, obtaining or if necessary reconquering Spanish Louisiana, which had been French until 1762. For this purpose, Napoleon would need St. Domingue as his staging and advance base, and gateway to the Caribbean and Gulf of Mexico.

As early as 21 July 1801, Louis Pichon, the French minister in Washington, had confided to Thomas Jefferson, the new President, that France intended to move against Toussaint when she could. Jefferson, unlike his predecessor, John Adams, had scant regard for Toussaint and was perfectly willing to see France regain the lost colony. His only reply to Pichon was "You must first make peace with England."(1)

Jefferson had no inkling of Napoleon's ultimate designs but he had a very clear idea of the interrelation between Louisiana - and thus St. Domingue - and France and the United States. On 18 April 1801 he wrote Edward Livingston, American minister in Paris, that New Orleans "is the one single spot, the possessor of which is our natural and habitual enemy . . . The day that France takes possession of New Orleans fixes the sentence which is to restrain her forever within her low water mark . . . From that moment we must marry ourselves to the British fleet and nation."

Now, in October 1801, the peace Jefferson had foreseen had come to pass. The British blockade was lifted. Napoleon did not waste an hour.

Throughout the dockyards and garrisons of France, Spain, and the Low Countries, the First Consul's staff officers distributed orders for assembly, embarkation, and movement of a powerful expeditionary force to St. Domingue. Within ten weeks, 20,000 picked soldiers of the Armies of Italy and the Rhine were at sea. With Talleyrand, on 15 November, Napoleon minced no words: he had resolved, he said, "to annihilate the government of the blacks in St. Domingue."

Watching these developments, Minister Livingston, on 30 December, wrote Rufus King, his American colleague in London, "The expedition, which has as its first object Hispaniola, will proceed against Louisiana if Toussaint does not oppose it." As Henry Adams would later add, "If Toussaint and his blacks should succumb easily to their fate, the wave of French empire would roll on to Louisiana and sweep far up the Mississippi."

The twenty-nine-year-old captain general whom Napoleon had chosen was his brother-in-law, Victor-Emmanuel Leclerc. The secret instructions Napoleon dictated were and are classic. Machiavelli or Nikolai Lenin could not have bettered them.

In brief, Leclerc's mission was to re-establish the *ancien régime*. His operations, directed the First Consul, would be divided into three phases: (1) seize the coastal towns and organize for further operations ashore ("If the first phase lasts fifteen days," wrote Napoleon, "all will be well; if longer, you will have been duped"); (2) smash organized resistance; (3) effect pacification by the use of mobile flying columns. Then Leclerc would restore slavery when he saw fit.

Your conduct [Napoleon directed] will vary with the three phases above-mentioned . . . In the first phase you will not be exacting: negotiate with Toussaint, promise him everything he asks - in order to gain possession of the key points and establish yourself in the country. This done, you will become more exacting. Direct him to reply categorically to your proclamations and my instructions . . . Win over Christophe, Clervaux, Maurepas, and the other black leaders favorable to the whites. In the first phase, confirm them in their rank and position. In the last phase, send them all to France . . . Toussaint will not be considered to have submitted until he comes to Le Cap or Port-au-Prince to swear allegiance, amid the French army, to the Republic. On that same day, without scandal or violence but with honors and consideration, he must be embarked in a frigate and sent to France . . . At the start of the third phase ship out all black generals, regardless of their conduct, patriotism, or past services . . . No matter what happens, during the third phase disarm all *noirs,* whatever their party, and put them to work..... Whites who have served Toussaint will be sent directly to Guiana..... White women who have prostituted themselves to *noirs,* whatever their rank, will be deported to Europe . . . No public instruction whatever shall be re-established in St. Domingue . . . Allow no temporizing with these instructions: and anyone protesting the rights of these *noirs* who have spilled so much white blood shall be sent to France, regardless of rank or past services.

"Rid us of these gilded Africans," Napoleon was later to say, "and we shall have nothing more to wish."

As bait for Toussaint, Napoleon sent with Leclerc the two sons Isaac and Placide - whom Toussaint had entrusted to France in 1797. Now they were to be returned, bearing a letter from the First Consul to their father:

> We esteem you and wish to recognize and proclaim the great services you have rendered to the French people. If their colors fly on St. Domingue, it is to you and your brave blacks that we owe it . . . Now that circumstances are so happily changed, you will be the first to render homage to the sovereignty of the nation which counts you among its most illustrious citizens . . . What can you desire? The freedom of the blacks? You know that in all countries we have been in, we have given it to those who had it not. Consideration, honors, fortune? After the services you have rendered and can still render, and with the esteem we have for you, you should not be uncertain . . . And General, know that if you are the first of your color who has attained such power and distinguished himself by his bravery and military skill, you are also, before God and us, responsible for their use . . . Count without reserve on our esteem and conduct yourself as one of the principal citizens of the greatest nation in the world ought to.

In early December 1801, beating into atrocious weather, French, Spanish, and Dutch squadrons sailed for St. Domingue from Brest, Rochefort, Lorient, Toulon, and Cadiz, with follow-up forces on the way from Cherbourg and Flushing - in all, 67 sailed under the flag of Vice Admiral Comte Louis-Thomas Villaret-Joyeuse. Embarked, besides Pauline and her court - artists, musicians, ladies' maids - and his infant son and the two Louverture boys and their cassocked tutor, Leclerc had 21,175 troops. They were of high quality and well commanded. The average age of the generals was thirty years and ten months; every one had earned his stripes under Napoleon. At forty-six, Rochambeau, Leclerc's deputy and senior division commander, was the oldest; at fifty-one, the admiral was nearly twice the age of the captain general.

Toussaint must have known that the French were coming. His intelligence service never failed him. Otherwise, why would he have been waiting at the Eastern end of the island, on the heights overlooking Samaná Bay, when Villaret made his landfall on 29 January 1802?

For a moment, when he saw the armada, even Toussaint's nerve faltered. "We are lost," he said; "all France has come to St. Domingue." Then, gathering his staff and sending messengers to his commanders, he spurred Westward.

They Have Cut off Only the Trunk

The force that daunted Toussaint represented only a fraction of the whole expedition. Because the December Atlantic had frustrated rendezvous plans of the widely dispersed movement groups, Leclerc had with him at Samaná Bay only 11,900 troops embarked hit-or-miss rather than combat-loaded and ready to land. Leclerc obtained a day's delay at Samaná while units reformed, gear was prepared for landing, and a frigate was sent ahead to Montecristi to co-opt native pilots capable of guiding the ships into the ports of St. Domingue.

Two more frigates, with General Kerverseau (one of several old hands in the expedition)(2) and 400 troops were detached to seize Ciudad Santo Domingo. Then, divided into attack groups for Fort Liberté (Rochambeau), the Cap (Leclerc and Hardy), Port-de-Paix (Humbert), and Port-au-Prince (Boudet), the force raised anchor and made sail.

Leclerc knew Toussaint had something over 20,000 soldiers throughout the colony. Therefore, rather than risk an opposed landing at the Cap, he planned subsidiary landings that would envelop the city from land while the main naval force feinted at the harbor entrance.

Toussaint's strategy - which Christophe at the Cap was preparing to implement - must have been clear to his lieutenants. Simple and ruthless, it would be to burn the towns, lay waste the habitations, kill the *blancs,* fall back into the mountains, wait for the climate to cripple the French, and massacre the survivors.

At midday, 2 February, with twenty-three warships and 5000 soldiers, Villaret stationed the force flagship, *Océan,* off the Cap. Before the admiral's barge was in the water, Henry Christophe had the arsenal making *lances-à-feu,* tar-headed firebrands for burning the elegant city he himself had largely reconstructed from the ruins of 1795.

When Leclerc's aide clambered onto the landing with Napoleon's proclamation ("Whatever your origin or color, you are all French and all free and all equal before God . . .") he was sternly greeted by Christophe: no warship could enter without clearance by the governor general.

Then commenced a kind of minuet that lasted three days, with Leclerc trying to bluff his way in and Christophe trying to bluff him out. Yet each bluff was in earnest: Leclerc knew Rochambeau was already landing at Fort Liberté and Hardy was off Port-Margot; Christophe for his part had tar barrels in his own mansion and torches for every soldier.

"I learn with indignation, Citizen General," stormed Leclerc, "that you refuse to receive the squadron and the army of France under my command, claiming that you have no orders from the governor general." Christophe replied: "The very ground underfoot will be on fire before your squadron drops anchor."

Toward evening on 4 February, a French ship, *Aiguille,* commenced replacing the buoys Christophe had removed. As she came within range, Fort Picolet fired a warning shot. *Aiguille* and her supporting frigates returned the fire. When Christophe heard the broadsides, he set fire to his own mansion and ordered the Cap destroyed. By midnight, while townsmen watched in horror from the Haut-du-Cap, the city was once again a sea of flames. Next morning, Villaret's pulling boats brought Napoleon's grenadiers ashore. Of 2000 houses, only 59 still stood: a hundred million francs had disappeared in flame and pillage.

Christophe held his troops in town only long enough to spike the guns at Fort Picolet, blow the magazines, and stand off agonized householders and merchants trying to protect their property from the flames. Then, with the soldiers crying "Mété feu partout! *Tué blanc-yo!* (Set everything afire, kill the whites!), he withdrew into the mountains, burning as he went.

What prompted Christophe's retreat was word that the French were already ashore on both sides of the Cap and closing in. The intelligence was correct. Hardy, Rochambeau and Leclerc were already ashore. By 7 February the captain general held the Cap.

While Villaret was landing fire pumps amid the ruins, Humbert and Boudet were storming ashore at Port-de-Paix and Port-au-Prince. At the former, Maurepas refused even to receive Humbert's *parlementaires,* blew up the forts, set fire to the town, and withdrew up the valley of Trois Rivières.

Port-au-Prince was spared because Agé temporized and because Lamartinière, the Haitian commander, an *homme du couleur,* decided he would fight the French without burning the city - which he did. On 5 February Boudet landed 3000 men at Lamentin, marched on Fort Bizoton, and swept North up the Grande Rue into the city.

But the French were not quick enough to save the white hostages Lamartinière had already arrested. As Boudet entered Port-au-Prince, the *blancs* were herded to Savane Valembrun (not far from today's Fort Dimanche) and massacred with machete and bayonet.

By 9 February, Leclerc was firmly ashore. And on that day, he reported to the Minister of Marine the disposition of his forces.

Santo Domingo 400; At the Cap: Rochambeau 1800, Hardy 1800, Desfourneaux 1400; Port-de-Paix 500; Port-au-Prince 2800

Then a situation report: insubordination and pillage by the sailors . . . Toussaint's estimated strength (17,000 soldiers and "a mass of cultivators") . . . trouble finding mounts for the cavalry and artillery . . . rations ("eight days of biscuit, after that we eat bananas") . . .and, more somberly, "Toussaint and his generals appear to me to have decided to burn down the colony and entomb themselves under the ruins before surrendering their empire."

Leclerc was right. At this very moment Toussaint was writing Dessalines: "The only resources we have are destruction and fire. Annihilate everything and burn everything. Block the roads, pollute the wells with corpses and dead horses. Leave nothing white behind you."

Dessalines needed no urging. Henceforth his war cry would be *"Coupé têtes! Broulé cailles!"* (Cut off their heads! Burn down their houses!).

In the South and in Santo Domingo, no heads were rolling and no habitations were in flames. With Boudet ashore at Port-au-Prince, the South, as in the days of the British, was again isolated. Laplume promptly made submission to the French and was confirmed in command. In Santo Domingo, Paul Louverture and Clervaux, neither of whom had much stomach for fighting, were easily persuaded to submit by the French bishop, Mauviel, who beneath his cassock was a secret agent of Bonaparte.

In the West and Artibonite the story was different. Before Boudet could take Croix-des-Bouquets, Dessalines burned it and retired on St. Marc, thus interposing himself between Boudet and Leclerc in the North. When Boudet pressed up the coast past Arcahaie, Dessalines, emulating Christophe, put the torch to his own home at St. Marc, killed some 200 white and *mulâtre* hostages, and struck inland to retake Port-au-Prince. But the city was vigorously defended by Pamphile de Lacroix, and Dessalines was repulsed.

Leclerc had learned his trade under Napoleon. He was barely more than half-strength and already short of funds as well as supplies which were supposed to have been embarked but through incompetence or jobbery were not. He had no field kitchens or mess gear; he had inadequate hospitals for a sick list already numbering 2000; and he was short 11,000 pairs of boots. Without hesitation, the captain general flung his columns into the attack.

As the French divisions began to close in, Leclerc sent Toussaint his sons, bearing Napoleon's letter in a sealed enamel case of blue and gold. Toussaint never wavered. To his credit, Leclerc let the boys make their own choice. Isaac, who because of his disposition should have been named Placide, said he could never fight against France. Placide, fiery and tempestuous, chose his father's lot. Then, on 17 February (the day his sick list hit 2000), Leclerc proclaimed Toussaint rebel and outlaw.

By 22 February, despite torrents of rain, Rochambeau, all energy and impetuosity, had thrust South through the mountains past St. Raphaël. Desfourneaux's French were near Ennery. With 3000 men, including his personal guard, Toussaint lay between. Holding a key defile, Ravine-à-Couleuvre (Ravine of the Serpent), Toussaint hoped to keep the French divided and beat them in detail. His position was strong: a precipitous gorge flanked by brush-covered mountains. (Afterward Leclerc would write: "You should see this country to form any idea of the difficulties we encounter. I have seen nothing in the Alps to compare.")

On the 23d Rochambeau launched the French grenadiers up the ravine. For six hours a bloody struggle ensued. But neither *Ogun*, god of war, not *Damballah* the Serpent could stop the bayonets of the Rhine, Italy, and Egypt. Toussaint had to abandon his position, leaving 800 dead, and fall back on Pont de l'Estère. Halting only to replenish ammunition, Leclerc threw Desfourneaux against Vernet trying to defend Gonaïves. After a stubborn defense the Haitians (3) had to retire, but not before the town was in flames.

Now it was Toussaint and Dessalines and Christophe against the invaders. By the beginning of March the only territory they controlled lay in the Montagnes Noires on the right bank of the Artibonite. Here Toussaint had cached his treasury and here, on a gently sloping elevation overlooking Petite Rivière de l'Artibonite, stood La Crête-à-Pierrot, a fort built by the English. The position, deceptively unimposing, covers the mouth of the Upper Artibonite Valley, the crossings near Petite Rivière, and the approaches to the summits where Toussaint and Dessalines still hoped to hold out. While Christophe's guerrillas and a mobile column under Toussaint slashed at Leclerc's rear, Dessalines concentrated at La Crête-à-Pierrot.

On 4 March, Debelle, down from Port-de-Paix, engaged Dessalines below Petite Rivière. As the French pressed them hard, the Haitian outposts fell back on La Crête. With Debelle at their head, French storming parties swept forward. Suddenly the guns of the fort loosed a murderous salvo of grape, accompanied by volley after volley of close-range musketry. Debelle and his second-in-command, Devaux, both dropped, and so did 400 attackers. The shattered division abandoned the assault.

A week later, the French tried again. Infuriated by discovery of 800 corpses of men, women, and children killed by Dessalines at Verrettes (4), Boudet and Lacroix (with Alexandre Pétion's *mulâtres* as the French advance guard) tried to seize the fort in a night attack. Once again they were repulsed.

Then the French divisions formed for a daylight assault. Inside La Crête, Dessalines took post beside the magazine with a lighted torch.

"If the French overrun the fort," he promised, "I'll blow it up." Time after time, the French swept forward; time after time, the fort's guns cut them down. One French subaltern gained the rampart, flung his kepi inside, and fell dead trying to follow it. Two more French generals - Boudet and Dugua - fell at the head of their columns. The captain general himself, up from Port-au-Prince, was hit by a spent ball. As night fell and the French again pulled back, mongrel dogs ranged the field, tearing the flesh of over 700 dead and wounded Frenchmen.

Since assault would not do, the battle lapsed into siege. Four divisions (Hardy, Rochambeau, Lacroix, and Burck) encircled La Crête. Pétion, an experienced artilleryman, set up a mortar battery that dropped shells into the fort day and night(just as, at Jacmel, he had been similarly punished by Toussaint's mortars). Amidst all the battle, from inside La Crête, the besiegers could hear Toussaint's bandsmen playing the "Marseillaise," "Ça Ira," and other French songs.

Yet the end was inevitable. Beginning on 22 March, the French bombardment intensified, Haitian ammunition ran low, and casualties (over 400) mounted. On orders from Dessalines, Lamartinière, the immediate commander (accompanied by Marie-Jeanne, the lovely *mulâtresse* who had shared the siege with him), silently evacuated La Crête-à-Pierrot by night on 24 March. Lacroix's verdict as soldier, participant, and historian, can stand: "The retreat the commander of La Crête-à-Pierrot conceived and executed is a remarkable feat of arms. We had more than 12,000 men surrounding him. He got away with the bulk of his garrison and left us only his dead and wounded."

Yet La Crête-à-Pierrot, Haiti's most glorious battle and, for Leclerc, a Pyrrhic victory, marked the end of organized resistance. It also signaled the successful conclusion of Napoleon's second phase. Before April closed, Toussaint (though still waging guerrilla war) (5) was in secret negotiation, via Boudet, with Leclerc. So also was Christophe. Dessalines alone had no thought of surrender.

On 25 April 1802, Christophe released 2000 white hostages, suspended hostilities, and met Leclerc at the Haut-du-Cap. Here, with his 1500 remaining regulars, he was confirmed with rank and command in the service of France. The balance of his force, some 4000 cultivators, resumed cultivation.

Eleven days later, assured by Leclerc that he had nothing to fear, Toussaint entered the Cap. Followed by his staff and 400 dragoons with drawn sabers, the governor general dismounted at the Place du Gouvernement and walked to await Leclerc, who joined him in Government House among the Haitian generals, his brother included, who had already submitted. When Paul sought to embrace him, Toussaint turned his back. Then, meeting with Leclerc, Toussaint, who had been promised rank as lieutenant general, agreed to retire to his plantation at Ennery. Belair, Dessalines, and Vernet were to be received into the French colonial forces, as were those of the honor guard who did not choose demobilization with their chief.

That night, Leclerc entertained Toussaint at dinner. The tone of the occasion may be gauged from the fact that Toussaint refused all food save a square trimmed from the inside of a cheese, and drank only from a water carafe that had already been tasted. Before the clock struck eleven he was on the road to Ennery.

At St. Marc on 23 May, accompanied by Belair, Lamartinière, and Gabart, Dessalines marched his demibrigades back into the town he himself had burned, and, by Leclerc's order, assumed command of the Artibonite. The struggle seemed over.

On 6 June 1802, Leclerc was uneasy. That day he wrote to the Minister of Marine in Paris: "Toussaint is not to be trusted . . . I am going to order his arrest . . . As soon as I have him safe, I shall ship him off to Corsica for imprisonment."

Leclerc at first thought Dessalines might be the man to do the deed. But he changed his mind and chose a French general, Brunet. On 7 June, Brunet, whose headquarters were at Habitation Georges, near Gonaïves, asked Toussaint to meet him for a conference.

It was a trap. Toussaint, his habitual suspicion inexplicably lulled, took the bait and went to Brunet, accompanied only by two officers and an orderly. Once inside he was arrested at sword's point and driven through the night by carriage under an escort of dragoons to Gonaïves.

Trussed like a convict, Toussaint was spirited aboard the frigate *Créole,* at Gonaïves, and conveyed to the Cap. There in the harbor awaited *Héros,* ship of the line, with Mme. Louverture and the boys, who had also been seized. With oars muffled, Toussaint was rowed on board and the ship got underway. The Haut-du-Cap, dropping behind the horizon, was Toussaint's last sight of St. Domingue.(6) To the captain *of Héros* he said: "In overthrowing me they have cut off only the trunk of the tree of black liberty. It will flourish again through its roots. They are many and deep."

These People Won't Surrender

Leclerc and the beautiful Pauline had settled into viceregal contentments divided between the breezy heights of La Tortue and the refurbished ruins of the Cap. The captain general, recounted Mary Hassal, a sharp-eyed American visitor, "ordered a superb service of plate, made of the money intended to pay the army....... Mme. Leclerc . . . a voluptuous mouth and . . . an air of languor.....is very kind to General Boyer." Miss Hassal, herself a close friend of Aaron Burr and perhaps no stranger to such arrangements, then went on to describe the setting of Mme. Leclerc's kindnesses:

A door, which stood open, led into the bedchamber. The canopy of the bed was in the form of a shell, from which little cupids, descending, held back with one hand, curtains of white satin trimmed with gold, and pointed with the other to the large mirror which formed the tester. On the table, in the form of an altar, which stood near the bed, was an elaborate figure representing Silence, with a finger on its lips and bearing in its hand a waxen taper.

Silence, however imperious in Pauline Leclerc's bower, could not still reports beginning to filter into St. Domingue of events abroad.

In April, before Christophe or Toussaint submitted, another French expeditionary force, under General Antoine Richepanse, had landed at Guadeloupe to reassert the authority of the First Consul. Even while Richepanse was at sea, Napoleon's new Minister of Marine (Denis, Duc de Decrès, an admiral, a figure of the *ancien régime* and an unbudging adherent of the old colonial system) was inditing a decree "to fix the status of the *noirs*" on Guadeloupe and St. Domingue as well as in colonies where they had never won freedom.

On 20 May 1802, Napoleon signed Decrès's draft. In Martinique, Tobago, Saint Lucia, and the Ile-de-France, slavery and the slave trade were overtly restored. On the face of the paper, Guadeloupe and St. Domingue seemed excepted. But as soon as word of Toussaint's surrender reached Paris, on 14 June Napoleon sent confidential copies of the decree to Richepanse and Leclerc. Each was authorized to restore slavery when the time seemed opportune. Richepanse did so immediately. Leclerc - by midsummer down to 8500 men fit for duty carefully locked away the decree.

At about the same time, mid-June, further edicts stripped *hommes de couleur* of equal rights, banned mixed marriages, and restored the color line. None of these decrees was published or executed in St. Domingue, but, by midsummer, word began to reach the colony of events on Guadeloupe.

More important, after the spring rains, the stagnant pools and coastal flats teemed first with larvae, then swarmed with *Aëdes aëgypti* mosquitoes. By May, the time of the Yellow Jack had come.

What it was to die of yellow fever (and most did: the mortality exceeded 80 percent) appears in the following contemporary account by a British doctor in the West Indies:

> When I entered the room, the patient was vomiting [coagulated blood], and was bleeding at the nose. A watery discharge was oozing from the corners of his eyes, and from his mouth and gums. His face was besmeared with blood. His abdomen was swelled, and inflated prodigiously. His body all over was of a deep yellow, interspersed with livid spots. His hands and feet were of ap livid hue. Every part of him was cold excepting about his heart. He had a deep strong hiccough . . Exhausted with vomiting, he at last suffocated with the blood he was endeavoring to bring up, and expired.

On 7 May, the day after Toussaint's surrender, Leclerc allowed himself to describe his situation to Napoleon as "brilliant." But even then, perhaps his brightest hour, he added: "Our death rate is dreadful." Well he might: the French were losing thirty to fifty men each day. The dead were being carted away by night. To hide the losses at the Cap, military funerals were suspended. Within a month, Leclerc was calling for eighty medical officers to replace those who had died. Thirty-five hundred sick lay sprawled on the foul mud floors of improvised hospitals.

On 11 June, Leclerc wrote Decrès: "If the First Consul still wants to have an army in St. Domingue by October, he had better begin mounting it out from France, because the ravages of sickness are simply indescribable."

Among the generals, Hardy and Debelle were gone. So were Leclerc's artillery commander and quartermaster. Every engineer officer was dead or on the sick list. Benezech, the civilian prefect, perhaps mercifully, was dead: by personal conviction, he abhorred slavery. By 6 July, Leclerc was reporting 160 deaths a day: June, he wrote, had cost him 3000.

Abed with malaria, which attacked those the Yellow Jack spared, Leclerc had still another problem. Although Toussaint's submission had brought peace to St. Domingue, the colony was nowhere near disarmed. Some 140,000 muskets remained in the hands of the blacks: they were not about to turn them in. With 8500 effectives on his 12 July morning report, Leclerc could well observe to Decrès, "Disarming the North will be touch-and-go." During the previous week, he added, there had been nighttime meetings of *noirs,* throughout the Plaine du Nord. Amid the beat of the drums and the hooting *lambis* and *vaccines* (7) echoed the words of Sonthonax: "If you mean to keep your liberty, take up your arms on the day the *blancs* call them in."

Limbé, Plaisance, and Grande Rivière du Nord were the first to resist. The bands of Scylla, Sans-Souci, Petit-Noël, Yayou, and Paul Romain retired to the mountains of the North. Throughout the West, Lafortune and Lamour Dérance did likewise. In the remote valleys behind Tiburon and Les Irois, Samedi Smith and Goman sent tremors through the Grande-Anse. Charles Belair, accompanied by his devoted wife, Sanite, vanished into the Matheux mountains South of the Artibonite and proclaimed himself general of the revolt.

By August, Leclerc had his hands full. In the hospitals at the Cap alone, a hundred Frenchmen were dying every day. On 6 August, the captain general told Decrès: "My position is no better, the revolt is spreading, and the sickness unabated. The blacks are persuaded . . . that we intend to enslave them, and I won't be able to disarm them without long, hard fighting. These people won't surrender . . ."

As French officers succumbed, Leclerc had to depend on his *noir* generals. "I have ordered them to make terrible examples and I always employ them when I have something fearful to do," he told Decrès on 9 August. "Dessalines," he confided to Napoleon on 16 September, "is my butcher." So he was: that very week, to avenge the killing of some French in the Artibonite, that man of blood coldly cut the throats of 300 *noirs* and *hommes de couleur.*

Dessalines, of course, had projects of his own. Belair had been his archrival in the days of Toussaint. In September, betrayed by Dessalines, Belair, with his wife, faced an all-Haitian court-martial at the Cap, presided over by Clervaux. On 5 October, side by side, the two Belairs were disposed of by a black firing squad.

Belair was not cold in his grave before Clervaux changed sides. On the night of 12 October, with his *mulâtre* demibrigades, Pétion had spiked the guns on the Haut-du-Cap and quit the Cap. His hand forced by Pétion, Clervaux, too, joined the rebels.

Christophe and Dessalines temporized. But when word reached Christophe of a new atrocity by the frightened French - 1200 disarmed black soldiers bayoneted and dumped in the harbor of the Cap(8) - his mind was quickly made up. Although an ancient enemy, Petit-Noël, led the bands around the Cap, Christophe, who feared no one, rode to join them at the head of his troops.

As Dessalines wavered, an attempt was made to trap him before Sunday dinner with the French *curé* at Petite Rivière. Warned in the nick of time by a servant, he sprang to arms and turned like a tiger upon the *blancs*.

As the volcano seethed underfoot, Leclerc desperately concentrated his European troops. Under Haitian attack, the garrison of Fort Liberté evacuated by sea and joined the defenders of the Cap, which by 16 October was surrounded.(9) Elsewhere, remaining French units retreated on St. Marc, Port-au-Prince, and the Môle.

Leclerc had good cause for alarm. Besides the appalling sickness and the new revolts, he had been abandoned. Replacements came in driblets,(10) supplies were nonexistent, and his war chest empty. Letter after letter to Decrès and Bonaparte detail the captain general's exigencies. On 6 July he wrote the Minister of Marine: "Except for 3000 pairs of shoes, I have received nothing, my army is naked . . . I am absolutely without funds."

Later the same day, in still another appeal to Decrès, Leclerc's patience snapped:

Citizen Minister, I haven't even heard from you since 11 April. . . Your utter neglect is cruel. I have asked for money, uniforms, medical equipment, ordnance supplies, artificers, and you have sent nothing, you have told me nothing. Not one of your letters has even said whether the Government is satisfied with my conduct. In my situation, one needs encouragement.

What Leclerc could not know was that Napoleon's attention had been diverted to a more grandiose enterprise. In June, satisfied that St. Domingue was his, the First Consul had secretly instructed Decrès to organize an expedition to proceed with the seizure of Louisiana from Spain. Ostensible reinforcements for St. Domingue were to compose the force. Leclerc would have to make do as best he could.

Nor was there any respite from the Yellow Jack. On 13 September, writing to Napoleon, the luckless captain general summed up the bill: total troops sent to St. Domingue, 28,000 - 10,500 Still alive (4500 on their feet, 1500 convalescents, 4500 in the pesthouses). Sailors dead in the fleet, 5000. "Thus," he concluded, "the occupation of St. Domingue has so far cost 20,000 men."

Leclerc must have known the game was up, or he would never, on 7 October, have written Napoleon what proved to be his last letter. If you reproach me, he said, blame the fever that destroyed my army, the premature re-establishment of slavery on Guadeloupe, and (not the last general to say so) the newspapers at home.

> Here is my opinion [wrote Leclerc]. You will have to exterminate all the blacks in the mountains, women as well as men. except for children under twelve. Wipe out half the population of the lowlands, and do not leave in the colony a single black who has worn an epaulet . . . Send 12,000 replacements immediately, and 10 million francs in cash, or St. Domingue is lost forever.

This letter, wrote Lothrop Stoddard in a memorable passage,

> . . . was Leclerc's last will and testament. He had written it in the flush of a new malarial crisis which prostrated him for some time, and scarcely had he shown signs of recovery when the first symptoms of yellow fever appeared . . . Leclerc has been much blamed for the French failure in San Domingo, but when, in the light of all the attending circumstances, we picture the Captain-General dragging himself from his bed in the flush of fever or the shiver of ague to pen his luminous dispatches, we must agree that it is a wonder he did so well.

It was on 22 October, with Christophe, Clervaux, Sans-Souci, and Petit-Noël at the gates of the Cap, that Leclerc knew he had yellow fever. Before midnight on All Saints' Day he was gone. Pauline Leclerc ("who had not loved him while living," noted Mary Hassal) cut off her luxurious hair and laid it in his coffin. ("She knows," sniffed her brother with equal cynicism, "that cropping will make it grow twice as thick.")

As provided by the First Consul's secret instructions to Leclerc, Rochambeau succeeded in command. The new general, wrote Miss Hassal, had "an agreeable face, a sweet mouth, and a most enchanting smile." Behind this facade the man himself was cruel, arrogant, whimsical, a caricature of the *ancien régime* and of its attributes which had ignited the French Revolution. Leclerc's estimate of his second-in-command was simple: "A brave and skilled fighter with no tact or political sense whatever, no character, and easily led."

Save that the French forces still held the Cap as well as, again, Fort Liberté and Port-de-Paix (which Rochambeau had promptly retaken - the one to assure supplies of Spanish cattle from the East, the other to safeguard the fever hospitals on La Tortue), Rochambeau was in the same fix as the British in 1797. His army was concentrated in the main coastal towns, and, despite pittances of replacements, he had nowhere near the troops needed to cope with general insurrection. To make matters worse for the French, the South, until then quiet under Laplume, joined the revolt in early 1803.

Late in the preceding year, Goman and Laurent Férou, a wealthy *mulâtre* proprietor, had sparked local outbreaks in the Grande-Anse. Cangé, another veteran of Savannah, was at large in the mountains behind Grand-Goâve. But it was Nicolas Geffrard, a *mulâtre* and former officer under Rigaud, who, freely acknowledging (like Pétion) the central authority of Dessalines, made his way into the South and brought the region to open war. Pétion, meanwhile, liberated Mirebalais and the Upper Artibonite.

But the war against the French was far from over.

By March 1803, Rochambeau had 11,000 effectives and only 4000 sick. The yellow fever had passed, and those still alive were immune. Napoleon, for his part, was at last shaping up 15,000 replacements for the summer and another 15,000 for a decisive campaign in the fall.

If Leclerc had in the end despaired of winning the minds and hearts of the Haitians, Rochambeau never gave the idea a thought. His cruelties seem unbelievable but have been amply recorded.

Maurepas, who had been seized before he had a chance to join Pétion and Clervaux, was lashed to the mast of a French ship at Cap Français. There, while his wife and children watched, with cocked hat set derisively askew, he had his epaulets spiked to his naked shoulders by the ship's carpenter. Then Rochambeau had the whole family bayoneted and dumped into the harbor.

At Port-au-Prince, Rochambeau, at his most charming, gave a grand ball in honor of the Haitian ladies. As midnight tolled, the women were conducted into a shrouded room where black-robed figures chanted a *Dies Irae* over coffins that lined the walls. "Ladies," announced Rochambeau, "you have just attended the funeral of your brothers and husbands." It was no joke: while the ladies danced, the men had been slaughtered.

Bloodhounds were purchased in Cuba to pursue rebels and *marrons*. On 6 April 1802, Rochambeau wrote a subordinate:

> "I am sending you a detachment of 150 men from the Cap, accompanied by 28 dogs *[chiens boule-dogues]*. These reinforcements should enable you to wind up operations. I need not remind you that no rations or ration allowances are authorized for the dogs. You will give them blacks to eat."

But the dogs proved to be trackers only and refused to eat the living flesh of naked prisoners staked before their kennels.(11)

After a fight at Acul du Nord, Rochambeau disposed of 500 prisoners by having them dig a pit and then shooting them on its brink. When word reached

Dessalines that evening, he repaid in kind: 500 crude gibbets were erected during the night, and at sunrise 500 Frenchmen were hanged under the eyes of Rochambeau's army.

The atrocities of Rochambeau, the *noirs'* fear of re-enslavement, the despair of *hommes de couleur* again stripped of their rights - all these accomplished what no ruler or régime in Haiti ever again achieved. For the first and last time in the history of the country, Haitians of all colors spontaneously united in a single cause.(12)

Only two years earlier, Pétion and Geffrard and the other *mulâtre* officers of Rigaud had fought Dessalines and Christophe to the last cartridge. Now they freely linked arms behind the fierce *noir* who had drenched the whole South with the blood of *gens de couleur*. Yet it was Dessalines himself who in the final analysis unified his countrymen.

Subordinating the perfidy, rancor, and cruelty that had dominated his actions and would do so again, Dessalines made himself the embodiment of the struggle for independence.

In the saddle night and day, like Toussaint before him, Dessalines was everywhere. In January 1803 he organized the North and Northwest. Then, leaving the West to Pétion (whom he now addressed as "*compère*"), he entered the South and met with Geffrard and the chiefs of the bands who had acknowledged him. Here, at Camp Gérard, outside Les Cayes, Dessalines first noticed an intense young *mulâtre,* Boisrond-Tonnerre, who had escaped through the French outposts and was soon to become his secretary and amanuensis.

By May it seemed to Pétion that the time had come for some formal act of unification, if only to secure the firm allegiance and effective collaboration of the *congo* chiefs.

Belair had burned Arcahaie in 1802, but it was still a lovely spot. Beside its beach and under its palms, the generals and the chieftains met on 14 May. With Christophe, Pétion, and Clervaux beside him, Dessalines hammered home the need for unity. Up to this moment the Haitians had fought under the flag of France. On 18 May, the last day of what was later to be called the Congress of Arcahaie, all swore allegiance to Dessalines. The table at which he stood was draped with the Tricolor. Seizing the flag, Dessalines rent out the white and ground it underfoot. As soon as the red and blue could be stitched together (by Catherine Flon, goddaughter of Mme. Dessalines), the Haitians had a flag of their own. (13)

But there was news the men at Arcahaie could not yet know. On 12 May, Pitt had broken the Peace of Amiens: Britain and France were again at war. Within a month, British cruisers were scouring the Windward Passage and were on station off Cap Français. Rochambeau was cut off.

Most Unhappy Man of Men

Between the green mountains and blue sea and sky of Haiti, April is very different from April in the Jura and the Franche-Comté on France's Eastern frontier. "The climate," says the *Encyclopedia Britannica* of the Jura, "is, on the whole, cold; the temperature is subject to sudden and violent changes, and among the mountains winter sometimes lingers for eight months. The rainfall is much above the average of France." In this forbidding place, within the ninth-century Fort de Joux atop 500-foot scarps of sheer rock, Toussaint Louverture - separated from his wife, his family, at last from his faithful servant, Mars Plaisir, was locked away to die. Even in those straits he would have savored the irony, could he have known it, that another cell in the same grim fort was at that moment occupied by an ancient foe. André Rigaud, shipped back from St. Domingue, had also been clapped into the Fort de Joux.

On 24 August 1802, Toussaint was admitted to the sinister fort. His cell was a stone vault twenty feet long by twelve wide. He never left it alive. His petitions and reports of his privations and indignities went unheeded. Napoleon had but two interests insofar as Toussaint was concerned: one was to keep him safely confined; the other, to discover where he might have hidden the treasure he was supposed to have cached in St. Domingue.

If the sickly season in the West Indies did for Leclerc, winter in the Jura killed his opponent. On 7 April 1803, Toussaint was found dead by his keeper, huddled over the ashes of his cold fireplace. The autopsy report listed the cause of death as "apoplexy-pleuro-peripneumonia." Very likely the surgeon did not know the forensic nomenclature for a broken heart.

> Toussaint, the most unhappy Man of Men!
> Whether the whistling Rustic tend his plough
> Within thy hearing, or thy head be now
> Pillow'd in some deep dungeon's earless den.
> O miserable Chieftain! where and when
> Wilt thou find patience? Yet die not: do thou
> Wear rather in thy bonds a cheerful brow:
> Though fallen thyself, never to rise again,
> Live, and take comfort. Thou hast left behind
> Powers that will work for thee: air, earth, and skies.
> There's not a breathing of the common wind
> That will forget thee: thou hast great allies:
> Thy friends are exultations, agonies,
> And love, and Man's unconquerable mind.

So wrote Wordsworth in 1802 (14), as Toussaint lay freezing.

Bonaparte reserved his verdict until later, when he himself was exiled, pinioned and dying by inches on a remote shore. To Las Cases, his secretary on St. Helena, Napoleon said, "I must reproach myself for the attempt on St. Domingue during the Consulship. It was a grave mistake. I should have been satisfied to govern by means of Toussaint Louverture."

Li Porté Fusils, Li Porté Boulets

Dessalines sorti nan Nord,
Vini compté Ca li porté,
Ca li porté.
Li porté fusils, li porté boulets,
(Chorus) *Ouanga nouveau!"*

"Dessalines has come from the North/Come see what he's brought/ he's brought guns/he's brought bullets/ a new *ouanga.*"A *ouanga* is a Voodoo charm or spell designed to achieve a specific purpose (for example, *ouanga-à-mort* is a death curse).

With this and other Créole marching songs on their lips, Dessalines's battalions swept against the French. "You had to have seen their bravery," remembered Lemonnier-Delafosse, "to have an idea of it . . . Their songs roared out in unison by two thousand voices, with the guns for bass, had a gripping effect . . . Those massed black squares, singing as they marched to death in the magnificent sunlight, stayed long in my memory; even today, after more than forty years, the imposing, grandiose picture comes back as vividly as in those first moments."

Laurent Férou occupied Jérémie on 4 August. Besieged by Gabart, with the British navy offshore, St. Marc held out until 2 September. Starved out, the French general, d'Henin, capitulated to the English. Jacmel had been under intermittent attack since December 1802 by the black colossus, Lamour Dérance, but commencing in June 1803, Magloire Ambroise and Cangé surrounded the city again; on 17 October the starving defenders were allowed to capitulate to the Royal Navy and evacuate to Santo Domingo.

Once again the noose was closing upon a European army. One after another, the familiar places fell or capitulated.

Under the guns of H.M.S. *Theseus,* Toussaint Brave recaptured Fort Liberté in September. On 3 October Port-de-Paix was evacuated; the little French garrison evaded the English and got away to Santo Domingo.

Sweeping across the Cul-de-Sac with fire and sword, Dessalines posted his headquarters at Habitation Frère (later the site of the Haitian Military Academy). Then, having shouldered the French out of Lascahobas, he attacked Port-au-Prince from the North. On terrain that would ultimately bear his name, Pétion extended Dessalines's left along the heights to Morne l'hôpital. Under Cangé,

5000 troops marched in from the South against Bizoton. Pétion personally
trained his mortars on the French hospital. When Croix-des-Bouquets fell, there
was no more food. Then Fort Bizoton was overrun: and, on 3 October,
Lavallette, the French commander, surrendered. Six days later the French were
allowed to embark and take their chances with His Majesty's cruisers, and
Dessalines marched down from Turgeau to take possession.(16)

By the end of October the only places left to France were Môle St. Nicolas,
held by Noailles, and Cap Français, where, with 5000 troops, Rochambeau was
at bay.

With 16,000 men (17), Dessalines marched North to finish the work begun
by Macandal and Boukman.

Rochambeau had ten forts and several batteries defending the Cap. Two -
Picolet and d'Estaing (a naval battery) - covered the harbor; the remainder, on
high ground, flanked the precipitous defile that leads from the Haut-du-Cap into
town.

Rather than institute formal siege, for which he lacked the artillery and which
he doubted his army could maintain, Dessalines decided to take the Cap by
storm. During the night of 17-18 November the Haitians emplaced their few
guns to bombard Fort Bréda, sited on the habitation whose former coachman
now lay buried within the Fort de Joux. Before dawn, Christophe and Romain
were silently moving to seize d'Estaing (today known as Batterie des Mornets)
from the rear. A storming column - the 9th Demibrigade under Capoix-la-Mort,
bravest man in a very brave army - massed to attack two mutually supported
positions, Butte de la Charrier and Vertières. In Haitian hands, either work
would envelop and permit neutralization of Bréda.

As the French trumpets sounded reveille, Clervaux fired the first shot. The
Haitian howitzers opened on Bréda, and the forts responded with a roar. On that
signal, Christophe and Romain swarmed over d'Estaing and turned its guns on
the town below. Capoix, mounted on a great charger, led his demibrigade
forward despite storms of grape from the forts on his left. The approach to
Charrier ran up a long ravine under the guns of Vertières. French fire tore gaps
in the Haitian column, but the Haitian soldiers closed ranks and clambered past
their dead, singing as they did,

"A l'assaut, Grenadiers!
ça qui mouri pas z'affaire yo.
Nan point mamans.
Nan point papas.
A l'assaut, Grenadiers!
Ca qui mouri, z'affaire yo!"'(18)

[Charge, Grenadiers!/Whoever gets killed, doesn't matter to you./You've got no
mothers,/You've got no fathers./Charge, Grenadiers!/Whoever gets killed, doesn't matter
to you!]

Capoix's horse went down. Capoix picked himself up, drew sword, and advanced on foot. Rochambeau, whose vices did not include cowardice, was watching from the rampart of Vertières. As Capoix plunged ahead, the French drums beat a sudden cease-fire. Like an arrested motion picture, the battle stood still. A French staff officer clambered stiffly down. "General Rochambeau," he shouted, "sends compliments to the general who has just covered himself with such glory!" Then he saluted the Haitians, faced smartly about, and the fight resumed.

To reinforce the spent battalions of Capoix-la-Mort, Dessalines sent in his reserve under Gabart, at twenty-seven youngest of the generals, and Jean-Philippe Daut. By midafternoon they had taken the Butte de Charrier. Inside Vertières the French magazine went up, taking with it the reserve ammunition; two thirds of the defenders lay killed or wounded. In the grand style of the Empire, Rochambeau's guard of grenadiers formed for a final charge. But Gabart, Capoix, and Clervaux - the last fighting with a French musket in hand and one epaulet shot away repulsed the desperate counterattack.

Then the heavens opened, and thunder, lightning, and sheets of rain drowned the battle. Under cover of the storm, Rochambeau pulled back from Vertières, knowing he was beaten and that St. Domingue was lost to France.

Next morning, the captain general sent his adjutant, Duveyrier, to obtain what terms he could. Before nightfall, the terms of capitulation were settled. Rochambeau got ten days to embark the remnants of his army and depart. His wounded would remain behind under safe-conduct until well enough for return to France. Dessalines issued a proclamation of safe conduct for people of all colors who wished to stay. Rochambeau presented his favorite stallion to Dessalines, and another horse to Capoix-la-Mort, "to replace the one the French had killed."

The captain general still hoped to outwit the British blockade, but Commodore John Loring was waiting when, at the last, "under a most tremendous squall, accompanied by thunder and lightning," the French had to sortie.

There was a second capitulation, this time to the British. Each French ship emptied her broadside in token of surrender, the Tricolor came down, and British prize crews took charge.

On 29 November the victors entered the Cap in triumph. Three days later, on orders of Dessalines, the French sick and wounded, 800 in all, were dumped aboard barges, taken to sea, and drowned (some accounts say bayoneted) off La Tortue.

At Môle St. Nicolas, Louis Noailles inscribed a brief and brighter postscript for France. Refusing to surrender to either the Haitians or the British offshore, Noailles managed to spike his guns in secrecy, get his people aboard seven ships, and evade the blockaders. Once at sea, he took station on the captured squadron of Rochambeau as it passed, sailed unnoticed amid the convoy, and, at the opportune moment, tacked clear and ultimately reached friendly Havana (17).

When Noailles cleared the Presqu'île du Môle on 4 December, the only French soldiers left in St. Domingue were dead ones, and these were abundant. If, as Tsar Nicholas I was later to remark, January and February were Russia's best generals, Malaria and Yellow Fever had proven to be Haiti's.

In the final twenty-two months, the days of Leclerc and Rochambeau, France, by Lacroix's count, had sent 55,131 officers and men to St. Domingue. Barely 10,000 ever saw France again. At least 10,000 sailors in the fleet died of yellow fever and malaria. Lemonnier-Delafosse says 50,270 men perished in 120 days.

Reckoning total deaths in the colony during Leclerc's time alone, Lacroix estimated 62,481. He gives up on the figures for Rochambeau. Fifty-five thousand dead French soldiers and sailors (including eighteen generals) comes as close to Bonaparte's final bill for St. Domingue as history can. Like the British before him, Napoleon in fact lost more casualties on St. Domingue than he had at Waterloo. Small wonder that, as he learned the full and final extent of the disaster, the First Consul burst out: "Damn sugar! Damn coffee! Damn colonies!"

As for Dessalines, the moment the last French ship cleared the Cap, he sent word to Etienne-Elie Gérin at Les Cayes: "There is no more doubt, *mon cher général,* the country is ours, and the famous *who shall-have-it* is settled."

The Haitian struggle for national independence and human liberty the only successful slave revolt in history - was ended.

For fourteen years, from the first musket shots of Ogé and Chavannes to the final sortie of Noailles from the Môle, St. Domingue had been battered by the French Revolution, torn in the struggles among Britain, France, and Spain, and wracked by one of the most cruel and bloody racial struggles the world has known. In 1789, the population of the colony, not counting whites, numbered at least 700,000. The first census of free Haiti in 1824 numbered 351,819 persons. It thus appears (no historian can ever know with certainty) that the revolution in St. Domingue devoured at least 50 percent of its children.

What had begun in 1789 as a revolt by *hommes de couleur* to secure rights guaranteed not only by the Declaration of the Rights of Man but even by the 1685 *code noir*, developed within two years into the first head-on collision in history between the notion of white supremacy and that of racial equality. After the revolt of the *noirs* in 1791, as Napoleon learned a decade too late, the page could never be turned back. From then on, the contest between whites and *gens de couleur* lost importance. By 1793 white authority in St. Domingue had collapsed, never, except briefly at bayonet point, to be restored.

From 1794 forward, Toussaint personified the Haitian struggle and with it the rise of black supremacy. In the next seven years the English were expelled, Rigaud was crushed, Santo Domingo conquered, and French authority nullified. When, shedding all pretense of republicanism, Napoleon tried to reconquer St. Domingue and reimpose slavery, his defeat not only lost France its richest colony but killed slavery and slaving throughout the Antilles. Moreover, the downfall of Leclerc and Rochambeau marked the collapse of Napoleon's aspirations in the Americas. Without St. Domingue as a stepping-stone, Louisiana exceeded his reach.

By the start of 1804, the whites had lost, the blacks had triumphed. The *mulâtres,* who began it all, did not yet know whether and what they had won - or lost.

Between the two races that remained- *noir* and *jaune* - Dessalines's *"who-shall-have-it"* was anything but settled.

FOOTNOTES - CHAPTER 4

1. One of Jefferson's first acts after taking office in 1801 was to recall the able Stevens from Cap Haïtien because of his "too great bias in favor of England."
2. Among many senior officers who knew St. Domingue, Leclerc had, beside Kerverseau, Rochambeau, Hardy, Boudet, Watrin, Brunet. In addition, aboard the frigate *Vertu* was a Haitian detachment, under Rigaud (still carrying French rank as brigadier), which included virtually all the *mulâtre* officers exiled after the war in the South: Pétion, Boyer, Villatte, Léveillé, Birot, Borno, Deléart, Dupuche, Brunache, and Dupont. If no resistance materialized, the First Consul ordered, the whole lot was to be sent directly to Madagascar and put on the beach.
3. Although Haiti as a nation will not appear until 1804, Haitians as a people were by now defending both their land and their freedom and will be so described.
4. Such brutality was not a Haitian monopoly. The captain of H.M.S. *Nereide,* at the Cap in March, reported 800 executions by the French. "They shoot everyone they catch," he added. A few days before the slaughter at Verrettes, Hardy's division came on a hundred white victims, throats cut and bodies still warm. At Coupe de l'Inde, Hardy caught up with the perpetrators and killed 600 on the spot.
5. "It is like warring against Arabs," Leclerc complained to Napoleon; "no sooner do we get through than the blacks occupy the woods on both sides of the road and cut out our communications." According to Lacroix, Hardy's division, marching North to the Cap from the Artibonite, lost 400 or 500 men from incessant ambushes and guerrilla swoops. These were the work of such *noir* chiefs as Scylla, Prieur, Petit-Noël, Gingembre, Sans-Souci, and Macaya.
6. Leclerc also seized key subordinates who had been closely associated with Toussaint, mainly as staff officers or members of his personal troops. These he deported in batches to Brest, to the hulks of Toulon and Ajaccio, and to Cayenne. One wretched draft of 880 shivering *noirs* was herded ashore in irons at Brest on 14 January 1803.
7. The *lambi* (conch shell) and *vaccine* (hollowed-out bamboo stalk) are musical instruments used in Haitian dances and ceremonies.

8. So many corpses washed ashore at the Cap that nobody would eat fish for weeks afterward.

9. With the insurgents hammering at the gates of the Cap, Leclerc ordered women and children withdrawn aboard ship. As the refugees streamed to the quay, Pauline surveyed them disdainfully. "You may go if you wish," she said to one. "You are not the sister of Bonaparte."

10. An example was the Polish Legion, 2270 Poles in exile under General Jablonowski, which reached the Cap - in Leclerc's words - "all but naked, badly armed, and due over three months' pay." His troops were hardly ashore before Jablonowski was dead of yellow fever.

11. Rochambeau's *boule-dogues* are not forgotten in Haiti. To this day, bloodhounds, mastiffs, boxers, and bulldogs are generically spoken of as *"dogues."*

12. Or nearly so. Petit-Noël and Sans-Souci, implacable enemies of Christophe, had to be gotten out of the way: the former taken and shot by Dessalines outside Dondon, the latter betrayed and bayoneted near Grande Rivière du Nord. Petit-Noël had earlier ambushed and beheaded Paul Louverture for having collaborated with the French.

13. The Arcahaie flag, of vertical blue and red, was blazoned by what became Haiti's national emblem - the palm tree surmounted by a Phrygian cap, with massed banners and weapons at its base. After independence, Dessalines and Christophe substituted black for blue, thus symbolizing in the two colors the union of *noir and mulâtre.* After finally unifying Haiti, Pétion restored the traditional red and blue, though horizontally arranged. But in 1966 François Duvalier reverted to the red and black. Upon Jean-Claude Duvalier's departure in 1986, the red and blue flag was restored.

14. Toussaint's life and struggle appealed deeply to the romantic imagination of the nineteenth century. John Greenleaf Whittier, who dedicated much of his life to the abolition of slavery, wrote a long poem, and Lamartine devoted a major play, as did Harriet Martineau a three-volume novel, to the story of Toussaint. In September 1977, London had a major opera, *Toussaint,* by David Blake.

15. Not all the French were lucky enough to get away. After assuring 300 prisoners at Croix-des-Bouquets that they would be treated humanely, Dessalines quietly told the escort commander to shoot them. "Aren't you forgetting your word of honor?" asked Bonnet, Dessalines's adjutant. "Shut up, Bonnet," growled Dessalines. "Since the revolution there's no more word of honor."

16. This is the strength worked out by the French military historian, Poyen. Historians Madiou and Corvington say 27,000.

17. For this exploit Noailles paid with his life. Along the North coast of Cuba he encountered a British corvette and, after a desperate fight, took her. Mortally wounded, the French commander barely lived to see El Morro as his flagship entered Havana.

Henry Christophe, King of the North, ruled with an iron hand. *Artist unknown*

Christophe's Sans Souci Palace was cooled by streams that ran beneath its marble floors. *Heinl Collection*

Henry Christophe's Citadel was built to fight a foe that never returned. *Heinl Collection*

CHAPTER 5

We Must Live Free or Die

1804-1820

In the emergence of societies, the chiefs of republics create the institutions and the institutions, in turn, create the chiefs.

- Montesquieu

WITH THE DAWN OF 1804, Haiti's highest hour has passed. St. Domingue - still bounteous, ever beautiful, utterly wrecked - represented the debris of the world's richest colony. Those who survived had won their freedom, yet were wholly unprepared to use it. Unwilling to be ruled by any foreigner, they were incapable of governing themselves.

There was a greater irony: the 1780s, when St. Domingue was a cornucopia of agricultural wealth, also witnessed the beginning of the Industrial Revolution. Coal and iron, foundries, mines, and factories would soon displace agriculture as a producer of wealth, reorder world trade, and create new markets for materials and products that Haiti neither knew nor had.

During the years just past, St. Domingue had played at center stage in the aspirations, clashes, and politics of the great powers. In the years to come, Haiti would encounter isolation, neglect, ostracism, and indifference.

Skin of a Blanc for Parchment

Gonaïves, original headquarters of Toussaint and now, in his stead, of Dessalines, was to be the cradle of liberty. Here, in December 1803, the generals assembled to ratify in ink what they had written in blood.

Besides the titans - Dessalines, Christophe, and Pétion - there were Clervaux, Geffrard, Vernet, and the brigadiers - Gérin, Férou, Bazelais, Toussaint Brave, and Yayou. Boisrond-Tonnerre (so named because he had been born during a thunderstorm) was secretary. Of thirty-four men who would soon sign the forthcoming declaration of independence, twenty-three were *mulâtres*, eleven *noirs*.

The army that had swept Rochambeau into the sea was dispersed to the principal towns. Before marching them off, Dessalines divided up the war chest, eight gourdes per man, so there was much celebrating.

Amid this national celebration the serious work proceeded at Gonaïves. Chareron, a staff officer, was directed to block out a declaration of independence(1) but none of it seemed to come out right. With Independence Day - 1 January of the new year - but twenty-four hours away, he produced his final effort. Read aloud for the benefit of many, including Dessalines, who could not read, the paper was greeted with silence. Unable to contain himself, Boisrond-Tonnerre burst out: "This doesn't say what we really feel. For our declaration of independence we should have the skin of a *blanc* for parchment, his skull for inkwell, his blood for ink, and a bayonet for pen!"

"That's it!" exclaimed Dessalines. "Boisrond," he commanded "take over! Make people know how I feel about the *blancs!*"

Dessalines had found the right man: Boisrond's prose smelled of *clairin* and gunpowder.

Townsmen and soldiers filled the streets of Gonaïves at dawn. Carrying provisions in baskets on their heads, barefoot *noirs* poured into town. At seven, after a brilliant sunrise from behind the mountains, the troops and officials formed. There was a momentary crisis when Boisrond and his effusion could not be found: the task finished, he had fallen asleep over his writing table and had to be shaken awake for the ceremony.

In what was then the *Place d'Armes* and later *Place de la Patrie* stood a platform, the *Autel de la Patrie* (National Altar), draped in the new flags. Surrounded by his generals and flanked by his demibrigades, Dessalines mounted the *autel* and quieted the drums and trumpets and the crowd. Then his great battlefield voice filled the square.

Like the speaker, few hearers knew more than a word or so of French, but they understood every syllable when, in the Créole of the mountains and canefields, Dessalines recalled the cruelties of the French and explained that this ceremony was to ensure that Haitians would forever after live free and die free. He paused and nodded; then Boisrond continued in the Jacobin French of 1792:

To the People of Haiti . . .We must live free or we must die . . . Citizens. look about you for your wives, husbands, brothers, sisters. Look for your children, your nursing babies. Where have they gone? They have fallen prey to these vultures . . . Whenever they near our shores may the French tremble, if not from the guilt of past atrocities then from our resolve to slaughter any person born French whose footprint henceforth contaminates our land of liberty . . . Peace to our neighbors. But accursed be the name of France! Hatred eternal for France shall be our cry..... Swear now, with clasped hands, to live free and independent and to accept death in preference to the yoke.

Then Boisrond produced a second paper, the Act of Independence, which the generals had all signed, renouncing France, declaring the country free, and giving it the new but ancient name of Haiti. This, too, he proclaimed.

"Long live independence!" shouted Dessalines. And the cannon began to boom and church bells pealed and the crowd roared.

Free at last, the world's first black republic, the hemisphere's second independent nation, Haiti, had been born.

Massacre of the French

After the ceremony, the generals returned to the headquarters and there swore a separate oath of personal fealty to Dessalines. Some accounts say they repaired to a *palais national* (national palace, or capitol), but, just as no government yet existed, so there was no capitol but merely a headquarters, probably the *hôtel de ville*.

Dessalines's title - the highest known in St. Domingue - was the same Toussaint had borne, *gouverneur-general-à-vie* (governor-general for life). The mechanism for governing consisted simply of Boisrond, the secretary, and the junta of generals who had signed the Act of Independence and the oath of fealty. Haitians in later times would recognize this arrangement under the familiar title of *gouvernement provisoire* (provisional government), and such it was.

As for the people themselves, they were, in the words of Dantès Bellegarde, "a crowd, not a nation, a multitude of slaves liberated pell-mell by violent means." Besides, Bellegarde added, they still had with them from the colonial past the notion that the master is the man who does no work, that to be free is to be idle.

Tired, at last at ease, and warmed that evening by rum, the generals asked each other what to do about the remaining French. After Boisrond's proclamation the question could hardly be brushed aside.

One opinion was for mass deportation. The second was that every French throat should be cut. Nothing was settled that night. For one thing, Christophe and Pétion, the two most powerful men in the room other than Dessalines, listened carefully but said little. Nor did Dessalines speak his mind. Next day, however, he annulled all French titles of property issued during the Leclerc-Rochambeau occupation. Returning in a day or so to their respective headquarters, the generals waited to see what might develop. So also, in deep foreboding, did the French *colons*.

If the French were looking for a sign, they had not long to wait. Some of the more fearful arranged to embark their goods, or sell out and take ship from the island. At Cayes, the Cap, St. Marc, and Port-au-Prince they were prevented from leaving.

What exactly lay in the minds of the Haitian leaders at this moment is harder to say than what they did. Many could neither write nor read: some could speak no French but only Créole. Those among them with education and literacy, like Pétion, Bonnet, and Boisrond, left no record of the events soon to take place.(2) Anyway, revenge speaks for itself.

"The murder of the whites began at Port-au-Prince in the early days of January," wrote a Frenchman who escaped,

> . . . but on 17 and 18 March, they were finished off en masse. All, without exception, have been massacred, down to the women and children. A young *mulâtresse,* named Fifi Pariset, ranged the town like a madwoman, searching the houses to slay the little children. Many men and women were chopped down by sappers, who hacked off their limbs and smashed in their chests. Some were stabbed, others mutilated, others bayonetted, others disemboweled, still others stuck like pigs."

Yet the butchery did not begin, as some have said, spontaneously. Popular fury there certainly was; but stoking that fury was the implacable resolve of Jean-Jacques Dessalines that Haiti must be cleansed of every French taint.

Thomas Madiou says that when, in February of 1804, Dessalines finally made up his mind to the extermination of the French, he was at Les Cayes. Geffrard was so horrified on receiving the order that, as soon as Dessalines left for Jérémie, he passed the job to his *mulâtre* second-in-command, Moreau Coco Herne, and went away on a tour of inspection. Of events at Jérémie, a full record exists in a contemporary account written by Pierre-Etienne Chazotte, one of the few Frenchmen who was spared.

On 9 March 1804, accompanied by a column of troops and his personal guard of 500 picked men, Dessalines entered Jérémie. All white males were rounded up and formed in the main square. Patrols ranged the town, searching every house for any who might be hiding. These were killed on the spot. Glittering in dress uniforms from Rochambeau's depots, Dessalines and his staff strode into the square and stared in baleful silence at the huddled French. Then the leader took a large pinch of snuff. "You *blancs* of Jérémie," he said in Créole; "I know how you hate me . . . The blood of all of you shall pay!" Dessalines then sorted out five doctors, a handful of merchants who factored foreign cargoes, and an American. These were placed aside and spared. Four hundred men of property were reprieved on condition of a ransom to be collected that afternoon. After dark, having paid up, all 400 were bound two by two, led away by Dessalines's axmen, and beheaded. Their bodies were stacked in a human cairn so that "the *cultivateurs* could look at their masters."

During the day, 200 *blancs* - including the white-robed vicar of Jérémie, who had been shot down at his altar - had already been slain. Bazelais, accompanying Dessalines, personally poniarded a French friend of earlier days. Before Dessalines left Jérémie, on 15 March all but a dozen of 1436 Frenchmen in the parish had been murdered. "On the Western road," Chazotte concluded, "upwards of 400 bodies lay heaped on one another in two high mounds. The blood flowing from beneath had made a rivulet crossing the road, forming a bar . . . The *noirs* from the country would not put their feet in this."

The only white men to be spared, other than the few selected by Dessalines, were the unhappy remnants of Jabolonowski's Polish Legion. At Boisrond's suggestion, they were given Haitian citizenship and absorbed into one of the demibrigades. Reporting to the Admiralty from Jérémie on 16 March, the day after Dessalines's departure ("with 25 mules loaded with plate and other valuables, all Plunder from Jérémie"), Captain Perkins of the frigate H.M.S. *Tartar* noted, "In hauling the seine the evening we came to our anchor, several bodies got entangled in it, in fact such scenes of cruelty and devastation have been committed as is impossible to imagine or my pen describe."

In the other cities it was the same. Dessalines reached Port-au-Prince late on the 16th. By midnight his squads were at work. Whites not killed in their houses were rounded up next day and herded off to Croix-des-Martyrs, where they were slaughtered in their turn. Haitian children with swords and daggers cut down white children in the streets. Behind the executioners stalked Dessalines's privy counselor, Balthasar Inginac, methodically sealing up the premises of murdered whites to prevent looting. In the words of Captain Perkins, "On General Dessalines' return [to Port-au-Prince] he ordered all the white men then remaining in the town to be immediately put to death. The order was executed without the least ceremony . . . In the span of 8 days no less than 800 were actually murdered by these assassins and their bodies thrown into the bogs and marshes to rot away."

His work completed on 25 March, Dessalines left Port-au-Prince and continued the bloodthirsty progress to Arcahaie, St. Marc, and thence (after resting a few days at Marchand) on to Gonaïves. Everywhere he went, the same horrors were re-enacted.

On 21 April Dessalines reached the Cap. Here, nearly 2000 Frenchmen still survived. In vain did Henry Christophe, the modernizer who comprehended Haiti's needs, try to stay Dessalines. The only concession he got was one that had been granted at Jérémie: English, Americans, and a few doctors and priests were spared. With guards to protect their homes, Americans, recounted one, ". . . at short intervals heard the pick-axe thundering at the door of some devoted neighbor, and soon forcing it. Piercing shrieks almost immediately ensued and these were followed by an expressive silence. The next minute the military party was heard proceeding to some other house to renew their work of death."

On the 22d no more French men were left. "If I die at this moment," exulted Dessalines, "I will go to my grave happy. We have avenged our brothers. Haiti has become a blood-red spot on the face of the globe!"

Up to this point, most of the victims had been men. Now came the turn of the women. At their breasts or in their bodies they bore future Frenchmen. To the tune of the "Marseillaise" and "Carmagnole," the distracted creatures were herded through the streets of the Cap and uphill to the Savanne de la Fossette. The deed seemed too horrible: the soldiers would not commence the slaughter. Then Clervaux broke the spell. Riding down a white woman, he snatched her nursing baby by the leg and smashed its skull against a boulder. As the sticky blancmange of blood and brains trickled to the ground, the soldiers roused themselves and fell to with saber and bayonet. What airs the band played when it was over, no historian has recorded.

Throughout the country similar scenes were re-enacted. At Les Cayes women were told they were being deported and were tricked into embarking with their children aboard a ship. At midnight they were roused, bound back to back, their ankles weighed with stones, and tossed into the sea.

But Les Cayes was also the scene of rescues engineered by Duncan MacIntosh, a Scottish-American merchant from Baltimore. MacIntosh was afterward credited by French refugees in that city with having saved over 2400 whites of all ages and sexes, mainly by spending most of his considerable fortune in bribing Haitian sentries, jailers, and officials to turn a blind eye as he smuggled whole families to safety aboard American merchantmen in harbor.(3)

In Jérémie, where the massacres had been launched, Laurent Férou received with revulsion the order to slay womenfolk. Thrusting the paper in his pocket, he kept it secret for two days. Meanwhile, he urgently ordered Gaspard, captain of the port, to embark every Frenchwoman and child he could aboard two ships in port and sail immediately for Cuba. Only after Gaspard had cleared the Grande-Anse did Férou disclose Dessalines's fearful warrant (while secretly prompting subordinates to shelter what women they could). A few killings took place: no command from Dessalines could be ignored. But when Gaspard returned from Cuba, enough survivors remained in hiding for him to make a second trip.

There were many other acts of mercy. Pétion saved many French in the West, including Mme. Campan, a lovely Frenchwoman who had shared his bed. Dessalines's wife, Claire-Heureuse, whose compassion and gentleness never flagged, interceded tirelessly whenever she could.

One final act of calculated treachery remained. Knowing that some French must have survived in hiding, Dessalines proclaimed that vengeance was complete and called on survivors to emerge and receive safe-conduct. Those who did were killed without pity.

So, because no more remained to be slain, ended the slaughter of the French. To the Sicilian Vespers and St. Bartholomew's Day, Dessalines had added 1804.

Dessalines set the seal on his revenge by a proclamation, composed by Chanlatte, which he published on 28 April 1804:

Yes, we have repaid these cannibals, war for war, crime for crime, outrage for outrage. I have saved my country, I have avenged the Americas. Never again shall colonist or European set foot on this soil as master or landowner. This shall henceforward be the foundation of our constitution . . . War to the death to the tyrants! This is my motto. *Liberté! Indépendence!* is our rallying cry.

Dessalines Reigns

The massacre was worse than a crime, it was a blunder. At one stroke, Dessalines had destroyed the foreign talent that men of vision, like Toussaint and Christophe, had recognized as essential for the reconstruction and administration of Haiti. Moreover, by launching the new republic on a sea of blood, Dessalines isolated Haiti beyond the pale of civilized recognition and provided arguments that would be used for decades to come to justify the international disdain and ostracism that were to be accorded the world's first experiment in black self-government.

Dessalines had liquidated the French, but in their stead he could offer only military dictatorship, corrupt, capricious, and grounded in enforced servitude.

The entire people, more than half of whom had been born in Africa, were to be divided into cultivators or soldiers. The former (including all women) were attached to the soil. The army, with 52,000 men on its rolls (a figure of speech only: illiteracy debarred paperwork) absorbed nearly 15 percent of the population. The first public work of the regime was to order construction of forts, most of which still stand, on the hilltops dominating the towns and harbors and the plains. The cultivators were to be moved inland, up the Artibonite and toward the central plateau, walled in from the outer world by mountains and forts. The coastal towns would survive only as entrepots. Dessalines even planned to abandon Port-au-Prince and relocate the city at Dérance, once the impenetrable *marron* stronghold of Lamour Dérance in the foothills of Morne la Selle.

The Haitians could not know the French would never return. On the other hand, they knew well that a French garrison remained in Santo Domingo and that the powers that ringed the horizon - France, England, Spain, and the United States - were all slave-owning. And it would be more than two decades later, in 1825, before a single country recognized Haiti as a sovereign state.

Dessalines was as incapable of vision of the future as of the outer world. For his purposes, government had only two goals: to prevent the return of the French or of any white man, and to forestall reintroduction of slavery. Behind both objectives, though not yet clear in 1804, lay visceral suspicion of all *mulâtres* who, after all, were descended from Frenchmen and, as landowners, had owned black slaves.

The administrative organization of the countryside, which would continue into the twentieth century, was that of the army. Haiti was divided into four districts, each commanded by a general: the North under Christophe, with Clervaux as deputy; the Artibonite under Gabart; the West under Pétion; and the South under Geffrard. There were two Ministers: Vernet, who could neither read nor write, for Finance; and Balthasar Inginac, a natural-born administrator, honest and indefatigable, for the Public Domains.

To repopulate the country (and, as he phrased it, "to bronze" the population) Dessalines authorized further imports of *cultivateurs* from Africa and tried to induce free American blacks to Haiti. His ultimate goal, never realized, was to bring over 500,000 *noirs* from Africa.

At Marchand, later to be renamed "Dessalines," the governor general ruled in despotic state, touring the countryside and flinging handfuls of silver to scrambling peasants, who hailed him as "Papa Jacques."

Of Dessalines, few contemporary descriptions and no authentic likenesses survive. To a visiting British naval officer in 1804, he was simply "a short stout Black." Charles Malo, writing in 1819, pictures him as:

> short in stature, but powerfully built, energetic and of undaunted courage . . . The respect he commanded came mainly from the terror he inspired. Yet sometimes he was open, affable, and even generous. His vanity led him to strange caprices. He was fond of gold lace and adornments and dressed magnificently: yet on occasion he would appear in public wearing the humblest clothing. It was Dessalines' pretense that he was an accomplished dancer; he always had a dancing-master in his suite who would give him instructions in leisure moments. The highest compliment one could give was to tell him he danced very well (although, quite different from most Haitians, he was very awkward at this art).(4)

Bellegarde adds a description attributed to the French adjutant general, Ramel: "Dessalines' face is hard. When he becomes angry, blood rushes into his eyes and mouth[sic]. He is the terror of the *noirs*."

When Dessalines learned, in August 1804, that Napoleon had been proclaimed Emperor he determined to follow suit. Boisrond and Chanlatte, his privy counselors, thereupon circulated petitions, stimulated acclamations, and attended to the preliminaries and preparations for a Haitian coronation. To no one's surprise, the generals unanimously urged the crown that Dessalines with undisguised impatience awaited.(5)

In October, accompanied by honor guard and suite, Dessalines proceeded in state to the Cap, where Christophe had all in readiness for the coronation of the first emperor in the Americas since Montezuma.

At three in the afternoon of 8 October - seven weeks before Napoleon would be crowned at Notre-Dame - Dessalines received the crown of Haiti under title of His Majesty Jacques I, Emperor. While cannon roared, Father Corneille Brelle, Capuchin *curé* of the Cap, anointed the emperor's hands, feet, and forehead with holy oil, and placed the crown upon his head. Afterward, in purple coronation robes and costumes rushed over from Paris houses still eager for the trade of St. Domingue, the royal party repaired from the Champ de Mars to a convent chapel: Notre-Dame, the church, was still roofless and ravaged from fire in 1802. As Dessalines knelt at an imperial priedieu, a Te Deum, punctuated by triple volleys of musketry and artillery, was chanted in thanksgiving. Then the cortege returned to Christophe's residence, where Télémaque, the aged mayor (who had nearly lost his head because of past association with the French), led the chorus in an ode set to a French vaudeville ditty, "The Village Fortune-Teller."

Comparable ceremonies were held in all the principal towns, including Port-au-Prince, the stronghold of Pétion, whose democratic (or, more accurately, republican) views had not escaped Dessalines.

Those who believed Haiti should be controlled by an oligarchy were quick to suggest that Dessalines create an imperial nobility. They were savagely rebuffed: "I alone am noble," replied the emperor. But the question would not stay still. Should Haiti's destiny lie in the hands of educated, philosophically democratic elitists (mainly *mulâtres)* or of black autocrats?

Invasion of Santo Domingo

The problems confronting Dessalines in 1805 closely resembled those that had confronted Toussaint in 1800. Ferrand and his grenadiers still held Santo Domingo; any Haitian who fell into their hands was automatically treated as a fugitive slave. Agriculture, despite Dessalines's system of servitude, continued to decline. The government, which Bellegarde described as "a military regime in full brutality," lacked even a constitution. Dessalines considered the public treasury his own, and sanctioned comparable attitudes on the part of his courtiers.

In February 1805, accompanied in the field by his favorite mistress, Euphémie Daguille, Dessalines launched 30,000 men in two columns against Santo Domingo.

The Haitian onslaught was swift. French and Spanish troops under a one-time *colon,* de Viet, made a determined stand near Azua at a fort called Tombeau des Indigènes. Gabart captured it in a swirl of cold steel. De Viet, captured, was led before Dessalines and flayed to death with thorn bushes. Before his body was cold, a soldier ripped open his belly with a machete, tore loose the quivering heart, ate it, and strung the entrails on a tree limb.

Santiago fell to Christophe on 25 February. In the words of Sumner Welles, historian of Santo Domingo and for years *eminence grise* of U.S. foreign policy, there then ensued rape, loot, and murder and when these pastimes palled, the more refined pleasures afforded by torture. The greater part of the inhabitants had taken refuge in the church. All these were slaughtered, and the priest officiating at the Mass, Don José Vasquez, was burned alive, the sacred books and vestments furnishing the fuel. The church itself, piled high with the mutilated dead, was then consumed by the flames . . . Children, whose bodies had first been mutilated, were literally torn to pieces: men and women were slowly sliced to bits with machetes. The body of one victim was first mutilated by strokes of the machete, and then lighted cartridges were placed in the wounds until at length the bleeding mass had been torn to shreds by the explosions . . . When they returned, the few inhabitants who had succeeded in escaping found the bodies of the members of the Cabildo. who had been taken captive by Christophe, naked and mutilated, dangling from the balcony of the *Casa Consistorial.*

On 7 March, the Haitian columns converged on Ciudad Santo Domingo. Under command of the resolute Ferrand, French and Spaniards alike prepared to sell their lives dear. Without artillery to breach the ancient walls, Dessalines determined to starve the defenders. On 21 March, when food was short and Ferrand was near the end of his tether, deliverance suddenly came from the sea. The French squadron of Admiral Comte de Missiessy appeared offshore. As soon as Dessalines saw the French ships with provisions, reinforcement, and heavy guns, he knew the game was up, and ordered a retreat.(6) On the night of the 28th, the besiegers silently withdrew.

The Haitians behaved worse in retreat than advance, although Pétion, and Geffrard, who commanded the Southern column during this phase, managed to moderate some excesses. Led back by Dessalines, the Northern force left pillage, slaughter, rape, and desolation in its wake. Whole towns, populated by black or *mulâtre* Dominicans, were destroyed, and their captive inhabitants marched off to work, until they dropped, on Dessalines's ring of forts and Christophe's citadel.

Horses, mules, and cattle were hamstrung, killed off, and left to rot. Among tens of towns sacked, burned, and gutted were some of the oldest in the New World and most illustrious of Santo Domingo. At Santiago, the sixteenth-century cathedral and four churches were burned and the entire clergy killed. Christophe alone took back some 1200 men, women, and children, including 318 girls younger than fifteen.

The differences between Toussaint's campaign of 1801 and Dessalines's in 1805 illustrate differences between the regimes and the men. Toussaint proclaimed liberty and unification, and revitalized commerce, administration, and even the road system of Santo Domingo. Where Toussaint came as liberator, Dessalines came as invader. So far as can be determined, the emperor had no desire to stay and no motive save to extirpate the last trace of French influence and to break Dominicans of all colors to his fearful will. What he achieved was to lay the foundation of unending fear, hatred, suspicion, and recrimination between the two nations of Hispaniola.

The Devil Himself Has Burst His Chains

Even while the Haitian army invested Santo Domingo, Boisrond and Chanlatte were at work on a constitution. By the time the campaign was over, in April, their draft had been approved by the emperor and, like the coronation petitions a few months earlier, was being circulated to the generals for signature. As usual, Dessalines was in a hurry; the generals were equally quick to oblige. On 20 May 1805, the emperor formally ratified Haiti's first constitution as a free nation.

In the tradition of Toussaint's constitution, this one was also despotic. All power - life, death, war, peace, punishment, and legislation -belonged to the emperor, who, like Toussaint before him, was to choose his successor. Administration was to be carried out by two councils - a Council of State, composed of all general officers, and a Privy Council, made up of the imperial secretariat (ancestors in direct line of later so-called *Musiciens Palais National*). There would be two Ministers, one of War and Marine, the other of Finance and Interior (and none for Foreign Affairs). Coordinating the Ministers was to be a Secretary of State, a post that Juste Chanlatte promptly nailed down.

Taking the very words from Dessalines's proclamation of April 1804, the constitution barred white men from possessing property or domain on Haitian soil. Should the French return, Article 5 of the constitution added: "At the first shot of the warning gun, the towns shall be destroyed and the nation will rise in arms."

The national colors were changed to red and black. Significantly, no gradation of race was to be admitted: all Haitians were to be known as *noirs*. Deviating from Toussaint's, Dessalines's constitution recognized freedom of religion (which, other than perpetual freedom from slavery, was the only freedom recognized). Yet the emperor controlled the religious establishment, such as remained. (Msgr. Guillaume Lecun, apostolic prefect of Haiti, had fled to Jamaica, disguised as a sailor, in February 1804). As *curé* of St. Marc, Dessalines appointed Félix, retired drum major of the *Légion Dessources*.

Whatever its imperfections, the constitution of 1805 reflected the actualities of Haiti under Dessalines. Yet there was one actuality that, by renouncing, the constitution underscored. This was the color line between *jaune* and *noir*.

In the scramble for and over the land titles Dessalines had revoked in 1804, *mulâtres* (who, in Dessalines's eyes, were merely the bastards of French *colons*) asserted claims to properties once held by French fathers or other relations *de la main gauche*. When the emperor heard this he burst out: "And the poor *noirs* whose fathers are in Africa they'll get nothing?" No indeed, Dessalines answered himself; what we spilled our blood together to take, we share equally. But to him, *noirs* were more equal.

To Dessalines, the racial equality he had in mind was the equality stated in the constitution: all Haitians were *noirs*. Probably even the reverse: only *noirs* could be true Haitians. So at least it seemed to Pétion and Geffrard and the *gens de couleur* of the South, who, just as the emperor considered himself heir of Toussaint, were equally heirs of Rigaud.

As if Pétion, sophisticated *mulâtre* of education and sensitivity, were available at stud, Dessalines proffered his daughter, Célimène. Pétion's dilemma was not eased by the knowledge (still hidden from Dessalines) that the girl was already pregnant by one of the imperial aides-de-camp (who subsequently paid for his peccadillo by having his brains blown out). Besides, Pétion had a voluptuous mistress of his own, now Choute Lachenais, to whom he was deeply attached.

Grasping the nettle, Pétion finally told Dessalines he was not of a mind to marry anyone. The reply sufficed; but neither could doubt what it implied.

Other tensions besides those of race were beginning to pull the regime asunder. The slave-master's whip was forbidden, but Dessalines scourged the *cultivateurs* with the *liane* and *cocomacac* instead. "Cultivators," he said with some personal knowledge, "can be controlled only by fear of punishment or death. I will lead them only by those means.(7)

St. Domingue had never been a very moral place, but the immorality of the emperor and his court was notorious. Surrounded like a sultan by mistresses of all colors, some chosen for delicate beauty, others wallowing in fat, Dessalines claimed the *droit de seigneur* in every town, so mothers would send away their daughters on the emperor's approach.

Amid all this, while the economy stagnated and sugar production declined, public funds lined private pockets. *"Plumez la poule, mais ne la faite pas crier"* (Pluck the chicken, but don't make it squawk) was the watchword from the emperor himself.

The army went unpaid, ill equipped, barely fed, and nearly unclothed. Officers diverted money appropriated for pay and rations. Despite every penalty, desertions spiraled upward. Drowning in corruption and loose living, Dessalines mocked his own troops for their sorry appearance. "You're as naked as a row of old bottles," he scoffed at an unhappy battalion drawn up for inspection. Only his honor guard, the 4th Demibrigade, was decently supplied, properly equipped, and paid on time.

But the discontents of generals are more dangerous than those of soldiers. Christophe's instinct for punctilio and dignity was offended by the loose and ludicrous scenes at court. ("Look at him!" Christophe incautiously snapped as Dessalines hopped through a ballroom figure, "isn't it shameful that we have to be ruled by such a caperer?") Pétion, Geffrard, and Férou, for their part, had long-standing grounds of color, region, and conviction to support a growing disaffection. In the Northwest, at Port-de-Paix, Capoix-la-Mort nursed equal resentment against the emperor and against his old rival, Henry Christophe. These leaders, strong in their home grounds, and many lesser generals, all joined in dislike if not detestation for the insiders of the secretariat: Mentor Laurent, the persuasive Martinique-born *noir* intriguer; Boisrond and Chanlatte, the extremist doctrinaires; and Vastey, whose first concern in auditing government accounts was the sack of gold pieces he received before pronouncing all in order.

Dessalines, whose suspicions never slept, sensed the growing alienation of the generals but did not act. At different times, he considered killing one or another or all. (In May 1806, when Geffrard suddenly died, the rumor of poison ran through the South and West. Dessalines merely grunted, "When God took Geffrard, He was in more of a hurry than I.")

August brought further bad news from the South, where the name of Dessalines already spelled hatred and fear. Hearing reports of wholesale peculation and disaffection, the emperor went in person to Cayes, where he presided grimly until mid-September. On his way back, at Petit-Goâve, Dessalines warned Lamarre, the local commander and one of his most loyal adherents: "Lamarre, be ready to march into the South. If the people there don't rise after what I've done to them, they're not human."

Within less than a month. Dessalines was proven right: On 8 October 1806, the South exploded. Led by one Mécerou, a *noir* proprietor, the principal men of Port Salut ambushed Moreau Coco Herne, Dessalines's *mulâtre* lieutenant who had succeeded Geffrard.

As the insurgents marched off Moreau to their camp at Taverny, near Torbeck. *Lambi* and drumbeat echoed from hillside to hillside throughout the South. *"Diable-la casé chaines"*, chanted the peasants in Créole, *"pou kimbé Dessalines"* (the Devil himself has burst his chains so that he can lay hold of Dessalines!) Cayes and its garrison went over. Gérin, Minister of War, was at Anse-à-Veau. Southerner and *mulâtre* as he was, he required little persuasion. At Léogane, Yayou was Pétion's man. With Gérin to his front and Yayou in his rear, Lamarre of Petit-Goâve needed no convincing. In just nine days, by 16 October, the revolt reached Port-au-Prince. Pétion threw off his mask and delivered the city.

The North, meanwhile, was quiet. Christophe had no love for disorders and had his countryside completely in hand. Although he was in close touch with events in the South and with Pétion, his sole reaction in early October was to arrest and execute Capoix-la-Mort, his rival and hero of Vertières, letting it be said, however, that the deed had been done by Dessalines.

Word of the risings in the South came to the emperor at Marchand on 13 October. Within forty-eight hours he was marching South with two battalions of the 4th Demibrigade. "My horse will wade in blood up to his breastplate!" he exclaimed. On the 16th, Dessalines halted at Arcahaie, picked up the third battalion of his imperial guard, and ordered a covering force to advance on Port-au-Prince. These troops, commanded by Colonel Thomas Jean and a Major Antoine Gédéon, were to halt North of the city at Pont-Rouge (a bridge with red handrails that was situated just West of today's Miliary Airstrip), and there await Dessalines.

Next morning, 17 October, 1806, exactly three years to the day from the French attempt to trap him at Petite Rivière, Dessalines took the road. The 4th Demibrigade, the best troops Dessalines had, halted without orders at Montrouis, supposedly to pick up supplies and equipment, without which they were not fit for field duty. The companies under Jean and Gédéon straggled anyhow along the dusty road toward the city.

Outside St. Marc, Delpeche, an officer who had escaped from the Petit-Goâve, spurred his horse to warn the emperor. Dessalines would not listen, and the bearer of bad news received his reward: Delpeche was bayonetted.

As the advance guard approached Port-au-Prince, the soldiers quickly learned what was afoot. When Pétion and Gérin met them at Pont-Rouge, they surrendered and turned coat. Colonel Jean demurred. Major Gédéon had no such scruples and was forthwith promoted colonel and given command. Then, to seal his new allegiance, he gave his scarlet tunic to an officer on Pétion's staff, who took post on the bridge amid the carefully laid ambush that awaited the emperor. Every cultivator on the Cul-de-Sac by now knew or suspected that the trap had been set. Not a single voice warned Dessalines as he rode South.

Not until the emperor was a few yards away did Colonel Léger, a *mulâtre,* recognize that the troops ahead were not those of Dessalines but the 15th Demibrigade, a unit from the South. His warning came too late.

The bayonets closed in, but no man dared pull trigger. In fury, Dessalines lashed out with his *cocomacac.* Finally, a young soldier named Garat fired his musket at the emperor's horse. As the charger pitched down, Dessalines was pinned to the ground. Then the generals swarmed forward. With fierce chops, Yayou stabbed him thrice. Vaval, a minor general, loosed his horse pistols into the writhing body. When Charlotin Marcadieux, a loyal *mulâtre* officer, tried to shield Dessalines, his head was blown away by a blast of musket shots. No other staff officer was as imprudent. Most of the suite took to their heels. A few, such as Mentor Laurent, joined in the melee.

Off came the gold-lace green coat. Soldiers ripped at the epaulets. Other hands tore away the breeches. Machetes hacked off ring fingers and then other members as well. Willing hands dragged the faceless cadaver into the city to be stoned and spat upon and defiled. And at last all that remained of Haiti's first emperor lay still in the midday sun.

When night finally descended and the sun dropped into the sea behind La

Gonâve, a madwoman called Defilée hauled away the body, cleansed and anointed it, and, with the help of a soldier burying-party, gave it sepulture in a nearby cemetery at Morne-à-Tuf.(8) Charlotin Marcadieux, the *mulâtre* who died for his *noir* emperor, was buried beside him.

Haiti Divided

By all appearances, Henry Christophe seemed the logical successor to Dessalines. On the day before the emperor's murder, Pétion had already proclaimed Christophe *"chef provisoire* of the Government of Haiti until such time as the Constitution, in conferring his august title officially upon him, shall have established his designation."

But, as Christophe soon learned, there was more to it than that. On 20 November 1806, elections were held for a Constitutional Assembly, and, when the returns were in, the majority of the delegates, brought in from hastily gerrymandered parishes of the South and West, proved to be *mulâtres* in the pockets of Pétion and his supporter, Gérin. Meanwhile, old scores were settled. Mentor and Boisrond, quickly arrested after the murder, were as quickly bayoneted in their cell. Little had it availed Mentor, as Dessalines was being hacked to bits, to shout *"Vive la Liberté! The tyrant is overthrown!"*

The Constitutional Assembly met in the cathedral at Port-au-Prince on 18 December. With time out for Christmas, the new constitution, already drafted by Pétion and his secretary and confidant, Jean-Pierre Boyer, was rammed through by the 27th. Haiti was declared a republic with a president, a Senate, and a rigid separation of powers between the two. The main effect of the constitution in this last respect, however, was to separate from the president, Christophe, almost all powers usually attributed to a chief executive and vest them in the Senate, whose presiding officer was Pétion.

When Juste Hugonin (who, with Ferrier from Le Cap, was one of Christophe's men at the convention) read the final draft, he reported to Henry: "If you accept this, you won't have the authority of a corporal." Christophe's response, even before the constitution was ratified, was to march on Port-au-Prince with the black demibrigades of the North and the Artibonite. Ahead, he sent a proclamation denouncing Pétion, Boyer, and their men as rebels and usurpers. "Once these rascals have attained their ends," Henry warned, "they won't even leave you the right to complain."

Halting only to arrest and execute leaders whose loyalty he suspected, and to appoint as chief of staff Bazelais, who had held the same post under Dessalines, Christophe was in Arcahaie by 28 December. That night, the Senate outlawed him and, in the style of ancient Rome, charged Pétion, ablest soldier among them, with defense of the capital.

Panic seized Port-au-Prince but not Pétion. Within the hour, he rushed off gallopers to Gérin at Anse-à-Veau and Yayou at Léogane, ordering them to bring up every soldier in the South. To Magloire Ambroise he entrusted the task of organizing Port-au-Prince for defense. Meanwhile, though heavily outnumbered by Christophe's 10,000, he himself advanced North across the Cul-de-Sac at the head of 3000 troops.

The date was New Year's Day, 1807. With independence only three years old, *noirs* of the North and the Artibonite and *jaunes* of the South and West were again at each other's throats.

Pétion hoped to surprise the army of the North, but he reckoned without Christophe. As Pétion's advance guard reached the Habitation Sibert, three miles Northeast of Croix-des-Missions, they discovered that Christophe, marching across country, was already behind them.

There could only be one result: after a confused melee, Pétion's force broke and ran. In the pursuit, Christophe's dragoons caught up with Pétion. As the cavalry closed in, a young captain, Coutilien Coutard, snatched the general's gilded chapeau and clapped it on his own head. The next moment, feigning his general, he suffered himself to be cut down while Pétion escaped, unnoticed. Someone brought in Coutard's body after the fight. He was buried at Morne-à-Tuf in the next grave to Charlotin Marcadieux's.

By the time the army of the North was again in hand outside Port-au-Prince, Yayou had thrown together a defense line at the Portail St. Joseph (then the Northern gate to the city), overlooked by Fort National. Lamarre, proscribed after the fall of Dessalines, was among the prisoners delivered from jail to man the defenses. Still wearing prison rags, he sought out his old command, the 24th Demibrigade, seized a sword, and led them in prodigies of valor.

Like Dessalines before Santo Domingo, Christophe had marched South without artillery. His only recourse now was a series of headlong assaults. All failed. On 8 January, frustrated and furious, Christophe withdrew, unpursued, to St. Marc, leaving flame and pillage in his wake. Secure again at the Cap, he lost no time regularizing his position in terms more agreeable than those proffered by Pétion's Senate. On 17 February 1807, Christophe's advisers created a new "State of Haiti" and turned Pétion's constitution on its head. Henry, denominated lifetime president, received virtually the identical powers Pétion and Boyer had vested in the Senate at Port-au-Prince.

The South and the West were not slow to reply. Less than three weeks later, on 9 March 1807, the Senate met in Port-au-Prince to choose a new president. The hotheaded Gérin (so sure of election that he had already bought an official costume) destroyed himself by an outburst against a brother senator. Guy-Joseph Bonnet, Pétion's respected henchman (and a widely influential Mason), thereupon lobbied the members for Pétion, who was handily elected. Now, having engineered the constitution of 1806, Pétion could try to make it work.

Betrayal and Dissension

The main problems that confronted Pétion were to administer the republic under arrangements that he, better than anyone, knew were unworkable; and to wage the civil war that now existed between the two divisions of Haiti.

To fortify his position with the important people - the *mulâtre* aristocrats of the South and the *anciens libres* planters who had owned land even in colonial times - Pétion quickly got the Senate to pass laws annulling Dessalines's despoliations and reimbursing owners for crops lost while their plantations had been expropriated. As further sweeteners for the elite, Pétion at the same time repealed the 25 percent share on every crop, ordained originally by Toussaint (and retained in his own system of *fermage* by Christophe), and proclaimed a crop-subsidy policy whereby in years of low prices the government would buy up surplus sugar and coffee.

If, however, Pétion had any hope of ruling by some kind of gentlemanly consensus, this hope was dashed. Gérin, not only ungovernable but rancorous, organized an opposition bloc in the Senate and set out to derail the regime. Allied to Gérin, but principled where he was opportunistic, was a faction of doctrinaire Jacobins who opposed virtually any government or measure strong enough to be effective.

The Gérin clique found a natural target in Bonnet, principal administrator of the regime - and, Gérin well remembered, the senator who had lobbied him out of the presidency. Bonnet managed to set up administrative and fiscal procedures that served well as long as he could supervise them himself. At his right hand was Inginac, another honest and therefore unpopular administrator.(9)

Calmly hearing their complaints, Pétion endured his Senate obstructionists until 1808. Then, showing an unexpected streak of Cromwell, he ranged his soldiers about the legislative building. When a quorum of senators hesitated to force their way through the bayonets, Pétion declared the Senate adjourned, blandly assumed its powers, and kept it adjourned until 1811. Then, with the republic deeply divided, he convened a nine-member rump (out of twenty-four original seats), which duly re-elected him for another four years.

But the uncompromising Bonnet was an early casualty: in 1810 Pétion threw him to the wolves and, with him, the uncomfortable notion that honesty was a requirement in the fiscal affairs of the republic. Himself irreproachably honest, Pétion would remark with gentle cynicism, "All men are thieves." Bonnet's reply (years later in his memoirs) was uncompromising: "In a country where corruption has hold of every branch of government, where everyone seeks to live off the public treasury . . . venality and misrepresentation end up as accepted norms. Every reform that tries to shut off graft by those who profit from this state of affairs stirs up a frenzy."

While government winked, coiners circulated debased coins ("*monnaie-à-serpent,*" peasants styled them). To make up its deficits, the regime issued 300,000 paper gourdes, redeemable only in future claims against state-owned lands. Distribution of the lands themselves was only a step away.

Meanwhile, without regard to internal affairs under either Pétion or Christophe, civil war ran its course.

Behind the Artibonite, backed in the mountains by the old Cordon de l'Ouest, Christophe enjoyed a defensible frontier with St. Marc as his outpost, but his flank was open in the Northwest.

Here, a spirit of separatism dated back to colonial times, when Cap François superseded Port-de-Paix as chief town of the French, and here Capoix-la-Mort, Christophe's chief rival, had ruled as satrap. In May 1807, led by a private named Rebecca, Capoix's former troops revolted at Port-de-Paix, thus inaugurating three years of sparring between Christophe and Pétion, which Haitians call the "Guerre du Môle." While Henry thrust South from St. Marc, Pétion, using British and American merchant ships for his navy,(10) put armies into the Northwest.

Rebecca, captured and beheaded, was no more, but one of Pétion's best generals, the rehabilitated Lamarre, contested the Northwest for two years against Christophe's efforts, and might have done even better had not Pétion been cramped by unforeseen developments in his own rear. Suborned by Christophe, Yayou, one of the old *congo* chieftains, waged guerrilla war against Pétion in the West; and, on the far Southern tip of Haiti, in the Grande-Anse, there broke out a stubborn insurgency under Goman that was to smolder on for thirteen years.

By October 1808, Christophe's big battalions had ejected Lamarre from Port-de-Paix.

Besieged inside the Môle, Lamarre hung on, but Christophe's navy, officered by Englishmen, had cut out his supply lines to the South. On 16 July 1810, resisting an attack, Lamarre was killed by a cannonball. When Christophe learned what had happened, he ordered his squadron to the Môle, where colors were half-masted in mourning, and a funeral salute fired to honor a brave adversary. Lamarre's aide-de-camp, a *noir* lieutenant named Faustin Soulouque, slipped through the lines, bearing Lamarre's heart, which he delivered to Pétion in Port-au-Prince.

The Môle fell on 28 September. Its surviving defenders were to perish toiling to build Christophe's Citadel on the slopes of La Ferrière.

Henry now held undisputed sway over the North, the Northwest, and the Artibonite, and could turn his mind singly to the problems of government and economic progress. Pétion, the republic deeply divided at his back, enjoyed no such respite.

The South Secedes

Six months before the Môle surrendered, on 7 April 1810, André Rigaud returned to Haiti. Since 1802, when Leclerc had packed him back to France, he had simmered in frustration at Agé and with Toussaint in the Fort de Joux under the watchful eyes of Fouché's soldiers. Now, conceivably with the secret backing of Bonaparte, he had eluded them and was back. Landing at Les Cayes, he received a hero's welcome.

"Proud, haughty, and cruel, and agitated by restless Ambition," had been Edward Stevens's vignette on Rigaud to the State Department in 1799. Nothing had changed save that Rigaud's former lieutenant, Pétion, now held top place, and that was insufferable.

Whatever his inward misgivings, Pétion received Rigaud with fair words and sent him to the South, with 5000 soldiers and instructions to pacify the rebellious Grande-Anse. Predictably, Rigaud did no such thing. Instead, he assembled electors at Cayes from all the parishes of the South (and a few malcontents from Pétion's West as well), and on 3 November 1810, proclaimed the State of the South (l'Etat du Sud) with himself its chief.

With more civil war on his hands than he could already cope with, Pétion was not prepared to open a new front against Rigaud on the latter's home ground. Instead, as no other living Haitian could ever have managed it, Pétion met his brother *mulâtre* at the bridge of Miragoâne on 2 December, suavely accepted the fait accompli, and asked only that Rigaud not betray the republic to Christophe and his *noirs*. Rigaud assented (not without one of his celebrated outbursts, during which he ran his sword through the foot of a staff officer), and the two shook hands.

Now Haiti was split four ways: Christophe's North; Pétion's West; Rigaud's South; and the insurgent Grande-Anse, under Goman, the *noir* guerrilla.

The detente of Miragoâne did not, of course, rule out intrigue. Before 1811 was very old, Pétion had engineered a revolt at Les Cayes, and Rigaud in turn was probing East toward Port-au-Prince.

But Rigaud's hour in the sun was short. During the summer he sickened, and, on his plantation, Habitation Laborde (where the Cayes airstrip now extends), the *Premier des Mulâtres,* aged fifty, died on 18 September 1811.

Rigaud's heir was Jerome-Maximilien Borgella, *mulâtre* son of that French Borgella who had been mayor of Port-au-Prince and had helped Toussaint draft the constitution of 1801. Borgella was brave, popular, and a Freemason of Cayes's old lodge, l'Heureuse Réunion, and his cause at first prospered.

Christophe had slackened the civil war ashore, but, better aware than any Haitian before of the uses of sea power, he continued to build and use his navy. In January 1812, he had a squadron cruising the Bight of Léogane to intercept commerce headed for Port-au-Prince. What Christophe did not know was that, headed by a *mulâtre* officer, mutineers bribed by Pétion were aboard the flagship, a frigate. Off Miragoâne they struck, captured the ship, and brought her in, as they thought, to Pétion there. But Borgella, Pétion's *mulâtre* rival, held the place. This was no impediment: the mutineers gave him the ship instead, and helped lure in Christophe's other two ships, whose officers and crews as quickly changed sides.

With its flagship, the frigate (renamed *Heureuse Réunion* for Borgella's lodge in Cayes), the South now had most of Christophe's navy but not for long. H.M.S. *Southampton*, standing West from Port-au-Prince, encountered the three ships off Miragoâne. Declining to recognize Borgella's flag, the British frigate ordered the Haitian squadron to heave to and be taken into Jamaica for adjudication. Augustin Gaspard, captain of *Heureuse Reunion,* said he would rather sink than surrender, and opened fire. In the murderous fight that ensued, the corvette and brig abandoned Gaspard. With his foremast and bowsprit shot away after an hour's battle, and a hundred dead and wounded, Gaspard surrendered to a British prize crew, which landed his casualties and then sailed the shattered frigate into Port Royal.

The annals of Haiti scarcely recall Gaspard's name or that of the *Heureuse Réunion,* yet the sea fight off Miragoâne was the most desperate, courageous, and well fought in the naval history of the country.

As for Borgella, his cause did not long outlast his navy's. On 7 March 1812, Pétion blandly stage-managed an almost bloodless sedition against Borgella in Les Cayes, and soon afterward magnanimously welcomed the South back into the republic as if nothing had happened. Borgella was allowed to remain one of the South's first citizens and, full of years and honors, died in 1844.

Henry, by God's Grace

Until 1811, when Pétion re-elected himself president of the republic, Henry Christophe had maintained, very thinly, the forms of republican government in the North. How thin they were, Bonnet, sent on a mission to the Cap (Cap Henry now, no longer Cap Français since July 1810), recounted: "One could hardly breathe for the atmosphere of aristocracy. The courtiers surrounding [Christophe] murmured 'Monseigneur' with respect and submission."

Once it was clear that the West would never choose him to supersede Pétion, Christophe put aside his pretense. On 26 March 1811, a Council of State proclaimed the North a kingdom and Henry I its king. Engrafting on the constitution of 1807 appropriate borrowings from Dessalines's imperial constitution of 1805, the council quickly fashioned for Henry a new constitution.

There followed the heady preliminaries of royal installation. On 5 April,

Henry created his nobility: four princes, eight dukes, twenty-two counts, thirty-seven barons, and fourteen Chevaliers of the Royal and Military Order of St. Henry. Corneille Brelle, the Capuchin who had anointed Dessalines six years earlier, was summarily raised to Archbishop and Grand Almoner of Haiti (word being falsely spread that he had been consecrated in Palermo).(11)

In *Almanach Royal*, Christophe promulgated in detail specifications for court dress and regimental uniforms. Princes and dukes would wear black cloaks faced with scarlet and gold over knee-length white tunics, white silk stockings, and red leather shoes with gold buckles; differing but equally gaudy plumage adorned each rank and regiment. The reality was sometimes less magnificent. A visiting British officer in 1807 described the officer of the guard at the Cap as "wearing the remnant of a French military officer's uniform, with the wreck of an epaulet on one shoulder, but neither shirt nor shoes nor waistcoat and his trousers in tatters."

A pair of royal crowns was already on order. Rather than rebuild Notre-Dame, still roofless and ruined in 1811 as it had been six years earlier, when Dessalines was crowned, Christophe now raised a new church on the Champ de Mars with an eighty-foot cupola beneath which the coronation thrones would be placed under a scarlet baldequin. Henry had already restored the liturgic pomp of the ancien regime: his seat and priedieu faced those of his wife, Marie-Louise, and one always set aside for Mme. Dessalines; ministers and officers of the government ranged respectfully to the rear on either side of the choir.

So, on 2 June 1811, Henry Christophe - twenty-one years earlier scullion, cook, and headwaiter of a Cap Français inn, La Couronne (was the name prophetic?) - was crowned:

Henry, by God's Grace and the Constitution of the State, King of Haiti, Sovereign of La Tortue, Gonâve and other outlying Isles, Destroyer of Tyranny, Regenerator and Benefactor of the Haitian Nation, Creator of her Moral, Political and Martial Institutions, First Crowned Monarch of the New World, Defender of the Faith, Founder of the Royal and Military Order of Saint Henry.

Then the bells pealed and the cannon of the forts roared in salute as King Henry I rode in his state coach over newly repaved streets back to the former presidential and now royal palace for a state banquet. When the captain of H.M.S. *Reindeer,* representing Britain at the coronation, pledged the new king's health, Henry replied with a monarchic toast to "Our dear Brother, George III, whose life may the Supreme Arbiter preserve to oppose invincibly the designs of Napoleon and ever serve as Haiti's constant friend."

The ceremonies were also attended by representatives from the North of Santo Domingo: the commandants of Santiago and La Vega, and others representing the Spanish blacks, whom Christophe had been carefully cultivating since 1807. (12)

Afterward, before the cheering ceased, Henry announced the members of his royal cabinet, among them his old friend Vernet (Prince des Gonaïves), Minister of Finance and Interior; Paul Romain (Prince de Limbé, where he had been born), Minister of War; Julien Prévost (Comte de Limonade), Henry's *mulâtre* secretary, now Foreign Minister; and Chevalier Alexis Dupuy (once secretary to Dessalines and, more memorably, first lover of Choute Lachenais, mistress of Pétion and Boyer), Royal Interpreter for a master who, though he could not read and could only just manage to sign "Henry," spoke French and English.

A few days later, work had already commenced on a new and magnificent royal palace, to be called "Sans Souci," located at Milot, where the mountain road surged upward along the dense green slopes of Bonnet-à-l'Evêque to La Ferrière.

The Kingdom of the North

The man who made himself King of the North had been penetratingly characterized by a British visitor at Cap Henry in 1818 as,

in his person what in England you would call a fine portly-looking man about 5 feet 10 inches. He is now growing stout, and on horseback, where he certainly looks his best, has much the appearance of old George . . . He is quite black, with a manner and countenance, when in good humor (and I have never seen him in any other), very intelligent, pleasant and expressive - his features are much that of his countrymen - his nose rather long but flat at the nostrils - his lips are not thick - his eyes, except when in a rage, rather small, but quick - his forehead, which gives so much character to his countenance,high. . . I am told by those who have seen him in one of his gusts of passion, that it can only be compared to a hurricane for its fury.

Long before ascending the throne, Henry had commenced the reconstruction and modernization of his realm. Dating from early collaboration with Vincent in the Petite-Anse, his system of *fermage*, with interruptions, went back to 1797: habitations owned by the state were let out to managers and worked by *noir* cultivators bound to the land; their lives were wholly regulated and their efforts as rigorously (if far more paternally) exacted as in the days of Dessalines or Toussaint.

Under Henry's Code Rural, overseers sounded the daily rising bell at 3:00 A.M. Following prayers and breakfast, work commenced in the fields at 4:30. Between 8:00 and 9:00 the cultivator had a pause for lunch, then three more hours until noon. From noon until 2:00 P.M., there was dinner and a midday rest. At 2:00, work resumed until sundown, ceasing only with the Angelus in the fields, after which, in the brief tropical twilight, the workers made their way back to their huts. Saturday was theirs for cultivation of their own plots and for the women to carry produce to market. Saturday night was a time of ease and sometimes of dance and drums, while Sunday, after church, was a day of rest.

The cultivator's wage was one-fourth the total yield, distributed by the planter-manager, who also had to feed, clothe, house, and care for the worker and his family.

To enforce this regime (and Henry, unlike Pétion, or Boyer in the future, or many another Haitian ruler, never set rules he could not and would not enforce) the king established his own combination of personal bodyguard and *maréchaussée*. Importing from Dahomey 4000 young *noirs*, Henry organized the Royal Corps of Dahomets, a rigidly disciplined, well-trained and well-rewarded national gendarmerie. Each of the kingdom's fifty-six *arrondissements* had a seventy man company of Royal Dahomets under an army officer who commanded the district and acted as justice of the peace.

Like the regime itself, the Royal Dahomets were incorruptible, and they made sure the people were equally so. Under Henry's express orders, they entrapped thieves by leaving money or valuables in the streets and arresting those who picked them up and failed to turn them in. Vagabondage was checked and punished, and peasants entering towns were required to be decently clothed. In place of the Frenchman's hated lash, *liane* and *cocomacac* rose and fell on the backs of idlers or transgressors.

Behind all this system and discipline, King Henry was everywhere, inspecting, punishing, rewarding, consulting foreign advisers, strengthening the currency (no *monnaie-à-serpent* in the Kingdom of the North!), improving marketing arrangements at home, negotiating with merchants abroad.

Then, as 150 years later, the Haitian cultivator broke his fields with shovel and hoe or more often merely with a pointed stick. Henry tried in vain to introduce the plow: a British demonstration team described by William Wilberforce as "the honest rustics and their apparatus" made no inroads in the traditional primitivism of the *noirs*.

In the words of the British visitor of 1818, "It is his mind, and his alone, that governs all; he has the ablest men of his kingdom employed about his person, but they are mere executors of his will. One proof of his being neither a very changeable or cruel man, is that almost all the great officers of the palace, who were there four years ago, are there now.

An example of Henry's mind for detail is found in a letter from the king to Marie-Louise, written in March 1813: "I have just seen the doctors,(13) my dear; they say that our daughter, Madame Première, has a badly coated tongue and is very much out of sorts. You will therefore have her take senna tomorrow, Sunday, and again on Monday, copiously. The doctors will be with you at Sans

Souci on Monday afternoon to give her another purge on Tuesday."

Yet the order, the industry, the flourishing prosperity of the North proved that Henry's attention to every detail and his economic system worked. (The annual revenue of the regime amounted to $3.5 million -the highest since 1791.) As Toussaint (and even Dessalines) had understood, it was the only system for a people without the remotest experience in self-government. It was founded on a mass of manual laborers and an elite that supervised them and ran the country. Its keystones were regularity, security, and obedience to authority.

Amid so many enterprises Henry had two preoccupations: building palaces and monuments, and the spread of education, without which Haiti could never raise herself from the state in which the French had left the blacks.

Commencing in 1816, with the aid of Clarkson and Wilberforce(14) the British abolitionists, Henry brought a succession of English schoolmasters to Haiti. By 1817 he had schools going at the Cap, Milot, Port-de-Paix, Gonaïves, and St. Marc. Typically, under rules set out by the king himself, truancy (first offense) was punished by a salutary week's confinement on bread and water.

When we think of Henry the builder, we think of La Ferrière - truly one of the world's wonders - and of Sans Souci. Yet Henry also built or at least began palaces at Limbé, Port-de-Paix, Jean Rabel, Môle St. Nicolas, Gonaïves, Fort Liberté, St. Marc, and that of 365 doors (one for each day of the year) at Petite Rivière de l'Artibonite.

How many thousands of prisoners and workers died hauling the great stones and guns of La Ferrière will never be known. The German military engineers who oversaw its building were never again allowed to step outside its walls, some of which rise sheer for 140 feet. The main gun gallery is 30 feet deep and 270 long. Its 200 guns were, as can still be seen from their markings, mainly English - taken from the Duke of York during his disastrous Low Countries campaign of 1794 and brought to St. Domingue by Leclerc as his siege train. With its thousands on thousands of cannonballs, and commanding embrasures jutting from its 2600-foot summit like the prow of a ship breasting a green wave, the Citadel-Henry embodies to this day the imagination, daring, pride, and power of its kingly author.

Papa Bon-Coeur

The last spasm of open war between Pétion and Christophe reached climax in mid-1812. Amid the torrential spring rains known as *"les Toussaints,"* Henry marched South for the last time and again laid siege to Port-au-Prince. Once again the defenders, commanded this time by Boyer, fought a delaying action on the Cul-de-Sac; once again, buying time, the troops of the West managed to hold Port-au-Prince against Henry's stubborn attacks.

Then there followed one of those conspiracies, at which Pétion excelled, to subvert a camarilla of Henry's officers into murdering the king during mass at St. Marc. But like so many Haitian conspiracies, this was betrayed. When Henry rode up to the church on 2 June, he took personal command of the honor guard, as Toussaint had done with the mutineers at the Cap in 1801. Slowly he intoned the names of the plotters and called them out of ranks. Ordering the guard to load with ball ammunition, he had them shot on the spot, and then strode in to mass while a burial party carried off the bodies and the soldiers cleaned their muskets.

There were other defections. The garrison at Mirebalais and the cultivators of the Artibonite, fed up with the rigors of Henry's stern benevolence, rose against the king. But disaffection was something Henry knew how to quell. Abandoning his fruitless siege, executing the disloyal (including *mulâtre* women of Gonaïves, whose only offense had been to pray for their brothers in the West and South), the king quenched the risings and once again retired North.

In the republic, Pétion's regime continued its effortless decline. Pétion's crucial decision, in retrospect his great mistake, had been to distribute land in small holdings. Beginning in 1809 (the first large-scale land distribution in the hemisphere) and continuing thenceforward, his regime already foundering in a sea of worthless paper and counterfeit coinage, Pétion parceled out the state's holdings to his soldiers. In addition to senior officers, who got large grants, every major got 35 *carreaux* (a *carreau* is an old French land unit, equal to 3.15 acres, used to this day in Haiti); captains received 30; lieutenants, 25; and sub-lieutenants, 20. Going down the line, by 1814, each soldier ended with his tiny Plot of 3 *carreaux,* and the republic, effectively, had become a nation of small-holding peasants rather than of serfs and plantations.

The effects of this policy, though not immediate, were fundamental. Production dropped, growth ceased, the economy stagnated, then declined. Fragmentation of the *latifundia* took out of production land used for money crops - sugar, coffee, indigo, and cotton - and put it into truck gardens and subsistence farming, thus further weakening the earning capacity of the republic. Coffee superseded sugar as the primary crop. Sugar called for mills, machinery, irrigation and hydraulic systems, intensive and disciplined labor, and close supervision. Coffee could grow wild on every hillside in Haiti. The peasant could strip the bushes, dry the beans, and bring them to market with never a care for pruning, fertilizing, or cultivation, and still produce the world's finest coffee.

In 1801, under Toussaint, Haiti had exported 13,250 tons of sugar; by 1822, her sugar export had plummeted to 326 tons, and from that year until 1916 sugar exports ceased entirely. In 1801, 14,750 tons of coffee went abroad; in 1822, the total had increased to 18,599 tons, and by 1860, Haiti was exporting

30,500 tons of coffee, a quantity barely short of that exported almost a century later, in 1952.

In March 1815 (this time with a rump of only five senators, down four from 1811), Pétion again re-elected himself. But the constitutional comedy had to end: within a year, at Pétion's behest, a committee sitting at Grand-Goâve produced a suitable replacement for the ill-starred constitution of 1806. Not surprisingly, Pétion was named *president-à-vie* (president for life), with power to choose his successor. The president would control all important executive powers. initiatives, and appointments. A Senate (fourteen members) and a lower house (twenty-nine members) would ratify the actions of the president.(15)

Except that it legitimized Pétion, the new constitution seemed to make little difference. In 1816, on revenues of 1.1 million gourdes. Pétion allowed the legislature to enact a 2-million-gourde budget. Apathy reigned, and so did graft and peculation.(16) Troublemakers, only if loud or conspicuous (such as Gérin, bayoneted at Nippes when "resisting arrest"), were, in the words of one historian (Brown), "disposed of by noiseless methods."

Through it all, available to all, good-hearted, calm, compassionate, philosophical, and permissive, Pétion sat under his colonnades, garbed in a planter's white suit and the madras headdress Toussaint had affected.

In all this drift, slackness, and micawberism, Pétion mustered the energy for one last good deed. Devoted to education, he founded the *Lycée* of Port-au-Prince (later *Lycée Pétion*) and a *pension* for girls. But here, no different in this respect from Henry's stern schools in the North, the children of the elite received an education that merely widened the gulf that already separated them from the illiterate black masses.

In 1816, rainiest year since 1812, the Cul-de-Sac was inundated. Sewage floated in the streets and gutters of Port-au-Prince. Malaria, yellow fever, and all manner of enteric diseases ravaged the country.

Toward the end of the year, under the onset of intermittent fever (probably, as Dr. Apollo Gamier concluded in a reconstruction of Pétion's medical history, the malaria from which he had apparently suffered since 1807), Pétion's health began to fail. All through 1817 and into the next spring, Pétion declined. Before daylight on 29 March. the candle flickered out. As word spread through Port-au-Prince and then out toward the plain and the mountains that "Papa Bon-Coeur" had died, the republic was plunged into deepest sadness. Pétion's body was embalmed and lay in state for three days: his heart, previously removed, was interred in Fort National. Every door was closed and draped in mourning.

From far and wide, Haitians made their way into the capital for the obsequies on 1 April. Among the funeral orations and prayers of grief, one simple mourner spoke for the country: "Pétion never once drew tears save by his death."

It is harder to assess Pétion in less emotional terms. Perhaps unwittingly, he had profoundly altered the society of his country. By 1818, the peasant, no longer serf, was secure on his own small plot. Discipline had vanished, inertia reigned, neglect was overrunning the habitations. But the elite - an elite of *hommes de couleur* not *noirs* as in the North - was firmly in charge and running the republic.

The ideal view of Pétion sees him as generous, well intentioned, politically liberal, concerned for the common man. Another view shows him as a realist, who recognized that after the convulsive years from 1791 to 1804 the freed slaves preferred poverty and security to discipline, production, and progress. Yet it is difficult to dispute a sharply different verdict by the historian James Leyburn on Pétion and his regime: "His country was rich when he came to power and poor when he died; united in 1806 and divided in 1818. Candor compels his admirers to admit that many of the calamities of the social and economic history of Haiti can be traced to Pétion's administration."

In his final decline, Pétion failed to nominate a successor. His body was hardly cold before the start of maneuvers to replace him.

Borgella of Cayes, popular and respected, probably represented the true favorite of the Senate. But Boyer, Pétion's secretary and commander of the Presidential Guard, held the *Palais National*. When the Senate wavered, Gédéon (the colonel, now a general, who had betrayed Dessalines) threw his ample bulk and local regiments into the scale and declared Boyer president for life, a verdict the Senate hastened to confirm unanimously.

Choute Lachenais (with whom, as Pétion ebbed, Boyer had discreetly consummated certain arrangements) never even vacated her apartments in the palace.

Goman in the Grande-Anse

Among much business left unfinished by Pétion was the Grande-Anse insurgency, dating back ten years to 1807. The mountains and valleys of the Grande-Anse are as remote and precipitous as any in Haiti. In this densely forested region within a region, a one-time *marron* of Corail, Jean-Baptiste Perrier, better known as "Goman," rose against Pétion in February 1807. Goman, proclaiming himself avenger of Dessalines against all *jaunes*, was a natural guerrilla. He could climb like a goat. Years of *marronage* had taught him every trick of terrain and fieldcraft. A soldier in the old Légion d'Égalité, he had later served under Rigaud against Toussaint and then, always in the mountains of La Hotte and Macaya that form the backbone of the Grande-Anse.

Goman's methods were classic. He carefully built an intelligence net. Disguised as cultivators, his agents not only spied on opponents but brought in produce from guerrilla areas and traded it in Cayes and Jérémie for ammunition, tools, and supplies. Every person in Goman's domain was either warrior or cultivator. To ensure productivity and peasant loyalty, his inspector of cultivation doubled as political commissar, moving ceaselessly by secret trails from stronghold to stronghold.

As a guerrilla tactician, Goman excelled. Never would he allow his forces to attack unless victory was assured. During combat, he himself kept clear, observing from some cliff or hillside with a spyglass, which was his most prized possession. The partisans would show themselves at Abricots; simultaneously there would be an ambush at Trou Bonbon; then, mysteriously, Goman with his main body would sweep down on Corail, only to vanish when the sweating government columns approached.

The cement of the Grande-Anse insurrection was peasant grievances, *noir-mulâtre* animosities, regional separatism, natural sanctuary areas, talented leadership, and a vast political and intelligence network.

Only once (at Habitation Beaumont, back of Corail, in 1808) was Goman ever brought to battle against his intentions. Here, Borgella fought the guerrillas to a standstill, taking one of Goman's lieutenants, Jean-Baptiste Lagarde, whom the government promptly suborned as a counterinsurgent leader against his former chief. Under Lagarde, on personal instructions from Pétion, who assumed charge of operations in June 1808, the republic organized a special corps of Eclaireurs (Scouts), mostly ralliers from Goman's ranks. Trap after trap, ruse after ruse, all failed.

When Rigaud entered the South in 1810, one of his few sincere efforts for the cause of the republic was to try to pacify Goman, whom he knew well. Goman promised everything to his old leader, but three months later he was not only still at large but had brought the whole corps of Eclaireurs back over in a body. Following this coup, in 1811 Christophe, impressed with Goman's troublemaking capabilities, dubbed him Count of Jérémie and *général de brigade* and supplied him with arms.

By 1812 Goman was at his summit. At Grand-Doko, beneath the mountains appropriately named "Les Mamelles," he had both headquarters and court, including a seraglio and a ceremonial dais and throne on which, adorned with triple-plumed chapeau, he held audience.

As chief of state, Pétion had shortcomings: as a soldier he had few. Goman's insurrection posed military and political problems that Pétion and his generals proved well qualified to solve.

As soon as Henry Christophe's 1812 foray into the West had been turned back, Pétion sent Bazelais into the Grande-Anse to subdue Goman. Pétion's instructions were typically politic: use minimum force, reassure the *noirs* that the republic did not intend a war of castes, and break up habitations and distribute land to disaffected peasants. Although Bazelais failed to snuff out the insurrection, he confined it. Moreover, by carrying out Pétion's sensible instructions and by lenient treatment and release of guerrilla prisoners, Bazelais laid the groundwork for ultimate pacification.

When Boyer succeeded Pétion in 1819, his first order of business was the Grande-Anse. Pétion's efforts, he felt, had in reality already accomplished three fourths of the job. "The element that remains to be subdued," he said, "should not be dealt with as enemies to fight but as *marrons* to be run down." Under Bazelais and Borgella, Boyer sent six regiments into the South. Methodically boxing in Goman, government columns worked their way up trails, stream beds, and ravines from Jérémie, Cayes, Tiburon, and Anse d'Hainault. Although Goman eluded them, they ravaged guerrillas' crops and overran their caches. Defectors were rewarded and in many cases shipped over in government ranks. As supplies failed and food ran short, Goman's bands began to dissipate.

At the end of May 1819, encircled at Grand-Doko, Goman was observed at bay on a cliff by a patrol of Borgella's. The soldiers fired and Goman jumped or fell - no one will ever know - into a jungle chasm a thousand feet below. His body was never found. Thus ended the thirteen-year insurrection of the Grand-Anse.

Haiti and the Outer World

Except to jockey for commercial advantage between the contending regimes, the outer world gave little attention to Haiti's internal struggle. According to their differing interests, only three powers - Britain, the United States, and France - took any notice of Haiti at all, and that in the most reserved and tentative fashion.(17)

The Congress of Vienna had, to be sure, outlawed the African slave trade, but the consensus of the powers was far from recognizing a nation that, after all, owed its origin to slave insurrection and the war of all peoples against all kings.(18) In Rayford Logan's perceptive analogy, "the specter of a free Negro republic that owed its independence to a successful slave revolt frightened slaveholding countries as much as the shadow of Bolshevist Russia alarmed capitalist countries in 1917."

Though not in fact, Haiti still juridically remained a colony of France in revolt. Until the relationship between the two countries could be made to coincide with the realities, no other nation (especially in the aftermath of Vienna and all it implied) was prepared to recognize Haiti as a sovereign, independent country. In 1806, America's John Randolph had called Haiti "an anomaly among the nations of the earth." Nine years later, Albert Gallatin was to write, "San Domingo must be considered as being neither independent nor part of the mother country."

With the war over and Bonaparte safe on St. Helena, Britain had two main objects concerning Haiti. One was to monopolize Haiti's trade. the other was to prevent the export of Haiti's slave revolt to the mutinous maroons of Jamaica and other British West Indian islands. The former called for active commercial relations, the latter for a diplomatic *cordon sanitaire*. While British merchants factored sugar, coffee, and cotton, and imported tools and weapons, British officials spoke of (and hardly to) "the two contending chiefs of Haiti, Generals Christophe and Pétion."

Yet in 1813 England's trade with Christophe alone totaled some £1.2 million. A year later Pétion accorded a 50 percent reduction in duties on all British imports and did away completely with duties on arms shipments.

The story of American relations with Haiti at this time and for a half century to come is that of merchants versus slave-owners. Northern merchants wanted to trade with Haiti. Southern slave-owners abominated Haiti and all it stood for. The planters prevailed. Haiti was to remain unrecognized by the United States for decades to come. In the words of Thomas Hart Benton to the Senate in 1826: "We receive no mulatto consuls or black ambassadors from [Haiti]. And why? The peace of eleven states will not permit the fruits of a successful Negro insurrection to be exhibited among them."

As early as 1803, American merchants had supported Dessalines. During the first six months of 1804 alone, some forty ships carried arms, ammunition, and supplies from New York to Haiti. In 1805, Dessalines recruited American and German armorers from Philadelphia. Under sharp pressure from Napoleon (and in return for his support in the U.S. dispute with Spain over West Florida), President Jefferson embargoed trade with Haiti in 1806. The embargo lapsed in 1809, but American trade did not recover. In 1810 it was but $109,000. The War of 1812 soon intervened. If, by 1821, after peace with England, American exports to Haiti had increased tenfold, they nonetheless amounted to but 3 percent of the total U.S. export trade, whereas in 1790 they had constituted 11 percent.

Diplomatic relations between the U.S. and Haiti were all but nonexistent. In 1802, Leclerc had expelled Tobias Lear, Edward Stevens's successor at the Cap. Not until 1813, when William Taylor held the position, was there even an American commercial agent at Port-au-Prince. Because of the British lock on Haitian trade and British wartime control of the sea, Pétion, Taylor reported in 1814, was "barely friendly.

In the North, Henry, Anglophile that he was, gave the United States even shorter shrift. In 1811, after a dispute over funds he had deposited in Baltimore, the king expropriated $132,000 worth of American cargoes at the Cap and, on various pretexts, declined to receive American ships or agents thereafter.

While Britain, France, and the United States sparred among themselves, Haiti's example was not lost on Spain's restive provinces in Latin America. Organizing his first (and ultimately unsuccessful) attempt to liberate Venezuela, Francisco de Miranda, in 1806, visited Jacmel, where Magloire Ambroise made him welcome and sent him on to Dessalines at Marchand. After Miranda had explained his plans at eloquent length to the emperor, Dessalines snapped: "*Écoutez!* To make a revolution and make it succeed, there are only two things you have to do - *Coupé têtes! Boulé cailles!*"

A decade later, in his darkest hours, Simon Bolivar sought and found shelter and support from Pétion's republic. Expelled from Venezuela in 1815 and made unwelcome in Jamaica, where he first sought asylum, Bolivar and his followers reached Les Cayes on Christmas Eve, 1815. There they were warmly received, succored, and, on Pétion's order, re-equipped. As soon as he could, in January 1816, Bolivar made his way to Port-au-Prince to meet Pétion. The sympathy between the two was instant. Pétion secretly directed that 4000 muskets, 15,000 pounds of powder, flints, lead, and - most telling weapon of revolution - a printing press be given to Bolivar. By way of ecclesiastical benefice, Pétion even installed Bolivar's chaplain, Padre Juan Marimon Enriquez, as *curé* of Petit-Goâve until the latter could return to Venezuela as a senator.

Before he sailed again for Venezuela, on 10 April 1816, Bolivar tried to thank Pétion. Pétion replied simply that the best thanks he could receive would be the liberation of every slave in the Spanish colonies. And, on 6 July, struck off by the liberator on his little press from Les Cayes, a decree by Bolivar, who had already manumitted the 1500 slaves of his family estates, proclaimed the abolition of slavery in Spanish America.(19)

Scarcely had Bolivar proclaimed freedom than he was again beaten. In mid-September he was back at Cayes. Once again Pétion helped him refit, and, on 28 December 1816, Bolivar sailed from Haiti for the last time. Hard fighting lay ahead, and an ultimate victory Pétion would not live to see.

When Haitians write this glowing chapter in their history, they tell of the handsome court sword Bolivar sent Pétion, of Bolivar's prophecy that Pétion would outshine George Washington, and of the fine statue eventually raised to Pétion in Caracas. What they omit is that Bolivar never even recognized Haiti's independence and that he refused to invite Haiti to the Congress of American States, held in Panama in 1826. They also omit the shameful ostracism of Haiti by Colombia, which in considerable part owed its liberation to Pétion's support, and by other Spanish-American republics during that congress, which had been organized by Colombia. Making Colombia's snub even more brutal, her Minister of Foreign Affairs bluntly asserted "great repugnance against maintaining with Haiti those relations . . . generally observed among civilized nations." Venezuela, at least equally indebted, did not even send a diplomatic representative to Haiti until 1874. And today, in the great Hall of the Americas in the Pan-American Union in Washington (where the bust of Dessalines, pallid in white marble, not black, is shoved back in a corner), no bust of Pétion is to be found amid the other liberators he inspired and supported.

Oblivious of what lay ahead, Pétion and, after him, Boyer nonetheless advanced the cause of liberty as best they could. In October 1816, not content with helping South American liberators, Pétion proffered three battalions and a supply of arms to Don Francisco Xavier Mina, the renowned Spanish guerrilla of 1808, who visited Port-au-Prince while mounting out a filibustering expedition against the royal authorities in Mexico. This ambitious arrangement fell through, but Pétion did find Mina some recruits before he left.

Five years later, in an act that shows the extent to which Haiti had become a worldwide symbol of liberty, partisans of Greek independence appealed to Boyer to support their struggle against Turkey. Boyer had neither the money nor the weapons the Greeks wanted, but he sent 25,000 pounds of coffee, which is not least among the sinews of war.

Pétion's ultimate monument is not his flawed rule of the republic, nor even his valor and brilliance as a soldier, but rather his place among the liberators of the Americas.

They Do Not Know the People I Have to Govern

Like Macbeth, Henry Christophe had "vaulting ambition" as his spur; but it was ambition for his people, his country, his posterity, and his race. According to the report of an English visitor during 1818, " He is certainly bringing that great question to a fair trial, whether the Negroes possess sufficient reasoning powers to govern themselves or, in short, whether they have the same capacities as white men. "

Toward the end of the king's life, his Scottish doctor, Duncan Stewart, recalled that Henry "seemed sensible that he had used his people harshly and that he ought to have been more liberal with his soldiers; but he had a very correct knowledge of the character of the people he governed and how necessary occasional severities were."

Earlier, in 1811, the king had asked a British naval officer, "Does your country think the laws I govern my people by, severe?" When the visitor answered yes, Henry rejoined, "They do not know the people I have to govern. "

A more harsh summary of the state of affairs in the North comes from Jonathan Brown, the Philadelphia doctor who wrote Haiti's earliest history published in America: "Christophe, who now [1819] might be denominated the Caligula of the blacks, was every day adding to the discontent and terror of his subjects. His soldiers were treated with extreme severity for every real or fancied fault,(20) and they sought for nothing so earnestly as for an occasion to abandon his service, and gain asylum within the territories of his rival."

While Henry, the black autocrat, enforced his rule upon the North, Pétion, the supple *mulâtre,* gave people what they wanted. No matter that the North flourished while the West and South declined. The cultivators of the North were unhappy; the peasants of the republic were at ease. Pétion's policy (and some might say that Pétion understood his people, and all Haitians, even better than Henry did) was simply to undercut King Henry and his absolutism by giving the peasants of the South and West license to settle into a congenial, unambitious style of life.

When word reached Sans Souci, with its great terraces and state chambers and spy holes through which the cooks could be watched to prevent poisoning, that Pétion was dead, Henry sent emissaries to Port-au-Prince urging unification. Boyer's answer was to put his army in readiness for renewed warfare and, as soon as he could, to subdue Goman, Henry's surrogate in the Grande-Anse. Meanwhile, Henry's cultivators in the Artibonite continued to vote with their feet by slipping Southward into the easier life of the republic.

The army had its vote as well; and the time was not yet to be for 140 years that a Haitian ruler could safely disregard the feelings of his soldiers and their officers.

Though Henry did not know it, two conspiracies were afoot. One was composed of aggrieved soldiers in the 8th Regiment at St. Marc. Their complaints were hard work, harsh discipline, and low pay; they were also resentful that their colonel, named Paulin, had been unfairly cashiered by the king. (Brought before Henry, Paulin had submitted impassively when stripped of his Cross of St. Henry; but as an adjutant reached to cut away his *galons,* he rounded in fury: "I won these epaulets on the battlefield. Nobody can take them away!") Paulin's life was saved only by intervention of Queen Marie-Louise. Instead of being executed, he was marched up the mountain to the dungeons of La Ferrière.

The other conspiracy was that of the generals. Typically, it was fueled not by grievance but by ambition. The junta - led by Jean-Pierre Richard, Duc de Marmelade, one of the king's most trusted officers and governor of the Cap - also included Paul Romain and Philippe Guerrier.

In mid-August 1820, age sixty-two, Henry Christophe seemed in vigorous health. In residence at Bellevue-par-le-Roi, a château in the hills eight miles East of Milot, he was joined by Marie-Louise, his family, and the court, to celebrate the queen's name-day, Sunday, 15 August.

The parish church of Limonade was decked for the occasion. The archbishop was to celebrate high mass before the king and queen. Kneeling in his priedieu, Henry watched the celebrant elevate the Host. Suddenly he was bathed in sweat and swayed giddily. A glass of water was pushed forward. As the king drank, he called for his carriage. William Wilson, English tutor of the king's children, watched as he tottered to his feet, then toppled. Outside, in the carriage, Dr. Stewart cut away his uniform, cupped, and then bled him. It was late afternoon before Henry could speak, and then only in the slur of an apoplectic: the cerebral hemorrhage had paralyzed his entire right side.

By nightfall, *telediol* was spreading the word: Henry Christophe was a powerless cripple.

Now came the hour of the plotters who had feared him and, because of that, had feared to trust each other. Yet it was 2 October before the conspirators mustered sufficient courage to strike. At St. Marc the soldiers rose up and slew the *général de place,* Jean Claude, chopped off his head. and sent it South in a gunnysack as an earnest to Boyer.

Lying paralyzed at Sans Souci, the king learned of these events on 4 October and, early on the 6th, ordered Marmelade to march South with every available soldier. Instead, Marmelade called the senior officers together at the Cap. Late that day the garrison troops were formed in the Place d'Armes. While the soldiers cried, *"Liberté! Indépendance!"* Marmelade tore off his Cross of St. Henry and said, "I am no longer Duc de Marmelade. I am the General Richard you have always known." Then, a pause before he shouted, *"Point roi! Point nobilité! Point tyrannie!"* (No king! No nobility! No tyranny!), "A *bas le tyran! A bas Christophe!"* thundered the soldiers. "All night," wrote Wilson, "the uproar continued."

Next day, amid the wildest excitement, the soldiers at the Cap looted, danced, and began to set fire to habitations of the plain. Richard and the officers gave them their head while deciding what they would do next.

Up at Milot, the king called for hogsheads of rum heated boiling hot and infused with the fiery pimento liquor that Haitians would later know as *sauce 'ti Malisse*. Bathing himself in this burning solution, Henry had attendants massage his crippled limbs. By supreme effort he rose, donned his uniform. and slowly dragged his way to the forecourt, where his 1200-man royal guard was paraded. As the soldiers watched with wonder and then horror, the king tried to mount his charger, shuddered suddenly, and collapsed.

Next morning (it was Sunday), Henry again had the guard paraded under its trusted commander, Jean-Baptiste Riché. Propped up by an aide-de-camp, the king spoke to them as best he could, then commanded a largesse of four gourdes per man. With four guns, under command of Noël Joachim (born Deschamps), Duc de Port Royal, the guard marched down toward the Cap.

Late in the afternoon, the king's troops reached the bridge at the Haut-du-Cap. Five thousand rebels were waiting; to the rear was Toussaint's Bréda. Joachim formed the guard in line and rode forward to read Henry's proclamation. His reply was a ragged volley. Behind, as he turned in the saddle, he saw the royal guard break ranks, throw away their muskets, and run forward to join the rebels. General Riche spurred past, not to rally the troops but, like Mentor Laurent at the Pont-Rouge, to throw in with the other side as quickly as he could.

When Joachim got back to Milot, Henry knew what he had to do. Donning a fresh uniform, he sent for Marie-Louise and the children. As the door closed and he was again alone, the king reached under his chair cushion for the loaded pistol that was always there. Duncan Stewart had shown him where his heart lay. There was a smoky flash and a muffled pop. Henry Christophe, dead at last, slumped over as blood gushed out of the powder-blackened uniform. If, as tradition says, the pistol ball was silver, the king had earned it.

By the time Dupuy, faithful unto death, Marie-Louise, and an unwilling huddle of body-bearers had the body buried in a heap of quicklime at La Ferrière, both the citadel and the palace below were overrun with looters.

Richard gave his protection to Marie-Louise and her daughters. As for Henry's fat princeling, Victor Henry, and his half brother, Eugène, they, with Joachim, Baron Dessalines (nephew of the emperor), and the arrogant Minister of Finance, Vastey, were bayoneted twelve days later in the prison at the Cap. The prince royal's corpse was left to rot on a dunghill.

With 20,000 men, Boyer reached the Cap (Cap Haïtien again, no longer Cap Henry) on 26 October in time to get hold of £11 million in the royal treasury and balk Richard of the fruits of his conspiracy. The North was thus reunified with the republic.

FOOTNOTES- CHAPTER 5

1. On 29 November 1803, an earlier declaration, signed by Dessalines, Christophe and Clervaux, was published at the Cap. Thomas Madiou questions its authenticity, but other historians accept it. The declaration's distinguishing characteristic was its moderate, even generous language toward French landowners, who would soon be butchered.
2. Juste Chanlatte's self-serving account, published in 1824, verges on fiction when he reaches 1804 and can be disregarded. Inginac the functionary, in his otherwise detailed and analytical memoirs (1843), omits the slightest reference to the massacres. No other Haitian principal has left an account.
3. MacIntosh was honored in Baltimore on 9 January 1809, by a banquet at which the French exile community presented him with a gold medal and a heartfelt recitation of firsthand testimony of his generosity, boldness, and ingenuity.
4. In pretended honor of Dessalines, Manuel, the imperial dancing master, invented the step known in Haiti for many years thereafter as the "the *carabinier*" and ultimately *the meringue* of the twentieth century. Actually, the first of Manuel's *carabiniers* was a hidden satire on the emperor. Never one to condone *lèse-majesté,* Christophe saw to it that Manuel was killed at the first opportunity after Dessalines's fall.
5. Unable to contain his eagerness, Dessalines had himself acclaimed emperor by his

personal guard (the 4th Demibrigade, which had slaughtered the women at the Cap) on 22 September. Subsequently, Madiou wrote, documents were antedated or otherwise doctored to make it appear that Dessalines's empire preceded Napoleon's.

6. Missiessy's appearance was wholly fortuitous. Ferrand had been cut off from metropolitan France for more than a year, and Napoleon did not even know French troops were still holding out in Santo Domingo. Missiessy's thrust into the Antilles was part of Napoleon's naval feint to draw the British fleet away from home waters during the planned cross-Channel invasion of 1805.

7. The *liane* is a tough vine that was used as a lash. The *cocomacac* is an iron-hard cudgel, the Haitian shillelagh, which also enjoys magical properties, including the protection of travelers far from home. The *cocomacac* is a symbol of power to be carried and wielded by a *gros nègre*.

8. This cemetery later became that of the Church of St. Anne, South of today's Penitencier National. Dessalines rested there under a modest tombstone until, in 1892, President Florvil Hyppolite ordered the cenotaph from France, which has since been reinstalled at the Pont-Rouge site. In 1926, President Borno reinterred Dessalines and Pétion in a single mausoleum in the Place Pétion, beside the *Palais National*. Ten years later, Vincent moved the cenotaph to mark the Pont-Rouge.

9. Inginac soon found himself as widely hated in Haitian government circles as the General Accounting Office in Washington. His first order was to make people present balanced books every month, but, he wrote, "Great God! what they said about me! What cutting remarks!"

10. In line with Britain's policy of supporting Francophobe Haiti, Robert Sutherland, English comprador in Port-au-Prince and gunrunner to Dessalines, not only lined up shipping for Pétion but acted as unofficial British representative in Port-au-Prince until his death in 1819. Typically playing off both sides, British ships and arms also supported Christophe.

11. Msgr. Brelle's checkered ministry was drawing to a close. In 1816, victim of palace and ecclesiastical intrigue, he lost the light of King Henry's countenance, and died a prisoner in the dungeon of La Ferrière, while his betrayer, Père Jean de Dieu Gonzalez, reigned in his stead. The latter, in his turn, is reported in church annals to have died of fright at the altar in 1820 on seeing the apparition of Msgr. Brelle.

12. Until 1808, the French, under Ferrand, stayed on in Santo Domingo like ghosts. In the summer of that year, supported by arms and money sent by Christophe, Don Juan Sanchez Ramirez revolted against Ferrand and raised the flag of Ferdinand VII of Spain. Beaten in a fight near Seybo, Ferrand killed himself rather than surrender. On 13 December 1808 Santo Domingo reverted to the Crown of Spain.

13. Henry's medical staff was headed by his friend and confidant, the able and sympathetic Scottish physician Duncan Stewart. The royal household had, subordinate to Dr. Stewart, three Haitian doctors with the incredible names of Sans-Façon (Maladroit), Sans-Souci (Careless), and Fatal!

14. Christophe and Wilberforce became faithful (and prolific) correspondents. Henry's first letter weighed 85 ounces and cost Wilberforce £37.10 postage - more than the price of a good horse in England. Wilberforce bettered the exchange by deluging Henry with a mountain of tracts intended to strengthen the king's Anglican leanings: Christophe forwarded the lot to Msgr. Brelle.

15. The constitution grandly provided universal suffrage by ballot, "except for women, criminals, idiots, or menials." By construction, however, "menials" included not only servants but peasants. Thus, only the elite and the army could vote at all - about 3 percent of the population.

16. Bonnet tells of a general caught operating his own do-it-yourself mint of *monnaie-à-serpent*. Haled before Pétion, the general replied that the matter had been greatly, exaggerated: all he was doing when the police broke in, he said, was to run off small change to send down to the market for provisions. Much relieved, Pétion dismissed the charges.

17. The curious negotiations of 1821-1822 between Boyer and Tsar Alexander I of Russia over a possible treaty of amity and commerce should not be overlooked. Boyer's objective (for which he was apparently prepared to offer Russia rights over Ile-à-Vache) was to gain Moscow's recognition of Haiti's independence and sovereignty as a makeweight in larger negotiations with France.

18. As late as January 1825 the Comte de Villèle, French Foreign Minister, was telling Lord Granville, the British ambassador (as the latter reported), "Recognition of a Black Empire founded on insurrection, and upon the Massacre of the White Population, would have a most pernicious moral Effect."

19. Bolivar's decree did not stick. It was 1846 before slavery finally ceased in Venezuela.

20. No substantiation can be found for the legend that, to prove their obedience, Henry marched a squad of grenadiers off the parapet of La Ferrière: but, as events would prove, his discipline was irksome and the royal yoke heavy.

Jean-Pierre Boyer ruled Haiti for twenty-five years. *Heinl Collection. Below:* When Emperor Faustin Soulouque smiled, the court chamberlin would command, "Smile, Messieurs." *Library of Congress*

CHAPTER 6

Chaos and Contentment

1820-1842

The fields of Haiti are dead. Cactus covers with its spines the canefields deserted by the hand of man; it invades the towns, flourishing amid the ruins.

- Victor Schoelcher, 1841

PRESIDENT BOYER'S first action was to dispose of the conspirators who had toppled Henry. Richard, accused of disaffection to the republic, was shot by firing squad in February 1821. Romain was bayoneted in August 1822. Dassou, one of Henry's surviving *noir* generals, was held at St. Marc and, as the *général de place* reported shortly after to Boyer, *"provisoirement fusillé"* (provisionally shot).

Henry's widow, Marie-Louise, with her daughters, Améthyste and Athénaïre, was allowed to leave Haiti for England. In 1824 they moved to Pisa, where they found the climate more salubrious. Neither daughter married, and both died prematurely. After Athénaïre's death in 1839, Marie-Louise wrote Boyer, requesting that she be permitted to return to her beloved homeland; heartlessly, Boyer ignored her and, in 1851, she died alone and in exile.

Immediate comparisons between conditions in the republic and the former kingdom were striking. Prince Sanders, (1) an American freedman who had served as one of Henry's foreign helpers, wrote Thomas Clarkson in early 1823: "Since the extension of what is called the Republic, all confidence is destroyed and is substituted by an almost unparalleled state of anarchy and disorder . . . The people of the South part of Hayti, who had lived under the governments of Pétion and Boyer, were at the least calculation twenty years behind the people of the Kingdom."

Henry's cherished projects for diffusion of education to the *noir* elite of the North, Sanders said, were already dead: "The numerous schools and academies which were established throughout the King's dominions are abolished, and most of the buildings themselves have been defaced or entirely torn down . . . I, in fact, have heard it asserted by some of the principal officers from the South that education must not be too general . . . "

Although Sanders did not make the point in so many words, Boyer's regime, composed mainly of literate *mulâtres* from the West and South, was already buttressing its elite status by denying literacy and education to the *noir* masses of the North and the Artibonite and, in general, to peasants and cultivators everywhere. The observation was by no means unique to Sanders. Only five years later, James Franklin, an English observer, remarked: "The present government seem to consider the poverty and ignorance of the people as the best safeguards of the security and permanence of their own property and power."

It took just three years for Boyer and the men of Port-au-Prince to run through the surplus inherited from Henry: in 1823 the republic's treasury was empty. In the following year the government spent more than it took in. A century would elapse before Haiti again enjoyed a balanced budget or a fiscal surplus.

Conquest of Santo Domingo

As seen by Boyer, two external obstacles still threatened the security of Haiti and blocked final consolidation of his own power. A European flag - that of Spain's Ferdinand VII - again flew over Santo Domingo *("La Partie de l'Est,"* Haitians called it). Worse still, Haiti's independence, though won at sword's point, remained unrecognized by France and therefore by the rest of the world.

In late 1821, Santo Domingo was splintered into four factions, one loyal to Spain, the second seeking independence, the third proposing union with Bolivar's Gran Colombia, and the last - mostly *noirs* in the North who had for years been cultivated by Henry Christophe urging union with Haiti.

Disregarding the gulf between the slave-holding East's Hispanic, monarchic, and Catholic institutions and Haiti's French, African, and Jacobin traditions, the two parts of the island could hardly have been more different. The population breakdown of Santo Domingo, for example, showed roughly 50,000 whites, another 50,000 mulattoes, and some 25,000 blacks.

On 30 November 1821, headed by Don José Nuñez de Cáceres, a junta declared Santo Domingo free of Spain and proclaimed a constitution under which the new state, "Spanish Haiti," united itself with Gran Colombia. The junta asked Haitian recognition and proposed a treaty of amity.

Like many others in those times, the president sought the advice of Guy-Joseph Bonnet. Replying to Boyer on 27 December, Bonnet conceded that annexation of the East had immediate advantages, not the least being that it would provide employment for idle and potentially seditious senior officers unemployed since the fall of Henry. But, warned Bonnet, the East has a migrant population of simple habits, eminently religious, habituated to civilian government. We would implant our spirit of rebellion and disorder, our military despotism, our antireligious principals. Our officers would bring along their concubines and force them into the society of Spanish families used to marriage. We would thus wound these people in their institutions, their usages, their convictions, and render them irreconcilable to us.

If Boyer were to go to Santo Domingo at all, concluded Bonnet, he should present himself as mediator, not conqueror.

Boyer's answer was to mobilize the army, one column commanded by himself to concentrate at Lascahobas, the other, whose command Bonnet reluctantly accepted, at Ounaminthe.

Bonnet had another reason for misgivings. Remembering Dessalines's expedition into the East, and looking about him at the state of the army, he had bluntly asked Boyer, "Do our soldiers have enough discipline to occupy friendly territory without misbehaving?" Answering himself, he said no.

That Bonnet's fears were well founded he himself soon learned. As the Haitians swarmed into Santiago, the soldiers began looting. Bonnet ordered them to re-form and continue the march. When they ignored him, he brought up a battery onto the town square, ordered the cannoneers to load with grapeshot, and repeated his command. This time he was obeyed. The advance resumed. The town was spared.

On 9 February, at the gates of Ciudad Santo Domingo, oldest town of the New World, Cáceres presented Boyer with the keys to the city on a silver salver while cannon roared salutes and the Haitian flag floated over the ancient cathedral and the bones of Columbus. Inside the cathedral, Don Pedro Valera, Archbishop of Santo Domingo, chanted a Te Deum; outside, in what is now the *Parque de Colón*, Boyer planted a palm to be known as a tree of liberty, symbolizing, for the second time, Haitian abolition of slavery throughout the East. Meanwhile, notes Père Cabon, a Haitian officer slipped loose a gorgeous collar of votive pearls from the neck of a Madonna and gave it to his mistress.

Before Boyer returned to Port-au-Prince on 10 March, he proclaimed the Haitian constitution of 1816 as the supreme law of Santo Domingo, including Article 38, Dessalines's prescription, in a country some 40 percent white, that all citizens were to be known as *noirs* and that no white man could own land or exercise domain. He also parceled out the country into *arrondissements,* each with a Haitian *général de place* and black garrison.

The date [wrote Sumner Welles] marks the beginning of a period of 18 years during which the Dominican colony slept a sleep which was almost that of death. No sooner had President Boyer returned to Port-au-Prince than he commenced the effort, which he consistently continued throughout those long years, of stifling every form of culture, and every feature of the Dominicans' proud inheritance, which from time to time glimmered feebly in the gloom . . . Agriculture came eventually to a standstill; commerce was non-existent . . . The University closed its door; the majority of the churches were left without priests.

There was still another grievance. Within three years, Haiti, forced by France to buy final freedom with a harsh indemnity, attempted to exact part of that price from Dominicans, who had never quarrelled with France.

As soon and as best they could, the upper classes, mainly but not entirely white, emigrated to Cuba and Gran Colombia. The archbishop, Don Valera, hung on in an uneasy relationship with Boyer until July 1830, when, vacating the primal see of Spanish America, he too departed for Havana.

Relations with France

Haiti could never find its place in the world until relations with France could be regularized. The notion of Haiti as the lost colony did not die soon or easily. Old St. Domingue hands nostalgically gilded the image of Antillean society and riches in the same way as impoverished Southerners in the United States later spun retrospective illusions of the antebellum South.

In 1808, Bonaparte had turned his mind back to St. Domingue. The year was not opportune: that July his army in Spain was swallowed up by guerrillas at Baylen; three months later, in an extension of the same war, Sánchez Ramírez overthrew Ferrand in Santo Domingo.

It has been asserted but never confirmed that Rigaud's escape in 1810 was engineered by Napoleon and that Rigaud's hidden objective was to re-establish the Tricolor over St. Domingue. However that may have been, it is certain that in 1813 the Emperor sent a secret agent, one Liot, formerly a *colon* of Port-au-Prince, to spy out the country. Under his thin disguise as an American, Liot was recognized. Where Henry would have shot him, Pétion profited by the occasion to take soundings. The message he sent back was that Haiti's independence was irrevocable.

As soon as Louis XVIII, fat and gouty, had been hoisted back on the throne of France by Talleyrand, it became clear that the Bourbons had indeed forgotten nothing and learned nothing. An instant clamor arose in 1814 for the reconquest Napoleon had been compelled to forgo. But France, leached out by two decades of war, could hardly take on a task that had defeated the First Consul at his zenith and cost him one of France's finest armies. Instead the king sent commissioners.

Jacques-François Dauxion-Lavaysse, a colonel, headed the mission and was specifically accredited to Pétion. Lieutenant Colonel Franco de Medina, a Spanish adventurer who owned land near La Vega in Santo Domingo and had collaborated with Toussaint, was to deal with Henry Christophe; Dravermann, husband of Borgella's white half sister, would approach his brother-in-law, whom the French, ignorant of Borgella's reconciliation with Pétion, thought to be ruling the South.

Stripped of circumlocution, the commissioners' instructions from Malouet, Minister of Marine and Colonies, barely differed from those of Leclerc: persuade Pétion and Henry to submit to France, restore slavery, pay off the elite by rewards and offices and a caste level "slightly below the whites"; and, in general, "to restore as much as possible the old order of things in the Colony."

The commissioners had mixed fortunes: in Jamaica, where they halted before entering Haiti, Dravermann was felled by a stroke and returned to France. Lavaysse and Franco de Medina both caught yellow fever but survived. Lavaysse was courteously received in October 1814 by Pétion, who repeated what he had told Liot, but conceded that reasonable indemnities could be arranged for the *colons* as part of a final settlement that included independence and recognition.

Franco de Medina entered the North from Santo Domingo in late October and was promptly arrested. When his papers were examined, Henry found a copy of Malouet's instructions: "It is essential," the minister had written, "that the most numerous class, the *noirs* . . . should remain in or return to their situation prior to 1789."

Henry read no further. Medina was clapped in irons to be judged as a spy and herald of re-enslavement. Frightened, as well he might be, Medina "confessed" to nonexistent plots and treaties between Bonaparte and Pétion and to French designs for using the republic as a base of operations against the Kingdom of the North.

The result was foregone. After a propaganda "funeral" in Notre-Dame (whose roof had finally been rebuilt), where the unfortunate commissioner was exhibited on a platform beside an open coffin while Msgr. Brelle obligingly chanted a requiem, Medina was brought before a military commission, headed by the implacable Marmelade, and sentenced to death.

In November 1814 he was executed in the prison at the Cap.(2) France's next demarche was conciliatory. In October 1816, two more commissioners - the Vicomte de Fontanges (former planter of Gonaïves and one-time commander of the Cordon of the West) and Sieur Esmangart - arrived in Port-au-Prince. The message they bore was of the French king's sorrow that his Haitian subjects, really his children, were still unreconciled. Aboard their frigate, *La Flore,* they brought, for judicious distribution, a thousand *Croix du Lys*, ten Crosses of Henri IV, and twelve Legions of Honor.

The commissioners' timing was poor. They had hoped to transmute Pétion from president to governor general, but a week after *La Flore* anchored, the newly ratified 1816 constitution redesignated him not merely as president, but, as *président-à-vie*. And Pétion would not negotiate in secret. At the Cap, Henry was even more difficult. When *La Flore* hove to off Fort Picolet and signaled for a pilot, there was no reply. Mindful of Medina's fate, Fontanges and Esmangart then relayed their proposals - addressed merely to "Général Christophe" - via an inbound merchantman. Reading no farther than the salutation, Henry returned the commissioners' letter with the endorsement: "Neither the French flag, nor any Frenchman, will be admitted to this kingdom until France recognizes Haiti's independence." After lying to for a few more hours, the frigate stood off and returned to Port-au-Prince.

On 10 November Pétion summed up Haiti's position: "The Haitian people have proclaimed their independence not just to France but to the whole universe. Nothing exists that can make Haiti retire from this unyielding resolution."

For eight more years negotiations dragged fruitlessly on. Pétion died in 1818: Henry in 1820. In 1822, as special envoy to Boyer, Louis XVIII sent Jacques Boyé, who had been one of Leclerc's most sympathetic officers. Boyé's diplomacy nearly dissolved the impasse: in July 1823 an acceptable agreement, calling for an indemnity of 100 million francs, came to the king for royal assent, but Louis would have none of it unless France were to retain control over Haiti's foreign relations. Then, in 1824, he too died, and Charles X, his brother, reigned in his stead.

Seized of divine right, imperious and impetuous (and under considerable political pressure from former *colons,* many of whom were living in poverty), Charles X determined to dispose of the matter. Disdaining further negotiations, the new king raised the indemnity by 50 percent (150 million francs,(3) to be paid in five years), unilaterally decreed the independence of Haiti on 17 March 1825, and conveyed his royal edict to Port-au-Prince in the hands of two admirals backed by the 494 guns of fourteen warships - every French man-of-war in the West Indies and Brazil.

On 5 July the French commander-in-chief, Admiral Baron Mackau, was received by the Foreign Minister, Inginac. "I showed them the royal ordinance," the admiral reported to the Minister of Marine in Paris, "and said that either . . . a new life of repose and happiness would begin for them or the large squadron would commence military operations."

Boyer had no choice. The day had passed when foreign fleets could be defied and Haitian soldiers could exterminate the armies of France. On 11 July - "with respect and gratitude," reported the French press - Charles X's ordinance was accepted, the squadron fired a salute to Haiti, the forts responded to the *Fleur-de-Lys*, and, in a fashion, Haiti was grudgingly allowed to join the family of nations.

Not only was the style of the transaction intentionally humiliating; so were its provisions. ("The form of it is not very gracious, nor the principal conditions very honorable to the magnanimity of the French Govt.," reported the U.S. minister in Paris.) Haiti was required to grant a 50 percent tariff preference to France, independence would be conditional until the whole indemnity was paid, and the grant was conferred not by treaty between sovereign powers (as Britain had conceded the freedom of the American colonies), but by unilateral edict from a throne no Haitian had ever recognized. Besides being a lien on Haiti's sovereignty, the indemnity was crushing. In order to pay even the first 30 million francs, Boyer had to mortgage Haiti's revenues at usurious rates to the moneylenders of Paris.

All this being at length settled, France reciprocated by sending to Port-au-Prince not an ambassador, not a minister, but a mere consul general. It would be 1847 before she deigned even to name a *chargé d'affaires.*

For the moment, however, all was joy. The week after Boyer's acceptance of the royal ordinance was marked by celebration. At the *Palais National* on 11 July Boyer held a dinner for the royal plenipotentiaries (who tactfully swallowed their surprise at being greeted on arrival by the Jacobin anthem "Ça Ira"!). Three days later, the French residents of Port-au-Prince - no more *grands blancs;* mostly hardy traders who had crept back - signalized independence by a banquet and a ball. As reported in *Le Télégraphe* of 24 July, Juste Chanlatte (who, twenty-one years earlier, in drafting Dessalines's proclamation, had anathematized the French as "cannibals") composed for the occasion and sang:

> *"Quel est ce Roi, dont la bonté*
> *Tarit les pleurs de l'Amérique? . . .*
> *C'est Charles-Dix qui, par sa loi,*
> *Est un Dieu pour l'indépendance.*
> *Vive Haiti! Vive la France!* (4)

Then, at nine, the ladies were admitted, the musicians struck up a quadrille, and the party lasted until dawn. Giving the officers a day to recover, the squadron sailed for France,(5) and Haitians could begin to reflect on what had really taken place.

Boyer, best of all, knew that the settlement represented no triumph for Haiti or himself. As Haitians realized the truth, they turned on the president. Furious over the capitulation of a *mulâtre* president and *mulâtre* Senate to the French *blancs*, the *noir* leaders made common cause against Boyer.

What did they owe the proprietors of St. Domingue? Nothing. And - on any terms at all - to compel the victorious slaves to pay off their former masters seemed an exaction in money for what had already been bought in blood.

The terms of Haiti's ransom were grinding. In 1826 and each year that followed, until 1830, Boyer, quite unable to pay, tried in vain to renegotiate the French debt on realistic terms. Charles X was unyielding. All the world knew the riches of ancient St. Domingue, and, most particularly, so did the former *colons,* who were both beneficiaries of the indemnity and stout supporters of the Crown. No, France would not remit a *sou.*(6)

By 1830, foreign debt and domestic bankruptcy had backed Boyer to the wall. In raising the first 30-million-franc installment, Haiti was required to pay 6 million francs' interest, deducted in advance; to make up this sum, Boyer in turn had to deplete the treasury of its liquid reserves. Futile to raise taxes (who paid when he could evade?), flood the country with printing-press gourde notes no better than *monnaie-à-serpent,* and run up arrearage in government salaries (but what official lived on his salary?).

In the "July Days" of 1830, Charles X was swept away by Louis-Philippe, the amiable Duc d'Orléans, and France found herself with a citizen king. From Haiti's viewpoint the change was fortunate: in 1831, but for Louis-Philippe, the Foreign Minister would have sent another squadron to Port-au-Prince to collect what in truth was uncollectible. (In the years 1825 to 1831 inclusive, Haiti's annual expenditures exceeded revenues by amounts ranging from 220,000 gourdes to 1.3 million gourdes: there was no blood in the turnip.)

That same year, 1830, Ferdinand VII of Spain thought the time opportune to reclaim the Partie de l'Est, and sent to Port-au-Prince aboard a Spanish frigate his agent, Don Felipe Fernandez de Castro, Intendant of Cuba. When Castro arrived, on 17 January, Boyer ordered the garrisons of Santo Domingo to war footing. However hollow the gesture, it sufficed: after two weeks' futile remonstrance, Castro departed empty-handed.

The ensuing five years were marked by continued sparring. France would not, could not, admit that Haiti was destitute, yet such was the condition of affairs.

In January 1835, still one more French agent, the energetic naval officer Aubert Dupetit-Thouars (who had distinguished himself in the conquest of Algeria), came to collect but stayed to find out the facts. Inginac opened the books of the republic from 1818 to 1834 and left Dupetit-Thouars to reach his own conclusion. When the admiral returned to France, his carefully prepared report convinced the most hardened doubters that both Haiti and French policy toward Haiti were bankrupt.

And so it came about that, on 23 January 1838, a final French delegation stepped ashore in Port-au-Prince from the frigate *La Néréide.* The opening words of its chief, the Comte de Las Cases, to Boyer were, "Our mission, Your Excellency, is one of conciliation and peace."

In this spirit, negotiating with a Haitian team headed by Inginac and Beaubrun Ardouin, later one of Haiti's most impassioned historians, the French drew up two treaties. One, superseding the hated ordinance of 1825, conceded without qualification the sovereignty and independence of Haiti. The second, after some dickering, reduced the remaining indemnity to 60 million francs, to be liquidated without interest over a thirty-year period.

Promptly the Haitian Senate consented and final ratifications were exchanged in Paris on 28 May. To Haiti's plenipotentiaries, Ardouin and Séguy de Villevaleix (stepson of Sonthonax), Louis-Philippe quietly said, "I hope the Haitians will recollect that they were once French and, however now independent of France, that France has been their *métropole*. On that basis we can maintain relations of friendship and mutual advantage."

Holland, Prussia, Sweden, Denmark, and Britain soon accorded recognition. The United States, its foreign relations hostage to Southern slaveholders in Congress, continued its ambiguous policy of dealing with Haiti through "commercial agents" while withholding political recognition. But the U.S. was hardly alone: not a single Latin American country sent so much as a consul to Haiti until, in 1865, Brazil broke the ice. And it would be 1934 and 1938, respectively, before Mexico and Peru finally accredited resident representatives to Port-au-Prince.

As for Boyer, his great success, the fruit of two decades of patient diplomacy pursued from weakness rather than strength, won scant appreciation. People remembered the humiliation of 1825 and disregarded the reconciliation of 1838.

To understand why this was so, it is necessary to follow the domestic vicissitudes of Haiti under Boyer.

What Disorder, What General Ruin

"Here is the capital. Foul public squares, ruined monuments, dwellings of plank and thatch, stove-in quays, tottering wharves, no names on the streets, no numbers on the doorways, no street lights at night, no paving anywhere: the ground underfoot composed of dust and excrement on which walking is impossible after an hour's rain. What disorder, what general ruin!"

This, wrote Victor Schoelcher, the French abolitionist and sociologist, was Port-au-Prince in 1841 after twenty-three years of Boyer's administration.

In the countryside things were no better. Where thousands of tons of sugar were produced under slavery, Haitians now grew only kitchen vegetables and bits of cane to crush into syrup for *taffia*. Never replanted, never burned off, never cleared, the fields produced only stunted, puny cane, which was invaded by the rampant cactus of what had once been the greenest land of the Antilles.

This deplorable state of affairs was not new. As early as 1827 Mackenzie, the British consul general, visited Habitation Laborde, outside Cayes, which had once belonged to Rigaud. In 1789, Moreau de Saint-Méry said, it had been worked by 1400 slaves and produced 6000 tons of refined sugar a year. Mackenzie found the place in ruins. Of three sugar mills, only the walls of two were standing; the roof of the third was in collapse. The once handsome stone dwelling houses were crumbling. No cane was growing; a handful of peasant squatters cultivated truck gardens- half-wild cattle grazed on overgrown pastures that had once been canefields.

"There are no bridges in the island," reported the Englishman James Franklin. "It is almost impossible to describe the state of the roads. Notwithstanding the heavy contributions levied for their repair, they have remained untouched since the revolution."

What had happened? Why had Haiti run down?

The dead fields and ruined towns noted by Schoelcher, Franklin, Mackenzie, and a host of other foreign observers represented the legacy of Pétion: whether he was a realist who accepted the inevitable, or an impractical dreamer who let national discipline and productivity slip through his fingers, will never be settled to the satisfaction of all.

To rescue Haiti from the trough into which it had slipped would have demanded leadership of more ability and imagination than Boyer, or conceivably any Haitian alive, possessed. When death intervened, even the stout back of Henry Christophe had begun to bend beneath the problems and pressures that were crushing Boyer.

Haiti's ruin and disorder were also the epitaph of history on Boyer's major attempt to put things right. By 1825, the president, his bureaucrats, and the elite of Haiti recognized that something had to be done. Their answer (Inginac was the main draftsman) was the *Code Rural*, which Boyer submitted and the Senate duly enacted on 1 May 1826 (somewhat ironically, as events turned out, the date of Haiti's annual *Fête d'Agriculture*).

The code, essentially, was an attempt to freshen up the *fermage* systems of Louverture, Dessalines, and, most recently, Henry. Its central provision was that all Haitians - except for categories briefly comprehended in two words, "elite" and "army" - were cultivators, and that every cultivator was attached to the soil and had an enforceable obligation to work it.

The army and a corps of inspectors were to enforce the code; another corps of bureaucrats was to manage the system and collect and distribute its proceeds. In his magisterial analysis of the code and its defects, Leyburn points out, "If every literate person in the state had been drafted for service, Boyer could not have filled all the offices provided by the Code." It was at best, said Leyburn, "a good piece of office-work."

What foredoomed the code (a system, after all, that had flourished magnificently under Toussaint and Henry) was that, by 1826, it was irrelevant. By breaking up the estates and parceling out the land into small holdings,(7) Pétion had already dealt the plantation system a mortal blow. Yet the underlying premise of the code was of large, efficient productive units grouping labor under tight supervision and, as required, military compulsion. But more than half the land was already in the hands of peasant freeholders (mainly former soldiers of the War of Independence, who had no intention of being legislated back into the serfdom and forced labor they had so spectacularly fought to escape).

No longer were Haitian peasants willing to trade liberty and the good life for discipline and national productivity. The rich fields might still be Haiti's great resource, but the other resource - manpower - could no longer be mobilized.

Another hole in the code - a reality its originators simply ignored - was that two thirds of the island, the Partie de l'Est, had never known *fermage* and was not about to accept it. In Santo Domingo, as indeed throughout most of Haiti, the code proved unenforceable.

Finally, greatest irony of all, just as the code was being drafted and promulgated, Haiti's most compelling pressure for national discipline -fear that the French would someday come back - was lifted by the ordinance of Charles X.

Some historians say that from this moment the army (nominally 45,000 strong) took off its pack and stood at ease. Leyburn quotes a trenchant passage (which he attributes to the Haitian historian Lepelletier de Saint-Rémy, though it cannot be found in the latter's work):

[The Haitians] never had more than a borrowed energy - that inspired by fear of French invasion - and when they saw themselves freed, by a solemn treaty, from all attack on their coasts, seemed to allow their arms to drop relaxed at their sides . . . . The soldier who until now had squeezed his body into uniform and had subjected himself to European discipline . . . now began to leave unbuttoned the uniform which choked him, dragged a mattress into his sentry-box so that he might sleep through his watch, and let his cross slip to earth never to pick it up again.

This analysis is not correct. In fact the army had been going steadily downhill, even under Dessalines and later in the Kingdom of the North. The stumbling performance of both sides in the civil war, their common inability to conduct successful offensive operations, the repeated mutinies and defections, the indiscipline, pillage, and disorganization of the Dominican forays of 1805 and 1822, and a mass of lesser evidence - all attest that in relying on the army to enforce anything, let alone defend Haiti, Boyer was, in Washington's phrase, "leaning upon a broken staff." Moreover, it had evidently been broken for at least fifteen years before 1825.

Schoelcher minced no words. The army, he wrote, "is assuredly the most miserable in the world. At reviews in Port-au-Prince, conducted by the president himself, I myself have seen soldiers ...bareheaded, others barefooted, still others with worn-out boots pulled together with twine; all, officers included, in trousers of diverse colors with torn and tattered blouses. I even remember a grenadier whose trousers had only one leg left . . . A review at Port-au-Prince is a masquerade."

And why not?

The private soldier, recruited by impressment, roped with other miserable conscripts, and herded to Port-au-Prince, received three gourdes every six weeks, providing his seniors ever let it reach him. His entire clothing-issue consisted of one blouse. The rest of his uniform and gear, as well as his sword or musket, he had to buy out of pocket from his commanding officer. Even in Port-au-Prince, let alone the back country, he was provided no barracks or rations and had to forage for himself, showing up only for pay call, occasional parades, or weeks on guard duty.

The officers had a good thing. Besides unlimited opportunities to pre-empt their soldiers' pay, army officers had power. Reinforcing Haitian traditions going back to 1804, when there was no government, only an army, officers ran most of the country. Each department came under a general; each town had its *général de place*. With unquestioned powers of life, death, and larceny, these worthies ruled all they surveyed. And the only provisions of Boyer's code that stuck were those that codified rural Haiti - the whole country outside the gates of Port-au-Prince - into the governance of the army.

If one result of Boyer's policies was to manumit the cultivators and the villagers to the army, another was a tacit division of spheres, along racial lines, between *jaunes* and *noirs*. The literate *mulâtre* elite monopolized politics, commerce, and bureaucracy. For an ambitious *noir,* on the other hand. usually without education, the army was the route to power and enrichment and (as in the United States more than a century later) to at least a limited social mobility.

But the era of Boyer was not one of social mobility; rather it was the reverse. The color line between *noir* and *mulâtre* was drawn sharply and permanently. It was not for nothing that a visiting American naval officer in 1831 attributed to Inginac "the looks, bearing, and manner of an old French marquis." In his acid frankness, Schoelcher reported, "The aristocracy of the high-yellow skin has been erected on the ruins of the aristocracy of the white skin."

Dr. Brown, writing in 1837, goes even further:

The prejudice of color existing among the mulattoes in relation to their fellow-citizens, the blacks, is almost as great as that once entertained by the whites of the colony against the class of mulattoes. Intermarriages between the two castes are extremely rare, and such unions are regarded by the mulattoes with absolute disgust . . . [but] the pure negro seeks to ally himself to the *griffe*, the *griffe* to the mulatto, the mulatto to the quateroon, the latter to a *mustif*, the *mustif* having an untraceable tinge of African blood in his organization, is uproariously indignant if he is accused of having any at all.

Far from evincing any desire to lift the *noirs* to a higher level or to bring them into the political process, Boyer's government (save for propitiatory concessions toward *noir* leaders) emphatically opted for the status quo. Like many another Haitian regime to come, Franklin noted in 1828, "the members composing the present government seem to consider the poverty and ignorance of the people as the best safeguards of the security and permanence of their own property and power."

With the failure of the *Code Rural*, Boyer and the people around him seemed to run out of steam. Temperamentally unreceptive to ideas not his own, Boyer found a hundred reasons to reject and ridicule suggestions for innovations. His witty, articulate tongue had a sharp edge of sarcasm and unkindness.

Sarcasm or not, the economic facts were grim enough. No finished sugar at all had been exported since 1820. In 1801, under Toussaint, Haiti had exported 9250 tons of raw sugar; twenty-five years later, under Boyer, raw sugar exports just exceeded 16 tons. Toussaint had exported 21,500 tons of coffee ; in 1826, Boyer managed 16,000. In 1801 there had been 1250 tons of cotton, in 1826, only 310. Indigo and molasses, once major products of St. Domingue, were no longer exported. (Indigo would never again become an export.)

"The government of Boyer," said Lepelletier de Saint-Rémy, "was a long sleep." But it was a sleep intermittently interrupted by catastrophes and calamities.

Two fires - in 1820 and 1822 - burned out nearly half of Port-au-Prince. The city had no fire engines or, for that matter, firemen. In the first conflagration, that of August 1820, over 500 houses were leveled, and 25 million francs' damage estimated (much of it due to looting and incendiarism by pillaging soldiers). Within a month, Port-au-Prince was lashed by one of its rare hurricanes, which at least quenched the ashes.

In February 1827, when a laborer in the national arsenal incautiously hit the iron hoop of a powder barrel with an iron hammer, the resulting spark touched off the magazine, blew down much of the waterfront, and caused $1 million damage. Guns in the water battery and artillery park, which no one had unloaded since Christophe's siege in 1812, went off at random for several days.

Cayes was nearly wiped out on the night of 12-13 August 1831, when a hurricane scourged the South and backed a tidal wave over much of the city, killing hundreds of townspeople before dawn. A year later, in July 1832, Port-au-Prince was swept by still another fire.

The worst disaster, perhaps of the century, occurred on 7 May 1842. That day an earthquake rocked Hispaniola from end to end. Santiago de los Caballeros was leveled, so were Fort Liberté and Port-de-Paix. At Cap Haïtien alone, 10,000 persons, including the poet Milscent (sometimes called Haiti's Béranger because of his political songs and verses), were buried in the ruins. When the peasants in the hills saw the fire and smoke swirling up from the Cap, they trooped down and looted the city as if the year were 1793.

Besides natural upheavals, Boyer's regime was, as it dragged on, subjected to political temblors of ever shortening periodicity and higher rating on the scale of intensity and magnitude. Boyer faced two kinds of opposition. One was *noir* discontent, especially in the North, with his *mulâtre* rule. The second, in an opposite sense, was the dissatisfaction and frustration among a rising generation of young *mulâtres,* some educated in France and charged with the effervescence of nineteenth century Europe. To stoke opposition, two anti-Boyer newspapers, *Le Manifeste* and *Le Patriote,* sprang up. Instead of addressing himself to the reforms they demanded, Boyer simply founded a paper of his own, *Le Temps,* edited by his friend, historian, and apologist, Beaubrun Ardouin.

Like Pétion before him, the president had weathered earlier risings from the North, from the South, from within the *Palais National.* Purely political attack. however, was a novelty.

The soul of *mulâtre* opposition to Boyer was Hérard-Dumesle, who had been Lamarre's secretary during the Guerre du Môle. In 1833, displeased over an indiscreet speech in the legislature by Hérard, Boyer simply excluded him from the legislature. Four years later he was back and promptly re-elected to his old post as speaker. In 1838 Boyer again expelled Hérard, this time accompanied by several supporters, and, to make his point. locked up Hérard. No sooner was he free (1842) than he and the others were again returned to the legislature.(8) This time, like Pétion in 1808, Boyer ringed the Chamber with soldiers and excluded his tormentors at bayonet point. For good measure, he barred almost the entire opposition (twenty-eight out of seventy-two deputies).

Backed by his aging, autocratic functionaries - Inginac, Bonnet, and José-Maria Imbert - Boyer had now alienated the rising, bright, eloquent *mulâtre* politicians as well as the South and West for whose elite they spoke. As Duraciné Pouilh put it sixty years later, in *La Ronde* (15 April 1902): "A quarter century had slipped by. Children had grown into men. From every side reforms were demanded . . . The National *Lycée* and the Covin School had launched a constellation of educated young men, impatient for the country to shed its isolation as progress passed it by. They had to speak up..."

In the streets and at the rallies now being held at the habitations throughout the South, the militant young sang Milscent's last song, composed before his death in the 1842 earthquake: "*Celà Me Contrarie*" (That Goes Against the Grain), a biting attack on the hypocrisy that confronted them.

Within six months after Boyer excluded Hérard and his other afflictors, the South was seething. In August 1842, at Habitation Praslin, Southwest of Cayes, owned by an older cousin of Hérard's, Charles Rivière-Hérard, a Society of the

Rights of Man and of Citizens was formed. Its charter was a list of grievances soon known as the Praslin Manifesto. When sufficient signers had been obtained, an executive committee, led by Hérard-Dumesle, was formed. Ready in the wings was Rivière-Hérard, formerly a soldier, who was prepared to profit by the oncoming revolt but not necessarily to uphold its principles.

Rivière-Hérard had not long to wait: on 27 January of the new year his outriders spilled out of Praslin across the plain. The revolt had begun. Borgella at Les Cayes had ridden out many such storms. Prudently, he temporized. Jérémie raised Hérard's banner. Lazarre, the general at Tiburon, threw in with the Praslinites and was given command of one of the ragged columns moving East on Port-au-Prince. On 11 February, at Mapou Dampuce, where the road leads out from Léogane to Port-au-Prince, the government formed its last army. There was a desultory exchange of shots, and within moments the defenders had faced about and were leading the march on the capital.

Boyer was in the grip of a miserable cold when the gallopers reached Port-au-Prince from Mapou Dampuce. Immediately he sent Ardouin to Thomas R. Ussher, the British consul general; certain arrangements were concluded with the commanding officer of the sloop *H.M.S. Scylla*, lying off Fort Ilet, and, by the time Ardouin returned to the *Palais National*, the president and his faithful consort, Choute Lachenais, were sadly packing their things. Had Ardouin completed the act of abdication they had spoken of earlier, asked Boyer? Only a few finishing touches were needed, was the reply, and Mlle. Lachenais found Ardouin a quill and inkwell to smooth it up while her equerry, the impassive Captain Soulouque, fumbled over the luggage.

On the 13th, just as the sun was dropping behind La Gonâve, *Scylla*'s gig and first cutter lay alongside the quay. When the trunks and boxes were loaded and Choute (now brevetted "Mme. Boyer") had been handed aboard by the boat officer, Boyer paid his last adieux and, accompanied by Inginac ("his friend," in Hérard's words, "his valet - and his master"), by Villevaleix, and by a few others, took final leave of the soil of Haiti. The straw-hatted bluejackets tossed oars, let fall, gave way smartly, and pulled with a will. As the distance lengthened, the dirt and shabbiness of Port-au-Prince diminished, and all they could see was the green face of Morne l'Hôpital, with the little city nestled at its base.

Behind, in the Senate chamber, while *Scylla* weighed anchor for Jamaica ("Pres. of Hayti and Suite," recorded the ship's log, "15 members, 13 children, and 4 servants of his family"), the president's brief message provided a dignified coda to Haiti's longest reign. "I have but one final wish," he concluded, "and that is that Haiti may be as happy as my heart has always desired it to be."

Later, in Paris, when he received Boyer, Louis-Philippe contributed a final grace note by addressing him as "Prince." Overwhelmed, Boyer demurred. "When one has governed a million people for twenty-five years," the king rejoined, "one has earned the rank of prince."(9)

Haiti in 1843

By 1843, when Boyer departed, Haiti had found its level. The fire had gone out.
Haiti was unified, its political traditions established, its place in the world fixed, its social structure solidified, and its economic life formed. If, however, the foregoing sounds like a recitation of progress. it is not. Stagnation and decline formed the leitmotif of the thirty-nine years from 1804 to 1843.

Though he ruled Haiti for twenty-five of those years, Boyer must be judged a failure. Not one of his programs succeeded. Give him ample credit for good intentions and for talent as a political prestidigitator; but he left behind him a country ruined, stagnant - and (except in limited, elite circles) contented. Himself a man of scrupulous probity ("a quality extremely rare among our rulers," tartly commented Dantès Bellegarde), he could nevertheless remark to a newly appointed collector of customs, "I've given you this job so you can make a little something out of it for yourself."

The plantations of Dessalines and Christophe had lapsed into a collection of truck gardens growing subsistence crops for a nation of peasant *noirs* with a static, village-based economy. Haiti had no need to develop a national market to unify or safeguard the traditional way of life. The sea provided highways to make up for the ruin of those built by the French. There was no requirement for a national economy or a nationwide transportation system. No economic, political, or social necessity was at work to challenge or modernize Haiti's primitive Africanized folkways. Power was now firmly vested in the elite and in the army, the one almost exclusively *mulâtre*, the other almost wholly *noir*. Each group was self-centered, self-serving, and self-perpetuating. Loyalties were personalized, paid to men not institutions. That there could be a public interest overriding individual interests was inconceivable. Writing of the men of these times, Jean Price-Mars remarked: "They were all, such as they were, the products of slavery, whether they had been slaves themselves or were *affranchis*. They were all habituated to trickery, dissimulation, lying, and vengefulness."

A measure of the political system these men produced is that, of the thirty-four signers of the Act of Independence in 1804, only five died natural deaths. Nearly all of them had repeatedly conspired, betrayed, or been betrayed, mostly by each other.

Such was to be the framework of Haitian politics for the next seventy-five years: intrigue, conspiracy, treachery, violence, coups, caste against caste, color against color, region against region.

FOOTNOTES - CHAPTER 6

1. Sanders (sometimes spelled Saunders) is said to have introduced vaccination into Haiti and vaccinated all of Henry's children.

2. Hubert Cole, Henry's able biographer, says Medina's life was spared, but Haitian accounts, contemporary and later, tell of his execution, as does William Wallis Harvey, a member of Christophe's British coterie.

3. The indemnity represented 115 million francs for the former colonial proprietors and 35 million francs to the French government for public buildings and fortifications - virtually all, by 1825, in ruins, and all of which, in any case, had already been taken or surrendered in war.

4. "Who is this King whose bounty/Dries the tears of America? . . . /'Tis Charles X who, by his edict,/Is a very God of independence./Long live Haiti! Long live France!" Charles Mackenzie, the British consul general, in 1827 described Chanlatte as "the honorary laureate of the republic."

5. Not all the squadron went home. Until final settlement of the question in 1838, the French maintained what the historian Beaubrun Ardouin described as "a naval station" in Haitian waters with French men-of-war continually covering the ports where France had representatives.

6. Anticipating the Haitian indemnity, the French Chamber of Deputies had promptly cut a juicy melon for the *colons* by voting them 625 million francs to settle outstanding claims for losses in St. Domingue

7. Between them, Pétion and Boyer gave away nearly half a million acres of public domain in approximately 12,000 grants, two thirds of them 15 acres or less.

8. The actual depth of political participation must not be exaggerated. In what contemporaries describe as the hotly contested election of 1842, Port-au-Prince, a city of about 40,000, cast a total of 284 votes for two opposing candidates, the winner, Lespinasse, receiving 221.

9. Boyer went first to Jamaica where, barely three months later, Choute, beautiful to the last, pined away and died ("a golden Diana of Poitiers," recalled one admirer). Soon Boyer was in Paris, long remembered from his days there with Rigaud. In 1844 when, in one of his last acts, Rivière-Hérard ungenerously confiscated Boyer's properties, the ex-president returned to Jamaica, whence for three years he tried to recover what had been his. But the spoils were never returned, and, in dignified poverty, Boyer finally returned to Paris, where, aged seventy-four, he died in his house on the Rue Castiglione, 9 July 1850. He was buried and lies today in Père Lachaise, that most elegant of the great cemeteries.

Fabre Geffrard, one of Haiti's most progressive presidents, tried and failed to rule by moderation. *Library of Congress*. Below: H.M.S. *Bulldog*, aground and under fire from batteries at Cap Haïtien, after sinking two Haitian warships (left) had to be abandoned and blown up. *Mansell Collection*

CHAPTER 7

Darkness Descends

1843-1858

What they are now. the freed Negroes of San Domingo will hereafter be: without peace, security, agriculture or property; averse to labour though frequently perishing of want; suspicious of each other and the rest of mankind: pretending to be free while groaning beneath the capricious despotism of their chiefs and feeling all the miseries of servitude . . .

- Bryan Edwards

BOYER WAS GONE; so were Bonnet and Inginac, the one dead of old age at St. Marc, the other penning his memoirs in Kingston, cursing the English typesetters who butchered his French. The power-hungry, educated young men who had turned them out now had their chance. What use would they make of the power and authority they had won? Would they get Haiti moving again, and in what direction?

These were questions being asked by people who mattered. For the time being, many who did not matter - yet - watched silently and, in the fashion of Haiti, waited for events to unfold.

Rivière-Hérard and the Downfall of the Mulâtres

It came as naturally as breathing that the men of Praslin would write a new constitution. But there were certain preliminaries.

Forty years old, handsome, dashing, balding - very much the man of destiny - Rivière-Hérard entered Port-au-Prince as soon as Boyer had departed. A few days later, accompanied by his cousin and other leading spirits, came the revolutionary army. Rivière moved into the *Palais National* and, in early April, got down to business.

On 4 April 1843, with self-abnegation worthy of ancient Rome, Rivière went through the motions of stepping down. Several figures, including Imbert (who, unlike Bonnet and Inginac, had ridden out the storm) and Guerrier and "one other" whom they would choose, were to compose a *gouvernement provisoire*. "As for me," Rivière concluded, "my work is done." Naturally, the "one other" selected by the junta proved to be Charles Rivière-Hérard.

A constitutional convention was to be convened in mid-September. Meanwhile, with sizable military escort, Rivière-Hérard took a swing to the North and over into Santo Domingo, where there were reports of disaffection: here Rivière disarmed the countryside and arrested several Dominican leaders. Arrests, however, were not confined to the East. The Salomon family, influential *noirs* of the South, were at daggers drawn with the volatile *jaunes* of Cayes. After a heated clash, the elder Salomon, accompanied by his twenty-eight-year-old son, Lysius, and numerous followers, retired under arms to Castel Père, the Salomon plantation two miles West of Cayes. When a messenger came from Hérard, ordering the Salomons' arrest, he was sent flying with a volley of musket balls. Lazarre himself, top general of the regime, hurried to Cayes at the head of a regiment and revoked the order. But as soon as the two Salomons incautiously left their stronghold, they were arrested anyway and hustled off by Hérard to exile at Neyba in the East.

Back in Port-au-Prince the spoils were being parceled out. Rivière-Hérard, who entered upon his new role as a major, was promptly promoted *général de division*. So was Hérard-Dumesle, who had no military background at all. David Saint-Preux, until then a lawyer and politician, and Elie Lartigue, from Jérémie, a peaceful planter (of course a politician too) contented themselves with colonelcies. Others were no less modest. "Vanity strutted forth," recorded Lepelletier de Saint-Rémy, "in a tide of cockfeathers; all you could hear in Port-au-Prince was the symphony of sabers, boots, and spurs rattling about the streets."

The sight of young *mulâtre* politicians dressing up in uniform and monopolizing promotions and top billets aroused what feelings can be imagined among an army whose leaders, *noir* and illiterate, had mostly won their *galons* under Dessalines and Christophe, especially when (a last straw) the *gouvernement provisoire* revoked Boyer's more recent promotions among their own.

Matters moved swiftly to a head on the bright moonlit night of 9 September 1843. With the complicity of Guerrier - old soldier and veteran of Vertières, Duc de Marmelade under Christophe, and a *noir* of the North (in short, everything the new regime was not) - the garrison at Fort National silently formed to march down on the *Palais National*. But as usual someone had betrayed the conspiracy. Hérard was up and in the streets with a soldier escort. As Dalzon, leader of the revolt, led his men down into the city, one of Hérard's soldiers let off a chance shot and killed Dalzon in Post Marchand, not far from the modern Ciné Capitol. Dalzon perhaps deserved better of the republic: it had been his stand in 1812 that had saved Port-au-Prince when Henry and the army of the North fell on the city.

Fugitives scampered for their lives, the troops marched stolidly back to barracks, and Hérard remained on at the palace. Guerrier, who had already proven himself politically bulletproof in anti-Boyer conspiracies of 1837, came through unscathed.

Over heated protest from Honoré Féry, a principled young *mulâtre,* that it just didn't look right, the first business of the Constitutional Assembly degenerated into a three-day squabble as to what pay and perquisites delegates should vote themselves.

The ensuing debate waned only in December, not because the delegates had transacted much business, but because Rivière-Hérard, an old artilleryman, pointedly positioned two 6-pounders in front of the meeting hall, had them shotted to the muzzle with grape, and laid to cover the veranda and open windows of the Chamber.

The natural result was that the new constitution was enacted on 30 December 1843; and, five days later, Charles Rivière-Hérard was inaugurated president.

But the men of Praslin and their man, Hérard, were by no means of like mind as to exactly how Haiti should be administered. The new constitution was a liberal and highly theoretical document. For example: under Pétion and, after him, Boyer, hardly anyone voted at all. The elite ran the towns, and the army ran the country. Now, under the new constitution, a swarm of civil and elective offices and jurisdictions mayors, prefects, municipalities - were brought into being and, previously unheard of, the vote was supposed to be extended to the peasants.

Even while Hérard was being inaugurated, officers and soldiers who were ranged around the Place Pétion for the ceremony kept interrupting the proceedings with ominous cries of "Down with municipalities! Down with prefects!" As murmurs rose, fears rose with them, and the crowd was bathed in panic. Adolphe Barrot, the magnificently uniformed French special commissioner, seated uneasily on the dais, began to wonder whether in a pinch he might make it safely to the harbor, where two French warships had been observing the constitutional process since September.

What hardly anyone knew was that Hérard, the new president, together with his supposedly ardent reformist cousin, Hérard-Dumesle, had secretly joined forces with the *noir* soldiery upon whom the Praslinite liberals were bent on imposing civilian (read, "elite *mulâtre")* supremacy.

Barely in office a month, Hérard soon found himself facing trouble in every direction. A good indication of the workability of the new constitution came at Petite Rivière de l'Artibonite, where one of the liberal *députés* and the local judge challenged the military authorities. When, with judicial backing, the *député* claimed constitutional immunity to arrest, the soldiers simply shot him - and the judge besides.

Worse was to come. As cathedral bells tolled Compline on the night of 27 February 1844, Juan Pablo Duarte, at the head of a band of patriots calling themselves "Trinitarios,"(1) seized the ancient fortress of Puerta del Conde in Ciudad Santo Domingo, proclaimed independence, and, before dawn, had wrested the city from its slothful, sleepy Haitian garrison. Because Hérard had presciently stripped the national arsenal during his 1843 visit, a fast-sailing brigantine was dispatched to Curaçao to fetch arms, gallopers were sent riding to raise the country, and homemade Dominican (or sometimes Spanish) flags blossomed over the capital.

Two days later, on advice of Commissioner Barrot, who seemed to turn up everywhere,(2) the Haitian *général de place* meekly signed the capitulation Duarte laid before him, and embarked aboard three ships for Jacmel. Eighteen years of Haitian misrule were at an end.

On 10 March Hérard took the field with 30,000 troops, who were to enter Santo Domingo via the traditional routes. Pierrot, Christophe's aged and eccentric brother-in-law, would march on Santiago from the North: a central column under Hérard, advancing by way of Lascahobas, would rendezvous at Azua with a third column attacking through the Cul-de-Sac and Neyba.

Before leaving Haitian soil, Hérard dissolved the assembly and called on all citizens to rally to the colors. When Dumai Lespinasse, of *Le Manifeste* and president of the assembly (and thus a double thorn in Hérard's side), objected, the president simply marched him off to prison between a file of soldiers. The lesson was not lost.

The fourth Haitian army to enter Santo Domingo in less than fifty years received a predictable reception: armed with pikes, machetes, and fowling pieces, furious Dominican peasants fought the Haitian invaders at every house and crossroads to cries of "Long live the Holy Virgin and the Dominican Republic!"

When Rivière-Hérard reached Azua on 19 March the city's greeting was a blast of grape: Dominican General Pedro Santana had sited two guns covering the narrow gateway to the town. As the Haitians recoiled with more than fifty dead, the defenders poured in volley after volley of musketry. But Santana, fearing the second Haitian column, thereupon abandoned the town and withdrew. With small stomach for pursuit, Hérard halted at Azua and called on Pierrot to march South and reinforce him. Hérard's order was meaningless: at Santiago, under General José-Maria Imbert, the Dominicans had already sent Pierrot reeling. Back at the Cap, and of no mind whatsoever to join Hérard, Pierrot took the only possible step. On 25 April, he proclaimed the North and the Artibonite separate from Hérard's republic and disclosed that his hard-drinking old friend Guerrier would head the new state.

Worse still, while Hérard marked time in Azua, disaffection burst forth at home.

Despite the grand promises of the Praslinites, the cultivators of the South had reaped no benefits. Into the place of Salomon, who had been packed off to exile, now stepped a *noir* chieftain of the old school. Louis Jean-Jacques Acaau, an old *congo* and later a junior officer in the army, rose against the government. In early April, at Camp Perrin, behind Les Cayes, Acaau called forth 2000 cultivators from the mountains and valleys. Armed with machetes, a few rusty muskets, and the homemade spears from which the peasants took their name, *"Piquiers"* (soon corrupted into *"piquets"*), Acaau's *armée souffrante*, as they called themselves, had two objectives: to overthrow Hérard and install a *noir* in the *Palais National*: and to loot the towns and divide up the properties of the rich *mulâtre* proprietors of the South.

Shaded by a conical straw hat, bare feet adorned by spurs, armed with a huge war machete and a brace of pistols, the giant Acaau presented a fearsome figure. The pride of his army was *Maman Pimba* (Red-Hot Mama), an old French 16-pounder.

On 5 April at Carrefour Quatre Chemins, a half-mile outside Cayes, government soldiers offered a quavering defense. The government's lone gun was overrun. After an hour of what contemporary accounts described as "desperate fighting," the defenders broke and ran. When Acaau counted his casualties he learned that the *armée souffrante* had suffered one man killed and three wounded. Government losses were comparable.

Locking up every *jaune* townsman they could catch, Acaau and his lieutenant, Dugué Zamor, thereupon entered Cayes in triumph. Watching anxiously from offshore, the captain of a British warship sent word to Acaau that if harm came to any foreigner he would bombard the town. Acaau replied ferociously, "Tell me which end you plan to begin with, and I'll set fire to the other."

Meanwhile, in the Grande-Anse, half-naked *piquets* burst into Jérémie and Anse-à-Veau and then struck East toward Miragoâne and Port-au-Prince. Like Wat Tyler's peasants in 1381, the Grande-Anse *piquets* had the same war cry, "Down with the bailiffs!", and no man of the law, be he bailiff or lawyer - or for that matter, any legal document, all of which were destroyed as found - was safe. In the eyes of the *piquets* the law and its agents signified, with no little justification, usury, exploitation, and expropriation.

In the flush of victory, Acaau had no way of knowing that his revolt was already done for. Two future presidents of Haiti - Generals F. N. Geffrard (son of that earlier Geffrard who died before Dessalines could get at him) and Jean-Baptiste Riché - had joined forces at Aquin and, after a lively squabble over command, on 10 April hurled back Dugué Zamor's spearmen.

Meanwhile, terrified by events in Cayes and the Grande-Anse, propertied

Port-au-Prince yielded readily to the suggestion, floated by Hérard's old foes, the Boyerists, that the only way to save the city would be to depose Rivière-Hérard and substitute an influential *noir*. Boyer's friend in the North, Guerrier, for example, would be ideal.

Guerrier was in his cups when a delegation headed by the elegant Beaubrun Ardouin found him. Momentarily fuddled, the old man, 87, at first refused the crown but quickly changed heart on hearing, from outside, cries of *"Vive Président Guerrier!"* On 3 May, backed by the bayonets of a friendly regiment from St. Marc, the new president duly took the oath, after - an early example of power coming from the barrel of a gun - Ardouin produced a suitable manifesto he had concealed in the bore of his musket.

Certain loose ends remained to be cleared up - and quickly were. Leaving behind a troupe of weeping mistresses, Hérard-Dumesle, the former president's regent in Port-au-Prince, was put aboard H.M.S. *Spartan,* corvette, for Kingston. Still marking time in Azua, Rivière-Hérard himself was notified that he was no longer president (though still a general with pay and pension guaranteed) and must return. He reached Port-au-Prince in time to be packed off in a sail boat and hoisted aboard the same British warship as his cousin. The two met acrimoniously on *Spartan's* quarterdeck, where Rivière-Hérard reproached Hérard-Dumesle for having let Port-au-Prince slip through his fingers. Then Ussher, the British consul general who had stage-managed arrangements, went ashore, and the ship weighed anchor for Jamaica.

Neither cousin saw Haiti again: the former president, like many another successor, was soon stripped of his pension by the new government, and died destitute six years later, hoeing a potato patch. The remnants of Hérard's army straggled home from Azua in the usual way, pillaging as they returned.

In the North, Pierrot quickly annulled his short-lived secession and adhered to his old crony, Guerrier, while at the same time prudently strengthening his hand as warlord of the North.

As for Acaau and his revolt, both had now fulfilled the purposes of the Boyerists behind Guerrier, and both could be dispensed with. The Grande-Anse *piquets* learned of Guerrier's ascendancy when they reached Miragoâne and, finding that the *armée souffrante* had been beaten at Aquin, immediately threw in with the new regime. Acaau enjoyed one final moment of triumph: after Geffrard and Riché withdrew, Dugué Zamor reoccupied Aquin and gave it over to the *piquets*. When a Haitian Barbara Frietchie, one Mme. Descotière, incautiously cheered the government cause from her balcony, Zamor had her stripped and beaten in the town square, raped her himself, and then passed her on to the *piquets*.

The *armée souffrante* simply petered out. By midsummer Acaau found himself in Port-au-Prince without his *piquets,* answering charges by a military commission: in August he was banished to St. Marc, where, on Guerrier's orders, he was permitted to console himself on the best of everything.

Yet Acaau had founded a tradition, if not a movement, that would outlive him. The *noirs* of the South would not forget, and the *piquets* would be heard from again. Also to be heard again - and again would be Acaau's biting dictum: "A poor *mulâtre* is a *noir*. A rich *noir*," he added, "is a *mulâtre*."(3)

Three Old Men

Philippe Guerrier, an *affranchi* of the olden times, born at Grande Rivière du Nord, had led one of the great charges at Vertières. He was brave, popular, kindly, illiterate, often drunk, and very old. In his simple terms, the elaborate constitution of 1844 was an irrelevancy. He governed by decree through a Council of State, and, behind him, the *mulâtre* establishment - the Ardouins and their set - pulled the strings: *"gouvernement de doublure"* (government by understudies) they called it.

Within eleven months, on 15 April 1845, carried away by his infirmities, Guerrier was dead at St. Marc. Though his funeral oration, pronounced by a French priest to the booming of minute-guns, compared him favorably with Titus, Marcus Aurelius, Trajan, Solomon, Aristides, Cincinnatus, and George Washington, Guerrier's achievements had been more modest. The regime is chiefly remembered because it established internal postal service and because Honoré Féry, Minister of Education, opened *lycées* (modeled on the *Lycée Pétion*) in Cayes and the Cap, where Guerrier proudly gave the North its first printing press since Christophe. The rest was silence, and Guerrier was buried at Fort La Source, behind Marchand, which was already being called "Dessalines-Ville."

Guerrier's successor, immediately chosen by the Council of State, was Jean-Louis Pierrot.

In selecting Guerrier, the elite had given first consideration to race: with Acaau and his *piquets* on the rampage, a *noir* president seemed clearly in order. Pierrot, an illiterate dotard of eighty-four and, like his predecessor, an *affranchi,* was not only a *noir* but also a patriarch of the North - a region whose separatist tendencies Port-au-Prince knew only too well. To propitiate the North and the Artibonite was the main reason the Council of State chose the brother-in-law of Henry Christophe as new president of the republic.

How bizarre their choice had been soon became clear. Within ten days after Pierrot, summoned from his beloved *Habitation* Lafond on the Bay of Acul, North of his birthplace, came to Port-au-Prince, the old man simply mounted his horse at the *Palais National* and rode out of town. As he passed through the Portail St. Joseph, he halted only to leave word with the guard that he was returning to the Cap.

A week later, still brushing off pursuing officials and bureaucrats, Pierrot was again installed at Lafond, whence he forthwith proclaimed Cap Haïtien the new capital of Haiti.

Amid the general confusion, the partisans of Rivière-Hérard made one last effort to regain the summit. On the night of 17-18 September. after a summer of plotting, some sixty Rivierists assembled at Croix-des-Martyrs, the bloody ground North of Port-au-Prince where Toussaint butchered Rigaud's officers. When the capital failed to respond, they spurred to Léogane. There, appropriating the public funds - 106 gourdes in the town treasury and 40 gourdes belonging to the republic - they raised the standard of revolt.

The reaction of the Council of State was prompt and savage. Commanded by General Lazarre, a 700-man column marched in pursuit. On the 20th, brought to bay in the streets of Léogane, the Rivierist cavaliers - some of the best blood of Port-au-Prince - were overwhelmed. General Pierre-Paul, the rebel chief, had his head chopped off and mounted on a pike at the entrance to town. Fugitives, swept up in the fields by government patrols, were shot en masse next day. Stripped of clothing, pocket money, and watches by the soldiers the carcasses were shoveled into shallow graves. Two brothers, Camille and Juste Plaideau, nearly made it back to Port-au-Prince, but were intercepted on the road. Naked, bound, and barefoot, they were yanked along by cords looped around their testicles. At Pont de Thor, outside Carrefour, where they collapsed from pain and exhaustion, they were sabered to pieces by the guards.

Still smarting from his drubbing by the Dominicans in 1844, Pierrot felt he had a score to settle. On 10 May 1845, even before he shook the dust of the capital from his shoes, the president had warned the "Citizens of the East": "National unity must be reconstituted . . . Never shall I renounce the indivisibility of the territory of Haiti."

Only the Dominicans took Pierrot seriously: in little more than a month, on 17 June, they attacked across the central frontier, burned and sacked Lascahobas and Hinche, and established a strongpoint at Cachiman, near Belladère. Roused to national fury, the Haitians poured troops into the remote Plateau du Centre, retook the towns, and, in a hot fight on 22 July, drove the invaders out of Cachiman. After that the war wound down, within a few weeks the remote hills and valleys were again quiet save for an occasional skirmish when a herdsman or his beasts drifted too far in one direction or another.

While Pierrot tilted at the Dominicans, Haiti's relations with France deteriorated. As usual, the French government was trying to collect the debt, in arrears since the revolution of 1843, and as usual Haiti was unable to pay. In September, a French druggist at the Cap was arrested and detained several days aboard *Rapide,* a corvette in Haiti's small navy. Following the druggist's release, the commanding officer of a French cruiser hauled *Rapide's* captain on board, triced him to a gun carriage, and had the master-at-arms give him thirty lashes. On the night of 10-11 November, when downtown Port-au-Prince was swept by fire, fire-and-rescue parties from the French warships stationed in Haitian waters were attacked in the streets as they helped fight the flames. Next month, after Christmas, Levasseur, France's imperious consul general, simply shut down his office and moved aboard the frigate *Thetis*, another ship in the French squadron, from which, to Haitian amusement, he sometimes sneaked ashore to Bizoton for exercise in the saddle.

Eleven months of Pierrot's senile vagaries proved enough. His attempt in January 1846 to reignite the border war fell flat. By carnival time in the spring, the streets were full of anti-Pierrot masks and songs and jibes. At the end of February, when the garrison at St. Marc received marching orders for the frontier, the men refused to march. Then, on the 28th, just as they had pulled down his mighty brother-in-law, the soldiers of St. Marc declared Pierrot deposed and sent emissaries to General Riché, who had been awaiting just such an invitation in Port-au-Prince.

There was a stormy scene in the *Palais National*, where Riché modestly opened the St. Marc manifesto, addressed simply to "The President of Haiti." Riché, too, was old (seventy) and by no means universally popular. Voices rose: blows and shoves were exchanged; then one general, a Riché man, leaned out the palace window and called to an artillery officer below: "Fire a salute and have the troops cry, '*Vive le Président Riché!*' " As the traditional 17 guns resounded, the town took up the cheers, and by that simple process, on 1 March 1846, Jean-Baptiste Riché, a one-eyed *ex-affranchi* (like Guerrier, from Grande Rivière du Nord), became president of the republic.

But Riché lost no time in taking hold: illiterate though he was, the same day he took office his first decree renounced the dictatorship of his predecessors and, with slight surgery, redesignated the Council of State as the Senate and summarily restored Pétion's constitution of 1816.

More surprises were in store. Acaau (whom Pierrot had restored to command and sent to Anse-à-Veau) had never forgiven Riché the defeat at Aquin. When word came to Acaau of Riché's incumbency, he set the drums and *lambis* throbbing for the *armée souffrante* to rise again. Corail, Pestel, Port-Salut, the Platons, Torbeck - all the old *piquet* country of the South - took up arms. But Riché had foreseen what was happening. Boldly entrusting an old enemy, Samedi Télémaque, with an army, he had troops in Anse-à-Veau within a week. On 12 March 1846, hemmed in like Goman before him, Acaau blew out his brains. Télémaque (who had routed the Dominicans from Fort Cachiman) proceeded energetically against the leaderless *piquets*, and on 24 June, accepted their surrender.

The condition in which Riché found the country was desperate. As described by an unidentified Haitian in August 1845, "Business is entirely dead. As for agriculture, don't speak of it. As of the moment. everybody is a soldier. The moral condition of the country is sad. People are in despair."

To try to right things, Riché called on the ablest of the elite and demanded that they do something for the country. After Télémaque pacified the South, he cut back the army (the first Haitian ruler to do so since Christophe) (4) and tried to balance the budget. But quickly he added, "Financial reforms aren't enough. We need more than that. It's time to establish our institutions on more solid foundations." These words, in a proclamation at Cayes, were not the literal ones of a president who spoke only Créole, but they represented Riché's ideas and his desires for Haiti. Unhappily for the country, other desires finished him: on 27 February 1847, Riché died from an overdose of the aphrodisiac cantharides, seeking, wrote Dorsainvil, "a vigor incompatible with his advanced age."

Ruin and Schism

"The Catholic Church in Hayti appears to be in a very disorganized state," wrote James Franklin in 1828. "Some of the priests are the most abject and miserable wretches I think I ever saw."

The Church's low estate was one dilapidation that cannot be laid at the door of Pétion or Boyer, for the Church in St. Domingue had never amounted to much. Casually established among adventurers, run-down aristocrats, transported convicts, and debauched planters, the Church had never been properly organized or manned. Save for the Jesuits, whom Louis XV expelled, St. Domingue never felt a strong religious authority, and, like many of their flock, priests who found their way to the Antilles were often shady adventurers.

Amid the wrack of St. Domingue, what survived of the Church after 1804 was rent by faction and schism. Msgr. Lecun, for example, apostolic prefect in Port-au-Prince since 1789, was a worldly politician who in turn had followed the British, served Toussaint, and welcomed Leclerc (besides being a reputed womanizer said to have seduced the wife of Juste Chanlatte). In the holocaust of 1804, where Dessalines spared some priests, Lecun, who barely escaped, said the Haitians cut the throat of every priest they caught.

Though the constitutions of 1806 and 1816 specifically re-established Catholicism as the religion of Haiti, hardly any of the original French priests were left. Under Henry in the North, the Church was firmly established on paper: the *Almanach Royal* for 1814 records dioceses, a numerous priesthood, and seminaries, The reality was different. Including Msgr. Brelle, the king's instant archbishop, there were but three ordained priests in the kingdom.

Boyer sincerely wanted a respectable, re-established Church, but he, and more particularly his anticlericalist advisers, Inginac and Ardouin, wanted it on terms the Vatican could not concede. The sticking point was who would control the

Church (and, not to be overlooked, its revenues) - the state (that is, the president) or the Vatican. In adamant Gallican, Jacobin tradition, the constitution gave Boyer power to name a bishop who in turn would ordain a priesthood. As the Holy See had not the slightest intention of creating a Haitian bishopric by rubber-stamping some nominee of Boyer and Inginac, there could be no bishop and hence no priesthood.

This impasse worried Boyer, who saw the problem not only in domestic terms but in terms of his long fight to win international recognition. It also worried the Vatican. The first solution was to extend the jurisdiction of the Spanish Archbishop of the Indies, in Santo Domingo. to include Haiti. Among many other defects, the arrangement foundered on the essential incompatability of Haiti and Santo Domingo. In 1819, 1834, and 1842, papal emissaries came to Haiti, but until 1842, returned frustrated by Haitian duplicity and obstruction. The 1842 negotiation, pursued by an American bishop, Msgr. Joseph Rosati, arrived at satisfactory answers and a draft concordat: but, before it could be ratified, Boyer fell. His successors had other projects of more immediate interest than ending a schism that had become part of the order of things.

From a practical viewpoint, the Church's overriding need in Haiti was to recruit zealous, fervent priests: by 1840 the Haitian priesthood had become an evangelical zoo.

Four years earlier, the *curé* of Port-au-Prince, Father Cazalta, had been unfrocked at home for having shot his father with a horse pistol. Cazalta's crony, another Corsican named Negroni, *curé of* Mirebalais, had been swept out of France for his high-living ways at Versailles. A third Corsican, Father Suzini, at Dondon, was a fugitive from the galleys at Marseilles.

Haiti still had no priests of its own. The first Haitian priest we have been able to identify was Father Georges Paddington, a *mulâtre* trained at Rome and ordained in 1837. Of the European priests, John Candler, who visited Haiti in 1840, reported: "The chief object of the ecclesiastics in Haiti is to secure gold and silver as quickly as they can. They encourage superstition in the people. Not content with baptizing children for gain, they baptize houses, boats, and door-posts."

While these unworthy servants bought and sold Christ and His Church, there went on, Candler noted, "widespread rites of heathenism, such as are practiced to this day in Africa." At funerals, he said, "heathen ceremonies are commonly resorted to, libations are poured out, and a table is spread for the dead, of common eatables."

In his report from Kingston, whither he had fled thirty-six years earlier, Père Lecun had indeed sounded a prophetic note: "The blacks have gotten hold of the debris of vestments and sacred objects, and, although most of them can't even read, have reached the point of miming the sacraments and even the celebration of mass. These wicked pretenders will pose grave problems for the first missioners who reenter this island."

Saints and Guyons, Rome and Old Dahomey

By the mid-1840s (but who could say exactly when?) strange goings-on had come to pass in the countryside of the West. During the presidency of old Pierrot, a pair of hitherto secret sects had surfaced openly and were at war with each other - one called "Guyons,"(5) the other, "Saints." The Guyons, much feared by the peasants, and also known as *"loups-garous,"* were avowed servants of evil, personified by certain grim spirits whose very names could barely be breathed. In their *macoutes* (country knapsacks) the Guyons carried *ouangas,* snakes, human bones, and, by wide repute, human flesh. They were supposed to be cannibals, or at least practitioners of human sacrifice.(6)

The Saints were fanatic believers who congregated in bands led by self-anointed frères (brothers), who exercised priestly functions in approximate forms of Catholicism intermixed with other liturgies every Haitian had in his bones. The frères - not just among the Saints of the West but in other parts of the country - were also known as *"prêtes savanes"* (hedge priests). Acaau's chaplain, for example, was a certain Frère Joseph, who marched about with lighted taper in hand, equally ready to chant a novena or invoke the primordial *loa* who had come to Haiti from Africa.

Whether devoted to light or darkness, both sects professed beliefs and knew mysteries of what would generically be called *"vaudou"* or, in English, Voodoo.

Amid the ruins of the Church, as Père Lecun had foreseen, religious practices had sprung up that commingled the rites of Rome and those of old Dahomey. Possessing no great churches, no hierarchy, no seminaries, no dogma, no credo, Voodoo yet possessed more than all these: it possessed the hearts and, on given occasions, the bodies of its people.

Voodoo, simple, instinctive - above all, authentic and fulfilling had become Haiti's folk religion.

Thomas Madiou (possibly an eyewitness) described what in 1846 may have been the first Voodoo service ever held openly in Port-au-Prince:

At eleven at night a dense crowd, howling fearfully to the lugubrious throb of drums, filled the street. A garlanded he-goat, led by a girl and a young man robed in white, emerged from the mob. Wailing and snorting in imitation of the victim, men and women swirled about the animal in indecent dances with voluptuous, snakelike contortions. With the immolation of the goat, the ceremony reached its climax. Even the agents of the police mingled with the crowd, dancing and chanting over the sacrifice.

Such a ceremony would never have been tolerated by Toussaint, by Dessalines, or by Henry Christophe. Paradoxically, all three of the great *noirs*, who understood Voodoo in its full ramifications (as the French planters never had) and remembered the secret meetings of Boukman the *houngan* and the slaves of the North, repressed, and conceivably feared, what would later become Haiti's true faith. Pétion and Boyer, educated *mulâtres*, conceived Haiti's destiny as French, not African, and simply ignored Voodoo. Probably mindful of Christophe's interdict, Guerrier would have none of it. What Voodoo can have signified in Pierrot's addled old head we cannot know, but at the least he tolerated it. Riché, on the other hand, tried to drive Voodoo underground. When the night wind bore the sound of certain special drumbeats or the chants of the sacred *hounsis*, Riché would set forth from the palace with *cocomacac* in hand and fall upon the unwary *houngans* and *mambos* and their votaries.

But all this merely touched the surface. By the time Riché became president, Voodoo's roots, like those of Toussaint's tree of liberty, were many and deep.

The Tranquillity of the Tomb

Based on their experience in manipulating Guerrier, Pierrot, and even Riché, the establishment *mulâtres* (mostly residuary legatees of Boyer albeit content to honor their lost leader in absentia) felt with some reason that they had arrived at a working formula for running the country.

It thus came about that, on 1 March 1847, after a series of deadlocked ballots in the Senate as to who should succeed Riché, a compromise was agreed upon. Born in Petit-Goâve in 1788 of slave parents new from Africa and the Mandingue tribe, the new president was a *noir* general who had commanded Riché's palace guard and was, in the words of Raybaud, the French consul general, *"bon, gros, et pacifique"* (good-humored, hefty, and peaceable). His name was Faustin Soulouque. Frédéric Marcelin, by no means an admirer, gave this description of the man:

His entire person breathed authority. He had frowns and haughty gestures that emphasized his will without phrase or discourse. But generally his expression was serene, as befitted a man who knew his own power. His forehead was high . . . His admirably fresh skin set off the dead white of his eyes and the sparkling white of his teeth . . . He was of medium height with a fine, well-formed chest - the breast of a chief who would create orders of nobility and so many decorations. A sculptor would not have scorned that head in a gallery of the Caesars.

Dantès Bellegarde has left an inimitable picture of Soulouque's discovery that, on the simple whim of Beaubrun Ardouin, who put his name up, he had become president of Haiti.

Through Bellegarde's eyes we see Soulouque resting after lunch in his hammock while the sea breeze caresses away the midday heat of Port-au-Prince. Then, just as he is well off, comes the orderly to say that a delegation of senators is in his office. Drowsy, in no good humor at being wakened, Soulouque tugs on his blouse, dons his cap, and simply refuses to believe his visitors when they greet him as "*Monsieur le Président.*" It is a bad joke, all the worse for having gotten him up in the bargain. Only after considerable explanation does the truth sink in: he, Faustin Soulouque - a man of no ambition who can barely write his name - is president. Still reluctant, he shakes his head and then, cryptically, grumbles to himself: "If I really am president, I will know how to conduct myself as such."

There runs a story that, during the days of Boyer, when Soulouque, still a lieutenant, was a palace equerry, the president had foretold days to come in which "any man in Haiti could become president, even [indicating Soulouque] that stupid *nègre* over there." In this tale, Soulouque replies humbly, "Please, Mr. President, don't make a fool of me."(7)

If this really happened (and Boyer did have a sharp tongue), the slight overlooked a career that to more perceptive eyes might have suggested qualities other than stupidity.

As a young soldier, Soulouque caught the eye of Rigaud, who made him an *affranchi*. Later, in the Northwest, Soulouque was aide to Lamarre, one of Haiti's most resolute generals. Then, when he brought back Lamarre's heart from the Môle for interment in Port-au-Prince, Pétion retained him in the Presidential Guard, a billet he held throughout the regime of Boyer. Somewhere along the way he learned French - no small achievement during an epoch when only about a thousand Haitian children attended any kind of school each year. Later a French visitor would report, "The most audacious subjunctive imperfects don't rattle him." Rivière-Hérard promoted him and gave him command at Plaisance. Finally, Riché, remembered for his able appointments, detailed this "stupid *nègre*" to the most sensitive military post any Haitian regime, then or now, could confer: command of the Presidential Guard. Having spent most of his career inside the *Palais National*, Soulouque might well say that he would know how to handle himself as president.

For the moment, Soulouque kept Riché's ministers and kept his thoughts to himself. The elite continued to pull the strings, and the new president responded. Céligny Ardouin, Beaubrun's politician brother, was heard to boast that he could make and unmake presidents as he pleased. When word of this reached Soulouque, he commented that he was not about to be disposed of like a change of linen. Then he added, "I know they are conspiring. Nobody can spit in Haiti without my hearing about it. . ."

Soulouque spoke the truth. While his ministers went through the minuet of *doublure*, the president had been silently gathering forces of his own. His successor in command of the palace guard was an old comrade, General Augustin Maximilien (called "Similien"), who, in the words of a foreign observer, "had an absolutely fixed hatred for *hommes de couleur.*" Under Similien, Soulouque lost no time in building a network of lower-class partisans calling themselves *"zinglins."* The *zinglins* were *noirs*. In the army, Souloque already had his power base - the *noir* generals and colonels from whose ranks he himself had risen. He appointed another crony, General Jean-Louis Bellegarde, as military governor of Port-au-Prince, and Colonel Dessalines (natural son of the great Jean-Jacques) became chief of police.

The first tremors were felt in July 1847. The North was restless and Port-au-Prince only slightly less so. Soulouque resolved to go to the Cap but, in the tradition of many another president, was unwilling to leave the capital with most of his ministers and potential rivals behind. When he announced that the chief among them would go along, they incautiously demurred and then more incautiously resigned. "Ministers or not," rejoined Soulouque, "you are not going to stay behind." And go they did, on 28 July, as hostages for the peace of Port-au-Prince.

Similien wasted no time in carrying out the secret orders Soulouque had given him. At Fort National, whose guns commanded the town, he doubled the guard, then sited two fieldpieces, port fires burning, to cover the entrance to the palace. Within the palace grounds he harangued the *noir* soldiers and assembled zinglin vagabonds from Bel Air and Morne-à-Tuf as to the "ingratitude" of the *mulâtres*. Mysterious fires began to break out in the houses of *hommes de couleur*. Fearful fugitives knocked furtively, or in some cases frantically, at the gateways of foreign consulates.

The events of August and September 1847 were but a rehearsal. As Lent of the new year drew in, David Troy, leading elite *mulâtre* politician, was caught with a house full of weapons. Together with his entire family and with Preston, a *mulâtre* deputy and richest businessman in Port-au-Prince, Troy was clapped into prison. By way of precaution, Soulouque's agents ranged the Cul-de-Sac and the mountains above the city, issuing ten rounds to every peasant, together with word that, at the sound of a signal gun from Fort National, all were to swarm into town with musket and machete and assemble at the palace.

On Sunday, 9 April, Consul Raybaud reported, "a band of *noirs* most extreme in their hate for the *mulâtres*" (actually the set of *zinglin* leaders who congregated at the *Palais National* every Sunday morning), pressed Soulouque to dismiss his *mulâtre* cabinet, and proclaim himself *Président-à-vie*. The president acceded promptly: within an hour he proclaimed a new government, in which, among other leading *noirs*, Lysius Salomon, the fiery young man of

Castel Père, became a Minister. On the second point, presidency for life, he said nothing.

One week later, at three in the afternoon next Sunday, the signal gun boomed. As the national guards milled in the streets and the Presidential Guard formed in the palace yard, the leading men - generals, senators, ministers, deputies, some *noirs* but mostly *mulâtres* - converged on the palace.

Imperious as ever, Céligny Ardouin strode up to the president to know what was afoot. Soulouque grimly accused him of being the soul of "*the mulâtres'* conspiracy" and ordered Bellegarde to arrest him. As Ardouin was marched off, someone tried to snatch away his epaulets. There was a scuffle, and two shots rang out. As if on signal, and perhaps it was, the gates of the palace clanged shut, the Presidential Guard faced inward and commenced firing from preloaded muskets into the crowd of elite politicians and merchants. Screaming with pain and panic, people hid behind corpses, scuttled for cover, cowered at the feet of soldiers, or tried to scale the iron fence, while other soldiers shot or bayoneted them. Within the palace similar scenes were enacted: Cérisier-Lauriston, deputy and former Haitian minister to Paris, lay in a pool of blood with his skull sabered in half. Ardouin, by some great luck, escaped with multiple wounds and was dragged off, bleeding, to prison.

Outside the town, as armed peasants began to surge in, the *mulâtres* (and propertied *noirs,* too) formed with backs to the sea at Place Vallière, while the French corvette offshore called away her landing force to try to halt the slaughter. Before the French sailors and Marines could get ashore, however, a messenger from the palace, the handsome *noir* Finance Minister, General Damien Delva, spurred up to the French consulate and told Raybaud: "What you are seeing is a family quarrel. *No matter what happens,* foreign nationals will be perfectly safe."

(Ussher, the British consul, had an appointment at the palace with Soulouque that Sunday afternoon and was conversing with the president when the first volley crashed in the courtyard. Ussher started up in alarm, but Soulouque laid his hand on his arm and told him not to worry: the government was merely settling accounts with some conspirators.)

Soldiers and guns were brought up to Place Vallière by Similien, with Bellegarde and Dessalines at his side. When Similien called on the *mulâtres* to lay down their arms, his reply was a musket shot. In return, the soldiers opened fire with a will. With the first volley of grape it was over: those who could move, fled; those who remained were already wounded or dead or would soon be. As night fell, survivors made it to the foreign consulates, and the French cruiser's landing force rescued some fifty, including Honoré Féry. Blackhurst, who, under Guerrier, had founded Haiti's postal service, crept in disguise through the cordon of *zinglins* that ringed every foreign mission and found safety within the French compound.

Next day the firing squads went to work. Doctors who had treated or harbored the wounded were hunted down by Bellegarde's executioners. So were the elegant professors of the *Lycée Pétion*, the lettered, disdainful, light-skinned men who would speak only French, never Créole. To the ugly crash of volleys throughout the town, wives and mothers sought to retrieve the bodies of their men. Those who reached the palace gates were turned away by Soulouque's guards while, in plain view behind the fence, the corpses in the yard swelled and began to stink. Only on the 18th, did the soldiers heave the dead onto tumbrils and dump them in a common ditch-grave dug out near the cemetery.

As at the Cap in 1842, peasant looters swept gleefully through stores, warehouses, and homes, crying out, *"Bon-Dieu nous donne ça!"* There was a bad hour when the Presidential Guard demanded to join the pillage, but the consuls prevailed on Soulouque to restrain them, and then, miraculously, a torrent of rain drenched out the looters' torches. Finally, on the 21st, the killing stopped and the turmoil subsided.

Meanwhile there was revolt among the *jaunes* in the South. Ironically, Soulouque's pretext for the events of 16 April had been reports of another rising at Aquin.

On 23 April, again leaving Port-au-Prince in the hands of Similien, Soulouque took the field. Calling to his standard the *piquet* chiefs Pierre Noir, Jean Denis, and Voltaire Castor, the president loosed them on the towns. At Aquin and Cavaillon, centers of disaffection, over 300 *mulâtres* as well as 184 *noirs* of means were shot, strangled, or otherwise disposed of. Raybaud, whose consulate in Cayes was sacked, later accused Castor of stabbing 76 victims himself, and then, because his arm was tired, finishing off 30 more with a blunderbuss.

When Soulouque entered Jérémie at the head of a raiding party of *piquets, zinglins,* and barefoot soldiers, it was as if Dessalines were back again. This time, though, the victims were Haitian. In the town square, 57 principal men - officials, merchants, planters - were ranged before the president and killed. Then Soulouque proclaimed: "My sword will never return to its scabbard while a man survives among the traitors who have plotted the betrayal of the country."

To prove his point and also to remind Port-au-Prince that he had not forgotten affairs at the seat of government, he sent a curt note back to Similien: *"Des la presente reçue, fusillez David Troy"* (On receipt hereof, shoot David Troy). Troy was dead in the prison courtyard before his friends or family even learned of Soulouque's mandate. The same fate awaited Céligny Ardouin: half-healed wounds oozing, he too was dragged before a firing squad and shot.

On 15 August when he returned to the capital, the *zinglins* received Soulouque with a traditional Haitian triumph: arches of palm and banana fronds woven with bougainvillea and hibiscus decked the roadside and the entrance to Port-au-

Prince. Even the potholes in the highway leading past Bizoton and Martissant and Fort Lerebours into town were hastily filled. Soulouque liked it all. *"Ca bon!"* he said.

Not all citizens of the city were equally pleased. One of the president's first measures on return was to forbid emigration from Haiti. Those who henceforth tried to leave without his permission would be shot. *Mulâtres* in Port-au-Prince were specially enrolled on a dread roster in the *Palais National*. On order of the regime, numerous commercial establishments and shops were padlocked, but then, so were some government offices, though for the different reason that many of Soulouque's new appointees could not read or write or keep books. Those who could read, however, found only slight comfort in practicing their art on the swirl of proclamations issuing from the palace, all (as one foreign observer remarked) seeming to begin with *"Quiconque"* (Whoever) and ending with the inevitable *"sera fusillé"* (will be shot).

Having neutralized the elite, Soulouque turned his attention closer home, for it was not his intent simply to eliminate the *jaunes* so as to make way for equally powerful *noir* king-makers.

Pierre Noir, *piquet* chieftain of the South, was first. Preying on foreign merchants more than happy to purchase protection, Pierre Noir became too prosperous, too powerful, and above all, too conspicuous. Silently making all arrangements in advance, Soulouque sent his agents to Cayes in November 1848, arrested Pierre Noir, and had him shot outside town.

Similien's turn came next. Confident, as he thought, of the support of the army, Similien began to aspire for higher office - an ambition he soon betrayed over a bottle of *taffia*. First enlisting the aid of Bellegarde and Dessalines, Similien's closest friends and therefore logical rivals, Soulouque one morning publicly relieved Similien at the end of guard mount as if he were the old officer of the day. When the general turned to the troops for support, not a bayonet stirred. The cell in which Similien ultimately found himself was that which had been occupied by David Troy. The date was 16 April 1849, exactly a year after the massacre of the *mulâtres*.(8)

Soulouque Invades Santo Domingo

Soulouque had now settled accounts with each element capable of opposing him: upper classes, *piquets, zinglins,* army - all in their turn had been brought to heel. The outstanding unsolved problem that confronted him lay in the East. With Pierre Noir dead and Similien under lock and key, the president could look afield toward Santo Domingo.

The incubus of insecurity that had possessed Toussaint, Dessalines, Boyer, Rivière-Hérard, and Pierrot now prodded their successor to try again to unify the island. Soulouque's uneasiness over affairs in the Partie de l'Est was not wholly imaginary. The liberated republic to the East had become a focus of great-power politics. France, England, and the slave-holding United States were jockeying for dominance. France felt that she had historic interests in Santo Domingo, going back to the days of Ferrand (Raybaud, besides, was the ardent advocate of an active Franco-Dominican policy that would offset the Soulouque regime he disliked and disdained).(9)

England, in the formidable person of Palmerston, wanted an independent Dominican Republic because this would deny France the protectorate she was seeking and would forestall U.S. expansionism, which was already making difficulties for the British in Oregon. The same American expansionists, in the mood of Manifest Destiny, were looking hard at Samaná Bay as a possible naval station and - with all-out support from Southern delegations in Congress spoiling to "protect white Santo Domingo" against black Haiti.

Haiti had been under special pressures from France as not a sou of the French indemnity, had been paid since 1843: the reserves Boyer had so dearly, earmarked for the indemnity had been pocketed or squandered by the Praslinites. (Léger, commenting in his able *Histoire Diplomatique d'Haïti* on "the incontestable bad faith which dominated Haiti's foreign policy after the fall of Boyer," wrote that "the liberals of 1843 had not exactly enhanced Haitian credit abroad.") In consequence, a new convention was ratified in October 1847, whereby Haitian customs revenues were hypothecated for the debt and M. Raybaud was to receive prompt and complete returns - a requirement that, by procrastination and by incomplete or meaningless accounts, Soulouque in the event evaded.(10)

To all the pressures that have been described, Soulouque's reaction was typical: asserting that, in order to pay off France, he would require the revenues of Santo Domingo's ports, controlled by "the insurgents" of the Partie de l'Est, he marched across the frontier on 9 March 1849 with 15,000 troops.

The Haitian scheme of maneuver not only had the advantage of novelty (it avoided both traditional invasion corridors - the Cul-de-Sac and Ouanaminthe-Santiago) but, more to the point, it at first succeeded handsomely. Under the inept presidency of General Manuel Jimenez, who, according to Jonathan Elliott, the American commissioner, spent his whole time "cleaning, training, and fighting cocks," Dominican arms were not at their most brilliant.

First at Cajul, then Las Matas, and again at San Juan de la Maguana, the Haitian invaders pushed aside the Dominicans. Azua, occupied and despoiled in 1844 by Rivière-Hérard, was again taken and pillaged by Soulouque. Despair reigned in Ciudad Santo Domingo; Jonathan Elliott reported on 24 April:

> The greatest consternation and alarm prevails here. The President of Hayti, Soulouque, is within two days' march of this city with 10,000 blacks. He declares extermination of whites and mulattoes . . . My house is already filled with frightened females . . . Almost all the extensive merchants have packed up their

goods and shipped them to the neighboring Islands, and [are] leaving with their
families . . .

The Dominicans' feelings were not exaggerated: only six months later,
Benjamin Green, U.S. agent in Ciudad Santo Domingo, would declare, "The
most bigoted Catholic here would accept the protection of Jew, infidel or Turk
rather than fall again into the power of the Haytians . . ."

In this desperate hour, General Pedro Santana, the Dominican patriot,
emerged, like Cincinnatus, from his *finca* in the remote Seybo, reached the
capital with 500 men, and advanced toward Baní, rallying and regrouping
fugitive soldiers as he marched. By the time contact was imminent along the dry
bed of the River Ocoa, Santana had 6000 men. In a spirited assault on 30 April
the Haitians, who still outnumbered their opponents nearly three to one, stormed
across the riverbed and were clawing their way up the opposite bank when, for
reasons that will never be known Soulouque suddenly lost his nerve and had the
buglers sound retreat. The attack faltered, broke, and then, as Santana struck
back, dissolved in disaster. Soulouque lost 6 guns (his entire artillery), 2 flags,
300 horses, over 1000 muskets, his baggage, and several hundred dead. The
retreat quickly degenerated into pillage, atrocity, and full rout. Azua and other
towns in the beaten army's path were looted and burned. Banana and mahogany
trees were cut down and canefields put to the torch. Only Geffrard, despite a leg
wound sustained at the Ocoa, brought his people back in any kind of order.

Soulouque's response to this debacle was simple: he declared victory. In a
proclamation Henry V could hardly have bettered, Soulouque apostrophized his
army: "You who have arrived safe home, you'll have much to tell those who
never reached these battlefields which shall be remembered with the glories of
our Ancestors."

Port-au-Prince was decked for a triumph, and on 6 May, accompanied, as
Bouzon wrote, "by the wreckage of his ragged army, amid the boom of gun
salutes and peal of church bells," the president returned to a conqueror's Te
Deum.

A New Emperor and His Court

In July 1849 *telediol* spread a mysterious word: the Holy Virgin (or was it
Maîtresse Erzulie?) had appeared atop a certain palm tree on the Champ de
Mars and signaled that God had anointed the president to become emperor of
Haiti.(11)

Within a month of this annunciation, circulated alike by army officers and
zinglins, Port-au-Prince was awash in petitions demanding that the Senate
elevate Soulouque to a throne. On 26 August, after thus learning the will of the

people, the entire Senate, mounted on horseback, proceeded as a body to the palace. Here, with great flourish, the president of the Senate produced a crown, fashioned the night before from gilded cardboard, clapped it on Soulouque's brow, and, as saluting guns roared (to the music of "a band that would give a dead man the toothache," reported Raybaud), conducted the new emperor to an extemporized coronation mass.

Less than a month later, on 20 September, a new constitution legitimized the proceedings. Faustin 1, and his progeny after him, would rule the Empire of Haiti. The Senate would be appointed by the emperor. Orders of nobility were created. On this last score, Raybaud caustically noted: "After four years in power, Christophe only created 3 princes, 8 dukes, 19 counts, 36 barons, and 11 chevaliers, altogether 77 noblemen. Soulouque, however, raised up, in the first batch alone, 4 princes of empire, 59 dukes, 2 marquises, go counts, 215 barons, and 30 chevaliers, all told, 400 titled persons."

As might be expected, the new nobility included some rare birds. Bobo, chief *zinglin* of the North (an unsavory *noir* Boyer had thrown into prison for atrocities amid the ruins of the Cap in 1842), now, for example, became "Monseigneur le Prince de Bobo." Bobo's counterpart in the South, the ineffable Voltaire Castor, was dubbed "Comte de l'Ile-à-Vache." Sanon, the *taffia*-loving *général de place* at Cayes and sometime army field-music, was "Comte de Port-à-Piment," and Jean-Claude, *piquet* chieftain in the South, held sway as "Duc des Cayes." This last worthy had only recently arrested two British officers ashore while they were taking meteorological observations: observing their barometer, the duke concluded that quicksilver in a glass tube could only be a device for divining buried treasure, which the *blancs* must be plotting to smuggle out.

Yet Faustin's nobility, widely mocked abroad, and especially in France (where Faustin himself was mercilessly caricatured by Daumier's contemporary, Cham, and lampooned by the magazine *Charivari),* (12) represented the people he had to work with and the only ones he felt he could trust. Those who condemn the *noir* racism of Soulouque and his largely *noir* nobility, however, overlook his reliance on some *mulâtres,* such as Dufrène, Duc de Tiburon, his able Foreign Minister, or Haiti's Thucydides, Thomas Madiou, whom Soulouque appointed editor of *Le Moniteur Haïtien,* the government's official journal.

In any case, monarchy (and with it estates of nobility) enjoyed ample precedent in Haitian, and, for that matter, African history. Faustin simply made the best use he could of people and devices that solidified what mattered most: power over his countrymen.

Faustin's investiture by acclamation, let alone the cardboard crown, would hardly do except for the moment, and a sumptuous coronation was elaborately planned. But arrangements dragged because Pope Pius IX was unwilling to provide a bishop until extensive matters outstanding between Haiti and the Vatican were set in order. Then, too, the French merchants who supplied the thrones, the crowns (50,000 francs for Faustin's alone), the scepter, the ermine robes, inconveniently demanded cash and thus protracted preparations.

Finally, on 18 April 1852, all was in readiness. In a pavilion erected West of the Champ de Mars (not far from the site of today's police station), following the exact ritual of Napoleon I's coronation, Faustin I and Adelina, his empress, mounted the altar to the strains of the episcopal "Veni Creator Spiritus," were there anointed with holy oil" by the Abbé Cessens, curé of Port-au-Prince, and donned crowns, this time of real gold.(13)

If I Were to Beat the Sacred Drums

Six years before his coronation. on the day Soulouque became president an odd thing happened. Ushered in state to the presidential *priedieu* for the customary Te Deum, Soulouque balked. Under the eyes of his ministers and of the diplomatic corps, ranged in the choir of the church, the new president shunned the priedieu and would not take his place.

Before nightfall, *telediol* was spreading an explanation: the priedieu was cursed by virtue of a spell cast upon it by a *bocor* in the service of Boyer - no man who occupied it would hold office longer than thirteen months. Moreover (this had been communicated to Adelina, a devout Voodoo initiate, by her *mambo),* there lay, in the palace grounds, a certain *ouanga* buried by Boyer. By virtue of this *ouanga* Soulouque's term was also numbered to thirteen months.

Possibly defuzed by the president's own *bocors* (chief among whom was General Bellegarde), the *ouanga* failed. Soulouque was destined to occupy the *Palais National* not thirteen months but nearly thirteen years and to die still later at the ripe age of eighty-five.

Pierrot had tolerated Voodoo. Soulouque openly practiced and encouraged it and, like most who do so, found nothing inconsistent between Voodoo and Catholicism. Voodoo came as naturally to Soulouque and Adelina as the air they breathed.

It was equally natural for Soulouque to install suitable spiritual advisers in the palace household. Like a certain mess sergeant in the Presidential Guard 110 years later, Bellegarde, the *bocor,* owed his rapid promotion in 1847 to ghostly rather than military powers. In addition, as *houngan* in residence, Soulouque brought in Acaau's onetime chaplain and *prête savane* of the *piquets,* Frère Joseph. Alas, after waxing great as colonel and baron, Frère Joseph eventually overreached himself and, *houngan* or not, one day found himself aboard ship bound for the airless dungeons of Môle St. Nicolas, from which no prisoner, Frère Joseph included, ever returned.

The fate of Frère Joseph served to remind people that no estate could withstand the power of Soulouque. Just as he had successively mastered elite, army, *piquets, zinglins,* so Soulouque mastered and exploited Voodoo as an element in his power structure (and an element no future ruler of Haiti could ever neglect in his own calculus of power). Yet Soulouque was at the same time a true believer, and he and the men of his regime practiced Voodoo openly and unabashedly for more than a decade.

It was surely no idle boast when a *mambo* of these times proclaimed: "If I were to beat the sacred drums and march through the city, not one from the Emperor downward but would humbly follow me."

Cimmerian Darkness

Anticipating that Soulouque would not give up his determination to reunify Hispaniola, Buenaventura Báez, now president of Santo Domingo, in November 1849 launched a series of naval raids against the South of Haiti. Commanded by a drunken French naval officer, Fagalde,(14) the Dominican squadron preyed on Haitian coasters, burned Anse-à-Pitre, bombarded Saltrou and Dame Marie, and burned Petite Rivière de Nippes.

That such harassment (likely the result of French prompting) would accomplish anything but to goad Soulouque into renewed war was a serious misreading of his obstinate and nationalistic character. Benjamin Green, the American "special agent" in Hispaniola, reported to Washington in June 1850: "He has sworn by the soul of his mother that he will not leave a chicken alive on the soil of the Dominicans, and he is one who will keep the spirit of his words . . ."

That very month, 10,000 Haitian soldiers again invaded the Partie de l'Est. The invasion soon wound down into inconclusive forays along the ill-defined frontier.

But Soulouque's dilemma regarding Santo Domingo was very real. On the one hand, if he invaded and attempted to unify Hispaniola by force, he would be jumped by the great powers. On the other, if he failed to intervene, foreign (most likely American) interests would establish a hostile slaveocracy in the Partie de l'Est. The consequences in 1850 were only too predictable: Britain and France (and, backhandedly, the United States) told Soulouque he could not pursue hostilities against the Dominicans and, on terms little short of ultimatum, "encouraged" Haiti to grant a ten-year truce to Báez. Throughout a year of intricate diplomatic maneuver, Soulouque and Tiburon adroitly manipulated the reciprocal jealousies of the three powers and, in the face of repeated naval flag-showing, (15) finally conceded a one-year truce. Then followed months of drift,

Haitian stalling, and, despite contrary reassurances, evidence that Soulouque was still bent on aggression, and, conceivably, even wider conquests than Santo Domingo.

On St. Thomas in early 1850, the authorities arrested a Haitian identified only as "Jacinthe" (Hyacinthe). Hyacinthe's papers revealed him as secret agent of Soulouque, who had sent him to St. Thomas to stir up discontent among the local blacks and report on the garrison and possibilities for invasion. Fantastic as this seems, it is also a fact that, during the disorders in Martinique in late 1851, mobs in the streets of Fort-de-France chanted " *Vive Soulouque!*", a circumstance that can hardly have been accidental.

Tiring of this game, London and Paris ordered, on 9 August 1851, ships of the British and French West Indies Squadrons to clamp a blockade on Port-au-Prince and the Cap. After ten weeks of this regimen, on 16 October, Tiburon assured his tormentors that Haiti entertained only "pacific intentions," and the cruisers withdrew.

During these foreign adventures, Soulouque ruled his subjects with a rod of iron. Fear was everywhere, for the emperor had spies everywhere. In 1851, caught out in a typical *Capois* conspiracy to detach the North from the empire, even the Prince de Bobo proved no match for Faustin's agents: with a price on his head, he took to the hills and was never seen again.

On the roads, such as they were, no traveler was safe. *Piquets* in the South and *zinglins* elsewhere established roadblocks where those who passed were systematically robbed. Anyone indiscreet enough to protest found himself under arrest as an enemy of the regime.

Other collections were even more systematic. Everything Soulouque undertook, invasions and coronations and royal pomp, cost money. Robert Walsh, the new American special agent (effectively *chargé d'affaires* or consul general), reported on 8 April 1851:

> The ceremony of the Chambers was performed with all possible parade . . . His Majesty and suite were robed for the occasion in costumes just arrived from France, making such a display as I have never seen rivalled except at Franconi's in Paris [the circus of Victor Franconi], and certainly none but theatrical magnificoes would venture to exhibit such varicolored and glittering splendor in any other metropolis however imperialistic. The toilette of Soulouque himself was quite wonderful.

To support such magnificence(16) (and to underwrite the fiscal pillage being conducted by all officials, from the emperor down), printing presses spewed money at a rate of 15,000 to 20,000 gourdes a day, more than $28 million in paper money during the whole thirteen years, according to historian Anténor Firmin. In two years, the dollar exchange rate for the gourde soared from 4 to 16. When Boyer stepped down, the Spanish silver piastre bought 3 gourdes; by

1859, it would buy 20.

Salomon, Minister of Finance, fought back by monopolizing export transactions in coffee and cotton, by channeling foreign imports through state monopolies, by steep import duties, and by levies on capital. As a result, smuggling - master-minded in true Haitian fashion by customs house *zinglins* - ran wild. Setting the example, Soulouque himself bought and imported (duty-free) all cloth and other findings for the uniforms and equipment of the army, and then - at fourfold prices - resold the same materials to the government. (17)

One immediate casualty, as so often before, was the French indemnity. Soulouque stopped payments in 1852. Next year, when Admiral Duquesne, the French squadron commander, threatened to bombard Port-au-Prince, if necessary, to restart payments, Soulouque fiercely rejoined: *"Je repousserai la force par la force"* (I will meet force with force), and Duquesne let the matter rest.

Duquesne was right. No bombardment could extract much from Haiti or from Soulouque. As Walsh left Port-au-Prince for Santo Domingo, accompanied by his colleague, Raybaud, he wrote Secretary of State Daniel Webster:

> The Haitian Government is a despotism of the most ignorant, corrupt and vicious description, with a military establishment so enormous that while it absorbs the largest portion of its revenue for its support, it dries up the very sources of national prosperity, by depriving the fields of their necessary laborers to fill the towns with pestilent hordes of depraved and irreclaimable idlers. The treasury is bankrupt . . The population is immersed in Cimmerian darkness . . . The press is shackled to such a degree as to prevent the least freedom of printing and people are afraid to give utterance, even in confidential conversation, to aught that may be tortured into the slightest criticism of the action of the Government.

The End of Empire

Faustin's last attempt to subjugate Santo Domingo began in November 1855. Losing deserters at every step, jettisoning equipment, half-starved before it even reached the frontier, the imperial army advanced in the traditional three columns.

Generaled by Santander, the Dominicans initially fell back. Then, on 22 December, they struck. At Santomé in the South and at Cambronal in the North, Dominican columns repelled the invaders. Only the fighting spirit and discipline of troops under Geffrard saved the Santomé battle from utter disaster. Two days later, on Christmas Eve, at Savana Mula, Santander attacked again: again the Haitians were defeated. Soulouque and his suite dragged their way North to Ouanaminthe for a third and final thrust. To raise morale, he had already begun shooting the generals: Voltaire Castor went first, then Dessalines, then Béliard, and after them a disconsolate file of beaten colonels.

All was in vain. On 24 January, at Savana Larga, the Dominicans once again prevailed. Soulouque withdrew the remnants of his army across the River Dajabón and never set foot on Santo Domingo again. This time, when Faustin returned to Port-au-Prince, there were no church bells or gun salutes or Te Deums. At midnight on 14 February, without so much as a drumbeat, he led the shattered, dispirited army through the darkened streets.

At last there was no further need for the great powers to nag Haiti: Soulouque had played out his string. At bay in the palace, the emperor had no one left to trust. In 1857-1858 world depression hit the prices of coffee and cotton, and there was no money left. Along the Grand Rue in Port-au-Prince, merchants shuttered their doors.

Up to the very last, Geffrard had enjoyed the confidence of the emperor. In December 1858, however, a whisper spread that he, too, was proscribed. Forsaking his dukedom of Tabara, Geffrard, accompanied by his son and two friends, slipped out of Port-au-Prince by night on 20 December aboard a sail boat and made for Gonaïves.

At Toussaint's old headquarters, a revolutionary committee was waiting, and, on the 22d, the empire was pronounced dead. The republic was again proclaimed, and the constitution of 1846 reinstated. Next day, almost an anticlimax, Geffrard was declared president. The Artibonite and the North immediately adhered to Geffrard. In Gonaïves and St. Marc, muskets were issued to the revolutionary army.

Geffrard's ground had been well prepared. Two key Ministers, Guerrier Prophète (Interior) and Louis Dufrène (War and Navy), were privy to events and simply waiting to see whether Geffrard would succeed.

While Geffrard organized, Soulouque temporized. Then, having first jammed the prisons with *mulâtre* hostages, including Geffrard's wife and daughters, on 2 January he marched North up the coast road toward St. Marc with, reported British Consul Byron, "a very inefficient force." The authorities in Jamaica diverted steam transport *Melbourne* to Port-au-Prince, with a draft of 300 Royal Artillery on board, to await developments. "Port-au-Prince is half deserted," reported the gunners' commanding officer, commerce at a standstill, universal distrust prevailing."

At Ravine Mary, near Montrouis, the emperor took his stand. The rebels attacked on the 5th while the imperial navy, before permitting itself to be driven off by Fort Bergerac, made the gesture of bombarding St. Marc. After inconclusive and mainly bloodless skirmishing during the next two days, Faustin bowed to a council of war and withdrew. On the 9th, Geffrard was in Arcahaie; on the 10th, at Croix-des-Bouquets. For four days longer, the armies minuetted before Port-au-Prince. Then it was over.(18)

"The late Emperor, with all his family, suite, and treasure were surprised at 4 o'clock on the morning of the 15th Instant" [wrote Consul Byron],"by the troops of General Geffrard, who . . . entered the Capital, took possession of all his forts, captured his Arsenal, and completely surrounded his Guards and his residence, and made him a prisoner in his own house. The whole town - persons of all claques and colours - at once rose with acclamation to welcome their favorite Chief and to proclaim the Republic . . ."

Protected by the victors (the imperial guard simply changed names and - still bearing Barton & Cie.'s badges - became the *Garde Républicaine*), Soulouque and his wife and daughters packed their things, including several heavy coffers of "personal" valuables.(19) Escorted first to the French consulate, where he signed an act of abdication, Soulouque - "very old & getting infirm, much broken in spirits," wrote Byron - walked slowly to Batterie St. Clair, where four of *Melbourne*'s boats lay at the quay. Accompanied by his family, by Damien Delva, so long his man-of-all-work, and, in Byron's words, "a few of his worst counsellors and most infamous Agents", Soulouque on 20 January left his empire behind. Aboard the transport, the captain and ship's officers gave up their cabins to the ex-emperor - a courtesy for which, on arrival at Port Royal, Soulouque presented them with £2000 from one of the coffers.

Kingston was so full of Haitian refugees that the police had to put down a riot, and at first no hotel-keeper would take the old man in.(20) Back in Port-au-Prince the police were not so vigilant. Guards were already pillaging the home of Delva (whose name became the byword in a Haitian saying: "Rich as Chancellor Delva"), and Soulouque's private house in Rue de la Réunion. In the streets, recounted Frédéric Marcelin, "Dukes, counts, marquis, chamberlains, all the noble train, scurried with panic like owls blinded by the light. You could collect carloads of Crosses of St. Faustin, marshals' batons, and bedizened outfits embroidered with silver and gold lace. They would do nicely for next year's Carnival."

This was the ridiculous side of it - of Soulouque, in Victor Hugo's caustic comparison, as a black Napoleon III. Ridiculous much of it was: and inefficient, corrupt, and bloodthirsty as he was, Soulouque managed to be something more. He was "*un authentique*" - a man of his time and people, who managed to hold the great powers at arm's length and, even in his unreasoning lunges to the East, won for Haiti Hinche, Lascohobas, and the fertile Plaine du Centre.

What Soulouque achieved or failed - or never tried to achieve - in and for Haiti was mordantly stated by Démesvar Delorme: "This imperial government whose very character was violence and which reigned by terror, had all possible power to set on foot reforms and administrative innovations that alone could change the face of Haiti and make it prosper. This government was absolute, it was obeyed to the merest gesture: it lasted ten long years. It undertook nothing, *absolutely nothing . . .*"

More profoundly, wrote Marcelin: "Empires fall when they can no longer sustain their principles. The principle of Soulouque's empire was fear, terror pushed to the extreme. It was the foundation of his political system. But terror cannot be called a system. It would be a century, precisely, before Haitians again knew such a system.

FOOTNOTES - CHAPTER 7

1. The Trinitarios took their name from the political trinity of their leadership: Duarte, Francisco del Rosario Sanchez, and Ramon Mella.
2. Barrot - exceeding instructions from Guizot, the French Foreign Minister - had in fact been in clandestine communication with Duarte and the Trinitarios, encouraging their revolt in the hope that, as in the days of Ferrand, they would seek French protection for the Partie de l'Est. Anticipating this possibility, Admiral Mosges, the French squadron commander, had shifted his force to Ciudad Santo Domingo so as to support Barrot if occasion demanded. Barrot and Mosges also wanted France to annex the Môle. Guizot, however, firmly disapproved any such forward policy on the correct assumption that it would reopen old *noir* hostilities and fears of French return and re-enslavement.
3. "Neg' riche cé mulat', mulat' pauvre sé neg'." Another version, conceivably equally authentic, is said to have been a virtual war cry of the *armée souffrante*: "Neg'riche qui connait li et ecri, cila mulat'. Mulat' pauvre qui pas connait li ni ecri, cila neg' " (A rich *noir* who can read and write, he's a *mulâtre*. A poor *mulâtre* who can't read and write, he's a *noir).*
4. In 1842, on a per capita basis, Haiti's standing army was more than twice the size of Britain's, as well as of most other major European powers.
5. No connection can be established between the seventeenth-century French mystic sect of Mme. Jeanne-Marie Guyon and the Haitian *Guyons.*
6. On the one recorded occasion when Saints and Guyons were brought into court (in Port-au-Prince in 1846) over the ritual murder of an aged woman Guyon said to have eaten an infant, the proceedings, according to Madiou, were abruptly halted by superior authorities for the reason that "nobody wanted foreigners to say that there were cannibals in Haiti."
7. This apocryphal anecdote, well cemented into the received history of Haiti, appears with no source or attribution in the works of Davis, Leyburn, and Rodman, all twentieth century foreigners. We have been unable to find it in any contemporary account.
8. Similien was not shot but might as well have been. "Turn him loose!" exclaimed the president when a petition for pardon was presented. "He can mildew away first." Later, when a report came that Similien's legs were turning gangrenous from the pressure of his fetters, Soulouque sent back word, "Tell him not to worry. When his legs drop off, I'll chain him by the neck." In 1853 Similien died (or was possibly starved to death) in prison.
9. Lambert, the French journalist who wrote of Haiti under the pseudonym "Paul Dhormoys,"described Raybaud as Soulouque's *"diable bleu "* and said he was "an object of terror and respect." According to Dhormoys, Soulouque even went so far on one occasion as to offer Raybaud 200,000 francs just to retire - a suggestion Raybaud dismissed with the reply that any successor would be cut of the same cloth. As a result,

noted Dhormoys, "the French in Haiti are respected like divinities."

10. One price for the convention that Haiti extracted from France was full and final diplomatic recognition. Although Haiti's independence had been conceded in 1838, the Quai d'Orsay had nevertheless refused to accord diplomatic status to Haitian representatives in Paris. Through the energetic diplomacy of Beaubrun Ardouin - who might well have shared his brother's fate had he been at home - Haiti's minister (Ardouin) was finally on 21 December, 1847, admitted to the diplomatic corps and accorded the right of legation in France.

11. 1849 was a great year for manifestations of the Virgin. On 16 July, to a peasant seeking a lost burro in a precipitous glen shaded by palms at Saut d'Eau (Ville Bonheur, 10 miles West of Mirebalais), the Virgin appeared beside the waterfall whose curative properties are now legendary in Haiti.

12. Cham in private life was the Vicomte de Noë, whose grandfather had owned *Habitation* Bréda where Toussaint was a slave. Cham portrayed Faustin and his court as monkeys. But the French press was not alone. The New York *Herald,* in articles on 14 and 15 April 1850, referred to him as "the nigger [sic] Billy Bowlegs, Faustin, Emperor the first . . . the big black nigger[sic]. . . the baboon."

13. Cessens, in Haiti's long tradition of religious imposture, let it be known, after a trip to Rome, that Pius IX had appointed him Bishop (Archbishop, he sometimes intimated) of Haiti and had personally given him the sacramental oil for the coronation. In acid tones, Père Cabon reveals that Cessens actually skipped Rome after being ordered by the Pope into arrest in a nearby monastery. As for the holy oil, Cabon sniffed, it was ordinary Marseilles salad oil.

14. Evidence of the length of Soulouque's arm came soon after Fagalde's victorious return from these depredations. In February 1850 he was murdered in a killing attributed to "Haytian influences."

15. The U.S. Government sent a three-ship squadron to Port-au-Prince in May 1850 to reopen claims for Henry Christophe's 1811 expropriations. As might have been foreseen, Haitian archives contained not a trace of the matter, and no money was ever collected. But, with one eye on the squadron's guns, Soulouque conceded consular status to the American commercial agents at Port-au-Prince, the Cap, and Cayes, and allowed the American colors to be flown over their offices for the first time since the days of Dr. Stevens in the Cap nearly half a century before.

16. In a typically cutting comment, Raybaud noted that, as early as 1847, Soulouque ordered from Europe a green costume costing 10,000 francs - exactly the amount, he said, budgeted that year for all public education in the country.

17. It was during this period that Dhormoys, attending a review of the palace guard, noted that the metal cap-badges of the grenadiers, purchased at fancy prices in France, bore the legend SARDINES A L'HUILE, BARTON ET CIE., LORIENT.

18. According to J. M. Ludlow, an English missionary, Port-au-Prince fell in the nick of time. Soulouque had ordered that the imprisoned elite hostages be killed off at 4:00 P.M. on 15 January. Geffrard's predawn coup de main preempted Soulouque by only twelve hours.

19. Twenty-eight boxes had to be left behind with the French consul. When the new regime eventually took custody, they were found to contain 27,000 *gourdes* in coin (not paper); large quantities of foreign specie; and the crown jewels, some of which still

remain in the hands of the Haitian government.
20. In a few years, memories faded, and, after the fall of Geffrard, in 1867, Soulouque was allowed to return in time to die, aged eighty-five, at his birthplace, Petit-Goâve, where he was buried.

Nissage-Saget was Haiti's only nineteenth century ruler to leave office alive and at the close of his constitutional term. *National Archives* Below: Boisrond-Canal, after leaving office, was mid-wife to new regimes for the rest of the nineteenth century. *National Archives*

CHAPTER 8

Black Republic

1859-1870

It is quite impossible, in this singular Country, to know what may, or may not, happen at any instant.

- Henry Byron, British consul,
Port-au-Prince, 24 January 1859

"OUR REVOLUTION has passed over without bloodshed," wrote Henry Byron to Admiral Stewart, British commander in chief in Jamaica,

&, what is more extraordinary still in Hayti, without any revival of those scenes of violence and butchery to which the passions and prejudices of party and colour here have, on all former occasions, given rise . . . [Geffrard's] extreme popularity and his great tact, and determination not to shed blood . . . contrasted with the extreme disgust felt in all quarters at the state of things that prevailed under the Empire that has fallen.

The able, agreeable man who had become president by acclamation (a formal election never occurred to anyone) took his oath of office on 23 January 1859.(1) Like his predecessor, Fabre-Nicolas Geffrard was a Southerner, from Anse-à-Veau, and a soldier, but there the resemblance stops. Educated, elite, posthumous issue of one of the *fondateurs*, the new president enjoyed a special advantage: son of a *mulâtre* father and a darker mother, Geffrard was neither black nor *jaune* - but what Haitians call a *"griffe"* - and therefore immune to the racism that gnaws at Haitian life and politics.

As seen by a British missionary when he took office, Geffrard was "... a grey haired man of fifty-four, rather short but slim in figure, of very pleasing countenance, and simple and gentlemanly appearance, dressed without ornament of any kind."

In a later report by the British minister, however, the acid in the etching bit deeper:

With all his amiable qualities, the President is vain and presumptuous, absorbed in himself and in his own superiority to the rest of mankind . . . There is not a subject on which he does not pretend to know more even than those whose studies have been special, as lawyers, doctors, architects and engineers. He seriously assures you that he discovered the use of steam by independent inquiries, and that he is prepared to construct a machine which shall solve the problem of perpetual motion . . .

Warts and all, this was the man - a former Praslinite and thus by bent a reformer - on whom Haiti's hopes now focused.

They Look upon Moderation As Weakness

For a man of large views like Geffrard, the deposed emperor was not difficult to succeed. So much needed to be done, and Geffrard immediately set to.

Overhauling the constitution - first project of every regime - was quickly accomplished. On 18 July 1859, complete with presidency for life, Riché's 1846 constitution, itself only lightly retouched from the 1816 model, was reinstated.

The army, which Geffrard knew only too well, cried out for reform. Only a soldier of his standing could get away with his first action, which was to cut the army in half (from 30,000 to 15,000). Thereafter, easing out Soulouque's palace guard, Geffrard formed his own - the *Tirailleurs*, 3000 strong, trained under his personal eye, with advice from European (apparently French) advisers, the first such to be brought to Haiti. Having thus ensured a capable Presidential Guard, he could and did leave the army unchanged.

Roads were improved. On 10 October 1863, it was Geffrard himself who got through a law reintroducing the long dormant colonial *corvée* requiring that the roads of the country be built and maintained by the inhabitants (2)- a law about which much was to be heard a half century later. Haiti's first steamboat, a small coaster, had entered service in 1843, but Geffrard obtained a fleet: five merchant coasters, operated on public subsidy by a Haitian company; and three small government steamers, which saw frequent service in moving *Tirailleur* detachments about the country to show that the president's reach was long.

Pastor Mark Bird, the indefatigable Methodist missionary who had labored in Haiti since 1840, even raised money in New York for a tiny gasworks, which, commencing in 1860, lighted the Methodist compound and the adjacent street. Like the plow in Christophe's day, however, gas proved too far ahead of the times: in 1862 Port-au-Prince citizens petitioned the regime to suppress the dangerous and mysterious novelty, and Pastor Bird sadly dismantled his gasworks. Writing in 1867, Bird recorded another setback: "They tried an electric telegraph in Port-au-Prince, but seeing it was not necessary, abandoned it."(3)

Other Geffrard initiatives met with only mixed success. He hired French engineers to restore the irrigation works of the Cul de Sac, untouched since 1812. Characteristically, the project ran out of money when half complete. Similarly, the Port-au-Prince water supply was improved, but never enough to fight the disastrous incendiary fires that swept the city in 1865 and 1866. With French foremen and instructors Geffrard instituted a national ironworks, but the foundry failed to outlast his government.

Another of Geffrard's ideas that deserved better was, as in the days of Boyer, to bring down black American colonists. Led by a black Episcopal priest, James Theodore Holly, a group of American blacks numbering nearly 2000 emigrated in May 1861 from New Haven to Haiti, where Geffrard settled them on the old *Habitation* Drouillard East of Croix-des-Bouquets.(4) Difficulties doomed the enterprise - inadequate logistics, floods and washouts, disease, cross-cultural shock, and stubborn animosity of Haitian peasant neighbors who wanted no part of the English-speaking *noirs*.

The efforts and achievements by which Geffrard remains best remembered, however, lay in a field where Haiti's rulers have more usually given lip service than produced results.

Public education, either neglected entirely or monopolized by the elite even under Christophe and Pétion, received immediate attention from Geffrard. Within five months after assuming office, in June 1859, the president founded a national law school and revitalized the medical school Boyer had started in 1838. For Geffrard's school of art and his naval academy,(5) both of which lapsed, evidently the time had not yet arrived.

Jean Simon and François Elie-Dubois, the first enlightened Ministers of Education since Honoré Féry, completely modernized the existing *lycées,* such as they were, and opened new ones in Jacmel, Jérémie, St. Marc, and Gonaïves, importing European instructors where they could. One of Simon's first projects was to rebuild Christophe's ruined school building at the Cap, an act that would have mightily pleased the great Henry. Geffrard also tried to introduce, in association with his foundry, vocational training; but this proved to be another uphill battle, one that has lasted throughout Haitian history. Because by definition no member of the elite works with his hands, the idea affronted perceptions of education as strongly held in Haiti of the 1860s as a century later, and therefore failed.

Geffrard himself conceived a system of national scholarships whereby the most promising young scholars (*noir* and *mulâtre* alike, but, by Acaau's formula, surely elite) were sent, as in the days of Toussaint, to France for advanced studies.

For all this progress - spurred by unremitting pressure from Geffrard - education remained an elite monopoly, widened and improved, no doubt, but still a monopoly. Writing with the authority of twenty-seven years in Haiti, Pastor Bird estimated in 1867 that, at any given moment, out of a population exceeding 700,000, no more than 10,000, including students in school, enjoyed what might be called education. "The fact is," Bird sadly concluded, "that the day has not yet arrived when the reigning powers of this Republic are sufficiently ashamed of national ignorance to undertake the education of every child in the country."

Conspiracy lies at the heart of all politics in Haiti. In the words of that astute observer, Marcelin, "Political intrigue is our mania, a trait in our national character. Every Haitian is born a conspirator . . ." Conspiracy was thus not slow to appear after Geffrard took office. Guerrier Prophète, Soulouque's Minister of Interior, a *noir* of the North, had originally betrayed Faustin on behalf of Geffrard and thus retained his portfolio. Within eight months, apparently supported from exile by Delva and Salomon, Prophète was working to overthrow the new president. Geffrard - realist enough to have immediately organized his own secret police - inevitably sniffed out the plot and, on 3 September 1859, packed off Prophète into exile.

The very next evening, as she sat reading by lamplight in her home across from the palace, the president's cherished daughter, Mme. Cora Manneville-Blanfort, newly married and pregnant, was shot down by an assassin's blunderbuss fired through the jalousies. When he heard the report, Geffrard, who frequently strolled across to visit his daughter, started up and would have rushed to the scene had friends not restrained him. Well that they did: the conspirators had laid an ambush outside and had murdered Mme. Blanfort simply to force her father into the street.(6)

Nine days later, Ussher, the British chargé, wrote Commodore Kellett in Jamaica that the murderer (a young *noir* named Timoléon Vanon) had been caught and had quickly betrayed his confederates. Out of some 900 principals, over 70 were already in prison. "Geffrard has evidently committed a great mistake and shown little knowledge of the character of his Countrymen," wrote Ussher, "by attempting to govern them by persuasion and conciliation. These people have so long been accustomed to an iron rule, that they look upon moderation as weakness, if not symptomatic of fear."

Within less than a month, Ussher had cause to revise his judgment. Of 23 plotters convicted, 16 were publicly shot in the place against the cemetery wall near the sinister fig-tree, "Maître Cimitière," long consecrated to the sepulchral *loa*, Baron Samedi, and his votaries.

Thus ended the first but by no means the last plot against Geffrard.

Goat without Horns

Catholic, enlightened, and elite, Geffrard predictably turned his back on the Voodoo that had permeated the regime of Soulouque. With obvious approbation, Pastor Bird noted that Geffrard had given Voodoo the most severe blows ever directed against it by any Haitian government. Don Mariano Alvarez, the Spanish *chargé d'affaires* in Port-au-Prince, reported in 1863, "President Geffrard, who is not afraid of the Vaudoux . . . with an energy that does him honor, has caused the authorities to throw down the altars, collect the drums, timbrels and other ridiculous instruments which the *papalois* use in their diabolical ceremonies."

The circumstances that caused Don Mariano and many others to be concerned over Voodoo arose from the famous *Affaire de Bizoton*, a case of ritual murder and cannibalism perpetrated on a six-year-old girl in Bizoton on New Year's Eve, 1863. Her murderers were a *bocor* and *mambo* named Congo and Jeanne Pellé, who, to deepen the horrors of a trial at which the child's skull and cooked flesh were introduced in evidence, proved to be their victim's uncle and aunt.

In the reverse of the 1846 decision to suppress proceedings against Guyons charged with having killed and eaten a child in almost exactly similar circumstance, Geffrard instituted a rigorous investigation and public prosecution of the Pellés and six of their fanatic accomplices - all reputed to have come originally from the African Mandingue tribe, which had a tradition of cannibalism.

The executions (at which untrained soldier firing squads took a half hour at close range before managing to finish off all eight accused) did not end the affair, primarily because Sir Spenser St. John, the new British minister, was to feature it prominently in his best-selling book on Haiti.

It is ironic that, for having taken the straightforward course of exposure and prosecution in open court, Geffrard undoubtedly incurred for Haiti the international notoriety and barbarous reputation Guerrier sought to avoid in 1846 by hushing up the crimes of the Guyons.

By Schisms Rent Asunder, By Heresies Beset

In Rome during March 1841, when he sent forth Bishop Rosati on his nearly successful mission to return the Church to Haiti, Pope Gregory XVI told the bishop, "I won't die easy if Our Lord doesn't give me the consolation of seeing this poor abandoned country become Christian again." His boon ungranted, Pope Gregory died in 1846.

Although obscured by a profusion of petty issues, the real difficulties that obstructed reconciliation between Haiti and the Church were these:
- The Haitian revolution, intertwined with that of France, had been deeply

Jacobin. The mentality of educated Haitians in the mid-nineteenth century (a generation behind the outer world) was that of Voltaire, Rousseau, and other anticlerics. Their favorite prelate was not the Pontiff, who loved them so specially, but Abbé Gregoire, who, as a schismatic bishop of 1793, had professed the Gallicanism that followed the Revolution and for a time sundered France from Rome. Haitian governments were at times eager to mend relations with Rome, but only on condition that the Church would be an arm of the state, which no Pope could accept.

- Suspicions that nurtured Gallicanist objections on the part of such minds as Inginac's were reinforced by the inescapable fact that Rome's approach to Haiti had to be pursued through a French-speaking, there fore largely French, clergy, and that the Bon-Dieu whose tidings they proclaimed was the French Bon-Dieu of the *blancs,* against whom Boukman had set his face in 1791.

- Practically speaking, the most resistant obstacle to reconciliation between Rome and Port-au-Prince lay in a scalawag clergy, profane and godless men from every religious order in Europe - and not a few jails - who had found a good thing in Haiti. Abetting elite opposition to a truly national (that is, *noir)* Haitian clergy, these fallen apostles feared nothing so much as the day of judgement when the Pope's writ and discipline would again run in Haiti.

The first phase of the Vatican's effort - fired not merely by solicitude for Haiti but by the mounting inroads of Voodoo (and, to Rome, worse, Protestant missionaries) - was to commission a zealous young French *mulâtre* priest, Father Eugène Tisserant, descended from General Bauvais, as apostolic prefect in Haiti. Tisserant quickly insinuated himself, in 1843, into the Praslinite circle but, like many coming new to Haiti, underestimated his difficulties and his built-in opposition.

Besides a cabal of ragtag cassocks viewing with hostility the advent of a young, zealous, papally designated superior, Tisserant encountered fierce opposition from Haiti's pervasive network of Freemasons, especially when, in accordance with Church doctrine, he began enforcing the interdict against Masonic rites, widely prevalent, at church funerals and burials. Backing the Masons, however, was a faction of priests called "Templiers," a schismatic crypto-Masonic order. Haiti was a refuge of Templiers, none anxious to have his priestly credentials scrutinized by regular ecclesiastic authority. All these, and others who simply favored the old, bad order of things, spun an impalpable web of intrigue around Tisserant, who, finally beaten when Guerrier succeeded to the presidency in 1845, retired from the scene.

A central figure in all this was Abbé Cessens, who, decked in bogus episcopal vestments, would anoint Soulouque with Marseilles salad oil. On Tisserant's departure, *"Le démon, Cessens,"* as Father Pierre Percin, one of Haiti's few good priests and a *noir* of St. Lucia, called him, wangled from Rome a caretaker designation as "Ecclesiastic Superior" of Haiti. With the promotion of this master of intrigue, the Vatican unwittingly returned the game to square one. During this time, Soulouque was pulling every possible string to find a bishop, any bishop (even, at various stages, from Santo Domingo or the Church of England), who would preside over the forthcoming imperial consecration. All efforts were vain. The Vatican was not going to celebrate the accession of a Haitian emperor until Haiti's religious house was in order. Moreover, Soulouque's widely reported terrorism as well as his continued attempts to reconquer Santo Domingo in the face of the great powers, inhibited the Vatican from legitimizing a regime so much of the world disapproved.

Simply because the Pope would not consecrate Soulouque with the pomp and rites reserved for Europe's oldest dynasties did not mean that the Sacred Propaganda had given up on Haiti. In May 1853, Pope Pius IX sent an Italian bishop who had long served in France, Msgr. Vicente Spaccapietra, as a kind of religious Hédouville, to find out what was really going on and, second, to do what he could, strictly in the spiritual sphere, to pull things together and curb abuses.

Capable and diplomatic though he was, Spaccapietra was defeated by the same forces and intrigues that had foiled Tisserant before him. Primed by Cessens, Soulouque would not speak to Spaccapietra or even allow him to celebrate mass publicly, let alone preach. To do either, Cessens warned the emperor, would constitute Haitian submission to Rome. When Spaccapietra tried to make contact with other clergy than Cessens, he was spied on, then restricted in his movements by Salomon, the implacable Minister of Interior. Finally, in July 1853, he, too, retired from Haiti.(7)

Seven years longer the Haitian church remained "by schisms rent asunder, by heresies beset." Then, in 1860, the darkness lightened. Realizing that no concordat could ever be negotiated in Port-au-Prince, Geffrard sent as plenipotentiaries to Rome Pierre Faubert and J.-P. Boyer, with instructions to iron things out. On 28 March 1860, an agreement, little different from Bishop Rosati's concordat years earlier, was signed. The long schism was finally healed.

Msgr. Testard du Cosquer, a former French army chaplain, was duly consecrated Haiti's first archbishop. With him he brought forty priests from the Congregation of the Holy Spirit (8) and a cadre of nuns. Under the archbishop's firm hand, and that of his eminent successor, Msgr. Guilloux, the country was at length purged of its bad priests. Whether Haiti would eventually belong to Jesus, or Voodoo, or both, none could say.

Geffrard's Diplomacy

Having learned firsthand on the battlefield the fruitlessness of Soulouque's (or any Haitian) policy of trying to subjugate Santo Domingo, Geffrard wasted no time in reorienting relations with the former Partie de l'Est. In February 1859, only his second month in office, the new president quickly proposed and negotiated a five-year detente with the Dominican regime of Pedro Santana.

Within two years, Geffrard had ample cause to regret his initiative. On 18 March 1861, in a gesture unique in the annals of colonialism, Santana delivered Santo Domingo back to Isabella II, the fat Queen of Spain. Once again Haiti had to contemplate its recurring nightmare - a European power installed on the other half of Hispaniola.(9) To this manifest breach of the Monroe Doctrine, the United States could only protest: Confederate gunners fired on Fort Sumter less than a month later. Only one other voice was raised. On 6 April, Geffrard "solemnly, and in the face of Europe and America [protested] against any occupation by Spain of Dominican territory," reiterated that Haiti would never recognize Spanish annexation, and declared that he would use all means in his power to assure Haiti's interests.

In practical terms, assuring Haiti's interests meant support for the Dominican insurgency, which immediately broke out. Commencing guerrilla war in May 1861 from sanctuaries in Haiti, Generals Cabral and Sanchez launched the struggle to expel the Spanish armies. Geffrard promptly dispatched Haitian "volunteers" (his own *Tirailleurs*) to serve with Cabral, while young Duraciné Pouilh, editor of *L'Opinion Nationale*, set up a Dominican political headquarters in his shop, printing communiques, manifestos, and even paper money, on *L'Opinion's* presses.

With characteristic inability to judge what the traffic would bear, the Haitian government unfortunately allowed its "volunteers" a triumph, in which they swaggered past the Spanish consulate general carrying flags captured across the frontier.

Spain was hardly of a mood to brook Haitian interference, and even less so when rubbed in by Geffrard's *Tirailleurs*. On the morning of to July 1861, Port-au-Prince awoke to see a Spanish squadron offshore, guns trained on the city. The commander, Admiral Rubalcava, presented Madrid's ultimatum: close the frontier to Dominican rebels and keep it closed, a $200,000 indemnity for past depredations, an apology, and a 21-gun salute to the Spanish flag (which Rubalcava would not return).

Had Soulouque still been in power, Rubalcava would have received the same answer as France in 1853. Instead, Geffrard backed down. Consul Byron's intercession with Rubalcava whittled the indemnity to $25,000, and the admiral consented to return the Haitian salute after all. But the Spanish punitive expedition achieved its purpose: Haiti for the time being had to drop its intervention, recognize Spanish sovereignty in the East, and again come to heel before European bullying. This last cut deepest: Haitians could not forgive Geffrard for a surrender they felt Soulouque would never have made. (10)

Within five months of humiliation by Spain, Geffrard reaped an important diplomatic gain as a result of the South's secession from the United States. On 3 December 1861, Abraham Lincoln told Congress: "If any good reason exists why we should persevere longer in withholding our recognition of the independence and sovereignty of Hayti and Liberia, I am unable to discern it."

With Southern members absent, legislation providing for U.S. missions in both countries handily passed and was signed by the Emancipator (who was ultimately destined to free seven times as many slaves as Toussaint) on 5 June 1862. On 27 September, Benjamin F. Whidden, a New Hampshire abolitionist, arrived in Port-au-Prince and presented his credentials as the United States first full-scale envoy to Haiti. (11)

Another milestone in Haitian diplomacy was the conclusion, in 1862, of a treaty of amity and commerce with Liberia, which led to the opening of diplomatic relations in 1864.

Other than Danish St. Thomas (where, one observer indignantly reported, Union naval officers spent their time "indulging in iced juleps and cock-tails"), Haiti was the sole place in the West Indies where the Stars and Stripes was welcome. Britain, France, and Spain were actively backing the Confederacy, building, manning, and harboring its commerce-raiders and blockade-runners, and exerting every effort to dismember the American Republic. It is thus no surprise that one of the first fruits of recognition of Haiti was Geffrard's permission for the U.S. Navy to establish a coaling-station for the West India Squadron at Cap Haïtien flanking the strategic Windward Passage. During a typical week in May 1863 the Navy had a store ship, a supply ship, and three combatant vessels at the Cap. Only five months earlier, with a warm welcome from the Spanish authorities, Raphael Semmes, commanding the Confederate raider *Alabama,* had based in Ciudad Santo Domingo and played hide-and-seek with Union cruisers unable to enter Dominican waters and fight. Confronted with such unneutral behavior, Whidden could only report to Secretary of State William H. Seward of "an untiring effort here on the part of the European Representatives to inspire prejudice against the United States, but facts and events proved too strong for their persistent efforts."

Sedition, Conspiracy and Attentat

Geffrard labored to restart Haitian agriculture. He stimulated exports and prohibited import of any articles or goods Haiti could produce, but at the same time reopened to foreign commerce the outlying ports Soulouque had closed.(12) Taking advantage of the dislocation of world markets resulting from the American Civil War and the blockade of the South, the president fostered cotton, imported gins and technicians, and, for the time being, did well. In 1861, Haiti exported $144,000 worth of cotton; three years later, exports had jumped twenty-threefold, to $2,892,000. Then the bottom dropped out: crops failed in 1865 and 1866, and by that time the U.S. was again exporting cotton. Sadly, the Haitian peasants returned to truck-farming.

The mysteries of fiscal practice and finance (other than personal) never unfolded to Geffrard. Commencing with a deficit in 1859 of 2 million gourdes, the president operated on a consistent and ever mounting deficit that by 1865 had quadrupled. Like Pétion and Boyer, Geffrard tried to balance his books with the printing press. Paper money again spewed out (and, while no one was looking, several million gourdes, printed in excess of the authorized run, spilled into the pockets of high officials).

Then came trouble with the legislature. In Haitian history's fatal way of repeating itself, Geffrard's problems of 1862 and 1863 seemed to repeat those of 1843: an impatient, elite youth, (13) national expectations out of all proportion to what any regime could deliver, balky, prickly, garrulous politicians in both Chambers. The president's attackers concentrated on two sore points: foot-dragging resistance to the concordat he had pushed through; and, even more touchy, his 1862 suggestion - a trial balloon - that it might be good for the country to ease the constitutional prohibition against foreign (that is, *blanc)* landownership in Haiti.

Under the constitution, Geffrard had the power to dissolve the legislature and, on 3 June 1863, he did. Anticipating the cry of despotism, he pointedly noted that although Haiti theoretically had over 200,000 qualified electors, barely 5000 of them ever voted in so-called national elections. The point was well taken but scarcely calculated to endear him to the elite handful who voted and therefore counted.

As might have been expected, the new legislature proved more ready to rubber-stamp whatever emanated from the palace, and the first order of business was therefore a generous presidential pay raise ($50,000 a year, augmented by $20,000 for secret police and $20,000 for contingencies). In addition, the legislature presented the president with two plantations. This munificence, St. John nonetheless reported, did not stop Geffrard from paying his food bills out of the *Tirailleurs'* ration allowances or charging the cost of palace champagne to the hospital fund. (Geffrard also established an importing firm, Fabre Geffrard & Cie., with offices in Paris, London, and Port-au-Prince, through which the government's European business was channeled.) *"Prendre l'argent de l'Etat, c'est pas volé,"* ("taking government money is not stealing") goes the proverb, and this of course was how Geffrard and most people saw it. St. John (admittedly prejudiced) claimed that no Haitian "seeks office except for the purpose of improving [his] private fortune."

When Geffrard drew attention to the minuscule number of voters, it was only to score a debating point. He knew as well as anyone that the locomotive of Haitian politics is not the ballot but the coup.

Commencing with the Guerrier Prophète attempt of 1859, the Geffrard regime - with a recorded total of fifteen coups in eight years - was subjected to a tempo of sedition, conspiracy, and *attentat* until this time unique in Haiti.

- The next rising against Geffrard took place in Gonaïves, when, during the night of 6 November 1861, conspirators under General Léon Legros tried to storm the arsenal. Government forces, alerted as so often by an informer, were waiting, and the attempt failed.

- Less than six months later on 1 May 1862, the turbulent Salomons of Castel Père, led by the exiled minister's elder brother, Senator (and General) Etienne Salomon, tried to rouse the *piquets* at Chollette, near Torbeck. But the peasants were of no mind to revolt, and Salomon, with six other generals and lesser fry, was taken and shot in Cayes.

- The man who had warned Geffrard in 1859 of Soulouque's plan to murder him had been Aimé Legros. Legros arranged Geffrard's hegira and accompanied him in the boat. Four years later all was changed. Bitterly opposed to Geffrard's tenderness toward foreign landownership, Legros (whose brother Léon had already tried and failed to seize Gonaïves) left Port-au-Prince for the Artibonite in June 1863. At Dessalines he fired the alarm gun, called the garrison to arms, and marched on Petite Rivière. Before he could read his manifesto, the cry went up, *"Vive Geffrard!"* and, amid a volley of stones, Legros went down, to be pinioned by the soldiers he had just marched in. On 19 June, he and eight confederates were shot in St. Marc.

- On 25 April 1864, while Geffrard, in Marcelin's acerbic phrase, "was on a military promenade in the North," the Port-au-Prince elite ("men of the best position in the capital," said St. John) made a clumsy attempt to seize the arsenal. "They had no organization," added Whidden, "and were readily overcome." The leaders were indeed of high station: Soulouque would have shot them down with relish. Geffrard flinched. After a tumultuous trial, in which the entire bank of defense counsel was jailed for protesting the inevitable death sentences, the president relented and commuted all findings to imprisonment or outright pardon.

- Port-au-Prince was barely quiet when word reached Geffrard that his one-time Praslinite coreligionist, General Ogé Longuefosse, was preparing sedition in the North.

- To review things in the North, Geffrard had to send his War Minister, Philippeaux, to the Cap, where, unknown to the regime, still another plot was brewing. Under leadership of their colonel, the local artillery regiment would rise, their signal being the assassination of Philippeaux, a project entrusted to a Major Salnave. One sultry evening in August, Philippeaux sat on his veranda playing a hand of bezique. From behind a bougainvillea Salnave leveled his carbine and fired: the bullet glanced; Philippeaux fell wounded but not dead. Salnave and other leaders escaped handily over the Dominican border.

- As 1865 dawned the *piquets* stirred in the Plaine des Cayes and in Goman's old hills behind Corail and Jérémie. Without Goman's generalship they were less fortunate: at Chollette, where Etienne Salomon had failed, government troops turned them back too. But the *piquets* were by no means extinguished. St. John recorded that, through 1865 and 1866, "bands of negroes were wandering through the South burning and pillaging, unchecked by the local authorities."

- There was no peace in Port-au-Prince either. On the night of 28 February 1865, fire broke out in the center of town. With no fire department, no water supply, and looters and arsonists helping along, the blaze consumed 350 shops and houses along the Grande Rue.

Geffrard had now held power for exactly six years. He had tried, not always judiciously but as best he could, to rule by conciliation, by reform, and finally by force. Had he known them, he might well have pondered the words of Edmund Burke: "Conciliation failing, force remains. Force failing, nothing remains."

Salnave's Insurrection

In his repeated sorties against the regime, Major Salnave had shown himself to be persistent and determined, not to say ambitious; in his attempt to bushwhack Philippeaux, desperate. All these characteristics and one other, potent demagoguery, shortly came into view.

On 7 May 1865, at the head of a band of Dominican freebooters from across the frontier, Salnave won over the garrison at Ouanaminthe and marched on the Cap. Entering the city two days later, at five in the morning, without a shot fired, he was enthusiastically received. The ground had been well prepared by one of his main adherents, the eloquent Démesvar Delorme, as well as by other leading figures, who immediately formed a revolutionary committee that, as so often before, proclaimed the secession of the North and bestowed on Salnave an accelerated promotion from major to major general.

Down toward the old boundaries of the Kingdom of the North, the regiments and leaders of the Artibonite and the North rallied to Salnave, but Geffrard had good soldiers too.

The first clash came at Puilboreau, a 3000-foot mountain pass North of Ennery, where on 15 May, a Salnavist column encountered government troops commanded by General Morisset. Morisset was wounded in an action whose fierceness recalled the War of Independence and foretold bitter civil war.

A week later, pressing North, Morisset encountered rebel forces entrenched on a hill at Chatard, South of Plaisance. As the May rains beat down, a bedraggled detachment of rebels appeared with white flag and asked to surrender. When Morisset went forward to receive them, a treacherous volley blew in his face. Then the assassins vanished into a cloudburst.

The Salnavists had reason to fall back: headed by Lupérisse Barthélemy, Geffrard's chief general, and a *mulâtre* general, Nissage-Saget, more than 10,000 government troops were marching North. Within a fortnight, Salnave was pinioned within the Cap, whose ancient forts had not seen action since 1803.

Now commenced a six-month struggle reminiscent of the siege of Jacmel, sixty-five years earlier. At the first whiff of powder, Salnave's committee, except Delorme, faded away. Salnave then went straight to his fellow *Capois*, and they rallied to a man.

When Barthélemy tried to capture the Barrière-Bouteille , gateway to the Cap, the attack was flung back, with its leader mortally wounded. To replace his fallen general, Geffrard himself took the field with his *Tirailleurs* and their French-trained commander, Pétion Faubert. Salnave in turn had at his side the incarnation of the North, General Pierre Nord Alexis, Christophe's nephew by marriage to the daughter of Pierrot. Thus, by August, when Geffrard reached the scene, four present or future presidents - Geffrard, Salnave, Nissage-Saget, and Nord Alexis - had joined the battle.

Yet nothing seemed to avail. "In vain," Marcelin wrote, "did Geffrard pile on the assaults, riddle the forts with bullets, in vain did he try to sow treason, to provoke uprisings from within, the insurgent city would not yield."

Commissioner Whidden found other reasons for the impasse. "The Government Army," he reported on 28 August, in a final dispatch before going home, broken in health, "is somewhat demoralized owing to the length of time that has elapsed since the rebellion commenced. The Army of Salnave, the Rebel leader, is much smaller than the Government army but is composed of very determined men."

Twelve days later, having visited the beleaguered city aboard U.S.S. *Wasp,* Peck, Whidden's successor, gave Washington a report from the other side of the hill. Salnave, he said, had about 500 soldiers reinforced by 1000 irregulars. He had run out of specie and was paying off in confiscated goods the blockade-runners who supplied the Cap. As for the government, Peck said that despite heavily superior forces (10,000 troops), "assaults upon the town are feeble and hesitating . . . peculation by military officers is carried on shamelessly . . . no man's life or property is safe." On 11 September, Peck added further somber tones, describing "horrible neglect in the Medical and Commissariat departments,"(14) then recording that mobs of Port-au-Prince market women had begun to attack government figures in the streets. He wrote: "The women, who are a power in Hayti, are very generally wearing turbans of a kind of handkerchief called 'Salnaves' -Revolution would have occurred before but Geffrard has . . for years been providing for the safety of his administration by expatriating or more summarily dealing with all the men of talent and force in the country . . . Untruth is so much the habit here that no man knows when to trust his neighbor."

The Royal Navy Intervenes

When Geffrard moved North, he set up headquarters at L'Acul du Nord, West of the Cap, opened the bay of Acul to foreign commerce, which Salnave barred at the Cap, and, employing his prized war steamer, *Voldrogue* imposed a blockade. Within a month, Salnave had broken the blockade: on 27 September, a swarm of barges and sail boats from the Cap stole upon *Voldrogue* in the piratical style of 1799, cut her out, and hoisted rebel colors. From this point on, the tables were turned. Recommissioned by Salnave under a new name, *Providence,* the steamer proceeded to blockade l'Acul with results that shortly provoked an international crisis.

Geffrard - who by report ultimately sank 100 million gourdes into suppressing the insurrection at the Cap - had been running in munitions and reinforcements aboard a charter British steamer, R.M.S. *Jamaica Packet,* which, on 18 October, Salnave's newly obtained flagship, *Providence,* pursued and tried to board. Observing all this, the British station ship off the Cap, the paddle-wheeler H.M.S. *Bulldog,* promptly intervened. To the indignation of the Royal Navy, the Haitian captain, Surprise Bien-Aimé, put his helm hard over and did his best to ram *Bulldog.* To underscore his approval of this act, Salnave, as soon as he learned what had happened, sent a file of soldiers to Her Majesty's vice-consulate at the Cap, smashed in its doors, plundered its offices, and removed seven asylees to the reeking dungeons of the town.

Already angered by Surprise Bien-Aimé's "insufferable impudence" [sic] in trying to ram a British man-of-war, *Bulldog*'s Captain, Commander Charles Wake, now proved himself more hot-headed than his antagonist. Without consulting higher authority (and disregarding the established principle of international law that consulates enjoy only by courtesy, if at all, the inviolable immunity of diplomatic missions), Wake proceeded to steam into the harbor of the Cap on the morning of 23 October, first bombarding Fort Picolet and then, even more rash, bearing down under full steam to ram the offending *Providence*, anchored 500 yards off Fort Picolet.

There was an unforeseen difficulty. Directly between the two ships, unmarked on any chart, *Agoué*, god of the sea, had raised a hidden shoal, and with a shudder and with a crunch *Bulldog* grounded hard at 9:00 A.M. in twelve feet of water.

Unable to believe their luck, the Haitian forts, until this moment silent, opened an intense fire on the hapless side-wheeler while, as the first order of business ashore, Salnave had all seven asylees dragged into the street and forthwith shot, leaving the corpses unburied in the square.

Undertaking too late what a more prudent captain would have done in the first place, Wake proceeded to sink *Providence* and "a revolutionary War schooner" by gunfire and tried without success to silence the forts, whose volleys of grape and roundshot (personally directed by Salnave and Nord Alexis) swept the topside of the *Bulldog,* staving in three boats, and killing and wounding fourteen sailors and Royal Marines. Expending as much ammunition as he could, Wake replied by bombarding the town. Then, calling his people to abandon-ship stations, he went below to the wardroom, where the gunner had laid a powder train to the magazines, downed a last glass of port, lit the fuze, and, under cover of darkness, pulled clear in the remaining boats as, to intense Haitian delight, *Bulldog* blew sky high.(15)

Salnave's victory was short-lived. On 7 November 1865, two weeks to the day after the *Bulldog* debacle, H.M.S. *Galatea* and *Lily* steamed into Port-au-Prince, embarked Spenser St. John for politico-military coordination, and proceeded at best speed for the Cap. Here St. John sent an ultimatum ashore to Salnave: he and the other offending rebel leaders were that day (8 November) to surrender themselves on board *Galatea,* to be transported to any point abroad they chose. Failing this, the British force would take whatever measures were required to obtain satisfaction.

Next morning, no reply having been received, the two warships this time with leadsmen in the chains sounding every foot of the way - entered the harbor and demolished the forts and batteries that had figured so prominently in the struggle against the French, coordinating their fire with the advance of Geffrard's besiegers.

As the British fire lifted from Fort St. Michel, General Alcantar occupied it. Then, under cover of the ships' guns, General Léon Montas successively took St. Pierre, Castelle, and Barrière-Bouteille.   When Fort Belair, the rebel stronghold commanding the Barrière-Bouteille, came under the British guns,

Salnave realized the jig was up. Accompanied by the faithful Delorme and what Minister Peck estimated to be "15 or 20" persons of importance, Salnave got aboard *U.S.S. DeSoto,* which transported the Haitian refugees to Montecristi.(16) Behind at the Cap, on Salnave's order, his remaining troops set fire to the town, while Geffrard's people tried to extinguish the flames, and looters from both sides and from the hills behind scrambled for plunder.

In all the tumult and shouting over the fall of the Cap and its six month siege, an interesting diplomatic development went unnoticed. Five days after the destruction of *Bulldog,* Salnave, at Delorme's prompting, sent via Captain Walker an offer to the United States of a naval station in Haiti. According to Rayford Logan, this was the first such offer ever made by Haiti, and it long anticipated any initiative by the U.S. to obtain a naval base in that country. Salnave, who blamed Geffrard for allegedly offering a base to the British, would doubtless never have made his own proposal had he not been in desperate straits. Henceforth, the tactic of dangling or proffering a base (usually the Môle) to foreign powers was to become a stock item of Haitian diplomacy as well as, in most cases, an indicator of difficulty, weakness, or particular need for external support.

His Hour Has Come

For the time being, Geffrard had disposed of Salnave, but at what cost. Financially, the insurrection was ruinous. Domestically - besides reopening old wounds and grudges between North and West and South - Geffrard's transparent exploitation of British gunboat diplomacy to defeat a popular nationalist rebel touched of widespread indignation. As Dr. Dorsainvil later wrote, "The country has never pardoned Geffrard." Though still very new at his post, Minister Peck put the underlying proposition exactly when he wrote Secretary Seward: "The people of Hayti are beyond measure, jealous of foreign interference in their affairs."

"After the revolt of the Cap," recounted Marcelin, "there was a great silence over all the country . . . What good was it to talk? What good was it to write, when the hour for deeds had come'?"

Geffrard, to be sure, had already taken, what to him had become customary actions. Arrests had been made, leading Salnavists had been shot, others had been shipped off to the oubliettes of Môle St. Nicolas, some few had been exiled or allowed to leave. And there was one new - and as it turned out double-edged - reprisal: to quiet some of the turbulent and impenitent young men from good families both at the Cap and in Port-au-Prince, the president put them in uniform as *Tirailleurs* -a measure that had earlier stilled several of the more independent journalists.

The lid stayed on exactly twenty weeks, though long enough for Secretary Seward, first American cabinet officer ever to visit Hispaniola, to stop off in Port-au-Prince during January 1866 (17)

Two months after Seward's departure, disaster (which Haitians tend to blame on incumbent regimes) dealt the capital a heavy blow. On the Feast of St. Joseph (19 March), as Msgr.du Cosquer was celebrating mass, he was interrupted by the cry of "Fire!": the convent and chapel were ablaze. It was the start of a $5 million conflagration, centered on today's Place Geffrard, that ravaged 30 square blocks including 800 houses and most business establishments in downtown Port-au-Prince. Once again, scenes of looting and incendiarism were repeated. At pistol point, St. John had to repel arsonists, torches in hand. "Few except the Europeans," he recounted, "cared to exert themselves, and when they brought out a fire-engine the mob instantly cut the hose and gave themselves up to pillage."

The ashes of Port-au-Prince had barely cooled when Minister Peck, describing affairs in "feverish state" and pleading for the presence of a U.S. warship, reported, on 4 April, local uprisings and attempts to burn both Jérémie and Gonaïves; to which latter place Geffrard had already sent a gunboat and "strong military force."

Geffrard's intelligence had served him well: in Gonaïves on 5 July, two generals (Victor Chevallier and Gallumette Michel) raised a pronunciamento against the government. Seizing a small war steamer, *L'Estère,* then in harbor, the garrison immediately defected. The president reacted energetically by embarking the *Tirailleurs,* under his own command, aboard the *Alexandre Pétion* (the former U.S.S. *Galatea,* sold as surplus by the U.S. Navy) and sailing for the Artibonite. When word reached Gonaïves that Geffrard was coming, Chevallier proclaimed a *levée-en-masse,* recusants and stragglers being forthwith shot. As suddenly as it began, however, the revolt was quelled, on 13 July, when General Léon Montas swept down from the North, barely failing to catch the leaders, who hastily retired abroad to Inagua in the Bahamas.

Within a month, the Artibonite was again in ferment. Salnave had emerged from Santo Domingo and was hammering at Mirebalais, though with no success. Repaying past obligations, reported Peck, Geffrard's old friend Cabral was "determined that the great agitator shall no longer have shelter on the Dominican side." At St. Marc, on 21 August, insurgents took the town hall and arsenal, but once again the government prevailed and, in Peck's phrase, "the assailants incontinently fled."

Prematurely, perhaps, but prophetically, in 1865 Peck had predicted Geffrard's downfall. *"His hour has come,"* he had reported to Washington. Now, less than a year later, he summed up the state of affairs in these words:

The President is thoroughly, but in large measure, unreasonably hated by the majority of the people. The government, as a whole, commands no respect, it rules

only by force . . . Under a thin crust of civilization there are lying dormant
superstitions, traditions. and prejudices . . . Ordinarily, the people are as mild and
orderly as any on which the sun shines; but their passions are easily aroused, and
then they know neither reason nor fear. And the excitements which now prevail are
bringing the fire fearfully near the magazine.

Peck's metaphor was more apt than he could possibly have known: five weeks
later to the day, on 18 September, 1866, at four in the morning, the national
arsenal, crammed with 30,000 pounds of powder, loaded shells, grenades,
primers, and pyrotechnics, went up like a volcano, bombarding Port-au-Prince
with flying projectiles and blowing down 200 houses that had escaped the
conflagration in March.

Stunned by this latest calamity, Haiti remained quiet for four months (though
Pastor Bird somberly commented that "the Republic had become one vast
military encampment").

Geffrard had failed to foresee the possibilities inherent in rounding up
recalcitrant young Salnavists and putting them in uniform. These educated, elite,
troublemaking draftees promptly set to work subverting the *Tirailleurs*, and the
result was soon forthcoming.

On the night of 22 February 1867,(18) stealthily surrounding the *Palais
National* before moonrise, the mutinous *Tirailleurs* loosed a massive volley into
the palace but, instead of killing Geffrard, merely awakened him. Supported
only by his three sons-in-law and a handful of aides-de-camp, Geffrard seized
a carbine and returned the fire so vigorously that the mutineers, a hundred
strong, hesitated. Meanwhile, led by a loyal officer, a rescue detachment came
running from the barracks and managed to regain control of the palace and its
grounds.

Deeply shaken though again victorious, Geffrard tried to stem the tide by
reforms and belated concessions. On 8 March, the president brought in a new
cabinet ("the best men the country could furnish,"said Peck), cut his salary and
allowances in half, even promised to clean the Augean stables of the customs
house, declared freedom of the press and general amnesty (save, of course, for
Salnave, Delorme, and Salomon).

All in vain. That very same day, Victor Chevallier and seventeen confederates
landed at St. Marc, to be received with open arms by Nissage-Saget and Léon
Montas, until recently the president's strongest supporters. A provisional
government was formed in the Artibonite, Salnave (in absentia, on Turks Island)
among its members.

"*Salnave, Victorin, et moi,*" exulted old Nissage.   "*Nous sommes trois
bandits!*"

Realizing the end had come, Geffrard took counsel with the French charge,
and, after spiriting his family and a few friends on board, himself donned

disguise, and at three in the morning on 13 March 1867, stole onto the French sloop-of-war *Destin,* bound for Jamaica and empty years of exile.(19)

What had gone wrong?

The government, never effective in fiscal matters, had gone broke. Crop failures in 1865 and 1866 had ruined agriculture. Forced to the wall by the expense and peculation of the Salnave insurrection, Geffrard first cut and then, in July 1866, defaulted on payments to France. In early 1867, called on for an emergency loan of 6 million francs, the business community sat on its hands.

But endemic peculation and crippling financial difficulties are the rule, not the exception, in Haitian public administration.

And why was Geffrard - personally popular. progressive, energetic, elite, and educated - the object of a drumfire of coup, sedition, and insurrection unequalled in the annals of Haiti? One answer (though this would apply with equal force to virtually any Haitian regime) can be found in the ruler's style. As Pastor Bird observed in 1867, "The chief magistrate, emperor, king, or president has up to the present been the master and not the servant of the country. He has worked his own will rather than that of the people."

Another answer is that, when Geffrard accepted *présidence-à-vie,* he trapped himself. He had no way to go but down, no constitutional machinery for transfer of power; in short, no exit. In these circumstances, pent-up political forces could vent themselves, as they did, only through revolt and subversion.

Commenting, in his harsh way, on the nature of these forces, St. John remarked: "Scarcely one of these plots and insurrections, by which the country has been bathed in blood, but was founded on the hope of office and the consequent spoils."

Peck,(20) a gentler but nonetheless penetrating observer, added, "There is reason to fear that when, in a month or two, the people have got rid of Geffrard, but have not got rid of their financial and other troubles, they will be more excited than they are now."

Salnave Président

Geffrard's accession to power had been next to automatic. It was not that simple for his successor.

In the vacuum left by Geffrard's abdication, political catalepsy seized Port-au-Prince while people waited to see what would happen. Catalepsy, however, did not mean quiet or order. (least of all, it would seem, in Cayes, where, Peck reported, "A plan to pillage the town was arrested only by the killing of many of the conspirators.")

Writing Secretary Seward in Washington on 27 March 1867, Minister Peck described conditions following Geffrard's exit:

> Business was suspended . . . Every man had a weapon in his hand, and gun and pistol firing was the order of the day. The property of the late President and his relatives was sacked with hardly an objection from any quarter . . The [*Tirailleurs*] seized an arsenal which had lately been filled with army stores, and took from it all its contents, and for days military equipments were being hawked about the streets for sale at any price. Every hour, troops of the disorganized and almost disbanded corps were making threats of further mischief.

The confused situation that existed was this: Geffrard had been faced down by Chevallier ("a man of violent and unreasonable temper, thoroughly 'red-republican' in his political principles" - Peck) at the head of a wild army of Artibonite *noirs*. When Nissage-Saget joined the revolution, Chevallier at least temporarily deferred to Nissage, whom Geffrard's still-surviving Senate promptly declared president. Nissage (prudently, as it turned out) declined the honor.

Meanwhile, after an initial check by General Lorquet, who did not know of Geffrard's departure, the populist revolution at St. Marc had spread to Gonaïves. A provisional government was shaped at St. Marc and set feverishly to work on a new constitution, simply detaining frantic delegations sent North by steamer from Port-au-Prince and blocking any movement or communication from the North into the rest of the country or the political process.

On 20 March, at the head of their Artibonite army, Nissage and Chevallier finally marched into Port-au-Prince, abolished the Senate and other remnants of the previous regime, set up a twenty-two-man *gouvernement provisoire,* in which Nissage finally consented to act, but only as provisional president. Chevallier, in turn, readily accepted the more ambiguous but prestigious title (going back to Praslin) of *"chef d'exécution."* The remodeled constitution, ultimately ratified on 14 June 1867, re-established a four-year presidency and otherwise took its lead from its predecessor of 1843.

None of these doings, however, filled the central vacuum awaiting a man of destiny, on whose identity there seemed little disagreement.

Somewhat out of touch with events, Sylvain Salnave had sortied from Turks Island aboard a schooner in mid-March, landed at Montecristi, again rallied his Dominican filibusterers, and set forth, as he thought, to recapture Cap Haïtien. On reaching that destination, he discovered to his astonishment that the revolution had already taken place - and he had won.

Stopping only long enough to kill off a few enemies and even old scores from 1865, Salnave raised a 4000-man army (headed by his favorite 30th Regiment of the North) and marched South on 10 April. Chevallier was at St. Marc to receive him; Nissage waited in Port-au-Prince. From Arcahaie South, the road was decked with flowers and branches, and the potholes were again newly filled. In triumphal progress, Salnave entered the capital on 20 April. Affecting the costume of the Dominican *carabinero* - panama sombrero, bright blue serape, great jackboots, and huge war machete - he rode along the Grande Rue in what *Le Reveil* next day described as "a rain of flowers." Then, at the Rue des Fronts Forts, he turned left, uphill to the cathedral, where, at the head of the clergy, Msgr. du Cosquer waited to welcome the hero and chant a Te Deum of praise and thanksgiving.

The delirious crowd cried, *"Salnave Président!"* but for the moment he simply took his seat in the *gouvernement provisoire* and awaited developments, which were not long in coming.

Seven days after reaching Port-au-Prince, Salnave denounced the junta for having failed the country, and resigned. Within hours, the *gouvernement provisoire* was dead: every member had read the writing, writ large, and resigned. That same day, executive power was assumed by the "Trois Bandits" - Salnave, Nissage, and Chevallier. That arrangement lasted forty-eight hours. On 4 May, Salnave allowed himself to be named "Protector of the Republic" - a development the legislature promptly ratified on 6 May. Two years had elapsed to the day since the protector's march on Cap Haïtien at the head of nine Dominican cutthroats.

Salnave's first actions were to declare St. John persona non grata and order the arrest of Léon Montas (21) Then, assenting to the new constitution and the expressed will of the assembly, he allowed himself to be named president and took oath the same day the constitution was ratified, 14 June 1867. Describing this event, Marcelin wrote: "The rain was falling in torrents. Thunderclaps drowned the traditional 17-gun salute. The cannon resounded more like a funeral knell than a demonstration of joy."

The object of this foreboding - *"a mulâtre brun,"* said *Le Reveil*: "a light-skinned *mulâtre,"* said Anténor Firmin, his son-in-law - was just forty-one. *Capois* to the bone, Salnave was headstrong and passionate. He had a way with people, especially soldiers and peasants. The elite, as with so many other regimes, held the new president at arm's length. Salnave had cordially reciprocated the distrust ever since that day, as the siege of the Cap commenced, when the support of his high-born committee melted away. Firmin said he had no preparation for the presidency or for anything else but soldiering. ("He was only a soldier," wrote Bellegarde.) But perhaps Salnave was a little more than that: he was honest and had no thirst for money. (22) In another way, too, he was honest, or at any rate authentic: his "connection with Vaudoux," reported St. John, "was notorious." The British minister was correct: Salnave distrusted the Church, resented the concordat, and made no secret of Voodoo leanings. (His trusted *houngan* and counselor was a *papaloi* named Jean-Pierre Ibo.)

Other notorieties reinforced the reservations of the elite. His personal habits were soon noticed to be wrong. Marcelin said he "scorned the most elementary conveniences in his domicile, and opened it freely to base and notorious intriguers. And, O Shame, women, compromised by debauch, haunted every corner." Yet, added Marcelin, Salnave himself was not a profligate. He had been swept into power on the shoulders of the mob without regard to the wishes of "the enlightened portion of the country" (of whom Marcelin of course was exemplar and tribune). The president's low associations, concluded Marcelin, sprang from demagogic necessity to maintain contact with the sources of his power. St. John's judgment was identical: "[Salnave's] main reliance was on the mob."

The first clap of thunder burst over the assembly on 11 October. Armand Thoby, fiery deputy from St. Marc, educated in France and England, moved the release of General Montas. As he reached peroration, onto the floor, revolver in hand, strode Chevallier. While the legislators shouted, one deputy ripped open his shirt front and challenged Chevallier to shoot him. The galleries took up the cries. "Revolvers, swords, daggers, flashed on all sides," said Marcelin. Nobody was stabbed or shot, however, and Chevallier was persuaded to leave.

But the imp was out of the bottle. Three days later, those same market women who had helped pull down Geffrard were again scouring the streets, armed with sticks, stones, and machetes, crying out, *"Vive Salnave! A bas la Chambre!"* At a certain moment, all converged on the assembly, where "these horrible negresses from the low quarters of the town" (Bellegarde's description) proceeded to smash the furniture, rip down the portraits of Pétion (the only *mulâtre* in sight) - not to mention those of the *blancs* Grégoire and Wilberforce - and ended up dancing and singing and drinking *taffia* amid the wreckage. Then, nailing shut the shattered doorways with Cromwellian signs reading *"Maison à Louer,"* (for rent) the women swirled out into the streets.

The portals of the assembly stayed shut. No legislative body again convened during Salnave's time. He had, in his way (the market women's outburst had of course been orchestrated by the regime), put aside ordinary politics. For the duration - his duration, it would turn out - Salnave's concern would henceforth be war.

The Cacos Revolt

Salnave's stormy passage through the Cap, followed by the imprisonment of Montas, boded ill for those who opposed him in 1865, and, rather than await the next blow, they set about organizing a counter-revolution. Not unlike those which had raged in the South for over a generation, this movement found fuel in the fears and aspirations of the *noir* peasantry, to whom it was represented that Salnave was a dangerous *jaune* bent on vengeance (as indeed he was) against all, peasants included, who had failed to take his side in 1865. In June 1867, while Salnave was savoring the adoration of the Port-au-Prince mob, the peasants of Vallière and Mont Organisé, remote villages in the mountains of the North, rose with fire and sword against the government. The movement and its partisans called themselves *"Cacos."*(23) Their leader (as distinct from *Capois* townsmen provocateurs) was the venerable Colonel Robert Nöel of Mont Organisé, whose original band numbered only twenty. Joined by more recruits from Vallière, the *Cacos* quickly seized a key defile, Monbin Crochu.

Throughout the summer and into fall, General Nord Alexis, commandant in the North and himself native to the disaffected region, mounted an effective and sagacious campaign of pacification. Dondon, St. Michel de l'Atalaye, St. Suzanne, all overrun by *Caco* bands, were retaken and pacified, with many *Cacos* rallying to the government. Much of the all-important coffee crop was also safely gathered in, as General Nord maintained pressure on the Vallière-Mont Organisé focal area ("a sort of hornet's nest," wrote François Légitime, then a junior officer, who would later be president) with columns based on Hinche, Ouanaminthe, and Grande Rivière du Nord. Outside this district the only remaining *Caco* stronghold was Fort Biassou, overlooking the Artibonite, opposite Bánica in Santo Domingo, built by the English in 1795 and afterward renamed for the mighty *congo*. In mid-September even Biassou fell, and its occupants fled across the frontier.

In January of the new year, as Nord Alexis, on Salnave's orders, tried to take Vallière by converging columns, *Cacos* ambushed and wiped out a covering force led by Colonel Bégeot Paret (whom they captured and executed). Blaming Nord Alexis for the botched operation, Salnave sent him into exile on Turks Island.

On 25 April, Nissage-Saget proclaimed himself general-in-chief of the Artibonite and provisional president of a Republic of the North. At Anse-à-Veau, General (and Senator) Normil Dubois announced on 1 May as "Chief of the Constitutional Army of the South," and a week later, from his stronghold at Les Cayes, Michel Domingue proclaimed the "Meridional State of the South." Then, to compound the confusion, Pétionville and Croix-des-Bouquets rose in arms under their beloved Boisrond-Canal, grandson of Boisrond-Tonnerre.

To outflank Nissage, Salnave loaded a steamer with troops and made for Gonaïves. The moment his back was turned, on 2 May, the elite of Port-au-Prince thought the time opportune for a coup. It amounted to little. In St. John's words, "A crowd of young men armed with swordsticks and pocket-pistols made a feeble attempt at insurrection but dispersed at the first fire." Returning immediately, Salnave gave the city's merchants and first families a brutal demonstration that he still reigned. Debarking at the Quai du Commerce on 5

May, the army, well fueled with *clairin*, systematically sacked commercial Port-au-Prince. At the height of things the colonel of one regiment was heard to caution, *"Z'enfants! Z'enfants! Pillez en bon ordre!"* ("Children, children, pillage in an orderly fashion!") Before the day ended the American legation (then on Rue du Centre) was jammed with 150 terror-stricken asylees, and in the estimate of the new U.S. minister, Gideon H. Hollister, over a million dollars' worth of property had vanished.

The elite did not miss the point. Not until the end did Salnave encounter trouble from Port-au-Prince. Before May was out, *Cacos* from the North and *piquet* armies from Jacmel and the South had the capital encircled. At bay in the palace, Salnave announced that he would burn the city before he would allow it to be taken.

Commencing 27 May there followed a week of attacks, first against Fort Bizoton; next, Portail St. Joseph (where the market women, screaming like furies, joined soldiers and townsmen in clawing the *Cacos* off the top of Bel Air), and then a series of probes at every vulnerable point. At sea, Salnave's navy, two steam sloops, defected to the rebels.

The president's prospects seemed poor indeed. But now came a minister, André Rigaud's son Numa (a *mulâtre* of the South who nonetheless had long-standing ties among the *piquet* chieftains), with a suggestion. The generals of the Southern besiegers - Normil Charles, Domingue, and J. P. Hector (or "Rebecca") of Jacmel - all represented elite elements. To subvert the *noir* peasants in their rear should prove easy. The emissary to convey this proposal to the South should be Salnave's son, Victor, who had the pure *noir* pigmentation of his mother rather than his father's lighter skin. Victor's message would be simple: now was the hour for the *piquets* to avenge Soulouque and smite the rich *mulâtres* of the South.

The *piquets* responded with alacrity. By mid-July, peasant hordes had overrun the Southern peninsula, except for the principal towns, infested the Plaine de Léogane in the besiegers' rear, and were at the gates of Jacmel. Numa Rigaud's stratagem had succeeded brilliantly.

The whole Southern wing of the Port-au-Prince besiegers melted to defend their towns and homeland.(24) On 15 August the siege of Port-au-Prince was lifted; two weeks later the *Cacos* fell back on St. Marc and made common cause with Nissage-Saget, who had been joined by Nord Alexis, back from Turks Island and thirsting for revenge. More significant than all, however, the intervention of the *piquets* had converted insurrection into civil war.

One Long Civil War

"I do not think it necessary," wrote St. John, "to do more than briefly notice the events of Salnave's presidency. It was one long civil war." Then he added,

"The year 1869 was one of the most disastrous .... in Haytian history."
     The British minister's assessment of Salnave's thirty months was correct; but his judgment that they were historically unimportant brushes aside the most deeply rooted, complex, and fiercely fought struggle among Haitians since the War of Independence.

     As 1869 began, Haiti, for the first time since 1820, was partitioned into three states: the Republic of the North, its capital St. Marc, headed by Nissage with Nord Alexis and Pétion Faubert at his elbow, the State of the South, its capital Les Cayes, under Domingue with Pierre Momplaisir Pierre as chief minister; and the republic proper, which Salnave was desperately trying to hang on to.
     Fragmented and entangled as this was, the factions, political motives, aspirations, interests, and forces arrayed against each other in the civil war now beginning ("Guerre de Salnave" or "Guerre des *Cacos*," Haitians usually call it) nearly defy categorization.(25)

     Despite extensive contrary misconceptions, there are two things this civil war was not. It was not, in Haiti's stereotype, a simple regional conflict between North and South. Though his legions were Accau's Southern peasants, Salnave came from the Cap. His enemy, Nissage, at the head of a *Caco* army of the far North, came from the Artibonite, while the latter's closest ally, Domingue, was from the South. Nor, again confounding tradition, was the civil war a typical war between the races. As Légitime pointed out, leaders on both sides were of both colors.(26)

     While holding off enemies of the North and Artibonite, Salnave's strategy was to try to reconquer the South and regain control of the sea. Having lost his fleet when his two steam sloops, *Liberté* and *Sylvain*, changed sides in May, he impatiently awaited the return, from a New York overhaul, of *Pétion,* which, on 19 September 1868, reached Port-au-Prince with a crew of American filibusterers.
     That same day, personally assuming control of the naval campaign, Salnave took *Pétion* to Petit-Goâve, then under siege by *piquets* who were being supported by both offending rebel warships. Standing in on 20 September with American colors flying (a lawful *ruse-de-guerre,* though it excited intense Haitian indignation) *Pétion* took station within easy range of *Sylvain,* hoisted Haitian colors, and opened fire. Riddled by the initial salvos, *Sylvain* rolled over and sank. *Liberté's* crew had time to get underway and steered straight for the beach as far as engines would carry. As they abandoned ship and burned her, Salnave went ashore and accepted the rebels' surrender. J. Frederick Nickels, the [former U.S. Navy] captain of *Pétion,* was thereupon breveted rear admiral in the Haitian Navy.

Warmed by victory, Salnave next attacked Jérémie, whose townsmen (commanded by a young general, Brice-ainé, formerly Geffrard's aide-de-camp) were stoutly resisting the *piquets* at their gates. Steaming down with *Pétion* and Admiral Nickels on 4 October, the president fired 575 shells onto the town and Forts Télémaque and La Pointe, but this time to no effect. When joined by a second U.S. naval vessel, the side-wheeler gunboat *Maratanza*, (27) the bombardment failed to budge Brice. Jérémie never yielded.

Then, continuing his amphibious campaign, Salnave struck the South coast at Aquin, which surrendered on 20 January of the new year. Cavaillon and Torbeck thereupon rallied to the government, thus completing the encirclement of Domingue in Les Cayes.

The siege of Cayes began on 4 February 1869, and until its end was marked by heavy naval bombardment from Salnave's fleet as well as by savage assaults on the part of *piquets,* whose chief and historic ambition since the days of Acaau had been to sack the town. The backbone of the defense, conducted by Michel Domingue, with his nephew, Septimus Rameau, beside him, was terror. Visiting Cayes in February aboard *U.S.S. Yantic* (which, with H.M.S. *Jason,* took out foreign nationals and women and children), Minister Hollister reported:

> Atrocities perpetrated by [Domingue] surpass anything I have seen on record. The murders in the prison on 3d inst. were committed without the form of a trial and without any notice given to the victims. The cells were opened and some of the prisoners were shot in irons but most were turned loose in the prison yard and killed by boys, 14 to 17, who were unskilled in the use of musketry and made a horrible butchery of the affair. General Mentor . . . compelled to see the business through . . . sick at the time and covered with sores from head to foot, was placed in front of a mortar at a distance of about four yards and blown to atoms with grape and canister . . . Domingue is in the habit of shooting the wives and children of deserters from his camp.

In an effort to lift the siege, Domingue suggested to Hollister that the United States annex the Meridional State, to which the American minister merely replied that he doubted that would halt Salnave.(28)

Cayes remained besieged for nine months. Salnave nearly carried it by storm in late May but ran out of ammunition, and then had to pull back when threatened by Momplaisir Pierre. All summer, from headquarters at Bourdet (or "Boudet"), two miles Northwest of the city, Salnave broke his teeth on Cayes to no avail. Finally, under the mounting pressure of disaster elsewhere, the president gave up the siege on 31 October, the traditional day of the dead, and fell back by night on Port-au-Prince.

The naval lessons of the war thus far had not been lost upon the rebels. In August 1868, emissaries of Nissage reached New York with the mission of acquiring a navy equal to the government's. The time was not propitious: at the height of negotiations resulting from Britain's having sent forth C.S.S. *Alabama* to destroy Union commerce in the Civil War, the United States could hardly afford to be caught fitting out rebel warships for Haiti. By dint of hard bargaining and intrigue, however, two paddle-wheeler merchantmen, rechristened *Mont Organisé* and *République*, were obtained and sent South to challenge Salnave's fleet.(29)

Groping for each other beyond the Môle, the two forces made contact on 14 September off Port-de-Paix. "Show your colors!" challenged an American filibusterer aboard *Salnave* (the former *Maratanza*). "*Merde!*" came *République*'s reply.

The only fleet action in Haiti's history ended inconclusively. Rammed on her starboard paddle-wheel, *Salnave* could maneuver only in circles, while *République* promptly lost all power from a hit that ruptured her main steamline. *Mont Organisé* (which stood so high out of the water, Légitime reminisced, that she looked like "a floating château") was hulled twenty-six times between wind and water by *Pétion* and left for sinking but never did. By mutual consent the fight ended off Le Borgne, with *Pétion* towing *Salnave* into the Cap while the two rebels luckily made it to Acul. All four ships were out of the war.

Like Jutland, in itself a draw, the battle off Le Borgne was in fact a turning point of the war. Salnave, who had made skilled use of his ability to strike from the sea, was now land-bound. Moreover, a lone prize taken off Anse d'Hainault in July, the steamer *Artibonite* gave Nissage the very advantages the government had heretofore enjoyed.

In a series of seaborne descents, Brice-aîné retook Miragoâne, his home town, then Petite Rivière and Petit Trou de Nippes, and finally Anse-à-Veau. By the end of October the old pirate coast of Nippes, Baradères, and Cayemite was Brice's.

Gonaïves, besieged by Nissage since April of the preceding year (1868) but supplied by sea, had to capitulate. Cut-off garrisons hung on in the North and Northwest while Salnave tried desperately to buy a new navy. The effort produced one more former U.S. warship (U.S.S. *Pequot*, renamed *Terreur*) and - a final purchase - another old ironclad, *Atlanta*, which, sailing for Haiti in December 1869, foundered in the winter gales off Hatteras, taking with her Salnave's hopes, all hands, and a purchase price of $160,000 gold.

Salnave, who at best had scant time for political affairs, was now drowning in them. In July one dollar purchased 700 gourdes; by December, reported the new American minister, Ebenezer Bassett, (30) the rate had soared to 3000 gourdes for one dollar. The usual Haitian solution, printing-press money, was mocked in the streets as "asses' ears". In vain did the president try to prop up the regime by a proclamation, on 16 November, of *présidence-à-vie* (until now merely implied) and by various warmed-over financial expedients remembered from Soulouque's time. When the Grande Rue began closing its doors for fear of violence or want of custom, Salnave decreed that any merchant shuttering his shop would be "considered an enemy of the government and treated as such."

But Salnave held one last card. Forces salvaged from Cayes and Gonaïves gave him means for a final play. While the North and Northwest toppled into Nissage's hands - Port-de-Paix on 24 October and, finally, on 14 November the Cap (together with Salnave's family twenty-two women and children) - the president concentrated his remaining troops against Jacmel in a single army under Chevallier. The outcome might have been foreseen, indeed, Chevallier could see it with perfect clarity. On 4 November, with his entire army, he joined the *Cacos*.(31)

Salnave's Downfall

At bay in his capital, with about 3000 defenders, Salnave made ready for his last fight. He had little time to wait. Under General Saint-Elia Cauvin, troops from St. Marc invested Port-au-Prince by land. Meanwhile, mounting out from Arcahaie, Brice and Boisrond-Canal crammed *Mont Organisé* and *République* (their battle damage repaired) and *Pétion* (surrendered at the Cap) with every soldier the three ships could hold.

At three in the morning on 18 December, Brice laid his ships alongside the Port-au-Prince quay and Fort Ilet (inelegantly known as "Fort Caca"), where the government's last and newest warship, *Terreur,* lay moored. Without a shot, Brice's *Cacos* took the sleeping ship, then deployed into the heart of the capital.

Within two hours, Fort Lacroix had fallen in the Northern outskirts, the prison had been opened, and, together with the prisoners, Port-au-Prince elite were somewhat surprisingly fighting side by side with *Cacos*.

Salnave defended Port-au-Prince street by street. There was ammunition enough though food was running low. That night the town caught fire, but the defenders managed to quell the flames.

Aboard *Terreur* the *Cacos* put a pistol to the head of Lieutenant Hall, once of the American navy and latterly *Terreur's* gunnery officer. The National Palace thereupon became Hall's target. Laying one of the 11-inch guns with special care, Hall yanked the lanyard. The round lit with a crash in the palace courtyard. Salnave, who knew better than most the contents of his palace (including 2000 barrels of powder in and under the main audience room), wasted no time. By the time the gun was reloaded, the president was outside the building and clear. Well that he was: Lieutenant Hall scored a target-hit on the throne room, and the palace blew up, "shaking the city," reported Minister Bassett, "to its very foundations." A third of Port-au-Prince was blown down or burnt up before the resulting fires were quenched, days later.

Accompanied by a few loyal soldiers and ministers, who could expect no mercy, Salnave spurred toward Pétionville (La Coupe), stopping momentarily at the American minister's residence, once a summer retreat of Soulouque's, at the top of Turgeau. The residence and the legation downtown now held 1800 refugees. As pursuers closed in, the fugitives made for the pine-forested mountains along the Dominican border.

Like Ogé and Chavannes before him, Salnave found no sanctuary. His luck had run out. Well into Santo Domingo on 11 January 1870, he and his followers were taken by Geffrard's old ally Cabral, who was then waging war against Salnave's friend Báez. Cabral wasted no time. As fast as an escort could take them back, he sent the forlorn Haitians to the frontier. At Anse-à-Pitre, with $5000 gold for Cabral, the *Cacos* were waiting. Some of the group (Alfred Delva, General Ulysse Obas, and the palace almoner, Abbé Buscail) were shot out of hand at Croix-des-Bouquets.

With slightly more formality, the deposed president, wounded in one hand, was brought to Port-au-Prince and, on the morning of 15 January, tried before a military commission headed by General Lorquet, on the encompassing charge of "having violated the constitution," which one not being specified. Within three hours Lorquet had done his work. (Two days earlier a grave had been conveniently dug in La Saline.)

Flanked by two priests, Salnave was marched through the streets by Boisrond-Canal to the rubble of the palace, where awaited a freshly painted blood-red stake and a firing squad. "People!" cried Boisrond. "You are about to be avenged of a traitor! *Vive la Constitution!*" Then, as the sun set, at 6:20 P.M., Sylvain Salnave was shot to death in his palace yard.

FOOTNOTES - CHAPTER 8

1. Various dates, ranging from the 18th to the 23rd, are given by Haitian historians for Geffrard's inauguration. But *Le Moniteur Haïtien*, 29 January 1859, not only a primary but an official source gives the 23rd and describes the ceremony in detail.
2. This legal obligation, known always in Haiti by its title in French feudal law as *"la corvée"* dated back to the Middle Ages and was specifically enacted into French statute law in the seventeenth century as *"la corvée royale"*. It enjoyed full force in colonial St. Domingue,
3. Dupuy, recalled in 1862 from exile in London, brought back equipment for a tele-

graph circuit to link the National Palace with headquarters of the Port-au-Prince garrison. Frédéric Marcelin said only two messages were ever transmitted: a query by the president as to the health of his favorite horse, and the veterinarian's reply. The poles and tattered wires stood for years afterward.

4. Father Holly, one of the earliest black Episcopal priests, had conceived the notion of Haitian colonization in 1856 and had visited Port-au-Prince and had been received by Soulouque. After the collapse of the Drouillard colony, Holly moved into the capital and built an Episcopal church and a school. On 8 November 1874, in New York City, he was consecrated Haiti's first Episcopal bishop, an office he filled until his death in 1911. Holly was the first black member of the American episcopate, and appears to have been the second black bishop consecrated in the Anglican communion.

5. The little naval academy is referred to in most histories as a "school of navigation," which it was. But the enabling decree clearly describes it as an "*école navale militaire.*" Founded to train officers and technicians for Geffrard's steam fleet, this institution was Haiti's first military academy.

6. Less than a year before, Geffrard's only son, aged eighteen, had died, apparently of a heart attack, during the excitement of his father's accession to the presidency. And a third child, his eldest daughter, was soon to die in childbirth.

7. Abbé Cessens lived only four months to savor his victory. On All Saints' Day, 1853, unattended and unshriven, he died. Had he lived a few days longer he would have received a fearsome denunciation indited by Pius IX himself, cutting him off from all ecclesiastic office and authority. Instead, he faced a higher judge.

8. This order, founded about 1840, was devoted to the evangelization of Haiti, Madagascar, and Africa, throughout which it was widely deployed. Collège St. Martial, for many years Haiti's leading secondary school for the elite, was founded by the Congregation. Père Cabon, magisterial historian of the Church in Haiti, was of the Congregation and produced his great works while teaching at St. Martial.

9. While there is no evidence that Spain intended or attempted to restore slavery in Santo Domingo, Haitians must have been well aware that, in Cuba, Spain's colony just across the Windward Passage, African slavery remained in force.

10. When the Dominican insurgency flared up again in 1863, Geffrard again supported the rebels, and his personal emissaries (Colonel Ernest Roumain, in the field with the insurgents, and Thomas Madiou, Haitian minister in Madrid) provided a channel of communication through which the Dominican revolutionaries finally negotiated their independence in 1865.

11. Whidden bore only the modest rank of commissioner and consul general. It was not until four years later, 20 August 1866, that his successor, H. E. Peck, was raised to the status of minister resident, apparently so that he could cope with Britain's energetic, aristocratic, racist - and markedly anti-American - Spenser St. John, who had been a friend of Palmerston and an intimate of Rajah Brooke in Sarawak.

12. On 12 May 1864, Geffrard activated Haiti's first modern aid to navigation, the lighthouse at Point Lamentin on the approach to Port-au-Prince. However, while the government was opening ports and encouraging navigation, silt was filling them up and restricting them. In 1864 *L'Opinion Nationale* called on the regime to procure a steam dredge and initiate a systematic program for upkeep and improvement of Haiti's ports - a sensible measure that, a century later, had not yet been undertaken.

13. The focus of opposition was the brilliant Démesvar Delorme, gifted journalist and master of *belles lettres,* who later became the intimate of both Hugo and Lamartine.

14. Sanitary conditions among both besieged and besiegers were fearful. Dysentery raged throughout Geffrard's camps and the fetid ruins and unswept, stinking streets of the city.

15. Commander Wake got his crew ashore at Limonade-Bord-de-Mer (just East of the Cap), whence he made contact with Geffrard's lieutenant, General Valentine Alcantar, who procured the Haitian corvette *22 Décembre* to transport the crestfallen British (save for eleven wounded transferred to the U.S.S. *DeSoto)* to Port Royal. With a searing endorsement on his action-report by Admiral Sir James Hope, British commander-in-chief at Jamaica, Wake was sent home to England to face general court-martial for the loss of his ship.

16. Captain W.M. Walker, U.S.N., commanding DeSoto, has been criticized for having refused to join Wake's attack and then refusing to stand in and tow off *Bulldog* (assuming she could have been gotten off). Walker's initial decision to keep out of the affair was justified by the fact that no American consular or diplomatic interest was involved, and also that, under international law, the British vice-consul at the Cap had no right to grant asylum anyway. When Wake sought help after running aground, Walker replied that he "could not interfere as an ally in a war so recklessly begun," but did send boats for Bulldog's wounded. The year was 1865 and probably the lowest point since 1812 in the state of U.S.-British relations.

17. The nominal purpose of Seward's West Indian trip was to recuperate from the painful injuries inflicted on him during Lincoln's assassination, but he was also scouting the West Indies for naval coaling-stations - a fact that St. John reported to the Foreign Office with concern after Seward told him, "We must have a Naval Station in the West Indies."

18. Most histories date this mutiny on 23 February, not 22, but contemporary diplomatic dispatches agree on the latter date, as does Pastor Bird.

19. Geffrard was never able to return. He died in Kingston on the last day of December 1878.

20. Peck and his family had been battered by tragedy. On Christmas Night, 1866, the American legation burned to the ground, destroying not only official papers and property but all family effects (the latter already depleted by the Pecks' shipwreck en route to Haiti, off Bermuda). Worse was to come: on 2 January in the new year, his daughter, Margaret, aged seven, died of "malignant fever." Peck had been the first American diplomat to bring his family to Haiti, and, in a letter not unworthy to be compared to Paul's recitation of tribulation (II Corinthians, 11:25-27), he told Seward: "I am satisfied my wife and children have done quite as much as I have to promote interest and respect for the name and institutions of our country. It is therefore, in a sort [sic], in the service of our country that my child has died." Even then, Peck's cup was not to pass: within six months, on 9 June 1867, aged forty-six, he died at his post of yellow fever.

21. The attempted interdict against St. John did not stick; that against Montas stuck only too well. One of Geffrard's best generals, popular though strict, tactful and generous, Montas had fought Salnave at the Cap in 1865. Imprisoned without charges for seven months, he died of apoplexy in his cell, if one could believe *Le Moniteur,* on 5 November.

22. The day he was shot, recounted Firmin, Salnave had five months' uncollected pay riding on the books.

23. The origins of the term "*Caco*" are obscure. Père Cabon speculates that it comes from *caraco*, a Créole word for a kind of peasant clothing worn in the mountains of the North. Many years later, when both the word and those who personified it became objects of solicitude by the U.S. Marine Corps, other possible derivations were advanced.

24. Rebecca exemplified the methods used for maintaining control in the beleaguered towns. On his return to Jacmel, noted *Le Moniteur* of 25 July 1868, he rounded up and shot over 200 politically suspect citizens, explaining simply that the constitution "demanded their death."

25. For the Salnavists an express term of opprobrium, *"zondolite"* (lizard), was reserved by their opponents; ninety years later, François Duvalier, a keen student of history, would revive the name to disparage his foes and thus associate himself with the old *Caco authentiques*.

26. Under Salnave, a dark *mulâtre*, served such lighter *jaunes* as Chevallier, Joseph Hibbert, Holophernes Lafond, and Thomas Christ. Under his opponent Nissage, who was likewise a *mulâtre*, came such notable *noirs* as Nord Alexis, Momplaisir Pierre, and Robert Nöel, who willingly took orders from Pétion Faubert, Nissage's *jaune* chief of staff.

27. *Maratanza,* which had home the same name in the U.S. Navy, had been sent to Haiti under American registry by Boston ship-brokers, who hoped to peddle her to Salnave. At the moment, in Jérémie, when the president closed the deal, *Maratanza* had U.S. Minister Hollister on board. To the latter's indignation and vain protest, the Haitian colors simply went up, the mercenary U.S. crew went to general quarters, and, with the American minister a helpless accessory, proceeded to join in the bombardment. Seward afterward rapped Hollister's knuckles for "very indiscreet proceeding."

28. Domingue's impromptu offer of the Meridional State to Hollister was not the only such proposition then being floated by the respective factions. Nissage offered Britain Môle St. Nicolas: Domingue made the same proposal to the British minister as he had to Hollister. France was approached in similar terms by both sides.

29. The two ships slipped out ahead of a U.S. Government detainer, the United States being pro-Salnave, and, in the style of Confederate blockade-runners of the Civil War, picked up their armament in international waters. They reached St. Marc on 18 July 1869.

30. Ebenezer Don Carlos Bassett, who reached Haiti on 22 June 1869, America's first black diplomat, was from Litchfield, Connecticut, and, so far as is known, the first black civilian presidential appointee of the U.S. Government. Bassett, who studied at Yale College, was a distinguished educator and polished linguist who spoke excellent French and quickly mastered Créole. He remained as American minister in Port-au-Prince until the Hayes administration displaced him in 1877.

31. Chevallier's defection was to no avail: in January 1870, on general principles, it would appear, the new government marched him before a firing squad at Fort Bizoton.

CHAPTER 9

Misfortunes without Number

1871-1888

If, since the proclamation of independence, Haiti had expended in serious study, in useful effort, one quarter of the energy it has committed to vain declarations, conspiracies, executions, revolutions . . . she would be the admiration of the world.

- Melvil Bloncourt, 1861

SALNAVE WAS DEAD, the war was over, but nothing had been settled. Along unchanging racial and regional fault lines, Haiti was divided as ever. To obscure these fundamental divisions, and also to perpetuate them, established political factions had begun to coalesce among the elite. Since Geffrard's time these had been as follows:

> *Liberals*: Moderate *mulâtres* who favored oligarchic (and hence mainly *mulâtre)* government.
> *Ultra-Liberals:* Hard-shell *mulâtres* who would accept no person in government or public authority save *jaunes*.
> *Nationalists* and *Ultra-Nationalists*: Moderate and radical *noir* factions, respectively.

As a general rule the label "Liberal" would henceforth mean *mulâtre:* and "Nationalist," *noir*.

These were the factions now picking over the debris, real and political, of Haiti's most disastrous war since that of independence.

A Mild, Humane, Religious Man

-The streets are broad but utterly neglected. Everyone throws out his refuse before his door so that heaps of manure, broken bottles, crockery, and every species of rubbish encumber the way and render both riding and walking dangerous . . . Ask Haytians why they do not mend their streets and roads, they answer, *"Bon-Dieu gaté li; Bon-Dieu paré li"* [God spoiled them, God will repair them] . . . Port-au-Prince is the filthiest town I have ever seen.

This, wrote Sir Spenser St. John, was Haiti after the fall of Salnave.
St. John wrote of physical conditions. Yet the institutions of Haiti, if one credits
Jean-Joseph Audain's *Gazette du Peuple* (6 April 1871), were little different
from the streets of its capital:

> For 68 years, ever since our existence, what have we accomplished? Nothing, or
> almost nothing. Our constitutions are defective, our laws have holes in them, our
> custom-houses are maladministered, our navy is detestable, our finances are rotten,
> our policies are ill organized. our army is in pitiful condition; the legislative
> function is not understood and never will be: primary elections are neglected and
> people fail to see their importance; public buildings are in ruins: public education
> all but abandoned.

In this milieu the triumvirate of Nissage, Domingue, and Nord Alexis (which,
with lesser figures, had proclaimed a *gouvernement provisoire* on 27 December
1869) sat down to restart government (by restoring the 1867 constitution),
arrange political futures for all concerned, and root out whatever remained of
the Salnavists. "The triumphant rebels," recounted Anténor Firmin, ". . .
celebrated victory by sickening hecatombs. For a month they shot and shot. The
most valiant generals, the most notable or redoubtable men of Salnave's government - not excepting the young, brave, and intelligent Alfred Delva - in all,
hundreds of victims, reddened the soil of Haiti with their blood."
     While the firing squads did their work, the leaders did theirs. Representing
the regional constituencies as well as the color spectrum of Haiti, Nissage *(jaune*
from the West), Domingue *(griffe* of the South), Nord *(noir* from the Cap) made
a deal.
     Nissage would be elected president by the assembly, which would convene in
March; Domingue would succeed him four years later; then would come the
turn of Nord.
     Jean-Nicolas Nissage-Saget, born in Port-au-Prince though a citizen of St.
Marc and by calling a tailor, seemed older than his sixty years. On 20 March
1870, as arranged, he was, in the words of the New York *Herald,* "named (it
cannot be said elected) president for four years." Some said his nine years in
prison had left him touched. (He had, for example, long held that the
constitution was the supreme law and must be obeyed.) Bassett, an acute
observer, simply described Nissage as "a mulatto of fair intelligence and . . .
a mild, humane, religious man."
     Touched or not, Nissage rightly viewed his task as one of reconstruction and
reconciliation, not to mention final pacification.(1)
     Like every predecessor, the new president soon fell afoul of the legislature,
which, elected as ever by a handful of elite ballots, no more than a few thousand

for the country as a whole, represented only the interests, ambitions, and divisions of their class. For once, however, the issue was substantive: how and on what terms to retire the infamous "donkey's ears" of Salnave, which by 1870 had sunk to the rate of 5000 gourdes for one piastre. In May 1871 the deputies brought in a vote of no confidence. Instead of dissolving them forthwith, in the usual style, Nissage, rolling his r's in a droll way he had, mildly remarked, *"Que chaque bourrique braie dans son pâturage"* (Let each jackass bray in his own pasture).

The upshot did credit to all parties. In August 1872, after raising the necessary funds by a domestic loan (the earliest voluntary loan ever floated in Haiti), the government acceded to the leaders in the legislature. Edmond Paul and Jean-Pierre Boyer-Bazelais (handsome grandson of Boyer and the first Bazelais) and bought in all paper money at a rate of 300 gourdes for one dollar of gold. A feature of this arrangement, which continued officially for more than a decade, was that the legal tender of Haiti became the metallic currency (gold and silver) of the United States.

Despite his even-handed policy of making appointments from a wide range of candidates,(2) as well as his welcome to many exiles whom the stormy years had stranded abroad, Nissage had three coups to quell.

The first was an attempt by old troublemakers - Gallumette Michel, Séïde Télémaque, and another of the turbulent Legros brothers - to seize the Port-au-Prince arsenal on 2 February 1871. Not its failure, but the way in which the twenty-one conspirators were dealt with, gives this small coup its place in history. Nissage simply turned over the malefactors, many taken with arms in hand, to the courts for trial by jury. In the astounded words of Edmond Paul's *Le Civilisateur* (30 March 1871), "This manner of referring to the ordinary criminal courts, for jury trial, jurisdiction over political cases, constitutes a veritable innovation and presents a striking contrast to that long-standing practice of the country of habitually referring trials of this nature to extraordinary jurisdictions."

The accused, all convicted, received nominal sentences and, in several cases, lived to conspire again.

On 15 March 1872, General Cinna Leconte, one of Salnave's original band, emulated his lost leader by emerging from Santo Domingo, where he had been lying low, and landed by night from a schooner at the Cap. Proclaiming himself "Jean-Jacques Dessalines II," he called on his "subjects" to "rally on the lightning sword of 1804!" More practically, Leconte also raised the ominous cry, deeply threatening to a *mulâtre* regime, of *"Vive Salomon!"*

But the *Capois* were wary. Next morning, when Nord Alexis beat the long roll, people stayed in their houses. Supporting the attack with his personal howitzer, Nord recaptured the arsenal and the prison (where Leconte had picked up recruits), scattered the rebels, and ran them down.

"Tonton Nord" was no Nissage. There were no juries at the Cap and not even any trials: Leconte and nine others (including a French adventurer and four Dominican mercenaries) were shot in front of the arsenal they had briefly seized; other executions followed briskly. Then, as surviving conspirators confessed, further arrests followed in the Cap, Gonaïves, and St. Marc. (At this last place including one plotter bearing a name, Benoît Batraville, that would be heard in future.)

The *noirs* of Gonaïves rose again (once again, and for the last time, it was Gallumette Michel, supported by the last surviving Legros, Jules; and by the elder Zamor, whose son would some day become president). In the night of 3-4 March 1873, at the head of some thirty rebels, Gallumette seized the powder magazine at Chevallier's old stronghold, Fort Bauteau, down by the waterside. But even with the potent rallying cry of *"Salomon!"* Gallumette was no match for the ferocious *général de place,* Montmorency Benjamin, who raised the town against the insurgents. Within twelve hours it was over, and all sixteen leaders, from Gallumette down, had either been chopped to pieces in the streets or marched before a firing squad. Until Nissage personally intervened a month later, Benjamin continued to arrest and execute without pity. Four years later, people still spoke of "the massacres of Gonaïves." Reporting these "frightful executions" on 6 May 1873, Bassett wrote: "Men were taken from their homes and led off to execution without ceremony and without warning...ceremony and without warning . . . The bodies of those who had fallen were allowed to lie unburied in the scorching sun to be devoured by ravenous animals . . . In one well-marked case these animals began their sickening work before the life of the victim was extinct."

Throughout all this, and throughout most of Nissage's regime, the capital remained tranquil. The reason was not the mildness of Nissage so much as the sternness of Lorquet, the city commandant. "Discussions tending to cast doubt on the stability of the regime," Bassett reported, were prohibited. Anyone abroad after 9:00 P.M. had to carry a lighted lantern and be prepared to justify his errand on pain of being summarily disposed of as an enemy of the regime.

Fire, not insurrection, continued as the scourge of Port-au-Prince. On 6 November 1871, downtown Port-au-Prince was consumed. Then, on the night of 9 February 1872, again came the cry *"Feu au Palais!"* and the new National Palace blazed with a fury that lighted hills and mountainsides for miles around. The French minister wrote: "The spread of the fire is impossible to convey. In six hours, from six in the evening until midnight, this completely new residence had been transformed into a heap of smoking ruins."

Next, on 27 April 1873, a child playing with matches touched off a can of lamp oil and with it, ultimately, four square blocks along Rue des Fronts Forts - over eighty buildings and a half-million dollars destroyed. Less than six weeks later, fire originating in Morne-à-Tuf burnt out forty buildings, including Father Holly's laboriously built Episcopal mission, while Catholic priests, marshalled sternly by Msgr. Guilloux, now the new Archbishop of Haiti, rolled powder barrels out of the nearby arsenal to prevent explosion.

Within two months, in August, came still another fire, which Minister Bassett reported vividly:

> High officials, generals, and other officers decked in cocked hats, plumes, and swords, dashed on horseback through the streets near the burning district. Ragged soldiers were stationed here and there and were now and then moved about under orders of serious-looking epauletted officers, as if they were on the eve of a battle: and shabby boys threw stones at the roaring flames as if to drive off an approaching evil spirit.

Following this summer of conflagration, a priest at St. Martial, Père Weik, organized a student hose company and, with contributions solicited from well-to-do parents, sent to the United States for a two-mule Amoskeag steamer and hose reel. The young vamps, representing some of the bluest blood in Haiti, reveled in *grand tenue* of red shirts, blue trousers, and burnished copper helmets. Their foreman, Philippe Sudre Dartiguenave, was destined for even higher place than the Compagnie des Pompiers.(3)

Annexation, Intervention, Gunboat Diplomacy

If the days of Nissage were marked by comparative tranquillity, Haiti's foreign affairs were jolted by difficulties with the United States over Santo Domingo, and with Spain and Germany on other grounds.

Manifest Destiny - both slogan and rationale of an American *mission civilisatrice* - had been running strong toward Santo Domingo for more than twenty years. Once in the White House, U. S. Grant, long interested in outright annexation (or, failing that, a base at Samaná Bay), wasted no time in negotiating a treaty of U.S. annexation (signed 29 November 1868) with Buenaventura Báez, dictator of Santo Domingo. Báez was in mortal contest with his enemy Cabral, and each had his Haitian partisans.

The threat of a foreign presence in the Partie de l'Est provoked instant fear and resistance in Haiti. Thus it came about that, with the backing of France and England (which had supported the rebels while the U.S. aided Salnave), Nissage-Saget, like Geffrard before him, in 1870 threw Haiti's weight into Dominican politics. This intervention (in a sense, remarked historian Ludwell Montague, Haiti merely applying its own "Monroe Doctrine" to Hispaniola) took the familiar form of Haitian sanctuaries for Cabral, printing presses for his manifestos, financial subsidy, *Caco* raids over the border, similar forays by

Haitian troops, and gunrunning from the national arsenal.

These activities by Haiti in support of a feeble pretender - Báez easily held the upper hand - constituted serious interference in the internal affairs of Santo Domingo. As viewed by President Grant, they also constituted interference in the affairs of the United States. Grant's reaction was what might have been expected from the conqueror of Vicksburg and Richmond. He ordered the Atlantic Fleet into Haitian waters with instructions to halt Haitian aggression against Báez. In the abrupt style of this school of diplomacy, Rear Admiral Charles H. Poor, U.S.N., delivered Grant's message to Nissage on to February 1870:

> "Any interference or attack . . . upon the Dominicans during the pendence of negotiations will be considered an act of hostility to the Flag of the United States and will provoke hostility in return."

It required fewer than seventy-two hours - Admiral Poor's flagship, aptly named U.S.S. *Dictator,* lay within easy range of the rebuilt National Palace - for the regime to assure Bassett that Haiti would observe "a strict neutrality as to the internal affairs of St. Domingo . . . and that it would use its power and influence to prevent any attempt at interference with the domestic peace of the Dominican Republic from being carried on through its territory or concocted within its jurisdiction."

This assurance - conceded under duress - was not made or kept in entire good faith. (As late as 24 October 1872, when Báez's dragoons swooped on Cabral's headquarters, they caught and killed the redoubtable *Caco* chieftain of Mont Organisé, John Lynch, acting as military adviser.)

But the U.S. Senate rendered the question moot. Responding to the eloquence of Charles Sumner (who, like his fellow abolitionists, had close and confidential relations with the Haitian legation in Washington),(4) the U.S. Senate, in a 28-28 vote, on 30 June 1870, withheld the two-thirds majority Grant's treaty of annexation required for ratification. Before rigor mortis set in, the corpse twitched a few times; but this was the effective end of the business. The result was a *froide glaciale*, if not a deep freeze, in Haitian-American relations until Grant finally abjured the project, while the legislature named a Port-au-Prince street for Sumner and hung his portrait in the Chamber beside the Amis des Noirs of 1789.

Haitian relations with Spain remained sour. The object of the Ten Years' War next door in Cuba was abolition of slavery, a goal Haitians enthusiastically supported. When Haiti gave shelter to a rebel gunrunner, S.S. *Hornet,* the Spanish navy blockaded her in Port-au-prince for eleven months until, in January 1872, the U.S. Navy defied Spain and escorted *Hornet* to Baltimore.

Still smarting over Haiti's unfriendly role during the Dominican struggle, Spain clearly hoped the *Hornet* affair might afford the pretext for a sharp blow at Haiti, but American diplomacy, pro-Haitian for a change, balked Madrid.

Within six months after *Hornet* and the Spanish cruisers were gone, German gunboat diplomacy made Spain's bluster and high-handedness seem deferential.

Haiti's outspoken sympathy for France in 1870 had not gone unnoticed by either the local German colony or the Wilhelmstrasse. It thus came about, on the morning of 11 June 1872, that two German corvettes, S.M.S. *Vineta* and *Gazelle*, steamed into Port-au-Prince on what was ostensibly a debt-collecting foray on behalf of German merchants, but was in fact a reminder to Haiti as to who had won the Franco-Prussian War.

Batsch, the German commodore, made a direct demand for indemnities totaling £3000 before sundown. When the government temporized, Batsch simply cut out and seized two Haitian warships that, in Firmin's account, were "anchored in the harbor with the negligence that characterizes our army and navy."

Only when, through St. John's offices, the money was hastily raised from the tills and strongboxes of foreign (non-German) merchants did Captain Batsch give Haiti back its navy. With the special finesse Hohenzollern diplomacy reserved for people of color, the German boarding parties left calling cards. When the Haitians were allowed back, they found their cherished flag spread out on the bridge of each ship, smeared with shit. It was, remarked Firmin, the republic's first contact with the methods of German diplomacy.

Haiti's indignant protest was ignored by Berlin, Captain Batsch retained his command, and - crowning indignity - he was, within seven months (by 19 January 1873), sent back with his ship into Port-au-Prince for a two-day "visit of courtesy."

Nissage Stands Down

With pride and a certain wistfulness, Haitian histories limn Nissage-Saget as a sort of philosopher-president whose constitutional regime ran its constitutional course and ended with tranquillity and good feeling.

This perception overlooks the incessant obstruction and bickering on the part of both houses of the legislature, which, as his term neared its end, tormented Nissage and his ministers. The underlying issue, often cloaked or misrepresented in a succession of parliamentary jousts, was simple: Who was to be the next president?

Nissage was committed on record to Michel Domingue ("that crafty, cold-blooded, determined aspirant," noted Bassett on 6 May 1873), while the Liberal majority in the legislature wanted the presidency for Momplaisir Pierre, the candidate of Boyer-Bazelais. Besides, waiting in the wings in Jamaica was Salomon, denied passport or visa but (Bassett again) "formidable candidate [of] great power and influence."

Against this background of intrigue and uncertainty, Bassett reported to Secretary of State Hamilton Fish (24 February 1874) that Nissage had set his cap at staying on after expiration of his constitutional term on 15 May. "It does not," Bassett perceptively observed, "appear to run in Haitian blood voluntarily to renounce authority once obtained."

In April 1874, with six weeks of Nissage's term remaining, partisans of Domingue and Boyer-Bazelais met secretly to try to arrange things, but to no avail. On 12 April Port-au-Prince had another fire, set, as always in times of political tension, by arsonists. As of the 17th, for once in unison, the ministers of Britain, France, Germany, and the United States asked their governments to send warships to Haiti.

On 9 May, at the head of a large escort, which established itself just outside the city, Domingue rode in uninvited from the South. Bassett reported "the greatest consternation," but still no word came from the National Palace. Two days later, still hoping to head off Domingue, the Senate petitioned Nissage to remain in office provisionally until his successor had been named.

On 12 May, with but three days to go, a self-appointed committee, headed by Thomas Madiou, waited on the aging president. In Bassett's report, "At first he would not listen to them and conducted himself in such an impassioned and boisterous manner that all were about to retire except Mr. Madiou, who with perfect self-command insisted on fulfilling his mission. The President finally listened and they then told him he must retire at the end of his term."

Nissage, mindful of Domingue and his army, faced the facts. Next morning, still in close secrecy, he appointed Domingue commander-in-chief of the army and then submitted his immediate resignation, thus bypassing the legislature and enabling the cabinet to function as a provisional executive.

Domingue, meanwhile, took no chances. On 14 May, wrote Bassett, "the capital awoke to find that several thousand of Domingue's troops had entered the city and stationed themselves on the Champ de Mars. I think I never saw a more determined looking set of men . . . Presently the drums were beaten and the fifes sounded, and the troops were drawn up in long lines through some of the chief streets, and almost everyone thought the critical moment had come."

Such a moment had indeed come, but this time at least not of revolution. Nissage's decision was proclaimed, and along the Grande Rue and Rue des Fronts Forts, merchants slowly began to unbolt their iron doors and shutters.

To the credit of each, Nissage and Domingue arranged the transfer of power with dignity and good order.(5) On the afternoon of 21 May, Bassett reported, Nissage, looking much worn and haggard, left the National Palace accompanied by a large escort of citizens, marched on foot, arm in arm with Gen. Domingue through long lines of military drawn up to do him honor, to the landing place at the seaboard where, after taking affectionate leave of many of his intimate friends, he was embarked for his home at St. Marc aboard the Haitian war steamer, Mount [sic] *Organisé*, with his family and all his personal effects . . . The voluntary retirement of a Chief of State and his open embarkation for his home amid the plaudits of his countrymen has never before transpired in the history of Haiti.

Tyranny and Its Reward

To no one's astonishment, the new Constituent Assembly unanimously elected Michel Domingue president of Haiti. The following Sunday (14 June 1874) he was inaugurated with the traditional Te Deum mass (at which Domingue, both anticlerical and adept in Voodoo, (6) received with stony silence Msgr. Guilloux's sermon of acclaim). Voicing the *ennui* of colleagues for generations to come, Bassett wearily remarked, "These services are felt by all, I think, to be exceedingly tedious, especially as the weather on that day was fearfully hot." Then, describing the new president, Bassett went on:

Domingue is a man of pure African blood . . . Even his grey hair and slight stoop in his shoulders are scarcely an indication of his more than three-score years and ten. In stature he is a little under height, not corpulent but solidly, compactly built, is now and always has been a man of abstemious habit...He is always neat and careful but never extravagant in his dress... French he speaks with ease and general correctness, though with intimate friends he sometimes seems to prefer the easy and flexible Créole . .

St. John's portrait of Domingue said as much about the British envoy himself as the President. The president, wrote the Queen's minister, was "an ignorant and ferocious Negro."

Anténor Firmin, the *Capois* editor, was ambivalent: "At once mild and decrepit," he wrote, "this aged general was capable of fearful decisions."

At the president's elbow, no longer in the shadows, stood his *noir* nephew, Septimus Rameau, one of the most feared men in Haiti. Educated, vain, cruel, suspicious, rapacious, and corrupt, Rameau, at forty-eight, was Haiti's true ruler.

Within two months, by 6 August 1874, the new constitution, based on the 1816 model, was out. The presidential term would run eight years, and there would be a vice-president (Rameau, of course), seized of plenary executive powers. Six days later the assembly authorized a loan of 3 million gourdes, but before this could be floated it was absorbed in a more spectacular transaction.

To establish a national bank, one of Rameau's long-standing ideas, there was now floated a French loan whose exact terms remain a matter of historical confusion.(7) What is in no way confused is that associated payoffs, commissions, *douceurs*, and lagniappe mounted so outrageously that in 1881 even the usurers of Paris (the Crédit-Général Français) felt impelled to remit 15 million francs back to Haiti. This scandal, so monstrous that it horrified even politicians and the elite, was accompanied by storm clouds of lesser scandal, cruelty, and arrests.

These doings were but a prologue to those of May. Under pretext of the traditional parades in celebration of the Fête d'Agriculture (1 May), Lorquet, an old hand at such arrangements, deployed the garrison of Port-au-Prince into three task forces. Their objective was to arrest the generals and erstwhile comrades - Brice, Momplaisir Pierre, and Boisrond-Canal - whom Domingue and Rameau feared most.

Brice, taking advantage of the holiday to clear up correspondence, was at his desk when the soldiers arrived. A glance told him what was afoot. Seizing a pair of revolvers, he dispatched his secretary to warn Boisrond, who was at his country place near Frères. Holding off the soldiers as long as he could, the hero of Jérémie, aged thirty-four, was shot down and mortally wounded as he gained the safety of the English legation. Momplaisir Pierre, better armed and equally resolute, killed seventeen soldiers and wounded twice as many more before a cannon was dragged up and blew him to pieces in his doorway. Warned by Brice, Boisrond rallied a handful of friends and put up such a stout defense that the troops fled. Then, before Lorquet could resume the attack, Boisrond and his brother made a dash for the American minister's residence at the top of Turgeau. Luckier than their fellow victims, they made it. All the soldiers (at times as many as 1200) could do was to ring the American compound, harass those who entered and left, and make the government's displeasure evident to Bassett, who, on 26 June wrote Washington, "Special orders are given to the soldiers around my house to keep up a noisy cry every night from early evening until the next morning for the express purpose of annoying me and my household."

Three weeks later, nerves frayed and patience for once exhausted, Bassett felt compelled to add: "After my long experience here and all efforts made in good faith and all sincerity to cultivate good will and carry out the considerate policy of our government, I am compelled to admit that my colleagues often have reason in dealing sharply with the unreasonable, conceited, and utterly hollow-hearted men who somehow always manage to get control of this government."

For five months, while Domingue and Rameau presided over a carnival of trials, executions, and banishments, the siege of the U. S. legation went on. Only after the Haitian minister in Washington was told that a U.S. warship was on its way to Port-au-Prince did Domingue relent. On 4 October 1875, Bassett was allowed to embark Boisrond and his brother aboard an American brigantine. The refugees ". . . according to a somewhat disagreeable French custom," reported Bassett, "embraced me and then permitted me to retire."

Despite all the regime's countermeasures, the barometer was falling. On 7 March 1876, General Louis Tanis, commandant at Jacmel (hard hit by a hurricane in September, 1875) proclaimed against the government. That very morning, apparently by coincidence, a filibustering expedition launched from St. Thomas by Boisrond-Canal stormed ashore at Jacmel, to be greeted on the quay by Tanis's guard and band and cheering townspeople. A week later, in another comedy of errors, a drunken captain missed Jacmel by 20 miles and landed Boisrond himself and his lieutenants at Saltrou, where the revolution had not yet taken hold. An ambush drove them back aboard ship and nearly killed Boisrond in the bargain. For the moment he retired to Kingston.

As the government concentrated troops on Jacmel, Croix-des-Bouquets, even closer home, revolted on 10 March. Then followed Baradères and Petit Trou. Rameau's response was to cram the jails with hostages, including women and children, and commence executions. Ordered with the government's new navy (8) to blockade and bombard Jacmel, the admiral promptly opened communications with Boisrond-Canal (while prudently saying that for the moment he would maintain the "semblance of blockade" until he had more news of how things were going) and secretly joined the revolution.

The North rose at the beginning of April. On the 12th, St. Marc joined in. Leading a column North from the capital, Lorquet got as far as Arcahaie, took a look at things, faced his army about, and, now the rebel vanguard, marched South on Port-au-Prince. When this news reached Rameau, he told Bassett "that he would put Port-au-Prince to fire and sword and fight over its ashes, that he would teach the whites and mulattoes that the blood of 1804 was still in vigor."

Next day, to prove he meant business, Rameau sent word to General Anselme Prophète, commandant of the arsenal, to lay powder trains and slow matches in readiness to blow up the magazines. Bassett, who learned this "by confidential communication," added that "orders had been given in the view of letting loose upon this and other cities the semi-civilized blacks of the mountains . . . to some of Rameau's favorite black regiments to attack and cut down in the streets or houses every white or colored person they could find, in case the revolution arrived at the gates of the city."

When Lorquet reached Cabaret, Rameau ordered the killing of all hostages, but instead (thus releasing not only the politicals but also 350 common criminals) the jailers threw open the jail and streaked for asylum. Rameau's reply was to announce that the seat of government was transferred to Les Cayes, and thereupon the final act began.

On the afternoon of Easter Eve, 15 April, with Lorquet's advance guard at Croix-des-Missions, Rameau and a few accomplices made for the *Trésor*, as people called his bank, a cast-iron edifice on the site of today's Catholic cathedral. There they began stuffing chests, moneybags, carpetbags, portmanteaux, and every sort of receptacle with money from the vault, and, as fast as they could, hauled their trove to the quay, where a schooner under Dutch colors was waiting. Then, as disorder mounted, Rameau returned to the now virtually deserted National Palace, where he found Domingue awaiting the French minister (Comte de Vorges) and the Spanish chargé, whom he had begged to come and escort him to safety. "The President and Vice President," recounted de Vorges "were huddled in a corner with their families, the objects of every sort of insult and menace by a hostile mob that had already burst in to pillage."

At 4:30, braving a furious crowd led by Momplaisir Pierre's son and Brice's devoted sister, Pauline, the two envoys linked arms with Rameau between them and Domingue clutching de Vorges. Sweating from terror and exertion, Rameau could barely walk: his boots, his pockets, his belt, his shirt front, were logged down with gold coin.

Fifty yards from the safety of the French legation, someone managed to trip Rameau. In a shower of gold pieces the tyrant stumbled and the crowd pounced. There was a sputter of shots, then the thud-crunch of musket butts on flesh and bone, and Pauline Brice, tears streaming, held aloft a handkerchief drenched in Rameau's blood. What was left, the crowd dragged by its heels through the streets, and left to rot in the Grande Rue, penis stuffed between teeth locked in rigor mortis.

The worse for a bayonet stab and a butt stroke, Domingue reached safety.(9) When the mob had done worrying Rameau's carcass, they marched on the home of Lorquet. The general had changed sides too late; his foes found him crouching in a privy and shot him on the spot.

Before the crowds finished looting, it was midday, Easter Sunday. The palace, the homes of Rameau, Lorquet, and their families were pillaged, and so was the *Trésor*, whose rusty iron doors gaped black and empty for twenty years afterward, until it was pulled down to make way for a new cathedral. What remaining money the crowds could not stuff into their pockets, they hurled into the sea.

Laissez Grainnin

On Easter Tuesday (17 April 1876), at the head of a hundred followers, Boisrond-Canal landed at the wharf from Jamaica. He was met by a cheering crowd, who carried him bodily to the cathedral, where Msgr. Guilloux was waiting at the portals to chant a Te Deum and improvise an eloquent sermon to the exceedingly apt Easter text, *"Surrexit sicut dixit"* (He is risen, as he said, Matthew 28:6). Within six days a provisional government was shaped up: besides Boisrond it numbered Florvil Hyppolite, Louis Tanis, and Louis Audain. Two powerful men whose names were missing were Jean-Pierre Boyer-Bazelais and (out of jail and already headed North) Nord Alexis.

More powerful than all, after seventeen years' exile, on 12 May Lysius Salomon stepped ashore in Port-au-Prince. Reporting this development, Bassett said: "Gen. Salomon, whose rare intelligence, commanding presence and manners, as well as his becoming use of elegant language, remind one much of our distinguished countryman, Frederick Douglass, is a black man of high character, of remarkable talents and culture . . . His very name carries with it influence and power . . . Salomon may loom up at no distant day as the star to guide and direct the destinies of this people."

Bassett's presentiment was evidently shared by others, but to them it was a foreboding: within two hours after the great *noir* of Castel Père had installed himself in his sister's home, (10) the national guard (preserve of the elite) stood to arms in the Place de l'Eglise while, in Bassett's words, "the blacks began to look grimly upon this treatment meted out by the hot-headed young mulattoes to the greatest man of their class."

Confronted with what Bassett described as "that most dreaded of all things in Haiti, an open collision between the blacks and mulattoes," the *gouvernement provisoire* temporized, and Salomon, who at that instant assuredly had it in his power to touch off civil war, agreed to withdraw to Jamaica for the time being.

Boisrond, however, faced other accommodations. Even before elections could ratify the latest transfer of power, Nord Alexis, once again secure in the North, revolted on 17 June, proclaiming "decentralization," catchword for secession of the North. Boisrond reacted forcefully. Taking the field himself, he moved two columns against the Cap, one via Gonaïves, the other inland by way of Hinche and Dondon, and sent *St. Michel* (one of the two new war steamers) to blockade and bombard the rebels. Having thus overwhelmed the revolt, Boisrond allowed Tonton Nord to leave his refuge in the American consulate and depart for foreign shores.

Accommodation in Port-au-Prince proved more difficult. The revolution that had swept in Boisrond-Canal was the first triumph of this kind expressly achieved in the name of the Liberal Party (though it of course partook closely of the same ingredients as the revolutions of 1843 and 1859), and as usual the victors were in disarray. Paris-educated Boyer-Bazelais, Geffrard's former aide, was the leader and hero of the Ultra-Liberals (hard-line *mulâtres)* and scoffed at Boisrond, a mere Liberal whose main (and best) school had been administering his large plantation at La Coupe.

It was widely reported that, besides scoffing, Boyer-Bazelais had tried to have Boisrond shot in Jacmel during the latter's botched landing in March 1876. That Boisrond in return sought to heap coals of fire on Bazelais's head availed nothing. When Boisrond offered Bazelais the portfolios of Finance, Commerce, and Foreign Affairs in the new government - in effect, coalition between the moderate and extreme Liberals - Bazelais would have all or nothing.

Boisrond, on the other hand, had the votes. The election was as free as any could remember. Now a very old hand with seven years at his post, Bassett reported to Washington: "In no previous election of any character in Hayti has there ever been any approach to the freedom of expression and choice allowed to the electors in this canvass. No one of them was . . . intimidated or driven or unduly influenced to vote or act against his own simple free will."

Then the American minister added a vignette of the president from Les Cayes, who had spent five months in his legation:

Canal is a mulatto about 44 years of age, in the full vigor of perfect health, of handsome face, erect carriage and manly form . . . A slight but constantly recurring impediment in his speech mars, but does not cover from view, his correct knowledge of his own language. Of a genial, happy temperament . . . he is personally very popular with all classes here, beloved alike by the blacks, the whites, and that ambitious passionate class, the aristocratic mulattoes . . . It is certain, however, that neither he nor any man can in the short space of four years materially change the fixed habits of this people or create this country into a paradise.

Beside fixed habits, there was also the constitution of 1867, and a national legislature determined to apply it in fullest force, not, perhaps, for the country, but certainly against the president. Anténor Firmin called the political situation "bizarre . . . that the same majority [in the legislature] that the country had sent to the Chamber to elect Boyer-Bazelais, then disregarded this imperative mandate by electing his opponent as President - and thereupon immediately lined up behind the former."

What this amounted to, as Firmin went on to say, was that the Liberals simply hamstrung themselves (not to mention the president) while the Nationalist *noirs* awaited the hour when Salomon would return.

Neither party (let alone Boisrond) had a program. As Dantès Bellegarde sadly observed, "In Haiti a political program has no value save that of the man who proposes it. In general, nobody asks a political leader his ideas: his name is enough, or the color of his skin, or the region of his birth."

Jean Price-Mars was more blunt. Of the party politics of these times he wrote: "The color of one's skin in this multi-pigmented country becomes in

Haitian politics a powerful and mysterious symbol which no one ever mentions officially but which is no less . . . a force for association or repulsion. "

During the next two years the legislature swatted at Boisrond and at his Ministers, some of whom, such as the waspish Armand Thoby, made excellent targets. Frustrated at every turn, Boisrond finally adopted Pétion's *laisser-aller*. His slogan, his habitual response, was the Créole phrase *"Laissez grainnin"* (Let the ripe fruit fall where it may; figuratively, Let things take their course).

"Nothing, absolutely nothing, has been done," reported French minister de Vorges. "Every project fails, whether from political crisis, bureaucratic jealousy, or lack of practicality."

Then de Vorges got around to the races:

> The *mulâtres* are more jealous of whites than are the *noirs*. They go on about peasant hatred for foreigners but that really only exists after the peasants have been fanaticized. The misfortune of the *mulâtres* is that their political debut came in 1793: even the way the officers wear their *chapeaux* evokes the volunteers of the Terror . . . In the end you get down to their most disgraceful characteristic, the absolute absence of probity . . . The *noirs,* those who have any hand in affairs, have contracted nearly the same faults as the *mulâtres.* However, lacking the brilliance and mischievous imagination of the *mulâtres,* they have more common sense and practicality, fewer ideas but stick to them. The mass of the people, little removed from a state of nature, are timorous and gentle when not stirred up.

One of the legislature's few constructive actions had been to probe the malodorous French loan of 1875, on which, with considerable justification, Haiti had suspended payment. In March 1877, nonetheless, France recalled de Vorges, who flounced out of Port-au-Prince without taking leave of the president, and replaced him with a mere consul, whose arrival coincided with that of a French warship. With some dignity the legislature replied by unilaterally recomputing the debt down to 21 million francs at the fair interest rate of 6 percent. A year later - it was no longer 1825 - France, which had with reason feared total repudiation of the loan, sent back a minister and recalled its cruisers.

The same year, 1877, was one of trouble with Spain. Madrid's grievance as before was Haitian help for Cuban rebels in the Ten Years' War. When Boisrond was in exile in Jamaica, he had become friendly with Cuban exiles, and, once president, he supported their cause. Haiti's record of aiding Spanish colonial rebellions went back to Pétion, and was of course a sore point with Madrid. In December 1877, accordingly, two Spanish warships steamed into Port-au-Prince, ostensibly to protest Haitian maltreatment of Spanish subjects (which was not inconceivable) but actually to present a bullying ultimatum and require Haiti to salute the Spanish flag. Under Spanish guns, Boisrond had no choice but to comply: as J.-N. Léger caustically noted, Cubans with British support were operating openly in and from Jamaica, but the Spaniards chose to present their ultimatum to Port-au-Prince, not London.

Earlier, in June 1876, Germany had raised the rank of her representation in Haiti and, for the first time, filled the post with a professional diplomat, one Dr. Bernhardt Graser. A year later, in August 1877, Liberia took a similar step, appointing, as consul general and *chargé d'affaires*, Vil Lubin, Soulouque's popular son-in-law.(11) That same month, after eight years in Port-au-Prince (the longest tour of duty by any American chief of mission in Haiti), Ebenezer Bassett resigned, to be succeeded by John Mercer Langston, former acting president of Howard University and later a U.S. Member of Congress. As Bassett sadly took leave on 27 November 1877, he spoke movingly to Boisrond of "this beautiful Hayti on whose soil and among whose people I have passed so many happy days."

Bassett had not been alone in his happiness. On the evening of 10 February 1877, Boisrond, a widower for twenty years, took unto himself an attractive new wife, Wilmina Wilson Phipps.

One of Minister Langston's first reports gives a picture of Haiti's life and commerce. Her imports for 1878 ($8,007,321 - barely less than her exports of $8,234,687) consisted of dry goods, ready-made clothing (American blue denims were sweeping the market), soap, tools (hoes, axes, machetes, picks), hardware, drugs and medicines, crockery, lumber, marble, coal, carriages, brick, butter, cheese, lard, flour, sugar, groceries, salt cod, and wines and liquors.

As 1877 wore into 1878, faction stirred sedition, and sedition soon led to insurrection. On 28 July 1877, Croix-des-Bouquets experienced what Bassett had routinely reported as "a brief insurrectionary attempt." On 10 September, General Diamant seized Fort Edouard and the arsenal at St. Marc, but was put to flight and soon captured. On 16 October there was a brief rising at the Cap. (12) These events were merely a prelude to 1878.

A less trusting chief than Boisrond-Canal would not, in such circumstances, have decided to leave Port-au-Prince for a swing through the South, but, on 18 January 1878, that was what Boisrond did, leaving the city in the hands of Louis Tanis, the military commandant.

On 15 March. word came to Boisrond in distant Jérémie that Tanis, who was a *noir,* and other high conspirators had tried and failed to storm the Port-au-Prince arsenal the night before and had then fallen back on Fort National. The president did not yet know that simultaneous insurrections had also popped throughout the North.

By the time Boisrond returned to the capital aboard *St. Michel,* the revolt was over. Tanis and his fellows were still holed up in Fort National but were ready if not eager to negotiate a stand down in which the insurgents would take asylum and then be eased into exile.(13)

No direct evidence can be found of a nationwide plot coordinated with the Tanis uprising, but it would otherwise be incredible that, within less than twenty-four hours of the latter, there should be revolts in Limonade, La Tannerie (near Milot), and St. Raphaël. All three risings, deep in old *Caco* country, apparently with some support from Nord Alexis in exile, were put down within a matter of days by two energetic generals in the North, Monpoint-jeune and Séïde Télémaque.

That the regime had thus survived its first major challenge may have gone to Boisrond's head: within ten weeks, in June, he asked the Chamber to amend the constitution so as to enlarge the powers of the president and, not surprisingly, extend his term in office beyond the prescribed four years. Boisrond had evidently forgotten that he himself had commanded the firing squad that shot Salnave on charges of tampering with that same constitution. The deputies' memory was longer: they rejected the amendments.

Boisrond had peace of a kind through Christmas and Independence Day (1 January 1879) but not for long. Adhering doggedly to his intention of trying to run the country by the constitution, however events turned out, the president held elections in January for the National Assembly.(14) The result was a hollow victory. By a deal with *noir* Nationalists, who quickly forgot an earlier flirtation with Bazelais's "Ultras," Boisrond won a coalition majority; its real strength lay in a Nationalist-Salomon majority. Even so, for unaccountable reasons, within less than a month there was a fresh *noir* revolt at Gonaïves by Montmorency Benjamin. Boisrond arrived aboard *1804* with fresh troops, rallied the terrified town, and drove Benjamin back into the hills.

Amid these political spasms, a conflagration on 17 February all but leveled Miragoâne, burning down 400 houses and the cathedral. More dreaded than fire, yellow fever revisited Port-au-Prince in April. No respecter of persons, the Yellow Jack claimed, besides uncounted humble dead, French Minister de Rouchechoart and Seguy de Villevaleix, recently the consul general of Peru.

Deadly as in the days of Leclerc, fever scourged Haiti all summer as heat and political tempers soared, too. At three in the hot afternoon of 30 June, tensions snapped among the deputies. Pocket pistols popped across the aisles between *mulâtres* and *noirs;* and, in Langston's words, "At once soldiers, policemen and ordinary citizens, armed, were seen moving in haste, greatly excited, to and fro, apparently in search of some object of attack.

Soon enough the situation clarified. With Bazelais, Hannibal Price, and

Edmond Paul at their head, some 500 liberals, including some of the best families of Haitian society, were in revolt against a liberal *mulâtre* regime. The elite, in a word, were committing suicide.

By nightfall the rebels had established a strongpoint around the Bazelais home on Rue Pavée near Rue du Centre. For three days this neighborhood was battered by desperate street fighting in which two brothers of Bazelais were killed. On 3 July Boisrond brought up artillery to cover sappers, who set fire to the Bazelais house and, for good measure, that of Edmond Paul nearby. The flames were impartial: within two hours the heart of Port-au-Prince was again burned out. Langston put damages at $500,000. The Ministries of Foreign Relations, Interior, Finance, and Commerce and all their archives, the town hall, and government printing office were wiped out. Over 150 persons, including leaders in both houses of the assembly, were killed. At the height of the uproar, under circumstances never explained, the war steamer *1804*, lying in the harbor, blew up with a tremendous whoosh, and, amid this pandemonium, Bazelais and other authors of the uprising slipped away into various legations and within a few days were aboard H.M.S. *Boxer* offshore.

Then in succession the Cap, Gonaïves, and St. Marc sprang to arms in what was race war rather than rebellion. Throughout the Artibonite and North, Nationalist *noirs* battled elite Liberal *jaunes* on nominal behalf of a *mulâtre* regime they were preparing to supersede. Bazelais got to Gonaïves, where he resumed insurrection. The struggle lasted until 17 August, when, with Gonaïves burned to ashes, Bazelais again eluded the government and escaped to Kingston.

Not exactly overthrown but rather pushed aside by his own class, Boisrond-Canal did the only thing he could. With a year of his term to go - after at least eighteen separate uprisings in three years, against the most moderate regime since the days of Pétion - he stood down.

On 17 July 1879, at six in the evening, accompanied by his family and his military suite, the luckless president walked from the National Palace to the quay, where boats awaited to take them aboard a French steamer for St. Thomas. People cheered him all the way (there was a sense he had done the best he could). He raised his hat and bowed left and right. Then, as the boats made for the steamer, the Nationalists made ready for the return of Salomon.

A Cheering Sound of Salvation

On 19 March 1873, in a pastoral letter, Msgr. Guilloux sternly warned the faithful of the pitfalls that surrounded them. Alluding to the "delirious impieties" of the French Revolution, then to the dangerous thoughts of Voltaire, the archbishop moved swiftly into the present: "In 1867 the Anglo-American sect calling itself episcopal took advantage of civil disorders to lay the first stones of a temple in this capital and even printed and distributed a French translation of the Book of Common Prayer. . . . They now flaunt the pretension of founding a national church to which they dare to give the incoherent appellation of a Catholic and Apostolic Haitian Church."

Protestantism was not new in Haiti. As early as 1815, Henry Christophe brought an unnamed Church of England missionary direct to the Royal College at Cap Haïtien and even printed and distributed a French translation of the Book of Common Prayer. In 1817, Pétion invited two Methodist teachers to found a school in Port-au-Prince. Their report described Haiti as "a land where Christianity is unknown, save through the disguise of Popery, and where no cheering sound of Salvation breaks through the horrid silence."

A year later, the Wesleyan Missionary Committee in London opened a mission in Port-au-Prince, which, with ups and downs, flourished over the years. When American Blacks came to Haiti in 1824 and 1861, they too brought Protestantism, Baptist and Methodist, from the United States. In that latter year came also the first Episcopal missionary, the Reverend J. T. Holly, originally of Washington but eventually a naturalized Haitian.

Father Holly, in Bassett's words, "from the very first, strenuously advocated and resolutely persisted in the important policy of raising up a national clergy in Haiti, a policy which never seems to have been thought of by any other religious denomination in this country."

Holly's mission attracted the notice of the American episcopate, which fostered what in 1874 became, with Father Holly's consecration, a Haitian Episcopal Church within the oversight of the parent American church.

The advent of Episcopalianism had obvious attractions for a Haitian government that, in the 1860s and 1870s, often found the concordat irksome and irritating.

With its essentially Catholic liturgy, Anglicanism seemed far less "protestant" and foreign to Haitians. Its dogmas of church-state relations were those from which the Gallicanism of Grégoire (and many prominent Haitians) were directly derived. It was weaker, and therefore less threatening, than the disciplined Catholic ranks of Msgr. Guilloux's archdiocese. As seen by the National Palace and some Haitian leaders, an Episcopal presence offered opportunities for the wedge driving that characterizes Haitian manipulation of competing foreign enterprises.

Besides, as Boisrond pointed out to the National Assembly in 1877, Haiti legitimately required "a body of native priests." Out of 93 Catholic priests (receiving annual government stipends ranging from 20,000 francs for Msgr. Guilloux to 1200 francs for a country curate) 91 were French. Only two Haitian ordinations had resulted from thirteen years' propagation of the faith and proselytization since the concordat, during which time the government was paying to maintain a Breton seminary, Pont-Château in France, for this express object.

Recording a grievance that would echo for years to come in relations between government and Church, Bassett observed, in 1877, "France lost open political control over this island in 1804, but by means of the Roman Catholic clergy she has maintained almost exclusive control over the religious affairs of these people." This issue - ecclesiastical colonialism on the part of the French church - involved fundamental principles as well as deeply felt Haitian sensitivities. On the other hand, just as, in future times, Haitians seemed to make poor communists, so few Haitians seemed inclined to the iron disciplines and austerities demanded by religious vocation. Then, too, in the background there remained the superstitious fear that black baptism might somehow not stick.

Despite recurring difficulties and government bad faith over the concordat, Msgr. Guilloux labored mightily in the Lord's vineyard.

Appointed to his archdiocese on 31 August 1871, after the virtual abdication of Msgr. du Cosquer,(15) Guilloux had, in addition to his own responsibilities in Port-au-Prince, four subordinate dioceses: Cap, Port-de-Paix, Gonaïves, and Les Cayes. There were 66 parishes served by 57 priests, boys' and girls' schools at Port-au-Prince and Jacmel, and of course, the Petit Seminaire, St. Martial, in the capital. By 1877, in spite of fever, fire, and revolution, Msgr. Guilloux had opened new schools in Port-de-Paix, Jérémie, Anse-à-Veau, and Cayes.

With all that was new, old customs died hard. As late as January 1879, Msgr. Guilloux himself had to "baptize" the new iron bridge (it finally collapsed in 1974) at Pont de l'Estère, complete with "godfathers" and "godmothers," while the president and diplomatic corps looked on.

Salomon at Last

When Salomon returned this time, on 19 August 1879, there was little doubt as to who the next president would be. In the wake of Boisrond-Canal's abrupt departure, a caretaker government marked time. Elections were scheduled, or, one might say, arranged, to fill vacant seats in the legislature. On 29 September the returns validated events. The Liberals were utterly defeated.

Within seventy-two hours, the elections were in turn validated by a coup d'état. Headed by General Richelieu Duperval, a loyal front-man for Salomon, a cabal of *noir* officers overthrew the *gouvernement provisoire* during the night of 2-3 October and had the two leaders under lock and key before dawn broke. Next morning, Port-au-Prince discovered it had a new *gouvernement provisoire,* whose chief minister was Lysius Salomon. Within three weeks, the National Assembly had fulfilled its two initial tasks: to revise the constitution so as to give the next president a seven-year term, and to select that official.(16) To no one's astonishment, on 23 October Salomon was chosen by a vote of 74-13.

Three days later, he was inaugurated.

The new president (promptly anathematized by the irrepressible Jacmelian, Alcius Charmant, as "that *Piquet*") has been evoked from childhood memory by a godson, André Chevallier: "A black giant with a bonnet of white hair (like the ogre in 'Tom Thumb') . . . a cottonheaded Goliath of glossy-black face, mountainous nose, he took me on his knees, patted my cheeks, gave me some candy, and slipped a gold piece into my hand."

This remarkable man, not always so avuncular in his dealings, was born in Cayes in 1815. He had been the nightmare of every Haitian regime from Geffrard's to Boisrond-Canal's. But in the words of J. C. Dorsainvil, Salomon was not "one of those ignorant *noirs* our criminal politics have too often hoisted to power . . . Salomon was a statesman of remarkable intelligence and education, honorable, who knew his people and his country from top to bottom, who won over every crowd, and, despite his age, a man of uncommon will power and uncommon energy.

Because of these very powers - and, of course, because he was a *noir* and had the *noirs* of the South in the palm of his hand (and because to the elite he bore the taints of Salnave and Soulouque) - Salomon had been condemned to twenty years' exile. After the fall of Soulouque, first as a private citizen, later (in the Haitian way) as ambassador-in-exile in Paris and London, he had read widely, studied deeply, traveled, and learned the world. In Paris he had married a Frenchwoman, Louise Magnus. Banishment and proscription had etched his character: Salomon's spirit was hard as iron, and, toward his enemies, the elite of Port-au-Prince, there was no mercy in his heart. Salomon had reasons: in the seventeen years since 1862, political foes in power had shot his two brothers, two uncles, his adopted son, and his brother-in-law.

Louis-Félicité Lysius Salomon-jeune (17) was the first president since Geffrard, his mortal enemy, to enter the *Palais National* with a program. He intended, if he could, to restart public education (an objective of Boisrond-Canal that Bazelais's elitist legislature had cynically balked), to put Haiti's finances on a sound basis, to restore agricultural productivity, to improve the army, and to upgrade public administration. Salomon, in short, was that rarity among Haitian chiefs of state, a modernizer, and, in his grim way, socially conscious as well. His aims (indeed, his methods) were those Henry Christophe would well have understood.

Eleven years as Soulouque's Finance Minister had not gone for nothing: the new president's first efforts were directed toward fiscal reform. "Our credit is ruined," Salomon bluntly told the country in a trenchant speech on 30 November 1879. Within four months the president had hammered legislation through the assembly to establish a national bank - no thieves' rathole like Rameau's *Trésor*, but a central bank of orthodox function, government depository, disbursing office, source of currency, and, it was hoped, an attraction for foreign capital. A consortium of seventeen French bankers with 10 million francs would capitalize and govern the enterprise. Léon Laforestrie, the Finance and Foreign Minister, was off to Paris in April. On 13 May 1880, *Le Moniteur* proudly announced receipt of a cable from France that his mission had succeeded.(18)

Salomon's solicitude for the national credit and his desire to regularize Haitian finances were realized through measures other than the *Banque*. In July 1880, he resumed payments to France not only on the Domingue loan (as revised) but on the 1825 millstone.

On the latter, the president managed to pay up all arrears and, before the very end of his regime, in 1888, liquidated the entirety. This performance (as well as the issue of a hard national coinage, authorized by law on 24 September 1880, and then struck in the Paris mint, of gold, silver, and copper) was one of the main factors influencing French financiers to underwrite the *Banque*.

Salomon the Francophile is revealed in his instinctive inclination to France (instinctive as, and not unlike, Henry's toward England) for help in modernization.

On 1 June 1880, Haiti adhered to the International Postal Union and, by a statute of 7 October of that year, authorized its first postage stamps, which, like the coins, were designed by Laforestrie and made in France. To make postal service a reality, Salomon obtained a mission of two French post-office specialists.

Besides bringing Haiti into the world postal system, the president also took up a project of Boisrond's, unattended since 1879: the grant of a concession to a British company to lay a cable connecting Port-au-Prince and Kingston. (Seven years later, in 1887, one of Salomon's last actions was to negotiate the contract for the cable linking Môle St. Nicolas with Santiago de Cuba.)

With the support of the French legation, the government recruited a cadre of French teachers for the *Lycée Pétion*, which Salomon refurbished, re-equipped, and brought to high standing. These teachers brought with them not only the classical standards of French public education but also its rigidities. Their influence was destined to carry over into the next century the dead hand of a system too inflexible and pedantic for even the mother country.

Working through French advisers and two able Ministers of Education (François Manigat and Pierre-Charles Archin), Salomon improved the other two *lycées,* at the Cap and Cayes, reopened numerous rural schools (though still not enough to begin to meet requirements; in 1877, there were but 19,250 pupils enrolled in all the public and private schools of Haiti), resurrected the defunct law school, and resuscitated the moribund medical school.(19)

A three-officer French military mission - the first such mission to come to Haiti - arrived in 1880. At their recommendation, on 6 October 1880, the president reorganized and enlarged the Armed Forces to a strength of 16,000, assigned to thirty-four infantry regiments; four artillery regiments; arsenals at the capital, Cap, Cayes, Jérémie, Gonaïves, St. Marc, and Jacmel; and, most important, an 1800-man Presidential Guard modeled on Geffrard's *Tirailleurs*, embodying the only mounted troops in the country. Like the military academy concurrently provided for by law, most of this force (save for its numerous generals and, of course, the Presidential Guard) remained a paper organization.

But the military mission left its mark (20) in uniforms and equipment, including the dread Belgian and French *mitrailleuses* - machine guns - which now entered Haiti's armament and were prudently sited to cover approaches, entrances, and interior passages of the National Palace. In addition, from this time on, a trickle of elite young men received appointments to St. Cyr, Saumur, and the Ecole Polytechnique in Paris. Here, for the first time, the army, hitherto largely a preserve of the *noirs,* began to have its officer corps infused with foreign-schooled elite *jaunes.*

Only thirteen years earlier, in 1867, the strength and grade distribution of the army had been reported by St. John as 6500 general officers and staff, 7000 officers of other grades, and 6500 enlisted men. *"Tout Haïtien qui n'est pas général de division, "* ran the phrase, *"est au moins soldat"* (Any Haitian who isn't a two-star general is at least a private). When Salomon took office, things had not changed. In his speech of 30 November 1879, the president admitted his embarrassment that "revolutions have made every Haitian a general." Writing of this time and phenomenon, Jean Price-Mars later observed, "For a century it had always been the army that had dominated the evolution of the nation. The result of this had been government by corporals."

In a long passage, abridged here, Anténor Firmin wrote more mordantly of the army:

Military service is a penalty inflicted only on the rural peasantry . . . The son of an elite family expatriates himself so as to evade military service and feels proud to tell of it in a Paris salon . . . With no instruction, illiterate. ignorant of drill or evolutions, our pitiful soldiers, able to march only in a body, comprise the pariahs of our demi-barbarism. They are neither quartered, clothed, nor cared for like human beings. They don't have barracks worth inhabiting, even in the capital: except on parade no clothing except miserable tatters bought out their own pockets. They are lucky to receive rations one day out of three while they labor without pay on jobs for the officers or their cronies . . . When a Haitian wearing epaulets says, "I am a soldier!" that only means he is ready to commit the most horrible crimes, to loot, to burn, or to kill, when ordered by a superior.

Only too well aware of the materials he had to work with, Salomon, accompanied by an imposing force of soldiery, set out to instruct the country in person, to make his presence felt, and to drive home - in a series of nationwide visits unprecedented on the part of Haiti's Port-au-Prince chiefs of state - his ideas for a new and better Haiti. In Jacmel, his own Cayes, throughout the North, he traveled from town to town with the same message: "Revolution must be forever blotted out. Revolutions have debased and destroyed the vitals of the nation." Sometimes the president spoke more sharply, as when he smelled disaffection at the Cap in March 1881: "Evil to you if a single musket goes off in this town . . . It will signal events beyond precedent in all our revolutionary annals. Once the people's anger is let loose, I will be powerless to recall them to their senses."

I Have Been Pushed to Extreme Measures

Salomon was no fool. He knew his countrymen and, above all, he knew his opponents. Toward the end of his regime, in 1888, Salomon remarked: "There is a difference between Soulouque and me, that the police used to come and tell him everything, whereas it is I who provide the police the information they need to keep watch on this individual or that."

Only four months after the inauguration Salomon's antennae quivered: the Kingston refugees were in communication with Liberal allies in Port-au-Prince, while the Cap, never happy under a president from the South, was uneasy. On 5 April 1880, without warning, Salomon arrested Nord Alexis and deftly swept up an assortment of opponents in both cities. Ten weeks later, during the night of 15-16 June, some "persons of prominent social position" (Langston), that is, mostly Bazelais *mulâtres,* were caught in another swoop whose most prominent and unexpected catch was none other than Richelieu Duperval, who months before had paved Salomon's way into office. (Duperval, popular in Port-au-Prince, was, like Toussaint, lured into the country on a false errand and seized.)

On 20 November, profiting by the president's absence on a swing into the South (where, as Salomon pointed out, he visited Saltrou, Marigot, and Bainet, towns no predecessor, and hardly any successor, ever entered while in office), General Mentor Nicholas broke house arrest in Port-au-Prince and headed for St. Marc. Nicolas ("whose criminal ways I know well," Salomon afterward remarked) had plans for a coup. Instead, when he reached his destination, he was met by General Turenne Levieux, town commandant, who had already locked up thirty-five of Nicolas's fellow conspirators and was simply awaiting the latter's arrival.

Yet on the horizon loomed certain clouds. For one thing, wrote Langston on 31 December 1880, "the government and country are without money." Salomon had drained every resource to pay off Haiti's ransom to France, where

Laforestrie's negotiations for the *Banque Nationale* were at a critical stage. Other engagements might go unheeded, but every *sou* of the French debt was being paid. In February 1881 the government suspended interest payments on all bonds but those of France. Then, a final slash: prudently excepting the army and police, Salomon stopped all government salaries until Laforestrie could return from Paris with the *Banque* in his portmanteau. To heighten hardship, the fall coffee crop of 1880, though bounteous and fine, was wasted on a poor world market.

On 24 June 1881, at 2:00 A.M., after a season of signs and portents, the heavens brightened portentously. Encke's Comet, reported Langston, "in the midst of a most magnificent tropical sky, was beautiful and impressive beyond description . . . Whence does it come? Where does it go? What is its mission? Is its augury good or evil?"

Such questions were not well received in the National Palace. People who recalled similar apparitions in the heavens that had preceded the fall of Soulouque were pointedly told to keep their recollections to themselves. At the Cap, which spent an uneasy night with the comet overhead, townsmen next morning found walls and houses bearing the legend "*A bas Salomon! Vive la Révolution!*" That very night in Port-au-Prince, Croix-des-Bossalles was illumined by earthly fire: the offices and barns of the new American horse-car company went up in flames. Within sixteen days there were four more fires, and on 29 August most of Cayes burned to ashes. ("It is proverbial here," wrote Langston, "that revolutionary movements are preceded by fires.")

Then, nurtured in filth and congestion, came smallpox. The first outbreak appeared in Port-au-Prince during December, and spread rapidly throughout the country. With many if not most cases admittedly unreported, Port-au-Prince authorities were nevertheless soon recording as many as 258 deaths a week, and Msgr. Guilloux wrote on 28 January of the new year that, not counting bodies dumped in La Saline, over 60 burials a day were taking place. Throughout the capital, every house seemed to display the white flag of plague ordered by the government. Nine days later, confirming his Catholic colleague, Pastor Picot, the Wesleyan missionary, reported: "I don't think there is a single home in town that isn't pest-ridden. Smallpox, scarlet fever, and typhoid rage simultaneously throughout every street in the city, and the roll of the dead is truly terrifying. They buried 105 today alone." Not until May 1882 did the epidemic subside; it would be 1883 before it was fully spent.

With sickness in the noonday came sedition by dark. In the night of 8 December 1881, Désormes Gresseau, fellow general and confederate of Mentor Nicolas, seized the arsenal at St. Marc and proclaimed revolution. Rising from a sickbed, Turenne Levieux again earned the president's thanks by retaking the arsenal and sweeping the rebels from town. Caught with arms in their hands, two of Mentor's brothers, as well as relatives of Armand Thoby, were summarily shot. But this was only the beginning. Declaring martial law in Port-au-Prince, St. Marc, and the Liberal stronghold of Jacmel, (21) Salomon made hundreds of arrests. Forty-eight of the chief prisoners were taken to St. Marc, tried in April 1882, and sentenced to death. The president reprieved twenty: the other twenty-eight, including Mentor Nicolas, were shot in batches at St. Marc and Gonaïves on 5 and 6 May. Those whom Salomon spared he retained as hostages to ensure the good behavior of antagonists in exile. In the words of *L'Oeuil*, a journal of the regime, on 20 May 1882: "Each pamphlet sent into Haiti will provoke the execution of one more of those condemned to death by the special military court of St. Marc."

The court in St. Marc was still grinding out death sentences when, on 12 April, the president, accompanied as always on such trips by his wife, by most of the cabinet, and by two shiploads of soldiers, moved into the North, where conspiracy and trouble were brewing. With Tirésias Simon Sam at their head, chief men not only of the Cap but of Port-de-Paix, Marmelade, Grande Rivière, and Fort Liberté, were brought before Salomon for an audience on 16 April. The president minced no words:

> I'm not here for the pleasure of visiting you but to perform a duty imposed on Me by the presidency . . . The situation of this city leaves very much to be desired . . . . Every time the post from the Cap arrives, I have to call together all My ministers, something I never have to do when I hear from the rest of the country . . . All by itself, the Cap obstructs the progress of the entire republic . . . I am the president of Haiti and not of just one part of the republic. Regardless of the price, I do not intend that there be two republics inside this country . . .(22)

Simon Sam broke in with protestations of loyalty. His reply was an icy rebuff: the president knew who his enemies were (out of forty-two young blades arrested at this time, wrote Firmin, twenty-nine were destined to be killed under Boyer-Bazelais at Mirogoâne, two years later.) Meanwhile, arrests continued and more regiments arrived from Port-au-Prince.

Exactly a week later (23 April), the president repeated himself to the assembled populace on the Champ de Mars

> *Mes amis*, I have come to break all horns . . III betide the Cap if a single shot is fired. That shot would be the signal for massacre, incendiarism, and, I will add, for I want to be truthful, pillage . . . Haven't I done more for the Cap than any other part of the country - Aux Cayes, for example? . . . Soldiers! Isn't it right you should be paid before civilian employees? The money has been sent here to pay you; if you haven't been paid, it is because the funds have been diverted to other pockets..... Wrongdoers have said I wish to have Myself proclaimed emperor..... If in 1848 it was an error to found an empire in Haiti, today it would be insanity .

. . Let us ensure that not a shot is fired here. Blood that flows from explosion of powder is a heady drink. Those who commence to drink of it are devoured by thirst . . . Let us be careful not to arouse the anger of the people . . . *Mes amis,* I pray, I entreat you, I adjure you - support Me in My work of pacification. Be My disciples, preach to all: Peace, Union, and Concord.

The foregoing conveys only the flavor of a 5000-word address in which Salomon carefully explained his program, defended the *Banque,* urged cultivation of the soil, replied, point for point, to calumniating pamphleteers, and balanced warm appeals for national effort and unity against the grimness that lay in his power.

That this was no mere rhetoric, Salomon then proceeded to demonstrate by extending his state of siege to the Cap, Fort Liberté, and Trou du Nord and summarily ordering forty-three more arrests. On returning to Port-au-Prince on to May, he said: "I have been pushed to extreme measures. Well, since I have had to begin, I shall continue. Peace is necessary, cost what it may."

The Liberal Insurrection

No one could say Salomon had failed to warn his enemies. More than any other ruler in the history of Haiti, he had gone untiringly to the country and made his voice heard in the land. They that have ears, he said, let them hear. Only the Liberals would not listen.

In one of the might-have-beens with which the story of Haiti is littered, Dantès Bellegarde was to muse:

> In the opposing factions were men remarkable for education, experience of affairs, integrity. Never before could Haiti have presented so fine a showing: Salomon, Boyer-Bazelais, Edmond Paul, Démesvar Delorme, Armand Thoby, Turenne Carrié, Louis Audain, Hannibal Price, Camille Bruno, Jean-Baptiste Dehoux, François and Guillaume Manigat, Victorin Plésance, Mathurin Lys, and a younger set which Geffrard's educational efforts had prepared for public life. By cooperation these men could have assured the prosperity and dignity of their country.

It was not to be. On 23 March 1883, the little American steamer S.S. *Tropic,* anchored in the secluded harbor of Mathewtown, Inagua, and embarked some seventy Haitian exiles. Next day the expedition, for such it was, rendezvoused at sea with a smaller British ship, *Albo,* from Jamaica, which carried a detachment headed by Jean-Pierre Boyer-Bazelais. As the rosters were excitedly checked off and arms distributed and test-fired, the party - Liberals all, some by conviction, others by opportunism - was seen to include such names as Désormes Gresseau (who had eluded Salomon in 1881), Boileau Laforest, Gélus Bien-Aimé, Mathurin and another Legros, no less than five Rigauds, two Chenets, and a host of other well-known persons, not to mention four pickup Cuban revolutionaries, who added color and, since they spoke little if any French, considerable confusion to the operation.

The objective was Miragoâne, chosen because it dominated the road net of the Southern peninsula and enjoyed communications across the mountains with Côtes de Fer, Bainet, and Jacmel, a region where the rebels had friends and sympathizers. Not least important, Miragoâne was old Boileau Laforest's home town, and *the piquets* of its hinterland had been his men.

Before dawn on 27 March the landing party scrambled ashore at Source salée, a mile West of the town. Not having much experience in such work, most of the participants simply took off their shoes in the boats or let them float out to sea, leaving this elegant force - surely the first Haitian army where all hands wore shoes - barefooted, a complaint (or, more accurately, a condition) that was to echo through the siege to come. (23)

By the best count, ninety-two rebels got ashore and were reinforced by sixty or seventy enthusiastic recruits from Miragoâne. The garrison had fled and the town was secured without resistance. Boyer-Bazelais's first act was to proclaim a Central Committee of the Revolution (the manifesto had already been printed in Kingston), with himself, after the manner of 1843, as *chef d'exécution*. Calls for support were sent to neighboring Nippes, Anse-à-Veau, and the Goâves, at all of which the local authorities prudently waited to see what would happen.

Salomon, always well served by his spies, had timely intelligence: the rebels' secrets had been ill kept. The president heard within forty-eight hours of the sailings from Kingston and Mathewtown; he knew the role of the *Tropic* (24)(which had sailed from Philadelphia carrying Boyer-Bazelais's arms); he was even able to estimate rebel strength as 106, a creditably close count. Commencing in March, Salomon doubled security and stepped up arrests.

Though momentarily repulsed, government forces now surrounded Miragoâne, and Salomon's navy lay offshore. Without the *Tropic,* retreat was impossible.

One clear chance remained: on 6 May, with the backing of the diplomatic corps, the president sent his crony and favorite, Burdel, the French chargé, to Miragoâne with a final offer: protection after surrender, safe-conduct into exile, and government assumption of the debts of the rebellion. Bazelais haughtily dismissed Salomon's emissary and thus sealed his own death warrant.

Although the main rebel force was hemmed in and would remain so, Salomon had ample reason to want to end the uprising as quickly as possible, for the Liberals had sympathizers in every town.

On 13 April, rising as they had against Salnave, the *Cacos* of Trou du Nord revolted against his inheritor. Now the government's precautions in the North paid off. The *Cacos* were brutally squelched. In the South it was another story. On 27 May, a Sunday of fierce fighting, which Charles Desroches, forlorn diarist of Miragoâne, called "the most terrible day we have endured," Jérémie rose. Assessing this development, Langston wrote: "Jérémie is as strong if not stronger in its natural defenses than Miragoâne, while its inhabitants, more intelligent, active, and determined than the people in any other part of the country, are earnestly opposed . . . to President Salomon."

Having first put down still another uprising in Aquin, Salomon, who had received a shipment of Gatling guns and repeating rifles from Remington and Winchester, sent troops and a ship to Jérémie. Then he declared the entire Grande-Anse, from Tiburon to Jérémie, in a state of siege and blockade.

Even as government troops tried without success to overwhelm the Jérémiens, they were repeatedly attacked from the rear by enemy forces, which had captured Pestel and Corail. Nor was the blockade effective. From Kingston, a merchant ship, S.S. *Alvena,* ran in a large cargo of arms to the defenders in Jérémie.

Worse still was to come. On 22 July, while the broken-backed Miragoâne siege dragged on in discouragement and dysentery, Jacmel exploded. The very night after Salomon's military secretary, Veriquain, had visited the city with Dessalinian warnings ("I will ride in blood," he said, "up to my horse's breastplate") forty-four bold Liberals, led by Barjon and Normil Chicoyé, seized the arsenal and military posts and threw Vériquain and all of Salomon's people into jail. The only man quick enough to get away was the indestructible Mérisier Jeannis, a hardy veteran of the fighting of 1868, who scrambled over a wall and out into the countryside before the elite young men could catch him.

With the *Cité vaillant, fière et libre"* (the evocation of Jacmel by Charles Moravia, half-British poet and editor *of La Plume)* went Côtes de Fer and Bainet. Salomon's reply was to send *800 piquets* volunteers whom Charmant scornfully called "va-nu-pieds" [barefoot vagabonds] swept up in Port-au-Prince - to Mérisier.

Armed only with spears, pitchforks, and machetes, the *piquets* made their first attack during the night of 2-3 August. In a desperate struggle that swirled around Jacmel's Masonic lodge, Parfaite Sincérité, and thus ever after known as the battle of Derrière-la-Loge (behind the lodge), the combatants hacked and blew each other to pieces. As dawn broke, with the assault thrown back, the Jacmeliens saw ". . . heaped-up wounded and corpses drenched in blood, chests smashed in, sides ripped open, eyeballs gouged, arms cut off, and skulls and stomachs laid open."

Every home in every quarter, Charmant said, had someone to mourn, and the city's rage was uncontrollable. At ten that morning, Vériquain and thirteen other government hostages (25) were dragged from prison to the Marché Geffrard and shot.

Led this time by Manigat, who had been recalled by Salomon from Miragoâne, government forces tried once more, on 17 September, to carry Jacmel by storm, but once again, despite another ferocious attack by Mérisier and his *piquet "rasoirs,"* crying " *Vive Salnave! Vive Salomon!,"* the defenders prevailed. After this, as at Miragoâne and Jérémie, Salomon determined to let hunger and blockade do what frontal attack could not.

Semaine Sanglante

By mid-September 1883, Salomon was fighting for life. Aside from the dire imperatives of rebellion, the struggle was also costing money, money the country needed if the president was ever to get on with modernizing Haiti.

Close to home, closer even than Jacmel, there were danger signals. In the night of 7 August Port-au-Prince suffered another raging conflagration, which burned down hundreds of houses in Bel Air.

Was 1883 a second 1869, questioned the elite, and Salomon merely another Salnave? Salomon knew well what they were saying, and had his answer prepared.

At ten o'clock on Saturday morning, 22 September, General Pénor Benjamin, town commandant of Port-au-Prince, was assassinated in his office by a troupe of twenty or thirty elite students from the schools of law and medicine (the latter a notorious nest of Bazelaisism). When the capital failed to respond to their cries of "A *bas Salomon ! Vive la Revolution!"* the young murderers made a run for the Spanish consulate (then located in what later became the Hotel de France).

Within an hour, troops stood to arms and *noir "volontaires" (zinglins* no longer) converged on the National Palace, where officers handed out weapons and ammunition. When a young *mulâtre* asked for a musket, he was ominously informed, "*On ne donne pas de fusils aux bourgeois.*"

On the steps of the palace, surrounded by ministers and flanked by Mme. Salomon and his fierce sister, Irma, stood the president. Shots began to resound; then came the cry of fire, and a pillar of black smoke rose up from the corner later occupied by the establishment of Henri Deschamps (Grand Rue and Bonne Foi). When Salomon saw the smoke, he was heard to murmur, "*Ah! On exécute mes ordres*" (They're doing what I told them to do).

The French minister, Burdel (26), saw general officers and members of the president's staff with kerosene and torches setting fire to the houses of their enemies. Caught in the act of lighting off a building adjacent to the French legation, one of Salomon's aides-de-camp was frightened away when Burdel and a clerk went after him.

All afternoon, soldiers, *volontaires*, and *noirs* of La Saline and Bel Air (homeless themselves from the fire of 7 August) rampaged through the business district, looting, burning, and, when victims were found, killing. "The amount of property destroyed was immense," Langston reported. "The very heart of the city, where the best and most valuable buildings, aggregating hundreds, were located, was left a charred and ghastly waste."

When the flames and smoke loomed over the capital, the men of the mountains and the Cul-de-Sac knew their hour had come. Into the city they swarmed, with old muskets, pikes, and machetes. French wine, fine rum, *clairin, taffia,* all were the same. To the throb of the drum and the hoot of the *lambi,* recalled one eyewitness, peasants danced the carmagnole as if it were 1793. As Sunday morning broke, the fury momentarily seemed to have spent itself. But still greater wrath was to come.

Soon after daybreak an angry rumor swept the city. For once *telediol* told truth: Henri Piquant, Salomon's Minister of War, had been mortally wounded by the Bazelaisists at Miragoâne, and the steamer bearing him back to the capital was at the wharf. Within an hour he was dead.

What now erupted made past violence seem like child's play. Supplied with kerosene, *lances-à-feu,* and muskets, rioters fanned through the remaining commercial streets and neighborhoods where the elite lived. Troops with cannon shelled residences (such as the sturdy Théagéne Poulle home, where numerous *mulâtres*, including Frédéric Marcelin, had gathered for refuge). Soon the whole Grande Rue was in flames, and mobs raged up Rue Fronts Forts, pillaged in Salnave's day and now the stronghold of Bazelais sentiment. *Mulâtres* were killed on sight, and elite ladies, Bazelais to the core, clawed cursing market women bent on the vengeance of Salomon.

Better prepared than the day before, the peasants brought in donkeys laden with straw sacks and panniers. When the holocaust reached the Magasin Alexandre Bobo, richest of the Paris importers, the mob battered in the iron shutters, surged among the counters, and only when they had been stripped were torches applied. Alfred Jean, an eyewitness, wrote:

One saw bolts of embroidery, rich carpets, on the backs of donkeys, dragging in the dust. Long after this saturnalia, the women of the plain wore French dressing gowns when taking part in Voodoo ceremonies . . . Some donned richly bedecked hats and shawls, while dead-drunk men were decked out with Gibus hats, overcoats, and open parasols. Women made off with umbrellas of every kind and price for Sunday mass at Croix-des-Missions . . . Scoundrels of the town staggered out, some with

boxes of shirts, packets of underwear, cashmere suits, hats, footwear from the great
establishments of Paris . . . while others lugged out pendants, jewels, expensive
watches, that fences bought for low prices - the ruin of Haitian business, by
Haitians!

As the fury fed itself, foreigners were lucky to escape with their lives. The
Reverend C. W. Mossell, Methodist missionary and an American mulatto, later
deposed:

> Our house was entered by soldiers armed with machetes, guns, revolvers, knives,
> clubs, and swords . . . We lost everything, furniture, clothes, provisions, piano,
> books, jewelry, records, and money. What they did not carry off they destroyed and
> burned. As we were leaving the house in the greatest distress, they pulled out of our
> hands all small packages containing valuables. [Then] they set the house on fire.

Under the eyes of Mossell's pregnant wife, soldiers shot down the midwife
and her son, as well as an eight-year-old who attended the mission school and
had sought safety with the Mossells. Mrs. Mossell delivered prematurely; the
baby died.

Surrounding the home of E. V. Garrido, Haitian chief clerk of the American
consulate, other soldiers opened fire when, like Mossell, he displayed an
American flag. Garrido dashed for safety under the roof of his distinguished
neighbor, the geographer Sémextant Rouzier, and there watched *volontaires* burn
his house.

Rolling flames consumed the Ministries of Foreign Affairs, Finance, and
Commerce; and all government records - effectively, the archives of Haiti -
were once again completely wiped out.

Salomon was now in a strange state. Burdel, who knew him well, went to the
palace and described the scene in a confidential report:

> The President was in bed, gripped by a fearful delirium *[transport au cerveau]*. This
> colossal man was thrashing about with despair, lashing out or smashing with
> powerful hands at anything within reach . . . Mme. Salomon, whom he did not
> recognize, huddled in a corner, restraining her anguish, while the sick man's friends
> made every effort to control him. Noticing on a table a vial of chloral I had sent
> him a fortnight earlier for the insomnia he complained of, I made him take a stiff
> dose, followed by two more. Then a dose of potassium bromide finally put him to
> sleep.

Late Sunday, watching from offshore, the captains of British, French, and
Spanish men-of-war (no U.S. ship was present) sent the senior officer, Captain
Courrejolles of the French cruiser *Chasseur,* ashore to his minister. In so many
words the naval officer told Burdel: "If you can't go to the palace and tell
Salomon to put a stop to this fire and pillage, we're going to land Marines and

bombard the Palace."(27) Burdel hastily assembled the diplomatic corps. The result was a terse communication, signed by the representatives of France, Britain, Germany, Belgium, Spain, Holland, Norway, and Sweden, (28) which read as follows:

> *President*: If the pillage, incendiarism, and murder being committed since yesterday in the capital by the soldiers of the Government, and particularly by the mob, do not cease before night, the vessels of war in the harbor will take such measures as they judge necessary; that is to say, they will find themselves under the necessity of sweeping the streets of the one and the other, but moreover will be under the dire necessity of bombarding the forts and even your palace, where sufficient troops should be found to restore the necessary order and tranquillity in the capital.

Salomon received this ultimatum at eight on Monday morning, even as the European landing forces debarked over the quay. By noon, as abruptly as it had begun, all disturbance ceased.

Even though the outburst lasted less than three days, the *semaine sanglante* (Bloody Week), as it became known, took uncounted lives (some Haitian estimates go as high as 4000, mostly *jaunes),* and, in foreign indemnities alone, ultimately cost the government $588,418. Worse still, as Dantès Bellegarde pointed out, "it evoked the most evil passions in all hearts. The most atrocious of all was the prejudice of color, which regained the virulence of 1804 . . ." In the words of Pastor Picot: "This struggle is a war of color, *noirs against mulâtres* - a war of extermination. Among all the merchants in the capital there weren't two *noirs.* Hence the government ordered the destruction of the business district of the city."

That an enlightened president - and Salomon was an enlightened man - could find, or feel, that he had to destroy the heart of his own capital and wipe out the lives and property of his country's most prosperous and best-educated citizens starkly illuminates the sad and profound division of the country, and indicates, in reality, that Haiti still amounted to two interlocking but irreconcilable nations, one elite and *mulâtre,* the other *noir* and primitive.

Malheurs sans Nombre

Salomon's terrible revenge broke the back of the Liberals. Barely a month later, on 27 October, worn out by siege, bickering lieutenants, and dysentery that would not stop, Boyer-Bazelais expired in the ruins of Miragoâne. Hemmed in by land, bombarded and blockaded by sea, his followers hung on.

Back in August the rebels had bought and armed an old British steamer (R.M.S. *Eider)* and renamed her *La Patrie.* For two months, despite Salomon's attempt to have her declared a pirate (which the great powers would not countenance), *La Patrie* ranged the Gulf of Gonâve and both sides of the Southern peninsula. In mid-November, after her complete purchase price had been paid in cash (a formality that had kept her immobilized at anchor for six weeks previous), Salomon's newly acquired *Dessalines,* under an American commander, put to sea and ran down *La Patrie* along the South coast. Although *Dessalines* failed to sink the Liberal cruiser, she drove her into Jacmel, full of holes and never to sail again. Salomon celebrated this victory on 19 and 21 November by naval bombardments of Jérémie and Jacmel. (From the latter the German warship S.M.S. *Freya* evacuated 150 women and children to Jamaica.) *"Des malheurs sans nombres vous attendent"* (Misfortunes beyond number are waiting for you), the president warned the Jacmeliens.

On 1 December the defenders of Miragoâne took a sad ballot: of fifteen leaders, nine voted to surrender, six to fight on. Four days later, Mathurin Legros, the Gonaïves lawyer now in command, asked the diplomatic corps to arrange capitulation. What Salomon would have welcomed in April, he adamantly rejected in December. Let them apply directly to him and to no intermediary, he replied. The meaning was clear: the siege dragged on.

Elsewhere, resistance was flickering. Jérémie surrendered on 26 December. That same day, led by Jean Vital, representing the United States, the consuls in Jacmel escorted Liberal emissaries through the lines to Manigat's headquarters. The terms seemed generous: exile for the leaders, amnesty for all others. The government army marched in on 31 December; four days later, "in a wholesale manner" (Langston), executions, not amnesty, were meted out. At least forty-seven persons were shot in batches.

On 8 January of the new year, the able-bodied defenders of Miragoâne, with Mathurin Legros and Boileau Laforest at their head, cut their way out and made for the hills, leaving behind 12 too weak to move; of whom 11 were promptly shot when the besiegers took possession. Pursued for their lives, the fugitives made contact with remnants from Bainet in the fastnesses of Morne St. Eloi behind Petit-Goâve. Down in the bay they could see foreign traders at anchor. On the 13th the survivors made a run for it, but the way to the ships was barred; the garrison had been forewarned, and only a handful slipped through. Boileau Laforest, like Goman, was never seen again; Legros was captured, interrogated, and shot. In a grim roster kept by Anselme Prophète's military secretary up to 3 February 1884, 113 executions were logged by name at Miragoâne alone, while at Petit-Goâve, where records were not so tidy, 25 rebels were either killed in action or shot impromptu, and 12 more were accorded the formality of a firing squad.

Thus, in utter futility as it had begun, ended the Liberal insurrection. On 17 January, Salomon embarked aboard *Dessalines* to visit the Goâves, Miragoâne, Jérémie, and Jacmel. Those who had survived the terrible year in the beaten cities seemed - at length - more ready to listen when the president spoke.

Inflation, Peculation, Reconstruction

In a perverse way, Bazelais had won. By clawing the country apart, by forcing the government to spend millions for arms and defense, by killing commerce, by polarizing society and the races, the insurrection inflicted wounds on Salomon and his programs - and on Haiti - that could never be healed.

Paper money and inflation followed on the heels of rebellion. On 6 October 1884, 2 million gourdes were contracted to be run off by an American banknote company for a fee of $45,000.

A second blow to the credit of the regime that fall was *l'Affaire des Mandats*, a gamy scandal in the National Bank that ultimately implicated its French director (Vouillon), its British chief accountant (Coles), alleged French and British confederates, and a ring of Haitian accomplices. When it turned out that Vouillon's testimony might embarrass the government, he was allowed to slip out of the country. Coles and a Frenchman, Clouchet, were convicted and jailed until British and French pressure secured their release. An unfortunate American lawyer retained by the *Banque's* Paris office suddenly found all charges extended to him as well as his clients, and spent 283 days in the common jail until, on forceful remonstrance by the American legation, he was released.

The modus operandi of the embezzlers could have succeeded only in Port-au-Prince.

Due bills *(mandats)* issued by government departments and redeemed by the *Banque* were, rather than canceled or mutilated, simply filed in a certain coffer. At the propitious moment during any given riot, insurrection, or conflagration, thieves would steal into the *Banque* and spirit away the coffer, whereupon accomplices in the streets would raise the cry *"Flambez la Finance!"* (Burn down the bank!). They, or ideally the mob, would thereupon put torch to the *Banque* and Finance Ministry, thus destroying all records and allowing the *mandats* again to be presented (some, the trial disclosed, for the third or fourth time around), and again stored away until the next outbreak.

Despite peculation, inflation, and the refusal of the peasants to modernize agriculture and use their land to grow export crops, Salomon toiled on. Ably assisted by François Légitime, now Minister of Agriculture, he conducted two national agricultural expositions, patterned on American state fairs and the first such gatherings in Haitian history. Two years earlier, he had opened the rebuilt National Palace, designed by Léon Laforestrie. It was a superb example of Port-au-Prince's nineteenth-century "gingerbread" houses, a few of which remained to delight foreign visitors a century later. Here, at his desk, Salomon conducted business with two loaded revolvers, as paperweights, in full sight and handy reach. His home, however, and chosen retreat, Villa Solitude, remained up the hill in cool Turgeau. It was described in 1886 by a French visitor:

> Each evening the little road from the Champ de Mars to the villas of Bois-Chêne and Turgeau (later to become Avenue Charles Sumner) presents an animated scene. During a good hour there is a continual *va-et-vient*, Panama-hatted businessmen, aides-de-camp in red coats. *Camionettes* alternate with horsemen, a few elegant tilburys are sandwiched between the escorts of the ministers . . . Peasant women of the mountains jog along with sacks of provisions atop little donkeys practically hidden in the long white robes that almost touch the ground. The battalion of the *Garde* that marches up each evening to protect the chief of state accents the picturesqueness of this green hill.

Here Mme. Salomon presided over the intimate, impeccably French dinners and *soirées* that provided the setting for her husband's adept manipulation of people and events. As Alfred Jean reminisced years later: "A Parisienne whose chit-chat charmed you, a tiny glass too much of Rhum Rossignol (which was in fashion in those days) - and there you were, caught in the president's snare."

Salomon and the Great Powers

It was in that ambiance just described, that Salomon, between 1883 and 1887, played out a three-cornered diplomatic game simultaneously involving, for the first time since Soulouque, France, Britain, and the United States. The background was France's attempt to dig a Panama canal and thus open a Pacific exit to the Caribbean. In geopolitical terms, the Caribbean's Atlantic gateway, the Windward Passage, would then become in effect the Gibraltar Strait of what Alfred Thayer Mahan would soon style "the American Mediterranean."

For a variety of reasons, going as far back as the Royal Navy's bombardment of Salnave at the Cap and as recent as British support for the Liberal rebellion (28) *perfide Albion* was Salomon's *bête noire*.

Salomon's first move, in May 1883, was an attempt to offset British hostility with American support. On 29 May, Salomon offered to cede La Tortue to the United States in return for what he circumspectly described to Langston as "the protection of [the U.S.] Government." Wary of overseas expansion and possible foreign entanglement, Secretary of State Frederick T. Frelinghuysen said no. Six months later, however, on 8 November, evidently feeling the pressure of his bitter struggle with the Liberals, Salomon reopened the matter with Langston, Salomon flatly offered Môle St. Nicolas or La Tortue, as the U.S. preferred, in return for an American guaranty of Haitian independence; for American good offices, backed if necessary by interposition, in resolving differences between Haiti and unnamed foreign powers (Britain and France of course); for assumption by the U.S. of Haiti's debt; and for two cruisers and two gunboats for Salomon's navy. This time the proposal reached the White House, where, after cabinet discussion, President Arthur instructed Frelinghuysen to refuse.

Salomon had made categoric offers to the United States. He may have made offers, and surely he entertained certain feelings, toward France. His diplomacy toward Britain was by contrast nervous, defensive, and primarily focused on forestalling apparent British designs and related claims, going as far back as 1875, on La Tortue. As in the case of France, the British negotiations were complicated by Haitian imprisonment, on 30 December 1885, of British employees of the *Banque Nationale* involved in the *Affaire des Mandats*, however warranted the imprisonment may have been.

What for many years had been known as "the Maunder claim" provided the basis for British interest in La Tortue, an interest that, of course, had been whetted by de Lesseps in Panama. Simply described, the Maunder claim arose from the lease of La Tortue, for a mahogany concession, to a British subject named Maunder and his wife of Haitian birth but British nationality. Local authorities violated the lease, maltreated the Maunders, and sent them packing. When a British warship was ordered to La Tortue in 1875, Mrs. Maunder's brother-in-law was thrown into Port-de-Paix jail, and left there until the gunboat departed.

In July 1886 and again in March 1887, a British envoy visited Haiti aboard H.M.S. *Canada,* to rescue Coles, the *Banque*'s late accountant, from jail, to collect assorted claims (including the Maunders'), and to have a look at La Tortue. This last mission aroused intense Haitian anxiety and some uneasiness in Washington and Paris. France promptly sent frigate *Minerve,* wearing the flag of Vice-Admiral de Vignes, "to keep an eye on the British," as the Haitian minister reported from Paris, and the United States sounded out the Foreign Office in London, receiving assurances from Sir Julian Pauncefote that Britain really had no designs on the lovely island. Salomon thereupon settled the Maunder claim for £32,000, and *Canada* steamed over the horizon for Barbados. Observing British methods, the new American minister, Dr. John E. W. Thompson, (who had succeeded Langston in June 1885, inheriting a thick file of uncollected U.S. claims) pointedly suggested to Washington that "some means [should be] devised by which [the Haitians] are impressed so validly that even constant evasion to recognize justice [sic] will be impossible." To round off the affair, in June 1887 when Callisthène Fouchard, the Haitian Foreign Minister, visited Paris and called at the Elysée Palace, President Jules Grévy, sent word to the Haitian president "that he could, under all circumstances, count on France."

Thus ended four years of intense and on the whole effective diplomacy, in which Salomon's long experience in that field, implemented by two able Foreign Ministers, Brutus St. Victor and then Fouchard, attained satisfactory results, not least being the shelter, at last, of the Monroe Doctrine.

Let Me Take My Soup in Peace

At the end of 1885 there had been a brief flicker of revolt: the Cap, thoroughly cowed in 1883, was the scene, on 11 September, of yet another attempt to storm the arsenal. Tirésias Simon Sam, the local commandant, was alert, and the attackers were put to flight. Three who failed to get away were dragged out to La Fossette next morning and shot. Sixteen arrests were subsequently terminated fatally at Gonaïves in January 1886, and Monpoint-jeune, who had only just been released from prison, thought it prudent to take asylum in the French consulate, which obligingly gave him a passport and passage to France.(29)

Nearly seven years had sped since Salomon took office. Now, burdened though he was, no more than any other Haitian president would the old man utter "Nunc Dimittis." Instead, the 1879 constitution was handily edited so as to remove the clause prohibiting self-succession and to substitute simply the words "and he is re-eligible." This formality attended to, Salomon was re-elected on 30 June 1886 for a second seven-year term, ending 15 May 1894.

The new term opened under a cloud. Cayes, ravaged by fire in late 1885, was inundated by flood in August the next year. Salomon went immediately to his old home with what resources the government had, characteristically reminding townspeople, *"Aide toi, le Ciel t'aidera"* (God helps them that help themselves). Then, on 23 September 1887, a heavy earthquake shook the North and Northwest and even Gonaïves and St. Marc, bringing down the new cathedral at Port-de-Paix.

Tremors were rumbling in Port-au-Prince, too. In his vivid language, Anténor Firmin described the state of affairs:

> There was no security for individual liberty, the press was gagged, legislative immunity was a vain word, the law gave way before the whim of a tyrant, whims all the more capricious and unpredictable because he literally applied, in their worst aspect, the precepts of Machiavelli. Internal espionage without precedent in the history of the Republic was carried on with abominable cynicism. No one dared express the most innocent criticism of the administration or policies of the government without being run down . . .

Fires began to break out, set, some said, by agents of the government, others supposedly by its enemies.(30) Worse than fire, gaps began to appear in the ranks. Fontanges Chevallier, who had taken Jérémie for Salomon in 1883, was the first to depart. Leaving a gap Salomon could not easily fill, Thomas Madiou, serene and judicious, had died in 1884. Even closer to the president, François Manigat and then Légitime would soon join Chevallier in banishment.

On 23 May in conversation with Dr. Thompson, Salomon assured the American minister that "he knew the malefactors, who were about twenty in number, that everything was perfectly quiet, and he had no anxiety."

Within less than twenty-four hours Port-au-Prince was in an uproar, touched off by the accidental discharge of a soldier's musket in the market. Troops were called out, ball ammunition issued, and the *Dessalines and Toussaint Louverture* got underway and took station broadsides-to, covering the city. When Thompson, accompanied by his British and French colleagues, went to the palace, they "found the grounds literally crowded with soldiers and armed citizens; a large mitrailleuse stood beside a heavy cannon, menacing the entrance . . ." The president said it looked to him as if a lot of people were tired of living and added that he was quite prepared to *"fusiller le monde en pile"* (shoot everyone in sight). As a further security measure, he had a cannon and detachment of troops sent to cover the home of Légitime, whom he suspected of harboring dangerous thoughts. (A week later, Légitime, accompanied by Manigat, thought it prudent to travel abroad for what *La Verité* called a *"changement d'air, "* and was allowed to do so by Salomon.) Thompson, making what appears to have been the American legation's first use of direct cable communications from Port-au-Prince, sent the following terse telegram to Washington:

SEND WAR VESSEL, REVOLUTION IMMINENT (31)

June passed uneasily. Random shots were heard about the city, and small disturbances flared. In a moment of weariness, the old president said plaintively: "I haven't been well these past days because I've been working too hard. I've been up day and night. And people keep on saying I should go . . . The complaints I have can't be cured abroad. I would have liked to get back to Europe to be rejuvenated, but you know perfectly well that [Europe] can't give you back your youth . . What I need is surcease. Just let me take my soup in peace and I'll get better and be always at your head."

Surcease and peace, asked the president, but there was no peace.

At high noon on 4 July, the second floor of the Chamber of Deputies on Rue du Centre and Rue des Casernes was set afire. Fanned by the sea breezes, the flames soon engulfed downtown Port-au-Prince. The Ministry of Interior, the Archives (one of Salomon's innovations), the town commandant's headquarters, the government printing office, law school (with its painfully acquired law library, collected abroad) and adjacent courts, and the Episcopal church and Bishop Holly's house - all, together with some 400 buildings, were completely gutted. Within three days incendiaries torched the Ministry of Justice (and, for good measure, the home of the Minister, Arteaud), ensuring a second conflagration. In aggregate, the two fires leveled at least a fifth of the capital and caused 12 million francs' damage. "At the fires," reported Thompson, "the smell of petroleum was noticed by all."

Succeeding days brought no letup. Fires were set and reset until little remained to burn. Salomon brought in regiments from the Artibonite, kept guards at every street corner, and set up roadblocks to keep townsmen who might remember the *semaine sanglante* from fleeing to the suburbs. Amid other readings on a falling barometer, two eminent figures of the regime, the opulent Callisthène Fouchard and his successor, Brutus St. Victor, separately sounded the American minister on possible arrangements for asylum. Fouchard and St. Victor were not alone: Mme. Salomon herself, as Thompson dutifully reported, "went so far as to inform Mrs. Thompson that already the private papers of the President, with other valuables, were placed in a small casket, that in a moment of danger the President had arranged to send her with such a casket to my private residence, there to remain - yet she is a French citizen." There was not much to be hoped, Thompson added, from the French or British legation.

> The British representative [Zohrab] is an intelligent, crafty man permeated with the sentiment of colonialization . . The French minister [Sesmaisons] is not as intelligent and subtle but is absolutely carried away by his great opinion of his own abilities . . . These gentlemen have been trying to convince me that these people are incapable of governing themselves and that Christianity demands that some other power make them subservient . . . Sesmaisons says that should the *Dessalines* fire one shot into the city, the French man-of-war would immediately sink her . . .

The diplomats had not long to wait. On 4 August Séïde Télémaque, commandant at the Cap, declared open revolt. The North responded to a man. Within twenty-four hours, Télémaque was on the road to Gonaïves at the head of an army.

By Thursday, Salomon could see the game was up. Sadly, he told Thompson he would resign. But events moved faster. Next morning, 10 August 1888, just after nine, Charles Héraux, a Port-au-Prince gentleman, dashed into the American legation, crying, "Mr. Thompson! Mr. Thompson! For God's sake go to the palace and save the old man's life!" As the message was delivered, the first rattle of musketry could be heard. Hérard Laforest, town commandant, and most of the capital garrison had joined the revolution.

Amid mounting disorder, Thompson pushed his way on foot to the palace, where Salomon was making distraught preparations to try to get aboard H.M.S. *Canada*. *"Quel malheur pour moi que vous n'avez pas un navire de guerre ici!"* (What a misfortune for me that the United States doesn't have a ship here!)

the president exclaimed. (The State Department for obvious reasons expunged the line from the published version of Thompson's dispatch.)

Then, while arrangements were made for carriages and boats and a landing party of Royal Marines from *Canada,* there was a conference at the French legation. Like an Impresario in the prompter's box, Boisrond-Canal materialized from Frères, while Laforest intimated delicately that he could control his men for an hour and a half exactly, but not two hours, and the three ministers - British, French, and American - joined by the Spanish consul, went to the palace.

> We descended from the Palace [reported Thompson] the President leaning on my arm. Lafontant, his private secretary, rushed up, saying, "Mr. Minister, I hear they refuse to take me. Do not desert me!" I placed [the President] in the first carriage where also was Lafontant, then Mme. Salomon. Mounting my horse, I rode on the left side of the carriage. The French minister rode ahead: the Spanish consul who was a little later joined by General Laforest, rode on the right side . . . an enormous populace and mob following us . . . some yelling "A bas *Salomon...... Vive la Revolution,* " and other incendiary cries. They were safely embarked . . .

The rest was anticlimax. Captain Beaumont of *Canada* (which only a year earlier had served as flagship and official yacht for a British envoy and suite) coldly announced he had no accommodations for the deposed president, and sent him, minus baggage, over to the immobilized hulk of a broken-down British merchantman S.S. Alps, where he and Mme. Salomon were held incommunicado in virtual custody of Zohrab, their old foe. When Thompson took a boat out next day, he was refused permission to come on board but did get a note from Salomon asking the whereabouts of their little daughter, Ida, for medicine, and for a change of linen ("We still have nothing but the clothes we embarked in," scribbled Salomon, "soiled, perspiration-soaked: if this is hard for a man, it is harder still for the ladies . . . I need my baggage. I want my child").(33) Then, almost to himself, he was heard to murmur, *"Si le pouvoir a des charmes pour eux, il n'en a plus pour moi. "* (If power holds charms for others, it no longer has for me).

Ashore, every legation bulged with fugitives, Boisrand-Canal sent a fast steamer to Kingston for Légitime, and Télémaque marched South from St. Marc, his ranks swollen with the government armies and generals sent North to oppose him.

To measure Salomon, we must look back to Henry Christophe. No intervening master of Haiti can stand the comparison. Indomitable, implacable, unswervingly bent on progress and national discipline, determined to make the best of his people and country, outward-looking and receptive to the world, ubiquitous and tireless in journeyings to the far corners of Haiti, Salomon would have been a fit collaborator for the mighty King of the North. Yet in the end, like Henry, Salomon failed.

Haiti's fierce antagonisms of section and color could not be overcome. Color prejudice had fused into class prejudice, and each masqueraded behind political labels. In these destructive battles - which time and again simply amounted to the clash between *noir* military autocracy and *jaune* oligarchy - just as in 1822 and 1843, the Liberals of 1859, 1870, 1876, and, to the bitter end, 1883, betrayed themselves and their proclaimed principles and squandered their opportunities. After Salomon became president, the Liberals never had another chance.

Edmond Paul, plunged into prophetic disillusion twenty years before the death of Bazelais, sadly blocked out the politics that lay ahead: "In office, the *mulâtres* are impolitic or powerless, the *noirs* unabashedly criminal or unqualified . . . They occupy the presidential chair in turn, the Machiavellianism of the minority serving as a step to the vandalism of the majority."

Working as best he could inside such a system, Salomon - like his enemy and *mulâtre* predecessor, Geffrard - found that, try as he would, he could not beat it: the cost was too high.

FOOTNOTES - CHAPTER 9

1. Salnave's *Göetterdäemmerung* had not ended fighting in the far South. Even as Nissage took office, Bassett reported, "Eight to ten thousand mountain people *[piquets]* are fighting . . . alike to avenge Salnave's death and to wreak vengeance on the aristocratic mulattoes of the cities." Tiburon, theater of fierce fighting during the war, held out against the new government until the end of March.
2. The president's policies on appointments (and on public finance) were expressed in words attributed to Nissage by Bellegarde: "Ask me for epaulets, and I'll confer as many as you want. But you'll never get at the key to the treasury!" Obviously, Nissage had no objections to epaulets or similar finery: during Holy Week, 1871, Samuel Hazard, the American journalist, described him as "gorgeous in diamonds, feathers and gold lace." The army, Hazard went on, was less gorgeous, being mainly uniformed in American Civil War surplus blues styled "van Boeckelens," from the name of the middleman who resold them to the government at a 600 percent markup.
3. For many years fire drill on the first Sunday of the month at 1:00 P.M. was one of the main social events and diversions of the capital. Sounding the alarm by bugle, led by the chief on prancing horse, the young firemen would go through their evolutions to the admiration of citizens. Eventually they obtained a second steamer, also quartered at fire headquarters on the Grande Rue, while outlying stations, each with a hand pump, were

located at Place St. Anne, Poste Marchande, and downtown on the Rue du Quai.

4. Stephen Preston, the *mulâtre* Haitian minister in Washington, was credited by Secretary Hamilton Fish with having disbursed $20,000 to sink the treaty. On 10 August 1872, Bassett reported to Fish that the legislature had voted Preston "several thousand dollars . . . as a sort of secret service fund." From the frequency of Preston's hurried trips to Port-au-Prince to replenish his slush fund, it may be surmised that not all was reaching intended American beneficiaries. "Mr. Preston's course," wrote Secretary Fish on 31 August 1872, "has not been such as to command respect or confidence in his character."[This from the Grant Administration!]

5. With a pension of 4000 gourdes, three aides, and a personal guard of fifteen men, Nissage lived comfortably in St. Marc until 2 October 1876, when, in an act of singular meanness, Domingue stripped him of pension and emoluments. Thereafter, increasingly addled, the old man lived in poverty until 7 April 1880.

6. In February 1875 the French legation reported an upsurge of Voodoo, including an account of a peasant discovered on the road between Léogane and Petit-Goâve, carrying in a basket on his head the freshly severed limbs and head of a young woman, which he said were for delivery to a Léogane *papaloi* for an impending service.

7. Firmin and historian Antoine Magloire say the loan was 60 million francs, to be repaid in forty annual installments of 7.5 million francs, a return of 400 percent. Bellegarde says 50 million francs, but that the Crédit-General in Paris was able to raise only 36.5 millions of which 26 million went to intermediaries and private pockets in Port-au-Prince and Paris, while the remaining 10 million francs were used to liquidate, at par, a mountain of worthless Haitian bonds bought up as scrap paper by European speculators. The Crédit-Général's commission alone exceeded 9.5 million francs.

8. Apparently unable to pick up any more war-surplus ships of the old Union navy,the government bought two new war steamers, *St. Michel* and *1804*, from Cramps in Philadelphia, and armed them with the guns of *Terreur*, *L'Union* (ex-Salnave), and *Mont Organisé*, described as "disabled and worn out."

9. Still under de Vorges's protection, Domingue was put aboard ship for Kingston, where he died, 24 May 1877.

10. Mme. Emile Pierre (née Salomon) represented and fiercely defended her beloved elder brother during his long years of exile. Deeply devoted to the family's cause, Irma Pierre kept Salomon closely informed on all events, often moving secretly about the Plaine des Cayes on his business. In the view of one French observer, Texier, she was "a veritable tigress." Not surprisingly, she herself knew exile and imprisonment and was once nearly executed.

11. Haiti and Liberia had concluded a treaty of amity and commerce in 1862. Two years later Liberia commissioned her first consul in Port-au-Prince, the American Reverend J. T. Holly, who served until his consecration as bishop in 1874.

12. We have been unable to find reports of any of the above three revolts in Haitian records or history. They are, however, reported in Bassett's dispatches to Washington of 28 July and 21 October 1877.

13. Emulating Nissage, Boisrond-Canal referred the cases of the few Tanis conspirators who had been captured to the ordinary criminal courts, where, in March 1879 ("to the great stupefaction," wrote historian Antoine Michel, "even of those accused") they were all released with what amounted to a Scotch verdict of not proven.

14. The National Assembly (as Americans would say, "the Congress") comprised under most constitutions the two houses, Chambre Legislatif (lower house) and Sénat, sometimes spoken of as *"le grand Corps."* When acting on constitutional matters the assembly was usually called the Constituent Assembly or "Constituante."

15. Msgr. du Cosquer, unwilling to accept or overcome the abuse and obstruction that had been his lot in attempting to give reality to the concordat, left Haiti in May 1867.

16. With soldierly impatience over red tape, the army had simply wanted to proclaim Salomon president without further delay on 3 October, but Salomon insisted that constitutional forms be followed.

17. It typifies the imprecisions of Haitian history that no two sources agree on Salomon's name. Some give him the added name Etienne, which in fact was that of his brother, the senator shot by Geffrard. His 1968 biography, subsidized by the government of Haiti, gives no less than five permutations, not to mention additions and subtractions, of the names Louis, Félicité, Etienne, and Lysius. Salomon's "official" name for the purposes of the present work, given above, is the version used consistently by Dantès Bellegarde. Jean Price-Mars, equally worthy of respect, reverses Bellegarde's order and calls him "Louis Lysius Félicité Salomon."

18. Under title of *Banque Nationale d'Haïti*, the institution opened its doors in mid-1881, with its Paris office at 66 Chaussée d'Antin.

19. By long tradition, graduates of the Port-au-Prince medical school were derisively dubbed *petits docteurs* in contrast with the so-called *grands docteurs,* who had their medical schooling in France or elsewhere abroad.

20. One other mark of the French mission, or at least of some of its advisers, survived in the names of two Port-au-Prince society units of the *Garde Nationale*, the *"Gioziens,"* named for their instructor, a Captain Giboze, and the *"Saint-Louisiens,"* who bore the title of Lieutenant Cicéron Saint-Louis.

21. Among those swept up in Jacmel was Alcius Charmant, who had infuriated Manigat, Salomon's Minister of Education, during an 1881 visit, by talking him down in a hot-headed exchange over the local *lycée*. After deciding to release Alcius, Salomon (whose practice with political prisoners was to require them to appear before him to express contrition prior to release) called the young man to the palace, talked to him like a Dutch uncle, and concluded: "Go home young man. I like you. But remember every day of your life what I say to you in our good old national patois, *'Toute mangé pas bon pour manger, ni toute verité pas bon pour di'"* (All food isn't good to eat, and not every truth is good to tell).

22. In his published text, as in other such papers and proclamations, Salomon employed the style and typographic form of divinity; that is, upper case for all pronouns referring to himself *(Je, Moi, Me,* etc.)

23. One of the few nearly complete sets of Haitian historical records is the headquarters correspondence of Boyer-Bazelais throughout the defense of Miragoâne. This was compiled in toto by Emmanuel Chancy (Pour l'Histoire, 1890), and gives fascinating details on an elite army, smothered in paperwork, whose atypical logistic needs included Noilly Prat vermouth, gin, French wines, mucilage, ink, shoes, kerosene, Epsom salts, and pencils, and one of whose members required an interpreter in order to converse across the lines with a government opponent who spoke only Créole!

24. The fact that *Tropic* was an American filibusterer has misled some American

historians, (for example, Rotberg) into asserting that the Miragoâne expedition had U.S. Government backing (". . . official American assistance," in Rotberg's words, on page *95 of Haiti, The Politics of Power).* Nothing could be farther from the truth. On her return to the United States in May, *Tropic* was promptly libeled by the U.S. attorney in Philadelphia for violating U.S. neutrality laws, and Rand, her master, together with his two mates, was prosecuted and convicted before the month was out. Subsequently, in the fall of 1883, the Treasury Department ordered the New York collector of customs to detain S.S. *Azelda and Laura*, another filibusterer being fitted out and armed to support the Haitian Liberals. Previous to any of the foregoing affairs, two other would-be Haitian filibusterers, *Mary N. Hogan* and *E. C. Irwin*, had been similarly libeled by U.S. authorities.

25. Charmant maintains that only five executions took place, but the report of the American minister on 7 August 1883 lists fourteen.

26. Burdel maintained that Salomon lost control of events and said that at one point the mob tried to shoot him as he dashed about the city on horseback. Be this as it may, when news of the *semaine sanglante* reached Paris, French and European indignation waxed hot. Subsequently reproaching Burdel for his passivity toward Salomon, Jules Ferry, the French Foreign Minister, is said to have burst out: *"Vous vous êtes laissé rouler par ce nègre!"* (You just let yourself get rolled over by that negro!).

27. Pleading the absence of a U.S. warship, the American representative abstained. He was also following long-standing U.S. policy, soon to be somewhat strained, neither to coerce Haiti politically nor to collect debts or claims, in the time-honored European style, by direct sanction of force.

28. H.T.C. Hunt, British consul in Port-au-Prince (ultimately declared persona non grata by Salomon), was on close terms with the Liberals and appears to have supported the 1882 outbreak. In 1883, there is little doubt British authorities winked at Haitian exiles' plans, preparations, and mount-out from Turk's Island, Inagua, and Jamaica. With Edmond Paul in charge, Kingston openly served as rear headquarters for the Boyer-Bazelais operation, and James N. Zohrab, the somewhat mysterious British consul at St. Thomas, was widely reputed to have been involved in the extensive gunrunning - almost exclusively by British merchantmen - that enabled the Liberals to fight as long as they did.

29. Indicative of unquenched French irredentism, the French legation and consulates had a standing policy throughout the nineteenth century of issuing a French passport and thus nationality to any Haitian, including fugitives on the run, who applied.

30. One politically impartial cause of fire was that almost all structures were wood, while the main illuminating agent was cheap kerosene possessing a dangerously low flash point. Characteristically methodical, Bassett, while Haitian consul general in New York, had flash-point tests run on various brands of kerosene exported to Haiti, and eventually persuaded the authorities to ban import of any below a given level.

31. As the explosive situation sputtered to short fuze that summer, Thompson sent seven of what today's diplomats would call "critic"s, each asking for a warship. In Washington's immemorial way of second-guessing men on the spot, all Thompson got for his pains (save for a couple of fleeting ship-visits) was an irritated reprimand from Secretary Bayard for supposedly having pressed the panic button. In some contrast, through the entire period in question, Britain and France maintained at least one man-of-

war in Haitian waters, and Spanish gunboats visited Port-au-Prince regularly.
32. Eventually reunited through Thompson's good offices with little Ida and their things, the Salomons made their way to Paris. The old man -he had been born in 1815 and was near seventy-four - had not much time. On 19 October 1888 he died and was buried in Passy Cemetery, where, up into the 1930s, visiting Haitians would leave cards at his tomb. His daughter, grown to womanhood as Mme. Ida Faubert, punctiliously returned her own card to each caller. In 1994, though the grounds-keeper denied all knowledge of a Haitian President's grave, the grave was located by one of the authors between sections seven and eight. Descendants have been buried there within the past ten years.

CHAPTER 10

Plots and Revolutions

1888-1911

> The history of the country is but a series of plots and revolutions followed by barbarous military executions.

— Spenser St. John

> Anything is possible in Haiti, particularly on the part of the government.

— Flesch to the Quai d'Orsay, 1891

AS HE DEPARTED, Salomon cryptically remarked (or so Marcelin said), "I have left them a cigar lighted at both ends."

Soon enough his meaning became clear. While the men of the West and South were rushing Légitime back from Kingston aboard a fast steamer, Séïde Télémaque, darling of the North, was marching South from the Cap at the head of 10,000 soldiers, picking up towns and adherents at every step.

For the moment, debonair as ever, Boisrond-Canal was in charge. "My fellow citizens," he advised Etienne Charles Laforestrie, Haitian minister in Paris, "have given me the responsibility of maintaining order until we can set up machinery for a transfer of power."

While Boisrond was keeping the lid on Port-au-Prince, Télémaque marched into Gonaïves with his old 30th Regiment from the Cap in the van. Behind followed General Bottex of Le Borgne, with several thousand volunteers and *Cacos* from the North and Artibonite.

The morning after Télémaque swept into Gonaïves (15 August 1888), S. S. *Albo* entered Port-au-Prince from Kingston. On deck, surrounded by a delegation sent to bring him home, stood the handsome, serious-faced *noir* of Jérémie, François-Denis Légitime, (1) who only two months past had departed in exile.

How it must have reminded Boisrond of 1876: the throngs at the wharf, the carriage and outriders to draw the new idol through the streets. "The city was a perfect bedlam," said Thompson. Commander Chester, captain of U.S.S. *Galena,* added, in more detail, "A grand salute took place from all arms. There being no blank cartridges for the muskets, fixed ammunition was used for an indefinite period, the firing generally taking place in the air. The result can be well imagined. The smallest estimate is, I believe, 5 killed and 25 wounded. Even the men-of-war in the harbor came in for their share, several shots having struck their decks."

So far - as seen by Légitime and his sponsor, Boisrond (and behind both the French minister, Comte de Sesmaisons, who stoutly supported Légitime, devout Catholic Francophile) (2) - So good. They held the capital - square one in Haitian politics - and Télémaque, for all his soldiery, was still in Gonaïves.

How to keep the armies of the North out of Port-au-Prince was the problem. Sesmaisons had a solution. Going to Gonaïves aboard a French warship, *Bisson,* under color (though without warrant) of his post as dean of the diplomatic corps, he urged Télémaque to leave his troops behind and come down to Port-au-Prince. Yellow fever was bad in the capital, said the minister untruthfully, and the soldiers would raise the danger of an epidemic. Télémaque's reply was curt: "Tell General Boisrond that as there are five thousand soldiers at Port-au-Prince, I will go there with ten thousand." In a note to Boisrond next day (17 August), Télémaque said that as soon as his troops were underway he would indeed come down by sea, aboard a coastal steamer he had prudently taken over at the Cap.

As it turned out, Télémaque changed his mind and moved South with his army. He entered Port-au-Prince on the 23d, and two of his divisions, under Bottex, pointedly bivouacked in front of the *Palais National.* Facing them, within musketshot, were Anselme Prophète's Presidential Guard, armed with cannon and the *mitrailleuses* inherited from Salomon. Port-au-Prince, in the words of Texier, the French journalist, was now "a vast bivouac."

Ragged peasant hordes from the North and the Artibonite camped in public buildings, parks, yards, and on people's porches. *Noir* volunteers, looters or sometimes just curious, poked through shops and homes of city dwellers, taking what caught their eye.

In this charged atmosphere the immediate task was to form a *gouvernement provisoire.* Whatever their rivalries, differing regions, and colors, Boisrond, Légitime, and Télémaque were men of intelligence and civility: quickly they agreed on a seven-man group - the three leaders, together with Florvil Hyppolite (the elite *Capois noir)* and three lesser figures. The constitution of 1867, as well as its subsequent progeny, were revoked by a stroke of the pen, and elections of a Constituent Assembly (to select the new president and get out another constitution) were set for 17 September.

Long before all returns were in, the ins were clearly out: Télémaque had won in a landslide. The North, Northwest, and Artibonite were solid for Séïde Télémaque; even Légitime's native South gave a majority to his *mulâtre* opponent. Only Boisrond's stronghold, the West, supported Légitime. On 10 October, the delegates (known as *"constituants"*) would meet. Then there would be a new constitution and a new president.

The day of 28 September was one of rumors. That night, said the *telediol,* there would be trouble.

Minister Thompson, who had decided to stay downtown in the American legation on Rue du Centre, was taking a final turn about the town as dusk fell, and stopped to chat with General Bottex, an old acquaintance, who was resting at ease outside his quarters.

At exactly 7:30, Thompson afterward reported, three shots rang out, "followed by a fusillade." Bottex sprang up, calling to his men, *"Courage, z'amis! Pas courri, z'amis!"*

"Amid bullets whistling and falling like hail-stones" (Thompson), the men of the North stood to arms and returned the fire. From the palace, the troops of Anselme Prophète, supported by some of the national guard under 'Ti Canal (Boisrond's impetuous son) and Osman Piquant, banged away. As the firing intensified, gunners on Fort National began discharging their old cannon in the general direction of Télémaque's headquarters on Place Pétion. Dominated by stuttering bursts from the palace *mitrailleuse,* Port-au-Prince was a battlefield.

Trapped in the middle of the fray, Dr. Thompson forgot diplomacy and reverted to his profession.(3) Though, as he related, without black bag and instruments, he rolled up his sleeves in Bottex's house and commenced dressing the wounded as they were dragged in, probably the only instance in American diplomacy in which a chief of mission has organized and operated a battle dressing-station.

About this time (9:00 P.M.) Télémaque appeared and advanced on the palace, when, in Thompson's report, "the *mitrailleuse* belched forth a volume of fire and lead, he pressed his hands to his abdomen, and said, "Nelson, [Nelson Desroches, his aide and secretary], they have cut through my entrails!' "

Assisted into the house, Télémaque was cared for by Thompson, by whose account (considerably blue-penciled in the State Department's published version), he moaned, "Those vagabonds, Boisrond and Légitime, have done for me."

Doing what he could, Thompson took time to note that Télémaque died in Desroches's arms at 12:15 midnight. The first reaction of the *gouvernement provisoire* (minus its foremost member) was to proclaim general amnesty and send gallopers and steamers far and wide, reporting Télémaque's "accidental" death and calling for calm and unity. It would not wash.

As always during turmoil in Haiti, the moment was opportune to settle old scores, and armed bands stalked the streets, pursuing and killing whom they could. Men of the North began quietly leaving town. Archin, one of their number and Minister of Interior, stayed on through 1 October, issuing travel permits to his friends. Then, like Hyppolite (who sent his resignation ashore from the German steamer for the Cap), he, too, went North.

As Sesmaisons and Zohrab waited upon Légitime with congratulations, the lines of civil war were being drawn. Everywhere North of St. Marc was in arms. At the same time, Mérisier Jeannis and his *rasoirs* spilled out of their valleys and took over Jacmel. Back at the Cap, Hyppolite donned the mantle of Télémaque and took command of the rebellion.

Légitime's response was predictable. On 16 October, convening a rump assembly (33 out of 84 original *constituants),* he allowed himself to be elected *chef du pouvoir executif.* That same day he proclaimed the Cap, Gonaïves, and St. Marc under blockade and ordered 10,000 muskets from the United States. "War is inevitable . . ." reported Thompson on 17 October. "Vengeance is the cry of the North."

I Will Give Them a Civil War

To the cry of the North, Légitime gave a defiant answer. "If they want a civil war," he said to Dr. Thompson on 18 October, "I will give them a civil war. I have more resources than they and will see the country totally destroyed before I allow these ignorant people to put me down. Before I [would] retire, I [would] prefer to see the country go into the hands of foreigners." (4)

As a *noir,* Légitime was a Nationalist, but he was, even more, a member of the elite. His opponent, Hyppolite, was also an elite *noir* Nationalist, but was the son of one of Soulouque's Ministers and had been Salnave's Minister of War, which put him squarely in the Soulouque-Salnave-Salomon antioligarchic line.

The *New York Sun's* stringer in Port-au-Prince wrote that Légitime was "as black as the ace of spades." More elegantly, the *Herald* described

a tall man, with a face of the purest African type. General Légitime is fairly entitled to be described as distinguished. He is erect as a tall pine and he moves with Gallic ease and dignity. His black Prince Albert coat was closely buttoned and his snug-fitting trousers ended over French *bottines* with pointed toes . . . His hands are long and slender and extremely well shaped. One of his favorite gestures is to close three fingers and to gently emphasize with the forefinger and the thumb.

On the face of things, Légitime's situation seemed impressive. He controlled the capital, the army, and the navy (which amounted to two ships but would soon be augmented by three converted merchantmen). His dilemma, which he never succeeded in surmounting, was that he could never claim to be *de facto* president when two thirds of the country was in arms against him, nor could he - the creature of a rump assembly -claim *de jure* standing.(5)

Légitime had arms and a navy, and the "Protestants" (as Hyppolite's men styled themselves) had none. The government's immediate strategy was therefore to try to prevent foreign (mainly American) gunrunning, and restrict rebel deployment by means of blockade, which Légitime had already proclaimed. But the first principle of blockade is that to be enforceable it must be effective. With two gunboats to start with, Légitime was asserting his right to blockade seven ports dispersed along some 200 miles of coast. This was ridiculous: even an efficient navy of comparable size could not have accomplished such a mission. In fact the government's ships wandered from port to port, closing none, sometimes congregating for coal and shore leave in Port-au-Prince, and thus abandoning any legal pretense of blockade.

Against this background the Haitian seizure of an American liner, S.S. *Haytian Republic,* off St. Marc on 21 October, kicked up a prolonged row between Haiti and the United States.

Incontestably, the *Haytian Republic* - in the course of her scheduled run - had earlier transported rebel troops between the Cap, Port-de-Paix, and Gonaïves, had delivered arms and regular cargo, and, when taken by gunboat *Dessalines,* had on board, as passengers from disaffected Jacmel, delegates, including Alcius Charmant, bound for Hyppolite's rival Constituent Assembly hastily convened at Gonaïves.

Heavily as these factors weighed in the mind of Légitime, none of them overrode the patent ineffectuality of a blockade, nor did they justify the government's action in convening a drumhead prize court, which seized and then disabled the *Haytian Republic.*

Only on arrival in Port-au-Prince of U.S.S. *Yantic* and *Galena* did the government, on 21 December, restore the unfortunate steamer, much the worse for wear (pilfered, stripped of parts, and battered from having been run aground), to American authority. (6)

While Légitime pursued his erratic course at sea, both sides concluded preliminaries for civil war on land.

Formally setting up shop under the name *République Septentrionale,* the "Revolutionary Committee of the North" proclaimed itself a provisional government on 27 November 1888, with Hyppolite its president. (Six days earlier, however, in a communication addressed to the assiduous Sesmaisons and Zohrab - who came to the Cap aboard *Bisson* to try to sway Hyppolite - the latter had already signed himself "Le Président Hyppolite. ")

At virtually the same time, Légitime finally was able, in form at least, to get himself lawfully elected president. The four Jacmel *constituants* scooped up on board the *Haytian Republic* gave the Port-au-Prince rump a quorum. They were thus too valuable to shoot, and to their amazement were received by Légitime at his most suave and were put up at government expense in a hotel. On 16 December, with three (7) Jacmel *constituants* stoutly voting nay, the Légitime assembly enacted the necessary new constitution and duly elected their chief for a seven-year term.

Légitime Attacks

While all this politicking went on, Légitime tried with mixed success to get the military situation in hand. One immediate disadvantage was that, though the rebellion was of the North, the "Protestant" army was mostly around St. Marc, where Télémaque had marched it before his death.

The war that now ensued closely followed the familiar lines of its predecessors.

With coastal support from his navy, Légitime directed his main effort against the Artibonite and, behind it, the North. Seesaw fighting and maneuvering went on against and around Gonaïves and St. Marc, with regiments and commanders turning on each other, shifting allegiance, or simply disappearing. Jean-Jumeau, the gnarled Artibonite *Caco*, turned over a shipload of Légitime's soldiers to Hyppolite, then vanished for a time, to reappear, after reflection in the wilderness, as one of Hyppolite's best generals.

To regain Jacmel, so often a thorn in the side of Port-au-Prince, Légitime sent two first-line leaders, Osman Piquant and Dardignac, an implacable *mulâtre* from Nippes who carried only his *cocomacac* in battle. On 27 October 1888, Dardignac took the town as Mérisier Jeannis, his old enemy, dashed for the consulates while Dardignac personally shot the prisoners.(8)

Depleted by the spectacular explosion of steamer *L'Estère* when a negligent watertender allowed her to blow up off Montrouis, the navy struck in December at Gonaïves and the Cap. As no one had thought to remount the guns or rehabilitate the forts after the British bombardment of 1865, the Cap was in a funk.

"Nearly 9000 persons fled," reported American Consul Goutier, . . . mothers with babes at their breasts, followed by children carrying small bundles of clothing; frantic women leaving their homes to sojourn under trees . . . some humane persons carrying out the sick, others leading the blind while the selfish majority took no concern." Then, lowering his tone several octaves, Goutier ended, "No great harm resulted."

While these events were in progress, Légitime, from before St. Marc, thrust boldly across the Upper Artibonite, into the Plaine du Centre, and thence to the Plaine du Nord, via its mountain back door. It was a region Légitime knew well from the Guerre des *Cacos* twenty years before.

By early January of the new year (1889), Anselme Prophète was poised to threaten Grande Rivière du Nord simultaneously with Le Trou. A few days later he seized Marmelade. Hyppolite's reading of the situation was clear: he immediately displaced his headquarters East from the Cap to Ouanaminthe with his back to the border. Ulises Heureaux, the Dominican dictator whose father had been Haitian, had had close ties with Salomon and therefore supported Hyppolite.(9)

Hyppolite's plight seemed desperate. Weakened by defection, his forces were shut up in St. Marc, Gonaïves, and the approaches to the Cap. Légitime commanded the sea. France and Britain, in the persons of their ministers, were pushing hard for his success. (Minister Zohrab personally procured and armed an old British steamer for Légitime, and then went to New York to recruit British officers, engineers, and gunners for the government's navy. When Hyppolite's roving ambassador in Europe vehemently protested equally unneutral behavior by the Comte de Sesmaisons and demanded his recall, the Quai d'Orsay coldly replied that Sesmaisons would be recalled only if the United States recalled Dr. Thompson.)

In this dark hour, from over the border who should materialize at Hyppolite's side but Nord Alexis and his long-time lieutenant, Turenne Jean-Gilles. These hardy sons of the North, asylees in the French legation since the death of Télémaque, had made an escape and, via the Bahamas, reached Santo Domingo.

In early April, at the head of 300 men, Anselme Prophète infiltrated his birthplace, Trou du Nord, set up a howitzer in the church door, and opened fire into the village. Tonton Nord and Turenne Jean-Gilles were waiting. With guns of their own, and even a *mitrailleuse,* they poured in a hot counterfire. Launching his soldiers for the final attack, Jean-Gilles said, "Advance with my blessing! By staying behind I am making a very great but necessary sacrifice." Then the rebels swarmed forward, carried the church with a whoop, and sent the invaders flying. *La Liberté,* reporting the battle two days later, said, "A rain of fire tossed men and horses, the altar and statues, alike into the air . . . a mass of flesh, mud, blood, and splinters."

But the church at Trou was no Haitian Alamo, nor, as slim casualty lists attest, were the battles of those days in a class with Borodino, Cold Harbor, Iwo Jima, or the Somme. As Texier would drily report in 1891, "These Haitian battles are not really murderous, each side, restrained by chronic fright, hesitates to advance, while the soldiers, like children terrified by the noise of a gunshot, bang away without looking."

Légitime's Downfall

After the debacle at Trou, Anselme Prophète took to his heels, halting only when the remnants of his army reached Port-au-Prince. In the Artibonite there followed an equally stunning reverse. Monpoint-jeune, all but out of ammunition and food in St. Marc, was resupplied by a blockade-runner bearing Alcius Charmant and a load of supplies from the Cap.(10) With these reinforcements Monpoint and Jean-Jumeau broke out and smote Osman Piquant at Dessalines on 6 May. On 14 May, Dr. Thompson reported, "Piquant arrived on the outskirts of this city with but a handful of disorganized, half-naked, almost starved soldiers . . . Five months of success in the field have been replaced by total rout in as many days."

Piquant was aboard a Spanish steamer in three days. Anselme Prophète hung on until 3 June: then he, too, decided to travel abroad. Thoroughly seasoned in such matters, Boisrond-Canal took the 14 June steamer for Le Havre, leaving Légitime on his own. Hyppolite thereupon returned from Ouanaminthe to the Cap, where, according to Admiral Bancroft Gherardi, now commanding U.S. forces in those waters, "he rode through the streets scattering money on all sides." He could afford to: the day before, a whole shipload of new paper money had arrived from New York for the rebel cause.

Tonton Nord mopped up the North he knew so well. Jean-Jumeau marched into the Cul-de-Sac. On 26 June he fell upon Thomazeau; less than a week later, Croix-des-Bouquets surrendered. As these disasters multiplied, Numa Rabel, son of Hilaire, the old warlord of Saltrou, declared for Hyppolite. Légitime sent Dardignac to the South coast. He never returned. On 3 August, Chicoyé and his Jacmelians and the Rabel clan smote Dardignac at Source Meyer between Jacmel and Cayes-Jacmel. Dardignac was slain by his escort. For years after, the peasants sang,

> *"Dardignac, coté ou pralé?*
> *- M' prale Carrefou' Cap Rouge,*
> *M' té rencontré Numa Rabel:*
> *Parole trop fort: machoi gonflé!*

[Dardignac, where are you going'? . . . / - I'm headed for Carrefour Rouge/I ran into Numa Rabel/I spoke too loud: my jaw's broken'.]

With Dardignac, Légitime's last fighting general, disposed of, the time had come for the South to rise. General Antoine Simon, the *noir* chieftain at Cayes, had thrown in with Hyppolite in July. Now he marched on the capital.

Texier, the acerbic Frenchman, saw Légitime - alone, honest, well-intentioned - "exploited by an indescribable rabble of persons without honor who pillaged the public treasury, ruined the government credit, stole money intended to feed the troops, and shoved the government to the wall. Then they swooped away like a flock of crows and made for the United States or Europe."

On the morning of August 20th, Légitime summoned the diplomatic corps and announced the inevitable: would they please, he then asked, intervene for the preservation of peace and order? With a long face, Sesmaisons said he thought Dr. Thompson was the only one Hyppolite would listen to, so it was agreed that, accompanied by Garrido, his Spanish colleague, the American minister would go to St. Marc to see what could be arranged. Légitime, Admiral Gherardi recorded, "seemed to be the most indifferent one of all, and certainly if he realized the great difference a few hours would make in his position, he gave no evidence of it.

When Thompson reached St. Marc by steamer at three in the morning, he was met by Commander Hamerton Killick, a dashing *mulâtre* in Hyppolite's navy, who took him to Firmin, Provisional Minister of Foreign Affairs. Then they all routed Hyppolite out of bed. Firmin quickly drafted a plan for peaceful occupation of Port-au-Prince under diplomatic supervision, and Thompson returned to the capital.

During the forenoon of 22 August, while the diplomats relayed Hyppolite's terms to Légitime, the *telediol* buzzed. Gherardi reported streets crowded with men and women, the former armed with the most modern rifles, and in many cases with revolvers; and from the excited manner of everyone, it was apparent that the end had finally come.

Once more as in the past, and finally, Sesmaisons put cruiser *Kerguelen* at Légitime's disposal, but time was running out. By two the mob had battered in the palace gates and were looting the lower rooms. Then, while the foreigners took counsel, Légitime sallied forth in his carriage, fist clenched around a rosary. *"Légitime vini!"* cried the crowd - the same crowd, he must have reflected (he was a thoughtful man), that had tumultuously acclaimed him one year and seven days ago; likely the same carriage, certainly the same wharf.

Finding it impossible to get him out of the carriage (Gherardi went on), there was only one thing left to do and that was to take the chance of getting him in safety to the wharf, where the French steam-cutter was in waiting together with our launch . . . We were fortunate enough to reach the wharf, followed all the way by the mob, which was joined by one quite as large, on our arrival. He at last embarked and a sense of relief was felt when he was safely afloat.(11)

Next day, while *Kerguelen* made preparations to get underway, Légitime could hear the cheers and drums and gun salutes as Hyppolite's three divisions entered town. Everything transpired as Firmin had planned, with most of the diplomatic corps and the consuls in attendance. Only Sesmaisons and Zohrab found themselves indisposed (". . . just as well," sniffed Thompson disdainfully, in violation of his Hippocratic oath). According to the American, all came off "in the most perfect order," but this was not quite so. In understandable if not excusable exuberance, Monpoint burned the Pétionville houses, each flying the Tricolor, of Sesmaisons and his secretary. Four days later, escorted by some 1500 cavaliers, Hyppolite himself came down to Port-au-Prince, went to the cathedral for the Te Deum, and then repaired in state to the *Palais National.*

Having promptly called, in full dress, on the new provisional president, Admiral Gherardi and staff returned on board U.S.S. *Kearsarge,* shifted from frock coats, fore-and-aft hats, epaulets, and swords to working uniform, and made sail North for a look at Môle St. Nicolas.

A Prophecy of Peace

To no one's surprise, Louis Mondestin Florvil Hyppolite was duly chosen president on 9 October 1889, and took the oath of office at Gonaïves on the 17th. In the usual way, with the victorious army "maintaining order," there had been a *gouvernement provisoire* to midwife the new regime; its leading figures included Firmin, Monpoint, and Nord Alexis. Under the skilled hands of Firmin and Léger Cauvin, a respected lawyer, the new constitution (modeled on that of 1879 and thus derivatively on 1846, but moderate, practical, and democratic) was adopted and promulgated on the day of Hyppolite's election. Destined to remain in force, or at least on the books, for twenty-nine years, the 1889 constitution still holds the record for longevity in a field where swift and early mortality has been the rule.(12)

The new cabinet was a good one, with Firmin at its head holding the portfolios of Foreign Affairs and Finance; Monpoint, War; and Cauvin, Justice. Its one concession to the South, and no bad choice, was the appointment of Rameau's nephew, Dantès, to Public Instruction. Young Rameau breathed life into the university, bluntly told the legislature that rural schools weren't worth talking about because they no longer existed, and set up still another technical school, Arts et Métiers, which survived exactly four years. (A more lasting landmark in education was the founding in 1890 by the Brothers of Christian Instruction of Haiti's second elite *lycée,* St. Louis de Gonzague.)

There was also a new face in the American legation. To replace Dr. Thompson, President Harrison sent Frederick Douglass, the most distinguished American black of his time. Sadly and somewhat down in the world, Ebenezer

Bassett, at $825 per annum, returned to Port-au-Prince as Douglass's clerk.

In Washington, too, there was a change of guard: the slippery Preston, Haitian minister for nearly two decades, was replaced by Hannibal Price, one of Haiti's most illustrious public men.

On 14 November, after Douglass presented his letters of credence, he described Hyppolite, then sixty-two years old, as "a man of about medium height, of dark brown complexion and gray hair. He has a well-balanced head, a clear steady eye, a calm temper and high intelligence. He is evidently a man not to be trifled with, and from what I have seen of him . . . I am led to think that his election is a prophecy of peace to his country."

That peace represented Hyppolite's purpose was promptly augured by a general amnesty, on 5 November 1889. (Typically, it was accepted mainly by lesser persons: as late as the following March, important figures, including Boisrond-Canal - in the British legation this time - remained in asylum or exile.) Three months later, on 3 February 1890, Hyppolite held a meeting at Thomazeau with Heureaux, the Dominican dictator who had supported him so effectively. Aside from window dressing, the important business was to reaffirm past agreements, made with Salomon and Légitime, that Haiti and Santo Domingo would keep hands off each other's internal politics and prevent fomentation within their respective territories of revolution against the other. (13)

Internally, the auguries seemed equally propitious. Although the public debt had soared to $20 million as a result of the revolution and of $4.4 million in paper money run off by Légitime or imported from New York by Hyppolite, logwood was booming, the coffee crop was bounteous, and world prices were up. In Firmin Haiti had an honest and capable Finance Minister: during his first year, Firmin reduced the debt by 13 percent and retired a million dollars' worth of paper by virtue of an equivalent loan floated on advantageous terms with the merchants of Port-au-Prince. Hyppolite, meanwhile, had promptly established the new Ministry of Public Works provided for in Firmin's constitution, and the air smelled of contracts, concessions. and prosperity.

'Ti Malisse Saves the Môle

After paying his first call on Hyppolite, Admiral Gherardi had noted: "He is quite reticent, seeming to weigh his words carefully, as though wishing to say no more than would suffice in conveying his thoughts."

The admiral was correct. Hyppolite had good reason to weigh his words, especially in conversation with the Commander, U.S. Atlantic Squadron.

A recurring gambit in Haitian diplomacy, originally dating from the tumultuous time of Salnave and repeated, on occasion, as late as the 1960s, has been to dangle naval-base rights (or a coaling-station concession, as the nineteenth century phrased it) under the noses of foreign powers.

In the desperate struggle for international recognition during the recent civil war, it was therefore not surprising that, in clutching for foreign support, both sides, regardless of actual intentions, made the most of the only negotiating asset Haiti had - its position beside the Windward Passage.

Back in 1868, U.S. Minister Hollister had been one of the first Americans to visit the Môle. As his report showed, he was deeply impressed:

> The harbor of St. Nicolas Môle is so out of the way of the ordinary works of nature that words cannot do it justice. The Môle proper must be more than three miles long, is almost of uniform height, and at a distance looks like some vast Roman wall. Cape St. Nicolas, on your right . . . is magnificently bold and volcanic-looking, and clouds always hide the summits . . . The cape rises in a series of natural terraces, at proper distances for the mounting of guns. The first three seem as level as a house floor, the others are more rugged. I think there are six in all. As you enter the harbor the Môle is on your left, and it stretches along between the ocean and the harbor, until it meets a little neck of land which protects the inner harbor . . . The outer harbor is..... protected from storms, and would hold all the fleets of the world...... The inner harbor has a sand bottom and I could see the tufts of sponge and little fish at a depth of eight fathoms . . . After you get in, you can hardly persuade yourself you are not on a little country lake surrounded by bold shores.

On 27 December 1888, when he was poised for the trek East to Ouanaminthe, Hyppolite had called in Goutier, the American consul at Cap Haïtien, and pleaded for U.S. support. In return, Hyppolite offered commercial preferences to American trade and shipping, and the use of Môle St. Nicolas as a naval coaling-station. But before Goutier could inform Washington, Hyppolite had second thoughts and asked the consul not to report the conversation. As a result, no word of Hyppolite's demarche reached the State Department until months later, and was then apparently ignored,

In backing away from his offer of naval-base rights at the Môle, Hyppolite did, however, instruct a diplomatic agent, Frédéric Elie, to present the commercial part of the Goutier package to the U.S. Government in Washington. Whether Elie in fact ever did so - directly or through American lobbyists - remains another obscure if not unanswerable question.(14) Later it was asserted by U.S. representatives that he had.

At virtually the same moment (21 December 1888) as Hyppolite was closeted with Goutier at the Cap, another of the former's agents, Dr. Nemours Auguste, was in Washington, warning the outgoing Secretary of State, Bayard, that Légitime had, through Sesmaisons, promised the Môle to France. Behind this smoke (for smoke it was) there soon appeared the color, or at any rate the look, of fire. In the spring of 1889 there circulated throughout Port-au-Prince the "text" of an agreement - very likely printed up by Légitime's enemies allegedly concluded on 7 March in Paris between Laforestrie, Haitian minister, and a purported representative of the Quai d'Orsay, a Marquis de Busigny (or in some references "Brésigny"). This document purported to cede La Gonâve outright to France and to grant a coaling-station at the Môle.

The agreement was a hoax, the transaction never took place. Sesmaisons, whom the Quai d'Orsay had sternly instructed "to observe extreme prudence and avoid any pretext for stirring up the susceptibilities of Washington," reported the *"soi-disant contrat" as "totalement fausse."* The French government disavowed all, pointing out, inter alia, that Busigny/Brésigny was unknown at the Quai d'Orsay. But the New York Times (21 May 1889) swallowed the story, which prompted Légitime's Minister Preston, then playing a very different game, to assure Blaine it was "forgery." What might have been intimated between Légitime and Sesmaisons is unknown, but the latter's reports to Paris give no evidence of any such transaction.

If the Marquis de Busigny was a phantasm, the Comte de Sesmaisons was a fact of life. (After all, had he not said, "Had I been minister in Port-au-Prince in 1883, Haiti would already be a French protectorate"') And France was digging, or trying to dig, a canal in Panama, which, if completed, would, like de Lesseps's canal at Suez, change a closed sea into a great highway.

The train of events precipitated by Dr. Auguste's warnings in Washington was (1) a reminder to France that the United States would brook no European colonization in Latin America, (2) consequent cooling in the French courtship of Légitime (France abruptly canceled a deal, only two months old, to provide the latter with a badly needed gunboat); and (3) on further American remonstrance a year later, French recall of Sesmaisons from Port-au-Prince.

To complete these complicated preliminaries and return to Admiral Gherardi requires one more sentence. Ludwell Montague, on circumstantial evidence admittedly, conjectures convincingly that, between March and August 1889, Preston subliminally dangled the Môle as bait to entice Blaine into recognizing Légitime. (15)

It is against this Byzantine background - a polysided, multidimensional chess game being played out between the United States, France, and contending Haitians - that American actions toward the Hyppolite government must be judged. In this as in preceding rounds of the game, the king, readily visible yet impalpable as ectoplasm, was the Cheshire Cat-like mirage of base rights at the Môle.

The 1890s were a decade of imperialism, intervention, and a European colonial fever that had begun to catch in America. With the change of administration in Washington in 1889 from Grover Cleveland to Benjamin

Harrison, U.S. foreign policy - especially with James G. Blaine at State - took an expansionist turn that, in the Caribbean and West Indies, meant Cuba and Haiti.

The upshot of all this (16) was that, on 25 January 1891, in company with U.S.S. *Kearsarge* and *Enterprise*, Admiral Gherardi brought his flagship, U.S.S. *Philadelphia* to anchor at Port-au-Prince and sent for the American minister to come on board.

It is unusual - bad manners, in fact - for an admiral, however puissant, to hail a minister or ambassador onto his quarterdeck, but Frederick Douglass well knew why he was being sent for. He also knew that had he been white, Gherardi would have come ashore and called on him.(17)

On returning to Port-au-Prince in December 1890, after home leave and consultation in Washington, Douglass bore instructions to open negotiations for the Môle. He was already aware through Clyde's man in Port-au-Prince that Gherardi, with President Harrison's special commission in hand, was on his way to Haiti to negotiate the lease of a coaling-station at the Môle.

Douglass lost no time in putting out feelers: on New Year's Day he found occasion to broach the subject with Firmin, and the ensuing conversation indicated no Haitian eagerness to proceed. Douglass (no doubt with Ebenezer Bassett's expert prompting) reminded Washington a week later, "There is perhaps no one point upon which the people of Hayti are more sensitive, superstitious and united than upon any question touching the cession of any part of their territory to any foreign power. They revolt at the idea of giving a foothold to any of the outside world."

Douglass's reporting, while impeccably accurate, was in no way what the State Department wanted to hear, and only confirmed the reputation he already bore, that of a black plenipotentiary accredited to, and therefore soft on, a black republic.

"In his peculiarly emphatic manner," Douglass later recalled, "the admiral made me fully acquainted with the dignity of his position,"(18) and told the American minister to set the stage.

On 28 April at the palace, flanked by Firmin, Hyppolite received Gherardi, Douglass, and Lieutenant Harry Huse, himself a future admiral and Gherardi's interpreter. Gherardi, admitted Douglass, "stated the case with force and ability, reminding the President of services rendered, of the friendship shown for his government by the U.S. Government, and of certain promises by the Haitian Provisional Government which it was now the desire of the government at Washington to have fulfilled."

As dusk fell on the three-hour interview, a Haitian tendency toward sparring seemed to appear. Was this simply a U.S. proposal, or was it the foreclosure of an asserted treaty obligation? The U.S. seemed to rely on initiatives by Elie, but his original instructions had been destroyed and were no longer of record. Yet at the end, though Firmin foresaw trouble, perhaps revolution, for any government that leased away the Môle, Hyppolite (as quoted by Douglass) said, "The Executive Department of the Haitian Government would grant the lease asked for, *subject to its ratification by the legislative chambers.*" (Italics supplied.)

Next Monday, having allowed a weekend (including a National Palace wedding, that of Hyppolite's daughter, Lozama, to Louis-Alexis Gauthier) to intervene, Gherardi and Douglass presented a formal note asking for the Môle. Firmin, Douglass noted, was his usual polite and cordial self but gave no assurance whatever that the lease would be granted.

That afternoon, the president and his suite came aboard the *Philadelphia* to return Admiral Gherardi's official call. Assistant Engineer E. L. Beach, just out of Annapolis and getting his first sight of Haiti, later reminisced:

President Hyppolite was accompanied by his "Secretary of State for Foreign Relations," M. Firmin, a solemn, small. elderly gentleman, dressed in a solemn high hat, a solemn long black frock coat, and solemn trousers . . . [and] by his personal staff of 29 strikingly uniformed military aides. Each wore a light blue long coat. flaming red trousers, military cap, and sword, all blazing with gold braid. Knee boots with spurs completed the outfit. The President himself was dressed with simple magnificence in a heavy black-blue jacket with gold trimmings. white linen trousers, military cap, and patent-leather hip-boots.

A week went by. The cabinet was reported to be "considering the problem." On 9 February, to loosen up negotiations, Gherardi took his ships a short way to sea and held a day of highly audible gunnery exercises off Iroquois Reef, while the afternoon breeze wafted pungent powder smoke shoreward through the jalousies of the palace. Another week passed. Beach continued: "Appointments were made and invariably broken. At most unfortunate times Hyppolite would be called into the interior. Once there was a threatened rebellion."

Then, on 16 February, Firmin blandly asked to examine Gherardi's credentials. After a few moments, in his courteous way he handed them back. Unfortunately, he said, the admiral's special commission was not quite *en règle*. It was signed only by Secretary of the Navy Tracy and not by President Harrison.

Only six weeks earlier (30 December) the new line tying in Port-au-Prince with the Môle cable, and thus with the United States, had been opened. Now its wires vibrated to a cipher dispatch from Gherardi to Blaine:

HAYTI WILL NOT TREAT FOR MôLE UNLESS I HAVE FULL POWERS
SIGNED BY PRES. OF U.S. . . .

While Gherardi chafed (and looked in vain for some pretext to land his Marines at the Môle and present all concerned with a fait accompli), Hyppolite left town for an extensive tour of the South, from which he did not return until after the American warships were out of sight.(19)

U.S. warships were not the only ones present. Early in March, the French squadron commander, Rear Admiral de Cuverville, fresh from the conquest of Dahomey and chastisement of its King Behanzin, brought in his flagship, *Naïade,* and another ship. Ashore, flushed perhaps by the minister's fine champagne, he told compatriots at the French legation (in the words of Gherardi's intelligence report), that "he would not hesitate to land men and use his guns; that he was accustomed to this sort of people from his experience of the African coast and knew how to deal with them."

Neither de Cuverville's saber-rattling (which of course immediately leaked into Haitian circles) nor persistent reports that France was preparing to support a comeback by Légitime deflected Firmin (Hyppolite's lone caretaker in town) from the business in hand.

Gherardi's revised powers arrived from the White House, but he withheld them for a purpose that became clear on 18 April. That day U.S.S. *Chicago, Atlanta, Boston,* and *Yorktown* steamed in to reinforce Gherardi. Three days later, even while Douglass was warning the Secretary of State that "the presence of our war vessels" had become a detriment, the admiral marched up to the palace, produced his new credentials, and asked Firmin for Haiti's answer.

On 22 April 1893, Firmin replied. The answer was no.

There could be no lease of the Môle because Haiti's constitution precluded any such alienation of sovereignty. Moreover, Haiti would not - could not - negotiate under the guns of seven foreign warships or, for that matter, under the bullying of the American press.

Expressed in Firmin's lucid French, the reply was dignified, firm, and logical-in Rayford Logan's phrase, "a masterpiece of *non possumus*".

Within forty-eight hours the Squadron of Evolution had its anchors up and catted and was underway for home waters. On the 27th, Admiral Gherardi (now, recorded Mr. Beach, "a solemn admiral") withdrew his ships. Later that day, Hyppolite reappeared in Port-au-Prince. Firmin - unfairly reproached for having even negotiated such a question - resigned his portfolio on 3 May. Douglass, as unfairly blamed by the American public for exactly the reverse reasons, requested home leave on 9 May and never returned to Haiti.

In terms of Haitian folklore, the 'Ti Malisse diplomacy of Port-au-Prince had, not for the last time, outmaneuvered ponderous Bouqui from Washington and New York.(20)

Without actually compromising an inch of Haitian soil, each party to the civil war had deftly exploited Haiti's one asset. Hyppolite and Firmin, called on to make good whatever gossamer commitments ever existed, had skillfully temporized, sidestepped, and, morally speaking, finally spiked the guns of the U.S. Atlantic Fleet.

Firmin's confidence in calling Gherardi's bluff was, however, not due to clairvoyance: we now know he was looking at the American cards. At some time in April (the date is illegible on the flimsy copy in the spidery hand of the Minister himself) the French Foreign Minister, Alexandre Ribot, sent a highly confidential enciphered telegram to Port-au-Prince:

BLAINE HAS SPONTANEOUSLY TOLD OUR MINISTER IN WASHINGTON THAT THE U.S. GOVERNMENT WILL NOT USE FORCE AGAINST HAITI. YOU SHOULD CONVEY THIS NEWS IN YOUR CONSULTATIONS WITH THE HAITIAN GOVERNMENT, WHILE UNDERSCORING ITS CONFIDENTIALITY AND WITHOUT DEPARTING FROM THE PRUDENCE ENJOINED UPON YOU.

Blaine's slip confirmed the acute judgment manifested by Hannibal Price in Washington. Dr. Logan, who enjoyed access to Haitian diplomatic archives no longer available, cites Minister Price's conclusion, from beginning to end, that the American public simply would not sanction such force against Haiti. Firmin accepted and acted consistently on this view, which the event (and the Quai d'Orsay's tipoff) proved absolutely correct.(21)

As for Blaine, Tracy, and Gherardi, the best that can be said is that they acted in what they thought to be their country's interest, never mind Haiti's. Ironically, the actions of Firmin and Price better suited the abiding interests of the United States than the short-sighted maneuvers of American statesmen and naval officers who fumbled for the Môle.

Panamam' Tombé

It was Fête-Dieu (28 May), 1891, and the president, attended by his suite, Ministers, and guard, was at mass in the cathedral, when a rising sputter of musketry was heard. Led by a General Sully-Guerrier and by François Gracia, an officer of the Presidential Guard, some seventy rebels were storming down Morne l'Hôpital and into Port-au-Prince. Their object was to deliver from the penitencier a large group of hostages gathered up by Hyppolite, who, rumor said, were to be ferried over to La Gonâve and there disposed of.

Making first for the prison, the attackers burst in the gates, armed their friends, and dashed for the arsenal and the Palais. For a short time, Hyppolite took cover inside the cathedral. Then he rallied his guards and counterattacked. The fighting ended in an hour, but Port-au-Prince was in an uproar that took days to subside.

While the rebels scattered, some for the consulates, others for the woods, Hyppolite, roused to insensible fury *"un accès de démence,"* wrote M. E. Flesch, the French minister),(22) began rounding up old enemies, suspected conspirators, and potential rivals. Describing the scene, Flesch went on: "On horseback with baton in hand, Hyppolite would strike unhappy victims at random and order them shot by the soldiers or *volontaires* . . . Following the President's example, the soldiers soon began killing for the pleasure of killing, or to settle old scores.

By the American legation's estimate "at least 150" conspirators and their friends and relatives were massacred. Sully-Guerrier and four confederates were hauled out of the Mexican consulate and shot in the street. Soldiers smashed their way into the archbishop's residence and searched it, over outraged protests from Msgr. Morice, after the latter had gone to the palace to remonstrate with the president over his *"grande férocité"* . A French merchant, Ernest Rigaud (typically described afterward by Haitian historians as "an adventurer"), made the mistake of protesting when Hyppolite tore down a French flag over his door. The president had him shot forthwith.(23)

The lesson sufficed: Hyppolite suffered no further coups.

Only two years before Hyppolite won power, Molinari, a French visitor, described the capital:

> Port-au-Prince is decidedly the most ruinous of capitals. But how could it be otherwise? During 40 years up through 1883, this unhappy republic and its capital have been continually buffeted and ravaged by riot and revolution . . . The waterfront, where the main commercial and shipping establishments are located, is littered with the wreckage of revolutions. The rest of the town is no better. Not a single public building stands intact. The Senate, the Chamber of Deputies, and the ministries are reduced to occupancy of wood shanties . . .

Hyppolite, however, had both the will and, with good times, the wherewithal to proceed with reconstruction. In June 1890 Douglass reported "manifold projects for improving streets, roads, and wharves, and the increasing number of private dwellings in process of erection . . . The sound of the hammer and trowel is heard late and early."

The president's projects included a domestic telegraph system, telephones, and waterworks in Port-au-Prince and a few other towns, markets and abattoirs, wharves (as well as a 700-ton marine railway at Bizoton), a new Chamber of Deputies, and, long overdue, a marble monument to Dessalines. Equally overdue, in September 1895 Port-au-Prince got its first ice plant and no longer depended for that precious commodity on sawdust-packed shipments from Europe or New England. For the first time in Haitian history, Hyppolite in 1892 brought to uninterrupted completion an important public work commenced by a predecessor - the iron bridge over the Momance River that stood until 1961 (when replaced by Bailey bridging supplied by the U.S. Naval Mission).

Besides this internal progress, much stimulated by the new Ministry of Public Works, Firmin as Foreign Minister reopened legations in London and Madrid, and established full relations with Berlin, Haiti's first minister to the Wilhelmstrasse being Démesvar Delorme. Another of Firmin's successes in 1892 was to secure from the Vatican Haiti's first apostolic nuncio, Msgr. Julio Tonti.

Many of Hyppolite's works still survived seventy-five years later: the Palais des Cinq Ministères in Port-au-Prince, the customs sheds, the charming Marché de Fer (inaugurated on 22 November 1891), which no tourist misses, the abattoir (replaced in 1961, thanks to the enterprise of an American entrepreneur, Mr. Bobby Baker). Among numerous ephemera was Jacmel's electric-light system (1895), which lasted only a year but whose monumental bronze fin-de-siècle lampposts stood until spirited away under the guise of "modernization" in 1985. ("It was nothing," observed one Jacmelien, "but a fine pretext for official pillage.")

That same Jacmelien, Rodolphe Charmant, son of Alcius, later reminisced: "Under Hyppolite in 1890, 1891, and 1892, there was a carnival of contracts in the Chambers. Every party regular, senator, minister, deputy, or former *volontaire de la révolution* had at least one in the bag . . . Handsome favors, to be sure, that Good Fairy handed out to the faithful who had just ravaged the four corners of the country with fire and sword."

The Mephistophelean master of these lucrative revels was Frédéric Marcelin, connoisseur not only of *belles lettres* but equally of dazzling contracts, concessions, and fine fiscal arithmetic. Marcelin had succeeded to Firmin's portfolio of Finance - an office of profit, though perhaps not trust, in which, for three years, he did extremely well.

Just after Marcelin's retirement to France in 1895 (when Haiti's public debt - $4.4 million in 1891 - had climbed to over $25 million) an enemy, Mathon, indignantly depicted the former Minister:

Monocle in eye, smiling with his lips, mustache pointed like the sting of a scorpion . . . Legislator, author, journalist, but above all, financial operator without shame, he soiled all he touched, and compromised and walked over every friend. That man who now parades his well-kept person through the scandalous halls of the Folies Bergères -need I name him? It is Monsieur Frédéric Marcelin.

Originally a protégé of Septimus Rameau, Marcelin had founded his fortunes under Salomon with a marvelous contract whereby in 1885 the government paid him as concessionaire and underwrote the charter of four French steamers to carry mail. For nearly two years, at a good profit, the ships carried freight and passengers but never a letter, until the deal collapsed when the shipowners protested to the French legation that they had never been paid.

While Finance Minister, said *telediol*, Marcelin was said to keep his accounts balanced by a tunnel which supposedly joined the ministry with the nearby *Banque Nationale*. When called on to exhibit assets, Marcelin is said to have trundled specie by cart through the tunnel from bank to ministry, and vice versa.

What must have been Marcelin's greatest coup, however, was the *Alexandre Pétion* caper of 1893, in which the aged gunboat of that name, reportedly carrying one and perhaps several of Marcelin's enemies (including Molina, the Dominican minister) sailed from Port-au-Prince with a cargo of crated bullion to liquidate obligations of Hyppolite to the Dominican dictator, Heureaux. At some point of voyage, for whatever cause, the old *Pétion* suddenly blew up and all that was ever seen of her, says tradition, were several stout cases, still sealed by the *Banque Nationale* and marked "Gold" - which floated ashore! (24)

But all good things come to an end, and, in a swirl of printing-press money and, in 1896, another French loan, so did the Hyppolite boom. If he looked up from the Folies Bergères, surely Marcelin smiled. Within the palace Hyppolite, like Pétion, openly kept his mistress, Mme. Victoire, whom the French minister characterized as "*ancienne fille publique du Cap.*" "She thinks only," he reported, "of making money and exploiting her position. The government budget is looted and any minister who stands up to her is ruthlessly sacked . . . She now takes the place of honor on public occasions, scandalizing the Apostolic Delegate, who pretends not to see her."

In 1896, as his term neared its close, Hyppolite, wrote Bellegarde, "just like all the others, had only one concern - to keep himself in power - and one fear: to see some other candidate capable of balking his ambition to stay on."

Hostages were again jailed, soldiers were camped in the streets and squares, and all the fieldpieces and ammunition of the city were lightered out of harm's way aboard the three gunboats.

Hyppolite kept the country in hand through a system of warlords known as "*députés militaires.*" Nord Alexis, naturally, presided over the North; bullet-headed Jean-Jumeau ruled Gonaïves and the Artibonite; and Antoine Simon held sway over the South. Only at Jacmel was the peace perennially disturbed by Mérisier. On the night of 15-16 March 1896, the old *piquet* and his *rasoirs* swooped on the town, caught sentries asleep, sacked the arsenal, drove the defenders in headlong flight, and then vanished back to Lafond.

This was too much: Hyppolite determined to teach Mérisier a lesson. As cocks were crowing and dawn was beginning to glow over Pétionville on 24 March, the president mounted his stallion and, at the head of an armed cavalcade, set out for Jacmel.

Just short of Portail Léogane, Hyppolite suddenly shuddered, slipped sidewise from his saddle, and fell with a thud - dead of apoplexy before he hit the ground. His great gold watch stopped on impact and Hyppolite's fine panama was trampled in the mud by the frightened horse. Afterward and to this day they sing the *meringue*

> *"En sortant la ville nan Jacmel . . .*
> *Panamam' tombé . . .*

Drift and Humiliation

General Tirésias Augustin Simon Sam, another *noir* of the North, enjoyed the best possible credentials to succeed Hyppolite: he was incumbent Minister of War and popular with the army; and he was Salomon's nephew by marriage and Séïde Télémaque's brother-in-law. Conceding that the general was universally liked, Pichon, French minister (and later distinguished Foreign Minister), quickly added, "Aside from military matters, he is an absolute incompetent." Described by an American naval officer as "a tall, very black, full-blooded Negro of good bearing," Simon Sam gained office in consequence of a three-way impasse among *mulâtres* seeking to restore Boisrond-Canal; an ultra-*noir* pro-French faction grouped around Manigat; and an anti-Manigat coalition headed by Callisthène Fouchard, one of the country's ablest men. Simon Sam was elected by the assembly on 31 March 1896. (Henry M. Smythe, the new American minister, reported a restless night on the 26th, when police and soldiers fired "perhaps a hundred thousand rounds" throughout the capital.)

Simon Sam took office without a program but with some momentum from that of Hyppolite. Public works continued. Now harnessed to wheezy little steam engines, the Port-au-Prince horse cars again clattered up the Rue des Miracles, work continued on the rail line to Thomazeau, and a new railroad, from the Cap to Grande Rivière du Nord, was commenced. Outflanking foreign-ownership prohibitions in the constitution, the prevailing instrument for such operations was a foreign concession, whose arrangements, typical of such enterprises, were summarized in disillusion by another American minister, William F. Powell, in 1899 as follows:

A railroad is to be constructed, water-works built, or an electric-light plant established. Some individual, either a native or a foreigner, secures from the government a concession to do such work, receiving in return all the emoluments from such enterprise, with an added subsidy from the government for a term of years, after which time it is supposed to revert to the government. The concessionaire, not having the money to conduct such an enterprise, takes his concession to Europe and parts with his interest in the concession to the highest bidder . . . In nearly every case the government becomes the victim, while the concessionaire is the victor.

In this time of drift - punctuated by yellow fever epidemics in November of 1896 and 1897 - Haiti was again brutalized by the Hohenzollerns.

As the century wore to its end (and increasingly until World War I), German commercial and political interests in Haiti had steadily expanded. Internal loans floated by the government on discounts as high as 40 percent were taken by German merchants, whose rewards included concessions for electric companies, ice plants, the Port-au-Prince wharf, and railroad franchises.

It was against this background that Emile Lüders, a half-Haitian German national and Port-au-Prince livery stable-keeper, became involved, on 20 September 1897, in an affray with the police over the arrest of one of his hostlers.(25)

Sentenced to jail and a fine, Lüders was released and deported in October on intervention by Germany's loud-voiced, overbearing minister, Count von Schwerin (who, Firmin later wrote, never allowed his wife to meet Haitians socially). Schwerin also presented demands, ignored by Simon Sam, for dismissal of the judges and police in the Lüders case. To exacerbate the matter, Schwerin insisted on trying to present the German protest directly to President Simon Sam, rather than through Foreign Minister Firmin, and, in the words of Ludwell Montague, pursued the president "like a process-server."

That the German government was adamant in pressing the case came home forcefully at dawn on 6 December, when two German warships, S.M.S. *Charlotte* and *Stein*, anchored off Port-au-Prince, and their commodore, Kapitän-zur-See August Thiele, sent word ashore that, commencing at 1:00 P.M., he would sink all Haitian warships present, destroy the *Palais National*, and bombard Port-au-Prince, providing the following terms were not acceded to: a $20,000 indemnity to Lüders and his readmission to Haiti; formal apology to the German government; a 21-gun salute to the imperial colors; and a reception at the palace for Count Schwerin. To the diplomatic corps's collective remonstrance, Thiele on his quarterdeck coldly replied that Berlin's orders allowed no deviations: unless the Haitian flag over the Palais was replaced by a white flag before 1:00 P.M., the bombardment would proceed.

Clutching at the Monroe Doctrine, Simon Sam asked the American minister whether any U.S. naval vessels were at hand. A negative reply left Haiti no more alternative than in the days of Batsch twenty-five years earlier.

Down came the colors; up went the white flag. By four o'clock the indemnity had been scraped up, and, an hour later, Lüders came ashore. At sunset, Fort National saluted the German flag. Schwerin, in full diplomatic tenue, stalked icily to the palace for the reception U.S. Minister Powell (26) called "an unpleasant affair."

Haiti's resentment over this painful humiliation did not engulf Simon Sam, on whom the French government quickly and pointedly conferred the Legion of

Honor, but the lines of Oswald Durand, Haiti's *Capois* laureate, bespoke the national anguish:

> *Non! Nous ne voulons plus, Allemands, Prussiens,*
> *Comme autrefois à Batsch, votre vil émissaire,*
> *Cracher l'argent, devant sa redoubtable serre,*
> *Ainsi qu'on jette un os aux chiens!(27)*

Despite France's show of sympathy and Simon Sam's Legion of Honor, the private conclusion of Meyer, the French minister, was that Haiti got what she had been asking for. Writing to the Quai d'Orsay, Meyer bluntly said Lüders's case was only a pretext, that Firmin while Foreign Minister had continually baited Scherwin and his predecessor, and that as late as forty-eight hours (4 December 1897) before the German gunboats arrived, Simon Sam had publicly threatened the diplomatic corps that if the Kaiser sent warships to Haiti, he would go back into the mountains and "Port-au-Prince would no longer exist."

Happily, the president's threat proved to be only the rhetoric of 1804. What on the other hand was very real was Berlin's ruthless display of an increasing special interest in the black republic.

Simon Sam Abdicates

Two weeks after the Germans departed with their booty,(29) the Haitian government laid the foundations of a scandal surpassing even those of the 1875 loans or the *Affaire des Mandats*. Under the worthy and ostensible object of consolidating the floating debt into a single series of obligations, a complex operation involving kickbacks and double payments to President Simon Sam, his family, his ministers, and French and German accomplices was consummated during 1899 and 1900. When, to the astonishment of all, the next president, Nord Alexis, initiated criminal prosecutions over *"les consolidations,"* the extent of peculation that was developed in evidence, probably only the tip of the iceberg, amounted to $1,257,993.(30)

Looking at Haiti's finances from 1890 to 1902, Louis Hartmann, for five years (1891 to 1896) an honest French director of the *Banque*, noted that the government had expended a total of 82 million gourdes (not including $25 million service on public debts) and asked what Haiti had to show for it. Taking the budgeted amounts for five ministries over the twelve years, Hartmann wrote:

LA GUERRE: 15 million gourdes. Are the army and national defense better than in 1890?

LA MARINE: 8 million gourdes. The navy no longer exists militarily.

L'INTERIEURE ET LA POLICE: 14 million gourdes. What improvements can be noticed? Is public safety any better?

TRAVAUX PUBLIQUES: 7 million gourdes. Public buildings are failing down. The highways are deplorable and getting worse, everything ought to be rebuilt.

AGRICULTURE: 3 million gourdes. National production has not improved. Coffee, notably, is at a standstill . . In no respect has any improvement been noticeable. The misery of the people is worse than ever.

Hartmann's question as to the army was well taken. Ever since 1804, for a century, the army had been the dominant institution of Haiti. "The country is governed by Generals," recorded Prichard, a visiting British journalist (30), seven years later, ". . . Generals of Departments; below them Generals of Arrondissements and of Communes. Lower again are Generals of subdivisions. Generals of *Postes Militaries,* and so it goes on. There is a General of the prison, and a General of the women's prison."

Although the generals numbered thousands," there were also junior officers and privates, whose numbers and pay laid a crushing burden on every government. Recruiting, as described by an American minister, was by press gang and *cocomacac.* "In the mountain districts they are hustled like wild animals and driven into the cities like a drove of cattle with their legs tied together with a rope sufficiently long to enable them to walk, their arms tied behind them . . . These people range in age from 14 to 65. If any resist or endeavor to escape, they are shot as they run.

Soldiers performed one essential civic function. They voted. In the words of the American minister, Dr. H. W. Furniss, in 1907: "The voters are the soldiers . . . In Port-au-Prince I have seen soldiers come up in companies and remain all day voting and repeating at command of their officers, while none of the better or middle classes were trying to vote, if indeed, it had been possible." (Furniss, who relieved Powell late in 1907, was the first American black to hold both an M.D. and a Ph.D.)

Thus, amid corruption and drift, the days of Simon Sam approached their close. As usual toward the end of a regime, restless outbreaks began to occur. On to September 1901, smelling sedition, the authorities at Jérémie arrested leading citizens and executed at least one. Turbulent Jacmel, with some thirty asylees already in consulates, was attacked on 11 April 1902, by insurgents seeking to depose Mérisier Jeannis, who since 1896 had been self-proclaimed *seul borome* (top man) of the town and region.(31) Despite treachery from within, the assault was bloodily defeated: forty assailants were captured, including their general. who, with six others, was executed in the streets. At the same time, in both Cayes and Port-au-Prince, waves of unrest were harshly countered by waves of arrest.

Simon Sam could read the omens as well as any other Haitian. On 12 May, three days before his term expired, the president abdicated - a maneuver meant to avert an election and throw the choice of a successor to the incumbent assembly (forty-eight of whose members were relatives of Simon Sam), where, generously bank-rolled by German merchants, (32) Cincinnatus Leconte had the electoral votes in his pocket.

The arrangement was too raw: Leconte, fellow Nordist and ally of Simon Sam, symbolized a regime whose mandate had run out. On the evening of 12 May, as the assembly prepared to vote, armed crowds gathered outside. Within, some hothead drew his pistol and fired. "In an instant," reported Minister Powell, "shooting commenced from all parts of the room. One or two were killed and the same number wounded. The members all sought shelter . . . under benches or desks. Others forgot the way they entered and sought exit by means of the windows. "
As in the days of Salnave, the mob swept the Chamber while others tried to storm the palace and arsenal. After bloody fighting that left a hundred killed or wounded, the Presidential Guard beat back the attacks, but the game was up. Next morning at six, Simon Sam and his cabinet placed themselves under protection of the diplomatic corps. Five hours later, escorted by the ministers and consuls, Sam and Leconte and their families safely ran the gauntlet to the wharf, and a steamer for France, where, besides a snug *pied-à-terre* at 39 Avenue des Champs Elysées, the outgoing president had $2.5 million consolidated in private accounts.

Firminist Civil War

Boisrond-Canal, veteran midwife of regimes, was at hand to assume his accustomed role. It was the last time: he would be dead in three years. (33) The usual Committee of Public Safety was cobbled together, political prisoners turned loose, and presidential hopefuls Fouchard and Momplaisir Pierre welcomed back from Jamaica. Of course it was not quite that smooth: on 15 May determined attacks were repeated against palace and arsenal, but were again beaten off.
Another candidate, Firmin, very embodiment of the neo-Bazelaisist aspirations of the educated, impatient oligarchist young, was already back at the Cap. Haitian minister in Paris, he had returned home with the body of Anna, his favorite daughter, who had died in 1901. Admiral Killick, for one, had left no doubt of his support for Firmin. The day Simon Sam departed, Killick, having thoughtfully diverted several thousand new Remingtons and a million rounds of ammunition from the arsenal, took the whole navy (his new flagship, *La Crête-à-Pierrot*, and gunboat *Toussaint Louverture)* North to the Cap to await

developments.

Firmin had not been inactive. Working in what seemed firm alliance with Tonton Nord, he had exacted a loan from the merchants of the Cap to finance a war chest for the army with which, on 18 May, Nord Alexis marched on Port-au-Prince, picking up the support of Jean-Jumeau of St. Marc. Killick in turn ferried to the capital the newly chosen delegates from the North, Northwest, and Artibonite, while Firmin remained with Nord and Jean-Jumeau and the army.

Boisrond and his heavily anti-Firminist junta were not insensible of the implications of a Northern army at St. Marc and an avowedly Firminist navy offshore. Their reaction was to persuade Firmin and Nord Alexis to come down to Port-au-Prince alone, while the army remained at St. Marc. At this point they tossed an apple of discord between Nord and Firmin by inducting the former but not the latter into the *gouvernement provisoire* proclaimed on 26 May.

Giving Nord Alexis $10,000 to pay expenses, the junta sent him and his army to the Cap "to maintain order." When Tonton Nord reached the Cap, it was with adamant intent to block Firmin and at long last gain the presidency.

In June the abscess burst. Led by Firmin's brother-in-law, Albert Salnave, Firminist troops clashed with those of Nord. Killick, impulsive as always, proceeded on 27 June to shell the Cap (not heavily: he had valuable properties in the town) and put ashore a landing force. He was no luckier than Galbaud 109 years earlier. Tonton Nord thrashed everyone in sight and chased the sailors off the beach, followed in hot haste by Salnave, and, improbably disguised as a sailor, Firmin. The moment *La Crête-à-Pierrot* had her anchor up, Nord Alexis loosed his men on Firmin's home.

"Everything," reported Minister Powell on 19 July "was destroyed, some of the costly furniture sold openly in the streets, his handsome library, the finest in the Republic, containing many rare books of priceless value, was destroyed . . . a work he was preparing for the press and near completion, styled 'The History of Haiti,' representing the work of twenty years, was given to the flames . . .

Even Joseph Jérémie, one of Haiti's most literate politicians and Firmin's most implacable (and ablest) foes, deplored the outrage at the Cap. Writing very privately to Firmin, the *mulâtre* Jérémie said, "The days of 28 and 29 June constitute yet another disgrace in our history. Do your enemies comprehend the extent of the crime they committed in scattering your records and burning your works? To blot out the works of the spirit is to proclaim the sovereignty of ignorance."

Less heart-rending but more ominous for Firmin, on 28 June *Toussaint Louverture* drove hard aground on the reefs off Caracol within ten miles of *Santa María's* grave. Now, bound for Gonaïves with Firmin, Admiral Killick had only one ship left.

The revolution never had a chance. Nord Alexis successively shattered the troops of Jean-Jumeau and Albert Salnave in pointless battles that burned Limbé, St. Michel de l'Atalaye, and Marmelade, and said Powell - other "slight engagements (called here a battle)." Petit-Goâve, defended by the irreconcilables of Jacmel, Miragoâne, and Aquin, went up in flames, a reprise of Miragoâne nineteen years earlier, when on 8 August government soldiers overpowered its defenders. Chicoyé, their leader, tracked down in the same mountains and woods as the men of Miragoâne, was shot beside the cemetery wall in Jacmel on to September. As Berrouet, his enemy and executioner, explained it, "General Boisrond is adamant . . . They won't forgive a bright *mulâtre* like you being a Firminist."

By the end of August, short of arms and compressed into the Artibonite flats of St. Marc and Gonaïves, Firmin realized that his only hope lay with Killick and *La Crête-à-Pierrot,* which still controlled the sea.

The Death of Admiral Killick

"The show ship," wrote Prichard of the Haitian navy, "is the *Crête-à-Pierrot.* She is a fat, white vessel with a yellow funnel and gold scrollwork upon her bows and stem, and over her floats the angry blue and red of the Black Republic." English-built, armed in France with a powerful battery, run by a British captain and engineer, *Crête-à-Pierrot,* acquired in 1896, had been Killick's pride and flagship ever since. As soon as civil war broke out in 1902, Killick proclaimed a one-ship blockade, and the government countered by proclaiming Killick pirate.(34)

On 2 September, cruising the Gulf of Gonaïves, *Crête-à-Pierrot* made prize of a German merchantman, S.S. *Markomannia,* running arms North to the Cap. Her cargo was swiftly unloaded at Gonaïves and jubilantly possessed by the Firminists.

The Imperial German Government reacted in Hohenzollern fury. Summoning the nearest warship, S.M.S. *Panther* (that same ship which, nine years later, was to precipitate the Agadir crisis of July 1911), the German chargé relayed orders from Berlin to seize or sink the offending Haitian gunboat.

On the morning of 6 September, her prognathous ram bow slicing the calm gulf, *Panther* tracked down *La Crête-à-Pierrot,* heedlessly anchored in Gonaïves, with the bulk of her crew ashore on overnight liberty. Admiral Killick, who had suffered the amputation of a finger the day before, was also on the beach. Punctuating his ultimatum with a warning gun, Fregaten-Kapitän Eckermann sent word for the Haitian ship to haul down her colors and surrender.

During the frantic scurry that ensued, Killick got into uniform, made his way out to his flagship, directed certain preparations, and ordered all remaining hands ashore. Alone except for his surgeon, Dr. Coles, who refused to leave,

(35) Admiral Killick, draped in the Haitian colors, touched his cigar to a powder train leading to combustibles in the magazine, and sat down in his cabin. Before the boats reached shore, an explosion and dense smoke erupted aft. Recognizing what had happened. Captain Eckermann decided to underscore the Wilhelmstrasse's point. He ordered Panther's four guns to open fire into the dying ship along her waterline. As flames reached the forward magazine, there came a second explosion, and *La Crête-à-Pierrot* rolled over on her port side and settled into the calm waters. Killick's blackened body was eventually retrieved - and, as a suicide, was denied Church rites by the local French priest. When word reached the Navy Ministry in Berlin, Kaiser Wilhelm II sent a personal signal: "Bravo, *Panther,* compliments!"

Tonton Nord, the Last Leaf

Firmin's cause went to the bottom with *La Crête-à-Pierrot.* Useless that Haitians of all colors and factions responded unanimously in grief, pride, and rage, when they learned what the Germans had done.(36) After a month of futile sparring, on 17 October Firmin boarded S.S. *Adirondack* bound for Montecristi and his retreat on St. Thomas, where, wrote foreign correspondent Stephen Bonsai in 1912 of Maloney's renowned bar, "ex-Dictators muse, and aspirant Presidents ply their followers with white rum."

After a few weeks spent in mopping up the North and the Artibonite, Tonton Nord marched South again, this time all the way to Port-au-Prince, and entered the capital on 14 December. Three days later, the army acclaimed its leader president and escorted him to the *Palais National.* Then the assembly convened briefly on 21 December and, with no dissenting voice, ratified the army's decision.

Pierre Nord Alexis, eighty-three, born in 1820 when Henry Christophe still ruled the North, was the last leaf in Henry's mighty tree. His wife, "Mère Alexis," daughter of Pierrot and a *mambo,* was the niece of Christophe. By no means an illiterate *noir,* as some have dismissed him, or an old simpleton either, Nord Alexis nonetheless disdained intellectuals (whom he styled as *"les intellects"),* feared and suspected foreigners and *blancs* and their intentions toward Haiti, and was consecrated to the point of obsession to three ideals - independence, La Patrie, and *"les aïeux"* (the forebears). Nothing else mattered.

Armed habitually with his *cocomacac* and not averse to using it, the old man, half-blind from an ancient powder explosion, still had eyes too sharp for malefactors. Like Christophe, he kept a private reader who read to him aloud. As he moved through the streets in the fashion of Dessalines, Soulouque, Salnave, and many another ruler of Haiti, Tonton Nord would toss small coins or bills to the cheering crowds. Seen by Frédéric Marcelin at a wedding in 1904, when he gave away the bride in the cathedral, "The President entered, very straight and very firm, and gave his arm to the bride. The vigor and the robustness of this man of eighty-seven are astonishing. His fine figure is no way bowed . . . He is well groomed, he wears his black suit handsomely."

It took only four months for Nord Alexis to tire of the maneuvers and obstructionism of a fractious legislature. On 30 March 1903, with a round of volleys, his soldiers dissolved the Chamber of Deputies. Financial problems were immediate and chronic. Simon Sam had borrowed from Peter to pay Paul (not to mention Simon): Nord Alexis, fearful of foreign debt-collecting forays, would not borrow from the *blancs*. Instead, he resorted to the printing presses of Boyer and Salnave. He had good reason to suspect the foreigners of the *Banque Nationale*, and one of his first actions was to launch the relentless investigation of the *Affaire des Consolidations* that climaxed in that cause celebre of 1904. In response to his probes, the *Banque*'s director, de la Myre-Mory (one of those later convicted) incautiously tried to cut off disbursements for the army. Tonton Nord's direct approach to the problem was to tell his officers that the *Banque* had their money and to go and get it.

Ever since the *semaine sanglante*, which had dealt a mortal blow to the Haitian merchant class, retail trade (with sidelines in usury) had been gradually taken over by an influx of Levantine immigrants, mainly Syrian and Lebanese, including many with cursory, or frequently fraudulent, American naturalization. In the words of a report to Washington by Powell:

> Up to a few years ago, one could see on the country roads, hundreds of country merchants or peddlers with their donkeys loaded with all classes of merchandise. going into the interior to trade with the country people. Today their places are supplied by these people [Syrians] who, instead of the donkey to carry their merchandise, employ natives to guide and porter them through the country.

In a time of poor coffee crops and unfavorable world prices, of printing-press money and foreign speculators who manipulated the exchange, it was not difficult to make visible scapegoats of the Syrians, and that is what the regime did. By June 1903, towns were flooded with handbills denouncing Syrian "birds of prey" and calling for their expulsion. In August, "for hygienic reasons that have absolutely nothing to do with race" (as J.-N. Léger solemnly assured foreign readers), the legislature obediently enacted a law virtually excluding Syrians from Haitian naturalization and, within a year, mobs led by soldiers - not only in Port-au-Prince but in Léogane, Arcahaie, the Goâves, and St. Marc - were plundering and burning the homes and shops of Syrians and stoning them and their families through the streets. Belabored in print by a newspaper explicitly called *l'Anti-Syrien*, batches of hapless Syrians caught with forged or irregular naturalization papers were expelled on three days' notice in February 1905; a month later, the government ordered all Syrian businesses closed by the end of March, and shoveled their owners out of Haiti in April.(37)

But the greatest preoccupation of Tonton Nord, as his regime neared midseason, was not the Syrians, the mounting economic distress, or the squalid peculations of the *Banque*, but the approaching centenary of Haitian independence. When in 1903 a politician incautiously suggested that observation of the anniversary might remind the world of what he referred to as *"nos turpitudes, "* the old man rounded fiercely and burst out *"Comment! Ne pas fêter le Centenaire! Ça serait plutôt la honte!"* (What! Not celebrate the centennial! That would be the most awful disgrace!).

The Centenaire

The approach of a centennial plunged Haiti into feelings of ambivalence and introspection. For the constellation of bright young men Massillon Coicou, Jean Price-Mars, Félix Magloire, Georges Sylvain, Charles Moravia, to name a few - limned with such fervor by another of them, Dantès Bellegarde, the gap between ideals and aspirations and performance was painful.

They could, for example, look in the street of the national capital and see such scenes as this market day, described in 1900 by a foreign visitor:

> Buyers and sellers spread themselves like an open camp into the streets around, the smell was appalling . . . In the (meat market] you can trace the evolution of the flesh-foods, the raw materials of your future meals. Pigs and goats, their legs tied together, raise their voices in expostulation as they lie in the sun. One has wriggled to a neighboring drain and is gulping the thick fluid . . .

Eight years later, little had changed save for the worse, reported the American minister:

> There are no sewers. The streets are full of all kinds of animals from a flock of sheep and several cows and goats which roam unmolested, they being the property of the President, to the ducks which swim in the gutter before the Legation and numerous pigs which wallow in the gutter . . . Personages of high social rank. owners of fine houses luxuriously furnished, find it quite natural to throw each morning the dirt. etc.. from their stables in the street within two meters of their drawing rooms . . .

Faced with these and other unappetizing realities, many able and sensitive persons did not feel it sufficed for Occide Jeanty to have composed his fierce "1804" centennial march, or for Justin Lhérisson to have written Haiti's stirring and evocative national anthem, "*La Dessalinienne*," or for the government to have erected a gingerbread *Palais du Centenaire* (Centenary Palace) at Gonaïves.(38) Marcelin, for one, was plunged in gloom.

> What folly to think of celebrating the *Centenaire*! What have you accomplished that you can be proud of? Show us the civilization you have created. Where is any accomplishment or concept to which you have attached your name? Will it be civil strife, your fratricidal slaughters, your social miseries, your economic ignorance, your idolatrous militarism that you are going to glorify on 1 January 1904? Marcelin's reply to his own question - the only possible reply - was simple: "We glorify an ideal that has permitted a tiny nation to remain free and independent - *l'Indépendance ou la Mort!*"

In the eyes of Dr. Rosalvo Bobo, the *mulâtre* nationalist physician of the Cap, Marcelin's answer was not good enough. Instead of celebrating the centennial, wrote Bobo, "the country should drape an immense funeral pall over all its territory and plunge itself into mediation on the follies of the past."

Dr. Bobo and other Jeremiahs of this time had good reason to call the people to repentance. The outcome of the Spanish-American War, coupled with the U.S. takeover of the Puerto Plata customs house (14 July 1904) followed early in 1905 by an American customs receivership intended to stave off European intervention in Santo Domingo - such signs and portents ought to have warned Haiti that its interests would be best served by what Ludwell Montague called "reform from within as a guard against reform from without."

To make the point abundantly clear, Haitians in 1904 need only have heeded Theodore Roosevelt's evocation of America's new-found *mission civilisatrice* in his message that year to Congress:

> If a nation shows that it knows how to act with reasonable efficiency and decency in social and political matters, if it keeps order and pays its obligations, it need fear no interference from the United States . . . Chronic wrong-doing, or an impotence which results in a general lessening of the ties of civilized society, may in America, as elsewhere, ultimately require intervention by some civilized nation, and in the Western Hemisphere . . . the Monroe Doctrine may force the United States, however reluctantly, in flagrant areas of such wrong-doing or impotence, to the exercise of an international police power.

Some Haitians did hear Roosevelt's words, and recognized how pointedly they could apply to Haiti. But most did not. For them the meaning and implications of the *Centenaire* were encompassed in the enormous gathering at Gonaïves, surely the greatest since Dessalines proclaimed independence, where - its four portals named Louverture, Dessalines, Pétion, and Nord Alexis - the *Palais du Centenaire* was nearly drowned in the throng of 250,000 that gathered to fête their country, their ancestors, and old Tonton Nord.(39)

Great Misery Prevails

Marcelin had advised Nord Alexis to mark the *Centenaire* by pardoning and bringing home every Haitian exile abroad. Instead, Tonton Nord marked the occasion in blood.

On 1 January 1904, while the very ceremonies at Gonaïves were in progress, Port-au-Prince was swept by rumors quickly confirmed by volleys. Caught in the home of General Maxi Momplaisir on Rue du Port, some thirty conspirators were surrounded by police and soldiers. Momplaisir, his son, and his coachman were executed on the spot. General Maxime Jacques broke his leg escaping but dragged himself to asylum. Not to be balked, the authorities seized his wife as hostage, whereupon he gave himself up. Following prolonged interrogation he was shot as he lay helpless in bed. Among widespread arrests ordered by Nord Alexis on return were those of General G. Destouches and Port-au-Prince's former mayor, C. Lafontant. At their trial, reported American Consul Terres, "the lawyers for the defense were not allowed to plead, the moment they commenced, their voices were drowned by the beating of drums and all kinds of disturbances . . . All were condemned to death as expected."

Suspicion, rarely dormant in Haiti, now took the reins. Jérémie and Jacmel were placed under curfew. Special permits were required by anyone seeking to travel outside Port-au-Prince. The cable company was made to submit copies of all traffic to the palace, and letters were closely scrutinized in the post office. In 1905 a New York detective agency (John G. Meehan, 42 Broadway) was hired for $3000 to keep tabs on Haitian exiles in the United States: other detectives were retained in St. Thomas.

Antiforeignism mounted. In June 1904 the French and German ministers and wives were stoned in their carriages by sentinels of the Presidential Guard for inadvertently taking a short cut behind the *Palais National*. Only three years later, Pichon, the French Foreign Minister (who had been French chargé in Port-au-Prince from 1894 to 1895), conveyed the sympathies of an old hand to his successor (who showed the letter to American Minister Furniss):

He [Pichon] was well aware of all the difficulties under which any diplomatic representative accredited to Haiti had to labor: he knew the treachery and duplicity of the Haitian officials; that if one performed one's duty toward one's government, he would become *persona non grata*, and, by intrigue and complaint, attempt would be made to have him recalled.

But diplomatic grievances were not one-sided: Vansittart, the British chargé, simply ignored the government. Ten months after his arrival, in 1903, wrote Powell, he still refused to meet or call on the president. In all this, the American legation (which had received its first typewriter in 1897 and - timeless Haiti! - its first clock only in 1900) got its first (and Haiti's first) military attaché.(40) Described in *Le Nouvelliste* as "*un noir au port correct et distingué* ." Captain Young of the 9th Cavalry was received in state at the palace in June 1904 while *(Le Nouvelliste* went on) "the champagne flowed and the Palace Band rendered the most entrancing morsels in its repertory."

On 29 April 1905, Powell sent a report to Secretary of State John Hay, which, simply redated, would have applied at any time during the next three years:

> The strength of the President is in the Army and the large amount of arms and ammunition he has under his direct control: but even this force is not altogether loyal as within a few weeks past, the President has stationed his regiment within the Palace grounds . . . Great misery prevails in nearly all the large cities . . . The President is almost unaware of conditions as he is almost a prisoner himself . . . He is surrounded by guards and it is only through those who have charge of the Palace that anyone can be admitted. When he goes out to Church or anywhere, he is surrounded by a guard numbering a hundred or more.

Despite all this and worse - unpaid government salaries, the printing-press gourde tumbling to 590 to the U.S. dollar - Nord Alexis made a determined effort to improve public education. Backing two able ministers, Murville Férère and Thrasybule Laleau, Nord tried to revive the rural schools (but the results were still feeble: in 1905, Out of an estimated 653,754 children of school age, only 30,000 were enrolled in all institutions, public and private). He also cooperated with the Church in establishing what appears to have been Haiti's first agricultural school - an experimental farm at Turgeau, opened in 1907 by the Brothers of Christian Instruction.(41)

Ever since the Consolidations convictions - especially as Britain and France had managed to pry their men out of jail - Tonton Nord had a score to settle with the *Banque*, which, with reason, he referred to as *"La banque friponne"* (the rogue bank). In 1905, he simply revoked its charter and carried on with no bank at all.

Fall 1907 saw more denunciations, arrests, more refugees in asylum, and more political trials. On 15 October, the inevitable executions followed.

After traveling through more than three fourths of the country on horseback, American Minister Furniss wrote a lengthy but prescient confidential summary. He found the peasants friendly and peaceable, with little interest in or knowledge of politics, wishing only to till their soil and avoid army service, which meant

seeking outside work in order to eat. Funds appropriated for soldiers' rations
seldom found their way down to the ranks. A general, Furniss recorded, called
regularly at the legation to collect his kickback from the soldier-sweeper
employed there. Yet, Furniss added:

> With all this the common people have no thought of revolution, they are forced into
> it by their commanding officers, yet once revolution is on with the accompanying
> burning and pillage, they get the fever and go on until they are stopped . . . Intrigue
> is so rife that one may be in high favor today and have others condemned to exile,
> prison, or even to be shot, and tomorrow fall victim to the intrigue of another and
> be treated as ignominiously as his own victims . . .

Though he knew no other ways to rule Haiti save those he had learned in a
very long life, Tonton Nord was not, as future generations would put it,
indifferent to Haiti's image or to fears of future U.S. designs. The day after
election day (3 November 1908) J.-N. Léger, the Haitian minister, had written
Nord Alexis a letter from Washington that set the old man thinking:

> M. Taft has just been chosen as the next President of the United States. I know the
> President-Elect personally. We can consider him as a friend. However I must tell
> you frankly that *I do not consider him inclined to allow neighboring Republics to
> continue the bloody game of civil war.* [Léger's emphasis.] What he has already
> done in Cuba and Panama [as U.S. Secretary of War] indicates clearly his future
> attitude.

For the time that remained, Nord Alexis, impressed and wary, carried Léger's
letter with him, showing it to politicians and generals alike. "My own son - if
I had one," he exploded one day with the letter in hand; "I'd shoot him down
without hesitation if I caught him conspiring."

Stormy 1908

January 1908 dawned stormy. Beginning on the 10th, deputies were to be chosen
who, it was widely asserted, would confer on Tonton Nord the second term he
now planned. Mère Alexis (or "CéCé," her Créole nickname) was behind it all,
people said. In another confidential report on 3 January 1908, the American
minister agreed: Tonton Nord would never have decided to succeed himself save
for "his wife, who, though uneducated, is a shrewd woman, wields an immense
influence and is the one who has to be 'seen' when any money is 'floating
around' for concessions, etc. Combined with Mme. Alexis is a coterie close to
the President who are rich from their stealings and plunder."

Dr. Louis-Joseph Janvier, Haiti's foremost constitutional scholar and late minister to the Court of St. James's, made the error of announcing his candidacy as a deputy for Port-au-Prince, a move that did not fit Tonton Nord's electoral game-plan. On 3 January he was arrested, dragged through the streets, beaten, and imprisoned. All that saved Dr. Janvier from a firing squad was his frantic promise to recall from circulation every copy of an imprudent electioneering pamphlet.

Despite the usual incendiary fires and minor disorders, polling was completed as planned; fifteen of Nord Alexis's relatives or godchildren were among those elected.

On 15 January, while the regime was congratulating itself on successful elections, a messenger dashed to the palace from the cable company: Gonaïves had been devastated by an earthquake and shocks were continuing. A phone call to St. Marc (Principal towns had now been linked by telephone, as well, in some cases, by telegraph of reasonable efficiency) seemed to confirm the tidings.

By late afternoon, even as relief ships were fitting out, the truth became known: the telegram and phone call were a ruse. Instead of an earthquake, Jean-Jumeau had slipped in by sailboat from St. Thomas, raised the banner of Firmin, and held Gonaïves and St. Marc. Throughout the Northwest, the Artibonite, and the *Caco* belt in the North, Firminist bands awaited only the necessary arms and Jean-Jumeau to lead them. Mérisier Jeannis, seventy but still hale, had slipped out of Port-au-Prince, where Tonton Nord had been keeping him in sight, and, bent on vengeance against his old foe, Berrouet, was headed across Morne des Commissaires for Lafond and Jacmel. Meanwhile, as government spies soon learned, Anténor Firmin himself, with twenty-five followers including his son, Albert Salnave, and Alcius Charmant, would at any moment arrive from St. Thomas aboard a British merchantman.

There was one fatal flaw: as yet unknown either to the government or to Firmin's followers, the U.S. Secret Service in New York had intercepted Firmin's arms and war chest - 2000 rifles, 100,000 cartridges, and $400,000. At one stroke, Firmin's logistics had been wiped out and his troops were empty-handed. He himself, blinded by the euphoria that envelopes exile invaders, assured the few who shared the dire secret that it was no matter: the country had already risen; they would be greeted with open arms and weapons in every hand.

It was not to be. Nord Alexis reacted by packing the would-be relief ships with soldiers under Cincinnatus Leconte and sailing them under forced draft for St. Marc. "The old nonagenarian was sublime," recounted Marcelin of the president. "He was on his feet day and night, imparting a youthful ardor to everyone."

On the 19th, after gunboats had shelled the town, Leconte took his soldiers ashore, chased the rebels out, or into the consulates, put the place to the torch, and prepared to march on Gonaïves, where Firmin was due to arrive on the 21st. (42)

When Firmin reached Gonaïves, he learned the truth: however widespread his support, there were no arms. Numbed by reality, he shut himself up in his room and - futile in the end as Bazelais - waited for what he knew must come.

Jean-Jumeau's response was characteristic. Arming 500 men with old swords, machetes, and every weapon and cartridge he could scrape up, he marched on Marchand (Dessalines) to meet the advancing government army. Next morning, at Carrefour Croix-Marchand, a half mile west of the village, he attacked. At first the fight went well; then, as ammunition ran low, Jean-Jumeau's men began throwing down useless rifles and melting away into the fields. At last, Jean-Jumeau had only seven men with him. Run down by pursuers, the old general was collared by a sergeant, trussed up, and led back into Dessalines to be shot.

He fell, pierced by six bullets [reported Furniss "on good authority"], but these failing to kill him. three soldiers were called from the ranks and ordered to chop him up with machetes. These soldiers, refusing, were shot and three others were called, who, fearing the fate of the first three, proceeded to hack him and mutilate his body.

Mérisier Jeannis fared no better. Before he could raise his *piquets,* word came that Jean-Jumeau was dead and Firmin in the French consulate at Gonaïves. As Mérisier tried to slip into Jacmel for a similar refuge, his luck ran out. Berrouet caught him at *Habitation* Desrue. Then - as reported by both the American and German consular agents and "verified by numerous eye-witnesses," Furniss wrote - Berrouet shot him, (43) ". . . had his head cut off and, with a soldier on each side holding an ear, the head was dangled through the streets and finally exposed on a pole in the market place at Jacmel."

Throughout these sanguinary doings, Port-au-Prince waited fearfully. Pauléus Sannon, biographer of Toussaint and Tonton Nord's Foreign Minister, surrendered his portfolio and repaired in haste to the French legation.

What forced Sannon into asylum was the question of asylum itself, a subject on which Haitian governments and politicians had deeply ambivalent feelings. It was Sannon's objection to the brutal executions in front of the American consulate in St. Marc that cost him his portfolio. The subject was touchy with the president. Nord Alexis felt himself balked of revenge against Firmin by the intransigence of the French minister, Carteron, who declined to subject France's asylees to the fate of the victims of Washington's misplaced confidence in Haitian due process. Speaking to Marcelin, Tonton Nord commented bitterly: "There isn't any justice. Jean-Jumeau was nothing but a poor man and he's shot dead. But the master-mind that pushed him out ahead will come through without a scratch. It's unjust!"

Yet only a year earlier, when the president had been similarly objecting to the French minister over another case, Carteron blandly rejoined that it might be best simply to abolish the entire practice of asylum and that he would so recommend to his government forthwith. At that, Nord Alexis, who owed his own life to asylum on at least two occasions, evinced great consternation and immediately dropped the matter. "The truth is," Furniss told the State Department, "the President fears to have asylum abolished for fear he may have to take advantage of it."

Not all the Firminists, at any rate, were safe in asylum, and especially not in Port-au-Prince, where Firmin was the idol of a circle of elite younger men headed, heart and soul, by the poet and playwright Massillon Coicou, Firmin's secretary in Paris and now professor at the *Lycée Pétion*.

On the night of 14-15 March 1908, betrayed by none other than Coicou's cousin, General Jules Coicou, town commandant of Port-au-Prince, the Firminists of the capital suffered their own Eve of St. Bartholomew.(44)

Starting at five in the afternoon of the 14th, with the seizure of Firmin's brother-in-law, Félix Salnave, and running through the night until dawn, Nord Alexis's "*Police du centenaire*" (latter-day *zinglins*) ranged the capital, rousting victims out of bed and dragging them off to the palace, to prison, or, in certain cases, directly to the cemetery wall. "Heavily cloaked," recounted journalist Jules Rosemond, "masked by huge straw hats with brims turned down, armed with revolvers, carbines, daggers and *cocomacacs*, furious, pitiless, they galloped the streets, hammering in the doors of surrounded houses to drag away citizens a moment earlier still asleep . . ."

Massillon Coicou was hemmed in beneath the statue of Dessalines on the Champ de Mars, beaten, then hauled off to the cemetery, where graves had already been dug.(45) His two brothers, Horace and Pierre-Louis, met a similar fate. Ten persons are listed by name as having been killed, but other accounts, both Haitian and diplomatic, give higher figures. Besides the killings, there were widespread arrests, mostly of the elite. Captain Laraque, proud graduate of France's St. Cyr and Saumur, and commander of the president's mounted escort, was thrown into jail. When her husband, a merchant who had importunately pressed unpaid claims, gained asylum in the German legation, a Mme. Gallette was arrested instead, stripped of her clothing, and trussed up naked in the men's side of the penitentiary.

Only on 16 March did the bloody rampage - a pogrom of the elite, unequaled since 1883 - come to a halt, when H.M.S. *Indefatigable* arrived and fired signal guns to communicate with S.M.S. *Bremen*, a German cruiser. At the sight of the warship and the sound of her guns, panic seized the government, and order was restored as quickly as it had been in 1883.

Several hundred people had fled to the legations, of whom seventy-eight alone were ferried to Kingston aboard the *Bremen*. Afterward, when Marcelin dared tax Nord Alexis with failing at least to go through a form of trial for the Coicous and their fellow victims, the president cut him short: "What do you mean? They earned what they got. They would most certainly have been condemned to death, and I would most certainly have shot them. So it's all the same anyway."

Amid all this decline and calamity, Port-au-Prince enjoyed the unwonted good fortune of an enlightened, energetic (and ambitious) mayor. Sténio Vincent, editor of *L'Effort* a few years earlier, gave the capital an administration so vigorous that he was remembered long after in the *méringue* "Magistrat Vincent":

> *Magistrat Vincent, nous contents:*
> *Magistrat Vincent, ou ap'fait bien.*
> *La ru' balé, rigol' nettié.*
> *Magistrat Vincent, nous contents.*
> *Quand ou fais bien, peup' toujours content.*
> *Lor' on agi' bien, gain younjour l'Va recompensé ou.*

(Mayor Vincent, we're content;/Mayor Vincent, you've done a good job./The streets are swept, the gutters clean./Mayor Vincent, we're content./When you do well, the people are always satisfied./If you treat the people right, there will come a day/When they pay you back.)

The people may indeed have been content but Nord Alexis was not: in 1908 he sacked Vincent for helping himself to the *recettes communales* (general funds).

After the ides of March 1908, the way led downhill for Nord Alexis. On 5-6 July, Port-au-Prince was ravaged by another fire, which leveled 1200 houses. Four days later, the Grand Rue, spared earlier, was almost consumed. When the government of Jamaica offered relief supplies, they were declined, reported the American legation, with the intimation that money would be more acceptable. This, to be sure, was no less than truth: government salaries were four or more months unpaid.

On 11 October, full of years, old CéCé died and Tonton Nord stayed on alone. No longer did he talk of succeeding himself. Now, reminisced Marcelin, "he was old, very old, no longer able to mount his horse; he was nearly blind and a few months would see the end of his term . ..Moreover, Port-au-Prince had had enough of General Nord . . ."

A month later, on 15 November, the old general, who still relished military ceremonies, dimly watched the Sunday morning parade from the palace balcony, then went inside and as always held audience. His theme this time -it would be his last - was the necessary fidelity and obedience of the army to the government. Then, as palace hangers-on chanted their usual *"Vive le Père de la Patrie!,"* he took his panama from the hand of a waiting aide, retired to a private office, and issued orders abruptly dismissing General Antoine Simon from his command at Cayes, where, for eighteen years, he had held peaceful sway over the South.

The lines were drawn: on the 19th, Simon - past seventy himself, with a snow-white imperial of the Third Empire, but a youth compared to Tonton Nord - prepared to march on the capital.

While Nord's gunboats aimlessly bombarded villages (46) of utter unimportance in the remote South, General Simon marched his *piquet* soldiery - many armed only with spears and machetes - Eastward. At Anse-à-Veau on 27 November there was a halfhearted fight from which the government army retreated. (The leader, the Minister of War, ended his retreat in a consulate at Miragoâne.) On the 30th Simon was at Léogane, and panic reigned in Port-au-Prince.

During the night of 1-2 December, the last regiments between Simon and the city declared for the revolution; before dawn, virtually the entire cabinet had found its way to the French legation. Save for the president and a few servants, the palace was already deserted. Marcelin made his way inside to tell Nord he must go. The old man was at his morning ablutions and would not budge. Finally, as Marcelin fumed, he emerged and with utmost reluctance consented to the final arrangements.

In time-honored style, not Boisrond-Canal any longer, but his son, 'Ti Canal, now a senator, materialized from Frères, convened a Committee of Safety, and confirmed that Minister Carteron would indeed assist Nord Alexis aboard the cruiser *Duguay-Trouin,* whose Tricolor could be seen from the shore.

It was midafternoon before the president could get ready to leave. Commander Shipley, U.S.S. *Des Moines,* at the wharf, described the scene:

People were in a state of great excitement, everybody was armed with rifles and had plenty of ammunition, soldiers and citizens alike. A perfect fusillade of firing ball cartridges in the air was kept up constantly The wharf, where [the President's] party met the French boats, was crowded with a howling mob of soldiers, citizens, and women. The French Minister and naval officers were waving the French colors in the faces of the mob and protecting the President as well as possible..... His clothing was cut through the back but his body was not touched...Part of the President's baggage was broken open by the rabble and it is reported that about $30,000 in gold was stolen.(47)

Commander Shipley's presence was no accident; having in 1884 finally
extended the Monroe Doctrine to Haiti, Washington had now applied its
"Roosevelt Corollary" and instructed U.S. naval forces in effect to exercise
general police power and provide protection to Europeans or other foreign
nationals who might be in trouble.

That night the town ran wild. Sémextant Rouzier laid the blame on "the
sovereign people," whom he drily defined as "the populace, the soldiers, and the
police." When 'Ti Canal felt things had gone a bit far, he sent in General
Poitevien with some troops who would still obey orders, and had a dozen looters
shot - an efficacious example that nonetheless failed to end a carnival of pillage,
mostly of Syrian shops, that went on until Antoine Simon reached the Portail
Léogane a day later.

In that interval - an indication of how the foreign community viewed Tonton
Nord's downfall - the gourde's dizzy rate of exchange subsided from 850 to the
U.S. dollar back to 500. In the words of one German banker, *"Le
Gouvernement tombe, la prime tombe"* (The Government falls and so does the
rate of exchange).

Délégué Simon

On 5 December, blinking at his own success, Antoine Simon entered Port-au-
Prince. Next day, to roll of drums and bray of bugles, he was proclaimed *chef
du pouvoir executif,* and, on the 10th, *Le Moniteur* announced that the assembly,
held over from Tonton Nord's elections in January, would reconvene to elect a
new president. This development, Furniss explained, "seems to show that he has
made arrangements with the congressmen [sic] for his election. Under the
circumstances they doubtless prefer to elect him and still be able to feed from
the public crib rather than oppose him and perhaps be shot . . ."

Like homing pigeons, exiles converged from Cuba, Jamaica, St.Thomas, and
Europe. Callisthène Fouchard... Sénèque Momplaisir Pierre . . . Cincinnatus
Leconte . . . Firmin...... the names were a political history of the past two
decades. Simon received them at the Palais as they returned, spoke them fair
and mild, and, in the logic of things as the man whose army held the capital,
received their assurances of support.

On 20 December at high noon, proving Minister Furniss a good prophet, the
Senate, prudently ringed with soldiers, cast 117 votes unanimously for Simon.
At next day's Te Deum, the archbishop, Msgr. Conan, counseled the new
president to be moderate, to respect the constitution, and work for the
upbuilding of Haiti."(48)

The archbishop's advice was appropriate and acceptable. François Antoine
Simon, who had begun his career as peasant *chef-section* outside Les Cayes, was

the grand old man of the South as Nord had been of the North, but with the difference that his rule as *délégué militaire* had been kindly, not stern. There were few executions, and, in the fashion of Christophe, he employed his soldiery in cultivating the fertile crescent of fine old plantations he had amassed. "He is a man of simple taste," Furniss reported, "good ideas and fairly good judgment. If he could have his ideas intelligently carried out, he would accomplish much for his country. As it is he is surrounded by a net of officials whose only thought seems to be to get their pockets full as quickly as possible."

In Cayes, his illiteracy and the fact that he could speak little but Créole had posed no handicaps. In Port-au-Prince, although they endeared him, as everywhere, to the humble, these limitations caused the elite to mock him. But Antoine Simon had one other bond with the people: he was a fervent devotee of Voodoo. Enlarging on this fact, Furniss wrote:

> The President and his family are full of superstition and are devotees of the voudeaux [sic] faith. This devotion is of long standing and while he was Military Governor in the South, he went so far as to have a mass said by the Bishop of Aux Cayes over a white goat which for a long time had figured as an emblem of the President's faith. The goat died and was brought with great pomp and ceremony to the cathedral in a closed coffin, and the Bishop, at the request of "Délégué Simon," not suspecting that the coffin contained a goat, said the mass. Later the Bishop found out what had been done and issued an order that in future no funeral masses would be said unless the corpse was exposed to the priest just prior thereto . . . Several priests have confirmed this story, and, when asked directly, the Bishop would not deny it.(49)

Briefly, the omens seemed favorable for the new regime. Simon's appointments - the accomplished Joseph Jérémie as War Minister, Dr. Edmond Héraux (a doctor of high probity) as Foreign Minister offered encouragement. For the first time in many years the president held a formal dinner for the diplomatic corps. This rare amenity was coupled with a full pardon to Simon Sam for his Consolidations peccadillo so that the former president might safely come home from the Champs Elysées, as he soon did.

For all this moderation, "Délégué Simon" soon found he could not rule Port-au-Prince (or, for that matter, the country) in the simple pastoral style of Les Cayes. Créole homilies delivered while the president reflectively picked his nose before Sunday audiences bored city folk and furnished ammunition for the spiteful wits of the elite. Do they disrespect and poke fun at me? he asked. Well, I will show them. In September he decreed that at his passing every knee must bow; all must remove their hats, and stop smoking. "When this is not properly done," wrote Furniss, "the offending party [is] arrested, clubbed, or placed in jail."

There were other oddities, mainly financial. A lucrative gunboat purchase was described three years later by the National City Bank's Roger L. Farnham, soon to become better known in Haiti's financial circles and annals:

> An instance of the way things were done under President Simon is found in the purchase during his administration of an old warship, the *Umbria*, from the Italian government. This ship, afterward christened the *Antoine Simon*, cost the Haitian government $26,000. Various deals were negotiated for armament and other equipment . . . Upon arrival of this ship at Port-au-Prince, nearly a year after she was purchased, her total cost to the Haitian Government was nearly $56,000.

In his entertaining memoirs, Jérémie wrote that when the *Umbria* was accepted by the government at Port-au-Prince, she was incapable of getting underway and her powder was so deteriorated that the captain refused to keep it on board, as a result of which it was landed and stored - where else? - in the palace basement arsenal, possibly a fateful decision. Only eleven months after reaching Port-au-Prince, never having gotten underway, *Antoine Simon* was sold to a Dutch ship-breaker for $20,000 gold.

Triumphal arches for the president's travels about the country provided welcome returns for those involved. (One such trip, however, provided something more, on 4 July 1909, when on the way to Ganthier, the presidential train collided head-on with another train, killing ten and injuring twenty in Haiti's first recorded train wreck.)

For eight roadside arches on a typical trip, the government allocated 20,000 gourdes. But the functionary in charge confessed to Furniss that they actually cost 1000 gourdes each, that he was being reimbursed at 1500 gourdes, and signing vouchers for 2000 gourdes - against an appropriated figure of 2500 gourdes. It is no wonder that Furniss wrote, "This matter of arches is always looked forward to by the faithful . . as a great opportunity."

For the president a still greater windfall happened in August 1910, when, "in appreciation of the eminent services rendered to his country by this Grand Citizen" (read the resolution), the assembly surprised Antoine Simon with a testimonial grant of $50,000 gold to acquire another plantation.

Not long before this bonanza, Louis-Edouard Pouget of the Cap, new Finance Minister (and, like Dr. Héraux, high-minded and patriotic), confided to the American minister, "Though he knew before he took charge of the Department of Finance, there were many connected with the Simon administration who were not above stealing from the Government, yet he did not know he would enter into a den of thieves."

In the same conversation Pouget told Furniss that the government had a special commission in Europe looking into the possibility of reconstituting the *Banque* and of extracting a new loan from France. Furniss asked why the mission had omitted Wall Street from its itinerary. Pouget laughed and explained that the trip was nothing but "a pleasure jaunt at government expense," and that, on their $12,000 allowance, the members would "spend their time in Paris on the Boulevards, at the Moulin Rouge, and like places dear to most Haitians."

FOOTNOTES - CHAPTER 10

1. As in the case of Salomon, it is difficult to say exactly what Légitime's name was. He habitually signed himself, "F.-D. Légitime," but some historians (for example, Dorsainvil) speak of him as "D. Légitime," and others (for example, Bellegarde) call him "François Légitime." Documents issued by his own regime spell his middle name "Denis" or "Denys," interchangeably, and still other accounts (for example, Rouzier) give him the middle name of "Deus."

2. Sesmaisons, with generous contingency funds from Paris, was reported to have been fishing for a French protectorate over Haiti. He was actively anti-American.

3. Dr. Thompson, one of the earliest black graduates of Yale Medical School, had also studied at the Sorbonne, where he learned the French that served him so well in Haiti. Born in Brooklyn, he had practiced in New York until his appointment as American minister to succeed Langston.

4. Légitime's reference to seeing Haiti in foreign hands was taken by Thompson to bespeak his known Francophilia, and he included in his report that Sesmaisons had sent a representative, M. Sylvie, to tell Goblet, the French Foreign Minister, that now was the hour for protectorate.

5. Légitime was promptly recognized by France and Britain, and would soon be accorded recognition by Portugal and Italy. The other powers represented in Port-au-Prince, led conspicuously by the United States and including Germany and Spain, declined to recognize either party.

6. Assertions that the *Haytian Republic* was repossessed by force are not true. As Admiral Luce's, as well as Thompson's, reports make clear, the ship was surrendered, without threat or duress (save that implied by the presence of two American warships), to a single naval lieutenant and a representative of the American legation. In his report to the Secretary of the Navy, the admiral commented: "According to a Créole proverb Haytians divide the world into two parties,'*Ça qui gagné canon et ça qui pas gagné canon*'; those who have guns and those who have none. The former they respect, the latter they despise . . . A claim against Haiti must be politely urged, for the Haytian is nothing if not courteous, the cannon's mouth should be concealed with studied negligence; but it must be there."

7. Typically, Alcius managed to talk himself out of Port-au-Prince on the eve of the vote, so in the end there were only three Jacmel delegates to pack the assembly. At this stage, however, no one was imprudent enough to suggest the absence of a quorum.

8. According to Prichard, the English journalist, Dardignac stumbled on an old enemy while traveling aboard one of the little coastal steamers. Dardignac had the ship stop, lashed fire bars to his opponent's feet, pushed him overboard, watched him gurgle feet first in the clear water to the bottom, had the captain get underway, and sat down to

breakfast.

9. Salomon and Heureaux carried the idea of Haitian-Dominican nonaggression a step farther by an understanding that neither would open his frontier to rebels seeking to overthrow the other, an arrangement destined to reappear perennially in the modalities of diplomacy between the two countries.

10. Alcius, last seen but not for long, in Jacmel, lost no time in getting into trouble and was soon again back in jail. When the guards burst into his empty cell, all they could find were his fetters and, on the wall, sketched in charcoal, the picture of a steamer disappearing over the horizon. The affair was satisfactorily cleared up when a dear friend and lady confederate explained to the authorities that she had seen a large white cat scuttle over the prison wall -obviously Alcius temporarily metamorphosed by a *ouanga.*

11. Légitime went to Paris, where he remained until 1896, after the death of Hyppolite. He thereupon returned to Port-au-Prince and not unlike Boisrond-Canal before him, lived many years as one of the capital's first citizens, until his death on 29 July 1935.

12. France, with thirteen constitutions between 1791 and 1875, is usually cited as world title-holder of instant constitutions, but Haiti, France's daughter, clearly outperformed the *métropole,* with fifteen from 1801 to 1889.

13. On 18 April 1893. in the manner of European sovereigns of the era, Heureaux and Hyppolite held a seaborne summit in Manzanillo Bay, where the common boundary meets the sea. Heureaux came in his yacht, *El Presidente,* and Hyppolite brought the *Dessalines,* escorted by *Défense,* crammed with soldiers. Heureaux greatly impressed the Haitians by taking the conn of his own barge and bringing it smartly alongside El *Presidente's* accommodation ladder.

14. William P. Clyde. owner of a U.S. steamship line that had heavily supported Hyppolite, was a crony and business associate of Benjamin F. Tracy, Secretary of the Navy at this time. Clyde was pressing hard for special concessions from Hyppolite (whose new regime owed the Clyde Line substantial sums). He also strongly wished. as did Tracy, not to mention James G. Blaine, Secretary of State, to see the American colors floating over Môle St. Nicolas. It is mainly on Clyde's somewhat dubious testimony that the allegation - it cannot be called a fact - of Elie's offer rests.

15. Montague gains support from a dispatch to the Quai d'Orsay, on 25 January 1891, by Flesch, then French minister in Port-au-Prince, that, while in power, Légitime had surreptitiously offered the Môle to the United States in return for recognition. Flesch added that Firmin, no disinterested witness, had written proof.

16. Two able diplomatic historians, Rayford Logan and Ludwell Montague, devote chapters to lengthy and fascinating exegeses of the Môle St. Nicolas affair, which, simply as detective work enriched by intrigue and gamy personalities, would support a book in its own right. The present account is a mere summary.

17. Gherardi must have had second thoughts about his rudeness, for, in his report next day (27 January), he fudged the facts to the Secretary of the Navy: "I have called upon the U.S. Minister. and received him with suitable honors upon his returning my visit."

18. Despite Douglass's understandable sensitivity at having been practically superseded, Gherardi, handsome for his sixty years, headstrong, brave, and decisive, was no Admiral Blimp. Nephew and namesake of the historian George Bancroft, founder of the U.S. Naval Academy, Gherardi was certainly one of the abler and more popular officers of the navy.

19. In a collateral report to the Secretary of the Navy, Gherardi said of the president's trip: "He has directed all the dangerously disaffected in the Capital to go with him, which they are said not to relish as they pay their own expenses and the trip is a long one."

20. Bouqui and 'Ti Malisse are central figures in an endless series of Haitian peasant tales wherein picaresque 'Ti Malisse perennially outsmarts, cons, or tricks slow-moving, slow-thinking, more prosperous Bouqui.

21. Haitians have asserted that French saber-rattling saved the Môle from the Americans - an assertion in no way supported by diplomatic correspondence in Paris, which was low-keyed throughout. A France that, on U.S. prompting, dropped Légitime like a hot potato and later recalled Sesmaisons was in no position to obstruct Blaine and Gherardi. What Napoleon III dared not in 1867, France in 1891 would not have contemplated.

22. Flesch made no bones of what he reported as madness. He told the Quai d'Orsay that the president had a history of insanity extending back several years, and that "he is subject to relapses when in the grip of violent rage." Haitian historians likewise picture Hyppolite as suffering periodic fits of madness characterized by ungovernable fury. Alcius Charmant (who witnessed one outburst in April 1892) said that when they occurred, Hyppolite assumed the surname and identity of "Mabial," a fact that strongly suggests that these seizures may have been *Crises de possession* of Voodoo origin. While not the name of any recognized *loa*, Mabial could readily have been a *loa de famile* who possessed the president from time to time.

23. Rigaud vainly protested French nationality. Hyppolite replied, "That doesn't concern me and means nothing." When Rigaud's nephew tried to rescue his uncle, the president had him shot, too, After stern protests, France exacted an indemnity for these executions.

24. More than a decade later, having dissipated his extensive holdings at the tables of Monte Carlo and in Paris, Marcelin, again Finance Minister, enjoyed a final opportunity to recoup, leaving Haiti for the last time with Nord Alexis in 1908.

25. Lüders had already served a jail sentence in 1894 for striking a soldier - no small offense in Haiti.

26. As soon as he learned, on 28 November, that German warships were on their way, Powell implored Washington to invoke the Monroe Doctrine and send a naval force to Port-au-Prince. For reasons never recorded (the Paris *Revue des Deux Mondes* said it was U.S. "designs on Cuba and Spain" that precluded antagonizing Germany), Washington did not respond. Powell poured out his exasperation in a dispatch that ended: This is the first time in my life I have ever had cause to be ashamed of being an American, or to have to blush for the flag that protects me." Underscoring Powell's point that same month (December 1897), Bismarck in Berlin sneeringly referred to the Monroe Doctrine as an "extraordinary insolence."

27. "No! We are no longer willing, Prussian Germans/As in the past to Batsch, your filthy emissary/To spit out money under your fearsome talon/As one throws a bone to curs!"

28. Germany's was not the only European mailed fist to be clenched at Haiti in Simon Sam's time: during March 1902 alone, two French cruisers collected a $75,000 claim, and an Italian cruiser extracted $30,000.

29. After a sensational trial in December 1902 the following were convicted of defraud-
ing the government: Simon Sam, Tancrède Auguste, Cincinnatus Leconte, Guillaume
Sam (the latter three, eventual presidents), Brutus St. Victor, Lycurge and Demosthène
Simon (both sons of the president), Rudolph Tippenhauer (German custodian of the
bonds), and two French directors of the Banque. None of those convicted (several in
absentia) is known to have served any part of the severe sentences meted out.

30. Prichard, correspondent of the *Daily Express*, reported that Simon Sam, an avid
checker-player, after triumphing over a particularly skilled opponent, dubbed him "general" forthwith.

31. Typical of Mérisier's Solomon-like justice was that in a case of adultery, in which
the accused woman vehemently voiced a counter complaint against her husband: *'Li pas
capab, Délégué!"* (He can't make it, Delegue!) When the husband as vehemently
contradicted the charge, Mérisier simply ordered him to prove it on the spot, which
being done, judgment was rendered against the wife.

32. Writing U.S. Secretary of State Bryan in 1914 from considerable inside knowledge,
Roger L. Farnham, concessionaire and president of the Chemins de Fer Nationales, said
that when Leconte made his 1902 try, ". . . he asked the Port-au-Prince firm of Keitel
& Co., a German house, to give him a credit of $300,000 gold, in return for which he
promised to give them very valuable mining concessions and as well . . . a coaling
station at and practical control of Môle St. Nicolas."

33. Boisrond, seventy-three and ailing, died peacefully of diabetes in Port-au-Prince on
6 March 1905. "There is general mourning among all classes," reported Powell; "he was
well liked by all."

34. France took Killick seriously enough to station a cruiser at Port-au-Prince during late
July and early August to prevent Killick from bombarding the capital. Later in the
month, that same ship, *D'Assas*, gave chase to *La Crête-à-Pierrot* off the North coast,
but Killick slipped into shallows where the Frenchman dared not follow.

35. Whether one or two others of the crew went down with *La Crête-à-Pierrot* remains
an open and probably unanswerable question. Some accounts say two persons stayed with
Killick; one contemporary description speaks of four. All agree that Dr. Coles was one.
A snapshot of the ship while actually under fire, before the second explosion, shows a
native boat close aboard, a few feet off the port bow, with two men in it. Conceivably
these may have been crewmen making a last-minute escape.

36. As word of the *Crête-à-Pierrot* immolation spread, Haitian streets were packed with
mobs crying, *"Tué z'Allemands! Tué blancs.!"* Typical of handbills circulated was one
hammered to the door of Herrmann & Co., a German firm in St. Marc:

> *Crions anathème au nom allemand.*
> *Jurons haine éternelle a l'Allemagne.*
> *Vive Haïti libre et indépendante!*
> *Vive l'Amiral Killick!*
> *Vive Firmin.!*
> *A bas l'Allemagne!*
> *A bas les enfants dénaturés d'Haïti.!*

(Cry anathema on the German name,/swear eternal hatred for Germany./Long live Haiti,

free and independent!/Long live [sic] Admiral Killick!/Long live Firmin!/Down with
Germany!/Down with all mixed-blood Haitians!) Very likely only the presence of two
more German men-of-war in Haitian waters precluded serious antiforeign violence.
37. Feeling against the Syrians ran so high that the handful of Italian fishermen who in
this era had begun to fish Haiti's bountiful waters stayed at sea in their boats for weeks
rather than run the risk of being mistaken for their Mediterranean neighbors.
38. One less noted but deeply appropriate observance of the *Centenaire* took place in
January 1904, when Haiti's indefatigable world-traveler and intellectual, Benito Sylvain,
of Port-de-Paix, presented letters from Nord Alexis to Ethiopia's Emperor Menelik II,
thus opening relations between the two states, which, before Sylvain's prodigious voyages to Ethiopia (four in all), had been practically ignorant of each other. Ironically, like
Columbus on return from the New World, Sylvain was mocked and disparaged in Haiti.
Nord Alexis, believing that Menelik's high decoration (Grand Cross of the Ethiopian
Empire) "as worthless compared with a European award" never bothered to wear it. *Le
Moniteur* did not even print the exchange of letters between emperor and president.
39. The modern cult of Dessalines, virtually neglected until re-entombed by Hyppolite
in 1892, dates directly from the 1904 centennial.
40. Captain Charles Young, U.S.A., an early black graduate of West Point. was the first
officer of his race to succeed in a Regular Army career. Young had mastered French and
was detailed to Haiti by then Secretary of War W. H. Taft, the first U.S. black military
attaché (as Bassett had been the first black diplomatic chief of mission before him).
Young's detailed maps (some of whose originals still survive in the National Archives)
were based on over a year of mounted reconnaissance. They represent, together with the
slightly earlier maps of L. G. Tippenhauer, a German engineer, the earliest modern
topographic surveys of Haiti. Young's mounted traverse, Hinche - St. Michel -Cerca la
Source - Hinche, mapped one of the most remote regions of Haiti and one probably not
surveyed by a foreign eye since the days of the French.
41. The Turgeau agricultural school lasted only four years, to be dissolved in failure by
that practical farmer, Antoine Simon, in 1911. Dantès Bellegarde said the site, wholly
unsuitable for farming, had been sold to the government by Marcelin, the Finance Minister, as the sine qua non for his support of the project. Even more of a handicap than the
uselessness of Marcelin's land, however, was the attitude of the elite students who
managed to corner the appointments. In the verdict of *Le Moniteur,* "They have, it
seems, a horror of agricultural labor. The parents maintain that their children should
never have to take part in the actual work in the fields."
42. At the height of the revolt, the State Department in Washington received evidence
that the American consul at St. Marc, a Haitian national, was also a leading Firminist
and a party to the uprising. Reacting with indignation, Secretary Elihu Root telegraphed
peremptory orders to Minister Furniss to dismiss the consul and deliver the St. Marc
asylees to the government - in the department's unctuous phrase - "for trial according to
the orderly operation of Haitian law." The process proved to be swift though hardly
orderly. When the American flag over the consulate was hauled down on 31 January,
Leconte's soldiers swarmed in and dragged out fifteen refugees. Within twenty minutes,
five leaders were shot in the street, and the remainder were hauled off to jail. This
transaction horrified foreigners, evoked pained remonstrance from Furniss (which the
department brushed aside), and sent shudders through the Haitian political community.

43. *Le Nouvelliste* confirmed most of this but said Mérisier's head was cut off "accidentally." Furniss wrote on 6 March, "It is said by officials that it was the intention to send the head here as a present to the President, but that the President, who, it is claimed, gave orders that the head be cut off, was persuaded to order it buried .... At the orders of the Military Governor [Berrouet] the son of Gen. Mérisier was cut up while yet alive."

44. A year later, meeting Marcelin in Santiago-de-Cuba (both now exiled), General Coicou recounted that, when he had gone to the palace to denounce the Firminists, the president and Mme. Nord heard him out in silence. Then Mme. Nord asked cryptically, *"Général Jules, qui Saints ou servi?"* (What saints do you serve?). Inclining to the dreaded CéCé, Coicou replied, *" M' servi tout Saints "* (I serve all the saints). Mme. Nord indulged in a thin smile and said, *"Ou servi bien depi hier ou te pou fusillé!"* (You have served them well since yesterday, otherwise you'd be shot by now!). This was her way of conveying that the alleged plot was already known and that Coicou would have been added to the list had he not cooperated with the regime.

45. In an eyewitness account, a year later, of the exhumation, funeral services, and reburial of the ten Firminist martyrs, *l'Impartial* (17 March 1909) reported that the bodies were "horribly mutilated," had broken limbs, machete-chops, and that Massillon Coicou had been decapitated and his head buried between his knees.

46. The largest of the gunboats, *Croyant*, ran aground in the treacherous waters off Jérémie and was driven ashore, a total loss, on 22 November 1908.

47. According to Marcelin, the president's luggage contained $41,000 gold, 20,000 to 25,000 gourdes, diamonds, and large quantities of jewelry, all lost to looters. Nord Alexis went to Kingston and died in 1910.

48. Echoing the plaint of Ebenezer Bassett and many another foreign diplomat, Furniss wrote: "Masses are a very frequent official function in Haiti ... It is often particularly disagreeable and fatiguing to go to an overcrowded, poorly ventilated church where anything else than order prevails. With numerous soldiers under arms occupying the aisles and the frequent blasts of bugles and roll of drums in the church, and cannon firing in front, there is not much appearance of a religious ceremony."

49. A typically embroidered version of the goat's funeral is in William B. Seabrook's *Magic Island,* page 118. The goat's name was "Simalo"; the bishop was Msgr. Morice. Simon's daughter, Celestina, was a widely reputed mambo, whose daughter, a half century later, was in turn to be one of the most powerful *mambos* of the Cul-de-Sac. Seabrook, much in the sensationalist Spenser St. John vein, also repeats a tale of Celestina's cutting the heart out of a human sacrifice behind the *Palais National* in 1909. Who knows? In November 1909 *Le Télégraphe* reported ". . . exhumations being carried on openly by night in the cemetery, for the past several weeks . . . It is said that thirst for power impels certain personages of high distinction to satisfy the demands of sorcery by these practices."

Salomon's palace (1882) was destined to be blown up in 1912. Note signs of progress: telephone poles and streetcar track behind sentry. *Library of Congress Right*: Salomon, Haiti's ablest ruler since Henry Christophe, ultimately found his country ungovernable. *National Archives*

332

Bust of Dessalines watches over Gatling gun (*mitrailleuse*) sited to discourage unannounced visitors to the president's office, National Palace, 1885. *Library of Congress Right*: The dashing Admiral Killick blew up his flagship, *La Crête-à-Pierrot*, at Gonaïves rather than have her captured by a German gunboat. The white priest at Gonaïves refused to bury him, claiming he was a "suicide". *National Archives Below*: *La Crête-à-Pierrot* at Gonaïves, seconds after Admiral Killick put a match to her powder magazine on 6 September, 1902 *National Archives*

Musiciens du Palais National pose in 1893 under leadership of Occide Jeanty (seated), one of Haiti's leading composers. *Library of Congress* *Below:* Tonton Nord (Nord Alexis) in presidential carriage on Champs de Mars, 1908. *Mansell Collection*

Two doughty old *authentiques*: Artibonite *Caco* Jean Jumeau and Mérisier Jeannis, Jacmel *piquet* beheaded in 1907. *Leslie's Weekly Below:* "A more non-descript collection could hardly be imagined": Oreste Zamor's *Cacos* enter Port-au-Prince, 1914, General Duchatellier mounted, with machete, in foreground. *National Archives*

CHAPTER 11

A Public Nuisance

1911- 1915

...qu'Il nous faut un Maître étranger ([it is said] that Haiti needs a foreign master).

- Joseph Justin, 3 December 1914

HAITI had changed hardly at all. But the world around her was changing a great deal. The Spanish-American War, essentially a war to expel Spain from the Caribbean, had put the seal of American hegemony over a region and a sea that U.S. editorial-writers, in the style of ancient Rome, were already calling "Mare Nostrum."

On the tether of the Platt Amendment, Cuba had twice been reoccupied and pacified by U.S. Marines and soldiers between 1900 and 1910. Puerto Rico was an American colony. So was the Panama Canal Zone. The United States had, or was attempting to negotiate, customs receiverships in Honduras, Nicaragua, and, next door to Haiti, in Santo Domingo.

The central concept that underlay U.S. foreign policy in "the American Mediterranean" was Theodore Roosevelt's corollary to the Monroe Doctrine: the United States would not brook European intervention in the Americas, and very specifically in the Caribbean, but on the other hand would help and if need be compel countries concerned to end the disorder, peculation, and misbehavior that invited intervention. Reinforcing the Roosevelt Corollary lay a related policy, an unacknowledged forerunner of the Alliance for Progress, soon to be known as "Dollar Diplomacy," stated by Secretary of State Philander Knox in May 1911: "to make American capital the instrumentality to secure financial stability, and hence prosperity and peace, to the more backward republics in the neighborhood of the Panama Canal."

Haiti, despite a century of freedom, more underdeveloped and unstable than any nation in the region, not only flanked the main Caribbean approach to the canal, but was also (or was widely thought to be) the object of foreign, particularly German, interventionist aspirations.

What a few Haitians and many foreigners were now asking was how long the United States could, or at any rate would, tolerate Haiti's mounting instability, her intrigues with German and French interests, and therefore her chronic vulnerability to European intervention.

Addressing this question on 10 June 1908, Jules Jusserand, France's long-time ambassador in Washington and intimate of Theodore Roosevelt, wrote Pichon at the Quai d'Orsay:

> The great American Republic will not tolerate outside intervention in the Black Republic. If that state should collapse as a result of international difficulties of such a character as to lead to foreign intervention, or in consequence of incessant troubles with outside powers, the Americans are not going to let anyone intervene and will take on the task themselves. But to believe they are seeking to provoke such a development, or that they are burning to add to the number of their black charges, I find impossible to credit.

Jusserand was fulfilling an ambassador's most important function. He was giving his own government a highly accurate, well-considered reading of the thoughts and intentions of the United States on matters where France felt she had abiding interests.

If, for the moment, none of the chanceries, save perhaps the Wilhelmstrasse, was prepared to hasten developments in Haiti, financiers and merchants were less cautious.

Banks and Railroads

Writing years later, Joseph Jérémie correctly said that President Antoine Simon's program was above all that of a peasant:

> Extensive cultivation of cotton and tapioca, both profitable exports, would, according to him, halt emigration to Cuba. Bananas and a rail net that would link the West, the Artibonite, and the North, would be the keystone. Incapable of realization save with American capital, this plan didn't fail to arouse alarm among Haitians . . . Moreover, reconstitution of the Banque couldn't be effectuated without a loan of which that institution would have to be the guarantor.

Whether old Antoine Simon saw things in so precise an overview may be doubted. He was, nonetheless, as Furniss pointed out, "a practical farmer," and what Jérémie summarized was what - with a little help from foreign friends - the Simon regime set out to do.

Through commercial and financial interests, Germany and France enjoyed greater influence in Haiti than anywhere else in the Caribbean. The United States, a late-comer in the worldwide imperialist free-for-all, already viewed

Germany, also a late-comer, as its most threatening economic and strategic rival in the region - a perception reinforced, as regarded Haiti, by a long record of German (not to mention French) interventionism in Haitian affairs and manifest Franco-German resistance toward increased American involvement therein.

French assets in Haiti were cultural, commercial, and financial. Francophone and, at least among the elite, Francophile Haiti had a French culture and system (warts and all) of education. The clergy - bastion of ecclesiastical colonialism - were French. France's *Petit Caporal* was Haiti's favorite smoke. The boulevards of Paris were the elite Haitian's paradise on earth.

Behind these intangibles, France was Haiti's best buyer: moving mainly through the import houses of Le Havre, two thirds of Haitian imports (including most of her coffee) went to France. In return even with the 50 percent tariff preference still in force from 1825, France exported only a tenth as much to Haiti, but that portion comprised highly prized and visible items, such as wines and liqueurs, perfumes and cosmetics, books, and precision instruments and tools. In this exchange, Haiti, which only got most-favored nation treatment from France, was dependent and vulnerable. Finally, until 1905 France had been Haiti's banker. The old Banque had been not only the central bank but the sole bank. Every loan from 1825 to 1896 was a French loan, so France still remained Haiti's chief creditor.

If France's cultural and financial weight was heavy, German commercial involvement in Haiti was at least equally powerful. Germans were now taking nearly a third of Haiti's coffee and were vigorously pushing German products across a wide front - hardware, for example, cement, beer, pharmaceuticals, and textiles. If France bought two thirds of Haiti's coffee, German ships of the Hamburg-America Line moved the same percentage (and much of the rest of Haiti's trade) to European ports.

The spearhead of German penetration was the Central Railway of Haiti, actually a holding-company owning and controlling the Chemin de Fer de la Plaine du Cul-de-Sac, or P.C.S. Railroad, the Port-au-Prince wharf and ice plant, and electric companies at the Cap and Port-au-Prince. The P.C.S., which also owned the Port-au-Prince tramway, ran from Thomazeau through the canefields, and in the other direction from Léogane, bringing sugar to the wharf. This structure, all but monopolizing the business of the island, was dominated by Gustav Keitel & Co., and, behind the Keitels, the bankers of Hamburg.

German merchants, moreover, had married (thus bypassing constitutional prohibitions against foreign land-ownership) and assimilated with Haitians and their society more successfully than any foreign group. In 1912, with financial help from the German government, a German school for "the descendants of Germans established in Haiti" was opened with impressive ceremony. So was a *Deutsches Verein* (German Society) for the Germans and Haitian-Germans of the country.

But the involvement of German merchants went deeper. It was German loans that bank-rolled each successive revolution. In the words of Furniss on 2 March 1912, "Everyone knows the complicity of the German merchants in Haiti in the Leconte revolution and they also know that the Germans financed the Simon revolution and others before it, and doubtless will finance all those to follow."

The way these arrangements worked was later described by John Allen, an American official in the soon-to-be-unveiled new *Banque*:

Revolutionary movements were financed by foreigners who, when approached by a leader of an incipient movement, would agree to lend funds and would buy so-called "revolutionary bonds" at perhaps ten cents on the dollar, with the understanding that if the revolution was brought to a successful conclusion, the bonds would be redeemed. They were not always liquidated at par, but they were paid at a figure which yielded a handsome profit. When one studies the history of Haiti, the revolutions and the participation of foreigners in its affairs that can properly be classified only as theft, the wonder is that the Haitians are as good as they are.

In 1912 and again in 1914, Washington believed that Germany, acting behind commercial surrogates, was trying to get naval coaling facilities in Haiti. Fueling Washington's anxiety (according to historian, and later President, Leslie Manigat), was word from the Haitian government, dating from 1911, that the German minister had inadvertently disclosed existence of a plan to make Haiti a German protectorate.

It was against this background of great-power rivalry that in 1910 the recrudescence of the *Banque* took place.

Several previous attempts (including a home-grown Haitian enterprise) had failed to fill the vacuum created by Tonton Nord's fiat.

In mid-1910 a Franco-German consortium, backed by the two governments and blessed in person by Pichon, proposed a new bank. This venture, which was presented to the Haitian government in July 1910 by a Dr. Treitel (who was the German minister's house guest), represented a modified version of the old *Banque*'s arrangements and functions with a 65 million franc loan, a sweetener to be secured in turn by bank control of customs.(1)

The purposes of the loan were monetary reform (retirement of paper currency) and replenishment of an exhausted treasury. The bonds were to be taken up by the consortium at 72.3 percent. (By comparison, bonds of the Dominican government next door, with its U.S. customs receivership, were going at 98.5 percent.)

By simple coincidence the Franco-German initiative was steaming a direct collision course with a competing American proposal, dating from 1909 but without official blessing and neither as well organized nor as intensively propagated.

The National City Bank, together with Speyer & Co., another New York firm, had in 1909 made an $800,000 loan to the P.C.S. Railroad, and, thus drawn into Haitian finance, had tried unsuccessfully to buy out the old *Banque*'s interests. In the very month (July 1910) when, on behalf of the Europeans, Dr. Treitel was obsequiously making the acquaintance of Haitian political leaders, the two U.S. firms disclosed that, if given the bank franchise, they would grant a $12.5 million loan and would actively promote introduction of American capital into Haiti. The guaranty conditional on the arrangement would be either Dominican-style U.S. customs receivership, if Washington concurred, or, alternatively, direct control by the banks.

There were immediate reasons why at first glance the Franco-German proposal seemed more attractive to the Haitian government. Besides providing for explicit support from two major powers, it traveled the familiar paths of French finance and German commerce in Haiti. Moreover, as the American embassy in Paris quickly learned, listing of the American group's bonds could and likely would be blocked on the Paris Bourse by both the old *Banque* and of course the powerful interests behind the Franco-German consortium. Besides, as Leslie Manigat drily noted, the latter had already seen to *"pots-de-vin opportunement et judicieusement distribués,"* whereas, unlike their European rivals, the American negotiators "had less knowledge of the way of people and things in Haiti."

On 5 September, Antoine Simon made clear that the Europeans had won. That day, with palace blessing, he sent the National Assembly their proposals and awaited legislation that would ratify the transaction.

Heretofore undecided as to the City Bank-Speyer initiative, the State Department reacted violently toward what it considered a Franco-German maneuver, through financial and customs control, to outflank the Monroe Doctrine. Washington cabled Furniss that it was an

ARRANGEMENT AT THE SAME TIME SO DETRIMENTAL TO AMERICAN INTERESTS, SO DEROGATORY TO THE SOVEREIGNTY OF HAITI, AND SO INEQUITABLE TO THE PEOPLE OF HAITI.

By confidential telegram on 24 September, the department therefore told Furniss:

U.S. WOULD SEE CONCLUSION OF THE BANK AND LOAN PROPOSITIONS WITH SUCH GRAVE APPREHENSION THAT IT WOULD BE COMPELLED TO RESERVE ALL OF ITS RIGHTS FOR SERIOUS CONSIDERATION IN ORDER TO DETERMINE ITS FUTURE COURSE OF ACTION . . . CONTINUE TO TAKE ALL PROPER AND DISCREET ACTION

... TO INDUCE GOVERNMENT OF HAITI TO REFRAIN FROM ADOPTING
THESE BANK AND LOAN PROPOSITIONS UNLESS PROPERLY MODIFIED.

Modifications Washington deemed "proper" - elimination of customs control
and banking monopoly, and adequate protection for all foreign claims, not just
French and German - would of course gut the European scheme. But, as the
State Department would belatedly realize, customs control and banking
monopoly were being just as eagerly pursued by the American group, though
such developments lay far downstream.

In any case, no amount of U.S. huffing and puffing seemed to sway Simon.
On 26 October, "bulldozed" by the palace, as Furniss put it, the deputies voted
the new franchise. But what Manigat called "the duel" was not yet over:
reluctant, franchise or not, to step in where America frowned, Paris extended
an olive branch. With German concurrence, the *Banque de l'Union Parisienne*
proposed American participation in the final deal, while, at higher levels, the
Quai d'Orsay, with a weather eye to the international storm clouds over
Morocco, privately intimated that, if necessary, France would make common
cause in Haiti with the United States.

The upshot - final defeat, though but dimly perceived, of French and German
designs, and ultimate American financial hegemony in their stead - was an
arrangement reluctantly approved by Secretary Knox on 11 January 1911, in
which American interests (led by the City Bank) took up 50 percent control and
participation in a new bank (to be called *Banque Nationale de la République
d'Haïti*, or *BNRH*) which, while maintaining treasury service, would keep hands
off customs and eschew monopoly. From Haiti's point of view the terms seemed
hard. On the loan of 65 million francs at 72.3 percent, the government realized
only 47 million francs, and of this, 10 million francs would be retained in
reserve by the BNRH for retirement of paper money. The new *Banque* would
receive government revenues, would service the external debt, and give the
government back what little was left. Instead of receiving interest on its
deposits, the government, incredibly, was to pay the *Banque* a 1 percent
commission for holding its money.(2)

Entwined, with the affairs of the BNRH, was the Chemin de Fer National, a
dormant venture revived in August 1910 by an American carpetbagger, James
P. McDonald. The National Railroad was to link the North, the Artibonite, and
the West, and was to finance itself from export duties on *figues* (fig bananas),
a Haitian delicacy McDonald was to cultivate on public land, ship, and export.
On a formula based on trackage laid and accepted (at $32,156 per mile of
track), the government would guarantee the railroad's bonds.

Amid other feats of high-binding, McDonald swung the contract by the
following tactic:

McDonald [went] to the President's daughter, Celestine [sic] Simon, who was also the head of a voodoo cult, and had a great deal of influence over her father . . . McDonald is said to have told Celestine Simon that all the crown princesses of Europe had collections of jewels and to have enquired, "Where is yours?" Upon Mlle. Simon's replying that she had none, McDonald is supposed to have reached into his pocket, to have taken out a box and, opening it, held up a string of pearls for Mlle. Simon to admire . . . He then told her the pearls were hers if and when her father signed the act granting the concessions. Antoine Simon signed that afternoon and the pearls are said to have been delivered that evening. The cost of the pearls was five dollars.

In light of later fortunes of McDonald and of the railroad, this string of fake pearls may have been an imprudent gift to confer upon a *mambo* of Célestina's long memory.(3)

Aside from what U.S. historian Hans Schmidt called "the frivolous character of the entire venture," the reasons why the railroad was on the track to bankruptcy were manifold. McDonald failed to develop his banana concessions (and the National City Bank, which with other foreign investors took over the project in 1911, never interested itself in *figues*). Construction consisted of three separate sections where the going was easy, but failed to link up across mountains(4) and thus never realized the road's prime objective of unifying the various regions.

Some Haitian writers contend that one reason the project was so bitterly opposed by the regime of Cincinnatus Leconte - who also had close connections with the American project's German rivals and held stock in the P.C.S. - was that it would facilitate swift penetration of the Artibonite and the North by government troops and thus strengthen the hand of Port-au-Prince and the West against ancient foes.

Frivolous or not, the immediately forthcoming years were not an encouraging time to be building or investing in Haiti, let alone backing a railroad, marginal at best; yet that is exactly what, in early 1911 , the National City Bank (together with Ethelburga, a London syndicate) did. Curiously, and significantly for events that lay ahead, the City Bank executive already serving as American vice-president of the BNRH was in 1913 appointed president of the National Railroad. His name - a name that for more than a decade would be synonymous with American financial interests in Haiti - was Roger L. Farnham.

A Great Many Will Die

Fifteen months of Antoine Simon and his contracts and concessions had made the country restive. In Port-au-Prince, for reportorial indiscretions during March 1910, the editors of *Le Bon Sens* and *L'Impartial* were imprisoned in chains.

When colleagues demurred, the government responded by hauling in another journalist, Nevers Constant, an assortment of Firminists, and the vociferous Dr. Bobo of Cap Haïtien, who, according to Furniss, "accuses the American Government of every crime in the Decalogue," but, more to the point, had raised his voice at the president in audience.

Later in the year, uneasiness mounted in Hinche and other remote towns of the Plateau Central while, on 9 January of the new year, bringing the government to the edge of panic, Anténor Firmin, aboard *S.S. Montreal,* tried vainly to go ashore but was sent to St. Thomas after a tense day during which the guns of Fort National remained trained on the ship, and the garrison stood to arms at the wharf.(5)

Even *délégué* Simon's South was astir. In January, reported American consular agent Villedrouin from Jérémie,

> people from the country are being arrested and sent to jail where they are so crowded that two died of asphyxia . . In the prison at Abricots, people of both sexes are so packed together that there have already been several cases of death by asphyxia among which are found pregnant women. These are arrested because their husbands or male parents cannot be found . . . I think a great many will die of hunger.

Although Antoine Simon professed to deplore them, a batch of nocturnal executions took place in February. Among those killed were "several prominent Haitians" (Furniss) in Port-au-Prince. Four days later (20 February) the British consul general told Furniss that foreign intervention was the only remedy for the "present reign of terror . . . to prevent annihilation of the only civilized Haitians."

During these months, Cincinnatus Leconte, back from exile, had been watching events from the Cap. Judging the time ripe, on 2 February, with strong support from Davilmar Théodore, *noir* senator from Ennery, and from the Zamor brothers (Charles and Oreste) of Hinche and Cerca-la-Source, Leconte allowed *Caco* generals to raise his banner at Ouanaminthe, where, in the old style of Salnave, Dominician auxiliaries could be most helpful. When this news reached Port-au-Prince it momentarily misled the government, Furniss reported, in the belief that the Dominicans had declared war.(6) "Soldiers were rushing through the streets, the population was rushing hither and thither, the doors and windows of the stores were being rapidly closed and there was a general air of alarm . . . the buglers having sounded the general call to arms."

When he learned the truth, Antoine Simon crammed a German merchantman and the *Nord Alexis* (whose name, for some reason, no one had remembered to change) with as many soldiers as they could hold, and, leaving behind several generals who missed ship, steamed for Gonaïves. There, the force debarked and, with the president in the van, marched into the North. At the head of another column, Joseph Jérémie marched over the mountains to Hinche, probing thence into the heart of the old *Caco* country past Cerca-la-Source, Mont Organisé, and Vallière.

Four days later, as Simon neared the Cap, Leconte left the revolution to shift for itself and prudently entered the German consulate. The government, having suddenly recovered its memory of 1904, issued a criminal warrant for his surrender as a fugitive *Consolidard* (one who participated in the Consolidation scandal) but the warrant was rejected.(7)

Antoine Simon seized Fort Liberté on 7 February and - ironically, in the same week as his own Cayes was swept by conflagration - gave over the North to pillage and slaughter. Joseph Jérémie by contrast burned nothing and pillaged little, a restraint that gave him subsequent credits in the central region with the Zamors and with another clan, the Péraltes of Hinche, one of whose leaders, Charlemagne, accompanied him on his march.

But Antoine Simon had only scotched the rebellion, not killed it. As soon as the invading government army was gone, the *Cacos*, indignant over burned villages and ravaged gardens, undertook new revolt. On 8 May, risings burst out through the North wherever the regime's troops had trod in February.

The government was not alone in its unpopularity. *Cacos* burned the railroad's sawmill and construction camps, fired into the houses of railroad employees, and cried "*A bas McDonald!*" - a sentiment no doubt inflamed by the fact that the railroad had surrendered its dynamite, powder, and blasting caps to the government forces.

Leconte had bribed safe-conduct out of the German consulate in March and was now in league with General Desiderio Arias, the Dominican frontier bushwhacker (whose 1916 rebellion would precipitate American occupation of Santo Domingo). Thus supported, Leconte hovered at Capotillo, while the president chartered a merchantman to haul troops North. (8) To fill his ranks, *délégué* Simon turned South. But the day was past when his *paysans* would chant, "*Antoine Simon, Ou cé lampe! Nous cé papillons!*" (You're the lamp, we're the butterflies!). Now the old president had only traditional methods of recruitment, ". . . forcibly taking men," Furniss reported, "from their homes at night, from the fields, on the road, or wherever they could find them, and thrusting them like animals into corrals . . . Every couple of days the General in charge would sort them out, sending the young men, in many cases boys, to Port-au-Prince to become soldiers. The older men were fined... in accordance with presumed financial condition."

While, as Bellegarde wrote, "these regiments melted away like ice in the sun," Antoine Simon let himself be hemmed in at Fort Liberté with a garrison, wrote a U.S. naval officer, "of ragged mendicants and half-starved wretches" in a hostile North. Finally, after narrow escapes, he made his way back to the capital by sea, arriving only in time to upset well-advanced plans afoot to prevent his return. During this critical time, the Zamor brothers, making use of Dominican byways, had swooped into Lascahobas and thence the Artibonite. At the Cap, on 20 July, as soon as Simon was out of the North, General Vilbrun Guillaume (who from his cousin, the late president, sometimes took the surname Sam) declared for his fellow *Consolidard*, Leconte.(9)

On 24 July Leconte entered his native Cap, to be proclaimed "Supreme Chief of the Revolution." Gonaïves and St. Marc had already passed over to the revolution, and, on the 25th, Jérémie joined in. On 1 August even Les Cayes rejected its ancient master. The capital was surrounded, with rebels in Pétionville able to control the water supply, which they promptly cut during the night.

Antoine Pierre-Paul, the president's secretary and amanuensis, described the final hours: bands of looters from Bel Air and Morne-à-Tuf racing through the streets, corpses lying in the threshold of the abandoned *douane*, Simonist adherents banging away with Remingtons and Gras rifles handed out from the arsenal, while "the sovereign people" hammered in the shutters of shops and pillaged Simon's country house.

It was midafternoon on 3 August when the president, fortified by the thought of $1.2 million on deposit abroad and surrounded by family, Ministers, and by the last of his trusty 17th Regiment from Les Cayes, set out for the wharf ("our wharf", wrote Herr Staude of the P.C.S. Railroad next day).(10) Firing pistols and rifles in the air and anywhere, the crowd closed in. Staude said Célestina was "furiously beaten and maltreated." She was also shot through the arm by a bullet that killed an accompanying député. At the wharf, the pier master and other Germans brandished the imperial Double Eagle, and the pursuers paused. Making their way out to a Dutch steamer, the party then embarked for Kingston under the guns of U.S.S. *Des Moines* and *Chester*, H.M.S. *Melpomene,* and S.M.S. *Bremen.*

The Best Haiti Has Had

There was a momentary flicker of Firminism. On 7 August 1910, for the last time, Firmin arrived aboard a French steamer, but Leconte was already there. Firmin's last sight of Haiti, so near yet never farther, preceded his death in exile on St. Thomas by five weeks.

At virtually the hour that Firmin was vainly striving to regain his native soil, Cincinnatus Leconte entered the city and repaired to the cathedral for mass. From Fort National the old cannon boomed a 21-gun salute as Leconte was proclaimed *chef du pouvoir executif.* On 14 August the National Assembly obligingly ratified events, and the great-grandson of Jean-Jacques Dessalines (born 29 September 1859) became Haiti's president.

Other than the brand of "*Consolidard*," the most noticeable label borne by Leconte seemed to be "Made in Germany." As a boy, he had been sent to school in Mainz; as a young man, he had worked in the German consulate at the Cap. German firms had bank-rolled his political rise, though not with entire disinterest: after the new president obtained an initial stake of 2 million *gourdes* from the German merchants, Perl, the German minister, was heard to gloat, "We will have control of the customs houses before the end of the year."(11)

Save perhaps Soulouque, no president of Haiti ever confounded more predictions than Cincinnatus Leconte. It was as if, marveled Dantès Bellegarde, "a new man had emerged."

Bellegarde could look back in wonder on Leconte's initial actions, but those on the spot were equally bemused. On 26 August, Furniss said the president's newly appointed collectors of customs were "without exception men who have the reputation for honesty and fair dealing." Reporting a conversation with Leconte, Furniss went on: "He intends to leave the details of business to the heads of the different departments. If he does this it will be the first time the Haitian government has ever lived up to its constitution."

Another first was a round of eminent judicial appointments in a system of courts that, from earliest times, had been a byword for venality, ignorance, and gross partiality. In Tertullien Guilbaud, new Minister of Education, Leconte brought to office one of Haiti's most distinguished men of letters and the law. Guilbaud, Furniss wrote admiringly, "represents the best type of his countrymen. He gives the impression of a retiring, polite, unassuming gentleman, a sound scholar, an upright citizen and an unassuming patriot."

Paris pince-nez quivering with energy, Guilbaud reactivated a corps of school inspectors, raised the pay of teachers (who were getting less money than jailers), revived the perennial project of a central vocational school, and set about resuscitating moribund rural schools, which, according to Edner Brutus, historian of Haiti's public education, "mainly served to support a class of illiterate sinecurists: political placemen, concubines, godchildren, bastards of deputies, senators, and generals."

Simultaneously shrinking the army and trying to improve it, Leconte rehabilitated the few officers whom the old French military mission had trained, organized a new formation styled "*La Réforme*" (housed in imposing new barracks built in 1912 and named for the president's great ancestor), and gave the army its first rifle range.

Not content with administrative reform, Leconte also cracked down on Voodoo, denouncing it as a "*culte grossier*", a gesture that prompted Joseph Pyke, the British minister, to report to London, "There is no doubt of the general practice of 'Vaudoux' among the peasants. I have myself seen within half a mile of Port-au-Prince a place of worship temple, sacred tree, sacrificial

stone and graves - with all the paraphernalia of daggers, skulls, pots of blood
and feathers and a priest in daily attendance. "

Conditions Leconte was trying to ameliorate had been well described, as of
late 1910, by John Laroche, soon to become the new president's Minister of
Public Works and already his son-in-law:

> Never having been kept up at any time, the streets, whether in the provinces or
> capital, become quagmires when it rains. Broken-down roads kill off the movement
> of goods. The bridges over our rivers are shaking with decrepitude and, when they
> collapse, cut all communication between country and towns. The jails are full of
> holes; some utterly stripped, without door or windows, invite escape. The iron
> markets that cost the country so much are rusting away for lack of maintenance.
> Telegraph service is at best mediocre . . . The wires have had more than 15 years'
> steady use. Water supply, even in Port-au-Prince, is rudimentary. The mains are
> broken. Public buildings need to be restored or rebuilt. The army posts look like
> abandoned shanties.

Streets and roads were repaired, thus permitting Haiti's first automobiles,(12)
now being observed with wonder, to chug about Port-au-Prince. Telegraph wires
were restrung and new lines constructed. Telephone service attained such a peak
during Leconte's presidency that Furniss, on one of his mounted tours into the
back country, was able in July 1912 to call Port-au-Prince long-distance from
Grand Gosier, with connections via Saltrou (renamed some seventy years later,
in an excess of poetic license, "Belle Anse") and Jacmel. Of flyblown Saltrou,
Furniss reported, "In passing upstairs I passed through a room containing five
kegs of powder doubtless for the iron muzzle-loading smooth-bore guns on a
decrepit mount in front of the Headquarters. There were about a hundred rifles
among which I noted three different makes and calibers and about 20 boxes of
cartridges. There were only 14 soldiers including Captains and lower officers."

The general, Furniss went on, was out rounding up recruits and deserters and
came in next day with "51 men tied arm to arm and carrying sweet potatoes,
corn and foodstuffs for themselves. There is no outside work for soldiers at
Saltrou, their pay is not sufficient to buy their food, there is nothing they can
steal, so to prevent them from starving to death they must from time to time go
up into the mountains where most of them have families". On 3 April 1912,
U.S.S. *Washington,* a new armored cruiser, brought an important visitor to
Port-au-Prince. Philander C. Knox, first Secretary of State to visit Haiti since
Seward, bore a message. It was essentially the message he had been delivering
in Costa Rica, Cuba, Santo Domingo, Guatemala, Honduras, Nicaragua,
Panama, and Venezuela: with the impending opening of the Panama Canal, the
time had come for the Caribbean republics to quiet down and behave. As Mr.
Knox put it in his reply to Leconte's address:

At a time when the obligation which my country has assumed . . . in creating a highway for international commerce is about to be realized, we are impressed with the conviction that the fullest success of our work is, to a notable degree, dependent on the peace and stability of our neighbors A community liable to be torn by internal dissension or checked in its progress by the consequences of nonfulfillment of international obligations is not in a good position to deserve and reap the benefits . . . such as are certain to come with the opening of the canal.

Knox's words were attuned to the hour, for in Leconte Haiti seemed to have a president determined to rise to the challenges of stability and progress.

The *Antoine Simon*, former Italian Navy ship *Umbria*, anchored in Port-au-Prince harbor in 1911. She never saw action, but her gunpowder, transferred for safekeeping to the Palace, exploded on August 7, 1912, killing President Leconte. *American Heritage Center - University of Wyoming*

Yet as always the horizon slowly darkened. Jérémie and Jacmel were uneasy. In Les Cayes, during April 1912, General and Senator F. P. Paulin, at the head of disgruntled Southerners, fomented a brief uprising featured by looting of the customs house. When the revolt was put down, the warehouses of a German firm yielded contraband arms and evidence of cash investments in the Paulin cause. Paulin himself made it to the German legation, where, for months to follow, he was given free rein, Furniss said, to use it "as his base of operation."

Other old friends besides the Germans were turning on Leconte. Chafed if not baffled by his new probity, the *Cacos* began to be heard from. Charles Zamor, now *délégué militaire* in the North, was their man, and his eye now rested on the *Palais National*.

Old Nord Alexis, who knew the *Cacos* well, was reported to have said, "Once you turn the *Cacos* loose, there will be no restraining them. There will be anarchy, pillage, insecurity. And then," he is supposed to have added, "some foreign army will intervene to protect life and property."

How and whether Leconte would have coped with the *Cacos* will never be known. At 3:00 A.M. on the hot night of 7 August 1912, Port-au-Prince was shaken by an enormous explosion, followed by a volcano of flame soaring skyward from the National Palace. Whether by accident or design, the *Antoine Simon's* Italian powder in the palace basement had finally gone off, taking with it a million rounds of ammunition and assorted other explosives squirreled away by presidents who felt safer with them under their feet than out of their sight. The entire floor of Leconte's bedroom dropped into the holocaust, and his daughter and son-in-law narrowly escaped out a window before the building collapsed. With that building, built by Salomon, also died the president's grandson, 300 soldiers of the *Garde Présidentielle*, and the hopes of many that Leconte might somehow be the leader who would bring Haiti into the new century. (13)

Roger Farnham, anything but a respecter of Haitian politicians or of the Germans to whom Leconte was linked, privately wrote the new Secretary of State, William Jennings Bryan, in 1914:

> The administration of President Leconte . . . probably was the best Haiti had for many years. A real effort was made to administer, honestly, the country. At one time during Leconte's administration, the management of the National Bank of Haiti estimated that fully 90% of the customs revenues were actually being collected. In one of my interviews with President Leconte he told me his life was being threatened by office-holders in different parts of the country because of his effort to collect all customs. These people told him he must loosen up some or he would be put out of office.

Tancrède Auguste

Before the palace rubble cooled, the National Assembly voted in a new president. Tancrède Auguste, fifty-six, a *Capois mulâtre* who then farmed a fine sugar estate at Châteaublond, site of today's International Airport, was - as who of any consequence was not? - another *Consolidard*. In Furniss's confidential biographic portfolio, Auguste nonetheless got high marks:

> . . . of small stature but well built . . . a man of force and character . . .He has a remarkable influence upon the people of the whole section contiguous to Port-au-Prince, and is very much liked and respected...has established free schools on his plantation at his own expense and compels his employees to send their children..

The extent to which Auguste owed his election to the Lecontists immediately became clear in the new cabinet: J.-N. Léger, the complex, some would say devious, lawyer-diplomat,(14) was, with Edmond Lespinasse, another able lawyer, the principal power. To reinforce these two high-born *mulâtres*, the president added still another, the ferocious Dr. Bobo ("a great charlatan in medicine [who] deceives his patients with high-sounding names and quack remedies," reported Consul Henry Livingston from the Cap), and the *noir* Guilbaud, Leconte's dedicated Minister of Education. *"Veux-tu la liberté?"* he had written in a spirited poem in *La Patrie;* *"Mets ton fils à l'école!"* (If you wish for liberty, put your son in school!).

Yet, for all Guilbaud's efforts and the new president's support, gains were little enough in the towns and nil in the countryside. Sir Harry H. Johnston, the British explorer and colonial analyst who visited Haiti in 1910, described the problem only too clearly:

Large sums of money are appropriated annually in the Haitian budget for schools . . . This appropriation is one of the many cruel tricks played on the Haitian people by its Government. In the beautifully printed *Budget général,* under the head of the Department of Public Instruction, there is a *cadre* providing for the education of Haiti . . . with a detail and completeness worthy of Switzerland or Germany. Yet much of this organization exists only on paper, and the funds appropriated for this splendid purpose find their way into the pockets of Government officials or possibly never leave the Treasury . . . I doubt if there are any rural schools at all, in spite of the fact that 500 are provided for in the budget; if they exist, they do so as a means of providing petty sustenance for some totally incompetent person. The plain fact remains that something like 2,500,000 out of 3,000,000 Haitians cannot read or write, and are as ignorant as unreclaimed natives of Africa.

Then Johnston goes on to speak of the fine education of the elite

"so highly educated, so clever with tongue and pen, so witty and well-read, such men of the world" - and his admiration descends to despair: The weak point in all this superior education is its utterly unpractical[sic] relation to a useful and profitable existence . . . France of today shows herself able to educate and send to Africa and Asia hosts of young men supplied with the most practical instruction . . . but the education she gives to the youth of Haiti is perversely useless in its nature. It is apparently only adapted to life in Paris or in a French provincial town . . . Lawyers can think of nothing but the meticulous intricacies of the *Code Napoleon,* and seem incapable of devising a simple civil and criminal jurisprudence applicable to the essentially African race which inhabits Haiti. As to other branches of science agriculture, forestry, zoology, botany, mineralogy, bacteriology - not a single Haitian interests himself.

Another science, though Sir Harry might not have so classified it, banking, was now pinching the government, and pinching hard.

Under the *Banque*'s charter, no obligation existed for the latter to release (except at the end of each fiscal year) revenues accumulated for the government. Given the hand-to-mouth necessities of Haitian finance, a monthly trickle was a necessity, and, in the tradition of the old *Banque*, Leconte had therefore sought a supplementary agreement or *"convention budgétaire"* whereby the new institution would continue this accommodation. To this request the BNRH turned a cold shoulder, with the equally chilling intimation that only if given some type of customs control would it put the government on a monthly allowance. While conveying this message, ostensibly from the "Paris Group," the *Banque*'s "New York Group" (Farnham and company) blandly assured the State Department that no such wicked thoughts of customs control had entered their heads. For the moment, however, due to efforts by the American legation (earning Dr. Furniss no thanks from the City Bank), a *convention* was worked out and, as a result of Leconte's unforeseen honesty and similar tendencies in the Auguste regime, the government fully covered the *Banque*'s advances and in fact ended fiscal year 1912-1913 with a balance of over $800,000. But this performance failed to mollify the bankers, who had already opened a second front.

The new *Banque* had held out 10 million francs in gold for retirement of debased paper *gourdes* printed mainly by Nord Alexis. In 1912, the assembly enacted a currency-retirement law, but, maintaining that the measure was insufficient, the *Banque*, which was using them as capital for loans at 12.5 percent, held on to its francs. Next year the assembly voted a law with no loophole that could warrant further stalling. The *Banque* thereupon changed tactics: without warning it called in past-due loans, refused further loans, and forced borrowers whose loans were current to pay a 1 percent tax thereon. This was more than a tight-money policy: it was commercial strangulation in which, during the next two years, the *Banque* would continue to tighten the bowstring. The only (and necessarily self-defeating) countermeasure for the government was to print more paper money in violation of the bank agreement and go to the German usurers.

Besides the bankers, Auguste also had the *Cacos* to reckon with. His election, a Port-au-Prince inside job, had been pulled off without regard to the *Cacos* or their ever more strident pretensions as king-makers. In December, paying them off, as Leconte had done, with arms and money, Auguste for the moment placated the chiefs -just in time to hear of trouble fomented by the Simonists in Les Cayes, where Célestina the *mambo* had quietly returned and was practicing her arts to no good purpose for the regime. Arrests followed at Cayes, as well as Jacmel and Jérémie, in February and March.

And the president's health was flagging. By April he was bed-ridden, and *telediol* (not to mention most future historians) told of slow poison. With professional exactness Furniss cabled:

PRESIDENT'S CONDITION NOW VERY SERIOUS. HE IS DELIRIOUS,
HEART ACTION IS BAD, AND HE IS UNABLE TO RETAIN NOURISHMENT.

Dr. Furniss had reason for his prognosis. On 29 April he had been asked to
participate in a consultation with the president's physician: the problem was not
poison but advanced anaemia. To Washington, Furniss reported clinically and
confidentially, "Samples of the President's blood give the characteristic reaction
for syphilis and it is doubtless due to having this disease in the third stage that
the anaemia is so pronounced and persistent."

At 9:00 P.M., 3 May, it was over. As his eyes closed and the rose-garnished
block of ice was lifted onto the dead president's chest, Port-au-Prince learned
that, for the third time in twenty months, another president had to be chosen.

The People Never Understood

Out of practicality in a tropical climate, the dead are buried promptly in Haiti.
Thus it was that President Auguste's state funeral commenced in the new
cathedral at 8:00 A.M., 4 May, the morning following his death, with the
diplomatic corps and all Port-au-Prince in attendance. The remains, escorted by
the *Musiciens Palais National* playing a dirge with drums muffled in black, were
placed on the catafalque, and in Furniss's account, "the Cabinet (the other
Musiciens), surrounded by armed officers, took their places." Amid the solemn
requiem, Archbishop Conan exhorted the living to respect the dead by peaceful
choice of a new president, then, censers fuming and swinging, and solemnly
aspersing holy water right and left, Msgr. Conan and the chief clergy descended
in processional from the high altar to give Tancrède Auguste their *viaticum* for
his final journey.

They had reached about midway,"recounted John Allen, the *Banque*'s
American manager,

when a low murmur peculiar to the people of the country took place, immediately
followed by a whistle of the same character. In less time than it takes to tell, the
Cathedral was in an uproar; simultaneously with this development came the firing
of guns from the instigators, who had ranged themselves on both sides of the
Cathedral, pouring their fire into the building, but with few casualties, so that it was
noise and apprehension rather than bullets that caused the panic. Pandemonium
broke loose. No one could run for safety because there was no chance to run. Every
bit of ground in the Cathedral was occupied. Neither would those near the doors go
out for fear of being shot as they emerged. As many of the people as could tried to
get close to the Archbishop and the other clergy, feeling that the nearer they were
to them the safer they would be. In this attempt to get close, the vestments and
clothes of the clergy were almost torn away.

Shouting "*A bas le Cabinet!*" and scattering the faithful, soldiers, firing all ways but mostly up, burst inside. With naval precision, the captain of U.S.S. *Nashville* took out his gold watch and noted that the time was exactly 8:30, and that a fusillade from three sides was being poured into the cathedral. Fortunately the windows are high enough that bullets flying inside were well overhead, and, so far as is known, no one was killed by ricochets.

In the words of H. P. Davis, who lived in Haiti and was later to write a history of the country, "It was evident that the time-honored preliminaries of a new election were underway."

As the coffin was snatched up and hurried across town to the Cimetière Extérieure through streets full of shouting, shooting soldiery, what had happened became clearer.

General Edmond Defly, military commandant of the capital and a presidential candidate, had surrounded the cathedral, and it was his soldiers who had broken up Auguste's funeral. Meanwhile, Beaufossé Laroche, also a candidate, had launched his own soldiers into the streets to head off Defly. All morning ("more by noise than bloodshed," related John Allen), the two factions contended, until Seymour Pradel, old Firminist and Auguste's Interior Minister, marshaled the commanders of *La Réforme* and the *Garde Présidentielle* and by noon got the cathedral and surrounding streets cleared so that shaken diplomats and clergy could retire safely to legations and presbyteries for a drink.

But Defly had not given up. At four, as the National Assembly convened to decide who should succeed Auguste, Defly's men charged the assembly, and battle again raged until La Réforme finally prevailed, and Laroche, during a lull, made for the German legation, where Dr. Perl welcomed him at the portal.

When the shooting stopped toward nightfall, the electors, choosing between the eminent lawyer, Luxembourg Cauvin, and Michel Oreste, also a lawyer and deputy, voted in the latter, and, to the surprise of history, after 109 years gave Haiti its first civilian president.

The election, however, had not wholly shattered precedent: each elector received Oreste's due bill for $600 gold, redeemable from the national treasury.

Michel Oreste, fifty-four, a *griffe* and one time Bazelaisist and Legitimist from Jacmel, was a man of popularity, intelligence, and brilliant reputation as professor of law, parliamentarian, and orator. Inaugurated on 12 May with a somewhat muted Te Deum, Oreste set out to do three things: reform the army; retire paper money; and make rural schooling a reality. (Himself of humble origin, self-taught and self-made, Oreste had scaled the ramparts of elite status by hard work and hard study.)

Besides the historical obstacles in the way of any such program, Oreste could count one more: for the second time, the *Cacos* of the North had been balked by a Port-au-Prince coup that, crowning affront, had conferred the presidency on a civilian parliamentarian from the West.

Everything Michel Oreste wanted to do earned him enemies. The army resisted reform by a civilian; sinecurists in the school system were outraged at the thought of being disturbed; the *Banque* had no intention of yielding up its 10 million francs for the currency-retirement law that Oreste got through on 26 August 1913; and the *Cacos* and the Zamors and their liegemen and Dominican friends liked no part of any of it. Concerning these last, Oreste made the mistake of continuing the payoffs of Leconte and Auguste and then abruptly cutting them off. This and other vacillations, reported Minister Pyke to London on 13 June, was doing Oreste "immense harm."

> The Cabinet [Pyke went on] which was formed with a desire to conciliate all parties meets with almost universal condemnation and is reported to be divided into two rival camps . . . The President is in daily receipt of threats and warnings for his personal safety: anonymous letters are pinned to his bed and his clothes: he refuses to use the throne set aside for him at the Cathedral and every Sunday, a chair is carried through the town from his residence and returned there after Mass . . . Mr. Pauléus Sannon, who apparently makes a habit of conspiring against each and every administration, has taken refuge in the French Legation.

One reform of sorts did get through. The brutal and high-handed *Police Administrative*, little more than institutionalized *zinglins*, were reconstituted as a Service de Sûreté and brought under ministerial control. Yet even this improvement raised suspicion. Reporting on a $60,000 gold special appropriation voted in the legislature, Furniss noted:

> "Secret Police" is the title under which large sums are appropriated and as no vouchers for its expenditure are required it becomes the source of a large part of the graft distributed by various administrations, usually by the President. In this case the money was withdrawn from the Bank as soon as the appropriation made it available, and was taken to the Palace, President Oreste himself removing the money from the carriage conveying it and placing it in his private apartments . . .

The palace was an interim structure. Auguste had done nothing to rebuild the Leconte ruin. Oreste extracted a $350,000 appropriation from the legislature in August 1913, after holding a contest in which the design of Georges Baussan, Haiti's leading architect, edged out French and domestic competitors. Work commenced on 20 May 1914, an event Michel Oreste was not destined to see.

As 1913 drifted to its close, Pyke wearily told the Foreign Office some truths in his annual report:

There has been no change except retrogressive . . . The proverbial apathy of the peasants, who are accustomed to suffer so much from their rulers - from the highest to the lowest - probably has prevented a repetition of the sanguinary revolutions of the last century, but it is the inherent distrust and dislike with which all Haitians regard the foreigner which forms a continued obstacle to that development of the country without which it will soon reach a state of bankruptcy . . . Procrastination and double-dealing continue to be the characteristics of Hayti's diplomacy, and the barefaced manner in which formal promises are habitually broken by responsible ministers makes it difficult to keep up the appearance, even, of cordial relations.

On 1 January 1914 there was an outburst at Thomazeau timed to coincide with an attempt, for once unsuccessful, to set Port-au-Prince afire. Rushed out in cane cars behind balloon-stacked little woodburners of the P.C.S., government troops surrounded Thomazeau, captured nineteen rebels and one general, and shot them on the spot.

Three days later the *Cacos* were heard from. Trou du Nord was seized in the night while, deep in the mountains near Vallière, so was Monbin Crochu. To confuse matters, not one but two factions were in arms: those owing allegiance to the Zamor family, the other to Davilmar Théodore of Ennery, the old Salnavist who had later become one of Leconte's political managers.

Because of doings at Thomazeau, the government was alert and for the moment reacted vigorously. Troops and arms were rushed by ship to the Cap and Fort Liberté, each arriving in the nick of time to chase out newly arrived *Cacos*: Zamorists at the former, Théodore's men at the latter. But the *Cacos* could not be contained; government troops soon joined them and, by 23 January, the entire North and Northwest were lost.

Elsewhere, too, the sands were running out: Port-au-Prince experienced fires, and, amid rising disorder, press gangs and firing squads combed Jacmel and Jérémie. Without precisely choosing up factions, the Môle, Port-de-Paix, and Gonaïves pronounced for revolution. Then, on 27 January, Charles Zamor landed at the Cap from exile and convinced Davilmar Théodore that the two *Caco* factions should make common cause.

"The last days of the outgoing administration," reminisced the *Banque*'s John Allen, "were full of interest . . . The Zamor revolutionary army had been working its way toward Port-au-Prince, going from village to village . . . There was no resistance; government troops, as the revolutionary forces advanced, would retreat, making no stand . . . It was customary to give the outgoing President time to take refuge in a foreign legation or vessel, the incoming leader knowing full well it would be only a question of time before he would be leaving under similar circumstances."

The night of the 26th, Oreste - *bon vivant* to the last - had a few friends in for dinner. Midway, an aide brought the fatal word that St. Marc had declared against the government. The president finished dinner, then announced he would resign next day. His last official act, according to Stephen Leech, the British minister, was to try to rent the National Palace to the American, German, or British legation as a residence or chancery, an offer all politely declined. Then he called for pen and paper and wrote a brief resignation: "History," he concluded, "will say I only sought, with great sincerity, the good of the Haitian people, and that I did all I could to realize it. The people never understood."

Promptly at 2:00 P.M. on 27 January 1914, a gun salute from the palace announced that Oreste was departing. The president's journey to the wharf - reported as if by TV commentators along the line of march - comes to us through three eyewitnesses: Leech, Smith (the new American minister), and Allen."

SMITH: The President, accompanied by his wife and several close friends, entered his landau and the march to the waterfront, almost a mile distant, began . . .
ALLEN: The German Minister was in the carriage beside him and they rode slowly down to the city along streets lined with the multitude . . .

LEECH: Mme. Oreste was at his side, accompanied by cavalry and a disorderly rabble of soldiers firing their rifles in the air and uttering strange yells . . .

SMITH: Large numbers of the populace joined in the procession, they also firing . . .

LEECH: Although Mme. Oreste displayed great courage, bowing and smiling to the crowd, the President in his fear lost all control of himself. On two occasions he rose and fired his revolver at his escort, suspecting treachery, with the result that the latter fired at the people and several were killed and wounded . . .

SMITH: Two soldiers were killed.

ALLEN: The President jumped into the street but he was quickly surrounded by the guard, who practically lifted him into his carriage, and between the Presidential Guard and the German Minister he was safely put upon a cutter of the German warship.

As an afterthought, while the diplomatic corps were paying their adieux, Oreste remarked that he "had taken no precautions to prevent disorder following his departure." As soon as he was gone, the ministers hastily called in British, American, French, and German Marines, the Americans bringing "a shore wireless," probably the first radio to operate from Haitian soil. General Edmond Polynice, head of the usual Committee of Public Safety, called the landings "a national humiliation," but there was nothing to be done about it, and the Marines stayed ashore until, with the arrival of the *Cacos*, the next act commenced.(16)

Prolonged Civil War Likely

Haitian and foreign historians generally bypass much of 1914 and 1915 with summary reference to *"présidences éphémères,"* as if by general consent Haitian history had been turned off with the fall of Antoine Simon and started anew with the dramatic happenings of mid-1915. Naturally, nothing of the sort occurred. Whirling vertiginously, events dizzied even their own participants as Haiti drifted, helpless, into an eighteen-month maelstrom.

With Michel Oreste out of the way, the Zamors and Davilmar Théodore, seemingly in close harmony, prepared to move South from their strongholds in the North. As an earnest of good feeling, Théodore entrusted the Zamors with a war chest to raise additional forces on an inland route of march via Hinche and Mirebalais.

When Théodore approached Gonaïves next day, he was astonished to find the Zamors already there. To heighten Théodore's surprise, he was greeted by a volley. What had happened, as Leech reported, was that "with the treachery, bad faith, and self-interest that characterizes Haytians, the Zamor brothers devoted [Théodore's] funds to their own purposes, and Théodore, on arrival at Gonaïves, found himself face to face with an opposing army under command of Oreste Zamor."

Interrupted by pillage and followed by fire, battle now joined. Leech went on: "Haytians are inexpert marksmen, and generally seem to fire in the air. When the tide of battle turns, the defeated combatants are apt to range themselves on the side of the presumed victor . . . This custom was followed at Gonaïves."

Théodore and a few followers straggled South from Gonaïves, whose flames could be seen from St. Marc. Charles Zamor cautiously pursued Théodore while Oreste occupied St, Marc. In Port-au-Prince, Zamor agents began spreading handbills, and Théodore people vanished into consulates.

Completing Haiti's first mass military rail movement, Oreste Zamor debarked his men from trains on 7 February and next day the army entered the city. John Allen saw the scene: "A more nondescript collection could hardly be imagined. Zamor rode a small native horse, with a number of bedraggled soldiers in tattered clothes, mostly without uniforms, strung behind, some with guns, some with swords, others with pistols, and several hundred trailers, men and women, and the usual accompaniment of burros, dogs, and roosters."

Within less than twenty-four hours the National Assembly, routed out of hiding, chose Oreste Zamor as president. Leech described the Zamors: "Oreste Zamor, a ferocious-looking Negro . . . seems to be a man of little education .

. . Charles Zamor is lighter coloured and of considerable refinement, and appears to be well-educated and intelligent, and is evidently the right-hand man . . . The third brother, B. Zamor, seems to be a weak creature with little if any intelligence."

The differences between the first two brothers were not a matter of color. Charles, the elder, had been educated at St. Martial before his Bazelaisist family fled Port-au-Prince during Salomon's time and settled in remote Cerca-la-Source. Oreste, born later, had only the education of the mountains and of Hinche. Rising to influence in the back country near the Dominican frontier, the Zamors were strong Lecontists with the usual Dominican ties.

Whether the Zamors would now be strong enough to rule remained to be seen. Minister Smith gloomily predicted, "Prolonged civil war likely."

On 5 February 1914 Davilmar Théodore and his men reached the Cap, which they looted and set afire. It would have gone worse but for the Marines of U.S.S. *Nashville,* whom Consul Livingston called ashore.

Like the psalmist lifting up his eyes unto the hills, Théodore occupied Grande Rivière du Nord and began organizing sanctuary areas among the *Caco* strongholds. Within less than a week, he also took over Port-de-Paix. As Charles Zamor slowly moved North, J.-N. Léger, again Foreign Minister, confided to Leech that the only obstacle to settlement was price: "Théodore," said Léger, "asked too much." (17) Any price would have been too much. The new regime, penniless to begin with, was on starvation rations. When Oreste Zamor sent for John Allen and asked for a loan (£750,000, said Leech), Allen replied there could be no loan without "proper control of customs" by the United States.

Lured South by the promise of 10 *gourdes* a day, the *Cacos* had not received a *centime.* The day Zamor was elected, when no pay was forthcoming, robbery and looting began. Within a week, hungry *Cacos* were fighting town police. When the former seized and looted the police stations, Leech wrote, "the police force entirely disappeared." Port-au-Prince, he went on, was "in a great state of alarm, excited crowds running aimlessly in every direction, while rifles were being fired off at random . . . The Palace and precincts were the scene of the wildest confusion. Every available space in the entrance-yard not already obstructed by Q.F. [quick-firing] guns was occupied by a vociferating crowd, everyone talking and no-one listening."

That the *Banque*'s unyielding stand reflected a hardening of Washington's position on customs control was demonstrated on 26 February when Minister Smith was instructed to tell Zamor he would be recognized by the United States after the State Department learned more about his disposition to accept American aid in customs administration and lighthouse service (important because of the new Panama Canal); and Washington received renewed assurance that no other power would be granted concessions at the Môle.(18)

Léger turned the discussion around by saying there could be no discourse on any matter until U.S. recognition opened proper channels. Bryan took the bait and extended recognition on 1 March 1914; Léger thereupon ignored further American overtures and gave no reassurances whatever as to the Môle.

In mid-March, Bryan again tried vainly to tighten the screws. Oreste Zamor personally turned out a mob in front of the *Banque* while Paris and Berlin told Washington they expected to share in any customs control and would resist any unilateral move by the United States. On the usual ruinous terms, the German merchants obliged the Zamors with 2.3 million *gourdes*, which quieted the *Cacos* but also demonstrated the truth of a U.S. Naval Intelligence report: "In Haiti, the Revolutionists fight for the promise of money, while the Government *must pay* in order to get men to fight for it."

In the North, the fighting dragged on. Money continued to come in to Théodore from Antoine Simon's prosperous Kingston dairy farm, weapons and recruits arrived from Arias, the turbulent cigar-maker of Montecristi. The *Nord Alexis* shuttled shiploads of Zamor's wounded back from the Cap, and press gangs scoured the streets of the capital.

Besides Antoine Simon and the Dominicans, Théodore had won another ally. From the French legation, that arch-*Consolidard*, Vilbrun Guillaume, in asylum for his health, had begun orchestrating support for Théodore against the German-Lecontist-oriented Zamors.

By the end of May 1914 the plain in the North between the Cap and Ouanaminthe was, wrote Livingston, "infested with *Cacos*." On 21 May, on instructions, Livingston made a roundabout pilgrimage to Théodore, via Montecristi to Ouanaminthe, in "a hired automobile," to see if some arrangement could be reached. Despite a warm reception (Théodore was on good terms with the consul), he was told that "they would rather see the country perish ten times and perish with it, than see the Zamors remain."

That Livingston had not overstated conditions was confirmed on 19 June when Farnham telegraphed Secretary Bryan:

REVOLUTIONISTS AT BAHON, GRANDE RIVIERE, LACOMBE. LACOMBE STATION ENTERED AND OUR AGENT FORCED TO LEAVE. TELEPHONE AND TRAIN SERVICE INTERRUPTED. HAND CARS HELD UP. TWO MEN SHOT. TODAY'S TRAINS NOT IN, PROBABLY CAPTURED . . .

Farnham was accurate: Trou had fallen the day before, leaving Charles Zamor all but hemmed in at the Cap. From the town, as in 1791, could be seen pillars of fire and smoke as *Cacos* surged over the plain, burning houses of Zamorist officials and sympathizers as they advanced. Against this apocalyptic backdrop Charles Zamor retaliated by shooting townsmen whose allegiance he doubted. Amid cries of *"Vive Zamor!"* prisoners were dragged up to La Fossette, where, on 25 June alone, fourteen hostages were shot, followed by uncounted others in days to come.

The situation in Port-au-Prince was precarious. Ross Hazeltine, an American consular officer, reported Zamor unpopularity rising apace with financial distress, and the city was full of Théodore supporters.(19) As early as 14 June, at Pont Beudet in the Cul-de-Sac, an American observer noted: ". . . Dominican rebels circulating freely among people at the [railroad] station . All rebels dressed in revolutionary style and wore the customary scarlet hat band or sash."

Thinking the time opportune in the capital, General Defly again mounted an *attentat*. After heavy street fighting on 17 and 18 July, culminating in an attack on the palace on the night of the 19th, the government prevailed, and Defly sought German hospitality while less fortunate supporters were run down and executed on the street corners. Among those who quickly joined Defly were old T.A. Simon Sam and three sons. Blind since 1908, the old man had come home to Rue Lamarre and was now investing some of his large remaining fortune in the future of his fellow *Consolidard* and cousin, Vilbrun Guillaume.

Reviewing reports of these events and of the gloomy military situation in the North, a Foreign Office official in London minuted a Port-au-Prince dispatch: "The present Haytian Govt are [sic] doomed." He was right enough, but the game was not quite played out.

Oreste Zamor got all the way to the Cap after some initial difficulties and swept the plain of *Cacos*, capturing Ouanaminthe on August 29th. Disguised as a woman, Davilmar Théodore barely squeaked across the border to Dajabón, where, Livingston reported, Desiderio Arias, like many another Dominican warlord before him, was now playing a double game, ". . . sheltering and openly aiding the revolutionaries at Dajabón, while protesting undying friendship for the Government, promising to aid them in consideration of a certain amount of money and a few hundred thousand rounds of ammunition when, through his aid, Ouananminthe should fall into their hands."

By ordinary rules, Théodore's rout should have signaled victory for the Zamors, but the times were not ordinary. The Zamors, absolutely strapped, were down to $62,000 cash on hand.

Consistent with past policy and future hopes, the *Banque* again declined to advance collected revenues before the end of the fiscal year.(20) Outbreak of war in Europe, almost as if the *Banque* had planned it, simultaneously tied up foreign-exchange transactions in Paris, which in turn provided ready-made excuses for tight money in Port-au-Prince. War-shipping dislocation and blockade cruelly impeded the export of coffee, and, hardest of all, France stopped buying Haitian coffee. By mid-October 1914, the Zamors' shoestring had frayed through.

Meanwhile, on 14 October, bolder than before, Dr. Bobo, whom Charles Zamor had somehow neglected to shoot despite his well known Théodore connections, tried to storm the prison at the Cap and deliver its rebel charges. The attempt failed, but the doors of the German consulate opened more easily and Dr. Bobo entered for what proved a brief stay.

During the momentary improvement of his fortunes in August and September, Oreste Zamor made himself scarce when the U.S. minister came North to reinforce Livingston's suggestions of U.S. customs control. Now Charles Zamor dropped all requests for a face-saving charade and guaranteed "to have the views of the United States government adopted" in return for U.S. assistance in keeping the Zamors in power. It was too late.

On 18 October, Charles Zamor evacuated the Cap by sea, and Oreste withdrew South over the mountains to Ennery. Next morning, as soon as the gunboats were out of sight, Dr. Bobo grandly emerged from the consulate, announced himself *chef civil de la révolution* and as such, greeted the advanced guard of Théodore. The latter, proclaimed president on the spot, appointed Bobo Minister of Interior. The only casualty in these proceedings was a donkey, whose rider, a rebel officer flushed with victory, tried to ride down a Marine sentry at the American consulate; with a bayonet thrust the sentry speared the unfortunate animal and unhorsed the general.

Oreste Zamor's soldiery forsook him at Ennery, whereupon the president made tracks for Gonaïves to join his brother. There, on 28 October, the Zamors boarded S.S. *Prins Willem V*, bound for Curaçao via Port-au-Prince, where certain loose ends remained to be tidied up.

Within hours, the *telediol* flew from Gonaïves to Port-au-Prince and thus (in the words of R. M. Kohan, the newly arrived British minister), "At 4 o'clock in the morning of the 29th October, a ... fusillade of machine-gun fire and rifle-fire announced the fall of the Zamor government."

Charles Zamor, hoping for a more orderly wind-up of the regime, later in the day debarked from the *Prins Willem V* to find the National Palace looted and his sister-in-law and children in refuge with the Dominican minister. Making hasty arrangements with the latter and with the French minister, whose hospitality he quickly accepted, Charles joined colleagues of the fallen cabinet at the French legation while General Polynice again shaped up a Committee of Public Safety.

On the 30th, as the *Prins Willem V* raised steam, the French and Dominican ministers loaded Mme. Zamor, the children, and baggage into two carriages for the journey to the wharf. The mob made no attempt to molest them, reported Bailly-Blanchard, but there was "a great deal of howling and personal abuse directed at Mme. Zamor . . As Mme. Zamor and children were being put on board, the maid, who was the last person in the party, was surrounded by the mob and a package she was carrying, said to have contained $4,000 in gold and which was wrapped in a Dominican flag, was snatched from her and its contents scattered over the pier. A part went overboard, the rest was taken by the mob."

Oreste Zamor, who, according to Minister Kohan, was "in a state of abject terror," never left the ship while *Cacos* of the town paraded the streets, pillaging shops and firing in all directions, awaiting the advent of Davilmar Théodore.

Un Maître Etranger?

As Davilmar Théodore's locomotive chuffed in from St. Marc on the afternoon of 6 November, the bells of Port-au-Prince rang and the old 3-inch muzzle-loaders at Fort National thumped out salutes. Yet how little there was to celebrate.

At age sixty-seven, the bullet-headed old *Caco* had, to be sure, finally reached the *Palais National*. Elected unanimously by the National Assembly on 7 November, he was inaugurated as soon as arrangements could be made, on the 10th (21) - but with the presidency, Joseph Davilmar Théodore's problems had only begun.

In haste to reap the spoils of victory, Théodore's *Cacos* had swarmed South, leaving behind large unsubdued pockets of Zamorists throughout the North and Center in old strongholds such as Hinche, Maïssade, Pignon, Ranquitte, and Vallière.

Foreign recognition was conspicuously lacking, especially by the United States, which had been on the verge of intervening to save the Zamors when their regime collapsed too soon for Marines to arrive. Other major powers, now thoroughly preoccupied with the World War, were likewise in no hurry over Haiti.

But Théodore's central problem was no different from what had brought down the Zamors. As succinctly explained by Livingston on 27 January:

[Théodore's] followers flocked to Port-au-Prince expecting to reap the rewards of ten months' struggle and hardships. The President found himself in a position where he was unable to satisfy the demands of his friends and had to suffer the consequences. As the revolution, like most of its predecessors, was made for money and nothing but money, the ignorant followers of the President became much incensed, refusing to believe that the head of a government was unable to find the means of meeting obligations toward those who had put him in power. His failure to supply these demands was attributed to cupidity and lack of good faith, and he immediately became the most unpopular man in Haiti.

The question of U.S. recognition and the more pressing one of funds were in fact closely linked. Woodrow Wilson's reformist instincts toward Central America and the Caribbean had long been offended by Haiti's bottomless problems and squalid politics and, more practically (through the medium of such rogues as Desiderio Arias) by the unhealthy interaction between Haitian affairs and those of the Dominican Republic, which the United States was trying to uplift and regularize .

Thus, with Wilson's personal approval, on 4 November 1914, Acting Secretary of State Robert Lansing mailed Bailly-Blanchard a lightly edited version of the so-called Wilson Plan, under which the United States had just imposed a semblance of constitutionality on Dominican politics - and which, prior to the downfall of the Zamors, Washington had hoped might just solve Haiti's difficulties. Vain hope. In the trenchant comment by Dana Munro, one of the State Department's ablest Latin American specialists and later a historian of the Caribbean, "The plan had worked in Santo Domingo, where there were organized political parties with a substantial following, but in Haiti the contending leaders were little more than chiefs of mercenary bands, and the ignorance and political indifference of the masses made a popular election practically impossible."

Then, on 12 November, dangling financial rescue and recognition, Bryan telegraphed Bailly-Blanchard a laundry list of demands covering practically all outstanding matters of interest to the United States: customs control, railroad and *Banque*, assurances about the Môle, settlement of private American claims, and so on. Once Haiti agreed to these conditions, the State Department promised to induce the *Banque* to slacken its grip.

Taking direction from the inapplicable Dominican experience and from Woodrow Wilson's moralistic Monroe Doctrine address at Mobile, Alabama, on 27 October 1913, the Lansing-Bryan thrust aimed at theoretically unexceptionable objectives: Haitian fiscal and administrative regularity; discharge of existing international obligations and disposition of pending claims, a near-utopian formula to achieve free and representative "democratic" processes; and an American tutelary role in all the foregoing.

Proof, if proof were needed, of Washington's ignorance of Haiti, these unrealistic goals called for performance beyond Haitian capacity, if not comprehension, and for concessions no Haitian politician could make.(22)

The extent to which questions of recognition and some special American role in Haiti were complicated by the private interests of the *Banque* was highlighted in November by a desperate attempt, on the part of the government, to outflank the *Banque* by printing up 16 million *gourdes*, in violation of the *Banque*'s exclusive right to issue currency. But the need for money, no matter what kind, seemed so pressing that, instead of waiting for the shipment from New York,

Haiti's Banque Nationale, 1910. A U.S. Navy gunboat landed Marines in 1915 to "protect" gold reserves from being used by the Haitian government. Taken to New York, the gold was returned after the U.S. occupied Haiti. *Heinl Collection*

364

The old North portal of Port-au-Prince (variously known as *Portail St. Joseph* and Fort Lamarre), through which invading revolutionary or *Caco* armies entered the capital from the North. *Heinl Collection*

the government ran off 8 million *gourdes* on newsprint at a local jobprinter's. Mocked in the streets as *"Bons Da,"* from Théodore's nickname, these bills were paid to hungry *Cacos*, who then forced them on merchants with machete and musket.

Théodore, who ran through five Finance Ministers in as many months, nonetheless had a fair grievance against the *Banque*, which was well stated by Joseph Chatelain in his history of the institution:

> It represented either a strange lack of logic or good faith on the part of [the *Banque*] to invoke for its own benefit the argument of *force majeure* [that is, wartime blockage of exchange transactions] to justify failure to carry out contractual obligations while at the same time demanding the government, victim of the same circumstances of *force majeure*, to respect its obligations rigorously.

But neither logic nor legality governed the actions of any party. Despite warnings from the United States, now openly the *Banque*'s protector (on 1 January 1915 the Tricolor was lowered over the offices on Rue Magasins de l'Etat and the Stars and Stripes went up), that the *bons da* would not be recognized, the government plowed ahead. At the same time - shades of Tonton Nord - officials muttered that the time had come for Haitians to take what was theirs.(23)

A raid on the *Banque* could hardly be ruled out: Théodore's unpaid *Cacos* were treating Port-au-Prince like a conquered town. It was therefore in a highly jittery frame of mind that the authorities in Washington and New York determined their next step.

After consultation with Bryan in Washington, New York officials of the *Banque* decided to withdraw from Port-au-Prince $500,000 of the currency retirement fund (known as "La Retraite"), which had been sent to Port-au-Prince. With the concurrence of the State Department, the bankers arranged to have the money shipped aboard U.S.S. *Machias,* an ancient gunboat. "The reason the money was brought from Haiti to New York in a warship," explained Roger Farnham, when asked in 1922 by a Senate investigating copmittee, "was because it was impossible to obtain insurance on it in the small ships of the Dutch Line which were then operating. It was after presenting that situation to the Secretary of State that it was arranged that the *Machias,* I think it was, should bring the money to New York. It was brought up and placed on deposit in New York and held there for the account of the retreat . . ."

In accordance with this arrangement, on 17 December 1914 a detachment of Marines landed during the somnolent noon hours, proceeded to the *Banque*, and ok the gold back without incident to the gunboat, which duly delivered its rgo to New York.

Legally, as the *Banque*'s eminent Haitian counsel, Seymour Pradel, so advised, the *Banque* had every right to transfer money from one pocket to another. It was, moreover, money that had only recently been brought into Haiti from New York. In New York, as (under the 1910 agreement) it had not in Port-au-Prince, it even earned interest. (24)

The Haitians, however, were in no mood for niceties. They saw the money as theirs, raised and secured by a Haitian bond issue, and clearly marched beyond their reach by foreign military force. Refusing to allow the law or the facts to get in the way of what were deeply felt to be principles of the case, Solon Ménos, Haitian minister in Washington, bitterly protested to Bryan what he described as "an arbitrary and offensive intervention . . . a flagrant invasion of the sovereignty and independence of the Republic of Haiti."

Behind Haiti's angry protests and the State Department's precisely drawn legalities, lay two questions. The first was whether the transfer really had to be made. Apparently none of the people on the spot Bailly-Blanchard; the new bank manager, W. H. Williams, who had succeeded John Allen, or the navy's senior officer present - felt convinced that the *Banque* was in clear and present danger of a raid, especially with three U.S. naval vessels and a regiment of Marines in Port-au-Prince harbor. The second question was simply how the whole affair looked, especially to Haitians. The short answer is that it looked bad then and, if only in terms of misreading and misjudgment, still does in hindsight.

Angered by the *Machias* incident and hard-pressed by *Banque* and commercial refusals of the *Bons Da*, the government hit back. On 23 December, the *Banque* was stripped of treasury service. Then, on the 28th, accompanied by a file of soldiers, a *juge d'instruction* strode into the *Banque*, writ in hand. Recognizing what was afoot, Desrue, the French assistant manager, leapt for the main vault, heaved the door shut, threw the tumblers, and spun the dial. Then, facing the *juge d'instruction* with Gallic aplomb, he courteously inquired if he could be of service.(25)

The cash drawers and lock boxes contained $66,910 in gold, and that was what the Haitians got. Inside the vault, placed under seal but beyond reach ("Bank" Williams guessed it would take five or six days to breach the main vault), lay $400,000 in gold, the remainder of La Retraite. With the *Banque* thus paralyzed, Haiti's finances were at a standstill, and default on the republic's foreign obligations, announced on 29 January 1915, was inevitable.

Beset as he was by troubles at hand, Davilmar Théodore could hardly refuse a request from Vilbrun Guillaume for the lucrative and powerful post of *délégué militaire* in the North and Northwest. The Cap was unsettled and uneasy. Unpaid *Cacos* continued to drift back from Port-au-Prince and into the arms of the Zamorists, headed now by Bussy Zamor and Charlemagne Péralte, Charles Zamor's brother-in-law and lately *général de place* at Port-de-Paix. Guillaume, still subsidized by blind old President Simon Sam, was, *telediol* said, chosen leader of this faction.

The rumor was confirmed soon enough. On 15 January Guillaume called together leading citizens of the Cap and, with the interesting preliminary announcement that he was a candidate for the presidency, disclosed that a *Caco* army was approaching and that the government had given him no means to resist. As printed up in next morning's *Le Cable,* the *Capois* then unanimously entrusted their destiny to *Délégué* Vilbrun, a move that virtually coincided with the appearance at Barrière-Boutielle of the feared and desperate *Caco* general Metellus (". . . a savage and the terror of the surrounding country," said Livingston), with a thousand men and several cannon. To the astonishment of all (or some, at any rate) Metellus simply paraded his bands in front of the cathedral, which he dutifully entered, and then marched around the town. There was no looting, no shooting. As Livingston reported with surprise, "This is entirely exceptional as a revolutionary incident."

Three days later, the 19th, Metellus's cannon banged out a 17-gun salute, and the cat was out of the bag: with the Zamorist generals behind him, Vilbrun Guillaume had proclaimed himself *chef du pouvoir executif.* Everything as far South as Gonaïves was his.

Instead of hastening South like Davilmar Théodore, Vilbrun Guillaume (who had begun to style himself Guillaume "Sam") tarried at the Cap to ensure that all would be safe in his rear. There was, after all, no hurry; the government was incapable of resistance. In a bemused dispatch to Washington on 27 January, Livingston explained:

> There has been practically no fighting at all. Not a single shot has been fired at Cap Haïtien or anywhere in the neighborhood . . . General Metellus, the famous *Caco* general . . . came into Cap Haïtien on Saturday morning the 16th with a thousand men and has remained here since to accompany General Guillaume to Port-au-Prince . . . Not a single act of disorder has been conducted here by him or his troops, and the general conduct has been such that the situation has more the appearance of a great holiday than of a revolution . . . Guillaume Sam is now considered the future president of Haiti . . . He will march to Port-au-prince without any opposition and . . . the Government of Théodore will fall without the firing of a single shot.

Revolution Is Flourishing

The very day Metellus's cannon were announcing a new *chef du pouvoir executif* at the Cap, the armored cruiser *Washington,* wearing the flag of Rear Admiral William B. Caperton, was rolling and bucking her way past Cape Hatteras. Descending the ladder aft, the communication orderly handed a half-sheet flimsy to the Marine orderly, who handed the radiogram to Admiral Caperton: PROCEED CAPE HAITIEN WITHOUT DELAY.

The *Washington* anchored outside the harbor (she was too big to go inside) on 23 January 1915, when she reached the Cap. Going ashore in his burnished steam pinnace, past the silent ruins of Forts Picolet and St. Joseph, and avoiding *Bulldog*'s coral-crusted bones, the admiral was greeted at the wharf by Livingston, who had forehandedly cabled for a warship the day Vilbrun Guillaume disclosed his presidential aspirations.

Haiti had changed little since Caperton's alert and thoughtful chief of staff, Captain E. L. Beach, had last been there with Admiral Gherardi in 1891. The Cap, wrote Beach, "presented the appearance of a ruined town. Business was at a standstill. The streets, still paved with cobblestones placed there by the French one hundred and fifty years ago, were uncared-for. Walls of buildings were cracked and crumbling and were left in disrepair. But one thing was flourishing, and that was revolution. "

Livingston quickly sketched the situation to Caperton, then suggested that he call on Guillaume. The resulting meeting, which took place on the 25th, was memorably described by the admiral:

> We were met at the door by a tatterdemalion soldiery, while inside a very gorgeous black gentleman, arrayed like a head bellhop at the Waldorf, directed us through a room and then up a pair of steps. He then suddenly disappeared, to appear again, still resplendent, at the head of the stairs, where he took our caps and gloves and ushered us into a large reception room, saying the General would be pleased to see us in a moment. Once upstairs in the reception room, a large portrait caught my eye. It seemed to be of some familiar face. In a moment General Guillaume Sam appeared. Greatly to my surprise, I recognized him as the bellhop; only this time he had discarded his coat for another but more elaborate one, and an enormous sword clanked around his heels. A glance at the portrait on the wall convinced me. It was also Guillaume Sam.

Taking no outward notice of this bit of theater, Admiral Caperton in due course extracted from Guillaume Sam a pledge that "he would not loot, or burn down the cities, or fire in the cities" - a large commitment for the leader of a *Caco* army, but one that Guillaume, not always enthusiastically, was destined to keep.

One reason for Vilbrun's restraint in what U.S. Senator William King later drily characterized as "electioneering by force" was described afterward by Caperton to a Senate committee:

ADMIRAL CAPERTON: I followed Mr. Guillaume Sam around the coast in order to impress upon him the importance of carrying on - I am trying to think of the word
THE CHAIRMAN: Civilized warfare?
ADMIRAL CAPERTON: Civilized warfare. That is the word . . .
THE CHAIRMAN: These were campaign pledges you were exacting of him?

ADMIRAL CAPERTON: Yes, sir. He gave me the first one in Cape Haïtien, but I was not satisfied with it. I met him at each [city], and so he finally laughingly said to me, "Every time I enter a city I find your representatives outside . . . asking me to behave myself." He promised to do so, and upon the whole he did very well, considering everything.

Since the *Washington* and her sister ship, *Montana* (carrying 650 Marines, whom the State Department had thought opportune to deploy into Haitian waters), were too large for any place but Port-au-Prince, Admiral Caperton ordered two smaller ships, gunboat *Wheeling* and cruiser *Des Moines,* to shadow Vilbrun Guillaume's march Southward and redeem his "campaign pledges" to the admiral.(26)

On 5 February Guillaume Sam entered Gonaïves to the acclaim of 21 guns from local warlord Mizaël Codio. In the capital, birds of ill omen flocked overhead.

Dr. Bobo, who had once so eloquently welcomed Théodore to the Cap and for his percipience been dubbed Minister, now became an ex-Minister and departed for the North, speaking darkly of a new revolution to come. On 12 February, reporting to Washington, Admiral Caperton told of being approached by a succession of politicians anxious to enter the National Palace under American auspices. That perennial hopeful, Defly, promised, in Caperton's words, that if allowed to head the prospective Committee of Public Safety, he would,

> . . . declare himself unable to maintain law and order and then ask me to land troops. Momplaisir has attempted to approach me with plans to join with Guillaume with the idea of their jointly asking that the United States intervene. A combination of ten Senators has attempted to approach me with the further proposition to prevent Guillaume from entering Port-au-prince so they might have a free election . . . their idea being that the U.S. support them . . . The better class of Haitians, while they express such views to us privately, are very careful to avoid publishing such ideas among their own people for fear of execution . . ..

It was Momplaisir's last hurrah: on 17 February, when Guillaume Sam's *Cacos* neared St. Marc, he was stabbed by his own men in a wild scramble to get aboard the *Nord Alexis* as she raised steam for Port-au-Prince.

Incapable though he was of opposing Guillaume Sam, the feeble old president could not bring himself to step down. As always in the final throes, related Captain Beach, the regime was "gathering volunteers with clubs and sending them to the North tied together with ropes." On the 18th, while Guillaume Sam, now fortified with $50,000 more from T. A. Simon Sam, was advancing into the fertile plain of Arcahaie, Hannibal Hilaire of Jacmel announced his own revolution and marched on the capital.

By 21 February Port-au-Prince was surrounded: Hilaire held Bizoton, Charlemagne Péralte, the Zamor brother-in-law, had materialized with 1500 men in the heights of Pétionville and cut the water supply, and Guillaume Sam was at Sibert. Inside the city, as General Defly, for the third time in two years, tried vainly to snatch power, rifle fire sputtered continually, while the *Pacifique* and *Nord Alexis*, forsaken by their crews, were boarded, looted, and stripped by *Cacos* of the town. Next morning, said Beach, Davilmar Théodore "mounted his horse, and, surrounded by guards, galloped about the streets of Port-au-Prince. Upon returning to his palace he resigned the presidency."

Fifteen minutes short of noon on the 22d, the guns of Fort National, echoed by those on the waterfront at Batterie St. Claire, told Port-au-Prince that another president was boarding a Dutch steamer for exile. Caperton described the event to the Senate Committee:

ADMIRAL CAPERTON: They made quite an imposing march down the street and wharf with their long frock coats and silk hats. [The president] was then going aboard the *Prins Frederik Hendrik* leaving the country I know it to be a fact that the old man, Mr. Davilmar Théodore, had hardly a sufficient amount of money to buy his ticket out of the country, as he appealed for money to help him go where he wished to go, and as it turned out he only went to Santo Domingo . . .

THE CHAIRMAN: In a plug hat, on a Dutch ship?

ADMIRAL CAPERTON: Yes, sir; leaving the city without any government whatever, and the only people with any authority were Gen. Praedel [sic] and Gen. Polynice, who appointed themselves a committee of safety . .

Three days later, Guillaume Sam entered the capital. Hilaire and Péralte (who had been surrogate for Charles Zamor until the latter emerged from the French legation) quickly accommodated to Sam's superior force and $50,000 gold, and joined in proclaiming him *chef du pouvoir éxecutif*. As rapidly as a National Assembly could be got together - 4 March it finally was - the legislature ratified the assize of arms, and, on the 9th, Vilbrun Guillaume Sam took office, to the boom of cannon and peal of a Te Deum and a reception in Casernes Dessalines. The gourde, which had skated to 12.5 cents gold in Théodore's last hours, promptly revived to 17.5 cents. After looking on for a day or so, Admiral Caperton took the *Washington* back to Guantanamo Bay, coaled ship, and steamed West for the Yucatan Straits, Veracruz and Tampico.

Action Is Evidently Necessary

Back in 1913, soon after he became Secretary of State, William Jennings Bryan had asked the *Banque*'s John Allen to stop by when on home leave and talk about Haiti. "We are very much interested in Haiti," said the Secretary. "Tell me about the country and who the people are." Then he paused abruptly and asked, "Where is Haiti?"

At the end of two hours, as Allen departed, Bryan shook his bald head and exclaimed, "Dear me, think of it! Niggers [sic] speaking French."

That Bryan never did acquire much more insight into the affairs of America's unmanageable island neighbor might be inferred from the ensuing succession of U.S. approaches to the possibility of intervening.

The notion that banana republics could be stabilized if not perfected through financial responsibility resulting from U.S.-imposed customs control was a Roosevelt-Taft hypothesis onto which Woodrow Wilson typically engrafted the corollary of civic uplift through the democratic process as he conceived it. "I will teach the Latin Americans to elect good men," he later said of Mexico, and it was this governessy attitude that informed Wilson and his no less evangelical Secretary of State whenever, as was increasingly the case, someone asked what to do about Haiti.

Behind the simplistic Wilson-Bryan view of Haiti lay not only ignorance such as John Allen described, but, in the case of Bryan, plausible misinformation acquired mainly from Roger Farnham. Farnham, a vivid raconteur who knew Haiti well - in some senses an American Spenser St. John - in his own words afforded Bryan insights "somewhat different from the view one obtains from the regular official reports." He was, besides, as Dana Munro remarked, "a dangerous counsellor." It gives ample testimony to Bryan's credulity that, arch--priest though he was of populism, he allowed his policies to be manipulated by a Wall Street banker who viewed Haiti across the ledgers of the National City Bank.(27)

A favorite theme of Farnham's was that European intervention could be forestalled only if Washington was prepared to pre-empt Paris and especially Berlin - a proposition that gained credibility from Germany's past brutalization of Haiti, from commercial penetration and political meddling, and hardly disguised German aspirations toward the Môle and at least a share in customs control.(28)

The synchronous opening in 1914 of World War I and of the Panama Canal heightened U.S. concern over the West Indies as well as American sensitivity toward what Germany evidently saw as its special position in Haiti. As the war went on, this sensitivity changed to suspicion.

Ever since mid-1914 (as in the case of many another potential Caribbean hot spot) the Navy Department maintained contingency plans for taking over Port-au-Prince. Such plans did not, however, indicate long-matured, secret designs on the part of the United States to subjugate Haiti, but merely that Haiti's instability, political degeneration, sanguinary history, and heightening interest in U.S. eyes made it a place of concern to planners who prudently anticipated events.(29)

Woodrow Wilson contemplated Théodore with increasing disapproval. On 13 January 1915, he wrote Bryan, "The more I think about [the Haitian] situation the more I am convinced that it is our duty to take immediate action there such as we took in Santo Domingo. I mean to send a commissioner there . . . and say to them as firmly and definitely as is consistent with courtesy and kindness that the United States cannot consent to stand by and permit revolutionary conditions constantly to exist . . ."

The President's instruments were John Franklin Fort (Wilson's predecessor as governor of New Jersey) and Charles Cogswell Smith, both of whom had conducted comparable negotiations with the Dominicans. Haiti, they quickly learned, was not Santo Domingo.

In part because of timing that could hardly have been more maladroit (they arrived in the interregnum between Davilmar Théodore and Guillaume Sam), the mission failed dismally. In no mood to welcome busybodies at such an hour, Ulrick Duvivier, new Foreign Minister, played Firmin's Refused Opening of 1891 and asked to see Fort's credentials. Incredibly, Bryan had neglected to provide any, whereupon Duvivier showed them the door. Appalled by the heat, the reeking gutters, and insects, Governor Fort, sixty-three years old, fled before the week was out, taking time only for a bad-tempered swipe at Minister Bailly-Blanchard, who was not to blame for any of this.(30)

Woodrow Wilson next selected a sophisticated New York lawyer, Paul Fuller, Jr., taking care this time to appoint him Presidential Envoy Extraordinary and Minister Plenipotentiary and giving him Wilsonian guidance besides: "Only an honest and efficient government deserves support. The Government of the United States could not justify the expenditure of money or the sacrifice of American lives in support of any other kind of government."

That Wilson and his advisers could imagine any such government in Haiti, then or to be, exposed the illusions that still persisted.

On arrival in May, Fuller proposed a treaty that would bind the Haitian government to take American advice in internal affairs, not to alienate the Môle to any other power, and to get on with arbitration of outstanding claims. In return, the U.S. would support the regime internally and externally. With the fate of Joseph Justin high in mind, Washington pointedly omitted the specifics of customs control. "The Haitian government's response," wrote Dana Munro in a passage based on long experience, "was typical of the methods of Haitian diplomacy. First it stalled, demanding formal [U.S.] recognition before making a reply." (This was the Léger Defense, whereby in 1914 J.-N. Léger had tricked Bryan into recognizing Oreste Zamor.) "Then it submitted a counterproject, omitting Fuller's proposal that an American Minister Plenipotentiary be appointed for the specific purpose of advising the government . . ." (the irrelevant counterproposal - Dr. Bobo's Gambit - bore down heavily on the regime's only real interest, U.S. financial support, and left out most features considered essential by Washington) "and accepting American help in maintaining order only on condition that the American troops be withdrawn at the first request of the Haitian government."

The final condition, stripping the agreement of any effective American power of intervention, proved to Fuller that the negotiation had no future, and on 5 June 1915, he too left. Nine days later, back in Washington, he told Lansing,

> Any concession made to the United States would be viewed by the public as selling out to foreigners, an accusation for which revenge would promptly be taken . . . The present Government in Haiti and a large majority of all classes are desirous of entering into a convention with the United States along the lines originally submitted . . . A majority of the honest Haitians would be willing to agree to a plan for indirect customs control and for turning over Môle St. Nicolas to the United States. Both the President and the Secretary for Foreign Affairs stated that they were not only willing to sign the guarantee regarding the Môle, but . . . to devise some legal method by which the United States could secure control of Môle St. Nicolas. I feel convinced that only fear of . . . personal violence now stands in the way.

So forcibly was Fuller impressed with the futility of negotiation that he concluded by posing the ultimate solution: land Marines and exact a treaty like the 1901 Platt Amendment, which governed U.S. relations with Cuba. When on 2 July 1915, he read Fuller's report, Wilson somberly minuted, "Action is evidently necessary and no doubt it would be a mistake to postpone it long."

The Worst Savagery

As Guillaume Sam took office, the omens briefly seemed favorable. The main reason was that he had money: some from Simon Sam and a shipload of Davilmar Théodore's New York banknotes, worth no more than *bons da* but authentic in feel and look and therefore negotiable. Because the *Banque* had lost treasury service, revenues now flowed into the *Palais National* and thus, in measure at least, into current expenses. No matter that much of this had been hypothecated to foreign creditors who could be expected to make difficulties; the short term augured stability.

Admiral Caperton had reported, "Guillaume is a strong man but feared by the better class of Haitians on account of his harsh methods." Pierre Girard, the French minister, later gave the same judgment on "this black in whom a marked sweetness of manner masked a nature authoritarian, vindictive, pitiless toward foes, cruel to those whose existence, rightly or wrongly, he considered a menace to his own security."

Admiral and minister were right: Sam's first act was to round up his enemies. When in March 1915 word came that Dr. Bobo, with the usual help of Desiderio Arias, was mounting an invasion, Guillaume Sam, like many another *noir* ruler, promptly began to seize hostages, mainly *mulâtres,* all elite. These, numbering at least 200 and representing the best families of the republic, were shut away in the old jail as bondmen for the tranquillity of Port-au-Prince. Besides Oreste Zamor, who had incautiously slipped back from Santo Domingo, and Dr. Bobo's Jamaican brother-in-law, Thomas Woolley, there were the three sons of Edmond Polynice, there was General Jules Préval, General Gaspard Péralte of Hinche, three Chatelains, and such names as Nau, Colcis, Lafontant, Alexis, Vincent, Turnier, St. Hilaire, André, Elie, Douyon, and Paret.

Guillaume Sam was not seeing ghosts; under the lead of Charles de Delva, Zamor's chief of police and now a refugee in the Portuguese consulate, a network of asylees linked with confederates in the city - Charles Zamor, the elder Polynice, veteran elite intriguer Gaston Dalencourt, among others - was indeed plotting still another coup and smuggling money North to Dr. Bobo.

By the end of April, Dr. Bobo's revolution had taken Fort Liberté, and on the 25th, amid a scramble for the consulates by Sam's friends, his advance guard entered the Cap. There, having looted the customs house, they welcomed the doctor on 5 May. By mid-May, when a government army had cordoned them in, Bobo's *Cacos* held a perimeter embracing the Cap, Fort Liberté, Terrier Rouge, Trou, Limonade, and Quartier Morin.

Whatever hope Sam may have had for a respite was now gone. To maintain the army in the North, with scant results to show, was costing the government 140,000 *gourdes* a week. Once again, recruiters were combing the villages, dragging old men and boys from humble huts, and clubbing them, roped and pinioned, to the army. In Port-au-Prince, the legations and consulates were packed.

The conflict in the North had become a stalemate. Bobo's control over his *Cacos* slackened. When he remonstrated, their reply was that they could easily "cross the bridge" [East] out of the Cap, head for the mountains, and find another leader.

To give the example, the *Cacos* beheaded two insufficiently enthusiastic *Capois* and shot others. Livingston saw the heads being paraded about the streets and called it the worst savagery in all his seventeen years at the Cap. The Paris-educated Bobo, campaigning as a "progressive," reproved a *Caco* general and

and called it the worst savagery in all his seventeen years at the Cap. The Paris-educated Bobo, campaigning as a "progressive," reproved a *Caco* general and was told in return that "Angels" had commanded the killings and "if there were a hundred people he would have killed them all."

The French cruiser *Descartes* arrived from Jamaica in time, on the 19th, to see a general breakdown, in which the *Cacos*, finally defeated at the Haut-du-Cap, threatened to clean out the consulates as a parting shot. *Descartes* landed marines and posted them at the consulates, the *Banque*'s branch, and the archbishop's house. Dr. Bobo, far from quenched, simply removed to Limonade and continued the revolution.

However welcome the *Descartes* was to consuls and clergy, her presence and that of her landing force ashore did not go overlooked in Washington. From the tall masts of the new navy radio station in Arlington, wireless orders reached the *Washington* at El Progreso, Mexico, that Admiral Caperton was again needed in Haiti. Trailing a thick plume of black smoke, the cruiser charged Eastward for Cap Haïtien on all sixteen boilers, one knot for each, with a bone in her teeth.

U.S.S. *Washington* Heinl Collection

One of the Bloodiest Crimes

When the *Washington* reached Cap Haïtien on the morning of 1 July 1915, Admiral Caperton's first action was to thank the French captain for *Descartes's* timely intervention and make clear that the United States would now assume charge. This was done with the exchange of gun salutes, official visits, ruffles and flourishes, and honor guards that characterized the naval etiquette of the day. When *Descartes's* captain called, the admiral reported, he observed that the French in Haiti "were anxious for the United States to intervene and establish a stable government so they might live and carry on their affairs in peace."

Caperton next sent Captain Beach ashore with a Marine squad to make contact, in their separate positions, with General Probus Blot, government commander, and with Dr. Bobo. Beach's message was simple: any further fighting was to take place well clear of the city; henceforth, the Cap was neutral ground. Beach never got to Dr. Bobo, but, with Livingston as guide, found Pierrot, one of the revolution's ministers, at Petite-Anse, East of the Cap, where Henry Christophe had once commanded as *général de brigade*. The look of Pierrot's *Cacos*, related Beach, seemed hardly reassuring: "A more villainous appearing set of men were never gathered together. All were but slightly clad, and each was armed with a musket, a pistol, a sword, and a long vicious knife . . . Each man looked to be a diabolical devil."

But appearances were deceiving. The "diabolical devils" got cane-bottomed chairs from the huts, put them in the shade for the *blancs* to sit on, and produced little cups of hot coffee and coarse sugar and oranges, sweet despite green skins. "It is not likely there ever was better coffee," Captain Beach commented. And when, after delivering Admiral Caperton's letter to Dr. Bobo, the mission departed, the *Cacos* gave them "a great, fat beautiful dressed turkey."

Thereafter, with gunboat *Eagle* well inshore and covering the bridge into town, and with twenty-nine Marines from the *Washington* operating a radio at the consulate and patrolling, the Cap remained neutral while Blot and Bobo skirmished about the Plaine du Nord.

As July wore on, Port-au-Prince seemed quiet enough. The goldbraided, cocked-hatted chief of police, General Charles-Oscar Etienne, well nicknamed "*Le Terrible*," kept tight rein on the steamy capital. Or so he thought.

Charles de Delva in the Portuguese consulate (and behind him, Charles Zamor in the French legation) knew otherwise, and, as tropical night fell swiftly on 26 July, their plan was complete.(31)

At midnight, under a full moon, stealing out of the consulate in Turgeau and then down the cavernous Bois de Chêne ravine that bisects Port-au-Prince and skirts the Champ de Mars, Delva assembled thirty-six heavily armed confederates, and, joined by another sixteen under General Ermane Robin, stealthily advanced on the *Palais National*. "Good cover in bed of this stream," Captain Young, the American military attache, had presciently noted in his 1907 map, and it was from this very spot that the conspirators, after whispered signals from allies among the guard, at 4: 00 A.M. opened a fusillade into the palace. As the stammer of machine guns joined the clamor, word spread that *Cacos* bivouacked in the yard had turned the palace *mitrailleuses* against their master. To the swell of musketry was soon added the glow of fire: outbuildings that cluttered the palace precincts were being doused with lamp oil and burned to provide light for the attackers.

For additional cover, one of the little tramway engines was tipped over in the street as a breastwork.

With a few faithful followers, the president and his family held out past daybreak. Then, clutching a carbine in one hand and a monstrous old key, Guillaume Sam led a dash through the haze and smoke toward an iron door in the ten-foot wall that separated the palace from the French compound.(32) Dodging and flinching as shots spattered about, the president tried to turn the stubborn lock: it was rusted tight. Agile with terror despite a leg wound, he clawed over the wall. Ironically, Charles Zamor, still waiting to see how things would come out, was at this moment in the legation and, according to H. P. Davis, actually helped Guillaume Sam inside. Girard, the French minister, quickly led his newest guest to his own bedroom, assisted the president into the adjoining bathroom, where he could bleed without messing up the rug, and sent for a surgeon. It was the work of moments to stanch the wound, little more than a graze and after powdering the dressing with pungent-smelling yellow iodoform the doctor departed.

Meanwhile, frantic pickaxes had breached the stubborn portal so that the family could get through, followed, in Girard's words, by

a fleet of women, of servants, of huge bundles stuffed with personal effects and household utensils swept up at the last moment. Then to finish, came four magnificent horses from the presidential stables, who pranced over the heaped-up rubbish despite the efforts of the grooms who tied them to our trees. They didn't stay there long . . . We saw them a few days later, already unkempt and hungry, for sale in the streets.

By now it was 8:30 A.M., and, from the safety of the Legation, Guillaume Sam sent a brief note to General Etienne, still holding out from the Bureau de l'Arrondissement in the lower town:

Mon Cher Oscar,
La partie est perdue, j'abandonne le pouvoir. Faites ce que votre conscience vous dictera.
/S/ VILBRUN GUILLAUME (33)

Whether Guillaume Sam knew it or not, Charles-Oscar Etienne had already done just that.

"Terrific firing down in the town" had awakened young Beale Davis, American *chargé d'affaires* (in charge while Blanchard was back in Washington on consultation). That same firing, echoing along Rue du Centre, had also aroused Charles-Oscar Etienne in the Arrondissement next door to the prison, as well as the hostages jam-packed into the sweat and urine-soaked cells. One prisoner, Stephen Alexis, still had his watch: when he awoke it was ten past four. Adjutant Chocotte, principal keeper, could be heard giving commands: "Fall in . . . Shoulder arms . . . Sound the bugle . . . Fifteen men, forward march!"

As the din intensified, another voice bawled, "The Arrondissement has given orders to shoot all military [that is, political] prisoners!" For a moment, it seemed, the officials hesitated. General Etienne, one prisoner said, started to expostulate, but was shouted down by Chocotte and jailers Hérard, Thrasybule, Hector, and Blain: "The president ordered us to start killing at the first shot." Horrified prisoners began to fumble on clothes, clasp hands, pray, and cower behind mattresses.

> A flash of red light entered our cell [recounted Stephen Alexis], my comrades were slaughtered, disemboweled, dismembered, reduced to a mass of flesh. "Finish me! Finish me!" shrieked a wounded man....I see a mass of dead bodies, huddled, faces on the ground, crouching in corners, horribly wounded . . . Bathed in blood a man came leaping from a neighboring cell - "Save me, *messieurs!*" he cried. "Go into the latrine," said Nemours Vincent. He plunged inside but then recoiled. "There's a corpse in there and besides they may find me." "Go down the hole," advised Nemours, and the man jumped in . . . A sepulchral silence descended. Those frightful voices ... were stilled. Cries of women came from the outer court.

Because he and a cellmate had connections with jailer Hector, Alexis lived to describe the fearful hours while guards shot, hacked, sabered, skewered, and clubbed terror-maddened hostages (among them Oreste Zamor) into carrion. Beale Davis reached the jail that forenoon; he described the scene:

> Bodies lay piled together just as they had fallen, and from their appearance it looked as if every sort of weapon had been used . . . [A survivor said] that even more vivid than the hours which he spent lying upon the floor soaked in his own blood and that of the dead men who had fallen across him, was the memory of the agonized prayers for death of a young boy whose cell was opened prior to his . . . The jailer, whose enmity this boy had incurred, before killing him, had taken a pair of tweezers [sic] and pulled out his teeth. one by one. and then gouged out his eyes.

Another eyewitness, Kohan, the British minister, reported: "They were found shot, hacked, mutilated, and disembowelled - the walls and floors of the prison were spattered with their blood, their brains, and their entrails."

The exact number of persons massacred is still in disagreement. Chargé Davis contented himself with "nearly 200." Girard reported 160, Kohan said 168, H. P. Davis (who was also there) gave 167, and still others say 169. Whatever the toll, 1915 had now taken its place with 1804, 1848, and 1883.

After one final volley - feigning to be rescuers, then finishing off the unwary few who stirred - Charles-Oscar and his accomplices quickly departed (he for the Dominican legation), leaving the jailyard to the dead and to the blue flies that buzzed slowly in the sun.

Events [wrote Minister Kohan to Lord Grey in London] were now taking the usual course of Haytian revolutions . . . the *"peuple souverain"* paraded the streets firing salvos into the air - a committee of safety was being organized . . . The *"peuple souverain"* marched to the prison to liberate the prisoners - a proceeding which forms part of the routine of a revolution. Then was discovered one of the bloodiest crimes in the blood-sodden history of Hayti. The criminals had already been released, but 168 political prisoners had been murdered . . . As news of the massacre was spread, the temper of the people became very ugly.

Well it might: not a family in the elite but mourned a victim, or, like Edmond Polynice and the Chatelains of Gonaïves, mourned three. As in 1848, survivors drifted through the town, seeking their dead. Beale Davis wrote: "An enormous crowd collected around the jail and everywhere that one looked in the streets could be seen little processions headed by two men carrying on a plank on their heads the body of some victim, followed by friends or relatives whose curses against the President mingled with those of the people who stood in the streets and watched."

After verifying what the jailers had done to his sons, Edmond Polynice left to others the task of recovering their broken bodies amid the enormous *pietà* at the prison. Garbed for the occasion, tradition says, in morning coat and gloves - he went to the Dominican legation, sent in his card to Charles-Oscar Etienne, and, when the latter appeared in the doorway, shot him three times very precisely, one round for each dead son.

Dragged into the street by the crowd, Etienne's body was " shot at, hacked at, and defiled by every passer-by," reported Kohan, "and by evening had become an unrecognizable pulp of flesh."

Next morning, someone doused the stinking remains with cooking oil and let fire cleanse the gutter of whatever bones and offal the dogs and birds of prey had left.

While Polynice was disposing of Etienne, the French legation had been surrounded by a mob shouting for Guillaume Sam. Breaking in a side entrance, a hundred armed men, mainly relatives of the massacred victims, tried to rush the two-story, verandaed residence but were halted by Minister Girard.

Charles Zamor ("brandishing a great machete," recalled Girard) led a knot of soldiers into the compound where for ten months past he had found asylum. Now, with tables turned and demanding the ex-president, he was blocked only by Alice Girard, the minister's pretty eighteen-year-old daughter, who had cared for and fed Zamor during his stay. Faced down by Mlle. Alice, Zamor lowered his machete and took the soldiers away.

Five times before sunset, similar sorties (but without Zamor) were repeated and narrowly repulsed. Through the long afternoon and night that followed, Girard was supported by Kohan and Davis and by his faithful Haitian clerk, Emile Rouzier.

The president meanwhile, Davis wrote, "was in a perfect frenzy of fear, creeping about the house like a hunted animal, so terror stricken that when passing an open window he would crawl on all fours for fear someone on the outside would see him."

Early on the morrow, 28 July, came the funerals and burials and, with them, the eye of the hurricane, an unnatural calm.

Then the storm broke.

Before Girard knew what was afoot, an enraged party of eighty men, the best blood in Port-au-Prince - *"tout en noir, le melon sur la tête"* (garbed in black, bowler-hatted), noted the minister - swarmed over a side wall onto the legation porch and burst inside. Answering Girard's protests with imprecations, the intruders, led by Charles Zamor, fanned through the building, overturning furniture, smashing doors, kicking open chests and closets, and threatening to burn the residence. A hapless servant resembling Guillaume Sam was all but strangled before someone vouched for him.

At bay in the W/C, its doorway camouflaged by the minister's high-backed bed, Guillaume Sam crouched as he heard the cries and tramp of the searchers. All might have gone well but for the iodoform on his dressing. One of the pack sniffed the aroma and, shoving aside the bedstead, nosed him out. His back to a rack of chamber pots, each immaculately polished, Guillaume Sam mustered all his courage.

"Messieurs," he said simply, *"achèvez-moi."* ["finish me"]

Who struck the first blow will never be known: Sam's face was already streaming blood when furious captors hustled the president past his wife and children. Elite social leader Paul Gardère, Girard reported, stabbed him fiercely with a poniard and was prevented from finishing the job on the stairs only when Rouzier pulled him away. Then, dragging their quarry downstairs by the heels, they flung him off the porch and onto the sharp gravel driveway.

As if drowning, Guillaume Sam locked an arm in the spokes of the minister's carriage and clung for a moment as assailants tugged at his feet. Someone whacked the straining wrist with a *cocomacac*. Shattered white bone poked through dark skin, fingers went limp, and, propelled by kicks and blows, the president neared the gate. Hérard Sylvain raised his machete and struck thrice. The third chop split the skull like a piece of firewood, and what followed next no longer mattered to Guillaume Sam.(34)

The stout lock and chain on the front gate no more kept Vilbrun Guillaume inside than, twenty-four hours earlier, another lock had kept him out. Over the wall, across the iron spikes and encrusted glass shards at the top, the mob heaved him. For a moment, like beef on a meat hook, the carcass dangled by a spike, but only a moment. Now came the turn of *le peuple souverain.*

> There was one terrific howl of fury [Davis wrote] . . . I could see that something or somebody was on the ground in the center of the crowd, just before the gates, and when a man disentangled himself from the crowd and rushed howling by me, with a severed hand from which the blood was dripping, the thumb of which he had stuck in his mouth, I knew that the assassination of the President was accomplished. Behind him came other men with the feet, the other hand, the head, and other parts of the body displayed on poles, each one followed by a mob of screaming men and women. The portion of the body that remained was dragged through the streets by the crowd.

During the ensuing hours, Guillaume Sam's torso, tied to a rope, was hauled about, riddled by shots, hacked, stomped, and defiled.(35) All Port-au-Prince, elite or ignorant, *noir* or *mulâtre,* joined in one vast spasm of rage. And that is what Admiral Caperton saw and heard from the bridge of U.S.S. *Washington* that forenoon when she entered Port-au-Prince bay, and dropped anchor a mile offshore.

The Situation Is Well in Hand

As soon as the boatswain's mates could get a steam launch into the water (the time was 11:50 A. M.) Admiral Caperton sent Beach ashore to the American legation and, immediately afterward, to the British and French legations. Captain Beach returned with Davis, Kohan, and Girard and let them tell the tale.

All three chiefs of mission agreed that no vestige of authority or government was left, and urgently asked, in the words of Kohan's report to Lord Grey, "that a strong force be landed at once." In Caperton's later recollection, the ministers "pleaded with me to land forces and do it as quickly as possible as they had no idea what might or might not happen on shore."

It was after four when the diplomats, accompanied again by Beach, left the ship.

As the barge headed to shore, boatswain's mates piped the word: "Prepare to land the landing force."

The immediate sequence of events, so freighted with consequence for both Haiti and the United States, that brought the 330-man landing force on deck and sent the diplomats and Captain Beach ashore with word that U.S. Marines and sailors were about to land was this:

2:00 P.M., 27 July, Beale Davis cables Lansing:

FRENCH LEGATION THREATENED AND A FORCIBLE ENTRY ATTEMPTED FOR THE PURPOSE OF TAKING OUT THE PRESIDENT. FRENCH MINISTER AND BRITISH CHARGÉ D'AFFAIRES HAVE TELEGRAPHED FOR SHIPS. SITUATION VERY GRAVE AND PRESENCE OF WAR VESSELS AS SOON AS POSSIBLE NECESSARY.

This telegram was apparently retransmitted by radio from Washington and reached Admiral Caperton later that day. Davis followed up his message with a longer report at six that evening, detailing the jail massacre.

During the forenoon of the next day, Wednesday, 28 July, a State Department memorandum records telephone conversations between the Office of the Chief of Naval Operations and the department's Latin American Division, resulting in a decision that "Admiral Caperton be instructed to land Marines . . . at earliest opportunity."

11:00 P.M., 28 July, Davis next cables Lansing:

MOB INVADED FRENCH LEGATION, TOOK OUT PRESIDENT, KILLED AND DISMEMBERED HIM.

It was 3:40 in the afternoon, however, before this was received and deciphered in the old State, War, and Navy Building (today's Executive Office Building), which then housed all three departments and thus the entire national security establishment of the government.

3:00 P.M., 28 July, Navy Radio Washington sends a message to Caperton:

STATE DEPARTMENT DESIRES AMERICAN FORCES BE LANDED PORT-AU-PRINCE AND AMERICAN AND FOREIGN [sic] INTERESTS BE PROTECTED . . . DEPARTMENT HAS ORDERED U.S.S. *JASON* WITH MARINES GUANTANAMO, CUBA, PROCEED IMMEDIATELY PORT-AU-PRINCE . . .

Caperton, however, did not receive this radiogram until 10:00 P.M. (Apparently communications between Washington and Guantanamo were much better: at 4:00 P.M., Admiral Caperton heard from Guantanamo that *Jason* was on the way with reinforcements, which the Navy Department assumed he would be landing.)

4:10 P.M., the chiefs of the foreign missions and Captain Beach leave for shore, bearing word that the landing has been ordered.

4:50 P.M., *Washington's* landing force shoves off for the beach.

5:48 P.M., Marines ashore at Bizoton.

What emerges from the foregoing is that all parties, both in Washington and Port-au-Prince, somewhat but not materially anticipated developments that in fact occurred.

When - with personal clearance from President Wilson - Admiral Benson, Chief of Naval Operations, sent Caperton his fateful orders to land, the final violation of the French (not to mention the Dominican) legation and Guillaume Sam's dismemberment were not yet known in Washington. On the other hand, the prison atrocities were known, and Beale Davis had reported mob attempts in progress on Tuesday afternoon to smash into the French legation. Faced with such information, the State Department can hardly be charged with overeager or premature action.

As for Caperton, although orders were on the air nearly three hours before the landing at Bizoton was effected, the admiral clearly acted in advance of receiving his final instructions. In this, however, he acted on the strongest urging of the local chiefs of mission, not only his own but of two other great powers. Moreover, even before the latter left *Washington* (and nearly an hour before the Marines started ashore), Caperton had in hand the Guantanamo Bay message whose text referred to and all but repeated the Navy Department's orders, which were not to reach him until that night and from which he could have drawn only one conclusion.

The U.S. authorities, from Woodrow Wilson down, may indeed have been eager to intervene in Haiti at an opportune juncture - Paul Fuller had bluntly so suggested only weeks before - but the final decisions were arrived at in response to events rather than anticipation.

Beach's immediate errand, meanwhile, was to find someone, anyone, ashore with authority. As he described the situation, "Crowds of citizens were rushing about, some shooting weapons pointed upwards. Soldiers wearing dungarees with red stripes on the collars, sleeves, and trousers, were running up and down, also shooting. Officers on small horses were dashing aimlessly through the streets."

At the *Palais National* he found Charles de Delva and his fellows, Polynice, Delinois, Charles Zamor, Dalencourt, Etienne, and General Robin. From the windows they could see the *Washington* close in, guns trained out. What Beach told them confirmed what they saw: U.S. Marines and seamen were landing at Bizoton; their intent was friendly but resistance would not be brooked. Would whoever commanded the local troops (this seemed to be Robin) try to get them into the barracks and keep people off the street and, most important, go with Beach out to Portail Léogane, and lead the landing force across town?

Beach later recalled Edmond Polynice as replying, "Tell the Admiral we thank him and that we accept his word that he is coming as a friend to help us. We need help and we need friendship. All you ask shall be done."

Kohan, however, reporting at the time, noted significantly that the Haitians objected to the landing if "for any purpose other than the protection of the Legations and Consulates."

There was no time for parley. Captain van Orden (head of the Marine detachment) moving through Martissant with his force, was disarming soldiers and civilians as encountered. At the Southern end of town, Robin and Beach made contact with the Marines walking point, then joined van Orden, and steered the advance through the city, dropping off guards for each of the foreign missions. At seven, just as the sun, dropping behind La Gonâve, silhouetted *Washington's* tall stacks, the main body bivouacked on the Champ de Mars and under cover in the Marché de Fer. There was no resistance except for a few shots fired as a Marine patrol took over Fort National.(36) The only U.S. casualties were two sailors of the landing force, who managed to get killed by wild firing. Kohan summed it up concisely for the Foreign Office: "The landing party put on shore at Port-au-Prince on the 28th July was not strong . . . A skilful show of strength was, however, made and by at once seizing all points of military importance, together with practically all Government arms and ammunition and disarming all Haytian military and civilians the landing force was able to anticipate any serious resistance which might have been offered."

Hayti Is a Public Nuisance

Robert Rotberg has correctly written: "The decision to intervene was no sudden, capricious response to Haitian political and financial destitution . . . It is more surprising that the Americans waited until 1915 than that they intervened at all." Yet the American intervention was no simple explainable act of dollar diplomacy.

American business interests in the country, the egregious Farnham their spokesman, to be sure exerted leverage on the State Department through Bryan, but economic penetration of Haiti, with or without U.S. support, had been negligible. In 1914, American investments in Mexico exceeded $800 million and amounted to $220 million in Cuba. In all Latin America, they totaled $1.7 billion. Of that sum, only $4 million was in Haiti.

U.S. political and strategic concern so disproportionate to investment can be explained in one further statistic: the day U.S. Marines landed, Haiti, at the

Atlantic gate to the "American Mediterranean" and the Panama Canal, had just experienced its eighth violent overthrow of government in less than seven years. If Secretary Lansing or Woodrow Wilson had had the time or the accumulated data ready in hand in July 1915, they would have learned that, of twenty-two rulers of Haiti between 1843 and 1915, only one had served out his term of office. Four had died in office. One had been blown up in his palace. One had been overthrown and executed. One had been torn to pieces by his subjects. Thirteen had been ousted by coup or revolution.

During these same seventy-two years (1843 to 1915), Haiti had been wracked by at least 102 civil wars, revolutions, insurrections, revolts, coups, and *attentats* - "Simply a succession," in the words of Paul Adam, "of bloody operettas."

Amid these tumults - not counting repeated acts of European gunboat diplomacy - the United States Navy had been compelled to send warships into Haitian waters to protect the lives and property of American citizens in 1849, 1851, 1857, 1858, 1859, 1865, 1866, 1867, 1868, 1869, 1876, 1888, 1889, 1891, 1892, 1902, 1903, 1904, 1905, 1906, 1907, 1908, 1909, 1911, 1912, 1913, and, during 1914, 1915, had maintained ships there almost without interruption.

If, as has truthfully been said, no American ever lost his life in any of these disturbances, possibly the nearly continual presence of the U.S. Navy may have been at least partly responsible.

The concatenation of events that finally put U.S. Marines ashore at Bizoton that afternoon on 28 July 1915, was not simple - few accurate or adequate explanations of human events are - yet a departmental minute by Alvey A. Adee, for many years the wise old, practically permanent Assistant Secretary of State in Washington, goes far to say why. Commenting on an 1888 dispatch from Consul Goutier at the Cap, Adee wrote: "Hayti is a public nuisance at our doors."

Nuisance could be tolerated, but when combined with utter disintegration - in a place and time where perceived American strategic interests could not allow collapse or vacuum - the hour for the Marines had come.

CHAPTER 11 - FOOTNOTES

1. Dr. Treitel served in this, as well as the ultimate transaction, as persuader-in-chief, paying out, as the German minister indiscreetly confirmed to Furniss, $175,000 in bribes to members of the government.

2. Americanization of the BNRH proceeded apace during 1911. First, U.S. representation in the European council of administration was sharply increased, and the City Bank became the BNRH's New York agent. In August, John H. Allen became the first American manager of any Haitian national bank, at first sharing responsibility with a French colleague, but later assuming sole charge. Soon afterward, Roger Farnham, vice-

president of the City Bank, became vice-president of the BNRH as well and assumed effective direction of the operations and interests of the American group.

3. After her father's fall, Célestina is said to have gone to Tiffany and tried to sell back the necklace, at which point the fraud was discovered. McDonald, apprised that Célestina was looking for him with a large knife, reportedly went into hiding.

4. Ultimately, 108 miles were built: one segment from the capital to St. Marc and Verrettes: another from Gonaïves to Ennery; a third linking Bahon, the Cap, and Grande Rivière du Nord. This triplification required three sets of rolling stock and motive power and maintenance backup. Other faults included slipshod right-of-way and high-binding American construction crews and foremen. One charge that recurred perennially but was finally put to rest by Dr. Georges Michel was that McDonald located the Port-au-Prince terminal two miles out of town. The station, surrounded in 1989 by a street market, stands well inside the city, where the Rue du Quai intersects the Rue des Césars.

5. The *Montreal's* reception differed sharply from that of S.S. *New York*, first cruise ship ever to visit Haiti (20 February 1911). The tourists were first shown through the *Palais National* and given champagne and a welcoming address while the *Garde* Présidentielle was issued new uniforms for the occasion.

6. Beginning in 1910, when the Dominicans commenced a frontier road in the remote Southwest region of Pedernales and Banane, a border dispute fueled a war scare that was eventually damped in January 1911 by a mixed commission from the two countries, headed, for Haiti, by Dr. Edmond Héraux. The controversy sputtered on but without further danger of hostilities.

7. As another means of extending its influence in Haitian political circles, Germany pursued a liberal policy of asylum in her legation and consulates, giving special hospitality to political aspirants she considered destined for future success. In 1910 the American legation reported: "It is now easy to cause trouble as there is always a safe place to run to. The German Consulates have always taken refugees, as they are always mixed up in the revolutionary movement."

8. The navy had sunk to lowest ebb: the *Liberté* (bought in New York for $15,000 and budgeted in Port-au-Prince at $126,000) had blown up on 24 October 1910. The costly *Antoine Simon,* whose aromatic Italian powder was quietly deteriorating in the palace basement, remained unable to move and *Nord Alexis* was no better. In this dark hour, apparently turning some $75,000 on the deal, McDonald produced a secondhand American yacht, which was duly consecrated on commissioning when a Voodoo baptism was held and a sheep thrown overboard for *Agoué.*

9. Guillaume Sam, as history knows him, had one of the gamiest records among the *Consolidards*. As Minister of War under Simon Sam, he purchased successive orders of nonexistent supplies and equipment, and then allocated to himself in repayment equivalent amounts in the so-called Rose Bonds (one series in the Consolidations). He was convicted, sentenced to life imprisonment and a fine of 500 *gourdes*. On appeal in 1905, he was fully pardoned on condition that he pay his fine and give the president six parcels of property he owned.

10. Simon had no diplomatic escort. Antoine Pierre-Paul says he refused an offer of safe-conduct from the French minister, and Herr Staude propagated the charge that the "famous American minister" had declined to participate.

11. The loan was urgently required to pay off revolutionary debts to the lenders and was really in the nature of refinancing. When Leconte took the field in May 1911, the German merchants had supported him, repayment to be made on the sporting odds of four dollars for one. Liquidating this debt was the first charge against Leconte's government.

12. In a letter of 13 July 1911, to *The Motor Age,* a Chicago magazine, Minister Furniss wrote: "To me is due the credit of introducing the automobile in Haiti. I was the first here to own a touring car and the first to demonstrate that a car could be run over the streets and roads."

13. While deterioration of the *Antoine Simon's* powder presents a more than plausible explanation for the palace explosion, Furniss confidentially reported the curious circumstances that, when Leconte's body was found, the head, arms, and legs were severed from the trunk, which of course suggests murder by enemies followed by detonation of the magazines. The most likely objects of such suspicion would be the Zamors and their *Cacos,* but it is also a fact that the death of Leconte came on the exact anniversary of his final expulsion of Firmin. As might have been expected at the time, public opinion widely attributed the explosion to those standing scapegoats, the Syrians.

14. Maître Léger, whose virtuoso casuistry was already known in Washington and would soon become even more familiar to American authorities, was the subject of a sharply etched vignette by Furniss: "While perhaps he would not exactly prevaricate, yet he would mislead in order to make his case more plausible." To the foregoing, in a dispatch of 14 January 1913, Furniss added: "His family considers itself superior to other Haitians, and they lead the Port-au-Prince social set ... This set is almost entirely composed of mulattoes and a very strong prejudice exists between them and the blacks..."

15. Madison R. Smith, sixty-three, a white former congressman, had succeeded Furniss as American minister in late 1913. Wilson had wanted to appoint another black, but William Jennings Bryan insisted that the new man be white "until affairs there could be straightened out" (as if Furniss had let things slide). The appointment was not brilliant: Smith had never been abroad, spoke no French, declined to mix with Haitians, knew nothing of diplomacy, bickered with colleagues, and by his own admission had suffered a serious nervous breakdown" before going to Haiti.

16. Michel Oreste left for Colombia aboard S. S. *Eitel Freidrich* on 28 January. He died, still an exile, in New York City on 28 October 1918.

17. Considering that the Zamors had filched his war chest, Théodore's terms were reasonable enough: $50,000 gold, government assumption of his revolutionary debts, and passports for himself and his leaders.

18. In 1913, Assistant Secretary of State Osborne, in Haiti on Knox's heels, had wrung from Michel Oreste the promise that no third power would be granted a foothold at the Môle.

19. Listed in official files only as "Consular Assistant on Special Detail," Hazeltine spoke fluent French and had come to Haiti in 1914. From his sharply focused reports and rapid movement to trouble spots, it may be surmised that he was on an intelligence assignment under consular cover.

20. Arthur Bailly-Blanchard, a new American minister (Smith lasted only six months), bore with him a draft agreement for customs control and financial advisership he was

told to press upon the Zamors. When Livingston brought up the matter with Charles Zamor at the Cap, the latter suggested that if trouble (for example, the Defly coup that day in progress) materialized at Port-au-Prince, the United States should land Marines and take over until, in his words, "the plan you have in mind may be put into execution." This action, Zamor explained, "would save appearances for the Government . . . and shift responsibility to the rebels for having provoked the landing of American forces."

21. Born in the North in 1847 - at Ennery, Fort Liberté, or Ouanaminthe, depending on which source one accepts - President Théodore, nicknamed "Fré Da," had, with no formal education, climbed the ladder from service at eighteen with Salnave, to senator in 1888, mayor of Ouanaminthe (with additional duty as Haitian consul in Dajabón), and president of the Senate in 1911. His allegiances, besides Salnave, had been to Salomon, Hyppolite, Nord Alexis, and Leconte. He died in Port-au-Prince on 13 January 1917.

22. How thin the ice was for any politician contemplating concessions to a foreign power was demonstrated on 3 December, when Joseph Justin, the Foreign Minister, was attempting to explain to the Senate the squeeze into which American demands were compressing the government. Justin said, "It has long been said the country cannot govern itself ... that our finances are disorganized": then, fatal words, "qu'il nous faut un maître étranger" (that we need a foreign master). "With cries of 'Vive la Liberté!' " Minister Bailly-Blanchard reported, "the audience with one accord, armed with canes, knives, and revolvers, surged toward the speaker. In the melee Mr. Justin received several blows. Except for protection offered him by other Cabinet members he would have been assassinated . . ." Next day, swept away by charges that he proposed "to sell out the country" (vendre le Pays) to the blancs, Justin resigned.

23. The Banque's holdings in Port-au-Prince now amounted to about $1 million gold, mostly in the disputed fund for currency retirement, together with smaller sums in collected government receipts that the Banque was refusing to release until the new fiscal year.

24. In his Senate testimony in 1922, Farnham said the interest for "part of the time" was 2.5 percent, and 3 percent for the balance. Paul H. Douglas, not to be disregarded, says it was 2.5 percent throughout. The money came back to Haiti, with interest, in 1919.

25. Long-standing tradition unanimously credits "Bank" (as he was known locally) Williams with slamming the vault shut, but Desrue appears in the reports.

26. Revisionists have charged that the U.S. Navy's flag-showing along Guillaume Sam's route was intended to display American support for the revolution, but no evidence of any such intention can be found; Caperton's testimony and papers disclose only concern that violence be minimized. In the admiral's words: "The cities were all undefended, and they were poor people." At another point he added: "Customary American Policy was based on considerate treatment of Haitian sensibilities and their sovereignty as a state," words that, however sincere in early 1915, would soon acquire an ironic ring.

27. In 1921 Farnham described his qualifications to a Senate committee: "What I know of this country was . . . gained by seven trips on horseback, one of 33 days, one of 30 days, and five of a fortnight each . . . I have sailed around the coast . . . and it is from these trips [the first in June 1911] that I have been able to observe conditions."

28. Without seriously crediting Robert Lansing's bit of Germanophobe apocrypha that. in 1914, only the outbreak of World War I prevented S.M.S. Karlsruhe from landing German Marines to take over Port-au-Prince, it is on record that von Tirpitz, the

Kaiser's Naval Minister, prodded the Wilhelmstrasse throughout the prewar period to obtain one or more Caribbean naval stations in Haiti, Santo Domingo, or St. John, to support possible German West Indian operations.

29. Civilian students, less familiar with military planning documents, have overstated the significance of these 1914 plans. Despite imposing binding and title ("Navy War Portfolio # 1 [Green] Haiti") the contents are nothing but a rehash of old reports prefaced by a lifted copy of the 5th Marines' landing plan hastily composed on the regiment's lone typewriter as *Hancock* plowed across from Guantanamo Bay in December 1914.

30. Dana Munro recalls the new minister as "a mild-mannered, elderly gentleman whose chief qualifications were a fluent command of French and long experience with the formal and ceremonial aspects of diplomacy in large embassies." Somewhat more acidly, his German colleague, Dr. Perl, reported on 27 April 1915 that at a meeting of the diplomatic corps, Blanchard "was so drunk he fell under the table." In 1921 the British legation depicted him as "a very hard drinker and not very much liked by Americans residing in Hayti." Blanchard had reason for becoming a man of sorrows; his heart's desire had been to remain second secretary in Paris; instead, he spent over eight years (1914 to 1922) at Port-au-Prince and never saw Paris again.

31. John Craige, later the U.S. Marine chief of police in Port-au-Prince, has left a vignette of Delva: "In him and his family were personified all the color and exotic flavor of Haiti in the old days. A magnificent figure of a man, six feet tall, powerfully built, very dark, mustachioed and handsome, he was very much the *beau idéal* of his section of Haiti's political class. Courtly, suave, intelligent, well educated, he would have appeared to advantage in any race or nation."

32. Most accounts say the wall was twenty feet high, but Captain Young, a meticulous observer, reported it as ten feet high and eighteen inches thick. The French property, once the home of Michel Oreste, was the legation residence, not the chancery, which was more than a block North on the Champ de Mars.

33. Several versions have been given of this note, which, in one form or another, was found in the pocket of Charles-Oscar Etienne. The wording herein is what the British legation reported as "the exact text." According to Lucien Chauvet, *Préfet de Police* of Port-au-Prince under Papa Doc and related to persons involved, Guillaume Sam sent either an earlier note or a verbal order to Etienne saying that though he (Sam) is from the North, Etienne is from the capital, and should thus use his own judgment.

34. Among many myths cultivated about the death of Guillaume Sam are (1) that he was politely escorted from the legation by a select committee who first paid their respects to the French minister: and (2) that he was killed by people of the streets, not the elite. The facts are otherwise. As depicted in the firsthand reports of Girard and his colleagues, the proceedings were savage and violent, and Sam was murdered in the legation garden by the elite intruders before his body reached the street.

35. That night, Girard recounted, a peasant brought an object, swathed in burlap, to the legation gate: it was the ex-president's head. "It's for Mme. Vilbrun Guillaume" he said in Créole. What could be reassembled (one main chunk of Guillaume Sam had been run the length of the Grande Rue, the other chivvied through Turgeau and Bois-Verna) was buried unshriven in a shallow grave outside the East gate of the Cimetière, "a place of desolation the most horrible I have ever seen," later wrote Girard.

36. It is now firm in the apocrypha of Haitian history that a single soldier (sometimes named Joseph Pierre, sometimes Pierre Sully) resisted the takeover of Fort National and was killed by the Americans. Although no confirmation of this can be found in U.S. reports of the landing, this man - if he ever existed - subsequently has been canonized in anti-American literature (for example, Jean Brièrre's *Le Petit Soldat*) resulting from the U.S. occupation.

Dr. Rosalvo Bobo, the red-headed *mulâtre* would-be president. "If I am cheated of my rights, I will leave the country and abandon Haiti to her fate. She can never survive without me!" *U.S. Marine Corps*

"I will permit Congress elect president next Thursday," radioed Admiral Caperton (center) shown here aboard U.S.S. *Washington* with new president Sudre Dartiguenave (third from left). At far right is American charge Beale Davis. *U.S. Marine Corps* Below: Charlemagne Péralte (center, in panama hat) surrounded by subordinate *Caco* leaders and bodyguard. *U.S. Marine Corps*

392

Only the assassination of Charlemagne Péralte finally quelled *Caco* resistance to the government put in place in Port-au-Prince. This photograph of his propped-up corpse, taken to prove Péralte's death to doubters, is cited as "evidence" that the U.S. crucified him. One Marine officer reflected on "the stong, the powerful, idolatrous hold that Charlemagne had on these people. Many, many good Haitians, strong followers of the Occupation, were sympathetic to the man." *U.S. Marine Corps*

Major John H. Russell served in Haiti from 1917 to 1930, eight years as American High Commissioner. *U.S. Marine Corps* Below: President Louis Borno, who accomplished much of Haiti's reconstruction during the 1920s. *U.S. Marine Corps*

Two presidents - Vincent and Roosevelt - sip rum punch in the Union Club, Cap Haïtien, 8 July 1934. *U.S. Marine Corps Below*: "Sieur Lescot," led Haiti during World War II. *Sumner Welles Papers*

CHAPTER 12

Occupation

1915-1934

We are not at war with the United States. We are at war with Humanity, which we have not ceased to offend for a century. The Americans are the foe of a sovereign, Despotism, and occupy the country to thwart his restoration.

- Charles Moravia, 1915

FOR AN EVENT so long considered, intervention in Haiti rather oddly seemed to have taken the U.S. Government by surprise.

With the Marines five days on the beach, Robert Lansing plaintively told Wilson: "The situation in Haiti is distressing and very perplexing. I am not at all sure what we ought to do or what we legally can do . . . I hope you can give me some suggestion as to what course we can pursue."

Whatever his faults, Woodrow Wilson could never be numbered in the ranks of the uncertain. Within twenty-four hours Lansing had his answer:

I suppose there is nothing to do but to take the bull by the horns and restore order . . .

1. We must send to Port-au-Prince a force sufficient to absolutely control the city not only but also the country immediately about it from which it draws its food . .
2. We must let the present Haitian Congress know that we will protect it but that we will not recognize any action on its part that does not put men in charge of affairs whom we can trust to handle and put an end to revolution.
3. We must give all who now have authority there or who desire to have it or who think they have it or are about to have it to understand that we shall take steps to prevent the payment of debts contracted to finance revolutions:

So much for the German merchants.

In other words [Wilson concluded], that we consider it our duty to insist on constitutional government there and will, if necessary (that is, if they force

us to it as the only way), take charge of elections and see that a real
government is erected which we can support.

What Wilson envisaged amounted to intervention, no more, and on the most
high-minded (however inapplicable) principles. Only the one phrase -"put men
in charge . . whom we can trust to handle" - suggested there might be more to
it.

Lansing (and Caperton, too, stewing over lack of guidance) found themselves
momentarily bemused by their own actions, but the pragmatic French had no
such difficulties. On the morning of 29 July, soon after van Orden's Marines
had eaten their first breakfast in Haiti, Jules Jusserand, France's masterly
ambassador in Washington, sent Laboulaye, his first secretary, down Sixteenth
Street from the French embassy and across Lafayette Square to the State
Department to find out exactly what was going on, and to convey a message.

Sitting in the Latin American Division's cool, high-ceilinged offices,
Laboulaye came quickly to his point:

> it was urgently desired [read the Department's "MemCon" of what he said] the
> United States take energetic action in Haiti. That if she did France would look with
> approval on her action and be willing to support her in every way, provided that a
> just recognition of French claims . . . was made by the United States . . . He added,
> however, that were the action not energetic but composed of half way measures,
> France would not look upon it with such approval.

No "half way measures." Wilson himself had spoken of "a long program."
Would simple intervention suffice?

While the *blancs* considered what ought to be done in and about Haiti, those
most immediately concerned, the elite, voiced their own reactions.

Only four months earlier, in April, Liberal leader Auguste Bonamy, in the
tradition of many another national prophet, had sounded what was to be called
a final call to repentance: "We are at the brink of an abyss. We cannot afford
another single dereliction: the country is slipping through our hands."

Now, as long foretold, it had happened, and, as they picked themselves up at
the bottom of the abyss, too dazed at the moment for recrimination, the elite
admitted their responsibility. In the words of Charles Moravia: "We are not at
war with the United States. We are at war with Humanity, which we have not
ceased to offend for a century. The Americans are the foe of a sovereign,
Despotism, and occupy the country to thwart his restoration."

Within three years, Moravia would be Haitian minister in Washington. Within
eleven years (founder and editor of *Le Temps,* since 1922 a beacon of Haitian

nationalism), he would be doing preventive detention inside the *pénitencier* - for having goaded the occupying Americans too far and too often.

Meanwhile, as Beale Davis had reported, "the better element of the natives and all foreigners in Haiti are in favor of American intervention . . . This belief is shared by most public men and the enlightened patriots of Haiti, also by the most prominent politicians. The latter, however, although readily stating their preference in private, are loath to admit it officially; in a word, they favor intervention provided they are not instrumental in or responsible for bringing it about."

The United States Prefers Dartiguenave

For the moment, Haitians and Americans cautiously tested each other. Until Wilson had spoken, Caperton of course had no intimation as to what Washington's long-range plans might be; until he had reinforcements, his 400-man landing force (including the Guantanamo Bay company) gave him only the most tenuous hold on a large city infested with at least 1500 Bobo *Cacos* as well as remnants of *La Réforme* and tag-ends of the army.

The *Comité Révolutionnaire* (Revolutionary Committee), Bobo to a man, was already prodding the National Assembly, whose members, emerging in the unnatural calm, seemed to have other choices in mind. When the deputies asked if they might proceed to elect a president, the admiral, temporizing, dissuaded them for the moment. The problem, as Caperton reported on 2 August, hinged on

professional soldiers called *Cacos*, organized in bands under lawless and irresponsible chiefs who fight on side offering greatest inducement . . . *Cacos* are feared by all Haitians and practically control politics. They have demanded election Bobo President, and Congress, terrorized by mere demand, is on point complying but restrained by my request. No other man can be elected account fear of *Cacos* . . . Stable government not possible in Haiti until *Cacos* are disbanded and power broken . . .

The *Comité*, now beginning to recover from shock, busied itself with politics as if nothing had changed. Heard to criticize the *Comité*, a senator, Joseph Dessources, was clapped in jail as if Guillaume Sam were still in charge; when word reached the *blancs,* they ordered Dessources freed. Then the *Comité* took over the telegraph offices and flooded the country with pro-Bobo messages, while closing the wires to all others. Caperton responded by assuming charge of communications. When the *Comité* began drawing and disbursing government funds from various depositories, the admiral withdrew every *gourde* and credited the money to a blocked account in the *Banque* (unfortunately designated "Admiral Caperton Account") with *Washington's* paymaster signing vouchers.(1)

The *éminence grise* behind these developments was Captain Beach.

While van Orden was disarming the capital (five wagonloads of weapons were the first day's haul), Beach had been ordered ashore with these words from the admiral: "Take up your quarters in the Legation . . . Give what orders you deem necessary...... Under no circumstances whatever, haul down any Haitian flag...... Find out where the government money is kept. Take any necessary measures to protect it. Find out what weapons and ammunition are in the city, and where they are . . . Send me word from time to time and come on board to report when you can."

Beach thus repaired to the legation, where the Marines had a field radio. On instructions from the State Department, Beale Davis ("a young gentleman of excellent judgment," the captain reminisced) put himself at Beach's disposal for the delicate work ahead.

Although the *Comité* seemed cordiality itself when they met Beach each morning, he soon observed that "while answering some questions, they would dodge others, and that they were chary of volunteering information. I could get nothing explicit about government funds, nor about the soldiers, and but little as to what the Committee was actually doing. But I learned one thing . . . the chief interest of this Committee was to convince me that Guillaume Sam had been eliminated for the purpose of having Dr. Bobo made president, and we Americans were in honor bound not to interfere."

Every afternoon and evening, he met with Haitians, all elite to be sure. But from these sessions, mostly in private homes, the captain began, often with the aid of Dr. Furniss (who had settled in Port-au-Prince and had a comfortable villa in Martissant), to understand people and events.

It has been asserted by some historians that, once vengeance had been wreaked on Etienne and Guillaume Sam, "perfect tranquillity" prevailed. For example, Dantès Bellegarde wrote, twenty-two years later, that "after the terrible days of July, the country recovered its calm." Contemporary reports paint a different picture. During the weeks after the massacres, Port-au-Prince was in almost constant uproar, with street robberies, assaults, and disorders on every hand, accompanied by wild night firing.

Caperton's first request had been for reinforcements. On 4 August, *U.S.S. Connecticut,* sister to the flagship, reached Port-au-Prince from Philadelphia Navy Yard with a Marine regimental headquarters and five more companies. The colonel, E. K. Cole, immediately assumed charge ashore. Eleven days later, bringing 1st Marine Brigade Headquarters and much of another regiment, U.S.S. *Tennessee* arrived with Colonel Littleton W. T. Waller on board. Waller took command of the 2029 Marines ashore in Haiti on 15 August.(2)

By the time Waller arrived, important political events had come to pass.

In simplest terms, Caperton's brief from Washington was to hold an election, make sure that a "suitable" candidate won with a respectable mandate, start government processes again, support the new regime by ending disorder, and conclude treaty arrangements whereby the United States assumed certain supervisory responsibilities over Haiti.

With Cole's 2d Regiment ashore, the first job was to demobilize the Port-au-Prince garrison. On 4 August, while Captain Beach blandly presided over a long-winded meeting of the *Comité*, Marines went to the casernes, arsenal, and other military billets, disarmed everyone in sight, loaded some 3000 rifles and 4 million rounds of ammunition into mule wagons, and demobilized the soldiers by hiking them out of town and paying off each man with a ten-*gourde* note. Having been recruited with rope and *cocomacac*, the soldiers were joyous, "tearing from their clothes," Beach recounted, "the red tape that had meant they were soldiers. But when they knew they were to receive the to-them huge sum of ten *gourdes*, pandemonium broke loose."

The *Comité* howled, too: "Each Committeeman jumped to his feet; wild, indignant protestations were shouted. The ground under them was being torn away. Their power had vanished . . . there was nothing they could do."

With the capital stabilized if hardly tranquil, the next step was to quiet the North and get Dr. Bobo, detached from his *Cacos*, down to Port-au-Prince.

To accomplish this, Beach (on the advice of J.-N. Léger) recruited a prestigious commission including Archbishop Conan, Légitime, and Charles Zamor. Shepherded by Lieutenant Coffey, Caperton's French-speaking flag lieutenant, the commission, "attired in black silk hats and topcoats," recalled Caperton, steamed for the Cap aboard the *Jason*.

After a day of high confusion, with assistance from landing forces of U.S. S. *Nashville* and *Eagle*, the commission sorted out contenders and candidates and embarked homesick demobilized government soldiers aboard *Nord Alexis*. *Jason*, with government figures quartered forward and Bobo supporters aft, then returned South. "She had," wrote Caperton,

> a notable gathering of Haitians, all bound for the capital to witness the election. General [sic] Bobo was on board with a staff of 26 generals, besides Generals Laroche and Bourand [ex-government generals]. Seventeen nuns also took passage. . . The Doctor talked incessantly about his plans for the regeneration of Haiti but had no specific cures. Coffey considered him unbalanced. To Coffey, Zamor and Chevallier confided that Bobo was crazy.

Zamor confided even more. In deepest privacy he disclosed to Livingston, [that]"He represented a group of politicians, including Léger, who had reached the conclusion that an arrangement with the U.S. was necessary, and that the candidate elected should be pledged to this beforehand; that he is the principal supporter of Bobo but that if the latter declined, he would be put aside."

YOU MAY EXPECT DEMONSTRATION WHEN BOBO ARRIVES,

Coffey had radioed the admiral, and it was with lively anticipation that the *Jason* was greeted when she stood into Port-au-Prince on 6 August. Caperton sent over a launch to bring Dr. Bobo, accompanied by four of his Ministers, on board the flagship. As the launch approached the *Washington,* the admiral watched with interest:

> I had my first glimpse of this famous red-headed mulatto. Attired in a frock coat and high hat, he arose. Assuming a commanding attitude, with one hand, Napoleon-like, stuck in his coat, tall and erect, he faced the *Washington* and gazed in a lofty manner at her. When they mounted the ladder it was observed that Bobo, and his four frock-coated followers, all carried dress suitcases upon which had been painted: "Dr. Rosalvo Bobo, Chief of Executive Power," "Dr. So-and-So, Minister of Interior," etc.

Beach, waiting at the head of the ladder, continues the narrative:

> Dr. Bobo mounted the gangway . . . with a rather slow stride, intended, perhaps, to be stately and majestic . . . On reaching the quarterdeck, with a grand air he removed his silk hat and held it extended, after the manner of potentates, from his side: and then he stood there in his Prince Albert coat, awaiting the salute of guns, and beating of drums, the blowing of bugles, the presenting of arms: courtesies and honors always accorded a visiting head of State.

It was not to be: the only honor Dr. Bobo got was a handshake, after which Beach led them below. Seated in the flag cabin (while Caperton, wishing not to involve himself at this point, observed unseen from behind the green curtain of his stateroom), Bobo, asked if he was a candidate for the presidency, rejoined, "Sir, I am more than a candidate; I am Chief of the Executive Power, I command an army in the North which is now unopposed. The presidency is already mine; the election is a mere formality!"

Captain Beach's reply was crushing: "You are not a candidate, because the United States forbids . . . You do not propose that the Haitian Congress have a free election, but with the menace of your troops in the North . . . you propose to force your election . . . There is to be no more revolution, ever, in Haiti, no more presidents made by force."

"Livid with rage," Caperton recalled, Bobo nevertheless then resigned as *chef du pouvoir executif,* signed telegrams to his men in the North, and went ashore a private citizen.

A private citizen? Well, not quite: from the context of events it is clear that, despite his words, what Beach really intended was to exact Dr. Bobo's resignation as *chef du pouvoir executif* and thus cool the situation in the North. When the doctor got ashore, he behaved very like a candidate. A crowd had been organized, there were speeches; then a progress through the city as Bobo "in a dilapidated carriage" flung handfuls of coins to scrambling urchins. "The whole country greeted its liberator, and proclaimed me President," wrote the doctor, savoring this moment in the sun:

> I was not an unknown, an improvised person made conspicuous by force of arms. The country had heard my conferences during twenty years, read my books, followed my correct attitude signalized by the most sincere patriotism and most perfect sense of honor . . . My program of public administration was in its hands and it was convinced of the excellency of the propositions contained therein . . . The delirious ovations given me had their foundation in these great things . . .

There is a Créole proverb that goes: *"Trop esprit, sòt pas loin"*(too many brains, madness not far).

While *Jason* was at the Cap, the Americans had been shopping for a candidate more to their liking.

Men of standing - Légitime, Solon Ménos, J.-N. Léger, all approached by various emissaries were not eager. Léger spoke for all: "I am for Haiti; not the United States, and I propose to keep myself in a position where I will be able to defend Haiti's interests."
Philippe Sudre Dartiguenave, distinguished *mulâtre* lawyer of Anse-à-Veau and president of the Senate, was, however, not so reticent. Popular among his colleagues, he had already emerged as the Senate's man. As early as 5 August Caperton reported: "From many sources hear Dartiguenave is man of personal honor and patriotism. Has never been connected with any revolution, is of good ability, and anxious for Haiti's regeneration, realizes Haiti must agree to any terms laid down by the U.S., professes to believe any terms demanded will be for Haiti's benefit."

Pressure was now mounting for an election, not only from the political hopefuls but from the country's simple need for a government. Elsewhere than the capital and the Cap, each tranquilized by Marines, anarchy reigned. The presidential choice seemed to lie between Bobo and Dartiguenave. To settle the matter, at least in his and the admiral's mind, Captain Beach arranged one more meeting. On 8 August to the American legation came the doctor, the senator (each with a Haitian second), and Beach. Beach moved quickly to the point. Addressing Dartiguenave, he bluntly asked, "Are there other Haitians as well qualified as you to be President of Haiti?"
"There are many better qualified," replied the senator. "This honor is not of my seeking, but I will not avoid it."

Now came Bobo's turn. To the same question, the doctor shot back: "No! I alone have sufficient honor and patriotism and intelligence. And I alone, of all Haitians, enjoy the love and confidence of my people. There is no other!"

Returning to Dartiguenave, Beach then put his second question: "Should Dr. Bobo be elected, will you promise to help him loyally in his efforts to secure the welfare of Haiti?"

"If Dr. Bobo or anybody else is elected," answered the senator, "I will exert myself to the utmost to help him. I will be loyal and faithful to him in all his efforts to benefit Haiti."

Would Bobo support Dartiguenave?

"Jamais!" the doctor burst out. "If *I* am not elected, it will be because the presidency has been stolen from me! By rights I am already President! If Dartiguenave is elected, I will not help him! If I am cheated of my rights, I will leave the country and abandon Haiti to her fate. She can never survive without me!"

On that note the meeting ended. There was brief talk afterward of another attempt to enlist Légitime as a compromise, but it came to nothing. Besides, Washington next day made its desires clear to Caperton:

ALLOW ELECTION OF PRESIDENT TO TAKE PLACE
WHENEVER HAITIANS WISH. THE UNITED STATES
PREFERS ELECTION OF DARTIGUENAVE . .

Josephus Daniels later wrote a friend, William Allen White, "... that this was equivalent to America making Dartiguenave President. The telegram by the Navy Department was sent at the suggestion of the State Department, which chiefly decided the policy . . ."

But the *Comité* had one last card. All day on the 10th, city dwellers and disarmed *Cacos* thronged the streets, shouting, "*A bas les députés! Vive Bobo!"* Next morning, when Port-au-Prince awoke, the capital was plastered with a decree by the committee, dissolving the National Assembly, proclaiming the *Comité* a provisional government with power to rewrite the constitution, and ordering that the doors of the Chamber, to which a copy was nailed, be sealed.

When Beach read the proclamation, he reacted swiftly. Summoning Dr. Bobo and all members of the *Comité* to the legation, he dissolved them on the spot. U.S. Marines ripped down the decree and shooed the committee's people away.

Now that the *Comité* had its marching orders, came the turn of the Assembly.

To the Théâtre Parisiana, behind whose charming gingerbread front Port-au-Prince had its nearest equivalent to the Folies Bergères, came the National Assembly, invited by Captain Beach and Beale Davis for what Beach later called an "informal meeting." For an informal affair, attendance was high: in fact, perfect: all 39 senators and 102 deputies were present.

Beach mounted the stage. When he announced the *Comité's* demise, no cancan could have excited wilder applause. Now the members of the assembly knew they would remain as ins, not outs. Then Beale Davis took the center. In his hand was a State Department telegram of the day before, whose contents the department had ordered to "be made perfectly clear." Davis did so in what was virtually the gospel of the occupation:

> First: Let Congress understand that the Government of the United States intends to uphold it, but that it cannot recognize action which does not establish in charge of Haitian affairs those whose abilities and dispositions give assurance to putting an end to factional disorders.
> Second: In order that no misunderstanding can possibly occur after election, it should be made perfectly clear to candidates . . . in advance of their election, that the United States expects to be entrusted with the practical control of the customs. and such financial control over the affairs of Haiti as the United States may deem necessary for an efficient administration.
> The Government of the United States considers it its duty to support a constitutional government. It means to assist in the establishment of such a government and to support it as long as necessity may require. It has no design upon the political or territorial integrity of Haiti: on the contrary, what has been done, as well as what will be done, is conceived in an effort to aid the people of Haiti in establishing a stable government and in maintaining domestic peace throughout the Republic.

Beach then closed the session with a final word: "This is the most important message Haiti has received. If you accept its provisions, Admiral Caperton directs that tomorrow you proceed to the election of your president. If you so proceed, the Admiral will take your action as formal agreement on your part that you do accept . . . The Admiral refuses to permit the election unless you agree."

The final message was indeed perfectly clear: the U.S. would allow Haiti to hold a "free" election subject to the one condition that the election hypothecate to Washington the freedom of Haiti.

The election proceeded without objection or delay. Marines were at every street intersection and cordoned the assembly. At their own urgent request, Caperton permitted senators and deputies to carry arms to the meeting "with the understanding," the admiral wrote, "that they would be free to shoot themselves while in session, but not others." Friends coming to the galleries were frisked by Marines, who netted in the process still another wagonload of weapons. Captain Beach enjoyed the freedom of the floor and mingled easily. As Dartiguenave saw it and later wrote, "The fullest freedom was assured to the National Assembly . . . Not a Senator, not a Deputy, was subjected to any act of pressure or coercion; each voted with perfect independence."

The assembly voted as Washington wished. It was Dartiguenave on the first ballot, 94 votes; Bobo, 16; the remainder scattered among lesser candidates. A third, 47, of the members felt free to vote for others than the U.S.-favored winner.

It would be easy to conclude that the election was at least pressured if not rigged - some historians have so concluded - yet this was not how Minister Girard viewed it. Reporting next day to the Quai d'Orsay, Girard said Bobo "found partisans only in the low elements of Port-au-Prince and had against him the great majority of those who had to decide the issue - the members of the National Assembly."

Whatever its failings as an electoral college, the assembly in any case enjoyed the nearest thing to legitimacy left in Haiti. Members, after all, had been in office since the days of Michel Oreste, four regimes back. It simply could not be admitted, Beale Davis later wrote of the *Comité*, "that a band of professional revolutionists had either the right or power, in furtherance of their own ends, arbitrarily to dissolve [the Assembly]."

How profoundly Dr. Bobo misread events and American purposes may be measured by the fact that, as soon as Dartiguenave was elected, he dashed for the British legation and implored asylum, which Kohan reluctantly granted.

Captain Beach immediately called at the British legation, where he found the doctor "in a small cabin in the grounds. He was quite disheveled but on recognizing [me], hastily drew on a pair of shoes, put on collar and necktie, and his Prince Albert coat." Bobo continued to refer to himself as President of Haiti, insisted he was surrounded by enemies seeking to kill him, and asked for a guard until he could embark for exile. A few days later, moving at night for fear of the enemies he still professed to see at every hand, Bobo, escorted at his own request by Marines, slipped aboard a French steamer, never more to return.(3)

The Only Thing to Do

Under stormy skies Dartiguenave took oath with an appeal for national unity and support. For the first time in memory (conceivably indicative of the Church's reservations as to the American presence)(4) there was no Te Deum.

There was one delay. Dartiguenave would not allow the inaugural procession to move until Beach, who was eager to get aboard *Washington* and report to Caperton, was beside him in the carriage. In innocence, the Americans took this for a gesture of respect and friendship; those who had seen the installation and demission of so many past regimes under personal safe-conduct of the diplomatic corps, recognized the measure of the new president's insecurity.

But there was no need. As Beach noted, "Everything quiet. Port-au-Prince had the appearance of being owned in fee simple by U.S. Marines."

Dartiguenave might well have suffered twinges of uncertainty. Besides being a civilian with no army behind him except a foreign one, he was the first elite *mulâtre* from the South to take office since 1876 - an office that, since the days of Boisrond, had been all but monopolized by *noirs,* generals, and men of the North and Artibonite. Not that he had no constituency: his constituency, like that of Haiti's presidents for the next thirty years, was the elite. Numerically insignificant, usually without lucrative occupation save politics, this was the group that, now more than ever before, events were propelling into a monopoly of office and, to the extent the Americans would permit, of entrenched power.

Dartiguenave's first cabinet meeting was held next morning (the 13th) in the bedroom of the house where, widower for many years, the new president had lived. Captain Beach was among those who squeezed into the room; when he told the group that a second Marine regiment was arriving, Dartiguenave murmured approval, only to be shouted down by his own Foreign Minister. Pauléus Sannon burst out, "By what right does Admiral Caperton presume to land troops in Haiti? If he wishes to do that, he should make a request of the Haitian government!"(5)

Four days later, Beale Davis paid his first formal call on the new president (whose regime still awaited U.S. recognition). In his attaché case the American chargé brought the draft of a treaty that the United States expected to be accepted "without modification." After delivering this document to Dartiguenave, Davis, as instructed, said Washington would extend recognition when the National Assembly had blessed the treaty, and authorized Dartiguenave to sign.

The draft Dartiguenave was expected to swallow represented a high-water mark of its kind among American treaties either proposed or concluded with neighbors in the Caribbean.

Taking departure from earlier arrangements proposed by Washington, this latest effort combined elements of the Platt Amendment and the customs receivership the U.S. was then trying to tighten on the Jiménez regime next door in Santo Domingo. Retreating only on Môle St. Nicolas (which the U.S. Navy no longer desired), the United States would nominate (no pretense of consultation) a customs receiver, customs personnel, and a financial adviser with extensive powers; would organize and officer a native *gendarmerie*; would (as in agreements with Cuba and Panama) designate American sanitary engineers to clean up Haiti; and would aid in development of Haiti's " agricultural, mineral and commercial resources." Besides accepting all this, Haiti, for its part, would be bound not to surrender any territory, under any condition, to any foreign power save the United States; and thus taking care of *Banque* and railroad and French bond-holders, to negotiate and settle outstanding foreign claims. All points involving discretion were left to the United States.

Yet even so inclusive a bill of fare, based on American interventions in three other Caribbean countries, still had gaps that would soon become evident: (1) the presence and status of U.S. occupation forces was not expressly recognized. (2) public education was not made subject to American advice or control, and (3) neither were courts and judiciary.

More fundamentally, as Ludwell Montague pointed out, the result was "a system that had neither the virtues of a treaty regime based on true agreement nor those of a clean-cut military administration like that established at Santo Domingo, but only the bad features of both . . . The regime in Haiti left the United States embarrassingly restricted by a treaty but was actually based on force."

These contradictions, however, were yet to become evident. The concern of the moment (at least Washington's concern) was to get the treaty accepted and ratified.

On 13 August, even before Davis broke the news to Dartiguenave, Secretary Lansing said as much to Woodrow Wilson: "I confess that this method of negotiation, with our Marines policing the Haytian capital, is high-handed. It does not meet my sense of a nation's sovereign rights and is more or less an exercise of force and an invasion of Haitian independence. From a practical standpoint, however, I cannot but feel that it is the only thing to do .

Wilson, mind made up, remained untroubled. "This, I think, is necessary" he wrote back, "and has my approval." Dartiguenave had become president (had been permitted to become president, Wilson, Lansing, and Caperton would have said) with a commitment to do what the United States wanted, but he also - especially with Sannon nipping at his heels - felt Haiti should have some say in a treaty that, if only in manner of presentation, was offensive to national pride. If Haiti were not to be allowed even to suggest modifications, said the president, he and his government would resign. But this was a bluff and was so recognized.

On 24 August Davis was instructed to warn Dartiguenave that he was playing with fire: if further stalling ensued, let alone rejection of the American package, Washington would either find a more cooperative regime or just establish straightforward military government - a prospect, Montague wrote, "fearful to patriots and unbearable to politicians."

To soften Davis's stern admonition, Lansing, aided by Acting Secretary of the Navy Franklin D. Roosevelt and by Captain Beach (on home leave because of his wife's ultimately fatal illness), drafted a personal message to Dartiguenave, on 25 August, over Beach's familiar signature: should Dartiguenave wish to dissolve the assembly, fire his obstreperous cabinet, and form a new government of "patriots," he would be fully supported.

Dartiguenave returned a soft answer. If only a few "details" in the treaty could be amended by "changes in phraseology" to create the illusion of mutuality and negotiation rather than American dictation, all would be well. On 27 August, however, when the Haitian "details" were submitted, they proved to be a general counter-proposal that undercut or simply omitted every provision of the original draft. This tactic - Dr. Bobo's Gambit, the unrelated counter-proposal - had worked after a fashion in 1914 and against Paul Fuller earlier in 1915. Now it no longer availed. Within forty-eight hours, Lansing sent word for Dartiguenave to conclude the treaty as written and be quick about it. By way of face-saving - it was Davis's idea - Washington agreed to drop the demand for a resolution from the National Assembly. Davis, wearing velvet glove, was also to "intimate" that if Dartiguenave got the ratification process moving, he "would not find the American government unsympathetic toward any proper effort . . .to place the Haitian finances on a sound basis."

Shortly before this, and intimately involved in both arousing and quelling the Haitian resistance that had created the impasse, two far-reaching actions had been taken by Admiral Caperton.

On 21 August, in accordance with prior orders from Washington, American naval paymasters began taking charge of all customs houses. Two weeks later, Caperton proclaimed martial law and press censorship throughout Haiti.

Customs control (which effectively meant financial control) had been one of the stated aims of U.S., and for that matter, all other proposed foreign intervention. It was not only inevitable; it was essential: there was no other source of revenue.(6) Eleven days earlier, Caperton had restored treasury service to the *Banque*, but without customs collections there was nothing to serve the treasury.

Thus the logic of customs control was irrefutable. Under instructions that revenues realized would be applied to public safety (organization of a constabulary), public works, and famine relief, demobilization of soldiers, and "supporting Dartiguenave government," U.S. Navy paymasters moved in as customs collectors and port captains at Jacmel, Cayes, Jérémie, Miragoâne, Petit-Goâve, St. Marc, Gonaïves, Port-de-Paix, and the Cap. On 2 September, capping the operation, Caperton took charge of the Port-au-Prince *douane*. At the admiral's urgent request, Paymaster Charles Conard, who had run the Veracruz customs house with marked efficiency in 1914, was, with ten junior navy pay officers, sent posthaste to Haiti. ("We have robbed every station on the East Coast," lamented Admiral Benson.)

If customs control was logical, and it was, the next step followed inexorably. As Benson explained in the same letter (25 August), enough Marines were on the way so that "you will be able to send a detachment with at least one machine-gun to each of the towns in which you control customs." Caperton agreed and, asking for three gunboats, rejoined,(7) "We cannot expect to seize and administer customs houses unless we take military occupation of town where it [sic] is located, with sufficient force to prevent trouble and insure order."

American assumption of customs control, however necessary and predictable, for the first time brought home to the elite (which in this context is to say all politicians) some hard practicalities of foreign intervention. For that class, much of whose livelihood had been the public treasury, the blow, square in the pocketbook, was disastrous. (8) The gathering opposition was not entirely venal. For many with sincere patriotic feelings, to whom 1804 was a holy word, the shock of *blancs* with machine guns assuming charge of Haiti's ten principal cities may be imagined.

Thus it happened at the most delicate moment of the negotiations that a storm of animosity broke and gathered force with each new customs house seizure.

It was this sudden gust of hostility, directed not only at the Americans but at Dartiguenave, their client (who himself had been present that day in 1914 when the Senate nearly lynched Joseph Justin for suggesting a *maître étranger),* that dictated Caperton's next move.

"We are having our own troubles here in Port-au-Prince," the admiral had written on 25 August, "and I may have to establish a military government."

What Caperton meant he later explained to a U.S. Senate committee as "increasing uneasiness at Port-au-Prince, the apparent inability of the Government to control conditions with which it was confronted, the propagation by newspapers and public men of inflammatory propaganda against the Government and American occupation; disloyalty of some Government officials . . ."

The conditions that worried Caperton had the same effect on Dartiguenave. On 2 September, the president secretly asked the U.S. authorities to "establish martial law as soon as possible."(9) And that, next day, is what Admiral Caperton did.

"Martial law" was the term used, but the reality (as Ludwell Montague convincingly argues) amounted to a circumscribed form of military government patterned on that improvised by the navy at Veracruz. Under its authority provost courts were set up for trial of political offenders and for anyone committing an offense against the occupation or American authorities. That political offenses were high in Caperton's mind comes through in a contingent decree directed at the press:

> Freedom of the press will not be interfered with, but license will not be tolerated. The publishing of false or incendiary propaganda against the Government of the United States or Government of Haiti, or the publishing of any false, indecent, or obscene propaganda, letters signed or unsigned, or matter which tends to disturb the public peace, will be dealt with by the military courts.

Such rules, not precisely spelled out to be sure, were of course not unfamiliar to any Haitian politician or journalist; indeed, this was the way of things under any Haitian government that expected to survive. But there was this difference: those who were making and enforcing the rules, and would do so for a long time to come, were *étrangers* and *blancs*.

No Velvet Glove

Whether he liked it or not, President Dartiguenave now knew the treaty must be signed. Caperton was only a step or two from outright military government, which would simply obviate Dartiguenave, National Assembly, and all. On 16 September 1915, therefore, Louis Borno (who had replaced Sannon) duly signed. Next morning, with Haitian colors at the foremast, U.S.S. *Washington* fired a 21-gun national salute, and Port-au-Prince learned that, with an exchange of official calls between president and admiral (who had been seeing each other all the time anyway), the new government had won American recognition. (10)

If Dartiguenave had made truce with necessity, the National Assembly had not, and it was the Assembly that had to ratify before the treaty could take effect.

In later years American officials would speak of the treaty as an "obligation" burdening the United States with heavy responsibilities and solemn duties. Perhaps.

If this were true, the lengths to which Washington now went, and the pressures applied, suggest eagerness inconsistent with commitments all that onerous, or with much sense of impending encumbrance.

- While the assembly stalled, Dartiguenave, increasingly strapped for operating expenses (including salaries), asked the Americans to let him have money. The answer: ratify the treaty.

On 3 October, after Dartiguenave had for the second time threatened resignation, he was told by Davis that "not one cent" of revenue would be released - particularly for overdue salaries of *députés* and senators, and for that matter, cabinet ministers and president - until both houses had ratified. Within seventy-two hours, defiantly attaching to the treaty a unilateral "interpretive commentary," the *députés* capitulated, 75 to 6.(11) Next day, Josephus Daniels radioed Caperton:

FURNISH HAITIEN [sic] GOVERNMENT WEEKLY AMOUNT NECESSARY TO MEET CURRENT EXPENSES . . . QUESTION BACK SALARY WILL BE SETTLED BY DEPARTMENT IMMEDIATELY AFTER RATIFICATION OF TREATY.

Ten days later, 13 October, still holding out back pay, Washington put the Haitian government on an allowance of $25,000 a week, to be doled out from customs receipts. Writing privately a few days earlier to his friend, Admiral Benson, in Washington, Caperton commented,

> These are the most deceitful graft seekers on earth and I really believe at times that the President's cabinet are all against him but they see that we are here for keeps and that we mean business, so they dare not do too much in opposition . . . The House of Delegates [sic] are with the President because he convoked an extraordinary session of two months, meaning $600 gold apiece to each of these gentlemen. The Senate got nothing extra, therefore they are on the fence.

- Now, in any case, it was the Senate's turn to stall, and, as opposition stiffened, the Americans became increasingly apprehensive that ratification might fail. As Caperton explained to Benson on 26 October, "Many Haitians who privately express themselves as being in favor of the treaty have publicly opposed it for political reasons."

Captain Beach was even ordered back from the bedside of his dying wife and set to work lobbying the Haitian politicians he now knew so well.(12) Despite Beach's tact and address, he made little headway. The opposition, he said, resulted from Dartiguenave's inability to bestow office or patronage and from the politicians' mounting resentment at being denied access to the public purse. Confirming Beach's diagnosis and heightening U.S. alarm, the Senate Foreign Relations Committee on 5 November adversely reported the treaty and, vain hope, urged that a new treaty be negotiated from the ground up.

. Now it was 11 November; time had run out. Flanked by Beach and Oberlin (Bailly-Blanchard, though in Port-au-Prince, had not yet presented credentials and does not seem to have been missed), the admiral went to the palace. What Caperton told Dartiguenave and his cabinet was simple. Treaty or no treaty, the United States intended to retain control over Haiti, pacifying the country to whatever extent might be needed and meting out to "those offering opposition" (a phrase clearly embracing senators) the treatment their conduct merited. This time there was no velvet glove.

- The Senate was sitting when word of Caperton's ultimatum arrived. At 5:50 P.M., after passionate oratorical fireworks led by Louis-Edouard Pouget of the opposition, the senators duly ratified the treaty 27 to 6.

One step remained - negotiation of a modus vivendi or stopgap working arrangement whereby the treaty could be immediately effectuated without waiting for American ratification. Here was a final opportunity for delay, and Louis Borno made the most of it. For nearly three weeks the Foreign Minister rejected various American drafts, until Paymaster Conard suggested a simple formulation which all parties accepted. Bailly-Blanchard ("using the stub of a lead pencil," Beach recalled) took down Conard's wording, and ultimately received Lansing's compliments for his negotiating and drafting. The date was 29 November 1915: now the United States was in Haiti to stay, and the Haitians knew it.(13)

Watching from the sidelines, Girard had musingly reported to Foreign Minister Théophile Delcasse in Paris the advent of *"Le Maître Blanc* whose very shadow can so readily madden these simple hearts . . . Then, peering ahead, the minister added, "In order to realize its programs, the United States may well have to undertake a campaign throughout the interior which will exceed anticipations and present difficulties."

Even as Girard wrote. reports coming in from the North depicted armed and quite unsubdued *Cacos* throughout those forbidding mountains Sonthonax had called "boulevards of liberty." At the mouth of the Artibonite, from Gonaïves to St. Marc, still other bands of irreconcilable *noirs* were coalescing to oppose the *blancs* and their *mulâtre* president from the South.

Not long before, twelve leading men among the elite were convoked by eminent lawyer Maître Georges Sylvain to hear an eloquent speech against American intervention. They then formed a committee - the *Union Patriotique* - that was to spearhead the adamant resistance of that class which until this moment had so confidently looked to each incumbent government for sustenance.

It was ironic, a contradiction never to be resolved, that the very interests, aspirations, and injuries that sparked the resistance of the elite to U.S. occupation were at the same time wholly adverse to, and bound to estrange them from, the mass of downtrodden *noir* fellow countrymen.

They Will Not Disarm

Resistance to Dartiguenave did not initially materialize in his native South. In the North, Northwest, and the Artibonite it was decidedly otherwise.

As early as 8 August, Livingston reported Bobo and Zamorist *Cacos* pillaging towns, burning plantations and murdering peasants. "It is not believed," he added gloomily, "they will disarm."

To safeguard the Cap, Caperton had kept a gunboat there from the beginning and, as soon as the *Connecticut* came down, in mid-August, the admiral sent the cruiser North with a Marine battalion under Colonel Cole, now Waller's second-in-command.

Cole's mission was to ensure the security of the Cap and pacify as much of the hinterland as his forces permitted. To accomplish this, the American plan was to demobilize *Cacos* willing to be bought in (100 *gourdes* for leader and weapon; 15 *gourdes* for ordinary *Caco* and weapon) and subdue whatever *Cacos* remained in the field. Neither objective could be realized until the Dominican frontier was sealed off, to deny sanctuary and arms from over the border.

Gonaïves was the first trouble spot. Beginning a blockade in September, Rameau cut the town water supply and then laid siege with 400 *Cacos*.

A Marine company led by Major Smedley D. Butler was moved to Gonaïves by gunboat with orders to lift the siege, reopen the water supply, and get trains running down the railroad from Ennery to ensure delivery of food. After an initial clash before dusk on 20 September, Butler's people caught up with Rameau and 500 *Cacos* at Poteaux. Rameau was glad enough to parley. Denying responsibility for anti-American fomentation with the truthful statement that he couldn't even read the handbills printed up over his name, he promised to behave and wistfully asked if he might not be given a portfolio in the new government. Alas, like his hopes, Rameau's promises were written in water. Five days later he led the *Cacos* in another foray, which proved to be his last: Butler and "Sunny Jim" Vandegrift, a blue-eyed lieutenant, caught him up the railroad, and, when the *Cacos* again surrendered, Rameau ("a sour-looking, vicious little devil," Butler later described him) was sent South for a sojourn at the newly rehabilitated prison.(14)

"Rameau has been completely subdued," Caperton wrote Benson. "We need to give the *Cacos* around Cap Haïtien a little of the same medicine.

That same day when Smedley Butler yanked Rameau off his horse outside Poteaux, and thus ended *Caco* depredations in the Lower Artibonite, was a bad one for Americans in the North. The situation there was later described by Colonel Waller: "They were stopping all food going to Cap Haïtien; they cut off the water supply, and were levying taxes on all market people and the business of the country without authority and were treating them brutally."

To break this siege, Colonel Cole promptly pushed out patrols. On 26 September, a Marine platoon was caught by *Cacos* at the Haut-du-Cap, and, when a second patrol and support from the Cap came to the rescue, these latter were attacked as well. Colonel Cole headed for the scene with the rest of his battalion. The *Cacos*, wearing red scarves of *Ogun*, banged away as if the French were coming. After killing two Marines, the *Cacos* retired to their base at Quartier Morin.

Next day, when Cole hiked a column from the Cap to Quartier Morin, the *Cacos* melted away. Only women seemed to be in the town, as well as a Dr. Fouché, claiming to be the *Cacos*' surgeon general, who, in Cole's account, "said the war was over; that they wanted to be good . . . that the day before had been a very severe lesson to them, and they realized it would not pay to attack us again." Those *Cacos* had indeed learned their lesson,(15) but other lessons remained to be taught. *Caco* bands were continuing depredations from sanctuaries located deep in the mountains, of which word gradually began to reach Colonel Waller, who had now determined to give the North his personal attention.

To close the gateway of the border, Ouanaminthe, Waller paid off and demobilized the ragged Haitian garrison (the majority of whom at the pay table claimed rank of *général de brigade* and were so paid), and installed a Marine company. This sealed the border. Next, Waller stationed a company at Grande Rivière du Nord and one at Fort Liberté, comprising, with nearly deserted Ouanaminthe, a triangle of key towns garrisoned between the Cap and Santo Domingo, and each place a base for intensive patrolling throughout the Plaine du Nord and into the mountains. "My idea," Waller said, "was to round up these people if possible in the mountains of the North and to find out exactly where their headquarters were. There were certain forts that . . . were used as points of incubation for these revolutions . . . It was very difficult to find out the exact location of these, so I ordered a reconnaissance made, which covered somewhere between 300 and 500 miles around. "

Major Butler was put in charge of a forty-man patrol with the mission of finding the *Caco* strongholds. Butler's route was traversed some of the most forbidding terrain in Haiti and much of it unvisited by any foreigner since the French. In describing the country, Butler later, and accurately, used the eighteenth-century simile, "Haiti looks like a crumpled-up piece of paper."

On the afternoon of 24 October, led by a Haitian guide, Butler at last came in sight of Fort Capois, seven miles South of St. Suzanne, reputedly the main *Caco* base. It was, Butler later said, "a mountain-peak about a mile away, towering 1000 feet above us. The cone-shaped peak was circled with rough stone walls and trenches. Every detail was outlined distinctly in the afternoon sunlight. Through my field glasses I saw men crawling over the ramparts."

This was a lot more than 40 men could handle, and Butler commenced what he hoped would be an unopposed withdrawal on Grande Rivière to the Northwest. It was not to be. After dark had fallen, a blast of rifle fire ripped out from the bush. Some 400 *Cacos* from Fort Capois and nearby Fort Dipitié, a lesser stronghold three miles East, had closed in. All night the Marines were surrounded and under steady fire.

When day broke, Butler attacked with everything he had. The *Cacos* retreated. Butler then returned to Grande Rivière and reported his adventures and findings to Colonel Waller, who now prepared to execute his general plan.

Starting on 1 November, the Marines began a Westward sweep - away from the Dominican frontier and toward the gorges of the Grande Rivière and the rail line South to Bahon - in small columns knifing systematically through *Caco* country. The main strongholds, virtually all of them ancient French forts comprising part of du Rouvray's Cordon of the West, were reduced one by one. As the Marines pushed in, *Cacos* abandoned Fort Selon, looking down the throat of Grande Rivière, then Fort Capois and Fort Berthol. And so, by mid-

November, the final remaining *Caco* citadel was Fort Rivière. "It was an old bastion fort," Smedley Butler related, "with thick walls of brick and stone, built in the latter part of the eighteenth century during the French occupation . . . on the peak of Montagne Noire, 4000 feet above the sea, midway between Grand Rivière, Dondon, San Rafael [sic] and Bahon. On three sides the masonry of the wall joined the rock of the mountain, thus forming a steep precipice into the valley. On the fourth side, a gentle slope led to the sally port."

Fort Rivière had already been located by a reconnaissance sent out by Colonel Cole, who entrusted the job to Major Butler. During the night of 17 November, three Marine companies converged on Fort Rivière over three trails and began the all-night climb to the crest of Montagne Noire. At daybreak the attackers had pushed in *Caco* outposts and were in position around the fort. On a whistle signal from Butler the assault commenced. To their consternation, on reaching the dead space under the walls, the twenty-four men in the storming party, led by Major Butler and two lieutenants, found the sally port bricked up. The *Caco* entrance was a slippery masonry drain four feet high, three feet wide, and fifteen feet long. Just inside, a *Caco* sentry was shooting at all and sundry.

Three Marines, including Major Butler, scrambled up as the *Caco* pumped shots down the tunnel. Miraculously, they reached the other end unscathed. Iams, Gross and Butler tumbled out as some seventy *Cacos* rushed them. Covered by the three Marines fighting hand-to-hand at the tunnel mouth, the remainder of the storming party scrambled into Fort Rivière. The *cacos* fought with machetes, sticks, and stones. General Josephette, the *Caco* leader, perhaps a devotee of *Baron Samedi*, was killed in his habitual garb - black frock coat, plug hat, and brass watch chain. Within a quarter hour, fifty *Cacos* lay dead in Fort Rivière, and the *Caco* movement in the North was dead with them. A ton of dynamite subsequently demolished the fort.

Trying to calm a Washington worried about the appearances of such exercises, the admiral wrote Benson on 21 November that *Cacos* were:

> ...bandits alike against the Haitian peasantry and Haitian government, simple ignorant people led by vicious chiefs . ... They do not pretend they are fighting for their country. They are fighting for revenue only, The *Caco* chiefs, assembled and individually, have made extensive demands on me and the Haitian government for money, agreeing to give up fighting if they are paid large amounts... The peasantry are beginning to till their fields and begging us for protection against the *Cacos* and are plucking up spirit on their own account. (16)

Caperton was not entirely off the mark. One of the bitterest opponents of the Americans, old Antoine Simon's political factotum, Pierre-Paul, in retrospect wrote, "[The *Cacos*] made a veritable industry out of insurrection and guerrilla war, creating and demolishing government after ephemeral government: government of nine months, of five months, and even of three months. The vandalism they made reign throughout our towns and countryside provided the pretext for the Yankee imperialists of 1915."

Pierre-Paul disapproved of *Caco* insurrections, but, as would become evident with the new year, he entertained no such qualms about uprisings by or on behalf of the elite against what one of them characterized as *"cet gros cochon d'Anse-à-Veau"* (that fat pig from Anse-à-Veau).

The occupation, wrote Déjean de la Batie, was by now bitterly opposed "by a hundred or so influential families who have lived on graft and for whom every revolution has presented a golden opportunity to fish in troubled waters."

Although these people had returned to authority through the installation of an elite president, they had, as they saw it, derived little or no power and none of the pecuniary gain to have been expected from the change.

Down in Les Cayes, where rich old Antoine Simon still held sway and Célestina unforgivingly remembered her fake pearls, the feelings of Port-au-Prince found support.

During the night of 4-5 January 1916, the darkness of the capital was shattered by what the French minister described as a *"vive fusillade"* directed against the casernes and the palace. Men dashed about the streets, crying, *"Vivent les Cacos!"* Marine sentries returned fire sparingly when they could make out targets, killing or wounding five men at various points before the uproar ceased and the assailants scattered.

What had taken place (later to be dubbed the "Pierre-Paul Revolution") was an *attentat* of the kind Salnave, Salomon, and Hyppolite had in their day so mercilessly crushed. Antoine Pierre-Paul, almost certainly financed by German merchants as well as by Antoine Simon, had gathered together a stock of arms, hired some *Cacos* and town riffraff with Mizaël Codio as general, and launched a night attack. Pierre-Paul apparently hoped somehow to seize the *Palais*, upset the regime and the Americans, and install Pauléus Sannon as president. The plot failed entirely. Codio, who the French minister said had been given 30,000 *gourdes* in expense money and had pocketed most, was pursued, eventually caught, and locked up. Pierre-Paul got away but later sought amnesty, which Colonel Waller granted with the unkind observation that Pierre-Paul was "politically dead" anyway.(17)

The affair that seemed so trivial in American eyes involved an extensive and typical conspiracy among the *noir* elite of the South running back to a former president and an ex-Minister (Sannon), both with long histories of such involvements in or based on Les Cayes. More acute than the Americans, the French minister, de la Batie, reported the affair thoughtfully, remarking that the "amenity and tact" of Caperton and Beach in dealing with Haitian sensibilities "will be taken for weakness by a people who from top to bottom respect only force . . "

Then, to underscore what he perceived as profound Haitian misreading of the situation, the minister quoted a contemptuous judgment on the Americans by no less than J.-N. Léger: "Believe me," Léger had told him in deep confidence, "two or three more outbreaks like this and they will leave. I was minister in Washington for a long time, and I know them: they are nothing but capons!"(18)

A Confused State of Affairs

American authority now had been established, *de jure* by treaty, *de facto* by the Marines. How the occupation would pursue its work and what it would accomplish remained to be seen. Also yet to be seen was how far Dartiguenave could serve two masters, between whom lay irreconcilable differences, the American authorities and his elite constituency.

The president was not alone in his dilemmas. Confronted by a unique task, largely if not entirely self-assumed, the American government still seemed unaware that Haiti posed no ordinary problems and that, to be well done, the work ahead - part military, part administrative, part diplomatic, part economic - would require some special organization in Washington - functionally, but never in name, a colonial office and, viceroy save in title, some single U.S. authority in Port-au-Prince. Instead, the State Department preferred to let the navy some- how carry on, while Josephus Daniels (who philosophically disliked the whole business) was well content to keep hands off as long as Marines kept the lid on.

Of the five "treaty services" provided for - Financial Adviser, Customs Receivership, Public Works, Public Health, and *Gendarmerie* the last came first. Public order has always been the crying need of Haiti, and 1915 was scarcely an exception.

Piecemeal demobilization of the army had commenced as the Marines landed. Concomitant organization and training of the *Gendarmerie* began in September 1915. The old army was forthwith disbanded and, on 1 February 1916, the new *Gendarmerie d'Haïti*, expanded to 1500, took over police responsibilities for the entire country. As a cadre of leaders, French-speaking Marine and naval officers were assigned to senior posts with *Gendarmerie* rank, while Marine NCOs and navy hospital corpsmen became junior officers. The first commandant of the *Ge- ndarmerie* was Major Butler, who for his new post was commissioned *général de division* by Dartiguenave. In Butler's later words, "That made me chief of police."

There was no difficulty getting recruits; many were ex-*Cacos*. Pay, promptly and fully paid, and decent rations sufficed to attract what Butler rated as "the best men in the country." Surplus Marine gear and old-model Krag rifles and carbines equipped them. From June 1916 on, when the *Gendarmerie* numbered

2553, with 115 American officers, the latter were seconded to the service of Haiti, bore Haitian rank, and, in addition to American pay, drew modest stipends from the *Banque*, an arrangement that in the long run ensured competition and thus selectivity for *Gendarmerie* assignment among the better officers and NCOs.

Pending organization of the other treaty services, the Marine and naval officers assigned to the *Gendarmerie* simply pitched in. Navy doctors set to work under conditions truly Augean: beggars afflicted with leprosy, elephantiasis, and open sores thronged the streets; 95 percent of the recruits selected for the *Gendarmerie* proved on examination to have malaria, yaws, or syphilis, and 85 percent had intestinal parasites. When Surgeon Garrison, the senior medical officer, looked for the daily allocation of ice (300 pounds) required by concession to be furnished the Port-au-Prince hospital, it turned out that the ice-plant manager was delivering it to the National Palace and residences of the cabinet.

The first financial adviser, Addison T. Ruan, an experienced U.S. civil servant, opened shop in Port-au-Prince on 9 July 1916. Almost immediately he came into conflict with Finance Minister Emile Elie: as in marriage, some of the bitterest differences arose over money. Not until 1918 did Ruan, at the cost of his own further usefulness, finally establish complete fiscal control.

By the end of August 1916, the naval paymasters were replaced at their customs houses by civilians under the receiver general, A. J. Maumus. Administering Haitian tariffs dating from 1872 proved not least among many difficulties; it would be 1926 before an up-to-date tariff could be enacted.

Public Works, had been by January 1917 turned over to a U.S. Navy civil engineer officer. Despite crying needs, his department was neither properly funded nor manned for three years to come. Meanwhile, using rough-and-ready expedients, including a revival of Geffrard's *corvée,* Marine district and subdistrict *Gendarmerie* commanders began the enormous job of creating roads, bridges, water supply, telegraph lines, and village markets - in short, a national infrastructure - where only ruins had lain. Of these young Marines, many of them corporals or sergeants or, in higher posts, captains or majors at most, an American civilian wrote in 1919:

> The Marine who becomes an officer in the *Gendarmerie* finds himself clothed with practically unlimited power in the district where he serves. He is the judge of practically all civil and criminal cases...He is paymaster for all funds expended by the national government, he is ex-officio director of the schools, inasmuch as he pays the teachers. He controls the mayor and city council [sic], since they can spend no funds without his o.k. As collector of taxes he exercises a strong influence on all individuals in the community.

Atop these activities and agencies, loosely coordinated at best, whether by Washington or Port-au-Prince, and occasionally at odds among themselves, were the Marine brigade commander and, paragon of ineffectuality, Minister Bailly-Blanchard. In the circumstances, what central authority existed therefore emanated from the brigade. Little wonder that American intervention soon began to be called "Marine occupation."

A disappointing consequence as well as example of the haphazard way in which the United States seemed to be exercising its responsibilities was the inability to organize the foreign loan that Haiti needed so badly to get its house in order and whose prospect had buoyed the hopes of those who looked to the United States for better times.

One of paymaster Conard's early projects, picked up and pursued in 1916 by Ruan,(19) had been to refund and consolidate, though not precisely in the style of Simon Sam and friends, Haiti's outstanding French debt from 1875, 1896, and 1910. The face value was about $23.3 million, but due to wartime weakness of the franc as well as the substantial discount quoted on Haitian obligations in the Bourse, it was purchasable for about $16 million. To buy in these bonds, redeem internal debt, resume service on the external debt (which had lapsed since 1914), and scrape up capital for urgently needed reconstruction, Conard and Ruan estimated that a U.S. loan of $30 million was needed. Alas, despite fair words of encouragement, and despite extension in 1917 of the Haitian-American Treaty until 3 May 1936 (a concession to assure bondholders the United States would stand behind their investment), Washington did not get everything together until 1922. This failure - partly owing to market conditions unfavorable to such a loan -embittered Haitians and their government toward the United States. Seven years after the Marines first landed, when the loan ulti-mately did materialize, seemed rather a long wait.

The central problem for the occupation was administrative: treaty service officials, independent functionaries, were acting in response to three different executive departments in Washington and, intermittently, the White House. Moreover, as Dr. Arthur Millspaugh, himself financial adviser in later years, pointed out, between 1915 and 1922 Haiti came under four senior naval officers, six Marine brigade commanders, four *Gendarmerie* commandants, and two financial advisers, not counting Conard.

At the Department of State, affairs were no better: the Latin American Division, with Haiti its responsibility, had during the same period six different chiefs or acting chiefs. "In general," Millspaugh fairly concluded, "a more confused, disorganized and unsatisfactory state of affairs could hardly be conceived."

Nevertheless, the occupation muddled ahead. As early as March 1916, for example, the highway from the Cap to Ouanaminthe had been rebuilt:

I know you would have enjoyed seeing the Catholic Bishop of Cape [sic] Haïtien. the American Minister and myself [Caperton wrote Benson] enter Ouanaminthe in a "Ford's" automobile. We made the distance of about 16 1/2 miles from Fort Liberté to Ouanaminthe in one hour and 50 minutes. As we neared the town, church bells began to ring and the people flocked to the main streets . . . There are now 1200 or more people in Ouanaminthe, whereas a few months ago, when we took possession, there were only nine.

Only two months later, de la Batie, the French minister, likewise noted progress. "The peasants, the pure *noirs* "he wrote, "are, like the tradesmen in the towns, delighted with the American occupation."

Dissolution and Dictation

The role of Haitian legislative bodies from the days of Pétion down has been a spoiling one, and Dartiguenave's was no exception. The legislature had become the rallying point for a disaffected elite. Revolution or coup, the traditional expedients of such factions, were, as Antoine Pierre-Paul could explain, out of the question. On the other hand, Dartiguenave no longer enjoyed access to equally traditional countermeasures that had been available in comparable situations to a Salomon, Hyppolite, or Soulouque.

Going privately to Caperton in February 1916, Dartiguenave and Borno explained their difficulties, which, they rightly pointed out, were exacerbated by American insistence on eliminating graft, reducing palace patronage, stopping double or triple pensions to single individuals, and ending fraud and kickbacks on government contracts. Fearful that a malcontent Senate might vote to impeach, Dartiguenave asked advance assurance that he would be supported if he dissolved one or both houses, and went for a new constitution to supersede that of 1889, still fitfully in effect. For the moment, his interest and that of the occupation exactly coincided: a new set of rules was what each needed - Dartiguenave to stifle opposition, the Americans, inter alia, to end the long-cherished (though often hotly argued) Dessalinian prohibition against foreign ownership of land and property.(20) Knowing Washington's mind, the admiral nodded.

On 5 April 1916 - it was Dartiguenave's initiative and contrivance, but Caperton did nothing to dissuade him - the president dissolved the Senate and locked the senators out of their Chamber, designated the *députés* a Constituent Assembly to rewrite the constitution, and convoked a hand-picked twenty-one-man Council of State (in reality an appointive Senate) to deliberate and advise the president.(21)

Now ensued a season of impasse, marked by impassioned rump meetings in private homes, by an attempt on the part of Légitime to conciliate, and, finally, by the *députés* simply sitting on their hands rather than going to work on the new constitution. On 22 September, at a dead end, Dartiguenave announced general elections for 15 January of the new year, and (according to Dr. Dorsainvil) set Edmond Héraux to drafting a constitution.(22)

Following a carefully supervised election unlike any in Haiti's past - *gendarmes* had to leave weapons in barracks and appear unarmed at the polls as ordinary citizens, while some districts in the North tried to elect Marines as their deputies - a new assembly came into being and convened on 21 April 1917. Its first order of business was the constitution.

The significant emendations in Dr. Héraux's draft that came back from Washington eliminated bars to foreign property-ownership; removed long-standing antiforeign discriminatory provisions so as to afford aliens equal protection of the laws; and - of overriding importance, based on American experience in Cuba - called for constitutional ratification of all acts taken by U.S. occupation authorities. In characteristically Machiavellian fashion, Dartiguenave, while assuring the Americans that he fully supported these changes, "deliberately spilled the beans" (the phrase was that of Cole, who had relieved Waller as brigade commander) to the National Assembly. Testifying in 1921, Cole went on: "[Dartiguenave] took this whole correspondence and sent it without comment, practically, to the national assembly. In other words, saying, 'Here is not our recommendation, but here is what practically amounts to dictation from the United States. Now, see what you can do with it.' There is not any question in my mind but what that was done with absolute malice aforethought, and it certainly did raise a rumpus."

As might be expected, the assembly bristled at the American suggestions" while Dartiguenave, covertly pouring gasoline on the flames, simultaneously insinuated to Cole that the problem could be solved readily enough if only the Americans would dissolve the assembly, a solution that would precisely suit his own political ends while placing its onus squarely on the *blancs*. General Cole's contemporary report (17 May 1917) says just that: "President Dartiguenave is not popular; he is and always has been . . . a consummate politician who is trying to stand well with both sides . . . He is trying to force the National Assembly into an attitude of opposition to the wishes of the American government in hopes that we will suppress the assembly."

During May, as this game was being played out, the assembly, led by its president, Sténio Vincent, backed in turn by Pradel, Sannon, Pouget, and Georges Léger (the brilliant young lawyer-son of old J.-N.), began writing a constitution of its own.

Cole's rejoinder to Dartiguenave was short: if the president wished to prorogue the assembly, he had ample power to do so; if, however, the Americans were forced to any such action in their own right, it would be not only the assembly that was suppressed this time, but with it the Dartiguenave presidency. Was full-scale U.S. military government what Haiti, let alone Dartiguenave, wanted?

Now the president was cornered. Deferring action on the Héraux draft, Vincent and his colleagues were rapidly enacting their own constitution, article by article, with Dartiguenave's own brother voting along with them.

On 16 June the president called in Cole for one last attempt to persuade the Americans to act. Cole was adamant, at least to Dartiguenave, but he thereupon confidentially radioed Washington:

UNLESS CONTRARY INSTRUCTIONS RECEIVED, IF NECESSARY TO PREVENT PASSAGE PROPOSED CONSTITUTION, I INTEND DISSOLVE NATIONAL ASSEMBLY, THROUGH PRESIDENT IF POSSIBLE; OTHERWISE DIRECT.

The Secretary of the Navy's reply (it was 18 June, and the assembly was half through its work) made clear that Josephus Daniels, as slippery a politician as Dartiguenave, was quite prepared to leave decision, action, and, above all, responsibility to the Marines:

DEPARTMENT VESTS YOU WITH FULL DISCRETIONARY POWER. ENDEAVOR TO ACCOMPLISH END DESIRED WITHOUT USE OF MILITARY FORCE. ACKNOWLEDGE.

Cole then drew up a proclamation in his Naval Academy French, carefully locking it in the brigade safe and, keeping this fact to himself, asked Dartiguenave whether he intended to proceed. The president ("He is willing to promise anything," Cole had previously commented) said he would.

Next morning, the 19th, when no decree was forthcoming, word reached Cole that the assembly, well aware that the climax was at hand, had shouted Charles Zamor off the floor when he tried to caution moderation, and was at that moment passing articles by batches and skipping others in order to complete the three required readings. Cole sent for Major Butler and ordered him to go to the palace and find out what had happened and whether the decree had been signed. As he departed, an officer telephoned urgently: "They've passed three hundred and twenty out of the three hundred and sixty articles. They're shoving them through ten at a time. It will be all over in a half hour unless you do something at once."

Butler, as he vividly told the story to American senators, was greeted in the palace hall by an aide "in bright red trousers and poisonous green coat" with word that Dartiguenave was sick but that he had ordered the *Gendarmerie* to dissolve the assembly. Expressing solicitude over Dartiguenave's malaise, Butler entered the president's office. Then, in Butler's words,

> [Dartiguenave] said, "I want the Assembly dissolved." I said, "All right, sir, then you must write a decree. I cannot use the *Gendarmerie* for that purpose without your written order." He said, "I give you my order." He said he could not sign a decree without the presence of the members of the cabinet, but that the Assembly must be dissolved. I said, "Then secure the members of the cabinet and sign the decree." He said . . . the simplest way would be for me to go down with the military force and dissolve it. I positively refused to do it. He then went out and secured four of his five ministers . . . and the President and his four cabinet ministers signed it.

In his memoirs Butler added: "The signatures were so small that one needed a magnifying glass to read them."

Now, with no time to spare, came the next moment of truth: Who would deliver the decree? Héraux gloomily said the bearer might be shot. By common consent, urging his capacity as a Haitian officer, the politicians nominated Butler. When the Marine entered the Chamber he was greeted with agitation and prolonged jeers and hissing. Before Vincent would read the decree from the tribune, Butler went on, he delivered "a vicious assault upon me and all other Americans, referring to us as foreign dogs and devils dissolving the Assembly."

As Vincent neared peroration, the *gendarmes* (mostly ex-Haitian soldiers and no strangers to such scenes) began to load rifles. Tables and chairs were upset while members, equally conscious of past events, took cover as best they could. To the surprise of all, however, Butler ordered the *gendarmes* to unload, and, after restoring quiet with the speaker's traditional dinner bell, Vincent finally proceeded to publish Dartiguenave's decree and, livid with fury, stormed out of the Chamber, dropping the decree (which Butler promptly pocketed).(23)

So the deed was done. The National Assembly dispersed, and Dartiguenave, with his Council of State, reigned in its stead.

After these high doings, enactment of the American-sponsored Héraux constitution, which required a year's paperwork between Port-au-Prince and Washington, amounted to anticlimax. Although Franklin Roosevelt was later to claim parentage of the document, it mainly represented the handiwork of Ferdinand L. Mayer, American chargé during one of Bailly-Blanchard's absences, and of various State Department luminaries.(24) The problem of getting the constitution ratified without a National Assembly was solved by a device until then new to Haiti, a national plebiscite. This idea, Chargé Mayer told Washington, was Dartiguenave's and "strongly urged" on the occupation authorities by the president.

To expect peasants from the hills to be able to entertain opinions on a constitution was farcical. Although in form and intent the ensuing plebiscite (held on 12 June 1918) was narrowly "honest", it is equally a fact, as Colonel John H. Russell, brigade commander, admitted, that his forces were proconstitutional, and any Haitian who knew enough to vote also knew enough to vote the way the soldiers voted. The elite, deeply opposed, simply stayed at home.

Reporting results (98,225 for; 768 against), Russell wrote, "It is thought all government employees voted at least once for it." Russell added that there might have been confusion as to the object of the process: some voters, he said, believed they were electing a president; one thought he was voting for a Pope.

The joker in the constitution lay in Title VIII, Transitory Provisions, which in effect permitted the president, without benefit of legislature, to govern indefinitely through the Council of State. The first election for the two Chambers, wrote the framers, was to be held "on 10 January of an even-numbered year," leaving the president to decide which, if any, year it would be.

This provision was no chance oversight; it guaranteed Dartiguenave and his successor(s) dictatorial powers free of legislative spoiling as long as it suited the Americans. This constitutional flimflam, for such it was, nevertheless did not, despite howls of the *Union Patriotique* and its allies in the United States, represent suppression of rights or freedoms previously enjoyed. Except that the dictatorship was being enforced by *blancs,* it departed hardly at all from the way of things in Haiti. While, on the one hand, Déjean de la Batie had accurately forecast the new constitution as "a disguised military government," he had earlier gone even nearer the heart of the matter: "The self-styled Haitian democracy for which they all wear mourning has never really been anything but an oligarchy imposing upon a people, described as free, a tyranny as abominable as it has been degrading."

The Occupation Is Not As Popular

The policies pursued by Caperton and Beach, even in the most difficult moments, had been those of conciliation. Reporting this in early 1916, Minister Girard had observed: "What has definitely not escaped the Haitians is the "engaging style" in which the American military authorities have wooed their sympathies . . . Admiral Caperton accepts invitations to the Cercle Port-au-Princien... and flings small coins along the roadside when he drives to Pétionville."

Danache, Dartiguenave's familiar, who detested the occupation and described Americans as "gross, brutal, always ready with boot or fist," said Caperton and

Beach spoke very correct French and had good manners. The admiral, Danache went on, "was a handsome man for his age, straight as a lightning rod, who irresistibly gained your sympathy. He was an indefatigable dancer, like all the other naval officers. People said that, after a waltz, you could see the print of his buttons on the bosom of his partner . . .

Then, one day in 1916, recounted Danache, Caperton and Beach were gone, ". . . the tactic of American diplomacy, with its vast reservoir of people, being to deploy representatives of the most refined manners and spirit, or, according to the end in view, torturers without scruple."

When Danache spoke of "torturers without scruple," he was thinking of Colonel Waller and Major Butler.

On 10 May 1916, responding to a crisis in Santo Domingo, Admiral Caperton had to move next door, leaving Waller, the Marine brigade commander, as viceroy. Two months later, Caperton was advanced to command the Pacific Fleet and never saw Haiti again. Henceforth, the senior U.S. naval commander remained as military governor in Santo Domingo, exercising increasingly tenuous authority over Haitian matters.

If Caperton and Beach had been men of address and conciliation, Waller was a man of war. Not that he was a stereotype blockhead colonel: he was energetic, practical, quick-minded, resolute, and extremely firm. He was also a blunt, out-spoken fighting soldier and no diplomat. The very qualities that enabled Waller, seconded by Cole and Butler and the regulars of the brigade, to subdue the North and the Artibonite in three months carried built-in defects insofar as the nuances of occupation and the Byzantine ways of Port-au-Prince were concerned.

None of this had escaped Caperton. In his final letter to Benson (at least from Hispaniola), he confided: "I am not at all pleased with the manner [of] Colonel Waller . . . When I left Port-au-Prince . . . there existed the warmest cordiality and cooperation between the Occupation and the Haitian Government. Judging from my own observations, my conversations, and from what people have told me, the Occupation is not as popular as it was, and this fact is much regretted by the better class of people . . . "

Whether Caperton was deluding himself as to "the better class of people," who had after all been obstructing him and the occupation in every way they could since 1915, is beside the point. There had indeed been a change of tone, and, in the disillusioning climate of mid-1916 following Dartiguenave's dissolution of the Senate, a soured atmosphere was inevitable. Only a fortnight after Caperton voiced his apprehension to Benson, Waller cabled a differing assessment:

GOVERNMENT HAS FAILED IN ALL ITS SOLEMN PROMISES, DENIES
MAKING THEM ALTHOUGH THEY WERE REPEATED IN ENGLISH AND
FRENCH. BORNO CONTROLS AND DOMINATES THE CABINET. AFTER
MONTHS OF INTIMATE ASSOCIATION WITH THEM, IT IS MY DUTY TO
REPORT THAT THE GOVERNMENT IS INSINCERE, UNSTABLE AND MOST
UNPOPULAR.

Caperton and Waller were both right. Soon after Waller sent his storm signal
to Washington, de la Batie, in unknowing echo, described the Marine
commander as "so disgusted by Dartiguenave's duplicity he no longer will
accept his word on a decision and demands written engagements on each
promise."

As for Dartiguenave, the French minister went on, "In any other country such
measures would be fatal to a Chief of Government, but in Haiti anything is
possible."

Waller's lack of finesse particularly infuriated the Haitian politicians.
Danache, their tribune, could at times barely restrain himself. To him, Waller
was one "who had never known common politeness, courtesy, or respect for
people . . . Such a man, at home, was certainly a professional lyncher
[professionel du lynchage] of poor Negroes seduced into the American Army."

Then, to prove Waller's "brutality," Danache quotes from a private letter the
Marine may well have sent Dartiguenave:

Mr. President, you correspond with me in amenities, but I know you send your
minister in Washington unfavorable reports on me for transmission to the State
Department. Quite simply, that is what we call hypocrisy. Let me remind you that
you are President because the Americans are here. If you continue to undercut me,
I will recommend that we pull our troops out for just 24 hours; we wouldn't be out
of sight of La Gonâve before you were thrown out of the National Palace.(25)

Brutal, yes: especially in retranslation from Danache's impassioned French
(the original in English has never surfaced). But Waller's true brutality lay not
in language, but, more wounding, in the harsh reminder of realities.

As *Gendarmerie* commandant, Butler set much of the tone of early American
contacts with most Haitians. Butler's contempt for the elite was outspoken, while
his feelings for the *noir* masses, as expressed in 1921, were affectionate but
paternal:

The Haitian people are divided into two classes; one class wears shoes and the other
does not. The class that wears shoes is about one percent . . . Ninety-nine percent
of the people of Haiti are the most kindly, generous, hospitable, pleasure-loving
people I have ever known. They would not hurt anybody. They are most gentle
when in their natural state. When the other one percent that wears vici [sic] shoes

with long pointed toes and celluloid collars, stirs them up and incites them, they are capable of the most horrible atrocities . . . Those that wear shoes I took as a joke.

After Waller was promoted and returned home to higher command in December 1916, he was succeeded by Cole -"more amiable and more conciliatory than his predecessor", commented de la Batie, but Butler - like most Marines, increasingly restive about getting to France - remained until March 1918, training the *Gendarmerie* and directing an intensive road building effort that would be associated with his name and also, later, with grave abuses.

After Waller's time, Butler involved himself in Haitian politics, attempting, for example, to bring pressure on Dartiguenave by making deals with his opponents, such as Charles Zamor and J.-N. Léger. After watching these maneuvers in 1917, de la Batie commented mordantly: "This officer, who without doubt has splendid military qualities and who especially distinguished himself in China, has blundered by involving himself in politics . . . Naive, self-assured, exceedingly optimistic, not speaking French, he has been readily duped by the politicians . . . In the present situation, because of his amateurishness, Major Butler is a veritable menace!"

Had it not been for World War I, which drew Waller and Butler (and eventually Cole) out of Haiti, their tensions with the elite could well have led to some final rupture, perhaps bringing on outright U.S. military government.(26) Instead, in December 1917, Cole was relieved by Colonel John H. Russell, the quiet-spoken Georgian who, except for one brief interval, was destined in one capacity or another to direct the American occupation for the next thirteen years.

Dartiguenave Balks

Dartiguenave was now well established - "a bachelor beau," one American writer called him, attractive to "pretty women of various colors . . . faultlessly attired in frock coat, pin-striped trousers, pearl-gray spats and patent leathers, twirling his imperial waxed mustache with kid-gloved fingers . . ."

This aplomb was no accident and was in fact the outward and visible sign of a new assurance emanating from the *Palais National* after enactment of the 1918 constitution.

Whatever else the new constitution did or provided, it took Dartiguenave's opponents out of play and, in thus freeing him from domestic constraint, left him corresponding maneuver room to take on the Americans.

In the new cabinet he appointed (24 June 1918) were such men as Louis Borno (Finance and Foreign Affairs), Eugène Roy (Public Works) and Dantès Bellegarde (Education, Agriculture, and Cults), as well as other like-minded persons. The bulldog he intended to set upon the Americans was Borno.

To lead the Council of State Dartiguenave picked Légitime - "with a powerful head like that of an aged Roman senator in ebony," wrote W. B. Seabrook - seventy-five, but ever at Haiti's service.

The government's proclaimed objects were enhanced freedom of action and an end to surrenders to the occupation. The terrain of battle was that issue which meant all to the elite, financial control.

The financial conflict, somewhat papered over in the harmonious relationship between Ruan, the adviser, and Dr. Héraux, Borno's predecessor, arose from the Haitians' irreconcilable feelings that they had hardly any of the national revenues within their control, and, just as adamantly, the American advisers' conviction that any funds remaining at the disposition of the government would be spent in the old improper, corrupt fashion. Both parties were right.

What became a two-year struggle between the government and the Americans and extended in the end beyond finance to the ultimate question of blanket American control over Haitian law-making had three phases of conflict, each of which ended in greater power for the occupation.

The earliest "encroachments," as with some justice the Haitians called them, seemed elementary and necessary to the Americans: beginning in 1916, treaty advisers took power to hire and fire all Haitians in the *douanes;* to receive not only customs but internal revenues as well; and to work out the budget, allocate funds between government and treaty services, and control expenditures by both. Then, on the heels of the 1918 constitution, Bailly-Blanchard, as instructed, extracted the further concession, on 24 August 1918, that "any project of law bearing upon any of the objects of the treaty, before being presented to the legislature, shall be communicated to the representative of the United States for the information of this Government and, if necessary, for discussion between the two Governments."

Soon after, in October 1918, frustrated by unchecked irregularities in the Finance Ministry, Ruan ("a pretentious, empty-headed megalomaniac," according to Danache) called on the *Conseil* to pass a law forbidding the Minister (that is, Borno) to approve any voucher without the adviser's "visa." Borno gagged; the *Conseil* stalled; worse still, when Ruan presented the new budget the *Conseil* rejected it and challenged the adviser's right to control expenditures at all. Now the fat was in the fire; without a budget the treaty services would, legally speaking at least, be without funds. Backed by his sword, Colonel Russell's pen gave prompt answer: on 13 November, the brigade commander simply directed the *Banque* to make no disbursements except by his order. Within the week, to make his point plain, Russell, with Bailly-Blanchard in tow, called on Dartiguenave to demand Borno's head. On 24 November, the Finance Minister resigned. Nine days later, the government gave up the game and conceded final authority of the financial adviser's visa on all payments.

During the month's deadlock not a *gourde* moved into the government's pocket. At the height of the clash, still vigorously protesting from the Washington legation, Solon Ménos dropped dead. The U.S. Navy returned his body to Haiti in pomp aboard a cruiser, but not a penny would Ruan authorize for his undertaker's bills or the travel vouchers of his children and widow - a circumstance not eased by outspoken pro-German attitudes of Mme. Ménos, daughter of one of the leading Haitian-German families. When Henri Chauvet, fiery editor of *Le Nouvelliste,* hopefully printed the *telediol* that Ruan had been disavowed and recalled (he had in fact resigned to take a similar post in Panama), he was waited upon by a file of *gendarmes,* marched off to provost court, fined $300, and locked up for three months. And *Le Nouvelliste* was shut down for the same term.

Ruan left for Panama in early 1919, and government paychecks again circulated. Ruan's successor arrived in March. Louisiana politician and Tabasco scion, wealthy intimate of Franklin Roosevelt, and a former U.S. Civil Service Commissioner, non-French-speaking John A. McIlhenny had only limited experience for a most demanding and sensitive post.

The new financial adviser was not, however, entirely new to Haiti. He had first come to the country in 1917 as Roosevelt's traveling companion on an adventurous Marine-escorted tour through the back country, including a visit to Fort Rivière. Until late in 1922, as Hans Schmidt has disclosed, Roosevelt and McIlhenny were to have their heads together on a scheme to set up a Haitian-American trading and factoring corporation tied in with development of plantations to be acquired as a result of foreign-ownership openings in the 1918 constitution. No evidence was to appear that either partner acted, let alone profited, improperly; but it is surprising to find an Assistant Secretary of the Navy, expressly charged with Haitian responsibilities of his department, collaborating with the incumbent U.S. financial adviser to promote plans (which to be sure never materialized) to make money out of Haiti.

When McIlhenny reached Port-au-Prince he was cordially received by Dartiguenave, who vouchsafed heart-warming assurance of forthcoming cooperation and receptivity to American advice. But euphoria dissipated as McIlhenny learned that, no sooner had he left the palace, Justin Barau, the Foreign Minister, pointedly notified both the Washington legation and Bailly-Blanchard that Dartiguenave had spoken only as an individual, not as president, and that his fair words were of no effect.

As 1920 began, the new financial adviser found himself locked in a three-sided wrangle with the *Banque,* foreign banks and mercantile houses, and the government (supported at points by the British, French, and Italian legations) over American proposals for foreign-exchange controls designed to preclude that time-honored speculation in *gourdes* which had enriched so many private parties at the expense of Haiti.

For the same reasons and in the same fashion, just as he had resisted Conard's similar steps to end currency speculation, Dartiguenave dragged his feet. In July 1920, McIlhenny thereupon simply pigeonholed the pending budget. A month later, when the government still balked, McIlhenny put the unsigned pay vouchers of the president, cabinet, and *Conseil d'Etat* in his pending basket and awaited developments.

The reason for the adviser's drastic action (which, although undertaken, according to Sumner Welles, on the basis of "certain oral and confidential instructions" by Lansing, had jolted the State Department) in fact had less to do with currency reform than with Dartiguenave's recent backsliding. Most particularly, he had initiated the enactment of objectionable laws without the laying-on of hands by the American minister, and sometimes even in the face of the latter's disapproval. Eleven such measures (including provocative limitations on foreign land-ownership) had found their way to the statute books in 1920. Not for three months, and not until all eleven laws had been rescinded or amended and four desired ones enacted, did the paychecks leave the pending basket and the president of Haiti again draw his own salary.

Even so, Dartiguenave successfully resisted the foreign-exchange curbs that had started the row. In vain, McIlhenny stalled two further annual budgets on the issue; the State Department bureaucracy, not as tough-minded as Lansing, deprived him of his one effective weapon, the paycheck embargo. And the adviser's influence was waning: justifying his absence by the difficulties of consummating the 1922 loan, McIlhenny left his seat in Haiti. Following over eighteen months in Washington without returning to his post, on 11 October 1922, he finally resigned.

What Dartiguenave gained seems hard to see. His 1918 campaign to bring the *blancs* to terms had provoked a disastrous response: American veto, nowhere intimated in treaty or constitution, over all actions by the government of Haiti. Henceforth the occupation would initiate and disapprove legislation, would at convenience treat as invalid pre-occupation laws of Haiti, and would enforce these prerogatives with the power of the purse or, at the stern heart of the matter, in the provost courts.

Corvée and *Cacos*

Back in 1916, when occupation authorities began to think about roads and economic development, and also of routes of penetration into *Caco* fastnesses, a cabinet minister showed the Americans a copy of the Code Rural in which, slumbering since 1863, Geffrard's *corvée* lay ready at hand:

Public highways and communications will be maintained and repaired by the inhabitants, in rotation, in each section through which roads pass, and each time repairs are needed.

Application and enforcement of this law were specifically assigned by the code to the police. Here, obviously, was one pre-occupation statute Smedley Butler was prepared to enforce. Commencing in July 1916, a nationwide *corvée* went quickly into effect: peasants nominated by *magistrats communaux* and *chefs de section* were notified by *gendarmes* to pay a tax or report for three days' work. As Butler later testified, "Nobody had any money, so they reported for work." Going on, the Marine reflected, "I was well aware that this thing was capable of tremendous abuse, and had been abused by Haitians previously."

To offset the possibility of just such abuse, peasants on *corvée* were to be fed, sheltered, and, as work proceeded, diverted by *bamboches* (described by Americans as "Voodoo dances"). Moreover, as part of the continuing push to get Dartiguenave out of the National Palace and Port-au-Prince and into those numerous regions where no president had previously set foot, Butler did his best to rattle the Model T presidential touring car out every week to some *corvée*, where, sharing the rations of *poix-et-riz* and *taffia*, Dartiguenave would remind the *paysans* that they were doing this for Haiti and their own good, and not as forced labor for the *blancs*.

And so, for a time, it went.

In 1915 only 3 miles of road usable by automobiles existed outside the towns. When Butler left in March 1918 the *Gendarmerie*-operated *corvée* had built or rebuilt 470 miles of highway at a cost of $205 per mile, mostly for local cement for culverts and food for the workers. On 1 January 1918, a through route linking Port-au-Prince and the Cap (180 miles) was opened by Dartiguenave and Butler in the president's Ford, which covered the journey, including six stops for receptions, in fourteen hours. Another important route of penetration, from Port-au-Prince across the Cul-de-Sac and over Morne-à-Cabrit to Mirebalais and Lascahobas, was opened on 23 February 1918.

So popular were some *corvée* camps on the Gonaïves-Cap Haïtien road in 1917 that workers stayed on as long as a month and finally had to be sent home by *gendarmes*.

The weak link in the system was that Haitian officials (and Haitian *gendarmes* still imbued with old traditions of the press gang and military high-handedness) had a hand in it. *Magistrats* and *gendarmes* soon found they could fill their pockets by exempting those who could pay, while impressing those who could not. When the *blancs* gave each peasant an exemption card after his annual stint, the *chef de section* would tear it up under the bearer's eyes and send him back to work with a thwack of the *cocomacac*. By late 1918 (significantly, after the departure of Butler, who, whatever his faults, ran a taut ship) it was not unusual to see peasants roped up for *corvée* in some distant place like conscripts for the old army. Nor was it only peasants who had to serve. Even more unfair, or so it seemed, some city-dwelling man of education was occasionally caught in the net: in 1918, so recounted Bellegarde, still outraged twenty-three years later, a *gendarme* knocked on the door of Jean Price-Mars in Pétionville and took him away for three days'*corvée*.

Thus it came about that the *corvée,* despite its benefits, however firm its legality, whatever its indisputably Haitian origin - matters in any case beyond the understanding of a roped peasant and of the *gendarme* who clubbed him - became a source of widespread resentment. Worse still, it formed the basis of *telediol*: the *blancs* are come hither to restore slavery; the *corvée* is only the beginning.

Butler's successor as *Gendarmerie* commandant, Major A. S. Williams (who caught much blame for subsequent events) , put the matter concisely:

The results of this exploitation of labor were two: First it created in the minds of the peasants a dislike for the American occupation and its two instruments - the Marines and the *Gendarmerie* - and, second, imbued the native enlisted man with an entirely false conception of his relations with the civil population. As the *corvée* became more and more unpopular, more and more difficulty was experienced in obtaining men; and this difficulty caused the *gendarmes* to resort to methods which were often brutal but quite consistent with their training under Haitian officials. I soon realized that one of the great causes of American unpopularity among the Haitians was the *corvée.*

On 1 October 1918, Williams acted on his misgivings and abolished the *corvée*. It was already too late.

Charlemagne Masséna Péralte of Hinche, brother-in-law of Oreste Zamor and thus sworn foe of the *mulâtre* Dartiguenave, was a man large in spirit, pride, intelligence, and ambition; in short, a *gros nègre*.(27) In early 1918 he had been convicted of complicity in a midnight raid on *Gendarmerie* headquarters at Hinche (where a $12,000 payroll had just arrived), and, caught at Ouanaminthe before he could skip over the border, was sentenced to five years' hard labor in the civil prison at the Cap.

To borrow Dr. Bobo's phrase, Charlemagne Péralte was no "improvised person." Educated (a graduate of St. Louis de Gonzague), natty in dress, intimate of Cadet Jérémie, a general in the olden time, *commandant de la place* at Port-de-Paix in 1914 and before that at Léogane, Charlemagne was soon to describe himself, somewhat expansively perhaps, as "a young man of family, belonging to the high society of Haiti, a devotee of progress and of civilization."(28)

Charlemagne was therefore no mere Zamorist *Caco* nor yet the charismatic primitive legend has depicted, but an opponent of Dartiguenave and adherent and supporter of Dr. Bobo, who from exile in Kingston was watching affairs closely and keeping in regular touch with opponents of the regime and of the Americans.(29)

For such a man to be set to sweeping the gutters of the Cap under guard was too much. On 3 September 1918, just twenty-seven days before Williams ordered an end to the *corvée,* Charlemagne induced his *gendarme* guard to join him in flight into the mountains behind the Plaine du Nord. Here he quickly rallied Dr. Bobo's old *Cacos,* soon joined by Zamorist bands from Hinche, and, exploiting the general grievance of the *corvée,* proclaimed war "to drive the invaders into the sea and free Haiti."

What he did not proclaim, but most Haitians understood and the Americans hardly at all, was that he was also mounting a traditional rebellion of the North and the Artibonite to topple Southern Dartiguenave and make way for Rosalvo Bobo.

Charlemagne's initial moves were shrewdly directed against outlying posts manned by small detachments of the *Gendarmerie.* As the *gendarmes* were the visible symbols of the regime and also of the *corvée,* these attacks served common purposes of resistance, discrediting the occupation, and acquiring modern weapons.(30)

On the night of 17 October 1918, a hundred *Cacos* stole down on Hinche. But the *Gendarmerie* had been warned. As the *Cacos* swarmed in, each wearing the scarlet badge of *Ogun,* the defenders opened fire. In a half hour it was over and the *Cacos* routed, with thirty-five dead; two *gendarmes* were killed. Reporting this first engagement of the *Caco* Resistance Colonel Russell, in a rare moment of misjudgment, commented, "This affair has no political or military significance whatsoever, and repetition of such raids by bandits hidden away in the hills on the frontier may be expected for some time to come."

Charlemagne's next strike was more successful. Before dawn on 10 November sixty *Cacos* hit Maïssade, the next garrison Northwest of Hinche, routed the ten-man *Gendarmerie* detachment, and sacked the town.

For the next four months the pot boiled higher. More than twenty contacts with large *Caco* bands were made by the hard-pressed *Gendarmerie.* On sober second thought, Russell estimated that Charlemagne had some 5000 active adherents. He himself was controlling operations in the North. Benoît Batraville, a *Caco* bearing Charlemagne's brevet as "Chief Minister of the Revolution," kept things hot in the Upper Artibonite, where once, as chief of police in Mirebalais, he had surrendered office when the *Gendarmerie* took over. Benoît, moreover (though the Americans would not know it until later), was also an adherent of Dr. Bobo, from whom he, too, heard regularly.

On 16 March, Colonel Williams admitted that he had a full-scale rebellion on his hands and the *Gendarmerie* was out of its depth. Williams therefore requested that the Marine brigade be committed to the campaign.(31)

Colonel Russell responded with what he had. Six small Marine companies were deployed to the hot spots: two to Hinche, two to Lascahobas, one to Mirebalais, and one to St. Michel. Twenty-five percent of the brigade was required to be on the trail, patrolling around the clock. Colonel Frederic M. Wise, was ordered from the States in mid-1919 to supersede Williams. Besides help from the Marine units in Cuba came a more portentous reinforcement - Haiti's first airplanes (seven HS-2 seaplanes, based at Bizoton, and six World War I "Jenny" land planes), which debarked at Port-au-Prince on 31 March 1919 and were soon flying. (32)

During the months that followed, April through September 1919, Marines and *gendarmes* fought 131 actions, ranging from skirmishes to pitched battles. Once Charlemagne's camp was overrun; three weeks later, Benoît Batraville's horse was captured. But Charlemagne and Benoît rode higher than ever.

How high Charlemagne was riding comes through in a letter he wrote about this time to Brigadier General Catlin, who briefly commanded the Marines until, in July, the lung half shot away in France at Belleau Wood invalided him home.

After flaying the Dartiguenave government, with evident inside knowledge of ministerial peccadilloes, Charlemagne went on in high style to the *Gendarmerie*,

> One of the most important institutions in the country. It is vain to hope for any progress without an organization to ensure law and order . . . Unhappily, the *Gendarmerie* is made up of ex-convicts, jitney-drivers, former house boys, and men of no account. It is commanded not by American officers who surely would have learned discipline . . . but by Marines dubbed officers for this purpose, having no capacity to discipline that evil creation called the *Gendarmerie*.

Slavery was already re-established, Charlemagne continued, accompanied by the rape of young virgins; property was nowhere safe (33), revolt smoldered in the heart of every Haitian. Were only Dartiguenave brought low, said he, "Haitians would then unite with avid enthusiasm to support the better American element which has already won its laurels in Cuba, Puerto Rico, the Philippines, and the Isles of Hawaii."

Having thus aligned himself on the side of law and order, as protector of property, and as firm supporter of imperialism and Manifest Destiny, Charlemagne got around to Dr. Bobo, "a man who affirms himself the greatest and most sincere admirer in Haiti of the Americans; a man who alone is capable, with the generosity that is legendary, of offering us the safeguards that we seek [sic]."

Catlin preferred to let the issues raised by Charlemagne be settled by the assize of arms, and simply filed the letter.

There were other letters as well, not from Charlemagne but to him from Port-au-Prince, where one of his brothers, Saint-Rémy, and his sister, Marie-Louise, acted as his agents. These letters, addressed under the code name "Maïs Goilte," provided a flow of intelligence spiced with *telediol*, transmitted funds and advice, and, rather oddly, recounted contacts with the British legation together with puzzling references to "an Englishman," never identified, who was or purported to be a foreign agent of the cause.

It was all so grandiose and at times mad: "the Englishman," on whom high hopes centered, would buy ammunition and have an interview with King George V, then "go to Japan, France, and Russia." (Marie-Louise had mortgaged a house to give him $2000 as expense money.) Nor must Voodoo be overlooked. For $500, Mme. de Thèbes, a *mambo*, would hold a *neuvaine* (novena) to cause the *gendarmes* to become "paralyzed and confused." But Charlemagne must first send by urgent messenger (he did) a pinch of earth from each commune in the North and Upper Artibonite, else the *ouanga* would fail. A delegation would shortly arrive from Port-au-Prince to treat with Charlemagne: "They will speak fair words; take them all prisoners."

On 6 October 1919, Charlemagne had a band of *Cacos* in the hills behind Cabaret, fifteen miles North of the capital. Here, using the style and title "General-in-Chief of the Revolution in the Republic of Haiti," he indited a manifesto to the British *chargé d'affaires*:

Monsieur le Ministre,

I have the honor to inform you that I am at the gates of the Capital with the Divisions which compose my guard. Without deploying troops who now garrison Vallière, Fort Liberté, Grande Rivière du Nord, Le Trou, the Cap, St. Michel de l'Atalaye, Gonaïves, Petite Rivière de l'Artibonite, Lascahobas and Mirebalais, my effective strength, including my general staff, is great. I would already have stormed the Capital... save that I do not wish to expose the house holders, the foreign residents, and the Capital itself to such harsh calamity . . . I now address you, *M. le Ministre,* as the protector of society and of the family, that you may concert action with your colleagues and the Papal Nuncio, to settle the situation and submit your reply before I am forced to change my mind

Receiving no reply by nightfall, Charlemagne launched his "divisions" - 300 *Cacos* - toward the city.

The Marines and *gendarmes* were ready. Within minutes after the *Cacos* began spilling into Port-au-Prince they came under sharp counterattacks. Soon the raid dissolved in pell-mell retreat.

Get Charlemagne

Suppression of the *Caco* Resistance was getting nowhere and promised to continue to do so until Charlemagne could be laid by the heels.

None knew this better than the new *Gendarmerie* commandant, Colonel Wise. Within days after he assumed command, he sent word to Major J. J. Meade, commanding the Department of the North: "Get Charlemagne." To "get" Charlemagne thereupon became the highly secret mission of *Gendarmerie* Captain H. H. Hanneken, a Marine sergeant in command of that *Caco* hotbed, Grande Rivière. As Wise later wrote, "It was a pretty big order. It meant running down one Haitian out of several millions of Haitians in a country as big as the State of New York [sic]. And that one Haitian was surrounded by his friends, operating in a country almost entirely sympathetic to him, was protected by a fanatical bodyguard, never slept two nights in the same place, and must be run down in a tangled maze of mountains and valleys, of which there were no accurate maps."

In August 1919, soon after Hanneken completed his plan, Jean-Baptiste Conze, one-time *Caco* general and lately resident of Grande Rivière, left town in the night after letting it be known he had had enough of the *blancs* and would henceforth be again found with the *Cacos*. A *Gendarmerie* deserter, Private Jean-Edmond François, went with him. Conze's destination and intended base of operations was Fort Capois, that same stronghold Major Butler had taken in 1915. Since Conze was well provided with rum, rations, and money, *Cacos* quickly rallied to his standard.

What none knew save Hanneken and Major Meade and Colonel Wise was that Conze was supported with Hanneken's out-of-pocket funds. Each week, or more often, Private François - on occasion even Conze himself - would steal into Grande Rivière for a secret meeting with Hanneken.

Charlemagne was suspicious, a trait to which he owed much success and continued survival. He was therefore slow to accept Conze at face value. However, after a carefully staged, purposely conspicuous failure of a *Gendarmerie* attack on Fort Capois, led by Captain Hanneken, Charlemagne sent Conze warm congratulations and a commission as *général de division*. Publicly crestfallen, Hanneken nursed a heavily bandaged arm stained with issue red ink. This, he reported, was a wound inflicted by Conze.

Conze now urged Charlemagne to join him in capturing Grande Rivière itself. Charlemagne assented: after his rebuff at Port-au-Prince, to take a town would be a great thing. On 26 October, accompanied by other generals and 1200 *Cacos*, Charlemagne arrived at Capois. The plan was to attack Grande Rivière in the night of 31 October. Charlemagne would stand by at Masère, a half hour South of town in the river gorge, to await the result.

While Conze and Charlemagne concerted plans for the 31st, so did Meade and Hanneken.

From the Cap on 29 October went a secret radio message: (34)

CHARLEMAGNE AT FT CAPOIS AND ALL PLANS MADE TO CAPTURE OR KILL HIM AND BREAK UP HIS FORCES. UNLESS VERY UNEXPECTED HAPPENS THIS WILL BE DONE . . .

Then, ensuring against the very unexpected, the Marine commander directed establishment of a chain of blocking positions on all trails across Charlemagne's line of retreat, from St. Raphaël to Vallière. The order concluded:

ABSOLUTE SECRECY AND QUIET MUST PREVAIL. CHARLEMAGNE WEARING BLUE SUIT, PANAMA HAT, RIDES MULE. SET UP FIELD RADIO STATION AT RANQUITTE.

On 30 October, while Grande Rivière slept, Major Meade brought in a strong *gendarme* reinforcement with a Marine machine-gun section, to lie close inside the caserne next day. Meanwhile, Hanneken briefed and disguised eighteen picked *gendarmes* and his own second-in-command, *Garde* Lieutenant (corporal U.S.M.C.) William R. Button, who, like Hanneken, spoke fluent Créole. Garbed as *Cacos* in worn denim (the two *blancs* being blacked with burned cork), the party slipped South, after night fell, to Masère and laid an ambush.

Some 700 unwitting *Cacos* filed by along the riverbed, but no Charlemagne. Then came Jean-Edmond François with news: Charlemagne had decided not to come down in person but would wait and see what happened. Once Conze had the town, he was to send a detachment to notify Charlemagne and lead him in.

Hanneken and his men thereupon became that detachment, toiling through the pitch-dark mountain trails toward the leader's camp. From below soon came the distant sputter of musketry interspersed with the hammer of Meade's heavy Browning; then the firing slackened and ceased.(35)

Six *Caco* outposts lay in their path, but Jean-Edmond François had the password - "*Général Jean*," in compliment to Conze. At the last outpost, in Hanneken's report, "the leader there was on the job" and tried to examine Button's "nice rifle" (a Browning automatic rifle or submachine gun). In Créole, Button snapped, "Let me go! Don't you see my *délégué* is getting out of sight!" and broke free.

By the light of a small fire François pointed out Charlemagne, dressed, just as intelligence had reported, in a blue shirt. Hanneken drew his pistol and put two .45 caliber slugs through Charlemagne's torso. The aim was true: the autopsy reported, "both bullets...penetrated the heart." A woman kicked out the fire. In the dark, Hanneken grappled the sticky, bloodsoaked shirt and stayed beside his quarry during intermittent counterattacks and shooting, which continued until dawn.

By morning light, the *gendarmes* found Charlemagne's correspondence, which betrayed numerous secret supporters. Trussed across a captured donkey, all that remained of Charlemagne was brought down to Grande Rivière, then immediately to the Cap. Abbé Pocreau, who had been his friend and confessor, identified the corpse and performed the last rites. The final word, however (at least until Charlemagne's subsequent reburial and state funeral),(36) came from a *blanc* - Major Meade - who, reporting all that had come about, almost musingly noted "the strong, the powerful, idolatrous hold that Charlemagne had on these people. Many, many good Haitians, strong followers of the Occupation, were sympathetic to the man."

After some mopping up that lasted until 2 November, the North now entered a time of peace and quiet unmatched since the days of Nord Alexis.

End of Armed Resistance

Charlemagne's assassination brought peace to the North, but the Center was far from quiet. Benoît Batraville was the cause.

Benoît (to whom as *Ministre en Chef*, Charlemagne's title had passed) was believed to have some 2500 *Cacos* in mountain fastnesses Southeast of Mirebalais, which 150 years earlier had been the stronghold of *marrons* from Santo Domingo.

Back in Haiti again after a brief interval at home, Colonel Russell, with a re-inforced Marine brigade (up to 1346 officers and men) and a battle-worthy *Gendarmerie* of 2700, prepared all forces, including the aviation squadron, for an all-out campaign against Benoît in January 1920.

Russell reorganized his staff, bore down hard on improved intelligence, and divided the *Caco* country into tactical areas of operations, with troops assigned to each. Russell instituted measures for harrying without letup every *Caco* band once located, "Little really drove us," recounted one Marine officer, later General G. C. Thomas. "We would come in from a 15-day patrol at daybreak, exchange our enlisted men and be off by dark."

Batraville's reaction to the Marines'offensive was characteristic of a leader whom Russell was soon to describe as "a much more aggressive man than Charlemagne but lacking in intelligence and leadership." Prompted by Dr. Bobo,(37) before dawn on the morning of 15 January 1920, Benoît marshaled more than 300 *Cacos* North of Port-au-Prince, some disguised in stolen *Gendarmerie* uniforms. This time there was no high-flown ultimatum to the diplomatic corps. Benoît could not write.

In the words of an eyewitness, Colonel Russell's son-in-law, who happened to be visiting the capital:

> The *Cacos*, advancing into town in columns and with flags and conchhorns blowing, divided . . . one column going along the waterfront and reaching town by way of the slaughter house, the other two columns turning farther inland and advancing around Bellair [sic] Hill, by the radio station. When the troops had nearly reached town our Marines opened fire with Brownings and machine guns, but the natives broke ranks and fired from around corners, and rushing into houses, fired upon the marines from windows . .

Russell's intelligence had not failed him. Marines and *Gendarmerie* reacted with speed and sharpness. By break of day, sixty-six *Cacos* were found dead and many more had been cut off, captured, or wounded, including the leader of the attack, Solomon Janvier, a man of Port-au-Prince who was found hiding in his own house. Surviving *Cacos* ever after referred to this night as "*la débâcle.*"

Following *la débâcle,* it became increasingly clear that Benoît's days were numbered. Various chiefs (including Benoît's secretary, Clément Dumortier, like Charlemagne an elite St. Louis de Gonzague old boy) began to surrender. As they did, Russell sent them into the field with patrols to prove their sincerity and manifest their change of heart to fellow *paysans;* the fact that these ex-generals were alive and well-treated by the *blancs,* and affirmed so, proved a powerful persuader.(38)

Benoît fought on, while Mme. Benoît, his handsome wife, posing as a market woman, pistol tucked under her dress, would freely ride her bay mule into Port-au-Prince or Mirebalais and pick up supplies and gossip. When larger quantities were involved, Mme. Benoît would organize a convoy of other *Caco* wives to accompany her.

At daybreak on 4 April 1920, Benoît scored his last victory. A small patrol, consisting of three Marines, led by Second Lieutenant Lawrence Muth, breasted the slope of Morne Bourougue,(39) near Lascahobas. Sighting a few *Cacos* ahead, they opened fire. Seconds later the whole hillside blazed with bullets from a powerful ambush laid by Benoît himself. Shooting their way out while aiding a wounded comrade, the remaining two riflemen left Muth for dead. Then Benoît and his men closed in and dragged him into the bush.

That afternoon a patrol led by Colonel Little himself made contact with Benoît's band and, after a hot fight, recovered all that was left of Lieutenant Muth.

According to a *caco* taken prisoner, Muth had momentarily revived after being hauled away. Too weak to stand (he had been shot in head and stomach), he was propped up while Benoît made a speech. Then, with his great war machete, and with certain ceremonies, Benoît (who was a *bocor)* cut off his head. What next followed was subsequently described on oath by Lieutenant Colonel R. S. Hooker: "They cut off his private parts, took out his heart and liver, opened up his stomach, and took out his intestines, and took two large strips of flesh from his thighs ... His heart and liver were eaten . . . This is from the testimony of four witnesses who were present, that I heard myself." Confirming Hooker, Methieus Richard, the captured general, said that bits of brain from Muth's cleft skull were smeared on each *Caco*'s cartridges "so that," he explained, "when we fire at Marines we do not miss them."(40)

Only forty-five days remained to Benoît. At daybreak, 19 May, on a peasant's tip, patrols closed in on his bivouac in the huge rocks atop Morne 'Ti Bois Pin, five miles Southeast of Lascahobas. When the *Cacos* opened fire, Benoît, still carrying Muth's binoculars, was cut down by a Marine automatic rifle. As he struggled to rise and draw his revolver, a sergeant finished him with a pistol shot. Thus ended the career of Benoît Batraville, and with it not merely the last armed *Caco* resistance, but the hopes of the red-headed *mulâtre* doctor for whose ambitions so many *Cacos* unknowingly had paid.

In fighting the *Cacos*, Marines and *Gendarmerie* sustained 98 killed and wounded. Claims for *caco* casualties vary greatly. Conservative estimates of casualties from 1915 through 1920 are 2,250 *Cacos* killed. Hans Schmidt estimates the number of deaths at 3,250. Roger Gaillard asks if

> total number of battle victims and *casualties of repression and consequences* [italics added] of the war might not have reached, by the end of the pacification period...somewhere in the neighborhood of 15,000 persons...This war, in many instances, must have resembled a massacre.

Whatever the final number, *Caco* guerillas were massively outgunned and paid the price. The wide disparity between *Caco* dead and opposing casualties is usually attributed to superior firepower and weapons-training of Marines and *gendarmes* (while both in fact were armed "only" with rifles, pistols, and a few automatic rifles and machine guns, weapons of this quality and quantity were largely unavailable to the *Cacos)*, or to unnecessary or indiscriminate killing by forces of the occupation. Certainly the Marines had the benefit of good weapons, reliable sources of supply, and good training.

The active *Caco* Resistance at most involved no more than one quarter of Haiti and a fifth of its population. Though never so recognized by the Americans, it was in some ways a traditional revolt of *noirs* of the North and Artibonite against a *mulâtre* regime of the South and West, typically abetted and manipulated by that regime's opponents in Port-au-Prince and in exile. Overlaying this well-worn template though was a new component - a rallying cry to oppose a common foreign foe. Though this anti-*blanc*, doctrinaire nationalist coloration originated in the literature of elite resistance groups of Port-au-Prince, who were indeed strongly animated by such sentiments, it was unquestionably fueled by the *corvée* and serious abuses stemming therefrom in the Plateau du Centre and Upper Artibonite. While the origins of those sentiments may have been in the elite, they were nonetheless credible on a gut level to a peasantry being subjected to forced labor. Even Smedley Butler admitted that the *Garde* was recruiting "the best men in the country" and that many of them were ex-*Cacos*. The revolt was never national - not a shot was fired or *piquet* banner raised South of the Cul-de-Sac, but its staying power was substantial. Only the assassination of its chief and his second in command brought an end to the guerilla war.

Indiscriminate Killings

Remote, forbidding, wild, Hinche lies far from Port-au-Prince. Across the Cul-de-Sac, 3000 feet up the face of Morne-à-Cabrit, past Mirebalais, over the headwaters of the Artibonite, through Lascahobas and the Montagnes Noires, thence to Thomonde and onto the Plateau du Centre, wound the highway newly cut through by the *corvée*. Over this road, perhaps, or traveling by other means, in January 1919 *telediol* came to Port-au-Prince that all was not well in Hinche: the *corvée,* said reports, though officially halted the previous October, still continued: peasants bolted to the brush when a *gendarme* came in sight; prisoners taken by the *blancs* were openly shot or simply disappeared.

When General Catlin heard these things, he directed Colonel Williams of the *Gendarmerie*, and the district commander, Major Clarke H. Wells, to investigate; he also sent his trusted subordinate, Lieutenant Colonel R. S. Hooker, to Hinche. On Wells's word, Williams told Catlin the charges were baseless. When Colonel Hooker got back, as General Catlin later related, he brought a different story: "He found *corvée* going on at both Maïssade and Hinche, and the *gendarmes* [had] used the natives so brutally that many had left their gardens and either joined the bandits or had come into the towns for safety."

Catlin went to see for himself. Painfully dragging his wounded, once magnificent frame over dirt roads and rough trails, the general visited St. Michel, Maïssade, and Hinche, talking to the priests, the *magistrats,* and to trembling peasants. Catlin later observed, "A Haitian, as a rule, will testify to whatever he thinks is to his best interests," but there could be little doubt where the truth lay. With evident sanction of Wells and local Haitian officials,(41) the *corvée* was in full force, prisoners had been shot ("escaping" was always the excuse), and Major Wells (falsely reporting to higher headquarters that his district was quiet when in fact *Caco* resistance and attacks were mounting) had made clear to subordinates that he didn't want to see or hear of prisoners.

Catlin forthwith relieved Wells and shipped him home, transferred every *Gendarmerie* officer out of the affected towns and ultimately out of Haiti, replaced the local *gendarme* force with units from elsewhere, and put Marine garrisons with U.S. commissioned officers in each town. Believing, so he later said, that the evidence, however damning, would not sustain courts-martial, he ordered no trials, and on this decision later charges of whitewash mainly gain credence. But for an accidental discovery, the business, bad as it was, might never have been heard of again.

In Washington, however, in September 1919, while reviewing a court-martial from Haiti, Marine Major General Commandant George Barnett was jolted to note a passing assertion by counsel that, in Barnett's later words, "practically indiscriminate killing of natives has gone on for some time."

Catlin had been invalided home, and Russell was back. On 27 September 1919, General Barnett wrote a stern letter headed "Personal and Confidential," which told Russell, "I was shocked beyond expression to hear of such things and know that it was at all possible that duty could be so badly performed by Marines of any class. I know you will take this up most seriously, and I cannot too strongly urge upon you the necessity of going into it personally and thoroughly . . . and let it be widely known throughout Haiti that this system will not be tolerated hereafter... I want every case sifted thoroughly and the guilty parties brought to justice."

Now began a rigorous and extensive series of investigations. Russell put the case in the capable hands of Hooker, backstopped by one of the sternest and most probing disciplinarians of the Corps, Major Thomas C. Turner. Based on the Hooker-Turner findings, which reflected and verified Hooker's initial conclusions, the Navy Department ordered Major General John A. Lejeune (whom Josephus Daniels called "the best military officer in America, and the wisest one"), accompanied by Smedley Butler, now a brigadier general, to go to Haiti for further, more formal, and broader investigations. The Lejeune-Butler report, filed on 12 October 1920, disclosed little more than had already been discovered, but again unmistakably confirmed what Hooker had reported eighteen months earlier.

Two days later, readers of the *New York Times* were as shocked as General Barnett had been a year earlier (and as he again now was) to read on page one the general's private correspondence with Russell, including that phrase, "indiscriminate killings," heavily played. Someone had leaked the story. With the 1920 U.S. elections at climax, the issue of "Indiscriminate killing" was ready-made for Republican opponents of Woodrow Wilson and of course for the anti-occupation constituency that had been gathering in the United States.

James Weldon Johnson, black adviser of Republican presidential candidate Warren G. Harding, and secretary of the National Association for Advancement of Colored People, for obvious reasons keenly alive to the occupation issue, counseled Harding to take immediate advantage of Haitian atrocity charges. "I could see," Johnson reminisced, "that he looked upon the Haitian matter as a gift right off the Christmas tree." Even without benefit of the latest revelations, Harding had already told election crowds, "Thousands of native Haitians have been killed by American Marines."

The Wilson administration's response was one final, full-dress investigation. Even more exhaustive than its predecessors, the Mayo inquiry (named after its presiding officer, Admiral Henry T. Mayo and dismissed in *the Nation* as "whitewash" before the court even reached Haiti or heard its first witness) arrived at similar conclusions but significantly added: "Considering the conditions of service in Haiti, it is remarkable that the offenses were so few in number..."

Sorting out these investigations as well as the antecedent events, several observations seem in order.

- Behind the smoke lay fire. Illegal executions did take place and so did acts of violence against Haitians. The *corvée* was continued in violation of orders and was flagrantly misused as a form of peonage for the benefit of Haitian officials. Major Wells and, following his orders, a handful of American subordinates, condoned and tried to cover up these misdeeds.

- Best evidence would indicate abuses were confined to the Hinche-Maïssade area and to a six-month period (December 1918 to May 1919). They were neither typical nor anything like nationwide. The Senate investigation of 1922, energetically pressed at home and in Haiti, established only ten illegal executions.

- A major guerilla war was in progress.

- General Catlin's decision not to press charges when evidence was fresh and all parties still in the service and in Haiti effectively foreclosed further prosecution. Six months later, when General Barnett reopened the matter, the trail was cold and guilty individuals were beyond legal reach.

- Although seen by some as "official whitewash" because they tended to vindicate American military conduct in Haiti, the successive investigations, pursued in every instance by officers of high standing, came through, a half century later, as fair and rigorous. That they failed to produce disciplinary results beyond courts-martial already completed or actions taken at first instance by Catlin resulted from (1) the unavailability to military courts of persons clearly guilty (Marines discharged on expiration of enlistment or, in one case, dead); and (2) unreliable and conflicting testimony of Haitian complainants.(42) Behind everything lies the evident fact that Haitian peasants simply didn't regard the

Marines as the sadistic oppressors and savage bullies so routinely depicted by the elite.

Months later in 1921, after the uproar had begun to die down, Colonel Little wrote a thoughtful letter to Edwin Denby, the new Secretary of the Navy:

> We have committed errors. The *corvée* was an error, for by unjust enforcement in certain localities it brought doubt into the mind of the Haitien [sic] of the altruism of our intentions. It is for this reason that our punishment of all offenses by Marines and *Gendarmes* against Haitians has had to be prompt and severe ... The countryman is mighty pleased to have the forces of the U.S. with him. It saves him from a compulsory service... little short of slavery, it enables him to work in the fields unmolested..... We may have had to kill in our engagements but it was to prevent the slaughter or ill treatment of many thousands more.

It remained for the British Foreign Office to extract a final lesson. Reading the reports from Port-au-Prince, and no doubt mindful of similar painful episodes of their own, such as the Amritsar massacre of 1919,(43) the Permanent Under Secretary minuted: "It is useful to remember cases of this kind when the U.S.A. take it upon themselves to preach to us about Mesopotamia or Persia."

Cacos de Plume

A central paradox of the occupation was that the specter of the *"maître blanc"* frightened Haitian peasants less than it scared and angered the elite. As early as 1917, Déjean de la Batie, reporting to the Quai d'Orsay on "the racial question which, here, takes precedence over all others", said that the oligarchy that had so long gutted the country now desperately feared possible reestablishment of a white society. Such fears were natural in the descendants of *affranchis* and all the more understandable in light of racial conditions then prevailing in the United States.

In supporting the *Caco* Resistance, the elite, characteristically at odds among themselves, had been playing with fire. Dartiguenave's enemies hoped to upset him, but the president and his faction, besides recognizing immediate political hazards, also perceived the danger posed for the elite order of things by a movement with so many *noir* generals.

Until the revolt was finally snuffed out, Dartiguenave seemed happy enough to collaborate with the occupation, but, in mid-1920, he again took on the Americans. His reasoning (buoyed by a progress through the Upper Artibonite and Plateau du Centre, where neither he nor any predecessor ever dared travel before) was, in Russell's view (December 1920), (a)That the Pacification of the country was complete and that he was in no personal danger; (b) That in view of the approaching American national elections the psychological moment was at hand . . He virtually threw off the mask, stepped into the arena, fought fiercely as the so called champion of the Haitian people and with the intention of posing as a martyr. The political situation at once became complex . . . Where formerly the scene of trouble had been in Central Haiti it quickly shifted to Port-au-Prince, which became the one sore spot in all Haiti.

Russell did not exaggerate. The terrain of resistance had shifted to the capital. In early 1920 an American socialist, journalist, and associate of the NAACP, Herbert J. Seligman, had briefly visited Haiti, and on return to New York, wrote for the *Nation* a purported exposé, "The Conquest of Haiti," which was the opening gun of a sustained Haitian-American campaign against the occupation. The tone and thrust of Seligman's article (which precipitated a sensation in July 1920 and typified the *Nation's* style in dealing with the Haitian question) may be judged quickly:

Five years of American Occupation, from 1915 to 1920, have served as a commentary upon the white civilization which still burns black men and women at the stake. For Haitian men, women, and children, to a number estimated at 3000, innocent of any offense, have been shot down by American machine-gun and rifle bullets; black men have been put to the torture to make them give information; theft, arson, and murder have been committed almost with impunity . . . by white men wearing the uniforms of the United States.

Seligman had not imagined his article. His source was that *Union Patriotique* formed in August 1915 by Georges Sylvain and associates. Five years later, the Union had expanded its ranks to include virtually every elite politician or intellectual who opposed Dartiguenave or the occupation, and claimed total membership of 30,000. Besides Sylvain, its leaders now included ex-Foreign Minister Sannon, Sténio Vincent, A.-N. Léger, Price-Mars, Seymour Pradel, Percéval Thoby, Pierre Hudicourt, Antoine Pierre-Paul, and the erratic editor, Jolibois *fils*. (In what surely must represent an apogee of self-deception, Ernest Gruening of *the Nation* claimed that these men - every one a presidential aspirant - were without ambition and that the Union was apolitical.")

More realistically, R. F. S. Edwards, the British minister, described the Union as a set of "disgruntled politicians who would do anything to obtain a government position," a judgment amply confirmed by past and, in some cases, future records of a number of the members.(44)

The Union also contained high-minded men - to name only one, Maître Georges Léger - but to protest its political chastity is to be blind to the realities and personalities of Haitian politics. In the sardonic phrase of a fellow countryman, these were *"les Cacos de Plume"* (*Cacos* of the Pen) who in 1920 took up the cause.

The American connection that gave the Union voice and support came through an interlocking relationship between the NAACP, the *Nation,* and an American front-group, the Haiti-Santo Domingo Independence Society, which, by Gruening's admission, "we at the *Nation* organized." *Amis des Noirs* reborn, the society recruited prestigious Americans for its letterhead, including at one time or another Eugene O'Neill, Walter Lippmann, Felix Frankfurter, and even H. L. Mencken (who, had he known, would surely have reveled in the political shenanigans of the Haitians). For the voices at the heart of all this - James Weldon Johnson, Seligman, and Gruening - *the Nation* was to afford a strident, unbridled, and unashamedly partisan pulpit during the decade to come.

If the *Nation* and other foreign critics of the occupation stooped to irresponsibility and untruth, the stream of invective and invention flowing from the *Union Patriotique* never faltered. "We live in an atmosphere of lying" Dantès Bellegarde once sadly wrote. "Telling the truth is not a quality the majority of Haitians possess."

Like Caperton before him, Russell was widely accused of peculation at Haitian expense. When Colonel Hooker went home in 1921, *Le Courrier Haïtien* wrote of "the fortune he had amassed" and charged he had come to Haiti "for the sole purpose of enriching himself." In *Les Annales Capoises* of 4 March 1921, Jolibois-*fils* signaled the expiration of Woodrow Wilson's presidency: "May he retire to private life followed by the maledictions of the Haitian people . . . May he never find a resting place upon this earth, and on his deathbed may he eat his own waste."

In August 1921, Sténio Vincent told a U.S. Senate investigating committee that 4000 prisoners died or were killed at the Cap from 1918 to 1920; that from the same prison, 78 bodies a day were "thrown into the pits" throughout 1918 (a total that would have amounted in one year to 28,470 deaths on an average prison population of about 400); that at Chabert from 1918 to 1920, 5475 prisoners died; that mortalities "just as high" occurred in the prisons at Gonaïves and Port-au-Prince."

Besides these statistical whoppers, Haitian accusers specialized in attributing to Marines kinds of behavior foreign to Americans but amply recorded throughout Haiti's own past.

Evidently remembering the saga of the *Antoine Simon,* an anonymous member of the Union, writing in a French periodical in October 1921, accused Admiral Caperton of simply selling the entire Haitian navy for $14,000 to a New York accomplice, who then resold the ships for $500,000 and split the proceeds.

Danache, for his part, said that when fire swept the Rue Fronts Forts that same year, American officers' wives (*"véritable gangsters à jupe"*) pillaged shops and houses. *Courrier Haïtien* and French journals elaborated this story by accusing the Americans of setting this and other fires in the first place.(45)

Citing a 1921 memorial by the *Union Patriotique*, the *Manchester Guardian* credulously detailed the killing of entire families by Marines; wanton burning of houses and villages; burning, hanging, and torturing of prisoners; and, 1804 updated, "outrages on pregnant women."

Bellegarde, for all his devotion to veracity, asserted as fact the crucifixion of Charlemagne Péralte and charged the occupation with "butchery of women and children, massacre of prisoners, use of man-eating dogs as in the days of Rochambeau, tortures of water and fire..."

Pursuing the same line, a colleague told French readers that Haiti's cities and villages had been sacked and burned by the Marines, and their inhabitants "devoured by war dogs imported from the Philippines."

Such vilification, carried on without cease by the *Cacos de Plume* and given a gloss of verisimilitude when filtered through the *Nation* and foreign periodicals, would continue for a decade. In the long run, save for a few canards such as those surrounding Charlemagne and one serious falsehood that has become firmly embedded as *histoire reçue,* this propaganda, however galling to the Americans, can be dismissed as the only resort of a group neither willing nor capable of pursuing resistance beyond the salon or the print shop.

The 1920 American elections, combined with the *Nation's* continuing campaign, served to light a fire under Congress, which typically reacted by an investigation. Convening in Washington on 5 August 1921, a Senate committee held exhaustive hearings on U.S. activities in Haiti and Santo Domingo. Running through 1842 printed pages of testimony and exhibits and ending with a final report nearly eleven months later, the Senate hearings, conscientiously chaired by Senator McCormick (Republican of Illinois), a cultivated Chicagoan who spoke fluent French, included every leading figure of the occupation as well as its main opponents, Haitian and American. To ensure fair play, the *Union Patriotique* and the NAACP were accorded adversary status, including rights of cross-examination and summing up; these were freely exercised both in Washington and subsequently in Port-au-Prince, which the committee visited in November 1921. The Union, although protesting "numberless abominable crimes," made only a weak case with testimony the senators frequently found to be gossip or hearsay where not obviously coached or suborned.

While the Senate hearings developed a mine of primary information, the results, in many ways foregone, disappointed those who expected Congress to bring forth much more than a mouse.

Forecasting the committee's finding that what was needed was improved administration, not withdrawal, Senator McCormick had written, in December 1920, "We are there, and in my judgment we ought to stay there for at least twenty years. " A year and hundreds of witnesses later, McCormick privately wrote Secretary of State Charles Evans Hughes of a "want of policy . . . no centralization of responsibility. "

Finally, to supply wanted policy , McCormick called on Hughes to create a new post, an American high commissioner with plenipotentiary powers who would supervise the lot: treaty officials, *Gendarmerie*, Marines, the legation, and all. And that, on 11 February 1922, was what President Harding did.

The idea had been in the wind for many months, not only among those who supported the occupation but also, for different reasons, among those who opposed it.

The Haiti-Santo Domingo Independence Society above all wanted a civilian for the post and thought his name should be James Weldon Johnson. On the other hand, with rare impercipience, Secretary Hughes all but settled on Smedley Butler - a catastrophe averted only when Dana Munro made common cause with McCormick and colleagues to torpedo the appointment. (46) As a result, to everyone's surprise, including that of the appointee himself, the lot fell to John Henry Russell.

Back in December 1920, at the very moment when Senator McCormick was decrying want of policy in and on Haiti, and urging that the United States face up to the responsibilities it had taken on in 1915, Colonel Russell had written confidentially to the Chief of Naval Operations: "The question naturally uppermost in everyone's mind is where this will lead the United States. Two people can ride a horse but one must ride behind. Is the United States in its dealings with Haiti going to ride behind? If so, it will soon be ready for a fall and would be much better to get off now. "

By 1922 the decision had been made: the United States would not get off.(47) Nor was Russell the man to ride behind.

Russell's Proconsulship

On 10 March 1922, while the old battleship *North Dakota* plowed steadily down the Gulf of Gonaïves toward Port-au-Prince, General Russell, aft in the flag cabin, removed his starched whites and then turned in as the land breeze brought Haiti's pungent presence - charcoal fires, dung, *frangipaniers,* overripe mangoes, and the distant tap of drums - in through the open ports. No doubt his mind dropped back to 1893, when, as a midshipman aboard U.S. *Atlanta,* he had first seen and smelled Port-au-Prince. "In my midshipman's journal," he later wrote, speaking of Port-au-Prince as "the dirtiest city I had ever seen and express[ing] the hope that [he would] never visit the country again. However, inexorable Fate decreed otherwise."

Next morning, the American High Commissioner went ashore. He was greeted by the *magistrat communal,* by a smart honor guard of *gendarmes* and the palace band, and the Port-au-Prince crowd that had cheered many another new ruler of Haiti. There was no Te Deum, but the mounted *Gendarmerie* escort and burnished Ford touring-car clattered authoritatively up Rue Fronts Forts, past the cathedral where the French Fathers watched impassively, and thence to the American legation. Out in the bay, following her gun salute for the high commissioner, *North Dakota* got underway. Ashore, Russell got down to work.

"The history of our intervention in Haitian affairs," Secretary Hughes had written in Russell's instructions, "is not viewed with satisfaction by this Government." It was with these words before him that the new proconsul issued his first directive.

As previously worked out in Washington, the treaty services were reorganized. All correspondence by treaty officials with the Haitian government, Washington, or each other would pass over the high commissioner's desk, as would Haitian demarches to the United States. No statement of policy, project of law, or budget item would issue save by Russell's writ. Not surprisingly, the organization and the way it functioned would resemble a military staff.

Honorific and prestigious as their offices and perquisites might appear - especially in the setting of Georges Baussan's gleaming new *Palais National,* completed in 1918 - the president, his Ministers, and the *Conseil d'Etat,* his creature, would not enjoy much power. Behind official pomp, invariably and tactfully sustained by the high commissioner, stood American officials, from Russell down, who would direct the affairs of Haiti.

An imperial analogy well known to Russell and other American officers of his day, whether serving in Haiti, Santo Domingo, or the Philippines, suited the case closely. It was expressed, by two studies of British administration in Egypt from 1882 until 1914: Milner's *England in Egypt,* and *Modern Egypt* by his successor, Cromer. In Cromer's words, "One alien race, the English, have had to control and guide a second alien race, the Turks, by whom they are disliked, in the government of a third race, the Egyptians." If applied to the Americans, the elite, and the peasants, the parallel was nearly exact.

Yet there was and would be another dimension. Back in 1920, with Benoît barely cold in his grave, then Colonel Russell had issued an order he was to reaffirm as high commissioner, which in abridgement reads as follows:

> Where the duty of officers and enlisted men brings them in contact with the Haitian people. such duty will be performed with a minimum of harshness . . . and a regard for decency and human kindness.

No people with any spirit can view the presence of troops of another nation in any light than as a heavy blow to their pride. Considerate treatment may soften the blow, but harshness is bound to harden into resentment that goes to defeat the larger interests of the intervening nation.

The Haitians are naturally courteous people and resent, and properly resent, rudeness and discourtesy. One rude act of an individual may undo much good work on the part of many others in the cause for which we are here.

/S/ JOHN H. RUSSELL

It was in this spirit, however masked by the necessary aloofness of command, that the high commissioner put his hand to the plow.

Dartiguenave, whose term expired in May 1922, wanted to succeed himself, but his presidency was at a dead end. Never truly popular with the country, let alone the elite, he had alienated the Americans by maneuver, untrustworthiness, and obstruction. Yet hope dies hard: after vainly seeking public endorsement from Russell (who said he intended to "preserve an absolute neutrality" so long as proceedings were "in accordance with the laws and Constitution of Haiti"), Dartiguenave declared in early April.

Public reaction showed rare unanimity. The press, *Union Patriotique*, and virtually every other organization in Port-au-Prince leveled its guns on Dartiguenave (even holding a mass in the cathedral for deliverance from his regime). The *Conseil d'Etat*, every man a Dartiguenave appointee, lowered its eyes. As Dartiguenave's support crumbled, there began a period of jockeying (and of private visits to lobby Russell). Although the leading candidate appeared to be Stephen Archer, Louis Borno - with financial propulsion from the already wealthy Jamaican-German entrepreneur O.J. Brandt suddenly pulled ahead. Borno's one disability, a question of eligibility based on nationality,(48) seemed to pale under Brandt's powerful persuasions, and, on the evening of 10 April (after Dartiguenave mustered only 4 out of 21 votes from his own *Conseil* and withdrew), Joseph Louis Borno was elected president.(49)

On 15 May 1922, for the first time since Nissage-Saget and only the second time in the history of Haiti, a constitutional transfer of power took place. With full honors, Dartiguenave surrendered office and Louis Borno was inaugurated.(50) The outgoing president's seven-year term equaled the combined terms of his seven immediate predecessors in office.

One-time editor of *La Patrie,* poet of distinction, keen botanist, fluent in English and Spanish, lawyer and legal scholar, ardent Catholic convert, diplomat and thrice Foreign Minister, Borno, at fifty-six, was a man of culture. In externals, described by an American visitor, "Borno was smaller of stature than one would guess from his pictures . . . but with a fine intellectual head. His brow had dominated his photographs but his eyes dominated the man; they were serious and rather arresting eyes behind his pince-nez with its dangling ribbon. He was a pale mulatto; he was clean-shaven except for a close-trimmed mustache... His thick, iron-gray hair ... receded from a high forehead. "

Borno had already demonstrated to the Americans that he was his own man. Now, in the frank collaboration he extended to the occupation, he was to demonstrate a pragmatism that would anger the elite and in the end, linked with Russell, result in what has been called a two-headed dictatorship. Speaking to H. P. Davis on the day of his inauguration, Borno said he was "confident that earnest efforts and sincere cooperation with the Americans . . . will secure to my people a large measure, if not all, of the benefits contemplated in the spirit of the treaty. "

It was with this common objective that president and high commissioner set to work. Russell held the high cards. Every Haitian knew that the high commissioner's views were backed by more than pure reason: behind him stood the Marine brigade. Yet Borno was not and would never be a figurehead or (as he has been demeaned in one history) a "client-president." In the words of Arthur Millspaugh, who knew him well:

> His attitude was by no means servile or unquestioning. He had ideas of his own, expressed them forcefully and in some cases insisted on their adoption. Some of his views were those of a politician rather than a statesman . . . But he was far from being merely a politician or a puppet . . . Thus, government in Haiti took the form of a joint dictatorship. It would have been difficult at any time to determine which was the controlling partner - Borno or Russell. There was understanding, friendship, and cooperation between them: each was ready to yield at times; and each needed the other.

Seven years later, in 1929, Edwards, the British minister, assessed the occupation (which is to say, the Russell-Borno regime): "What has America done for Haiti in the fourteen years since the intervention? Primarily, maintained peace and allowed the peasant to work in safety.

To Edwards, an Englishman inclined to condescension , little else save overelaborate public buildings and a few roads ("not comparable," he sniffed, "with those of Jamaica") had been the result. Viewing Haiti six decades after the end of occupation, one might suppose Edwards had been right.

The facts, however, are otherwise. Financed entirely from efficiently managed Haitian revenue - foreign aid was a concept then unknown to the United States, and "dependencies" were expected to pay their own way - the material achievements of the Russell-Borno years belie the British minister and can be summarized before we return to the politics, the problems, and shortcomings that occupy the other side of the ledger.

- In 1929, the year of Edwards's assessment, the *Travaux Publiques* (directed by a handful of U.S. Navy civil engineer officers) had built and were maintaining over a thousand miles of all-weather roads suitable for traffic by the 3000 motor vehicles that had followed in the tracks of Furniss's original 1913 touring-car. There were 210 major bridges; there were airfields at Port-au-Prince, Gonaïves, Les Cayes, Jacmel, Cap Haïtien, Port-de-Paix, Hinche, Jérémie, St. Marc, and numerous auxiliary landing fields in more remote places.

    In 1920, the lighthouses of all Haiti amounted to three kerosene-burning relics at Port-au-Prince and one at the Cap; nine years later, the republic could boast fifteen automatic acetylene lighthouses, fifty-four buoys, ten harbor lights, and extensive aids to navigation in the modernized smaller ports. At the Cap, Gonaïves, St. Marc, Jérémie, and Les Cayes, whose harbor had been dredged, modern reinforced concrete docks had replaced aged, tumbledown timber wharves, thus enabling tramp freighters to ply these ports. Weekly first-class steamer service for Port-au-Prince on the Panama Line's New York-to-Colon run had been arranged by Russell; in 1929, Pan American clippers from Miami commenced service to seaplane ramps constructed near the site of old Fort St. Clair.

- About 1912 the French telephone system and the telegraph had sputtered into silence; ten years later, Port-au-Prince could take pride in the first automatic telephone exchange in any city in Latin America, which was soon followed by a second such system at the Cap. By 1929, there were 1250 miles of telephone long lines connecting twenty-six local exchanges, the telegraph had been completely rehabilitated, and the national communications were paying for themselves and showing a profit. (On one sample day that year, Port-au-Prince logged 27,574 local calls.) Jacmel's famous street lights shone again, as did those of the capital, the Cap, and Gonaïves. In 1926, Haiti's first radio station (HHK) went on the air at Port-au-Prince.

- Ten towns enjoyed potable running water, and 64 villages had clean wells or springs (Port-au-Prince also had pressurized fire mains). Eighty-two miles of new irrigation canals had been dug in the Artibonite Valley. Notable among a wide range of agricultural reforms were national forests, extensive mahogany and pine reforestation, and soil conservation. Sisal was introduced into Haiti, and, for the first time in decades, sugar and cotton again became significant exports.

- "The U.S. Naval Medical Service stands alone and far ahead of all American services. The devotion to duty of the U.S. Naval doctors is a great credit to the profession. The 'cleaning-up' of the country is proceeding steadily in spite of opposition from ignorance and inertia."

    Thus in a rare moment of approbation Minister Edwards wrote Sir Austen Chamberlain in May 1929. Fourteen years earlier, Haiti had been rotten with hookworm, tuberculosis, filariasis, leprosy, malignant malaria, enteric diseases,

Written in Blood

yaws, syphilis, smallpox, and typhoid. "The whole country," recorded Captain Kent C. Melhorn, the able naval Medical Director of Public Health, "teemed with filth and disease . . . The few so-called hospitals were miserable shacks to which more miserable human wrecks were brought to die."

The *Service de Santé Publique* responded by building and operating 11 modern hospitals, staffed by 2222 persons (all but 2 percent of them Haitian), and 147 rural or traveling clinics. In addition there were 4 other hospitals: U.S. Naval Hospital, Port-au-Prince (later the famous Hotel Oloffson and setting for Graham Greene's novel *The Comedians);* military hospitals at the Cap and Port-au-Prince; and St. François de Sales, the Catholic hospital in the capital.

In 1929, 1,341,596 consultations and treatments were conducted, and nearly half the country's 159 physicians worked for the Service de Santé. From 1926 on, the government allowed the occupation, with a Rockefeller Foundation grant, to take over and reorganize the National Medical School, which, with a hospital corps and dispensers' school, for the first time enabled Haiti to produce doctors and technicians with up-to-date professional qualifications.(51)

- None of these achievements could have been accomplished without the public order that the *Gendarmerie,* backed by the Marines, had brought about by 1920. With Marines entirely withdrawn to Port-au-Prince (except for a detachment at the Cap), the *Gendarmerie* (on 1 November 1928, renamed *"Garde d'Haïti"*) pursued its nation-building tasks: police, fire, prisons, customs and immigration, emergency communications, lighthouse service, rural medicine, and communal advisership. Enforcing firearms-control laws more drastic than those of the United States seventy years later, the *Garde* drained Haiti of private arsenals - a healthy condition destined to prevail until the early 1960s. Military marksmanship was raised to professional standards - an improvement dramatically underscored, to great national pride, when a Haitian rifle team, competing in the Olympics for the first time in 1924, tied France for second place.

The occupation would later be criticized because it allegedly made only perfunctory efforts to train Haitian officers for the Garde, yet an Ecole Militaire in 1922 was one of Russell's first projects. While a few candidates got through, the story was not unlike that of Haitian seminarians in France or *boursiers* at the old Turgeau agricultural school: the elite found military discipline, the hard work required of junior officers, and having to serve outside Port-au-Prince too demanding a way of life for persons of their class. Nonetheless, among those who stuck it out were such officers destined for national distinction as Jules P. André, Démosthènes Calixte, Gustave Laraque, and Franck Lavaud (the last two top shooters of the great 1924 rifle team). By 1929, just under 40 percent of the officers were Haitian. When complaint was raised a year later that no Haitian had yet risen higher than captain, Russell rejoined: "The reason for the efficiency of the *Garde* is due in large measure to the fact that the promotion of

Haitian officers has not been rapid... It is impossible to take an officer and run him rapidly through the various grades and then have an efficient service... If this is true in countries where the officer personnel is of high standard, how much more must it be true in a country which has been one of the most backward in the world?"

- The most far-reaching and controversial of American programs was that of the *Service Technique de l'Agriculture et de l'Ensignement Professionnel*, organized in April 1923 (usually referred to simply as the "*Service Technique*"). Its functions, stated by Russell in his 1924 report, were "higher agricultural education for the training of experts, research workers, teachers of farm schools, and farm advisers; rural farm schools . . . advice to adult farmers . . . direct aid through animal clinics and demonstrations . . . experiments in all phases of agricultural activity . . . and vocational industrial education."

In more general terms, the goal the *Service Technique* set itself was creation from among the peasants of a class of *noir* yeomanry - obviously a matter of extreme social sensitivity for the elite. Leaving, however, the resulting controversy for later, it is enough to recite undeniable achievements: agricultural experimental stations, a cattle breeding station at Hinche, the school of agriculture at Damien ("a miniature Tuskegee," Rotberg called it), demonstration farms and extension service. Plantation Dauphin at Fort Liberté (for years the world's largest sisal acreage), reintroduction of tobacco as a money crop, nationwide soil and resources surveys, and veterinary clinics, which healed more than 100,000 sick beasts. That so many good intentions and, for that matter, good works should have ignited such hostility, so deepened divisions, and, in the end, left so little behind was not least among the tragedies of intervention - and of Haiti.

Quite Unqualified to Colonize

No sooner had Louis Borno occupied the National Palace than his enemies ("mostly those who had been affected by his election," Russell commented) began plotting against the regime; it would not be Haiti, the high commissioner said, if they had not. Like many another president, moreover, Borno periodically rearranged cabinet and *Conseil*, inevitably enlarging the ranks of outs and thus of opponents. Yet the opposition was divided and uncertain. Throughout 1924, rumors of "Macandalism" (in this instance meaning mass poisoning of *mulâtres* by *noirs*, and ominous whispers of Dessalinian atrocities, also by *noirs* against *mulâtres*) troubled the elite. These rumors coincided with *telediol*, prompted by news that the Marines were to leave Santo Domingo and that they would leave Haiti too, a prospect that simultaneously elated yet unnerved those who could remember earlier times. When President Borno made his first official progress throughout the South, in 1925, Antoine Pierre-Paul and fellow *noir* irreconcilables of Les Cayes tried, but failed, to drape the city in black, sent messengers among the peasants to tell them the visit had been canceled, and stove in the drums of countrymen planning *bamboches* for the presidential visit.

With the 1926 election approaching, candidates jockeyed hopefully. Archer Wainwright, just out of jail for having killed his brother-in-law; Emmanuel Thézan ("one of the most dangerous characters," said Russell); and Gaston Dalencourt led the pack. To spice the preliminaries, a leading *mambo,* Mme. Lespasse, revealed that should the *Conseil* re-elect Borno, one member would then drop unconscious and die in the *Palais,* and Borno would be killed soon after. Pressed for her authority, Mme. Lespasse quoted a sister *mambo,* Mme. Savain, who had learned it from the spirits. "Madam Savain," drily commented General Russell, "is the mistress of Dr. Gaston Dalencourt, and unquestionably the spirit in this case is Dr. Dalencourt. I shall take means to have Dr. Dalencourt placed under observation in the event of Mr. Borno's reelection."

Spirits or no, Borno dropped easily into the pattern first set by Dartiguenave in 1916. No dates for legislative elections were proclaimed in 1924 or 1926, thus continuing rule by *Conseil.*(52)

Then followed one further shakeup of the *Conseil d'Etat*: Borno sacked eighteen of twenty-one incumbents. With one member absent and another casting a blank, the new team re-elected the president by a vote of 19 to 0.

The Borno-Russell regime had accomplished much since 1922, but progress had been uneven. New problems had arisen, old ones went unsolved, and original promises (and premises) of occupation remained unfulfilled.

Seven years after American assurance of a quick solution, the long stalemated, tangled skein of Haitian finance had been finally unraveled. With Borno's cooperation , $16 million in Haitian bonds were floated in 1922 by the National City Bank at a record 96.50; all French loans (worth $21.4 million in 1915 francs) were refunded for $6.04 million, leaving $10 million working capital for the government. Denominated in *gourdes*, $5 million more in bonds were given out to foreign and domestic claimants to pay off awards of the claims commission, and over $2 million in government bonds were exchanged for those of the Chemin de Fer National.(53)

That albatross, the Chemin de Fer National, was thus loosened from the government's neck, and a belated attempt was made to convert the road into a viable carrier. Yet at this time when the company was making only $85,000 a year, Roger Farnham, its absentee president and subsequent receiver, was getting $25,000 a year while his New York legal friends, Sullivan and Cromwell, drew down a $20,000 annual retainer as counsel. In the verdict of a distinguished economist (later U.S. Senator) Paul H. Douglas, "Mr. Farnham was an expensive luxury for the Haitian peasants to support."(54)

Many hopes of the first years of occupation had stemmed from the belief that Haiti held hidden resources that American capital might quickly exploit. The truth, as disclosed by U.S. geological surveys, was that Haiti had little or nothing except bauxite at Miragoâne and marginal copper deposits . As it was in the beginning, agriculture was the country's only resource. Yet plantation agriculture, based on large-scale foreign land-acquisition and consolidation, would outrage national feelings, and, in the absence of good titles, which Haiti has never had, could not be safely backed by investors. Peasants forcibly resisted occupation projects to conduct a cadastral survey bound to threaten tiny immemorial freeholds. (In 1926, after Marine aviators had made extensive aerial photographic coverage for such a survey, the building housing the negatives mysteriously burned down.)

By 1930, despite attempts to diversify into cotton, castor beans, and pineapple, with sugar and sisal significant but failing, Haiti still depended on coffee as its money crop. Among several large American enterprises only two had survived. While U.S. investment in Haiti waxed almost fourfold, from $4 million in 1913 to over $14 million in 1930, it had nonetheless mounted far faster in neighboring unoccupied countries during the same time, refuting dollar-diplomacy theories as to American intervention.

The inevitable chagrin of U.S. businessmen at Haiti's not turning out to be a bonanza recoiled on Russell and the State Department. The former in 1927 particularly offended the American Chamber of Commerce in Port-au-Prince by emphatic rejection of that group's request to advise the high commissioner, as a matter of right, "on proposed legislation and other matters under discussion with the Haitian government." The author of this impertinence was H. P. Davis, backed by HASCO, which then and in future conducted its own foreign policy in Port-au-Prince. Davis, before he wrote his history of Haiti, was for years local stringer for the Associated Press and is probably responsible for much of the American journalistic tone toward the occupation.(55)

Borno and Russell experienced common and continuing difficulties with the press. Edited in the polemic tradition of France, Haitian journals had only secondary regard for dissemination of news and none at all for truth. Enjoying freedom and security unknown before the occupation, they delighted in attacking it with irresponsibility and scurrility licensed by courts that refused to convict an editor. Through part of 1925, for example, a paper opposing Borno's reelection carried a standing notice:

BY ORDER OF THE SANITARY SERVICE, THE STINKING REMAINS OF LUIS [SIC] WILL BE REMOVED IN 309 DAYS [number changed daily] FROM THE MAUSOLEUM TO THE CITY DUMP.

Another paper urged readers to poison Borno.

With such media, Russell's original plan to hold regular press conferences quickly foundered. Terms of preventive detention meted out under a 1922 law provoked domestic and international howls. (56) Howls or not, Jolibois *fils* was in and out so often that Dana Munro remarked he "spent most of his time in jail by preference," and Ernest Chauvet, fat and flamboyant editor of *Le Nouvelliste* and one-time Brooklyn Eagle reporter, was periodically locked up by Borno; by Seabrook's account, "He enjoyed himself hugely, devoured whole roast turkeys, drank champagne, and thumbed his nose at the wide world outside."(57)

   If, as Chauvet conceded, detention represented no Calvary for Haitian newsmen, it provided endless ammunition for opponents of the occupation and of Louis Borno.

   The roots of the above and numerous other problems reached beyond the treaties into the courts, one of the few institutions the occupation, despite continual efforts, utterly failed to change, let alone reform.

   "The maladministration of justice," reported Minister Edwards in 1929, ". . . is the chief cause of trouble in Hayti. The majority of the judges are thoroughly bad and some are well known to be blackmailers." He also commented that though a black foreigner might win his case against a Haitian, a white man stood little chance and a white American none at all.

   While the Cour de Cassation (supreme court) and the two courts of appeal - benches occupied by some of Haiti's most distinguished lawyers - were more even-handed and correct, the 136 lower courts (First Instance *Tribunaux de Paix*), where most cases originated and were tried, differed little, if at all, from predecessors a half century earlier. Besides venality so ingrained as to be regarded merely as a court cost, enormous and unwarranted judgments were routinely returned against the government or anyone else considered able to pay. Such awards were, aside from the fragility of land titles, one main reason why foreign capital avoided Haiti in favor of its neighbors. The high-handed remedy of successive financial advisers was simply to disapprove payment of judgments considered improper, which further undermined the judicial system and only whetted its bias. Criminal justice was erratic in the extreme. Numbers of murder cases, for example, ended in acquittal on the sole defense that the victim had been a *loup-garou* (werewolf). Yet who could blame ignorant *juges de paix* for so construing a penal code that proscribed sorcery as a crime and recognized *zombiism* as a phenomenon?

   The abysmal and vexatious performance of Haitian courts constituted the main justification - aside from that of *force majeure* - for continuation of American provost courts and the technical state of martial law they were prepared to enforce.(58)

Like preventive detention of editors and agitators, provost courts and martial law presented a continuing embarrassment to the United States and a handy stick whereby opponents could belabor the occupation.

In fact, however, provost courts were only exceptionally employed, descending sharply from 911 cases in 1920 to a handful of cases in immediately subsequent years and no cases at all from 1926 to 1929. This had been Russell's policy from the outset, a course strongly encouraged by a nervous Washington. Of both courts and Marines, it was aptly remarked in 1927 by the American chargé, Christian Gross, "So long as they are there, there is no need for their being there."

One of the occupation's most serious mistakes - a mistake of ignorance - was to permit the *Garde* (and thus by implication the American authorities) to be used in ill-advised attempts to stamp out Voodoo. Borno was deeply anti-Voodoo, and the elite, with whom U.S. treaty officials and senior Marines had most contact, further confused the Americans with traditional condescending attitudes giving the impression (whatever their inward beliefs) that Voodoo was superstitious rubbish capable of causing trouble among the lower classes. It is a measure of the occupation's lost opportunities, during nearly two decades in Haiti, that no evidence can be found that senior American officials ever seriously comprehended Voodoo in its impressive totality as Haiti's national religion.

The *garde* arrested and prosecuted (and Borno's judiciary sentenced) Haitians for such "crimes" as preparing *"mangé pour les saints"* (consecrated meals to propitiate the *loa)* or conducting various Voodoo services. To American officers of the *Garde*, it seemed only that they were enforcing anti-Voodoo provisions of the Code Pénal(59) (and to most foreigners Voodoo was prima facie "witchcraft" or "black magic"). That a Haitian might draw no distinction between lighting a candle in the cathedral and lighting one at the foot of the giant fig tree, *Maître Cimetière*, overshadowing the gate of the Port-au-Prince cemetery, never seems to have penetrated. On the part of the *Garde's* Haitian officers, there was comprehension and tolerance, as indeed there occasionally was on the part of individual Americans, such as Lieutenant Wirkus, who bore the portentous Christian name Faustin and was widely publicized as the "White King of La Gonâve."

In social relations with Haiti, the occupation mirrored colonial attitudes of the day - paternal toward the masses, aloof and condescending toward the elite, who cordially reciprocated. As if Haiti were West Africa or British India, the Americans had their club in Turgeau, which no Haitian ever entered except as a servant. From 1918 on, no U.S. officer was admitted to the *Cercle Bellevue*.(60) Some of this distance has been blamed, no doubt correctly, on

American racial attitudes and particularly those of the wives of the lower-ranking among the 250 treaty civilians and the less numerous noncommissioned officers who served as junior officers in the Garde.

Edwards, never at a loss where American failings were concerned, in 1929 donned the mantle of Kipling: "I do hate to see one's own colour and race behaving in a way that brings discredit to the whole white race. What respect can an educated Haitian have for a race that allows its women to get so drunk that they have to be taken home in the bottom of the car? And all that before native servants. One can only put it down to lack of tradition and education."

Only six months later, unable to contain himself further, Edwards rendered a final verdict: "The American in Hayti has shown himself quite unqualified to colonize at all."

In a larger sense than a person of his mind-set would readily have comprehended, quite possibly the British minister was correct.

Southerners to Handle Haitians?

A recurring theme in reports of Minister Edwards during his years in Port-au-Prince was stated in an April 1927 dispatch to the Foreign Office: "The U.S. Government has sent about 75 percent Southerners to Hayti as they are supposed to know how to handle coloured people."

The charge was not new. Its earliest appearance was not in Haiti but in a October 1920 *New York Times* interview with Harry Franck. How Franck substantiated this assertion, or where he found it, are unknown. It might have surfaced during the 1920 U.S. presidential campaign, when James Weldon Johnson was advising Warren Harding; conceivably it could have sprung from the fertile imagination of the *Cacos de Plume* (though this seems unlikely because the 1921 *Union Patriotique* memorials, pulling out every stop, made no use of what would have seemed a particularly telling charge and one, as history shows, nearly impossible to refute).

Following enunciation by Franck, the charge that the Marine Corps deliberately exported American racial prejudices to Haiti was echoed in 1927 by Emily Balch and Paul Douglas. In 1941 the sociologist Leyburn (who admitted subsequently that he could not substantiate the assertion) gave the proposition his considerable weight by writing, "The United States government in the early days had sent Marines from the Southern states to Haiti, on the theory that they would, from long acquaintance with Negroes, know how to 'handle' them."

In 1954 Selden Rodman reinforced Leyburn; two years later Edmund Wilson did the same. In 1954 *Time* magazine stated the charge as fact.

Curiously, this accusation cannot be found in the extensive contemporary anti-occupation writings by Haitians or their American claque. It was never raised, either in testimony or reports, by the McCormick Committee of 1922 or the Forbes Committee of 1930. Bellegarde's comminatory *Résistance Haïtienne* (1937), otherwise an anti-occupation litany, is silent on this count. By 1950, many years later, Danache - apparently the first Haitian to do so - said Marine officers were chosen from *"les Etats négrophobes du Sud des Etats-Unis."* Hogar Nicolas, writing in 1956, echoed Danache, and, by the late 1950s, the assertion had become a commonplace of *histoire reçue* by Haitians claiming to remember it.

Analyzing by name against U.S. Census data the record of every Marine officer on duty in Haiti from 1916 to 1932, a Wellesley College Researcher found (1) that the proportion of Southern-born officers in the Corps as a whole during this period was lower than the percentage of Southerners in the national population; and (2) that in thirteen of the nineteen years of occupation, the percentage of Southern Marine officers in Haiti was below the percentage of Southern officers in the Corps.

While accepting these findings as far as they went, critics have demurred that the research covered only officers and did not consider Marine NCOs breveted to junior ranks (captain and below) in the Garde. But partial data on such cases confirm the researcher: in 1930, one year when complete statistics covering the *Garde* were compiled, only 24 of 116 officers, including ex-NCOs, 20.6 percent, were Southern, at a time when 23.4 percent of all Americans were Southern-born.(61)

The authors, despite a lifetime of familiarity with the Marine Corps, were unable to find any trace in records or recollection that any such policy ever existed.

While the foregoing facts are incontrovertible, there remains a very important question of what may be called atmospherics.

Though he served in Haiti less than two years and departed in 1917, Colonel Waller of Virginia was a conspicuous, and very Southern, figure of the occupation. Anywhere Waller served, he set the tone. "I know the nigger[sic] and how to handle him," he wrote in June 1916 to Colonel Lejeune. A further sample of Waller's attitude comes loud and clear in another letter: "They are real niggers[sic] and no mistake - There are some very fine looking, well educated polished men here but they are real nigs beneath the surface."

General Russell was a Georgian, yet no critic ever caught him in act or attitude suggesting racism. He and his wife, who spoke polished French, mixed unself-consciously with, and entertained, Haitians throughout their tour. Mrs. Russell conquered even Danache, who described her as "a great lady . . . of tact and high courtesy."

Several treaty civilians (Wilson appointees under a Southern Democratic administration) were Southern. Yet, as Dana Munro documents, these and lesser

Southern civilians were carefully sifted for qualifications by Wilson, and, with the exception of McIlhenny, worked out well.

In short, no evidence has surfaced of a Southerners-only policy for Marines which in any case would not only have foundered on the rocks of administrative practicality, but would have left recorded tracks, which do not exist. Nonetheless, as Paul Farmer has pointed out in *Aids and Accusation*, "...a few Wallers, especially in top positions, can go a long way."

Children's Crusade

The *Service Technique*, which Russell organized in 1923, was no mere agricultural extension program as known in Kansas; it was in fact an attempt to make good what Rayford Logan called "an almost inexplicable omission" in the original treaties, failure to include education in the ambit of the occupation.

In 1915, Haiti already had two school systems: (1) the network of graft-engulfed government schools, enrollment about 30,000, preponderantly nonexistent except on paper, manned if at all by illiterate spoilsmen; and (2) the flourishing, mainly Catholic, religious schools (roughly 12,000 students), exclusive preserve of the elite except for about a hundred "presbyteral" schools, in which back-country Breton priests imparted rudimentary smatterings to a few thousand peasant children.

No matter by whom conducted, education in Haiti had inherited, and still has, unique problems. Haiti's peasants were apathetic; its elite rightly feared uncontrollable social consequences resulting from enlightenment of *noir* masses (in the 1920s they also feared that those masses might bestow greater loyalty on *blancs*, who were demonstrably bettering their lives, than on Haitian masters who exploited them). The almost insoluble Créole-French language barrier was another obstacle: teachers, clawing their way upward, persisted in using French, language of social cachet, rather than Créole, understandable to *noir* pupils. And teachers in Haiti, even the best, were, and are, among the poorest-paid (when paid at all) of all public servants.

Behind these Himalayan barriers to enlarged education lay still one more. Clutching at any shred of power not monopolized by the occupation, Haitian politicians - headed by one of the most unyielding opponents of the Americans, the talented Dantès Bellegarde - rallied to education as a national redoubt against further foreign encroachment.

The Americans saw Haitian education as hopelessly misdirected, preparing elite children for white-collar jobs that did not exist, turning out swarms of lawyers, other professional men, and votaries of *belles lettres,* while shunning vocational practicalities so desperately needed. These very perceptions had long been accepted by thoughtful Haitians. Joseph Justin, for example, had written in 1915: "As for the commonplace trades and manual arts, we hold them in holy horror; they are beneath us ... Our school system is not only defective, it constitutes . . . a real social danger."

How insoluble the problem really was may be questioned. Keeping Haitian peasants ignorant supported the interests, conformed to the natural inclinations, and quieted the insecurities of the elite.

Regardless of how correctly the Americans perceived the situation, their solution was foredoomed. To head the *Service Technique*, which was to be not merely the font of agricultural improvement in a country supremely agricultural, but also the vehicle for a third competing school system aimed at the masses, the director, Dr. George F. Freeman, was a poor pick. Assessing Freeman and his work in late 1929, another British minister, John Magowan, wrote:

> Dr. Freeman's *Service Technique* has not a friend in the island. He himself is regarded even by the Americans as of doubtful competence: his right to the title of Doctor is disputed: his previous career as a cotton expert as well as his six years in Hayti furnish, it is said, no evidence of suitability for any post demanding initiative, resource, tact, and organizing ability, as well as theoretical knowledge. Worse . . . . his personnel is made up to a great extent of men and women who neither speak a word of French nor have any special qualifications as "experts," but who have been dumped upon the unfortunate Haytian budget at unnecessarily high salaries.

Magowan's verdict (especially his identification of what could be called "foreign aid mission syndrome" before its time, with high-paid foreign "experts" incapable of disclosing their insights save through interpreters) is confirmed by a cloud of witnesses.

The fuse that was to detonate the coming explosion the *blancs* had so unwittingly, even haphazardly, prepared had been lighted in 1925.

That year a young scion of the elite who was pursuing engineering at Zurich had delighted the *Union Patriotique* by a fiery letter asking to be enrolled. This brilliant young *mulâtre* was a grandson of Tancrède Auguste; his name was Jacques Roumain. When he returned to Haiti in 1927, he flung himself into the intellectual resistance by launching a literary magazine, *Revue Indigène*. When, in 1928, this went the way of most literary reviews, he soon founded a less arcane journal, *Le Petit Impartial,* calling itself "Organ of the Masses" and specifically the voice of a student organization, Ligue de la Jeunesse Patriote Haïtienne, brought into being by Roumain. What was then known to few Haitians and no Americans was that Roumain had been recruited in France by the Communist Party.

The time was ripe for Roumain, for his ideas, and for those of the volatile elite students he set out to politicize. Reporting the mid-1929 desecration of Dessalines's statue by youths of the Ligue, an officer of the *Garde* commented: "These people, mostly aged up to 22 years, are ANTI EVERYTHING, even

Dessalines. Their attitude is strictly anti anything that might have caused the present condition of Haitian politics . . . They are against their parents, the Government, the opposition, and the Occupation."

After fourteen years' occupation this was the disaffected mood of a class whose parental bases of self-respect and pride, identification with French culture and condescension alike toward American materialism and ignorant *noir* culture, had been so undercut. Roumain's feelings, voiced in mordant verse, were even more bitter:

> *pour en finir*
> *une*
> *fois*
> *pour*
> *toutes*
> *avec ce monde*
> *de nègres*
> *de niggers*
> *de sales nègres.*

Seeking an issue, the Ligue, in April 1929, seized on an alleged confrontation at St. Louis de Gonzague between a French priest and a Haitian one, to demand a student boycott.

The *Service Technique* show window was its Central School of Agriculture at Damien. Here, in a program intended to create a cadre of teachers, students were taught agronomy. In the way of things in Haiti, and more particularly because such studies required literacy and prior preparation, the students came from elite families, though, alas, with no more appetite for the dunghill side of agriculture (let alone for going out into the country to instruct peasant *noirs)* than their predecessors at Turgeau. To overcome such reservations, there was adopted a system of scholarships, or *bourses,* whereby each student received the not inconsiderable sum of $25 a month and, as Dr. Freeman was later quoted in the *New York World,* was "virtually hired to go, by means of scholarships." This incentive notwithstanding, student *boursiers* concentrated on academic work while hired peasants dug ditches, cleaned stables, slopped hogs, and shoveled manure.

The above arrangement might have gone on indefinitely but for the fact that 1928 was a bad year for coffee, and 1929 ended as a bad year for everything. The concatenation of these economic circumstances led to a series of financial cutbacks of which the *Service Technique* was forced to accept its share.

Like many other presidents, Louis Borno, as his second term waned in 1929, became increasingly reluctant to stand down. He also (despite earlier commitments for a 1930 popular election) had doubts, shared by General Russell and by policy-makers in Washington, as to whether Haiti was ready to elect a National Assembly.

Marshaled by Seymour Pradel (who had not forgotten himself as a presidential possibility) and trumpeted by the opposition press, another league - the *Ligue Nationale d'Action Constitutionnelle* - sprang into being and launched a violent anti-Borno campaign that in its nature was automatically anti-occupation and anti-American.(62)

It was at the height of this uproar that Dr. Freeman, confronted with the need to reallocate funds, made a three-way decision: to reduce by $2000 the $10,000 set aside for Damien *bourses;* to divert this amount to peasant students at Hinche and other experimental stations in the interior; and to take up the resultant slack at Damien by requiring that *boursiers* do their own bucolic labor rather than hiring peasants as in the past.

As Magowan commented, "Dr. Freeman's motives were doubtless sound," but on the other hand, as Russell later wrote, "The proposition of being paid less or not at all to attend school for a free education displeased the students." Displeased is a mild word: simultaneously stung in pocketbook and *amour-propre,* the students were outraged.

On 31 October at 3:00 P. M., all 215 students at Damien, accompanied by Haitian instructors,(63) struck and trooped into town, thus launching the first serious disturbance in Haiti in nearly a decade.

Within less than ten days, the elated students, inflamed by Roumain and Pradel and the two respective leagues, were being treated like heroes. Backed by sympathy strikes in the American-run J. B. Damier industrial school in the city, in the schools of law, medicine, and applied science, as well as the normal school, "the action of the students," reported Magowan, "was lauded to the skies as signifying the re-awakening of the Haytian national soul. Assemblies were held at which flaming orations were declaimed; street processions and demonstrations of the strikers were organized."

Strikes were swiftly orchestrated at the Cap , at Jacmel (where a Damballah banner of green snake on red background became the student flag), at Gonaïves, and at St. Marc. When bands tried to play the *"Dessalinienne",* student leaders howled it down and called instead for Occide Jeanty's fierce "1804."

As November wore on, the capital was plagued by demonstrations, mobs, and spot strikes at the *Banque,* at the wharves, and at the ever-turbulent *douanes.*

The reaction of the authorities (with General Russell applying brakes to keep Borno from locking up every politician in sight) was initially restrained. Parade permits were freely issued to strikers (though parade routes selected by the *Garde* took barefoot students through the hottest, narrowest, and flintiest cobbled streets, an expedient that tended to make parades melt away). As the strike metastasized from student disturbance into general protest against the occupation and began to lap at the doorways of the treaty services, the authorities became less sanguine. Borno's announcement (after backstage American arm twisting) that he would not be a candidate in 1930 seemed to have little effect. Russell, who three weeks earlier had few qualms, on 3 December telegraphed Secretary of State Stimson:

> LOYALTY OF THE GARDE NOW VERY QUESTIONABLE. IT IS THEREFORE REQUESTED THAT STRENGTH OF THE BRIGADE BE IMMEDIATELY INCREASED BY 500 UNTIL AFTER INAUGURATION OF THE NEW PRESIDENT IN 1930.(64)

While Stimson and Washington officials fussed over Russell's request and suspected he had lost his head, events moved swiftly. Within twelve hours after the high commissioner asked for reinforcements, on the morning of 4 December, the *douaniers* walked out, in the process manhandling an American collector of customs. When the collector fought back, the *douaniers* rampaged, bashing another American with a steel bar when he tried to phone the police. As crowds gathered in the Rue du Quai, employees at the nearby financial adviser's office joined the strike. Russell, once again very much the general despite his civilian clothes, reactivated martial law, proclaimed a curfew, and ordered the Marine brigade to take charge of Port-au-Prince.

The elite protest against the occupation found an echo in the South. Emissaries from Port-au-Prince had early reached Les Cayes as well as other towns, including Jacmel, Miragoâne, and the Goâves. The day *the douaniers* erupted in the capital, stevedores and *douaniers* at Cayes halted the unloading of two ships.

Next morning, 5 December, the commanding officer of the *Garde* at Cayes reported disturbances "getting rapidly out of hand." Soon afterward, telephone lines were cut (as were lines leading into Jacmel, where intelligence reported the landing of a shipment of weapons from Guatemala). Amid these developments, the peasants of the Plaine des Cayes, hard-pressed by a poor harvest, resentful of higher taxes on alcohol (and the opening of a competing distillery in Port-au-Prince, which had cut into profits on local *clairin),* had grievances of their own for which the agitators from the towns provided slogans. At Torbeck and Chantal, home grounds in olden times of the Salomons and of Acaau, *noir* mobs, armed with sticks, machetes, and spears, and chanting, "A *bas Borno! A bas Freeman!"* all but overran the tiny *Garde avant-postes* and, fueled with *taffia,* hatred of the town, and expectation of loot, marched, as so often in times past, against the city.

Outside Cayes a crowd encountered a section of Marines with an automatic weapon. For half an hour, the 1500 man crowd milled, hurled stones, and tried without success to creep past in the cane, then twice turned back when the twenty Marines fired overhead. A leader, stepping forward across the narrow interval to parley, suddenly grappled with and bit a Marine. As another Marine prodded the assailant off with a bayonet, the *piquets* charged. This time the Marines fired for effect, expending 600 rounds. Abandoning twelve dead and twenty-three wounded, the mob evaporated.

This, as the *Nation* quickly dubbed it, was the "Cayes Massacre."

The issue went beyond any justification of self-defense: the killing of a single Haitian, let alone twelve Haitians, by a single Marine or by twenty, was at this juncture an event the occupation could not stand, for, in the later words of Dean Acheson, "A free people cannot long steel itself to dominate another people by sheer force."(65)

On 7 December, even as the strike quickly collapsed in face of the Marines' show of force and a round of flag-showing by U.S.S. *Galveston,* a venerable cruiser sent over from Guantanamo Bay, President Hoover (who since inauguration in March 1929 had been searching for a way to get out of Haiti) asked Congress to establish a commission to determine, as he soon afterward said, "When and how we are to withdraw from Haiti [and] what we shall do in the meantime."

Within ten days, martial law and curfew were lifted, papers were again published, the Damien dispute - which, almost overlooked at the end, had been narrowed to trivia - was settled, and Dr. Freeman (who would be dead in nine months) (66) was on his way out. "Throughout the Republic," Magowan wrote in epilogue, "order is good and spirits calm."

A Palliative, Not a Remedy

Back in 1915, Admiral Caperton had written Benson in the Navy Department: "For the love of anything good or bad, do not send any politicians down here yet awhile. I would like to say, never send them."

Now, fifteen years later, the old admiral's nightmare was being realized.

In fulfillment of his promise of December 1929, Herbert Hoover, on 7 February 1930, named a five-man Commission for the Study and Review of Conditions in Haiti. The commission was named for its senior member, W. Cameron Forbes. Forbes - distinguished Boston lawyer, former governor-general of the Philippines, and recognized colonial expert - wryly confided to his diary, that what his mission was to be "was laid out for me in no uncertain terms."

Mr. Hoover, a Quaker humanitarian by background, had come to the presidency with little sympathy for U.S. Caribbean politico-military policies, which, in the words of his Secretary of State, Henry L. Stimson, had "been left to each succeeding Administration by the Wilson Administration."(67)

Hoover's distaste for Wilson's bequest was exacerbated by one from another administration - the then five year old war in Nicaragua.

The Forbes Commission arrived in Port-au-Prince on 28 February, 1930. It was welcomed by a 19-gun salute, banners (courtesy of the *Union Patriotique*) calling for an end to the occupation, and a special English language edition of *Le Nouvelliste* taking a similar line.

The next afternoon, General and Mrs. Russell held a reception for the commission, a function boycotted by a number of invited Haitians. Although invitations required no acknowledgment, some recipients (as well as others not even invited) chose the columns of *La Presse* to print replies whose tenor can be judged from that of Roumain: "*Nègre* Jacques Roumain does not deign to associate with whites".

The Forbes Commission, White House marching-orders in hand, took twelve days of testimony. The nature of hearings may be gauged from the following: charges against the occupation were in every case heard by the full commission, but rebuttals, when heard at all, were taken by single commissioners or staff members; no treaty official was allowed to appear as witness during the first week of proceedings; no opportunity to cross-examine witnesses or publicly refute charges was ever accorded Russell or treaty officials; and 90 percent of the hearing-time was allocated to those opposed to the occupation.(68)

Maître Georges Léger, then and for many years to come Haiti's most distinguished lawyer, had orchestrated a deafening case. "The same banners," reported the commission, "scarcely varying a word from Port-au-Prince to Cape Haïtien, waved everywhere . . . The same agitators were often seen in the crowds in distant parts of the Republic." Noting in his diary the English of the placards ("Suppression of Borno . . . Withdrawal of Marines . . . Down with the High Commissioner") Forbes reflected, "Always the same and usually shown by people who had not the remotest idea of what it all meant."

Behind these effervescences seethed a powerful head of steam - the determination of the opposition to bring down Borno on the spot.(69)

As early as 6 March, Russell confidentially warned Forbes that the opposition leaders had the bit in their teeth and were prepared to stop at nothing. Russell then put forward a plan, worked out with Colonel F. E. Evans, the astute commandant of the Garde, to ease Borno out in favor of a transitional, politically neutral provisional president to be chosen by the *Conseil d'Etat*, who would then call for legislative elections and, by agreement, step down in favor of the National Assembly's ultimate choice. On Forbes's nod, the general went to Borno, who, with feelings that may be imagined, acceded. Russell, in coming back to Forbes, underscored that, to have the least chance, such an idea must appear to have originated with the commission, and they must sell it to the opposition as their own. So, after cabled approval from the White House, Forbes and his colleagues sent for Maître Léger, Pradel, Hudicourt, Justin Sam, and Antoine Rigal, representing the *Ligue d'Action Constitutionnelle* and other opposition groups. Then, as Fletcher recounted,

We informed the opposition leaders that we had been assured that M. Borno was not seeking re-election and was willing to accept a neutral non-partisan as his successor. We said we were willing to help find such a man. They all doubted that he could be found. M. Hudicourt asked with an air of finality: "Where are we to find this white blackbird?" But they agreed to think it over . . . and asked us what we had to propose. We then suggested that . . . they should prepare a list of five neutral men, any one of whom they would accept as Provisional President. Borno would be asked to prepare a similar list, If one man's name appeared on both lists, he would be the *merle blanc.*

After a discussion somewhat protracted, Forbes recorded, by Antoine Rigal's insistence that he alone was more neutral than anyone and should therefore be transitional president, the leaders assented and prepared their slate.

Borno never drew up a list. When he looked at the opposition names, his eye stopped at Eugène Roy. It was then agreed that, on 14 April, the *Conseil* would duly elect that highly regarded elite exchange-broker (whom Forbes remembered as "a man of dignity, white-haired and quite black") as provisional president to succeed Louis Borno on 15 May.

There remained only the communique and press release, the final calls, and of course the report to be written as *Rochester* steamed Northward.(70) The main thrust of the report was clear enough: the United States should liquidate the occupation as expeditiously as possible, meanwhile rapidly "Haitianizing" treaty services and the *Garde* and reducing American interference in Haiti's internal affairs. The first and foremost step in this process would be to wind up the office of U.S. high commissioner after election of Roy's successor, and replace the Marine general with an American minister. For Russell, the report had only condescending praise: it noted his whole-hearted and single-minded devotion to the interests of Haiti, as he conceived them. (71)

The central conclusion, however, was beyond argument: "The failure of the Occupation to understand the social problems of Haiti, its brusque attempt to plant democracy there by drill and harrow, its determination to set up a middle class - however wise and necessary it may seem to Americans - all these explain why, in part, the high hopes of our good works in this land have not been realized."

When the commissioners reached Washington, they repaired in a body to President Hoover, who, after looking through the report, said, "This seems to be along the lines I would like to move. I think we might accept it now."

To his credit, Forbes replied that "the Commission harbored no illusions, that I thought we had offered a palliative and not a remedy. That conditions were fundamentally thoroughly unsound in Haiti and that we did not feel that after all these changes had been made there was any guarantee that the new government would be able to carry on."

On 28 March Hoover announced acceptance of the commission's recommendations as American policy toward Haiti.

The one-sidedness of the report, as well as the accompanying press coverage, were deeply wounding to General Russell. As the *New York Times* reported a year later (28 June 1931), Russell's rebuttal to the commission, which he asked to be made public, was withheld from the press and ignored in the report, because it was "controversial," or, as the *Times* said, because "it would have been politically disturbing in the United States."

On 26 May, Russell sent the Secretary of State a final thirty-one-page reclama for the record. Well constructed, in places devastating, this *cri de coeur* rightly lays at the doorstep of American policy the shortcomings of the United States in Haiti. When Cotton read it, he minuted: "This report should go to the Secretary *and then be locked up.*"(72) As if in echo, though written earlier, a British analyst had commented: "Hayti is sorely troubling to the American conscience . . . The United States has got itself into a most unfortunate mess."

In the margin, a Foreign Office reader penciled, "One need not wonder at the result of a visit to the Augean Stables."

France, the Church, and the Occupation

In 1891, telling the Quai d'Orsay about an ecclesiastic contest among the Fathers of the St. Esprit and between their order and the secular clergy in the back country, Flesch, the French minister, set out some penetrating observations on the Church in Haiti: "The secular clergy of this country are composed exclusively of French priests recruited in Brittany, every man imbued with warmest love of country and therefore strongly inclined to profess that the interests of France and of the Catholic Church are inseparable in the Black Republic."

Then Flesch went on:

The essentially French orientation implanted up to now among the Catholic clergy in Haiti will be lost . . . as will the invaluable moral preponderance we enjoy here from support of the small army of priests, brothers, and nuns deployed throughout Haiti, where, obedient to the impulse of France, they labor without cease to imbue all classes of the Haitian people with French instruction and education, with ideas and tastes that foster sympathy for France and strengthen the bonds between the two peoples (and also promote the sale of our products, and our commercial enterprises).

During the first decade of occupation, France, preoccupied with larger and more immediate interests in Europe, pursued a waiting policy in regard to Haiti (73). This was the period in which the *Service Technique* began to take shape, whether so intended or not, as an American challenge to French and Catholic educational and cultural institutions of Haiti, thus generating head-on collision between the Breton priests who still ran Haiti's schools and parishes and the practical men, largely Protestant, who worked for Dr. Freeman. While these latter maintained that they were merely agricultural and vocational specialists, the *Service Technique* cut square across the grain of French Catholic education and willy-nilly set out to supplant primary schools by American-style, vocational-training schools. The result, whose symptoms first appeared in 1927, was the beginning of subterranean opposition by the Church to the American presence and all its works. American Brothers of Christian Instruction, brought to Haiti to teach during this period, were virtually ostracized and eventually sent home by French ecclesiastical superiors(74)

By 1929 opposition became less subterranean: the Church's support of the students and their strike was well known, and intelligence reports came to Russell that the French legation had been suborning both priests and strikers. These developments, moreover, coincided with arrival in 1929 of a new French minister, Ferdinand Wiett ("thick set and round faced"), whose actions and attitudes, Russell wrote, signaled "a decided change in attitude. It could only be concluded that he was acting under instructions and that France's policy toward the Intervention had changed."

That Russell was correct was soon proven when Wiett began making openly anti-occupation speeches to the Alliance Française and other groups.

What were did France's interests in sabotaging the American occupation?

One answer would be that cultural irredentism impelled Paris, the Church its surrogate, to undermine American incursion into a one-time French preserve.

The proximate cause, however, was the *Service Technique*, which uniquely provoked the Bourbon displeasure of France, the Church, and the elite, all of whose intersecting interests it maladroitly threatened. In the thoughtful verdict of Magowan,

> Brother Hyppolite, the little Breton friar who for twenty years has been walking up and down the mountains of Hayti, seems to have routed Mr. Colvin (Dr. Freeman's acting successor] with his batteries of experts in Buicks and his promise of prosperity on the Illinois model. If the *Service Technique* had been instructed by the same ideas as the Haytian Ministry of Education, the troubles of October-November 1929 and the subsequent revision by the United States of her policy here would probably never have occurred.

Borno Departs

Neither side quite knew how to end the Borno regime (or, more largely, the occupation) with dignity, let alone grace. No sooner were *Rochester* and the Forbes Commission beyond the horizon than the opposition, though it had won everything it wanted, gave in to the temptation to flout Borno even at the price of bad faith. On 20 March, at the Théâtre Parisiana, Borno's foes convoked a meeting whose proclaimed purpose was to "elect" Roy provisional president and thus render moot the prearranged, constitutional election by the hated *Conseil d'Etat*.

Borno, for his part, made one final attempt to clutch the power that was slipping away. Word was spread that the Roy deal was unconstitutional and, banish any such thought, Borno would therefore have no part in it. At that point - it was now early April, with only a month of the president's term to go - General Russell, for the last time, used his iron hand, telling his old friend and faithful collaborator that, if matters came to it, the United States would simply install Roy as president on 15 May. On 21 April - rammed home by a final shakeup to replace ten intransigents - the *Conseil* thereupon met and elected Eugène Roy.

The remaining weeks passed in a flurry of sedition and disorder: scurrilous handbills papering Port-au-Prince with mourning notices (*La bête est morte... foudoyée par le plan Hoover ...*") for Borno's forthcoming "funeral," and a rash of fires such as the capital (75) had not known since 1915.

On 15 May 1930, Haiti had its third constitutional change of power in 126 years. Eugène Roy took the oath of office at the Autel de la Patrie, then went to the cathedral through cheering streets for a very grand Te Deum such as the hierarchy had never given his very Catholic predecessor, and returned to the *Palais National*, where, with full honors and gun salutes by the *Garde*, Borno received the new president and took his leave. As he passed through the palace gates, he was roundly booed by the crowds that had acclaimed Roy.(76)

Recessional

President Roy has made a completely clean sweep of the Borno Administration, and has, in fact, made some appointments that render competent observers uneasy about the future . . . This policy is being pursued regardless of any arguments based on efficiency of administration.

Thus did Magowan report developments a few weeks after Borno departed. American chargé Stuart Grummon in turn succinctly described the new cabinet as "largely composed of black Haitians of extreme anti-American antecedents." But Roy's appointments, except as they symbolized the end of the *dictature bicéphale* (two-headed dictatorship), were of little consequence: as caretaker, his function was to arrange and preside over the forthcoming election of a permanent president in the fall, and this he did with fairness and competence.(77)

All summer the campaign rolled on in a welter of *taffia,* cockfighting, and *bamboche;* but despite the impassioned speeches, apathy prevailed, and no wonder: only a half dozen out of any hundred voters could read, write, or speak French. All candidates and factions alike ran against the occupation; otherwise, the underlying issue was as old as 1804 - whether *mulâtre* Liberals or *noir* Nationalists were to get control. Evidently new to Haiti, the American vice-consul at the Cap said, "Bitter hatred has developed between the Black people and the Mulattoes . . . "

In the event, when elections for the two Chambers were held on 14 October 1930, it was what Magowan called "the appeal to the black man's blackness" that carried the day. The Nationalists won in a landslide.

The reaction of the defeated *mulâtres,* who had labored so long, and often so mischievously, to release this imp from the bottle, was surprise and dismay. Two eminent elite visitors (Hannibal Price and Robert Ewald) told Grummon that "they consider it inevitable, unless matters change radically during the next years, that it will be but a brief time after the date of withdrawal of the Intervention when political strife and dissension will again break out, and Haiti will revert to the chaotic condition which obtained in 1915."

There followed frantic jockeying, culminating on 18 November when, on the fourth ballot, Sténio Vincent - ironically, the lightest-colored man in the Chamber save perhaps the distinguished Fombrun - prevailed over Pradel and Jean Price-Mars and in so doing assured continuance, for a time at least, of *mulâtre* hegemony. Jolibois *fils,* alumnus of three lunatic asylums, was elected president of the *députés.* (78) The first piece of business of the new legislators was to vote themselves a monthly expense allowance of $100, retroactive to November of the year previous. The next - a resolution that both Vincent and the American legation simply ignored - was to declare the treaty of 1915 invalid.

Vincent's cabinet - who pointedly referred to themselves as *"un ministère de combat"* - included Sannon, Foreign Minister; Percéval Thoby, Finance; and Auguste Turnier, representing one of Jacmel's most distinguished *noir* families, Interior.

It had been the American expectation that the remaining period of occupation and tutelage would be devoted to a nicely regulated, fine-tuned, orderly retrocession of authority to carefully prepared Haitian officials during the years until 1936, when the treaty expired. Vain hope. The Vincent regime felt obligated to repudiate Borno and an his works, and the best way to publicize this policy was noncooperation with the *blancs* (a tactic both Vincent and Sannon blunted under the table whenever it was possible to work with Dana Munro without being caught at it). When, in May 1931, as a result of a squabble unrelated to *"désoccupation,"* as the process was being called, the National Assembly forced out Vincent's entire cabinet, cooperation became still more difficult.(79) As 1931 reached its close, E. D. Watt, Magowan's successor, summed up the legislature's performance as "a Punch and Judy show where the rabble met daily either to approve some of the impossible projects put forward in very exciting language . . . or to jeer at some sensible remark made against any of these projects by one or more of the responsible members."

Fortunately, more progress in Haitianization had already been brought about by General Russell than the Forbes Commission had taken the trouble to find out. As early as 1928 the high commissioner had intensified programs for training Haitians to take over key jobs in the treaty services.

It was well that this solid groundwork was already complete, for little more could be accomplished in any constructive spirit. Egged on by a press whose editors, insofar as the occupation was concerned at least, need no longer fear Borno's prison,(80) ministers and legislators vied in jabbing at treaty officials and the occupation as a whole, a process, Munro pointed out, that took considerable heat off Vincent. But the point was clear enough: Haiti wanted the Americans out, as in truth by now the Americans did also save for the nagging thought of $16 million in bonds still unredeemed in 1930 - a U.S.-guaranteed obligation which demanded financial control, and thus other tutelary controls, until expiry of the treaty.

Thus the *désoccupation* became one long wrangle in which it seemed increasingly advantageous to the Haitians to provoke continuous controversy because they knew they could make the exercise of American treaty rights profitless and bothersome, and in the end usually obtain further concessions. This process caused a disillusioned Munro to write Washington in June 1931: "I cannot see that it is any part of .our duty toward Haiti to assist the Government in power by lending ourselves as a target for abuse."

The first step toward *désoccupation* was complete Haitianization in August 1931 of the Travaux Publiques, Service de Santé, and the broken-backed *Service Technique*. In addition, for the first time since 1918, Haiti could enact its own laws without submission to the American legation, and the *Banque* could again pay government *mandats* without the visa of LaRue. Though not provided for in the agreement, Colonel Little, back in Haiti again as the popular and tactful brigade commander, not only put a final end to martial law, but personally ordered that the tall flagpole at the casernes, from which the Stars and Stripes still flew, be shortened until it was lower than the palace flagpole and the Haitian Flag(81).

The essential final steps that remained were negotiation of a treaty to replace the odious predecessor of 1915, thus settling future relations (including fiscal controls) between the United States and Haiti, and the drafting of a new constitution to supersede that of 1918, with its smell of 1915.

Constitution came easier than treaty. While presented as liberal and de-Americanized, the draft enacted in 1932 perpetuated Borno's 1927 amendments and further concentrated power in the *Palais*. (Ironically, with cosmetic changes in language, it even retained the once-controversial section permitting *blancs* to acquire and own land. But few had done so anyway.)

There was a great row in which, on a tide of nationalism, the assembly rejected a treaty that had been signed by Dana Munro and Foreign Minister Albert Blanchet. The way out was to renegotiate the essentials - Haitianization of the *Garde*, stand-down of the Marines, and future fiscal controls - in terms least offensive to national pride and to set out the result not as a treaty subject to the caprice of press and politicians but an executive agreement between the two presidents. Norman Armour, the new American minister, was able to get through such an agreement, signed on 7 August 1933, which in effect ended the occupation.(82)

Like Borno before him (who was the first president ever able to leave the country for a foreign trip while in office), Vincent visited the United States in the spring of 1934. He was feted at the White House, by the Pan-American Union, and at a brilliant diplomatic dinner given by Sumner Welles in his Massachusetts Avenue mansion (now the Cosmos Club). The visit was returned on 5 July 1934, by Franklin D. Roosevelt, who put in at the Cap aboard U.S.S. *Houston,* en route to Panama and thence the Pacific.(83)

The President, clad in white pongee, debarked over the wharf in a temperature that was close to 100°. After what FDR later said was the longest walk he had made since being stricken with polio, the two presidents drove through dense crowds to the Union Club, where, amid toasts drunk, at Roosevelt's request, in that greatest of rums, five-star Barbancourt, the memorandum of understanding was agreed to. Then, not forgetting a special word with Ernest Chauvet and André Chevallier, who had been his interpreters in 1917 - Roosevelt delivered a short speech in French and returned to *Houston,* his coat, Armour recollected, now wringing wet.

The main result of the historic meeting (which a plaque in the Union Club still recalls) was that U.S. Marines would be out of Haiti by mid-August.

Already orders had been issued dispersing the American officers of the *Garde* to such far corners of the world as San Diego, Bremerton, Quantico, Shanghai, and Peking. Like Rochambeau leaving his horse for Capoix-la-Mort, (84) the Marines (by authorization from Washington) left behind the American weapons, ammunition, and military equipment with which, on long-term loan, the *Garde* had been equipped. On 7 July 1934, the Chief of Naval Operations radioed Colonel Little:

THE PRESIDENT HAS DIRECTED COMPLETE HAITIANIZATION OF GARDE BE COMPLETED I AUGUST AND THAT WITHDRAWAL OF MARINE FORCES SHALL TAKE PLACE DURING THE FORTNIGHT FOLLOWING,

Soon afterward, supply ships began shuttling out forward echelons of the brigade and its gear. On 28 July the last of the wives, children and pets set sail aboard U.S.S. *Chateau Thierry.*

Nineteen years to the moment since American troops set about taking over Haiti, on 1 August as ordered, while President Vincent, the cabinet, Norman Armour, and 10,000 Haitians watched, a smart battalion of the *Garde d'Haïti* swung onto the Champ de Mars to the lilt of "Angélico" from drums and bugles, and Colonel Démosthènes Calixte proudly accepted command from Colonel Vogel.

On 14 August before sunset , with a company of the *Garde* facing a company of Marines on opposite sides of the flagpole, the American colors came down for the last time at brigade headquarters(85) while the band played "The Star-Spangled Banner" and Fort National boomed out 21 guns. Then to the inexpressible joy of Haiti, 21 more guns and the "*Dessalinienne*" rang out, the cherished scarlet and blue flag rose to the peak and billowed grandly in the evening breeze.

Next morning at eight, the Marines paraded for the last time, and, behind a *Garde* band that in nineteen years had well learned "Semper Fidelis" and "The Halls of Montezuma," marched down to the waiting transports.(86)

What many Haitians made of it was expressed in *Le Temps* by Charles Moravia, who, from initially welcoming the occupation amid the chaos of 1915, had soon become its most unyielding opponent and had known the inside of the prison for his patriotism. Yet his verdict was measured and generous:

> No sentiment of enmity was manifested on the occasion of the departure of the Marines, either here or at Cap Haïtien. The Military Occupation had so tempered itself that it became unnoticed . . . There was no longer more than a suffering of patriotic pride, of wounded national self-esteem, for the Occupation had long since ceased to intervene in private life or injure private interests, and *there remains nothing for which we can reproach the Marines.* (Italics his.)

Little Better Fitted

Once again, 131 years since 1803 yet so differently - for history never really repeats itself - the *blancs* left, and it is proper to ask what they left behind.

Haiti before 1915 had been isolated from the surrounding world for more than a century. Thus, the overriding impact of American occupation was modernization. Any comparison of the Haiti of 1915 with that of 1934 would support this conclusion overwhelmingly - even though 1995 might not.

Yet the essential Haiti had been changed so little; in only nineteen years to be sure, little enough should have been expected. The Americans - reversing the cliche that the United States always tries "to export democracy" - had laid no foundations, were really not allowed to lay foundations, for Haitians to rule themselves save in the old ways. Writing bleakly to Forbes in 1930, Russell went to the heart of it: "While tremendous advances have been made in the material rehabilitation of Haiti, and the happiness and prosperity of the mass of the Haitian people have been decidedly increased, the Haitian people are, today, but little better fitted for self-government than they were in 1915." Little real change had in truth been wrought.

Item: In March 1934 (wrote the British minister), Vincent breathlessly apostrophized on inauguration by the *Nation* in December 1930 for "his love of liberty and his ardent belief in self-government" - "is becoming more and more an admirer of the dictatorship principle and considers Haiti quite unsuited to parliamentary government. "
Item: Elie Lescot of the Cap, late Minister of Interior and now Haitian minister in Ciudad Trujillo, in July 1934 secretly ordered five gross of special military buttons from an American firm. The buttons were for the uniforms of himself and personal staff when, later in the year, conjecturally with the support of Rafael Leonidas Trujillo, he planned to fly into Port-au-Prince and take over the presidency.
Item: By the end of 1932, doctors of the newly Haitianized *Service d'Hygiène* were already diverting so many government drugs and medical supplies into private hands that pharmacists complained they might be run out of business.

Leyburn, who knew his Haiti so well, said afterward that the occupation failed because the Americans never recognized the social situation in Haiti, and their labors were thus in vain. To this might be added that the elite, like the Bourbons forgetting nothing and learning nothing, for their part proved unable to rise to the greatest opportunity ever vouchsafed Haiti by history.
What the occupation did and tried to achieve or build - from infrastructure to creation of a *noir* yeomanry or a career civil service, even the Garde, it matters not - turned out to be built on sand. The few legacies that did last were indirect: a degree of modernization, and cultural echoes of a prolonged and, for a while - before it too went the way of other *blancs* - dominant foreign presence.

At the very end, a Marine officer, who during two tours in Port-au-Prince had been a tenant of Georges Léger, came to tell him the Americans were leaving and to bid *congé*.
"You'll be glad to see us go and the occupation end," said the Marine.
"Yes," replied Maître Georges, who had done so much to bring this about. "I will be absolutely honest. We know how you have helped us in many ways

and we appreciate that. But after all, this is our country and we would rather run it ourselves. "

Footnotes - Chapter 12

1. Within less than a year, propaganda broadsides making play with the "Caperton Account" were shrieking, "Admiral Caperton has already placed to his personal credit the sum of $216,000 as his share of the pillage of the Treasury."
2. Haiti presented few new problems to Colonel Waller. A dynamic Virginian with thirty-three years' service, he had been with the British in Egypt, served in the Boxer Uprising, conducted the initial pacification of Samar in the Philippines, and commanded Marine brigades in the Cuban Pacification (1906) and Veracruz (1914). In the tactics of pacification and of what was then called "colonial infantry," Waller probably had no peer among American officers.
3. On 15 August Bobo sailed for Santo Domingo, where he was refused permission to remain, and thence went on to Cuba. Eventually, after some years in Jamaica, where he had a large medical practice, Bobo ended up in Paris, still intriguing for the presidency. There he died on 3 December 1929, and lies, suitably interred, he would have considered, in Père Lachaise cemetery.
4. Reporting the Church's "continued disquiet," Déjean de la Batie, who had succeeded Girard as French minister, said the Catholic hierarchy perceived the Marines "as the advance guard of an invasion of Protestant pastors."
5. Sannon lasted less than a month, during which he continually attempted to block ratification of the treaty that would establish the new order of things. B.Danache, Dartiguenave's cabinet secretary, later wrote that Sannon accepted his portfolio only as a pulpit from which to proclaim hostility to the United States. On 7 September, with Sansaricq, Minister of Public Works and the other die-hard, Sannon was eased out and replaced by Louis Borno, who, besides ability and intelligence, brought considerable diplomatic experience. Minister Girard saw Sannon's eclipse as no disaster. Besides being viscerally antiforeign, Girard reported, Sannon was *"un esprit chicaneur"* whose previous time in the Foreign Ministry had been characterized by *"une grande faussete."*
6. Even with customs collections, little enough was available. In 1915 Haiti's public debt amounted to $25 million (estimated market value, $19.875 million). On a coffee export tax of $3.00 per hundred pounds, $2.53 were legally earmarked for the three French loans (1875, 1896, and 1910), and 28 cents more represented liens for various interior loans and contracts. This left the Haitian government 19 cents out of $3.00 revenue for ordinary operating expenses - assuming total honesty and efficiency in the *douanes.*
7. Within a month, realizing that to be effective, customs control required control of smuggling, of coffee particularly, Caperton was asking the Navy Department for coastal patrol forces, still another logical if unforeseen corollary of customs takeover. Smuggling thereupon ceased to be a problem.
8. Adding injury, Paymaster Conard promptly stabilized the *gourde* in a fixed (5 to 1) exchange rate for the dollar, thus at one stroke putting out of business the currency speculation, both Haitian and foreign, that had so often gutted the treasury. Emile Elie, Dartiguenave's Finance Minister, pled in vain to Conard that all his friends had been

accustomed to make their living from a floating *gourde* and "it would be an economic crime to ruin their business."

9. Carrying water on both shoulders, Dartiguenave then promptly instructed Solon Ménos, Haitian minister in Washington, to protest imposition of martial law, which Ménos heatedly did.

10. France, as might be expected, took its time re-recognizing Haiti, while for its part the Dartiguenave government tried to get out of the public penalties Paris sternly demanded. The Haitians, for example, told the French no gun salute could be rendered because the Americans wouldn't let them have any powder. Finally, on 25 November, after president, cabinet, and general staff had paid a call of contrition on the French minister and finally rendered the salute, France restored diplomatic relations. Until then a French cruiser was stationed in the harbor and (somewhat to American annoyance) French Marines were kept ashore. One sidelight from Quai d'Orsay archives is that the French navy cracked Caperton's codes, and, from 2 September onward, the communication staff of cruiser *Conde* were intercepting and reporting classified U.S. radio traffic to and from Port-au-Prince.

11. The interpretive commentary - seven pages in typescript - had as its main objects retention of the president's patronage power to appoint employees in the *douanes* (thus gutting customs control): a Haitian veto over American appointment of treaty officials; and definition of the American role as advisory to, rather than binding on, the Haitian government. The United States simply declined to accept the commentary, on the technicality that it was not couched as an express reservation, and in due course sent the treaty, minus commentary, to the U.S. Senate for ratification. Thereafter, when in a forlorn hope Borno delayed final exchange of ratifications while trying to negotiate the commentary into reservations and thus into the treaty, Lansing pointed out that the U.S. Senate had never considered, let alone ratified, the commentary - and there the matter rested.

12. Three days after Beach returned, Davis, suffering from then dread "blood poisoning" (septicaemia), was invalided home by steamer under care of a navy surgeon. During the next fortnight, until Minister Bailly-Blanchard was finally sent back, the American legation, in an arrangement probably without precedent in U.S. diplomacy, remained in charge of Caperton's bright French-speaking engineering officer, Lieutenant Oberlin.

13. The U.S. Senate ratified the treaty on 28 February 1916, without debate, by unanimous consent. Ratifications were finally exchanged on 3 May of that year, whereupon the treaty superseded the modus vivendi and took effect.

14. An unforeseen problem encountered by Marines at the prison was a chronic surplus of prisoners. Every time an outside work-detail checked back in, it would contain a few volunteers glad enough to live in as long as the Americans fed them regularly. Another attractive aspect of incarceration, U.S. style, was that each discharged inmate was allowed to keep the converted tin can issued to him as cup and mess gear.

15. Cole got on friendly terms with both leaders and later spoke warmly of them. Pétion, a friend of Charles Zamor, he described as "a man of a great deal of intelligence," who settled into peaceable ways and prospered handsomely in logwood, which was then in world demand. "Most of the *Cacos* I ran into I rather liked," Cole said in 1920. "They were more sincere. The Haitian politician, I never had much use for."

478 Written in Blood

16. One of Charles Zamor's first proposals to Caperton, on 27 August, had been that he be given $200,000 gold and sent into the interior to buy in the *Caco* chiefs and their men. The admiral said the sum was "preposterous" and noted in his journal, "It was obvious that a large part of the sum suggested by Zamor would be pure graft."

17. In an account written forty years later, Antoine Pierre-Paul said his force numbered 800 and that his own "column" had routed "150 American Marines," leaving the streets blocked with "numerous corpses of dead Marines." Nothing remotely resembling this took place: there were no American casualties. Pierre-Paul blamed his defeat on treachery, which may not be wholly wrong. Colonel Waller later testified that Dartiguenave had ample advance warning. And only three days afterward Caperton accurately reported the main outlines of the "plot covering Port-au-Prince, Les Cayes, and South Haiti generally."

18. Léger's true feelings did not entirely escape the Americans; in February, Waller wrote, "One of the greatest agitators against us and this Government is Léger. Léger is very quiet but very active."

19. On his return to the United States, Paymaster Conard was seconded to the State Department for some months to help with the financial and economic problems of the occupation.

20. *"Vendre le pays aux blancs!"* was a cry no politician could ignore, but sophisticated persons - notably Frédéric Marcelin, and, going back to 1860, Alexandre Bonneau - had long argued that Haiti would never attract foreign capital for development until land-ownership restrictions were relaxed.

21. The *Conseil d'Etat* has been labeled an American gimmick to enable Dartiguenave to bypass an obstreperous legislature. In fact it represented a suggestion by Dartiguenave and was an ancient constitutional organ that dated back to Dessalines's constitution of 1805 and reappeared six times between 1805 and 1874.

22. Colonel Waller, not for the first time, seems to have been at odds with Caperton in allowing Dartiguenave to dissolve the Senate. Testifying in 1921 , Waller said, "Personally, I was bitterly opposed to it," and went on to describe his efforts to "reestablish them," which, he stated, were thwarted at every point "by the President of Haiti and his secretaries."

23. Haitian accounts of these proceedings, such as that advanced by the *Union P-atriotique*, are at extreme variance. Vincent in 1921 said Butler and American officers "burst into the hall . . . with their revolvers" and that the decree in question had never been published. Other accounts (for example, the statement of the NAACP at the Senate hearings) charged that U.S. Marines had closed down the assembly by force and that no decree ever existed - an assertion Butler demolished by producing the signed original. As for the "revolver" charge, Butler testified that the only weapons in the hall were those of *gendarmes* posted there, at the request of the speaker, to keep order.

24. In a speech at Butte, Montana, on 18 August 1920, Roosevelt, then running for the vice-presidency, expansively remarked,"You know, I have had something to do with running a couple of little republics. The facts are that I wrote Haiti's Constitution myself and, if I do say it, I think it a pretty good Constitution." Warren Harding, soon to be elected on the opposing ticket, took Roosevelt at face value and rejoined, "I will never empower an assistant secretary of the Navy to draft a constitution for helpless neighbors in the West Indies and jam it down their throat at the point of bayonets." Both politicians

were wide of the mark: Sumner Welles put the facts straight in 1927: "Although Franklin Roosevelt claimed . . . the Constitution had been written by him, his statement was not accurate, since it was drafted in the Department of State." In the same letter Welles added that the constitution "was practically forced upon the Haitian Congress in a manner which was unwise and undoubtedly open to criticism." None of this dented FDR: as late as 1933, as the latter recalled, he regaled Henry L. Stimson with an account of high jinks in writing the Constitution of Haiti.

25. Waller had more immediate sources than the State Department. By 1916, as Waller testified, U.S. cryptographers were decoding Dartiguenave's instructions to Solon Ménos in Washington, which were, Waller said, often "exactly the reverse of his promises."

26. Haiti declared war on Germany on 12 July 1918. As an intended slap at the United States in 1917, the legislature had declined to join the war although Dartiguenave and Borno saw such action as opening the way for an American "war loan" and a seat at the peace table - expectations they so adroitly supported that the State Department, which realized that Haiti's hopes could not be fulfilled, applied the brakes as long as it could.

27. In the way forceful men sometimes convey an impression of bigness, Charlemagne has been remembered as a man of powerful physique. His autopsy report and prison medical record, however, show that, at 5 feet, 9.5 inches and 140 pounds, he was of middle height and spare in weight. He was born in 1886.

28. One of history's ironies was that only three years later, Charlemagne's successor at Port-de-Paix under the occupation was Lieutenant H. H. Hanneken, with whom Charlemagne had a rendezvous yet unforeseen.

29. A confidential report of 25 May 1918 shows agents systematically combing the North to tabulate the location and strength of each *Gendarmerie* detachment on behalf of Charles Zamor and Dr. Bobo. Further confirming the ambivalent relationship between the two, however, the report noted "some discord between Zamor and Bobo." This report also accurately predicted subsequent *Caco* tactics of picking off small posts initially and then working up to larger efforts.

30. The *Cacos* were poorly armed. Colonel Russell reported that they had only 200 to 300 old rifles (for which they adapted captured or stolen cartridges by wrapping string or goatskin around the base). Otherwise, they carried machetes, spears, knives, and an occasional pistol. This time, there were no weapons to cross the frontier and no German merchants to finance gunrunning. As the *Caco* cause seemed to prosper in 1919, however, more and newer arms began to leak into guerrilla hands.

31. By later standards the designation of brigade would be a misnomer: the entire Marine force numbered only 948 officers and men, barely the strength of an infantry battalion during World War II.

32. Haiti's first airfield, a dusty grass strip extending due East from Pont-Rouge, where Dessalines was massacred, later bore the name Bowen Field (for Second Lieutenant James G. Bowen, U.S.M.C., killed in 1920 in the country's first aircraft crash, outside Port-au-Prince) and as such in the late twentieth century remained the base of the Corps d'Aviation.

33. As to the insecurity of property, Charlemagne was on solid ground. A typical report at this time (of his attack on Plaisance on 3 May 1919) read in part: "The *Cacos* robbed everyone they met, pillaging all houses and taking all the men they found."

34. Throughout these operations the Marines communicated only by primitive field radio or by courier. Use of Haitian telegraph or telephone systems was expressly forbidden. That the *Cacos* and their friends were not unaware of the need for secure communications was disclosed in a *Gendarmerie* report of the discovery of a block of fifty carrier pigeons operating for supposedly commercial purposes by the German firm of Reinbold.

35. The area traversed by Hanneken, though familiar to him and even more to his *gendarmes*, was as yet unmapped. Therefore, the exact location of Charlemagne's camp (and thus of his death) remains something of a mystery. Hanneken's report simply placed Charlemagne "in the mountains between Grande Rivière and Fort Capois on the top of a high hill." To reach the camp, he went on, required "three hours' difficult mountain climbing." These clues suggest the camp may have been on Morne Celestin or Morne Dulonay, about four miles Southeast of Grande Rivière. But Haitian tradition locates the site near Morne Pompée, seven miles South of the town, where a steep ravine bears Charlemagne's name.

36. To convince other *Cacos* that Charlemagne was indeed dead, his body, laid out on a door, was photographed at Grande Rivière, a circumstance that gave rise to the canard, widely accepted decades later, that the *blancs* had crucified him to a door, a charge that the autopsy report completely dispels. To prevent necromancy or Macandal mythos, Charlemagne's body was buried in concrete at Post Chabert (between the Cap and Fort Liberté), but after the end of the American occupation, he was reburied with a state funeral at the Cap, an occasion depicted in a 1946 painting by Philomé Obin, and regarded as his masterpiece.

37. Methieus Richard, one of Benoît's generals who was captured by the *Gendarmerie* in April 1920, stated under interrogation, "Benoît told us very often he was fighting for a man named Bobo. Benoît attacked Port-au-Prince upon receiving a letter from Bobo." Richard added that Benoît "receives letters very often from Port-au-Prince."

38. U.S. Marine Corps archives (Box #23, file #6) contain a veritable *Who's Who* of ex-*Caco* leaders who had surrendered as of September 1920 and were either at home cultivating gardens or encouraging further surrenders.

39. Official reports call the site of Muth's ambush Morne Michel, but Methieus Richard, one of Benoît's generals who took part in the action, emphatically called it Morne Bourougue. Neither appears on the map or in Rouzier's geographic dictionary. On the assumption that Richard knew the country better than occupation officials, we have chosen Bourougue.

40. Although other cases of cannibalism were reported in the press (for example, the Washington *Times-Herald* of 3 January 1921) or variously charged in books, the ritual cannibalism practiced on Lieutenant Muth appears to be the only well-verified instance of this practice by the *Cacos*. On the other hand, horrifying mutilation of prisoners or dead was virtually the rule. Hooker, an experienced officer who commanded in the North and later investigated serious charges of corresponding offenses by Marines and *gendarmes*, testified to numerous cases of which the following are only examples: a *gendarme* captured outside Thomonde "cut up in small pieces and distributed along the trail"; a *gendarme* at Lascahobas, "head cut off, arms cut off at the elbows"; body mutilated"; *gendarme* at 'Ti Montagne, "head cut off, heart cut out, and body horribly mutilated." These atrocities were not confined to *gendarmes* but were routinely inflicted on peasants as well.

41. Colonel Hooker found one fifty-man *corvée* serving under *gendarme* guard as a labor force on the farm of the *magistrat communal* at Maïssade.

42. Court-martial charges were preferred against Major Wells but had to be withdrawn short of trial because of insufficiency of evidence. The report of the 1922 Senate hearings on Haiti included the following: "The Committee finds every evidence of sincere and energetic investigation of charges against Major Wells."

43. On 13 April 1919, British Ghurkha troops opened fire with rifles and machine guns on political demonstrators in the Jalianwala Bagh, a park in Amritsar, killing at least 400 and wounding some 1200 more. This tragedy, exactly contemporaneous with the alleged "indiscriminate killings" at Hinche-Maïssade, did not inhibit members of Parliament from loudly condemning American actions in Haiti in 1920.

44. Joseph Jolibois *fils, noir* editor of *Le Courrier Haïtien* and sometime president of *the députés,* had a police pedigree richly spiced with civil and criminal charges. Subsequently exiled to Argentina in 1928, he was promptly detained in an asylum, and died mad in 1936 at Pont Beudet, Haiti's lunatic asylum. The year before his death the press published a letter from him asserting that the sun was composed of geometrical blocks of ice shining by reflected light and inhabited by a species of beings resembling Laplanders.

45. *Pompiers,* with their twelve buglers, leaky two-mule Belgian steamers, and members who went home to change into uniform before responding to a fire, were not originally under the *Gendarmerie.* In the wake of a series of fires beginning in September 1918 (and coinciding remarkably with the fortunes of the *Caco* Resistance), an experienced American fireman was brought down to be an adviser, but the *pompiers* would have none of him. The Rue Fronts Forts conflagration in the spring of 1921 persuaded even President Dartiguenave (foreman though he had once been of the *Pompiers du Petit Séminaire*) that the time had come for a change. Fire service was assigned to the *Gendarmerie,* the merchants chipped in to rehabilitate or buy apparatus, and eventually the *pompiers* ended up with four motorized steamers, two gasoline pumpers, two hose wagons, and a chemical rig, as well as an effective water-supply system. When the first fire to occur under the new regime was knocked down in minutes, the press said the American fire chief had set it in order to show off.

46. Because of his singular maladdress in a 1918 episode at the Cercle Bellevue, Haiti's most exclusive social club, Butler caused all invitations to, and memberships of, U.S. officials to be withdrawn, as well as establishment of a house rule that no officer wearing U.S. uniform would be admitted. Not until 1960 was a U.S. Marine officer again elected to this distinguished club.

47. To nail down U.S. policy of continuing the occupation, the Senate, by a vote of 43 to 9, rejected an amendment by Senator King, seconded by Senators George Norris (Republican of Ohio) and William Borah (Republican of Idaho) to eliminate from the 1922 naval appropriations all funds to support U.S. forces in Haiti.

48. Watt, the British minister, reported of Borno's citizenship status, "The question is a very complicated legal one as it would appear that while according to French laws M. Borno's father would be French, according to Haitian law he would be a Haitian." Setting aside the juridical intricacies of the issue - which was raised against Borno throughout his presidency - it is fair to point out that he lived his life and spent his career as a Haitian in the mainstream of Haitian politics.

482

As the occupation took hold, the fires that had been so often the scourge of Port-au-Prince lessened. Merchants chipped in to buy motorized equipment such as the steamer shown here. *Heinl Collection*

49. It has been frequently charged, in Robert Rotberg's words, that "the Americans simply replaced [Dartiguenave] with Borno." Other than unsupported statements to this effect, no evidence has been found to justify the conclusion. Given Dartiguenave's declining usefulness to the occupation, not to mention (but in hindsight) Borno's future cooperation (which the United States could hardly have anticipated), the change proved welcome. But, on the known record, the forces that put Borno in office were not American machinations (and Russell, unlike Beach, avoided all contact with the electoral process) but rather Borno's political astuteness and 0.J.Brandt's purse.

50. Dartiguenave had only four years to live. Like Nissage, he retired to his native town, Anse-à-Veau, where, in 1925 (possibly owing to the pipe he inveterately smoked), he was smitten with tongue cancer. He died there on his estate during the night of 7-8 July 1926.

51. One product of this program, a twenty-seven-year-old Port-au-Prince student who got his original interest in medicine doing chores at the naval hospital, graduated in the last American-supervised class, 1934. His name was François Duvalier.

52. Describing Haitian politics, American chargé d'affaires George R. Merrell explained: "There are two political groups: the pro-Government and the anti-Government A political party in Haiti is like a group of clients in ancient Rome. A political aspirant with money gathers his own supporters, and when he has spent all his money, or failed to gain office, the clients go to another leader."

53. Despite the windfall of buying in for only $6 million debts amounting to over $21 million, hindsight critics scored Financial Adviser McIlhenny for (1) neglecting to refund before the franc had recovered after World War I (thus allegedly "losing" a million dollars): and (2) not foreseeing and awaiting the later collapse of the franc, thus "losing" still more - and of course allowing critics a victory either way.

54. Dying by inches, the Chemin de Fer National expired in the 1960s, its last function being to haul cement from the Fond Mombin factory to Port-au-Prince. The Plaine Cul-de-Sac survived as a canefield line for HASCO, with industrial sidings in Port-au-Prince for the wharf. Vintage engines and ancient National Railroad rolling stock treasures for the railroad buff - remained abandoned at St. Marc, Verrettes, and the Cap and were sold piecemeal for scrap. One tonton macoute explained to an onlooker who had the temerity to question his title to the rails he was having removed from the abandoned right of way that they were a "gift" from Maman Simone [Duvalier]. This and other bits of arcana are recorded in a splendid book by Dr. Georges Michel, "Les Chemins de Fer de L'Ile d'Haïti". During an otherwise uneventful life, Haiti's third railroad, Chemin de Fer Central, provided the country with its most disastrous train wreck in 1917, near Lamentin, where over a hundred passengers were killed.

55. In 1929 Davis surfaced on Sumner Welles's doorstep in Washington, seeking to replace General Russell as high commissioner. When news of these maneuvers reached W. W. Cumberland, who for four years had been the no-nonsense financial adviser, the latter wrote Dana Munro: "No worse calamity could befall [the occupation] than having Mr. Davis connected with it."

56. Visitors were told (and naively believed) - an outcry the U.S. press quickly took up - that Haitian editors were being "denied the right of habeas corpus," a process unknown to the Code Napoleon and unheard-of in Haiti.

57. Chauvet served some years as secretary-interpreter for the *Gendarmerie* and had ardently supported the occupation until his father-in-law, Stephen Archer, fell out with Borno. "His views," unkindly reported the British minister, "are unpredictable without knowledge of his paper's sources of income."

58. During his 1921 testimony before the McCormick Committee, Smedley Butler went to the heart of the question of provost courts and martial law: "If you raise martial law down there, while there are any United States troops at all in Haiti, you are going to have some of them murdered . . . Wherever the flag goes, we have got to have protection for the soldier."

59. Article 409 of the Code Penal expressly proscribed "makers of *ouangas,* practitioners of Voodoo, *macandalisme,* and other witchcraft ... All dances and other practices calculated to foster fetichism and superstition shall be deemed witchcraft and punished accordingly."

60. The Cercle Bellevue became more than ever a symbol of elite resistance in January 1928, when, in protest against the detention of editor-members, the club canceled its grand ball for Carnaval. Retribution struck quickly: Borno padlocked the club on 31 January (employing an American officer of the *Garde* to execute the decree). Not until eighteen months later, when Eugène Roy, a founder-member of 1905, became president, was the edict revoked.

61. A sibling charge often lodged by Haitians was that the American *Garde* officers were ill-educated, raw rankers, an accusation that during World War I, when the best Marines of all ranks were going to France, was probably true. But Russell's earliest effort was to upgrade this class of officer not only by stringent selection but by a three-month indoctrination course before the officers were passed for duty with the *Garde.* In 1930, 49 *Garde* officers were college graduates; 51 had high school diplomas or some college courses. That same year, 85 spoke French and 92 also spoke Créole. The entire group, 116 Americans in all, averaged over four years in Haiti and thirteen years in the Corps.

62. Opportunely founded in the fall of 1929 was one of the most inflammatory of the anti-Borno and anti-occupation dailies, *La Presse,* edited by Placide David, with Jacques Roumain a leading contributor. David, a *noir* and well-known Voodoo practitioner, had, though secretly working against Borno, been the latter's *chef de cabinet* until one day he was caught placing cornmeal *"vèvès"* (cabalistic tracings) as a *ouanga* in the cabinet room and on the president's chair. In the words of Russell's report, Borno entered the room, "kicked the cornmeal aside, brushed it off his chair, and sat down. The explanation of Mr. David regarding this incident was not satisfactory, and he accordingly resigned."

63. Haitian teachers had a grievance of their own, the disparity in pay between what they received as compared with Americans doing similar work. Rayford Logan, for example, cites the 1926 case of Haitians in the *Service Technique* drawing $35 a month for the same duties as Americans receiving $150. Moreover, he goes on, Haitian teachers at the J. B. Damier school got $732 a year, while teachers in the *lycées* averaged $408 each.

64. The so-called brigade had been run down to an enlisted strength of 452 Marines in order to provide replacements for the active campaign in Nicaragua against Sandino. Five hundred reinforcements would still have left it below the size of an infantry battalion of the 1990s.

65. The clash at Les Cayes provoked a perhaps not altogether spontaneous shudder from Jacques Roumain's allies in New York, the American Communist Party, who fielded 500 demonstrators on 14 December to oppose the occupation and battle New York's finest. Dr. Gruening, now removed to the Portland *Oregonian,* was again heard from, as was the *Nation's* steady drumbeat. Secretary Stimson, who had been so hasty in attributing to General Russell the panic felt by high officials in the State Department, Stimson included, calmed himself sufficiently to apologize to Russell in a handsome message of commendation on 31 December 1929.

66. Freeman dropped dead in Puerto Rico in September 1930. His death was celebrated at Damien by a mock wake organized by students whose extreme bad taste seems to have offended both Haitian and foreign adult communities.

67. Hoover (as well as his long-time associate and man at the State Department, under Secretary Joseph P. Cotton) had even less desire to see the United States represented by the Marine Corps, against which he had long-standing animosities going back to an altercation, when he was a young civilian in Tientsin, with a Marine lieutenant, Smedley D. Butler, during the Boxer Uprising in 1900. In 1931 - 1932 Hoover was balked only by public and congressional resistance from abolishing the Marine Corps outright and transferring its members to the U.S. Army.

68. When, toward the end, a delegation from the Borno party, the National Progressives, appeared before Forbes and one other commissioner, the former told Colonel Auguste Nemours, the respected spokesman, that there would be no need for a statement as the commission "had already made up its mind."

69. Minister Magowan commented on 12 March: "The strong anti-American feeling of last November has been replaced ... by a narrower current directed particularly against the person and *entourage* of President Borno. " Two days later, Forbes noted in his diary, "The more thoughtful people, particularly the candidates for President, of whom they are legion, all want the retention of the Marines. They do not trust the capacity of their own people, their own Garde, to maintain order."

70. Secretary Cotton, whom Forbes correctly suspected had been undercutting both the commission and General Russell, tried to order the group to stay in Port-au-Prince until President Hoover had their report, but Forbes would have none of it, recording, "so we up anchor and left anyway. Five buccaneers running away with a U.S. warship against orders." That Cotton was going out of his way to disparage the performance of Russell and the Marines is confirmed in a report by the British ambassador in Washington (Sir Ronald Lindsay), stating that Cotton had said. "The regime of the U.S. High Commissioner in Haiti had done pretty badly."

71. Privately, Forbes complained to Cotton about "the injustice done to Russell," whom he described soon afterward as "a competent, conscientious official who has rendered great service to Haiti under very difficult circumstance. General Russell deserves the thanks of the American people and the credit for great achievements."

72. The original of Russell's reclama was never seen again after it presumably left Mr. Cotton's desk. The carbon copy now in the National Archives was rescued in 1933 after prolonged search by a dutiful secretary who, by the evidence of accompanying memoranda, felt the files on Haiti would be incomplete without it.

73. The Quai d'Orsay archives dealing with Haiti, so revealing up to this point, were, at the time of the writing of the first edition of this work, closed after 1918; so it remains

for future historians to set out with full authority the exact workings of French diplomacy in and toward Haiti after that point.

74. The Catholic Church in Haiti as of January 1930 comprised 1 archbishop, 5 bishops, 205 priests, 105 Brothers of Christian instruction, and 366 sisters (Filles de la Sagesse, St. Joseph of Cluny, and Filles de Marie). The brothers (83 French, 10 French--Canadian, 9 Spanish, and 3 Haitian) operated seventeen large schools. In this numerous clergy, Haiti was represented by a total of 11 priests and brothers - a considerably feebler show of Haitianization over two thirds of a century than the *Garde* that same year, with 40 percent Haitian officers after fifteen years' existence.

75. Much of the arson was anti-American or supposedly so (but the fire marshal's investigation of the blaze that razed the home of Colonel Cutts, the brigade commander, disclosed faulty wiring in a primitive icebox as the cause). Attempts were made to burn the residences of two other Marine officers and of Dr. Colvin. Yet there were other targets - a Syrian pawnshop, the charming Théâtre Parisiana, and, most senseless of all, the Cercle Bellevue, newly reopened by founder-member Eugène Roy. Magowan, puzzled, commented, "There seems to be no satisfactory explanation of this outbreak of terrorism." Jolibois *fils*, mad as ever, said the Americans were responsible.

76. Borno (the first ruler of Haiti to depart by airplane rather than Port-au-Prince Wharf) left by Pan American clipper for Havana and New York and, with his family, departed for what Magowan called "a recuperative voyage to Europe." On eventual return he lived in Pétionville (outlasting Eugène Roy by three years) and died on the morning of 29 July 1942. Among the few who left the presidency alive and constitutionally, Borno is the only incumbent who neither sought nor was granted a pension.

77. Roy returned to business and honorable retirement, died at home in Pétionville on 27 October 1939, and received a State Funeral. Just before the election, his work concluded, General Russell left Port-au-Prince quietly, without pomp or fanfare. By his own request, his escort and honor guard were composed only of U.S. Marines. Four days after Russell's departure, Dr. Dana G. Munro presented his credentials as American minister on 16 November. Russell went on to become one of the Marine Corps's most distinguished commandants and died in 1947.

78. But not without misgiving: in September 1930, when the financial adviser suggested that suitable arrangements for the interim president's pension might be left to the new regime. Roy burst out that he "would not think of leaving his case to a government of bandits such as may result from the forthcoming elections."

79. In the eighteen months preceding 1 July 1931, Haiti had six Foreign Ministers, a record as bad as that of the American officials in the early days of the occupation.

80. While open season continued for vilifying the occupation, things otherwise soon returned to normal. When, on 6 August 1932, *Le Courrier Haïtien* charged that Vincent "gorged himself on rejuvenating old wines to enable him to continue the capers of youth" and took "five doses of aphrodisiac a day," the president promptly locked up the editor, his old *Union Patriotique* colleague, Jolibois *fils*. At the same time, he also suppressed five other newspapers. As for the *Union Patriotique*, it was already eight months dead: in November 1931, a moment of supreme irony, Vincent dissolved the Union on the grounds it had become "a political association."

81. China soldier that he was, Little also enlivened Port-au-Prince by a series of gymkhanas and horse races, which promoted social contacts among races, classes, and

nationalities of those who enthusiastically attended. Educated in France, Little spoke better French than any civilian treaty official.

82. When the Haitians realized that the new American president would be Franklin D. Roosevelt, remembered for his role in the early occupation, replacing Hoover, whose decision had ended the occupation, they began negotiating more amenably with Armour, who replaced Dana Munro in 1932. Edmund Watt, British minister and old Haitian hand, vignetted his two American colleagues at this moment: "[Armour is] a man of unusual charm. Haitians find him satisfactory not only on this account but because it flatters their Francophilism to recognize in him a Europeanized diplomat. Dr. Munro, however well liked he may have been, was an expert in Central American affairs and his appointment had connotations of schoolmastership. Mr. Armour is a man of the larger world and his appointment seems a tacit recognition that Haiti has grown up. Mrs. Armour, formerly the Princess Noroff, emphasizes the European flavor with her own rather sub-acid charm."

83. Arrangements for this first visit to Haiti by an incumbent American President were nothing if not complicated. *Houston* drew too much for Port-au-Prince, but could anchor at the Cap to permit debarkation of the President, whose infirmity made the landing difficult and painful. In response, the Haitian government actually proclaimed the Cap national capital for the duration of President Roosevelt's stay, the legislators not forgetting to vote themselves what Third Secretary Gerald A. Drew (to be Ambassador a quarter of a century later) noted as "a rather handsome travel allowance for the trip." The day before *Houston* was to arrive, Armour collapsed with dengue, but struggled North in a Marine airplane whose sergeant-pilot flew high enough to get Armour's temperature down to 102. He collapsed again aboard the cruiser, but Drew, an unflappable young man who spoke excellent French, took charge and carried on.

84. Little did just that, giving his horse to one of the capital's leading equestriennes, Mme. Clément Magloire. In an unrelated grace note, Vincent invited the Littles to dine at the *Palais*: ". . . *au moment du coktail, il me sera très agréable de vous remettre le diplôme de Grand Croix de l'Ordre et Mérite pour les bons et loyaux services que vous avez rendu au pays.*"

85. The brigade headquarters, soon to become the American legation and later the embassy, remained under the American flag until 1961, when a new embassy opened on the bay front.

86. The small remaining detachment at the Cap departed on 6 August after the Department of the North, last of the departments to Haitianize, had been turned over to Major Kébreau Desvesin on 25 July. The *Capois*, some with moist eyes, raised their hats to the American colors as the Marines marched to the wharf. When their ship, U.S.S. *Woodcock*, so long the brigade's Guantanamo-based tender, pulled clear, the *Garde's* band struck up "Auld Lang Syne."

Dumarsais Estimé takes the presidential oath behind the electoral urn, 1946 *Heinl Collection* *Below:* Magloire and Trujillo in a pistol-packing embrace. *Heinl Collection*

CHAPTER 13

Second Independence

1934-1957

When they reach their forties, all good Haitians have a higher objective than a seat in the Senate.

- Paul E. Magloire

Sténio Vincent set Tuesday, 21 August 1934, as the day of the second independence, when *désoccupation* would be celebrated, but it was expecting too much to ask people to wait. Parties began on the 18th: a grand ball at the Cercle Bellevue, next night another at the Port-au-Princien, and of course the whole capital - no, the whole country in delirious *bamboche*.

The evening of the 20th, President Vincent gave a diplomatic dinner - the white palace ashine, like the Champs de Mars, with festive illumination. To the diplomatic corps and special ambassadors (including rather conspicuously the Dominican vice-president at the head of a heavily medaled delegation), Vincent's first toast was to Franklin D. Roosevelt, to which, in polished, easy French, Norman Armour replied.

At the stroke of midnight, while the guests sipped champagne on the balconies of the *Palais*, a gun boomed from Fort National, cheers and tumult echoed from Bel Air to Morne l'Hôpital, and the great *fête* began.

The diplomats had little time to sleep: by daybreak, like Gonaïves 130 years before, the city was throbbing with tens of thousands of humble Haitians who had been told they were free again; free of exactly what, may not have been very clear to some - but *"libre"* is the most intoxicating word in the Haitian vocabulary. Had not Dessalines himself on that first day of liberation proclaimed, *"Ou vivre libre ou mourir"* ?

At 8:30, true to the Church's promise, Msgrs. Conan and Le Gouaze celebrated a glorious Te Deum (at which, to be sure, the clergy were white and the altar boys *noirs*). Then, as church bells pealed from Pétionville to Bel Air, followed a presidential progress, with fistfuls of new printed *gourde* notes fluttering from Vincent's limousine right and left into the rejoicing crowd. First the president stopped to lay wreaths at the statues of Toussaint and Dessalines, the latter's bronze saber ever aloft in warning to *blancs* who might come to re-enslave the *noirs*. The next destination was the Place de l'Indépendance and the common tomb of Dessalines and Pétion monument. Doubling back to the casernes, Sténio Vincent himself ran up the colors.

Now it was 11:15 and time for a *vin d'honneur* at the palace with more speeches and then, in the palace yard and forecourt, a review of the *Garde*, including a unit constituted the day the Marines left - a new *Garde Présidentielle*, four strapping rifle platoons and one of heavy machine guns, commanded by Major Durcé Mrmand, intimate and kinsman of the president. Colonel Calixte, the new commandant, led the assembled officer corps in a moving oath of personal fealty to Vincent (also an innovation - the old oath prescribed by the *blancs* had been only to the constitution and the Haitian people), gave the president an iridescent gold-hilted sword of honor, and led the smart battalion past the gleaming white portico, to the crash of "1804." When dusk fell there were such fireworks as Port-au-Prince had never seen and *bamboche* that continued until dawn.

Nothing Stands Still

Comparisons with 1804 are irresistible. Yet obvious and powerful as are similarities between January 1804 and August 1934, the differences are even more striking.

In 1804 Haiti was wrecked and ravaged; in 1934 the country was modernized, solvent, and thriving, with a national infrastructure surpassing anything in its history.

Few if any states have been born with less preparation for nationhood than Haiti in 1804. By contrast, in 1934 Haiti was a going concern with functioning bureaucracy, disciplined apolitical forces of public order, and an incumbent administration, not of former slaves but of educated men constitutionally in power. This hegemony, unlike that of 1804, was *mulâtre,* not *noir.*

Haiti of 1804 was disdained and ostracized. That of 1934 was an object of solicitude and good wishes. On the other hand, Haitians had not defeated or massacred anyone or swept any foreign armies into the sea. The conquerors had departed unconquered.

In physical aspects the country seemed to have been reborn. As the *New York Times* reported less than a year later, "Port-au-Prince today is spic-and-span. Her public buildings glisten and every morning her streets are carefully cleansed. Thoroughfares are no longer used for garbage, or gutters for sewers. It is as healthy a capital as can be found in the Caribbean."

Yet nothing stands still; the millennium had not dawned simply because the *blancs* were gone. To begin with, there was the *Banque.* Neither the National City Bank, its owner, nor the Haitian government, its prime client, felt easy in the present situation. The City Bank, acutely aware of the American stand-down, saw itself increasingly exposed and vulnerable in Port-au-Prince.(1) Nor could any Haitian, especially a nationalist like Sténio Vincent, much enjoy the idea of a national bank and treasury owned in New York.

Then there was the *Garde,* seven eighths of its NCOs and privates *noir,* its officers mainly *mulâtre* under a *noir* commandant. Would this new-model armed force stay out of politics? Was it adequate to counterbalance the efficient, heavily armed forces of Leonidas Trujillo, the new Dominican strongman? Could the *Garde* maintain its discipline and professional edge? (2) What were the implications of the new *Garde Présidentielle* commanded by a Vincent favorite (who had been sternly reprimanded in 1931 for political activities, and who, only two months on the job, in October 1934, had already cautioned Colonel Calixte: "When you wish anything for the *Garde* from the President, see me first")?

Could parliamentary government work? Were legislative nonfeasance, obstruction, and spoiling capable of remedy? Or did the remedy - as pro-government papers were already hinting - demand that Haiti follow the trend toward dictatorship, especially fashionable in Europe?

What was the commercial future of Haiti in a world depression? The departing occupation had taken with it a $700,000 payroll, a large sum (equal to 10 percent of the national budget) in a small economy. (The first casualty of the Marines' departure was that Brasserie La Couronne, Haiti's only brewery, shut down and operated for the next forty years only as an ice plant.)

What were to be Haiti's relations with the Dominican Republic, whose chief of state was already manifesting heavy-handed friendliness toward Vincent? Not content with sending a large delegation to the *désoccupation* celebrations, Trujillo followed up with a state visit in November, described by Norman Armour in a letter to Sumner Welles:

> He arrived after many delays, a picturesque figure of the Richard Harding Davis type, moving from place to place entirely surrounded by Dominican officers openly carrying Thompson submachine-guns. Even at the receptions and dances, when the Generalissimo takes the floor, as he has done on occasion, to tread the light fantastic, he is followed around the room by his officers with hands pointedly resting on an ominous bulge in their hip pockets . . . The whole thing has been a comic opera of the very first class . . .

When not treading the light fantastic, Trujillo engaged in some very frank talk with Vincent, the only other person present being Lescot. The ground they covered was familiar: mutual reinsurance along the frontier and continued surveillance over each other's refugees and enemies. Trujillo (one of whose ships lay in Port-au-Prince sending ashore daily alms to the poor) grandly put his two-gunboat navy at Vincent's disposal to prevent arms-smuggling into the

North, where, it appeared, the *mulâtre* president from the West was regarded with reservations.(3)

Thus, in general the ongoing business and new problems of the second independence - do we say new? Not really: these were hardy perennials, old problems in new bottles.

But the most pressing business that engaged President Vincent was how he might succeed himself and prolong a term in office that, by the constitution of the moment, would end in May 1936.

The president's solution (which he confided to his new friend, Trujillo) was straightforward enough: dissolve the legislature early in 1935, rewrite the constitution agreeable to his new ideas, and put this to the people for ratification, using that device first instituted by Dartiguenave, a national plebiscite. With new constitution in hand, including express provisions for self-succession, Vincent would then hold elections at the regular time, in January 1936, for a legislature to be composed exclusively of good men and true.

His scheme, atypically, worked almost exactly as planned. As a trial run, Vincent set out to acquire control of the *Banque*, a project for which the time seemed ripe. Content to be rid of its Haitian operation, the City Bank agreed to sell out for $1 million, the institution's independence to be safeguarded by the vesting of control in majority directors appointed in New York. What seemed good to Vincent, however, did not suit the Senate (each member of which, or nearly, a presidential aspirant). When it became clear that the transaction would never pass the Senate, Vincent organized a plebiscite that, in February 1935, to the agreeable tune of 454,357 to 1172, transferred to the palace exclusive control over all economic matters. Thereupon he closed the sale as proposed, not overlooking in the process to remove eleven senators (including Price-Mars, hot-blooded Pradel, and, another colleague in the *Union Patriotique*, Pierre Hudicourt). The senators' opposition, Vincent blandly explained, put them "in rebellion against the popular will."(4)

A new constitution was the next business. While spontaneous petitions, in the manner of those preceding Dessalines's coronation, began urging Vincent to stay on, a draft was prepared by a special committee and was presented to the country by plebiscite on 2 June 1935. To no one's surprise the people obediently ratified a charter that allowed the president to dissolve the legislature and govern by decree, abolished the separation of powers, proclaimed the executive "sole authority of the State," and, for all the world like Borno with the *Conseil d'Etat*, gave Vincent outright power to name ten of twenty-one senators, the remainder to be chosen by him from slates presented by the legislature. Most important, a "Unique Article" invested Citizen Sténio Vincent with a second term commencing 15 May 1936. "The entire referendum," reported the British minister on 25 June, "was even more of a farce than most popular votes in this country."

But it was not quite that easy. No bigger than a man's hand, in March 1935 had arisen the first plot against the presidency: Lucien Hibbert, Foreign Minister and Jacques Roumain's brother-in-law, made overtures to Colonel Calixte; the colonel promptly informed the president; and Hibbert was dismissed into house arrest while pining for permission, never granted, to leave for Paris. There were also disturbances in the North, stage-managed by René Auguste, wealthiest of the senators, who aspired mightily for the office his father, Tancrède, had once held. In January 1936, while the sentry slept, bandits hit the *Garde's avant-poste* at Limonade, cut telephone lines, and decamped with weapons (quickly recovered by Colonel Calixte, who stormed North, made fifty arrests, canceled all leaves, and relieved subordinates responsible). There was also a midnight foray into Milot by a mounted band on 14 April. This time, stinging under Calixte's lash, the *Garde* was alert, returned fire, and drove the marauders off.

That, however, was all. On 15 May 1936, with the usual ceremony and pomp, Sténio Vincent succeeded himself. No one, reported George Gordon, the new American minister, was killed or wounded anywhere in Haiti throughout the day. Vincent, now at midpoint, was assessed by Shepherd, the new British minister:

> Though his general principles have been good, the President is not himself a clever man and he has not been fortunate in his choice of advisers. His choice is made difficult by his own intolerance of advice once his mind is made up, and men of an independent habit of mind will not submit." Shepherd depicted the personal side of his man in another report: "Suave, reasonably intelligent, patriotic, but reputed to be somewhat lazy and fond of the good things of life (5); He is a bachelor, and the hostess at the National Palace is his sister (Mlle. Rézia Vincent), till fairly recently French mistress in a ladies college in the United States."

The first two years of the *libération* had not been kind either to Haiti or its president. World depression had reduced by 40 percent the average annual earnings of the coffee crop prior to 1931 ; the harvest of 1935 had been a bad one, all the worse for devastating floods in October 1935, which put eight feet of water over downtown Jacmel, washed away bridges and houses throughout the Grand-Anse, and drowned at least 2000 people throughout the country. Logwood exports were at a standstill. The Haitian Pineapple Company, thriving in 1932, had gone to the wall. In fact, of the American agricultural ventures so hopefully begun a decade earlier, only HASCO and the Dauphin Sisal Plantation at Fort Liberté still survived. The one success Vincent could show was a highly successful banana monopoly worked out in 1935 with Standard Fruit Company, whereby the latter would buy Haiti's entire crop of succulent *figues-bananes,* tramping fruitboats to all ports (in itself an economic and commercial boon), rebuilding or expanding wharfage at St. Marc and Les Cayes, and opening a 2500-acre plantation in the Artibonite (though most bananas came directly from peasants). The results seemed miraculous: from an export of 1600 stems in 1927, that ten years later was 1,363,176.(6) Finally, although the surpluses accumulated by American advisers and husbanded by de la Rue still wiped out deficits, there was no easy money for anything but, perhaps, the *Garde*, in which, to the concern of Calixte, Major Armand played a larger role from the *Palais*. (7) As if all this weren't enough, complained de la Rue in a letter to Sumner Welles, garbage was no longer being regularly collected in the suburbs.

Money was the problem. The government needed more money than it could raise in order to do things it felt necessary (including providing for the livelihood of that segment of the elite in favor with the regime). Besides, as Georges Léger (soon to become both Foreign and Finance Minister) so often pointed out, continuance of American fiscal control was incompatible with an independent government. Yet the only way to get rid of the fiscal representative was to pay off the 1922 bonds. To solve both problems, borrowing from Pierre, so to speak, to pay Sam, Constantin Mayard, Haitian minister in Paris, was instructed to see how French bankers would like to make Haiti a loan that would refund the 1922 debt and, of course, include some margin for current requirements. It could almost have been 1875: at the end of 1935 negotiations collapsed of their own weight in scandal, Mayard was recalled, and his cabinet ally, Frédéric Duvigneaud, was summarily demoted to mayor of Port-au-Prince.

Other attempts to coax money out of Europe soon followed. In 1936 and later, turning to Hitler's Reich, government emissaries dickered with Hjalmar Schacht for a blocked-mark loan in which German companies and engineers would take over all public works in Haiti. December 1937 saw a renewed bid for French money in which Georges Léger - fruitlessly, as it turned out - went to Paris for secret negotiations with the Delbos government, looking to French investment of state-controlled trust funds in Haitian bonds. In both deals, surrender of control over the newly purchased *Banque Nationale* was proffered as part of the package. (When Léger arrived home empty-handed after being turned down in Paris, the French legation and French Chamber of Commerce in Port-au-Prince spread word throughout the country that Haiti's economic plight was all the fault of the Americans.)

One reason French bankers hardened their hearts toward Haiti was that certain of their clients - bitter-enders still holding out for payment of the 1910 bonds in 1910 gold francs - had prevailed on the Quai d'Orsay to tighten its screws now that the Americans had left. Although, with some fanfare, France in 1935 had renewed its commercial treaty with Haiti, the ink was hardly dry before the 1910 loan came up. Haiti was not friendless: Sumner Welles called in the

French ambassador and suggested that pressure on Haiti "would prove highly prejudicial" in trade negotiations then pending with the United States. But Washington underestimated both the stubbornness of France and concurrent heavy pressure against a tottering franc.

In March 1936, in one of the cruelest economic blows ever dealt Haiti, France abruptly denounced the commercial convention, raised duties to levels that effectively closed French markets to Haitian imports (the Havre coffee market, on which Haiti had depended since the days of Boyer, was where it hurt), and cut the black republic adrift. Within a year, prodded by de la Rue, Haiti had raised production standards for an American trade that, until Brazil dropped the bottom out of the market in 1939, was buying 35 percent of the harvest, while the rest went at good prices into Italian *espresso* and other European blends.

No reader of the Haitian papers could have learned much about the difficulties besetting Vincent. The country had been under a "state of siege" almost since the Marines left, and the tightly controlled press emitted only sycophantic paeans for the success of what Vincent called "my program." In fact, the program singlemindedly followed by the president was a smooth transition, behind due facades of legality, from representative government to dictatorship. Thus, the September elections of 1936 - the country's first general elections since *désoccupation* - presented voters with unopposed government candidates for every seat in the Chamber of Deputies, and with preprinted government slates (which voters were forbidden to alter) of members for the electoral college. This body, under the new constitution, was to nominate to the president the eleven senators he did not directly choose himself. As Vincent was soon to tell Calixte, "The Government makes the Constitution, the Laws, the Regulations and Agreements; such instruments could not handicap its activities and it must dispense with them, whenever measures deemed necessary for the maintenance of the Government rendered such a decision necessary."

In other words, the president seemed to be saying *"L'Etat, c'est Vincent,"* and by the end of 1936 it was. The masses remained disenfranchised under an authoritarian *mulâtre* oligarchy with little to show other than its own perpetuation in power. The evil old distinctions of class, region, and color were again operating full force.

There were other signs of slippage as well, not least, despite Colonel Calixte's best efforts to preserve the legacy of the Marines, reports of deterioration and politics within the *Garde*. To seasoned observers in Port-au-Prince, storm signals could be perceived ahead.

Communists and Griots

While Haiti was effortlessly slipping back into old politics and old ways, Haitian intellectuals, grouped as of old on opposite sides of the fault lines of class and color, were reexamining the country's problems in search of cultural justification and forms of politics that would be new, not old. One such group, stimulated by the worldwide intellectual infatuation with Marxism, nowhere stronger than in France, was communist.

As early as 1926, overlooking no possibilities, Jolibois *fils* made a written overture to Moscow, which the Comintern wisely seems to have ignored. Four years later, under sponsorship of the French party, the Haitian Communist Party was organized in 1930 by Jacques Roumain in concert with Max Hudicourt. Only a short time after *désoccupation,* in fall 1934, President Vincent had locked up Roumain for revolutionary activities, releasing him two years later. Speeded on his way by a presidential decree of 19 November 1936 that outlawed the communists and all their works, Roumain returned to France. In 1940, as the Nazis approached Paris, he fell back on New York, where he had friends at Columbia University. (Among Americans closely associated with Roumain was poet Langston Hughes, who in the 1930s preached communism and proletarian revolution as Haiti's ultimate solution.)

Roumain's Haitian associates throughout the decade (and until his subsequent death) (9) included Jacques Alexis (cofounder with René Depestre of the radical review, *La Ruche),* Jean Brièrre, the wild-eyed young poet of the Grand-Anse, and Jules Blanchet of Port-au-Prince. All these elite literary intellectuals of much talent were communists and would be heard from again. Also, like virtually every Haitian communist of any significance in the years to come, they were, with the conspicuous exception of Alexis, *mulâtres.*

The radicalized offspring of the elite were not the only Haitians goaded by national frustration, quest for image, and of course hard times. French Marxism, so congenial to Roumain and his fellows, had little appeal for a new breed of bourgeois *noir* intellectuals and bureaucrats, products of the occupation (and, though they would hardly have admitted it, of General Russell's effort to create a *noir* middle class), who, at the time communism first germinated, were seeking and finding Haiti's roots in Africa. The leaders of this movement, which was to coalesce in 1937 under the name of *Les Griots,*(8) were Jean Price-Mars, whose ethnographic studies had illuminated Haitian religion (Voodoo), language (Créole), and folklore; Lorimer Denis, the tall, forbidding, Voodoo-steeped, black-clad professor from the Cap with his stout *cocomacac;* and Dr. J.-C. Dorsainvil, author of the *Manuel d'Histoire d'Haïti,* read by generations of schoolchildren long after his death. Another *Griot* was François Duvalier, an ultranationalist young doctor already steeped in Haiti's history, who was writing obscurantist articles in equally obscure publications.

The self-assumed mission of the *griots* was to re-examine Haiti in the light of African origins, consciously turning their backs on European heritage and seeing in Voodoo, (sometimes politely called "folklore") essential sources of Haitian literature, art, and folkways. This movement had various names - *"indigènisme"*, *"Africanisme, "Haïtienisme"* - and its votaries, virtually all *noirs,* spoke of themselves as *"authentiques, "* in slighting contrast to *mulâtres,* who were not *noirs* and could therefore never be *authentiques.* Within a decade, Jean-Paul Sartre had given this African-West Indian phenomenon a title, *"négritude. "* It expressed profoundly the impulses that animated the *Griots.*

Both communists and *Griots* were heavily literary in makeup. Roumain, for example, was Haiti's greatest novelist. His works explored the folkways and social plight of urban and rural masses. Just as the *griots* were a counterfoil to the communists, Roumain's novels took departure from the romanticized ethnological writings of Price-Mars. Denis and Duvalier coauthored a series of labyrinthine works.'

Although neither group could perceive it, they were already in competition for a power base among the urban poor and such peasants and villagers as had attained political perceptions. The *griots* and their followers, however, were avowedly anti-elite and anti-*mulâtre*, and thus a true movement of masses against the classes, something, because of its members' elite origins, the Communist Party could never quite become.

In contrast to its elite, Haiti in the 1930s was not ripe for communism, nor were the rigors of communism - self-discipline, self-sacrifice, and self-denial - any more congenial to most Haitians than the same demands in the vocations the Church so infrequently found on Haitian soil. In addition, as a people all but impervious to the written word and speaking Créole, an indigenous and private language, the Haitian masses were, as long as they remained illiterate (the transistor radio was still twenty-five years away), uniquely insulated against propagandization.

On the other hand, the *griots* and their heirs and followers were to realize at least one revolution and for some thirty-five years, in peculiarly Haitian fashion, inherited the earth.

Another Grim Chapter

Back in 1929 in a treaty of 21 January of that year, Horacio Vasquez, president of the Dominican Republic, had joined Louis Borno in ironing out the interminable frontier controversy. Boundaries were surveyed and marked, and Haiti gained a few thousand acres in the readjustments that ensued. To refine and complete this settlement (and, it was widely rumored, to induce President Vincent to cease harboring certain Dominican exiles who were causing General Trujillo anxieties), a further advantageous readjustment was negotiated in 1935 and signed in 1936.(10) To cap previous fulsome advances - marked, as we shall see, by concurrent subornation of leading Haitians - Trujillo, on the basis of the frontier settlement, in 1936 personally nominated Vincent for the Nobel Peace Prize.

Besides coffee, cheap labor, primarily for canefields in Cuba and Santo Domingo, had long been a Haitian export. However miserable this peonage, for the Haitian peasant it had represented opportunity. The pigmentation of Eastern Cuba had long been darkened by Haitian emigrants until, in 1937, to restore jobs and increase wages, dictator Fulgencio Batista expelled every Haitian he could catch.

The tortuous, remote, ill-defined frontier between Haiti and the Dominican Republic has always been porous, and it was across this border, impelled by population pressure and attracted by sugar jobs in Santo Domingo, that thousands of Haitian peasants (some estimates exceeded a hundred thousand) had seeped next door. By 1937, to an even greater extent than in Cuba, Haitian cane-cutters were the fieldhands of Dominican sugar estates. Employers welcomed them as pathetically cheap labor but, whether on economic or racial grounds or both, no one else did. One subject that had come up during the numerous Vincent-Trujillo summits was repatriation of Haitian laborers and better control of line-crossers; there is no indication that the Haitian government ever did (or could have done) anything about it.

The Massacre River, which separates Ouanaminthe from its Dominican twin, Dajabón, defines the frontier for some forty-five miles in the North, emptying into Manzanillo Bay beside Fort Liberté. The river's name dates from 1728 and commemorates the last stand and slaughter that year of a band of *boucaniers* whom outraged Spanish colonists caught and killed following a foray into the East.

On 21 October 1937, the *New York Times* ran a brief report, filed by a United Press stringer in Kingston, of a "border clash" on the frontier in which "several Haitians" had been killed. Based on this and other rumors, *Collier's* magazine sent reporter Quentin Reynolds to Hispaniola. Lunching a few days later over Lanson 1928 champagne with General Trujillo, Reynolds was told, "Yes, it is true. A few Haitian farmers crossed the border up North and tried to steal some goats and cattle from our farmers. There was a fight - very regrettable - and several were killed on both sides."

When Reynolds crossed into Haiti and reached the hospital at the Cap, he found over 400 patients suffering from machete chops, knife slashes, and hideous clubbing. In flimsy aid stations at Ouanaminthe and elsewhere, thousands of other battered peasants were dying on straw mats or the floors of huts.

By 10 November, despite heavy Trujillo censorship, newspaper readers were beginning to learn what confidential diplomatic cables had been reporting to Washington, London, and other world capitals since early October. The Massacre River and other localities in Santo Domingo had witnessed scenes of slaughter unsurpassed since 1804.

For three days and nights, from 2 October, on orders from Trujillo, the Dominican army and Policia Nacional had systematically butchered some 15,000 to 20,000 Haitians not only along the Massacre but as far away as Samaná Bay, Barahona, and San Pedro de Macorís.(11)

The first outbreak of this fearful bloodbath took place at Bánica, ten miles Southeast of Cerca-la-Source, where 300 Haitians were shot and hacked to death. In Santiago, some 1900 poor souls were herded into a barracks compound. Here - on express orders to use clubs, machetes, or primitive weapons, not firearms - killer squads hacked and flailed indiscriminately at women, children, men, until their arms were tired and fresh executioners replaced them. Army trucks, hauling mutilated dead into desolate ravines of the countryside, left trails of stinking, stale blood along streets and roads. At ports and coastal areas, charnel convoys unloaded bodies onto commandeered fishing boats and coasters, which shuttled them offshore to swarming shark and barracuda.

At Montecristi for three successive nights, moaning files of Haitians were herded to the end of the customs wharf, to be clubbed or bayoneted and kicked into deep water alongside. Other droves of victims, never to emerge alive, were marched inside the gloomy fort and later buried by night in and beyond the moat. Elsewhere, bands of "deportees" (like the French women of 1804 at Cayes) were led to the sea "to board ship for Haiti." But there were no ships, only bludgeons, bayonets, machetes, and finally the sharks. Some were first put through a perfunctory process of deportation to provide cover for their disappearance, and afterward taken into desolate stretches of frontier no man's land and there killed. Others were hauled from huts, driven to some isolated spot, and there murdered. Detachments of soldiers manned the crossings and the banks of the Massacre, cutting down peasants seeking safety beyond the frontier.

In a chilling personal report to Sumner Welles, the able American minister in Ciudad Trujillo, Henry Norweb, wrote:

> The drive was conducted with ruthless efficiency by the National Police and Army. The technique used is of special importance in that it was designed to give the Dominican government an opportunity to disclaim all responsibility. Following a house-to-house canvass of Haitians resident in the area between Dajabón and the

sea, all who had not previously fled were rounded up and cited for deportation proceedings. Their papers were examined and they were passed through immigration control offices which in turn reported that persons so indicated had been deported to Haiti. The Haitians were then murdered by the Dominican troops . . .

Throughout, as Norweb's British colleague reported, "care was taken not to molest Haitians working or living on foreign-owned property or in towns where foreign witnesses might be."

Dessalines was no more savage; Joseph Stalin or Adolf Hitler could have been no more efficient.

Why Trujillo unleashed this "spontaneous" pogrom, so evidently long prepared and closely planned, is by no means clear. It has been variously speculated that he was angry with Vincent for incautiously having liquidated several Dominican agents in Haiti; or that he was piqued at a sullen reception by ex-Haitians in the border village of Restauración, ceded to the Dominican Republic; or that he acted out historic racial fears and hatreds going back to 1822; or that, as Vincent told Shepherd, the British minister, the massacre was a pre-election ploy by Trujillo to goad Haiti into invasion and disaster or otherwise provide a pretext for Dominican intervention; or that - deeply ambitious (as his own Foreign Minister later confided to the American minister) to unify and rule all Hispaniola - Trujillo chose this moment to teach Haiti a lesson. No answer is satisfactory. The act must speak for itself.

Vincent's reaction was supine. The Haitian government said not a word until 9 October when Evremont Carrié, minister in Ciudad Trujillo, timidly raised the subject with Trujillo, conveying Vincent's personal doubt that the Dominican government could have had anything to do with the killings. Six days later the two governments concluded a secret joint declaration "energetically condemning" the asserted facts, noting " searching investigation" on the part of Trujillo, and reaffirming the unshaken friendship and "patriotic labors" of those "illustrious statesmen," Trujillo and Vincent. This astonishing document, freely signed by Haiti, was subsequently made public by Trujillo to demonstrate that there really was no international controversy worth the hemisphere's time and that Haiti was satisfied.

Under pressure from aroused world opinion as well as mounting complaints among his opposition, Vincent on 12 November asked for inter-American mediation. Trujillo stalled at granting access to the commission, which consisted of Argentina, Guatemala, and Peru. Meanwhile, however, intensive and very private bilateral bargaining commenced. As a result, by 12 January 1938, the commission - not to mention a surprised Haitian delegation to the negotiations - found it had nothing to do: Trujillo had settled out of court. The Dominican indemnity was to be $750,000 - $30.00 a head for 15,000 murdered Haitians -

a figure subsequently whittled down to $525,000 cash, following a secret visit to Port-au-Prince by Anselmo Paulino-Alvarez, later Trujillo's secret-police chief, with a suitcase containing $25,000 in $10 and $20 bills.

Whether the final payment was $30.00 or $17.50 is perhaps irrelevant; Crassweller quotes an unnamed Dominican negotiator who told of widespread payoffs to Haitian public figures. With what was left over, he said, the Haitian government compensated survivors at about "two cents a head." At this time, a good pig would have brought $30.00 in the market.

"I think," U.S. Minister Ferdinand Mayer wrote his friend Welles, "the whole thing is pretty venal." Then Mayer went on to quote rumors that Vincent was striving to avoid difficulties because of "sums of money accepted by him from Trujillo before the incident."(12)

Setting aside the deeply suspect flavor of the settlement, it must in fairness be recognized that Haiti, with its small, lightly armed, and, alas, rapidly politicizing *Garde*, was no match for a heavily armed Dominican Republic under the tigerish Trujillo. Moreover, it must not be forgotten that the massacre involved "only" peasant *noirs*.

Commenting on this fact, Minister Shepherd reported to the Foreign Office:

> Educated Haytians have preserved an admirable balance in a difficult situation [but] . . . this otherwise admirable attitude is in a large measure due to the contempt in which the educated Haytian holds the peasant, whom he regards as belonging to a race apart, and with whom he has little real sympathy. The Haytians are willing to admit that their peasantry abroad are difficult to manage, dishonest, lazy, and extremely exasperating, and they are not prepared to complain of occasional murders among workers which are understood to occur fairly consistently in Santo Domingo.

Shepherd, of course, was right: it was only too easy for a *mulâtre* regime of the South and West to preserve its balance when the only victims were *noirs* of the North.

Little more can be said save to add that the Dominican Foreign Ministry once again took the occasion to suggest to the Nobel Prize Committee in Oslo that Trujillo and Vincent share a Peace Prize for having settled what Mayer described to Welles as "another grim chapter . . . in the bloody history of Dominican and Haitian relationships."

The Garde Politicizes

The frontier still swarmed with vagabond robbers ready enough to raid either side. Even so, given the tensions following the massacres, it seemed strange that, on 4 December 1937, a mixed band of some hundred Haitians and

Dominicans swarmed down on Thomonde, twenty miles inside Haiti, chased off the corporal and three soldiers of the *avant-poste*, and took over the town, eventually retiring back into Santo Domingo. Ten days later, the same crew, augmented to 200, made a swoop on Hinche, where the *Garde* had strength to resist and pursue them to the border, capturing several wounded Dominicans. The raiders were led by one Excellent Desrosiers, calling himself "general," a Haitian exile among several whom Trujillo had been harboring. Why these raids, undoubtedly armed, sanctioned, and launched by Trujillo, took place at this moment is obscure, unless we assume that they were intended to induce even worse jitters than those Port-au-Prince was already suffering.

What was even more puzzling was that, after the Thomonde raid, when Colonel Calixte alerted one of the *Garde's* mobile companies to reinforce Hinche and press pursuit, Major Armand refused to issue ammunition from the palace basement, and thus held up the column forty-eight hours, until Calixte appealed personally to the president.

Trouble lay within the *Palais*, and its instigator was Armand.

Mulâtre intriguer and Vincent relative, Armand had not only carved out a private army in the *Garde Présidentielle* (which by 1938 numbered 550 picked men) but had control of the heavy weapons and ammunition reserves, the fighting sinews of the *Garde*. At least since early 1937, and probably before, Armand had been undercutting his commandant, Colonel Calixte, by intimating to Vincent that Calixte was disloyal.

Armand was also undercutting his master: in conspiracy with Frédéric Duvigneaud, the slippery Interior Minister, as well as a Captain Merceron, *chef de la maison militaire,* the major was plotting the assassination of Vincent, together with Calixte, at which point Duvigneaud would seize the presidency and Armand would take over the *Garde*. Late in November 1937, Calixte learned he was to be bushwhacked on the Pétionville road while driving home; he was forewarned, and surprised and arrested the ambushers. A few days later, in an abrupt cabinet shakeup, President Vincent replaced Duvigneaud. Calixte accused Armand of complicity, but Vincent's only reaction was to call in Armand and tell him "not to be foolish." Armand later snarled a savage warning to Calixte.

On the evening of 12 December, when Armand and Captain Merceron were enjoying a glass of rum in front of the Café Rex at the top of the Champ de Mars, a taxi cruised by, carrying five persons. Abreast of the two officers, the cab slowed. There was a blast of pistol shots, and Armand and Merceron toppled to the sidewalk, spilling their rum. The taxi - someone caught the license, P-3031 - gunned its engine and tore off into the dark.

Armand and Merceron were only wounded. The cab, stolen earlier, was soon found. Its occupants had been Lieutenant Bonicias Pérard and four other junior officers of the *Garde*. Pérard, a *noir*, was Calixte's nephew.

Next day there was a *"courri,"* that spasm of panic that signals crisis in Port-au-Prince. People and cars dashed hither and thither; Syrians on the Grand Rue began putting up iron shutters; *marchandes* scooped up their little stocks; parents snatched children from school and kept off the streets. At street corners, reported Shepherd, appeared *"gendarmes* armed with shaky rifles."

Vincent's first act was to lock up his archenemy, Seymour Pradel, and as many other opponents as he could lay hold of, including one plotter young but already steeped in intrigue and opportunism, Arthur Bonhomme, a leading *griot*. Then, as the dragnet tightened, a lieutenant talked. It was an attempted coup, he told Armand and Vincent, by Calixte and the *noir* officers of the *Garde*. Ultimately, sixteen lieutenants were implicated.(13)

On 9 January, telling the American legation all evidence pointed at Calixte, Vincent sent him to Nice with the post of Inspector of Consulates, and appointed Colonel Jules André, the soldierly *mulâtre* assistant commandant, to take command. André understood the situation: henceforth, Armand enjoyed a free run.

Vincent Restores Dictatorship

Alluding unkindly to the president's "wobbly chin," a State Department analyst observed, in February 1938, "Vincent is not of the stuff from which dictators are made." Within ten months, almost to the day, wobbly chin or not, Sténio Vincent declared Haiti a dictatorship.

In a speech at Les Cayes (whose "tone and highlights are essentially Hitlerian, " reported Mayer) Vincent on Sunday morning, 18 December announced an end to plebiscitary selection of presidents (a feature of the 1935 constitution), told the people their mentality was too "arrested" for democracy, flayed the elite as "tourists" in their own country, and - shades of the *corvée* - said Toussaint's system of forced agricultural labor was perfectly valid for twentieth-century Haiti.

Going on to express ideas that twenty years later would seem pointedly apposite, Vincent extolled the diplomacy of Toussaint as "subtle, fluctuating, shady," exploiting "antagonisms of the epoch." "I suppose it has rarely happened," Mayer commented, "that a dictator has so abruptly and brutally taken down the screen which has shrouded his autocracy."

The American minister may have been surprised, but the facts and the situation were already well known. (Foreign Minister - and Francophile poet - Léon Laleau, for example, said he "saw nothing of particular note" in the Cayes speech.)

Only a month before, Vincent had dismissed and jailed five influential senators for alleged subversive activities. At the same time, he cashiered eleven more officers of the *Garde* and locked up a selection of opposition journalists, one of whom, Louis Callard, suddenly died in prison, it was given out, of "appendicitis."

During virtually the entire administration of its self-proclaimed "Second Liberator," Haiti had been under constitutional state of siege. The press was tightly controlled. Mail censorship and interception were commonplace. The president's nonaccountable secret-police fund, which in 1931 had been 2500 *gourdes* a month, had quintupled. Free speech and public assembly had been abolished. The supposedly coordinate branches of government, legislature and judiciary, had at Cayes been expressly proclaimed subordinate to the president. Personal enemies of Vincent, such as the irrepressible Milo Rigaud, were sent to prison on trumped-up charges or no charges at all, and kept there.

The regime was thoroughly corrupt. In the words of Mayer, writing in 1940, "Seven years [sic] after dis-Occupation they have succeeded in reestablishing as venal a public administration as one could find anywhere."

Vincent, for example, had gone to Washington in 1939 on the invitation of the U.S. Government, all expenses paid; yet he claimed and collected (and banked) 100,000 *gourdes* for the trip. The Haitian legation in Washington, not to mention the Foreign Ministry in Port-au-Prince, had attracted the attention of American authorities by a thriving trade in Haitian passports and naturalization certificates to foreigners (mainly European refugees); by sale of diplomatic passports; and by spurious accreditation in claimed diplomatic status of numbers of persons, including non-Haitians, to Haitian diplomatic missions abroad.

De la Rue in 1940 said "communal revenues have been pirated" and estimated that 50 to 75 percent of such collections had "gone into the pockets of the administration's friends."

These were but samples. Underlying all, of course, was lack of money, whether over or under the table, aggravated, after war in Europe commenced in 1939, by dislocation of Haitian exports and markets.

In mid-1938, the U.S. Export-Import Bank advanced Haiti - in the first of a series of loans that would eventually total $24 million - $5 million for secondary roads, irrigation and drainage systems, agricultural development, and port facilities. The J.G. White Engineering Company, which undertook this program, quickly came under strong pressure to hire Vincent favorites and fire qualified Haitian engineers, while the government sought to gain control of disbursements and thus get directly at this alluring prize.

Vincent's apologists could rightly point to the multiplication of schools, at least in towns; to redevelopment of part of the Port-au-Prince slum, La Saline, into modern housing, naturally dubbed "Cité Vincent"; to allocation of national lottery proceeds to public health, housing, and schools; and to the unceasing good works of Mlle. Rézia Vincent, the president's sister and hostess. Alas, when measured against the popular mandate and the machinery he had, unparalleled in Haiti's history, - not to mention eleven years in office - these results seem little enough: what Vincent frittered away was not to be regained.

Under pressure of war in Europe, Britain ended first her purchases of sugar, then of Haitian cotton. The Japanese consul in Port-au-Prince thereupon quietly bought in the British share and more. (14)

After the fall of France in 1940, even her most assiduous journalistic apologist, Gérard de Catalogne of the Cap (who in 1941, however, quickly foreswore France to become a naturalized Haitian) could find little to say, and the German legation strutted as of old. But the Germans, and also the Italians, were not merely strutting. They were also putting money into the war chests of Haitian presidential aspirants: Duvigneaud was the favorite of the Italians, Antoine Carré, of the Nazis.

The United States was sinking no money into Haitian politics but, with something less than enthusiasm, it was watching Vincent (just like President Roosevelt, people insisted on repeating) lay the groundwork for a third term. Expressing impressions that had been building up for some time, Mayer privately wrote Welles in 1939 about Vincent's "fundamental anti-Americanism":

> Vincent is really a xenophobe, and I believe loathes - I use the word advisedly - the United States with an enduring passion . . . Only recently, when commenting on his great hero Toussaint L'Ouverture, he eulogized with a real gleam in his eye Toussaint's strategy of pretending, as Vincent said, to be friendly with *"les blancs,"* but only to drop this mask at the proper moment and destroy them.

If the State Department's view of Sténio Vincent had darkened, one reason was that the Haitian minister in Washington, Elie Lescot, had ever since 1938 been intimating to Sumner Welles and other officials his increasing divergence from Vincent's anti-American attitudes and policies while at the same time hinting at bargains that existed whereby he would succeed to the presidency whenever Vincent stepped down.

Besides sweetening American connections, Lescot was even more closely connected with the Dominican Republic; he was, in fact, on Trujillo's payroll,(15) and was El Benefactor's hand-picked nominee for the *Palais National.*

But Vincent was far from out of the way. Sparked by his late Foreign Minister, now Senator Alfred Nemours, both houses of the legislature, on 28 January 1941, spontaneously passed resolutions calling on the president, never mind constitutional prohibitions, for another five years. One of the few members who abstained was ex-minister and new Senator Lescot.

Down to the wire, hoping against hope, Vincent kept his forces together, but the sands of time had run out. Washington could still cast the deciding vote. In late March - election day was 15 April 1941 - the American legation frowned, and on 5 April, pleading ill health, Vincent told the leaders of the two Chambers that he did not wish to be considered. The way was clear for Elie Lescot.

John Campbell White, the new American minister, described the electoral proceedings:

> The voting was done on little scraps of paper which were put into two urns, one of the urns being emptied into the other. One Senator and one Deputy read them out and then the ballots were passed around for scrutiny by a sort of Committee of Control. One ballot was reported blank and another contained a vote for President Vincent. All the remaining 56 were for Lescot, his name being inscribed in various forms - sometimes the bare name, and sometimes there were appropriate sentiments, in one case, I believe, a short poem . . . After the results were made known the *Garde* rushed forward with sub-machine guns and surrounded M. Lescot.

Max Hudicourt later ascribed the electors' rare unanimity to prior beatings, electric shock, and widespread torture, but no evidence supports any such allegations. Jean Price-Mars, still seeking the presidency, did have his printing press shut down when he had the temerity to make his candidacy public; that was about it.

Thus, on 15 May 1941 - Haiti's fourth peaceful and constitutional transfer of power since 1915 - Elie Lescot succeeded Sténio Vincent. Inaugurals on this model would not soon be seen again.(16)

Another State of the Union

The inauguration was a grand affair, which, because of wartime prices for French champagne, cost the government 10,000 *gourdes* more than budgeted. Reporting this to Washington, Minister White mused, "I am afraid there are terrible times ahead for the poor Haitians, in view of the growing scarcity of necessities of this kind. I also hear that Messrs. Lescot and Dennis [Haitian minister in Washington] were very unfavorably impressed by the American champagne which they found being consumed in bars, night clubs, etc., in the United States. I trust Haitian-American relations will not suffer as a result."(17)

The suave and patrician *mulâtre* who had become president was a man of commanding personality and ability. Born in 1883 at St. Louis du Nord of a respected *Capois* family (his mother had as a young lady been lady-in-waiting to the Empress Adelina; his grandfather lifelong *magistrat communal* of the Cap), Lescot, besides extensive diplomatic experience, had held the portfolios of Interior, Justice, Agriculture, and Education. Raconteur, *bon vivant,* seldom without a fine Havana cigar, he was (save for that one peccadillo - "the golden cord," Crassweller called it - the Trujillo connection) a Haitian of impeccable distinction. As early as 1934, Norman Armour had spotted Lescot as a future president (remarking, on pure hypothesis, "Lescot would, from Trujillo's point of view, be the perfect choice for President of Haiti"). Then Armour wrote, "He is a true son of the North, where the Christophe tradition of discipline and the iron hand as the sole method of effective rule in Haiti still persists . . . He loves a good fight, has unlimited confidence in his own abilities, and is somewhat naive."

Two years later, the British minister penned an equally penetrating description: "Managed to retain office under both Borno and Vincent, a unique achievement... of imposing appearance and extremely affable. Efficient and shrewd, has every intention (and a very good chance) of becoming President. If he does, he will undoubtedly work hard for his country while not neglecting to provide for his old age."

Lescot stated his program in unexceptionable terms - "Peace, order, and hard work, based on broad social justice." The new president's political formula was simple and concrete: secure the loyalty of the *Garde*, emasculate an already compliant legislature, profit by wholehearted loyalty to the United States, and rule Haiti with an iron hand.

His first step, proclaimed on 6 June 1941 at a review of all troops in the capital, was to assume title as "Commander-in-Chief of the Armed Forces" and, in the fine print of the implementing decree, place both *Garde Présidentielle* (no effective change, to be sure) and Port-au-Prince police under his direct control, leaving the chief of staff of the *Garde* merely an administrative functionary. (18) Within less than a year, by February 1942, he extended the jurisdiction of military courts to all offenses and persons, and established military tribunals at Port-au-Prince and headquarters of the departments.

During summer 1941, a heavy-handed campaign was mounted against Voodoo. *Houmforts* were raided and smashed, as were drums and other sacred objects. Since Lescot blamed the Catholic clergy (and they blamed him) for these excesses, it is hard to tell how they began - ambivalent feelings toward Voodoo are as deep-rooted in the Church as among the elite. What is certain is that the president was dissatisfied with the Church. Not without reason, he considered the French clergy political, at least where French interests were concerned; besides, he now told Minister White, and soon after wrote Welles, that the priests in Haiti were largely Vichy-oriented and, in his phrase, "pro-Nazi."(19)

What the president wanted was to introduce American priests into Haiti. With the diocese of Les Cayes opportunely vacant in September 1941, he asked Welles to suggest an American ecclesiastic whom he in turn could nominate to the Vatican for the post. With discreet help from the American hierarchy, Welles found the right man, and, in February 1943 (over obdurate opposition from archbishop and nuncio), Lescot installed Msgr. Louis Collignon, an American Oblate Father, at Cayes.(20)

De la Rue had been a marked man ever since he had embarrassed Lescot over the rifles in 1940 and, although nearly $8 million of the 1922 bonds were still outstanding, the president moved swiftly to negotiate the fiscal representative out of a job. On 13 September 1941, the United States agreed to close out the office in lieu of a fiscal department in the *Banque,* which in turn would take on responsibility, under the steady hand of "Bank" Williams, that man of iron who had piloted the *Banque* since 1914, for preparing the national budget and maintaining limited fiscal supervision over the government.(21)

A month after gaining increased control over Haiti's finances, on 14 October 1941, Lescot further consolidated his position. Abolishing the prefectural system in use since 1918, he created six regional *délégués* (at the Cap, Port-de-Paix, Gonaïves, Jacmel, Cayes, and Jérémie), each wielding sole local authority as in the olden time and answering in turn to Interior Minister Gontran Rouzier, a man of heavy hand.

The attack on Pearl Harbor in December 1941 evoked an immediate response from Port-au-Prince. On 8 December, Haiti declared war on Japan; four days later, as the *Garde* rounded up Germans and Italians and packed them off to Fort National, declarations followed against the European Axis; and on Christmas Eve Haiti added Hungary, Bulgaria, and Rumania to the list.

With the first declaration of war went a companion state of siege. On 7 January of the new year, when German submarines were beginning to sink merchant ships in sight of Haiti, the president sequestered enemy property, having the day before offered to raise 20,000 troops and 50,000 farm laborers for service wherever the United States might desire. However valued as moral support, the offer could not practically be accepted: Savannah was not to be repeated during World War II.

At the president's prompting, the legislature on 14 January obediently conferred "extraordinary powers" on the executive for the duration of the war. Exercising these powers to the full, on 23 February Lescot simply suspended the constitution. Remarking that war "demands swift and radical measures," he instructed the *Garde* to be alert for saboteurs and arsonists, who, Lescot went on, "should be tried, condemned, and promptly shot."

Having thus rendered himself secure at home (22), Lescot repaired to Washington to see what belligerency and alliance held for Haiti.

On 6 April 1942, after a week of Washington's Rock Creek springtime at the windows of his deluxe suite in the Shoreham, Lescot and his friend Welles (whose cellars on Massachusetts Avenue still contained ample reserves of French champagne), initialed a memorandum of understanding covering several points of extreme interest to Haiti.(23)

Replacing Japan, the United States would buy Haiti's entire cotton crop (of which Britain had originally been primary purchaser) for the duration. The Export-Import Bank would credit Haiti with $2 million to support the *gourde* and for other purposes. Sisal was to be stepped up to meet war needs. Finally, good news for the *Garde*: Haiti would receive Lend-Lease artillery, military aircraft, and a U.S. Coast Guard detachment to base at Bizoton.

The immediate military results were as follows:

A U.S. Coast Guard detachment with five patrol boats for local antisubmarine operations took over Bizoton, modernizing the yard and later constructing a marine railway. In 1945, with the Atlantic battle won, the Coast Guard withdrew, leaving a well-trained *Garde-Côtes* (organized on 28 July 1942) and a trim 83-foot flagship well named *Savannah*.

Arriving in May 1942, a U.S. Field Artillery detachment sited cannon for harbor defense of Port-au-Prince, the Môle, and the Cap, and, training Haitian gunners, finally armed the *Garde* with artillery.

Most important, however, was the arrival during summer 1942 of six Douglas O-38s to base at Bowen Field. These aircraft were unsuitable (all six would be wrecked or unserviceable within a year), but they nonetheless marked the debut of the *Corps d'Aviation*, which, eventually brought to proficiency by a U.S. Army Air Corps detachment of fifty officers and men, procured more appropriate planes and came into being as a separate unit on 9 September 1943, under command of Captain G. Edouard Roy, who thus became Haiti's first aviator. One of Roy's earliest perceptions was of the usefulness of air transportation in a country still possessing a built-in network of airfields laid out by the Marines. Under his leadership, most but not all the old Marine fields were eventually rehabilitated. Regular air mail and transport service was established in June 1943 and what finally became the first national airline, COHATA - operated by the *Corps d'Aviation* - was duly launched.

All these doings from 1942 to 1945 were stage-managed by Lieutenant Colonel Thomas H. Young, U.S.A., the energetic military attaché who, with a small staff, operated a *de facto* military mission. Alas for Young: his energy and wide-ranging operations aroused the antagonism of Armand, who in September

1943, for wholly contrived reasons, provoked Lescot into abruptly ordering Young's recall.

Colonel Young's expulsion was one of very few anti-American acts by Lescot. In a decision that must have rocked Firmin in his grave, the president encouraged the American minister and U.S. officers to reconnoiter the Môle in May 1942, having just earlier said the United States could have it on any terms or for any duration as a permanent base.(24) In November 1942, surpassing himself, Lescot told a visiting delegation of U.S. officers: "For the duration of this war I would like your government to think of Haiti as another state of the Union of which I am governor."

Vive la Liberté, A bas Lescot

In October 1943, journeying to Canada to accept an honorary degree at Quebec, the president embarked on a triumphant progress that took him to Montreal, Ottawa, Washington, New York, and thence homeward via Havana. Including a stay at the White House as guest of President Roosevelt (who warmly described Lescot to Welles as "a very old friend of mine"), President Lescot's trip ranks as one of the most impressive and distinguished, and surely the grandest, foreign trip ever made by a sitting president of Haiti.(25)

Roosevelt, old Haiti hand that he always considered himself, had a long visit with Lescot, much of it in French, leaving Edward Stettinius (who had just replaced Welles) floundering, and launched expansively into a favorite idea: rebuilding the Môle as a free port. At the end, never far away from politics, FDR said he thought they ought "to get up a list of two or three items that President Lescot could take home as having accomplished here." Stettinius promptly suggested that both presidents would want to know that from 1938 to 1946, either already paid out or projected, the U.S. Government would have put $40 million into Haiti, specifically including a handsome credit for rubber development by an American enterprise that hoped to produce latex from a weed, *Cryptostegia,* that abounded in the South. Then - for the last time - they parted, and with Mme. Lescot and entourage Lescot went to luncheon with the Nelson Rockefellers at their place on Foxhall Road.

One shortfall of the occupation had been American failure (more expressly, the failure of Freeman and the *Service Technique*) to live up to the 1916 treaty commitment to help Haiti to develop its agricultural resources - which, besides natural beauty and good climate, in truth comprise the sum of Haiti's resources.

In 1941, as Japan rampaged into Southeast Asia, it appeared that Haiti's time had arrived to provide America with sisal as a substitute for hemp, and, even more exciting, to become a prime source of rubber. "Corne-cabrite," the peasants' name for that weed the two presidents had spoken of, had a high latex content and was expected to yield a generous output. This, at any rate, was the confident assertion of Thomas A. Fennell, an American agronomist who, in early 1941, first winning the confidence of Dartigue, Lescot's Minister of Agriculture, then prevailed on the Export-Import Bank in Washington to extend a $5 million credit for Haitian sisal and rubber as well as for a wide range of lesser agricultural and forestry operations. The vehicle for these developments was to be forever remembered as *SHADA*, short title for *"Société Haïtenne-Americaine de Développement Agricole"*(Haitian-American Partnership for Agricultural Development). SHADA was set up with extensive monopoly and concessionary status in late 1941 on that first $5 million (an Ex-Im Bank loan guaranteed by Haiti) and later fortified, in the urgent days of November 1942, by a direct U.S. credit of $7 million.

Twelve million dollars - exponentially more than the *Service Technique* had to work with over the life of the occupation - could and ought to have done a great deal for agriculture. Unfortunately, the effect was negligible, in fact negative: *SHADA* was a flop. Overruling the advice of competent Haitian agronomists such as Georges Héraux (one of the Damien rebels of 1929 who had gone on to serious work at the University of Illinois and eventually to direct Damien), Fennell and *SHADA* ran roughshod over peasant proprietors, condemning choice agricultural plots, bulldozing huts, even sacred *houmforts,* standing crops, coffee bushes, cashew, avocado, and banana trees (an estimated million fruit-bearing trees and shrubs in all), paying pittances to , and rehiring as day laborers expropriated peasants who had been subsistence farmers. Everything Fennell touched went badly. Not his fault, to be sure, that 1942 to 1945 were exceptionally dry years and thus wretched for sisal. A first shot at trying to get rubber from hevea, the Brazilian rubber tree transplanted to Haiti, failed, as local agronomists had predicted. The main effort - which by 1943 had gobbled up over 100,000 acres, or more than 5 percent of Haiti's best land, and was temporarily employing 92,000 peasants - went to *corne-cabrite*. By 1944 the worst was known: *SHADA* had failed miserably. Only five tons of rubber ever resulted; in May of that year work was abandoned. Nearly 40,000 families had been shoveled off land, only half of which had even been planted, that was now ruined for years to come. *SHADA* employment had dropped to 16,000, and in many cases returning peasants could no longer even identify, let alone repossess, old holdings whose landmarks had been obliterated. Fennell left for other employment - ironically, like Dr. Freeman before him, in Puerto Rico. Under new management, *SHADA* worked more realistically for a few years in sisal, which did better, and in timbering Morne la Selle's magnificent Fôret des Pins. The Haitian government, for all this, found itself with $5 million in added debt.(26)

The *SHADA* fiasco was the only one of Lescot's American transactions that went sour, but failure of such evident magnitude was a serious blow to an increasingly autocratic regime whose popularity had begun to slip. "Nowadays," commented Ambassador White (27) in May 1943, "persons who take too firm a stand in opposition to President Lescot's views are increasingly liable to fall into disfavor."

That such was true was perhaps best known at the jail, whose walls had begun to enfold journalists, politicians, people of talkative habits, either on sentence by military courts or, on what amounted to *lettres de cachet,* as "prisoners of State."

On 19 April 1944, pleading worldwide emergency, the National Assembly rewrote the already well-rewritten 1935 constitution to the following further effect: (1) no elections would be held until peace had been concluded with all enemy powers, even unto Bulgaria; (2) the presidential term was extended from five to seven years; and (3) first ratifying en masse all actions, past or future, during his incumbency, Citizen Elie Lescot would succeed himself as president for a new term extending until 15 May 1951.

Lescot's decrees now began to be prefaced *"Nous, Elie Lescot."*

As a gloss on the remodeled constitution, the president's inaugural address of 15 May 1945 set out certain political conclusions: "We know that people seek to exercise the Four Freedoms. Naive and impoverished people . . . We have decided to extend the Four Freedoms only when the Haitian people have learned how to use them.

These developments were not unanimously acclaimed. In July there was a plot in the *Garde.* It miscarried, and seven enlisted men were taken to Fort Dimanche and shot. Colonel Armand, suddenly dispensible, was ordered to Mexico City as Haitian *chargé d'affaires.* Then came the still more disturbing rumor that Trujillo had withdrawn the light of his countenance. More tangible evidence quickly followed.

In early October, on a tip that the Dominican consul at the frontier town of Belladère, one Ferrando Gomez, had imported thirteen Smith & Wesson .38s and ammunition in the diplomatic bag, the *Garde* (under a new chief, Colonel Franck Lavaud) pounced on the recipients. Excellent Desrosiers, that old *Caco* of Trujillo's who had raided Hinche in 1937, was the leader. Interrogation brought quick confessions, confirmed when the weapons were traced to American military-assistance stocks received by Trujillo. Desrosiers and two others were shot; the remaining conspirators disappeared into prison.

In the event, Trujillo's pen proved more deadly than his Smith & Wessons: in June 1945, as delegates assembled in San Francisco to sign the charter of the United Nations, each found at his place a handsomely printed glossy pamphlet containing the unabridged Lescot-Trujillo correspondence since 1937.(28)

The president put on an uncompromising face through 1945, but murmurs were rising. A student journal, *Zinglins,* had the poor judgment in May 1945, to call for freedom of the press. The Interior Minister, Gontran Rouzier, suppressed it quickly enough, but the cry was picked up by the most strident and troublesome of all voices of the young, *La Ruche*. René Depestre, who, with Théodore Baker, was editing *La Ruche*, now brought forth *Etincelles*, a collection of revolutionary poetry that sold like hotcakes. On 1 January 1946, not very obliquely, *La Ruche* saluted the new year as "the year of victory over certain hostile forces . . . the triumph of Democracy over all forms of fascist oppression!"

Then came four flaming lines of verse:

Down with all the Francos!
Long live Democracy on the march!
Long live Social Justice!
Long live the World Proletariat!

Not for nothing had people come to speak of the president as "Sieur Lescot" (Sire Lescot). Within forty-eight hours, the editors of *La Ruche* were inside the old police station on the Champ de Mars and their paper was suppressed.

In the words of Hogar Nicolas, "This was the drop of water that overflowed the vase."

It could have been 1929 again, and many of the faces, though more lined, were the same. First the medical students took to the streets, then the rest of the university, then the *lycées,* and finally boys and girls, some as young as ten, trooping over the Champ de Mars, crying, *"Vive la Liberté! Vive la Démocratie! A bas la Dictature!"*

The *Garde* replied with *cocomacacs:* heads were broken but not the strike.

For four days tumult mounted. On 7 January, headed by Jacques Stephen Alexis, Depestre, and Baker, a new political party - *Parti Démocratique Populaire de la Jeunesse Haïtienne* - trumpeted demands for release of political prisoners, immediate elections, and freedom of the press. On the 8th and 9th, first the government clerks, then the teachers, and finally the shopkeepers struck. As iron shutters began to clang shut on the Grand Rue, President Lescot went on the air. But his speech, delivered, he said, in his capacity of commander-in-chief, was anything but conciliatory: he would remain in the palace and, "My final warning," he thundered: "the most drastic measures will be taken to reestablish order; the nation is warned; the entire world put on notice!"

The next two days, 10 and 11 January, were frantic with demonstrations and with Lescot's attempts to form a new government that could forestall events. Meanwhile, Jacmel, Léogane, Les Cayes, and Miragoâne seethed with demonstrators. At two in the afternoon of the 11th, Jacques Alexis and Dr.

Georges Rigaud (a deep-voiced dentist who had formed a popular front of intellectuals and bureaucrats), went to the Manoir des Lauriers and told the president he must step down.

Finally at bay, Lescot lowered his eyes and replied softly, "You must realize this has taken me by surprise. I have no private means; I need a little time to put my affairs in order." (29)

Without reply, the delegates stalked out. Two hours later, the saluting battery on Fort National boomed three times. Within minutes, those who had radios heard the solid voice of Colonel Lavaud announce that the *Garde* had assumed power, that the president was under house arrest at Manoir des Lauriers, and that elections would be held as soon as possible. As the streets rang with *"Vive la Liberté!"* and *"A bas Lescot."'* the presidential flag was hauled down over the *Palais National.*

An Example of Professionalism

Calling themselves the *Comité Executif Militaire*, the *Garde* junta that, with genuine reluctance, had taken hold of what looked like a runaway situation, was headed by Colonel Lavaud, a hefty professional from Jérémie, seconded by Major Antoine Levelt of the Artibonite (a trim, chic officer and master raconteur) and the compact, decisive commander of the *Garde Présidentielle*, Major Paul E. Magloire, of Quartier Morin.

Lavaud and Levelt were *mulâtres;* Magloire was a *noir.* All three enjoyed the respect of the *Garde.* Levelt, who had been the immensely popular commandant of cadets at the Académie Militaire, had the junior officers in the palm of his hand.

Colbert Bonhomme, who wrote the best-known account of all this, euphemistically described the next two days by saying the people breathed in liberty with full throat and lungs. Jean-Pierre Gingras was more blunt: "A heterogeneous mass of people - human robots," he wrote, "sacked Port-au-Prince." The first targets, as might be expected, were the homes of officials, notably including Gontran Rouzier, who barely escaped to the Cuban legation. Next came the Syrians, whose shops were pillaged as if it were 1904. While the *peuple souverain* thus amused themselves, politics and political organization absorbed the elite and began to worry the *Comité.*

Political parties bloomed like a hundred flowers. Besides a Committee of Public Safety and a United Democratic Front - each seeking to supersede the *Comité Militaire* - a dozen other parties and labor unions surfaced before the end of January. Exiles of all stripes flocked back. Among numerous declared presidential hopefuls were Dr. Price-Mars, Percéval Thoby, Senator Marcel

Fombrun, Frédéric Duvigneaud, and Dumarsais Estimé. Besides Thoby and Duvigneaud, another person of the past to return and reappear in the hustings was Colonel Calixte, no very welcome sight to the *Comité Militaire*. Strikes popped like firecrackers: against *SHADA* and Plantation Dauphin, among the workers on the wharf, and at the electric company, and at HASCO, where the firebrand *noir* leader was a former mathematics teacher, Daniel Fignolé, whose every sentence intoxicated Port-au-Prince workers. Fignolé of course had a party, *Mouvement Ouvriers Paysans (MOP)*; his secretary general was a taciturn, unsmiling *noir* M.D., that Dr. Duvalier who had been writing political tracts a decade previously, under the pen name Abderrahman.

One common thrust in all this activity was race. On every hand, *noirs* *("mangeurs-mulâtres")* they called themselves) were breathing threats and hatred toward *jaunes*. The respected Pierre Liautaud, an eminent *mulâtre*, felt constrained to resign deanship of the law school. Dr. Elie Villard, one of the country's ablest and most popular physicians, similarly stepped down at the *Hôpital Général*. Riots and disorder, accompanied by looting and arson, continued sporadically at Jacmel, Marigot, St. Marc, and Port-de-Paix.

On 4 May 1946, the *Nation* scolded American readers: "It is fantastic to say that the unrest in Haiti is of communist origin... The Communist party in Haiti is not actually a Marxian party. It is a strong Socialist movement to end the oppression of the working classes and the corruption in the government."

That the *Nation,* in distant New York, felt obliged to raise the question only confirms what more and more observers (including American Ambassador Orme Wilson) were reporting: a vigorous and well-organized communist effort was afoot to profit from, and give direction to, the turbulence that followed Lescot's fall and had decompressed Haitian politics with such a whoosh.

As early as 14 January, written only seventy-two hours after the event, Pravda editorialized warm approval ("The Haitian people have just given the world a lesson in democracy") of an uprising - widely popular, to be sure - in which communists had conspicuously acted as midwives. The names of those who brought down Lescot - Depestre, Baker, Juste Constant, Max Hudicourt hammering away in New York, and a whole nimbus of articulate intellectuals (Edris Saint-Amant, Georges Petit, and Adrien Chevallier, to list only a few) - constitute a *Who's Who* of vanguard Haitian communists, some with records going back to the 1929 strike and the party's debut in the 1930s. And the bellwether of the February strikes was Jacques Alexis, now head of the leather-workers' union (the *Syndicat de l'Industrie de Cuir*).

As of 4 February 1946, three avowed communist parties were in existence: two influential popular-front committees were dominated by communists or cryptocommunists; and - leaving out *La Ruche* - the movement could boast two newspapers. *Le Combat,* the official party organ, and *La Nation,* edited by Max

Hudicourt, back from exile in New York. The two most influential party elements were Max and Pierre Hudicourt's *Parti Socialiste Populaire*, an elite group working closely with the Cuban Communist Party, and the more proletarian segment, the *Parti Communiste d'Haïti (PCH)*, in which Father Juste Constant, transferred from his long-time post as secretary general, attempted to broaden the communist base by recruiting *noirs* and other non-elite converts. Besides these two, there was also an ephemeral *Parti Communiste Manchoutiste*, apparently a Maoist splinter, of which little is known.

The first communist-influenced popular front was Dr. Rigaud's Unified Democratic Front, which had joined with Jacques Alexis in demanding Lescot's abdication; the second, the *Comité de Défense Nationale* (Committee of National Defense), which surfaced in May 1946 under the leadership of Dr. Rigaud's brother, numbered eleven avowed communists among thirty-two signatories of its manifesto.

It is against this background, barely perceived by many Haitians at the time, that the military coup - in hindsight a preventive if not preemptive action - and the subsequent policies of the junta can best be measured.(30)

In a perverse sense Haiti's first coup since before the occupation restored the country to normal. The *Comité Executif Militaire*, carrying out the traditional role of *gouvernement provisoire,* now had to face the disorders and vexations encountered by such bodies in the past.

The first act of the junta was to dissolve the Lescot legislature. Next - a decision of equal popularity - was to appoint Haiti's greatest athlete, the legendary Olympic track star and genial owner of the Café Savoy, Sylvio Cator, as mayor of Port-au-Prince.

Even as these decisions were being made, violence, directed by elements calling themselves "the proletariat" against a class dubbed "the bourgeoisie" (that is, elite *mulâtres),* mounted steadily. Shops, including the large Bata department store, continued to be looted. Momentarily the soldiers' nerve seemed to fail: the *Comité* offered to transfer its power to the *Cour de Cassation*, an honor the jurists quickly declined. Then, in early April, with recognition as *de facto* government from six Latin American nations and the United States, the junta, a cabinet finally cobbled together from *Garde* officers, regained its feet and set about the work to be done.

The most important job was to restart the political and constitutional machinery, and this the *Comité* promptly did. Elections for twenty-one Senate seats and ninety-seven deputies were proclaimed for 12 May, under the no-nonsense electoral procedures of 1930.

The rules were sternly enforced. Armed persons were disarmed and barred from polls, sales of *taffia* and *clairin* were closed down the night before, and political speeches shut off at the same time. There were no disorders worth mentioning. The communists, who had opened an office just off the Grande

Rue, failed to do as well as they had hoped, but did get Max Hudicourt and Dr. Rigaud elected to the Senate. Daniel Fignolé, the Port-au-Prince spellbinder, was defeated. As soon as returns were announced next day (and sign of things to come), Fignolist supporters erupted in a fierce riot, which the *Garde*, armed with *cocomacacs* and tear gas, broke up handily. Similar disorders at the Cap were likewise taken in hand and quelled.

Now the legislators, sitting as National Assembly, set to work on a constitution. As Dantès Bellegarde later described them, discussions were "unbridled, interminable, violent and demagogic." Until the *Garde* threw them out in late June, mobs packed the galleries and stormed here and there about the legislative precincts, setting upon enemies and shouting for what Hogar Nicolas called "a left-oriented" constitution. Left-oriented was mild: the resulting draft was a longwinded Jacobin-Marxist tirade.

Meanwhile, in streets and cafés, Dr. Rigaud's *Comité de Défense National* began beating up opponents and talking up another general strike. *"Rouleau dehors!"* (Watch out for the steamroller!) would be the cry, and merchants too slow with their shutters would find themselves looted clean.

With *Comité* backing, alarmed moderates moved to resurrect the liberal 1932 constitution so quickly dispensed with by Vincent. On 12 August 1946, this compromise carried, and elections were thereupon scheduled four days hence. The chief candidates were Bignon Pierre-Louis, Edgar Néré Numa, Colonel Calixte, and Dumarsais Estimé.(31) At ten o'clock in the morning of the 16th, with a company of the *Garde Présidentielle*, the palace band, and all five of the *Garde's* armored half-tracks drawn up across the street, the National Assembly met in the *Palais Législatif*, whose Chamber and galleries were conspicuously posted at intervals by *Garde* officers with submachine guns in their laps. This time no poems were allowed; only names written on slips by senators and deputies.

On the first ballot, Estimé - a lower-middle-class Artibonite *noir* and, perhaps more significantly, a friend of Major Magloire's with Vincent connections and a war chest from the distiller Alfred Vieux took the lead with 25 ballots, trailed by Pierre-Louis with 8, Numa (candidate of the *Parti Socialiste Populaire*) with 7, and Calixte, 6. The remaining votes were scattered in all directions among the fifty-odd parties that had sprung up.

With time out for a bit of jockeying, the second ballot commenced. When the slips were tallied, Estimé had an ever greater plurality, 32 - against 14 for Numa and the left, and 10 for Pierre-Louis - and was thereupon declared winner. The officers brought submachine guns to the ready and closed ranks around the new president.

Following the speeches, the half-tracks coughed authoritatively, clanked to the head of the procession, and led the presidential sedan to the cathedral for a Te

Deum. The crowds, Fignolist to a man, watched silently from the sidewalks. Afterward, at the palace, there was a little ceremony in which Lavaud, flanked by Levelt and Magloire, standing at ramrod attention, returned executive power to a duly elected president. Estimé in his reply precisely caught the significance of the moment: "At one and the same time you were the head which commanded and the arm which executed. It would have been easy enough to revert to dictatorship. But you made a promise and you kept it . . . giving an example of professionalism which will never be forgotten." It was, conceivably, the *Garde*'s finest hour.(32)

The Noirs Return

To gauge Dumarsais Estimé by his enemies, especially in Port-au-Prince, would lead to self-canceling conclusions. The elite *mulâtres,* deposed after twenty-one years' power and violently denounced as "*nonauthentiques*" by Estimé, let alone Fignolé, were fearful and embittered.(33) On the other hand, Fignolé and the Port-au-Prince mob, besides outflanking Estimé on the left, felt cheated by an election in which Calixte, the Fignolist candidate, had mysteriously won almost no votes at all. As in May, the MOP therefore took to the streets, smashing electric lights and fixtures, pulling down utility poles, and venting fury on anything in its path, retiring to La Saline when nothing remained to smash.

Dumarsais Estimé was an ulcer-afflicted Artibonite *noir* who, as a child, had frolicked around the hulks of the abandoned locomotives rusting outside his native Verrettes. Born on 21 April 1900, schooled by the Christian Brothers at St. Marc and then in the *Lycée Pétion* at Port-au-Prince, he taught mathematics for a time until, inopportunely crossing Borno's bow, he lost both job and platform. Vindication came in the 1930 elections, when he was elected deputy, rising to presidency of that Chamber and then to successive portfolios under Vincent.

Remembered by Milo Rigaud (no compliment, considering the source) as "*élève de Vincent*" (Vincent's disciple), Estimé was depicted by Minister Mayer in 1937 as "the silent, somewhat surly President of the Chamber of Deputies."

Viewing the new president from other perspectives, Katherine Dunham, legendary American dancer and choreographer who came to know Estimé intimately, would write

I have thought of Estimé when looking at bronzes of Benin, at Bambara, and Baule masks: the head large for the body, because there in the head the ancient artists of the kingdom of Benin placed the spirit, soul and intelligence of a man . . . At times brusqueness, impertinence, aloofness and rude manners seemed to govern his actions; these were the times when an intense timidity, a hypersensitivity, were in danger of exposure and would have to be hidden behind the defense which served him best.

In a metaphor Miss Dunham would have been the last to deny, a senator, Alphonse Henriquez, marveling at Estimé's ceaseless energy, murmured drily, "a motor in a pair of pants." But Estimé was by no means all work and no fun: he was a snappy dresser, and the tan presidential Oldsmobile was, according to one lady, known about Port-au-Prince as *"le tombeau des vierges"* (last stop for virginity).

As Robert Rotberg has pointed out, Estimé's victory was "the victory of the *folklorique* movement of black intellectuals . . . who had long sought political power." Rayford Logan put it in slightly different terms when he called the election the advent to power of the *noir* elite.

The goals and principles Estimé announced transcended those of any past president: restoration of independence to legislature and judiciary, ending of American financial control, establishment of political parties with the right to criticize the government, free press, trade unions, improved and wider public education. To proceed with these and other social programs, the new president could start from an economy that since 1944 had been booming: besides coffee, bananas and sisal were doing well on the world market, a thriving trade in mahogany handicrafts had sprung up - and - one of *SHADA*'s successes - a new industry, that of essential oils extracted mainly from the Haitian herb *vetivert*, had come into being. Government revenues and trade balance of 1946 were the highest independent Haiti had ever attained.

But first there must be a new constitution, and that meant fireworks. Estimé, stirred like much of the Third World by the liberal rhetoric of World War II, and a reader and admirer of Henry Wallace, backed a document whose initial drafts described Haiti as "socialist," restored bans on foreign land-ownership, effectively prohibited foreigners from owning or conducting business, nationalized the clergy, and specifically legitimized trade unions. This was heady stuff, but, under protests by the United States, Britain, France, Switzerland, and the Vatican, not to mention the business community, most of it was eliminated in the final constitution as enacted on 22 November 1946.

Estimé's politics thus amounted to a kind of peasant populism tinged with Vincent's antiforeignism and with fierce *"mangeur-mulâtres"* black racism. Yet Estimé, the self-made doctrinaire intellectual, was, if only on past performance, also a highly effective politician. Including in his cabinet two of his most outspoken rivals, Fignolé (Education) and Dr. Rigaud (Commerce), the president allowed these fiery spirits to collide and cancel each other, and then in October 1946 sacked the entire cabinet, simultaneously creating new places for the deserving and shelving old foes. To pay off the *Garde*, Estimé gave Lavaud a well-earned promotion to *général de brigade* (Haiti's first general since 1915) and quickly took steps in May 1947 to obtain U.S. military assistance credits. On the other hand (a political decision that shattered much of its mystique) Estimé, on 29 March, redesignated the *Garde* as *"Armée d'Haïti"* and, on paper, split off its police elements into a Rural and Urban Police, the latter a theoretical reform that failed to stick. Thereafter, in a moment of rare misjudgment, he proffered Lavaud, Levelt, and Magloire distant ambassadorships in Washington, Santiago, and Paris (where incumbent Placide David had just been caught by the French in large black-market operations). Politely, the three officers declined.

Under the 1935 Standard Fruit contract, Haiti's fine little bananas had risen to an export of 7.3 million stems and the second largest income earner in the economy. Standard Fruit ships were plying Haiti's ports, and the company was spending money for wharves, buoys, roads, and even schools.

It was too tempting. In September 1947, refusing to renew Standard Fruit's monopoly, Estimé nationalized the industry, parceling it out into seven concessions to seven political friends, including Colonel Magloire.(34)

What then followed is one of the saddest stories in Haiti's economic history. The concessionaires cut prices paid to peasants, thus increasing profits but discouraging production. Worse still, the government-hired shipping, replacing Standard's vessels, turned out to lack refrigeration, so cargoes arrived spoiled and stinking. Both production and exports dived in 1948 and ceased entirely thereafter. In the words of missionary Père Roger Riou of La Tortue, "Estimé wreaked the worst possible harm to his country by nationalizing Standard Fruit. The Americans had proper refrigerator ships and outlets. The Haitians had no ships and chartered Greek and Panamanian vessels without refrigeration. In a few months the whole business was washed up."

Estimé's apologists said he had gutted Standard Fruit not out of greed or antiforeignism but because his reforms demanded money and the new men in power were in a hurry.

In the days of Frédéric Marcelin, they would have gone to Paris, but France of 1946 was impoverished and dreary, so in December that year a financial mission pled Haiti's case in Foggy Bottom, where the State Department had just moved.

The Haitians' Christmas list was simple enough: a moratorium on, or even forgiveness of, the 1938 Ex-Im (J. G. White) loan; U.S. credits for an assortment of projects; a moratorium on amortization of the bonds. That they were seeking all this at a time when Haiti's financial position was stronger than in many years was not thought to be a fair or even relevant rejoinder by the State Department or the unsympathetic money men of the Ex-Im Bank.(35)

After the mission returned empty-handed, the Haitian ambassador in Washington, Joseph D. Charles, bitterly told an American newsman: "Every time the United States has tried to help us, they have increased our poverty and confusion instead of lessening it."(36)

It was in this recriminatory spirit that Lucien Hibbert (whom Estimé had appointed rector of the university) came to Washington for another try in September 1947. After he asked the Ex-Im Bank for $20 million, he was immediately told that any such money must be conditioned on a well-justified and thought-out project. "Such an approach is impossible for the Haitian government," Hibbert flared back. At the end of an unproductive mission, he burst out that the Bank was "slamming the door in Haiti's face," and flounced home.

All was not lost: Norman Armour had now risen to the high places of the State Department and, old Haitian hand that he was, set out to smooth feelings and find ways to help. The upshot, resulting from less stormy and better focused negotiations, was a better Christmas gift. On 29 December 1948, the Ex-Im Bank gave Haiti $4 million on easy terms for a project with a long future - the development of the Artibonite Valley as a source of power and agriculture.

Looming like a giant *mapou* on the horizon, what looked like a new-found money tree now beckoned. While the United Nations was still in temporary quarters at Lake Success in 1947, Ernest Chauvet, Haiti's delegate, convinced Secretary General Trygve Lie that the U.N. should (in the words of the *New York Times)* adopt Haiti as its laboratory model, "as a demonstration of how it was prepared to tackle the problems of technical aid to underdeveloped countries."

Mr. Lie was delighted. Announcing that Chauvet's request had given the U.N. its very first opportunity to make a "test case," the secretary general mobilized experts in health, agriculture, education, public administration, and finance, who deployed South as the fine fall weather set in. The era of solving Haiti's problems by foreign survey team had dawned.(37)

Manfully the experts wrought, surveying Haiti from Cap to Cayes, plumbing its offshore waters, poking into its schools, and discovering that university French enunciated with a Scandinavian accent conveyed little to peasant coffee-growers back of Grand-Goâve. The result, a year later, was 327 pages of what was wrong and what needed doing. Malaria, yaws, tuberculosis, and parasites must be eliminated. Twenty-six separate agricultural recommendations covered but the top priorities. Mining - it mattered not that Haiti had hardly any minerals - should be pressed. Besides hydroelectric power, said one expert, Haiti should develop windmills; swamps should be turned into fishponds; and the educational system should be reorganized, modernized, and expanded.

In these and other recommendations (save perhaps for the fish ponds and windmills, which were new) the U.N. report was one General Russell could have dictated any Friday afternoon. Attaining these results, as Russell could have explained, was another matter.

When the question of money came up in late 1948, the Haitian government was dumfounded to learn that the U.N. really had none. Perhaps, suggested the experts, the United States would like to finance it all? Or the Ex-Im Bank? Or the International Monetary Fund? Or the Bank for Reconstruction and Development? Unfortunately, when smitten, none of these rocks gushed forth. The last that was heard for the time being was M. Chauvet telling the General Assembly in 1949, "Haiti insists that practical action be taken on the Haitian survey by the U.N."(38)

No matter, Haiti's budget - fattened by a good harvest and, Estimé's unwelcome gift to the elite, the country's first income tax - hit $13 million in October 1949. Six hundred thousand of those dollars, nearly 5 percent, went for the transformation of Belladère, a humble frontier post on the highway from Santo Domingo, into a modern new town complete, like a toy village, with bank, theater, *hôtel de ville*, a restaurant, new church, hotel, and so on. The reason, with no economic justification whatever, was to upstage the thriving Dominican town, Elias Piña, just across the border. Trujillo, no more friendly toward Estimé than Lescot, silently watched the new buildings go up. A few weeks after Belladère's grand opening, El Benefactor simply closed the highway and rerouted traffic into Haiti via Jimaní and Malpasse on the Cul-de-Sac, leaving Belladère to crumble into a ghost town, or, in the metaphor of a critic, to melt away like ice cream in the sun.

Belladère was only a curtain-raiser to a more costly failure: the 1949-1950 International Exposition held to celebrate the 200th anniversary of the founding of Port-au-Prince (which, for purposes of the fair, was officially dated 1749). At a budgeted cost of $6 million, and, despite a gambling ship sailed down from Miami, the poorly planned, mismanaged, and underpatronized exhibition proved a tourist fiasco. As seen on opening day by Edmund Wilson, "One found almost nothing there. The Palace of Tourism as yet had nothing in it but murals, at which people were staring through locked doors. The aquarium housed no fishes and was not yet even equipped with tanks . . . Many buildings were hardly begun.(39)

But the exposition could boast artistic triumph - the inspired performances by Katherine Dunham and her troupe of Haitian dancers, and the debut of what would soon be the sunburst of Haitian art on the world scene. In addition, through the medium of *folklorique* dances, Voodoo for the first time began to come into public (that is, tourist) view.

(Under a *noir* regime with Lorimer Denis one of its begetters, Voodoo had regained its central place. In 1946 Estimé's Minister of Education outraged Church and elite by presiding over a university function in the Ciné Rex that featured Voodoo chants and dances. When the Catholic *Action Sociale* then called for a new anti-Voodoo campaign, it was suppressed and its editor jailed; while Père Foisset, a French priest whose articles had charged Voodoo involvement in politics, was expelled.)

"Life in those days," later reminisced the journalist Edith Efron, "was one long debate. Jean Brièrre would write a new poem and it was a social event."

Içi la Renaissance

> *Beaux Arts:* The fine arts are generally neglected. There are a few musicians and artists with remarkable talent, but, unfortunately, they receive very little encouragement.

Thus disposing of *"les beaux arts"* in the 1890s, Sémextant Rouzier, Haiti's geographer-historian, undoubtedly never gave a thought to the intricate cornmeal vèvès being traced on the floors of countless *houmforts,* or considered the rhythm of elaborately carved *Petro and Rada* drums as music in its purest form.

Music has always flowed through Haitian veins; toddlers swing instinctively to the beat of a *compas.* A *bamboche* without music is to a Haitian like a repast without wine to a Frenchman. Turn-of-the century poets flowered profusely. How many other countries have published a special map of their poets? But the language of the early poets was French, and the style that of Victor Hugo and Lamartine.

In July 1927, Emil Roumer, Jacques Roumain, Daniel Heurtelou, and Philippe Thoby-Marcelin founded the *Revue Indigène,* and Haitian literature and poetry achieved an exciting new dimension. Novelists wrote of, if not for, the people. Jacques Roumain's *Gouverneurs de la Rosée (Masters of the Dew)* received international acclaim and was widely translated. The Marcelin brothers became the first Haitians to win the Latin American novel contest in 1943. Dr. Jean Price-Mars's *Ainsi Parla l'Oncle (Thus Spake the Uncle)* awakened his country's pride in its own rich folklore, its wise yet pungent Créole proverbs, and its Voodoo songs. Jean Brièrre's spontaneous poems prepared the way for other intensely Haitian poets, such as Hamilton Garoute and Paul Laraque - two officers of the *Garde* as well as poets of the avant-garde.

The renaissance of Haitian art did not unfold until after World War II, when DeWitt Peters, a California artist who came to Haiti during the war to teach English, founded the Centre d'Art in 1944.

Until that time, Port-au-Prince artists with a degree of formal training still tended to the hearts-and-flowers, gondola-by-moonlight style, while in the country, chicken feathers were being dipped into cans of house enamel to create curving Damballahs on *poteau mitans* or mystical symbols on *houmfort* altars. Just as the artisans of Chartres and Europe's other Gothic cathedrals worked solely for the greater glory of God, these peasant artists were painting to please their *loa,* and the *loa* must indeed have been pleased.

The Centre was not the first venture of its kind. Henry Christophe imported an English drawing-master to his court, and one painting, said to be the work of a young page named Desroches, survives. It shows a flourishing Sans Souci with gingerbread houses set against a backdrop of jagged mountains that might have been painted by Philomé Obin.

Peters's original plan had been not so much to promote primitive art as to provide a gathering place for the educated artists who still continued, in Rouzier's words, "to receive very little encouragement." Peters was at first unaware of being surrounded by Haitian Douanier Rousseaus, including his own chauffeur, Rigaud Benoît, and his yardboy, Castéra Bazile, whose *Baptism of Christ* was destined to become one of Holy Trinity Episcopal Cathedral's most famed murals.

Hector Hyppolite, one of Haiti's great early painters, first attracted Peters's attention through his brilliant birds and flowers painted on the walls of a small roadside café prophetically named "Içi la Renaissance." Hyppolite, a *houngan* from St. Marc who had been informed by the *loa* of his impending fame, was the first Haitian primitive to achieve international recognition and a one-man show in Paris, in 1947. He died a year later, some say because he neglected the *loa* who had bestowed good fortune upon him.

Philomé Obin, stern old man of the North and a practicing Baptist, had received, as a youth, some training in art at the local *lycée.* While working at other trades in his native Cap, he continued to record in paint the turbulent history that unfolded before his eyes during almost half a century. *Loa* don't speak to Baptists, so Obin manipulated his own destiny. He sent the Centre his magnificently detailed painting of Franklin D. Roosevelt's 1934 visit to the Cap and was immediately placed on salary. Heretofore the largest sum he had ever received for a painting was one dollar.

Selden Rodman's *Miracle of Haitian Art* tells the full story of how the bare walls of Holy Trinity Cathedral gradually bloomed with scenes from the New Testament uniquely and unforgettably Haitian. Rodman, in 1949 codirector of the Centre d'Art, was distressed to see the finest works leaving the country almost before the paint was dry. His suggestion that Haitian artists paint murals for the buildings being erected for Port-au-Prince's bicentennial went unheeded by almost everyone. This was fortunate as it turned out, for many of these buildings have ceased to exist. Haiti's Episcopal bishop, the Right Reverend C. Alfred Voegeli, one of the earliest connoisseurs of Haitian art, was, however, more receptive.

The project did not flow as smoothly and readily as the wine in Wilson Bigaud's sparkling *Miracle at Cana*, which now covers part of the transept. Money had to be raised, the roof of the cathedral repaired, and a medium found that would enable the murals to withstand the rigors of the tropics.

A tryout on the walls of the Centre d'Art developed a bitter rivalry between "advanced" and "primitive" painters.

The artists who had been trained suffered agonies of indecision. Rodman writes:

> Downstairs the "Primitives," once coaxed into the initial effort, attacked their wall spaces with abandon. The briefest of charcoal sketches, then on with the paint. Talent immediately revealed future muralists. Benoît, Bazile, Toussaint Auguste, Wilson Bigaud, Gabriel Levêque, and Obin alone in his library, simply translated to the wall space those formulas for easel pictures which had been monumental in their simplicity. That month there appeared on the Centre d'Art privy a derisive pencil scrawl in a primitive hand: *"Les artistes de l'étage qui se disent des avancés ne sont pas mêmes des préliminaires primitives"* (The artists upstairs who call themselves advanced are not even preliminary primitives).

The work on the walls of the cathedral began in fall 1951. New rivalries developed. One communicant, on seeing Auguste's *Adam and Eve*, remarked: "Surely the Creator could have done better than that in the beginning." Tourists wondered why the only white man in Obin's *Last Supper* was Judas Iscariot. Préfét Duffaut's inclusion of a luscious *Maîtresse Erzulie* shocked the faithful. One night, vandals (some say disgruntled rivals) streaked three partly finished murals with pitch.

Bishop Voegeli never wavered in his faith in the artists. To complaints that conceptions of Christ varied widely he would reply, "After all we have four versions of the Gospel." The completed murals raised the curtain on Haitian art and have remained a leading tourist attraction.

Haitian artistic talent surfaced in many forms besides painting. Haiti's mahogany begged to be carved rather than consumed in charcoal fires. To coffee tables and salad bowls prized by visitors were added the vibrant peopled landscapes of Odilon Perrier and the driftwood sea monsters of André Dimanche. Masks, clearly African in inspiration, flooded the market.

A Croix-des-Bouquets blacksmith, Georges Liataud, who for many years had added Voodoo flourishes to his cemetery crosses, went on to produce weird and wonderful two-dimensional figures and found a new school of metal art.

The American sculptor Jason Seley discovered Jasmin Joseph, then a shy twelve-year-old, whose delicate yet apocalyptic figures seemed to Seley strangely Etruscan. Joseph molded the ventilating grilles inset with figurines, which so well replace windows in the cathedral and in the Théâtre de Verdure, the latter the work of Albert Mangonès, an architect and artist of great skill and talent, though no primitive.

Many names became justly famous during the sixties and seventies, including that of one outstanding artist, André Pierre. A *houngan* iconographer who for years had depicted the *loa* on *houmforts* throughout the Cul-de-Sac, Pierre was, in 1961, persuaded to sell his work - mostly *coués* (Voodoo icons) - through the gift shop of the Episcopal cathedral. Had he not had an earlier misunderstanding with the Centre d'Art, he would almost certainly have been one of the muralists.

Today Port-au-Prince and Pétionville are awash with art galleries, and aspiring artists peddle their wares on every corner. Haitian art is hawked throughout the Caribbean, often at handsome markups. The fruits of the movement that started in the basement of the Centre d'Art five decades ago now adorn the salons of the world.

Down with Estimé

Just as Toussaint and many another Haitian ruler feared that enemies would strike through Santo Domingo, so, from earliest days, Rafael Trujillo believed the Dominican Republic could never be secure unless it controlled all Hispaniola. It was this which drove Trujillo so many times to manipulate governments in Port-au-Prince, enterprises facilitated by the fact that his secret-police chief, the unsavory Anselmo Paulino, had a Haitian wife and had served as Dominican consul at the Cap and subsequently as minister at Port-au-Prince. (One reason for the grudge between Trujillo and Estimé was that the latter, with what subsequently would appear good reason, had refused consent when Trujillo in 1946 proposed Paulino for a second tour as minister.)

Throughout 1949 the Dominican strongman launched his most violent attacks, involving plots to poison Estimé, fomentation of sedition and insurrection, and, finally, invasion. Trujillo's instrument was the *mulâtre* Astrel Roland, former colonel in the *Garde*. A familiar of Paulino since 1937, Roland had taken refuge in Ciudad Santo Domingo in 1948. Working closely with Roland was Dr. Alfred Viau, a Haitian educator. one of whose sons had been killed by Estimé's police. The first manifestations of the Roland-Viau vendetta were a series of inflammatory broadcasts beamed at Haiti over La Voz Dominicana, coupled with dissemination by mail and even air-drop (from Dominican planes) of revolutionary tracts. Besides being subversive, the broadcasts were vulgar and overheated, detailing alleged crimes by Estimé and charging him with keeping a mistress and four extraterritorial children in Paris. In kind, Port-au-Prince radio replied, "Aha, Roland the Shameless, shut your mouth!"

But more passed between the two countries than insults. As an investigation verified in 1950, Trujillo (in what came to be called the "Dupuy-Roland plot") provided money and guns for killer-teams which were to infiltrate Port-au-

Murals in the Episcopal Cathedral in Port-au-Prince bespeak a Haitianized Church and the explosion of artistic creativity that began in the nineteen-forties. *Heinl Collection*

Prince; assassinate Colonel Magloire, Major Prosper (chief of police), and the president if possible; put the city to the torch; and link up with an invasion column to be led from Jimaní across the Cul-de-Sac by Roland. The plot, dead serious and on the verge of execution, was foiled only when, in bizarre circumstances, on 26 December 1949, it was betrayed to Estimé's Foreign Minister by the Dominican ambassador in Port-au-Prince.

While Estimé, aided by luck, was barely fending off Trujillo from the right, his regime was simultaneously being penetrated from the left by forces that had overthrown Lescot and expected to profit thereby.

No serious assertion that Estimé was a communist could be supported (although his representatives in Washington felt obliged in 1946 to take notice of such charges, their denial being somewhat weakened by the fact that Dr. Rigaud was a member of the delegation present). Nonetheless, emergence of a self-conscious, self-styled, often Marxist left, a new phenomenon in Haitian politics, did characterize the Estimé regime.

Trade unions, with their governmental counterpart, the Ministry of Labor, were showpieces in Estimé's program, but the movement was initially all but captured by Fignolé (who after all was a practicing unionist at HASCO). By hastily pumping up a government-fostered central labor movement (*Fédération des Travailleurs Haïtiens, or FTH*) Estimé contrived to outflank Fignolé, but the FTH, as reported both the *New York Times* and American embassy dispatches, was communist-dominated, and its leader, Edris Saint-Amand, was, on public record, a top signer of the national Communist Party manifesto of March 1947.

Besides this communist presence in the new labor movement, Estimé, no doubt ensuring himself against the far left, employed at various times, as Ministers or principal advisers, Dr. Rigaud, Minister of Commerce; Lucien Hibbert, rector of the university; and Jean Brièrre, Minister of Tourism.

These developments and much accompanying noisy rhetoric, had raised a degree of apprehension sufficient to impel the government in 1948 to outlaw the Communist Party, but not the Cuban-supported Popular Socialist Party, and in January that year all avowed PCH members were stripped of office. The PSP, however, remained unhindered and, in the opinion of the American embassy, continued to be a significant political force.(40) Based on political muscle duly noted in November 1949 by the *New York Times* however, a new, non-communist union, the *Fédération des Chauffeurs-Guides*, was beginning to emerge as a powerful supporter of the government. Dr. Duvalier, secretary general of Fignolé's MOP, was now Minister of Labor under Estimé and was already forging ties with the *Chauffeurs-Guides*.

By 1949, with a year to go in office, Estimé's days were numbered. He had talked and dreamed big. He had also blundered. The American development loans, though concentrated logically enough in Estimé's own Artibonite, were doing nothing for other regions. Standard Fruit's contribution to national earnings and government revenues had been thrown away. In March 1949 - a new device and as unpalatable to the masses as income taxes to the upper classes -the government required every worker to invest 15 percent of his pay in 3 percent bonds supposed to mature in 1959. The peasants then simply quit work and ate mangos.

Faced thus with discontent on left and right, and menaced externally by Trujillo with the Caribbean's largest army, Estimé kept Haiti under state of siege throughout 1949 while at the same time working to prolong himself in office.

July 1949 saw the inevitable preliminary: a proposed constitutional revision to erase 1952 as the end of Estimé's term, coupled with deletion of the often-expunged provision that no president may succeed himself. During November 1949, at PSP incitation, a general strike was called, centering mainly on the university but extending throughout a wide range of splinter parties, including the Fignolists. Estimé thereupon suppressed seven newspapers and the parties concerned (Fignolé gaining the Argentine embassy by a hair's breadth), proclaimed general censorship, and put his face to a rising storm.

When the legislative Chambers convened on 18 April 1950, the Senate, by a thirteen-man majority, balked at the constitutional revisions that an Estimé-packed lower house had passed. During sixteen days of mounting tension, the senators would not be budged. Then the dam burst.

Crying *"Vive Estimé! Vive la ré-élection!"* a mob formed in the Marché Vallière and roared down onto the Senate, manhandling fleeing members, wrecking the premises, burning archives and portraits (even that of Charles Sumner), and parading fragments of furniture through the streets. In a message broadcast that night by radio and printed next day by *Le Moniteur,* Estimé applauded his supporters' hooliganism: "Your eloquent attitude this morning," he said, overlooking 1867 and other similar occasions, "which is without precedent in our history, bears witness to your political maturity and your direct participation in the affairs of the state."

The elite (notably including the newly rich *noir* elite Estimé had fostered) shuddered as the mob surged past heavily shuttered shops and sacked the homes of recusant senators. On 9 May Estimé called in the principal officers of the army for a declaration of fealty. All professed loyalty. Meanwhile, however, led by such figures as the pitiless Lucien Chauvet, other mobs began to paint the walls and shout *"A bas Estimé! Vive la Révolution!"*

At 9:00 A.M. on Wednesday, 10 May, the general staff, headed by Lavaud, Levelt (though Magloire, *primus inter pares,* had emerged as the strongman), and Marcaisse Prosper, the stuttering chief of police, waited on the president. In their hands was a proclamation announcing his resignation. One hour later, on the stroke of ten, Fort National boomed a salute, and Port-au-Prince learned that the junta that had steered the republic through the stormy hours of Lescot's fall was again at the helm.(41)

Most Civil of the Military

Whatever else might be said, the army had become overtly political. Having once, in 1946, tasted the fruit of the Tree of Good and Evil, it had now returned four years later for a second bite. Regular soldiers that they were, the men of the junta still accorded due respect to rank and precedence. Lavaud's name appeared at the top of the list, but it was Magloire who assumed the portfolio as Minister of Interior and National Defense and thus stood forth as the *gros nèg'*.

The first action of the junta, after immediate dissolution of the legislature, was to appoint, mainly from the Senate and chaired by Dantès Bellegarde, a *Conseil Consultatif*, privy counselors who, besides providing general advice window-dressing, were to recommend electoral procedures and, natural as breathing, a new constitution. At a press conference, another innovation, Colonel Magloire had observed, "The Constitution is in caretaker status." Also in caretaker status, in jail, though perhaps less publicized, were several active Estimé partisans as well as leading members of the mob that had sacked the Senate, quietly arrested as the junta took charge.

"The first thing to do," remarked Colonel Levelt, suave as ever, to a *New York Times* reporter, "is to let the minds of people cool off."

By 3 August, hardly the year's coolest day, the process had nonetheless proceeded so well that the *Conseil*, under Bellegarde's steady hand, had produced a decree that, for electoral purposes, amounted to an interim constitution: national elections for a new legislature and for the presidency - Haiti's first direct presidential election, with suffrage for all men over twenty-one - would take place on 8 October.

Even as the new decree was proclaimed, Colonel Magloire resigned from the junta and announced for president. His post was immediately taken over by the distinguished *Capois* lawyer Maître Luc Fouché.

Magloire's only serious opposition - fierce but limited - came from the communists, marshaled by Néré Numa and Georges Petit, using the latter's *L'Action* as their pulpit. Even Fignolé, fire-eater though he was, knew which way the wind was blowing: when he began to spout about "the will of the people," Magloire cheerfully replied, *"Mon cher, de qui peuple ouap palé moin? Nan pays ça, cé dé force qui gaignin, l'Armée et la bourgeoisie!"* (Mon cher, what people are you talking about? In this country there are only two forces that count, the Army and the elite!)

In the event, the sole opposing candidate, an obscure architect running as Estimé's executor, never had a chance against the confidence and bonhommie that radiated from the handsome, broad-shouldered soldier who circulated about the country in well-cut civilian clothes. With Church (42), army, elite, and (very discreetly) the American embassy behind him, Magloire could hardly lose. On election day, despite rains that flooded towns and roads, people trudged through mud or rode burros to over 600 polling places strictly supervised by the army under the 1930 rules that had served so well.

Returns from Port-au-Prince told the story: Magloire, 25,679; Fénélon Alphonse (the opponent), 7; Papa Legba, 3. On 10 October, to no one's astonishment, Magloire was pronounced winner by 99 percent of the vote. Estimé's men, most of whom had boycotted the polls, muttered the predictable recriminations. Nonetheless, in the words of *Newsweek* (23 October 1950), "There is little doubt that the one-sided result reflected popular opinion. Magloire is far and away the most popular man on the island among all classes. He seems even to have transcended the rivalry between the Negro masses and the mulatto aristocracy which is the traditional dividing line in Haitian politics."

Climaxing three days' party, Magloire took office on 6 December 1950. That day, to the slam of gun salutes and peal of bells, General Lavaud again handed over power to an elected president. (Sitting, with a sense of historical fitness, at Gonaïves, Dantès Bellegarde and twenty-one other eminent colleagues had meanwhile completed the new constitution and secured its adoption by the legislature on 28 November. The Estimé interdict against serving officers assuming political office was pointedly missing.(43)

The charismatic, forty-two-year-old *noir* from Quartier Morin who now entered the palace was direct, authoritative, fond of order, and given to show (one of his first actions was to suit out the *Garde Présidentielle* in resplendent dress blues). Like Toussaint, Magloire loved horses, and the army stables out past HASCO soon boasted a handsome set of officers' chargers and nimble mares. Whatever else he was, the president was no *mangeur-mulâtres:* his associations cut across the racial divide as no Haitian ruler's ever had. He was also, to the delight of high and low, a great *bambocheur,* moving ebulliently from party to party, more often than not without guards or escort, tarrying sometimes at one of the clubs for poker or bridge. Sundays, at the president's hideout in La Boule, old army friends and leading politicians would gather for baccarat and whiskey, whose plenteous flow soon evoked a popular song: *"Tout le jou, m'sou, cé wisky m'boué, nan sein maman moin cé wisky m'boué!"* (Every day, I'm plastered, it's whiskey that I drink, even at mother's breast I sucked whiskey!).(44)

However late he partied, Magloire the soldier was up each morning with the roosters, working out on an exercise machine, getting a rubdown and an eye-opener of pungent coffee, then dressing immaculately in white linen or gray gabardine with favorite gray suede shoes, and getting to work in the little second-floor private office of the *Palais* in time to see guard and band execute morning colors as the "Dessalinienne" blared out on the stroke of eight.

The president's policies can be quickly summed up: harmony and reconciliation among the classes and colors (which Estiméists sourly dismissed as *"doublure"* with Magloire as cat's-paw for the elite); internal development; and friendly relations with the two powers that counted: the United States and the Dominican Republic.(45) Magloire's assets were considerable. The country still enjoyed relative stability; if the economy had been stagnant under Estimé, it was comfortable stagnation. The *gourde* was sound. After four years of Estimé, people had had enough social tinkering. Land reform, a burning issue elsewhere in the underdeveloped world, had for good or ill been completed a century and a quarter earlier.

Yet the central problem, too little land, too many people, grew inexorably with Malthusian certainty. Scarcely less critical were uncontrolled deforestation and soil erosion. Bananas and cotton were dead; sugar and sisal were at the mercy of fluctuating markets. The budget still represented the take from an archaic system of import duties (70 percent); income taxes from a few thousand elite and Syrians (10 percent); and a grab bag of hit-or-miss levies to make up the rest. There was no budgetary system.

If there was to be a central plan, as Magloire believed there should be, it must focus on agriculture, on efficient use of government revenue, and on encouragement of foreign capital to enhance development. And this is what the president set on foot.

By July 1950, Magloire had negotiated a U.S. Point Four agreement covering soil conservation, cattle farming, irrigation and drainage, and sanitation. Picking up Estimé's haphazard Artibonite Valley project, Magloire went to the Ex-Im Bank for $14 million added to Haiti's $6 million for construction of a great dam, 225 feet high and 1075 feet wide, at Péligre on the Artibonite. When completed, the dam would irrigate 80,000 arid acres and would ultimately (nearly two decades later, as it turned out) provide 40,000 kilowatts of scarce power.

Besides emphasis on agriculture, Magloire wanted to build or improve 300 miles of roads, including blacktop from Port-au-Prince to Cap Haïtien, with an asphalt extension to Fort Liberté. Not forgetting his own North, he planned a $7 million modernization of wharves and harbor at the Cap.(46)

All the foregoing programs and many others were incorporated in a five-year plan costing a staggering $40 million to be raised by stimulated revenue, by U.S. loans, by some United Nations aid, and by the attraction of foreign capital, an augury of which was the 1953 opening at Miragoâne of the Reynolds Metals bauxite mines. One other attraction for foreign capital was Magloire's short way (he could quickly enough put on his *cançons fé)* with strikers and syndicalists. When, in 1951, he found the *Parti Socialiste Populaire* fomenting strikes against American firms, he shut it down for good, and Fignolé's MOP to boot. With this he also silenced two gadflies, the communist *La Nation* and the Fignolé mouthpiece, *Chantiers.*

The United Nations, which had little to show for early rhetoric in aid of Haiti, now deployed more purposefully. Coordinated by a U.N. resident representative permanently assigned to Haiti, a cadre of some ten to twenty specialists, with skills ranging anywhere from public administration to fisheries, provided advice, administered programs and funds, and backstopped Magloire's sustained push for development. Under U.S. aegis, besides numerous other programs, was SCISP (Service Cooperatif Interamericain de Santé Publique), a nationwide effort to wipe out malaria, parasite diseases, and in particular, Haiti's endemic yaws,(47) which at any given moment infected 90 percent of the population.

In addition to aid from the United States and U.N., Haiti benefited further in December 1954, when, with encouragement from Magloire (who provided a colony of old Standard Fruit quarters for the purpose), Dr. and Mrs. William Latimer Mellon opened their *Hôpital Albert Schweitzer* at Deschappelles, near Verrettes, a project that would earn world attention as the years went by.

Another American program of long-range importance was the mapping of Haiti. This began in 1953, under the Inter-American Geodetic Survey, and resulted, a decade later, in high-grade topographic maps covering the entire country, an essential for future land-use planning, public works, and even the beginnings of cadastral survey.

The times were vibrant with modernization. Haiti, like its energetic president, was on the move. Things were happening.

There were state visits - not the court affairs of Sieur Lescot, but occasions instead for celebration and *bamboche.* In April 1952, Hector Trujillo, brother of El Benefactor, came over for four days from Ciudad Santo Domingo. Next year, in August, came old General Anastasio "Tacho" Somoza, president of Nicaragua. Then, in November 1954 -Haiti's first visit by an African chief of state - Liberia's William Tubman spent three days as Magloire's guest. And Sir Hugh Foote, first governor of Jamaica to set foot on Haiti since Henry Morgan was shipwrecked and imprisoned 279 years earlier, visited Port-au-Prince in February 1954, laid wreaths on all monuments, and, as *Time* reported, "gamely accommodated his swooping waltz style to the intricacies of the *meringue. "*

Nor were the politicians alone; Haiti, already discovered by foreign intellectuals during Estimé's time, now swam into the ken of the smart set. Haitian weekends became the thing, while the improbable gingerbread-style Hotel Oloffson, last seen as the Marines' hospital during the occupation, assumed its later role as *de rigueur* watering-place for writers ranging from Nöel

534 Written in Blood

Coward to Truman Capote (and of course Graham Greene, who limned it so vividly a decade later in *The Comedians*).

None of this would have happened if the world economy had not smiled on Haiti. By the end of 1954, tourism (not including regular visits by U.S. warships and free-spending sailors) had (48) expanded threefold over 1950. Coffee exports went up 20 percent a year during the same period, and, sisal, ever a war crop, benefited from the Korean war. Bank deposits were rising steadily. A few light industries began to take root. These included a French cement factory, a Texas-owned flour mill (both subsequently nationalized), and an Italian shoe factory.

To sweeten the economy still further, in July 1952 France resumed purchase of Haitian coffee. The terms were extortionate: besides tariff concessions on French wines and luxury items, Haiti was compelled to liquidate the trumped-up claim for gold redemption of the 1910 bonds (whose provenance, through successive refinancing, went back to the grinding reparations of 1825, but the immediate benefit was undeniable).

In this booming atmosphere it was inevitable to want to celebrate: after all, Estimé had had his exposition. So 1954, sesquicentennial of independence (christened "*Le Tricinquantenaire*") was ordained a festal year.

(There was one essential preliminary. Again donning *cançons fe,* the president locked up some twenty-three troublemakers, notably Fignolé and veteran communist Rossini Pierre-Louis. A third, Marcel Hérard, slipped past the dragnet and was delivered to the Mexican embassy, rolled cocoonlike inside a rug. Magloire also took the occasion to shut down Fignolé's new paper, *Haïti-Démocratique,* and Georges Petit's newest, *Le Constitutionnel,* in each case confiscating type and smashing presses.)

The *Tricinquantenaire* was splendiferous.

At dawn on 1 January saluting guns thumped out their opening salute to the throngs in Gonaïves. Here, in the new cathedral, set on the Place de la Patrie, gleaming in modern architecture and stained glass, echoed the grandest Te Deum since 1934, after which the president unveiled a memorial obelisk with bronze bas-reliefs while General Levelt, a debonair Boisrond-Tonnerre, intoned the original declaration of independence, complete (if hardly Levelt's style) with the *blanc's* skin for parchment, his blood for ink, and skull for inkwell. After lunch Mme. Magloire led a pilgrimage of ladies to the tomb of the gentle Empress Marie-Claire Heureuse, and, that night, amid brilliant illuminations, Jean Brièrre and Jacques Alexis declaimed original works while dinners were digested.

Next day, via Bréda for hommage to Toussaint, the presidential progress moved to the Cap, and on the morrow came the long-awaited re-enactment of Vertières, on the very battleground. As thousands of peasants watched breathless, cadets of the Académie Militaire and soldiers of the army, costumed for their roles, fought the famous assault to the last blank cartridge and saluting charge. At one point, when the Haitians were momentarily thrown back by "French" defenders, the peasant spectators rose with a fierce outcry and surged into the Haitian ranks, to make sure Dessalines would win.(49)

That night, as evening cooled, the president and Mme. Magloire held a state dinner for 700 guests on the floodlit esplanade of Sans Souci Palace with La Ferrière brooding overhead against the moonlight. Backed by a superb Haitian choir, Marian Anderson brushed the stars with her incomparable voice.

The grand finale, a ball on 4 January, attended by 3000 guests at the *Palais National*, preceded that day by unveiling of statues of the Fondateurs on the Champ de Mars, rang down the curtain on a glorious celebration that did honor to Haiti and its president. How proud Tonton Nord would have been.

Two days after the great doings in Port-au-Prince, the *New York Times* headlined: HAITI'S POOR CROPS CUT DOWN TRADE. Coffee had not turned out well, and the *Banque* had had to buy in nearly a million dollars' worth of government bonds to provide operating cash to support a budget now over $30 million. (Even so, for fiscal year 1954-1955, the *Banque* could report a surplus of $3,460,000 against a prior-year deficit of $2,788,000.)

Other tremors were felt. As always, there were fewer places than claimants: outs were beginning to murmur against ins. The president's brothers, Jacques and Arsène, seemed to be making rather a good thing out of the "nonfiscal" *Régie du Tabac*, that Estimé monopoly whose books, if they existed, were exempt from audit or disclosure. Prosper, the toothy police chief, completed a palatial mansion (cost, $250,000)on monthly pay of $350.

On 11 October 1954, howling over slate-gray seas, eighty-knot winds lashed up from the South. Hurricane Hazel hit the coast at Port-à-Piment, ripped viciously past Cayes, all but destroyed Jérémie, leveled villages, killed at least a thousand victims, denuded 40 percent of Haiti's coffee bushes, flattened irretrievably the new Magloire-sponsored banana plantations, and uprooted half the country's cacao trees. Nan Mapou, a prosperous village outside Port-à-Piment, was converted into a mile-long lagoon. Malaria and sickness stalked Hazel's wake.

The world reacted generously. U.S.S. *Saipan,* aircraft carrier, was on the scene within twenty-four hours, as was H.M.S. *Vidal.* Contributions in funds and in goods came from the International Red Cross, the United States (with grants ultimately totaling $4.925 million), Venezuela, Cuba, Jamaica, Ghana, and Guadeloupe, to name only a few. Years afterward, visitors to outposts in the back country would stumble on private hoards of relief supplies in army storerooms, prefectures, and of course shops. And the word "Hazel" entered

Haiti's vocabulary: henceforth, mink wraps worn by officials' wives were styled *"les Hazels".*(50)

Besides questions raised by Hazel, the Artibonite project appeared to be consuming funds at greater rates than anyone had anticipated. In 1955, with completion of the dam still over a year distant, the Ex-Im Bank had to increase its $14 million to $21 million, then to $27 million. (The total cost, when the Péligre dam was finished, without generating equipment, in September 1956, amounted to $40 million; the 1951 projection had been $18 million.) Haiti's debt to the Ex-Im Bank for Artibonite loans ended up exceeding all the country's other debts combined.

Yet the regime still enjoyed momentum. In 1954, Magloire paid visits to Venezuela, Colombia, Nicaragua, Panama, and Puerto Rico. Early in 1955, in what *Time* rightly called a "commanding performance," the president climaxed his travels with a state visit to Washington that included an impressive address to a joint session of Congress, on 27 January 1955. The peroration, Hogar Nicolas pointed out, amounted to an exorcism of 1915: "No doubt from time to time," said Magloire, "clouds darken the atmosphere of confidence [between the two countries] . . . But for better or for worse, we believe our destiny is closely linked with that of the great American democracy." Accompanied by Mme. Magloire, by General Levelt, and by Daniel Théard, his elegant and witty *chef de protocol,* Magloire thereupon proceeded to captivate Washington and New York. When General Eisenhower, admiring his guest's wide assortment of decorations, asked where he had gotten them, Magloire unhesitatingly - and truthfully - replied, "On the Champ de Mars, *mon général."*

In New York there was a ticker-tape parade laced with real snow in freezing weather, Sunday mass, luncheon with Cardinal Spellman, and, covering all bases, evening prayer in Harlem with the Reverend Adam Clayton Powell, Jr., at his Abyssinian Baptist Church. Equal triumphs followed in Canada and Jamaica, whence the presidential party were conveyed home aboard the British aircraft carrier H.M.S. *Triumph,* on whose flight deck Magloire became the first incumbent Haitian chief of state since Toussaint at the Môle to receive a British guard of honor. Well might he savor the cheers of his people as he and Mme. Magloire landed at the Wharf de Colombe. Never again would they ring so loud.(51)

Throughout 1955 events moved downhill. Blasted by Hazel, the coffee crop was the worst in years. Complaints of graft mounted as the regime ebbed. The *Nation,* never content with affairs in Haiti, began to zero in on the regime and afford a foreign mouthpiece for the enemies Magloire had earned among the left. Then, as in the days of Simon Sam and many another outgoing president, controversy began as to when the president's term lawfully ended. By exegetic

The Magloires and Eisenhowers chat before a state reception in Washington. *Heinl Collection*

reading of various constitutions, Estiméist foes as well as new hopefuls claimed that Magloire should leave either in May or, at the latest, in December 1956. Magloire, taking departure from the effective constitution (his own, to be sure, the Bellegarde opus of 1950), said May 1957. But from May 1956 on, there was no peace.

On 17 May, *lycée* students at Les Cayes and Jacmel surged into the streets, as did those of *Lycées Pétion* and *Toussaint Louverture* in Port-au-Prince. The latter was the scene of student insurrection: barricading entrances against police, pitching furniture from windows, hurling stones, books, inkwells, shrieking *"A bas Magloire!."* schoolboys and teachers fought police from corridor to corridor and each schoolroom. The city was suddenly flooded with tracts originated by a *"Comité Révolutionnaire* (Revolutionary Committee)." Hospitals filled with injured students and police alike. Magloire promptly proclaimed a state of siege for the capital and the other two towns. Calm returned, but it was a tense calm in which Magloire and his foes and also the jockeying candidates waited for each other to make the next move.(52)

Later in May, various unions, including the increasingly muscular *Syndicat des Chauffeurs-Guides* (originally fostered by Dr. Duvalier) staged strikes. Police chief Prosper blamed Duvalier for these and the student disorders. Two leaders of the *Comité Révolutionnaire,* both Duvalierists and communists, Paul Blanchet and Lucien Daumec, were arrested and jailed, along with some fifty others, including journalists. Once again, there was surface calm. Beneath that surface there was also intense politicking. Even so, Magloire, confident as ever, remained strong enough to visit the United States in September for a medical checkup in Philadelphia and then a few days at Niagara Falls, after which he returned to preside over the national homage for Jean Price-Mars on his eightieth birthday.

Greeting the president on his return was a mounting campaign of audible opposition centered on *Le Souverain,* journal of the students and their less youthful prompters of 17 May, who were openly appealing for a return to "the revolution of 1946," a year whose events few if any student protesters had any clear recollection of. At the same time, Magloire continued to talk as if he meant to step down in 1957, commenting openly on the candidacies of Duvalier, Jumelle, Fignolé, and Déjoie. "When they reach their forties," he observed with a grin, "all good Haitians have a higher objective than a seat in the Senate."

By November the atmosphere had turned edgy. Terrorist bombings - a new phenomenon - began to take place in public places. Random shots fired among the market women in the Marché de Fer would quickly lead to a *courri* through the waterfront mercantile district and the ominous sound of iron shutters creaking shut. Though it was not then suspected, the bombings and terrorism were the work of Dr. Duvalier's agents. That this was so would become dramatically apparent within five months, when, in April 1957, a bomb factory was uncovered in Martissant by the police, two of whom were mortally injured when one of the products detonated. The fabricator, who survived, implicated Duvalier as well as one of the latter's principal lieutenants, Clément Barbot. A second arms cache was found in the home of a lady Duvalierist in Lalue. Daniel François, the bomber, admitted in detail the November and December bombings that Duvalier had piously disavowed.

What was then even less suspected than the Duvalier connection with the bombings was that since July or earlier - originating among a group of ambitious junior officers discontent with slow promotion, some still lieutenants after twelve years or longer - an army plot was forming. The hopes of "*notre groupe*," as one of the plotters called it, were focused on a likeable *noir* colonel, Léon Cantave ("'Ti Cantt" to friends), and a soldierly *noir* major, Pierre Armand.(53)

As the month wore on, conditions worsened. There were more bombings; Fignolé was ambushed by night on the road to Léogane but luckily survived. Magloire, always a man for order, thereupon rounded on all the candidates, even his own dauphin, Jumelle. Afterward, the mild-mannered Duvalier issued a statement deploring all disorder or subversion. The statement had no effect: on 4 December, the main reservoir serving downtown Port-au-Prince was dynamited, killing or wounding five people. Soon afterward, another bomb went off among the market women at Marché de Vallière.

Enough was enough. That same day, the president clamped down on all political meetings, broadcasts, and publications. The announced candidates, all nineteen of them, then published a defiant round robin of protest. Magloire's rejoinder was to assume personal command of the Casernes Dessalines and call in his officers for a loyalty check. Only two demurred: Colonel Cantave, the quartermaster, and Major Paul Corvington, the handsome professional who directed the Académie Militaire. Cantave was forthwith arrested; Corvington, an erstwhile Magloire favorite, was not. Magloire then sent for American Ambassador Roy Tasco Davis, and asked if it might not be wise to postpone elections for a while to let things cool. Davis was noncommittal but not for long. The next day, accompanied by Msgr. Luigi Raimondi, papal nuncio and thus dean of the diplomatic corps, the Ambassador returned. Their blunt answer was that Magloire had lost public confidence, no longer enjoyed a mandate, and should plan to leave on schedule. Now it was Magloire who was noncommittal.

On 6 December - it was Thursday - the president assembled his cabinet, the general staff, and what amounted to the national establishment. To this group and listeners of station Radio Commerce Magloire announced that, six years having elapsed since he took office (there was no mention this time of the Gonaïves constitution), he now stood down. Since, under Chief Justice Nemours Pierre-Louis, the Cour de Cassation, nimble-footed as in 1950, had again declined the honor, the army ("always the vigilant protector of the people's rights") had again accepted its responsibilities. Then came the clear, familiar voice of Levelt: the army, guardian of patriotism and public order, now called on its senior soldier, Major General Paul E. Magloire, to accept the heavy burden of provisional president "to avert crisis and take all necessary measures."

"It is my duty," slowly replied General Magloire, "and I must, if reluctantly, accept." Thereupon, as if he had previously considered this contingency, the general proclaimed a state of siege ("in order," he said, "to assure the most rapid possible return to normal political life") and dissolved the legislature.

But the *cançons fe* had worn thin. They were in fact only khaki drill. Magloire had but seven days left. On Monday morning another *courri* erupted. Then - seemingly as planned, and led by Alain Laraque, a businessman of the same family as the two lieutenants in the army plot - the business houses failed to reopen. Employees of the *Banque* stayed home; so did schoolteachers. Filling stations dispensed no gas, but that hardly mattered because the Duvalierist *Chauffeurs-Guides* had every cab and *camionnette,* and any other vehicle they could catch, off the streets and immobilized. Peasants, alerted by *telediol* that *loups-garous* were abroad in Port-au-Prince, brought no food to market. Accompanied by his staff, submachine gun cradled in his arms. Magloire walked the waterfront. Shops opened as he approached, then closed as he passed. The submachine gun was a sham; Paul Magloire was no man to shoot down fellow Haitians in cold blood.

For two more days, with support from all candidates, Déjoie especially, the strike continued. On Wednesday, Magloire turned again to the chief justice. This time Nemours Pierre-Louis accepted executive power, and Magloire ceased to be *président provisoire.* (But there was this little catch: Citizen Paul Magloire also held a commission as *général de division;* General Magloire therefore simply walked out the palace back gate, across the parade ground, and opened headquarters in the casernes.)

It was too much. Crying out *"Li pas bon! Li pas bon!"* (He's no good!), the mob now demanded that Magloire go. A delegation of pistol-toting young officers waited upon the general. Their leaders, Captains Pasquet and Dominique, told him the time had come. Magloire drove up Avenue Charles Sumner to the cool of Turgeau and began to pack.

Next day, announcing that the army would remain in barracks awaiting orders from civilian authority, General Levelt submitted his retirement. Colonel Prosper, disguised as a pipe-smoking market woman, sought the French embassy. So did Colonel Cantave, taking no chances when the gates of Fort Dimanche swung open.

Next day, Lieutenant Auguste was sent to tell the Magloires that one of the army's DC-3s would be waiting at Bowen Field. Taking what he could with him, imperturbable and self-possessed to the end, Haiti's ablest president since Salomon climbed, with his wife and a few associates, aboard the plane, greeted the pilot, Major Roy, as if embarking for an inspection, and watched sunset gild

the mountains and green slopes and sleepy Jacmel as he flew South over the
darkening sea to Kingston and to exile.(54)

They Have Gone Mad

The day Magloire left, work stopped - not by decree, but in the mysterious
way things stop, run down, die, or vanish in Haiti - on the new Port-au-Prince
abattoir that was to have replaced the bloodcrusted relic built so long ago by
Hyppolite. For years after, the rusting, gaunt frame reproached successor
governments, which would neither touch the project of a predecessor nor even
move the remaining building materials from curbside and street, where they had
been stacked in 1956.

So it was with Haiti: all the stability, development, modernization, prosperity,
panache, and pleasure *("six ans de kermesse!"* [six years of carnival!], burst out
one indignant critic) that had been Magloire's were suddenly dissipated, with no
more trace than Soulouque's orders of nobility.

What was to follow for nine kaleidoscopic months was a dizzying succession
of provisional regimes and arrangements signifying in themselves absolutely
nothing. Within six months alone, five governments were to rise and fall while
Haiti, in the words of Leslie Manigat, "exhausted all the forms of transitory
government that had been used throughout the nineteenth century: provisional
constitutional presidency, provisional revolutionary presidency, collegial
government, provisional military government, and the unavoidable Constituent
Assembly in a kind of *bas-empire* competition."

Unlike the *"gouvernements éphémères"* from 1911 to 1915, which participated
in and were produced by deep struggles over control of the country, the truly
ephemeral governments of 1957 represented surface phenomena while the real
contests went on below the surface.

Three, or at most four, serious presidential candidates - Déjoie, Jumelle,
Duvalier, and Fignolé - battled for the succession. The army which would
ordinarily have settled matters, was itself split into factions, one of which
supported the new chief of staff, Colonel Cantave (who emerged, rather
ingloriously, to take up his appointment by Nemours Pierre-Louis), the other -
mostly *mulâtres* as the former were mostly *noirs* - supported Louis Déjoie.

The candidates can be quickly described:

- Louis Déjoie: wealthy aristocratic *mulâtre* planter and dealer in essential
oils, with extensive holdings outside Cayes and Jacmel, choice of the elite, of
the South, and of one army faction.

- Clément Jumelle: educated (Fisk and Chicago universities), self-made
Artibonite *noir* Finance Minister under Magloire, and inheritor of Magloirist
political assets. A strong believer in planning and development, Jumelle had at

one time been the bureaucratic superior and close friend of another candidate, François Duvalier, whom Jumelle had sheltered when he was in hiding in 1954.

- Daniel Fignolé: *noir* Port-au-Prince syndicalist and demagogue whose urban proletarian MOP could at will disrupt the capital and government but had never been able to gain and hold national power. Fignolé, fiery, erratic, stinging in debate, slim and handsome, has been called a Haitian Castro. His harsh, witty, exciting Créole speeches anticipated by some thirty years those of another champion of the urban masses, Jean-Bertrand Aristide, in attaining the uttermost limits that that *piquant* language can reach.

- François Duvalier: Port-au-Prince *noir* physician and ethnologist, political and intellectual spokesman of Les *griots* and the *folkloristes,* and self-proclaimed inheritor and apostle of Dumarsais Estimé.

Of the four men, two - Fignolé and Duvalier - spoke of their candidacies as "revolutionary." To Déjoie, the idea of revolution was abhorrent; to Jumelle, it was distasteful, but more to the point, not pertinent.

These - together with three soldiers, Cantave, Armand, and Kébreau - were the personalities whose tug and ebb and flow and polarization finally combined to produce a solution unforeseeable by any participant save one.

Joseph Nemours Pierre-Louis, whom the *New York Times* described as "a pleasant middle-aged man with a legalistic temperament," lasted fifty-five days. Entering office on 12 December 1956, and resigning on 4 February 1957, the fifty-six-year-old *Capois* bachelor judge (and also member of The Hague Court) never really had a chance. His pickup cabinet, composed of cronies, and of surrogates for Déjoie and Duvalier, omitted representation of Jumelle or Fignolé and thus automatically mobilized those factions in opposition. In addition, the major left party (*Parti du Peuple Haïtien*) called stridently for a "revolutionary" program; that is, immediate return to the principles of Estimé. A second PPH demand was for proscription of Clément Jumelle on grounds that, as Magloire's Finance Minister, he should be made to explain the empty treasury. The *Parti du Peuple,* while neither communist nor a communist front, embodied substantial communist elements (Rossini Pierre-Louis, Etienne Charlier, Georges Rigaud, and Edgar Néré Numa, to name four). It also represented a significant segment of Dr. Duvalier's support.

Throughout January 1957, PPH terrorist squads, calling themselves commandos, hunted down, beat up, and expelled from office known Magloirists throughout the government - a process described as "people's justice." Bombings also continued: on 10 January at O.J. Brandt's margarine factory, and more seriously, fifteen days later, when a bigger *"engin,"* as the papers described it, blew in the North portal of the Legislative Palace and broke windows in downtown Port-au-Prince. By the end of January, disorganized by spot strikes, shaken by *engins,* and prowled by commandos, government and capital alike were at a standstill. The coup de grace came on 1 February, when Déjoie members of the cabinet, maneuvering for the moment in unlikely concern with the PPH and Duvalier, resigned en masse over the Jumelle issue. Simultaneously, orchestrated by Déjoie, came another general strike.

There were, for the moment at least, no *engins,* no gunfire, no bloodshed. Again there was no gasoline; again the Chauffeurs-Guides stopped everything on wheels. Damien shut down, and so did the Hôpital Général. With every shop closed, the business district was like a tomb, and so was the National Palace. On 4 February Pierre-Louis resigned.

Now followed days of aimless riot, uncertainty, and intense jockeying as adepts of constitutional divination debated fiercely as to who should succeed Pierre-Louis. With more practicality than constitutionality, General Cantave finally got the leading presidential candidates together at army headquarters - but Déjoie boycotted this meeting -and secured an agreement that the choice of a new provisional president should be thrown into the National Assembly. The vote - 23 against, 13 for all other contenders - went on 7 February to a forty-six-year-old fervent Catholic lawyer and journalist from Grand-Goâve, Franck Sylvain. Maître Sylvain was also a supporter of Dr. Duvalier. He lasted fifty-two days.

Electoral disorders seethed; behind such turbulence, old scores were settled. Riots and shooting erupted at Jacmel (where Duvalier was stoned, an occurrence the *"cité fière et vaillante"* would later regret), at Cayes, Jérémie, Léogane, Gonaïves, and of course Port-au-Prince. In early March, on the rumor that Fignolé had been arrested, the proletariat stormed the Champ de Mars, attacking the police station and the palace itself. Thrown back by the police, the mob surged through the downtown, smashing, looting, and, a new tactic, stoning out street lights.

Amid all this, Sylvain tacked and jibed uncertainly, first banning political broadcasts, then announcing elections for 28 April, next dissolving the legislature (29 March), then ordering sequestration of Jumelle's property (whereupon, to avoid arrest, Jumelle went into hiding as partisans demonstrated wildly). Still another strike was called, this for 1 April. Where would it end?

Quite unexpectedly, the answer came on 2 April, when an astounded capital learned that, following discovery of the Martissant bomb factory, with its fatal consequences for two police officers, President Sylvain had resigned and was under house arrest on charges that he had known about the bombs and bombings and, worse still, had prior knowledge of a plot to assassinate the principal candidates in their homes. One candidate apparently not on the bombers' list was Dr. Duvalier. This was hardly surprising, because the four persons directly implicated were his close supporters, a fact the "mild-mannered doctor" (as the *New York Times* and other U.S. media kept describing him) blandly denied.

Now was confusion confounded. General Cantave's solution was to try to set up a "collegium" of representatives designated by each candidate. As might have been predicted, any such arrangement was foredoomed. With elections reset for 16 June, candidates popped in and out of hiding, their representatives flounced in and out of council sessions, arrests multiplied, and general strikes on behalf of this or that cause halted the economy. Every night and many days, shots could be heard. Another sound heard nightly was a lugubrious din called "beating the *ténèbres,*" wherein people would hammer iron light poles or fuel drums with rocks or skillets to produce atonal tintinnabulation indicating discontent or mourning.(55)

With bar and bench on strike and the *Banque* closed, *Le Matin* could well report, on 25 April: "The country is without a government and on the verge of anarchy. The army is the only possible arbiter."

On 30 April Alain Laraque (who, like his army kinsmen and *"notre groupe,"* had turned anti-Cantave) launched still another commercial strike, aimed this time at the overthrow of General Cantave. Taking up headquarters inside the fortresslike casernes, 'Ti Cantt broke the strike after five days.

People were too young to remember 1889, but the simultaneous convulsions of color, class, and region were no less furious: mobs attacked schools; arch-*mulâtre* Jérémie (invaded at one point by *10,000 piquets)* was in flames; the Cap, Gonaïves, and St. Marc were taken over by old-style "Committees of Public Safety." Brandishing machetes, St. Marc peasants heaped up boulders and tree trunks in the defile South of town so as to prevent traffic (and food) from reaching Port-au-Prince.

Cantave took soldiers and bulldozers North, cleared the sixty-foot roadblock, and was, somewhat surprisingly, cheered by the townspeople. They opposed the council, already being derided as *"le college croupion,"* or rump college, but were not yet ready to take on the army; yet before Cantave was back in the casernes, the barriers were up again.

Even as this was happening, sixty-six years almost to the day of the Fête-Dieu *attentat* against Hyppolite in 1891, the cathedral, celebrating Flag Day (Fête de Drapeau, 18 May) was again the scene of carnage. As the government, comprising what was left of the council, accompanied by a nervous diplomatic corps, entered the basilica for the traditional Te Deum, Fignolist mobs from nearby Bel Air converged on the cathedral, roaring, " *A bas le collège croupion!"* and were held at bay outside only when police fired into them, killing two and wounding many more.

In the aftermath, the collegium, now truly a rump, demanded Cantave's resignation and appointed police chief Armand to succeed 'Ti Cantt. Cantave promptly rejoined by dismissing the *collège,* while supported by still another general strike - Armand debated whether to take up his new appointment, and, more important, how?

Prompted by his friend Louis Déjoie, Colonel Armand finally decided to assume command of the army on 25 May, and his method was nothing if not direct. Concentrating the units under his banner - cadets, aviation, police, the artillery battery - at Bowen Field, Armand seized Radio Commerce, proclaimed Cantave deposed, and sent the one flyable airplane, piloted by Henri Wiener, a civilian, on a leaflet-strike to convince the (as he thought) unpaid army to join in.(56) Following this, the airplane (an aging DC-3), returned to Bowen Field and rearmed for a second sortie. As Port-au-Prince watched, palpitating, the capital underwent its first air raid. Roaring low, with engines wide open, the DC-3 swooped past the palace; then, over the casernes, through the side door, rolled a bomb, which tumbled over and over, hit the parade ground with a bounce, and skidded, unexploded, to rest beside the brig: in the excitement, nobody had thought to fuse it.

Meanwhile, the artillery, three old 105s, clattered onto the upper end of the Champ de Mars and commenced firing on (or, more exactly, since most of the rounds lit in the bay 2000 yards over, at) the casernes.

Alas, the gunners had neglected the axiom "A battery seen is a battery lost"; they had also neglected the equally fundamental precaution of organizing a ground defense. Even as the howitzers banged away, Captain André Fareau, emulating Charles de Delva in 1915, was leading a squad down the Ravine de Chêne. When the patrol reached the Club Port-au-Princien, within 200 yards of the battery, the riflemen set battle-sights on their Springfields and within minutes picked off three officers and two cannoneers and wounded several others. At that point, the remaining cannoneers abandoned their guns, which Fareau promptly took over while massed crowds cheered from the adjacent Champ de Mars grandstand.

Amid the turmoil, mobs and looters surged through the city, overturning and stripping cars, and stealing or demolishing what they could. Three radio stations (all anti-Fignolist) were wrecked; so were two newspapers *(Le Jour and Le Matin);* besides seventeen officers and soldiers killed, there were numbers of civilian casualties. The Armand coup had clearly failed. Since neither side was inclined to march on the other for a final showdown, Msgr. Augustin, backed by Archbishop Poirier, shuttled between the two camps. The result was a cease-fire and the agreement that both Cantave and Armand would retire. Simultaneously, the three *noir* candidates worked out a political fix: joining ranks to the exclusion of Louis Déjoie, they agreed on Fignolé as provisional president with a coalition cabinet. Next day, the officers of the reunited army met at the Palace for the investiture of Fignolé, shook hands all around, and applauded when Cantave and Armand embraced. Afterward, by way of reinsurance, Colonel Armand packed his bags and moved to the Spanish embassy.(57)

On Sunday, 26 May 1957, Pierre Eustache Daniel Fignolé ("tall, slender, ruggedly handsome," said the *New York Times*) took office. Improbably clad in well-fitting striped trousers and cutaway, the forty-three year-old provisional president and father of seven seemed to have come a long way from his native Pestel, or, for that matter, even Bel Air and La Saline. His inaugural address to 10,000 followers was a restrained appeal for democracy and unity; but the heroes he invoked included Soulouque, Goman, Acaau, and Rameau.

Fignolé's all-important choice to take hold of the divided army was another father of seven: the department commander at Les Cayes, Colonel Antonio Kébreau, five years older and (though unnoted at the time) a friend of both Trujillo and Duvalier.

The first moves of the new president - to get shops open, to restore stability, to restart the country - were all to the good. But there were others less promising: mass transfers in the army, directed not by Kébreau but by the palace, the commissioning of Fignolé henchmen as officers, and, above all, the fact that Fignolé unabashedly continued to run for a permanent term. (Already, Bel Air was clamoring for a six year extension of their leader's provisional term without the bother of an election.) Amid all this, when, without consulting Kébreau or the general staff, the president pointedly announced a 100 percent pay raise for all enlisted men, the high command knew time was running out. That evening - 14 June, the nineteenth since Fignolé took office while the Port-au-Prince garrison raptly followed a new Western being screened at the casernes, a group of officers led by General Kébreau marched upstairs in the *Palais*, slammed open the door of the council chamber, silenced the cabinet with a look, and marched off the president before even he could utter a word.

Stopping only to obtain Fignolé's signature on a brief letter of resignation, Kébreau drove the ex-president to Bizoton, where another group was waiting with Mme. Fignolé, the children, and her baggage. A *Garde-Côtes* cutter had steam up; the party was hardly aboard before lines were cast off, and Daniel Fignolé, in the manner of Toussaint, had a last look over the stem at the dimming view of his former Capital.

Their destination was the Môle. Here, at the airstrip built by the Americans on the Presqu'ile during the war, waited the same DC-3 that had bombed the casernes. As the doors shut and seat belts were tightened, the engines coughed, roared momentarily to check magnetos, and then lifted the airplane Northwest over the Windward Passage and Cuba toward Miami.(58) Shortly afterward, the social columns of *Le Nouvelliste* murmured solicitously, "We hope their stay in New York will prove to be a pleasant one for M. and Mme. Daniel Fignolé."

Kébreau was nothing if not thorough. Before the Western and its gunsmoke had vanished into the setting sun, the cabinet were on their way to jail, there to join some twenty Fignolist bosses who been simultaneously picked up. Next morning at 10:30, as Fort National's battery boomed a salute, the general announced that again the army had taken charge. "We soldiers," he told the press afterward," are the fathers of the family. We aren't politicians; we simply want to restore order and conduct elections from which will emerge a legitimate President. "

Bel Air and La Saline had a last word. On the night of the 16th, as the *ténèbres* began to reverberate after eight o'clock curfew, came a new sound like the roaring ocean: Fignolé had been secretly executed, said *telediol,* and the response of the slums was overwhelming.

With the ferocity of 1791, the *rouleau compresseur* swept across Port-au-Prince, leaving a pall of darkness, as street lights were broken, followed by a pillar of flame. *Pompiers* had apparatus smashed and hose slashed. Fort Dimanche, under attack from La Saline, responded with machine guns. Then, behind half-tracks and light tanks, the army moved in. Machine-gunning streets and whole blocks of flimsy huts, soldiers and police fired point-blank into stone-throwing, torch-bearing mobs. All night and into the morning furious battles took place throughout the lower city. Finally, as the army gained the upper hand, trucks began picking up littered corpses, and the *pompiers,* after wetting down fire-desolated areas, hosed away whatever blood and guts the dogs left. The official casualty list gave 50 dead and 250 injured. In his book, Maurepas Auguste says over 500 died; in *Papa Doc,* Diederich and Burt put the carnage at 1000. Kébreau thereupon invoked an iron-handed state of siege, which continued without further disturbance until election day, set at last for 22 September.

Whatever else six months'chaos had done to the country, it had sorted out the electoral contest. Fignolé was gone; Jumelle, however attractive his qualifications, had been skillfully discredited; and Déjoie, though campaigning and intriguing with equal vigor, was on the defensive. At center stage, Duvalier, with an ally in command of the army and the junta (and a growing Duvalierist cell among the officers), was also discreetly propagating the notion that he had American support.(59) Isolating the elite Déjoie from the masses, Duvalier went to the people with a farrago of nationalism, mysticism, Estimé racism, and they-against-us demagoguery, delivered in rambling nonstop sentences where Créole fused with sciolistic French. *"They have gone mad"* was his leitmotif on one celebrated occasion:

They dare to keep Duvalier, most popular of the Candidates, in outer darkness . . . *They have gone mad.* Masses of the Northwest, the North, the Artibonite, peoples of the Southwest, the Grand-Anse, middle classes of Port-au-Prince, intellectuals,

Masters of thought and art, professors, teachers, students: they have decided to ignore you. *They have gone mad . . .* The mad coalition has decided that you and I have nothing to say . . .

Then the peroration,

Men and Women of Duvalier, You my thousands and ten thousands, You of the heroic North, worthies of Dérac, Phaëton, Maribaroux, You of Vallière and Monbin Crochu. You of the Cap, Fort Liberté, and Ouanaminthe, renowned valiants of Limbé, thousands from the Northwest. You of Port-de-Paix, the Môle, of Jean-Rabel, unconquerable phalanxes of the Artibonite, invincible all, and You of Belladère, Hinche, Mirebalais, Lascahobas, Oh, my cohorts! Marigot unyielding, Cayes-Jacmel, Côtes de Fer, well-named Jérémie which evermore adorns the steely poems framed from love of Estimé, Dame Marie, Anse d'Hainault, lucid South of Cayes, of Cavaillon and of Aquin, lucid South of Nippes, Coteaux, have You understood? They would decide without us. *They have gone mad.*

(Why Duvalier omitted La Gonâve cannot be explained: in the forthcoming election. its few hundred inhabitants were to deliver 18,000 votes.)(60)

Perhaps because Kébreau administered it, the state of siege seemed to inhibit all candidates save Duvalier. The press, whose saturnalia since the fall of Magloire had gone unchecked except when its plants were sacked or burned, was sharply curbed, thus evoking a sententious editorial that demonstrated how little the New *York Times* understood Haitian politics and journalism: "The Haitian press and radio have been responsible and restrained. Each paper has its particular candidate, but they have not preached violence and revolution, and they would not do so. Why then impose a censorship?"

Two days before the election, Jumelle resigned a contest hopelessly lost. Luc Fouché, Magloire's able lieutenant, stood down from a senatorial race in his native Cap, remarking drily: "After careful scrutiny of the realities of the hour, I do not cherish any illusion about the outcome.

On Sunday, 22 September, some 950,000 Haitians went to the polls for a vote that had been thoroughly organized by the army. In what author Jean-Pierre Gingras called "the perfect peacefulness of fixed bayonets," the elections came off smoothly enough. Duvalier received 679,884 votes, Déjoie trailed with 266,992. Duvalier candidates made a clean sweep of the Senate and won two thirds of the *deputés.* Only in Port-au-Prince, stronghold at once of the elite and Fignolé's masses, was the little doctor decisively beaten.

As results came in, Duvalier told *New York Times* correspondent Peter Kihss that the biggest issue was honesty. For his part, Déjoie said, "Eighty-five percent of the election was crooked."

To himself, perhaps, the president-elect might have agreed. One of his favorite Créole sayings had always been: *"Nèg ap trahi nèg dèpi nan Guinée"* (From time immemorial in Guinea, every man betrays his neighbor).

FOOTNOTES - CHAPTER 13

1. As early as July 1930, an official of the National City Bank predicted to Francis White at the State Department that "we will scuttle from Haiti, in which event the Bank wants to scuttle also."
2. It had been assumed that a small American military mission of Marines would stay on, and the *désoccupation* agreement so provided, but for reasons never stated, Vincent declined to avail himself of this option.
3. Showing how little had changed, de la Rue, the American fiscal adviser, was soon to be approached (in March 1937) by two leading politicians of the North, Senator René Auguste and General Alfred Nemours, feeling out U.S. views on partition of Haiti into two realms, the 1889-model in which the quid pro quo would be base rights in the North for the U.S. Navy.
4. Within the year Vincent would expel a French priest who had the temerity to give Pradel lunch when the senator was visiting his parish, and - how times had changed - complain when Dr. Gruening bustled into Port-au-Prince and visited Hudicourt, an act, in the president's view, that constituted meddling in Haiti's internal affairs.
5. Shepherd left no doubt as to the "good things" he had in mind when he bluntly characterized Degand, *préfet de Port-au-Prince,* as "pander to the President."
6. In 1939, Haiti not only exported over 2 million stems of top-quality bananas but ranked tenth among Latin American countries in banana production, surpassing, among others, Brazil, Ecuador, the Dominican Republic, and British Honduras.
7. As early as mid-1935, Armand was proposing that the *Garde* organize artillery and aviation units, a combination of arms the Marines had attempted to forestall by taking home their aircraft squadron and the lone artillery in Haiti save for the saluting battery at Fort National. One of the first moves by the regime after *désoccupation* was to begin buying weapons, including light artillery, on the international market. Once acquired, however, the new arms, together with all crew-served weapons and the *Garde*'s reserve ammunition, were placed under control of the Presidential Guard and soon, as if Leconte's immolation had been forgotten, were again in the palace basement. When Calixte tried to draw weapons and ammunition for training, his requests were denied.
8. *"Griot"* is the name of an African sect (or member thereof) whose propensity is wisdom and an ability to foresee the future. It is also similar in sound but not spelling to *"grillot,"* a Créole word for a highly spiced morsel of broiled pork, one of the most piquant delicacies of the Haitian cuisine.
9. Roumain returned to Haiti in 1941, but was immediately packed off into exile by President Lescot, as Haitian *chargé d'affaires* in Mexico City. There he appears to have developed relations with the Mexican Communist Party, which, as of the 1960s, had operational control of the Haitian party. Aged thirty-six, Roumain died prematurely, on 17 August 1944.
10. The signing ceremonies were complicated by the fact that, after original signature in Ciudad Trujillo, the Haitian copy of the treaty was lost when the Foreign Minister and

his car were swept away, axle over tincup, by a flash flood near Ganthier while he was returning in state from Santo Domingo. This disaster required a re-signing ceremony, this time in Port-au-Prince, on the occasion of Trujillo's visit (his third since 1934) for Vincent's second inauguration in May 1936. The generalissimo arrived aboard gunboat *Trujillo,* distributing free food as always and thousands of personal photographs to the masses. In return, Vincent renamed the Grande Rue "Avenue Trujillo."

11. Because of Trujillo's massive coverup and the inability (or unwillingness) of the Haitian government to marshal full statistics, precise numbers of those killed will never be known. The figure used here, 15,000 to 20,000, is most frequently accepted. Similarly, the exact duration of the bloodbath remains undefined. The American legation in Ciudad Trujillo reported three days: the British legation, six. Crassweller, Trujillo's able biographer, says it was over in thirty-six hours.

12. In a 1940 memorandum referring to the massacre, de la Rue recalled "the curiously disinterested attitude of President Vincent and his government" and went on to speak of rumors, "never cleared up," that money had changed hands between Trujillo and Vincent.

13. Calixte's nephew was court-martialed and shot by firing squad at the Fort Dimanche rifle range and died bravely without talking. The remaining officers drew long prison sentences.

14. Like its Axis partners, Japan had begun to take a sharpened interest in faraway Haiti. As reported by American naval intelligence, the Yokohama Specie Bank in late 1940 quietly closed a deal for the *Banque* to take over Japanese accounts in New York and receive remittances from South America, acting on instructions from Tokyo concerning these funds and thus evading ever-tightening U.S. restrictions.

15. In August 1940, for example, Lescot, who had received $31,250 for the purchase of rifles for the *Garde,* was unexpectedly called to account by de la Rue and could produce neither money nor rifles. In this dire emergency he telephoned Trujillo for help, which the Dominican minister in Washington, Andrés Pastoriza, thereupon provided. In his haste, Lescot simply endorsed the Dominican check over to the Minister of Finance. From Lescot-Trujillo correspondence subsequently made public, it appears that Lescot had been receiving money from Trujillo ("my great and good friend," he addressed him) at least since 1937.

16. Vincent left Haiti immediately after his successor's inaugural. Feeling against him had soured to such an extent that Lescot felt it necessary, in the old style, to escort Vincent personally to the wharf. He remained abroad in virtual exile until 1943. On his return to Haiti, the former president lived quietly in Port-au-Prince until his death in Pétionville, on 3 September 1959 (surviving his sister, Mlle. Rézia, by less than two months). He was buried in the Cimetière Exterieure.

17. Washington held little fear as to U.S.-Haitian relations under Lescot. In a personal memo to President Roosevelt on 11 January 1941, Welles described the departing Haitian minister as "a thoroughly loyal friend of the United States . . . If he is elected President, his administration will cooperate very closely with us."

18. Lescot must have entertained these changes long before taking office, It was his idea, at the "second independence" ceremonies of August 1934, that the officers of the *Garde* swear personalty fealty to the president on that gold sword of honor (Lescot's suggestion, too) they had presented Vincent.

19. Lieutenant Colonel Thomas H. Young - Haiti's first American military attache since Captain Charles Young of earlier days - disagreed forcibly. In 1943, the colonel described the French priests as "ardently pro-Ally" and went on, "insinuations often repeated in Haiti to the effect that most French priests are pro-Nazi and Vichyites is a base calumny."

20. Collignon brought with him, in effect, his order. The Oblates, specializing in agriculture, thus became the first non-French religious order to assume duties in Haiti.

21. With $5 million outstanding on the bonds (and with the government in excellent financial condition as a result of mounting receipts from 1944 to 1947), in July 1947, spearheaded by a "Committee for Economic Liberation," an internal loan was floated that paid off the last 1922 obligations. Thereupon ended American responsibility for Haiti's foreign debt, and with it the participation of Americans in the administration of the *Banque*.

22. In December 1941, mindful, as he told at least one American official, of the fate of Leconte, the president paid $80,000 for a handsome private home in Bourdon, Manoir des Lauriers, for many years the property of Edgar Elliott of HASCO, and then the French embassy residence. Lescot observed to Colonel Dumont of the U.S. Military Mission that the constitution required him to live at the palace but not to sleep there.

23. Pointedly emphasizing the harsh realities of war, a German U-boat sank the ship carrying Lescot's baggage, laden with hard-to-get items carefully accumulated in Washington and New York for the long pull ahead.

24. The offer seems not have been seriously considered. Despite its highly strategic location, the Môle by mid-twentieth century offered little that Guantanamo Bay could not surpass, and besides was too small and too open for the requirements of modern operations.

25. Not only did Lescot undertake foreign travels never before surpassed by Haitian presidents - he also welcomed to Port-au-Prince a steady stream of distinguished visitors, including the presidents of Chile and Venezuela. Princess Juliana (later queen) of Holland, André Maurois, W.E.B. Du Bois, Alfred Métraux, and Jacques Maritain.

26. At the prompting of Nelson Rockefeller, who had become Roosevelt's Coordinator of Inter-American Affairs, the U.S. Government extended $300,000 in credit, mainly for farm instruments, seeds, and other necessities to help peasant reconstruction after the devastation of *SHADA*.

27. As a result of President Roosevelt's decision to upgrade all American legations in Latin America to embassies, White became the first American ambassador (and first representative of ambassadorial rank from any power) to be accredited to Haiti. This took place on 14 April 1943.

28. Later in the year El Benefactor dropped the other shoe. Port-au-Prince, all literate Haiti in fact, was treated to the widely circulated text of a letter of 1 November 1943, in which Trujillo, reproaching Lescot for alleged ingratitude, recapitulated every loan and favor ever extended, together with details of services rendered in return.

29. Accompanied by thirteen members of his family, on 13 January 1946, President Lescot flew by chartered aircraft (for which Pan American demanded $2500 in advance) to Miami, and proceeded thence by train to Montreal, where the entire party was hospitably lodged in the capacious guest house of the Redemptorist Fathers in nearby Aylmer. Contrary to widespread reports, Lescot left office in modest circumstances and

for a time was close to poverty while in exile. On eventual return to Haiti, the former president lived quietly in La Boule, where he died on 21 October 1974, receiving a state funeral and burial in the Cimetière Exterieure.

30. The members of the *Comité Executif Militaire* were under no illusions. Major Levelt told Ambassador Wilson on 1 February that the reason the junta had not broadened its base by adding civilian members was that the communists were strong enough to demand a portfolio.

31. Fignolé, who could have won any popular ballot, was too young for the presidency, and therefore used Calixte as his surrogate, an odd marriage between the conservative and correct former *Garde* commandant and the Port-au-Prince demagogue.

32. No member of the *Comité* or the military-officer cabinet drew extra compensation for his governmental duties, receiving only *Garde* pay and allowances throughout.

33. Commenting in 1947 on the *mulâtres'* downfall, American Ambassador Harold Tittmann observed, "The proportionate size and political effectiveness [of the *mulâtre* elite] is probably no greater than that of a European nobility."

34. In 1948 Estimé likewise nationalized sales of tobacco, creating a state monopoly, *Régie du Tabac*, for the purpose. The beauty (and the catch) in this device was that the *Régie's* books were exempt from scrutiny and outside the budget and thus ideal for many special projects.

35. At one point, Dr. Rigaud (who, on his outspokenly anti-American record, made an odd member of the delegation) justified an agricultural loan because, he said, it would benefit some 40,000 young intellectuals of good education who were currently unemployed!

36. Omitting to explain to U.S. audiences that the indebtedness mainly represented French bonds advantageously refunded for Haiti by Dr. Cumberland, Ambassador Charles went about making speeches (such as the one on 4 February 1947) in which he said, "Haiti labors under debts to American banks which total more than eleven million dollars at six percent."

37. In the political milieu of the U.N., Estimé discovered new assets. One of Haiti's first important votes was against the State of Israel - a position reportedly arrived at after Syrian merchants had delivered a sizable sum to the *Palais National*. Subsequently, displaying a maneuverability that was to become a byword in international organizations, and after vigorous lobbying by the articulate, attractive (and Jewish) American journalist in Port-au-Prince, Edith Efron, Estimé switched sides and left the Syrians holding the bag.

38. In April 1950 the U.N. International Children's Emergency Fund - a singular source for such a cause - did put up $300,000 to eradicate venereal disease in Haiti. Despite billions of units of penicillin dispensed by some ten mobile units over two years, VD was not eradicated and in time became the stalking horse for its deadlier companion, AIDS.

39. *Time* (22 February 1954) said the exposition finally cost $26 million, of which $10 million were never accounted for. But the fair and its buildings face-lifted Port-au-Prince, replacing squalid slums with the graceful open-air Théâtre de Verdure and providing new tourist hotels, such as the Ibo Lele and El Rancho. One landmark to go (as Pan American had stopped flying seaplanes) was the seaplane ramp.

40. Jean Brièrre, ardent votary of Marx, held his portfolio throughout the Estimé regime and continued in the first succeeding cabinet, that of Magloire.

41. Estimé and his family went to Jamaica, where like Soulouque, Katherine Dunham recounted, they were shunned by the exile colony. From there they went to New York and lived for three embittered years at the old Franconia Hotel on upper Broadway. Estimé died on 20 July 1953 of uremic poisoning, a circumstance telediol quickly rendered as poisoning. Paul Magloire, Estimé's successor, had the remains returned to Port-au-Prince for a state funeral with full honors (ironically including obsequies in the *Palais Legislatif*, which Estimé mobs had sacked in 1950). On 22 November 1968, with highest honors and a eulogy, another successor, François Duvalier, re-interred Estimé in an elaborate multicolumned memorial sited beside Port-au-Prince bay. Earlier, in July 1959, Duvalier had appointed Mme. Estimé, Haiti's first woman envoy, as minister to Belgium.

42. Taking advantage of his strong relationship with the Church, Magloire, in 1953, ninety years after the concordat, was able to nominate the first Haitian Catholic bishop, Msgr. Rémy Augustin, who, after consecration on 31 May 1953, became auxiliary to Msgr. Le Gouaze.

43. Having twice presided over *gouvernements provisoires,* General Lavaud may claim a place near those of Boisrond and Légitime. Following Magloire's accession, Lavaud stood down from the army and was appointed Haitian ambassador in Paris, where he served some years before retiring in *la ville lumière.*

44. If Estimé's time had been, as Edith Efron recalled, "one long debate," Magloire's seemed to be one long party. Every evening there would be brilliant dinners and dances at the palace or one or another of the clubs (the Bellevue relocated to sumptuous new quarters in Bourdon on 22 December 1952, with president and papal nuncio presiding). Then, after squiring wives home, the gentlemen would rendezvous with other ladies, most often at Dan Allen's, a durable American pub in the Cité de l'Exposition, which was a favorite retreat of the president's.

45. In February 1951, just three months in office, Magloire had already patched things up with Trujillo. The two chiefs had a meeting shared between Elias Piña and Belladère, refurbished with new paint, after which they signed a joint communique affirming solidarity and anticommunism and promising to re-ensure each other against exile movements. When the two embraced in friendship, each could feel the hard bulk of the other's hidden pistol.

46. But Magloire, like Salomon, was national-minded. Not only did he pick up and continue sound programs from Estimé; he allocated over two thirds of development to regions not his own: mainly the Artibonite and Center, and as far afield as Léogane, which, for example, received electrification.

47. Yaws, syphilislike but nonvenereal, was a plague of the West Indies from the earliest times and in those days contributed to the conventional medical wisdom that "90 percent of Haitians suffer from syphilis." It was under steady attack by Dr. Melhorn and other medical authorities during the occupation, and was the object of another American-supported campaign in 1943 (when Dr. François Duvalier, then a rural practitioner at Cabaret - two decades later to be renamed "Duvalierville" - was employed by the U.S. Sanitary Mission). Because yaws, like syphilis a spirochete disease, was difficult to cure by old arsenicals and other drastic remedies, no serious progress was registered until 1950, when penicillin burst onto the scene. Undertaking a house-to-house program, foreign and Haitian doctors and technicians by 1954 had injected 2,623,141 peasants with massive antibiotic doses and effectively eliminated yaws from Haiti.

48. An American embassy economist calculated that every U.S. bluejacket ashore in Port-au-Prince or the Cap spent $17 a liberty, mostly on soft goods.

49. The Vertières sham battle was staged by the already distinguished Major Paul Corvington. Among junior officers assigned key roles were Captain Marcel Colon, Lieutenants Franck Bayard, Robert André (Haiti's first signal officer), Antonio Doublette, F. M. Arty, and - prophetically - Claude Raymond, who acted the role of a Haitian general. All these names would be heard again.

50. Hazel was the greatest but not the only natural disaster of the time: on 27 October 1952, Anse-à-Veau, which had recorded over eighty temblors since 1909, was shaken by a violent earthquake that took numerous lives and caused extensive damage.

51. In April 1955, returning Magloire's visit, Vice-President Richard Nixon came to Port-au-Prince in time to stay at the Magloires' new mansion in Turgeau, grander even than Prosper's, or Lescot's Manoir des Lauriers, where, in the tradition of Franklin Roosevelt, he personally compounded a round of his favorite daiquiris, using Barbancourt.

52. The principal candidates were Louis Déjoie, a wealthy *mulâtre* planter and a great-grandson of Geffrard; Clément Jumelle, Minister of Finance and widely viewed as Magloire's chosen inheritor: and Dr. François Duvalier, who had left employment with the American SCISP and gone into hiding in 1954. Duvalier emerged in August 1956 and became an overt candidate as Estimé's heir.

53. Among other officers linked in this affair, many to be heard from in future, were Captains Victor Blanchet, Antonio Kébreau, and Lieutenants Maurepas Auguste, Franck and Paul Laraque, Adrien Blanchet, and Claude Raymond.

54. From Jamaica, the Magloires journeyed to New York, eventually settling in a pleasant home in middle-class Queens. While there seems no doubt that, like many Haitian political leaders, Magloire made ample provision for retirement, repeated subsequent charges that he had absconded with the entire Haitian treasury, to the tune of some $21 million, were never verified despite a probing investigation by American lawyers retained by the Duvalier government to recapture Magloire's asserted gains.

55. "*Ténèbres*" was a pun on the French word for gloom or deep shadows and on the ecclesiastical name for an evening service conducted during Holy Week in mourning over the Crucifixion.

56. It was not known in the Armand camp that the Cantave (and for the moment, therefore anti-Déjoie) forces in the casernes had just received $46,000 back pay mysteriously provided from the pockets of Dr. Duvalier.

57. Not counting Magloire, since 15 December 1956 the army, with a total strength of about 350 officers, had lost 67, mainly but not entirely due to political purges (2 brigadiers, 15 colonels, 5 lieutenant colonels, 15 captains, and 30 lieutenants). Accompanied by comparable enlisted losses, this heavy attrition of experience would be painfully felt and would contribute in great measure to the weakening and eventual disintegration of the Armed Forces in the 1960s.

58. Among conflicting accounts as to the Fignolés' movements following the coup, we have here followed that of Maurepas Auguste, who would certainly have been well informed. After being landed at Miami, Fignolé went to New York, where he lived in exile until the overthrow of Jean-Claude Duvalier in 1986. He thereupon returned to Haiti and died shortly thereafter.

59. Afterward, people would say the United States put Duvalier in power, which is not wholly true. During the campaign, the astute American ambassador, Gerald A. Drew (who had learned his Haiti as one of Dana Munro's juniors), had serious reservations as to Duvalier. Drew, however, was unable to restrain an uncritical AID director or the widely respected American Episcopal bishop, both of whom gave ostentatious support to Duvalier and undoubtedly contributed to his subsequent election.

60. La Tortue, Haiti's next largest island, was destined to do almost as well: out of 900 registered voters, wrote Père Riou, La Tortue delivered 7500 ballots for Duvalier.

François Duvalier survived numerous attempts to overthrow him. In the so-called "Sheriff's Coup" of 1958, this Palace bust of Pétion was the most prominent government casualty. *Heinl Collection*

Ambassador Drew (who had been first posted to Haiti during the occupation), General Gaither, and Col. Heinl confer with François Duvalier. Colonel Max Dominique, standig at left, was Duvalier's son-in-law, but from 1967 on destined to spend most of his life abroad. Both guards hold concealed submachine guns. *Heinl Collection Below*: François Duvalier (far right) surrounded by *macoutes* and *VSN* with fingers at triggers of ancient mausers. *Heinl Collection*

557

Mme. Max Adolphe, sadistic warden of Fort Dimanche, presided over horrors worthy of Buchenwald. Her demand for safe-conduct to the U.S. caused furious protests in the State Department. Here shown in uniform as "*Fillette Lalo*'" (woman *macoute*) *Associated Press/ Wide World Photos Below:* Clément Barbot (right) ruled with an iron hand while Papa Doc lay in a coma in 1959, but gave back power when he recovered. Later, he went underground with his brother, Harry (left). Six weeks after this photo was taken, they were gunned down near Port-au-Prince. *Associated Press/ Wide World Photos*

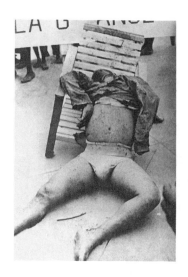

Bloated corpse of Captain Yvan Laraque was exhibited for three days by Duvalier opposite entrance to Port-au-Prince airport. *Heinl Collection* Below: "I was the first to have a pen in one hand and a gun in the other," said François Duvalier, shown here at his desk with tools of governance. *Allan Blanchard*

559

Tonton Macoute. Heinl Collection Below: Cemetery wall execution of *Jeune Haïti* invaders Numa (left) and Drouin in 1964. Officer with pistol is probably Franck Romain. *Heinl Collection*

An enfeebled Papa Doc passes the mantle to his only son and successor, Jean-Claude, February 2, 1971. Confounding all prognostications, the son ruled longer than the father. *Heinl Collection*

CHAPTER 14

I Am the State

1957-1971

Je Suis le Drapeau Haïtien, un et indivisible
[the Haitian Flag and I are one and indivisible]
- François Duvalier

IF, when second independence began in 1934, comparisons with 1804 were inevitable, how would the year 1957 - twenty-three years later - compare with 1827?

The answer is that 1957 and 1827 hold far more in common than 1934 and 1804. The condition of 1827 has been described as "general ruin." The fields were dead, French roads and bridges gone, cities ruined, seaports decayed or closed, economy at a standstill, the army in miserable deterioration, political institutions deadlocked, *noir* and *mulâtre* at each other's throats.

By 1957 the modernized Haiti of two decades earlier seemed to have glimmered away like a mirage. Exports, mostly agricultural, had declined by 20 percent between 1946 and 1956 and were still going down. American-built roads and bridges had ceased to exist. (In 1934 one could drive from Port-au-Prince to Jacmel in less than two hours, in 1957 it took nine hours by jeep in good weather.) Communications had collapsed; the telephone system was dead. Ports were silted, unlighted, and obstructed by wrecks, docks had crumbled. Desperately ill patients lay on the floors of stinking hospitals. Sanitation and electrification were in precarious decline. Political institutions and army were in shambles; races, classes, and regimes contended bitterly.

In the words of the new president-elect, Haiti, two decades after the occupation, was "rotting in poverty, hunger, nudity, sickness, and illiteracy."

The Americans had modernized everything but Haiti and the Haitians. By 1957 Haiti had retrogressed to normal. These were the fruits of the second independence.

The soft-spoken, slight (five-feet-six, 150 pounds) *noir* physician-ethnologist who had just attained the National Palace was the son of a Port-au-Prince *juge de paix*. Born in the capital on 14 April 1907, during Tonton Nord's last years, François Duvalier had first attended the tin-roofed *Lycée Pétion* in Bel Air (where Dumarsais Estimé taught him mathematics) and then gone on to medical school. Like Dessalines, Dr. Duvalier married a *mulâtresse,* Simone Ovide Faine, a nurse, who bore him four children: Marie-Denise, Simone, Nicole, and one son, Jean-Claude. He had worked with American public-health missions in the 1940s, had taken (and failed) public-health studies at the University of Michigan in 1944, had followed Estimé into politics, first as director general of public health, then as Under Secretary of the new Labor Ministry, and finally as Minister of Labor and Public Health. With Estimé's fall, he went over to opposition and stayed underground ("in the *maquis,"* he often later called it) from 1954 to 1956.(1)

As seen by the world (and not a few Haitians), Duvalier was a bourgeois professional man of modest tastes, innocuous habits, and something of an intellectual, who had held and left office no richer than he started. He was a civilian, no soldier, a fact that immediately endeared him to Washington and to the enlightened men who would soon be shaping the Alliance for Progress. His very dress, always a black suit, white shirt, dark tie, black shoes, and black homburg, together with owlish thick-rimmed eyeglasses, gave him the look of a conservative family practitioner.

But Duvalier was also deeply steeped in the history and folk culture of Haiti and was committed to the proposition that Haiti should wipe away its French veneer and proudly acknowledge its African origins. His master, Lorimer Denis, was dead at the Cap (later, some would say Duvalier fed the soul of Denis to the *loa),* but in Duvalier, even more than Estimé, the *griots* had finally come into their own. Rejecting any goal of assimilation into Euro-American cultures, Duvalier was determined that his government would become the political expression of that Africanist mystique, *négritude.*

He was of course an adept of Voodoo, almost certainly a *houngan,* and, most believed, a *bocor.* In addition, he was deeply versed in the labyrinthine esoterics of spiritualism, astrology, and *onomancie,* a Haitian kind of magical numerology from whose divinations Duvalier became convinced that the number 22 would confer upon him high and sinister powers. Amid these mysteries, he was a student of Machiavelli (Clément Barbot, so long his familiar and lieutenant, said he kept a tattered copy of *The Prince* in his pocket during those years on the run). He admired Nasser, Lenin, and Nkrumah, and would subsequently compare himself with Dessalines, Mao Tse-tung, Ataturk, Charles de Gaulle, and Christ.

Duvalier's complex, multifaceted paranoid personality (which none would ever plumb completely) had above all a need for violence, a need that in 1957 the inaudible voice and halting manner still masked. It was not for nothing, however, that he often reminded Haitians that they had become a nation only through violence.

As for those conservative black suits and black hat, those unblinking eyes behind heavy spectacles, they were, as any peasant instantly recognized, the very cerements and earthly trappings of *Baron Samedi*, that most feared *loa* who kept the gates of the grave.

It was not only *Baron* whom the new president personified. In 1893, writing of Toussaint, Castonnet de Fosses had said: "Toussaint realized he could confide in no one save himself. Ever suspicious that he was being hoodwinked, he felt a need to render himself impenetrable; dissimulation was the cornerstone of his nature. None ever knew what he did, whether he stayed or departed, or where or whence he went or came."

Still earlier, in 1811, Gilbert Guillermin, who had known Toussaint, probed even deeper: "Mistrustful and crafty like an African, even among those who appeared to enjoy his confidence, Toussaint was deeply secretive and guarded . . . The cruel ways of this singular man well bespoke a fierce and suspicious heart where not God, but Machiavelli, held sway."

Yet behind Toussaint, behind even Lorimer Denis, there lay a young man, poor, black, desperately ambitious, determined to claw his way out of the abyss, who in 1934 in his convoluted, turgid rhetoric scrawled both *défi* and *cri de coeur:*

> *Eh bien!* When like me, Abderrahman, you spring from that class of youth despised as misbegotten, rejected in mistrust and contempt simply because you emerge from the lower depths of the real Haiti - like me, Abderrahman - repressed back into the nameless hordes of the homeless and the hungry, crushed back every day by the pangs of misery, spattered each day by the impudent arrogance of the elite, the insulting well-being of those Johnny-come-latelies *[néo-arrivistes]* . . .

Here were fires that underlay the burning lava of the volcano that would soon erupt.

For a simple country doctor - so he still called himself when talking to foreign reporters - Dr. Duvalier had already assembled a decidedly mixed team. Basking in the sunlight were his fellow *griots*, headed by the venerable Jean Price-Mars, as well as long-time medical colleagues such as Dr. Aurèle A. Joseph, who had fought yaws in the Marbial Valley beside Duvalier in the 1940s. There was a brain trust including Roger Dorsinville (one of the Estimé men who early rallied to Duvalier) and Lucien Daumec, Duvalier's brother-in-law and speechwriter. There were other communists: the Blanchet brothers, Jules and Paul; Hervé Boyer, with his French wife; and, until 1960, René Depestre.

The army had a fervent cell of Duvalier activists headed by Major Jacques Laroche, with Captain Claude Raymond not far behind.(2) Among the Haitian clergy were priests like Père Georges, who secretly applauded the new president's outspoken strictures against a Church still dominated, in hierarchy and numbers, by Frenchmen. Clémard-Joseph Charles, who had found the

$46,000 to pay off Cantave's soldiers in May 1957, was banker and bagman. Another bagman was the young deputy from Cabaret, Luckner Cambronne, a student fund raiser from university days.

Besides all these, Duvalier's men had from the beginning included a hard-eyed fringe whom he found opportune to disown during the campaign but would soon pardon in a general amnesty: Temistocles Fuentes-Rivera, a Cuban terrorist and explosives technician; Fritz "Toto" Cinéas and Charles Lahens, confederates of Fuentes; and the Dominican Johnny Abbes-García, who slipped effortlessly in and out of Port-au-Prince on orders from Ciudad Trujillo. There were also educated men harder to classify except as they were attached to Duvalier: the Olympic medalist André Théard, the Grandguignolesque Lucien Chauvet, the bloodthirsty Dr. Jacques Fourcand (palace physician and head of Haiti's Red Cross), the slippery *griot* Arthur Bonhomme, and the saturnine Morille Figaro. less conspicuous but nonetheless influential was a foreign legion: Gérard de Catalogne, the Corsican publicist with his French police pedigree; the American Herbert Morrison (known among Haitians as " 'Ti Barbe," for his little beard, and to authorities in the United States by his real name, Jerome Breitman); and, a kind of privy counselor, Dr. Elmer Loughlin, severed from the U.S. Public Health Service, who would eventually earn an American prison sentence for illegal activities on behalf of his fellow doctor Duvalier.

Atop all these - scholars, soldiers, priests, politicians, terrorists, scapegrace foreigners, as well as many a Haitian nationalist who saw progress and redemption in the soft-voiced doctor - there was one man who could be called the new president's alter ego. He was a St. Marc *noir* named Clément Barbot. Barbot, a slim, fine-featured former schoolteacher, slightly taller than Duvalier, had as a boy been caned by a French priest for daring to defend Dessalines as Haiti's greatest hero. At each stroke of the rod, the Frenchman grunted, *"Dessalines! . . . Dessalines! . . . Dessalines!"* Clément Barbot never forgot.

Robespierre of the Duvalier revolution, nationalist to the core, *noir* of *noirs*, capable of any deed yet man of his word and kindly father and husband, Clément Barbot would in the end prove how true it is that revolution devours its children.

I Have No Enemies

François Duvalier selected 22 October as inauguration day. Seated *en banc* behind a plywood rostrum in the Salle des Bustes of the *Palais National*, the new president, flanked by General Kébreau and Hugues Bourjolly, president of the Senate, received the sash of office from Kébreau. Then, as the gun salute thumped from Fort National, he drove to the cathedral for his Te Deum. Back at the palace, Duvalier unhesitatingly occupied the accursed presidential chair that had daunted Soulouque a century earlier, and uttered his first pronouncement: "My government will guarantee the exercise of liberty to all Haitians and will always give them the necessary protection in that exercise . . My government of national unity will evenhandedly seek to reconcile the Nation with itself."

At his first press conference, he said, "I have no enemies except the enemies of the Nation."

My enemies are enemies of the nation. Louis XIV could hardly have put it more succinctly.

There was, of course, the inevitable new constitution. This set the end of the president's term as 15 May 1963. And there were other first steps: an amnesty, which somehow seemed to release Duvalierists and skip Déjoieists: sequestration of Magloire's remaining holdings; and retention, at a fee of $150,000, of a New York public-relations firm headed by John Roosevelt, son of FDR, who had been especially invited down for the inauguration. Those who smelled Hyppolite-era wheeling and dealing in the Roosevelt retainer had their instincts confirmed as figures of the regime, including Barbot and, very notably, Arthur Bonhomme, began huckstering concessions and contracts for a grandiose series of public projects or monopolies: the razing and relocation of La Saline (which would displace and disperse several thousand Fignolists); new airports at the Cap and Port-au-Prince; (3) and numerous tourist hotels.

A $4 million "loan" was negotiated with Cuba's Batista (no matter that Batista's enemy, Prio Socarras, had given candidate Duvalier $20,000 and the professional services of Temistocles Fuentes), in return for which Haiti agreed to harbor no Batista opponents, quickly deported Fuentes, and slipped Batista's middlemen a $1 million kickback. The lucrative gambling concession of the International Casino, originally negotiated by Estimé, was revoked. This elicited protests by the Italian government on behalf of the displaced Italian concessionaire. Rome might have saved its breath: after further, ever more lucrative, transfers, the concession came to rest full circle in the hands of the Mafia.

Trujillo, who had a long memory, somewhat sourly recalled Duvalier as an Estiméist, but two important figures, Kébreau and Barbot, enjoyed relations with *El Benefactor* (through a mutual friend, Abbes-García) that soon bore fruit. Arrangements were made for the orderly export of Haitian cane-cutters across the frontier for a head-charge to Duvalier said to have been $8.00(4) plus half the daily wage ("to be held until return") - a practice that, save during an interruption while Juan Bosch was in office, netted millions of dollars for the Duvaliers.

The above arrangements were not pursued at leisure. The new regime was hard-pressed on every front. Above all, the treasury was empty. In the chaos of the previous year, tourism had dried up. Coffee production was down 43 percent from 1956. American aid programs had shut down because Haiti could not pay its token share of joint expenses. The U.S. Government - no fault of Duvalier's, to be sure - was grimly indignant over the police murder, in September, of a naturalized American-Lebanese, Shibley Talamas, who had been beaten, without cause, to crow's meat in the Pétionville police station - an outrage for which the United States ultimately extracted a $100,000 indemnity.(5)

Before October was out, Déjoieists called a general strike of the kind they had so often wielded. This time the weapon turned in their hand. Duvalier activists - muscular *noirs* with dark eyeglasses and pistol bulges under their jackets - persuaded shopkeepers to stay open. In a few cases, cutting tools opened steel shutters on the Grande Rue, and police invited "shoppers" to take their pick. (It was legal: a law had been passed giving police authority to reopen strike-bound premises and "redistribute" merchandise to "needy persons.") Joining Clément Jumelle and Clément's two older brothers, Ducasse and Charles, Louis Déjoie thereupon went underground. The business strike would not again be used while Duvalier held the National Palace.

Using police and those same *noir* toughs - outcasts of the Port-au-Prince slums whom Soulouque's Haiti would have recognized as *zinglins* - the regime was counterattacking in all directions. Within two months, at least a hundred political prisoners were in the penitentiary or Fort Dimanche, an equal number were in hiding, and asylees were beginning to slip into embassies. At the center of these happenings was Barbot, steely-eyed, pitiless toward Duvalier's enemies and toward the elite and their foreign clergy, whom he perceived as exploiters, no better than slave-holding *colons,* of nine out of every ten Haitians. Barbot's men (whom the elite, perhaps recalling the French terrorists of earlier years, were already calling *"cagoulards"*) had in January 1958 chilled both elite and journalistic communities by kidnapping, beating, and sexually abusing Yvonne Hakim-Rimpel, a feminist editor and activist. Despite widespread outrage, police did nothing.

Kébreau, who, after all, had put Duvalier in office, seemed unaware of the tensions that were rising. Going about the country in style, junketing over to visit Trujillo, the general (whom Duvalier in the fashion of Estimé had promptly given a six-year appointment as chief of staff) sensed nothing amiss even in early March, when Duvalier pointedly underscored to *New York Times* correspondent Paul Kennedy that he was "constitutionally and in fact" commander of the Armed Forces. Five days later (10 March), the president abruptly transferred twenty of Kébreau's key officers to such strategic localities as Hinche, Cerca-la-Source, La Gonâve, and Banane. At 5:30 on the afternoon of 12 March, while driving up the Pétionville road, the general was startled at that hour to hear the boom of Fort National's battery. At the thirteenth gun, the salute ended. There could be only one explanation: quickly Kébreau ordered the driver to cut directly across the back road via Musseau to the Dominican embassy. Within four days, on Trujillo's safeconduct, he reached Ciudad Trujillo, where he received another decoration, a Mercedes-Benz, and other emoluments from *El Benefactor*.(6) Kébreau was succeeded by Colonel Maurice Flambert, whom Duvalier soon dubbed *général de division*. Kébreau's sacking was widely interpreted as, and indeed was, a sign that the diminutive president intended to maintain civilian supremacy over the military.

La Voz Dominicana, Trujillo's high-powered radio station, did not approve. Before long, a clandestine transmitter, Radio Liberté, began broadcasting Jumelliste news and sentiments.

There were more immediate problems with the media. *Haiti Miroir, Le Patriote, Le Matin*, and *L'Indépendance*, each for its own reasons out of tune with the regime, underwent midnight visitations or bombings that wrecked their plants. Georges Petit, that hardy troublemaker whose *Petit Impartial* of 1929 had printed young François Duvalier's first article, was clapped in jail for the sins of his *L'Indépendance*, as was Jacques Alexis.

In this jittery atmosphere, the loud bang on 30 April of another bomb factory, a hut in Mahotières, near Carrefour, galvanized the government into action. Déjoie and the Jumelles, publicly condemned as responsible on general principles, were outlawed, and on 2 May, the legislature voted Duvalier a state of siege, a curfew, and press and communications censorship. Through the night, tourists, waiting for the next ship or plane out, could hear the noise of shooting and of *engins*. Amid all this, Louis Déjoie reached safety in the Mexican embassy, whence, after touching bases in Mexico, the United States, and Santo Domingo, he settled in Cuba's Oriente province, peopled by some 120,000 Haitians whom he set out to recruit. The Jumelles, not so lucky, really did hide in the *maquis*.

In midsummer 1958, rumors reached Port-au-Prince through overseas informants, whom Duvalier was already beginning to shape into an intelligence net, that a Florida-based filibustering expedition of Déjoieist or Magloirist provenance might soon be heading for Haiti. The warning was not taken seriously, or at any rate not seriously enough.

On the night of 28 July, the 55-foot Key West fishing boat, *Molly C,* outward bound from Marathon Island in the Florida Keys, lay off the pretty little inlet at Delugé, just North of Montrouis. The *Molly C* carried three former Haitian army officers: Alix "Sonson" Pasquet, the leader: his brother-in-law, ex-lieutenant "Phito" Dominique; and another ex-lieutenant, Henri "Riquet" Perpignand. The Haitians, all high-flying young *mulâtres* with records of past intrigue, were accompanied by five American soldiers of fortune, retained at $2000 apiece - three ex-deputy sheriffs from Miami and Buffalo, and two others. Earlier they had put into Montrouis and Kyona Beach, posing as tourists. Tonight, they were unloading weapons in the lee of a cabana owned by the unsuspecting Robert Nadal, one of Haiti's most wealthy and generous figures. If all went according to plan, sixteen friends in Miami would at the same time be loading weapons and ammunition for 150 men aboard a World War II airplane, cleared for the Dominican Republic, at a shabby little private field outside town.

But no plan, as the elder Moltke observed, survives contact with the enemy. The Miami doings were at that moment closely observed by a detachment of U.S. customs officers staked out in response to a tip; the landing party at Déluge had been reported to the *chef de section* by an alert peasant; and a three-man patrol embarked in a jeep was heading for Déluge from St. Marc.

When the jeep rattled over the railroad crossing on the side road to the Nadal beach, the filibusterers stopped unloading and their outpost thumbed down safety catches on weapons. The jeep stopped and its occupants tumbled out, firing at the *Molly C* and the dim figures visible by moonlight on the beach. The return blast felled all three intruders, but not before Arthur Payne, a swashbuckling thirty-four year old Dade County deputy, was hit in the thigh. Stanching his wound with a first-aid packet, the others quickly finished unloading, drove the jeep out to the highway, and halted the first vehicle to come along.

The blue *camionnette*, "Ma Douce Clairemène," license number 8028, blazoned with two singularly appropriate inscriptions "*Malgré Tout*" (in spite of everything) and *Dieu Maître*" (God is Master) - was pressed into service by the Haitians, all wearing army uniforms, and the little convoy headed South. Even though word got through to Port-au-Prince of some trouble outside St. Marc, General Flambert, for reasons still unaccountable, failed to alert the garrison or government and instead lay in wait on the Champ de Mars, apparently hoping to intercept the invaders.

Near Arcahaie the jeep gave out, but springless *Ma Douce Clairemène* - with Payne cursing or moaning at each bump -jolted ahead. Whatever Flambert expected to see, the humble *tap-tap* escaped him - wheeling around the corner into the main gate of the casernes, Number 8028 braked down. As the sentry came to port arms, Pasquet, who, like the others, knew the casernes inside out, announced he was bringing in five *blanc* prisoners, and the guard presented arms and passed them on. Turning left to the headquarters offices, they scrambled inside, shot the officer of the day when he reached for his pistol, and then cut down the officer and sergeant of the guard as they ran across the parade ground.

It was the work of moments for the submachine-gun-armed filibusterers to awaken and confine fifty groggy soldiers in their squad rooms. Incredibly, the plot seemed to have succeeded, but success, as often happens, had outrun the plan.

Now would have been the time, not losing an instant, to dash through the back gate between the casernes and the palace, seize control, and confront Port-au-Prince with a fait accompli. Though they didn't yet know it, the weapons the attackers expected to find in the casernes had already been transferred by a prudent president to the palace basement.

Instead of thrusting ahead, the filibusterers frittered their time (and, as it happened, their lives) away. Ringing up army installations on the uncertain phone, even ringing the palace to announce their presence, they wasted their two commodities, surprise and time. President Duvalier meanwhile packed his luggage with greenbacks and stood ready for a dash to the Colombian embassy. Dawn was less than an hour away.

At about 5:30 A.M., after an assortment of soldiers and officers had made their way to the Champ de Mars, the palace siren sounded the alarm. As in the days of Soulouque and Salomon, the regime's men swarmed up from the slums and down from the hills, and milled and ducked and cried out with every burst of fire that came from automatic weapons inside the casernes. Word was out that 300 invaders were inside.

At the height of this, cheerful little Riquet Perpignand wanted a smoke and collared a frightened soldier with orders to go outside and buy a pack of the *Régie du Tabac's Splendides*. But Lucien Chauvet was at the gate, and the soldier never got back; instead, dissolved in terror, he found himself explaining to Chauvet that the invaders numbered only eight.

Four more hours were required to organize an attack, but finally a motley troop - Barbot, Chauvet, General Flambert, two Ministers (Duvigneaud and the able Marc Charles) and the president himself at the head of a mob of Duvalierists and soldiers - advanced across the parade ground with machine guns firing overhead, to the flanks, and every which way. With a shower of grenades, they dashed up the barracks steps and inside.

One grenade blew in Sonson Pasquet's skull, and the one-time champion center forward of the army soccer team slumped into a pool of his own brains and blood. Five others were killed in another room. Exactly how they died would be hard to tell: mortuary photographs show massively abraded, smashed bodies riddled with bullet holes. Lying on a mattress with oozy stale dressings already stinking, Payne was shot and pummeled to death. Walker, the *Molly C's* skipper, had his legs broken and his genitals pounded into blood-soaked hamburger. Riquet Perpignand, wounded, escaped from the casernes but was run down by a mob, which found him hiding in a chicken coop. Kersten, one of the mercenaries, was also caught outside. The two shared the fate of Guillaume Sam: stabbed, shot, kicked, gouged, trampled, twisted, all but dismembered, their bodies were dragged naked through the streets, tugged into the palace, shown in triumph to the president, and then hauled about under the blazing sun until police gathered up the carrion and dumped it at the morgue.

Inside the palace, a cold-eyed Duvalier, still wearing an army helmet and two .45s, received the press beside the bust of Pétion, which, not unlike the late

Captain Pasquet, had a bullet hole in the forehead and a large exit hole in back. Beside Duvalier stood young Captain Claude Raymond and the savage-faced soldier-*bocor*, Lieutenant Gracia Jacques. There was no pity on any of the three faces.

The performance of the army - most of which sat on its hands during the deputy sheriffs' coup - did not heighten the president's confidence in his soldiers. Ostensibly to revitalize the *FAd'H* (which in truth had become no better than a small banana army), Duvalier had eagerly pursued negotiations, originated by Kébreau in 1957, to obtain an American military mission composed of Marines. The need for an American military mission to rehabilitate the army required no documentation; even before Duvalier's election Kébreau had put out a feeler for this purpose. To Kébreau it seemed logical that the U.S. Marine Corps, which had forged the modern Haitian Armed Forces, should be asked to put them back on their feet.

Characteristically thinking far past Kébreau, it was François Duvalier who immediately discerned the political mileage to be obtained from the return to Port-au-Prince of even a few U.S. Marines in uniform and conspicuously at the side of a shaky regime. Few decisions more clearly illuminate Duvalier's essential Machiavellianism than that the-self proclaimed *"nationaliste farouche"* (fierce nationalist) whose writings all but canonized Antoine Pierre-Paul, Codio, Batraville, and Péralte - should immediately ask for the return of the Marines. But it was to be Duvalier also, who on at least four occasions while president, invited the United States to establish a base at Môle St. Nicolas, so perhaps we need not be surprised.

For contradictory reasons the mission's efforts were to earn only suspicion and grudging thanks if any, whether from Duvalier or his enemies. The last thing the president really wanted was a professionally capable *FAd'H*, led by Marine-trained and indoctrinated officers and NCOs. Moreover, fundamentally anti-American as he was beneath the surface, Duvalier deeply feared the potential impact of Haitian officers and NCOs being sent to the United States for training.

On the other hand, Duvalier's opponents perceived in the mission a device to strengthen the regime both psychologically and by revitalizing the *FAd'H*,(7) and also - a refrain they never ceased to echo - a secret means whereby for obscure reasons the United States was supposed to be training and arming *tonton macoutes*. "Is it true," superciliously asked one of the elite, "that you Marines are teaching the *tonton macoutes* how to give beatings?"

"Haiti doesn't need foreign instructors to teach Haitians how to beat other Haitians," was the reply.

All this was in the future - a future which Dr. Duvalier with his knowledge of Voodoo may have been able to divine, but which was hidden from

Washington. The Haitian army's track record, despite the debacles of 1957, was a good one: it had frequently assured or restored stability and had midwived four constitutional elections since 1934. To resuscitate it in 1958 seemed a good idea (not least to Ambassador Drew, who could remember the *Garde* in its prime), especially since the United States was by then betting heavily on Dr. Duvalier.

In January 1959 the first echelon of what would eventually comprise some seventy officers and men of the U.S. Marine Corps, Navy, and Coast Guard, commanded by one of the authors of this history, arrived in Port-au-Prince. The Marines had been carefully selected. (A Foreign Service inspection team visiting Port-au-Prince was chagrined to discover that the military mission had more, and more highly qualified, French linguists than the American embassy and aid mission put together: the skilled civilian language instructor largely responsible has since made his mark in higher endeavors as a member of Congress.)

They set to work in what Rotberg afterward rightly called "the most impossible and contradictory of situations." To be sure, the contradictions were still obscured by Washington's conviction that Duvalier was the man who could best cure Haiti's ills and was therefore most worthy of support.(8)

Just before the arrival of the U.S. Mission, the president - like Soulouque dismissing Similien in 1849 - abruptly changed the guard, retiring Flambert - second Armed Forces chief of staff in fourteen months to feel the Duvalier ax - one brigadier, ten colonels, and forty lieutenant colonels. To replace Flambert, the president selected the quiet, efficient *mulâtre* police chief, Pierre Merceron, who could be relied on to take orders from the palace. Rather than consolidate power through close alliance with the Armed Forces (like, for example, Trujillo), Duvalier now chose the riskier path followed by Adolf Hitler, who also came to power with an army he did not trust: from mid-1958 on, he set about creating a paramilitary counterpoise organization answerable directly to the National Palace. This group -in the fashion of the brownshirts versus the *Wehrmacht* in Germany - could offset the military and could also provide an activist Duvalier political cadre throughout the country.(9)

The organization was built on the Port-au-Prince *cagoulards* and those rural headmen, the *chefs de section,* whose appointment, until 1958 a long-standing army perquisite, had been quietly taken in hand as a function of the palace, thus at a stroke creating two chains of authority into the back country - one, the army's, the other, the president's. As the *cagoulards* came out into the open, people soon began to call them "*tonton macoutes*" or just "TTM"'s.(10) They were subsequently described in the *New Republic* as follows: "A *Tonton Macoute* is a Duvalier activist. In 99 cases out of 100 he is black. The civilian TTM can be recognized by his sharp clothes, dark glasses, pearl-gray homburg, and bulge of a pistol on his hip . . . This man is an informer, neighborhood boss, extortioner, bully, and political pillar of the regime."

The man Duvalier charged with creating this organization was Clément Barbot, who about this time made one of his rare mistakes by printing up calling-cards identifying himself as "Chief of Secret Police." In the words of Bernard Diederich, "Whenever an opponent to the regime was arrested, Barbot did the interrogating and he was savagely efficient. Prisoners talked or died, sometimes both."

One more step followed on 15 December 1958. After sacking General Flambert, the president abolished the old *Maison Militaire* and in its stead re-established the *Garde Présidentielle* as his personal army within the Armed Forces, answerable only to the president and not the chief of staff or *Grand Quartier Général* (Armed Forces Headquarters, or GQG). Here again, on Haiti's miniature scale, was a Hitlerian solution: the creation of an elite, autonomous armed body (like the *Waffen SS* of Hitler) answerable only to the chief of state and very pointedly above both the regular army and its paramilitary rivals.

It was to the *Garde Présidentielle* - *noir* to a man - and its commander, Major Claude Raymond, that François Duvalier entrusted the keys to those cellars under the central wing of the *Palais National* where the heavy weapons and most of the army's ammunition were again being stored. And, instead of being quartered in the casernes, for the first time since Leconte the *Garde* was again barracked inside the *Palais* itself.

The months following the July *attentat* had been ones of rising tension. Over a hundred more persons were arrested. Radio transmitters in private hands were confiscated. As if it made a difference, the death sentence, theoretically long outlawed, was revived as a legal penalty. Hot on the trail of Clément Jumelle, whom the government indiscriminately blamed, along with Louis Déjoie and Paul Magloire, for the various bombings and the Pasquet foray, Captain Jean Beauvoir, a leading TTM within the army ran down Ducasse and Charles Jumelle. Both were shot to death while asleep in bed, after which their bodies were dragged outside and posed like gangsters for photographers, with planted pistols in cold hands.

Clément Jumelle had seven months to live.

Early in April 1959, after twenty-one months on the run and desperately ill with uremic poisoning, he dragged himself in from the cold to the Cuban embassy, where, with his wife at his side, he fought for life under intense medical care provided by the ambassador. On 11 April he died.

Next day, in a scene memorably evoked by Graham Greene in *The Comedians,* as the funeral cortège, followed by hundreds of sympathizers, turned up Avenue Charles Sumner toward the Sacré Coeur Church, spectators at the Rond Point were horrified when a police car, siren screaming, screeched ahead of the hearse and halted it. Police and TTMs with submachine guns held the crowd at bay while a detail, led by Captain Beauvoir, knocking down wreaths and mourners alike with *cocomacacs,* snatched the coffin from its bier, and heaved it with a thud into the bed of a truck. Sirens again wailing, the ghastly convoy roared North without stopping to St. Marc. There, at the cemetery beside Portail Montrouis, spurning the offices of a priest (Jumelle had been a devout Catholic), *tonton macoutes* buried Clément Jumelle with Voodoo rites in a shallow grave.(11)

Nor were foreigners immune where TTM interests arose. In 1959, after a dispute with a *macoute* leader over an alleged debt, Atherton Lee, an American horticulturist whose Châtelet des Fleurs at La Boule was not only a prosperous flower-exporting enterprise but a tourist attraction, had his property wrecked overnight - plants uprooted, greenhouses smashed - a scene of irretrievable ruin.

None of these events or many others of similar character were happening in a vacuum. As the *New York Times* accurately headlined: HAITI REGIME HAS FIGHT FOR ITS LIFE. Both Fignolé and Déjoie were in Cuba and had good relations with Fidel Castro, newly come to power in early 1959. The well-heeled Déjoie (already sentenced to death in absentia by a military court) got a training camp, an 800-man Cuban detachment, and a Havana headquarters - not to mention three nights a week of Haiti-beamed Créole broadcasts over Radio Progreso - only to lose out when Duvalier and Castro arrived at an underground accommodation. (In the new setup, Major Raymond, a graduate of the Venezuelan military academy and thus fluent in Spanish, served as liaison officer and bagman.)

Even as Clément Jumelle was dying in Cuba's embassy, a band of six Déjoieists on 9 April hijacked one of COHATA's DC-3s, killing the pilot after takeoff from Les Cayes, and forcing the copilot to fly to Santiago de Cuba.

Within a month, however, François Duvalier faced a deadlier test than any foe could possibly have arranged: on 24 May 1959, the president suffered a cardiac arrest, which, in conjunction with a never fully explained misdiagnosis and therapeutic blunder on the part of Dr. Fourcand,(12) kept him in deep shock and coma for nine hours while his life hung by a thread, and incapacitated him until midsummer.

Duvalier was laid low but Clément Barbot ruled with a rod of iron. The full seriousness of the president's condition was suppressed for over a fortnight while Barbot ran the country. It was a commonplace of diplomatic speculation that the St. Marc strongman would never relinquish power and that Duvalier was finished. Barbot's opportunity was unlimited; it says much for his integrity that, by early July when Duvalier could raise his head, Barbot handed the country back - a decision that, four years later, cost Barbot *his* head.

Besides internal troubles on every front, political and economic, Haiti was at the center of a Caribbean whirlpool of tension and conflict. Cuba and the Dominican Republic were at each other's throats. (With the defeat of Castro's abortive 14 June invasion, Cuba had launched and failed in three consecutive attempts to intervene in Santo Domingo.) Fearful that Haiti would be used as a staging base for his numerous enemies, Trujillo worked out a traditional reinsurance agreement with Duvalier, signed at a frontier meeting at Malpasse on 22 December 1958 (at which Duvalier infuriated *El Benefactor* by keeping him waiting for two and a half hours in the hot sun - a calculated putdown Duvalier often used). Throughout the intense summer of 1959, Dominican warships and aircraft were in and out of Haitian waters and air space, while Trujillo continually nagged Port-au-Prince over transborder security.

During this dangerous time, bombings in June and July 1959 reached the highest level ever sustained. On 15 June, seventeen persons were killed or wounded by a bomb on the Casino dance floor. Soon after, Interior Minister Jean Magloire was injured in an attempted bombing-assassination. Worst of all, forty-two people were hurt when a large bomb went off on 26 July in the middle of the traditional Feast of St. Anne. Amid all this, on 21 June, one wing of the casernes was burned out by a highly suspicious fire. Shots in the night - often accompanied by cries of "A *la porte!*" - were common; empty fuel drums went out at sundown each evening to prevent uninvited landings on Bowen Field or other airfields. The Senate became restive: two senators, Episcopal priest Yvon Emmanuel Moreau and Victor Nevers Constant, launched an attack on the government but backpedaled in time. A more impetuous colleague, Jean David, allowed himself to be carried away. Within hours he was handed an economy-class ticket, diplomatic passport, and commission as ambassador to Tokyo - where Haiti had no embassy.

Cuba's ambassador to Port-au-Prince - Rodriguez-Echazabal, that one-time butcher whose downtown shop, the Oso Blanco, hid a clandestine radio that was contributing so effectively to Haiti's jitters was attacked twice by Barbot's men but survived.(13) Castro thereupon sent him an embassy guard of four green-fatigued Cuban *barbudos,* who, with machine pistols and grenades in their belts, enlivened Port-au-Prince and thoroughly discouraged *tonton macoutes.*

Rodriguez's *barbudos* were not the only soldiers Castro sent to Haiti that summer.

During the night of 12-13 August, a sailboat on passage off Cap des Irois was overtaken and boarded by a small diesel coaster out of Baracoa, an obscure port on Cuba's Northeast coast. Under the guns of a Cuban boarding-party, all of whose members bore the uniforms and weapons of Castro's army, the sailboat took on board a thirty-man Cuban platoon headed by a Créole-speaking Algerian

Frenchman, Henri d'Anton (or Henry Fuertes), who had lived in Haiti and married into the Déjoie family and later served as a soldier of fortune under Fidel Castro in the Escambray Mountains.

On dawn's light breeze, the sailboat eased into Les Irois, headed up as the shallow beach approached, flung over the rusted engine block that served as anchor, and dropped its flour-bag mainsail as the invaders, giving the skipper Cuban cigarettes, quickly went over the side.

A few shots routed the four-man *avant-poste* (though one man escaped to Anse d'Hainault), after which d'Anton engaged guides from the willing villagers, each of whom was given Déjoieist "liberation" insignia. Then the column struck off into the interior toward Goman's ancient strongholds in the Massif du Sud.

The initial reaction in Port-au-Prince was panic. On the advice of the just-arrived Marine officers, however, immediate steps were taken to institute air and seaborne reconnaissance and to contain, find, and fix the invaders. With Marine advisers, units from the casernes were airlifted to Jérémie and went into the field. Two sharp contacts ensued, after which the Cubans, who had suffered appreciable casualties, separated into small parties that were run down and killed or captured by the Haitian force or by *paysans* (whom Barbot offered the enormous sum of 500 *gourdes* for each dead invader). D'Anton was run to earth and killed in a cave; five boyish-looking young Cubans were eventually brought in alive, roped together as in olden times. On 22 August it was over. (14)

September 1959 marked the end of two turbulent years in which, virtually at bay as he took office, François Duvalier had, through political judo, managed to survive against internal and external forces by dividing politicians and citizens into opposing factions, by maintaining and exploiting tension, insecurity, fear, and suspicion, by knocking opponents off balance, and by disposing of potential rivals. No longer could the question remain as to whether he would survive, but rather what he intended to do with power now he had it.

An intimation of the future came on 9 October when - in emulation of his long-time mentor, Sténio Vincent(15) - Duvalier, on various unproven or unspecified charges, declared six of Haiti's twenty-one Senate seats vacated. Five of the six senators were already in asylum or exile abroad. The sixth, Father Yvon Emmanuel Moreau, was imprudent enough to remain in Port-au-Prince and continue in open though law-abiding opposition to Duvalier. Within a year, Moreau was arrested by *macoutes*, never to be seen again.

For a look inside the heart and mind of the oblique, formidable man who would now move swiftly to consolidate the power he had won, we have the words of a proclamation issued by him on 5 August 1958:

I have mastered the country. I have mastered power. I am the New Haiti. To seek to destroy me is to seek to destroy Haiti herself . . . No earthly power can prevent me from accomplishing my historic mission because it is God and Destiny who have chosen me.

A further step remained. One evening in 1959 as dusk was settling over the Cul-de-Sac and charcoal fires and kerosene lamps flickered in a thousand huts, truckloads of soldiers deployed stealthily around Croix-des-Missions and Croix-des-Bouquets, Voodoo's heartland. During the hours ahead, pouncing without warning, detachments picked up every *houngan* and *mambo* in the region, packed them into trucks at gunpoint, and drove them off into the night.

The convoys converged in the inner courtyard of the *Palais National*. At midnight, herded up the darkened spiral backstairs of the palace into the Salle des Bustes, *houngans* and *mambos* faced François Duvalier, standing alone and menacing in the blood-red robe of the Secte Rouge.

"Never forget," he told them, "that I am the supreme authority of the State. Henceforth, I, I alone. I am your only master."

Then, wordlessly, he dismissed them.

Repression Will Be Total

Within a year, at the start of 1960, the doors of Dantès Bellegarde's modest, book-lined home in downtown Port-au-Prince were slammed open. Doyen of living Haitian historians, embodiment, over the decades of enlightenment, patriotic nationalism, and intellectual lighthouse of the elite, this upright, courtly *mulâtre* septuagenarian found himself facing the muzzle of a Sten gun. Backed against the wall by the *noir* intruders, whose identity or authority he had no need to ask, white hair standing *en brosse,* even stiffer perhaps than usual, Bellegarde, in one of the latter scenes of his distinguished career, saw fellow Haitians systematically rip through his papers, overturn his books, and, as if it worked, yank his telephone from the wall. Then with a final cuff or two, trampling the mess of papers and dismembered books, the TTMs stalked out. Not a word had been spoken.(16)

Dr. Elie Villard, the good physician Estimé's men had forced out of the *Hôpital Général* in 1946, was subjected to a savage beating that cut his head open, broke his nose, and marked his kindly face with hideous scars for the rest of his life. What his crime had been, neither he nor anyone else knew.

Niccolo Machiavelli could have provided an explanation: the most efficacious cruelties, he wrote, are those practiced at the outset of a reign to assure the security of a new prince. And François Duvalier was indeed "a new prince." But he would hold power only as long as he could keep his opponents divided and humbled; and, in the definition of ethnologist Rémy Bastien, his opposition would include "the whole conscious population minus one citizen - the president."

To terrify the elite required little more than such episodes as those described above. However they hated the regime and despised it, henceforth they feared it more.

The press, already cowed where not corrupt, posed few problems. The main opposition papers had already been suppressed and troublesome journalists jailed or beaten into silence. From mid-1958 until its seizure in 1960, the Catholic *La Phalange,* even though under orders to report only those political matters covered in official government statements, remained effectively the only voice of opposition. The papers that were left were easily controlled by government subsidies (or lack thereof); by assignment of TTMs to editorial positions; by access to electricity, newsprint, and labor; and by the force-feeding of boilerplate editorials and articles. In addition, Duvalier's   Minister of Information, Paul Blanchet, ran his own government-subsidized *Panorame,* and Gérard de Catalogne, with his well-edited, utterly venal *Nouveau Monde* at the Cap, enjoyed the favors of the government in abundance, especially after having been refused a bribe (to "foster American-Haitian goodwill") by the American embassy. (17)

The foreign press, following a brief honeymoon of presidential press conferences and interviews, was obstructed or harassed by expulsions, censorship of outgoing cables, and occasional suppression of whole issues from abroad (or postal scissoring of offending articles from incoming periodicals such as *Time,* the *New York Times,* and the *Miami Herald).*

Labor, despite Estiméist genesis and roots, came under suspicious observation by a president who had been one of Estimé's Labor Ministers. Demonstrations planned for May Day, 1958, by the *Comité Intersyndicale* were canceled by Duvalier personally.(18) Early in 1959, after arresting the president of the *Union Nationale des Ouvriers Haïtiens,* Duvalier told a delegation: "All popular movements will be repressed with utmost rigor. The repression will be total, inflexible, and inexorable."

That Duvalier was not joking would be abundantly proven. One by one, unions were destroyed, driven underground, or simply taken over by *macoute* leaders. By 1960, Haiti's weak unions were paralyzed or moribund; by 1963 they were dead. There was but one exception, the *Syndicat des Chauffeurs-Guides,* fostered years earlier by Duvalier and by 1958 mother lodge of the *macoutes.*

The business community, particularly the Syrians, were hardly strangers to extortion, bullying, and coercion. The once-feared commercial strike was dead. That Duvalier had the upper hand was clearly indicated, for example, by the actions of weathervane O. J. Brandt, who had financed so many past presidents. In 1960, showing once again his infallible sense for good investments, Brandt bought for his own interest the entire $1 million government bond issue being floated to repave the Grande Rue. Two years later (after Duvalier, to be sure, had just driven an oaken stake through the heart of organized labor by his *Code du Travail*), HASCO similarly chose to pay the government $400,000 in advance taxes covering the forthcoming year's estimated payments.

To prevent merchants from publicly showing any lack of confidence under unsettled business and political conditions, Duvalier also prohibited declarations of bankruptcy, commercial default, or closing by any business or individual, without prior private approval by the Palace.

Plucking the chicken in the style of Dessalines, the regime had, from the beginning, levied so-called spontaneous contributions from the business community. These arrangements were soon regularized when the Chamber of Commerce was given the task of levying such contributions on merchants. Even the slightest reluctance, let alone refusal, to pay up was an invitation for bad trouble on the part of the individual concerned.(19)

The ultimate institutionalization of the business shakedown came in early 1961 with the launching, under sponsorship of Luckner Cambronne, up-and-coming *député* representing Arcahaie, Cabaret, and La Gonâve, of a nationwide *Mouvement de Rénovation Nationale (MRN)*. It was Cambronne who told the legislature on one occasion: "A good Duvalierist is ready to kill his children, or children to kill their parents."

The project with which the MRN is most closely associated (and certainly best remembered among Haiti's merchants) was the building of a new town, a pilot city adjacent to Cabaret, whose name, just as, 157 years earlier, Marchand had been renamed Dessalines, would be eliminated in favor of a new title, Duvalierville. The choice of Cabaret for this honor was not without sentiment. The president had for a time practiced in Cabaret and once reminisced, "Only yesterday it was here in Cabaret I came to practice as a country doctor. I can still see the tiny clinic, the old road, even the stream where I bathed after caring for my peasant patients."

When it had been four years building, Graham Greene remembered the place less sentimentally: "On the flat shoddy plain between the hills and the sea a few white one-room boxes had been constructed, a cement playground, and an enormous cock-pit which among the houses looked as impressive as the Coliseum. They stood together in a bowl of dust which whirled around us in the wind of the approaching thunderstorm: by night it would have turned to mud again."

As a fund-raising device, Duvalierville was more impressive. Commencing in early 1961, the project was the object of the most intensive shakedown of the decade. Not only businessmen but government employees. schoolchildren, the military, even members of the legislature, were solicited for monthly contributions to the MRN. Cambronne set $5000 apiece for the starting price in Port-au-Prince business circles; in the provinces a merchant could get by with

$1000. (One contributor enjoyed the novel sensation of finding on his canceled check for Duvalierville the endorsement of Cambronne's mistress.) Like Soulouque's *zinglins* before them, *tonton macoutes* put up tollbooths on the highway at Cabaret to help finance Duvalierville. As Diederich and Burt recount, Cambronne next hit upon the idea of billing Port-au-Prince telephone-holders at several hundred dollars apiece for the decade that service had been dead: the money, he said, would eventually be used to restore service.(20) The collection effort, even against foreigners, was merciless. When Britain's blunt-spoken, high-principled ambassador, Gerard Corley-Smith, protested maltreatment of foreigners by the MRN in early 1962, he was summarily expelled from Haiti, ostensibly for having uttered, in the teeth of the *macoute* Foreign Minister, René Chalmers, the still unutterable phrase "*tonton macoute.*" Whitehall's memory is long - thirty-three years later, Haiti still has no British Ambassador.

Watching the extortions of the MRN, another foreign diplomat mused, "Duvalier is at war with the commercial and productive classes of Haiti."Duvalier was also at war with the diplomatic corps. It was utterly characteristic of his neo-Dessalinian isolationism to suspect and hold foreigners at arm's length, and to demonstrate to Haitians that he was strong enough, when it suited him, to bully and harass (and, in the style of Soulouque, hoodwink) foreign powers and their *blanc* ambassadors. Showing his disdain for the latter - he never gave a diplomatic dinner during fourteen years in the *Palais* - he expelled more foreign chiefs of mission than had been expelled during the whole of Haiti's history. By 1963, Duvalier's thin diplomatic corps (down to twenty-odd resident missions) bore the scars of outright expulsion or hasty departure of a papal nuncio and of chiefs of mission from Great Britain, Chile, Cuba, Venezuela, the Netherlands, the Dominican Republic, and of two American ambassadors. To this distinguished list within less than a year would be added the resident representative of the United Nations.

Besides these, Duvalier routinely expelled lesser foreign representatives and all stripes of religious on a scale likewise without precedent. While some of these expulsions defy, and were probably meant to defy, explanation, it was generally perceived that foreigners who successfully penetrated Haiti's closed society beyond the limits of Port-au-Prince excited anxiety and suspicion on the part of the regime and were suddenly called on to depart.

The elite, diplomats, the business community, the press, even the unions, terrified, crushed, dislocated, had not presented very formidable obstacles to Duvalier because none had means for striking back. The institutions that remained - army and Church - could fight back.

At the beginning of the regime, the army, (21) politicized and factionalized, had degenerated steadily for a quarter century. Its military proficiency was lower than at any time since 1915; it was deeply divided, not only along predictable lines of color and (as May 1957 had shown) politics, but also on generational lines. Senior officers had been at or near the top a long time and represented the last of the Marine-trained lieutenants of the early 1930s. Immediately below these elders chafed a middle group, dominated by the 1941 Académie Militaire class, calling itself "*La Promotion Flambeau.*" The *Flambeaux* had spent long years as junior officers, had realized nothing from the Magloire good times, entertained a high opinion of themselves as destiny's children, and eagerly awaited their hour on stage. A number had attended advanced U.S. Army schools in the United States or Panama, and had learned many things about nuclear weapons, armor, artillery, air power, and the theory of modern war, all of which was intoxicating but utterly irrelevant to Haiti.

Duvalier's army house-cleaning at the end of 1958 brought the *Flambeaux* to the top, created block vacancies in lower ranks (which Duvalier proceeded to infuse with young *noirs)*, put the officer corps under his thumb, and prevented (by eliminating at the stroke of a pen every Marine-trained officer remaining on the active list) the new U.S. Marine mission (due to arrive in January 1959) from attaining too effective an independent relation with the *FAd'H*. At last on their own, Duvalier correctly reasoned, the *Flambeaux* would be little inclined to take much initial guidance or interference from a *blanc* mission.

As a deep student of Haitian history and politics, the president was keenly aware of the pivotal role historically played by military kingmakers. In all but a handful of power transfers since 1806, it had been generals who called the tune; and it was Duvalier's determination that, whatever had befallen his predecessors, the *FAd'H* would never end his term. As a result, taking a characteristically original tack, Duvalier shoved aside the *FAd'H* (whose potential he still feared and whose loyalty he suspected), and set about building a second army while at the same time undermining the prestige, disorganizing the leadership, drawing the teeth from, and hamstringing the capabilities of the *FAd'H*. These processes were by no means clear in 1958, but, as events soon showed, had been consistently afoot.

In late 1959, using the *Garde Présidentielle* as a parent organization, Duvalier began recruiting from the slums of Port-au-Prince what he at first designated "*La milice Civile,*" a blue-jeaned militia armed with old weapons from the palace basement. Later redesignated "*Volontaires de la Sécurité Nationale*" *(VSN)*, this force within two years would be double the size of the *FAd'H*. Its rural platoons in every village of the back country - led by peasant *gros nègres* giving orders to *FAd'H* opposite numbers - wore the red sashes of *Ogun* and big straw hats of the old *Cacos*, whose latest descendants they were, and were meant by Duvalier to be.

A critical turn in these developments came in June 1961, when Colonel Claude Raymond was ordered by Duvalier to take over the Military Academy (where the president sniffed disaffection). Raymond's relief in command of the palace guard was Gracia "Gros Gra'" Jacques, sinister former mess sergeant and *bocor*.(22) But the Académie Militaire was not long for this world: regarding it as a source of *FAd'H* elitism and of the very professional qualities he was seeking to quench, Duvalier in 1961 simply closed the academy, never to reopen during his presidency.

By this time the *FAd'H* had lost, or at any rate yielded, its ability to protect its own members - a state of affairs previously unheard of - against the *macoutes* or the new *milice* (who were simply uniformed TTMs). One of the first victims in 1959 had been Major Pierre Holly, grandson of the great bishop. Now followed a series of reliefs, shakeups, forced retirements, and arrests of *FAd'H* officers. The *Flambeaux* were quickly divided, turned against each other, and neutralized. By the time they belatedly realized that the American military mission wanted nothing more than to help the *FAd'H* weather the mounting storm, it was too late. In still another shakeup, General Merceron was abruptly relieved on 6 September 1961 and exiled to Paris as ambassador. Merceron's successor, a cool-headed straightforward *noir,* Colonel Jean-René Boucicaut, lasted but eleven months. His downfall resulted from his brave attempts to maintain the status and integrity of the *FAd'H* and its officer corps against ever more truculent TTM incursions, a particularly brutal example of which was the unprovoked and unpublished murder at Hinche in November 1961, by the local *macoute* headman, of Colonel Max Deetjen, one of Haiti's most popular and capable officers. Bleakly summarizing the situation in 1962, the chief of the U.S. military mission wrote: "The practice on the part of individual *miliciens* or their leaders of establishing themselves as vagrant law officers exercising police authority with little if any training and education, and no sense of responsibility, has had a degrading effect on the regular Armed Forces . . . [who] appear to have lost control over the ill-defined police functions asserted by *miliciens* and are unable or unwilling to reassert control."

By this point, alas, the observation was superfluous: the *FAd'H* cowed, disorganized, factionalized, enfeebled, and all but disarmed (the "rearming" of the *FAd'H* by the U.S. Mission, which had attracted attention from the media and politicians, was in fact minimal: only about 10 percent of the U.S. military assistance to Haiti, slightly over $1 million in all, had been allowed by the Marines to find its way into weapons or ammunition) had become impotent in the face of Duvalier's special brand of civilian supremacy over the military. The *milice/VSN*, numbering some 12,000 rural and urban members, had in turn usurped police authority and become the regime's instrument of nationwide political enforcement.

Even more significant, these loosely controlled bands of armed *noirs* not only repressed fellow *paysans* but terrified the propertied elite as they had not been frightened since the *semaine sanglante*.(23)

On 1 August 1960 the Port-au-Prince *milice* staged an anniversary demonstration and parade, during which the capital was mysteriously plastered with handbills. The mostly illiterate *miliciens* of course had no way of reading what the handbills said. But, as they fearfully watched the rifle and machete-armed, *taffia*-reeking, blue-jeaned bands troop past the palace to the throb of "1804", the quaking elite could read on every wall and hoarding the terrible words of Sonthonax in 1793 to his own *noir* militia: THESE MUSKETS ARE YOUR LIBERTY! IF YOU WANT TO KEEP IT, MAKE GOOD USE OF THESE ARMS . . .

Both François Duvalier and Clément Barbot had scores against the Church. Some of the president's earliest writings had been in favor of a national clergy and - what else? - expulsion of the French. Barbot would never forget that childhood caning for the sake of Dessalines. Neither man was prepared to overlook the hierarchy's unanimous support of Louis Déjoie.

As perceived by many Haitians, moreover, the Church, with its French hierarchy, its Breton seminary, its foreign (overwhelmingly French) clergy,(24) represented a prime example of ecclesiastical colonialism that clearly neither France nor Rome was in any hurry to set right. Internally, the Church was aligned with the elite and, while spiritually ambivalent toward Voodoo, bitterly opposed the Estiméist *folklorique* politics of Voodoo so ardently espoused by Duvalier.

One of the earliest targets of the regime's animus against the Church was, logically enough, the outspoken Père Etienne Grienenberger, blue-eyed Alsatian headmaster of that nursery of the elite, St. Martial. Père Grienenberger, who was also chaplain of the Boy Scouts, had been in Haiti since 1945 and was a religious figure of high visibility. Another target, Père Joseph Marrec (curé of St. Marc for thirty years; it is tempting to wonder whether it was he who caned Barbot) was a well-known French provincial priest. On 16 August 1959 - charging connivance with subversives on the part of Grienenberger and omission of customary prayers for the president by Marrec - the government ordered immediate expulsion of the two priests.

Msgr. François Poirier, Haiti's stern and unbending French archbishop, reacted with a stiff pastoral letter ordering nationwide prayers for Père Grieneberger and Abbé Marrec and, for good measure, "for all other French priests who can now regard themselves under threat, any fine day *[du jour au lendemain]*, of being deprived of the guaranties of security and stability required for exercise of their ministry."

Late on the afternoon of 18 August, over a thousand communicants and most of the local Catholic clergy were gathered in Port-au-Prince cathedral, chanting prayers and a rosary for the departing priests, when suddenly an uproar burst out. Led by Barbot with his submachine gun, phalanxes of *cocomacac*-swinging *tonton macoutes* waded into the congregation while another group made for the altar, knocking down priests and sacred objects alike. As TTMs swept worshipers out onto the street, police outside arrested some sixty, including numerous broken-headed wounded still bleeding in the aisles of the basilica. Later that day, attempting to justify this sacrilege, the ordinarily softspoken Minister of Cults, psychiatrist Louis Mars, told the *New York Times's* Homer Bigart: *"Jésus Christ, lui-même, prit son fouet une fois pour chasser les pêcheurs de Temple"* (Christ Himself took a scourge to expel the evildoers from the Temple).

Ever since 1929, rebellious students had looked to the Church for counsel and support in strikes that had ultimately toppled regimes (Lescot, Estimé, and Magloire, not to mention the American occupation). Thirty years later, against a François Duvalier who had changed sides, students with backstage religious coaching supported secondary schoolteachers in a 1959 strike against TTM infiltration into teachers' ranks. The government for once capitulated but, as Barbot said, for the last time.

In September 1960, the regime struck back: twenty student leaders were secretly picked up by *macoutes* and hustled off to prison on charges of communist conspiracy. After two months' agitation, on 21 November, students at the university and the *lycées* went out on what would prove to be an eighty-eight-day boycott.

Duvalier responded by abolishing all youth groups down to and including Père Grienenberger's Boy Scouts, and, as bombs began to explode about town, ringed the university and all schools with police. In the president's perception, not unjustifiably, the students were the offspring of his enemy, the elite, egged on by a hostile foreign Catholic clergy.

The president's next move was therefore even bolder: early the next day, 22 November, catching the archbishop before he even had time to shave or put in his false teeth, police swooped into the archiepiscopal palace, allowed Msgr. Poirier just long enough to throw on a cassock, and cuffed him aboard the early plane for Miami, where, with one dollar in hand and no false teeth, wearing only cassock and underclothes, he was eventually succored by American priests. The charge that supposedly justified Poirier's banishment (like Abbé Lecun in 1804, *"sans linge et sans argent"*) was that he and "communist priests" had contributed $7000 for communist infiltration of the student movement.

By the end of 1960 the strike had begun to crumble. Duvalier prohibited all private teaching or tutoring or home study, ordered jail sentences for parents of striking students, had TTMs take university roll calls and report absentees, and declared prized university places vacant so that young Duvalierists could be enrolled (a process that was later to be paralleled by refusal of exit visas to elite sons, thus precluding their obtaining abroad the education denied them at home). In January 1961, as the university strike flared for the last time, the regime again turned on the Church. During the night of 10 January, Msgr. Rémy Augustin, Haiti's sole native bishop (whom the Vatican had appointed apostolic administrator after Poirier's deportation), was shaken awake and carted off to Fort Dimanche, and four other French priests were rounded up and expelled. Next day, *La Phalange* was seized by the government, and, as the strike petered out, a quiet descended on Port-au-Prince not unlike Soulouque's "quiet of the tomb." After a few days' meditation in Fort Dimanche, Msgr. Augustin was removed from prison to nearby Bowen Field and shoved onto the first plane for New York.

Msgr. Augustin's ouster finally stirred the Vatican to excommunicate Dr. Duvalier (the first excommunication of a Latin American chief of state since that of Juan Peron in 1955), but this notably failed to faze him, and certainly did not mitigate the government's anti-Catholicism. Within a month, Bishop Robert of Gonaïves, an uncompromising old Breton in Haiti thirty-nine years, including a quarter century in his bishopric, was expelled from his diocese for refusing to say prayers for the excommunicate president. As *macoutes* looted the diocesan warehouse and guzzled sacramental wine, Bishop Robert was hauled off to Port-au-Prince, where, before his eventual expulsion, he found asylum with the apostolic nuncio, Msgr. Giovanni Ferrofino.

Behind, in Gonaïves, the chief *macoute* and noted *bocor*, Zacharie Delva, held a public *Cérémonie Bois Cayman* in the cathedral portals, complete with a chalice of warm pig's blood.

There now followed a parade of expulsions of rank-and-file religious, which was to continue for the next three years and eventually extend to leading Protestant figures, and including Duvalier's friend from earlier times, Episcopal Bishop C. Alfred Voegeli, and Baptist missionary Wallace Turnbull. This culminated in February 1964 - two centuries after their first banishment from St. Domingue - in eviction of the entire Jesuit order.(25) These purges not only debilitated the Church but, as in the case of the *FAd'H*, opened up vacant livings to be filled by the president with men of his own choosing. The result was a cadre of *macoute* priests of a type not seen since the days of Dessalines: Père Jean Hilaire, who celebrated mass with pistol on hip; Père Bouillaguet, swaggering chief of the Léogane *milice*; and Père Albert Dorélien, who earned instant promotion from parish priest to cathedral canon by publicly pronouncing that, in his dealings with the Church, Duvalier had "brought 1804 up to date," which was true enough.(26)

No more than Soulouque was Duvalier prepared to risk challenge from within the ranks of his supporters. With the hypersensitized antennae of paranoia, it was perhaps his supreme attribute, as it was also Soulouque's, to sense not merely disaffection but competition far ahead. The obvious case was Barbot. Clément Barbot had been the president's best and certainly most loyal friend. The two families, who had shared homes, were equally close. Barbot had run the country during Duvalier's heart attack and had willingly restored power. He was, however, the only man around Duvalier who had a power base of his own, not to mention a wide range of independent financial arrangements. He had also earned his reputation as a strong and efficient administrator and a man who could get things done.(27)

On the evening of 14 July 1960, as he and Mme. Barbot were returning from the French embassy, a *Garde Présidentielle* roadblock halted them. Within a week he was in Fort Dimanche, where, for sixteen months in a lightless, fetid cell, he was allowed to rot on a diet of sour mangos and overripe bananas.

The fall of Barbot, who took with him at least a dozen powerful supporters (including several wealthy Syrians in his extensive commercial constituency), marks the point at which Duvalier, dropping the pilot, fully grasped the helm. Henceforth, like the Javanese Upas-tree, he would poison all who reposed in his shade.

One provision that had been tinkered into the 1957 constitution was that, on expiry of their current terms, the two houses of the legislature would be merged into a unicameral fifty-seven-man National Assembly, a change that would even further facilitate rapid assent to the president's actions where required.(28) Thus it came about that, on 8 April 1961, President Duvalier dissolved the two Chambers and decreed elections for the new body on 30 April. The ballots, which were forthwith printed up, like many official papers were headed:

République d'Haïti
Dr. François Duvalier, Président de la République

Below, in appropriate position, were listed the names of legislative candidates. The turnout on election day was mixed: at the Cap, for example, the *préfet* not only required all government employees and prisoners in the jail to vote, but swept up Canadian, American, and other foreign residents, French priests, missionaries and their wives, and marched them all to the polls under guard so that they too could vote the local slate. Even so, as both the *New York Times* and *Time* reported, the returns were sparse.

Sparse the returns may have appeared, but, out of an estimated 1 million Haitians eligible to vote, 1,320,748, according to the government, exercised the franchise, sweeping in the all-Duvalier slate. More to the point, in a stratagem surely without precedent in the history of electoral politics, on 9 May voters and the world were told that, to everyone's surprise save perhaps one man, Haiti had not only elected a new legislature, but, by a vote of 1,320,748 to 0, had re-elected François Duvalier, unopposed, for a second six-year term, commencing 22 May 1961.

What could the president do but accept? Idle to protest (none inside Haiti did) that this "re-election" for a constitutionally forbidden second term even more expressly contradicted Duvalier's own constitution of 1957: "The term of the present President of the Republic, who was elected on 22 September 1957, shall end on 15 May 1963." François Duvalier bowed his head and softly replied, "My enemies can reproach me only with one crime - of loving my people too much. As a revolutionary, I have no right to disregard the voice of the people."

Neither had he disregarded experience: not for nothing had Duvalier seen Vincent, Lescot, Estimé, and Magloire, his four predecessors, each overthrown as a result of last-minute attempts to prolong waning presidencies. With characteristic astuteness and boldness, Duvalier therefore re-elected himself while two years remained to run.

Failing to appreciate the genius, let alone the sheer farce, in the April election, the *New York Times* on 13 May gasped "Latin America has seen many rigged elections in its history, but none more outrageous than the proceedings of May 7 [sic] in Haiti . . . [which] is saddled with Dr. Duvalier and his henchmen for six more years. It is not a pretty picture . . ."

But here again, the president had the last word. "Haitian democracy," he replied, "is neither the English nor the French version, and still less the American democracy." He was of course perfectly correct.

Extraordinarily Resistant

The surreal election of 1961 shocked Washington at least as strongly as it did Port-au-Prince and heavily underscored a favorite observation of Ambassador Drew that no country in the world is more difficult to help than Haiti.

The United States had (despite Ambassador Drew's reservations), in 1957, looked to the Duvalier regime with high expectations. The advent of a constitutionally elected civilian president of middle-class professional background and extensive past associations with Americans seemed too good to be true, and indeed it was; but the sequence of events that by mid-1961 reduced the United States to frustrated disillusion needs to be set down, if only because François Duvalier's Soulouquian manipulation of his most powerful neighbor marks one of the most intriguing themes in the history of this remarkable man and his regime.

When Duvalier came to power in 1957 the Gorgon's head that faced him was an empty treasury. Quickly and correctly he concluded that the United States, which had so often helped Haiti in the past, was the logical source of replenishment.(29)

Duvalier's hopes found sympathetic hearing in Foggy Bottom among those officials who, under the enchantment of distance, could still regard Fidel Castro and François Duvalier as standard-bearers of Caribbean democracy. And Duvalier's first move seemed encouraging: on American advice, and saying he intended to "clean up the mess," he took on in 1958 a U.S. consulting firm, Klein and Saks, to undertake a $338,000 top-to-bottom financial and fiscal survey of the government. Nobody could then know that he had not the least intention of following the exhaustive recommendations, which, like so many others by American experts, were doomed to gather dust.

Besides being at a very low financial and economic ebb, Haiti in 1958 had reached the limit of its capacity to service hard loans. (The country already owed the Ex-Im Bank $25 million on the thus-far unproductive Artibonite Valley project - an enduring grievance since the government felt it should not be compelled to maintain endless interest payments for a project, whatever the reasons, still incapable of producing new revenue.) The first American loan, $4.3 million to restart the Artibonite development, was therefore handled by the Development Loan Fund (DLF, a "soft-loan" U.S. agency) in an effort to convert the Artibonite from a burden to an asset.

Going still further, the United States simply gave Haiti $3.5 million for budgetary support, mainly to pay salaries and even Haiti's nominal share of projects already jointly in progress. By the end of 1961, in budget support or economic assistance grants - outright gifts Duvalier had received $24.4 million from Washington. Besides this, he also got $7.2 million in technical assistance and $4 million in American foodstuffs - a four-year total of $40.4 million. This sum, all to Duvalier, equalled two fifths of all U.S. aid to Haiti during the preceding twenty-five years.

It should not have been expected that Duvalier would be grateful; although the aid was desperately needed, as Rotberg says, "he knew he could do better by being difficult." In addition, of course, the greed of Ministers involved (for example, Bonhomme) caused them to short-circuit DLF procedures, as in the 1958 Port-au-Prince airport fiasco and the subsequent Port-au-Prince to Cayes "Road to the South," in each instance cutting deals with carpetbagging contractors the U.S. Government would not approve.(30)

Besides mere venality and peculation, in March 1960, only a year after work in the Artibonite had been resumed, Duvalier, abruptly flouting the agreement that personnel must be hired with joint U.S.-Haitian approval, unilaterally dismissed key Haitian employees and replaced them one and all with deserving *macoutes* (one of whom Duvalier had just released from the penitentiary after doing eight months for embezzlement and malfeasance). This was but one example of such tactics wherever U.S. aid was within reach of Duvalierist manipulation. In the Artibonite case - which cost Haiti suspension of the Artibonite loan by the DLF and of two other pending loans - Duvalier's immediate (and typical) riposte was to expel the American aid directors who had been so presumptuous as to complain of the original purge.(31) Other sharp disagreements continued over Haitian misuse of American-supplied equipment, which, under agreements, was not to be diverted to unspecified uses without U.S. consent. It was galling to the United States when, for example, in 1962, Duvalier stripped the Artibonite of U.S. engineering gear and packed it down to Cabaret for Cambronne's Duvalierville, where much of it simply rusted apart. Even worse was the president's diversion, in the teeth of American protests, of tens of U.S. AID trucks to haul peasants to Port-au-Prince for the 22 May celebration of his sleight-of-hand re-election, which the United States disapproved and refused to recognize.

To rub salt into U.S.-Haitian relations, and of course to maintain pressure on the United States, Duvalier coupled bad faith and systematic misappropriation of aid with a highly skilled war of nerves intended to keep Washington on the defensive and exploit American nervousness over communist successes in the Caribbean.

Duvalier's speech at Jacmel of 21 June, 1960 - ever after called "*Le Cri de Jacmel*" - had been such an example. Dedicating the new coffee wharf, itself built by American benefactions, the president said, "For thirty-three months, My Government and people have lived on promises, smiles, encouragements, recommendations, hesitancy, lengthy delays and lack of understanding . . . A massive injection of money is needed . . ."

Communist Information Minister Paul Blanchet, a Duvalier fixture who distributed and widely publicized the speech, intimated that $150 million might suffice. Then, in language no doubt attributable to Blanchet, the president threatened: "Haiti has to choose between the two great poles of attraction in the world today to realize her needs."

In 1960, year of the *Cri de Jacmel*, American aid totaled $9.3 million, equal to 30 percent of Haiti's budget. As a percentage of a recipient country's budget, this was the third highest level of U.S. aid extended anyplace in the world: what Duvalier really wanted, of course, was aid on his own terms, which, unhampered by governessy American conditions, could be applied for maximum internal political benefit to the regime. It was when he realized that the United States would never (at least as long as John Kennedy was in the White House) extend aid on any such basis that the honeymoon ended.

Duvalier's way with the United States was highlighted by the events of January 1962. On the *Fête des Aïeux* (Ancestors' Day, 2 January), sneering at President Kennedy's Alliance for Progress, Duvalier said the United States had failed either to understand or meet Haiti's needs, and demanded massive amounts of aid without strings. That afternoon, the president conspicuously received Aleksandr Bekier, the Polish trade representative, for a discussion as to how the Warsaw Pact might help Haiti. (Save for a few Czech automatic weapons brought in for the *milice* Civile, it never, however, did.)

On the larger hemispheric scene, where the United States was attempting to contain Fidel Castro, the Organization of American States on 21 January convened a meeting of Foreign Ministers to consider that subject at Punta del Este, Uruguay's lovely seaside resort. Here Haiti again displayed the mobility for which its diplomacy has become well known.

On 27 January, to the surprise of the American delegation, headed by Dean Rusk, Foreign Minister Chalmers abruptly delivered a pro-Castro address that all but promised Haiti's swing vote (needed for the two-thirds majority to effectuate sanctions against Cuba) to Castro. Soon afterward, as recalled by Arthur Schlesinger, Jr., a participant, Chalmers sidled up to Rusk in the lobby of the San Rafael Hotel and not so cryptically remarked that he represented a poor nation in need of aid, a need that could not but influence Haiti's vote. Rusk, inscrutable as always, turned away from the *macoute* Foreign Minister but later conveyed word that, since Chalmers himself had linked Haiti's vote and U.S. aid, why yes, future aid would indeed by scrutinized with that crucial vote in mind. Haiti thereupon promptly joined with the United States. Within a few weeks, to the surprise of those who had not followed developments, the Port-au-Prince airport loan came back to life. Back in Foggy Bottom, desk officers grinned over the quip that Secretary Rusk's expense account on the 28th read:

Breakfast $2.25
Lunch with Haitian Foreign Minister $2,800,000.00 (32)

The American courtship of Haiti's vote at Punta del Este was in stark contrast to relations between the two countries on the ground in Port-au-Prince. The Marines' adamant refusal to train or in any way support the *milice* or *VSN* had precipitated the first open rupture with Duvalier. In July 1961 it was learned that a group of *milice* leaders had been hastily commissioned in the *FAd'H* and were being nominated as bona fide officers for training at American military schools. When these nominations came in, they were vetoed *en bloc* by the mission chief. Duvalier's response was to cancel all pending United States training or courses for *FAd'H* officers.(33)

From this time forward, relations between the palace and the Marines became increasingly strained. In the words of the Marines' commander, "After four years of ever-increasing obstructionism and, at the last, of overt Duvalierist anti-Americanism, I felt like a doctor transfusing blood into one arm of a failing patient while another M.D. - Dr. Duvalier - had a suction pump on the other."

Duvalier's increasingly open sabotage was a roundabout compliment to the military mission's effectiveness. It was even more a result of the larger duel in progress between Duvalier and John F. Kennedy.

It was only natural that the father of the Alliance for Progress should be sensitive to an intractable tropical Appalachia in the backyard of the United States. Moreover, from the beginning, some of Kennedy's advisers (notably A. A. Berle) had ties with exiled opponents of Duvalier and were eager either to reform the regime in Port-au-Prince or find a new one.(34)

In keeping with the evangelical climate of the New Frontier, Haiti -just as it had in 1947 to the United Nations at dawn on Lake Success - seemed the very place to demonstrate notions on human improvement subsumed under the generous and stirring phrase "nation building."

As then Secretary of State Dean Rusk was to write in 1975, "We were very concerned about Haiti . . . In the first place it appeared to be a kind of political and social cesspool here in the Western Hemisphere. Poverty, illiteracy, superstition, inadequate public services of the most minimum sort, human rights - make your own list. One could not think of Haiti without being concerned about the miserable condition of the Haitian people."

Rusk went on to say: "We felt that the Duvalier regime in Haiti constituted an open invitation to attempts to establish a Castro-type dictatorship in that country. Many Americans felt that Batista had prepared the way for Castro in Cuba and that the same thing could happen in Haiti. In any event . . . it seemed clear that Haiti constituted a major problem and my Latin American colleagues and I discussed it many times in private."

If only from a strategic viewpoint, any Pentagon planner could see on his maps that the Windward Passage, already flanked on one side by Fidel Castro's Russian submarine bases, was flanked on the opposite side by Haiti. Two thirds of the traffic entering or leaving the Caribbean, much of it bearing South American raw materials vital to the United States, moves through the Windward Passage. For these sound strategic reasons, rendered urgent by Castro's evident interest in Hispaniola, Haiti - so vulnerable yet paradoxically not vulnerable at all - deeply preoccupied Washington. The Kennedy administration would have been happy in truth to see a new regime in Port-au-Prince but (with the Bay of Pigs fresh in mind) could never decide how such a change might be brought about, or whether for that matter any other occupant of the National Palace would be much of an improvement over Duvalier.

"I would add," reflected Rusk, "that we made all sorts of efforts to bring about changes in Haiti. We used persuasion, aid, pressure and almost all techniques short of the landing of outside forces, but President Duvalier was extraordinarily resistant." Mr. Rusk's allusion to " all sorts of efforts . . . and almost all techniques" was vividly confirmed in November 1975, when a U.S.

Senate investigation disclosed that the CIA - presumably in the early 1960s insurgencies and probably in the 1968 exile landings - armed and supported attempts to overthrow Duvalier.

At any rate, the above and like preoccupations on the part of Washington were heightened and underscored by dawning recognition by mid-1961 that Duvalier was essentially unfriendly, more and more openly anti-white - a projection of anti-*mulâtre* racism few *noir* leaders of the past had cared to take on - and gave signs of fostering internal communists as a means of blackmailing the United States. As a senior American official then in Port-au-Prince later put it:

> The reasons for American dissatisfaction with Duvalier are simply stated: the regime is unconstitutional, uncooperative, unreliable, unresponsive, unfriendly, inhumane, insincere, and ineffective. American citizens have been maltreated, illegally arrested, held incommunicado and deported without explanation. American businessmen have been shaken down for heavy contributions by the notorious MRN . . . . American diplomatic and consular officials have been harried and insulted in the conduct of business.(35)

The foregoing perceptions crystallized after the May 1961 "reelection." From that day until his death, Kennedy withdrew the American ambassador from Port-au-Prince for Washington consultation so that the United States would not be represented at the anniversary celebrations held to rub in the claimed legitimacy of the regime. On each of these fêtes, peasants by tens of thousands were herded onto confiscated *camionnettes* (not to mention U.S. AID trucks) and driven to the capital like livestock, billeted in schools, parks, front yards, and not infrequently returned to the wrong villages. One of the authors noted in her diary on 24 May 1961: "*Camionnettes* returning to the country. Strong stench everywhere."

Also holding its nose, Washington had authorized a $7.3 million aid program to Haiti for 1962, but insistences that key personnel be approved by the AID Mission were adamantly rejected by Duvalier. Added to the latter's long record of bad faith and noncooperation, this broke the camel's back: in August 1962, Washington began closing out its once-grandiose aid program, Punta del Este airport and all. By January 1963, the former seventy-man AID Mission was down to eight caretakers administering a holdover malaria-eradication program and supervising distribution of U.S. surplus foods. In the final analysis, like so much other past foreign aid to Haiti, it had gone for nothing, "as if," wrote Robert Crassweller, "an ocean liner had plunged to the bottom, leaving only an oil slick and a brief pillar of air bubbles."

The U.S. military assistance program died too, but more dramatically, in a pillar of fire rather than of air bubbles.

The terminal issues were long-standing: Duvalier's continued attempts to infiltrate *macoutes* into American training courses and his parallel attempts to divert what few arms and ammunition the U.S. military mission had actually furnished the Army into the *milice*. As a riposte for what he considered the Marines' obstructionism on these counts, Duvalier, increasingly uneasy about the numbers of Haitian military going to the United States, in June 1962, abruptly canceled all seventy U.S. military scholarships previously accepted. Although warned that this step would cost him further materiel aid, the president was characteristically unbudging. So were the Marines: on 25 June, the mission chief halted all deliveries of equipment and, with his government's concurrence, terminated the program.

By Washington's decision, the Marines stayed on nearly a year as tension mounted throughout Haiti. Any possibility of patching up relations with the regime ended on 20 July, when, again on instructions, the Marine commander presented a stiff memorandum characterizing the *milice* as "a militarily superfluous organization [with] an explosive potential" and recommending its disbandment or dissociation from police or military functions.

The result was certainly explosive. Called on by Duvalier to disavow publicly or rebut the devastating study, General Boucicaut refused to do so, resigned, and on 8 August took asylum with his family in the Venezuelan embassy.

When the Cuban missile crisis exploded in October 1962, Duvalier quickly aligned Haiti with the United States but characteristically continued government subsidy for Paul Blanchet's Moscow-line *Panorame,* which throughout the crisis vehemently attacked the Americans and extolled Castro and Khrushchev. He also opened Haiti's ports and airports to U.S. ships and forces - an invitation that, possibly not without malice, the United States promptly accepted by landing a Marine battalion in full combat gear one morning for an "exercise march" from the wharf to Bizoton. Prearrangement was intentionally minimal. The first Duvalier learned of it was when the leading companies were ashore under the Foreign Minister's windows; the president's reaction was to load his limousine with bulky black suitcases and prepare to make a run for the Colombian embassy.

Duvalier's revenge was typical. Early in the new year, after due consultation with spiritual advisers, the president donned his magical Secte Rouge scarlet robe and, assisted by Dodo Nasar, chief *bocor* of the *Palais National*, made two dire *ouangas-à-mort:* one for the Marines' commander, the other for John F. Kennedy. (36) Missing no options, he then initiated diplomatic steps for the former's recall, which was effected in March 1963. Within two months the U.S. Naval and Air Missions and the American ambassador, too, were out as

Duvalier faced his greatest crisis. It would be almost precisely six months before the stalemate broke.

On 22 November - what other date? asked Haitians - John F. Kennedy died in Dallas. When word reached Duvalier, champagne was served in the *Palais National*.(37)

In early 1964, one evening toward dusk, a special emissary of François Duvalier drove over to Arlington Cemetery and walked alone to the tomb of President Kennedy. His errand was to secure a bit of earth from each corner of the grave, a withered flower, and, in a bottle he had brought from Port-au-Prince, a breath of grave-site air. The pilgrim's object was not sentimental but practical: by means of the ingredients obtained, Duvalier hoped to "capture" the soul of Kennedy, render it subject to his will, and thus control future American policies toward Haiti.

In a sense, the trip was not necessary: Haiti and, in his perverse way, more particularly Duvalier, had engaged, baffled, and frustrated John F. Kennedy since 1961.

The Terror

On the night of Boukman's dread anniversary in August 1962, the president had presided over a *Cérémonie Bois Cayman* at which, under his cold eye, the cabinet and leading *macoutes* gulped warm blood from a chalice to whose rim stiff hairs from the slaughtered pig's throat still adhered.

Duvalier's sense of history never misled him. The two years ahead were to be among the bloodiest in all the blood-drenched annals of Haiti.

Tattered though it was, the constitution of 1957, written after all by Duvalier himself, required that the president announce new elections on 15 November 1962 and hold them the following 10 February. The psychologically critical period, as Duvalier reckoned it, would run through these months until 15 May 1963, when, by the constitution at any rate, his term expired (and when, that same date, underscoring "the realities of power solidly established," as he put it, he could simultaneously celebrate the second anniversary of his 1961 re-election). If trouble were to come, it would, as so often before, show itself in April and May.

At first the terror seemed random and formless. A watchman at the *Travaux Publiques* was found swathed in a cocoon of rusty barbed wire, hung up in the night to bleed to death outside his shack. Another watchman, this time in Pétionville, was crucified beside the cemetery wall. Jean Chenet, a lively intellectual who loved chess, was called out into the dusk and, after being mercilessly beaten, was gunned down on his doorstep at Arcachon beside the bay; led by the pitiless Major Franck Romain, *macoutes* prevented Chenet's American wife, Winnie, from succoring him or moving the body until next day.

By October 1962, conditions had intensified to the extent that the OAS Commission on Human Rights asked permission to visit Haiti for a look. The first request was simply ignored. To a second inquiry, on 9 October, Chalmers, the *macoute* Foreign Minister, brusquely replied that any such probe would violate Haitian sovereignty and would not be tolerated.

About this same time, apparently to emphasize Haiti's neo-Dessalinian isolation, diminish foreign contact and influence, and cut off people from any sense of outside support, the government commenced harassment against a wide range of foreign welfare and charitable agencies long active in Haiti.

Haitian consuls abroad began refusing shipping documents for relief supplies or food destined for starving peasants (38) Shipments by CARE, Catholic Relief, and Church World Services were held up on the Port-au-Prince docks for weeks, allowing tons of donated food to spoil or be stolen. Illegal customs duties and fees were demanded. Despite express treaty exemptions for such shipments, road taxes and tolls were levied on foreign charitable distributions. Large shipments of clothing, collected at Marine bases throughout the United States and sent to the military mission for distribution, were stopped at the ports: further donation of such clothing was banned by Haitian authorities as "unsanitary."

These inhumanities, continuing throughout 1963 and 1964, being inflicted by a regime whose people were starving, naked, and miserable, and whose estimated average annual per capita income at that time was about $65. To an American friend, a Haitian confided: "Duvalier has performed an economic miracle. He has taught us to live without money and eat without food."

Other storm signals began to fly. Since 1958, emigration from Haiti had never been easy. Now, like Soulouque in 1848, Duvalier converted Haiti into a prison. Lists of persons applying for exit visas went directly to the president's second-floor office in the palace. Here, in his own spidery hand, François Duvalier crossed out the names.(39) Few got by. "Everyone," Graham Greene was to write, "is some sort of prisoner in Port-au-Prince."

At the opposite end of the *Palais*, on the basement corner, was another sort of office. This room, with a direct side entrance opening, ironically, toward the Place de l'Indépendance, was the *tonton macoutes'* receiving and interrogation room for persons arrested. Its floor and walls to shoulder height were painted rusty brown, a color that does not show bloodstains.

Breitman/Morrison, who would have known, in 1963 told an American reporter that an antechamber contained, among other implements, a coffin-shaped Iron Maiden, its interior spiked with stiletto blades. General Merceron, a former police chief and thus no stranger to violence, was reliably said to have vomited in that room at the condition of Eric Brièrre, a young man tortured to death in 1961, for a plot to assassinate Duvalier.

There were other such chambers, perhaps not so elaborately equipped or fastidiously painted, in the *pénitencier,* the new police headquarters, and, above all, Fort Dimanche. Here, reported survivors, the raw flesh of beaten prisoners was rubbed with citrus juice, red pepper, or, according to one account, a dilute solution of sulphuric acid.

The grim atmosphere was heightened by nightly "blackouts" due to the inability of the *Compagnie Electrique* to handle peak loads without cutting off power, an hour at a time, to major districts of the capital. In the blanket of darkness could be heard shots and outcries, or sometimes transistor radios blaring the *tonton macoutes'* alert-signal, the unforgettable song *"Feu nan caille-la!"* (House afire!).

Perhaps to warn off Juan Bosch, who had succeeded Duvalier's Trujillo friends in Santo Domingo, nocturnal assassins in January 1963 cut the throat of the Dominican consul at Les Cayes. The unfortunate consul, Senor Gerardo Blanco, had reportedly been helping *mulâtres* of the South (for a fee) to slip away with Dominican papers. Others unable or afraid to risk escape began to make arrangements with the Latin American embassies for eventual asylum, thus providing a good thing for ambassadors, who in some instances were able to turn as much as $50,000 on a single case.

On 10 February 1963, the day the constitution prescribed for elections, foolhardy students distributed anti-Duvalier leaflets and went out with paint cans and scrawled Port-au-Prince walls with the obscenity *"Caca Doc"* (Doc is shit). This proved a mistake: some thirty students and their relatives, including several university professors, were arrested, beaten, and tortured; several, after personal interrogation by the president in his basement room, were executed.

Nor was trouble confined to the towns. Under new levies established in March, wretched peasants were taxed on rice and even on the homemade chairs and tables in their huts. When strapping market women protested, the *milice* beat them down. And *macoutes* themselves turned ferociously on each other in Gonaïves, when a carload of Eloïs Maître's Port-au-Prince TTMs clashed with local braves of Zacharie Delva and Charlotin Saint-Fort. Next morning the battered bodies of the Port-au-Princiens were found, genitals stuffed in mouths, again profaning the church portals where, after Msgr. Robert's expulsion, Delva had celebrated Bois Cayman.

While tension mounted within, François Duvalier was facing his most serious challenge from abroad. His chief opponents were the United States and the Dominican Republic, backed by the Organization of American States and the Vatican. Friends and supporters he had none.(40)

Trouble with the Dominicans began on 17 February 1963, when Juan Bosch was inaugurated president in Ciudad Santo Domingo. In the words of the perceptive American ambassador there, John Bartlow Martin, "While Trujillo lived, Duvalier was comfortable. After Trujillo fell, Duvalier became uneasy." Duvalier's uneasiness was justified: the excitable, volatile Bosch, whom Duvalier subsequently called *"ce fou irresponsable,"* was viscerally hostile toward him, and, like most Dominicans, toward all Haitians. (Almost as soon as he was inaugurated, Bosch began to talk of nudging the Haitian military toward a coup. "We want to give hope," he said, "to the Haitian people.") Duvalier reciprocated in the style of Trujillo: [1] he helped to arrange an assassination plot against Bosch (it failed), and [2] he invited four members of the Trujillo family from Spain to Port-au-Prince, accompanied by former officers of SIM (Trujillo's secret police). Their arrival in Port-au-Prince on 28 April heightened the already serious internal and foreign crises pressing upon Duvalier during those weeks.

The United States had by now burned its bridges to Duvalier. While not actively intriguing with his enemies, the U.S. Government was looking about alertly for any possible successor but was finding no one in sight.(41) Like Duvalier, Washington was also looking toward May 15 without any reliable forecast as to how events would turn out.

Early in April, a group of colonels in the *FAd'H* felt the moment had arrived. Headed by Colonel Lionel Honorat, a well-educated, slightly-built *mulâtre,* the plot included those of the patriotic senior officers who still survived, perhaps eight to ten in all. In the usual way of such intrigues, however, there was a leak: on 10 April, D-day, it was Papa Doc who struck. Five of the leaders most implicated made it with their families to the Brazilian embassy.

One who did not flee was Charles Turnier, a handsome, upright, soldierly *noir* from one of Jacmel's fine families. On 14 April Turnier was arrested and taken to the casernes and beaten all night. *"Fai pié-li pédi té"* (Make his feet leave the earth) was the command.(42) Next morning, to end Turnier's agony, another officer shot him through the head. For a week after, just as Soulouque left dead enemies' bodies to rot in the open, what remained of Charles Turnier was allowed to decompose into a heap of offal in the hot sun in the middle of the dusty parade ground.

During the next ten days Duvalier dismissed sixty-nine officers, roughly one third of the officer corps. Virtually all of them, as well as most of the plotters, had received American training. At the same time, there began systematic arrests and roundup of retired or former officers and their families, who were thrown into Fort Dimanche as hostages for the future behavior of the Armed Forces. While this was going on, about 15 April, Clément Barbot, who had been living very quietly at home since release from prison, slipped out of his house in Déprez and, joined by certain trusty friends of earlier times, went underground.

April 22, 1963 opened a new national fête, the Month of Gratitude, during which the Haitian people were called upon to express their gratitude to François Duvalier for all the good things he had done.

A first, if unexpected, expression of feeling toward the president came on 26 April. That morning, as a palace limousine delivered two Duvalier children, Simone, aged fourteen, and Jean-Claude, eleven, at the Methodist Collège Bird, where they went to school, another car slowed alongside. Three shots were fired: each found its mark, killing the driver and two *macoute* bodyguards. The children, who ran inside the schoolyard, were not fired on.

Clément Barbot, the one man who knew enough of Duvalier's methods to fight him, had struck his first blow. With characteristic precision - he loved children and knew the Duvalier youngsters well - he had shot the *macoutes* only.

The spasm that seized Duvalier can be compared only with the insensate rages of Hyppolite. The events that followed can be likened only to 1915. Soldiers and TTMs combed Port-au-Prince, arresting at random, firing weapons in savage panic. Under shoot-to-kill orders with regard to any retired or former military officers, they gunned down Captain Albert Poitevien, former *Garde-Côtes* commandant, on his doorstep. Many hundreds of arrests were made of men, women, and children; all were hustled off to Fort Dimanche. Hardly any ever emerged. One among many never seen again was Colonel Edouard Roy, Haiti's pioneer aviator. Motorists driving cars of the same make as the original attackers' were shot in the streets and their vehicles riddled.

At the height of his frenzy, Duvalier, not yet aware that Barbot was involved, conceived the idea that the marksman who had picked off the *macoutes* could only be former Lieutenant François Benoît, one of the stars of the recently abolished rifle team, who was among those purged in the preceding days. That Benoît had been in asylum inside the Dominican embassy when the attack was executed was ignored. Commanded by the sinister Major Romain, a swarm of *macoutes* and Presidential Guard dashed up to the Benoît home in Bois Verna, opening fire as they deployed. The first bursts of automatic weapons gunned down Benoît's aged father, a retired judge, and his mother and a friend on the front porch. The servants and even the family dogs were killed. The house, battered by hundreds of rounds, was doused with kerosene and then set on fire. Benoît's baby son, Gérard, died in his crib as flames consumed the old gingerbread house. Mme. Benoît, still teaching school though advanced in pregnancy, was warned and got away to the Ecuadorean embassy before *macoutes* attacked the schoolhouse. Balked of their prey, the TTMs stormed, looted, and gutted the home of Lieutenant Benoît's brother. An elderly lawyer, Maître Benoît Armand, was killed because his first name was Benoît.

Belatedly learning that Benoît had been in asylum the whole time, but no less convinced of his guilt, the *Garde Présidentielle* then moved against the Dominican chancery on the Delmas road. Setting up machine guns to cover the building, where they mistakenly thought Benoît had taken refuge (together with twenty-two other fugitives, he was actually in the residence, not the chancery), they ransacked the premises and maltreated the lone woman secretary. This was the first occasion since 1915 that Haitians had violated a foreign diplomatic mission.

Their fury somewhat subsiding, the Duvalierists then invaded the grounds of the Dominican residence but were driven out by the *chargé d'affaires*, Francisco Bobadilla. In sullen rage they ringed the residence with troops and weapons while Benoît and his fellows inside wondered whether their fate might be that of Guillaume Sam.

Besides abhorrence throughout the hemisphere, the savagery in Port-au-Prince evoked two reactions: [1] the Caribbean Ready Amphibious Squadron of the U.S. Atlantic Fleet, complete with the 4th Marine Expeditionary Brigade, was ordered at forced draft to the Gulf of Gonâve(43), [2] Juan Bosch put the Dominican Armed Forces on war footing, sent his navy to sea, massed 3000 troops at Dajabón, Elias Piña, and Jimaní, sent Duvalier an ultimatum demanding withdrawal of troops surrounding the Port-au-Prince embassy, and invoked the Rio Treaty.

Duvalier never blinked. His response the same day, 28 April, was to break relations with Bosch while welcoming the Trujillos and their secret policemen to Port-au-Prince that afternoon on Pan Am flight 431A.

Even as the OAS council was voting to send an investigating team (the OAS ambassadors from Chile, El Salvador, Ecuador, Colombia, and Bolivia) to Port-au-Prince, Dr. Jacques Fourcand, the *macoute* surgeon whose past manipulations of Red Cross aid had caused Haiti to be disaccredited by the International Red Cross, was preparing what in effect was Duvalier's Dessalinian answer.

With revolver at his hip, Fourcand, in a memorable Month of Gratitude oration, lashed out at "Haiti's great and powerful neighbor" as "a democracy of sluts," accused white Americans of raping Negro girls and loosing mad dogs against blacks in Alabama, and in his peroration warned the world what would happen if any foreigner tried to topple Duvalier:

> Blood will flow in Haiti like a river. The land will burn from the North to the South, from the East to the West. There will be no sunrise and no sunset, just one great flame licking the sky. There will be a Himalaya of corpses, the dead will be buried under a mountain of ashes. It will be the greatest slaughter in history.

When Fourcand finished, Duvalier, who had been raptly listening, embraced him.

Seconding Fourcand, Luckner Cambronne called on all Duvalierists to keep their rifles and machetes ready. To set the stage further, after ignoring two telegrams from the OAS, Duvalier abruptly proclaimed out-of-season Carnaval and, as police scraped up the decomposing corpses still surrounding the ruins of the Benoît home, began issuing *taffia* and orders that revelry be unconfined.

The morning the OAS commission reached Port-au-Prince, 30 April, the president had filled the city with *clairin*-soaked peasant mobs (photographs of the enormous sea of faces before the palace that day confirm Duvalier's claim that they numbered 150,000). While drums throbbed and *lambis* and *vaccines* hooted and crowds ululated, the president received the OAS representatives. Behind every ambassador stood a *macoute* with cocked weapon.

For a quarter hour Duvalier sat silent and motionless, unblinking as *Baron Samedi*. Then he addressed them (Diederich and Burt in their *Papa Doc* say he cursed them "in foulest Créole"). When they replied in French, he answered only in Créole. Then, after herding the delegation onto a balcony from which they could see the seething masses packing the Place de l'Indépendance, Louverture, and Dessalines, the president spoke in furious Créole:

Listen carefully, people of Haiti: it is only once every forty years a man is discovered capable of embodying an ideal. Once every forty years. I am the personification of Haiti. Those who seek to destroy Duvalier seek to destroy our fatherland. I am, and I symbolize, a historic moment in your history. God and the people are the source of all power. Twice I have been given power: I have accepted it, and I shall keep it forever . .

Now mixing his words, stuttering angrily sometimes in French, then back to Créole, Duvalier continued with mounting passion:

Bullets and machine guns capable of daunting Duvalier do not exist. They cannot touch me . . . Haitian people, lift up your hearts to the spirit of the Ancestors, prove that you are men, put marrow in your bones, let the blood of Dessalines flow in your veins . . .

Reaching climax, the dictator flung down his *défi*:

I take no orders or dictates from anyone, no matter where they come from. No foreigner shall tell me what to do. As President of Haiti, I am here only to continue the traditions of Toussaint Louverture and of Dessalines. *I am even now an immaterial being . . .*

Then, as the crowd roared and the sacred drums hammered, Duvalier related that, for the first time - inside his head, who knows? - he heard cries of

"Duvalier! Duvalier! Président-à-vie! Duvalier! Duvalier! Président pour-toujours!"(44)
   "Moi," he replied. *"Moi, je suis prêt"* (I am ready).
After fifty-six hours of insult and affront more uncompromising even than Soulouque's defiance of Duquesne, the OAS council went away sorrowing. They knew that 103 persons had so far taken refuge from the terror in foreign embassies; estimates of hostages confined ran as high as 2000. As Graham Greene would report in the *New Republic:*

> Travel on the island is almost at a standstill. The roads were always a deterrent, but now there are roadblocks around Port-au-Prince to the North and controls at every small town to the South. Within a circuit of a few kilometers from Port-au-Prince I was searched four times, and it took me four days at the police station to gain a two-day permit for the South . . .

Then, reflecting on what it was all about, Greene went on,

> There have been many reigns of terror in the course of history. Sometimes they have been prompted by warped idealism like Robespierre's, sometimes they have been directed fanatically against a class or race by some twisted philosophy surely never has terror had so bare and ignoble an object as here.

During these events, Bosch in Ciudad Santo Domingo had, in Ambassador Martin's words, "deliberately whipped up a war atmosphere," but American and OAS restraints (and apparently cold feet on the part of the Dominican military) were holding off the threatened invasion. With his usual spoiling diplomacy, Duvalier, knowing this would goad Washington, had meanwhile outflanked the OAS and taken his case out of the hemisphere to the U.N., where the *macoute* Chalmers delivered a racist appeal aimed at African votes, saying Haiti was defending the cause of black peoples everywhere.(45)

On 12 May, emerging from the *Palais National* for the first time in over two weeks, the president dedicated a new public building (appropriately enough, a new office for the tax bureau, within sight of the Palace), the *Bureau des Contributions* on Rue des Casernes, where Maison Bellegarde had stood and seen so much history. But the engrossing question - was Duvalier preparing to leave the palace for good in three days? remained unanswered.
   The first rumors were that reservations had been booked with KLM for the 15th to fly a Duvalier party to Curaçao and thence to New York. This was amended on the 14th when the CIA confirmed, correctly, that Pan American had Duvalier reservations for space to Paris and thence, via Air France, to Algeria, where Ahmed Ben Bella was supposedly expecting them.

During the night of the 14th, in an atmosphere of anticipation and tension, Foggy Bottom issued its instructions: if Duvalier departed, he might well do so in the *Götterdämmerung* foretold by Fourcand; alternatively, he might unloose the *noirs* in another *semaine sanglante* and remain to preside. In either case, the Marines, who would remain close offshore, would go in to protect the U.S. and foreign communities and put a stop to violence (and Duvalier). The American embassy, coordinating with the Latin American ambassadors, would then bring into being a non-Duvalierist *gouvernement provisoire,* which the Washington planners visualized as being quickly reinforced by the more respectable among returning exile politicians. The OAS and even the U.N. would be asked to bless and support the resulting new regime. Meanwhile, every radio (including not a few aboard the naval flagship) was tuned to Port-au-Prince for news of Duvalier.

Everything in Washington's (and the American embassy's) calculus was sound except that it left out one major eventuality - that, to foreclose any pretext for international intervention, Duvalier might abruptly tune down the terror and stay put.

While the American ambassador offered rum punches to twenty-two foreign reporters on the hilltop lawn of the American embassy residence with its Howard-Johnson white walls and orange roof, the naval amphibious task force took station the next morning under their eyes, and the world waited.

Radio-Commerce, usually so strident, played Tschaikowsky and Massenet interspersed with such soft and lilting favorites as "Choucoune." Gone were the bloodthirsty provocations, and so, mysteriously that morning, were the roadblocks. With every sensible Haitian indoors on this bright May day, Port-au-Prince seemed enveloped in a delicious spring calm punctuated only by the breeze rustling through the scarlet flame trees.

At two in the afternoon Duvalier held a press conference at the palace in the second-floor *Salon Jaune,* where diplomats were usually received. "Fresh pink roses," reported *Newsweek,* "had been placed on every table; on the chandeliers, the motif of the moment was cobwebs. "

Smiling his inscrutable smile through *Baron Samedi* eyeglasses, the president of the republic nodded to his guests and delivered a brief statement: "Haiti will continue under my administration. The country is calm and peaceful . . ." Then he continued: he had no plans to leave - it was all "an Aesop's Fable" (the Haitian consulate general in New York was at that moment canceling Duvalier reservations for Paris and collecting a $6000 refund); there was no crisis save that artificially manufactured by the U.S. Government; as Chief of the Revolution (a title he now assumed), he had merely taken necessary steps to resist subversion and prevent invasion; Haiti had no special relations with any communist country nor plans to declare itself a socialist state; as for the OAS, it had no power to intervene to prevent domestic turmoil . . . "If such a right did exist," Duvalier went on, "why has it not been invoked in Birmingham where there are not only possible threats of violence but actual violence? I sincerely sympathize with the President of the United States in what must be an extremely difficult situation for him."

Then, pleading press of business, François Duvalier inclined his head, again smiled slowly, and retired to his office in the next room.

Nonplussed reporters went down to the cable office to file their stories, the American ambassador's servants brought the chairs and empty glasses inside from the lawn, and Marines offshore took off their packs.

As the unconstitutional second term began, Venezuela and Costa Rica did sever relations (so did the *New York Times,* which editorialized,"Duvalier is sailing a pirate ship. . ."); the United States simply "suspended" relations and withdrew its ambassador (whom Duvalier declared persona non grata and refused to allow back to pick up his household effects). On 3 June, sailing North in the wake of Admiral Gherardi while the State Department "reappraised" its position, the amphibious task force withdrew from the Gulf of Gonaïves.

Looking back on the whole fiasco (which in Washington's terms it was), John F. Kennedy ruefully asked Ambassador Martin, "Wouldn't it have been better if we'd let Bosch go?"

The few discordant notes in that superbly orchestrated performance of May 1963 came from the crack of rifle and pistol shots and the thud of bombs aimed by the one man Duvalier feared.

Clément Barbot had left his calling-card on 26 April. Now, early in May, with Rhéa, his cherished wife, and four children safe inside the Argentine embassy, he was ready to take the field.

In rapid succession, as only he could, Barbot harried and fooled *macoutes* and *milice,* shooting them down from ambush, killing them by tens at a time. Privy even to the mysteries of the telephone system, he got an open line to Duvalier's ornate white phone and warned the president that his coffee was poisoned (Duvalier's reply: "Clément, you will bring me your head . . ."). While Major Jean Tassy, his successor and one of the cruelest men in Haiti, relentlessly combed Pétionville, Barbot raided Fort Dimanche and emptied the armory. A closer call came when pursuers found his Martissant hideout not far from the bomb factory of 1957. But Barbot escaped - all they got was a weapons cache and a black dog who vanished in the night. Haitian suspicions were confirmed: Barbot could at will, as had been widely said, change himself into a black dog. Word went out from Duvalier: shoot black dogs on sight. Barbot's answer was to leave a personal note on Duvalier's desk in the *Palais.*

On 21 May, as Duvalier herded in 50,000 peasants to celebrate the climax of the Month of Gratitude, Barbot's forces (now bearing the title "*Comité des Forces Démocratiques Haïtiennes*") bombed the *Lycée Pétion* and the Collège

St. Pierre (the Episcopal primary school), both co-opted to billet rural militia, and failed to blow up the HASCO fuel dump only because the grenades he used were high explosive, not thermite incendiary. During the night, while mysterious fires reddened the sky over the Cul-de-Sac, rifle fire of a predawn ambush and shootout echoed for hours from Déprez to Martissant.

Meanwhile, on the dark night of 19 May, a daring American reporter, the *Washington Star's* Jeremiah O'Leary, made contact with Barbot himself at a canefield sanctuary near Cazeau, South of Damien. Here for two hours Barbot talked of his struggle, called Duvalier a "madman," said the president had expressly ordered that 300 persons a year be killed by TTMs, and asserted that Duvalier had accumulated more than $1.5 million in a Swiss bank.

"Duvalier," said Barbot in his soft-spoken intense way, "is not a communist, a democrat, or anything else. He is an opportunist."

Then O'Leary was guided out through drenching rain and back to Port-au-Prince.(46)

On 14 July the end came. With ammunition running low, Barbot and his pediatrician brother, Harry, and several followers were betrayed by a peasant. Led by Gracia Jacques, the *Garde Présidentielle* and assorted *milice*, under Eloïs Maître and Luc Désir, ringed the Cazeau hideout and set the cane afire. When flames finally drove them out, the Barbots broke cover and were mowed down in blasts of automatic-weapons fire. Afterward, pictures of their riddled, mutilated corpses were triumphantly displayed throughout Port-au-Prince. It was months to come before any black dog was safe.

The Barbot insurgency, mounted exclusively by *noirs authentiques* striking expertly at the vitals of the regime, imperiled Duvalier to a degree never previously or later attained by his enemies. Nonetheless, the sixteen months following the Barbots' deaths were punctuated by a succession of incursions and guerrilla infiltrations that managed to plunge Haiti into an abyss of violence and terror.(47)

While all eyes focused on the capital, General Cantave, who had returned to the Dominican Republic, was, with some support from the local military, training and organizing a force, at one time 210 strong, for invasion of the North. The Cantave "invasion" materialized during August and September 1963 in a series of piecemeal and fruitless raids and probes, most of which had been betrayed in advance or otherwise compromised.

Ably supported (until a heart attack felled him in the field) by Colonel René Léon, who had fought the Castroites in the hills above Les Irois, Cantave successively took or tried to take Fort Liberté, Ouanaminthe, Mont Organisé, Croix Rouge, and Terrier. In no case did the invaders have munitions or staying power (or frequently the stomach) to get an insurgency going. Cantave's last hurrah was a disastrous frontal attack on the barracks at Ouanaminthe (typically betrayed in advance) on 22 September. Among the dead was former *FAd'H* Captain Blücher Philogènes. On express orders of the president, Philogènes's head was chopped off with a machete, packed in a fast-melting bucket of ice, and flown back to the National Palace. Here, with spiritual counsel from *houngan* Dodo Nasar, Duvalier interrogated the spirit of Philogènes and conversed at length with the head.(48)

Duvalier's spiritual entourage, who assisted him in the rites over Philogènes's head and on other similar occasions, included not only Colonel Gracia Jacques and Dodo Nasar, but *macoute houngans* Zacharie Delva and Edner Day, and the president's food-taster, Pierre Novembre. The coordinator of these *houngans* and *bocors* was Colonel Gabriel Gamier, often referred with the bleak sense of humor that Haitians have perfected as "Ministre des Rélations Occultes."

An immediate sequel to the Barbot and Cantave operations and related Dominican connections was Duvalier's decision to close the border and create a "war zone" some three miles deep along the Haitian side. Commencing in June 1963 and working all summer, *miliciens* expelled peasants, burned their huts, herded off their livestock, and thenceforth shot any person found in this cordon of scorched earth.

In June and July 1964, a year later, Père Georges, in some relationship with the Dominican authorities and also with his fellow anti-Duvalier priest, Père Gérard Bissainthe, was able to organize, train, arm, and land a guerrilla band of elite youths and some former *FAd'H* personnel calling themselves "*Camocains*," who entered Haiti by ship over the beach at Lagon des Huitres East of Saltrou. The *Camocains*, twenty-five strong, were led in the field by Captain Fred Baptiste, one of the best of the officers who had served with Cantave the year before. Taking to the Fôret des Pins and the rugged Morne la Selle, the Camocains readily eluded and frequently ambushed pursuing detachments of the *FAd'H* and *milice*, and excited peasant sympathy by capturing and executing rural TTMs. But the Camocains were finally driven back to the Dominican Republic from a region that had harbored so many *marrons* two centuries earlier because the people, near starvation and scrabble-poor, could not feed them, and the water sources on slopes heavily eroded by Hurricane Flora were all but nonexistent. Another equally critical reason was that the weapons smuggled to the *Camocains* from New York were intercepted by a Haitian communist cell in the Dominican Republic, led by poet Jacques Viau (son of Alfred Viau, who had intrigued with Colonel Roland against Estimé in 1949). Communist sabotage of a promising anti-Duvalier guerrilla movement reinforces questions often raised during the mid-1960s as to the precise nature of Duvalier's relationship with the communists.(49)

The measure of the president's alarm at this time was that he put on the khaki battle dress he had not worn since 1958. Savage reprisals were now the order of the day. At least seventy-three executions, mainly of Fort Dimanche hostages, were reported. Among these, said the *New York Times,* twenty were believed to have been personally shot by Duvalier in the palace basement. Widespread jailings, beatings, and arrests ensued in Jacmel, Port-au-Prince, and throughout the Cul-de-Sac, where rumor falsely told of Camocains. For a week *miliciens* terrorized Croix-des-Bouquets and environs because, it was said, someone had reported seeing a Camocain photographing the strategic police station. To drive home the lesson, two peasants were crucified and left to rot in the sun. Relatives of anti-Duvalier exiles, especially of former *FAd'H* officers in New York - even grandmothers and children - were swept up and in many cases never seen again. Ten members of a single family, including an eighteen-month-old baby, kin of Captain Claude Edeline were arrested and butchered. The warden of Fort Dimanche and leading *fillette-lalo'*(female *macoute*), the sadistic Mme. Max Adolphe of Mirebalais, daily presided over horrors worthy of Buchenwald or the Gulag.(50)

But the guerrilla epic of these times was that of thirteen young men, mostly *mulâtres* from Jérémie, all elite, who landed on 5 August 1964, at Cap Dame Marie on the far tip of the Southern peninsula. Their leader, Gusle Villedrouin, a tall, handsome, twenty-four-year-old erstwhile U.S. airman, was the son of one of the most distinguished former *FAd'H* officers, Colonel Roger Villedrouin, who had been killed during the carnage of May 1963. It has been said that this operation was mounted by the CIA, and it is true that the group, calling itself *Jeune Haïti,* had been associated with the CIA in New York, but the agency's estimates of its chances at this moment were so pessimistic that every effort was made to dissuade the fiery young men from going ahead, to no avail.(51)

As distinguished from all other such landings, *Jeune Haïti's* was at least well prepared; its members were versed in guerrilla weapons and tactics (several had served in the U.S. Armed Forces), and they had a thought-out political concept of trying to win over peasant support. Yet the resemblances and inescapable weaknesses of this neo-Boyer-Bazelais landing in the South by elite invaders who wore shoes doomed *Jeune Haïti* as certainly as Miragoâne.

Foredoomed it may have been, but *Jeune Haïti's* eighty-three-day anabasis to death was nevertheless the most hard-fought guerrilla campaign Haiti had seen since the days of Péralte and Batraville. Balked of their initial objective - to seize Jérémie and raise the standard of revolt in the South - the brave thirteen marched East along the spine of the Southern peninsula, through the crags and fastnesses of Goman and Siffra. Sweeping to the North and South coasts, evading and ambushing government forces in at least ten serious engagements, shooting down a strafing aircraft, and marching well over 200 miles throughout some of Haiti's most difficult and remote terrain, *Jeune Haïti* soldiered on indomitably even while Hurricane Cleo ravaged the South and converted mountain valleys into torrential death traps.

The strategy of Port-au-Prince in response was to cordon off the peninsula at Miragoâne, send in the *FAd'H* Tactical Batallion from the casernes, and flood the hills with rural militia, using the *Corps d'Aviation* for armed reconnaissance.

Each engagement exacted its toll, and there were no peasant recruits. The last stand took place on 26 October 1964. Run to ground at Ravine Roche, near l'Asile, Villedrouin, accompanied by the remaining two survivors (Roger Rigaud, son of Dr. Rigaud, and Réginal Jourdan, kinsman of Hector Riobé), stood off the attackers to the last round, then fought with rocks until they were cut down. Their heads were chopped off, delivered to Duvalier, and photographed so that, on the president's orders, they could be seen on the front page of the next morning's *Le Matin*. Whether Duvalier conversed with the heads is not known.

The simultaneous though wholly uncoordinated campaigns of *Camocains* and *Jeune Haiti* goaded the terror to spasms not attained since the spring of the previous year. Jérémie, historic birthplace of Audubon and Alexandre Dumas (and of most of *Jeune Haïti*), was savaged as in the days of Dessalines and Soulouque. Duvalier simply gave over *mulâtre* Jérémie to the *noir Milice*. Whole families were slaughtered - Villedrouins, Drouins, Guilbauds, Laforests, Sansaricqs, and others. The Drouin and Sansaricq families were stripped naked and herded through the town to execution. Homes and shops belonging to suspected families were looted and then burned, a process the government called "nationalization." At least a hundred prominent Jérémiens died (Peter Benenson, the British lawyer who investigated the Jérémie atrocities for Amnesty International, said "hundreds"), and the *New York Times* reported 200 to 300 victims elsewhere, many of them university and high-school boys, in a "wave of killings" toward the end of August.

Among the chief executioners at Jérémie were Saint-Ange Bontemps, a bloodthirsty *macoute*, and Captain "Sonny" Borges, one of the cruelest of Duvalier's young army officers, whose previous specialty had been running tank treads across the arches of prisoners' feet. According to *Haïti Observateur* (17 March 1978), when in tears tiny Stephane Sansaricq asked to "*faire pipi*" amid the slaughter of her family, Borges said he would wipe her eyes and did so - with the hot end of a lighted cigarette. Then he slashed her to death with a dagger. The balance was redressed on the night of 8 June 1967 when Borges was among these executed by Duvalier at Fort Dimanche as a crony of Max Dominique.

To give a grisly example to Port-au-Prince (which Duvalier reportedly told assembled *miliciens* he was prepared to burn if opposition was not quelled), the body of former Captain Yvan D. Laraque, killed during a rearguard fight at Préville, was flown to the capital. There, on public view, facing the Grande Rue exit from the airport, the swollen, flyblown corpse, flung over a wooden chair, clad only in jockey shorts, was left to rot in public view. Across the street a large sign told tourists: WELCOME TO HAITI.

One final example remained. Two of the thirteen - Louis Drouin and Marcel Numa (lone *noir* among the band) - had fallen into government hands alive. After fearful tortures, at seven in the morning of 12 November, Drouin and Numa were driven by jeep to the cemetery wall where Massillon Coicou had died, pinioned to pine posts beside their graves, and shot by a nine-man firing squad personally commanded by newly promoted Colonel Franck Romain.(52) The proceedings were televised and rebroadcast daily for a week, but there was hardly need: Duvalier had declared a public holiday, closed all shops, and bussed schoolchildren down to the Cimetière. Afterward, reported *Time,* "the crowd was marched to the National Palace, where Duvalier, acceding to its 'solicitations,' appeared on the balcony to smile and wave."

Thermidor

> Man talks without acting. God acts without talking. Duvalier is God.
>
> - Duvalierist slogan

Early in 1964, just as in the days of Dessalines so long ago, army officers began circulating petitions that François Duvalier heed the voices demanding he become president for life. Almost simultaneously that spring, a commission under Ulrick Saint-Louis, appointed to launder the 1957 constitution into conformity with later realities, brought in a memorable draft appointing Duvalier (like Toussaint) *président-à-vie* with power to name his successor and referring to him throughout as "the Sovereign." This the unicameral National Assembly ratified on 25 May.

The process failed to keep up with events. On 1 April, with Dessalinian haste, Duvalier installed himself as lifetime president of the world's first hereditary republic. "It is not easy," the president explained, "to find a man who has complete confidence in himself and in his country, and who determines to maintain its dignity and its prestige; such a revolutionary is found only once every fifty or seventy-five years . . . I have a holy mission to fulfil, a mission which will be fulfilled entirely."

The constitution, with its new dispensations, he announced, would be submitted to the people for ratification by plebiscite on 14 June. In the meantime, carrying through one of the rare measures on which the country had balked in 1958, the *président-à-vie* discarded the horizontal blue and scarlet flag designed by Pétion, and adopted, as part of the new constitution, a black and red design blazoned with *lambi* and *pinone*, said to have been used by Dessalines and Christophe. The black was placed beside the staff because, in the words of Député Pierre Armand, "black is the color of the true Haiti." Père Albert Dorélien, Duvalier's priestly thurifer, officially consecrated the new colors on 21 June 1964.(53)

About this same time, official decrees and pronouncements emanating from the palace began capitalizing, in the prerogative of deity, personal pronouns referring to The Sovereign. The press quickly caught on: in June, shortly before the plebiscite, *Oédipe* ran a half-tone of Christ with his hand on the shoulder of Duvalier. The legend: *"Je Lui ai choisi"* (He is My chosen one.)

On the day, reported the government, exactly 2,800,000 Haitians casting ballots pre-printed "Oui" ratified the new order of things. The 3234 who voted *"Non"* were mostly arrested on charges of defacing a ballot.

To set the tone of years ahead, Paul Blanchet issued to Duvalierist faithful a *Catéchisme de la Révolution*, which, like the Jacobin blasphemies of Sonthonax, mocked the form and liturgy of catechism.(54)

Q. Who are Dessalines, Toussaint, Christophe, Pétion, and Estimé?

A. Dessalines, Toussaint, Christophe, Pétion, and Estimé are five distinct Chiefs of State who are substantiated in and form only one and the same President in the person of François Duvalier.

In place of the Lord's Prayer, Duvalierist children were bidden to say, "Our Doc, who art in the *Palais National* for life, hallowed be Thy name by present and future generations. Thy will be done in Port-au-Prince as it is in the provinces. Give us this day our new Haiti and forgive not the trespasses of those antipatriots who daily spit upon our country; lead them into temptation, and, poisoned by their own venom, deliver them from no evil ..."

On 22 May 1964, for the first time since 1960, an American ambassador was in Port-au-Prince and felicitated the *president-à-vie* on his ascension to ultimate office. In the person of Ambassador B. E. L. Timmons III, the American government in 1964 resumed cordial relations, which Washington, fooling no one, kept describing as "cool and correct." On 8 April, a week after Duvalier's investiture, Lyndon Johnson told a new Haitian ambassador, André Théard, "This Government looks forward to close cooperation and solidarity with the Government of Haiti."(55)

These were no idle words: the State Department, which had been discouraging American tourists and businessmen from visiting and investing in Haiti, suddenly ceased frowning. Swallowing hard, the Inter-American Development Bank found it had $2.6 million to lend Duvalier for "waterworks repairs." The U.S. Navy quietly resumed liberty visits to Port-au-Prince and the Cap. The Kennedy economic cold war (which all but broke Duvalier's back in 1962-1963) was thus allowed to thaw.

It has been suggested that one reason for Washington's abrupt turnaround from Kennedy hostility toward Duvalier was the latter's prompt retention after Lyndon Johnson's inauguration of an American lobbyist with major Texas accounts (including the all-powerful Murchisons, who owned Caribbean Mills, the U.S. milling enterprise in Haiti), and with ties to Mr. Bobby Baker, the convicted Johnson protégé who had invested heavily in HAMPCO, a Croix-des-Missions meat packing venture.

Setting aside perhaps oversimplified conclusions prompted by the above and similar evidence, the State Department, which in 1965 would feel the fierce heat resulting from U.S. intervention in the Dominican Republic, had in any case concluded by 1964 that a showdown with Duvalier (who after all had votes in the OAS and the U.N.) was not really necessary and ought at least to be deferred. Policy therefore veered toward the "cool and correct," which in practicalities meant nursing Duvalier along much as, for similar reasons of expediency, Washington had propped up Trujillo until near the end of his days. Working mainly through various indirect channels, American aid was thus resumed.(56) It was, together with international aid from the U.N., Canada, West Germany, the Inter-American Development Bank, and American charitable agencies whose help was once again welcome, to continue until the death of Duvalier. It was a curious process: as Rotberg remarked. "He managed both to display enmity toward foreign benefactors and shamelessly to take advantage of their generosity."

Along with fulsome praise for Marx, Lenin, Ataturk, Nkrumah, and Mao Tse Tung ("I associate myself with them," Duvalier said in 1967), he rarely omitted to refer to Lyndon Johnson as "my great colleague."

Even while the regime was thus taking in foreign aid exceeding $5 million a year (about ten percent of the national budget), Duvalier was collecting, and concealing in the malodorous "nonfiscal accounts" originated by Estimé. about $10 million annually, which never saw the budget. This sum came mostly from the *Régie du Tabac*, which under Duvalier extended its original monopoly to cement, dental products, air conditioners, flour, sugar, condensed milk, automobiles, textiles, alcohols, perfumes, matches, and electronic equipment. Where the money went (save into the *Banque Commerciale*, run by Duvalier bagman Clémard-Joseph Charles) was never explained, but the best conjecture is that it was primarily used to pay or reward top *macoutes*. It was the measure of Duvalier's extraordinary force of character that no nation or agency rendering aid to Haiti ever openly challenged the nonfiscal accounts during his presidency.

Reversing history, the Pope was soon to make his journey to Canossa over a road at least as rocky as that just traveled by the United States.

At the height of the terror, in early 1964, Duvalier, excommunicate and caring not, had dealt the Church his heaviest blow. On trumped-up evidence, after arresting two priests for an alleged "attempt against the security of the Republic," the president expelled from Haiti the entire Jesuit order. In the words of their Superior, the Canadian Father Gérard Goulet, "In 1763 [the Jesuits] were considered to be too devoted to the religious welfare of the enslaved *noirs*. In 1963, they were considered too influential and perilous for the security of the state. Basically, this represented the same traditional calumnies under new pretenses."

Effective the same day (15 February 1964) the government locked up Villa Manrèse, the Jesuits' Turgeau retreat house, disestablished the Jesuit parish at Quartier Morin, and, in a gesture resembling the closing of the Académie Militaire, shut down the *Grand Séminaire*, bringing home fifty-two young seminarians, with orders to report daily to the police. The Canadian Foreign Minister protested vigorously. The Vatican had no one left to protest: in 1962, Msgr. Ferrofino, the apostolic nuncio, had been withdrawn.(57)

In late 1965, however, through negotiations entrusted to Adrien Raymond, the sophisticated diplomat brother of Colonel Raymond, Duvalier intimated to the Vatican that the time had come to patch things up. His price was simple enough and, historically speaking, a worthy one: an end to the centuries-old ecclesiastical colonialism of France over the Catholic Church in Haiti. Specifically, what the president wanted was a Haitian episcopacy.

What he also wanted the Church to swallow were bitter memories of the expulsion of Msgrs. Poirier, Augustin, and Robert, and of the Jesuits; of repeated persecutions, abuse, and expulsions of other priests, nuns, and religious, Haitian and foreign; of the suppression of *La Phalange;* of *macoute* profanation of the cathedral; of the blasphemous abominations of Delva in Gonaïves; and of the elevation of Voodoo to very nearly official status as a religious establishment.

To err is human, to forgive divine. So reasoning, Pope Paul VI acceded to further discussions in early 1966 that led a Vatican delegation, as in days before the concordat, again to Port-au-Prince. Headed by Msgr. Antonio Samoré, the clerics put best face onto a protocol of 15 August 1966, that, after reservation on certain choices, accepted Duvalier's nominations for a native hierarchy, withdrew decrees of expulsion against the three bishops (but not the Jesuits), and ultimately returned an apostolic nuncio (Msgr. M. J. Lemieux) to Port-au-Prince. Bishops Poirier and Robert were pensioned; Msgr. Augustin was grudgingly allowed to return but only as coadjutor without right of succession, to the rural see of Port-de-Paix. *La Phalange* remained shut. François Duvalier's excommunication was lifted. Henceforth, conspicuous behind the president's desk (was it an icon or was it a trophy?) there would stand a silver-framed inscribed photo of the Supreme Pontiff. This time, the holy oil truly came from Rome, not Marseilles. Where even Soulouque had failed, Duvalier had prevailed.(58)

The five new Haitian prelates were François Wolff-Ligondé, Archbishop of Haiti; Claudius Angénor (whom Duvalier had arrested in 1965 for praying for political prisoners), Bishop of Cayes; Emmanuel Constant, Bishop of Gonaïves; Jean-Baptiste Decoste, Bishop of Port-au-Prince; and Carl Edward Peters (descended from the great Bazelais), auxiliary at Cayes. They were not, drily commented the redoubtable anti-Duvalierist Raymond Sapène, "chosen exactly by chance." Would not Ligondé subsequently assure the president: "Excellency, your authority partakes of the Divine"?

The consecrations took place in a grand service in the cathedral on 28 October 1966. Msgr. Samoré presided; among the consecrants, emerging briefly from retirement at his beloved Cap, was Msgr. Jan, for so many years French bishop in the North. Enemies of Duvalier would say the Church had been *"macoutisée"* or, worse, *"zombifiée."* Yet the fact remained: any *noir* altar boy might henceforth aspire to the archbishop's miter and cathedra; never again would a French *blanc* stand between Haitians and the throne of Bon-Dieu.

After 1964, despite intermittent political tremors that never seriously threatened the regime, Duvalier's worst disasters were natural. On the heels of Hurricane Flora in 1963 - which had killed 5000, left 100,000 homeless, and wiped out 95 percent of the cattle and over half the coffee in the South - had come Cleo in 1964, Inez in 1966, which killed thousands and all but razed Jacmel, and then devastating floods at the Cap in 1968. The international community, and particularly the United States, reacted with generous aid. The main responses of the government were to try to collect as much foreign disaster-relief as possible in cash; to keep a close eye on the U.S. Navy's rescue helicopters to see that they weren't landing Marines; and to declare periods of national mourning.

By 1965, Duvalier had survived and prevailed. He had mastered Haiti, stamped down internal enemies and rivals, fended off invasion by exiles, and brought the United States and the Church to heel.

Through it all, the face of Haiti remained little changed. *Time* reported in May 1966: "Phone service is dead. Lights wink on and off fitfully. Main waterfront roads are pot-holed or sometimes buried in six inches of muddy ooze. Business is grinding to a halt . . ."

To the *New York Times's* Richard Eder, one of Haiti's most perceptive observers, a visiting African diplomat confided: "If in fifty years my country is in a condition like this, I would wish we had never won our independence." Duvalier could have rejoined that Haiti had never enjoyed the advantages of being colonized.

The only ways of escape were essentially those open to slaves in bygone St. Domingue: suicide or *marronage*. The new *marronage* was exile, sometimes legal, sometimes by secret flight, often to the Bahamas by open boat. Unwanted by the newly independent Bahamian government, Haitian refugees, when caught, were harshly treated by their fellow blacks and deported back. (There were widespread charges that Duvalier suborned high officials of the Pindling government in Nassau to pursue these inhumane tactics, which for not a few deportees amounted to death.) By 1970, it was estimated that, legally or illegally, close to 35,000 Haitians were in the Bahamas.

The measure of the exodus was that, in 1976, 150,000 Haitians were in New York City alone, with large colonies in Montreal, Chicago, and Washington. Robert Rotberg said that, by the mid-1960s, 80 percent of Haiti's qualified professionals (doctors, lawyers, engineers, teachers, and public administrators) were in the United States, Canada, or Africa. By the same year, 1963, over a thousand Haitian professionals were in the Congo. Colonel Paul Corvington, one of the best professional officers of the *Garde*, was a senior officer in Mobutu's army; Rigaud Magloire was a principal fiscal adviser in Kinshasa. Of 70 schoolteachers trained by U.S. AID, none of whom Duvalier would hire, 38 went to the Congo - to fight illiteracy. In Ghana an exiled Haitian Episcopal priest had risen to an Anglican bishopric. By 1963, over 300 Haitian professionals were working in Guinea. Joseph Déjean became counselor in Sekou Touré's Ministry of Foreign Affairs. In 1975 Ulrick Joseph received one of Togo's highest awards for brilliant successes over eight years in combating illiteracy. Over 300 Haitian specialists - primarily doctors, teachers, public-health nurses, engineers, and even judges - had been hired by or through the United Nations for jobs in the Congo, Dahomey, Guinea, Togo, Rwanda, and Burundi. With the lowest per capita income and literacy rate in the Western hemisphere, Haiti nonetheless was contributing more technicians to the U.N. Technical Assistance Program than any other Latin American nation.

Aside from Duvalier's dead-end social policies, which in effect rendered Haiti's professional people jobless exiles within their own homeland, Haitians fulfilled two invaluable political requirements for the U.N. in Africa: they spoke French and they were black. By 1970, there were more Haitian physicians in either Montreal or New York than Haiti. Montreal had ten times more Haitian psychiatrists than Port-au-Prince. Of 246 medical-school graduates from 1959 to 1969 from the University of Haiti, only three could be found in practice in the country in 1969. Some 50 public-health nurses, trained by the United States, were all lost to Africa. The Organization of American States and the U.N. had more Haitian economists on their payrolls than the government of Haiti.

The creation of this new diaspora of Haitians was ultimately to have significant consequences both economic and political for Haiti and the United States.

The departure of these intellectual, articulate, aspiring people was, regardless of brain drain, not unwelcome to Duvalier. At home, each in his own way would have focused discontent and potential turbulence. Better to have them abroad, out of the way; Haiti, at least by Justin Bouzon's measure, would be quieter.

On Ancestors' Day, 1966, François Duvalier proclaimed Thermidor. "The time has come," he said, "to put an end to the explosive phase of the Duvalier revolution."

Within four months the president was more explicit. In a rare press conference within the palace he scarcely left save in secret or by night, Duvalier said the time had come "for every Haitian, wherever he is, to come home . . . The Haitian soil belongs to every Haitian." Then he went still further: "In every democracy we should have an opposition. Otherwise, it would be what you call a graveyard."(59)

Graveyard or not, foreign tourists, who were the real targets of Duvalier's appeal, could see differences.(60) *macoute douaniers* at the airport no longer shook out the briefcases and toilet articles of arriving visitors. Curfew was lifted. Roadblocks disappeared. Newsmen were no longer followed as they left the Oloffson Hotel; they were even allowed to file uncensored reportage via the cable office. Every foreign travel agent, promoter, or carpetbagger received a hearty welcome. *Miliciens* no longer guarded street corners. Two Miami public-relations firms were retained. The new Minister of Tourism, the slippery de Catalogne, affably received reporters, wrote Richard Eder, "on his flower-bordered terrace, his considerable bulk covered by blue silk pajamas."

At the height of what the *Washington Star's* Jeremiah O'Leary called Duvalier's "charm period," came a state visit on 24 April 1966, from no less a personage than Emperor Haile Selassie of Ethiopia, accompanied by his sister, Princess Sophia Dhesta. The Lion of Judah declined to stay overnight but his day-long visit was marked by two long Duvalier addresses and somewhat briefer replies in Amharic, a palace luncheon, a reception where decorations were exchanged, and a joint communique. It was rhapsodically described by Duvalier in his memoirs as "an enormous success in the domain of diplomacy." In a relative way, it was: Haile Selassie was the only chief of state to visit Haiti during Duvalier's fourteen-year reign (save for a short stop in 1965 by Nigeria's Azikiwe). For Port-au-Prince, the visit meant a general cleanup and street repaving along the emperor's itinerary as well as the filling of every pothole between the newly opened jet airport (built finally with internally generated funds by Haitian engineer Alix Cinéas under the watchful eye of Clovis Désinor) and town. Unlike Tonton Nord, Duvalier boasted of receiving Ethiopia's Grand Collar of the Order of the Queen of Sheba: Benito Sylvain would have been happy.

In June 1966, receiving the Detroit News's Allan Blanchard and three other U.S. reporters, Duvalier, after denying the existence of press censorship (that day, the incoming *New York Times* had been scissored before delivery to subscribers), pronounced: "In Haiti we have a democracy. Papa Doc is not a dictator, he is a democrat . . . I am a scientist." While he rambled on in halting English, the journalists were fascinated by his desk paperweight, a huge .45 revolver.(61)

Blanchard inquired about the pistol. In professed amazement, the president looked down at his desk. Then he gingerly lifted the weapon between thumb and finger as if it were a dead mouse and, giggling through gold teeth, ordered an aide, "Take it away."

Almost unbelieving, Milan Kubic of *Newsweek* summed up:

"Duvalier impressed me as Big Brother masquerading as the Mad Hatter."

The president's view of himself naturally differed. Atop the reviewing stand on the Champ de Mars each night flashed an illuminated sign with six-foot letters:

JE SUIS LE DRAPEAU HAITIEN. UN ET INDIVISIBLE.
- DR. F. DUVALIER

Duvalier was right. The state, like the flag, had become his own.

The Year Ten, and After

In August 1963, the respected International Commission of Jurists, a Geneva-based organization dedicated to peace through law, had flayed the Duvalier regime:

The rule of law has been replaced by a reign of terror [Haiti] has become the poorest country in Latin America as a result of the incompetence, inertia, and corruption of its government . . . The reprehensible dictatorship of François Duvalier has a unique character. In today's world there are many authoritarian regimes. Generally speaking, they are the reflection of some ideology. The tyranny that oppresses Haiti does not even have that excuse; its only object is to place the country under tribute in order to ensure the future affluence of those in power.

In September 1967 the commission condemned Duvalier in, if possible, even stronger terms:

It is difficult to describe the present state of affairs with any accuracy. The systematic violation of every single article and paragraph of the Universal Declaration of Human Rights seems to be the only policy which is respected and assiduously pursued in this Caribbean Republic. The rule of law was long ago displaced by a reign of terror and the personal will of its dictator, who has awarded himself the title of Life President of the Republic, and appears to be more concerned with the suppression of real or imaginary attempts against his life than with governing the country. He is leading his nation not in the direction of prosperity but towards the final disaster that can be seen in its political, social, and economic collapse.

These and other such comminations had been well earned. Yet the Haitian situation was especially baffling because, in peculiarly contradictory and typical ways, Haiti under Duvalier met (while simultaneously mocking) every goal advanced by reformist liberals for Latin American development and progress.

- Was it civilian supremacy over the military? Who could be more civilian or more supreme than Dr. Duvalier?

- Was it land reform? Pétion and Boyer had carried through the first agrarian reform in the Western hemisphere: within thirty years after independence, two thirds of the population were landowners.

- Was it a docile, non-feudal, non-landowning Church with a native hierarchy, sticking to spiritual matters, eschewing temporal? Haiti had it.

- Was it self-development? Duvalier would point to Luckner Cambronne and Duvalierville, and the millions undoubtedly raised by the MRN.

- Was it popular redress against a selfish, haughty elite? No other elite in Latin America save Cuba's had been so thoroughly chastened and chastised.

Over Duvalier's first decade - described by him as "the decade of development" - the economic regression of Haiti had been staggering. Socially and morally, the country was mired in apathy and despair.

As the United Nations has pointed out, Haiti was the only nation in the world experiencing almost no growth during most of the 1950s and 1960s (while the expanding birth rate had caused the individual gross national product to slump by an annual rate of 2.3 percent between 1961 and 1967). At the same time, the cost of living (assigning an index of 100 to 1943) had spiraled from 112 in 1957 to 135.2 ten years later. Agricultural production had declined 13 percent; generation of electricity had dropped 4 percent; cement production, an index of housing construction, was down 43 percent. Internal debt, $4 million in 1946, was $52.1 million twenty-one years later.(62)

When *New York Times* correspondent Henry Giniger stopped by Port-au-Prince in August 1967, he reported:

Haiti's economy is showing no forward movement . . . Even casual study of the economic situation shows no parallel for the state of the Haitian economy anywhere in the Western hemisphere. Every other country is showing some economic growth. It is generally agreed here that Haiti was probably better off two centuries ago when French colonists were efficiently exploiting her as a source of colonial products . . . . Projects to develop farm production entail turning the clock back. Efforts are being made, for example, to restore roads and irrigation ditches to the condition they were in during French colonial days.

This was the condition of Haiti in 1967, advertised and proclaimed as *l'An X de la Révolution Duvalieriste.*

The Year Ten was to be celebrated by four days special Carnaval marking Duvalier's sixtieth birthday (14 April). The impresario of these and other doings was the president's *mulâtre* son-in-law, Luc Albert "Prince Albert" Foucard, married to Nicole. Foucard's sister, the ambitious and attractive Francesca St. Victor, was Duvalier's private secretary and, in the words of Diederich and Burt, "more than just a secretary."

Duvalier's other son-in-law, Colonel Max Dominique (at six-feet seven, the tallest man ever to graduate from the Académie Militaire), was married to Marie-Denise, the old man's favorite. He was also at daggers drawn with the Foucards, as for good cause also was Mme. Duvalier, supported by her son, young Jean-Claude.

On 15 April, while nine beauty queens were being slowly towed past the palace on floats, there was a heavy detonation and the ice-cream peddler's pushcart, where the bomb had been planted, disappeared in a vanilla-strawberry cloud of splinters. Four people were killed and forty injured. Soon afterward, an explosive charge went off under a *camionnette* laden with musicians playing a Duvalier *meringue.* The bombs were Max Dominique's way of dampening the festivities organized by his rival, Prince Albert.

Near midnight on 8 June, a messenger aroused *FAd'H* chief General Gérard Constant from his heavy slumber. With eighteen other senior officers, including Colonel Dominique, the general was summoned to the *Palais.* Characteristically, the president let them wait two hours. Then, in the noon of night, with a phalanx of *macoutes* brandishing submachine guns, Duvalier appeared. Without explanation the officers were herded into a large truck, which under escort jolted across town to Fort Dimanche.

When the convoy halted beside the butts of the rifle range, the officers realized with mingled horror and relief why they were there. Bound to nineteen stakes stood nineteen brother officers, ten from the *Garde Présidentielle,* each an intimate of Dominique's. Off to one side, *Baron Samedi* incarnate, stood the black-clad president. With a *macoute*'s submachine gun at each man's back, the nineteen senior officers were handed rifles with one round in the chamber, and formed, under the macabre glare of headlights, into a firing squad, each man facing an old friend. On Duvalier's high-pitched *Guédé* command, the officers raised their rifles and leveled them at the figures in front of them. On the president's word, a volley stuttered in the night. Then Duvalier had the executioners file slowly past each crumpled figure for a long final look, and sent them back to bed. Few slept soundly.

By sunrise there was a rush for the Latin American embassies. That day at least 87, some said 108, Haitians took asylum: before the month was up, the total neared 200, not including 3 Haitian ambassadors who defected abroad. Conspicuous among the refugees was the grand inquisitor, Jean Tassy, who thoughtfully took into the Brazilian embassy 20 relatives (but not his brother, Harry, who had died at Fort Dimanche) and a complete set of secret-police dossiers as well as Duvalier's meticulously kept execution records, all of which eventually reached the files of the CIA. Other notable fugitives were Lucien Chauvet and palace chaplain Père Hilaire. Those not fortunate enough to reach embassies included the *macoute* Ministers of Interior and Justice, Jean Julmé and Rameau Estimé (who were never again seen after entering Fort Dimanche), and Clémard-Joseph Charles, the rags-to-riches banker, who was eventually released, penniless, after having turned over a sheaf of signed blank checks on each of his Swiss accounts.

On Mme. Duvalier's intercession, the Dominiques and their children were allowed to go abroad to that sinecure of exiles, the Europe-based post of inspector of embassies. Before the aircraft carrying them was out of sight, Colonel Dominique's chauffeur and two bodyguards were seized by TTMs and shot. Dominique's aged father was arrested at home and died of maltreatment at Fort Dimanche. With his old ferocity, Duvalier is said to have cabled Dominique: GIVE ME BACK MY DAUGHTER AND I WILL GIVE YOU BACK YOUR FATHER.

Confronting the packed embassies, Duvalier took one further step. On 1 August of the Year Ten, Haiti deepened its alienation from the hemisphere by denouncing existing treaties that provided for the right of asylum.(63)

It mattered not: Duvalier cared no more for OAS or Latin American opinion than he had for the Church. He had already flouted the OAS charter by assuming life presidency. In 1967, when the Inter-American Commission on Human Rights again asked for information on political atrocities and prisoners, Duvalier and *macoute* Chalmers again ignored them.

One voice to which Duvalier, not to mention thousands of his subjects, listened more attentively originated in New York. There, at 6:00 A.M., as dawn hit the Caribbean, a young Haitian journalist, Raymond Alcide Joseph, would sip strong coffee in the Madison Avenue studio of Station WRUL and broadcast highly informed Haitian news briefs interspersed with sharp jabs at Duvalier and his men.

Joseph was the voice and intellectual sparkplug of the *Coalition Haïtienne*, a moderate group of exiles mainly supported by Paul Magloire. The coalition eschewed filibustering and violence: not for them the Florida Keys fiasco of 1966, Operation Nassau, when, with CBS reporters handing out money and writing the script, Père Georges and Cuban gunrunner Rolando "El Tigre" Masferrer were restrained by federal agents from a maladroit attempt to invade the North on CBS Evening News. Appropriately, one initial press account of Operation Nassau appeared in *Variety*, which treated the affair as a showbiz happening.

No Haitian with a transistor would miss "Six O'Clock Mass," which, broadcast in Créole, was a hairshirt for Duvalier. Since, on White House instructions, the Voice of America had discontinued Créole broadcasts, Radio *Vonvon* (Vonvon= Bug, Joseph's signature) for over three years provided the only competition for René Depestre's two daily hours of Créole over Radio Havana. Using jamming equipment whose export was mysteriously licensed by the U.S. Government, Duvalier worked hard to jam *Vonvon* but never Radio Havana.(64)

Duvalier's relation to Haitian communists remained ambivalent as ever. From the beginning, he not only maintained communists in his cabinet and inner circle (Paul and Jules Blanchet and Hervé Boyer) but countenanced continuing clandestine contacts between the regime and Fidel Castro and with the French and Mexican Communist Parties. And Duvalier made skilled use of these connections to needle Washington. Lucien Daumec was, for example, allowed to attend a propaganda school in Rumania; while, in November 1961, Duvalier sent Jules Blanchet on a secret mission to Warsaw and Vienna to try to negotiate Russian aid for Haiti.

In a 1963 Scripps-Howard interview, the American ambassador aptly characterized Duvalier's tactics: "I don't believe President Duvalier himself is a communist but he finds it useful to throw them in our face, and so far he seems to have them under control. We also know that the communists here maintain links with Castro in Cuba and with the international communist base in Mexico . . . The longer it goes on, the better is the chance the Commies [sic] will get control."

Speaking more bluntly that same year, a State Department spokesman in Washington said Haitian communists came from two sources: "the people's misery and Duvalier's extraordinary tolerance of them."

Duvalier, however, never tolerated communists when he felt they represented a threat. Back in 1960, *noir authentique* Jacques Alexis (son of Stephen Alexis, author of *Le Nègre Masqué*) had left Haiti for world travels that took him to Moscow, Peking, and Cuba, as official representative of the *Parti Entente*

Populaire, a communist group founded in 1958. In April 1961, sailing from Baracoa (origin of the 1959 Castro "invasion"), Alexis, with four Haitians and $20,000 in cash, landed at the Môle. Here, instead of being greeted as liberators, the revolutionaries were trussed up by peasants, handed over to the garrison, and thrown into slime-coated *oubliettes* at Fort St. George, where in their day Similien and Bellegarde had languished. After several days' beating and torture, the five were led out under the ramparts and, on orders from the president, stoned to death by the peasants they had come to save.

Although officially outlawed, domestic communist activity had, however, been sanctioned since Duvalier took office. Besides the PEP mentioned above, the elite, headed by *mulâtre* René Depestre, who cordially detested Jacques Alexis, in 1958 organized their own *Parti Populaire pour la Libération Nationale*. Like Estimé, Duvalier toyed with both, shutting his eyes when it suited him but also killing Alexis, as well as, in 1966, PPLN leaders Mario Rameau and Jacques Ambroise. In December 1968, following long negotiations, the two parties finally merged to form a single *Parti Unifié Communiste Haïtien (PUCH)*, which *Tass* on 31 March 1969 duly hailed: "The united party will guide the struggle of the proletariat to . . . seize power and build socialism in Haiti."(66)

The newly unified party (fired to imprudent action, it was said, by Cuban precepts) had not long to await its first test. On 17 April 1969 (referring to a *macoute* shootout with communists at Boutillier on the slopes of Morne l'Hôpital on the 14th), Radio Moscow "Peace and Progress" reported arrests and summary executions of Haitian communists. Another clash a week earlier at Cazale, near Arcahaie, had claimed the life of Alix Lamaute, veteran communist organizer and syndicalist. At the Cap (if we are to believe a letter from Graham Greene to the *Times* of London), not only communists and anti-Duvalierists were killed by TTMs, but the impoverished dwellers of La Fossette were shot down by "indiscriminate machine-gunning." On 2 May, *FAd'H* units and *miliciens* surrounded a house in Fontamara, outside Port-au-Prince, shot the building to pieces with automatic weapons and grenades, and, after some seven hours' battering, reported the death of twenty-two (some accounts said thirty-five) communist defenders, including Joseph Roney (who had led the student strikes in 1960) and Gerald Brisson (whose sister was communist Minister Hervé Boyer's secretary). In what had become a commonplace of the regime, over twenty mangled bodies were publicly exhibited outside Fort Dimanche.

Ramparts, a U.S. magazine, later reported that the PUCH had launched "an underground guerrilla campaign" against Duvalier, but that there was an informer on the party's central committee and "more than 200 PUCH cadres were slain in the Duvalier counteroffensive."

Why Duvalier struck the communists so hard and so suddenly nevertheless remains unanswered. *Combattant,* so often well informed, said the communists were merely a pretext for another of Duvalier's purges, and charged that hundreds of victims - denounced as "agents of internal Communism" - were killed, tortured, or arrested, and their homes looted by *macoutes*. Another surmise, not inconsistent, was that the communists were conspicuously targeted as part of a charade to set the stage for the July visit to Haiti by U.S. presidential representative Nelson Rockefeller (which in the event did result in final melting of official American disapproval of Duvalier).(66)

That Duvalier had lost none of his power to strike or strike back had been demonstrated against others than communists. On three occasions, in 1968, 1969, and 1970, he repulsed and survived exile-supported attempts to overthrow him.

Duvalier's military vitality was not as surprising as it might seem. As early as September 1964 - when the U.S. Government apparently winked at the illegal export to Haiti of military aircraft (two T-28s, one R4D, and two SNBs) - Washington had been quietly helping him rebuild the *Corps d'Aviation*. Subsequently, the United States without publicity licensed the export of an additional F-51 fighter and in some fashion funded commercial overhauls in Miami of all five Haitian F-51s and the other hitherto grounded military planes of the *Corps d'Aviation*. In November 1970, the Nixon administration dropped all pretense of a ban on arms exports, granting licenses to arms-sales firms for a variety of light weapons and six 65-foot patrol boats for the *Garde-Côtes*. By 1971, over $1 million in private U.S. arms sales to Haiti had been approved.

Not only because of the political cycle but also because it is the end of the coffee and sugar harvests, when peasants are laid off and money and food grow short, May is the season for coups and invasions. On 20 May 1968, after a morning leaflet-strike on Port-au-Prince (in which someone forgot to untie the packed propaganda leaflets), two Bahama-based aircraft landed at the Cap and disgorged a landing force of some thirty-five invaders garbed in jungle-camouflage suits labeled "Big Game: Styled by Broadway." One of the aircraft took off to shuttle in reinforcements while the invaders began a spirited attack across the salt flats toward the Cap.

Duvalier's immediate response was to execute numerous (the *Coalition Haïtienne* said fifty-seven) hostages at Fort Dimanche and order all members of his cabinet and chief *macoutes* to repair to the palace and stay there under guard, sleeping at night, Mafia style, on mattresses in the council chamber. Then he sent two sinister messengers, Colonel Romain and Major Monod Philippe, to the North with soldiers and *miliciens*. For good measure, he ordered Zacharie Delva North from Gonaïves to take charge of the Cap and crush any murmur of sedition or unrest, a task he performed with murderous zest.

But the invaders' game was already up. The aircraft that flew away for reinforcements never returned: the pilot got cold feet. And the seaborne follow-up echelon, nearly a hundred men with heavy weapons and supplies, never left the Bahamas because, incredibly, their small ship was accidentally allowed to sink. The rebels held the air-field and outskirts of the Cap for forty-eight hours, until units of the *Garde-Côtes* steamed up from Bizoton and shelled them into submission. Several insurgents were killed, ten were taken, and a few vanished toward Santo Domingo. The remaining aircraft, a World War II B-25, was claimed as a war prize, like the *Molly C,* and eventually joined the *Corps d'Aviation.*

On 4 June a year later, Port-au-Prince had another air raid, this time by an aged Constellation carrying, as it later proved, Colonel René Leon, a second Haitian, and several U.S. and Canadian mercenaries. Dropping improvised incendiaries, which (like every other bomb so far dropped on Port-au-Prince) malfunctioned, the plane nonetheless reduced the capital to panic. In the wholesale *courri* that ensued, palace antiaircraft cannon sprayed the skies, over thirty serious auto accidents took place, fire engines and ambulances raced mindlessly from street to street, professors and students at the medical school jumped out the windows, and tellers at the new tax office took advantage of the moment, as in bygone days of *mandats,* to decamp with the day's proceeds.

It came to nothing. On their return to the Bahamas, the airplane and crew were caught by officials of Duvalier's collaborator, Mr. Pindling, and eventually deported to the United States.

In April 1970, again smelling sedition, Duvalier conducted wholesale arrests, retired more officers, and replenished his supply of hostages. Unusual for him, he missed certain key men. On 24 April, sortieing from Bizoton, all five ships of the *Garde-Côtes,* commanded by *noir* Colonel Octave Cayard, for years a staunch pillar of the regime, took station off the city and commenced shooting at (but not hitting) the *Palais National.* Pandemonium again ensued, but the essential ingredient of the *attentat,* an army uprising to be coordinated with the ships' gunfire, never materialized. With *miliciens* at the back of every cannoneer, soldiers got one of the famous 105 mm guns (last fired in 1957) into action on the waterfront near the site of old Batterie St. Claire, but their gunnery was, if possible, worse than the fleet's. When the lone flyable F-51 was ordered to attack the ships, it was found that on palace orders the airplane had been stripped of its ordance and the guns were nowhere to be found. For two days, in complete stalemate, land fought sea and vice versa, but without casualties on either side. Then, with fuel running low and no response from confederates ashore, Cayard took the squadron Northwest to Guantanamo Bay and, with him, the entire *Garde-Côtes,* into asylum.(67) Thus, like its predecessors, ended unsuccessfully the last of at least nine invasions, coups, and insurgencies directed against the extraordinarily durable, bizarre man who had ruled Haiti for thirteen years.

Guinée

When Nelson Rockefeller, smiling wide, was photographed virtually embracing President Duvalier on 1 July 1969, what the cameras failed to catch was that the broad-shouldered New York governor was all but holding up a frail and debilitated Duvalier. Rockefeller staffers afterward confirmed that Duvalier, who had not appeared to the public, even from his palace balcony, since early May, was ill and weak and literally had to be supported by Rockefeller.

On May Day, Duvalier had proved unable to read his speech and handed the script over to Paul Blanchet; his hands and ankles were swollen, his face puffy. Nine days later, he complained that he could barely breathe and that he felt an intolerable weight, like a heavy stone, across his chest. Heart specialists were summoned. Papa Doc hardly needed to be told: he could diagnose congestive heart failure as well as any of them. Digitalis, diuretics, indomitable will to hang on and hold power pulled him through for the time being. Then on 20 May the president faced another foe: in the old French hospital, St. François de Sales, where he had interned so long ago, he secretly underwent excruciatingly painful and debilitating surgery, long overdue, for a prostate mortal as that of any other sixty-three-year-old man. Confined to a hospital bed in the palace, Duvalier convalesced feebly until he forced himself to rise for Rockefeller.

The Rockefeller visit and its sequelae proved a tonic. A new American ambassador - this one black, the first since Dr. Furniss, and a voluble and convivial supporter of the regime - publicly called for new American loans and told reporters they would be "symbolic of a new official attitude toward Dr. Duvalier . . . I think the feeling in Washington is quite favorable." Within months, Port-au-Prince would be styling the pliant ambassador an honorary *Tonton Macoute*. De Catalogne put it more positively. "Ambassador Clinton Knox," he purred to foreign reporters, "is a man who understands this country."

Now there were more tourists, even some light industry (all the baseballs in the United States were being sewn by Haitians). In summer 1970, as the young trooped back from school abroad (a few chosen Haitians, some Syrians, and assorted foreigners), Duvalier noted disquieting changes. Suddenly one morning in the manner of King Herod, the president had *macoutes* sweep up every male teen-aged returnee. After they had spent interminable hours in the police station, barbers suddenly appeared, and each shaggy head or beard or high-style Afro was shorn. Next morning, herded into the *Grande Salle* of the palace by submachine gun-armed TTMs, the chastened youths and fearful parents found themselves facing Duvalier. In the manner of Toussaint delivering a discourse, the white-haired president spoke like a bishop on public morality: he would, he said in conclusion, hold the youths, and their parents, fully responsible for acceptable future dress and behavior in all respects. "As you know," he murmured softly after a long pause, "I do not like to have to say the same thing twice."

On Armed Forces Day (18 November, 167th anniversary of Vertières), the president conducted the usual review, delivered a typically delphic and diffuse speech in the mixed French and Créole reserved for such occasions, and pinned decorations to the tunics of the faithful, including General Constant, now eight years in servile command.

The exertion was too heavy. Next day Duvalier spoke of dizziness and intolerable headache. He had trouble standing, and his speech, never clear in conversation, seemed to have a slur. Now he knew with certainty, as he had in 1962, that certain preparations must be undertaken.

The first to learn of the president's resolves was General Constant. Early in December, the well-upholstered *noir* chief of staff was abruptly replaced by Duvalier's trusted godson, Claude Raymond. On Ancestors' Day, there was a short speech: when the time came, Duvalier told a silent audience, he would step aside for youth, and he promised Haiti "a young Leader." Next day, *Le Nouveau Monde* observed, "That a Duvalier may one day succeed a Duvalier . . . should alarm no one."

The National Assembly could take a hint. Ulrick Saint-Louis, still leader, flanked by *Macoute* bodyguards with submachine guns, proposed that the constitution be amended to lower the minimum age for the presidency from forty to eighteen. The assembly so voted, and asked the president to hold a plebiscite of ratification.

22 January was declared a public holiday. Just as on execution days, schoolchildren were let out and marched downtown. Bands were mobilized and fueled with *taffia*; obedient peasants were hauled in, given their one-*gourde* paperbacks and *clairin*. When the president stepped uncertainly onto the palace balcony, the familiar cries rose high as ever. His son was beside him.

In a half-hour speech - by Duvalier's terms, brevity itself - the president announced that his successor would be Jean-Claude. "He will succeed me not only as Chief of State," said Duvalier, "but as Chief of the Duvalierist Revolution . . . Good luck, My Son, Jean-Claude Duvalier." As he spoke, the old man placed his hands on the boy's shoulders. He could barely remain on his feet.

Within moments, on cue, the streets began throbbing to the beat of Duvalier *meringues* while the schoolchildren cheered and sang songs and the peasants obediently roared. One month later to the day, the Haitian people voted on the following proposition:

Citoyen Dr. François Duvalier has chosen *Citoyen* Jean-Claude Duvalier to succeed him as *president-à-vie de la république*. Does this choice respond to your aspirations and your desires? Do you ratify it?

The vote was 2,391,916 to 0, yes.

Even as the plebiscite was in progress, more important decisions were being taken inside the *Palais*: to guide the young leader and prepare him for new responsibilities, a council of advisers was named. Headed by Cambronne, the regents included General Raymond, his brother Adrien in attendance to advise on foreign affairs, Antonio André of the *Banque*, and Hervé Boyer. There was no need to specify Mme. Duvalier or her strong-willed daughter Marie-Denise (who since 1969 had superseded Mme. St. Victor in the secretary's office and could be seen striding about the palace with submachine gun cradled in her arms).

On 16 March there was another brief appearance. Duvalier's face was pinched, his features sharp under a skin of taut, dark parchment, his brow creased as if by constant pain.

A few days later - the date is uncertain - the blinding headache returned. This time the president lost consciousness. Like Christophe, when he came to, one side was paralyzed and he could hardly speak. But there was no silver bullet for the .357 Magnum.

Early in April, reporters began to gather in Port-au-Prince. In his high-pitched, Maurice Chevalier English, de Catalogne assured them there really was no story: "He takes a rest, he is very quiet, and everything is perfect." Then, almost reflectively, he added, "He is president for life. Five minutes before his death, he will still be president."

Duvalier's sixty-fourth birthday fell on 14 April. With Jean-Claude impassive at the palace balcony, there was another massive official celebration, but there was no Papa Doc, not even a radio message to his people.

"I see him every day," de Catalogne rattled on; "I have told him to relax, not to work so hard, but I don't know whether he will obey me."

It was all lies. François Duvalier lay dying.

In the evening hours of 21 April, after the sun had plummeted behind La Gonâve and night had fallen, the president seemed restless and tried to speak, but the words were not clear. Minutes later the term of the *president-à-vie* had reached its end.

Now came the time of the houngans. In the houmforts of the Cul-de-Sac it was whispered that to Edner Day fell the task of performing the last rite called Déssounin. First tracing on the floor a large cross in maize flour the length and breadth of the body, then climbing past the silent doctors and nurses, under the dead president's sheet and astride the frail and wasted little corpse, the houngan now implored Duvalier's loa, the Maîte-Tête who had so often driven away the Gros Bon Ange, to retire and leave the dead in peace. Only then could the soul be shriven and the Maîte-Tête safely transferred to the head of Jean-Claude, standing mute and awed by the light of the candle at the foot of his father's bed.

When the body seemed to shudder ever so slightly, some thought it tried to rise and shake its head: they knew the Maîte-Tête had departed. Papa Doc had gone to Guinée.

Nothing had been overlooked. Even a refrigerated glass box, complete with fluorescent lighting, had been secretly brought in so that the president could lie in state, spectacles carefully in place over unseeing eyes.

Close at hand, as people filed by in an endless stream, were his collected works. Standing watch over the body was a guard of twenty-two soldiers and twenty-two *miliciens*. All day Radio Commerce played classical music, with a Mozart mass at noon. At five that afternoon, they closed the palace gates and began preparations for the morrow.

On Saturday, 24 April, day of *Baron Samedi*, François Duvalier was buried. The day dawned very still and very hot. No one could remember such heat in April; peasants said it was the doors of hell opening wide.

In the *Salle des Bustes* at the top of the great stairs inside the *Palais*, Archbishop Wolff-Ligondé, flanked by his bishops, Haitian to a man, commenced intoning the solemn pontifical requiem mass. Outside, every church bell tolled throughout the city, while Fort National fired a 101-gun royal salute, one gun every two minutes through the forenoon. At an organ was Guy Durosier, the internationally famous Haitian tenor flown from Paris. Amid the incense and the liturgy, Durosier, accompanied by the cathedral choir, sang words set to the choral movement of Beethoven's Ninth Symphony:

"François, we thank Thee for loving us so much
Thy star will be shining in the firmament."

Outdoing even Durosier and Beethoven, Judge Félix Diambois of the *Cour de Cassation* proclaimed in funeral oration, "This man was the Messiah!"

Down the steps, borne by sweating officers in heavy dress blues, through the mass of tophatted diplomats, black-robed judges, pistol-packing *Macoutes* in black sunglasses, white-cassocked priests, blue-denimed *miliciens* with ancient Mausers, ladies in chic miniskirts, and fat *députés* in shiny black Duvalier suits, bobbed the bronze casket, its hinged top sealed at last. Outside, for the last time, the *Garde Présidentielle* presented arms as the casket was loaded into the black Cadillac hearse. At each corner of the *Palais*, low in the shrubbery, a .30

caliber machine gun and crew were emplaced to command the gathering and, should occasion demand, mow down the funeral.

As the guns boomed sullenly from Fort National and the band struck up a dirge, the procession filed slowly out the gates. Preceding the hearse marched a phalanx of officers, each bearing on a scarlet cushion one of the decorations Duvalier had amassed; now they were more meaningless than ever. Past Dessalines and Pétion, commingled in their common shrine, along flower-strewn Rue Guilloux and down Rue Oswald Durand, the cortege, a black serpent, wound its way. The heat was overpowering.

At the gate of the Cimetière, sentry post of *Baron Samedi*, a mysterious event transpired: suddenly from nowhere, with a fierce howl and dark coil of dust, a mighty wind swirled up from underfoot and obscured the sun. There was a shriek of horror. Musicians dropped instruments; mourners trampled each other to escape they knew not what; *miliciens* fired rusty Mausers in the air.

Duvalier has burst the grave, men cried, *and is loosed upon earth. There is no hiding place.*

All at once the wind twisted out to sea. Again it was very hot and very quiet. The procession hesitantly reconstituted itself and picked its way slowly inside the sun-baked old cemetery packed tight with the dead. In the cream-colored mausoleum with aquamarine tile steps he had built for his parents, the little doctor who ruled Haiti fourteen years and died in bed was shut away from the living.

Now he was alone with the Ancestors. Or almost alone: at the portal as the last mourner straggled out, a fearful sentinel remained lest any seek to spirit Papa Doc away and enslave him as a *zombi*.

Duvalier was in every respect a remarkable man. Like no predecessor save Pétion and Riché, he served his full term and died naturally in the palace.

He was a master of calculated obscurity. He was a connoisseur of human weakness and contradictions, and his unsleeping suspicion played ceaselessly on people and governments like radar sweeping the skies.

It was to sleepless suspicion that Duvalier owed his full term in office; and, of course, to betrayal. He readily forgot friends but never an enemy.

It would have surprised even Duvalier to be compared with Adolf Hitler. Yet the two dictators - one white and racist, the other black and racist, each a supreme megalomaniac - shared much in common. Neither man, in fact, had much more than the attributes they shared: cruelty, suspicion, fanaticism, superstition, racism, and megalomania.

Power. Yes, that was the thing. Papa Doc never had enough of it. There was also another thing. Duvalier knew everyone and everyone's secrets. Most of the peasants and not a few *houngans* believed the *loa* made Papa Doc their familiar. Possibly indeed the *loa* did.

Speaking to foreigners (whom he delighted to chicane and mislead) Duvalier would refer to himself as an ethnologist (which he was) and to Voodoo as "folklore." But no Haitian could ever truly dismiss Voodoo as mere folklore. For Voodoo is in Haiti's bones. And Haiti was in the bones of Duvalier.

He was unbelievably cruel while ruling a simple, kind, cheerful people; negative and destructive in every act and policy; a symphonist who consummately orchestrated human divisions, weakness, venality, and cynicism. He was a xenophobe who duped the great powers and their U.N. and Organization of the American States; a mighty Ozymandias whose monument proved to be misery and ruins.

But Duvalier was no less a profoundly Haitian figure in the historic mold of Toussaint and of Dessalines. Black (as so many of the titans had been) and not a *mulâtre,* and touched, too, with madness, knowing his people better than they knew themselves, Duvalier breathed and articulated the aspirations of his countrymen. It was their tragedy, and his, and Haiti's, that he betrayed them all - people, aspirations, and himself.

FOOTNOTES - CHAPTER 14

1. "Underground" and *"maquis"* (bush) are both relative terms in Duvalier's case: at first he hid out with neighbors on the Ruelle Roy, where the family lived within a few doors of the Clément Jumelles, who gave Duvalier food, shelter, and money. Dressing himself as an old market woman (a favorite disguise), he subsequently moved nearby to the home of Père Jean-Baptiste Georges, where, in the Canada-educated priest's library, he spent long hours reading and writing.
2. Other notable army Duvalierists included Colonel Georges Danache; Majors Frédéric Arty, Edner Nelson, and Franck Romain - this last to gain a certain fame as the original for Graham Greene's Captain Concasseur in *The Comedians* - Lieutenants Monod Philippe, Jean Tassy, and Gracia Jacques *(houngan, bocor,* and former mess sergeant).
3. Bonhomme's pursuit of fly-by-night entrepreneurs to build the Port-au-Prince jet airport, largely on land owned by the Augustes at Maïs Gaté, so soured the transaction that the U.S. Government, which wanted nothing more than to help Haiti in building the airport, dropped the project.
4. In 1964, an AFL-CIO official, Andrew McClellan, who specialized in inter-American labor matters, asserted that, every year since 1957, Duvalier had supplied 30,000 cane-cutters for the Dominican canefields. Duvalier, said McClellan, got $15.00 apiece for each laborer plus a further cut of 50 percent of wages paid, thus realizing some $7 million a year from this peonage.
5. Talamas, another Syrian as far as Haitian authorities were concerned, had been guilty only of breaking curfew at a touchy time, going for an obstetrician to deliver his wife. A police Captain had given American Consul Thomas W. Davis. Jr., his word of honor that Talamas would not be molested. Subsequently, over the incredibly battered 300-pound corpse, Haitian doctors solemnly assured U.S. representatives that Talamas had died of a heart attack.

6. After a cooling-off period, Kébreau came home to accept appointment as Haitian ambassador to the Vatican - a congenial post for one who had spent five years as a seminarian before entering the *Garde*. On his recall to Port-au-Prince in 1962, he died suddenly of a heart attack or, some said, poison, hours before an appointment with one of the authors of this history.

7. Duvalier did take steps to rearm the Armed Forces. Collecting a month's pay from every soldier and government employees ($74,940) and $60,000 from the *bord-de-mer*, the president sent agents to Italy to buy up war-surplus arms, including old M5 light tanks, several hundred rebuilt M1 rifles and automatic rifles, several aging half-tracks, and quantities of ammunition and spare parts. These were paraded in Port-au-Prince on 18 November, anniversary of Vertières and designated Army Day.

8. The nearest thing to a specific statement of mission ever given to the Marines' commander came from a State Department deputy under-secretary. "Colonel," said he in January 1959, "the most important way you can support our objectives in Haiti is to help keep Duvalier in power so he can serve out his full term in office, and" - a portentous pause - "maybe a little longer than that if everything works out. Good luck."

9. Throughout François Duvalier's regime, rumors persisted that he had one or more former Nazis as secret advisers. These rumors were never solidly confirmed - or disproven.

10. "*tonton macoute*" (literally, in Créole, Uncle Knapsack) is the Haitian child's antiperson to "Tonton Noël" (Uncle Christmas): good children get presents from Tonton Noël at Christmas: bad ones are whisked away into the cavernous *macoute* of Tonton *macoute* and are never seen again. How apt this soubriquet was for the regime's partisans would soon and frequently be demonstrated.

11. Conceivably the Jumelle outrage may have triggered the June 1959 Voodoo desecration of the grave of Duval Duvalier, the president's father, who had died in August 1957. The corpse was dug up at night, the heart was reportedly removed (some accounts say the head was cut off and stolen), and the body, coffin, and tomb were daubed with feces.

12. Duvalier's attack, whatever its exact etiology, was initially diagnosed as diabetic coma by Fourcand, who administered a massive insulin injection, which seriously aggravated the heart condition. Barbot, acting on a second medical opinion, quickly obtained glucose to neutralize the insulin and probably prevented Duvalier's death. As soon as the president's illness became known, the U.S. Naval Mission, with approval of Ambassador Drew, brought in a navy cardiac team by air from Guantanamo Bay. The team attended Duvalier around the clock for more than a month and ensured his survival. Of the medical background and questions surrounding this episode and its consequences, Rotberg (pages 219 to 220) has by far the most authoritative analysis,

13. In May 1959, TTMs tossed a live grenade inside Rodriguez's car. The old butcher, tough as some of his meat cuts, threw it back in his assailants' faces, with fatal results. A month later he was waylaid after midnight on his return home from an evening on the town. Despite a blast of submachine-gun fire that put over fifty holes in his car, he ducked behind a door (which he had thoughtfully inlaid with an armored panel) and drove off the attackers with well-aimed .45 caliber pistol fire.

14. For differing reasons of political delicacy there was reluctance on the part of the United States, Cuba, or (at first) even Haiti to admit the fact of this landing. But the

weapons, papers, uniforms, and the prisoners themselves were incontestably Cuban, and the last were eventually repatriated in 1963. The U.S. Marines involved are probably the only United States troops to have engaged in ground combat with forces of Fidel Castro.

15. Vincent, who died, aged and blind, at Canapé Vert Hospital on 3 September, had long advised Duvalier. It has been credibly stated that, after his election to the presidency was confirmed, the first person Duvalier visited was Vincent.

16. In late 1963, Bellegarde was again subjected to Duvalierist brutality. For the offense of having assisted the U.S. Information Service in editing a commemorative pamphlet following the death of John F. Kennedy, whom the old historian admired, he was called into the office of the *macoute* Foreign Minister, Chalmers, to be cuffed and cursed by the infamous secret-police chief, Major Jean Tassy.

17. The Haitian press could in any case hardly be considered a national institution of strength or respect. As of 1969, Haiti had but six daily papers of all stripes aggregating 25,000 circulation (top individual circulation, *Le Nouvelliste,* 6000), a fluctuating number of weeklies, and fourteen radio and one TV stations. In 1930, speaking of the paper traditionally claiming place as doyen of Haiti's press, British Minister Magowan had written, "The tone and level of *Le Nouvelliste* are one of the most glaring indictments of the Haytian elite to be found in the island." Newspapers, Magowan continued, "are merely daily pamphlets for or against the government." Forty years later, nothing had changed, save that only the government side appeared.

18. After running through a series of name-changes and reorganizations, the communist-dominated *Comité* became the *Union Intersyndicale d'Haïti.* Among its leaders were Ulrick Joly and Alix Lamaute, the militant communist who would be killed in disturbances at Cazale in 1969. It maintained active and fraternal relations with the labor organizations of East Germany, Czechoslovakia, Rumania, Bulgaria, Poland, and China. It was dissolved, as its historian recounts, "on pretext of communist activity" in 1963.

19. Cromwell James, a Jamaican storekeeper over sixty years old, objected to government shakedowns and was arrested and held incommunicado while being mercilessly beaten. Released after the British embassy intervened on 22 November 1960, James died of gangrene from hideous, uncared-for wounds.

20. By 1972, under successor president-for-life, Jean-Claude Duvalier, telephone service was indeed restored.

21. In mid-1958, for essentially cosmetic reasons, the army (formerly the *Garde*) changed its designation to the more grandiose *Forces Armées d'Haïti* or *FAd'H,* as it will be referred to hereafter.

22. The hulking Jacques (original of Graham Greene's "Fat Gracia"), who would stand at the president's side on every public appearance holding a cocked .357 Magnum revolver, signalized his assumption of command by surgical removal of a huge mole that dominated even his Himalayan nose. His one humane trait, fondness for animals, prompted a brother officer to say he treated animals better than human beings.

23. Living in the quiet of retirement at La Boule, old President Lescot told friends at a lunch in January 1961 that the *semaine sanglante* could reoccur at any moment. Within less than a month the government's Radio Haiti was reminding listeners of that dread event and underscoring that it could indeed be repeated.

24. By 1962, out of 416 priests, only 113 - mainly *mulâtres* of elite background were Haitian. Of the remainder, 180 were French and the rest were mostly Canadian or American.

25. Between 1959 and 1964, Duvalier expelled the Archbishop of Haiti, two Catholic bishops, one Episcopalian bishop, some forty priests, and several nuns. The foregoing figures do not include the Reverend Yvon Moreau, Episcopal priest and former senator, who was never again seen after his arrest in 1960.

26. Duvalier's initial stance toward the Church presented every appearance of conciliation. In appointments without past precedent, he named Père Jean-Baptiste Georges Minister of Education, and included two other priests, Père Hubert Papailler and Père Gérard Bissainthe, in subsequent cabinets. Of these, Pères Georges and Bissainthe eventually moved into opposition and were expelled, but Papailler, apparently seduced by this world, is reported to have abandoned his vocation and become a Haitian ambassador.

27. Barbot had nonetheless earned Duvalier's suspicions: since early 1960 he had been in touch with U.S. officials, making no secret of his dismay over the president's mounting misuse of American aid and conveying seemingly sincere doubts as to Duvalier's mental condition (misgivings being independently expressed at the same time by Dr. Loughlin, another long-time Duvalier familiar). In June 1960, speaking with alarm to an American official, Barbot told of bizarre scenes inside the palace and said Duvalier "had never been the same man" since his heart attack and prolonged coma. Barbot's overtures were not reciprocated by the United States. He was told that Washington was determined to support constitutional governments, even Duvalier's, and that his terrorist past would make Barbot difficult if not impossible to recognize, let alone support.

28. One of the few measures that failed to sail through the existing legislature was a Duvalier favorite: to change the cherished blue and scarlet flag of Dessalines and Pétion to the black and scarlet design, with vertical subdivision, as used by Henry Christophe. Later, in 1964, the president succeeded in effecting this change.

29. Duvalier as usual was right: between 1945 and 1964, the United States was to give Haiti $100.8 million in aid. As of the latter year, Haiti tied with Panama for third place among ten Central American and West Indian countries that had received U.S. assistance since 1945.

30. A necessary condition for funding the Road to the South was an engineering study that the DLF offered to have undertaken for Haiti at a $35,000 fee. Instead, Haitian senators signed a contract with a little-known firm for $80,000. Not only did the study cost over twice as much; it failed to meet DLF standards and set the loan back by months. The transaction finally died when the government attempted to throw the contract to an obscure but high-bidding firm which the DLF declined to approve.

31. The Artibonite dismissals ought not to have taken anyone by surprise; as early as 1958, postal service all but collapsed when Duvalier purged long-time employees in favor of TTMs unable to read, whose main and gainful preoccupation, once installed, was soaking postage off letters and reselling the stamps.

32. Mr. Rusk, perhaps restrained by the discretion of years as Secretary of State, demurs from the implication given here. "It is inevitable - but cynical -" he wrote in September 1975, "to oversimplify these two things and put them together as a form of bribery."

33. Ironically, as it happened, more than half the cancelations were of American hospital residencies for Haitian medical officers, which the doctor in the *Palais* unhesitatingly sacrificed in efforts to get weapons-training for *macoutes*. Unfortunately, when, this time, Duvalier yielded, funds for the residencies had been allocated to other Latin American countries and were no longer available for Haiti.

34. On the basis of presumed special expertise in Haitian affairs, one of Berle's first moves in 1961 was to engineer the replacement in Port-au-Prince of Robert Newbegin, the cool-headed veteran Foreign Service officer who had relieved Drew as ambassador. Newbegin had made the mistake of intimating to Berle that Haitian problems were not so subject to simplistic remedies, as Berle's friends were fond of asserting. Newbegin would be missed.

35. More than ever anxious to break contact between the *FAd'H* and the Marines, Duvalier had sent an emissary (Colonel Edner Nelson) to the United States with instructions that Haitian student officers then in training at Quantico should foment difficulties and precipitate an open breach. This took place in the fall of 1962, when a Haitian officer publicly insulted and provoked a fist fight with a Marine officer. Duvalier then recalled all military students remaining in the United States, alleging "blatant American racism."

36. President Kennedy was not the last U.S. President to be targeted by a Duvalier *ouanga-à-mort*. In December 1977 (reported in *Haiti-Observateur*, 6 January 1978, and subsequently by the Washington Post later that month) Zacharie Delva, the *macoute houngan* of Gonaïves, entombed a bull alive bearing a photo of President Jimmy Carter around his neck. This ceremony was intended to kill Mr. Carter and thus put an end to human rights pressures being exerted against Haiti by the Carter administration.

37. *Horoscope,* a Paris journal of astrology Duvalier subscribed to and read closely, had predicted during that summer that Kennedy would be assassinated on 22 November 1963. Duvalier was therefore unsurprised by the event, and in private moments credited his *ouanga* with Kennedy's death. Given the date, 22 November, few Haitians ever doubted it. Almost unbelievably, one of the Warren Commission's leads on the Kennedy assassination actually took investigators to Haiti but proved groundless.

38. In early 1963 the Haitian consul in New Orleans declined to issue documents on a large supply of Church World Services food for Haiti, but relented to the extent of offering no further difficulties if he were paid $800 for "consular services."

39. Those lucky enough to get out were still not beyond the tyrant's reach. Through extensive use of private detective firms in the United States, Canada, and Europe, Duvalier kept track of the movements and actions of Haitians abroad and of any non-Haitians he considered suspect. In 1964, the U.S. Attorney General's office, responding to a congressional inquiry, listed four detective agencies in Washington, D.C., New York City, and Miami on Duvalier's payroll. In May of that year, Joseph Thévenin, a Haitian Voice of America translator, was murdered in Port-au-Prince during a visit, because of anti-Duvalier remarks overheard by agents in New York. In his memoirs, Duvalier later referred to these gumshoes as *"Ma haute police internationale."*

40. In his revisionist memoirs, Duvalier later claimed support from Ghana, Uruguay, and France, none of which in fact supported him.

41. About this time, with or without Juan Bosch's personal knowledge, a Déjoieist--Fignolist coalition was training Haitian revolutionaries in the Dominican Republic with

support from the Dominican Armed Forces. With its built-in instability, cemented only by opportunism, this band did not seem to present possibilities of serious political or military success.

42. For an ordinary beating, the usual Créole command is *"Réflechi-li, pe-z-à-pe"* (Make him think a bit). For more severe treatment, the phrase goes *"Réflechi-li, mais pas lever lageuil"* (Make him think but don't stir up his pride). "Make his feet leave the earth" means death.

43. Britain likewise ordered H.M.S. *Cavalier,* with a detachment of Royal Marines, to station in Gonave Channel, where she was joined by a Canadian destroyer, H.M.C.S. *Saskatchewan.*

44. Dr. Duvalier's recollection of this day in his memoirs differs widely from our account. He concedes that he received the OAS team with *"hauteur, "* but says that he delivered a scholarly, wide-ranging rationale of Haiti's position, lasting over an hour: whether in Créole or French he does not say.

45. About this time, looking at the aircraft carrier U.S.S. *Boxer* and Marine Expeditionary Brigade just offshore, Duvalier taunted, "If the OAS claims the right to intervene because of repressive internal conditions, why don't they land troops in Birmingham?"

46. Twelve years later, in April 1975, O'Leary wrote in the *Washington Star* that members of the Marine Mission, during its last days in Port-au-Prince, had supplied Barbot with small arms, ammunition, and grenades. This account was strongly denied, both privately and officially, by Colonel R. J. Batterton, chief of the mission from March to May 1963.

47. In a kind of reprise of the Barbot insurgency, a group of young Port-au-Princiens led by Hector Riobé, whose father and family Duvalier had killed, fought a three-day battle in caves behind Kenscoff, where they had secreted weapons. The Riobé stand, finally overrun by overwhelming *FAd'H* forces, inflicted some 100 casualties on government attackers on 18 July 1963. Riobé killed himself with his last round rather than be captured.

48. A convinced spiritualist, Dr. Duvalier frequently joined in rites whereby the spirits of Dessalines, Toussaint, and Henry Christophe were called up for consultation, and would on occasion refer openly to occult conversations with the Ancestors. His similar credence in astrology led the CIA to put up a substantial sum to buy space, so to speak, in an astrological forecast column avidly read and believed by Duvalier in the French magazine *Horoscope.*

49. While Viau and his communists were keeping ammunition away from the Camocains, Duvalier's methods of ammunition-supply were subsequently described by the *New York Time's* Richard Eder: "Last June, one visitor was shown how Haitian military logistics operate. He was sitting with Duvalier in his office when an aide came to tell the President that guerrillas had landed at Saltrou and the Army needed ammunition. Silently the President took a gold key from his pocket and took out a revolver. He got up, tiptoed to the door and cocked the revolver, opened the door and peered out. A secretary appeared and he gave her the gold key . . ."

50. One particularly awful feature of Fort Dimanche was the "special cells." These oubliettes were a yard wide, five feet high, and six or seven feet deep, and were used to confine as many as four persons simultaneously. In February 1978, Amnesty Interna-

tional asserted that the mortality of political prisoners in Haiti was the highest in the world.

51. In a chance meeting in the lobby of New York's Henry Hudson Hotel, Jacques Wadestrandt, a Harvard contemporary of Teddy Kennedy's, engaged former President Harry Truman in conversation, telling Mr. Truman he was "a revolutionary" who hoped to liberate Haiti. Truman listened attentively to the attractive, impulsive young man, then put his hand on Wadestrandt's shoulder and replied, "All right, my boy, but don't get yourself killed," which is exactly what Wadestrandt did.

52. The marksmanship of Haitian firing squads appears to have been as bad as during the nineteenth century: *Le Matin* reported "three volleys of Springfields and submachine guns, and three coups de grâce," a somewhat extravagant use of firepower to kill two men twelve paces distant.

53. Rémy Bastien explained the new design as follows. Black proximity to the staff signified *noir* superiority, the *lambi* (which called the slaves to rebellion in 1791) signified massacre, and the *pintard,* most alert of fowl, stood for perpetual *noir* watchfulness against whites and *mulâtres.* The vertical repositioning of stripes instead of the former horizontal striping follows the thesis of Dr. Arthur Holly that the latter is in opposition to occult forces that will not be propitiated until the stripes are vertical.

54. Showing doctrinal eclecticism, Duvalier in 1967 compiled a Chairman-Mao style chrestomathy, *Bréviare d'une Révolution,* complete even to pocket size and red cover, containing 177 pages of selected Duvalier thoughts. The preface, by Gérard Daumec, said the compilation should be "breviary and Bible for the citizen, the intellectual, the statesman, in their quest for liberty, justice, equality, and the common prosperity."

55. Duvalier was neither so cordial nor so solicitous to Mr. Timmons. When the latter reached Port-au-Prince in January 1964, he was kept cooling his heels for five weeks before the president deigned to receive him. After Duvalier eventually noticed Timmons, he received him glacially: "I hope you are up to your job; your three predecessors have given me no satisfaction whatsoever," and then went on to calumniate John F. Kennedy. Having thus publicly bullied Uncle Sam and thereby demonstrated his strength to Haitians, he thereupon grudgingly accepted the U.S. aid supinely tendered by Timmons. According to the *Washington Star,* during the thirty-month period between January 1964 and July 1966, Duvalier allowed Timmons to see him only six times.

56. On 20 March 1969, Edward T. Long, a U.S. AID representative, told the Haitian Subcommittee of the Alliance for Progress: "AID is currently providing far more assistance to Haiti than seems to be generally realized . . . It may be of interest that in 1964-1968 AID has given $15.2 million, all grants of course." Thus had the Kennedy aid cutoff been converted by Lyndon Johnson and the State Department into a sham.

57. The Episcopal Church was also leaderless: on 23 April 1964, while he was shaving, *macoutes* at gunpoint arrested and deported the Right Reverend C. Alfred Voegeli, Bishop of Haiti since 1943, Maecenas of Haitian primitive art who had commissioned the glorious murals of his cathedral, and who had resolutely Haitianized his Church and clergy. All but three of some fifty Episcopal priests were Haitian.

58. How well Duvalier kept the bargain is arguable: on 16 August 1969, on the charge that they were propagating communism, he expelled the entire faculty of St. Martial, all Fathers of the Holy Spirit (including the Superior, Père Adrien, Pères Paddy Poux, Déjean, Smarth, and others). These priests, all Haitian and regarded as some of the

ablest, were superseded by *macoute* professors under a *macoute* priest, and St. Martial became a government institution. Msgr. Wolff-Ligondé was not allowed to see the priests before deportation.

59. Perhaps unintentionally, the president's metaphor was apt. Exiles who returned, like the French survivors who emerged on Dessalines's invitation in 1804, were imprisoned where not executed. One wary exile in Santo Domingo compared the situation to Aesop's fable of the lion who invited the sheep to lunch in his cave: "All the footprints lead in; none go out."

60. The tourist trade, which in 1958-1959, hardly a banner season, brought Haiti $5 million, had dwindled in the 1965-1965 season to $500,000. Out of 1200 tourist rooms in the country's hotels, only 400 were operated let alone occupied. Empty hotels were looted of furniture and air conditioners.

61. Besides his desk pistol (usually a .45 revolver as in this case, or sometimes an automatic), Duvalier kept a .357 Magnum revolver in the cushions of his overstuffed office chair. Perhaps the weapons were at least partly symbolic. One afternoon in 1967, holding discourse with a chosen group of young officers of the *Garde Présidentielle*, the president asked the group a question: *"Do you know why I have succeeded where other intellectuals, such as Firmin and Bobo, failed?"* Duvalier paused for a moment, then answered his own question: *"I was the first to have a pen in one hand and a gun in the other."*

62. At the end of 1966 the Alliance for Progress reported that Haiti had the lowest life expectancy (forty years) in the hemisphere, lowest per capita intake of calories (1780), lowest per capita income ($73), lowest literacy, and lowest percentage (6 percent) of children in school.

63. Since the asylum conventions required at least one year's notice of denunciation,it proved possible to negotiate the terrified asylees out of the country before they could be seized and slaughtered. In a future attempt to minimize foreign influence in internal affairs and cut off foreign contacts with Haitians, Duvalier in mid-1968 abruptly revoked accreditation of some ten honorary consuls of countries otherwise unrepresented in Haiti.

64. To back up *Vonvon* in print, the Coalition put out an equally lively and informed weekly, *Combattant,* which ran until the late 1960s. The *Vonvon* operation lasted until July 1969, when, with political jamming that succeeded where electronic gear had failed, Haitian government protests and sharp pressure from Washington caused WRUL to cease carrying the broadcasts. An effort was made to continue broadcasts from Guatemala, but this too petered out.

65. By far the best and most detailed account of Haitian communism, no doubt owing authority to official sources, is found in Diederich and Burt, *Papa Doc,* pages 332-335.

66. At the end of a disastrous Latin American circuit on behalf of Richard Nixon, mobbed, hissed, and execrated in every capital, Mr. Rockefeller was cheered in Port-au-Prince by peasants mobilized for the occasion while de Catalogne's *Nouveau Monde* trumpeted: "Haiti will never become a communist spearhead." At the 1 July climax of a brief, Haile Selassie-style stopover, Rockefeller appeared arm in arm on the palace balcony with Duvalier. Within a fortnight, Radio Vonvon was silenced and *Combattant* forced to suspend. Eight months later, with U.S. blessing, the international economic blockade against Duvalier officially ended.

67. The ships were eventually returned to Haiti by the United States (after appreciable U.S.-funded repairs). When they were, Duvalier erased the faithless *Garde-Côtes* by a stroke of his pen on 8 October and designated the revived force *"La Marine Haïtienne"* (Haitian Navy).

Jean-Claude and Simone Duvalier at François Duvalier's bier. "Nothing had been overlooked. Even a refrigerated glass box, complete with fluorescent lighting, had been secretly brought in so that the president could lie in state, spectacles carefully in place over unseeing eyes" *UPI/Bettman Archives*

Chapter 15

Riding the Tiger

1971 - 1986

"Anyone can ride the tiger. The trick comes in being able to dismount without
being eaten." - African Proverb

"When a government lasts a long while it deteriorates by insensible degrees."
- De Montesquieu

NO one thought he would last. Emerging groggily from the political stupor
into which they had been willed by the master *bocor*, Papa Doc, Haiti's elite,
both *noir* and *jaune*, began to indulge in the kind of political speculation which
had been so long proscribed and for which the penalties had been so draconian.
It was not a question of "if", most agreed, but rather "when" Jean-Claude
Duvalier would be ousted. The only other Haitian leader audacious enough to
publicly anoint an heir had been Henry Christophe, and his son had been
bayonetted and left to rot on a Cap Henry dung hill within twenty-four hours of
Henry's death.

Such musings were perforce conducted with a discretion learned under
fourteen years of Duvalierism. The regents Duvalier *père* had appointed - a
summons from anyone of whom would have induced fear in all save the bravest
- concentrated their efforts, disparately and without coordination, for Papa Doc
had discouraged any coordination below the top of the pyramid, on steps that
would ensure the maintenance of the status quo.

Popular opinion did not matter. Those in the inner circle who had been
imprudent enough to show anything less than heartfelt approval of the old man's
succession plans he had purged ruthlessly, demonstrating for the last time

Duvalier's maxim that gratitude was cowardice. Constant, who had failed to salute Jean-Claude on Vertières Day the preceding November, had been replaced as Chief of Staff by the more obliging Claude Raymond.

Clovis Désinor too had voiced misgivings about entrusting the "Duvalierist Revolution" which he had so long served to a nineteen year old and found himself stripped abruptly by Papa Doc of his post as Minister of Finance.

But now with François Duvalier dead, the remaining core - all of the Duvalier family, the Raymond brothers, Madame Max Adolphe, Gracia Jacques, Antonio André and the thousands of others with a vested interest in the regime's continuance - could only hope for the best.

Few outside the Palace really knew the new president, though many thought they did. Jean-Claude Duvalier had been barely five years old when his father had entered the Palace. He, like many younger Haitians, had never known any other president. But, unlike other Haitians, he had the opportunity to observe the operating methods of Papa Doc first hand.

A robust six feet tall, Jean-Claude Duvalier favored his mother in coloring, and disposition. His growing-up had been a lonely affair. As friends he had been permitted the company of a few chosen children of Duvalierists, and occasionally in the early days of the U.S. Naval Mission that of sons of senior members of the Mission (1), yet he learned early the transitory nature of such friendships as the parents of his friends fell out of favor with the Palace.

One of the few people to whom Papa Doc had entrusted his children was Clément Barbot, to whose house in Pacot Jean-Claude would be driven on hot afternoons for a solitary swim in the Barbot pool. Yet it was Barbot who had orchestrated the attack on the car carrying Jean-Claude to school in 1963, provoking Papa Doc's volcanic rage. The target, to be sure, was not the Duvalier children, whom Barbot had known and been fond of since their infancies, but the attack had nonetheless made deep impressions on the youngster sequestered in the Palace.

Duvalier *père* had loved his family, but the fighting between the alliances brought about by the marriages of the various daughters had gradually taken its toll. Too, Duvalier's appetites of all kinds were constrained by his various physical ailments so that life in the Palace was both cloistered and relatively (compared to the Magloire days) abstemious. Presiding over lunch in the Northeast corner of the second floor living quarters, Papa Doc could have been mistaken for any well-off *noir* family man, dishing out various delicacies (all tasted by a designated taster) to his family in a room littered with toys, books, and papers. Ironically for a regime that presided over the dismemberment of what was left of Haiti's railroads, an electric train set sat off in one corner.

Those around him felt no such constraints and partook in various sins of the flesh. The Duvalier daughters were assiduously courted by various young *noirs* (*mulâtres* never even tried) sensing their chance. If the father disapproved, a young officer could find himself abruptly assigned to Hinche or Ouanaminthe or cashiered. Sometimes, as in the case of Max Dominique, the daughters themselves went after the object of their desires, even if he was already married.

Duvalier *fils*, at first too young to enjoy the adult pleasures pursued by his sisters, took on early a certain girth which caused many to dismiss him as lacking in intellect or self-discipline.

To Papa Doc's annoyance, his only son had no great interest in the arcana of Haitian history that so fascinated his father and was an indifferent scholar. One of Jean-Claude's nicknames about town was "basket-head" - a Creole term indicating someone of limited intelligence.

At recess in his grade school, the children had all been cautioned to never, ever, repeat their error of shouting, as they had after Jean-Claude once fell, the fatal words "*Duvalier tombé*". His teachers, afraid of Palace opprobrium, gave him passing grades year after year and breathed sighs of relief when unburdened of their intellectually unambitious young charge.

All these assessments were based on limited observations. He had been much indulged from early childhood and often ignored by his father, whose favorite was eldest daughter Marie-Denise (2). He was shy and insecure. He liked music, playing the viola. Like many another teenager in the sixties, he had confrontations with his father when he played his stereo too loudly. He had a passion for things mechanical and was already learning to drive by age ten, weaving in and out of the courtyards of the Palace in flashy sports cars. Motorcycles followed, as well as a taste for hunting - anything that would, as he grew older, enable him to escape, even momentarily, the stifling atmosphere of the Palace.

Ironically, even as his father, the ultimate *noiriste*, was decimating the ranks of the elite, Jean-Claude found his lot often thrown together with the scions of the very group whose stranglehold on Haitian society the father sought to break. At Collège Bird and elsewhere, Jean-Claude met those whose family circumstances were such that they could have the toys he had grown to like, and a freedom he could only dream of. Not for him the suppressed rage of his desperately poor, *noir* physician-father with a hatred of those lighter-skinned and better off.

Deprived of steady companionship, witness (at least at a distance) of unspeakable horrors conducted in the torture chambers of the Palace basement, the young man took refuge in acquiring things, often seeking to one-up friends who sported a new watch, suit, or car.

He had been abroad only once, staying some six months in France in the late sixties, this as a consequence of the family feud in which Papa Doc had exiled Max Dominique after executing most of the officer's best friends.

What he did not wish to be was president.

Surrounded by Hyenas

The pictures published in January of 1971 showing an ailing François Duvalier next to his son gave notice to Haiti and the world what those in the inner circle already knew - change was imminent. Now that the old man was gone, it was up to those left to make do with what they had.

Jean-Claude Duvalier was quickly sworn in on April 22, 1971. The ceremony was private, orchestrated by Simone Duvalier, who had in hand the list of those to be named to the cabinet. The new President was in shock, grieving not only for his father, but for the loss of what little freedom he had had. With the crisis upon him, an already placid temperament had been pushed over the brink into stupefaction, abetted by liberal doses of tranquilizers freely and willingly administered by Palace physicians at Simone Duvalier's command. He did not accompany his mother and sisters in the funeral cortege that bore Papa Doc's remains to the family mausoleum.(3)

Ceremony dispensed with, the family returned to the Palace. Port-au-Prince was awash in journalists, all of whom were looking for one more piece of copy to file before flying on to their next crisis. Cable submissions were uncensored, and a number of reporters had not been reticent about reporting the speculation in Port-au-Prince about the longevity of the new president's term.

After a day's rest, Duvalier *fils* met the assembled foreign press corps, introduced by Cambronne right-hand man Fritz Cinéas, newly designated Minister of Information. Some wanted a full-fledged press conference, but sterner heads prevailed, so after reading a statement in French in which he expressed hope that "objectivity" would characterize their reporting about Haiti, the "boy president"(as some dubbed him) shook hands and disappeared through the side door into what was now *his* office.

Constituencies more vital to the regime than the foreign press were not overlooked that Monday as Duvalier visited police, army, and *macoute* posts throughout the city. With Constant's fate in mind, those visited were not restrained in declarations of fealty.

The next hurdle was an address to the National Assembly on Thursday, gathered dutifully by Ulrick St. Louis, to speak about "his program". Hopes ran high for a political amnesty of some sort. After attending a memorial mass at Notre Dame, he was driven through large, cheering crowds to the Assembly Building.

Duvalier spoke in a voice so low it could not be heard in some portions of the chamber - a device his father had employed to compound confusion about what he was saying. No pardons, no tolerance of "Communists or troublemakers" was to be permitted. "The United States will always find Haiti on its side against communism", he said, music to Richard Nixon's Washington and helpful to an American Ambassador dubbed an "honorary *macoute*".

Ambassador Knox, more experienced at giving press conferences than Duvalier, had opened the week with one of his own, suggesting that Haiti was ripe for other than the diet of "humanitarian" aid to which it had been limited by the U.S. since the falling-out with President Kennedy. Others too, sensing opportunity, had begun to put forth their ideas for overdue change.

The financial team, Francisque as Minister of Finance, André at the *Banque*, knew that certain of the more blatant practices of the regime would have to have facelifts if the spigot of international aid was to be turned. In particular, the channelling of so much of the tax receipts to the unaudited (at least by the public) *Régie du Tabac* had been a long standing gripe of various would-be donors. In their efforts though, they ran straight into the very forces on whose support the regime was so dependent, and to which the coffers of the *Régie* had always been generous - Luckner Cambronne, Simone Duvalier and the whole *VSN/macoute* structure throughout the country.

There was, mercifully, more to play with than before. The new jet airport was bringing in tourists in numbers not seen since the heyday of the Magloire years. A new type of tourist was appearing in Haiti. Package tours offering what quickly became known as "quickie" divorces were being hawked by New York travel agents. For $1200, one got a two day trip to Haiti, Haitian "legal representation" with a minimum of fuss, food, hotel, and a divorce decree as a souvenir to bring home to an often-surprised spouse who had not been offered the chance to contest the decree. The now thoroughly Haitian Catholic clergy offered only the faintest of protests.

Further fattening the regime's treasury were the remittances of the one Haitian export that had multiplied under Papa Doc - economic and political refugees. These refugees sent home some $14 million in 1971 alone. In 1970 Haiti enjoyed its first balance of payments surplus in many years.

Hearkening back to balmier days as well, generators were finally installed at Péligre Dam, begun under Magloire, and came on-line in July, ending the chronic blackouts that had been so long a fixture of Port-au-Prince life. (4) Factories, assured at last of steady supplies of power, were being set up by foreign investors on the outskirts of Port-au-Prince to profit from Haiti's cheap labor, providing by mid-1971 some 7,000 sorely needed jobs.

The prospect of jobs hastened the flight from the countryside of peasants who could no longer eke out subsistence livings from the eroded plots divided, split, and divided yet again that had been given their great-great-grandfathers by Pétion. Port-au-Prince, whose infrastructure (an inheritance from the occupation) could barely support its 200,000 population in 1957 was, by 1971, bursting at the seams with nearly a million inhabitants. The World Bank, in yet another study, opined that "Haiti's future was destined to be urban".

Representatives of the U.S. Agency for International Development made an official visit to Port-au-Prince that summer as well, demonstrating that Ambassador Knox'es pleas had not gone unheard in Foggy Bottom. Further evidence of this was to come in the Fall with the approval of a $750,000 Agricultural Development loan on soft terms. Haiti, it would seem, had shed its label of pariah.

Knox and other Duvalier advocates in the international arena were aided by demonstrable changes in the government's tone. The fiercest *Tonton macoutes* kept low profiles, at least in public. *The New York Times* reported optimistically that they had been "partially disbanded". To serve as an adjunct to the *Garde Présidentielle*, a new brigade of elite "counter-terrorist" troops, the Léopards (5), began training and were a part of the formal Army structure. Yet those who thought the *macoutes* had been tamed or disbanded were wrong. True, they had gone to ground, but, like pythons napping after the ingestion of a particularly plump goat, they were too busy participating in the new prosperity to revert to old ways.

Cambronne's hand was everywhere. Some went so far as to say it often touched that of the so-called "First Lady of the Revolution", Simone Duvalier. Still strong with that bastion of Duvalierists, the *Chauffeurs-Guides* (who now had tourists to chauffeur and guide about), he owned travel agencies, plantations, and was instrumental in establishing a thriving trade of the export of Haitian cadavers for use by foreign Medical schools. The cadavers were said to be much-prized in the U.S. and Canada because their lack of fat made them easier for medical students to dissect.

Not even the few remaining operating spurs of the Chemin de Fer National escaped his predations - honed ten years earlier in the "*Mouvement Rénovation National*" that had so successfully raised money when the U.S. Government had turned off the aid spigot. Passenger service had long since been abandoned (6), but cane was still hauled by train from as far West as Léogane, through Carrefour, along the waterfront, and into the HASCO refinery. The track and roadbed that led to St. Marc and East to Croix-des-Bouquets still saw occasional use. To the North, just outside the Cap where the railroad station had once stood, sat in lonely majesty the hulk of one steam locomotive - sole remnant of the line that had run all the way to Bahon only fifty years earlier.

The rail system that had been such a horn of plenty for so many over the course of eighty years did provide one final opportunity for peculation. With Simone Duvalier's blessing (7), the rolling stock (save that too rusted out to be of use) and anything that could be used was sold, mostly abroad. Some of the rails are today employed as fenceposts on beachfront villas on the road North to St. Marc.

Busy as the various guardians of Duvalierism were making money, they were not too busy to snipe at one another. Without Papa Doc to regulate the flow of power and patronage, infighting was not slow in coming. In late July - with the old man dead barely three months - Cambronne pounced, arresting Max Dominique's cousin on charges of passport counterfeiting. Marie-Denise Duvalier, asserting her position as Jean-Claude's private secretary, demanded the release of her husband's kinsman as well as Cambronne's ouster.

Presented with his first crisis, Jean-Claude sought advice from his Mother and heeded it, for a glum-looking Marie-Denise and Max Dominique soon thereafter left for Paris where Dominique resumed his Ambassadorship. Marie-Denise's functions as private secretary were filled by Duvalier's St. Louis de Gonzague classmate Auguste ('ti Pouche) Douyon. Loyal, a gifted raconteur, Douyon knew his friend's limits and came quickly to handle all manner of personal errands that Duvalier chose to delegate - from procurement of women to banking.

The young president, increasingly confident, began to resume his forays from the palace, lightly guarded, if guarded at all, to the houses of friends. In those years it was not uncommon for the driver of a sports car on the Pétionville or Delmas roads to find himself in a late-night impromptu race with the Chief of State at the wheel of one of a rapidly expanding stable of muscle cars of various pedigrees. A wave or blink of the headlights usually signalled the end of the contest.

Attentive to his mother's advice, Duvalier grudgingly acceded to her demand that he study law when the academic year began in October. Tutored in turn by three of Haiti's most eminent lawyers, he would quickly doze off while his professor continued his monologue. A "secretary" (Simone Duvalier's insurance against the inculcation of any radical ideas) took notes. The tutors left promptly at the time designated for the lesson's end whether their young charge was awake or not. His stock line for foreign journalists was, "Not a night passes that I don't fall asleep with my books."

As year XIV of the revolution came to a close, Simone Duvalier and others must have breathed sighs of relief. A record number (more than 90,000) tourists had come including such gliterati as Arthur Ashe and Mohammed Ali. Aid, including the $750,000 Ambassador Knox had lobbied so hard for, had reached $8 million. The foreign press was indeed being appropriately "objective". So far, so good.

Seeking a "family" Christmas, Simone summoned home Marie-Denise and Max Dominique from Paris for the holidays and was put out when Max found the climate of Acapulco more salubrious than that of Port-au-Prince. One of the first bits of business of the new year was to strip him of his Ambassadorship. His brother found himself recalled home from his demanding post as press attache in Rio, while a chum lost the taxing sinecure of consul in Le Havre.

As the young president read in flat tones set pieces prepared for him in stilted, oratorical, French, raced motorcycles, hunted, and tried to enjoy being a twenty year old, Cambronne - Richelieu behind the throne - was busier than ever. Shuttling back and forth to Miami (now only 90 minutes away by jet), his various commercial interests demanded more and more of his time.

In addition to the cadaver business, a new line, plasma sales, had been developed. Every morning, lines of the poorest of the poor formed in front of the Port-au-Prince offices of a company called Hemo Caribbean. From their blood was extracted plasma, for which they were paid a few dollars. The blood products were then exported to the U.S. at a handsome profit. Cambronne was estimated to net some $25,000 a month for his role as middleman. "The 'plasma cows'", one Haitian doctor observed to writer Herbert Gold, "are rather tired, but they don't have jobs anyway."

For those who found life under the Duvalierist economic revolution too taxing, Cambronne had a home-grown panacea. On a well-tended plantation near Arcahaie, *paysans* busily cultivated high-grade cannabis both for local consumption and the beginnings of what was to become a lucrative export trade.

March found Cambronne, Foreign Minister Raymond, and Finance Minister Francisque making the rounds of official Washington on what the *New York Times* described as a "self-initiated goodwill mission." Offered lunch on succeeding days by Secretary of State Rogers and the Pentagon, the visitors pressed Haiti's case for increased aid on all fronts.

The team's visit coincided with the publication of articles two days running in the *New York Times* detailing Haiti's, and more specifically, Cambronne's relationship with a Miami-based company called Aerotrade. Aerotrade, the *Times* revealed had been designated by Haiti as its agent to purchase arms in the United States and had hired ex-Marines to assist in the training of the *Léopards*.

In response to press inquiries about the export of arms to a country which had been subject to a U.S. arms embargo since 1962, Foggy Bottom quietly let drop the news that the embargo had actually been lifted without fanfare by President Nixon in late 1970, some seven months before Papa Doc's death.

Cambronne's presence at the Pentagon therefore surprised no one in the know, nor did his request for an evaluation team to take stock of Haiti's military needs, eerily reminiscent of the minuet Papa Doc had danced with the U.S. government in 1957. Typically, the request for advice was accompanied by a detailed shopping list for some $1.5 million in ordnance that Haiti had been starved for over the previous decade.

The *Times* article went on to say that the Nixon administration was disposed to give "favorable consideration" to Cambronne's request. Not only Washington, but Ottawa and Paris, as well as the World Bank, OAS, and InterAmerican

Development Bank all were quietly engaged in conversations with Port-au-Prince, seeking appropriate development vehicles to showcase their largesse.

Aid projects began to be parceled out to various countries like prize job assignments. The French were to tackle, yet again, a road for Jacmel (8), the Canadians the road to the Cap - the list was endless. As in the time of Antoine Simon, the smell of money was in the air, of *"pots-de-vin, judicieusement distribués"*. The fly in the ointment was that most, if not all, of the incoming aid seemed at some point always to pass through the hands of the man who was becoming known around Port-au-Prince as the "Premier" - a post not provided for in the Haitian constitution.

Tourists disembarking at the François Duvalier jet airport were greeted with a picture of the latest president for life on which was emblazoned the following quote:

"My father made the political revolution.
I, I will make the economic revolution."

To many in Port-au-Prince it seemed that the primary beneficiary of the economic revolution was one of its main fighters - Cambronne himself.

On April 22, 1972, expectant crowds gathered outside the Cimetière to watch the *Jeune Leader* mark the first anniversary of Papa Doc's death. It cheered as a stolid Jean-Claude, accompanied by his mother, Cambronne, and the rest of the Cabinet paid their respects. After taps was played, the convoy roared back to the land of the living as quickly as it had arrived at the city of the dead.

Cambronne's March pilgrimage to Washington bore fruit in July. An ambiguously named "technical team" of U.S. Officers whose mission was to assess the future needs of the Haitian Armed Forces slipped quietly into Port-au-Prince. That same month, in a move that would have gotten no approval from the newest occupant of the Duvalier mausoleum, the *Académie Militaire* was reopened after an eleven year hiatus, albeit only with carefully vetted officer candidates.

Port-au-Prince, and selected pockets of the rest of Haiti seemed to be waking up. New hotels were being opened and old ones re-furbished as hoteliers saw occupancy rates unknown in fifteen years. The telephone system, long dormant, had been coaxed back to life by Canadian engineers who, in their thoroughness, saw to it that even a legendary leak in the roof of the Central Telephone Exchange was repaired. (9)

Quietly, many Haitians who had spent years abroad began returning, at first as visitors, then as residents. Those who had been shoved onto Pan American flights by *Tonton macoutes* had little hope of returning while a Duvalier occupied the *Palais*, but others, for whom exile had been more a matter of prudence rather than necessity, now found the climate far more to their liking and returned, often with fortunes and families fledged abroad.

Portents of change were everywhere, and irony of ironies, nearly all the change was being brought about by Duvalier's alliance with those very forces his father had sought to neutralize - the Army and the elite.

Predictably, exemplifying the Chinese maxim that "the nail that sticks out gets hammered down", the high-flying "Premier" who had engineered the Dominique's exile was about to have the tables turned on him. The agent of change was Roger Lafontant, an early devotee of Papa Doc whose willingness to traduce his fellow student strikers in 1961 had earned him a place in the Duvalier hierarchy. While Simone Duvalier was in Miami visiting her third daughter, Lafontant managed to convince Jean-Claude that Cambronne was guilty of "disloyalty". Suddenly denied access to the *Palais*, Cambronne - no stranger to such maneuvers - deduced what was afoot and sought refuge in the Colombian embassy. In the time-honored manner of such things, a few days later he found himself in Bogota. *L'Inspiratrice*, returning quickly from Miami after word reached her of the doings in Port-au-Prince, was too late to undo the damage done by Lafontant.

Somewhat truculently, the president turned a deaf ear to his mother's pleas to soften his views about Cambronne. In reality, he had already begun to outgrow the constrictive role which the elder Duvalierist *noirs* had designed for him. Ever a realist, Simone set about to put the best face on things, and the outside world was informed of a "change in the cabinet" resulting from Duvalier's alleged "distaste" for some of Cambronne's business activities, particularly plasma farming.

Hemo Caribbean closed its doors, while the divorce law that had proved so lucrative was modified slightly so that both parties had to be represented.(10) As further evidence of the regime's new-found probity, it was announced that all revenues from quickie divorces would henceforth go into "official" accounts - a backhanded way of acknowledging that such revenues had heretofore been funnelled straight into Cambronne's pockets.

A number of Cambronne acolytes such as Fritz Cinéas, Secretary of State (former bomb maker in 1957) for Information, followed their master into "exile" in the following months. Unlike Papa Doc's days, these periods of "exile" were short, providing time for reflection, after which the offender was allowed without fanfare to return home. Duvalier, donning his inherited mantle of "Spiritual Leader of the Nation" spoke feelingly of the need for "morality" in government.

As the nation approached its second Christmas without Papa Doc, more political prisoners were either released or had their sentences shortened, lending credence to reports that the new Duvalier government was liberalizing.

Bolstering such a view was a newfound license in the press, and more importantly in largely illiterate Haiti, on the airwaves. Criticism of local problems - which once guaranteed a visit from the TTM's and a smashing of one's presses or transmitter - was now allowed, provided always that it was couched ever so carefully.

Appearances mattered, for the regime was moving into a position that Papa Doc had never allowed - it was becoming dependent on foreign aid. In particular, the once "cool and correct" relationship with Washington had grown steadily more cozy since the succession, but certain cosmetic changes were required to allow the U.S. administration to sell domestically the notion that things were improving in Haiti.

It was thus of particular concern to both countries when just before Mardi Gras in 1973, the U.S. Ambassador (after nearly four years in service, a veteran), "Honorary *macoute*" Clinton Knox and his First Consul were kidnapped by three gunmen demanding the release of several political prisoners as well as $500,000 ransom. Compounding the confusion was the fact that several of the prisoners whose freedom was being sought had not been on what had been thought to be an authoritative list of such prisoners issued by the government a few weeks earlier.

This slight contradiction was overlooked in the scurry to resolve the crisis. With the mediation of the French Ambassador, twelve prisoners were released from Fort Dimanche and put on board a Mexico-bound Air Haiti DC-6 with the kidnappers and $70,000 in ransom money. An exile group in New York - the Coalition of National Liberation Brigades - claimed responsibility for the affair and warned that more violence could be expected.

Such contretemps were infrequent however, and nothing like the air of almost ongoing siege that had characterized Papa Doc's early years was allowed to mar the feeling of *bonhomie* that seemed to be the hallmark of the rule of the son.

That rule was very nearly cut short in a fashion quite familiar to several of his predecessors. One procedure that had remained unchanged was the storage of nearly all munitions in the basement of the Palace. Access, whether by gold key or some other system, was strictly limited. From causes unknown, a fire roared through the basement on, of course, July 22nd. Huge explosions reverberated throughout the city as ammunition exploded.

The regime quickly sought help from the American Embassy, discarding advice from Haitian firefighters (who, to be fair, may well have not known just how explosive the contents of the palace basement were) to let the fire burn itself out. Experts were brought in from the U.S. Naval base at Guantanamo Bay, and under their direction, the blaze was soon doused. How much of the stock lost had been procured as a result of the Nixon administration's shift in policy was unclear.

Initial reports had the building largely destroyed like its predecessors in 1912 and 1883, but Paul Baussan's structure proved hardier than early edifices, so that while substantial repairs had to be made, the *Palais* remained Port-au-Prince's most imposing building. As the principal occupant of the building was away for the weekend, little official comment was made on the matter, though this did not dampen elaborate conspiracy theories from being propounded around the city.

With Cambronne and the Dominiques gone, the remaining Regents sought, in their disparate fashion, to continue to assert their influence. To their dismay, Jean-Claude Duvalier was increasingly inclined to seek the advice of those who had shown him kindnesses while he was growing up, or "apolitical" (i.e., non-*noir*, politically neutral) individuals whose expertise was needed.

One such returnee, Lucien Rigaud, had actually come home in the waning months of Papa Doc's rule. An astute businessman, Rigaud took one look at the wharfage system in Port-au-Prince and knew major changes would have to be made. The customs sheds were by then eighty years old, and the wharf, jutting far out into the silt-laden bay to Fort Caca (which, with the increasing amounts of ordure being dumped into the bay ever more justified its name), had been built under Tonton Nord.

Rigaud pitched the concept of containerization to an enfeebled and suspicious Papa Doc who was, like Dessalines before him, suspicious of a Rigaud returning from exile with new ideas. In this instance though, the old man gave his assent, with the result that by 1973, in partnership with Sea-Land containers, new facilities were being constructed to draw Haiti into the world's transportation web. The new project was completed just in time to serve the expanding needs of new assembly plants erected on the Northern fringes of Port-au-Prince.

It was through Rigaud that Jean-Claude Duvalier had been introduced to a staffer for Congressman Daniel Flood ("Dapper Dan") of Pennsylvania who had appeared in Port-au-Prince bearing a letter of introduction from his boss and seeking an audience with the president. Stephen Elko was granted his audience and soon thereafter, Rigaud and a Haitian Air Force Major were dispatched to Washington to make a plea for increased aid for Haiti.

Lodged in the same apartment building as Flood, during a two week visit the duo made the rounds of Capitol Hill under the tutelage of Elko and Flood. What Flood's colleagues did not know as the thirty year veteran of Congress called in chits and importuned them on poor Haiti's behalf was the nature of the understanding between Port-au-Prince and Flood. In return for his services, Flood received veto power over which U.S. companies were to get contracts for Haiti-related projects and in turn got kickbacks from those companies.

The Rigaud/Cazeau mission quickly bore fruit. Before Congress adjourned for Christmas, U.S. aid to Haiti was more than doubled as President Nixon signed into law a $26 million aid package for the island.

The international aid that the regime was becoming so dependent on was all conditioned on the regime's continuing "liberalization". This was evidenced to the outside world's satisfaction by incremental loosening of press controls, periodic freeings of those prisoners hardy (or lucky) enough to have survived time in Fort Dimanche and tolerating visits by various human rights groups. The latter was especially galling to the old line Duvalierists (referred to as the "dinosaurs" by younger, lighter-skinned members of the government).

After a few initial mistakes, the government perfected its routine in this regard, emptying cells at Fort Dimanche, painting them, and substituting felons and even soldiers three or four to a cell for dozens of skeletal carcasses that had been crammed in before an investigating commission's arrival. Much like the Nazi charade at Theresienstadt, all of this was done with the utmost cynicism. Beneath the surface, however, there was a change in tone.

Few were arrested on mere whim, and fewer still subjected to the elaborate tortures once routinely conducted in the Palace basement. Extortion, bribery, cruelty, all still held sway as they had always done in Haiti, but compared to the previous decade, "liberalization" was indeed prevailing.

Spring

Not only did Paris, Washington, and other major capitals (London, the sole holdout, still withheld its blessing as a result of its Ambassador's ouster in 1962) buy the story, but the man on the street in those countries did as well. François Duvalier Airport, celebrating its tenth year of service, received some 200,000 tourists in 1973.

Jumbo jets poured in from Europe with those seeking "something different". Nor were the beautiful people forced to congregate solely on the veranda of the Oloffson (11) and listen to the cajoleries of Graham Greene's model for Petit Pierre, Aubelin Jolicoeur.

In an article entitled "A New Retreat for the Rich - Surrounded by Misery", the *New York Times* chronicled the opening at the beginning of 1974 of a set of colonial ruins rebuilt into an hotel with a series of surrounding villas, each with its own pool. Christened *Habitation* Leclerc, the project's publicists maintained that this property had once belonged to Napoleon's sister and that she had lived there while her husband was trying to re-take Haiti.

History does not record Pauline venturing further South than Dondon, but no one had the audacity to ruin such a splendid fiction with any taint of veracity. George Hamilton, Alexis Smith, Barbara Walters and numerous Palm Beach and New York socialites mingled with Haiti's rich in buildings designed by Albert Mangonès. "Baby Doc" failed to show as promised, but sister Nicole breathlessly gushed "Finally, Haiti has something no other country has."

Unfortunately, what had been several leagues South of Port-au-Prince in the eighteenth century had since been enveloped by one of its more insalubrious slums. Arriving guests were driven in dilapidated jitneys over potholed roads, dodging naked children, market women, pigs and chickens only to reach the oasis of *Habitation* Leclerc, its calm guaranteed by high walls topped with shards of broken glass. There, for $150.- a day (roughly the per capita income of the average Haitian in that year), their material wants were ministered to.

Those who cared to venture outside the compound could partake of simpler and cheaper pleasures in the capital's conveniently close and shabby red-light district. One of the more renowned Madams, seeking to cash in on the tourist boom, had re-christened her establishment as a "guest house". Still on display for all to see though, were the framed diploma from the University of Nebraska (by correspondence) in taxidermy and the various animals she had had her girls stuff in idle hours in years past. It was the closest thing Haiti had to a museum of natural history.

While newcomers may have been startled by the poverty, clamor and chaos, a visitor returning in 1974 after ten years could not help but be impressed by the changes. At the airport, all was calm. No frisking by *macoutes*, no fights between taxi drivers over fares. Jolting (some things remained constant) along the Boulevard Hailie Selassie from the airport, one passed the Parc Industriel which housed so many of the new assembly factories.

Travel within the country was relatively easy, the necessary permits obtained in one stop. A trip to the Cap occasioned multiple detours as road crews, thanks to a Canadian grant, worked the length and breadth of the road to rebuild and resurface the route linking the two cities. North of St. Marc, one had to swing inland. After ninety years' service, the bridge at l'Estère whose "baptism" ninety years earlier had occasioned such laments from the Church had finally collapsed.

Telephones worked. There were few blackouts. Quietly, many were willing to speak on subjects they would not have confided to their confessor at the height of the terror. Many things endured, though somehow institutionalized and seemingly (to foreign eyes) softened. The *VSN* blue denim was no longer regarded as an oddity, but as part of the established order. It had been so long since anyone had been allowed to walk on the sidewalk in front of the Palace that many assumed it had always been that way.(12)

Duvalierism had become institutionalized - some of its most savage proponents grey haired, pot-bellied and hugely invested in the status quo. When threatened, they still reacted fiercely, but for the sake of the international community, Duvalierism was on its best behavior. Indeed, sniffed one observer, if Papa Doc had spent much of his life in the *maquis*, it seemed that Jean-Claude was spending it in the *maquillage*.

Maquillage though was what it was, and like all makeup, only skin deep. Madame Max Adolphe might truck out members of the *VSN* on weekends as part of a tree planting campaign (13), but she had lost none of her abilities to order torture or beatings. Outside Port-au-Prince, away from the glare of publicity, the chef sections ruled as they always had, with an iron hand. Nobody around Gonaïves talked about liberalization as long as Zacharie Delva was still practicing black magic and coercing unwilling peasant lads into his bed.

Fort Dimanche might have less prisoners, but this was scant consolation to those caught up in the net. Scions of *jaune* families who had grown up abroad and took the regime at its word with regard to a new mood in Haiti found themselves hustled aboard the next flight back out or worse, in Fort Dimanche, for some indiscrete association or utterance in New York or Paris that had been picked up by the well-oiled Duvalier intelligence machine. Between Fort Dimanche, the Dessalines barracks, and the police station in Port-au-Prince, some four hundred political prisoners were held in conditions designed to snuff out their lives. Those who survived initial interrogations at the *Casernes* were consigned to Fort Dimanche, there to perish from tuberculosis, malnutrition or madness. The machine was still in place, still functioning, still turning Haitian against Haitian, demonstrating the evil genius of its creator. "Jean-Claude Duvalier", one diplomat, "is a pleasant young man surrounded by hyenas."

How much of the nastier aspects of running his government the president was aware of initially is unclear. Most of the torturing was done away from the Palace, either next door in the *Casernes*, or at the downtown police station known as the "*Cafétéria*".(14) He never came to share his father's relish for the exquisite agonies inflicted on the regime's prisoners, but neither did he curb those who enjoyed such activities.

Just as a new generation of technocrats was on the rise, so too was a new generation of police and army officers well skilled in the means necessary to allow the regime to keep its grip. Some of the older *macoutes* such as Luc Désir made tape-recordings of interrogations they conducted, apparently savoring them in quiet moments.(15)

While the more distasteful aspects of the regime were conducted away from the public eye, Duvalier circulated easily, partying with friends, giving lavish gifts (cars - Volvos - and wristwatches were special marks of favor) and doling out patronage. He saw a number of different women, and, rumor had it in Port-au-Prince, fathered a son by one of them, but no special love interest captured his attention.

Occasionally, some peccadillo would be too much even by the relaxed standards set by the regime for its public servants, and the normally relaxed president was forced to act. Such was the case in 1975, when several well-placed individuals (including, it was said, Nicole Duvalier, whose cut was touted at some $4 Million) colluded to have a very limited edition of commemorative postage stamps produced in Europe for the collector's market. The stamps' bona fides were certified to International Postal authorities by a copy of the official gazette, *Le Moniteur*, of which one copy had quietly been produced for just such purposes.

The plotters had not reckoned on Haitian stamp collectors, one of whom received an advertisement for the issue from Europe. As he was also highly placed on *Le Moniteur*, he went to his superiors in some puzzlement.

Word began to leak out, and a show trial was held which purported to identify and punish the malefactors. Port-au-Prince was riveted by the process and wondered how close to the palace prosecutorial zeal would take the investigators. None of the principal culprits were fingered, and those who actually did time were later rewarded for their silence.

One factor in the decision to lift the curtain on this affair was a severe drought that was taking its toll on already dwindling traditional agricultural exports such as coffee and sugar and which had caused failures of the rice and corn harvests. The government, more dependent than ever on its international benefactors, was forced to listen to advice from various foreign chancelleries.

Some of the foreign missions had inserted themselves deep into the running of the government. Just how proprietary official Washington was about its links to the Palace was illustrated starkly to one young foreign service officer. Posted to Haiti (he was the third generation in his family to have served there either in the Marines or Diplomatic Corps, and the second to have lived there as a child), in his first week he was summoned by a Senior Official in the embassy. The Official minced no words. "I know you knew the president when he was a boy. You are not to contact him or approach him in any way. He's mine."

In a meeting in 1975 with one of the authors, Jean-Claude Duvalier asked after this individual and his brothers by name, and looking puzzled and a bit hurt, said "he's never gotten in touch with me, but I know he's here."

That same year, drought, aside from showing to the world pictures of swollen-bellied children suffering from malnutrition (it was estimated in 1974 that some 75% of school age children suffered from some degree of malnutrition), also reduced the amount of electricity generated by Péligre. Oil-powered generators partially filled the gap, but the return of occasional blackouts reminded some observers of just how thin the veneer of prosperity was.

At odds with the image of drought and poverty was an odd new subterranean structure with volcano-like roof vents one block from the Palace. It had been finished in the middle of 1975 at a cost, it was reported, of between three and five million dollars. Intended as a mausoleum for Papa Doc, it sat empty for months, generating speculation about the Palace's reasons for not wanting to disturb the old man's remains. Some said that he had never been buried in the cemetery at all - that his corpse was kept in the Palace in the event a quick exit was required by the living. Sitting unused in a city teeming with humanity, it provided ironic commentary on the regime's claims about the economic miracles of Duvalierism.

One businessman told a New York Times reporter (not for attribution of course - liberalization had its limits), "A few people are making a lot of money, but very little spills over to the masses. You can't really talk about economic recovery."

Still, with new roads open to the Cap and the South, foreign aid, tourists pouring in and generally benign press treatment, those with such views were dismissed as cassandras. Life was good for Duvalier and those around him. Simone Duvalier placated the "dinosaurs", yet enough "liberalization" was under way to satisfy Haiti's patrons in the international community, so there prevailed an odd kind of stasis - one that permitted Jean-Claude Duvalier to delegate many of the more tiresome chores of ruling to an increasingly light-skinned and young group, seasoned here and there by holdovers from his father's rule.

One of the most durable of the dinosaurs, though certainly not a *noir*, the aptly named Paul Blanchet, found himself without portfolio for the first time in many years as a Cabinet shuffle on the eve of the president's fifth anniversary in office removed him from his post as interior minister. One or two other tremors briefly interrupted Port-au-Prince's agreeable torpor as executives from a Dallas real estate firm testified before the U.S.Senate about the efforts of "a small black man who resembled a grade B Hollywood gangster" to extract a $200,000 bribe for "the widows and orphan's fund" of the president in return for permission to proceed with a development scheme for La Tortue. The widow and orphan, the executive revealed, were Simone Duvalier and her son. Rather than cave in, the company took its lumps, receiving, it revealed, "little help" from the U.S. Embassy.

Just as a prescient Léger had seen fit in 1908 to warn Tonton Nord from Washington of President Taft's likely attitude toward Haiti, so disquieting rumblings began to be heard from the U.S. as the Summer of 1976 turned to Fall. Keen observer of the U.S. political scene, the Government watched the candidacy of Jimmy Carter with alarm, reminiscent as he seemed of John Kennedy.

Two widely disseminated Jack Anderson articles that appeared immediately after the Democratic convention lambasted both the amount of U.S. aid to Haiti and the uses to which it was being put. Pouring salt in the wound, Anderson revealed that the regime (shades of Hurricane Flora in 1960) was refusing donations of used clothing on the grounds of "sanitation" reasons for the drought-stricken Northwest, by then suffering through a second consecutive year in which the rains had failed.

The government had not helped its international image with the July disappearance of a crusading young journalist, Gasner Raymond, who had pushed the government's tolerance of a limited free press to its limits with his investigation of labor unrest.

With an eye to the North, Duvalier decreed his Christmas amnesty earlier than usual - in fact in early October - announcing that some 261 prisoners would be released on November 17th - a few days after the American Presidential elections. "Some" were political, the regime announced, prudently declining to give specific figures, as even the innumerate were finding it increasingly difficult to square the periodic release of more political prisoners with its insistence that it held none.

The Port-au-Prince amnesty seemed not to sway the American electorate one whit, and euphoria over early Republican victories turned to consternation as Democrats chalked up successive wins later in the evening. By 1976, every nuance of U.S. electoral politics was trapped from space by the satellite dishes that had begun to sprout in Pétionville's more prosperous neighborhoods. Thus Haiti's "haves" realized immediately that the Democratic outsider who won the U.S. Presidency seemed to threaten the U.S.-Haitian entente that had endured since Papa Doc ordered champagne served on November 22, 1963.

Not all the satellite dishes were in the posher sections of town. Shortly after Jimmy Carter's election, a Baptist preacher, Luc Nerée, took it upon himself to write his co-religionist and president-elect about the human rights problems in Haiti. Carter, in what was to prove the first of a long series of sallies into matters Haitian, promptly wrote back pledging support and offering to preach in Nerée's church.

The correspondence quickly became known, and putting on its *cançons fer*, the government arrested more than 100 people in the capital as the year came to an end. As always, a shroud of mystery surrounded the fates of those arrested. Appointments announced by the incoming U.S. administration, drawing as they did on cadres of veteran U.S. Civil Rights workers, made for a somber New Year's celebration. Andrew Young's nomination as U.N. Ambassador elicited pronounced distaste in Port-au-Prince.

Mindful, perhaps, of the prevailing winds, the regime that had arrested one-hundred in December announced the release of ninety in January, again to no avail. Amnesty International, piercing the veil of secrecy that had heretofore surrounded such matters had been doing its sums with a mathematical exactitude unseen in Haiti since the days of "Bank" Williams. It announced that the majority of prisoners released were non-political. In any case, Amnesty added, few of those on the list had actually been seen free in Port-au-Prince or anywhere else.

In reaction, the Duvalier family circled its wagons, judging the time appropriate to bid Marie-Denise to rejoin yet again the inner circle. Despite pleas from Marie-Denise, the time never seemed quite right or circumstances desperate enough to invite Max Dominique home with his wife. Once, at the beginning of 1978, he was so confident of going home that he actually had his car shipped back from the U.S. To bolster support among the up-and-coming generation of army officers, Simone Duvalier orchestrated the marriage of Nicole Duvalier to Acedius St.-Louis, commander of the *Léopards*, in a match reminiscent of that of the Dominique's a decade earlier. St. Louis's ascent in the army was blocked though by Gracia Jacques, that most venerable of Duvalierist "dinosaurs"and commander of the presidential guard. Rumor had it around Port-au-Prince that St. Louis sought to remove the last obstacle to his promotion by having a *ouanga* placed on Jacques, himself a noted *bocor*. On several mornings Jacques arrived at his office to find various traces of black magic.

Even as the residents of the Palace sought other-worldly help in their power struggles, the Gods continued to frown on Haiti's Northwest, by 1977 baking in a third year of drought. Péligre's catch basins were at their lowest level in twenty years, forcing EDH (Electricité d'Haïti) to cut power in Port-au-Prince to five hours a day. Observers worried that permanent climate change might have been wrought as a result of the progressive de-forestation of the once lush island, as precious moisture-retaining soil was washed by what rains there were into the sea. "Haiti", remarked one observer, [has]"a big brown dirt mark around (it) in the blue Caribbean - like a dirt ring in a bath tub. That is the topsoil going to sea."

Into the breach poured various aid organizations, but while their penetration
of all levels of Haitian society bought temporary peace for the regime, it
mortgaged even further the autonomy which François Duvalier had so zealously
guarded.

High on the international hit list was the *Régie du Tabac*, that piece of fiscal
fly-paper to which a portion of all revenues seemed to adhere and then
disappear. Despite promises of "reform" and "fiscalization" of the *Régie* that
had been made as early as 1971, the Duvaliers continued to operate it as their
private piggy bank, as they pled poverty to the International community.

"Jean-Claudist" bumper sticker c. 1977 - *Heinl Collection*

Even the French, tpraditionally indulgent of their former colonies, expressed
impatience with a regime which collected $12 million a year in taxes earmarked
for the "discretionary fund" of the President of the Republic. One World Bank
report announced that approximately half of the 1975 Government revenues of
$95 million was credited to "special accounts" whose purposes were "unclear".
A series in *Le Monde* entitled "Blank check for Haiti" lashed out at
"administrative carelessness, incompetence, peculation of public funds, and [the
reliance on] torture" of the Duvalier regime. Clearly some re-packaging of the
regime was in order.

On the sixth anniversary of his father's death, Jean-Claude Duvalier startled
the country by abandoning the stuffy set pieces so carefully prepared for him

and addressed the nation in Créole. In what was described as a "pungent" piece, he announced the birth of a new ideology - "Jean-Claudism" - whose goal was to complement the political liberation of the masses that had happened under his father with economic progress to boot. In one sense, his mission was already accomplished - Haiti's political and economic maturation were in no danger of outpacing one another - both were in an appalling state.

Mindful of the increasingly reproachful foreign chorus, the regime set to organizing the parades of May 1st, Workers and Agriculture Day, with a special zeal. Parading before the Palace for all to see were thousands of enthusiastic "workers" fueled by the *clairin* and cash doled out liberally on such occasions. Yet the device had lost much of its effect on a foreign community whose workers were now insinuated into the remotest nooks and crannies of Haiti and who could report the facts to their home offices.

More telling was the remark of one foreign agricultural expert that "you could give money to everyone in Haiti to buy food, and some would come home empty-handed, for the country's food production is now insufficient to feed its masses." Underlining that statement was the stark fact that Haiti, which in the 18th century provided ALL of France's sugar and much of that needed for the rest of Europe, was now forced to import sugar for its domestic needs.

As the masses scrambled for food, the regime continued to try to at least appear responsive to its foreign sponsors, voting in Grenada on June 22d for a human rights resolution which called on Western Hemisphere countries to abjure torture, arbitrary arrest, and execution without due process.

Haiti's vote gave no solace to the inmates of Fort Dimanche. Lucien Rigaud, instrumental in opening the U.S. aid spickets three years earlier, by 1977 had himself fallen prey to the system he had helped bolster. Imprisoned on a trumped-up murder charge, he was luckier than most of his cell mates. Bribes paid regularly had secured him a better diet than most of his fellow inmates, and he was able in early 1977, to secure a temporary transfer to the prison wing of the General Hospital so that his wife could visit him. Using drug-laced soft drinks and bribes supplied by his Swiss wife, Rigaud managed a daring escape and bolted straight for the sanctuary of the Mexican Embassy, taking with him numerous documents related to the various projects and individuals whose fortunes he had helped advance.

The regime was furious. Rigaud's escape could not have been more inopportune, and several of Rigaud's erstwhile jailers found themselves consigned to the tender mercies of the institutions they had been running.

Ignoring such unpleasant matters, U.S. Ambassador Heywood Isham gave a valedictory press conference on July 6th, bemoaning the "gulf" between foreign perceptions and what was actually happening in Haiti. Isham praised the regime's progress in correcting "certain" excesses and abuses. Isham's recall spared him the duty of hosting a Carter appointee with whose views he could not have been much in sympathy.

Andrew Young, the Carter administration's ambassador to the U.N. and human rights tribune was scheduled to stop in Port-au-Prince on August 16th as part of a hemispheric tour. Anticipating that Young would not, as one foreign ministry wag put it drily, "be another Clinton Knox", the government launched what was quickly dubbed "operation bluff". More political prisoners were to be freed, the screws loosened further on the press, and a smiling face put on Duvalierism.

Washington announced Isham's replacement before Young's visit. William Jones, a career diplomat, like Bailly-Blanchard sixty years earlier, was to leave the City of Light, where he had been accredited to UNESCO, for Port-au-Prince. Black, 49 years old, a member of the California Bar, he was indeed unlikely to be "another Clinton Knox."

The new Ambassador wasted no time in taking up his post. On hand as Andrew Young's plane landed in Port-au-Prince after the short hop from the Dominican Republic were the Haitian Foreign Minister, Edner Brutus and other grim-faced representatives of the government. The tone had been set just before Ambassador Young's arrival by an airport press briefing given by a U.S. official.

"The United States intends to communicate clearly and distinctly to the Government of Haiti the Carter Administration human rights policy... the situation [despite the release of some prisoners] remains very serious."

Underlining his priorities, Young spent his first night on Haitian soil with a Baptist preacher and his congregation, whose prayers he sought for his meeting with President Duvalier on the morrow.

Underscoring the message of changes afoot in Haiti's U.S. relations, the next morning's *New York Times* carried an image destined to become familiar to the world, but which was then novel. A rickety wooden sailboat, crammed to the gunwales with Haitian refugees was shown being towed by the Coast Guard into Miami after being intercepted off the Florida Coast. Sixty-one people had been at sea for a month. Impatient with diplomacy, the "boat people" of Haiti began turning up, unbidden and unwelcome, on America's shores.

After a long day of meetings with the full panoply of Haiti's rulers, Young startled his hosts and reporters with a candid press conference at which he blasted Haiti's record on human rights, adding that "the imprisonment of voices of dissent, denying of access to families and the denial of the most fundamental due process" could no longer be tolerated. And then, like so many who sought to put their own imprint on Haiti, he was gone, flying off to the next stop on his itinerary.

Young had encountered, it was said, "a recalcitrant" attitude among Haitian officials whom he sought to lecture on human rights. Duvalier had received coolly a list of twenty prisoners who were "special cases" and promised to "look into them", but no tangible progress had been obtained. To make matters worse from the regime's point of view, the dirty laundry was being aired in front of the at least partially unmuzzled Haitian press - its own freedom the result of concessions to Washington.

Angry recriminations resounded through the Palace that night, with the "Dinosaurs" demanding the end of any more concessions while younger "liberals" sought ever-greater change.

Against this somber backdrop, the regime marked on September 22, 1977, the observance of twenty years of Duvalierism. The press had been reminded in a none-too-subtle fashion by the Palace in a release from the Minister for Information, Pierre Gousse, that a "...Campaign of MOTIVATION for the urban and rural populace through the publication and broadcast of SLOGANS exalting the political, cultural, economic and social conquests of Duvalierism to the benefit of the Haitian people from 1957 - 1977" would be undertaken, and that this would constitute an opportunity for all to "renew their attachment [not only] to the Chief of State, but to the First Lady of the Republic, her excellency Simone Ovide Duvalier, Vigilant witness on duty on nights of watchfulness and meditation of the illustrious departed, counsellor to the Chief of State."

Heeding begrudgingly the admonitions from its able Ambassador in Washington, Georges Salomon (a direct descendent of the great president), the government stated that it had freed 104 political prisoners to celebrate its twenty years in power. Then, letting the other shoe drop, it announced that it held no more political prisoners. Those whose family members had disappeared were now free to apply to judicial organs to regularize the status of the deceased.

Predictably, the move only intensified the light shone on Haiti's human rights policy generally.

Hoping to capitalize on what they viewed as a window of opportunity created by the Young visit and the concessions made by the government that loosened the fetters of the press, three young journalists - Marc Garcia of Radio Métropole; Guy Meyer of Radio Haïti; and Bob Nerée, the son of the courageous Baptist pastor who had written Jimmy Carter the previous year, of weekly *Hebdo Jeune Presse* - made their way across the border to the Dominican Republic. There, on October 18th, they outlined the state of Haitian press freedom to the annual Inter-American conference on Freedom of the press.

The picture they painted was a somber one. Fresh in many minds still was the murder some months previously of *Le Petit Samedi Soir*'s Gasner Raymond after an article in which he limned in painful detail the exploitation of workers by the state-owned flour mill. One foreign observer in Port-au-Prince was quoted as saying that "anyone in Haiti who takes the Government's assurances on press freedom at face value is playing Russian Roulette."

What the three young reporters did not suspect was that the voice that had thundered so sternly in August seemed to be, even as they were making their dusty progress East from Port-au-Prince to Santo Domingo, quietly extending an olive branch to Port-au-Prince.

It was a startled group of delegates that heard the official American delegate to the conference, Terence Todman, fresh from a four day visit to Port-au-Prince, declare that "My government has noted with much satisfaction a series of Haitian Government measures which contribute to the amelioration of the fundamental human condition." Todman's speech in fact did not represent administration policy, but no rebuttal or clarification was forthcoming from Washington.

As the Carter Administration was apparently softening its rhetoric, other voices quickly filled the vacuum. Several prisoners who had been released in the August and September amnesties described in minute detail the conditions of their incarceration and quickly put the lie to the regime's statement that it was holding no more political prisoners.

In Montreal, Marc Romulus stated that

> on entry to Fort Dimanche one [is] stripped naked, examined like a beast, and [then thrown up against a wall] to await the baptism of fire from the commandant, Enos

St. Pierre. 'Communist! Shit! Screw your mother! Duvalier himself put me here for this very purpose!'

At 2 A.M., it's shower time. There are between 25 and 33 to a cell, and each cell has exactly five minutes to wash beneath a pipe a quarter inch in diameter from which trickles a stream of water. At 5:30 A.M. each prisoner is given a mug of coffee and a stale roll At least 45 to 60 percent of the prison population has tuberculosis..."

The airwaves though were more powerful than the pen, and many foreigners believed Jean-Claude Duvalier, when, in an interview given to Canadian Television in mid-October, he declared "there is not one single political prisoner in Haiti." The *Miami Herald* noted what it called an "Easing of U.S. Human Rights Pressure on Haiti's Duvalier. Saying that American diplomats were "satisfied with the human-rights progress made in Haiti over the past several months", it quoted one U.S. official to the effect that "If we push him too far, he might get mad and fall back into repression".

The regime subscribed to the *Herald* too and quickly tacked. Those within its grasp who had had the audacity to test the limits of its tolerance were the first targets. Acting on instructions from the president, a working group consisting of, among others, the Minister of Defense, Aurelien Jeanty and Minister without portfolio, Henri Bayard sought to deal with what Duvalier referred to as "intolerable attitudes" of the "so-called 'independent press'".

Two newspapers in Port-au-Prince, *Oedipe* and *Regard*, were closed, the first as it prepared its inaugural issue.In the provinces, away from the glare of the international spotlight, *VSN* members had resumed old habits, beating schoolchildren, extorting money and creating what *Jeune Presse* in Port-au-Prince had had the audacity to refer to in an article published at the beginning of December as "a climate of insecurity".

Retribution was swift. With his son was in Europe, *Jeune Presse* publisher Luc Nerée (the Baptist preacher who had corresponded with Jimmy Carter) found himself set upon, beaten, and left for dead by *macoutes* acting on orders of the Interior Minister. Nerée had been summoned several times by Jeanty who had warned him to soften the tone of his articles. After his assailants decamped, Nerée, though in a coma, stirred enough to encourage his congregation to demand his transport to the *Hôpital Général*. There, he came to the next day and was soon sent home for a slow convalescence.

The furor stirred by the Nerée incident was less quick to die down. Son and associate editor of *Jeune Presse* Bob Nérée quickly returned from abroad and fed daily health bulletins to a concerned international community, recognizing that in publicity lay immunity. In Washington, the Black Caucus (a group of Black members of Congress) cancelled a visit scheduled for December. In the face of all this, the government's description of what transpired was terse: an auto accident had been followed by a fight.

The Haitian press rushed to the defense of the beleaguered Nerées, using its limited license to condemn the attack. *Le Petit Samedi Soir*, so often in the vanguard of government critics, warned bleakly of the possibility of other "accidents befalling those who inquire[d] too closely about the regime's affairs." The attack took its toll: *Jeune Presse* suspended publication, while *Le Petit Samedi Soir* muted somewhat its voice.

Prevented by the international community's watchfulness from taking further overt action, the government turned to home-grown remedies. Zacharie Delva, feared *bocor* and pro-consul of the Gonaïves region, very publicly ushered in 1978 in Gonaïves by presiding over a voodoo ceremony at which a bull bearing Jimmy Carter's picture was sacrificed. For good measure, light-skinned members of Jean-Claude's cabinet (such as Henri Bayard) who had incurred the wrath of various "dinosaurs" were targeted too, leaving little doubt that the recourse to magic had been ordered by the chief "dinosaur" herself, Simone Duvalier.

In the first weeks of the new year, processions of goats, pigs, and bulls dressed for sacrifice were sighted throughout the Artibonite, Northwest, and North. An upsurge of thefts of sacred objects such as chalices and consecrated hosts from Parishes moved the Church to warn priests to exercise special vigilance to prevent those "practicing Satan's dance" from obtaining holy objects for use in black magic.

Simone Duvalier, it was said, believed that *Guédé*, long the protector of the Duvalier family, had turned his back on it. More alarming still, this view seemed to be shared by increasing numbers of Duvalier stalwarts - the *houngans* and *mambos* who had for so long formed the backbone of regime support. Only drastic measures could propitiate the angry *Guédé*.

To add to the dinosaurs' sense of anxiety, events several thousand miles to the West were giving fresh impetus to the heretofore ignored cries of the exile community in the U.S. for a close examination of U.S. aid to Haiti. One exile paper's article chronicling various expenditures of the regime lamented that "mostly it's our [U.S. taxpayers] money." It was right. The Haitian diaspora, a mere handful of mostly elite and political exiles before the Duvaliers, had grown into a dynamic, well-established community scattered around the world that numbered nearly a million. Many of these exiles had citizenship, most paid taxes, and were increasingly learning how to make themselves heard politically. Haitians overseas managed to find outlets at home for new ideas acquired in their travels. One young *noir* seminarian studying abroad whose article was published in 1979 in the Port-au-Prince Catholic paper, *Le Bon Nouvel*, was destined to be heard from again: Jean-Bertrand Aristide.

The bribery conviction of a Congressional aide in a Los Angeles court seemed to have little bearing on matters Haitian until the Associated Press deduced that the aide in question was the same Stephen Elko who had appeared in Port-au-Prince in 1973 as an emissary for "Dapper Dan" Flood, the Pennsylvania Congressman who had been so helpful to Lucien Rigaud. In return for a reduced sentence, the aide provided stories of sacks full of cash, secret trips to Port-au-Prince, and corruption in a series of projects that had nothing to do with Haiti. The normally somnolent House Ethics Committee was goaded into action and convened hearings on influence peddling by Congress.

All of this seemed to confirm what Lucien Rigaud, still holed up in the Mexican Embassy, had been saying all along. The U.S. Justice Department sought safe passage from Haiti for Rigaud to the U.S. to enable him to testify, but Haitian officials balked, knowing too well how damaging his testimony could be. Rigaud's Swiss wife had reluctantly left Haiti the previous year, concluding that with her husband safe for the moment under diplomatic protection, she should get her children out of the country. Prudently, she had arranged on Rigaud's instructions to make photocopies of most documents relating to Rigaud's efforts on behalf of the regime, and it was this trove that interested the U.S..

Impatient, Rigaud managed to slip by his captors, and, though he had never sailed before, commandeered a small sailboat into the Gulf of la Gonâve and sailed towards Cuba. Rescued by the U.S. Coast Guard, he was whisked to Guantanamo Bay for medical treatment and then to the U.S. for debriefing. The cat was out of the bag.

To the dismay of the palace, when the story finally broke it was featured in no less a forum than the Sunday *New York Times* Magazine. Entitled " 'Baby Doc's' Haitian terror", it laid out the Rigaud affair in great detail and asked "Why have we resumed sending foreign aid to Haiti?"

Perhaps mindful of the negative press, the regime appeared very receptive to the aid program suggested by the American ambassador when he met with the president in mid-summer. Aid would double under the suggested structure, but the regime would have to undertake "demonstrable and permanent" reforms both fiscally and in the human rights area. Ambassador Jones' first year had had a topsy-turvy quality to it. Arriving in time for Andrew Young's visit, he found his hard line stance on human rights undercut by Terence Todman's speech two months later in Santo Domingo.

That speech, it turned out, had been the result of a high-level struggle in the Carter administration over its shotgun marriage of human rights and diplomacy. Many argued that a doctrine so unevenly applied was inherently flawed, while idealists fought hard to differentiate administration policy from that of its predecessors. All winter and spring the debate raged, with the idealists, headed by Under Secretary of State Warren Christopher, gaining the upper hand. Terence Todman found himself reassigned to other duties - a move applauded by *The Nation* in an editorial entitled "The Good Riddance of Terence Todman".

In response to international pressure, Duvalier sought to carry water on both shoulders. Max du Plessy was allowed in the beginning months of 1978 to found a "Human Rights League" which purported to lobby against the regime's abuses. Only twenty people were courageous enough to openly sign up, though many others indicated their tacit support of the task the league set out to perform.

Workers at HASCO were given the nod to elect their own union bosses after they complained that their existing stewards were "stooges of management". Striking interns at the State Medical school who were protesting inadequate supplies were startled to receive a visit from the Chief of State, who listened attentively to their pleas. Leaving the scene, he was cheered.

In this flurry of activity designed to sate the appetite of the international community for signs of "progress" on the human rights front, the regime even announced elections for the Unicameral National Assembly for March. To be sure, only Duvalierists were allowed to run, and at that the Deputies' powers were limited at best, but for a country which had had nothing even like such an event in several years, it seemed like progress.

Two people who had the temerity to take the government at its word on the openness of the electoral process came up against the harsher realities of Duvalierism - Françoisist and Jean-Claudist. Sylvio Claude, human rights crusader and constant thorn in the side of the government presented himself as a candidate in Mirebalais to run against none other than Madame Max Adolphe, head *macoute* and former warden of the notorious Fort Dimanche. For his efforts, he got beaten and shoved on a plane to Bogota.

What the regime could do in the hinterlands, it hesitated to try at the Cap. Chafing always at Southern domination, the feisty *Capois* fielded an "opposition" candidate - a heretofore obscure customs clerk   Alexandre Lerouge. Lerouge spoke out openly in favor of change (stopping just short of the taboo subject of the Presidency for Life), and to the delight of the *Capois*, was not arrested, beaten, or deported, but allowed to continue his campaign.

Mesmerized *Capois* listened as Lerouge got air time to express his views while the regime's candidate, Claude Vixamar, got none. Unbeknownst to the electorate, Duvalier had decided to let the Cap seat be fairly contested as a show of independence from the dinosaurs. Last minute efforts by the dinosaurs to reverse what looked sure to be an electoral rout availed not, nor did attempts to spirit the ballots away to Port-au-Prince for a "special" count. Lerouge, the outsider, swept the field with 34,800 votes out of 37,200 cast.

Fire, so often a portent of a crisis of Haitian regimes, in March struck downtown Port-au-Prince, narrowly missing a major pharmacy that had recently received a large shipment of chemicals. All too apt a metaphor, the roof of the Chamber of Deputies collapsed in mid-July with a huge explosion that minded old-timers of bombing campaigns that had typically ushered out regimes. To the further consternation of the conservatives, Grégoire Eugène, briefly the young Duvalier's professor, published a tract entitled "In Defense of Political Parties in Haiti". When the expected reprisals for the article did not materialize, two groups - the Haitian Christian Democratic party and the Christian Democratic party of June 27th - set up shop on July 5th, two days after the president's twenty-eighth birthday. The dinosaurs were right to be worried.

Seeking to reassure them on the twenty-second anniversary of the regime, Duvalier praised the *Milice* and *macoutes*, referring to them in a speech as "the first line of my defense."

By late 1979, as the weakness of the Carter administration in the face of world events had begun to become apparent, the government felt confident enough to pass new regulations restraining the press, finishing the work begun against the Nerées two years earlier."Offenses"(undefined) against the Duvalier family were punishable with prison time as were articles that "disturbed the public peace".

To emphasize the tough message, the government sent in *macoutes* to break up a meeting of the year-old human rights league. As Gérard Gourgue began to speak to a record crowd of 6,000, the TTM's waded in, truncheons swinging. Reporters, foreign embassy staff - no one in the crowd seemed immune from the blows that were rained down on the heads of those in attendance. To foreign protests, the government issued a tepid statement of "regret" for any harm that had come to foreign observers at the meeting.

Those who had maintained that "Jean-Claudism" was fundamentally different from old-line Duvalierism found their task made more difficult still by the announcement of yet another cabinet change only four days after the breakup of the rights rally. A roster full of dinosaurs was capped with the appointment of Papa Doc's godson, Claude Raymond, as Interior Minister. Never before in either Duvalier government had an army man held a cabinet portfolio. "Spring", said one observer, "is over."

We Don't Know Where It Goes

The average Haitian, city dweller or peasant, was far too caught up in the struggle to survive to be interested in the struggles and capers of the ruling class, even if he or she had known about them in any detail. Duvalierism was so institutionalized by 1978 that a numbed population that had never known anything different accepted it with resignation. Far more important to this group was the ability of the regime to provide jobs, roads, security - things that even a population with such reduced expectations as Haiti's expected their government to provide.

But crucial shifts, long in the making, were transforming the country in ways that would only be visible in hindsight. Like the *ancien regime*, the Duvaliers sat atop a volcano, insensitive to the trembling beneath them, but trembling there were.

The surface veneer of prosperity that the "new" Duvalierism had ushered in was built on very shaky foundations, but to a casual observer, progress was visible in many sectors. Aid money had come cascading in over several previous years, with the international community engaging in what seemed like a bidding war to secure for itself the privilege of sponsoring this road, that dam, or some other project.

New roads, as yet unbedeviled by that traditional third world problem, lack of preventive maintenance, stretched from Jacmel to the Cap, and West from Léogane to Les Cayes. Jacmel's traditional charms were being rediscovered by a new generation of tourists who could make their hotel reservations from overseas on the revitalized phone system. The trip from Port-au-Prince took an hour (as in the 1930's) instead of eight. With paved roads appeared bicycles -

now ridden instead of painstakingly walked around myriad potholes and rim-bending rocks - and other indications of prosperity.

Port-au-Prince, now thoroughly captive to the technology of containerization set up by Lucien Rigaud, thrived as increasing numbers of assembly factories disgorged their production for consumption by Haiti's richer North American neighbors. Baseballs, circuitry, clothes, wicker furniture - anything that required manual dexterity and a docile, cheap labor force seemed to be coming from Haiti. Some 250 assembly plants provided jobs - albeit low-paying ones - to nearly 60,000 people. One economist estimated that a third of the population of Port-au-Prince - some 300,000 people - benefitted directly or indirectly from these jobs.

Tourism continued to thrive. The new roads opened up provincial towns long cut off, and "economic tourism" provided by the multiple delegations from international aid organizations served only to swell the government's coffers. Club Med opened a branch along a pretty stretch of beach 50 miles North of the capital. There, with imported foodstuffs, tourists could bask in the sun and claim they had been to Haiti, all the while safely insulated from the poverty and squalor that lay just beyond the compound's chain link fence.

The factories in Port-au-Prince served to exacerbate the exodus from the provinces to the capital. What had begun under Papa Doc as political strategy - the isolation and slow death of any place he could not constantly watch - now gathered momentum as peasants voted with their feet by leaving the countryside.

Agriculture, long hobbled by inefficiencies inherent in Pétion's division of land into subsistence plots, became increasingly tenuous as holdings were divided, sub-divided, and divided yet again among heirs. The same population explosion that caused a multiplicity of heirs for every plot drove peasants ever-further in search of wood for charcoal. The machetes that hacked the trees down for fuel hastened erosion, reducing yields and rendering whole sections of the country such as the Northwest susceptible to increasingly violent climactic shifts.

The land was simply played out. Haiti, the major exporter of sugar to eighteenth century Europe, two centuries later became a net importer of sugar. Coffee exports in 1977 amounted to 450,000 bags - half that exported in 1910. A hurricane in 1979, long the scourge of the South, destroyed many of the coffee bushes that had managed to survive increasingly frequent droughts. More menacingly, peasants began to hack down coffee bushes and mango trees, once sacrosanct, in their ever more desperate search for fuel. In Miragoâne, Reynolds aluminum struggled to extract increasingly marginal deposits of bauxite from the uncooperative land while dealing all the while with an ever more restive labor force.

To add to the burden, a swine virus that had originated in Africa appeared in 1978 in the Dominican republic, threatening to spill over the porous frontier into Haiti. Pigs, in a largely non-cash rural economy, constituted reserve savings accounts that enable peasant families to weather bad times. To try to stop the infiltration of the virus, Haitian authorities, acting on foreign advice, cleared a wide swath along the frontier of all pigs, further devastating the rural economy. Farmers elsewhere watched in trepidation as pigs were slaughtered wholesale for minimal compensation.

What nature, abused by man, did not do, man did directly. The lack of a cadastral survey, long a disincentive to foreign investment, now encouraged land grabs by Duvalierists of plots held by families for generations. Illiterate, unable to read what few pieces of paper (if any) that attested to title, those who dared protest were beaten into submission and joined the throngs heading for the towns and the beaches where those rickety sailboats destined to become so familiar to the world were being built with the last few precious scraps of wood available.

The regime, spurred on by the international community, engaged in wholesale reforestation efforts, but it was too little, too late. The president acknowledged in a speech "Once we exported mahogany. Now we import formica." The Northwest, always the most marginal agriculturally, by 1978 was virtually under caretaker status from various international aid organizations.

Once productive areas elsewhere in the country stagnated too. The regime announced the ceding of 19,000 hectares near Fort Liberté that had been the property of Port Dauphin, once the world's largest sisal plantation, to Marie-Denise Duvalier for "tourist development".

Sweetheart deals to various regime favorites, echoes of Estimé's banana decision, strangled other sectors of the economy. Cocoa exports, which had provided $3 million a year in revenue to the economy, dried up as deteriorating relations between Marie-Denise Duvalier and still-exiled husband Max made their jointly held monopoly the subject of a marital property fight. "We have stopped our purchases till this is cleared up," said one trader in New York as Marie-Denise warned foreign traders not to deal with her husband, "Max Dominique ... was always the guy that made all the decisions." *Ciment d'Haïti* and other state companies were rocked with scandal as wholesale diversion of resources for private ends was reported by a partially but not wholly muzzled press.

What writer Herbert Gold referred to as government by "kleptocracy" continued unabated. On a salary of $24,000 a year, the president purchased a $1 million yacht, ranches, and a $3 million villa in Monaco. Years later, in an interview with Barbara Walters, Jean-Claude Duvalier seemed genuinely puzzled at the notion that his money and state money should not be commingled.

But the regime, dependent on remittances from Haitians abroad and the goodwill of the international donor community, found itself hostage to international opinion as never before. Pressure mounted, as in the early 1960's for a full audit of government revenues, some 50% of which were estimated to flow into "private" accounts. In 1975 alone, the World Bank reported, some $45 million was unaccounted for, this at a time when the Haitian government professed itself unable to pay even its very modest part of international projects. The abiding object of the donor community's ire was the *Régie du Tabac*, into which so much money flowed, and seemed to disappear. Calls for "fiscalization" of the *Régie* were met with foot dragging and resistance, but the international community was wising up.

As bidding wars for projects were replaced by consultation between donors, aid packages came with conditions which François Duvalier had been able to reject as an affront to national sovereignty but which his son was increasingly forced to accept.

Looking at the paucity of results in relation to the sums expended, foreign officials increasingly admitted that Haiti did not have the infrastructure to absorb properly the amounts being funnelled into it. "We simply", one foreigner said, "don't know where it goes."

"Why couldn't He Have Married a Haitian?"

The young president continued steering by his own star, showing much of his father's skill in dismissing ministers or officers whose power was judged to be a possible threat, handing out largesse to friends and allies, and continuing to associate with the elite his father had so ruthlessly suppressed. *Mulâtre* "Minister without Portfolio" Henri Bayard had immense influence with Duvalier, and it was largely due to younger *mulâtre* technocrats that demarches in certain areas such as family planning began to enjoy some success.

A Dominique family feud, exacerbated by Marie-Denise's long separations from Max, who was still unwelcome in Haiti, finally became public in 1978 when Marie-Denise hired one of the leading lawyers in Port-au-Prince to arrange a divorce. Max, she let it be known around town, had squandered much of "her" fortune. Gossip had it too that an affair was underway between Max and Marie-Denise's younger sister, Simone, in Miami - a rumor both stoutly denied.

Marie-Denise's continued stay in the capital throughout 1978 (before 1977 she had refused to stay away from her husband more than three months at a time) gave heart to the dinosaurs, who saw in her the legitimate heir of François Duvalier. With her around, they reasoned, they could more effectively fight the influence of Henri Bayard and his technocrats. Without the baggage of Max Dominique, might she finally prevail?

The dinosaurs' hopes were soon dashed, as Marie-Denise Duvalier managed to wear out her welcome within a few weeks of the divorce announcement. The president, wilier than his opponents gave him credit for being, was not about to let her changed marital status become a vehicle around which opposition to him might coalesce. Despite his mother's pleas to let his sister remain in Haiti, she was soon asked to resume her travels abroad. (14) Employing another of his father's favorite maneuvers, Duvalier reshuffled his cabinet, keeping all off-balance, and - perennial casualty to power politics - preventing those few capable appointees from developing too much expertise.

The constant game of musical chairs slowed accord on the new aid agreement. The Haitian side, having promised much, now balked at the fine print. Inflation, which was beginning a dramatic rise in the U.S., hit Haiti too now that its economy was so closely linked to that of its neighbor. Rice prices - a bellwether gauge - crept up as drought caused reduced rice yields in the Artibonite. The workers at HASCO who just months before had been allowed to elect their own union leaders, found a strike for increased wages quickly and brutally broken by the army and *macoutes* who cited an anti-strike bill hurriedly promulgated by the regime in an attempt to foster Haiti's image as pro-industry.

The regime continued to take its lumps on the foreign policy front at a widely-publicized encounter between Ambassador Salomon and disgruntled American investors that took place at a trade forum in Atlanta. Busy touting Haiti's advantages as a tax haven, Salomon found himself in an impromptu debate about shortcomings of Haiti's legal system with the Texas group that had hoped to develop La Tortue as a tourist resort. Only the intervention of the moderator saved the diplomat from further embarrassment.

The news was no better domestically. Alarming reports began to filter in that despite the slaughter of 27,000 pigs along the border in the summer, the cordon sanitaire had failed with the result that the first cases of African Swine Fever began showing up in Haiti's breadbasket - the Artibonite valley. The country plunged into its usual end-of-year celebrations, but in the Palace the mood was decidedly somber.

Conscious ever of both the rewards and threats stemming from its increasing dependence on the outside world, the government sought, like Solomon (or Salomon) to please all sides. Tourists coming to Haiti had, for several years, only to show minimal identification to gain entry. Tourism had indeed swelled, but some goats had wandered in with the sheep. Journalists, Haitians who had taken American citizenship, and "undesirables" carrying fake North American documents - all used liberalized entry requirements to slip quietly into the country, often bringing unwelcome ideas and views with them.

Ignoring protests from the Tourist Office, the Interior Ministry announced that after March 1, 1979, all visitors to Haiti would have to present passports for entry. The foreign travel industry predictably protested, causing the government to make an embarrassing volte-face - first delaying the effective date of the law until June 1st, and the rescinding it altogether for Canadians and Americans.

Despite the burdens of office, Jean-Claude Duvalier still found plenty of time for pleasure, hunting, motorcycle racing, and partying. In stark contrast to his father, he ventured out with few guards and startled several ambassadors by leading them on a long tour through the Artibonite to look at conditions there, stopping without warning to query villagers on various matters and taking the wheel himself." These days," one critic said, "the main danger from a presidential convoy seemed to be getting run over."

Anxious for her son to settle down, Simone Duvalier and other elders preached the virtues of a more mature life style. Some were more philosophic, arguing that a twenty-seven year old should be allowed some pleasures. Further, in a society so closely run, the question of who the president could marry vexed many. He had dated many of the eligible women in Port-au-Prince and bedded some number of the married ones as well, but the "dream" match was nowhere in evidence.

The President's social life, which occasioned clucking of tongues by older Duvalierists, was in many ways quite typical of that of an upper class Haitian of his age. Disposing of wealth and power, Duvalier was nonetheless formal in asking women out, working through intermediaries, and took no action when the object of his attention declined. Drugs did not figure in the circle, though dancing, drinking, and outings both to the "ranch" at Croix-des-Bouquets (in reality a great walled compound on land that had in the eighteenth century been

one of the great sugar estates) and the beach provided a welcome respite from
life in the Palace.

His companions in these outings were those he had grown up with or who had
come to be close to since taking office. In this context, it was unremarkable that
the president should come into contact with the two daughters of Ernest Bennett,
a wealthy *mulâtre* merchant. Alarm bells started to ring though when the older
daughter, Michèle, kept appearing by Jean-Claude Duvalier's side. Long-haired,
vivacious, the young woman who was dating the President had first met him at
Collège Bird in 1962. Her father, whose financial dealings had earned François
Duvalier's disapproval(and a jail sentence), shipped the young woman overseas
for schooling.

There, she had met and married the son of Alix Pasquet, one of the leaders
of the 1958 "Sheriff's Coup". When they parted ways in 1978, she had borne
Pasquet two sons. After working as a secretary in New York's garment district,
she returned to Haiti to work for her father. Foreign life had done nothing to
quiet a headstrong streak, and soon she began making the rounds of the party
circuit in Port-au-Prince. Free with her favors, in due course she found herself
in the company of her old schoolmate, whom she set out assiduously to woo.

Jean-Claude Duvalier, impassive, restrained, hard to read, fell hard. Smitten,
consumed with passion, he sought to accommodate her every whim, which
became increasingly demanding. Old line Duvalierists were horrified, and the
president's peers were not much happier. Simone Duvalier, her entreaties to her
son availing nothing, ordered *macoutes* to take "Michou" to the airport and put
her on the next plane. Michou protested loudly, and getting through on a private
line, told an astonished president what was afoot. Immediately rescinding the
order, Jean-Claude Duvalier engaged his mother in a furious row, showing
resolve that few had seen before.

Bennett became increasingly possessive, demanding that the president see only
her, and berated him in front of guards and staff alike if she thought he was
being unfaithful. These tantrums quickly became staples of gossip and were
dubbed *"Michelbé"* (a play on the Creole word *"shelbé"* - caper). Port-au-Prince
was treated to the unedifying spectacle of the young president, of whom many
were genuinely fond, being wrapped around the finger of someone it did not
approve of. Franck Romain, long-time *macoute* and Army officer, made the
mistake of trying to limit her access to the president and found himself quickly
cashiered. Even Claude Raymond, François Duvalier's godson, Chief of Staff,
with unimpeachable Duvalierist credentials found himself curtly dismissed when
he tried to dissuade his young chief from pursuing his obsession.

When the president accompanied the head of UNESCO on a trip to the Cap to raise funds for the preservation of the Citadel in March, 1980, Michèle Bennett appeared unannounced and unbidden to demand accommodation in the honeymoon suite of the hotel in which the official party was lodged. Dressed down for her "impertinence", she quickly got her way after a call to the Palace and was installed for all to see during the president's visit. It was becoming clear that Michèle Bennett was a force to be reckoned with.

On April 29th, Tele-Haiti announced what those in the inner circle had dreaded - the president would marry. The news hit Port-au-Prince like a bombshell, sending the *telediol* into overtime. Fiercely opposed to the union, Simone Duvalier had grudgingly put on the best face possible as she acquiesced in a marriage about which she had dreadful presentiments, even agreeing to serve as Matron of Honor. Her consent had been secured only when old friends made the argument that the continuing row between mother and son over the marriage could cause the regime's collapse.

Not all the old Duvalierists were as accommodating as Simone Duvalier, nor, it quickly became apparent, was their approbation as valued. Michèle Bennett used the guest list to avenge old slights - real or perceived - and many stalwarts were shocked to suddenly find themselves on the outside. Some, whose approval she initially sought, such as Clovis Désinor, refused outright to attend the wedding, further exacerbating the rift of color and generation that the marriage was demonstrating. Désinor, who ten years earlier had made no secret of his view that he was the legitimate political heir of François Duvalier, felt the marriage was "stupid politically".

At the urging of Tourist Office Head Jean Saurel, the government decided to "package" the event as a great *bamboche*. Always obliging, Duvalierist Archbishop Wolff-Ligondé, was to marry the young couple, Michèle Bennett's divorce notwithstanding, in a solemn high mass to be sung in the Port-au-Prince Cathedral. Ligondé explained to those troubled by the spectacle of a twenty-seven year old divorcee being married at the high altar that since her first marriage was in the Episcopal Church, it could be ignored. In return, the Palace pledged funds to restore the barnlike wooden eighteenth century cathedral that sat next to the more modern edifice inaugurated at the turn of the century. The Monsignor's theological dilemma also yielded to family ties - Michèle Bennett was his niece.

Haiti - at least the Duvalier's Haiti - was going to party. 2,000 invitations went out around the world. Thousands of cases of champagne and other delicacies were imported, as were $100,000 worth of fireworks for the amusement of Port-au-Prince's poor. Those same poor were to be able to watch the wedding on television as they swigged rations of rum and food dispensed by the government to ensure goodwill. Unable in tropical Haiti to find enough flowers to their liking, the young couple-to-be arranged for three florists to fly in from Miami with rare flora to decorate the Cathedral and the ranch at Croix-des-Bouquets. Under a sodden sky, the president of Haiti, on May 27, 1980, took unto himself a wife. Emerging from the cathedral, the young couple walked between an honor guard of *milice* and army whose drawn swords formed a canopy of steel over the young couple. They were going to need it.

The marriage was a public relations fiasco. The foreign press contrasted the scenes inside the Cathedral with the poverty of Port-au-Prince and mused about the appropriateness of spending $5 million on a wedding when the government was receiving most of its budget as foreign aid. Satellite dishes ensured that this adverse foreign comment was carried into homes all over town. The TV's set up by the government for the occasion in parks and neighborhoods in the poorer quarters of the city showed the largely *mulâtre* crowd decked out in Paris fashions enjoying themselves in a world that was inaccessible to the man in the street. Mutterings were heard throughout the country, evidencing just how thoroughly François Duvalier's *noirisme* had rooted itself, "Why", asked many, "couldn't she have married one of us - a *Haitian?*"

The Gathering Storm

The young bride wasted little time in cleaning house. As the summer progressed, old retainers around the palace found themselves abruptly cashiered after years of loyal service. All had managed somehow to incur the wrath of Michèle Duvalier, and nearly all of them had some tie to Simone Duvalier. A mysterious automobile accident abruptly took the life of the half-Jamaican English translator (disliked by the new Mme. Duvalier) who had served Jean-Claude since Papa Doc's death. To his chagrin, Jean-Claude found himself put on a strict diet by his new wife. Dire recriminations were threatened to any who fed him on the sly.

Under the circumstances, a preoccupied government had little inclination to deal with "troublemakers" such as rights activist Sylvio Claude, and it moved quickly in July to shut down his newspaper, *Verité Su Tambu* after only one issue, betting correctly that a U.S. administration increasingly with foreign policy crises in Iran and Afghanistan and an election underway would have little appetite for disciplinary action in Haiti. In these assessments the government was aided by its Foreign Minister, Georges Salomon, who had been brought home to Port-au-Prince from Washington to take up his portfolio late in the previous year. Salomon's years in Washington made him an astute observer of the American scene, and his views commanded respect.

To add to the climate of tension, nature weighed in with Hurricane Allen on August 6th. Packing walloping 175 mph winds, the storm devastated the Southern peninsula to an extent not seen since Hazel in 1954. Even Port-au-Prince, normally shielded by Morne-la-Selle, was not exempt. The populace received four hours notice from the government - barely time enough to batten their flimsy shanties against the eighty miles an hour winds on the storm's edge. As usual, Cayes and Jacmel were in the direct path of the storm, which left two hundred dead and more than 150,000 homeless. Worse still, coffee bushes and other crops which had taken years to recover from pummelings in the fifties and sixties were again destroyed, further eroding an already weak agricultural base.

This time, the storm occasioned no outpouring of aid from a sympathetic world, for the world was already heavily invested in Haiti and didn't much like what it saw. An IMF report in 1978 had criticized all the usual aspects of the regime's finances - the lack of a unified budget, the unaudited *Régie du Tabac*, the slush funds, but had a new and disturbing aspect. Future IMF funding was tied to discrete progress. By mid-1980 Haiti had been able to draw almost none of the money and was forced instead to turn to commercial banks with commercial interest rates to finance its debt. A *Wall Street Journal* article quoted planning Minister Edouard Berrouet on the subject of corruption:"We aren't angels. We know there is corruption, but we must learn to live with corruption." The international community was less philosophical.

In the face of natural and man-made disasters, increasing numbers of Haitians voted with their feet, hocking everything they had to pay $800 or $1000 for a risky journey across the straits of Florida. U.S. Coast Guard cutters off Florida found numerous boats drifting empty, while startled citizens of Miami Beach awoke some mornings to see bewildered Haitians trudging toward them from a just-beached sailboat. Some captains seized the chance to make quick money, dumping their charges on uninhabited islands after they collected the fares. In one such episode, 102 refugees were forcibly repatriated from the Bahamas by the Bahamian government after being stranded for a month on a deserted island called Cayos Lobos. The Haitian government's response was to look the other way, and when critic Grégoire Eugène criticized the government's handling of the affair in print as a "national disgrace" he found himself bundled aboard an American airlines flight to New York. He had a lot of company.

In November, American voters overwhelmingly repudiated Jimmy Carter and in the process his governessy brand of foreign policy. The Duvaliers threw a lavish gala to celebrate the incumbent's defeat and moved aggressively to, as *Time* put it, "jail the news". All told, some forty newsmen including such hardy veterans as Radio Métropole's Marc Garcia were rusticated to Miami, there to contemplate their sins. Repentant, they would gradually be issued the entry visas that would allow them to come home, but the action had the desired effect - those remaining in Port-au-Prince tempered their words.

Despite government admonitions, the news refused to stay jailed for very long. By year's end, confidence was shaken by the revelation that foreign exchange reserves had dwindled by some $40 million over the previous year. Rumor had it that a good portion of the deficit had been caused by the president's withdrawal of $20 million for personal reasons - to fund the shopping sprees abroad of his new wife. The *gourde*, for many years interchangeable with the U.S. dollar at a rate of five to one, began to trade at rates of six and even seven to one.

The government, buoyed by the election results in the U.S., took an aggressive stance towards the foreign donor community even as it held out its hand. Meeting with officials from all the principal donor countries, Minister ("We"re no angels") Berrouet drowned the speech of an official from the lame-duck Carter administration who sought to make references to human rights abuses. Ringing a hand-bell, Berrouet intoned that human rights statements were "not acceptable" and ordered the official to "pass to the technical part of your speech." Cowed, all present made no further disagreeable allusions, indeed agreeing to a 20% increase (to $170 Million) for 1981 of Haiti's dole from the international community.

Every penny was needed. Already cash-strapped as a result of a decline in tourism and the failure of crops due to Hurricane Allen, the government was forced to propitiate the cupidity of the newly-empowered Bennett clan. Ernst Bennett, once imprisoned for shady business dealings by Papa Doc, was riding high. With a finger in every pie, Bennett and his cronies set about to siphon off what few dollars were left in the Haitian economy. Oil provided at concessionary prices by Mexico to help Haiti was sold to petroleum-starved South Africa. Only an astute guess by Interpol kept the $7 million in profits from that transaction from going into Bennett's pocket. Haiti Air, a 727 wet-leased from Aer Lingus, did a thriving freight and passenger business shuttling between Port-au-Prince and Miami. Mysteriously exempt from export taxes that formed the backbone of government revenue, Bennett managed to corner what was left after Hurricane Allen of the coffee crop, buying it cheap from desperate cultivators to hold until world commodity prices recovered. He alone had the credit to do so.

In the palace, Michèle Duvalier managed routinely to overspend her $100,000 a month allowance. Palace officials sought, ever so delicately, to re-package her, teaching her the finer points of makeup, decorum, and manners. This process was observed in glacial silence by the "First Lady of the Revolution", Simone Ovide, who was forced on all public occasions to share top billing with her new daughter-in-law. The first lady was finding the house in Canapé Vert where her octogenarian mother lived increasingly to her liking. Her son's wife began issuing ever-lengthening lists of Duvalierist stalwarts who were to be denied entry to the Palace. Deeply unhappy, Simone Duvalier even refused to eat for a time until coaxed into doing so by her mother. In the conflict between the two, Michèle Duvalier gave no quarter. Various members of the Ovide clan, long used to roaming the corridors of power, found themselves keeping company with radicals such as Sylvio Claude and Grégoire Eugène on the Northbound flight to Miami.

Michèle Duvalier wanted to be not only "First Lady" in fact, but in title. Having seen to the exile of much of the Ovide clan, having engineered repeated and public snubs to François Duvalier's widow, she finally badgered the president into granting her wish. The actual task was delegated to the Deputies, but no one was fooled as to what was going on when the wire services announced that henceforth the president's wife would be first lady, and his mother, "first lady of the revolution." Michèle Duvalier had won.

The final blow for Simone Ovide was the death of her mother, Clélie, a month later. Jean-Claude had loved his grandmother (who had refused to give her blessing to his union with Bennett), and after the marriage she bolstered Simone's spirits in adversity. Now, she too was gone.

Further North, Haiti's new ambassador to Washington, Georges Léger (grandson of the great lawyer) was finding it heavy going. An increasingly skeptical liberal group on Capitol Hill was making common cause with unlikely allies - Southern conservatives - in demanding that the new Reagan administration attach conditions to Haitian aid. The conservatives, normally at home with right-wing foreign leaders, were beginning to hear about Haiti from their constituents, who either saw footage on television of the "boat people", or worse, found them on their doorsteps in Southern Florida. Haiti was becoming a domestic policy issue for Americans, including sizeable numbers of naturalized Haitians and their children.

As if the almost daily interception of pitifully overloaded boats were not reminder enough of Haiti to all Americans, the issues surrounding the care, and ultimate disposition of this new wave of refugees flared up in ways guaranteed to rub raw nerves in many different communities. Though it could hardly say so openly, the Cuban population that had so long prospered in Florida's salubrious climate wanted nothing to do with a new wave of poor, *Créole-*

680 Written in Blood

speaking, black immigrants. At the same time, the Cuban community, important politically to the Reagan administration, insisted that the door to the U.S. remain open to *all* Cubans, who were of course fleeing communism.

Cries of "double standard" and racism began to be heard from various quarters. The administration explained that the Haitians were "economic" refugees, and were consequently ineligible for the asylum given their lighter-skinned brethren from two hundred miles further West. Refugees having a "well-founded" fear of persecution, the government explained, would be permitted to stay in the U.S. The argument didn't wash. The problem, as the refugees knew better than anyone, was that the hearings which determined refugee eligibility were conducted by inspectors who didn't know Créole, didn't know Haiti, and were under pressure to send the boat people home and away from the eyes of the U.S. electorate. Predictably, few refugees' fears were judged to be "well-founded".

Into the breach poured volunteer lawyers from all over the country. Some of New York's poshest law firms took on cases on a *pro bono* basis, with individual lawyers taking responsibility for five or ten cases each. Coordinated by activist priests such as Antoine Adrien and Gérard Jean-Juste of the Haitian Refugee Center in Miami, the informal network proved very effective in preventing repatriation. To relieve overcrowding in the barbed-wire Krome detention center (which looked to the average television viewer remarkably like a concentration camp) and, some said cynically, to remove the refugees from contact with the activist network which sustained them, the U.S. government began farming refugees out to camps throughout the country. This move too drew criticism.

Faced with a backlog of more than ten thousand refugees in detention and hundreds more landing every week, the U.S. administration quietly entered into discussions with Port-au-Prince. The result was announced by President Reagan on September 29, 1981. With immediate effect, a U.S. Coast Guard Cutter was to be stationed off Haiti permanently. Assisted by other rotating Coast Guard vessels, a *cordon sanitaire* was to seal off Haiti. No longer would Americans have to reconcile the cherished standard of the "melting pot" with ingredients many weren't comfortable adding to the brew. Howls of protest came in from many quarters, not least the U.N., which publicly questioned both the legality and ethics of the administration's policy. It mattered not - the U.N.'s views didn't count much at the Reagan White House.

The price for Haiti's acquiescence in this pact became quickly clear. In Washington, a group of senior Haitian officials wrangled through October with their U.S. counterparts over the exact definition of thirty pieces of silver. At the beginning of November the deal was made public: U.S. aid, it was announced, was to continue, even increase, after "categoric assurances" had been received from Haitian authorities that none of the returned refugees would face punishment. Veteran Edouard Francisque, leading the Haitian delegation to Washington, announced that "We have the feeling that the United States will really cooperate with Haiti." Blaming "bad press" of the past several years for a souring of U.S.-Haitian relations, he went on to push the Reagan administration's hot button: "Only the U.S. can save Haiti from Moscow."

Agreement with the U.S. gave consolation in the wake of a December Socialist victory at the polls in France. Previous French governments had held their noses over some of the less attractive aspects of the regime and given foreign aid generously, valuing *Francophonie* above all. François Mitterand signaled a break with his predecessors, roundly condemning the Duvalier government's rule as "...catastrophic for Haiti".

In what proved to be another betrayal of its people (though perhaps one about which it had no choice, given that some of Haiti's major aid donors were involved), the regime in July had signed a protocol with the Inter-American Institute of Cooperative Agriculture. The protocol called, in Herodian terms, for the slaughter of all Haiti's pigs within two years on the theory that this would prevent African Swine Fever from reaching the North American mainland. Peasants were to be compensated, and "plans" called for foreign pigs (*"cochons blancs"*) to be imported to replace the native ones, but in the short term, all the cultivators saw was the forced liquidation of the closest thing many had to a savings account, often at distress prices. Some took pigs into hiding. Others preferred to sacrifice their pigs to their own Gods rather than the *blancs*, so that an upsurge of pig offerings to the *loa* was reported throughout the country. Within a year, rural school registrations had dropped 30% as the pig traditionally kept in the yard to pay for books, fees, and uniforms was no longer there. Not since the *SHADA* fiasco forty years earlier had the Haitian peasant had to pay so dearly for the theories of foreign agronomists.

In the face of heavy weather, the regime veered right, sentencing Sylvio Claude to fifteen years at hard labor for his political activities. Continuing to "clean house", the new first lady succeeded in banning even the president's long-time friend and private secretary Ti-Pouche Douyon from the Palace. He had held the job for ten years. Jean-Claude Duvalier continued to use him discreetly for certain delicate matters, but always at a cautious remove.

The makeover of Michèle Duvalier was proceeding apace. As Fall progressed, like Evita Peron, she was seen everywhere doing good works, always impeccably and expensively clad. A gushing Mother Teresa was photographed with the first couple and announced that she had received "a lesson in humility" after having seen "the closeness of the first lady to her people." A foundation was to be established in the first lady's name that would benefit children's causes throughout the Republic. Even Rev. Nerée, following more closely his original vocation of Minister after his near fatal flirtation with journalism, received a visit from Mme. Duvalier and a $2,000 check for his work with orphans.

Those few who had the wherewithal brought in the New Year with the customary celebrations. On the 179th anniversary of 1804, the traditional masses were sung at the Cathedral with the full complement of participants from the first family on down. Some two hundred miles North, an exile group had decided to mark 1982 in a different, and for Jean-Claude Duvalier a newly disturbing, way. Led by Bernard Sansaricq (uncle of the two year old Sonny Borges had blinded with a cigarette in Jérémie in 1964), half a dozen exiles landed on La Tortue on January 9th, having embarked from grand Turk island ninety miles north.

The regime's ability to respond to such forays had grown rusty, and it was thus several days before a coordinated response involving the *Léopards* and other troops from the *Casernes Dessalines* could be mounted. Indeed, *miliciens* on the scene initially turned their fire on the government troops when they arrived, assuming they were invaders. Led by Henri Namphy and Williams Regala - two names destined to be heard from again - government forces ultimately prevailed, killing or capturing (and executing shortly thereafter) those of the band who had not managed to escape after initial reverses. Interior Minister Jean-Marie Chanoine's radio boasts of quick suppression were belied by the temporary airlift of all surgical residents of the Hôpital Général to Port-de-Paix, not, *Haïti Observateur* noted drily, to tend wounded rebels.

In addition to the publicity attendant to the La Tortue landings, Haiti garnered other notices in the foreign press. Jesse Jackson, self-anointed tribune of the oppressed everywhere, denounced the INS detention camp in Miami as a "scar on the face of democracy" - a remark that was quickly picked up and repeated on editorial pages around the U.S. On a related theme, the *Philadelphia Inquirer* detailed how "Skill, U.S., Keep 'Baby Doc' on Top".

Less exacting editorially was an article in the March *Town and Country* which carried all the usual pictures of art galleries and beaches. Nostalgically reminiscent of the "fluff" pieces of the early nineteen-seventies, it was one flickering candle in a darkening pall. Tourism had been steadily declining since the first pictures of "boat people" seared themselves into the consciousness of would-be tourists, creating a foreign exchange crisis.

Part of the agreement worked out with the U.S. administration and other donors the previous Fall had been the appointment of a finance minister with impeccable credentials who would tackle the intractable structural problems which so vexed donors. Not without trepidation, the regime had agreed to the appointment of a Haitian who had spent most of his career outside Haiti, Marc Bazin. Smart, fluent in English, the new minister had been promised carte blanche in his efforts to clean the Augean stables. With him, Bazin brought in other young World Bank technocrats of Haitian origin such as Leslie Delatour, who were destined to leave their mark. The government's pleasure at having so deftly dealt with the *blancs* turned to consternation when it realized that the new cabinet minister took his mission seriously.

First, a special levy on imported cars was announced, and worse still, collected without exception. Grumbling turned to outrage as "Mr. Clean" (as he was quickly dubbed by nickname-loving Haitians) attempted to collect overdue taxes from various members of the elite. Then earning still more enemies, Bazin cancelled a short-term note issue of some $3.7 Billion that had been planned by his predecessor. Designed to get the government over the hump of any near-term exchange problems, the loan had loomed like a horn of plenty on the horizon of *gourde*-rich individuals, many of whom happened to be senior officials in the government. To Bazin, the thing had looked too much like some of the 19th century loans which Haiti had struggled so long to pay off.

From an international perspective, Bazin's efforts came not a moment too soon. A GAO study in February declared that the U.S. aid channelled to Haiti in such copious amounts over the preceding decade had been a "failure". Domestically, the murky quarrel between the dinosaurs and technocrats grew more pronounced as the *Cour de Cassation*, Haiti's supreme court, overturned Sylvio Claude's sentence of the previous Fall as "too harsh". Knowing full well that the justices would not hand down such a verdict without some signal from the Palace, observers awaited developments with interest.

Giving renewed hope to the "liberals", the president on April 21st announced to the deputies assembled to fete the eleventh anniversary of his Presidency that "free and honest" municipal elections would be held. Few were churlish enough to point out that no date had been given, preferring instead to focus on the positive.

Into this characteristically rich brew was then added the ingredient of family politics. The first brother-in-law, Franz Bennett, was apprehended by U.S. officials in Puerto Rico in a cocaine sting operation. Bennett offered a capability which U.S. officials had long suspected but of which they'd never had such good proof - the use of Haiti as a transhipment point for large amounts of cocaine. The conversation was taped. Thrown into jail, Bennett *fils* yelled for help from his sister. To her intense anger, she found that long-time counsellors such as Henri Bayard and Washington ambassador Georges Léger (who had heard the tapes) recommended that the president stay well away from the affair.

For his opinions, Bayard found himself sacked, after six years' service as Chief Mandarin. Michèle Bennett had managed in weeks what Simone Duvalier and Zacharie Delva's *ouangas* had not been able to do in eight years - the ouster of the most powerful *mulâtre* from the Cabinet. Bazin and his entourage were not long in following. Taking his mandate too broadly, he had incurred Michèle Duvalier's wrath by dunning Bennett *père* for some $1 million in back taxes. "Mr. Clean" had lasted only six months. Out of office, in New York, he wasted little time in letting friends know that his duties had included finding up to $15 million a month in state accounts for siphoning into the first couple's Swiss bank accounts.

Into the vacuum created by the *mulâtre* exodus came Roger Lafontant ("a dog that bites will do it again") who had undone Luckner Cambronne a decade earlier. His appointment as Interior Minister sent shivers up many spines. Another appointment that summer had great, though unforeseen at the time, consequences for Haiti. A thirty year-old divinity student, fresh from philosophy and psychology studies in Italy and Israel was ordained in the Catholic Church by Bishop Romélus of Jérémie. The date was Jean-Claude Duvalier's twenty-ninth birthday, July 3, 1982. The priest was Jean-Bertrand Aristide.

Adroitly avoiding what was sure to be another collision with the international community, the president exercised "executive clemency" for Sylvio Claude, his daughter, and a number of other casualties of the post-Reagan election roundup. After having his sentence of hard labor overturned, Claude had been scheduled to be retried in September - a trial which a number of watchdog groups had promised to monitor closely. Negative publicity was the last thing the government needed.

Slowly, like a cloud on the horizon which looms ever larger as it approaches, a "story" had been building that would do more damage to Haiti's economy than scandals, human rights violations and boat people combined. In the Spring of 1981, a few newspapers around the United States carried short accounts of a new illness that seemed to hit gay men with particular virulence. Dubbed "GRID", or Gay Related Immune Deficiency Syndrome, the virus within a year had a new name and a much longer list of victims. Re-titled AIDS (Gay men having been quickly proven to not be the only affected group), the disease was invariably fatal, and its etiology mysterious. Numerous theories abounded about its transmission, but there was little hard fact. "Tainted" blood was thought to be the culprit, but questions abounded. An American population which had been treated to cover stories on herpes was panicked by the advent of this new disease so many magnitudes worse.

In such a climate, any observation, no matter how small a population it was based on or however faulty the science, was granted widespread publicity. Thus it was that when physicians in South Florida noticed that a good number of heterosexual AIDS cases involved Haitian immigrants, the Haiti AIDS "linkage" was born. Randy Shilts noted in *And the Band Played On* that

> ...There was talk of voodoo rituals that might allow blood transmissions. Investigations were made difficult by language barriers and the suspicions Haitians had of anything governmental... Were these people really gay, having picked up the disease from visiting New Yorkers? Had they given it to gay Manhattan men on holiday? Was the disease spread through ritualistic scarring that might engender blood transmission?

Given local anti-Haitian sentiment in South Florida, it took little for the story to catch fire. Haiti was soon being portrayed as a breeding ground of this deadly new disease, and Haitians in the U.S. were asked not to give blood. Luckner Cambronne's plasma-farming was noted, as were Voodoo practices involving the drinking of blood from freshly slaughtered animals. Tourism, already battered by U.S. inflation, recession, boat people, and human rights publicity simply died overnight. In the 1982-1983 season, the total of all visitors to Haiti was 10,000, compared with some 200,000 a couple of years earlier. One businessman returning to New York was asked by the passport inspector to "open your passport - I don't want to touch it." With bitter humor, Haitians began calling AIDS "4H" - Homosexuals, hemophiliacs, heroin-addicts and Haitians.

The government quickly closed the few guesthouses that had catered to foreign gays, but this had more to do with publicity than public health. Homosexuality was not common in conservative Haiti, but some young men had resorted to homosexual prostitution with foreign tourists for purely economic reasons. Studies showed that once introduced, transmission models in Haiti most closely followed those of heterosexual urban Africa (see Farmer's *Aids and Accusation*), and that the virus had most likely come to Haiti from North America rather than the reverse. But logic was in the future. Blaming the messenger, the world began to shun Haiti. Well might Simone Duvalier think that *Guédé* had turned his back.

Importing basic foodstuffs, losing tourism revenues, without the fiscal discipline of "Mr. Clean", the government ended the year on a dour note - Haiti's exports and imports were out of balance by some $40 Million. Accentuating the gloom, a bomb exploded on New Year's eve near the Palace. Out partying, the Duvaliers were unharmed, but for security reasons the traditional Te Deum for the next day was cancelled for the first time in memory.

Hoping perhaps for Divine Intervention, the Duvaliers had managed to persuade the peripatetic Pope, John-Paul II, to include Haiti on a March trip through Latin America. The Haitians had been lobbying for the trip since the late seventies, but the Curia held out until it got its price - retrocession to the Vatican of the right to name bishops and the archbishop. Port-au-Prince was worth a mass, and so it was announced that on March 9, 1983, the Pope would visit Haiti for one day.

Michèle Duvalier loved nothing so much as a party and pomp, so she threw herself into preparations for the pontiff's arrival with gusto, pausing only briefly to deliver an heir on January 31st. Anxious as any father, the president was gowned, scrubbed, and at his wife's side as Nicolas François Jean-Claude Duvalier came into the world at 7:22 A.M. The line was secure.

As the first lady recovered, she badgered ministries to contribute to a face-lift for Port-au-Prince from the slush funds she knew they all kept. Playing *doyenne* of public morality, she insisted that Roger Lafontant marry his mistress as the price of meeting the Pope. Catering arrangements were made with Miami firms, diverting already scarce dollars. Unbeknownst to the government, the Vatican had rather a different agenda for the Papal visit. It had noted with disquiet the increasing popularity of Liberation Theology in Latin America. There were few places that seemed to offer such fertile ground to such doctrine as Haiti, and the increased militancy of many young priests in the movement known as "*Ti l"Egliz*" (little church) had attracted Vatican attention. Only by reclaiming the Church'es moral authority from the *Macoute* Bishops could Rome hope to forestall a move by the masses to alternatives.

Nou ka rete SIDA
sou rout li,
ak tout lot maladi nou ka trape nan fè bagay!

"Renmen, fè bagay, fè pitit, tou sa se reskonsabilite nou."

After ten years, both alphabetized Créole and AIDS were such facts of life that by the mid nineteen-nineties, posters such as the one above were effective tools in fighting the epidemic. *Heinl Collection*

Tens of thousands of Haitians gathered at the newly spruced up Port-au-Prince airport to watch the Pope's Alitalia DC-10 land after a two hour flight from Guatemala. Monsignor Ligondé and the Nuncio (le *Nonce* - nicknamed by some "*le Monstre*" for his chumminess with the regime and the lavishness of the newly-built nunciature) went on board to greet the Pontiff. Shortly thereafter, garbed in his traditional white cassock, the Holy Father emerged from the aircraft, stepped off the red carpet imported for his visit and kissed Haitian soil. Responding to a speech from the president, the Pope, in front of millions of Haitians clustered around radios and televisions, greeted the masses in Créole. Twisting his tongue around the unfamiliar groupings of sounds, in nonetheless comprehensible Créole the Pontiff lashed out against misery, hunger, and fear in Haiti. Then, in words which reverberated around the country, he thundered,"*Fok sa Chanje*" (things must change!).

The airport, closed for the day to all save the Papal flight, became an instant stadium as the Pope celebrated Mass in the open. Declining the food brought in by the government at such expense from Miami, the Holy Father took instead a simple repast in the company of Haitian priests. Stopping at the Palace long enough only to bless the newest Duvalier, one month old Nicolas, his message to the Haitian people was unmistakable - the Pope was siding with them. Port-au-Prince snickered as it reveled in the details of the untrodden red carpet, the spurned repast, the marriage in vain of the *macoute* minister. "What could you expect?", old ladies mused - Michèle Duvalier had not even worn a hat!

Firmer than a Monkey's Tail

Shaken, the government resumed its business. The "free and honest elections" promised by the president the previous April were scheduled, finally, to be held everywhere except Port-au-Prince in April, and May. The capital, bursting at the seams with a population of more than a million, was to be last, in June. The first balloting in the Northwest, in April, went well enough, with the regime's candidates winning as expected. In May, with the mayorship of the ever-troublesome Cap being contested, the government took the precautionary measure of detaining the sole opposition member of the Assembly, *Capois* Alexandre Lerouge, for the duration of the campaign. Security forces were thwarted in their attempt to lock up Sylvio Claude who had opted to go to ground for a few days rather than enjoy government hospitality.

To the intense annoyance of the government, the maverick *Capois*, in a replay of the Lerouge election, opted for the "independent" candidate - Wilson Borjella. Nothing could be done about the election at the Cap, but away from the snooping of the international press, the regime moved decisively. Roger

Lafontant, demonstrating his credentials as a Duvalierist, *pur et dur*, invalidated the election results in dusty St. Raphaël and in Petit Goâve on the basis of "irregularities". The Port-au-Prince elections were postponed.

Other portents of change began to manifest themselves that dusty Summer. Skilled as Kremlin-watchers, the elite began speculating about the meaning of three changes to the constitution that the president announced in August. First, he obtained the right to appoint an interim president in case he decided to travel abroad. Then, though his *dauphin* was still in swaddling clothes, he had the constitution amended to give him the right to nominate a successor - there was no mention of "interim" this time. Since foreign travel was more symptomatic of the end of a presidential term than its *entr'acte*, the telediol buzzed about possible presidential maladies that might require attention abroad. Nothing likely to trouble a thirty-two year old seemed to fit the bill. Second, the new and improved constitution also created a "super cabinet" that was to preside over the bloated cadre of ministers.

Comprising the key portfolios of Finance, Foreign Affairs, and Interior, the "super cabinet" in microcosm demonstrated the contradictions that were pulling the government apart. Roger Lafontant disliked intensely the Finance Minister, Frantz Merceron, *mulâtre* technocrat that he was. Merceron was adept and obliging enough to do what Bazin had balked at on principle - routinely transfer millions from state coffers into private accounts - so he stayed. Michèle Duvalier disliked Lafontant. The president was trapped in the middle, swaying first one way, then another. Continuing the long Duvalierist policy of "preventive rotation", the president also announced in October a nearly clean sweep of the Army high command. The incumbents learned of their retirements from a midnight television broadcast. To an habitually suspicious public, it seemed that the president was paving the way for a change.

Impolitic enough to print what was topic A around Port-au-Prince, *Le Petit Samedi Soir*, ever in the vanguard, ran in December an article that listed eleven possible successors to the Presidency. Not for Interior Minister Lafontant the harsh measures of the early days of the revolution. No presses were smashed. Instead, the issue simply vanished from newsstands. Some subjects were still taboo.

As if frozen in mid-action, the country took time out for the habitual Christmas celebrations. At least those who could afford it did. With the dawning of the New Year, all eyes were focused on the legislative elections on February 12th. The first couple made a number of progresses throughout the country to urge their fellow citizens to vote. A year early because of the president's decision to dissolve the chamber before its term had expired, elections were sure to provide clues to the regime's direction - if there was any. There were few opposition figures of any prominence remaining and fighting in Haiti. Alexandre Lerouge, the customs clerk from the Cap who had bucked the trend five years earlier was warned against running for a second term. Grégoire Eugène was barred from returning from his four year exile in the U.S. until the elections were over.

Sylvio Claude barely hung on. Released on Christmas eve from yet another stint in prison, the former schoolteacher was under "house arrest" in the modest cinderblock structure that was his home outside of jail. Recovering from beatings administered during his latest encounter with the State, within earshot of the omnipresent *macoute* who barred most visitors, he told reporter Jock Hatfield that "while I'm here, Jean-Claude has someone to worry about." Dismissing the imminent elections as a "show put on for the United States", the Christian Democrat reflected wearily on the seven imprisonments and twenty-two arrests he had endured since 1979, all for a party that would not even be permitted to run.

More than three hundred candidates contested the fifty-nine seats that had become vacant by presidential fiat. Inasmuch as opposition to the government's programs was impermissible, most candidates satisfied themselves with declarations of fealty to the regime. Despite preliminary vetting, a few contests actually heated up, allowing the electorate some semblance of choice. In one such race, Ed Racine, one-time mayor of Croix-des-Bouquets, was pitted against incumbent Edner Cadet. Racine had spent most of the sixties in the United States, there raising his family with his attractive and intelligent wife. In the way of such things, despite personal ties with such figures as Marc Bazin and Père Adrien, he had made a degree of peace with the second Duvalier government. Apparently he had made enough peace to run, but not enough to win, for when regime candidate Cadet began trailing seriously, the government simply stuffed the ballot boxes. Despite the fact that nearly two-thirds of the incumbents were replaced, the resultant body looked identical to the one it replaced. The elections were indeed, "just a show put on for the United States".

The regime put on less of a show than it had during the previous American presidential elections. Four years earlier, it had still been worried about Jimmy Carter and had trimmed it sails accordingly. Now, with Ronald Reagan's re-election looking certain, fewer gestures were necessary. After delivering a speech in favor of "press freedom" on May 5th, the president allowed his first minister only six days later to ban all political activities and political pamphleteering (save of course those related to Jean-Claudism). The American

Secretary of State, George Schultz, was at the same time certifying to Congress that there had been enough demonstrable progress in the human rights area to justify the continuance of U.S. aid to Haiti.

Lafontant's political antennae may have been more keenly tuned than those of foreigners. Birds of ill omen were circling. In Gonaïves, sitting just to the North and West of the Artibonite breadbasket, the rains had failed and people were hungry. The rains that had failed Gonaïves had also failed Péligre. With little water to turn the turbines, electricity in Port-au-Prince was fitful at best. No pigs rooted about in peasant courtyards to buffer nature's calamities - all had been slaughtered. In the Cap, no cruise ship had docked for eighteen months, with a withering effect on the economy of that proud city. Some eighty-two thousand children in the Cap region alone were dependent on CARE and other organizations for a meager daily ration of grain to keep them alive.

On a day-to-day basis, Lafontant seemed to be running the country. Rumor had it that the First Couple were enmeshed in domestic difficulties. Michèle Duvalier had demanded that her husband sack Lafontant, whom she cordially detested and who returned the favor. Lafontant though represented Jean-Claude's links with old-style Duvalierism - links that he was not minded to repudiate, and links that were essential whenever the regime needed to get tough. At one point Michèle Duvalier, again with child, presented the president with an ultimatum: Lafontant or me. Jean-Claude Duvalier picked Lafontant. Momentarily humbled, Michèle Duvalier skulked back to the Palace and took refuge in shopping and the cocaine that her father was so instrumental in importing. The president's tough stance may have been facilitated by the rumor making its way around Port-au-Prince that the child due shortly had been fathered not by him but by, appropriately enough, the Minister for Social Affairs, Théodore Achille.

On May 20th, officials at the CARE warehouse in the Cap loaded some food that had been spoiled in the course of the long journey from the U.S. onto trucks. The food, a small portion of the amounts held in the storehouses, was destined for farm animals at an agricultural station nearby. As the trucks pulled out, a rumor swept the market that supplies were being diverted to the black market, and an angry mob stormed the warehouse. *Miliciens* called to the scene fought a pitched battle that lasted four hours. Three were killed - none of them *miliciens*.

Perhaps it was the news of disturbances at the Cap, broadcast over Catholic Radio Soleil. Perhaps the *telediol* carried the news. But by the next day, violence erupted elsewhere. In Gonaïves, a group of residents marched on police headquarters to protest the beating death of a pregnant woman. Refusing to stop at barricades around police headquarters, crowd members were clubbed with rifle butts and *coco-macaques*. Instead of passively submitting to the beatings, the crowd fought back. Over the next two days, thousands protested, managing in the process to loot food warehouses of various international groups. Dozens were injured, but most sought no medical aid, fearing that the lone hospital, such as it was, would turn the injured over to police. Only the arrival of machine-gun toting reinforcements from Port-au-Prince finally quelled the sullen, hungry mob.

Shocked, government ministers (including Social Affairs minister Achille and the Agricultural minister) sent to investigate reported that the riots had metamorphosed from food riots into anti-government riots. Marking Jean-Claude Duvalier's marriage as a turning point in national fortunes, rioters were calling for his divorce and expulsion of the Bennett clan. The message was unwelcome, and five cabinet ministers found themselves sacked for bearing bad tidings, as did most of the local government in Gonaïves. The riots marked the first broad public resistance to Duvalier rule since the student strike in 1961.

Grégoire Eugène, home barely three months, told the press: "The people were eating dog and overripe fruit. The Government turned a deaf ear. But Gonaïves and Cap Haïtien used a language that was loud enough to be heard in Port-au-Prince." Even Aubelin Jolicoeur, consummate survivor of nearly thirty years of Duvaliersm, put down a marker. "It was", he told the press, "the movement of hungry people who got angry. The food was there but it was not distributed. They have CARE here, but they don't care."

Far North, events in Haiti were being followed with interest by the U.S. Congress, which had voted to make 1985 aid to Haiti contingent on "certifiable" progress in the Human rights area. The government's response was to add Grégoire Eugène and Haitian envoy to UNESCO Hubert de Ronceray to the list of those under house arrest. For good measure, *Le Petit Samedi Soir* editor Dieudonné Fardin was hauled into the Dessalines barracks for a few hours to allow time for reflection.

Pursuing a program of circuses, if not bread, the regime did authorize the expenditure of more than half a million precious dollars for the rights to air the European Cup soccer matches over a two week period. Those urban poor lucky enough to have access to both a television and electricity could momentarily assuage their hunger pangs with sports. The last such experiment in outreach to the masses had been the Duvalier-Bennett marriage.

That Summer, at the party held annually every August by Mme. Max Adolphe at her Pétionville home to honor the *Milice*, the president and all his cabinet (including the *mulâtre* finance minister, Merceron) appeared in *gros bleu* - the regulation denim uniform of the *milice*. The message was unmistakable. In times of trouble, the government reverted instinctively to its old power bases.

School enrollment, one of the few reliable barometers of social welfare, plummeted for a second year in a row as the effects of the pig purge continued to manifest themselves. Small merchants throughout the country found themselves with surplus stocks of school supplies as *paysans*, stripped of their savings, kept their children home. By year's end, six years after the first pig slaughter along the Dominican border, the first foreign pigs, or *cochons blancs* began to be delivered to hamlets throughout the country under the second phase of the swine virus eradication program. The new pigs, unlike the hardy Haitian stock, could not survive by rooting about in garbage piles, but instead required expensive feed and cement pigpens. "These pigs", one peasant commented bitterly, "live better than we do." Nothing could better symbolize the failure of foreign aid to Haiti.

Into this Haiti - sullen, hungry, and angry - Jean-Bertrand Aristide returned in January of 1985 from two years "study" (in reality Church-mandated exile) in Montreal. He had gone unwillingly, and from abroad had avidly followed events at home. Now, after considerable negotiation with his superiors, he was allowed to take up duties at a parish in one of the poorest quarters of Port-au-Prince - St.-Jean-Bosco. Other members of the Church felt called to serve the urban poor as well. Port-au-Prince was the scene of a protest march in January led by Catholic priests. The crowd of 30,000 shouted "Down with Misery and Hunger." The rising tide of protest had begun to lap against the capital.

The ferment the young priest saw was being duplicated throughout urban Haiti. On the fourteenth anniversary of his succession to power, the president had relaxed a bit Lafontant's ban on pamphleteering and political parties. Still in the thrall of his dark angel, he negated any positive effects his announcement might have had by announcing on June 29th a referendum. The vote, Lafontant's brainchild, would ask Haitians to: allow the creation of a new post of Prime Minister and legalize "opposition" parties - both subject to the electorate's approval of the Presidency for life. The vote, thought Lafontant would dispose of the issue of whether or not the president enjoyed a popular mandate.

Clumsily conceived, the vote was greeted with widespread apathy. Aside from a few polling stations where free *clairin* was being passed out, few bothered to vote. The electorate had been encouraged in its passive resistance by the priests of the *'ti l'egliz* movement. "Only Jesus Christ is forever!" thundered one preacher. Radio Soleil carried this message nationwide. Opting yet again to "jail the news", Lafontant promptly ordered the expulsion of three foreign priests associated with the broadcasting operation. In protest, more than two-hundred priests and religious workers marched in Port-au-Prince, vowing not to be silenced.

Putting the best possible face on things, the government announced that 99.9 % of the electorate had voted "yes". "The opposition", announced Press minister Chanoine, "must cooperate or retire". 1985 though was not 1961 or 1971, and the plebiscite device no longer worked. The final blow to the regime's credibility was dealt by one of its own. Clovis Désinor, once faithful minister to Papa Doc, deprived, he felt of the presidency that was legitimately his, decried the fact that "fifty percent of the nation has never had the privilege of electing a leader." He would, he said, found his own political party.

The vote intended to "settle" matters had instead inflamed them, and for this, Roger Lafontant was bundled on board a flight to Montreal. From there, as Canada's winter set in, he spent most of his time on the phone to Port-au-Prince, plotting (in calls that were recorded and delivered to the Palace) to insinuate himself back into power as he had done so many times before. Coalesced now around the president were all those who felt a stake in Duvalierism's survival - Merceron, Madame Max Adolphe and her *macoutes* and *milice*, the Bennetts - even *'ti Pouche Douyon* was again allowed inside the tent.

Such a caucus violated a fundamental precept of François Duvalier's. He had never let the various groups that owed their existence to him make common cause. It was inevitable as Fall progressed that those circling the wagons began to talk among themselves. Two parallel dramas were taking place in Haiti. On the streets, a disenfranchised, gunless, hungry populace was increasingly in ferment. Capitalizing on that discontent, younger priests were organizing and giving the masses a real voice that they had not enjoyed in a generation.

Watching this radicalization with increasing apprehension were all the institutions that had worked so long with the regime but no longer saw their interests as congruent - the army, the new rich in the elite, and the non-liberation theology church. With at first tacit, then overt encouragement by an American administration that had no desire to see a "people's government" take root on its very doorstep, there began to build a plot.

The army, quiet for so very long, had once been the traditional hatchery of such arrangements until emasculated by François Duvalier. Since his death, it had been allowed, albeit on a short leash, to regain some of the status it once enjoyed. In its ranks, among the drug dealers and grafters, were some honest and capable men. A number of officers who had made careers there by keeping their low profiles had found themselves arbitrarily cashiered as a result of some clash with the Bennett clan. Others, survivors of the sixties and seventies, were newly energized by the excesses, even by Duvalier standards, of life in the Palace. Some of the young *noir* officers whose careers had prospered until the arrival of the lighter-skinned Bennetts also had grievances. The army could spearhead change, but who? An unlikely alliance between the Army commander and a younger *noir* officer formed the nucleus of the cabal.

Henri Namphy, the Army Chief of Staff, was born to a *mulâtre* family in the Cap in 1932. Receiving his commission as second lieutenant in 1954, he was old enough to remember a Haiti that worked, and one where the Army had a pivotal role in society and government. Known as *'ti Blanc* because of his light color, he survived the fall of the Magloire government and the purges of the officer corps conducted by Papa Doc. Duvalier *père's* brand of populism appealed to Namphy enough so that he never became enmeshed in the various army plots to overthrow Duvalier in the sixties, preferring instead hard drinking and womanizing. A "soldier's soldier" was the description given of him by one foreigner who worked with him. His career prospered under Jean-Claude Duvalier who promoted him to Brigadier General in 1981, and then Lieutenant General and head of the Army in 1984.

Namphy was known to take care of his troops, and also had refused on several occasions to order those troops to fire on the people. In an Army that had been repeatedly compromised over nearly three decades, he had relatively clean hands.

His partner in this venture could not have been more different. Williams Regala was five years younger than Namphy but was a total product of the Duvalier regime. Graduating in one of the last classes of the Académie Militaire before its ten-year shutdown, he had watched his fellow officers fall by the wayside. *Noir* to Namphy's *mulâtre,* he had served in all the key positions - the presidential guard, the Dessalines battalion, and as head of the *Léopards.* For two years he had been inspector-general of the Army and was consequently well-placed to know where pockets of discontent might lie.

Cautiously, the two gradually widened their circle. While, disaffected army men were in plentiful supply, pivotal to any arrangement was the elimination or at least neutralization of the *Macoutes* and *Milice.* Unlike the army, they stood to lose much if the regime changed, and their opposition would mean either outright failure or civil war. Cannily, the duo sought out the one person who was disaffected but whose credentials with the dinosaurs were impeccable - Clovis Désinor. Skulking outside the halls of power for fifteen years after voicing his dissatisfaction over the choice of Jean-Claude Duvalier to lead the "revolution" he had fought so hard for, Désinor alone could safely approach Madame Max Adolphe, the *VSN/Macoute* head.

To their relief, the conspirators found Désinor in agreement with their aims. Not only did he agree to talk to Mme. Max, but he offered useful insights on the logistics of pulling off a coup. While Désinor sought out Rosalie Adolphe in her Pétionville home, the army men met with the Americans. First with junior officials, then the ambassador, they put their case. Duvalier's excesses had undermined the confidence of key pillars of the regime. Only the Army had enough standing and the cohesiveness to pull together a post-Duvalier regime. Failure to act could result in a bloody civil war and the ultimate installation of a radical government unsympathetic to the U.S. To underscore their point, the Army men had only to draw attention to the demonstrations in Gonaïves and the *'ti L'Egliz* movement. Would the U.S., having supported Jean-Claude Duvalier's government in varying degrees, at least remain neutral if a change were attempted?

Watching the deterioration in Port-au-Prince and the provinces, Foggy Bottom came quickly to the conclusion that an arranged transfer of power was infinitely preferable to the high-minded but far more dangerous policy of non-intervention. It signed on. The devil, though, was in the details. Madame Max, fierce devotee of the regime, was initially appalled by Désinor's pitch. After reflecting for a few days, she gradually came round, but for a price. Certain key *macoutes*, including herself, would have to be guaranteed safety. The rest could not be told until the last minute, or they had the means to abort the entire exercise. Elaborating, she demanded a U.S. visa so that she could live with her daughter and grandchildren in the U.S.

This demand, roughly like the Allies giving safe-conduct to Himmler in 1945, made the Americans gag. Only when Mme. Max threatened to betray the entire operation did the U.S. consent, over the vigorous protest of several of those close to the operation. By the beginning of January 1986, the pieces were beginning to fall into place.

None too soon, either, for while the traditional constituencies in such matters were making their arrangements, the situation on the ground was worsening rapidly.

Turbulent Gonaïves, the flashpoint fifteen months earlier, had erupted at the end of November. Crowds carrying signs reading "down with misery" and "long live the Army" had grown violent after riot troops shot three school children in cold blood. An uneasy order was reestablished by the dispatch and permanent stationing of a unit of *Léopards*, but all waited tensely for the next act. Jailing the news, the president ordered Catholic Radio Soleil to stop broadcasting. But the *telediol* carried what the airwaves could not - the feeling by all that a sea change was occurring.

Or nearly all. In an awesome display of indifference, with her country starving, Michèle Duvalier that December flew to Paris with several friends on Concorde to do her Christmas shopping. The $1.7 million she spent on furs, jewelry and other baubles so depleted the national coffers that there was no money to pay an oil tanker that docked at Port-au-Prince with desperately needed petroleum. Denied payment, the captain upped anchor and sailed off with his precious cargo into the Gulf of Gonâve. As *tap-taps* ground to a halt and generators sputtered out, Haitians in horrified fascination began to realize that the regime's cupidity had literally and figuratively drained them dry.

Trying at the eleventh hour to jettison much of the baggage that had brought him to this pass, the president put together a new cabinet. Gone were Merceron, Chanoine and the other feckless young men. In their places were old-line Duvalierists - Alix Cinéas, Pierre Merceron (who, so long ago had been chief of staff), and most importantly, Georges Salomon. The scion of *Castel père*, grown weary of defending a regime that he knew had betrayed its people, nonetheless agreed to take up the traces one more time. This time, he did it for the Haitian people, for Georges Salomon too realized what nearly everyone in Haiti save the occupants of the Palace knew - "*Fok Sa Chanjé*" - things must change.

Even the clergy - the *'ti l'Egliz* by definition had long since signed on - the mostly (save for the courageous Bishop Romulus of Jérémie) compromised Episcopacy, was climbing on board the bandwagon. To the stupefaction of the first lady, who wondered out loud how a family member "could do this" to her, Msgr. Ligondé delivered a Christmas sermon whose message was "Yes to Liberty and Justice. No to Lies and Servitude." A stunning indictment of the status quo, the message that was read from pulpits across the land gave the Church'es imprimatur to the gathering momentum of change.

At the beginning of January, thousands of students failed to go back to school, in the process foregoing their one sure meal a day. Realizing, perhaps for the first time, the true extent of this massive civil disobedience and what it portended, Jean-Claude Duvalier belatedly did what his father would have done long ago - he consulted the gods. Gathered in the Palace a few days later was a delegation of eight *houngans* and a *mambo* led by the dapper Max Beauvoir. Beauvoir, a university graduate, had made money by staging "voodoo ceremonies" for foreign tourists in a *peristyle* cum nightclub on the Léogane road, but behind the showmanship the truth was more complex. Like Lorimer Denis, Milo Rigaud, and François Duvalier, Beauvoir was an educated man who recognized that voodoo was part of Haiti's lifeblood, and had studied it accordingly. At some point he had made the transition from scholarship to belief.

Now, standing before his president, Beauvoir and the others delivered the news of just how bleak things were. The Gods, said Beauvoir, had wanted Duvalier to leave for nearly a year. Duvalier was surprised, and then depressed as the enormity of what he had heard sunk in. Dismissed, the bearers of the bad tidings made their way back to their peristyles at Léogane and Croix-des-Bouquets and braced for what was to come. A few days later, the association of industrialists added their voices to the chorus demanding change. *Guédé's* seeming desertion the president could take in stride, but when the industrial community, whose fortunes he had done so much to advance, joined in, his depression turned to anger.

Unaware of the plotting going on beneath his nose, the president played a card which sealed his fate. Seeking to buy time, he ordered the dismissal of several of the more odious army officers and the re-installation of several others who had run afoul of Roger Lafontant or Michèle Duvalier. Unknowingly, he delivered the command of key army units to people who would not support him when the crunch came.

Throughout the country disturbances reverberated. Cayes, the Goâves, Jacmel, Léogane - all were rocked. Tellingly, many demonstrators waved small American flags. In the fashion of *piquets* sacking Cayes or *paysans* looting Port-au-Prince in the 19th century, mobs did not forego the opportunity to sack food and medicine warehouses throughout the country. By now, 800,000 children depended on the foreign organizations that owned those warehouses for survival. Regional army commanders received orders from the Palace to fire on rioters - orders quietly countermanded by Henri Namphy. Mobs began to target property of *Macoutes*, who in increasing numbers were fleeing to the relative safety of the capital. The Army had either stood by passively or actively intervened to disarm local *macoutes*. Not in a generation had the its stock been as high.

Long ago, echoing a truth so well known to generations of Haitian leaders, Papa Doc had said, "You can beat them in Port-au-Prince and bribe them in Gonaïves, but when the Cap riots, pack your bags." On January 28, 1986, the army stood by as rioters looted the CARE warehouse at the Cap. Emboldened by their success, the demonstrators toppled a statue of Papa Doc while shouting "*Vive l'Armée!*" The noose was drawing tight.

Arrangements were largely in place. It remained only for someone to bell the cat. Vacillating, Duvalier variously favored leaving or fighting, depending on who he listened to. A delegation of deputies, convened to ratify a state of siege decreed by the president, instead found uncharacteristic courage. Waiting on Duvalier, they asked him to declare elections, only to meet an icy rebuff. On January 31, the Duvaliers were so resigned that they headed for the airport where a chartered plane waited for them. Changing his mind en route (some said he drew encouragement from Prosper Avril), the president returned to the Palace in the early dawn, determined to make a stand.

From the Palace, Duvalier drove the few blocks through deserted streets to the studios of Radio Nationale. There, Haiti heard its president describe the rumors of his departure as "...nonsense. The president is here and standing firm - *firmer*", he added, using an old Créole proverb, "*than a monkey's tail.*"

Washington, with communications temporarily jammed, assumed that the presence of the aircraft at the airport meant that the transfer it had sought to engineer was taking place and so announced to the world. Celebrations broke out among Haitians in Miami, Montreal, and Chicago, only to turn to despair when it became clear that it had been a false alarm. Red-faced, the U.S. administration back-pedaled throughout the day. Port-au-Prince too had broken out in premature celebration - celebration that quickly died when the first couple stopped at several points around the city.

At 1:00, wearing a khaki safari shirt and standing behind a lectern, the president read a set piece written for him by Salomon. "I know many of you are extremely disturbed by the waves of violence that have swept the provinces... our institutions must work together... I reaffirm my mission to realize socio-economic benefits for the majority of the nation." Going on to declare a state of siege throughout the country, he walked off-camera. Just behind his left shoulder stood a *noir milicien* in *gros bleu*. The contrast between the light-skinned president and the jet black *milicien* spoke volumes about the odd coalition that had sustained this regime.

Despite the state of siege, mob violence continued throughout the weekend as crowds burned government buildings and tried to settle accounts with the hated *macoutes*. Roadblocks manned by machete-wielding *paysans* throttled traffic throughout the country. With Mardi Gras only ten days off, many of the crowds looked like carnival celebrants until one read the signs - "long live the army; down with Duvalier; we want liberty."

Only in Port-au-Prince, swollen with *macoute* refugees and bristling with guns could the regime be said to be in control. Phone lines to the provinces were cut, but word of scores dead and hundreds injured reached the citizens of Port-au-Prince. Using a tactic unseen in twenty years, shops hat had shut early over the weekend had their doors broken open by Duvalierists. Produce prices soared as peasant women voted with their feet and stayed home, depriving the city of food. On Monday morning, repeating their performance of Thursday, the first couple, foreign press frantically scrambling behind, made a well-publicized progress throughout the city. Asked point blank about plans to leave, the president said, "I am *Président-à-vie.*"

Satellite dishes and VCR's did double duty as bootleg tapes of the latest utterances by U.S. officials were circulated around town. The coup de grace to a regime hanging on by a thread was delivered Wednesday morning by Secretary of State George Schultz, on *Good Morning America*. Answering questions about the Haiti situation, he opined that it would be better if Haiti had "a government put there by a democratic process." The regime had lost the mandate of heaven.

Schultz'es remark pushed the regime over the edge. Diplomacy of the airwaves had been accompanied by behind-the-scenes representations from the Jamaican Prime Minister, Edward Seaga, who had some personal ties to the Duvaliers. Concerned about the effect that violence in Haiti would have on Jamaica, a Seaga envoy had urged the president to step aside during two long private interviews early in the week.

The tempo quickened. As squads of increasingly tense *miliciens* roared around town in jeeps, feelers from the Palace went out to countries that might be willing to offer the Duvaliers refuge. Air Haiti's lone cargo plane, loaded chock full of Bennett possessions, flew out Wednesday afternoon. The senior Bennetts were not slow in following. Passengers on outbound flights found themselves yanked out of their seats as ministers scurried to secure places for family members, mistresses - anyone who might be in danger. The smell of panic was in the air.

Bowing to the inevitable, Thursday morning Jean-Claude Duvalier abruptly told a startled Salomon that he wanted to leave that night. The French and U.S. Ambassadors were summoned to the Palace at noon and informed. Scrambling, the U.S. and France quickly agreed that a U.S. Air Force C-141 aircraft from Charleston would take the first couple and (what else?) twenty-two others to France. The stay in France was to be temporary pending permanent arrangements with another country. The lights burned late in the Palace as the Duvaliers tried to cram as much as possible into their Gucci and Vuitton luggage.

Finally, almost casually, the president agreed to see Henri Namphy. He still had no idea of the intricate web that had been woven around him in the preceding weeks. Namphy and Regala showed their hand to the Duvaliers in the president's office. As the outlines of what had really taken place became clear, Michèle Bennett began to scream hysterically. Here was a moment of supreme danger. The Palace was full of *macoutes* still unaware of the drama that was unfolding. Prosper Avril, restored to the Army and promoted to full Colonel only the week before, delivered a stunning left hook to the First lady, temporarily knocking her out. The time for niceties was over. As Michèle Duvalier came to, whimpering, arrangements for the transfer of power were quickly finalized.

The president made a video-tape to be played after his departure. The tape, aired the next morning at 8 a.m., said what people by then already knew. Sitting in the office bequeathed him by his father, a dark-suited Duvalier spoke to his countrymen:

My dear compatriots. In recent days I have looked in vain for any sign that would suggest a way out of this nightmare of blood. Desiring to enter history with my head held high and a tranquil and clear conscience, I have decided tonight to pass the destiny of the country over to the Armed Forces....

Somber, short, it was the finest speech Jean-Claude Duvalier ever gave.

The first lady, her head bound with a turban so as not to show her wound, decided to invite a few friends to the Palace to consume as much champagne and cocaine as possible until it was time to leave. "There were", said one participant, "no tears".

At the airport, Salomon and others breathed a sigh of relief as a convoy of BMW's and luggage-laden trucks zoomed through the side gate just past 3 A.M. In the third car came Jean-Claude and Michèle Duvalier with their children and two army officers. Taking a long drag on her cigarette, Michèle Duvalier looked right through the press, radiating an icy calm. Simone Duvalier followed in another vehicle.

U.S. Airmen and Haitian soldiers loaded the aircraft. All the passengers save the first couple had to submit to frisking by U.S. airmen - a bracing indication of how their lives were about to change. Then, at 3:47 a.m., Friday, February 7, 1986, doors secured, the C-141 lumbered onto the runway, taxied, and headed East to Puerto Rico. After refueling, it flew into the dawn towards France. Telephones started ringing - "the bird has flown". Nearly three decades of Duvalier rule were over.

With the ejection of the Duvaliers, Haiti brought to a close a remarkable chapter in its history. Poor but proud when François Duvalier assumed power in 1957, the country had been brought, by 1986 to depths of misery and desperation that would have shocked even Papa Doc. Nature was calling in its bills. An overworked land with a population problem of Malthusian dimensions, its lot had been worsened by the avarice, short-sightedness, and indifference of its rulers. The Duvaliers changed forever the face of Haitian society by creating through their politics a diaspora which reached far beyond the elite. By 1986, one out of six Haitians lived abroad. Papa Doc, the ultimate nationalist, sowed the seeds for an internationalization of Haiti that would go far beyond anything achieved in the U.S. occupation.

Haitians, who had been grateful in 1971 that Jean-Claude Duvalier was *not* his father, by 1986 realized that Duvalierism was Duvalierism no matter which Duvalier was at the helm. Yet the Duvaliers did not create the attributes which so gnawed at the vitals of the Haitian people. They played on them, they institutionalized them, they channelled them, but they did not create them. Jean-Claude Duvalier, ultimately, was as much manipulated by the system as he was the manipulator of it. Thrust unwillingly into a job for which he had little training and even less inclination, he defied all predictions by managing for fifteen years to ride the tiger.

At the moment of reckoning though, he had neither the blood lust nor the ideological fire in his belly to continue the game. Papa Doc saw money as a means to get power. Jean-Claude Duvalier saw power as a means to get money and was ultimately used by the powerful to get money. To his surprise, when the mechanism ceased functioning, he was discarded. What only a few could realize in 1986, and even they only dimly, was that in ridding themselves of the Duvaliers, Haitians had barely begun the task of addressing the Duvalier legacy. As in 1804, the "who shall have it" was anything but settled.

FOOTNOTES - CHAPTER 15

1. One American youngster, invited to spend the day at the palace with Jean-Claude, roamed too far. At the door of the basement arsenal, a soldier aimed his rifle directly at him. Indignantly he burst out, "My daddy says you're never supposed to point a rifle at someone unless you mean to shoot them!" He survived.

2. Burt and Diederich maintain that Papa Doc briefly considered trying to install Marie-Denise as his successor, but concluded that male chauvinist Haiti wouldn't buy it. Too, Marie-Denise's marriage to Max Dominique had alienated certain parts of the Duvalier power base.

3. In 1986, mobs sacking the Duvalier family mausoleum found nothing. The Duvaliers were very aware of the dangers of corpses being stolen. Thieves had stolen Duval Duvalier's corpse. Many believe that Papa Doc's body did not leave the Palace until the Duvaliers fled to France in 1986 and that the "funeral procession" was for show purposes.

4. As Paul Farmer points out in *Aids and Accusation*, none of the peasants dislocated by Péligre's building and the subsequent flooding ever got any of the electricity for which they had paid so dearly.

5. Few foreigners thought to recall either West Africa's dread secret society of "Leopards" who kill their victims while wearing leopard skins and using the actual claws of the animal, or the widely held belief that certain men can turn themselves into leopards at will and thus kill with impunity.

6. Herbert Gold has a particularly good description of his ride on a Haitian passenger train in *Holiday* Magazine.

7. Described in Georges Michel's *Les Chemins de Fer de L'Isle d'Haïti*.

8. This time, by literally taking the high road, the French avoided the criticsms leveled at past roads - that they had been too susceptible to flooding. This time the road climbed up the hills and stayed there until a dizzying drop into Jacmel at the end. The flooding problem was promptly replaced with a new one - landslides.

9. With the repair of telephones came to an end a whole subculture of communication. One clerk told of being startled to hear Papa Doc's voice on the other end of a normally dormant phone line. It was a wrong number, but Duvalier engaged the clerk in conversation for some minutes out of curiosity. The lines to the *Casernes* always worked.

10. Haitian divorces had become so notorious that by 1984, a Washington divorce lawyer professed wonderment at hearing that a couple had actually been *married* in Haiti.

11. Greene, with his sure sense of what made the best reading, picked an atypical hotel, even by Port-au-Prince standards. Had the plot been set amidst

the Eisenhower era architecture of the El Rancho, a very different book would have emerged.

12. Given the Clinton administration decision to restrict access to Pennsylvania Avenue, the Duvaliers may have been merely guilty of being ahead of their time.

13. Many of the saplings were planted in inappropriate places or were not watered. Those few that made it to maturity were quickly hacked down for charcoal.

14. The *Caféteria* received its name from its original function - a feeding station for the urban poor during the Magloire era.

15. Along with the clearly audible crack of bones breaking, relatives of victims were able to identify loved ones by listening to their howls of agony.

Jean-Claude and Michèle Duvalier drive through the gate of François Duvalier Airport to a waiting U.S. Air Force aircraft, February 7, 1986 *AP/Wide World Photos*

Chapter 16

Paper and Iron

1986 - 1995

Constitution se papier, baïonet se fè
[a constitution is paper, a bayonet, iron]

- Créole proverb

"The blow by which kings fall causes a long bleeding."

- Corneille, *Cinna*

"Never came reformation in a flood"

-Shakespeare, *Henry V*

A solitary church bell that began ringing insistently at 5 A.M. performed for the poor of Port-au-Prince what telephones were doing for the rich: announcing that the "bird has flown". Soon it was joined by others as sleepy sacristans, rubbing their eyes, mounted Church towers to let their bells peal forth the news. *Telediol* had one advantage over the telephone. Its circuits could not be overloaded. As the pre-Lenten sun rose from behind Morne l'hôpital, Port-au-Prince debouched into the streets in a spontaneous demonstration of joy. There were that morning throughout the country *macoutes* and *miliciens* so unconnected that they had no idea of what had happened while they were sleeping. Donning their *gros bleu*, strapping on their revolvers, they were quickly and rudely brought up to date, and as the morning progressed a remarkable sartorial shift occurred. The only people still in denim were either dead, barricaded and fighting for their lives, or being paraded around by angry mobs.(1)

The metamorphosis from jubilation to anger was swift and thorough. Reports began coming in of *macoute* heads being paraded around on spikes. *Macoutes* were stoned to death or, borrowing a page from South Africa, "necklaced" with old tires and set afire. The necklaces soon were known by the name of Haiti's largest tire importer - *Père Lebrun*. As always, it became a time to settle old scores. Throughout the country, homes and businesses of anyone associated with the Duvaliers came quickly under attack. From the piney heights of Fermathe to the dust-blown *Parc Industriel* by the airport, nothing was immune. Bennett properties were targets of particularly intense wrath. From the Port-au-Prince Toyota dealership (unbeknownst to the crowds, Bennett had prudently sold it to an unwitting buyer before skipping the country two days earlier), Tele-Haïti showed crowds carrying office furniture, light fixtures, toilets, floor tiles - anything that could be pried loose. To the cheers of onlookers, cars were pushed off showroom floors and down hills in hopes of jump-starting that for which they lacked ignition keys. Many contented themselves with a less dramatic assertion of their sense freedom, opting to join the crowds milling about in front of the *Palais National*. There, like children freed from the thrall of a tyrannical teacher, they reveled in their freedom to walk unchallenged on the sidewalk - an act forbidden for a generation. In their jubilation, many waved green branches stripped from the few trees that Port-au-Prince still afforded. The scene was the same throughout the country. Long-hidden flags of blue and red emerged to be carried triumphantly by marchers. Some, lacking cloth, used body makeup to daub blue and red on their faces.

The army was golden that morning. The soldiers stationed shoulder to shoulder along the inside perimeter of the Palace fence watched with bemused looks as people handed them flowers, sought to shake their hands, or even kiss them. Cries of "*Vive l'Armée*" were heard everywhere. In the midst of jubilation though, some noticed that the "liberating" army had moved in to protect certain properties (like Simone Duvalier's home in Canapé Vert) of regime associates from any mass action.

The spiritual domain was not ignored either that morning. Seeking to avenge themselves against Papa Doc as his enemies had done with his father's corpse in 1957, an angry mob descended on the *Cimetière* before Henri Namphy's videotaped announcement of the change in regime had been even broadcast. Using rocks, bits of pipe - the crudest of tools - the frenzied crowd broke through the final layers of cement to find nothing. François Duvalier's tomb was empty.

Leaving nothing to chance, the Duvaliers had spirited Papa Doc's coffin out of the country with the rest of their luggage. Speculation, never slow to arise in Port-au-Prince, had it that the coffin had never left the Palace until it was shipped to France. Even from the grave, Papa Doc had outwitted his opponents. Deprived of their quarry, the crowds disinterred Gracia Jacques, who, alive, might have forestalled these events, and burned what was left of him in a celebratory bonfire.

Throughout neighborhoods in Port-au-Prince, the scene was repeated. Houses which people had once been afraid even to look at were suddenly the target of intense hatred which could now be manifested. Cabinet ministers, *macoutes*, the targets were many. Luc Désir's house yielded tape-recordings of torture sessions over which the bible-toting Baptist had presided. Désir's pleasure of an evening, like an oenophile surveying his cellar, had been to replay tapes of sessions in which bones could be heard snapping as victims screamed. When some of the confiscated tapes were played on the radio, horrified relations of people who had disappeared without a trace years previously came forward to identify the voices of loved ones in their terminal agonies.

Madame Max Adolphe's house in Pétionville was sacked, its contents revealed to a curious crowd of tele-voyeurs. They were not disappointed. The sixty-one year old grandmother with a daughter in St. Louis had literary tastes that buttressed the claims of those few lucky enough to have survived or escaped her predations at Ft. Dimanche. Dog-eared titles such as *Tyrannical Mistress* predominated in the private library of the doyenne of national security. Thanks to the newly-respectable Créole orthography, there appeared in print in the accounts of that morning's doings a word new to urbanites - *dechoukaj*. Long familiar to farmers, it meant to uproot, and was quickly appropriated to describe the process going on throughout Haiti the morning of February 7th.

The objects of the *dechoukaj*, those who had not been given shelter in the rapidly filling Dessalines barracks or were already abroad, found themselves in increasingly perilous situations. The abruptness of Jean-Claude Duvalier's decision to leave had left many in the lurch. Even Madame Max, informed just after the American and French ambassadors, had arrived at the *Banque Nationale* too late in the day to withdraw her substantial holdings. She asked for and was given refuge in the caserne long before the mobs reached her home in Pétionville. In Bel-Air, Edner Day was less fortunate. The *bocor* who had performed the voodoo rituals that had ensured the return of Papa Doc's spirit to *Guinée* fifteen years earlier found himself and a coterie of cohorts under siege from an angry mob. Armed to the teeth, he managed to fend them (by killing four) off until rescued by the army.

Day was not the only *bocor* to be attacked that morning. Given the Duvalier reliance on voodoo to rule, *hounforts* and *houngans* throughout the country were *dechouké*. Max Beauvoir barricaded himself in his house on the Léogane road - an option not available to those of more modest means - and there received grim reports of killings of *houngans* throughout the country. In succeding days, as what became known as "the voodoo wars" progressed, Church encouragement moved from silence to overt encouragement. Evangelical protestant figures went on Radio Lumière with Elmer Gantry-like denunciations of anything related to voodoo, and encouraged their flocks to uproot all "associated with Satan". Their flocks responded with zeal. In response to foreign creeds, Haitians were again destroying part of their collective heritage.(2)

Anything with the Duvalier name on it was subject at least to an impromptu paint job to erase the letters. The "eternal" flame that flickered in front of the statue of the *Nègre Marron* statue opposite the palace was quickly doused, while bronze plaques describing its dedication by Papa Doc were ripped off the base.

Mobs toppled the statue of Christopher Columbus on the waterfront, scrawling the graffito "*pas de blancs en Haïti*"(no foreigners in Haiti) on the now naked plinth. Cité Simone, the bastion of poverty and resentment by the bay, became Cité Soleil. François Duvalier Airport became, temporarily, *Maïs Gaté* (spoiled corn - the name of the area in which the airport was built), before taking on the more bland "International Airport". The airport, closed to commercial traffic, did open temporarily to allow Eastern Airlines and Air Canada aircraft in to evacuate foreigners who wanted to leave. Streets reverted to old names not used in a generation.(3)

Après Nous, C'Est Nous

The videotaped abdication that was aired at 8 A.M. on Tele-Haïti had been immediately followed by the reading of a proclamation. In a live broadcast from the Palace, a spokesman stepped up to a lectern and intoned "Proclamation of the day, National Council of Government, Lt. Gen. Henri Namphy". Backing away from the lectern, he bowed to the khaki-clad general to his right. The general and five others rose from their chairs and Namphy strode forward to address the country:

> *Conseil National du Gouvernement*, proclamation. For many months our country has known an exceptionally grave situation...In all the provinces, popular demonstrations have claimed innocent victims. The spectre of civil war is raised. The Haitian Army reiterates to the nation that now, more than ever, it has no political ambitions and remains at the service of the country.

The bulldog-faced general folded his paper and introduced Haiti to its new rulers:

> Henri Namphy, president of the Council; Col. Williams Regala, *FAd'H*, Member; Col. Max Vallès, *FAd'H*, Member; Engineer Alix Cinéas, Member; Mtre. Gérard Gourgue, Member; Col. Prosper Avril, *FAd'H*, Counselor. Namphy's verbal cues during the presentation were telling. When introducing Cinéas, he started to give him Haitian Army rank, only to stop in mid-sentence. Avril's name and title were almost whispered in a tone that seemed to say, "oh, by the way...".

The members of the *CNG* (as it quickly became known) trooped out to the front steps of the Palace to raise the colors (still black and red) while the other *musiciens palais national* played the national anthem. As the stirring tones of *La Dessalinienne* came to an end, an off-screen announcer gave the *CNG*'s order number one - all schools, businesses, and government offices were to be closed that day. The *CNG* went back inside the palace. On the streets, with crowds dancing, car horns honking, it was obvious that order number one was superfluous. "I have already had my cocktail", one smiling Haitian announced to a reporter.

Long used to reading between the lines, Haitians and foreigners who had watched on TV or listened to the radio began to remark that for a government of national liberation, the *CNG* was oddly composed. Three of the five "members" were army men - six if you included "counselor" Prosper Avril. Vallès was commander of the presidential Guard. Avril (Papa Doc always referred to him as "*l'intelligent Avril*"), was reputed to have been Jean-Claude Duvalier's bagman - the only person other than the Duvaliers themselves with signature authority over their foreign accounts. Of the two civilian members, Alix Cinéas had served the Duvaliers for more than twenty years, rotating in and out of cabinets as required. Only Gourgue, lawyer and founder of the human rights league during Jean-Claude Duvalier's term, was an outsider. Back inside the palace, the group began to address the himalaya of issues before them.

At the top of the list was the preservation of public order. In the week before Duvalier left, many *macoutes* were lent army uniforms and made their way to Port-au-Prince. Most were in hiding - a good number, including Madame Max, in the barracks behind the palace. They still had their weapons and many, increasingly fearful, were minded to use them. A counter-coup was a real possibility. Reports of decapitations and necklacings only increased tensions. The main hospital was jammed with dozens of wounded - both Duvalierists and non-Duvalierists. By mid-morning, the *CNG* decided enough steam had been let off and announced a 2 p.m. to 7 a.m. curfew to quiet things down. Under the cover of night, some of the more messy aspects of governance could be attended to.

The other tasks the *CNG* faced were no less daunting. First, a time bomb of rising expectations that could not possibly be met by a government of angels, let alone men, was ticking. The mobs in Port-au-Prince and other cities that had served the purposes of the real forces behind the coup - the Army, the Church, and the United States - were still on the streets. No one new better than the *CNG* how quickly approbation could turn to denunciation, but there was no easy way to put the genie back in the bottle. Second, the balancing act that had allowed the coup, for such it was, to be pulled off, threatened to fall apart as people turned twenty-nine years of wrath on the *macoutes* who had been so casually sacrificed by Madame Max and others. Cornered, armed, they had nothing to lose in countless confrontations that were going on all over the country. Many were being hidden inside the *Casernes Dessalines* under Army protection, even as crowds outside were shouting support for the Army. They would have to be disposed of quickly and very quietly. Third, the country was broke. The Duvaliers had left less than $2 million in the treasury. The succession of economic crises of ever worsening severity that had rocked the country since 1980 had as their root cause not only incompetence and natural disaster but the gradual exclusion of all save a very small group from the patronage whose distribution ensured the Duvalier power base. Money, from foreign friends, was imperative. Fourth, within the coalition that staged the coup, disparate players had very different and sometimes directly conflicting agendas. The Church, with its tame *macoute* Episcopacy still in place, was looking with scarce-concealed anxiety at the specter of ever-growing power for the '*ti l'Egliz* movement. At the same time, it rightly perceived an opportune moment to try and redress the balance between it and Voodoo through the medium of the peoples' anger. As it presided over this rich brew, the *CNG* had to keep itself in power long enough to hand over power to a popularly elected government (its stated goal) or to an "appropriate" government (its unstated goal).

With the country under curfew, the soldiers and two civilians huddled to produce a cabinet, whose nineteen members were announced on Saturday. The lineup was carefully scrutinized. As a cabinet of national reconciliation, it contained some odd players. Gérard Gourgue's credentials as a human rights campaigner were impeccable. His appointment as Minister of Justice as well as that of Rosny Desroches as Education Minister gave the cabinet respectability. François Latortue was named Foreign Minister. Attracting the most criticism was the role of Prosper Avril, who was too closely linked to the ousted regime in he popular view. Max Vallès was named Information Minister, but far more importantly, held on to command of the presidential Guard. The key post of interior Ministry went to Williams Regala, Namphy's *noir* co-conspirator.

Other crucial decisions were made that weekend. The thoroughly discredited National Assembly was dissolved, while the tattered constitution, more honored in the beach than the observance, was suspended. The *CNG* announced that it would rule by decree. Some political prisoners were set free, but to decide who should be set free, the *CNG* required an accurate tally of who was being held and why - a task made impossible by the flight of the jailers.

In masses of Thanksgiving across the country that Sunday, messages from the Bishops were read that urged their flock to respect life and property. The rash of necklacings with its underlying implications of popular empowerment had rattled the Church badly. Under the cover of curfew, the Army mounted a rescue operation for many *macoutes* across the country, spiriting them to safe-houses in preparation for flight abroad. By doing so, it hoped to defuse the potential hotspots that occurred by the presence of the no longer immune *macoutes* cheek by jowl with the populace it had so thoroughly oppressed. The Army's task was made easier in some ways by the fact that the deterioration of things in the provinces in January meant that great numbers of regime stalwarts had already sought the protection of the capital - the only place still under regime control. Finding homes abroad for the most notorious and then spiriting them out under the very noses of a suspicious mob would be difficult, but in the weeks that ensued, the *CNG* successfully managed to expatriate those most in danger and those who knew the most. Madame Max popped up overseas having variously, depending on who one listened to, escaped disguised as a nun (reports do not mention which order) or in a crate of mangoes destined for export. Albert (known as '*ti Boule*, or "little flame", because of his effective use of cigarette lighters during interrogation) Pierre, the hated chief of Police, was aided in escaping to Brazil. Lafontant was of course already in Canada. Others, such as Eloïs Maître, Lyonel Wooley, and Luc Désir, many enjoying Army protection, were busily seeking ways to extract themselves, roundly cursing the regime that had so quickly deserted them.

Optics were not ignored. Following what street crowds had already put into effect with makeshift banners of blue and red, the *CNG* restored the beloved red and blue flag, with Namphy himself hoisting the colors to their place of pride above the Palace. Cité Simone, named after Simone Ovide, was promptly re-christened Cité Soleil in honor of Radio Soleil that had done so much to bring about these changes. The station itself had gone quickly back on the air, with priests appearing at the windows of the studio with a poster of the Blessed Virgin and waving at crowds outside.

The work of governance continued in earnest the following week with the formal installation of the new cabinet. Taking advantage of the gathering, Namphy announced that the *CNG* was committed to the development "of a real and functional democracy". Left unstated was just how and when the elections that would facilitate that handover would be held. Meeting with the foreign press a few hours later, the *CNG* made several other statements. The *TTM*'s were, they announced, abolished immediately. Popular pleasure at this bit of news was seriously dampened when Prosper Avril, in response to questioning, conceded that many *TTM/VSN* members could be incorporated in the army - a statement that sent shivers up many spines. Regala, unused to the scrutiny of the press, made the mistake of telling the truth, stating that many *TTM*'s had been rounded up "for their protection."

While Namphy led the news conference, the confidence with which other *CNG* members spoke raised questions in many minds as to who the real powers were. Under the structure inherited from the Duvaliers and still in effect, all the soldiers on the *CNG* had independent power bases that reported directly to the top. The hydra-headed government looked like an unwieldy tool with which to rule.

With time out for a much-restricted carnival, the government sought to get the country back to some semblance of order. Schools, closed for more than a month, were reopened, as much to allow the feeding programs that the country's youth was so dependent on to resume as to educate them. Factories, whose coveted positions generated the paychecks that so much of Port-au-Prince was dependent on, reopened. Slowly, the realization dawned on both the governors and the governed that they were adrift without a compass.

Its appetite for revenge unsated, the masses waited for the *CNG* to take further steps toward justice for the *macoutes* while the *CNG* tried to figure out how to put the imp of popular participation back in its bottle. Occasionally, the crowd took matters into its own hands. When Luc Désir sought to board an outbound Air France flight on February 24th, a ticket clerk at the airport quickly phoned Radio Soleil. At the station's urging, a crowd of several thousand quickly descended on the airport, threatening to burn the aircraft if Désir was not taken off. A visibly frightened Désir and his defiant wife were hustled off by Army troops. Thwarted of revenge against the Duvalierist, the mob contented itself with *deckoukéing* both of his elaborate villas.

While some concentrated on getting out, others were coming back in, aching for a glance of Morne l'Hôpital after years in exile. By the end of March, both Paul Magloire, (4) still hale and hearty, and Daniel Fignolé, dying of cancer, returned home. Less well-known exiles flocked home by the thousands, bringing welcome cash. Most, after trips down memory lane, returned to the lives they had so painstakingly carved out over so many years in the diaspora. Indeed, a new Créole word, *"diaspo"* grew up to describe those living abroad.

In this volatile climate, everyone was edgy. In the Port-au-Prince suburb of Martissant, a *tap-tap* driver overtook and passed an army captain's staff car - an act of daring that would have been unthinkable under the old regime. Reverting to form, the captain promptly arrested the man, causing protests by large crowds. The *Léopards*, called in to restore order, fired for effect, and within minutes five civilians were dead, and many others beaten. It had taken the *CNG* only six weeks to draw its first blood.

Justice Minister Gourgue, uncomfortable with his bedmates in the *CNG*, resigned to protest the killings as well as the blind eye the *CNG* was turning to the escape of so many *TTM*s from the country. Using the opportunity to do some housekeeping, the *CNG* invited and received the resignations of Cinéas and Avril as well. Avril, now out of the limelight, did keep the all-important job of Chief of Staff of the Army. The three remaining members of the Council were all military.

Those who saw ill omens in the changes had their worst fears quickly confirmed. On April 26th, a crowd of several hundred marched peacefully to Ft. Dimanche after attending a mass in memory of political prisoners who had died during the Duvalier years. As the crowd approached the mustard-yellow barracks that had been the scene of so many atrocities, one of the march organizers, the young parish priest of St.-Jean-Bosco, Jean-Bertrand Aristide, offered live commentary on Radio Soleil. Unbeknownst to the crowd, Ft. Dimanche commandant Pognon had mounted machine guns on the roof and lay in waiting. When the crowd got within range, he and his men fired. The first casualty was a high-tension electric wire overhead which, cleaved by a bullet, fell to the earth. There it electrocuted several of the marchers. Meanwhile the bullets were by now directly claiming marchers. Aristide, his mike still open, provided running commentary to a country riveted in horror. The protesters scattered, and when the dust settled, six lay dead and fifty wounded. Interior Minister Regala, sounding for all the world like a member of the government he had overthrown, opined to a journalist that this sort of thing happened when "people demonstrated and didn't behave properly." That same day, after a quarter century in exile, Professor Leslie Manigat returned to his native land. As an announced candidate for the presidency, he was puzzled that no members of the press greeted him at the airport. He didn't realize that they were all at Ft. Dimanche where he had once been incarcerated.

On the cultural front, Port-au-Prince was flocking in record numbers to see an old movie that starred Lillian Gish. At least it was old as far as the rest of the world was concerned. *The Comedians* had never, for obvious reasons, been shown in Haiti before. Enjoying yet another fifteen minutes of fame, Aubelin Jolicoeur explained to foreign reporters that he, like Petit Pierre on screen, had not been killed by the Duvaliers because he was "too famous".

While the government was receiving a well-deserved black eye on its human rights record, it was taking less fair knocks on other fronts. Leslie Delatour, the University of Chicago-trained economist who had briefly served under Marc Bazin five years earlier was laboring mightily to get the economy started again. Haiti had no lack of studies or prescriptions - indeed, it was one of the most studied countries in the world. The trick though was implementing the remedies. All had attendant costs in terms of alienated constituencies or ripple effects in an already fragile economy. A balanced budget? Revenue was what was needed. Fiscal austerity? What could be more austere than having no money in the treasury. Furthermore, how can one reign in spending when one doesn't even know where all the accounts are? Lower inflation? By cutting the cost of imported products, native producers are undercut, raising charges of American "plans" to make Haiti an agricultural dependency of the U.S. (which it had already become long since). In the weeks following the coup, Port-au-Prince had filled up with missions from international lending agencies such as the IMF. In some cases, IMF technocrats were effectively providing the only leadership some parts of the government had. In closing down the state agency that ran the cooking oil monopoly, ENAOL, Delatour was immediately picketed by employees who had lost their jobs. It availed him absolutely nothing to explain that the monopoly and the taxes it funnelled into the Duvalier's pockets (a phenomenon known as *le siphonage* - the "siphoning") cost the man on the street precious dollars. When the price of cooking oil dropped 30% after the market was opened, he received no thanks.

As the *CNG* staggered from crisis to crisis, its nominal head took to his bed, pleading "extreme fatigue". The *telediol*, never slow to comment where the peccadilloes of Haiti's leaders were concerned, had it that Namphy had resumed his heavy drinking, leaving Regala to take the lead on a day-to-day basis. In such a climate, even stasis, let alone restoration, seemed almost impossible.

Nature, ever Haiti's enemy, weighed in with her own blow in June. Record flooding in the Cayes area cut road connections with the rest of the country as crucial bridges, many fewer than five years old, were swept away. Relief efforts, never the "Republic of Port-au-Prince's" strong suit, were not improved by the chaos of the central government.

The civil unrest in urban areas had tangible costs. In the four months following the coup, nearly twelve thousand, or twenty percent, of Port-au-Prince's assembly plant jobs had disappeared as foreign investors sought more docile and dependable labor forces overseas. Unions, revived after so many years of subservience to the government, were demanding a doubling of the minimum wage from $3.12 to $6.24 a day. Such demands elicited howls of protest from the country's industrialists and quickly dissipated any residual inter-class good will left over from the coup. The government, knowing who its constituency was, quickly sided with the industrialists. Employees seeking to organize assembly plats found themselves locked out or replaced. Others were set upon by thugs hired by plant owners. The thugs bore remarkable resemblances to *Tonton Macoutes*. Eyeing the omnipresent violence, presidential would-be Bazin mused out loud that "we will have to go back to the basics of an organized society."

In the country, things were no better. In many areas the dreaded *Chefs Sections* still held sway, ruling in tandem with the army as virtual satraps. Regional ports such as St. Marc or Gonaïves, long tightly controlled by the central government, were now wide-open. Local officials took advantage of the vacuum of central authority by allowing smugglers to bring in vast quantities of consumer goods as well as bulk quantities of U.S.-grown rice. The "miami rice" as it quickly became known, pitted city dweller against farmer, with the latter setting up roadblocks throughout Haiti's breadbasket, the Artibonite, to protest the undermining of their livings. Beset with chaos, Haiti staggered into the Fall.

Suspicious of anything sponsored by the *CNG*, voters greeted an October, 1986 "special election" with apathy. Designed to elect writers of a new constitution, the polling attracted barely 5% of eligible voters. To everyone's surprise, the "constituents" as they became known, set to with a will, producing what was widely considered to be a good document in the space of only four months. The draft, in what the Left, ever suspicious, promptly branded a "ruling class trick", was to be submitted to the people for approval the following Spring.

It called for elections of increasing degree of importance, leading up to a presidential election in November of 1987. The winner would take office on February 7, 1988, two years after Jean-Claude Duvalier's departure. It created a post of Prime Minister, in the process sharply limiting the powers of the president, and banned prominent Duvalierists ("architect of the dictatorship") from participation in national political life for ten years. It also, to the consternation of the *CNG*, deprived the army of the right to conduct elections, creating an electoral council for just that purpose. Foreign diplomats, fearing that it might prove unworkable on a day to day basis, tactfully described it as "a useful healing document."

Less than healing was the October announcement by a group of Duvalierists that they too intended to sit at the table of democracy. While the October 30th news conference got little coverage outside Haiti, its participants, Claude Raymond and Clovis Désinor among them, attracted a lot of attention within the country. "The Party for National Togetherness" had a French acronym - PREN - that sounded too much like the Créole word for take. Fearing that the Duvalierists intended to do just that, crowds took to the street to protest. In Port-au-Prince, 50,000 marched on the Palace, while smaller demonstrations occurred in the provinces. Radio Soleil weighed in with comments critical of the government, and suddenly, two weeks later, PREN announced its dissolution, saying that the time was "not yet opportune" for such a party. Perhaps it had taken General Namphy at his word when he made a public statement on November 12th that he "would choke at birth" any movement that tried to halt the march back to democracy.

Abroad, ten days later, Namphy showed less patience with democratic process. After speaking at the U.N. and meeting with Ronald Reagan, he complained to the foreign press that "we have a hundred one man parties" in Haiti. Actually, the reckoning of the "constituents" just then gathering in Port-au-Prince was that the number was more like seventy, but the General had made his point.

Returning home after his few days away, Namphy had found things as chaotic as ever. Finance Minister Delatour, to his chagrin, had found that his own ministry employees were busy netting some $400,000 a month in a scheme whereby ministry checks were reissued (echoes of *l'Affaire des Mandats*) with new payees and amounts. Further up the hill, somewhat chastened after the botched launch of PREN, a reflective Claude Raymond looked back over the past year. Talking with a *New York Times* reporter, François Duvalier's godson, well ensconced in a mansion whose appointments suggested a comfortable retirement, concluded that "Jean-Claude Duvalier never cared about the country."

The country's current leadership, mindful of the dismal turnout in the fall election for constitutional delegates, brought in the new year with a plea to the masses to participate in the upcoming referendum on the constitution. The *CNG* had clearly not yet seen the final fruits of the assembly's labors. Having thrown a bone to democracy in the future, the Council then requested and received the resignations of its four most liberal members, including Justice Minister Latortue and Education Minister Desroches. One tradition of the Duvalier years - rapid Cabinet turnover - endured. After absorbing the setback of the PREN dissolution, the Duvalierists were again stirring. Widely suspected of providing the impetus for the government lurch to the right, they became increasingly confident. Grinning, one *macoute* went so far as to boast, "*Après nous, c'est... nous!*"

But elsewhere in Port-au-Prince that month, other stirrings were underway. In what was the largest such forum in Haiti's history, more than one thousand delegates from some three hundred center and left organizations met as the National Congress of Haitian Democratic Movements. The debate did not go unnoticed by the constituents, by then well into their labors. At the end of five exciting days, the Congress set up a permanent standing body, KONAKOM, which was to be heard from time and again over ensuing months.

As the first anniversary of its year in office approached, Haitians wanted nothing so much as to have done with the *CNG*, but no one saw any realistic way to accelerate the process that would culminate in November elections. Marc Bazin, Leslie Manigat, and Louis Déjoie fils ('ti Loulou) were all strong candidates, but none had the broad mandate needed to heal their shattered society. For the moment, reflected the *Christian Science Monitor*, there was simply no alternative to the *CNG*.

The government continued to be the beneficiary of good will from the international community. U.S. aid for 1987 was to double to more than $100 Million, much of which would go for the purchase of precious oil. The IMF, expressing satisfaction with the efforts of Minister Delatour, promised some $25 million over three years for "structural readjustment", $10 million of which was to be available for immediate drawdown. The money was needed, for, as one Haitian commented, "freedom doesn't fill empty stomachs."

The anniversary occasioned a spate of articles on the high style in which Jean-Claude Duvalier was living in his "temporary" exile in France. Eating at many of the numerous three star eateries to be found in such profusion around Lyons, the former president was frequently on the phone to Port-au-Prince, enriching France Telecom by as much as ten thousand dollars a month. In a display of domestic flexibility that occasioned comment even in an otherwise preoccupied Port-au-Prince, the household over which he presided frequently included Michèle Bennett's former husband Alix Pasquet, so long too an exile.

Within weeks of taking power, the *CNG* had commissioned a New York law firm, Stroock, Stroock and Lavin to go after the Duvaliers and the money they had expatriated, much as François Duvalier had sought to retrieve part of the money put aside by Magloire for his retirement. Of course the scale was different. Estimates of the amounts netted by *le siphonage* went from $300 million to $800 Million. Everywhere the New York firm probed, it ran into roadblocks. A U.S. court agreed to the freezing of a number of accounts at

Irving Trust, but French courts refused American jurisdiction. Swiss bankers justified their well known penchant for discretion, and in Haiti itself, the *CNG* seemed to be paying little more than lip service to the principle of recovering the lost funds, most of which had been in the form of aid from other countries anyway.

A Constitution is Paper

Once the final draft of the constituents was produced, Henri Namphy must have regretted his get out the vote speech of earlier in the year. It was, in the words of Mark Danner:

> ... an extraordinary document: a constitution that, in its litany of absurd and brilliant and, finally, Machiavellian provisions must have surprised the people of Haiti as much as it surprised the government, which had thought that everything was under firm control and now found itself presented with a populist and wildly popular document that stripped the officers of the one power that was the only power in Haiti - of the *parenthèse* - the right to conduct elections.

The Church gave its blessing, saying that the constitution "seems a good guarantee of freedom... despite gaps and contradictions. "
Reflecting the success, finally, of the campaign to make Créole a viable written language, this constitution was written in Créole and French, so that the man in the street could ponder the implications of just what he was voting on. "Créole", said ex-minister Latortue, has become the political language." The linguistic walls with which Haiti's elite had so long kept the populace at bay were beginning to crumble.
Anticipating approval of the constitution, the *CNG* in March battened down the hatches, prudently awarding a General's star to Williams Regala in case his army career should be abruptly ended. The number of generals at the top of Haiti's 7,500 man army now stood at seventeen.
The fears of the officers were amply justified. This time, on March 29, 1987, more than 50% of the electorate turned out. In a vote observed by numerous foreign organizations (which concluded that the vote was "fair"), more than 99% voted aye. With that vote, the clock started ticking on a thirty day period, at the end of which Haiti's new charter would become the law of the land.
Euphoria over the constitution's passage was quickly dissipated by concern over bread-and-butter issues. In April, HASCO closed its doors, laying off more than 3500 workers in the process. The smuggling which was ruining the rice farmers of the Artibonite was having a like effect on sugar, as Haiti, the world's

leading eighteenth century sugar producer, found itself unable to compete with an avalanche of sugar pouring in from abroad. Feeling pinched, perhaps because of notoriously generous subsidies to U.S. sugar producers, the Reagan administration submitted a draft budget to Congress in which it asked for a $20 million reduction in aid to Haiti for the next fiscal year.

Preferring to be abroad when the new constitution came into full force, General Regala spent two weeks abroad shopping for new toys for the army. His travels took him first to Venezuela and ultimately to Israel, whose arms makers had a catholic view of their potential markets.

He returned to a Haiti whose governance was codified in a new constitution. People were proud and protective of what they viewed as "their" document. But like proud parents with a frail child, they were on the lookout for signs of trouble. Two weeks into its run, the Church, shedding increasingly its *macoute* roots, sent up a flare. In a statement from the Bishop's conference (whose members contained radical Jérémie Bishop Willy Romélus as well as the thoroughly compromised Wolff-Ligondé), it underlined the necessity of elections. Its prescience was quickly proved.

Prodded by an alliance of many in the elite as well as most surviving Duvalierist elements, which stood to lose everything if the populism embodied in the new constitution swept a candidate of the *peuple souverain* into office, Henri Namphy made an attempt in June to grab back what had been ceded in March. On June 22, he challenged the authority of the electoral council (*CEP*) called for in the constitution to run elections, saying instead that the army would play its accustomed role. As the *CEP* had been one of the charter's main selling points, reaction was predictably strong.

Into the streets poured demonstrators intent on protecting "their" constitution. Having tasted blood in March, the *CNG* was not reticent about shedding it in June, and scores of demonstrators perished. When the fallen were replaced by others, Namphy finally backed down, giving a televised pledge on June 30 that the elections would indeed be held as scheduled. He had noted perhaps too a statement from Foggy Bottom the day before that U.S. aid was dependent on a continuing transition to democracy. Buoyed by its success, the *peuple souverain* kept on demonstrating, taking as its war cry the theme of a sermon given by Bishop Romélus - "*Raché manyok, ba'é té-a blanche!*" (pull up the roots, sweep the fields clean) demanding the resignation of the *CNG*.

This the *CNG* had no intention of doing. The opposition and its demands were embodied in the so-called "Committee of 57" - an outgrowth of *KONAKOM*. Led by long-time activist priest Jean-Claude Bajeux, around it coalesced other important figures such as Sylvio Claude and head of the Moscow-oriented Unified Haitian Communist Party (PUCH), René Théodore. In the sweltering July heat, each side hardened its stance. The Army rank and file declared its support for the *CNG* and for the most part gave it, despite instances of troop defections in Port-de-Paix and Jérémie. By July 7th, after troops tear gassed a peaceful march of 25,000 on the Palace, even Radio Soleil began to speculate that the protests would be hard to continue. A stalemate of sorts was beginning to emerge.

Even the Church was split. The radical faction looked to Bishop Romélus and his lieutenant, Jean-Bertrand Aristide, for leadership. Conservatives (a relative quality) favored the more conciliatory stance of Bishop Gayot, head of the Bishop's conference and thus effective head of the Church in Haiti. In the troubled days of July, the army took note that increasing numbers of disaffected urban dwellers trooped to hear the fiery sermons of the parish priest of St.-Jean -Bosco who had vaulted to national prominence by staying on the air during the Ft. Dimanche massacre. *Père* Aristide, who had once dubbed capitalism "a mortal sin", minced no words. "We won't solve the country's problems by voting. The candidates can't bring change...[the] elections are in the hands of the oligarchy who use them to undermine popular demands."

Into this uneasy atmosphere was introduced a new element. Under cover of darkness, squads of *Léopards* as well as *macoutes* began conducting night time raids on the poorer quarters of Port-au-Prince, terrorizing the inhabitants and killing a select few. Wearying of it all, hotelier Suzanne Seitz (her husband Al dead of cancer) finally surrendered her lease of the Oloffson, scattering veteran correspondents to other hostelries throughout the city. Selling even the furniture and the rickety piano on which Mick Jagger had banged out tunes in better days, the survivor explained that she wanted some time to give to her family.

That the *CNG* had taken off its gloves (if indeed it had ever had them on), was brought home with a new ferocity as reports began to filter in at month's end of horrible doings in the Northwest. Near the town of Jean-Rabel, a left wing peasant cooperative, Tet Ansamn (Heads Together), was in virtual trench warfare with a group of *macoutes* who had stolen land as well as more conservative landowners and peasants unsympathetic to calls for redistribution of land.

On July 23rd, a peaceful march of Tet Asanm members was set upon by machete wielding paysans as well as *macoutes*. More than three hundred were killed, and many more wounded. Those wounded who sought succor from primitive local medical facilities were in many cases subsequently abducted, never to be seen again. Access to the area, difficult at best, was blocked for several days as *macoutes* sought to cover up the evidence of the orgy of murder. By the 31st, the Haitian Red Cross got through and confirmed both the scope and intensity of the massacre. The Bishop's conference warned of the specter of Civil war as Haiti was at daggers drawn in the struggle over "who shall have it."

The heat did not abate, nor passions cool in August. In a clumsy attempt to divorce *Père* Aristide from his power base, the Port-au-Prince Bishopric ordered

720 Written in Blood

his transfer to a church at Croix-des-Bouquets, fifteen miles distant. Long a bastion of prosperous *macoutes*, Aristide was unlikely to elicit the kind of response from his new parishioners that he had gotten at St.-Jean-Bosco. Predictably, protests sprung up, culminating in the occupation of Port-au-Prince's Cathedral by 100 protesters who vowed to stay until Aristide's transfer was revoked. Unwilling to be seen evicting some of its most ardent communicants from God's house, the hierarchy backed down. Duly noting the event, the Army and its henchmen made other plans.

On August 23, near Pont Sondé, Aristide and three other priests (including *Père* Adrien) were ambushed as they returned to Port-au-Prince from meetings in the North. Only quick thinking and some good driving by one of the four enabled them to escape being killed. Five days later, spotting an unfamiliar parishioner in their midst, the faithful at St.-Jean-Bosco exercised some muscular Christianity, in the process finding a concealed handgun. Aristide, if he had needed notice, now knew that he was a marked man.

The country entered the Fall in a sour mood. The Finance Ministry was unable to collect taxes. Despite a good corn crop, farmers were losing ground overall to smuggled foodstuffs. Urban dwellers were subject to nighttime terrorism. Their better off brothers fared little better as daytime robberies by men in fatigues made the elite increasingly chary about venturing downtown. State employees were receiving their paychecks irregularly, and were finding out, deprived of *le siphonage*, just how meager they were. Professionals, heretofore largely sheltered from the effects of the economic and social chaos, were being hit too. Faced with the prospect of a November election whose outcome would most likely beget more violence, those who could afford it voted with their feet, spending more time in the Miami condos which so many had acquired as boltholes over the years.

In the Palace, the once seemingly genial Namphy, who only a year earlier had threatened to "strangle at birth" any movement that tried to thwart democracy, was at daggers drawn with the leaders of what had become known as the "popular movement". Embittered by his summer of confrontation, seeing nothing but trouble ahead, the General presided over a campaign of terror designed to disrupt the elections scheduled for November 29.

The nightly predations of the killing squads continued, while the *CEP*, funded by cash grants and equipment from Haiti's foreign friends (including $7 million from the U.S.) got no help whatsoever from the government whose enmity it had incurred at birth. In an episode so brazen it startled even Haitians, a recently returned "diaspo" lawyer and presidential candidate, Yves Volel, was gunned down in front of cameramen (whose film was promptly confiscated) after demanding to see a client who had just been hauled in by the police. Another *CNG* opponent, Daniel Narcisse, found himself bundled on board an Air Canada flight against his will. Election season was open.

Would-be candidates had a week to register, starting on October 8. After a slow start, hampered by the lack of telephones and other logistical support, the *CEP* extended the registration period for a second week. Under the leadership of respected Methodist elder, Alain Rocourt, buffeted on all sides, labored on under impossible circumstances. Thirty-five candidates announced. Of these, some number were at least tainted (in the view of many) by past associations with Duvalierism. At the core of this group was a small nucleus of hardcore Duvalierists whose names were all too familiar to the electorate.

Claude Raymond, Franck Romain, even Papa Doc's old bagman Clémard-Joseph Charles, threw their hats into the ring, not withstanding the explicit article in the constitution that forbade their candidacies. Doyen of them all, Clovis Désinor announced, saying that "no piece of paper can take away my rights, not even a constitution." Désinor even appeared on Sixty Minutes at the beginning of November, consenting unwisely to be interviewed in English (in which he was less adept than he realized) by Mike Wallace. There, he unashamedly stated his loyalty to Duvalierism, unaware that his idealized version would not be understood by the audience.

All eyes were on the *CEP*, which after some hesitation, announced on November 2 that twenty-three candidates had met all the requirements. Emerging as front runners were Louis Déjoie ('ti Loulou), Leslie Manigat, Marc Bazin, Sylvio Claude, and Gérard Gourgue. In a masterpiece of indirection, left unsaid but obvious to all, was that the twelve Duvalierist candidates had been disqualified.

Retribution was not slow in coming. The very night of the announcement, *CEP* headquarters were set on fire. A few days later, the offices of candidates Bazin and Manigat were riddled with gunfire in drive-by shootings. The presses (echoes of the fifties) of the printer contracted to produce the ballots were smashed in the middle of the night, requiring the ballots to be printed in Venezuela.

Two weeks before election day, real doubts persisted in many minds as to whether elections would take place at all. Registration hovered at 50% of the electorate. Requests for protection of *CEP* facilities by Alain Rocourt went unanswered by the Palace, as did pleas for help in transporting ballots to 6,000 polling stations, many of them remotely located. In Gonaïves, an attack on the *CEP* office was thwarted only by volunteer action of what were becoming known as *brigades de vigilance* (watchdog brigades). Looking to the future, the head of the *CNG*, General Namphy, appointed himself to a three year term as commander in chief of the Army, ensuring, he thought, his continued presence on the scene.

As election day drew near, the tempo of violence increased. The *Marché Salomon*, one of Port-au-Prince's oldest markets, was torched. On the highways, various groups set up roadblocks, harassing candidates and extorting money. On

November 23, the Army sat on its hands as gunmen, shouting "*vive l'armée, A bas CEP!*" attacked the council's offices.

That same night, non-candidate Clovis Désinor was given air time by the *CNG*. Addressing his countrymen over thousands of flickering screens, he urged them to observe "*Abstention totale* [and to not] participate in the criminal operations of the *CEP...*[which is] conniving with foreigners." In its use of *langage*, the rhythmic chanting créole and oratory, it was a piece familiar to all Haitians as vintage Duvalier. The line had been drawn.

By election eve, with foreign observers (including Jimmy Carter) blanketing the country, the toll of dead stood at eight killed. Ominously, the Army, heretofore silent, broke into scheduled television programming to scroll a message across the screen:

> The situation has been aggravated by the appearance of groups of peasants known as *comités de vigilance* which ... only serve to sow confusion and to render the task of the forces of order more difficult... in these conditions, the Minister believes it is his duty to remind that the maintenance of public order is the direct and exclusive responsibility of the armed forces of Haiti... Major General Williams Regala."

Election day, Sunday, dawned hot and still. Some polls in the provinces had opened as early as 6 a.m. Those up early in Port-au-Prince came upon a number of corpses, the result of the previous night's terror. Anyone searching for news of the latest incidents would have been frustrated. With the exception of Radio Métropole, the airwaves were, in the words of Mark Danner, "utterly silent." In the night, by means of grenades and machine guns, agents of the *CNG* had sabotaged the radio stations most likely to give any trouble.

In front of the Palace, the other set of *musiciens* thumped out the *Dessaliniene* as the colors were raised. From behind the palace, convoys of troops were dispatched to various parts of the capital. Five blocks away, where the Avenue John Brown begins its gentle progress up the hill towards Pétionville, voters were gathered in a school converted for the day into a polling station. A gang of men armed with machine guns and machetes, after chatting briefly with an Army convoy that had stopped and then moved on, closed in on the several dozen voters waiting inside. In scenes reminiscent of 1915, the party slew everyone in sight, finishing with machetes that which their machine guns had not accomplished. When their work was finished, some twenty lay dead, dismembered and riddled with bullets.

The sound of the gunfire had drawn foreign correspondents to the scene. Staggered by the hecatomb before their eyes, the witnesses (for such they had become) found themselves the target of gunfire from four *macoutes* who had not counted on company. Photographer Jean-Bernard Diederich, whose father had penned such brilliant vignettes of François Duvalier, managed to escape over a wall. One cameraman lost his life. It became abundantly clear that no elections would be held that day. Some speculate that in the hours before the strangulation at birth of the elections, Gérard Gourgue, to whom Namphy entertained an almost pathological dislike, was ahead. No matter. Again, as if a weary people needed reminding, the Army had proved that "a constitution is paper, a bayonet iron."

Addressing a Port-au-Prince where nothing moved (*le silence d'un tombeau*), Namphy, in the staccato speaking style that he used to overcome a stutter, glowered into the television camera. The *CNG* had "put an end" to the *CEP* and its election so that Haiti could have a democratic president installed on schedule who was "freely elected by the Haitian people." Stunned, the American embassy announced through its spokesman Jeffrey Lite that all aid was suspended.

Reaction was not slow in coming. The opposition called for a general strike in the days that followed the election massacre, but it did not materialize. The Church condemned the slaughter, only to receive a tart reply from Namphy about how little it had helped the Haitian people. Opposition figures went into hiding or, like Louis Déjoie, back abroad. Dispirited, fragmented, and demoralized, the opposition was no match for the *CNG*. Desroches, once the *CNG*'s partner as Education Minister, said "Democracy is very difficult." By contrast, the disqualified Duvalierist candidates maintained a united front, in effect collectively shrugging their shoulders and saying "what did you expect?"

No longer beholden to anyone, the Army set its course. In the succeeding days, impervious to the opprobrium that rained down on its head, the army moved to continue its "clean up". The sound of gunfire was the music of the night throughout the capital. By day, efforts to legitimize a new election scheduled for January 17 continued. Bazin, Déjoie, and Claude announced that they would boycott the new contest. Other candidates, sensing opportunity, were slower to rule themselves out. Haiti that Christmas had even less to celebrate than usual.

Conjoncture

With the commencement of the new year, Haitians began contemplating the next election. Many if not most of those eligible to vote would stay home, honoring the boycott announced by the "major" candidates. No matter. There was no quorum requirement to transact this business, especially in a country whose first century had been characterized by elections in which no more than a total vote of a thousand people decided who would govern.

Those willing to collaborate with the *CNG* included Hubert de Ronceray, one time minister in Jean-Claude Duvalier's government; Grégoire Eugène, and Leslie Manigat. Of the three, the fifty-seven year old Manigat stood out intellectually. Author of numerous analyses of Haitian history written during more than two decades of exile during Duvalier rule, he had little illusion about the sharks with which he would be swimming. That much he had made clear in a televised speech given in the dying days of the old year. In essence, he condemned as hothouse politics the refusal of the so-called "major" candidates to work with the army, arguing that, like it or not, it was a force that would have to be reckoned with.

After a day of very light turnout at the polls (independent observers thought 5% of the electorate, the *CNG* said 35%) the *CNG*-sponsored electoral council retired behind closed doors to count the ballots. To no one's surprise, the well-upholstered *noir* intellectual had won the election. The margin, at 50.27% of the vote, seemed contrived. Sworn in on February 7, 1988, two years after the ousting of Jean-Claude Duvalier, the new president seemed almost lost amidst the sea of uniforms and medals around him.

It took him nearly two weeks to cobble together a government. At the first cabinet meeting of his administration, he drew easily controlled enthusiasm with his recommendation that all present take a 10% salary cut and that a number of ministries be consolidated. Those who hoped a Manigat presidency would open the valves of foreign aid were destined to remain disappointed. The donors from which Haiti had received so much largesse hardened themselves against any approaches from the Manigat government. After two months of negotiation, the Japanese government did contribute some $16 million in aid, but in kind, not in cash. While the Japanese four-wheel drive vehicles were much sought after for those who had to contend with Haiti's deteriorating roads, the gift did nothing to solve the larger problems by which the new administration was beset.

State companies were clogged with patronage appointments, while Army commanders sought to profit from smuggling everything from rice to cocaine. To add to his litany of woes, Manigat got word that Roger Lafontant was just two-hundred miles to the East in Santo Domingo, seeking yet again to engineer a coup that would bring him to power. Cruel irony for an intellectual of impeccable pedigree, Manigat was forced by his clients to order the dismantling of Catholic Créole literacy efforts which had been having too much success in the view of those interested in the status quo.

In mid-March, a Miami grand jury returned a multi-count indictment for drug dealing against the commander of the *Casernes*, Col. Jean-Claude Paul. The indictment was more symbolic than real as there was no danger of extradition, and inasmuch as the United States had already cut off most aid, the stick with which it had to beat the Haitians was a slim reed at best.

Economic bad news continued as well as smugglers, dominated by the army that supposedly guarded against smuggling, turned key crossing points at the Dominican border into vast transshipment depots. Eyeing the mess, ever more factory owners called it quits, with the result that by mid-1988, the number of assembly jobs in Port-au-Prince had declined a further 20%, aggravating the misery of the extended families that depended on those paychecks to survive.

Fire, ever the outrider of trouble in Port-au-Prince, hit several businesses in late May. The army-run fire department arrived one and a half hours late.

Boxed in all sides, already compromised in the eyes of those with whom he had spent most of his life, Manigat did what any tactician would do. He made an alliance. That he chose as his partner the even more disgraced Col. Paul was perhaps an unfortunate choice, but unlike the Pope, Col. Paul did indeed have the divisions. Opportunity came when Namphy, perhaps sensing that something was afoot, ordered Paul's transfer. In response, Manigat had Namphy put under house arrest. The alliance was short-lived. Angering Namphy subordinates (and, some said, Prosper Avril, whose hand they saw behind all this) who had initially sat on the sidelines while Namphy was removed, within two days Manigat had the tables turned on him.

Namphy, angry and depressed, was in his cups when informed of the sudden resurgence of his fortunes. Not even taking time to sober up, he made an angry TV announcement in the early hours of the morning to a weary nation that the army was taking over in name as well as in fact. Leslie Manigat, having been in office barely four months, was promptly packed over the border to Santo Domingo, there to ponder the vagaries of Haitian history in the relative comfort of the Concord Hotel. Engaging in a postmortem on his government, the professor revealed that General Namphy had never read the 1987 constitution. In an interview with *Le Figaro*, Henri Namphy declared that "constitutions weren't made for Haiti".

With the resumption of outright military rule, any hint of restraint that had been exercised to try to package the Manigat government for outside consumption disappeared. Foreign aid continued to be withheld, and the killing squads roamed freely in the capital and provinces, eliminating, as at the height of the 1964, anyone who incurred their displeasure.

Other members of the regime in addition to Col. Paul were tarred with the drug smuggling brush. A 727 leased by *Haiti Trans Air* (the successor operation to the Bennett airline) yielded some 50 kilos of high grade cocaine to observant customs officers in Miami. The trail seemed to lead back to Williams Regala.

In early September, the officers judged the time right to complete the task they had undertaken a year before. Still installed in his parish of St.-Jean-Bosco, Jean-Bertrand Aristide was packing them in with his fiery rhetoric. Under orders from Franck Romain, the *macoute* mayor of Port-au-Prince, a large party of gunmen poured into St.-Jean-Bosco on Sunday, September 11, 1988, during mass. As in the election day massacre ten months earlier, this was hardly a surgical strike, but to the intense annoyance of the *macoutes*, their main target, *Père* Aristide, miraculously escaped. Again, machete-wielding thugs followed those who had done the shooting, mutilating and decapitating. When they had finished their work, a dozen parishioners lay dead. For good measure, they then burned down the church.

This was too much even for the army. A week later, younger, lower-ranking soldiers packed Namphy off to Santo Domingo, where he took a suite in the Concord Hotel on the floor below professor Manigat. Franck Romain sought and received asylum in the Dominican Embassy, and from there waited to see how events would pan out. Having gotten rid of Namphy, the putschists were unable to agree on who should lead the new government. Prosper Avril, anathema to the *peuple souverain* two and a half years earlier because of his Duvalier ties, now emerged as top man.

Avril was no stranger either to the corridors of power or to the U.S. He had been class valedictorian of the 1961 class at the *Académie Militaire* - the last class to graduate before François Duvalier, considering it a hotbed of sedition, closed it down. He had been on training courses sponsored by the ill-fated U.S. Naval Mission before it too incurred Duvalier's wrath, travelling several times to the Marine Corps Officers School at Quantico, Virginia. He joined the *Garde Présidentielle* in 1969, and was consequently in a key position to profit from the shift of power from François to Jean-Claude Duvalier in 1971.

He profited handsomely from weapons procurement and other programs in the nineteen-seventies and was entrusted by the Duvaliers with management of much of their overseas portfolio. His wife, a captain in the Army Medical Corps, became the Duvalier family nurse after Jean-Claude Duvalier's marriage in 1980. He was a sworn enemy of Roger Lafontant. A more thoroughly Duvalierist product would be hard to imagine. Unlike Namphy though, he was restrained in his personal life, and he did not have the blood lust that seemed to possess so many of the *macoutes*.

Briefly, despite Avril's antecedents, the auguries seemed favorable. After pledging to take Haiti on the road to "an irreversible democracy", the new government got to work. First business for any incoming regime was a reshuffling of the army. Williams Regala, Jean-Claude Paul (who had gone unpunished for his June indiscretions) and several other officers, including Cecilio Dorcé, were retired. Avril refused to give Franck Romain the safe-conduct he sought to make his way to Santo Domingo. Some prisoners were released, and the death squads reined in. Avril even promised investigations into the Jean-Rabel massacre and the violence surrounding the aborted elections of the previous year. In one of those ironies with which Haitian history is replete, Avril named sharpshooter François Benoît (whose parents and relatives had been killed by an enraged François Duvalier a quarter century earlier) as his ambassador to Washington.

All of these steps were taken with an eye toward international opinion. Col. Paul's sudden death (several said after eating poisoned pumpkin soup) several weeks later removed yet another irritant in Washington/Port-au-Prince relations. Relenting somewhat, Foggy Bottom released some $15 million in aid that had been suspended. Still held back was an additional $70 million - the real prize that Avril was angling for. France, suspicious, decided to await developments before she opened her pocketbook.

In taking these actions, Avril was gambling. The drug trade was greatly profitable for many in the army. Too, the officer corps had grown increasingly confident in its ability to withstand external pressures for change. More than a thousand people showed up for Col. Paul's funeral, many of them key army figures. In December, when it became clear that no further aid would be immediately forthcoming, Avril relented and allowed Franck Romain, author of the St.-Jean-Bosco massacre to slip into exile.

That month, the Salesian order, taking its signals from a Rome fed up with the fire breathing Haitian cleric's brand of radicalism, expelled Jean-Bertrand Aristide, accusing him of "inciting violence and class struggle ." Aristide's description of senior church hierarchy as "imperialists in cassocks" had done nothing to endear him to the Vatican either. This time, no protest marches or sit-ins could reverse the verdict. Expelled from the order, but still a priest, *'tiTid*, as (because of his slight stature) he was becoming known, retreated to the orphanage he had set up for Port-au-Prince street urchins, there to ponder his future.

At the beginning of 1989, continuing his attempts to please conservatives, foreigners and democrats, Avril proposed the formation of an "electoral forum" which would lay the groundwork for a new *CEP*. Predictably, the opposition was divided in its response. Bazin, de Ronceray, Latortue and several others felt that the vehicle put forward was the most practical way to get to elections. Adamant in their opposition were Sylvio Claude and Louis Déjoie, who merely intensified their calls for Avril to step down.

In attempting to placate the left, Avril inevitably brought on the wrath of the Duvalierists. Ideology may not have been the only component in this campaign. At the beginning of February, the government announced a number of measures intended to curb the widespread smuggling that had so drained the treasury of taxes. Demonstrations, believed organized by Roger Lafontant from across the border, swept the Cap, Gonaïves, the Goâves, and other ports which had profited from lax enforcement of the rules. The slogan of many of the marchers was *"Avril verra-t'il Avril?"* (will "april" see april?).

Reshuffling his cabinet in mid-February, Avril brought in former *Léopards* commander Acedius St. Louis as interior minister. The move parallelled in public what had been happening in private over a number of months. As the left was increasingly muzzled, numbers of former Duvalierists were slipping quietly back into Haiti, there to quietly enjoy the fortunes they had made in better times.

On March 13, still seeking the legitimacy that eluded him, Avril reinstated part of the constitution that had been so thoroughly trashed by General Namphy. Omitted, on the quite reasonable (at least from Avril's point of view) grounds that they were incompatible with military government, were some 37 articles. He had managed to adopt the form, while dispensing with the substance. Expressing annoyance at the lack of positive response to his reinstitution of the charter, Avril complained on television that "the first six months have been Ok, but all they do is resume wheat shipments."

Using the issue of the gutted constitution as a cover, the soldiers of the *Casernes* and the *Léopards* made an *attentat* on April 2. The real concerns were pay and U.S. efforts to stamp out another lucrative source of income, the drug trade. It is possible that some of the mutineers were indeed uncomfortable with suspension of some of the constitution's articles, particularly the one that protected them against arbitrary dismissal.

After a week of spasmodic struggle, Avril triumphed, but at a cost. He was more than ever indebted to the officers who had stood by him, leaving him less maneuvering room than ever. In an immediate post-*attentat* gesture, he did constitute his own version of the *CEP* but grew impatient with a dearth of results as the months went by. Despairing of ever reaching sufficient internal consensus to move forward on elections, Avril invited outsiders to impose it. The August visit of a high-level CARICOM (Caribbean Common Market) delegation that included concerned foreign ministers of several countries seemed the perfect vehicle. Following meetings with the Avril-denominated *CEP*, the delegation announced that it had learned that elections would be held in November of 1990, there being "insufficient time" to organize them in the three months that remained before November, 1989. Hearts sank at the prospect of eighteen more months of military government, but some political operatives began cautiously to seek alliances in advance of next year's elections.

The Avril government took little solace from the passage of an additional $60 million in U.S. aid in June. Shepherded through Congress by Delegate Walter Fauntroy, the legislation tied aid to specific steps such as full restoration of the 1987 constitution, and effective reform of the army. "If General Avril wants the money, he's going to have to put up with Uncle Sam looking over his shoulder", remarked one observer. Even had he wanted to, Avril at this point didn't have the maneuvering room to pull off such reforms.

As the Fall progressed, Haiti descended ever deeper into the abyss of anarchy. In Washington, President Bush declined to extend the $10 million food program that Avril had complained about in March.In addition, Washington despatched an energetic new, Créole-speaking ambassador, Alvin Adams. Ambassador Adams, whose command of Créole included a way with proverbs, drew General Avril's ire even before his credentials were presented. Shortly after his arrival, he commented to the press that the need for democracy in Haiti was very urgent because *"bourik chaje pa kanpe"* (a heavily-laden donkey can't wait). Port-au-Prince promptly nicknamed him *"bourik chaje"*. The ambassador was kept waiting for some weeks before being allowed to present his credentials.

In October, looking ahead to the second anniversary of the Nov. 29 election massacre, Louis Déjoie, Evans Paul, and two other opposition leaders called for civil disobedience and a mass march on the palace. Paul and the two others were severely beaten and then, in bloodied shirts and bandages, shown on national television. Déjoie and a number of other opposition leaders promptly went into hiding. "This", said Déjoie, "is the beginning of Duvalier III."

Observing the almost complete collapse of the Haitian economy, one economist commented, "in most countries the rich subsidize the poor. Here, it's the other way around."

After nearly fourteen months in power, Prosper Avril had yet to succeed in restoring the flow of foreign aid to Haiti. Desperate, he sought to play Haiti's China card. Previous governments had skillfully used the rivalry between the Chinese government in Beijing and that in Taipei to their advantage. Beijing regarded diplomatic recognition as a trophy, particularly in the days before it had been accorded full U.S. recognition or a seat in the U.N. Taiwan, eager to maintain "embassies" in as many countries as possible, was not slow in rewarding with development aid those who stood by Taipei. The roster of countries with full embassies in Taipei tended to reflect those regimes which were ideologically more comfortable with Kuomintang (Chinese Nationalist) than Chinese Communist doctrine.

From a practical point of view, Taiwan was a good friend to have. Bursting at the seams with foreign exchange, it also manufactured a variety of consumer goods that were by definition of interest to smaller, undeveloped economies.

By 1990, having stanched the flow of diplomatic deserters to Beijing, the Taipei government was far less keen to simply buy recognition outright. Into this situation, at the beginning of 1990, flew Prosper Avril.

Preliminary signals from Taipei to Port-au-Prince had led Avril to believe that some $40 million in aid would result from an Avril visit. The General promptly embarked on the long trip across the Pacific. Arriving jetlagged in a chilly Taipei, Avril was livid to find that his arrival had been anticipated by a telex to the Taiwan government sent by opposition leaders while he was in mid-air. The gist of the telex was that any agreement reached would not be considered binding on the Haitian people.

The Chinese put on a welcome befitting a head of state - treatment the General was delighted to receive - but behind closed doors, the going was much tougher. Instead of an agreement with a specific amount, or better yet, a wire transfer, he found himself presented with a vague promise of yet-to-be-defined aid, the quid pro quo for which was his signature on a joint declaration in which he promised to hold democratic elections in Haiti. Confronted with a diplomatic fait accompli, the now sour Avril cancelled a planned press conference and embarked, empty-handed, on the long trip home.

Back in Port-au-Prince, the opposition had hoped to use Avril's absence to gin up enough disturbances to prevent him from returning home. A call for a general strike on January 12 failed, and just to underline how real the government (left in the charge of Gen. Fritz Romulus while Avril was away) power still was, the offices of the Christian Democratic Party and the most powerful union, CATH, were smeared with excrement the night before Avril's return home.

Showing its ideological roots, the regime had mustered a welcome-home demonstration at the airport by forking out three dollars a head to everyone who showed up. In a hungry Port-au-Prince, many took the bait. Home, Avril denounced the senders of the Taiwan telex as "vile and unpatriotic".

Other signs of fraying were appearing. In Washington, Ambassador Benoît announced his resignation, saying that he had come to the conclusion that "free elections are impossible with Avril." Benoît's disillusionment stemmed from the November arrests and beatings of opposition leaders.

Within two days of Avril's return, unknown assailants murdered a Colonel in the *Garde Présidentielle*, André Neptune. After a chaotic weekend which included power outages and a blackout of news as well, the government took the bit in its teeth and declared a state of siege on January 22. In Miami, two of the more prominent opposition leaders, Louis Roy (one of the 1987 constituents), and Hubert de Ronceray related to the press corps the details of their sudden expatriation.

Also picked up in sweeps conducted by the government was Antoine Izméry, a prominent Haitian merchant of Palestinian origins and a known critic of the regime. A Ministry of Information decree imposed censorship on all radio and television stations, whereupon most non-government stations ceased broadcasting. The protest may have played into the government's hands, for Haitians were unable to hear an angry denunciation of the state of siege issued by Bishop Romélus in Jérémie.

This time though, the lucky number 22 didn't carry through. By the beginning of February the state of siege was ended with, sources whispered, some tightening of the screws by Ambassador Adams. Roy and de Ronceray were soon back in Haiti, and over several weeks, there evolved enough consensus among the opposition to issue a joint declaration calling for Avril to resign. The signers of the declaration were a veritable Who's Who of Haitian politics, including Louis Roy, Marc Bazin, Hubert de Ronceray, René Théodore, Sylvio Claude, and the redoubtable *Père* Adrien. All in all, some eleven parties signed the manifesto.

To underline the urgency of matters, shops shuttered, schools closed, and people took to the streets. Inevitably, there were casualties, among them an eleven year old girl killed by a stray bullet while studying. Three days later, at the request of Ambassador Adams, Prosper Avril met with the American envoy.

Adams, invoking the Nixon resignation (and, more practically, threatening that Avril's U.S. bank accounts would be frozen), prevailed on Avril to step down in order to avert further bloodshed. At 2:40 p.m., on Saturday, March 10, issuing no public statement, Prosper Avril was taken by motorcade to his Pétionville home.

At 3 p.m., General Hérard Abraham, the acting Army Chief of Staff went on television to announce Haiti's fifth change of government in four years. In a one minute speech, Abraham announced that the Army would act as caretaker for seventy-two hours while, in accordance with the 1987 constitution, an as yet unnamed Supreme Court Justice took power until elections could be held. There then ensued three days of confusion.

While agreeing to step down, Avril had not agreed to leave the country, and while there he would inevitably act as a lightning rod for disaffected rightists. To complicate things further, the Justice in line for the Presidency, Gilbert Austin, was regarded as far too close to Avril to be able to govern. Austin disqualified himself, eventually opening the way for Ertha Pascal-Trouillot, the youngest (at forty-six) member of the court. She had been appointed to the *Cour de Cassation* by liberal Justice Minister François Latortue during his ten month stint with the *CNG*. Avril, prevailed upon again by the good offices of *bourik chaje*, was whisked Monday in the early dawn with his family by U.S. Air Force jet to Florida.

Nou Se Lavalas

Ertha Pascal-Trouillot was sworn in as interim president on March 13, 1990. Haiti's first woman president received the sash of office from General Abraham who declared that "the Army will stay in its barracks". To a wildly cheering crowd, the new president, in a white linen suit, declared "I have no ambition but for the singular service of my country." For the first time in two and a half years, Haiti was back on the road to democratic government.

The new president spent the next twenty-four hours mulling over cabinet choices and preparing decrees that would reestablish normal life by opening schools and abolishing censorship. She was under no illusions as to the difficulties that lay ahead. In addition to the army, in its barracks for the moment, but restless, were the *macoutes*, still armed, still out of power. Looking over her shoulder, with power to veto her every move, was a nineteen-member Council of State, many of whose members could be expected to harbor ambitions for the elections now scheduled for December.

Within a week, in fact the very day of the installation of *Madame Présidente*'s (as she quickly became known) cabinet, a group of *macoutes* wielding machetes and guns took hostage a group of six elderly nuns at St. Rose of Lima. After administering beatings, the attackers disappeared. The motive, other than terrorizing the populace at large, was unclear.

As the weeks passed, it became clear that whether by necessity or choice, *Madame Présidente* intended to reign, but not rule. Relations between her and the Council of State quickly deteriorated. Viewed as powerless, she seemed unable to stem violence that was again on the upswing. She made few public appearances. Ominously, the *New York Times* reported on May 15 that General Abraham's soldiers had gone unpaid.

The government's finances remained as precarious as ever. 1989 exports had plummeted to $153 Million from a high of $223 Million in 1985 - Jean-Claude Duvalier's last full year in power. In another echo of 1985, unable to muster the foreign exchange to pay for a tanker of oil, Haiti went without petroleum for ten days in August.

Another ill omen was the return from Santo Domingo of Roger Lafontant. Kept at bay as long as his mortal enemy, Prosper Avril, was in the palace, Lafontant lost no time in returning once Avril was gone. By October, he was rallying Duvalierists throughout the country. After announcing his candidacy, he was disqualified by the Trouillot-appointed electoral council. He and others who were barred by the 1987 constitution from running for office immediately clamored for a change in the rules with the implicit threat that if they did not get their way, the 1990 elections would be disrupted in the same manner as those three years earlier.

Among those eligible, none seemed to capture the popular imagination. Marc Bazin, polished, accomplished, was regarded as "America's man" and thus discredited in the eyes of many. The leading leftist candidate, Victor Benoît, was regarded as lackluster. None of the remaining nine candidates had enough name recognition to govern even if they received a plurality. In many minds, there existed the real possibility of a Lafontant-Bazin contest. That prospect threw the left into a frenzy, for it new that Bazin would inevitably emerge victorious from such a race.

At the eleventh hour, on October 18, the liberation theologian whose principal preoccupation since his expulsion from his order had been the running of his orphanage made an announcement that electrified the race. Jean-Bertrand Aristide became the candidate of the FNCD(which had quickly discarded Benoît once Aristide became available). Running under the banner of *Lavalas* (the créole word for gully-washing torrents that sweep all before them) he electrified the country with his Créole oratory and petrified the elite. His program, he said, could be summed up in three words, "participation, transparency, justice." Nowhere, many noted, was there a call for reconciliation. One businessman described him as "a cross between Fidel and the Ayatollah" and declared that given a choice between polar extremes, he would reluctantly back the ultra-right.

Foreign investors, already at a premium, put any investment decisions on hold, pending the December 16 vote. Duvalierist forces stepped up the intensity of their attacks. A grenade attack on an Aristide crowd on December 5 narrowly missed the firebrand priest. The attack, which killed seven and wounded fifty-three, resulted in a ban on any large rallies for the duration of the campaign. By radio, Aristide told his followers, "Take heart. Dry your tears. On the 16th of December the *macoutes* will disappear from Haiti." And still the Army stayed in its barracks.

In preparation for the election, more than a thousand foreign observers from the U.N., the OAS, and private groups and yet again, former President Jimmy Carter, swarmed into Haiti. As election day dawned, officials of the electoral council arrived at polling places to find large crowds already lined up. Mindful of 1987, many appeared apprehensive but determined to cast their ballot for "*Kok Kalité*" the rooster that was the symbol of *Lavalas*.

Other than logistical snafus, this election went relatively smoothly. Ballots arrived late in many places including Cité Soleil, but anxious residents were reassured that the polls would stay open until all who wished to vote had been able to do so. In Port-au-Prince and other cities, the fashion of the day was a red thumb - the indelible ink kept voters from going back for another vote. True to its name, the *Lavalas* torrent swept all before it. When the vote was counted, Aristide had captured sixty-seven percent of the vote - three times as many votes as the runner-up, Marc Bazin. Bazin demanded a recount in the West, alleging irregularities, but the trend was clear. Haiti's president-elect was a liberation theology priest.

Holding its nose, the U.S. government, in the person of Ambassador Adams, met immediately with the victor in a show of support. "It was", said one State Department official, "important to send a signal to the Duvalierists and the army that there was no wink or a nod" for them to undercut Aristide.

Aristide, for his part, tried to reassure nervous foreigners by stating "foreign investors are always welcome in Haiti." His disclaimer did little to comfort those who had heard the story of his visit, on election day, to the home of a wealthy Haitian. Aristide, impressed with the size of the house, remarked that it "could be home to a dozen families". The elite braced itself. More pointedly, in a Christmas Eve statement, Roger Lafontant vowed that "Attila the hun will not enter the gates."

Echoing the elite's sentiments, Msgr. Wolff-Ligondé chose as the theme of his independence day sermon on January 1 the "coming regime of political authoritarianism" and wondered if Haiti could avoid "the social bolshevism rejected by countries of the East".

Spurred on by the bishop's blessing, Roger Lafontant gathered his men for one final *attentat*. On the evening of January 6, three weeks after the election, he and a group of *macoutes* seized the palace, President Trouillot, and broadcast facilities. Appearing grim-faced on television, he announced that he had seized power. Counting on the army to rise up in support, he was shocked when troops stayed loyal to the interim government and counter-attacked at noon the next day. Arrested, Lafontant was hauled off to the penitentiary to which he had consigned so many.

Public response was immediate and visceral. In echoes of the first waves of *dechoukaj* following Jean-Claude Duvalier's ouster, mobs went after all *macoutes*. Pitched battles were fought around Lafontant's Delmas home and his political headquarters. Followers who emerged were beaten to death or necklaced, while others who jumped down a well to find sanctuary drowned. In a message whose nuances were not missed by the elite, crowds looted then burned the Lalue supermarket, whose "Syrian" owners were alleged to be *macoutes*.

Associating Msgr. Wolff-Ligondé with the *attentat*, the vengeance-bent crowds burned down Port-au-Prince's eighteenth century cathedral whose restoration had been Ligondé's *quid pro quo* for performing the marriage of Jean-Claude Duvalier ten years before. The oldest building in Port-au-Prince and one of the oldest in the Caribbean was now no more than a pile of embers.

For good measure, crowds sacked the Papal Nunciature and beat the nuncio's secretary. It was all over in a matter of hours, but with thirty-seven dead and scores wounded, it did nothing to reassure anyone about the path ahead. Nor did the president-elect's response give much comfort to those seeking solace. While referring on the radio to the "hideousness" of the destruction, he urged followers to be "vigilant without vengeance". Going further, he said that "I take note of your will to catch powerful *macoutes* today so that they don't destroy you tomorrow. It is legitimate." His speech was seen by many as tacit encouragement of further mass action against the macoutes.

Madame Présidente, freed, promptly declared three nights of curfew, while the army, in good odor for once, affirmed that Lafontant and the fifteen accomplices being held would be turned over for civilian trial.

In the days that followed, Radio Métropole received threats of lynching following a news reader's condemnation of the destruction of the cathedral. The news reader was accused of "opposing the people's will." When a reporter for *Haïti Observateur* asked a question about street violence at a January press conference, the president-elect prefaced his response by saying, "It is not today that I started observing you. I am asking the Haitian people to observe you too." Later in the same news conference, Aristide confirmed that his remarks were "very serious."

The second round of elections for the legislature and other offices went off on January 20 without a hitch, though turnout was light. Having elected Aristide, many voters had apparently given no thought to the notion that an opposition-dominated legislature could effectively thwart much of the *Lavalas* program. And still the army stayed in its barracks.

As February 7 drew closer, nerves in Port-au-Prince were increasingly on edge. On January 27, *telediol* had it that there was a plot afoot to free Lafontant and his associates from jail. Barricades and burning tires promptly appeared in Port-au-Prince's poorer quarters. Mobs lynched four *macoutes* and attacked a police station in Carrefour. Only radio announcements from Mayor Evans Paul and the Army High Command affirming that Lafontant and his cronies were still in custody cooled things off. Six were killed as the army restored order.

Displaying remarkable *sang-froid*, *Père* Aristide left as planned for two days of meetings in France with François Mitterand and other officials.

While Aristide sought aid from one of Haiti's two largest aid donors, France, his chief backer in the elite, Antoine Izméry, was busy trashing the other, the United States. A forty-seven year old Haitian of Palestinian origin who had made millions importing goods for the elite *Père* Aristide so despised, Izméry seemed an unlikely soul mate for the new president. Speaking to the *New York Times*' Howard French, Izméry claimed that Ambassador Adams had provided the impetus for the Lafontant coup attempt and that Jimmy Carter had tried to get Aristide to concede the election before the first votes were counted. He said that Haiti was "like a whore, a safe house for bandits with a Mafia organization controlling it, and the boss of the Mafia is the United States."

Under the circumstances, George Bush could be excused for declining to attend Jean-Bertrand Aristide's inaugural on February 7. The United States was represented by its Ambassador, Alvin Adams, and the Secretary for Health and Human Services, Dr. Louis Sullivan. They, along with Jimmy Carter and scores of dignitaries from around the world looked on as the thirty-seven year old *noir* from Jérémie took the oath of office before the Senate. After taking the oath, Jean-Bertrand Aristide accepted the blue and red sash of office from a peasant woman.

As supporters blew on conch shells, the newest president of Haiti went to the Cathedral for the traditional te deum from the Church with which he had so often been at odds. The embers of the eighteenth century church a few hundred yards away had barely cooled.

Then, in front of the Palace, he delivered an inaugural address that mesmerized the thousands gathered on the lawn and behind the palace fence. In what one diplomat called "a very astute political move", he retired six of the army's eight remaining generals, thanking them for their service to the nation. Another move that would prove to be freighted with consequences was the appointment of an up and coming *mulâtre* officer, Raoul Cédras, as Army chief of staff. In an implicit rebuke to the outgoing administration, he immediately forbade outgoing President Pascal-Trouillot, her entire cabinet, and senior electoral officials from leaving the country for a month. The next day, in a move whose symbolism no Haitian could miss, he vistied Fort Dimanche, which he announced would be turned into a museum.

The Aristide government started with a large reservoir of good will as well as concrete committments for aid from the international community. Donors were chary though, having incorporated the expensive lessons of the Duvalier years, of providing funds on anything but carefully-designed projects with realistic goals. In practice this meant that pending the Haitian government getting its act together, little money would be coming in. This in turn translated to no substantial change in the plight of the urban or rural poor in the first months of the government, despite the great expectations of those classes.

By the terms of the 1987 constitution, much of the power that had been traditionally concentrated in the hands of the president devolved to the prime minister and the cabinet. It was thus with great interest that Haiti and the international community looked to the appointments announced on February 9. Many hoped that Aristide would, in a national unity move, appoint Marc Bazin as prime minister. Others who thought they deserved a place at the table included Port-au-Prince Mayor Evans Paul whose FNCD party had allowed Aristide's last-minute entry into the race, and Jean-Claude Bajeux whose KONAKOM support had been so important.

The president's choice for prime minister was a forty-eight year old bakery owner with European training as an agronomist, René Préval. Devoid of previous political experience, Préval had been a close Aristide confidante and another survivor of the Romain raid on St.-Jean-Bosco in 1988. The choice, widely viewed as a way of side-stepping the constitutional controls on the presidency, occasioned one of the newly-elected senators to comment "He probably thinks it will be easier to pass his own program with his own man as prime minister, but if he intends to rule with a pertsonal clique, we might as well go back to a dictatorship." Doubting that the necessary approval would be forthcoming for his choice of Préval, Aristide simply omitted to submit the nomination - a poor start to his relationship with the legislators.

Other appointments followed the same pattern. As if to underline that the omission of Evans Paul and other FNCD members was not accidental, the new president set about immediately to transform *Lavalas* into a sort of super party of his own, much, some reflected, as François Duvalier had done some three decades earlier.

Referring to the *Lavalas* activists, one diplomat described them as "straight from another era. Their political models were Paris in 1968 and the Cultural Revolution in China." As there was no absolute majority in parliament, Aristide was required to "consult" the National Assembly, but in practice could find many ways to sidestep it, and did. For the all-important Washington embassy, Aristide appointed Jean Casimir, whose tact went a long way in smoothing feathers ruffled along the Potomac by some act or another in Port-au-Prince. None to soon either, for in early March the Aristide government demonstrated its independence from Washington by sending a Haitian youth group to Cuba - the first such open move by a Haitian government in many years.

Like many of his predecessors, Aristide was not above showing some muscle when frustrated by the legislature. An insufficiently compliant Senate was the object in early April of a visit from a mob shouting, "*Aristide à Vie*". April was also memorable in that, Ertha Pascal-Trouillot, only two months after handing over power to Aristide, was charged with being a co-conspirator in the January *attentat* rather than being a victim of it. Briefly imprisoned in the *Pénitencier National*, she was soon released for lack of evidence, but the truculent action on the regime's part gave pause to many. Also bundled into the *Pénitencier*, though for far more reason, was Isidore Pognon, the Fort Dimanche commander whose 1987 ambush had pushed *Père* Aristide onto the national stage.

Mass action was again in evidence at the July trial of Roger Lafontant for that same *attentat*. Crowds outside the court paraded tires ("Père Lebrun") about while waiting for the verdict. Lafontant received a life sentence - illegal under the '87 constitution as Greg Chamberlain points out - which Aristide did nothing to commute, instead declaring an impromptu national holiday. By all accounts though, actual necklacings during Aristide's first period in power amounted to no more than a few dozen - certainly a much lower level of violence than that of most Haitian governments.

Irregularities in ordnance acquisition caused Aristide to replace General Abraham that July with General Cédras, the latter just five months into his job as chief of staff. The Cédras appointment, like all senior army appointments Aristide had made since taking office, was conditional, not permanent. Aristide believed that by making such senior appointments in this manner, the appointees were more likely to behave accountably. While the army had been on its best behavior since the inaugural, fundamental issues of restructuring the army, disarming the *macoutes* (for the moment at bay) and creating a civilian constabulary had still not been addressed by the new government.

The government was encountering problems with the legislature which sought, in August, to pass a no-confidence measure on Prime Minister Préval. Two thousand *Lavalas* supporters gathered outside the Assembly building, harassing and intimidating legislators as they went in.

In the wake of the Abraham dismissal, Aristide, survivor of three assassination attempts and innumerable threats, decided to form what was described later, depending on who painted the picture, as variously "a small security force" or "private army". To be totally independent of the *FAd'H*, the

738 Written in Blood

proposed force sounded curiously like the route taken by Papa Doc, who created the *VSN* to deal with the army.

Alarmed, the army protested, especially as the size of the proposed force grew with each telling. As he left in September to address the U.N. in New York, the president knew that this was a problem he would have to address on his return. In New York, he was accorded a hero's welcome by a crowd of nearly 300,000 Haitians, members of what he had come to refer to as "the 10th Department" in recognition of the fact that by now, one in four Haitians lived overseas.

While he was gone, there coalesced in the army and the elite enough support for an *attentat*. As always, the grievances were varied, and the agendas often personal. Many civilians who had been willing to give Aristide a chance in February had been dismayed by many of his actions since. The army's complaints were predictable. The senior command felt threatened by the lack of permanent appointments. The institution felt threatened by the proposed "security force", at that point still in embryo. Also, an order that the *Chef Sections* report to the Justice Ministry rather than the Army exacerbated army fears that it was losing any say in the conduct of national affairs. More venally, the Aristide government's efforts to clamp down on smuggling and drug running were putting a dent in many officers' life-styles.

Trouble began September 29 at the military base at Frères, just outside Port-au-Prince, and at the *Caféteria*. Radio stations went off the air, while in Cayes, Sylvio Claude, survivor of so much Duvalierist horror, was burned to death after emerging from a political meeting. The next morning, Aristide's home in the Port-au-Prince suburbs - where he was resting for the weekend after his hectic visit to the U.S.- came under fire. By noon, loyal soldiers managed to get an Armored Personnel Carrier to the house. Accompanied inside by the French Ambassador, Jean-Rafaël Dufour, the president made the six mile trip to the Palace. The convoy was fired upon en route, but sustained no serious damage. At some point during the day, Roger Lafontant was killed in the *Pénitencier*. Some said later that Aristide ordered Lafontant's killing in his last act as president.

By 5:30, the mutineers stormed the palace, taking Aristide hostage. Initially, there was a move to hang him on the spot, but calmer heads prevailed, and he was instead hustled the short distance across the square to *FAd'H* headquarters. From there, the Army negotiated with the international community, finally agreeing to allow their prisoner to leave the country. By 10:30, he was on his way to the airport and was met there by the U.S. and Venezuelan ambassadors. Surrounded by several score jeering soldiers, Aristide retained his composure while waiting for a Venezuelan Air Force plane to arrive, which it did just before 3 A.M. After the short flight to Caracas, he was flown to Washington, there to confer with those elements of his government still under his control.

A Bayonet is Iron

It was a shaken and tired president who conferred in Washington in the succeeding days with those members of his government that managed to escape Haiti or who had had the good luck to be abroad when the boom was lowered. In Haiti's elegant, fin-de-siècle Massachusetts Avenue embassy, Aristide conferred with his able Washington envoy Jean Casimir. In Washington, the president enjoyed the good will and the resources of the Washington Office on Haiti, an independent center-left group that had been established in 1984 and whose analyses commanded considerable respect.

In New York and other cities across North America, the emigre apparatus, long-used to life in opposition, was newly energized under such veterans as *Père* Adrien. At the U.N., his tribune Fritz Longchamps stood ready to defend the interests of what was rapidly becoming a government-in-exile. Hurried and frequent conversations with the State Department and White House also ensued, concluding with a rousing address from Secretary of State Baker to an emergency session of the OAS convened on October 2. Baker's words in support of a government with which the U.S.administration had been so uneasy, were unequivocal:

> ...this junta will be treated as a pariah, without friends, without support, and without a future. This coup must not succeed...It is imperative that we agree for the sake of Haitian democracy, and the cause of democracy throughout the hemisphere, to act collectively to defend the legitimate government of President Aristide.

The applause of the assembled delegates gave heart to the Haitian president, as did George Bush two days later, who affirmed to the press that "we want to see President Aristide restored to power." Following the U.S. lead, the OAS cobbled together language that called for an embargo against Haiti. More concrete actions taken by the U.S. such as freezing access to all Haitian government assets in the U.S. by anyone save the exiled president and a few aides guaranteed that Aristide would not starve.

On the ground in Port-au-Prince, no one was vouchsafed such certainty. The coup had been fronted by General Cédras, General Biamby, and Major Michel François. Cédras, at forty-five, was to many the face of the coup, but it was said that it was François, driven both by ambition and fear for his career under Aristide, who was the driving force behind the coup. Biamby's inclusion (reportedly as a counter-weight to the popular François) made the coup a family affair. Biamby's ties to the Cédras family reportedly included claims on the affections of Mme. Cédras. Both François and Cédras were reputed to have amassed considerable fortunes, while Biamby lived austerely, taking care of his troops first.

While real power was in the hands of Cédras and his fellow officers, the putschists quickly found allies in other key constituencies. Many of the most pro-Aristide deputies had gone to ground, leaving a rump parliament, composed of ambivalent or openly anti-Aristide deputies that continued to sit. The coup leaders declared the Presidency vacant, and following the form, if not the substance, of the 1987 constitution, offered it to Supreme Court Justice Joseph Nerette, who accepted. The deputies then ratified (an option they had been denied, they quickly pointed out, by Aristide) Nerette's choice of Prime Minister, agronomist Jean-Jacques Honorat. It went without saying that the Army and Duvalierists supported Cédras, and in the first days of October, many in the elite came around as well.

Securing their base domestically, the officers handed back the weapons that had been confiscated from the *Chefs Sections* and re-established their reporting line to the Army. The *Chefs* lost little time in re-asserting their authority, taking good care to avenge slights, perceived or real, that they had suffered during the past eight months. *Lavalas* organizers, activists, anyone identified with forces for change was driven underground. There quickly developed around Haiti an underground railway (the most efficiently run railway in the country's history) that gave succor to up to 300,000 internal refugees. In several cases, severely threatened people of prominence were smuggled abroad with the help of foreign commando teams.

Internationally, the picture was more clouded. No one argued that Aristide, for the moment, held the moral high ground. Almost no one. Alone in the world, the Vatican conferred recognition on the regime which had replaced the contentious priest-president. The officers and their allies however held Haiti, and moral suasion was unlikely to dislodge them.

Hard on the heels of the emergency OAS session at which Secretary Baker had so ardently championed Haiti's cause, a delegation visited Port-au-Prince in an attempt to persuade the junta of the error of its ways, and more pointedly, of the barriers to its remaining in power. While there, the delegates received views of the deposed regime somewhat at odds with those being disseminated in Washington. Ambassador Adams, whose load had grown heavier in the preceding months, made sure that the delegates heard about some of the less attractive aspects of the Aristide regime. In so doing, he promptly earned the condemnation of many who had been pre-disposed to believe that the U.S. had somehow had a hand in the coup.

The French Ambassador, fresh from his harrowing journey to the Palace in the Armored Personnel Carrier with the now-deposed president, was, according to Kim Ives, "denied access" to the OAS delegation by Ambassador Adams. Whatever the range of opinion they had been exposed to, the delegates returned to Washington to advise Aristide to enter into negotiations with the rump parliament.

However practical the advice may have been, it was received with easily-controlled enthusiasm by Aristide, particularly as the OAS conversion in Port-au-Prince seemed to be echoed in Washington. At best, the political heirs of Ronald Reagan had been ill at ease with a government whose leader had once described capitalism as a "mortal sin". Putting the best face on things, it had nonetheless sought and achieved a modus vivendi with the government whose legitimacy sprung from the very election the United States had worked so hard to bring about.

Now, with that government brought low, the naysayers emerged from the gloom to which they had been consigned for some months. Echoing the "practical" views emerging from the OAS delegation, renewed attention was given to "mob rule" and necklacings during the Aristide presidency. The Bush administration began in its own mind and the public eye to separate democratic rule in Haiti from the person of Jean-Bertrand Aristide. Press secretary Fitzwater, just a few days after the Bush-Aristide meeting let drop that "The U.S. supports the rule of democracy in Haiti... we don't know if President Aristide will return to power."

The tenth department entertained no such doubts. On October 11, some 100,000 Haitians marched in support of Aristide in downtown New York, even as the UN was voting its support of the proposed OAS sanctions. At the heart of any such sanctions was an oil embargo. Unable to afford a "strategic reserve", Haiti would not "be able to last more than a few days" in the face of an oil embargo. An oil and trade embargo were imposed by the OAS on October 23, and by November 5, George Bush had ordered U.S. compliance. From the outset, the concept was fatally flawed. First, while the Western hemisphere had signed on, not all of the U.N. felt bound by the embargo. Second, Haiti enjoyed a long and porous border to its East with a conservative government whose sympathies were scarcely calculated to run to Père Aristide. Overlooked, these two details vitiated the embargo's effect and were to keep doing so for nearly three years.

In October of 1991, few prophesied this course of events. Buoyed by the demonstrations and pressured by Washington, Aristide agreed reluctantly to meet a delegation of pro-coup parliamentarians in Colombia in November. The embargo, though leaky, did give Aristide leverage. While not its targets, Haiti's poor were first to feel the embargo's effects. As the Fall wore on, transportation costs soared with the cost of petroleum. Ripple effects were felt in agriculture, where fertilizers, gasoline for pumps, and the cost of anything else imported was immediately passed on to farmers. Foreseeing nothing but bad times, villagers started pooling their savings to finance the building of boats.

The tide of boat people, which had almost disappeared during Aristide's time in office, began to rise. In the first two months of the coup, nearly seven thousand refugees were intercepted at sea. Reluctant at first to return them to the arms of the regime which it had so recently branded as a pariah, the U.S. set up a temporary camp at Guantanamo Bay. As the tent city mushroomed, it quickly became apparent that this measure could not be sustained. With a presidential election less than a year away, the pressure was on to find some sort of solution.

Feeling its oats, the junta expelled the French Ambassador, Jean-Rafael Dufour, who had been so instrumental in saving Aristide's life the day of the coup, just a few days before the Colombian talks. The delegation that left Port-au-Prince for Cartagena had clear marching orders: end the embargo and work out some sort of arrangement that legitimizes the junta. In view of the great power "flexibility" that had characterized Haiti's relations with the outside world since Duvalier's fall, Port-au-Prince could be forgiven for thinking it had an even chance of success.

By the 1987 constitution, the key was the office of prime minister. The president was chief of state, but it was through the prime minister that he ruled. With Aristide away, the question of who would rule in his stead became paramount. In the back of everyone's mind, not the least Aristide's was the fact that the president served for a five year non-renewable term. While the 'non-renewable" label had not bothered many of his predecessors, it weighed heavily on Aristide. Every minute that he was away from Port-au-Prince and there was no regent on the throne, was a minute for the opposition to dig in further. The junta, through the rump legislature, had appointed Honorat, but without recognition from abroad, the appointment enjoyed little legitimacy.

While the junta enjoyed possession, their prize was worth little unless they had the approbation, however grudging, of the outside world, and the concomitant loosening of sanctions. Aristide, dealing from a position of weakness, conferred on the Port-au-Prince delegation the legitimacy it sought by agreeing to negotiate with it. Having won points by being allowed to come to the table, the junta's representatives had no incentive to compromise quickly.

Negotiators, as in the time of Borno, began early to search for someone who might satisfy both sides Discarding a number of names, attention began to focus on René Théodore and Marc Bazin. Sole survivor of a bloody purge of Haiti's communists in the late sixties, Théodore's ideological fires had been banked by age and the tropics to the point where he actually seemed to represent a middle road between Aristide and the military.

The difficulty lay in such an appointment - indeed, in the entire process of negotiation - lay in the fact that at the extremes of left and right lay groups which believed their leaders had no business negotiating with the other. Aristide balked, especially when the quid pro quo offered by the junta neither reaffirmed his presidency nor offered a specific return date. "Intransigent" was the adjective used by Washington in December to describe Aristide. His difficulties were not eased by the statement of his mentor, Bishop Romélus, still holed up in Jérémie, that the Haitian people had no desire to see René Théodore as their prime minister.

On January 8, feeling heat from Washington, Aristide agreed to have Théodore's name put forward as prime minister. The howls of outrage from both ends of the spectrum were extreme. By the end of the month, the assassination of one of Théodore's bodyguards and the beating of the nominee himself finished what three weeks of polemics had started - it sunk the nomination. The elite, bolstered by several renegade tankers of petroleum, wanted no part of a solution that involved Aristide.

Pouring salt in the wound, the Bush administration announced a "fine-tuning" of the embargo at the beginning of February that allowed some goods manufactured by assembly plants in Port-au-Prince to enter the U.S. Useless it was to argue about the more than 50,000 jobs lost from the assembly sector since the embargo's start, or that the leaky embargo hurt poor Haitians far more than the elite. Worse still, Elliott Abrams, perennial villain of the left in the nineteen-eighties, was by nineteen ninety-two acting as a lobbyist on behalf of some of the companies most hurt by the embargo. In a March piece in the *National Review*, Abrams, whose faults did not include intellectual flaccidity, put the U.S. government dilemma squarely.

...What attitude should democratic countries take toward governments that come to power in free elections, but then undermine democratic institutions? The embargo [Abrams went on to say] left the U.S. Government in the untenable position of attacking Haiti's economy, destroying jobs, creating emigrants - and then telling them "No!" when they sought a haven in this country.

Abrams concluded that the U.S. would have to continue muddling through, seeking a middle path, but that it might well regret its earlier embrace of Aristide. *Père* Adrien, who, as a Catholic priest knew cynicism when he saw it, denounced the U.S. policy as "the most cynical thing".

The refugee crisis grew worse. With Guantanamo (at 12,500 refugees)nearly full, the Bush administration began returning boat people to Port-au-Prince. The richer parts of Port-au-Prince, the *Times* and the *Post* noted, were doing just fine. To provide additional generating capacity at Péligre, water was being diverted from the Artibonite, further crippling agriculture, but in Pétionville the elite dined well off French wines and Norwegian salmon.

The holes in the embargo were being widened by the increasing traffic over the Dominican frontier. Thirty-five miles East of Port-au-Prince, the aptly

named town of Malpasse had been largely off-bounds for most Haitians since
Duvalier's troubles with the Dominicans in the sixties. The sole exception to this
had been the thriving but (for understandable reasons) unpublicized traffic in
bodies that went on every year when Haiti furnished the wherewithal to harvest
Dominican sugar cane.

Beyond Croix-des-Bouquets, hardtop turned to flinty rock, and the rutted
track that limped toward the border was ill-suited for the increasing amounts of
traffic it began to carry. Bowing to economics, the junta managed to scrape up
the funds to macadamize the entire unpaved stretch of road to the border,
demonstrating that *it* did indeed know how to build roads for Haiti.

A month after the beating of Théodore, a new OAS-backed proposal was put
forward. It improved on previous puts in that it affirmed Aristide's title as
president, but set forth no date certain for his return. It also legitimized acts
undertaken by the regime since the coup, and offered amnesty to the officers.

Again, *bourik chaje* lumbered into the fray, urging approval in Port-au-
Prince. Again, the vessel of practicality was smashed against the rocks of
emotion. The rump parliament, it became clear, could not muster enough votes
for passage. Right-wing members brandished arms in debate, and fisticuffs
ensued between those few still brave enough to urge a centrist path and their
diehard opponents. Men of principle were appalled. Conservative Senator Guy
Bauduy, no Aristide lover, lamented that "repression in the countryside is
severe."

In the countryside, livestock prices fell as the means to take cattle (pigs were
still too scarce to be a significant factor) to market became ever more dear.
The rich, noted the *New York Times*, increasingly forsook reliance on the
sputtering power grid for private generators. While they could not avoid
travelling on the ruined roads whose upkeep they refused to pay taxes for, their
discomfort was eased by the purchase of four-wheel-drive vehicles. With gas at
ten dollars a gallon, traffic had so dwindled that the drive from Pétionville
downtown was, marvelled one old timer, "just like the good old days". The four
wheel drive vehicles were useful too to drive over the mountains of uncollected
garbage that were beginning to accumulate at principal intersections in towns as
heretofore sketchy municipal services vanished altogether.

Aristide supporters still in Haiti daily took their lives in their hands, playing
a deadly game of cat and mouse with their opponents in the junta." Ministers"
in the Aristide cabinet were that in name only, with their lives threatened if they
tried to exercise their functions. To underscore the point, each night saw its
share of shootings in the poorer sections of town. Not even the more prominent
were immune.

In May, the assassination of Georges Izméry, brother of Aristide financial
backer Antoine, some two-hundred yards from the police station in broad
daylight revealed just how lawless things were. The violence was not confined

to Aristide supporters. Soldiers from various army units used the cover of darkness to even old scores, and many mornings, the harvest of fresh corpses included some soldiers.

Some of the murders were committed by a smoldering but increasing Aristide resistance. Retribution was swift and brutal, with whole neighborhoods torched in return for a single death. The undercurrent of tension was fed by pro-Aristide shortwave broadcasts and Lavalas pamphlets showered on Port-au-Prince from private planes. Haiti's army was becoming an occupying army in its own country.

In the U.S., Aristide sought to bolster his position with key constituencies, addressing rallies in Central Park and working with the Congressional Black Caucus. Sensing opportunity, Arkansas Governor Clinton declared himself to be "appalled" by the Bush policy of repatriation of refugees.

In the wake of the collapse of the Winter efforts to reach an accord with the outside world, those left ion Haiti tried again to form some sort of government. As a result of meetings at the end of May and the beginning of June between the Army, President Nerette, and Prime Minister Honorat, both of whom were being referred to in Creole as the "de-faktos", there emerged a call for a "government of consensus". In theory, such a government would include both Lavalasiens and Duvalierists - a noble sentiment, but one which ignored reality on the ground.

As de-facto Prime Minister, Honorat had been unable to garner desperately-sought international support. Now he stepped aside in favor of Marc Bazin. Bazin's presence, the junta felt, would lend legitimacy to the de-factos. To some degree, the gambit worked. François Benoît, pressed into service as de-facto Foreign Minister, by September was meeting in Washington with *Père* Adrien. The meetings were greeted with howls of indignation from those who wished to keep their perceived moral high ground as coup victims untainted by any dealings with the coup-makers. As a token of good faith, Adrien put forward a suggestion that a number of OAS "observers" take up positions in Haiti as a step to defusing tensions there.

Just before the thirty-fifth anniversary of François Duvalier's 1957 revolution, the observer team hit the ground in force. All eighteen. A five hundred man team had shrunk to eighteen, a force that René Théodore, his name officially still in play as Aristide's nominee for prime minister, called "truly negligible." In view of the paucity of results from a Summer of negotiations, the hardliners in Lavalas felt vindicated in their anti-negotiation stance. "If we have learned one thing", said a pro-Aristide Senator, "it is that for all those involved in supporting the coup, the return of Aristide signifies a total failure."

What the alternatives to negotiation were, no one was willing to publicly say, least of all the delphic president-in-exile. Brave talk of "popular resistance" played well in slick New York leftist journals, but those advocating it were staying well clear of any line of fire. Nobody, at least not yet, was willing to touch the third rail of Haitian politics - to call for foreign military intervention, though UN debates were certainly headed in that direction. Nor had any calls gone out for a cutoff of overseas remittances from the diaspora - at $250 Million a year the largest source of foreign exchange. Rather, as Fall progressed, increased hopes were put on a change of administration in Washington rather than one in Port-au-Prince.

On November 3, those hopes bore fruit as the first Democratic administration since that of the ill-omened Jimmy Carter was voted into office. A Democratic administration looked hopeful for several reasons. First, Gov. Clinton had campaigned on a promise to change the Bush administration's refugee policy. Second, the incoming administration, on the face of it, seemed a lot more in harmony with the ideological bent of the Lavalasiens. Finally, the Black Caucus in Congress had gained key influence because of the slimness of Governor Clinton's margin, and could consequently expect to be listened to in the new government. The Black Caucus numbered several legislators who had in-depth knowledge of the refugee situation in particular and the Haitian situation in general. The omens seemed briefly favorable with the nomination of Warren Christopher, Carter veteran, to the post of secretary of state.

Disappointment was therefore doubly keen, when President-elect Clinton, reversed his position and announced that the new administration would continue the Bush policy of repatriating refugees. Swallowing his disappointment, President Aristide made good on a previous promise to make a broadcast to the Haitian people in which he asked them to stay put rather than taking to the seas. *Père* Adrien, less constrained than Aristide, stated quite rightly that "mixed signals" from the U.S. were at the core of the inability to resolve the situation in Haiti.

With Aristide's words echoing in their ears, Haitians witnessed the arrival in mid-January of yet another OAS team, this time led by veteran diplomat Dante Caputo. Caputo hoped to revive the plan to station five hundred OAS observers around the country, but found himself almost captive in his hotel because of demonstrations by throngs of coup supporters. While managing to meet with Raoul Cédras, the *mulâtre* general nominally in charge of the factionalized and restive Army, he was prevented from making any serious progress. The mission, in the words of one diplomat "was a total bust".

Wearying of drawing factions at daggers drawn together, perhaps nudged by Washington, Marc Bazin resigned on June 8, having labored for nearly a year. His departure occasioned a flurry of activity that seemed to have promise. The UN, as a result of skillful diplomacy by Ambassadors Casimir and Longchamps, made the leaky hemispheric oil embargo global in mid-June. The move was long overdue. Mindful that plowshares alone might not suffice to resolve the conflict, the body also put in place an arms embargo, but with less optimism as to how effective it would be.

Armed with resolution 841 (the resolution which made the oil embargo global), Dante Caputo, now wearing a UN hat, invited Gen. Cédras and President Aristide to New York. There, on an island in New York harbor (access to which would be restricted, given the size of the diaspora population nearby) the parties would try, so the script went, yet again to cobble together an agreement that would solve the "Haitian impasse".

Even in New York's summer heat, things were sufficiently frosty that the delegations that ultimately responded to the U.N. invitation on June 27 never actually sat down face to face. Instead, over three days, envoy Caputo shuttled proposals and counter-proposals back and forth. What emerged from the discussions, like three drops of corn likker from a still of sour mash, was what came to be known as "The Governors Island Accord".

Presidents Aristide and Clinton meet the press after one of many meetings in 1993. *Embassy of Haiti*

The principles of the accord addressed all the same tired issues. As scripted in New York, Aristide would name a prime minister, the sanctions would be lifted, "reforms" would be made in the army, the coup-plotters given amnesty, and Aristide would return. The army and police "reforms" would occur under the watchful eye of a UN "peacekeeping" force. The date set for Aristide's return was October 30, 1993.

It took very little insight to realize that Aristide, pressured by the international community, had agreed to give up his only weapon - the recently toughened sanctions - in return for an iou to be filled later. Nothing in the Junta's previous behavior gave anyone any hope that they would fulfill their bargain, but without even a de-facto Prime minister on the ground, Aristide felt obliged to put his shoulder to the wheel yet again.

In Port-au-Prince, a returning Cédras was given a tumultuous welcome by a crowd looking forward to a renewed flow of oil and goods through normal channels. For his prime minister, President Aristide put forward the name of Robert Malval. Mary McGrory described him as looking like "a better-fed Peter Lorre" with "sad eyes" and a "self-effacing manner". He had studied in the United States and marched in the historic civil rights marches at Selma, Alabama. Well-educated, thoughtful, Malval was the successful owner of one of Haiti's largest printers and publishers, Imprimerie Natal. A member of the elite, he seemed well positioned, if anyone could, to bridge the gap between Pétionville and Washington. Announcing his acceptance of the post in mid-August, Malval noted that he would stay in the job only until December 15. By then, with the president home, someone else could take over. Sworn in in Washington and Port-au-Prince successively, Malval would have done well to note the actions of a fellow member of the elite, Fritz Mevs. Within days of Malval's taking office, the scion of the conservative family which so despised Lavalas broke ground outside Port-au-Prince on a mammoth oil tank farm.

Those looking for storm signals had not long to wait. On September 11, a mass was sung at Sacré Coeur in memory of those killed by Franck Romain's *macoutes* at St.-Jean-Bosco five years earlier. In attendance, courageously, was Antoine Izméry, still grieving for the brother assassinated the previous year. In a move whose message could be mistaken by no one, *macoutes* marched into the church, removed Izméry at gunpoint, and killed him on the very spot where Clément Jumelle's corpse had been hijacked thirty-four years earlier.

Key to Aristide's return on October 30 was the landing of a U.N. force that could keep the peace. The concept, deeply troubling to those with memories of 1915, was reluctantly regarded as a necessary evil by most Aristide partisans if the cycle of army-sponsored violence was ever to be broken. Predictably, with the embargo suspended and oil flowing, the sensitive issue of foreign "peace-keepers" on Haiti's soil was used to rally those already ill-disposed to see the final parts of the Governors Island Accord fall into place. Under the banner of

FRAPH ("Front for Advancement and Progress of Haiti" - the name, not by coincidence, sounded exactly like the Creole word for "hit"), a band of second and third generation *macoutes* (typified by "Toto" Constant, forty year old son of the former army chief of staff) coalesced to give the shadowy terror a more public face. Many of *FRAPH*'s younger members had been to school in the U.S. and were fluent in English. Familiar with the use of the media, they were able to organize demonstrations in just the right numbers to assure a spot on the nightly news in the U.S., along with an accompanying soundbite.

The U.S. public was the target of these demonstrations. *FRAPH* members watched CNN like many others, and thus were aware of the Clinton administration's growing discomfort with its ill-defined Somalia mission - an inheritance from the Bush administration. A number of casualties in Mogadishu firefights in early October had done nothing to ease the administrations qualms about the possibility of having to open a second international police operation in its own back yard.

Steaming toward Haiti in the second week of October, the USS Harlan County carried a contingent of lightly armed U.S. and Canadian troops who were to form the vanguard of the U.N. force. In Port-au-Prince, telediol buzzed with rumors that the troops would not be allowed to debark. FRAPH rallies for several days before the October 11 landing had grown in size and boisterousness, and were, thanks to frequent and efficient advance work on FRAPH's part, well-covered by the U.S. media. As the *Harlan County* hove to, a group of one hundred or so FRAPH members gathered with placards and weapons in the dock area of Port-au-Prince. Diplomats trying to pass through the crowd to observe the disembarkation of the troops were jostled, manhandled, and in some cases blocked.

Washington, after consulting at length with the U.S. embassy while the troops waited on board ship, decided not to attempt an "opposed" landing, and ordered the *Harlan County* to set course for home. Incredibly, one-hundred *macoutes* had bullied the international community into submission. Questions immediately arose as to whether the administration's heart had ever been in the project, or if the landings had been quietly sabotaged by a Pentagon not in love with either Clinton or Aristide. At a Washington cocktail party, Deputy Under Secretary of Defense Walter Slocombe was alleged to have boasted that he "had saved the United States from a small war". The Pentagon, he said, would not risk soldiers' lives to put "that psychopath" back in power.

Whatever the impetus of the change of heart, the following days brought a rash of anti-Aristide stories "leaked" by the Republicans. Senator Helms, surely William Jennings Bryan's spiritual successor in ignorance on matters Haitian was at the vanguard of those attacking Aristide's psychological health.

With the *Harlan County* episode, U.S. credibility in Haiti sank to zero. The junta in Port-au-Prince celebrated its victory by removing yet another critic. On

October 14, Guy Malary, an able young lawyer from one of Haiti's distinguished families and Aristide's justice minister was shot dead.

Seeing that the Governors Island accord was dead, President Clinton reimposed the embargo, putting teeth in it by ordering U.S. naval vessels to patrol Haiti's perimeter. The junta, of course, had taken good advantage of the suspension of the embargo to bunker as much petroleum as possible. Malval, officially Prime Minister, labored on in Port-au-Prince, almost in isolation. He and his colleagues were in most cases even unable to gain physical access to what were nominally their own offices. It would have availed them little. Most of them had already been stripped of fixtures of all kinds, even down to the toilet bowls.

Seeking to make yet another fresh start, Malval proposed at year's end a grand conference in Port-au-Prince of all the parties to the conflict. Received well in the international community, the idea was vetoed by Aristide, who feared a repeat of the Governors Island fiasco. The Washington Post chided, "Mr. Aristide's limited view of his own role and responsibilities is troubling. He seems to consider it someone else's job to restore him to power... It apparently has not occurred to him that it's up to him to devise a strategy to bring about his own return."

In Port-au-Prince a frustrated Malval offered his resignation. He had, he said, promised to stay until December 15, and with the date upon him, was doing what he said he'd do. Prevailed upon to stay on in "caretaker" status, Malval was sharply ordered by Aristide not to undertake any new initiatives.

Haiti stumbled toward its third Christmas of embargo bloody but unbowed. One poor city dweller in Port-au-Prince told the *Times'* Howard French, "Either do what is needed to bring our president back, or have the honesty to say that you have failed, and leave us alone." At the other end of the economic and political spectrum, his sentiments were echoed by a member of the elite. "You are trying to coerce a bunch of people who have no sense of nation and no sense of patriotism. They don't care what happens to the ordinary Haitian. They don't even care what happens to Haiti." This was the group that held Haiti hostage, the group writer Herbert Gold came to dub "M.R.E.'s" - Morally Repugnant Elite.

Delivering yet another fierce-sounding ultimatum, the "four friends" (the U.S., Canada, Venezuela, and France) closed the year by threatening to expand the embargo if Cédras did not step down by January 15. The junta's reply was defiant - large parts of Cité Soleil were torched, nominally for the killing of FRAPH leader Issa Paul, but the officers knew all too well that Washington was watching their actions. As Laënnec Hurbon was to comment later, "The main effect of the gangsterized society that the coup d'etat of 1991 reimposed was to dissolve virtually all social values. Staying alive in Haiti [had become] a favor granted by the whim of men with guns."

A Powerful Persuader

Annoyance at Aristide's perceived intransigence carried over into the new year. Even President Clinton, normally careful to conceal what could be a strong temper, let slip that "his own prospects are clouded by what happened with Malval." "Where we go from now", said the president,"is something we're really going to have to sit down and think through and reassess."

President Aristide had done nothing to mend fences with the Washington administration by calling at mid-month for the revocation of the agreement which gave the U.S. legal cover for its refugee repatriation. His call prompted a State Department representative to walk out in anger. *Bourik chaje*, never unladen, had been replaced as U.S. ambassador by a Clinton appointee, William Lacy Swing.

In Haiti, emboldened by these and other signs of disarray in the opposition camp, the junta turned up the heat. The morning harvest of bodies increased, and, in a weapon calculated to outrage Haitian society, rapes as a weapon of political retribution. The campaign, with all its Duvalierist trademarks, was the handiwork of Michel François, who by now held the job of police chief in Port-au-Prince.

The junta's boldness masked a deteriorating situation. Business, once strongly on the army's side had begun to reassess. Some still held out for what another scoffed at as a "dream solution", but the mood was better summed up by one businessman who said "It is clear that what we have to do to get out of this crisis. Aristide will have to come back, and the army is going to have to change."

Everyone agreed that this was the solution except the army and the *macoutes*. Warren Christopher, normally diplomatic, was expressing increasing exasperation at this most intractable situation. Further, the standoff created friction between the U.S. administration and domestic allies such as the Congressional Black Caucus whose cooperation was needed on more important issues. Criticism was coming from unexpected quarters too. Even the Army War College, not normally known as a hotbed of liberalism, scored the administration for "vacillation and confusing actions" that "had been interpreted in Haiti as indecisive." The sixty page report went on to say that "good intentions are not enough. One must have clearly defined and realistic goals, the means of attaining them and the will to persist." Less diplomatically, the head of the powerful House Appropriations Committee, David Obey, called for a U.S. invasion.

Three years into a five year term, Aristide and his advisers grew increasingly suspicious that Washington's intent was to let him serve out his term in exile. Playing the one remaining card he had, Aristide gave the six month termination notice required by the 1981 refugee treaty. The notice was accompanied by a well-crafted public relations campaign that had been devised in consultation with his sagest advisors such as Casimir and Adrien, as well as the Black Caucus. In mid-April, Trans Africa's Randall Robinson launched a hunger strike in protest of administration policy. On April 20, eschewing niceties, President Aristide himself lambasted Washington's refugee policy as "a cynical joke. It's a racist policy. It's really aa way to say 'we don't care'". Going further, he said that if Clinton had "done just half what he promised", the situation would have been long since resolved.

National security adviser Anthony Lake and Deputy Secretary of State Strobe Talbott scrambled to do damage control. The administration, they announced, had just completed a three week policy review and intended to tighten the embargo. Their statement did nothing to mollify six democratic congressmen, including Joseph P. Kennedy, who allowed themselves to be arrested after staging a well-publicized sit-in in front of the White House.

Stung by the barrage of criticism, President Clinton moved decisively. Lawrence Pezzullo, a veteran diplomat with excellent credentials, was replaced as point man on Haitian policy by William Gray, former Congressman and head of the United Negro College Fund. At the UN, Ambassador Madeleine Albright began circulating a draft policy change that would, on paper, radically toughen the embargo. In response to these moves, Randall Robinson, after twenty-seven days, ended his fast.

Thumbing its nose, the junta named a new *de-facto* president, octogenarian Emile Jonassaint. At the UN, Ambassador Albright had secured passage of Resolution 917 by the beginning of May. On the heels of that resolution, William Gray paid a visit to the Dominican Republic. There, President Balaguer had averted his eyes, such as they were, from the booming border traffic in illicit goods. Allegedly acting from concern about the effect enforcement of the embargo would have on the poor in Haiti, Balaguer was not unaware of the money being made by key army men from embargo-busting. Gray's timing was good. Balaguer had just won reelection in a vote that had been somewhat irregular. He was consequently more amenable than before to moral suasion from the U.S. In a flurry of well-publicized activity just after Gray's visit, the Dominicans clamped down on the bustling border trade. In companion moves, on June 10, the U.S. banned all remittances to Haiti of more than fifty dollars a month as well as all commercial airline flights. In these actions it was joined by Canada. The two countries accounted for three-quarters of the flights in and out of Haiti. U.S. embassy dependents, as well as some one hundred employees were to be withdrawn as well, Washington announced, before the flight ban went into effect on June 25. The tempo was beginning to quicken.

Port-au-Prince began to react. Families packed children and others off to the provinces, jamming the few buses that were still running on eighteen dollar a gallon gas. The elite, emulating the poor, sent children off to relatives overseas.

Marines rotating into the U.S. embassy in Port-au-Prince as embassy guards had helmets and bulletproof vests confiscated at the airport. In Santo Domingo, the brother of Michel François, a member of Haiti's diplomatic delegation there, alleged in a radio interview that his brother was "willing to make the necessary concessions". De-facto President Jonassaint, on television, declared a state of emergency, claiming that Haiti was in danger of "invasion and occupation". Envoy Gray, on ABC, downplayed the declaration, saying that he didn't "know what it was all about."

As usual, the Haitians knew what they were talking about. Gray's disclaimers notwithstanding, the administration had been in quiet consultation with the rest of the hemisphere. Many Caribbean countries were strongly urging the U.S. to intervene. Some urged outright intervention, some under the fig leaf of UN authorization. Pressed on the matter, Ambassador Gray said, "Those whose house is adjoined, next to Haiti, are very concerned and don't want to debate how many buckets of water will be thrown on the fire per minute."

Missing from the chorus was the endorsement of the object of all this international solicitude, Jean-Bertrand Aristide. Fearing, with considerable justification, that his endorsement of military action would alienate many of his supporters, he waffled. At the beginning of June, he had gone so far as to ask for a "surgical strike", emulating the operation which had deposed Manuel Noriega five years earlier. In the face of outcries, he backed off, by the end of the month telling National Public Radio that he would "never" allow himself to be returned by force. Some began to voice suspicions that the quixotic president preferred life in opposition, a though that had been voiced earlier in the year by Robert Malval. "Even if we were to find a way out of this crisis," he said in an interview, "I think Aristide would find a way to keep it from happening."

Notwithstanding Aristide's coyness, events began to take on a momentum of their own. On July 11, the Jonassaint government expelled 104 UN "human rights monitors" who had trickled back into Haiti over the previous few months. The sole remnant of one of the many UN initiatives to resolve the crisis, the monitors had provided a window to the oppression occurring in the countryside. Their effect was debatable. One person complained that the only consequence of their presence was that "the Army now beats us at night rather than during the day."

Nonetheless, the UN reacted strongly. By July 29, even Aristide had signed on, and Resolution 940, authorizing U.S. intervention on behalf of the UN, was passed. Anticipating passage, the U.S. had already begun to muster its forces. The Pentagon scanned its database to find Créole-speaking personnel and was pleasantly surprised to find that there were quite a number of young Americans of Haitian descent. Orders went out transferring these people on TDY to Fort Bragg and other bases. Paratroopers from the famed 82d airborne at Fort Bragg began training exercises with Haiti in mind, while in the Bahamas, the Marines rehearsed for forced evacuation of Americans from Port-au-Prince.

While international and particularly regional opinion (Cuba's Castro, for obvious reasons, was a loud exception) mitigated toward a military solution, President Clinton had still, in an election year, to prepare American public opinion. "Our preference", sighed one State Department official, "would be to get a phone call from Cédras and company that they are leaving." Cédras, however, gave no sign of playing ball. Interviewed by Peter Jennings on ABC, he said "I am the pin in Haiti's hand grenade. If pulled, an explosion will occur." As if to underscore this hard line, *macoutes* on August 28 murdered Jean-Marie Vincent, a fellow priest of *Père* Aristide who had narrowly escaped assassination during the Jean-Rabel massacre of 1987.

Speculation, which the White House did nothing to dampen, grew about possible dates. Almanacs were consulted to see when moonless nights (favored by paratroopers) would occur in August. Behind the scenes, Washington sent messages to the junta in Port-au-Prince that they would be well-advised to take this one last opportunity to get out. Obdurate to the last, they refused. The MRE's, *Newsweek* reported, seemed resigned to an invasion. "It is my country that is dying", said Fritz Mevs. "I am already saved."

On September 15, President Clinton addressed America. Noting the murder of Vincent, the rapes, the misery, he said that "We must act." Commenting in Port-au-Prince on the Clinton speech, General Cédras responded, "I would rather die, and if I die in the next few hours or the next few days, that would be better than leaving my country in dishonor and leaving my children with a dishonorable name."

Consulting calendars, many noted that the following week would meet tidal and lunar requirements for what some were already calling the "intervasion". As President Clinton addressed his fellow citizens, nine navy warships were already off Haiti with an 1,800 man Marine amphibious task force on board. Nine more ships were en route as well as fourteen cargo vessels. Hospital ships prepared to take station in the Gulf of Gonâve while the carrier *Eisenhower* steamed South with combat elements of the army's 10th Mountain Division. The pieces were falling into place. No one expected much resistance from the Haitian army. One observer predicted that "there will be more Haitians hurt by the butts of rifles the soldiers throw down than by Americans firing on them." Outriders of disaster, television crews began massing in Port-au-Prince for the show, in the meantime enjoying Haiti's good rum and the view from the Montana hotel.

Into this charged situation strode the ex-president of the United States, Jimmy Carter. Aping earlier actions in Somalia and North Korea where he had, with the most reluctant support from the Clinton administration, appointed himself extraordinary envoy, he descended on Port-au-Prince at the head of a troika which also included Senator Sam Nunn of Georgia and retired Joint Chiefs of

Staff Chairman Colin Powell. The presence of the latter two individuals brought credibility to their mission - to make one last stab at brokering a peaceful settlement.

With the clock ticking towards a landing in the wee hours of Monday, the trio met at length with the junta, breaking off at 2 a.m. Sunday morning. After a few hours of rest, the group met with Aristide supporters, President Jonassaint, and then Gen. and Mme. Cédras. At noon, Carter broke off to get additional time from President Clinton, who agreed to three more hours. Talks with the junta went on all afternoon. President Clinton gave final approval to Secretary of Defense Perry to commence operations at 12:01 a.m. Monday.

Throughout Sunday afternoon, as additional ships and aircraft took up station in Haiti's skies and off her shores, Carter kept talking. At one point, perhaps carried away by the moment, he told Cédras that he was "ashamed" of American policy. Finally, at 6:30 p.m., Clinton told Carter he had thirty minutes left. The junta agreed to the terms presented by Carter, who then faxed what was in effect a fait accompli to the White House. After some debate as to whether Jonassaint could sign an agreement since the U.S. did not recognize his government, President Clinton accepted. The invasion, to be replaced the next day with a "permissive entry" by U.S. troops, was called off.

Haitians got the news from President Jonassaint, at eighty-one old enough to remember the last occupation. Just before midnight, he went on TV to appeal for calm. "You can go to sleep knowing that there will be no invasion...We couldn't let the annihilation of Haiti happen without any reason, hence we signed an accord. Many people will not be happy, but will see from the results of the accord that we were right."

The deal brokered by Carter allowed Cédras to stay in command until October 15, when President Aristide would return. During that time, parliament was supposed to vote "a general amnesty." As Michael Kelly pointed out in the *New Yorker*, Carter achieved his goal "by the simple ploy of giving away the farm, or, at least, a large chunk of it; backing down on issues important to America's friends and enemies and betraying promises made by the American government."

Nothing in the agreement addressed the fate of any members of the junta, who in theory could have stayed in Haiti, been pardoned, and run for office. Jean-Bertrand Aristide, who had been kept briefed by Ambassador Gray (to the degree *he'd* been informed by the freelancer in Port-au-Prince) greeted the new agreement with all the enthusiasm of a boy who got socks for Christmas. An adviser put it bluntly. "His dilemma is how to make clear the dangers it poses without appearing to be ungrateful to the United States."

Many members of the diaspora were equally concerned, noting that the "thugs" of President Clinton's Thursday night address had become the "honorable" (Carter's word) partners of Monday. International reaction was favorable. The French, always ambivalent about America's role in Haiti, had declined to send any troops, but promised to send one hundred *gendarmes* later. Carter quickly flew back to the U.S., in Kelly's words "upstaging the President with a long interview on CNN hours before he was due to join Clinton for a press conference in the East Room." While the skirmishing was underway in Washington, the "intervasion" of Haiti had begun. "Superior force", Winston Churchill had noted some years earlier, "makes a powerful persuader."

Second Occupation

The first American troops landed at Port-au-Prince's civilian airport at the relatively civilized hour of 9:30 a.m. Monday. Disgorged in full battle gear from army choppers, the soldiers, fierce and combat-ready, were startled to see thousands of cheering Haitians pressed against the airport fence. Port-au-Prince was clearly not going to be Kuwait City.

In the vanguard was Lieutenant General Henry H. Shelton, Commander of the American troops in Haiti. While his troops were busy setting up camp at the Eastern end of the runway and in nearby structures that had, in better days, housed some of the assembly factories that had provided precious jobs, Gen. Shelton conferred with Ambassador Swing. Then, Shelton (Haitians quickly nicknamed him "Shelltox" after Haiti's most efficient pesticide) was driven to Military Headquarters near the palace to discuss with General Cédras the logistics of landing and billeting some 15,000 American troops. The meeting was described as "cordial". Over the next few days, troops landed at the Cap and fanned out across the country. In many cases there was no one to surrender to them. The army had, for the most part, shifted into civilian clothes and tried to melt back into the population, leaving barracks and government buildings empty.

Port-au-Prince Mayor Evans Paul emerged from hiding for the first time in three years as did thousands of others. At the airport, still closed to civilian traffic, flights bearing legislators home from exile in the U.S. competed with C-130 cargo planes for ramp space. The U.S was determined that there would be the necessary quorum in parliament to enact whatever legislation was necessary. Haitians watched with awe as tent cities went up with miraculous speed. Pandemonium erupted when it was discovered that some of these *blancs* (the term startled the non-créole speaking black troops, but not those of Haitian descent) not only spoke Créole, but were women.

Under rules of engagement announced by the Pentagon, U.S. troops were not to interfere in Haitian-on-Haitian violence. The rules were quickly modified after several well-publicized incidents in which Haitian police beat protesters while

U.S. soldiers stood by. One reporter asked a Haitian policemen why he was beating a man. Taking time out to reply, he responded "I'm doing my job." "What exactly is your job?" "To intimidate the populace".

The fact that the American troops were in effect working with the very people they had set out a few days before to conquer was the cause of more than a little unhappiness in many quarters. "How", asked one resident of Cite Soleil, "can we feel safe if the United States does not take away guns from those who have killed us for three years?"

Many were restrained in their celebrations, fearing that Cédras and others would manage to outwit the Americans and abort Aristide's return. Others were more bold though, and Aristide posters, smudged and creased, appeared magically around the city.The accord was much the same as Governors Island, though, as Secretary of State Christopher noted dryly Sunday night, there would be 15,000 troops on the ground this time to enforce it. One Aristide partisan was quoted as saying, "We just hope this is not another betrayal by the Americans, who always wanted to save the army."

By Thursday, U.S. soldiers had taken over the dreaded Camp d'Application, where most of Haiti's heavy weapons were stored. They expected to find a more intimidating collection of hardware than they did. Most of the weapons and vehicles were unserviceable. The place, said one soldier, "looked like a junk yard."

Even as the American troops consolidated their hold, Cédras, perhaps encouraged by Jimmy Carter's accolades in the U.S., told CBS news that he had no intention of leaving Haiti. In the streets, cries were beginning to go up to "handcuff Cédras". *Le Nouvelliste*, in a Thursday editorial, commented "The Haitian elites are in a state of shock. Already one accuses the other for the historic responsibility for this new occupation." Some in those elites were willing to confess a certain relief. "Things could not have gotten much worse", said art gallery owner Johnny Saba.

By Monday, with troops on the ground a week, General Shelton felt compelled to assign some 1,200 MP's to "monitor" the Haitian police. In many cases, they found themselves doing primary police work as well, for the police and army had vanished. Retired policemen were brought in from the U.S. under contract to the State Department and quickly adjusted to the realities of Haitian justice. One policeman, retired after twenty years on the Dallas police force, sauntered into the *Roi Christophe* one evening in October with a happy look on his face. Asked at the bar what he was smiling about, he explained. He had been dispatched to pick up a man accused of murder in a village near the Cap, he said. The man had been in jail for several weeks, and no one knew what to do with him. Finally, a justice of the peace decided to petition the Americans in the Cap. When he arrived to remove the prisoner, a menacing mob seemed ready to take justice into its own hands. The prisoner, much relieved not to be wearing a necklace, looked puzzled as the American, through an interpreter, said, "Now I'm going to read you your rights." He continued, "You have the right to sing the blues, and the right to suck air." "I've wanted to do that for twenty years" he said, sipping his rum punch.

For Port-au-Prince, the defining moment came with the occupation of the hated Caféteria by U.S. troops. Crowds milled outside, hurling insults at the few Haitian policemen inside. Between the two, a thin line of MP's kept the peace. Penetrating to the holy of holies, fifty special forces men bivouacked alongside Haitian army troops in the *Casernes Dessalines*. Their rifles were of less use than wrenches and mops, which were needed to clean up the fetid barracks and get the showers and toilets functioning.

All eyes were fixed on October 15, the day set for Aristide's return. On October 4, U.S. troops raided *FRAPH* headquarters, arresting a number of people. They also took the opportunity to spirit away some 60,000 pages of documents, fearful perhaps that some of them might be embarrassing to the U.S. This last matter was not revealed to the public for nearly a year. What was revealed quickly, fueling the worst suspicions of those who felt that the U.S. had had a hand in the 1991 coup, was that Toto Constant had been on the CIA's payroll in Port-au-Prince as an informer for several years.

Michel François decided to decamp for the Dominican Republic just after the *FRAPH* raid, taking care before leaving to arrange the rental of his house to the Dominican ambassador. Shortly thereafter, the parliament voted the amnesty called for in the Carter agreement, limiting it however to "political matters". On one of the white sentry booths on the Northeast corner of the palace, someone spray painted a graffito that read "Americans in Haiti for fifty years".

On October 10, in a ceremony outside army headquarters, Raoul Cédras stepped down. The porticoed building was surrounded by U.S. troops, and just beyond them, thousands of Haitians jeered the man they viewed as responsible for so much misery. With General Shelton by his side, Cédras passed the flag of command to Jean-Claude Duperval. Several in the crowd shouted to Shelton "You are taking away a thief and leaving another." A thrown rock shattered the rear window of Cédras' car as he left with a U.S. escort, but shots fired in the air by U.S. troops quickly restored order. Arrangements had been put in place to have both men fly to Panama before Aristide's return.

In the U.S., Jean-Bertrand Aristide was preparing his return. Accompanying him would be two planeloads of dignitaries, many of whom had sustained him in his three year exile. While crews scurried to clean up Port-au-Prince, President Aristide attended an OAS reception in his honor, a memorial service for Guy Malary, and one final meeting with Bill Clinton.

Few Haitians saw Haiti's president step onto Haitian soil at mid-day other than on television. The airport was cordoned off, and in any case, helicopters quickly whisked the president off to the Palace. There, crowds had massed expectantly since dawn, straining for a glimpse of '*tiTid*. The diminutive president, surrounded by burly security men, walked across the lawn to the palace steps, and there, from behind a bulletproof plastic shield, addressed Haiti and the world. After quoting Martin Luther King, Jr., he said "Today, in our beloved Haiti, the dream of democracy has become a reality. This restoration of democracy brings reconciliation for all, and respect for every single citizen...We all want peace. Let all weapons be silent." Then, shaking hands with General Duperval, he reviewed an honor guard. The celebrations went on late into the night.

The Haiti Jean-Bertrand Aristide returned to was even worse off than the one he had left. The Palace had been stripped of telephones, toilet bowls, air-conditioners and light fixtures. It made an appropriate symbol for the plight of the entire government. In Aristide's pocket were pledges of nearly $One billion in foreign aid over five years, but these loans would take from three to six months to materialize. In the meantime, it took approximately $15 million a month to run the government. Fortunately, USAID was able to immediately provide $15 million for operating capital.

Weapons - some estimated some 200,000 small arms of one kind and another - were still in the hands of the *macoutes*. A prime minister to relieve the long-suffering Malval had to be selected, and other appointments made. Commerce and industry had to be jump-started. For several days, Aristide stayed in seclusion, not even venturing out to Mass on Sunday.

When the appointments did come, they were good. To replace Malval, Smarck Michel was chosen. Leslie Delatour, much seasoned since his brief stint under the Duvaliers thirteen years earlier, was chosen as Governor of the Central Bank. Other cabinet appointments were broad-based. Constantly, Aristide preached the need for reconciliation and calm.

Civilian flights were restored, and Haitians poured in from abroad. American Airlines had to shrink wrap hand baggage at checkin in Miami and New York to prevent additional items being crammed into bags already bursting at the seams. As the terror, thanks to the omnipresent American troops, abated, a subdued optimism took hold.

Again though, mother nature weighed in. "Tropical Storm" Gordon, which barely grazed other islands whose eco-structures were more intact, devastated Southern Haiti on November 14. At least five hundred lives were lost, while tens of thousands were made homeless. The pretty town of Jacmel, which so often bore the brunt of these storms, was devastated by a wall of water that cascaded from the denuded watershed at its back.

Troubles, said Shakespeare, "come not singly like spies, but in battalions". After only four weeks in command, the new Army commander, Jean-Claude

Duperval, was caught skimming receipts on gun licensing fees. Forced to sack Duperval, Aristide turned to one of the few generals left - Gen. Bernard Poisson, commandant of the fire department. The scandal augured ill for the Armed Forces.

There were other tremors too. Toto Constant, the FRAPH head who had been picked up in the early October raid on *FRAPH* headquarters, failed to show up for a magistrate's hearing in early December. To the consternation of many, he showed up in New York, having entered the U.S. on a valid tourist visa. Those who were disposed to do so saw the hand of the CIA, unable to believe that a great power could act in so uncoordinated a fashion.

As 1995 began, President Aristide could well have been forgiven for wishing he was back in exile. The year literally started with a bang as dozens of former army men, angry about delays in their pay, tried to take army headquarters. There was some exchange of fire with U.S. troops, but the disturbances were quickly quelled. Not only the Duvalierists were restive. Feeling, like many of his predecessors, the heat of media scrutiny, the president moved to replace the head of the state-owned television network, only to find himself embroiled in a labor dispute with all the reporters.

The urban poor grew tired of being urged to "drink the coffee of conciliation" by Aristide, preferring to see a bit more of "the filter of justice". Impatient at the snail's pace with which judicial reforms were moving, the president replaced justice minister Mallebranche. Other institutions were long in their convalescence as well.

With legislative elections scheduled for June, the new electoral council lacked telephones and pencils. Confidence in the *CEP* was not increased when its head, Anselme Rémy, admitted in May that some one million voter registration cards seemed to have gone astray. Squatters took over any empty buildings they could find, even roosting in the shell of Ft. Dimanche. Mayor Paul lamented that there was no legal apparatus functioning to dislodge them.

In February, the Carter troika returned to inspect its handiwork. The reception it got was cool. There was no official welcoming party at the airport, and graffiti had sprung up in the city that read "Carter - Fake Democrat" and "Carter go Home". The horn of plenty of aid money that had beckoned so invitingly seemed to be always just out of reach. Burned by their experiences in the nineteen seventies, where nearly a billion dollars seemed to have been poured down a hole, international organizations tied disbursements to verifiable performance tests, often difficult for the government to meet. In particular, the IMF, in keeping with its tough prescriptions throughout the rest of the world, demanded privatization of money-losing state enterprises such as the electric company and the flour mill. Efforts to trim bloated payrolls in these companies were met by protests of Aristide's "neoliberal" program. Critics protested that the only ones who stood to gain by such sales were the elite, who alone had the capital to invest, and foreigners. Paranoia about U.S. intentions of plucking the supposedly ripe fruit of Haitian economic riches off the vine ran rampant.

Aristide continued to whittle down the army, purging the officer corps in February of four generals, and thirty-nine colonels and majors. The army was now down to a fifth of its former strength - fifteen hundred men. With all the former army men at loose ends, it was inevitable that trouble should occur. Williams Regala and Franck Romain were called in by the international police force and told to mind their p's and q's. Deprived of some of their more draconian methods of policing, Haitian police fought a losing battle against crime control. A crime wave hit Port-au-Prince. More shocking was the assassination in broad daylight of Mireille Durocher-Bertin. Fluent in English, a U.S.-schooled lawyer, she had often served as spokesperson for the junta. Three days before President Clinton was due to arrive, she was gunned down in her car. FBI agents dispatched to aid Haitian police quickly discovered that the trail went back to interior minister Mondesir Monbrun, appointed to his post after the army purge a month earlier. Aristide refused to do anything.

The U.S., its gamble having worked, was anxious to get its troops home and turn command over to the U.N. Even before Christmas, the number of American troops had been much reduced. The formal turnover was scheduled for March 31, and President Clinton came to Haiti for one day for that event. That day, despite all its troubles, Haiti, led by its president, turned out to say "thank you". When the brief visit was over, the normal chaos resumed.

Finally grasping the nettle, in April Aristide dissolved what was left of the army, leaving only the palace band. Into that vacuum trickled the first class of graduates from the kinder, gentler police academy. All 370 graduates carried a copy of the 1987 constitution in their pockets. Their presence was keenly needed. In June, after a mammoth logistical effort which inspired pride in Haitians, Haiti hosted an OAS foreign ministers meeting at the former Club Med near Montrouis. Haiti's Foreign Minister, Claudette Werleigh, was held up while driving from the capital to the conference.

As June's elections approached, the split between the FNCD and LAVALAS, in the making before the '91 coup, became final. In the initial round of voting, which the *Washington Post* described as "a triumph of muddling through", Port-au-Prince Mayor Evans Paul was defeated by communist singer Manno Charlemagne. The opposition, unhappy with the results, demanded that new elections be held, which Aristide refused to do. The Washington Office on Haiti, back to its watchdog role, concluded that the contest was "marred, but free and democratic." Aristide did use the occasion to sack *CEP* chief Rémy, who protested that he was being made a scapegoat.

Two more rounds of elections remained. The second, scheduled for December, was for Aristide's successor. There was huge sentiment in Port-au-Prince and elsewhere for the three years that the president had spent in exile to be added to the end of his term. Even some of his fiercest opponents, preferring the devil they knew, began to speculate along these lines. Such a move would, however, go directly against all promises Aristide had made to the international community and might cause political problems for President Clinton. Also, with 45% of his budget coming from foreign aid, Aristide could hardly afford to break his promises. Aristide remained mum.

At the end of September, Lavalas swept the parliamentary elections, taking seventy-one out of eighty-three seats. Marking the one year anniversary of the U.S. effort in Haiti, the Fort Lauderdale *Sun* noted that the operation had cost U.S. taxpayers nearly $600 million. U.S. troops were down to 2,000. In Washington, the restive republican congress voted to hold up further aid until receiving a "satisfactory" explanation of the Durocher-Bertin murder. In frustration, Aristide played a card from Avril's deck, sending his foreign minister off to Taiwan in an attempt to pry open their coffers and lessen slightly his dependence on the U.S.

A U.S. delegation led by Vice President Al Gore was on hand to help Aristide celebrate the October 15 anniversary of his return, and to remind him of his promise to step down as scheduled. Gore's visit was overshadowed by the resignation of Prime Minister Michel after the cabinet failed to approve steps needed to privatize state enterprises. Aristide had remained aloof from the debate, further fueling speculation about his intentions. After the swearing-in of the newly elected Lavalas-dominated parliament on October 16, the president submitted the name of his foreign minister, Claudette Werleigh, as the new prime minister. Approved, she was sworn in with her new cabinet on November 7. Aristide still had not tipped his hand. Fidgeting, several of the major parties announced that they would boycott the elections even if they were held. Former president and candidate Leslie Manigat went so far as to call the entire exercise "a hoax".

Leaving the palace after the installation of the new cabinet, two of the newly-elected parliamentarians were shot after stopping at a bank. One, a cousin of the resident, Jean-Hubert Feuillé, died of his wounds. Though the money disappeared, police suspected *macoute* involvement - a suspicion that grew when Prosper Avril, long back from Florida, made a dash for the Colombian embassy just before police arrived at his residence. The government grew furious when it learned that Avril had been in the company of an embassy official just before deciding to bolt. The embassy's bland explanation that it felt the need to routinely touch base with all sectors of society did not sit well.

At Feuillé's funeral, Aristide took off his gloves. In an impassioned eulogy, delivered in front of a grimly attentive diplomatic corps, he urged followers to "go to the neighborhoods where there are big houses and heavy weapons to disarm [the occupants]... Do not sit idly by, do not wait." Gazing at the diplomats, particularly the head of the U.N. mission and Ambassador Swing, he said "I am reminding you that until further notice there are not two or three heads of state, but just one."

Broadcast repeatedly over radio and television in the ensuing days, the eulogy had a predictable effect. Perceived opponents of the president had their homes burned, and a radio station found itself under attack. Foreigners in Gonaïves and Limbé were attacked too. The *Nouvelliste*, reflecting on the violence, said that a "shadow" had been cast on the upcoming elections. The *gourde*, already shaky, dropped by a further 16%.

Aristide rattled the international community further still on November 24 when he told a "national reconciliation" meeting at the palace that he might consider staying on. National security advisor Anthony Lake, dispatched hurriedly by Washington to take a first-hand reading in Port-au-Prince, was in the palace when riots broke out in Cité Soleil, killing four. After conveying Washington's displeasure, Lake flew North. The president broke his silence on November 27, announcing that he would indeed depart on February 7. The elections would be held as scheduled on December 17.

Fourteen candidates had registered with the CEP, representing Christian Democrats (Sylvio Claude's old party), KONAKOM, and a number of smaller groups including the Paradise party and the Virgin Mary party. The candidate of the latter declined to give biographical information, stating that it would be supplied "if heaven wished it". The heavy favorite to win was René Préval, the agronomist and bakery owner who had served in Aristide's pre-coup government. Fifty-two, Préval had been educated overseas after his parents left Haiti in the early years of Papa Doc's government. Before taking up portfolios in the government, he had played active roles in various Aristide charities such as Lafanmi Selavi - the Aristide orphanage.

Curiously, the president did not stump for the man described as his "alter-ego", but remained relatively aloof. Finally, two days before the election, in Jacmel to dedicate a bridge that replaced one washed away a year earlier by Gordon, he urged people to vote. Whether three elections in one year were too much, or whether people just assumed Lavalas would win, only 28% of the electorate exercised its franchise. Préval got some 88% of the votes cast. As a mandate, it was less than overwhelming. The election proved yet again that Haitians place loyalty in people, not institutions. In the words of Michel-Rolph Trouillot, Lavalas today "remains a loose amalgam of factions united around Mr. Aristide but unable to mature into a viable political party... The next president will also need to build support among all Haitians, not just a faction of fervent supporters. His legitimacy will depend on his willingness to include people of all classes in a debate on the country's problems."

René Préval is scheduled to be inaugurated on February 7, 1996. Foreign troops will have left the country before the year is through. In 1997, the constitutional prohibition that bars Duvalierist candidates from running for office will expire. Somewhere today, in Haiti, Santo Domingo, New York, or Paris, is a Haitian who feels that he alone can right things in his country. Whether by the constitution, or the second occupation, or the quirks of fate, he feels that that which should have been his has been deprived him. For the sake of the nation, he will feel bound by the assize of arms to take up weapons to seize his country's leadership.

Daniel O'Connell once said that the history of Ireland could be traced like a wounded man through a crowd, by the blood.

That is the history of Haiti.

Are the Haitian people, living endlessly in a perverse continuum, oblivious of their past, doomed always to repeat a history that is written in blood?

FOOTNOTES - CHAPTER 16

1. In one memorable episode, a crowd carried around a dog dressed in a *milicien's* cap and scarf. As the dog looked quite calm amidst the disturbance going on around him (it was a *milicien's* uniform, not *fillette lalo'*), one may assume that it was his master's shoulders on which he sat and that neither he nor his master were in peril.

2. One consequence of the destruction in the "Voodoo Wars" was the demand, granted nine years later by President Aristide, that Haiti have a national *péristyle* consecrated to the conservation and preservation of objects that formed so important a part of the national patrimony.

3. Curiously, Rue Lorimer Denis, a small side street on the way to the airport, kept its name despite the role Denis had in teaching Duvalier about some of Voodoo's finer points. Perhaps the fact that he had died at the outset of the regime kept people from making the connection.

Appendices

———

Voodoo

Chronology

Glossary

Voodoo

It is a mystery religion of great complexity and splendor, and those who are its priests are powerful men.

- Francis Huxley

Except for their chains, all that the slaves of St. Domingue could carry from Africa came in their hearts. Here they brought with them old rites and beliefs and sure and certain knowledge of a pantheon of gods whom they called *loa*. *Papa Legba*, guardian of the crossroads; *Damballah* the serpent; *Agoué*, god of the sea; *Ogun Badagris*, god of war who protects his followers from bullets - these and myriad other loa came to St. Domingue aboard the slave ships from Guinea and above all Dahomey. The manner of their worship was summed up in a Dahomean word *"Vodun,"*(1) meaning "God" or "Spirit."'

But Voodoo, deeply African though it is, is not simply the transported ritual of Guinea and Dahomey. In the New World the slaves were taught by Catholic chaplains, the *curés des noirs,* about a certain God of the *blancs* whom they addressed as *"Bon-Dieu."* Among the saints who served *Bon-Dieu* were beings who possessed the attributes of the *loa* and thus could be similarly propitiated. In the slaves' minds there appeared no contradiction in coming to terms with powers, whether African or Christian, who they believed ruled the universe.

To read the history of Haiti while ignoring Voodoo would be comparable to studying the Middle East with no prior knowledge of Judaism, Christianity, or Islam.

Legba

The Cross and the Snake

One immediately associates Haiti with Voodoo. But Voodoo also journeyed throughout the islands of the Caribbean, to the Southern United States, and to South America. However, apart from Brazil, where Macumba (a Brazilian variant) flourishes, Haiti continues to provide Voodoo its most fertile soil.

Voodoo as it now exists of course did not spring into being all at once. It evolved and took form during the decades of Haiti's isolation after the great revolt of the slaves had won them their freedom.

An animistic religion, Voodoo is a tenacious blend of West African beliefs and practices infused, by historical coincidence, with hedge Catholicism. It acknowledges one God above all but works through a vast army of tutelary spirits, or *loa*, credited with power to control the forces of nature and the universe and affect the health, wealth, and happiness of all mortals.

The *houngan* (Voodoo priest) and *mambo* (Voodoo priestess) are the interpreters and servants of the *loa*. Each is hierarchic head of his or her *société* (following) and *houmfort* (cult center) and deals directly with the spirits served.

In the manner of all religions, Voodoo helps its followers over the hurdles of life: being born, dying, and the infinite variety of obstacles that lie between. It has the added bonus of giving a voice to the departed. In the *wêté mò nan d'lo* (bringing back the dead from under the water) ceremony, the soul returns to complain in no uncertain terms if its wishes have not been carried out.

Voodoo worshipers believe that God is present and all-powerful, but too concerned with the affairs of the universe to be approached directly; hence the *loa* who form His cabinet. *Bon-Dieu-Bon* (God is good) and *si Dié vlé* (God willing) are frequent and fervent phrases on the lips of peasant and townsman alike.

Numerous Haitians shun and deplore Voodoo, yet cannot ignore its existence. Some, at least atavistically and subconsciously, fear it but Voodoo turn to it for help in extreme situations. It has frequently been said that Voodoo has more enemies in public and more friends in private than anything else in Haiti.

Although many Catholics want no part of Voodoo, Voodooisants have no difficulty in commingling Catholic practices and liturgy with their own. Saints and Virgins, as well as the *loa,* are regularly invoked at the beginning of a Voodoo *service* (ceremony), and chromolithographs of them hang over Voodoo altars. The brightly hued posters are, however, valued primarily for the loa with whom each saint is identified. The Virgin Mary is equated with *Maîtresse Erzulie,* goddess of love, St. George on his charger with *Ogun Badagris,* god of war. The great feasts of the Christian year are closely syncretized in Voodoo. If one God reigns supreme, why not use all possible approaches to him?

*Damballah
and Aida Wedo*

Damballah the Serpent

A small cake of flour: a little bit of butter; if you obey the snake you and
yours shall thrive.

- Proverb of the Snake tribe in the Punjab

Live snakes seldom play a part in Voodoo ceremonies today. They have been
virtually eliminated or relegated to a purely ceremonial role. However, the
importance of *Damballah,* the snake god, has not diminished.

Moreau de Saint-Méry described Voodoo of the eighteenth century as the cult
of a supernatural being incarnate in the form of a nonvenomous serpent whose
oracles were interpreted by a priest or priestess and who was the focal point of
all slave gatherings.

Ophiolatry, the worship of snakes, plays an important part in the mythology
of many cultures, but it was in West Africa that the nonvenomous python was
especially venerated for its strength, its markings, its putative wisdom, and the
belief that its bite afforded protection against poisonous snakes. Wydah, today
part of Guinea, became a huge slave emporium after its conquest by the
Dahomeans in 1724. It was the center of African ophiolatry and the site of a
temple to *Dangbé,* the good serpent. Thousands of slaves were shipped from
Wydah annually, packed in the fetid holds of slave ships to make the dread
Middle Passage to an unknown destination. Those disembarking in St.
Domingue, an island of nonvenomous snakes, may have felt some measure of
hope and reassurance to find that *Dangbé,* or *Damballah,* the serpent *loa,* had
not forsaken them.

Marassas

The Voodoo Pantheon

The *loa* love us, protect us, and guard us; they tell us what is
happening to our relatives, who live far away. . .
- Haitian peasant.

Damballah and his wife, *Aida-Wédo,* were not the only *loa* to come to the New
World. The slaves - Congos, Bantus, Fons, Ibos, Yorubas, Mondongues, Aradas
- all imported their own tribal beliefs, customs, and rituals, some similar, others
varying widely (2). The acknowledged predominant Dahomean influence on
Haitian Voodoo has been attributed to the Fons, who were noted for their
bravery and intelligence. *Vodun* is a word of the Fon dialect.

Basically there are two groups, or families, of *loa,* "Rada" and "Petro." A
further existing subclassification, *"Congo," "Ibo," "Mondongue,"* and others,
is too esoteric for general consideration.

Rada stems from the ancient kingdom of Alladah or Dahomey, and includes
most Nigerian and Dahomean *loa. Petro* takes its name from Dom Pedro, said
to have been an eighteenth-century *houngan* of ill repute in St. Domingue who
later became a *loa* in his own right. Most *Petro loa* are indigenous to the New
World, whereas *Rada* came with the slaves from Africa.

Milo Rigaud, one of Voodoo's greatest authorities, claimed a hundred-page
volume would not suffice to catalogue all the *loa.* Like the manner in which they
are *servi* (served or worshiped), they vary from region to region and from
houmfort to *houmfort.* New *loa,* some the spirits of powerful dead *houngans* or
mambos or influential members of the community, appear without warning.

Others are forgotten or retire to a permanent ancestral niche *nan guinée* (in African Guinea).

There are *loa*, especially the *Guédés* (spirits of death), with improbable names such as *Guédé-'ti-Pêté* (Little-Fart), *Guédé-Bon-Poussière-de-la-Croix* (Good-Dust-from-the-Cross), or *'ti-Puce-nan-dlo* (Little-Flea-in-the-Water). A Southern *loa*, *Taureau-trois-grènes* (Bull-with-three-balls) causes those whom he possesses to immediately display triple powers by leaping on the nearest bystander.

Général Cleirmil, a *mulâtre*, is the special protector of light-skinned children born to darker parents and has been known to possess and punish men who doubted their wives' fidelity. There is even a U.S. Marine *loa*, recruited during the American occupation. When he makes an appearance, he speaks with a strong American accent and demands bourbon and corned beef.

Of the *loa* in the Voodoo pantheon, *Legba* is invoked first. Like the Lares Compitales of the Romans, he is *Maîte-Carrefours* (Guardian of the Crossroads). It is he who opens the gate and points the way to communication with the other world. He is always called on first by *houngan* or *mambo*, who, shaking the *asson* (sacred rattle), chants: *"Papa Legba, ouvré barrière pou' moin!"* (Papa Legba, open the gate for me!). *Legba* is represented as a lame old man with a crutch, but his great physical strength is demonstrated in the violence of his possessions. He is one *loa* common to most African tribes, and was also long popular in Louisiana, where he was known as *Papa Lebat*.

As in all animistic faiths, Voodooisants are convinced that the elements must be specially propitiated. The sea, as well as all those who go down to it in ships, is the domain of *Agoué*. Archibald Dalzell, an English slave-trader writing a firsthand account of eighteenth-century Dahomey, refers to *Agoué* as the generic title of the general-in-chief of the armies. In Haiti, *Agoué* is depicted wearing the uniform of an admiral. His symbol is a ship, and sacrifices to him are frequently made at sea. He is revered by all seafarers who look to him for protection. His followers understood that visiting foreign men-of-war that fired gun salutes in Port-au-Prince harbor did so in *Agoué's* honor.

Agoué's female consort, *La Sirène*, is represented as a luscious mermaid rising from the depths, fish in one hand and *lambi* (conch shell) in the other. Some consider her as an aspect of the great *Maîtresse Erzulie, or Erzulie-Fréda-Dahomey,* the most powerful of the female *loa*, who symbolizes at one and the same time beauty, love, jealousy, and vengeance. *Erzulie* frequently demands marriage of the young men who serve her, and woe betide the human wife who tries to claim her husband's attentions on days sacred to the *loa*. Some *houmforts* have a special chamber set aside for *Maîtresse,* where the bed is always made up with fresh, hand-embroidered linen sheets, and the dressing table is set with her favorite toilet articles, cosmetics, and perfumes.

There are other *Erzulies* less fortunate. *Gran' Erzulie,* though well disposed, is bent by age and crippled by arthritis. *Erzulie-gé-rouge* (Erzulie of the red eyes) is a hideous hag who deals primarily in evil. The features of those whom she possesses are contorted beyond recognition, and they claw at themselves drawing blood in their frenzy.

Ogun is the god of war in Haiti, as in Nigeria and in Brazil (where any piece of scrap iron may be considered an incarnation of him). He may appear as *Ogun Féraille, Ogun Badagris* (for the African town captured by the Dahomeans in 1783), *Ogun Balindjo, Batala,* or others; some consider each *Ogun* as a separate and distinct *loa.* Those possessed by *Ogun* (whose color is red) don a scarlet kerchief, shirt, and kepi, brandish a sword or machete, chomp on cigars, and call loudly for rum.

Cousin Zaca's special province is agriculture. He wears the *gros bleu* (heavy blue denim) of the Haitian peasant, carries a *macoute* (knapsack) in which he gathers herbs with magical healing powers, and puffs on a clay pipe.

The *Guédés* are a large family. The distinguished Haitian scholar Louis Maximilien links them to the cult of Osiris. Others feel that they are exclusively *loa pays (loa* belonging to the country). They are mischievous and salacious beings who frequently appear uninvited at *cérémonies.* They dress in black, their voices (like Dr. Duvalier's on occasion) are high-pitched and nasal, and their dances are unabashedly erotic, sometimes emphasized by the use of a gigantic wooden phallus. An altar to the *Guédés* is usually set apart from the rest of the *houmfort.* Occasionally it is a simulated tomb on which offerings are placed.

Outside Haiti, *Baron Samedi* has become the best known of the *loa* because of his widely publicized association with François Duvalier (or vice versa). In the 1960s the somber dress and owlish glasses of *Baron Samedi*/Duvalier were a commonplace in the world press although the then president usually wore a black homburg rather than the tophat or bowler dear to *Baron. The Barons* (there is also *Baron La-Croix and Baron Cimetière)* are closely identified with the *Guédés* and often thought to be part of the *Guédé* family.

Baron's emblems are a skull and crossbones, his tools those of the gravedigger. There is a legend that a woman who dies a virgin must be deflowered before burial or she risks rape by the *Barons. Baron Samedi* lives in cemeteries, and traffics with the souls of the dead. Possessions by him are not uncommon during funerals.

Not only Voodooisants, but the other *loa* recognize the importance of *Damballah.* They salute him as they pass and ask his permission to grant favors sought by humans. The *poteau mitan* (central post of the *houmfort)* is sacred to him and is frequently painted with intertwined snakes or with his colors.

Marassas (twins), living or dead, are said to have great power for both good and evil and must be properly propitiated. During ceremonies they are called on immediately after *Legba,* for they too belong to Africa and are able to point the way. A family with twins is obliged to hold a special *service* for them at least once a year. *Marassas* are always served first. Their special dishes are kept on the *pé* (altar) before a picture of Cosmas and Damian, the martyr twins.(3) It is well to keep a few pieces of candy or roasted peanuts in these dishes at all times.

If displeased, the *Marassas* behave like spoiled children and delight in afflicting their parents with a variety of ills.

Marassas are also capable of affecting cures. Odette Rigaud tells of a remarkable recovery from a serious illness made by a small girl whose grandmother had complied with the *Marassas'* demand for a tureen of soup made with a whole chicken, thus proving the interfaith efficacy of chicken soup.

The bad Voodoo spirits are less well known than the great *Rada loa,* or *mystères.* People who have dealings with them incline to secrecy. Mainly *Petro, Congo,* or *Mondongue loa,* they are said to be extremely powerful, and the price for their services is high. *Angelsou* has earned the nickname "Bucket of Blood" as those whom he possesses are destined to become murderers. *Marinette-Bwa-Chech* (Marinette-ofthe-dry-arms) appears in the form of a screech owl, dwells in the depths of the forest, and delights in boasting of her evil deeds. *Général Mounantiou* (man-in-the-hole) demands, in return for his favors, a *Mondongue* ceremony at which a dog is sacrificed according to his blood-curdling specifications. The rites of *Loa Criminelle* are as violent as he himself.

Some Voodooisants believe the evil *loa* turn themselves into *bakas* from time to time. *Bakas* are ferocious, red-eyed creatures capable of assuming whatever form they fancy. The noted anthropologist Harold Courlander tells of a *baka* who changed himself into a bicycle and was seen traveling alone, at night, on the road from Port-au-Prince to Léogane. A rumor current in Port-au-Prince in the 1960s had the Liberian ambassador metamorphosing himself nightly into a black cat and prowling the town. A startled housewife who seized a broom and attempted to shoo the animal out of her house was reproved by her husband with: "No, no my dear, we must treat *Monsieur l'Ambassadeur* with more respect."

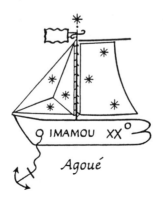

Agoué

Voodoo

Country *houmfort*, nineteenth century, at Grande Saline, with pictures of the *loa. Library of Congress Below:* Voodoo sacred objects, left to right: *govi*(jar in which spirits live); *coué* (calabash ikon) of *Général Mounantiou; hounsi* beads; *paquet congo* (magic package with feathers); embellished cross; *coué* of *Maîtresse Erzulie; asson* (sacred rattle, in front of *Erzulie*). *Coués* are by renowned primitive painter and *houngan*, André Pierre. *Heinl Collection*

Houngan and Houmfort

Sanctuary, clubhouse, dance-hall, hospital, theater, chemist's shop, music
hall, court and council chamber in one.

- J. Jahn

In rural areas the *houmfort* is the center of the community clustered around
it, and the presiding *houngan* or *mambo* may be called on to provide roughly
any of the services one might seek in the places Jahn mentions. The task is an
arduous, though frequently lucrative, one.

At the turn of the century Eugène Aubin (4) wrote: "The foundation of
Voodoo is found in the family. Each family head, clothed with a family
priesthood, honors the spirit of the ancestors and their protecting *loa.*"

The assumption of the *asson* marks the elevation to the priesthood. The role
of *houngan or mambo* can be, but is not necessarily, hereditary. A *hounsi*
(initiate and assistant) may rise from the ranks, the call may come in a dream,
or the *loa* may announce their intentions at the birth of a child. A breech birth
is considered the omen of an exceptional career. Superior powers are essential
for those who wish to take the *asson*, notably the gift of *quatres gé* (four eyes),
which indicates the ability to see into the future.(5)

The would-be *houngan* makes his wishes known to an already established
priest and must submit to a period of detailed instruction followed by ceremonies
of purification and initiation.

Some *houngans* set themselves up in business claiming to have received full
connaissance (second sight) and training directly from the *loa.* They are
regarded as decidedly suspect by those who have traveled a more orthodox
route.

Once established, *houngan* or *mambo* reigns supreme in his or her own
houmfort, though remaining on good terms with colleagues and frequently
attending services at other establishments. The greater the knowledge and power
of a *houngan* is reputed to be, the more followers will be attracted to his
société.

Speculating on the motivation for becoming a Voodoo priest, French
anthropologist Alfred Métraux felt that faith, ambition, love of power, and greed
each plays a part, but added: "Priestly vocation is none the less interpreted as
a call from the supernatural world which cannot be disregarded with impunity."

First assistant to the *houngan* is the *laplace* (from *général de la place* or local
commander-in-chief). He is responsible for maintaining discipline during
ceremonies and leads all processions brandishing sword or machete.

The *hounsis* are the servants of the temple. They perform necessary chores,
make preparations for and take part in services, and obey the commands of

houngan or *mambo* with a humility that might be expected of a novice in a convent. If their conduct fails to meet requirements, the loa, acting through the *houngan* possessed, may reprove them sharply, though *mambo* and *houngan* can also be stern disciplinarians in their own right.

Top *hounsi* is the *houngeniçon* (choir mistress), whose task demands no little musical knowledge and talent. She is responsible for all singing during ceremonies, recognizes the *loa* as they appear, and indicates the appropriate songs in their honor.

Houmforts vary widely according to the degree of prosperity and renown enjoyed by their leaders. The distinctive feature is the *peristyle,* a shed, sometimes partly walled or banked by benches on three sides, protected from the elements by a roof of thatch or corrugated tin. The roof is supported by the *poteau mitan,* a large wooden post down which the loa descend during ceremonies. The *poteau mitan* has great ritual significance. It is the focal point of all services, and around it are traced the vèvès (symbolic designs) of the *mystères* involved.

The *caille mystère* (sanctuary) opens directly onto one end of the *peristyle.* This is the abode of the *loa* served, and one enters only on specific invitation from *houngan* or mambo. Inside are one or more *pés,* some with special sinks for *Damballah* and the water *loa.*(6)

To the uninitiated eye the *pé* (altar) is covered with a truly eclectic collection of objects: govis (earthenware jars) symbolizing the *loa; cruches* (pitchers) from which holy water is poured; *pots têtes* (covered jars) containing hair and nail parings of initiates; *pierres-tonnerre* (thunder-stones - actually Arawak stone ax-heads reputed to have magical powers); the flags of the society; the multicolored necklaces of the *hounsis*; the sword of *laplace.*

If *Ogun* is served, his sword may be stuck in the earth in front of the *pé.* On the wall above are prints or paintings of the *loa* or of the saints with which they are identified - St. Patrick for *Damballah,* St. Anthony of Padua for *Legba,* St. George for *Ogun.* In one *houmfort* a large photo of Admiral William F. Halsey (U.S.N.), in full uniform, was puzzling until identified as *Agoué.*

Bottles of wine and liqueurs to suit the varied tastes of the *loa* are also provided in the more opulent *houmforts;* champagne for *Maitresse Erzulie, clairin pimenté* (white rum with hot peppers) for the *Guédés,* the best Barbancourt for *Ogun.* Mme.Ile-de-Vert, prosperous *mambo* of the Cul-de-Sac region, with a large following in Cuba, the Dominican Republic, and the United States, always kept several bottles of Manischewitz in readiness, though she was unable or unwilling to reveal which *mystère* had this particular preference.

Country *houmforts* are usually surrounded by a courtyard planted with *arbres reposoirs* (sacred trees), around which certain ceremonies are held and at whose bases offerings are made. The trees are easily recognizable by their protective circle of large stones and strips of colored cloth tied to their branches.

Everyday life centering on a large *houmfort* provides ample material for a
Haitian Breughel. Mothers wash babies in tin tubs, laundry hangs over the sides
of the *peristyle,* women pound corn or prepare vegetables. *Hounsis* sweep and
garnish while the *houngan* is offering a visitor a cup of coffee. Small boys kick
around a greatly prized empty Clorox bottle. Perpetually hungry dogs sniff for
scraps. Tethered goats and chickens watch, blissfully unaware of their destiny.
There is no suggestion of the bloody or the bizarre. Yet bloody and bizarre are
the religious esoterica that have earned Voodoo its sinister reputation.

Ogoun Badagris

Blood Sacrifice

Ye shall eat the flesh of the mighty, and drink the blood of the princes of the
earth, of rams, of lambs, and of goats, of bullocks . . .
- Ezekiel 39:18

The greater efficacy of a blood offering as measured against one consisting of
the fruits of the field is demonstrated in the story of Cain and Abel, and the
pages of the Old Testament are drenched with sacrificial blood. According to
anthropologist E. 0. James: "The fundamental principal throughout is the same;
the giving of life to preserve life, death being merely a means of liberating
vitality." Sacrifice played a dominant role in early Hindu ritual, too. The Vedas
recommend that the rite be unending lest the gods be offended. African tribes
included both animal and human sacrifices in their rituals. Prisoners of war
continued to serve as thank-offerings long after the slave trade provided a
profitable alternative for disposing of them. Arriving in the New World, the
Spaniards found human sacrifice on a monumental scale among the Aztecs,
Mayans, and Incas.
    Voodoo does involve the sacrifice of animals ranging from doves, chickens,
and turkeys to pigs, goats, sheep, and, sometimes, a bull. *Cérémonies* are

frequently referred to as *mangé-loa* because they provide food for the gods, but also for the humans who serve them. Some *loa* are content with a *mangé-sec,* in which no blood is spilt.

Haitian writers react with hypersensitivity to the very mention of human sacrifice and indignantly dismiss the trial of Jeanne and Congo Pellé and the *Affaire de Bizoton* as isolated incidents. Yet it would be strange if sacrifices involving "the goat without horns" had not sometimes occurred.

In 1889 Sir Spenser St. John (former British minister to Haiti whose *Black Republic* is a vivid farrago of half-truths and hearsay laced with unfriendly though sometimes painfully accurate and penetrating judgments) gave the *Affaire de Bizoton* international notoriety that has never wholly quieted down. St. John propagated two notions that have dogged Haiti and Voodoo ever since: (1) that Voodoo is a dark and bloody rite whose central and dominant liturgies involve human sacrifice; and (2) that cannibalism was rife in Haiti. Neither idea is true, but, in the context of the nineteenth century, each appeared believable.

Until the French occupation of Dahomey in 1894, large-scale human sacrifice occurred regularly at the funerals and anniversaries of all persons of rank. According to a French government report, the victims were beheaded and their warm blood spread on the tomb of the ancestor to be honored. When a king died, his wives, sometimes as many as 600, would poison themselves so that he might avail himself of their services in the next world.

The word "cannibal" stems from *"canibalis"* or *"caribalis,"* recorded by Columbus for the man-eating Carib Indians of the Lesser Antilles. Of the slaves brought to the New World, Moreau de Saint-Méry wrote that the *Mondongues* were fierce cannibals greatly feared by the other tribes. It would, however, seem unlikely that they were the only group who ever partook of human flesh.

Alexander Murray, British minister to Haiti in 1910, helped perpetuate the "goat without horns" legend by reporting to the Foreign Office that on special occasions children were sacrificed; he wrote that a Haitian colleague justified it to him as follows:

> You condemn our human sacrifices, but Abraham was about to sacrifice his son when he saw the ram caught by his horns in a thicket; we also sacrifice a goat instead of a child on ordinary occasions. We have our solemn feasts at which we eat human flesh; your priests tell you to believe that it is the body of Christ that you partake of at Communion.

J.-N. Léger, one of the most outraged Haitian denunciators of foreign reports of anthropophagy (ritual cannibalism), maintained that Haitians "are not given to cannibalism because they are too hospitable." Verschueren, a Belgian priest who spent his life in Haiti, rejoined, "No doubt they are hospitable, but it is in the Haitian character to move with ease from extreme goodness to the greatest excesses."

Cousin Zaca

Possession

Among most uncivilized populations, as among civilized peoples, certain
ecstatic conditions are regarded as divine possession or as union with the
Divine.

- James H. Leuba

Like sacrifice, possession is neither a new nor a unique phenomenon. We
speak of it routinely. "He is very self-possessed" (in control of himself and his
actions). Or "she acts like one possessed" (unaware of what she is doing or
under control of a supernatural force).

The Christian saints who sought union with God through prayer, fasting, and
meditation, who heard voices, had visions, received the stigmata, and levitated,
were considered to be imbued with the Holy Spirit. Others less fortunate, or
more flamboyant in their manifestations, were pronounced possessed by the
Devil and were burned at the stake. The decision as to whether the voices heard
were those of God or the Devil was an ecclesiastical one fraught with human
fallibility.

Voodooisants generally fear and avoid possession by evil spirits but welcome
the *loa* in good standing. The gods are happy when the people are happy, and
they show their approval by appearing with increasing
frequency.

Possession takes place when the *loa* mounts his *choual* (literally horse; in this
case human subject) and the personality of the mount is subordinated to that of
the rider. The term was in common use in Europe during the Middle Ages,

when, at a witches' Sabbath, the Devil would mount his victims. It remains current among the *Zars* of Ethiopia, many of whose beliefs, customs, and traditions are strikingly similar to Haitian Voodoo.

The *loa* may choose to manifest themselves anywhere, at any time, but a *service* obviously provides an inviting setting.

Take the interminable hours consumed by the chanting of the *Action de Grace* (Litany of the Saints), a habitual preamble to most services, the hypnotic beat of the drums, the heat, the fumes of *clairin*, the general atmosphere of excited anticipation; add long hours of fasting to the pervasive malnutrition found in the Haitian peasant - and you have the ingredients clinically necessary to produce a state of modified consciousness.

Dr. Louis Mars and Dr. J.-C. Dorsainvil, both of whom have done extensive research on the subject of possession, see it respectively as a "schizoid process of mystical appearance," and a form of neurosis to which certain members of the same family will have a marked predisposition. Others fascinated by the phenomenon regard it variously as a need for self-transcendence; an attention-getter; an opportunity to act out fantasies; a chance to shed responsibility (a *houngan* whose advice, given while possessed, goes sour, can blame it on the loa), mass hysteria, or masochism (in some cases the *loa* will violently punish his horse). Aldous Huxley adds:

> In primitive religions prolonged rhythmic movement is very commonly resorted to for the purpose of inducing a state of infra-personal and sub-human ecstacy . . . Sporadic outbursts of jigging and swaying . . . generally occur in times of trouble following wars, pestilence, famines and are most common where malaria is endemic.

Voodoo is a danced religion, and Haiti has never known more than a brief period of respite from the Four Horsemen.

When a *loa* is about to appear, his *choual* is seized with violent convulsions, lurches, groans, staggers, becomes drenched in sweat, and has to be restrained from falling. The *gros bon ange* (good big angel) that dwells regularly in all beings is driven out to make room for the *mystère*. Once the identity of the new arrival has been established, the *houngeniçon* directs the *hounsis* in the appropriate songs to the accompaniment of an intensified roll of the drums. If *Agoué* is present, he seizes the paddle kept in readiness for him and appears to be rowing vigorously. *Ogun Badagris* will call for rum complaining, *"Grènes moin fret"* (My testicles are cold), proposition any attractive woman who catches his eye, or grasp a red-hot iron from the fire without flinching. *Damballah* hisses instead of speaking so that the *houngan* must interpret his message. He either writhes on the ground or swarms up the nearest tree. At a *cérémonie* near

Arcahaie two of the authors witnessed a *Damballah* possession where the *choual* slithered rapidly up a seventy-five-foot tree and lay coiled in the vines at the top. Possessions last everywhere from a few minutes to several hours, sometimes with one *loa* succeeding the other. The *loa* make no sexual distinction in their choice of mount. A frail *hounsi* may appear as an obscenity-spewing Ogun, or a capricious *Guédé* may make his subject don women's clothes and stick a *calabasse* (large gourd) under the skirts to simulate pregnancy. Once the *loa* has departed, the mount appears fatigued and bewildered.

Maîtresse Erzulie

A Thin Veil of Secrecy and Discretion

While few, if any of the white men who are at present on the island have witnessed the sacrifice of "the goat without horns," it is the easiest thing in the world to assist at the preliminaries of a Voodoo feast.

- Stephen Bonsal

What was true for Bonsal in 1912 remains amply so more than eighty years later, despite the relish with which foreign visitors describe their Voodoo experiences as unique. Attendance at an actual *cérémonie* does require an introduction from a friend of the host *mambo* or *houngan*. A favorite con game is that of the chauffeur-guide who will offer, always for a substantial fee, to take the visitor to a highly secret rite never before witnessed by a *blanc*, then, with the connivance of a *bocor*, whip up whatever erotic absurdities he thinks will suit his client's fancy.

During the occupation, the Marines - with strong prompting from elite Catholic presidents Dartiguenave and Borno - interpreted literally and enforced Article 408 of Haiti's Code Penal prohibiting Voodoo practices, and the *loa* went underground, or under water. They were forced to beat an even more vigorous retreat in the 1940s, when the Catholic Church, in conjunction with President Lescot, also an elite Catholic *mulâtre,* mounted an all-out campaign against the *houmforts.* Temples were destroyed, artifacts burned, and drums silenced, but not for long. With the advent of President Estimé, the dancers and drummers of the Troupe Folklorique gained enthusiastic local and later international acclaim, and the *loa* returned triumphant. Voodoo dances have since been a feature of virtually every nightclub act in Port-au-Prince, while a greatly curtailed but reasonable facsimile of a *service is* regularly staged for tourists in the capital. It includes drumming, singing, frenzied dancing, sacrificial chickens, *hounsis* chomping on glass bottles, and a variety of possessions, some of which are no doubt real. In 1995, President Aristide, the former priest, even agreed with the demands of those who demanded the establishment of a national *peristyle* to preserve voodoo artifacts against increasing forays by intolerant foreign missionaries.

Commitment to the *loa* begins in the womb. A woman consults a *houngan* as soon as she is aware of her pregnancy, offers a *mangé-sec* for a safe delivery, and may request a charm for protection against the evil eye. After parturition, all of the family *loa* are invoked. On Christmas Eve, babies are brought to the *houmfort* to be dedicated to the *Gran' Enfant Jesus* (Great Christ Child) as well as to their guardian *loa.* The service is one of great poignancy: the naked infants are presented to the *houngan,* lifted to the four points of the compass, then dipped in a bath of freshly pounded, sweet-smelling herbs and grasses.

Participation in the affairs of the *société* does not cease with death and the important *dessounin* ceremony that liberates the *loa maite-tête* (principal *loa*) from the head of the deceased. A further step comes a year later, when the soul of the dead is called back from its sojourn under the water, sometimes compared to a period in purgatory. After that event ancestors who fail to become *loa* must be fed, nurtured, respected, and consulted in important family matters.

There are services of supplication, services of *remerciement* (thanks), services of atonement, *lavé-tête* (ceremonial washing of the head in initiation), *kanzo* (highest rank of *hounsi* reached by ordeal through fire). There are *mangé-yams* (feast of the yams), *mangé-morts* (feast for the dead), *mangé-Marassas.* A most important ceremony is the one at which the drums are baptized. The rites are almost as numerous as the loa served and there are many regional variations and interpretations.

An important *service* for *Cousin Zaca* held near Croix-des-Bouquets in March of 1960 typifies such an occasion in a wealthy *houmfort.* The *cérémonie,* attended by *houngans* and *mambos* from as far away as Thomazeau and Verettes, lasted three days and three nights, during the course of which six chickens, a goat, and a bull were sacrificed.

At nightfall the faithful gather in the *peristyle* for the *Action de Grâce.* As the name of each saint, virgin, or *loa* is chanted by the *prèt savane* (hedge priest) the congregation responds, *"Priez pou nous"* (Pray for us). Cornmeal *vèvès* are traced around the *poteau mitan* and greetings exchanged between visiting *houngans and mambos* and their host. The salutations are highly stylized, accomplished in a dance form that has strong traces of the minuet and inspires an eerie deja vu of house slaves watching their French masters dance far from the court of Versailles.

Greetings accomplished, the *hounsis,* preceded by *laplace* waving his sword, emerge from the *caille mystère* bearing the richly embroidered flags that are the pride of each *société.* The choir chants as the flag party salutes the *poteau mitan,* the cardinal points of the compass, the drums, and all visiting dignitaries. The sword is presented to each guest, who kisses the hilt as a sign of respect and fidelity.

Libations are poured by the visiting priests to the *vèvè,* the drums, and the *poteau,* which each priest kisses three times.

Possessions may now occur at any time. They are carefully watched and controlled by the *houngan,* and uninvited *loa* may be asked to leave. As the moment of sacrifice approaches the tempo of the drums increases and possessions multiply.

The sacrificial animal has been carefully chosen, prepared, bathed, scented, and draped in the colors of the *loa* to whom it is being offered. The sacrifice cannot take place until the bewildered beast has eaten some of the food placed on the *vèvè.* The manner of sacrifice is determined by the rite. Goats, pigs, and bulls are first castrated; then their throats are slit. Some of the blood is caught in a bowl, later to be mixed with various spices and fed to each member of the family offering the *service.* The legs and wings of fowl are generally first broken and their heads wrenched off. Afterward they are plucked and cooked by the *hounsis.* The first and choicest portions of all food must be buried for the *loa.*

Marriage to a *loa* is a serious undertaking though not a solemn occasion. The human bride or groom promises to set aside one day a week for the *loa* who has chosen him or her. A typical wedding service took place at a *houmfort* in La Saline on 11 November 1961, when a *hounsi* became the bride of *Guédé-Nibo.* The ceremony was performed by a suitably vested prèt *savane,* who read the marriage contract and advised the couple as to their martial duties. The bride wore purple *(Guédé's* color) and carried a bouquet of yellow roses. The groom *(houngan* Nicolas possessed by *Guédé-Nibo)* was resplendent in a purple silk shirt, cowboy hat, and boots. At the reception that followed, the guests were served a large yellow wedding cake, champagne, *cremas* (a thick sweet drink popular in Haiti), and salted coffee. With the pop of each champagne cork, new *Guédés* appeared to join the fun. *Guédés* are never restrained in their behavior, and the possessions left little to the imagination. The party ended when the bride and groom withdrew into the *caille mystère*.

Dessounin is the ceremony at which a person's principal *loa* is released from his head after death and transferred to another member of the family, to a *govi* or *pot tête*, or set free. Opinions on this vary widely, but it is agreed that the *loa* must be released from the body or vengeance will be wreaked on the family. Preferably the *service* takes place immediately after death.

Wêté mò nan d'leau is celebrated a year after death, when the soul of a powerful *houngan* or other person of distinction in the community is called back from a temporary sojourn under the water to speak with and be consulted by the living. Once returned, the soul is placed in a *govi* and may later become a *loa*. At a 1962 *wêté mo* for a drummer famous throughout the Cul-de-Sac, a tub of water mixed with herbs and liquors was placed under a small tent next to the *poteau mitan*. Following the usual preliminaries, permission to make contact with the dead was asked of *Baron Samedi*. Drumming and singing filled the air until midnight, when a line of white-clad *hounsis* emerged from the *caille mystère*, swaying and chanting as they held on their heads draped *govis* prepared to receive the returning soul or souls. (Extra *govis* are provided for strange spirits who may present themselves and ask for help, in which case a collection is made and given to the *houngan* for their salvation).

Prostrate on mats before the tent, the *hounsis* held their *govis* under the flap while they themselves were completely covered with sheets. The *houngan*, seated on a small chair, had his head inside the tent. The drumming ceased and all lights were extinguished simultaneously. An oppressive silence was broken by a gurgling, gasping sound: the soul had returned. After exchanging amenities with the officiating *houngan,* the late drummer proceeded to berate his daughter for failing to visit him in the hospital. Her sobbing *"pardon papa"* was grumblingly accepted. Other relatives were praised or reprimanded and detailed instruction on the care and feeding of the drums was given.

The foregoing are but a random sampling of *cérémonies* attended by the authors. There are detailed, firsthand accounts of virtually every type of *service* by anthropologists, both Haitian and foreign. Katherine Dunham, a true Voodoo initiate, writes autobiographically of her *lavé-tête* (baptism). It remains for a native-born *houngan or mambo* to publish his or her memoirs - maybe a literary *loa* will materialize to guide his or her pen.

Baron Samedi

Magic and Spells

It is singularly difficult to define the frontier where religion ends and magic begins.

- Jean Price-Mars

Most houngans *sé deux mains* (serve with both hands) or are at one and the same time priest and magician. Despite attention paid to the dead, Voodoo is essentially a religion of the here rather than the hereafter. If *a houngan* is thought to have the power to make life on this earth more bearable or pleasant, then he is worth consulting and his methods should not be questioned too closely. He must be able to counteract spells placed on his followers or to turn the spell against the rival who conjured it. Under such a system one man's meat cannot fail at times to be very literally another man's poison. The average Voodooisant believes implicitly in magic yet claims to make a distinction between white magic, supposedly harmless, and black, which is acknowledged to be evil. Little is said about the infinite shades of gray that lie in between. White magic provides love philters, offers insurance against failure (whether in the cockpit, the political arena, the marketplace, or the boudoir), furnishes amulets to ward off the *mal d'ioc* (evil eye), and guides the hand that picks out the winning number in the national lottery. Lack of success merely indicates that someone else's magic was more potent, or that the *loa* did not approve.

Black magic per se, at least in theory, is more the province of the *bocor* than the respectable *houngan*. It includes *ouangas-à-mort (death* curses), sending the souls of the dead on questionable errands, and trafficking with *bakas* and *zombis*. Some *loa*, mainly *Rada,* prefer white magic. Others, notably *Erzulie-gé-*

rouge, 'ti Jean-Petro, Kita-démembré, and Marinette-bwa-Chech, are more than willing to assist sorcerers.

Ouangas are spells *rangé* (cast or worked) by *houngan* or *bocor* either for the protection of a supplicant or to harm (though not always fatally) the supplicant's enemy or rival.(7)

Sudden death, apparently psychogenic, is a worldwide phenomenon. The knowledge that a man has been bewitched, cursed, has had the bones pointed at him (as among Australian aborigines), has unwittingly violated tribal taboos, or has had a *ouanga-à-mort* placed on him seems sufficient to cause some of the healthiest victims to falter and fade away. Almost everyone in Haiti claims personal knowledge of at least one case of this kind.

A favorite *ouanga* is a doll effigy, made of cloth and stuffed with the hair or nail parings of the intended victim, that is then mutilated by having a pin stuck into the heart or other parts of the body. This is in the tradition of West African wooden images pounded with nails.

Not all magical practices in Haiti are African in origin however. France of the seventeenth and eighteenth centuries was steeped in the occult. Many noble families kept an in-house astrologer who, it was hoped, was also versed in alchemy and at least knew how to discover the elixir of life. Clairvoyance, spiritualism, and mesmerism also had numerous devotees. Copies of *Le Grand Albert* (so named for supposedly containing the secrets of the great Albertus Magnus), *Le Petit Albert and La Poule Noire,* the how-to-make-your-own-magic handbooks of the Midlle Ages, traveled in more than one trunk to St. Domingue and were handed down from generation to generation. The liberated slaves into whose hands they eventually fell assumed that the books themselves to possess an aura of magic.

No doubt the scandalous rumours surrounding the Marquise de Montespan also drifted across the Atlantic to spice plantation gossip, The marquise, Louis the XIV's mistress, is said to have consulted an infamous sorceress, La Voisin, in order to gain the king's affections. Later La Voisin was arrested for arranging black masses at which live children were sacrificed, the naked bodies of ladies of the court serving as altars. Some of de Montespan's sisters under the skin in St. Domingue may have been tempted to emulate her methods, thus further melding European magic with that of Africa.

Zombis, loups-garous (werewolves), *djabs, bakas,* and *demons* all have a time-honored place in Haitian folklore. They form a tangled skein related directly or indirectly to the *Sectes Rouges.* The *sectes* have various names: *Cochons Gris, Zobops, Bisangos, Vin'-Bain-Ding* (blood-pain-excrement). Their members are strictly consecrated to black magic. In the countryside they are feared and spoken of in hushed tones even by nonbelievers. Human sacrifice and cannibalism are among the crimes attributed to them.

Tales of *Sectes Rouges* midnight orgies, where a red-clad assemblage (summoned by the clashing of stones audible only to the ears of initiates) dance wildly around a candlelit coffin, provide fuel for sensationalists. The existence of the *sectes* appears nonetheless undeniable. Numerous passports issued to members, or, for a fee, to peasants wishing to travel by night, were confiscated during the anti-Voodoo campaign of the 1940s. They continue to surface from time to time, and traces of mysterious ceremonies are found at crossroads, bridges, and in cemeteries.

Members of African sorcerer societies believe themselves capable of turning into animals, or of sending their soul to inhabit temporarily the body of an animal who will do their bidding. *Sectes Rouges bocors* are credited with the ability to become *baka* at will.(8)

Courlander describes a *zombi* as "A human being who has 'died' and been resurrected from the graveyard by members of the Zeaubeaup [zobop] Society, by a wicked sorcerer, or by some other person who has the power to perform this act."

Zombi stories abound - a woman long buried appears thirty years later wandering down the main street of her native village; fieldhands, after tasting salt (said to restore the memory), realize they are the living dead and try frantically to scratch their way back into their graves.

Wicked plantation owners are accused of buying *zombis* from *bocors* and using them as beasts of burden who toil tirelessly and mindlessly in the fields.

According to the American writer Elsie Clews Parsons, some *zombis* are turned into animals, slaughtered, then sold as meat in the marketplace. The good *loa* are supposed to protect their devotees from eating *zombi* flesh unknowingly. Vansittart, British consul to Port-au-Prince who was mysteriously stricken in 1908, is reputed to have eaten *zombi* meat. He himself reported to the Foreign Office that he attributed his illness to having inadvertently eaten human flesh, which, he said, "is hawked in the streets."

Apart from bodies stolen for various necromantic purposes, there have been cases where a poison-induced (a toxin from the puffer fish is generally believed to be the agent) lethargy was mistaken for death. Burial is, of necessity, quick in a tropical country where embalming is little known so the possibility of awakening Juliets exists.

Werewolves flying through the air at night, leaving sulphurous trails and threatening especially the lives of infants or of the fetus in the womb, appear at a glance to be straight from *Dracula* - a reasonable assumption, for vampires and *loups-garous* were long dreaded in many parts of Europe. They continue to be greatly feared in the Haitian countryside, and protective charms for pregnant women are deemed of the utmost importance.

The role of the foregoing potpourri of beliefs and customs in shaping the history of the Haitian people cannot be ignored. Voodoo continues alive and well in Haiti. Protestant and Catholic missionaries labor in their tropical vineyard caring for minds and bodies as well as souls. A native clergy, who understand the *loa* as no *blanc* ever can, walk a fine and often hazardous line between Jesus and *Legba*. The *loa* are renounced and rejected, especially by converts to the Protestant sects, but they continue to permeate Haiti's soil. Their roots are as deep, as strong, and as tenuous as those of the sacred mapou tree. For better or for worse, Haiti is a magic island, and the laughter of a thousand African gods echoes through her hills.

FOOTNOTES - VOODOO

1. "Vodun," "Vaudun," and "Vaudou" are all ways of rendering the title of the religion we speak of and refer to in its common English form as "Voodoo."

2. In terms of today's Africa, the slaves of St. Domingue came from what are now Senegal, Mali, Guinea, Liberia, the Ivory Coast, Ghana, Dahomey, the Congo, Angola, and Nigeria.

3. Cosmas and Damian, patron saints of physicians, were doctors of medicine in Asia Minor during the third century. Famed for their medical skills and their Christian charity, they were imprisoned, tortured, and beheaded during the persecutions of Emperor Diocletian (circa 303).

4. Eugène Aubin is the better-known pseudoym of L. Descos, who was French minister in Port-au-Prince from 1904 to 1906.

5. Northern Siberian tribes consider the possession of supernatural gifts a prerequisite in their choice of a *shaman* (priest).significance. It is the focal point of all services, and around it are traced the veves (symbolic designs) of the *mystères* invoked.

6. The late great houngan Joe Pierre-Gilles, at his *houmfort* near Croix-des-Bouquets, had a swimming pool-sized *bassin for La Sirene,* the walls of which were decorated by André Pierre, the now famous artist.

7. Reba Stevenson, a long-time family friend who grew up on Maryland's Eastern shore in the 1920s, well remembers the "Hoodoo man" whose spells resulting in crippiling and death were known and feared for miles around.

Chronology

1492 December 6: Columbus lands at Môle St. Nicolas.
1508 King Ferdinand of Spain sends first official cargo of African slaves to New World.
1665 February: Ogeron appointed Governor of St. Domingue, establishes settlement at Port-de-Paix.
1679 First slave insurrection against French led by Padrejean.
1697 Treaty of Ryswick; Spain recognizes France's claim to Western St. Domingue.
1734 September 20-21: Cap François burned to ground.
1751 Macandal leads insurrection against the French.
1758 Macandal captured and executed at Cap François.
1779 France sends troops from St. Domingue to support Americans in War of Independence. Troops fight at Battle of Savannah, October 8.
1789 July 4: French National Assembly votes to seat six delegates from St. Domingue.
1790 October: Ogé and Chavannes take up arms against French in North.
1791 May 15: French National Assembly declares all free-born men of color eligible to be seated.
August 14: Ceremony of Bois Cayman.
August 22: Revolt of slaves.
September: Toussaint Louverture joins slave revolt.
1793 June: Cap Français pillaged and burned. White refugees flee.
August 29: Sonthonax decrees liberation of slaves.
September: British troops land in St. Domingue.
1794 February 5: Mixed delegation from St. Domingue seated at Paris National Convention.
1796 March-April: Toussaint marches into Cap; is declared lieutenant governor by Laveaux.
1797 March: Sonthonax appoints Toussaint commander-in-chief of French forces.
1798 August 31: British troops evacuate Môle.
October 23: Toussaint enters Cap in triumph. Hédouville forced to sail for France.
1801 January: Toussaint invades Santo Domingo. Declares slavery abolished.
July 8: New constitution promulgated. Toussaint declared governor general for life.
1802 February 1: Christophe refuses Leclerc permission to land at Cap; sets

fire to town.
March 4-24: Battle of La Crête-à-Pierrot.
June: Toussaint betrayed and sent to France.
November 2: Leclerc dies of yellow fever. Rochambeau assumes command.
1803 April 7: Toussaint dies in captivity in France.
May 18: Dessalines rips white from French Tricolor at Arcahaie; Haitian flag is born.
November 18: Battle of Vertières. French evacuate Cap.
December 4: French withdraw from the Môle.
1804 January 1: Haitian independence declared by Dessalines at Gonaïves.
January-March: Massacre of French.
October 8: Dessalines crowned Emperor Jacques I of Haiti.
1805 February: Dessalines launches unsuccessful invasion of Santo Domingo.
May 20: Dessalines ratifies Haiti's first constitution as a free nation.
1806 October: Revolt against Dessalines. Emperor betrayed and killed at Pont-Rouge, October 17.
December: Haiti declared a republic. Christophe refuses presidency; marches South against Pétion.
1807 February 17: Christophe proclaimed president of newly created State of Haiti in North.
March 11: Pétion elected president of republic of Haiti.
1810 November 3: Rigaud declares L'Etat du Sud.
1811 June 2: Christophe crowned King Henry I of Haiti.
1816 June 2: Pétion declared president for life.
1818 March 29: Death of Pétion.
March 30: Boyer elected president for life.
1820 October 8: Christophe takes own life.
October 26: Boyer enters Cap, which is renamed Cap Haïtien. Haiti reunited.
1822 February 9: Haitian army reaches Ciudad Santo Domingo; receives keys to city from Cáceres.
1825 April 17: France grants independence to Haiti.
1838 June 9: Treaty in which France recognizes Haiti's final and complete independence.
1842 May 7: Earthquake destroys Cap, Port-de-Paix, and many towns and villages in North.
1843 March 13: Boyer abdicates, sails for Jamaica. Provisional government headed by Rivière-Hérard.
1844 March 10: Rivière-Hérard invades Santo Domingo.
April: *Piquet* uprising in South. Acaau heads *armée souffrante*.

May 3: Rivière-Hérard deposed. Guerrier sworn in as president.
1845 April 16: Council of State elects Pierrot president, following death of Guerrier.
1846 March 1: Pierrot deposed. Riché declared president.
1847 March 1: Soulouque elected president following death of Riché February 27.
1848 April 16: Soulouque massacres in Port-au-Prince.
1849 March: Soulouque invades Santo Domingo; retreats before reaching Ciudad Santo Domingo.
August 20: Soulouque proclaimed Emperor Faustin I.
1859 January 15: Soulouque abdicates.
January 18: Geffrard takes oath of office as president. Empire declared dead, constitution of 1846 reinstated.
1860 March 28: Concordat between the Vatican and Haiti signed.
1862 June 5: United States recognizes Haiti.
1863 May: Salnave insurrection and siege of Cap.
1867 March 13: Fall of Geffrard. Nissage-Saget declared president of provisional government, March 20.
June 14: Salnave sworn in as president of Haiti. New constitution ratified.
1869 Guerre de Salnave or Guerre des *Cacos*.
1869 December 18: Port-au-Prince invaded by rebel troops. National Palace blown up. Salnave flees.
1870 January 15: Salnave tried, condemned, and executed.
March 20: Nissage-Saget elected president.
1872 February 9: National Palace burns to ground.
June 11: Germans seize Haitian navy in Port-au-Prince harbor.
1874 June 12: Domingue succeeds Nissage-Saget.
1876 April 15: Domingue deposed.
July 17: Boisrond-Canal elected president.
1879 July 17: Boisrond-Canal steps down.
October 23: Salomon elected president.
1883 March 23: Boyer-Bazelais and followers land at Source Salée, seize Miragoâne.
September 22-25: *semaine sanglante*.
1884 January 8: Miragoâne falls to government troops.
1888 August 10: Salomon steps down; sails for France.
September 28: Télémaque killed in Port-au-Prince uprising. Outbreak of civil war.
December 16: Légitime declared president.
1889 October 17: Hippolyte sworn in as president after victory over Légitime.

1896 March 31: Simon Sam elected president following death of Hippolyte, March 24.
1902 May 12: Simon Sam abdicates. Mob uprising in Port-au-Prince.
July 26: Firmin civil war errupts.
September 6: Sinking of the *Crête-à-Pierrot* by German gunboat *Panther* at Gonaïves.
December 17: Nord Alexis acclaimed president.
1904 January 1: Centennial of Haitian independence.
1908 December 20: Downfall of Nord Alexis. Antoine Simon elected president.
1911 August 14: Antoine Simon deposed; Leconte president.
1912 August 7: National Palace blown up; Leconte and 300 soldiers killed.
August 12: Auguste inaugurated as president.
1913 May 12: Death of Auguste; Oreste inaugurated.
1914 January 27: Oreste resigns; leaves country.
February 8: Zamor elected president.
November 7: Théodore elected president following departure of Zamor.
1915 February 22: Théodore steps down.
March 22: Guillaume Sam takes oath of office as president.
July 27: Sam orders slaughter of political prisoners in penitentiary. Takes refuge in French embassy. Is dragged out and killed by mob next day.
July 28: U.S. Marines land to maintain order in Port-au-Prince.
August 11: National Assembly elects Dartiguenave president.
August 21: Americans take charge of Haitian customs houses.
September: *Cacos* revolt in the Artibonite and the North.
November 17-18: *Cacos* in the North defeated; Fort Rivière destroyed.
1918 November: *Caco* Resistance in the North.
1919 October 30-31: Death of Charlemagne Péralte. End of *Caco* war in the North.
1920 May 19: Benoît Batraville killed. End of *Caco* Resistance in the Artibonite.
1922 February 11: Russell appointed American high commissioner.
April 10: Borno elected president.
1929 October: Student strike at Damien followed by general strike, December 4. Martial law declared.
December 5: Cayes demonstrations and "massacre."
1930 April 21: Roy assumes powers as provisional president.
November 18: Vincent elected president.
1934 August 14: End of American occupation.
August 21: Haiti's second independence day. Celebration of

désoccupation.
1937 October: Dominican massacre and deportation of Haitian citizens.
1941 May 15: Lescot succeeds Vincent.
December 8: Haiti declares war on Japan, followed by declaration of war on Germany, Italy, and all Axis powers.
1946 January: General strike; fall of Lescot; army assumes power.
August 16: Estimé elected president.
1949 Port-au-Prince International Exposition.
1950 May 10: Estimé deposed, army assumes power.
December 6: Magloire inaugurated president.
1956 December 12: Magloire falls; goes into exile. Pierre-Louis takes over as provisional president.
1957 February-June: Ephemeral presidencies of Sylvain and Fignolé.
October 22: Duvalier inaugurated as president.
1958 July 28: Attempted invasion and takeover of palace thwarted (deputy sheriffs' coup).
1959 August 13: Attempted Castroite invasion in South fails.
1961 April 30: Duvalier maneuvers new six-year presidential term.
1963 April: Start of Barbot insurrection.
August-September: Cantave invasion attempt.
1964 April 1: Duvalier declares himself *president-à-vie.*
June-July: Camocain invasion, Saltrou.
August 5: Jeune Haiti landing in South.
August 11: Beginning of Jérémie "Vespers" (Massacre)
1967 June 9: Mass execution of *FAd'H* officers at Fort Dimanche.
1968 May 20: National Palace bombed; invasion attempted at the Cap.
1971 January 22: Duvalier announces Jean-Claude will succeed him.
April 21: Death of François Duvalier.
1972 *Académie Militaire* Reopened; Raoul Cédras in first class
Haiti passes law facilitating "quickie" divorces.
Franck Romain named Mayor of Port-au-Prince.
1975 American Foreign Aid Quadruples
Drought hits Northwest
Stamp scandal
1977 Club Med opens, signals burgeoning tourism
Drought
1979 "Boat people" begin appearing in U.S. waters
1980 May 5: Jean-Claude Duvalier Marries Michèle Bennett
Nov : Ronald Reagan elected U.S. president, portends easing of U.S. Human Rights stance.
1981 Marc Bazin has brief stint as Finance Minister
1982 Michèle Duvalier's brother arrested as Drug Smuggler in U.S.

Press begins articles on AIDS, Haiti mentioned
1983 Pigs slaughtered throughout country to eradicate swine fever - popular discontent. Reynolds closes Bauxite mine at Miragoâne.
March : Pope visits, rebuffs Duvaliers
1984 February 1: "Elections" held for legislature
1985 U.S. aid reduced by 25%
July : Plebiscite held by Jean-Claude Duvalier, life presidency "approved" by 99% of vote.
November : Anti-regime riots in Gonaïves
December: Old Duvalierists rally to try to save regime.
1986 January: Students strike, Episcopacy calls for change
February 7: Duvaliers leave Haiti for France, Henri Namphy and Junta take charge
October: Elections for Constitutional Delegates
1987 March 29: New Constitution Approved by Huge Majority
July: Hundreds of landless peasants killed near Jean-Rabel
Nov. 29: Elections aborted after Army-Duvalierist violence
1988 Jan. 17: Election organized by Army elects Leslie Manigat
Feb. 7: Leslie Manigat sworn in as president
June 20: Manigat ousted by Namphy
Sept. 11: Massacre at St.-Jean-Bosco
Sept. 17: Namphy ousted, Prosper Avril assumes power
1989 April 4: Coup Attempt fails
1990 January: Avril declares state of siege, lifts it after nine days
March 10: Prosper Avril resigns, Supreme Court Justice Ertha Pascal-Trouillot sworn in as interim president, first woman president
Dec. 16: Jean-Bertrand Aristide sweeps polls, garners 67% of vote after late entry into race
1991 January 6: Roger Lafontant attempts to seize power, fails
February 7: Jean-Bertrand Aristide sworn in, purges army
Sept. 30: Jean-Bertrand Aristide ousted by army coup, flees to Venezuela; Roger Lafontant dies in prison during turmoil
Raoul Cédras heads junta
Oct. 23: UN Votes embargo against Haiti
1992 Embargo impacts Haiti's poor, farmers, more than elite
June 10: Marc Bazin nominated as Prime Minister
November: Bill Clinton defeats George Bush with strong diaspora support.
1993 January 14: Bill Clinton announces continuation of Bush policy on refugees
March: 250 man UN civilian mission deployed
June 27: UN invites Aristide, Cédras to negotiate under UN auspices

at Governors Island, New York
June 30: Governors Island agreement approved
Aug. 15: Robert Malval sworn in as Prime Minister
Oct. 11: U.S.S. *Harlan County* turns tail because of *FRAPH*
presence at docks in Port-au-Prince
1994   March 18: Aristide threatens to revoke refugee agreement with U.S.
April 26: Clinton replaces Pezzullo with Gray
June 7: Commercial airline flights to Haiti stopped. Remittances from
U.S. limited to $50.- a month
July 31: UN resolution gives U.S. authority to intervene
Sept. 18: Jimmy Carter announces deal with junta, avoiding armed
conflict
Sept. 19: "Intervasion" begins
Oct. 15: Aristide returns
1995   March 31: President Clinton visits Haiti, UN takes command of
foreign troops
Oct. 15: Al Gore visits Haiti for one day to celebrate anniversary
of Aristide's return, urges December elections be held on schedule
Nov. 7: Claudette Werleigh replaces Smarck Michel as Prime
Minister. Latter had resigned in October after cabinet refused to
back privatisation of state-owned enterprises.
Dec. 17: René Préval elected to succeed Aristide. 28% of electorate
votes, 87.9% vote for Préval

Glossary

NOTE: This glossary contains most of the Créole words used in the text, together with French words and usages peculiar to Haiti.

Agoué Voodoo god of the sea
Aïeux Ancestors
Anpile A lot of, a great many
Arret Magic charm against evil
Action de Grâce Catholic ritual prayers which precede Voodoo services
Affranchis Freedmen
Arbres reposoirs Sacred trees in which the *loa* live
Arrière-pays Back-country
Asson Voodoo calabash rattle
Authentique Truly Haitian
Bagaille Any object or thing
Baka Evil spirit
Bamboche Party or get-together
Banda African dance
Banque friponne Rogue bank
Baron Samedi Voodoo *loa*
Bocor Wizard
Bon-Dieu-Bon God is good
Bord-de-mer Downtown mercantile area of Port-au-Prince
Bossal Wild or unbaptized Voodoo *loa*
Bourse Scholarship (not to be confused with financial mart of same name)
Cacos de plume *Cacos* of the pen
Caille House
Caille mystère Inner sanctum of *houmfort*
Calabasse Gourd
Cançons fé Iron pants
Casernes Barracks, usually referring to the *Casernes Dessalines* behind the National Palace
Cayman Alligator

Cérémonie Any one of a number of Voodoo rituals
Chef du Pouvoir Executif Chief of Executive Power
Choual Horse Loa mounts his *choual* or person he possesses
Clairin Cheap white rum
Cobs small coins
Cochon Gris Secret society (literally: gray pigs).
Cocomacac Sturdy Haitian stick said to have magical powers; nightstick
Combite Cooperative peasant group for work on land
Congo loa Special group of *loa*
Connaissance Special knowledge of the supernatural attributed to *houngans*
and *mambos*
Corvée Forced labor on roads levied by law
Cour de Cassation Supreme Court
Courri General panic
Cousin Zaka Loa whose special province is agriculture
Cruche Pitcher
Culte grossier Vulgar cult
Curés des noirs Slave-chaplains
Damballah serpent *loa*
Dechoukaj - to uproot, the term describing efforts to eradicate traces of
Duvalierism.
Délégué Delegate
Démon Evil spirit
Désoccupation End of foreign occupation
Dessalinienne Haitian National anthem
Dessounin Ceremony at which principal *loa* is liberated from head of the
deceased
Dictature bicephale Two-headed dictatorship
Djab Devil
Doublure See *Gouvernment de*
Dogue Large fierce dog (especially mastiffs, Alsatians, boxers, bulldogs)
Drogue Magic charm
Engagés Indentured immigrants
Engagement A contract between man and a wicked spirit
Engin Bomb or homemade explosive device
Enragé Enraged. mad
Erzulie The most important of the female *loa*. Sometimes appears as
Maitresse Erzulie. Erzulie-Freda-Dahomey or *La Sirene*
Erzulie-gé-rouge (Erzulie of the red eyes) an evil *loa*
Etrangers Foreigners
Fête de Drapeau Flag Day (18 May)
Fête des Aïeux Ancestors' Day (January 2)

Fondateurs Founding fathers
Forces Armées d'Haïti (FAd'H) Armed Forces of Haiti
Général Cleirmil loa
Gens de couleur free *mulâtres*
Gens de sac et de corde Burglars (literally: people of rope and bag)
Govi Earthenware jar in which spirits live
Gourde Haitian currency
Gouvernment de doublure Government by proxy; manipulation of black regimes by *mulâtre* advisers
Grand Quartier General (CQG) Armed Forces Headquarters
Grands blancs Powerful whites
Gréffier Law clerk
Grève Strike
Grillots Highly spiced pork
Griot An African sect whose initiates have an ability to foretell the future
Gros bleu Heavy blue denim worn by Haitian peasants
Gros bon ange One of two souls that Voodooisants believe to inhabit all bodies
Gros nègre (gros neg') Powerful black
Guédés Loa who are also the spirits of the dead and who speak in high, nasal, singsong voices
Habitant Peasant
Houmfort Voodoo cult center
Houngan Voodoo priest
Hougeniçon Voodoo choir mistress
Hounsi Initiates who assist *houngan or mambo*
Ibo loa Special group of *loa*
Lambi Conch shell used as musical instrument
Laplace (général de la place) Voodoo master of ceremonies
Lavé-tête Ceremonial washing of the head in voodoo initiation
Legba (Papa Legba) Loa who is the guardian of the gate
Liane Haitian vine whose stalks were used for whips
Loup-garou Werewolf
Macoute Knapsack, or generically, a Duvalier thug
Maître-Carrefours Guardian of the crossroads
Maître-Tête Principle *loa* in a person's head
Maitresse Erzulie (see Erzulie)
Mal d'ioc Evil eye
Mambo Voodoo priestess
Mangé-sec Voodoo food offering which does not include animal sacrifice
Mangé 'ti moune Feast for the children
Mangeurs-mulâtres Mulâtres-eaters

Mapou Large tree with magic and tutelary powers
Marassas twin *loa*
Marchande Marketwoman
Maréchaussée Mounted gendarmerie
Maringouin Mosquito
Marronage Practice of slaves escaping and living free
Marrons Escaped slaves
Meringue Haitian dance
Merle blanc White blackbird
Mondongue loa Special group of *loa*
Mornes Mountains
Musiciens Palais National National Palace Band, or (colloquial) Port-au-Prince politicians
Mystères Voodoo gods or spirits, same as *loa*
Nan Guinée African Guinée. Voodooisants think of it as a sort of nirvana
Nationaliste farouche Dedicated nationalist
Négritude Blackness, pride in
Ogun Badagris God of war. Other *Oguns* are all related
Ouanga Voodoo spell or curse
Ouanga-à-mort Death curse
Papaloi Earlier name for *houngan* or Voodoo priest
Pé Altar in sanctuary
Peristyle Part of houmfort where ceremonies are held
Petro loa Special group of *loa* who take their name from *houngan* Dom Pedro or Petro
Petits blancs Poor whites
Pierres tonnerre Ax heads used by Arawaks and reputed to have magical powers. (Literally: thunder-stones)
Pintard Guinea hen
Plaçage A conjugal relationship without marriage
Poix-et-riz Rice and beans, a favorite dish
Pots têtes Covered jars containing hair, nail parings, etc., of Voodoo initiates
Poteau mitan Post in center of peristyle by which the loa enter
Prèt savane Hedge priest
Rada Special group of *loa*
Ra-ra Lenten carnival, not to be confused with pre-Lenten Mardi Gras
Récolte Harvest
Réforme, La A body of special troops who intermittently served as presidential guards
Régénerés Slaves enlisted by Sonthonax in the Republican forces. (Literally: regenerated)

Régie du Tabac Originally State tobacco monopoly, ultimately large unaudited slush fund.

Rouleau compresseur Steamroller, slang term for roving bands of looters that sacked Port-au-Prince shops in the 1940s and 1950s

Salle des Bustes Hall of statues in the National Palace

Sang-mêlé A person of mixed blood

Sectes Rouges Secret societies whose primary concern is evil

Servi To serve or worship

Service Voodoo ceremony

Si Dié vlé God willing

SIDA French acronym for *AIDS*

Société soutien Support society for *houmfort*

Splendides Haitian brand of cigarettes

Taffia Raw (and nasty!!!!)rum

Tap-tap Public bus

Tonton Macoute (TTM) Name given Duvalier thugs. (Literally:Uncle Knapsack)

Telediol Rumor, grapevine

'Ti moune Child. (Literally: small person)

Vaccine Hallowed bamboo used as musical instrument

Vèvè Voodoo tracings honoring loa

Vin d'honneur Ceremonial gathering and toast

Voilier Sailboat

Vonvon bug

Zinglin Noir supporter of Soulouque

Zombi Living dead

Acknowledgments

First acknowledgments must go to the great archives and libraries and their people, without whom this work could never have been written: foremost, to our incomparable Library of Congress and the National Archives in Washington: the Public Records Office and British Museum Library in London; the Bibliothèque and Archives Nationales, and especially the Archives of the Quai d'Orsay, in Paris, the New York Public Library: the Boston Public Library; the Archives and Library, U.S. Marine Corps Historical Center; and the university libraries of Yale, Virginia, and Howard, as well as those of the U.S. Naval and Air War colleges.

Equal though individual thanks must next go to those who, bearing the heat and burden of the day, have read and commented on all or part of this work in draft. Among these, we are grateful above all to Rayford W. Logan, who has gone over every page with the ripeness of five decades' scholarship and the flinty eye so well known to many a student. Only short of Dr. Logan, however, we must thank other readers for equally penetrating criticism and insights: Ambassador Gerald A. Drew; Dr. Dana Munro: Ambassador Robert Newbegin: Ambassador Gerard Corley-Smith: Colonel Henry H. Reichner, Jr.: Kenneth T. Ripley; and Dr. Hans Schmidt.

For access to the papers of Sumner Welles, we are deeply grateful to our friend and neighbor Benjamin Welles. For similar access to the journals and unpublished manuscripts of Captain E. L. Beach, we are equally in debt to his son, Captain E. L. Beach, Jr.

Others, among so many, to whom special thanks are due include Igor Allan, Dudley Ball, Jim Cartlidge, Alice Child, Robert Cowley, Ambassador Roy Tasco Davis, Senator Paul H. Douglas, the Reverend W. D. Dennis, Charles B. Everitt, Colonel J. J. Farley, Colonel Angus M. Fraser, Rowland Gill, Colonel Robert E. Gruenler, Dr. Archibald Hanna, George Kapelos, the Very Reverend M. J. Lemieux, M. Lionel Laviolette, the Countess of Longford, the Reverend Frère Lucien, Rear Admiral Samuel Eliot Morison, Major General F. P. Munson, Barbara Norwood, Lt. Cdr. Gerard O'Donoghue, Agnes Pouillon, the Honorable Dean Rusk, W. S. Sartain, Commander R. F. Schreadley (for access to his able but unhappily unpublished study of the American occupation), General L. C. Shepherd, Jr., Robert Sherrod, Major J. C. Short, Brigadier General E. H. Simmons, the 10th Mtn. Division, Sister Florence Weston. Lieutenant Colonel Gary Wilder, and William C. Wilson.

The above list would of course be incomplete without mention of Haitian friends, living and dead, who contributed so much to this work but preferred to remain unidentified.

The title of this book was suggested by Charles W. Thomas, FSO-1, who served in and loved Haiti.

Maps and cartographic work are the product of Samuel H. Bryant.

Photographic credits are shown with the respective illustrations.

Bibliography

Abbott, Elizabeth. Haiti: *The Duvaliers and Their Legacy.* New York, 1988

Acheson, Dean G. *Present at the Creation.* New York, 1969.

Adams, Henry. *"Napoleon I at St. Domingue,"* Historical Essays. New York, 1891.

d'Adesky, Anne-christine, *Under the Bone,* New York, 1994

Advielle, Victor, *L'Odyssée d'un Normand a St. Domingue.* Paris, 1901.

Alaux, Gustave d'. "L'Empereur Soulouque et Son Empire," *Revue des Deux Mondes.* Paris, 1860.

Albertus Parvus (spuriously attributed to). *Secrets Merveilleux de la Magie Naturelle et Cabalistique du Petit Albert.* Lyons, 1758.

Alexander, R. P. "Haiti's Bid for Freedom," *Nation,* 4 May 1946.

Allen, J. H. "An Inside View of the Revolution in Haiti," *Current History,* May 1930.

Almeras, Henri d'. *La Franc-Maconnerie et l'Occultisme au XVIII siècle.* Paris, 1904.

Ambroise, A. L. "Magloire Ambroise," *Revue de la Société Haïtienne de l'Histoire et de Géographie,* January 1951.

Antoine, Jacques C. "Literature from Toussaint Louverture to Jacques Roumain," in Cook, Mercer, Haiti. Washington, D.C., 1951.

Antoine, Max A. *Louis-Etienne Lysius Felicité Salomon Jeune.* Port-au-Prince, 1968.

Ardouin, Alexis Beaubrun. *Etudes sur l'Histoire d'Haïti.* Paris, 1853-1860, 2 vols
. *Géographie de l'Ile d'Haïti.* Port-au-Prince, 1856.

Ardouin, Charles Nicolas Celigny. *Essais sur l'Histoire d'Haïti.* Port-au-Prince, 1865.

Aristide, Jean-Bertrand. *Aristide.* Orbis Books, New York, 1993

Armbrister, Trevor. "Any Hope for Haiti?" *Saturday Evening Post,* 15 June 1963.

Arquin, Florence. "Contemporary Popular Art in Haiti," *Pan-American Union Bulletin.* January 1948.

Arrendo y Pichardo, Casper de. "Memoria de mi Salida de la Isla de Santo Domingo, 1805," ms. published in *Clio* (Ciudad Trujillo), no. 82, 1948.

Aubin, Eugène (pseud. L. Descos). *En Haïti.* Paris, 1910.

Aubourg, Michel. "Le Drapeau Dessalinien," *RSHHG,* no. 4, 1958.

Audain, Léon. *Choses d'Haïti.* Port-au-Prince, 1916.

Auguste, Jules. *Quelques Verités a Propos des Recents Evénements de la République d'Haïti.* Paris, 1891.

Auguste, Maurepas. *Genèse d'une République Héréditaire.* Paris, 1974.

Ayala, Juan de. *Report to Ferdinand and Isabella.* Translated and copyrighted, 1961, Otto Kallir.

B., C. M. A *Glimpse of Hayti and Her Negro Chief.* Liverpool, 1850.

Bach, Marcus. *Strange Altars.* New York, 1952.

Badinel, J. *Some Accounts of the Trade in Slaves from Africa as Connected withEurope and America.* London, 1842.

Baker, C. S. "Some Colorful Haitian History," *U.S. Naval Institute Proceedings,* 24 May 1916.

Balch, Emily Greene. *Occupied Haiti.* New York, 1927.

Baskett, James. *History of the Island of St. Domingo, From Its First Discovery to the Present Period.* London, 1818.

Bastien, Rémy. "Anthologie du Folklore Haïtien," *Acta Anthropologica*, 1:4. Mexico, D.F., 1946.; *Vodun and Politics in Haiti.* Washington, D.C., 1966.

Beach, Edward L., Jr. *The Wreck of the Memphis.* New York, 1966.

Bellegarde, Dantès. *Au Service d'Haïti*, Port-au-Prince, 1962.

Dessalines a Parlé. Port-au-Prince, 1948.

Haïti et ses Problemes, Port-au-Prince, 1941.

Histoire du Peuple Haïtien (1492-1952). Port-au-Prince, 1953.

La Nation Haïtienne. Paris, 1938.

Pages d'Histoire. Port-au-Prince, 1925.

"Pétion et Bolivar," *RSHHG*. October 1941.

Pour une Haïti Heureuse. Port-au-Prince, 1928.

La Resistance Haïtienne. Montreal, 1937.

Bellegarde, Windsor. *Petite Histoire d'Haïti 1492-1915.* Port-au-Prince, 1921.

Benjamin, Georges J. *La Diplomatie d'Anténor Firmin.* Paris, 1960.

Berle, Adolf A. "Is Haiti Next?" *Reporter,* 23 May 1963.

Bervin, Antoine. *Benito Sylvain.* Port-au-Prince, 1966.

; *Louis-Edouard Pouget.* Port-au-Prince, 1945.

Bila, Constant. *La Croyance à la Magie au XVIII siècle en France.* Paris, 1925.

Bird, Mark Baker. *L'Homme Noir.* Edinburgh, 1867.

Bloncourt, Melvil. *Des Richesses Naturelles de la République d'Haïti, et sa Situation Economique.* Paris, 1861.

Bogat, Fortuné L. *Ideés et Réminiscences.* Port-au-Prince, 1970.

Boissonade, Prosper-Marie. *Saint-Domingue à la Veille de la Révolution.* Paris, 1906.

Bonafede, Dom. "*Haiti Employs U.S. Spies.*" New York Herald Tribune, 4 June 1964.

Bonhomme, Colbert. *Les Origines et les Leçons d'une Révolution Profonde et Pacifique.* Port-au-Prince, 1946.; *Révolution et Contre-Révolution en Haïti de 1946 à 1947.* Port-au-Prince, 1957.

Bonnet, Guy-Joseph. *Souvenirs Historiques* (documents collected and edited by Edmond Bonnet). Paris, 1864.

Bonsal, Stephen. *The American Mediterranean.* New York, 1912.

Bouchereau, Madeleine Sylvain, *Haïti et ses Femmes.* Port-au-Prince, 1957.

Bouzon, Justin. *Etudes Historiques sur la Présidence de Faustin Soulouque.*Paris, 1894.

Brand, William. *Impressions of Haiti* (pamphlet). The Hague, 1965.

Breda, Jérémie. "Life in Haiti: Voodoo and the Church," *Commonweal*, 24 May 1963.

Bridges, George W. *The Annals of Jamaica.* London, 1828.

Brown, Jonathan. *The History and Present Condition of St. Domingo.* Philadelphia, 1837.

Brudnoy, David. "Letter from Hispaniola"

Brutus, Edner. *Instruction Publique en Haïti, 1492-1945.* Port-au-Prince, 1948.

Brutus, Timoleon Cesar. *L'Homme d'Airain.* Port-au-Prince, 1946.

Buell, Raymond Leslie. *The American Occupation of Haiti.* New York, Foreign Policy Association, 1929.

Bulletin of the International Commission of Jurists. Geneva, August 1963.

Burney, James. *History of the Buccaneers of America.* London, 1816.

Burt, Edward. *Historical Notices of St. Domingue.* Bath, 1844.

Cabon, Adolphe. *Histoire d'Haïti.* Port-au-Prince, 1921, 3 vols.

L'Histoire Réligieuse d'Haïti. Port-au-Prince, 1933.

Monseigneur Alexis-Jean-Marie Guilloux. Port-au-Prince, 1929.

Calixte, Démosthènes Pettus. *Haiti: The Calvary of a Soldier.* New York, 1939.

Candler, John. *Brief Notices of Hayti.* London, 1842.

Carneiro, Edison. "Les Cultes d'Origine Africaine au Brésil," *Decimilia.* Rio de Janeiro, Ministerio da Educacao e Cultura, 1959.

Carteau, F. *Entretiens sur les Evénments qui ont opéré la Ruine de la Partie Française de Saint-Domingue.* Bordeaux, 1802.

Castonnet des Fosses, H. L. *La Révolution de Saint-Domingue.* Paris, 1893.

Cauzons, Th. de. *La Magie et la Sorcellerie en France.* Paris, 1910.

Celestin, Clément. *Compilations pour l'Histoire.* Port-au-Prince, 1958-1959. 3 vols.

Cercle Bellevue. 1905-1955. (privately printed, author unknown), Port-au-Prince, 1955.

Chamberlain, Greg. *Dangerous Crossroads*, South End Press, Boston, 1995; "Haiti's Underside", *Manchester Guardian*, 17 April, 1977

Champlain, Samuel de. *Voyage to New France,* transl., Michael Macklem. London.1971.

Chancy, Emmanuel. *Les Evénements de 1902 .* Port-au-Prince 1902.

L'Indépendance Nationale d'Haïti. Paris, 1884.

Pour l'Histoire. Port-au-Prince, 1890.

Chanlatte, Juste. *Histoire de la Catastrophe de Saint-Domingue.* Paris, 1824.

Charlevoix, F. X. de. *Histoire de l'Isle Espagnole ou de S. Domingue.* Paris, 1730-1731, 2 vols.

Charmant, Alcius. *La Mort de Chicoye .* Le Havre, 1907.

Charmant, Rodolphe, *La Vie Incroyable d'Alcius.* Port-au-Prince, 1946.

Chatelain, Joseph, *La Banque Nationale.* Port-au-Prince, 1954.

Chauvet, H., and Prophète, Raoul, *A Travers la République d'Haïti.* Paris, 1894.

Chauvet, Lucien. *8 Mai 1950* (pamphlet). Port-au-Prince, 1956.

Chazotte, Pierre-Etienne. *The Black Rebellion in Haiti* (ed., Charles Platt). Privately printed, 1927.

Chevallier, André F. *Remembrances.* Port-au-Prince, 1936. Cipriano de Utrera, "Aniquila el Batalon Fijo de Santo Domingo," *Boletin del Archivo General de la Nacion.* Ciudad Trujillo, no. 2, 1938.

Coffey, R. B. "A Brief History of the Intervention in Haiti." *U.S. Naval Institute* Proceedings, August 1922.

Cole, Hubert, *Christophe, King of Haiti,* New York, 1967.

Conard, Charles. "A Year in Haiti's Customs and Fiscal Service." *U.S. Naval Institute Proceedings,* April 1923.

Cook, Mercer. *An Introduction to Haiti.* Washington, D.C., 1951; "Mountains and Manuscripts," *Americas,* September 1951.

Corvington, Paul. *Bataille de Vertières* (pamphlet). Port-au-Prince, 1954.

Coulthard, G. R. "The French West Indian Background of 'Negritude,' *Caribbean Quarterly,* December 1961.

Courlander, Harold.
The Drum and the Hoe: Life and Lore of the Haitian People. Berkeley, 1960.
Religion and Politics in Haiti. Washington, D.C., 1966.

Craige, John H.
Black Bagdad. New York, 1933.
Cannibal Cousins. New York, 1934.

Crassweller, Robert D. *The Caribbean Community.* New York, 1972.
Trujillo: The Life and Times of a Caribbean Dictator. New York, 1966.

Cromer, Earl of. *Modern Egypt.* London, 1908.

Crouse, Nellis M. *French Pioneers in the West Indies.* New York, 1940.
; The French Struggle for the West Indies. New York, 1943.

Dalencoeur, François. *Alexandre Pétion devant l'Humanité.* Port-au-Prince, 1928.
; La Fondation de la République d'Haïti par Alexandre Pétion. Port-au-Prince. 1944.

Dalzell, Archibald, *The History of Dahomey* London, 1793.

Danache, B. *Le Président Dartiguenave et les Américains.* Port-au-Prince, 1950.

Danner, Mark. "Beyond the Mountains", 3 parts, *New Yorker,* 27 Nov., 4 Dec., 11 Dec., 1989

Davis, H. P. *Black Democracy: The Story of Haiti.* New York, 1928 (revised 2d edition, 1936).

Delince, Kern, *Quelle Armeé pour Haiti?,* Paris, 1994

Del Monte y Tejeda, Antonio. *Historia de la Isla de St. Domingo.* Ciudad Santo Domingo, 1853.

Deleage, Paul. *Haïti en 1886.* Paris, 1887.

Delorme, Demésvar. *Réflexions Diverses sur Haïti.* Paris, 1873.*; Réflexions Diverses sur Mgr. Alexis-Jean-Marie Guilloux.* Port-au-Prince, 1929.

Denis, Lorimer, and Duvalier, François. "L'Evolution Stadiale du Vodou," *Bulletin du Bureau d'Ethnologie d'Haïti, 1944.*

Depestre, Edouard, et al. *Discours Parlementaires.* Port-au-Prince, 1911.

Deren, Maya. *Divine Horsemen: The Living Gods of Haiti.* London, 1953.

Descourtilz, M. E. *Histoire des Désastres de Saint-Domingue.* Paris, 1795.
Voyage d'un Naturaliste en Haïti, 1799-1803. Paris, 1809. 3 vols.

Desroches, Charles. *Matières Li Réflexions.* Port-au-Prince, 1884.

Dewey, Loring D. *Correspondence Relative to the Emigration to Hayti of the Free People of Colour in the United States* (pamphlet). New York, 1824.

Dhormoys, Paul. *Une Visite chez Soulouque,* 2d edition. Paris, 1864.

Diederich, Bernard, and Burt, Al. *Papa Doc.* New York, 1969.

Dorsainvil, J.-C. *Histoire d'Haïti.* Port-au-Prince, 1942.
Lectures Historiques. Port-au-Prince, 1930.
Manuel d'Histoire d'Haïti. Port-au-Prince, 1934.
Psychologie Haïtienne: Vodou et Magie. Port-au-Prince, 1937.
Quelques Vues Politiques. Port-au-Prince, 1934.
Une Explication Philologique du Vodou. Port-au-Prince, 1924.

Vodou et Nevrose. Port-au-Prince, 1931.

Dorsinville, Roger. *Toussaint Louverture, ou la Vocation de la Liberté*. Paris, 1965.

Doubout, Jean-Jacques, and Joly, Ulrick. *Notes sur le Developpement du Mouvement Syndical en Haïti* (pamphlet). 1974.

Douglas, Paul H. "The American Occupation of Haiti," *Political Sciencce Quarterly*, June and September 1927;"Political History of the Occupation," *Occupied Haiti* (ed., E. G. Balch). New York, 1927.

Douglass, Frederick. "*Haiti and the United States*," North American Review. September-October 1891.; Lecture on Haiti. Chicago, 1893.

Douyon, Lamarque. "Phenomenologie de la Crise de Possession," *Revue de la Faculté d'Ethnologie*, no. 12, 1967.

Dubuisson, Paul E. *Nouvelles Considerations sur Saint-Domingue*. Paris, 1780.

Dumas, François Ribadeau. *Dossiers Secrets de la Sorcellerie et de la Magie*. Paris,1961.

Duncan, G. A. *The Public Works of Haiti* (pamphlet). Port-au-Prince, 1930.

Dunham, Katherine. *Island Possessed*. New York, 1969.

Du Tertre, R. P. *Histoire des Antilles* Paris, 1667.

Duvalier, François. *Face au Peuple et à l'Histoire*. Port-au-Prince, 1961. *Mémoires d'un Leader du Tiers Monde*. Paris, 1969; (under pseud. Abderrahman). *Souvenirs d'Autrefois*, 1926-1948. Port-au-Prince, 1968?

Edouard, Emmanuel. *Recueil General des Lois et Actes du Gouvernement d'Haïti*. Paris, 1888.

Edwards, Bryan. *An Historical Survey of the French Colony in the Island of St.Domingo*. London, 1801.

Elie, Louis E. *Histoire d'Haïti*. Port-au-Prince, 1944-1945, 2 vols.; *Le Président Boyer et l'Empereur de Russie Alexandre 1er*. Port-au-Prince, 1942.

Engels, George L. "Sudden and Rapid Death during Psychological Stress," *Annals of Internal Medicine*, May 1971.

Esquemeling, John. *The Buccaneers of America*. London, 1684.

Fagg, John Edwin. *Cuba, Haiti and the Dominican Republic*. New Jersey,1967.

Faine, Jules. *La Philologie Créole*. Port-au-Prince, 1937.

Fievre, Michel. "Nissage-Saget, 1810-1880," *RSHHG*, July 1933.

Farmer, Paul. *Aids and Accusation*. U.C. Berkeley Press, 1994
    The Uses of Haiti, Common Courage Press, Maine 1994

Firmin, Anténor. *Diplomates et Diplomatie*. Cap Haïtien, 1899. *Une Défense*. Paris, 1892.*L'Effort dans le Mal*. Reprinted, Port-au-Prince, 1962. *Lettres de Saint Thomas*. Paris, 1910; *M. Roosevelt Président des Etats-Unis et la République d'Haïti*. Paris, 1905.

Fletcher, Henry P. "Quo Vadis Haiti?" *Foreign Affairs*, July 1930.

Foner, Philip S., *Frederick Douglass*. New York, 1964.

Fortescue, John. *The History of the British Army*. London, 1906.

Franck, Harry C. *Roaming Through the West Indies*. New York, 1920.

Franklin, James. *The Present State of Hayti*. London, 1828.

Frazer, James G. *The Golden Bough* (vol 1, abridged ed.). New York, 1958.

Froude, James Anthony. *The English in the West Indies*. London, 1888.

Gaillard, Roger. *Les Cents Jours de Rosalvo Bobo*. Port-au-Prince, 1973.

Gallatin, Albert. *Writings of Albert Gallatin* (ed., Henry Adams). Philadelphia, 1789.

Gardner, W. J. A *History of Jamaica*. London, 1873.
Garnier, Apollo. "Autour de la Mort de Pétion," *rshhg*, January 1932.
Garron-Coulon, J. *Rapport sur les Troubles de St. Domingue, fait au Nom de la Commission des Colonies*. Paris, 1798.
Gastine, Civique de. *Histoire de la République d'Haïti*. Paris, 1819.
Georges, J. *La Diplomatie d'Anténor Firmin*. Paris, 1960.
Gingras, Jean-Pierre 0. *Duvalier: Caribbean Cyclone*. New York, 1967.
Girard, Pierre. "La Révolution d'Haïti, Juillet, 1915," *Revue Hebdomadaire*, July 1925
Girod, François. *La Vie Coloniale de la Société Créole*. Paris, 1972.
Gold, Herbert, "Americans in the Port of Princes," *Yale Review*, Autumn 1954- "Caribbean Caudillo," *Nation*, 5 February 1955. "Haiti: Hatred Without Hope," *Saturday Evening Post*, 24 April 1965. "Progress in Haiti", *New York Times Magazine*, 12 Mar. 1972. *Best Nightmare on Earth*, New York, 1991
Gordon, Nancy (pseud. of Nancy G. Heinl).
"Bishop James Theodore Holly," *The Cathedral Age*, Summer, 1975.
Is Papa Doc's Death a Windfall for Haiti's Voodoo Priests?" North American Newspaper Alliance, 11 May 1971.
Gouraige, Ghislain. *L'Indépendance d'Haïti devant la France*. Port-au-Prince, 1955.
Greene, Graham. *The Comedians*. New York, 1967. "Nightmare Republic," *New Republic*, 16 November 1963. Letter to the *Times* (London), 12 January 1970.
Griggs, E. L., and Prater, C. H., eds. *Henry Christophe and Thomas Clarkson*. Berkeley, 1952.
Gruening, Ernest. "The Conquest of Haiti and Santo Domingo," *Current History*, March 1922.
Guillermin, Gilbert. *Précis Historique des Derniers Evénmens de Saint-Domingue*. Paris, 1811.
Halliday, Fred. "New Black Magic," *Ramparts*, January 1973.
Hambly, William D. "Serpent Worship in Africa," *Field Museum of Natural History*, Chicago, 1931.
Hartmann, Louis. *Haïti, les Budgets, Situation Financière*. Paris, 1903.
Harvey, William Wallis. *Sketches of Hayti*. London, 1827. *the Horrors of St. Domingo*. Philadelphia, 1808.
Hayti, Royaume d'. *Almanach Royal*, 1811 to 1820.
Hazard, Samuel. *Santo Domingo, Past and Present, With a Glance at Hayti*. New York, 1873.
Heinl, Nancy G. "America's First Black Diplomat," *Foreign Service Journal*, August 1973. "Col. Charles Young," *Army Magazine*, March 1977.
Heinl, Robert D., Jr. "Bailing Out Duvalier,"*New Republic*, 14 January 1967.
"Haiti," *New Republic*, 16 May 1964.
"Haiti: Next Mess in the Caribbean?" *Atlantic Monthly*, November 1967.
"Papa Doc Angled for JFK's Soul," *Washington Post*, 5 July 1964.
Soldiers of the Sea. Annapolis, U.S. Naval Institute, 1962.
Herring, Hubert. "Dictatorship in Haiti," *Current History* , January 1964.
Herskovits, Melville J. *Life in a Haitian Valley*. New York, 1937.
Hicks, Albert C. *Blood in the Streets*. New York, 1946.

High, Stanley. "Alien Poison," *Saturday Evening Post,* 31 August 1940.

Hilliard d'Auberteuil. *Considérations sur l'Etat Present de la Colonie Française de Saint Domingue.* Paris, 1776-1777, 2 vols.

Holly, Arthur. *Les Daimons du Culte Vodou.* Port-au-Prince, 1918.

Howland, Charles P. *Survey of American Foreign Relations.* New York, Council on Foreign Relations, 1929.

Hudicourt, Max L. *Haiti Faces Tomorrow's Peace.* New York, 1945.

Hurston, Zora Neale. *Tell My Horse.* Philadelphia, 1938.

Huxley, Aldous. *The Devils of Loudun.* London, 1952.

Inginac, Joseph B. *Mémoires.* Kingston, 1843.

Inman, Samuel G. *Through Santo Domingo and Haiti: A Cruise with the Marines.* New York, 1919.

Ives, Kim. *Dangerous Crossroads,* South End Press, Boston, 1995

Jahn. Jahneinz. *Muntu: An Outline of the New African Culture,* translated by Marjorie Greene. New York, 1961.

James, C. L. R. *The Black Jacobins: Toussaint l'Ouverture and the San Domingo Revolution.* London, 1938.

James, E. 0. *The Ancient Gods.* New York, 1960.

. *Origins of Sacrifice.* London, 1933.

Janvier, Louis-Joseph. *Constitutions d'Haïti.* Paris, 1886.

Jean, Alfred. *Il y a 60 Ans, 1883-1943.* Port-au-Prince, 1944.

Jérémie, Joseph (Cadet), *Haïti Indépendant.* Port-au-Prince, 1929.

Mémoires. Port-au-Prince, 1950.

Jessup, Philip C. *Elihu Root.* New York, 1938.

Johnson, James Weldon. *Along This Way.* New York, 1923.

. "The Truth About Haiti," *Crisis,* 20 September 1920.

Johnston, H. H. *The Negro in the New, World.* London, 1910.

Jones. Edward A. "Dantès Bellegarde, Miracle of Haiti," *Phylon,* vol. 11, no.1, 1950.

Joseph, Raymond A. "An Exile Forecasts Chaos in Haiti," *Wall Street Journal.* December 1970.

Junot, Laures. *Home and Court Life of the Emperor Napoleon.* London, 1893.

Justin, Joseph. *Exposé Général de la République d'Haïti.* Port-au-Prince, 1892.

; Les Réformes Nécessaires: Questions Haïtiennes d'Actualités. Port-au-Prince, 1915.

Kelly, Michael. "It All Codepends", *New Yorker* 3 October 1994

Kitching, A. L. *On the Backwaters of the Nile.* London, 1912.

Kobler, John. "Land of Misfortune," *Saturday Evening Post,* 16 April 1960.

Korngold, Ralph. *Citizen Toussaint.* Boston, 1944.

Kreiger, H. M. "Aborigines of the Ancient Island of Hispaniola," *Annual Report of the Smithsonian Institution.* Washington, D.C., 1929.

Kuser, J. D. *Haiti: Its Dawn of Progress after Years in a Night of Revolution.* Boston, 1921.

Labat, Jean-Baptiste. *Nouveau Voyage aux Isles de l'Amerique.* Paris, 1742. 8 vols.

Lacombe, Robert. *Histoire Monétaire de Saint-Domingue.* Paris, 1958.

Lacroix, François-Joseph-Pamphile de. *Mémoires pour servir à l'Histoire de la Révolution de Saint-Domingue.* Paris, 1819.

LaForest, A., and Osson, R. *Le General A. Simon dans le Sud.* Port-au-Prince, 1910.

Lamaute, Emmanuel. *Le Vieux Port-au-Prince*. Port-au-Prince, 1939.

Langston, J. M. *From the Virginia Plantation to the National Capital*. Hartford, 1894.

Large, Camille. "Goman et l'Insurrection de la Grande Anse," *RSHHG*, January 1940.

La Selve, Edgar. *Le Pays des Nègres*. Paris, 1881.

Las Casas, Bartolome de. *Historia de las Indias* (ed., A. Millares Carlo). Mexico, 1951.

Laujon, A. P. M. *Précis Historique de la Dernière Expédition de Saint-Domingue*. Paris, 1805.

Laurent, Gerard M. *Le Commissaire Sonthonax à Saint-Domingue*. Port-au-Prince, 1965. *Pages d'Histoire*. Port-au-Prince, 1960. "Toussaint Louverture et l'Indépendance de Saint-Domingue," *Le Document*, 20 May 1946.

Leclerc, Victor-Emmanuel. *Lettres de Saint-Domingue* (ed., Roussier). Paris, 1937

Léger, Abel-Nicolas. *Histoire Diplomatique d'Haïti*. Port-au-Prince, 1930.

Léger, Jacques-Nicolas. *Haïti: Son Histoire et ses Detracteurs*. New York, 1907.

Légitime, François-Denis *Histoire du Gouvernement du General Légitime*. Paris, 1891. Souvenirs Historiques," *Revue de la Société de Legislation*, August, November, December 1907; January-May 1908.

Leiris, Michel. "La Croyance aux Genies Zar en Ethiopie du Nord," *Journal de Psychologie*, Paris, January-March 1938.

Lemonnier-Delafosse, Marie-Jean-Baptiste. *Seconde Campagne de Saint Domingue*. Le Havre, 1846.

Lepelletier de Saint-Rémy, *Saint-Domingue*. Paris, 1859. 2 vols.

Voyage aux Isles de l'Amerique. The Hague, 1724.

Le Pers. *La Tragique Histoire des Flibustiers: Histoire de St. Domingue et de l'Ile de la Tortue*. Reprinted, Paris, undated.

Leslie, Charles. *A New History of Jamaica*. London, 1740.

Lespinasse, Pierre-Eugene de. *Gens d'Autrefois*. Paris, 1926, reprinted in 1961.

Leuba, James H. *The Psychology of Religious Mysticism*. London, 1925.

Lewis, I. M. *Ecstatic Religion*. Harmondsworth, 1971.

Leyburn, James G. *The Haitian People*. New Haven, 1941.

Logan, Rayford W. *The Diplomatic Relations of the United States with Haiti, 1776-1891*. Chapel Hill, 1941. *Haiti and the Dominican Republic*. New York, 1968. "Education in Haiti," *The Journal of Negro History*, October 1930.

Lokke, Carl Ludwig. "Jefferson and the Leclerc Expedition," *American Historical Review*, January 1928.

Lubin, Maurice A. "En Marge du Recensement en Haïti," *RSHHG*, January 1950.

Ludlow. J. M. "Geffrard, President of Haiti, *Good Words*. London, 1862.

Lundahl, Mats. *The Haitian Economy*, New York, 1983

McCormick, Medill. "Our Failure in Haiti," *Nation*, 1 December 1920.

Mackenzie, Charles. *Notes on Hayti, Made during a Residence in that Republic.* London, 1830, 2 vols.

Madiou, Thomas. *Histoire d'Haïti*. Port-au-Prince, 1847. Madiou, Thomas (fils). *Histoire d'Haïti*. Port-au-Prince, 1922-1923. 3 vols.

Magloire, Auguste. *Histoire d'Haïti*. Port-au-Prince, 1909. 4 vols.

Magloire, Jean. *Dumarsais Estimé: Esquisse de sa Vie Politique*. Port-au-Prince, 1950.

Malo, Charles. *Histoire de l'Ile de Saint-Domingue*. Paris, 1819.

Mangonès, Edmond, and Maximilien, Louis. *L'Art Précolombien d'Haïti*. Port-au-Prince, 1942.

Manigat, Leslie F. *"Le Délicat Problème de la Critique Historique,"* RSHHG, October 1954. *Haiti of the Sixties, Object of International Concern.* Washington, D.C., 1964. *Politique Agraire du Gouvernement d'Alexandre Pétion, 1807-1818.* Port-au-Prince, 1962. *Statu Quo en Haiti?* Paris, 1971. La Substitution de la Préponderance Américaine à la Préponderance Française en Haïti au Debut du XXe Siècle," *Bulletin de la Société d'Histoire Moderne,* October 1960.

Manning, William R. *Diplomatic Correspondence of the United States Concerning the Independence of the Latin-American Nations.* New York, 1925.

Marcelin, Emile, *De l'Enfance à la Jeunesse.* Port-au-Prince, 1934.

Marcelin, Frédéric. *Bric à Brac.* Paris, 1910.

Choses Haïtiennes. Paris, 1896.

Ducas Hyppolite. Paris, 1878.

Une Evolution Nécessaire. Paris, 1898.

Le Général Nord Alexis. Paris, 1905-1908.

L'Haleine du Centenaire. Paris, 1901.

Marcelin, L.-J. *Haïti - Ses Guerres Civiles.* Paris, 1892.

Marcelin, Milo. *Mythologie Vodou.* Port-au-Prince, 1949.

Mars, Louis. *La Crise de Possession dans le Vaudou.* Port-au-Prince, 1946.

; *Témoinages I.* Madrid, 1966.

Martin, John Bartlow. *Overtaken by Events.* New York, 1966.

Mathon, M. E. *M. Frédéric Marcelin.* Port-au-Prince, 1895.

; *Révolutions de 1888-1889.* Port-au-Prince, 1890.

Mathurin, Augustin, *Assistance Sociale en Haïti, 1804-1972.* Port-au-Prince, 1972.

Mauviel, Guillaume. *Anecdotes de la Révolution de Saint-Domingue.* Paris, 1885.

Maximilien, Louis. *Le Vodou Haïtien.* Port-au-Prince, 1945.

Melhorn, Kent C. *The Health of Haiti.* Baltimore, 1930.

Mennesson-Rigaud, Odette. "Etude sur le Culte des Marassas en Haïti," *Zaire* (Louvain), 6 June 1952.

Mennesson-Rigaud, Odette, and Denis, Lorimer. "Cérémonie en l'Honneur de Marinette," *Bureau d'Ethnologie,* July 1947.

Metral, Antoine. *Histoire de l'Insurrection des Esclaves dans le Nord de Saint-Domingue.* Paris, 1818.

Métraux, Alfred, *Haïti, Poètes noirs.* Paris, 1951.

; *Voodoo in Haiti.* New York, 1959.

Michel, Antoine. *Avènement du Général F. N. Geffrard à la Présidence d'Haïti.* Port-au-Prince, 1932.; *La Mission du General Hédouville à Saint-Domingue.* Port-au-Prince, 1929.; *Salomon Jeune et l'Affaire Louis Tanis.* Port-au-Prince, 1913.

Michel, Georges, *Les Chemins de Fer de L'Ile d'Haïti*, Port-au-Prince, 1985

Michel, Henri Adam. "Toussaint Louverture et la Liberté Général des Esclaves," *RSHHG,* vol.5, no. 14.

Millspaugh, Arthur G. *Haiti Under American Control, 1915-1930.* Boston, 1930.

Mims, Stewart L. *Colbert's West India Policy.* New Haven, 1912.

Molinari, M. G. de. *A Panama-La Martinique-Haïti.* Paris, 1887.

Montague, Ludwell L. *Haiti and the United States, 1714-1938.* Durham, 1940.

"La Navase," *RSHHG*, April 1940.

Moore, O. Ernest. *Haiti, Its Stagnant Society and Shackled Economy.* New York, 1972.

Moreau de Saint-Méry, M. L. E. *Description Topographique, Physique, Civile, et Historique de la Partie Française de l'Ile Saint-Domingue.* Philadelphia, 1797-1798. 2 vols.; *Lois et Constitutions des Colonies Françaises de l'Amérique Sous le Vent.* Paris, 1784-1790. 4 vols.

Morison, Samuel E. *Old Bruin.* Boston, 1968 ; "The Route of Columbus Along the North Coast of Haiti, and the Site of the Navidad," *Transactions,* American Philosophical Society, December 1940.; (trans. and ed.) *Journals and Other Documents on the Life and Voyages of Christopher Columbus.* New York, 1963. and Obregon, Mauricio. *The Caribbean as Columbus Saw It.* Boston, 1964.

Morris, Joe Alex. "Cruel Beauty of the Caribbean," *Saturday Evening Post,* 17 November 1951

Morse, Richard. *Views Of Twelve Haitian Leaders,* Wilson Center, Washington, 1988

Moynahan, Pat."A Day in the Country with Baby Doc", *London Sunday Times,* 21 Aug. 1977

Munro, Dana G. *Intervention and Dollar Diplomacy in the Caribbean, 1900-1921.* Princeton, 1964. *The United States and the Caribbean Republics, 1921-1933.* Princeton, 1974.

"The American Withdrawal from Haiti," *Hispanic-American Review,* February 1969.

Nau, Emile. *Histoire des Caciques d'Haïti.* Paris, 1955.

Nemours, Auguste. *Histoire Militaire de la Guerre d'Indépendance de Saint Domingue.* Paris, 1925.

Nemours, Alfred. *Les Présidents Lescot et Trujillo.* Port-au-Prince, 1942.

Nevins, Allan. *Hamilton Fish: Inner History of the Grant Administration.* New York, 1937.

Nicolas, Hogar. *L'Occupation Américaine d'Haïti: La Revanche d'Histore.* Madrid, 1955.

Niles, Blair. *Black Haiti, a Biography of Africa's Eldest Daughter.* New York, 1926.

Nina-Rodriguez. *L'Animisme Fétichiste des Nègres de Bahia.* Bahia, Brazil, 1900.

Noel, Ascensio A. *Les Responsables des Vêpres du 25 Mai.* Port-au-Prince, 1957.

Notes Historiques, Armée d'Haïti (author unknown). Port-au-Prince, 1954.

Nowell, C. E. *A Letter to Ferdinand and Isabella.* Minneapolis, 1965.

Numa, Edgar. *Antoine Simon et la Fatalité Historique* (no date or publisher given).

O'Leary, Daniel Florencio. *Memorias.* Caracas, Venezuela, 1879.

Paret, Timothée. "Toussaint Louverture," *RSHHG,* vol. 4, no. 12.

Parham, A. *My Odyssey: By a Créole of St. Domingue.* New Orleans, 1959.

Parsons, Elsie Clews. "Spirit Cult in Hayti," *Journal de la Société des Americanistes de Paris,* vol XX, 1928.

Pattee, Richard. *Haïti: Pueblo Afroantillano.* Madrid, 1956.

Paul, Edmond. *Questions Politico-Economiques.* Paris, 1861.

Perkins, Dexter *The Monroe Doctrine, 1867-1907.* Baltimore, 1937. ; *The United States and the Caribbean.* Cambridge, 1966.

Perkins, Samuel G. *Reminiscences of the Insurrection in Saint-Domingo.* Cambridge, 1886.

Pétion, Roy. *En Marge de l'Histoire.* Port-au-Prince, 1942.

Phareaux, L. C. *La Vie Contemporaine.* Port-au-Prince, 1953.

Pierre-Paul, Antoine. "Les Contrats de Banque et d'Emprunt du Gouvernement d'Antoine Simon," *RSHHG,* April 1951. "Les Contrats de Chemin de Fer et de Figues-Bananes," *RSHHG,* April 1951.

Les Contre-Verités d'une Thèse. Port-au-Prince. 1963.

La Première Protestation Armée contre l'Intervention Américaine de 1915. Port-au-Prince, 1957.

Placide, Justin. *Histoire Politique et Statistique de l'Ile d'Haïti-Saint Domingue.* Paris, 1826.

Pollet, Georges. *Saint-Domingue et l'Autonomie, 1629-1730.* Paris, 1934.

Pompilus, Pradel. Manuel Illustré d'Histoire de la Litterature Haïtienne. Port-au-Prince, 1961.

Pouilh, Duraciné. "*A la Mémoire de M. Eugène Bourjolly* (pamphlet). Port-au-Prince, 1896.

Poyen, H. de P. *Les Guerres des Antilles.* Paris, 1896; *Histoire Militaire de la Révolution de Saint-Domingue.* Paris, 1899.

Pratt, J. W. *America's Colonial Experiment.* New York, 1930.

Pressoir, Catts. *Le Protestantisme Haïtien.* Port-au-Prince, 1945-1946.

____; "Quelle est l'Origine du mot gourde?" *RSHHG,* July 1947.

Prevost, Julien. *Rélation des Glorieuses Evènemens qui ont porté leurs Majestés Royales sur le Trône d'Haïti.* Cap Henry, 1811.

Prewett, Virginia. "Duvalier Spies Operate in U.S.," *Washington Daily News,* 4 May 1964. "When Duvalier Dies," *North American Newspaper Alliance,* 24 February 1971.

Price, Hannibal *(fils) Dictionnaire de Législation Administrative Haïtienne,* 2nd edition. Port-au-Prince, 1923, 2 vols.

Price, Hannibal. *The Haytian Question.* New York, 1891.

Price-Mars, Jean. *Ainsi Parla l'Oncle.* Paris, 1928.; *Formation Ethnique, Folk-Lore, et Culture du Peuple Haïtien.* Port-au-Prince, 1939. *Jean-Pierre Boyer-Bazelais et le Drame de Miragoâne.* Port-au-Prince, 1948. *Une Etape de l'Evolution Haïtienne.* Port-au-Prince, 1937." Henry Christophe," *RSHHG,* January 1934.Les Origines et le Destin d'un Nom," *RSHHG,* January 1940." L'Unité Politique de l'Ile d'Haïti," *RSHHG,* October 1937.

Prichard, Hesketh. *Where Black Rules White.* London, 1900.

Rainsford, Marcus, *A Memoir of Transactions That Took Place in the Spring of 1799* London, 1802; *An Historical Account of the Black Empire of Hayti.* London, 1805.

Ramel, Jean-Pierre. *Journal de l'Adjudant-Général Ramel.* London, 1799.

Ravenscroft, Kent, Jr. "Voodoo Possession: A Natural Experiment in Hypnosis, " *The International Journal of Clinical and Experimental Hypnosis, vol.* 13, no. 3., 1965.

Raynal, G. T. *Histoire Philosophique et Politique des Etablissements et du Commerce des Européens dans les Deux Indes.* Geneva, 1787. ; *Histoire Philosophique et Politique des Isles Françaises dans les Indes Occidentales.* Lausanne, 1784.

Redpath, James. *A Guide to Hayti.* Boston, 1861.

Reynolds, Quentin. "Murder in the Tropics," *Collier's,* 22 January 1938.

Richardson, James D. *A Compilation of the Messages and Papers of the Presidents, 1789-1897*. Washington, D.C., 1899.

Riesman, David, *La Foule Solitaire*. Paris, 1964.

Rigaud, Candelon. "Histoire d'Haïti et Histoire de Port-au-Prince,"*RSHHG* October 1934.

Rigaud, Milo. *Contre Vincent*. Paris, 1946; *La Tradition Voudou et le Voudou Haïtien*. Paris, 1953.

Riou, Roger. *Adieu la Tortue*. Paris, 1974.

Roberts, W. A. *The French in the West Indies*. New York, 1942.

Robertson, William Spence. *France and Latin-American Independence*. Baltimore, 1939.

Roc, Gesner, *Haïti: Tournant apres Duvalier*. Quebec, 1968.

Rodman, Selden. *Haiti: The Black Republic*. New York, 1954.

The Miracle of Haitian Art. New York, 1947.

Renaissance in Haiti. New York, 1948.

"A Mural for Wilson Bigaud," *Magazine of Art*, October 1951.

"Murals for Haiti," *Art in America*, December 1951.

Rodriguez-Castro, Jose. *Cosas de Haïti*. Ponce, 1893.

Rodriquez-Demorizi, Emilio. *Invasiones Haïtiannas de 1801, 1805, y 1822*. Ciudad Trujillo, 1955.

Rosemond, Jules. *Affaire du 15 Mars 1908*. Port-au-Prince, 1910.

; Davilmar Théodore (unpaginated pamphlet). Port-au-Prince, 1914.

Rotberg, Robert L. *Haiti, The Politics of Squalor*. Boston, 1971.

Roumain, Jacques, *Gouverneurs de la Rosée*. Port-au-Prince, 1944.

Rouvray, Le Marquis et la Marquise du. *Une Correspondence Familiale au Temps des Troubles de Saint-Domingue* (eds., M. E. McIntosh and B. C. Weber). Paris, 1959.

Rouzier, Sémextant. *Dictionnaire Géographique et Administratif d'Haïti*. Port-au-Prince, 1928.

St. John, Spenser. *Hayti, or the Black Republic*. London, 1884.

Saint-Remy. *Pétion et Haïti*. Paris, 1854; *Vie de Toussaint Louverture*. Paris, 1850.

Salomon, René, *Etudes Politiques*. Port-au-Prince, 1948.

Sannon, H. Pauléus. *Histoire de Toussaint Louverture*. Port-au-Prince, 1920.

Sapène, Raymond. *Proces A: Baby Doc*. Paris, 1973.

Sanders, Prince. *Haytian Papers*. Boston, 1819.

Sargant, William. *The Mind Possessed*. London, 1974.

Scelle, Georges. *Histoire de la Traite Negrière*. Paris, 1906.

Schlesinger, Arthur, Jr. *A Thousand Days*. Boston, 1965.

Schmidt, Hans. *The United States Occupation of Haiti, 1915-1934*. New Brunswick, 1971.

Schoelcher, Victor. *Colonies Etrangères et Haïti*. Paris, 1843.

Seabrook, William B. *The Magic Island*. New York, 1929.

Seeman, Bernard. "Haiti's Economic Bondage," *American Mercury* January 1947.

Seley, Jason, "A Sculptor in Haiti," *Las Americas,* November 1953.

Sénat, Franck. *Feu Contre Papa Doc*. Paris, 1971.

"Shaky SHADA," Unsigned. *Fortune,* February 1946.

Shilts, Randy. *And the Band Played On*, New York, 1987

Simpson, J. M. *Six Months in Port-au-Prince.* Philadelphia, 1905.

Skertchley, J. E. *Dahomey As It Is.* London, 1874.

Sondern, Frederic, Jr. "Haiti Doesn't Like Dictators," *Reader's Digest* April 1957.

Steel, Ronald. "Haiti," *Atlantic Monthly,* September 1969.

Steele, Martha. "Constitutions of Haiti, 1804-1951," *RSHHG,* vol. 23. no. 84.

Steward, T. G. *The Haitian Revolution.* New York, 1914.

Stimson, Henry L., and Bundy, McGeorge, *On Active Service in Peace and War.* New York, 1948.

Stoddard, T. Lothrop. *The French Revolution in San Domingo.* Boston, 1914.

Stowe, Leland. "Haiti's Voodoo Tyrant," *Reader's Digest,* November 1963.

Street, John M. *History and Economic Geography of the Southwest Peninsula of Haiti.* Berkeley, 1960.

Sylvain, Georges, *Dix Ans de Lutte pour la Liberté, 1915-1925.* Port-au-Prince, 1925.

Taft, Edna, *A Puritan in Voodooland.* Philadelphia, 1938.

Tansill, Charles C. *The United States and Santo Domingo, 1798-1873.* Baltimore, 1938.

Texier, C. *Au Pays des Généraux.* Paris, 1891.

Thoby, Armand, *Jacques Bonhomme d'Haïti en Sept Tableaux.* Port-au-Prince, 1901.

Thomas, Ian, *Bonjour Blanc,*

Thomas, Lowell, *Old Gimlet Eye,* New York, 1932.

Thomson, Ian. *Bonjour Blanc,* London, 1992

Trouillot, Ernst. *Démesvar Delorme.* Port-au-Prince, 1958; *Prospections d'Histoire.* Port-au-Prince, 1961.

Trouillot, Michel-Rolph. "Haiti's only Hope is More Hope". *The New York Times,* 16 Dec. 1995

Vaissière, Pierre de. *Saint-Domingue: La Société et la Vie Créole sous l'Ancien Régime (1629-1789).* Paris, 1909.

Val, Jacques (pseud.). *La Dictature de Duvalier.* Paris, 1972.

Vandercook, John W. *Black Majesty.* New York, 1928.

Vastey, Pompée Valentin. *Notes à M. le Baron Malouet, Ministre de la Marine et des Colonies.* Cap Henry, 1814.

Vaval, Duraciné, "L'Abbé Henri Grégoire," *RSHHG* November 1931.

    "Pétion: l'Homme et sa Vie," *RSHHG,* July 1932.

Velie, Lester. "The Case of Our Vanishing Dollars in Haiti," *Reader's Digest,* March 1962.

Verna, Paul. *La Verdad Sobre Duvalier* (pamphlet). Caracas, 1962.

    Robert Sutherland, Amigo de Bolivar en Haïti. Caracas, 1966.

    Grand 'Anse, Patrie des Poètes," *Conjonction,* December 1947.

Verschueren, J. (pseud.). *La République d'Haïti.* Paris, 1948, 3 vols.

Vigoreux, G., "Recits Historiques," *Haïti Littéraire et Sociale,* 20 February, 5 June, 20 June 1908.

Vincent, Sténio. *En Posant les Jalons.* Port-au-Prince, 1939.

    La République d'Haïti. Brussels, 1910.

    and Lhérisson, L. C. *La Législation de l'Instruction Publique de la République d'Haïti (1804-1885).* Paris, 1898.

Wallis, William. *Sketches of Hayti,* London, 1827.

Warren, H. G. "The Origin of General Mina's Invasion of Mexico," *Southwestern Historical Quarterly*, July 1938.

Washington Office on Haiti. *Haiti: Barriers to Justice and Democracy*, Washington, 1986

Waxman, Percy. *The Black Napoleon*. New York, 1931.

Weil, T. E., and Munson, F. P. *Area Handbook for Haiti*. Washington, D.C., 1972.

Welles, Sumner. *Naboth's Vineyard*. New York, 1928.

Wilentz, Amy. *The Rainy Season*. New York, 1989. "Lives in the Balance, Letter from Haiti", *New Yorker*, 26 Dec. 1994

Williams, Joseph J. *Voodoos and Obeahs*. New York, 1932.

Wilson, Edmund. *Red, Black, Blond, and Olive*. New York, 1956; "The Marcelins - Novelists of Haiti," *Nation*, 15 October 1950.

Wimpffen, F. A. S. Baron de. *A Voyage to San Domingo in the Years 1788,1789, 1790*. London, 1797.

Winkler, Max. *Investment of U.S. Capital in Latin America*. Boston, 1928.

Wirkus, Faustin, and Taney, Dudley - *The White King of La Gonâve*. New York, 1931.

Unpublished Sources

Atcherson, Lucille, "History of the Principal Events in the Political Relations of Haiti and the United States." Division of Latin American Affairs, StateDepartment. 1923.

Armour, Norman. "Notes re My Recollection of the Visit of Franklin Delano Roosevelt to Haiti, July, 1934." Undated, privately held.

Beach, Edward L., Sr. "Admiral Caperton in Haiti." 1919. Privately held.

; "Annapolis to Scapa Flow." 1919. Privately held.

Butler, Smedley Darlington. The Smedley Darlington Butler Papers. U.S.Marine Corps Historical Division, Washington, D.C.

Caperton, William. The William Caperton Papers. Library of Congress.

Daniels, Josephus. The Josephus Daniels Papers. Library of Congress.

Drew, Gerald A. " FDR Comes to Haiti: 5 July 1934. " Undated. Privately held.

Forbes, W. Cameron. The W. Cameron Forbes Papers, Library of Congress.

Gruening, Ernest. Draft memoirs. 1972. Privately held.

Heinl, Michael "Haiti notes 1974-1995", Privately held.

Heinl, Nancy G. "Haiti Journal, 1959-1963." Privately held.

Heinl, R. D., Jr. "Haiti: Impacts of American Occupation, 1915-1934." Paperread at Haiti seminar, Harvard, 1969.

Howard, Donnell. "Chaos in the Caribbean," U.S. Air War College ResearchReport 33771. April 1969.

Howard, Thomas. *Journal in St. Domingo, 1796-1798*, in Boston Public Library.

Hurst. Ann. "Southerners to Handle Haitians?" Undergraduate term paper,Wellesley College. 4 May 1964.

Lejeune, John A. The John A. Lejeune Papers. Library of Congress.

Little, Louis McCarty. The Louis McCarty Little Papers. U.S. Marine CorpsHistorical Division, Washington. D.C.

MacLeod, Murdo J. "The Soulouque Regime, 1847-1859: A Reevaluation."Paper presented to M.I.T. seminar, 1969.

Marine Corps. Haiti Papers. U.S. Marine Corps Historical Center, Washington, D.C.

Matthieu, Joseph B. "Saint Domingue dans les Relations Internationale." Dissertation, Institute d'Hautes Etudes Internationales, Geneva, 1964.

Mills, Herbert E. "The Early Years of the French Navy Department. General Records. National Archives.

Ravenscroft, Kent, Jr. "Spirit Possession in Haiti: A Tentative TheoreticalAnalysis." B.A. thesis, Yale University, 1962.

Russell, John H. "History of Haiti." U.S. Marine Corps Historical Center,Washington, D.C. A Marine Looks Back on Haiti." U.S. Marine Corps Historical Center, Washington, D.C.

Schreadley, Richard L. "The American Intervention in Haiti." Ph.D. thesis,Fletcher School, Tufts University, 1969.

Sergeant, N. Diary 1900. Manuscript Division, Library of Congress.

Stimson, Henry L. The Henry L. Stimson Papers. Yale University Library.

Welles, Sumner. "Journals" and other papers. Privately held.

Wilder, Harry. "Haiti, Duvalier and the Coming Crisis." Thesis, U.S. NavalWar College, 1970.

Public Documents

Great Britain. *Calendar of State Papers, Colonial Series, America and WestIndies, 1693-1696.* Public Records Office. London.

Haiti, Republic of. *Le Moniteur,* 1845-1971. Official Government Journal.

Organization of American States. *Report by the Investigating Committee of the Organ of Consultation.* 13 March 1950.

United States. *American State Papers, U.S. Commerce and Navigation.* Washington, D.C., 1832.

; *Annual Report of the American High Commissioner at Port-au-Prince.* 1922-1929. Washington, D.C.

Foreign Relations of the United States. 1866-1945. Washington, D.C.

Hearings before the House Committee on International and Foreign Commerce. 91st Congress, 1st and 2d Sessions. Washington, D.C. ; *Hearings before a Select Committee on Haiti and Santo Domingo.* 67th Congress, 1st and 2d Sessions, 1921-1922. Washington, D.C. ; *Naval Documents Related to the Quasi-War between the United States and France. 1799-1801.* Washington, D.C., 1936, 5 vols. ; *Report of the President's Commission for the Study and Review of Conditions in the Republic of Haiti.* Washington, D.C., 1930.

Source Notes

ABBREVIATIONS

Adm	Admiralty, London
AmMin	American Minister
ArchNat	Archives Nationale, Paris
BrMin	British Minister
CT	Cuidad Trujillo
DipRels	*Diplomatic Relations of the United States*
FO	British Foreign Office
FornRels US	*Foreign Relations of the United States*
Gd'H	*Garde d'Haïti*
GOH	Government of Haiti
GPO	U.S. Government Printing Office
HO	*Haïti Observateur*
HQMC	Headquarters, U.S. Marine Corps
LC	Library of Congress, Washington, D.C.
MGC	Major General Commandant, USMC
MemCon	Memorandum of Conversation
NA	National Archives, Washington, D.C.
ONI	Office of Naval Intelligence, Washington, D.C.
NYT	*New York Times*
PauP	Port-au-Prince
PRO	Public Records Office, London
QDO	French Foreign Ministry Archives, Quai d'Orsay, Paris
RSHHG	*Revue de la Société Haïtienne de l'Histoire et de Géographie*
WO	War Office, London
WP	*Washington Post*
WSJ	*Wall Street Journal*
WT	*Washington Times*

Chapter I A Very Great Island p.11

Introduction :

Samuel E. Morison (transl. and ed., *Journals and Other Documents on the Life and Voyages of Christopher Columbus* (NY, 1963), 110-43, 212-13. S. E. Morison, "The Route of Columbus Along the North Coast of Haiti, and the Site of Navidad," *Transactions,* American Philosophical Society, December 1940. Judge, Stanfield, Marden & Lyon, *Columbus and the New World,* National Geographic, November, 1986. S. E. Morison and M. Obregon, *The Caribbean as Columbus Saw It* (Boston, 1964), 75-89.

The Rape of Quisqueya:

James Burney, *History of the Buccanneers of America* (London, 1816), 7-14, 18-27. 30. Bartolome de Las Casas, *Historia de las Indias,* ed., A. Millares Carlo (Mexico, 1951), ii, 346. G. T. Raynal, *Histoire Philosophique et Politique des Etablissements et du Commerce des Européens dans les Deux Indes* (Geneva, 1787), iv, 18. F. X. de Charlevoix, *Histoire de l'Isle Espagnole ou de S. Domingue* (Paris, 1730), i. 268-69, 287-88, 333, 341-47. Morison, "The Route of Columbus Along the North Coast of Haiti, and the Site of the Navidad." S. Rouzier, *Dictionnaire Géographique et Administratif d'Haïti* (PauP, 1928), iii, 169. C. E. Nowell, *A Letter to Ferdinand and Isabella* (Minneapolis, 1965), 45. H. M. Kreiger. *"Aborigines of the Ancient Island of Hispaniola,"* Annual Report of the Smithsonian Institution (Washington, D.C., 1929), 478. Emile Nau, *Histoire des Caciques d'Haïti* (Paris, 1894), 52-53. Marcus Rainsford, *An Historical Account of the Black Empire of Hayti* (London, 1805), 37. G. T. Raynal, *Histoire Philosophique et Politique des Isles Françaises dans les Indes Occidentales* (Lausanne, 1784), 1-5.

The Boucaniers of Tortuga :

Pierre de Vaissière, *Saint-Domingue; La Société et la Vie Créole, 1629-1789* (Paris, 1909), 6n, 7-10. Nellis M. Crouse, *French Pioneers in the West Indies* (NY, 1940), 24-26, 29-30, 81-84. Burney, 36-46, 49-51. Baskett, 55-56, 65. Raynal, *Isles Françaises,* 154-58. R. P. du Tertre, *Histoire des Antilles* (Paris, 1667), i. 415. Rainsford, 40-44. J. B. Labat, *Nouveau Voyage aux Isles de l'Amérique* (Paris, 1742), v, 79-84, 86-110, vii, 81. Nellis M. Crouse, *The French Struggle for the West Indies* (NY, 1943), 122-28. W. A. Roberts, *The French in the West Indies* (NY, 1942), 57-58. Samuel de Champlain, *Voyages to New France,* transl., Michael Macklem (London, 1971), 32-34.

I Have Given a Hand to Everyone :

L.Stewart Mims. *Colbert's West India Policy* (New Haven, 1912), 68-71, 201209, 251. Charlevoix, ii. 57-65, 78-79, 82-98, 100-101, 108-109. Labat, vii, 38-39. Vaissière, 18-19, 22, 24n. Burney, 57-58. Baskett 74-75, 77-90, 101. Rainsford, 51-54. John Esquemeling, *The Buccaneers of America* (London, 1684: reprinted 1951), 259-66. Crouse, *Struggle,* 128-34, 141-45. Roberts, 59-62. Raynal, *Isles Françaises,* 159-66.

La Partie Française de St. Domingue :

Vaissière, 16, 19-20, 24n, 27-31, 40-44, 52-53, 58, 70-71. Charlevoix, ii. 19598, 206-20, 222-24, 229, 236-37, 240, 256-60, 263-81, 285-91, 294-97. *Calendar of State Papers, Colonial Series, America and West Indies, 1693-1696 PRO* nos. 1113. 1236, 2021. Burney, 130-31, 293-307, 320-24. Raynal, *Isles Françaises,* 167-73, 179-85. Baskett, 80-83, 87n, 85-94, 98-100. Labat, vii. 95-108, 113. Thomas Madiou, *Histoire d'Haïti* (PauP, 1847), i, 19-20. R. P. Le Pers, *La Tragique Histoire des Flibustiers.- Histoire de St. Domingue et de l'Ile de la Tortue* (reprinted, Paris, undated), 204-208. Charles Leslie, *A New History of Jamaica* (London, 1740) 26-63. W. J. Gardner, *A History of Jamaica* (London, 1873), 101-104. George W. Bridges, *The Annals of Jamaica* (London, 1828), 312-24. Crouse, *Struggle,* 134-35, 146-47, 176-79, 190-98, 200-211, 218, 244. Roberts, 76-83.

Pour les Ancêtres :

Vaissière, 155-56, 164, 182-83, 189-94, 229, 234-38, 247-48. Charlevoix, ii, 235-36, 482, 498. P. M. Boissande, *Saint-Domingue à la Veille de la Révolution* (Paris, 1906). 2 1. Georges Scelle, *Histoire de la Traite Négrière* (Paris 1906), i, 122-31, ii, 182-83. Madiou, i, 20, 25, 29; iii, 442-51 (Code Noir). Alexis Beaubrun Ardouin, *Etudes sur l'Histoire d'Haïti* (Paris, 1853-1860), 1, 42-47. Dantès Bellegarde, *Histoire du Peuple Haïtien (1492-1952).* (PauP, 1953), 25. M. L. E. Moreau de Saint-Méry, *Description Topographique* (Philadelphia, 1797-1798), i, 23, 25-34, 694; ii, 497-503. Louis E. Elie, *Histoire d'Haïti* (PauP, 1944), ii, 164-65, 174-77, 180-85. Pompée Valentin Vastey, *Notes à M. le Baron Malouet, Ministre de la Marine et des Colonies,* (Cap Henry, 1814), 6. F. A. S. Wimpffen, *Voyage à Saint-Domingue* (Paris, 1797), ii, 10-12. Rouzier, i, 65. C. L. R. James, *The Black Jacobins: Toussaint l'Ouverture and the Revolution* (London, 1963), 5.

Rich as a Creole :

Vaissière, *55, 151-52,* 216, 28o-81, 297-300, 330-31. Baskett, 102. Michel-René Hilliard d'Auberteuil, *Considérations sur la Colonie de Saint-Domingue* (Geneva, 1799), ii, 169. Rainsford, 60-65, 81, 85. Adolphe Cabon, *Histoire d'Haïti* (PauP, 1921), i, 76. Bryan Edwards, *An Historical Survey of the Island of Saint Domingo* (London, 1801), 30-31, 230-31. Moreau de Saint-Méry, i, 11. Wimpffen, i, 274-75, 277; ii, 8. Elie, *Histoire,* ii, 289. Madiou, i, 25. Rayford W. Logan, *Haiti and the Dominican Republic* (NY, 1968), 86-88. Georges Pollett, *Saint-Domingue et l'Autonomie, 1629-1730* (Paris, 1934), 224-30, 248-56, 258-62. H. P. Davis, *Black Democracy* (NY, 1936), 23-26. Victor Advielle, *L'Odyssée d'un Normand à St. Domingue* (Paris, 1901), 46. Paul E. Dubuisson, *Nouvelles Considérations sur Saint-Domingue* (Paris, 1780), Pt ii, 32.

Loaded Barrels of Gunpowder :

Vaissière, 164, 217, 222-23, 230. Moreau de Saint-Méry, *Description Topographique,* i, 68-89. Justin Placide, *Histoire Politique et Statistique de l'Isle d'Hayti, Saint-Domingue* (Paris, 1826), 145. Madiou, i, 24,49. Baskett, 110-12. Elie, *Histoire,* ii, 190-91, 197-205, 209-10, 289-91. Edwards, 30-40. Cabon, *Histoire,* ii, 397-400. Washington to Philip Schuyler, 24 November 1779, in *Writings of Washington* (Washington, 1937), xvii, 176.

Chapter 2 Bois Cayman and Carmagnole p.37

Introduction :

Cabon, *Histoire,* ii, 9, 20, 44-45. *Le Moniteur Universel,* 27 June, 3-4 July, and 22 October 1789; 8 and 28 March 1790. S. G. Perkins, *Reminiscences of the Insurrection in St. Domingo* (Cambridge, 1886), 14-15. Edwards, 65-70, 72-74, 235-44. Clarkson, *Notes,* ii, 246-58, 304-306. C. M. B., *A Glimpse of Hayti and Her Negro Chief* (Liverpool, 1850), 57.

Bois Cayman :

Edwards, 92-102, 103n. S. G. Perkins, 17n. Ardouin, 226-31, 234-45. Madiou, i, 70-73. Cabon, *Histoire,* ii, 70-71. F. Carteau, *Entretiens sur les Evénments qui ont opéré la Ruine de la Partie Française de Saint-Domingue* (Bordeaux, 1802), 87-88. Antoine Métral, *Histoire de l'Insurrection des Esclaves dans le Nord de Saint Domingue* (Paris, 1818), 9-25. Hubert Cole, *Christophe, King of Hayti* (NY, 1967), 52. Letter, British officer, name unknown, 24 September 1791,ArchNat D-xxv, 79. A. Parham, *My Odyssey: By a Creole of St. Domingue* (New Orleans, 1959), 31. Letter, Marquise du Rouvray to her daughter, 4 September 1791, *Correspondance Familiale du Marquis et de la Marquise du Rouvray* (Paris, 1959), 27.

France Must Renounce All Hope :

Debates of the National Assembly, 7 and 11-15 May 1791. Wimpffen, 49-51. Letter, Moreau de Saint-Méry, quoted in T. L. Stoddard, *The French Revolution in San Domingo* (Boston, 1914), 119. *Adresse de l'Assemblée Provinciale du Nord de St. Dominque à l'Assemblée Nationale,* 13 July

1790. Rouzier, i, 322. Joseph Saint-Rémy, *Pétion et Haïti* (Paris, 1854), i, 23-24. Rouzier, iii, 310, 371.

Think This Over:

The two speeches in full are given in Madiou, iii, 451-53.

Kill, Sack, Burn :

Cabon, *Histoire*, ii, 85-88. Deposition by French merchant captain, December 1791, ArchNat D-xxv, 87. Report by Colonial Assembly to Paris, 28 January 1792, ArchNat D-xxv, 62. Pamphile Lacroix, *Mémoires* (Paris, 1819), i, 13743, 194. Edwards, 118. Stoddard, 372n. Madiou, i, 97.

Ruins, Solitude, and Scattered Bones

Cabon, *Histoire*. ii, 82-83, 89, 105-24, 147-49. Madiou, i, 74-76, 94, 131, 139-40. Rouzier, i, 309; iii, 59, 151-52, 438-39; iv, 75. Letter, Jean-François and Biassou to commissioners, 12 December 1791, ArchNat D-xxv, i. Stoddard, 173-74, 191-209. J. Garron-Coulon, *Rapport sur les Troubles de St. Domingue, fait au Nom de la Commission des Colonies* (Paris, 1798), iii, 299315. J.-N. Léger, *Haïti: Son Histoire et ses Detracteurs* (NY, 1907), 52n. Letter, Rigaud to commissioners, 24 June 1793, ArchNat D-xxv, 16. Parham, 51, 71. J.-C. Dorsainvil, *Manuel d'Histoire d'Haïti* (PauP, 1934), 85-86. Edwards, 134-36.

C'est la Fin du Monde :

Edwards, 134-37, 142-45. Madiou, i, 135-38. S. G. Perkins, 36-44, 61. Cabon, *Histoire*, ii, 150-56, 172. ArchNat D-xxv, 47-48, 79-84. H. de Poyen, *Les Guerres des Antilles, 1793-1815* (Paris, 1896), 31-33. Gérard M. Laurent, *Le Commissaire Sonthonax à Saint-Domingue* (PauP, 1965), i, 66, 139-50, 155-58, 161. Letter, Sonthonax to Michel-Ange Mangourit (French consul, Charleston) 8 July 1793, in New York Public Library. Lacroix, ii, 209. Rouvray, *Correspondance, 102.*

The Evangel of France :

Proclamation by Sonthonax, 29 August 1973, in Cabon, *Histoire,* ii, 178-8 1, and in Garron-Coulon, iv, 59-64. Letter, R. Marie to Thomas Millet, 18 March 1794. Sonthonax to Convention, 9 September 1793, in ArchNat D-xxv, 12. *Le Moniteur Officiel.* 3-4 February 1794. Madiou, i, 145, 171-78. Jean Price-Mars "Les Origines et le Destin d'un Nom." *RSHHG,* January 1940.

Chapter 3 I Am Toussaint Louverture p.61

Britain and Spain Intervene :

Edwards, 169-77. Cabon, *Histoire, III.* 192-95, 199, 203. Madiou, 90n, 133-38, 165. Lacroix, i, 25. Report, Capt John Ford, RN, to Admiralty, September 1793, Adm 1/245, in PRO.

The British Advance :

Edwards, 172, 178-86. Cabon, *Histoire,* ii, 200-206, 212-16. Poyen, 36-38.

I Am Bent on Vengeance:

Dantès Bellegarde, *La Nation Haïtienne* (Paris, 1938), 70-71. Rouzier, iii, 215, 469. Ralph Korngold, *Citizen Toussaint* (Boston, 1944), 100. H. Pauléus Sannon, *Histoire de Toussaint Louverture* (PauP, 1920), 2, 139, 165-68. Madiou, i,139, 193-96, 199. *Le Moniteur Universel*, 20 January 1799. Edwards, 187-90. *Cabon, Histoire.* 240-41. Percy Waxman, *The Black Napoleon* (NY, 1931), 106.

After God, Laveaux :

Edwards, 195-200, 203n, 222, 384-86. Cabon, *Histoire*, ii, 252-53, 357-59, 261, 283-84, 289-91. Madiou, i, 197. Korngold, 116. MajGen Sir Adam Williamson to War Office, WO 1/61/62, PRO. Laveaux to Committee of Public Safety, 14 January 1796, in Bibliothèque Nationale, Paris, ff. 12104. Lacroix, i, 308-309. *Le Moniteur Universel*, 18 November 1794. Charles C. Tansill, *The United States and Santo Domingo, 1798-1873* (Baltimore, 1938), 6, 8. Jefferson toMonroe, 14 July 1793, Jefferson Papers, LC, vol. 97. John Fortescue, *A History of the British Army* , iv, 545-46. Rainsford, 204-206. Thomas Howard, *Journal in St. Domingo, 1796-1798*, in Boston Public Library.

Toussaint Consolidates :

Lacroix, i, 309, 312-16. Cabon, *Histoire*, ii, 287, 308-312, 315-22, 347, 352-57. Toussaint to Laveaux, 1 June 1798, in ArchNat. Sonthonax to Minister of Marine, 23 July 1796, in ArchNat D-xxv, 45. Rigaud to Corps Législatif, 21 October 1796, ArchNat AF-iii, 208. Cole, 50. BrigGen Sir Thomas Maitland, letter. 23 July 1798, WO 1/70, PRO.

A Brigand Island :

Nouveau Larousse Illustré (Paris, 1902), v, 59. Cabon, *Histoire*, iii, 370-71, 374-76, 389, 395. *Dictionary, of National Biography* (London, 1893), xxxv, 374-76. Madiou, i, 306, 309, 312-13, 322-25. Catts Pressoir, "Quelle Est l'Origine du Mot Gourde?," *RSHHG*, July 1947, 67ff. Maitland to Dundas. March 1798, WO 1/69, PRO. Edwards, 385-86, 396, 400, 402. Maitland to Dundas, 23 July 1798; MajGen the Earl of Balcarres to Maitland, 6 July 1798; Maitland to Dundas, 31 July 1798; Adm Sir Hyde Parker to Maitland, 30 July, 7 and 27 August 1798: Maitland to Parker, 23 August 1798; Maitland to Dundas, 31 August 1798, WO 1/70; Maitland to Dundas, 28 August 1798; BrigGen Spencer to Dundas, 3 October and 13 November 1798, all in WO 1/70, PRO. Fortescue, iv, 565.

Hédouville Fails :

Maitland to Dundas, 26 December 1798; Spencer to Dundas, 13 November 1798; both in WO 1/70, PRO. Cabon, *Histoire*, iii, 396-97, 400-401. Rayford W. *Logan, Diplomatic Relations of the United States with Haïti* (Chapel Hill. 194 1), 65-66. Lacroix, i, 346-47. Madiou, i, 310, *312. Le Moniteur Universel*, 27 December 1798. H. de P. Poyen, *Histoire Militaire de la Révolution de Saint-Domingue* (Paris, 1899), 67.

Civil War

Roume to Minister of Marine, 11 February 1799, in ArchNat, AF-iii, 2 to. Cabon, *Histoire*, iv, 25-26, 41, 46-50. Madiou, i, 333-34, 345. Kornold, 173. Rouzier, i, *353-54; ii,* 15. Toussaint to Christophe, 15 July 1799, in Madiou. i, 346. Lacroix, i, 376-79. Capt Patrick Fletcher, USN, to Benjamin Stoddert, 14 August 1799, in U.S. Navy Department, *Quasi-War with France*, ii, 243; i, 30; ii, 479. *American State Papers, Commerce and Navigation* (Washington, 1832), i, 24. Mentor

Laurent, "*Toussaint Louverture et l'Indépendance de Saint-Domingue,*" in *Le Document,* 20 May 1946 (PauP). Stoddert to Capt Christopher R. Perry, USN, 3 September 1799, in *Quasi-War,* iv, 149-50. Higginson to Pickering, 20 September 1799, 209. Liston to Grenville, 31 January 1799, FO 5/25, PRO. Hamilton to Pickering in *Works of Alexander Hamilton* (NY, 18501851), vi, 395. Tansill, 12.

War in the South :

Stevens to Pickering, 13 February, 4 April, and 16 March 1800, in *Quasi-War,* v, 183, 383, 312. Letter, U.S. Naval Officer, USS *General Greene.* 4 April 1800, *Quasi-War,* V. 250. Rouzier, iii, 50-54, 57-59.Samuel E. Morison, *Old Bruin* (Boston. 1968), 16-21. Toussaint to Stevens, 21March 1800, *Quasi-War,* v, 336. Ritchie to Pickering, 3 May 1800, *Quasi-War,* v, 473. Proclamation by First Consul to Citizens of Saint-Domingue, 25 December 1799, in ArchNat. Lacroix, i, 373-94. Ardouin, iv, 176. Sannon, ii, 188-99. H. L. Castonnet des Fosses. *La Révolution de Saint-Domingue* (Paris, 1893), 211, 213.

Santo Domingo Occupied :

Castonnet des Fosses, 218-22, 224-25. Lacroix, ii, 1-20. Stevens to Pickering, 16 March 1800, *Quasi-War,* v, 311 Cabon, *Histoire,* iv, 133-35, 139-40, 143-47, 149-53. Chanlatte to Minister of Marine. in Ardouin, iv, 161. Sannon, ii, 205209, 218. Sumner Welles. *Naboth's Vineyard* (NY, 1928), i. 20-21, 26-27. Gilbert Guillermin. *Précis Historique des Derniers Evénmens de Saint-Domingue* (Paris. 1811), 372.

Toussaint Reigns :

Edwards, 257. Becker to Minister of War, ArchNat, Ministry of War, iv, A. Unknown officer to Minister of Marine, ArchNat, AF-iv, I 212. Castonnet des Fosses. 232-33, 235, 238-40, 245, 260-62. Rouzier. i, 248. Lacroix, ii, 25, 30-32, 46-49, 51. Dorsainvil,*Manuel,* 124. Charles Mackenzie, *Notes on Hayti* (London, 1830), ii, 298. Madiou, 95, 104-105, 119-24. C. L. R. James, 182. Louis-Joseph Janvier, *Constitutions d'Haïti* (Paris, 1886), 7-23. Martha Steele, "Constitutions of Haiti, 1804-1951. "*RSHHG.* vol. 23, no. 84, pp. 17ff. Cabon, *Histoire.* iv, 163-70, 201-204. Sannon, iii, 25-29. Alphonse Marie Louis de Prat de Lamartine, *Toussaint Louverture: Poème Historique.*

Chapter 4 The Death of St. Domingue p. 95

Introduction :

Pichon to Talleyrand, 22 July 1801, ArchNat, Affaires Etrangères (E.-U.), vol. 53, 177-84. Tansill. 78-81. Lear to Madison, 17 July 1801, Consular Dispatches. NA. Napoleon to Talleyrand, *Correspondance de Napoleon,* vii, 307. "*Notes pour servir aux instructions à donner au Capitaine Général Leclerc,* " *31* October 1801, ArchNat, AF-iv, 863. *Correspondance de Napoleon,* vii, 322ff, and Napoleon to Leclerc, 1 July 1802, vii, 503. Poyen, 87-90. Lacroix, ii, 63.

They Have Cut off Only the Trunk

Poyen. *Histoire Militaire,* 96-97, 103-104, 107, 137-49. Cabon, *Histoire, iv,* 211, 2csl;-Sg. Sannon, iii, 48, 62-63, 107. Leclerc to Christophe, 3 February 1802. in *Lettres du Général Leclerc* (Paris, 1937; unless otherwise noted all Leclerc letters are from this source). Lacroix, ii, 6s-66, 74, 76-77, 96, 149-54, 164-65, 172. Leclerc to Minister of Marine, 9, 15, I7, and 27 February 18O2. Rouzier.

i, 376-77. Madiou, ii, 146-52. 194. Mauviel to Napoleon, ArchNat, AF-iv, 1187. CO, HMS Nereide, to Admiralty, March 1802, Adm I/252, PRO.

These People Won't Surrender :

Mary Hassal, *Secret History, or the Horrors of St. Domingo* (Philadelphia, 1808), 17, 24, 51. Decree by First Consul, 6 April 1802. *Correspondance, vii,* 430. Decrès to Leclerc, 14 June 1802. Stoddard, 332, 346. Laurés Junot, *Home and Court Life of the Emperor Napoleon* (London, 1893), ii, 342. Edwards, 201n. Leclerc to Napoleon, 7 May and 16 September 1802. Poyen, *Histoire Militaire,* 239-42. Cabon, *Histoire,* iv, 276, 280. Lacroix, ii, 209, 218. Napoleon to Decrès, 4 June 1802, *Correspondance.* vii, 617. Baskett, 284. Timoleon C. Brutus. *L'Homme d'Airain* (PauP, 1946), i, 241-42, 274-75. Mauviel Guillaume, *Anecdotes de la Révolution de Saint-Domingue* (Paris, 1885), 116-19. Rainsford, 336-38. Madiou, ii, 328-30; iii, 14-15, 469.

Most Unhappy Man of Men :

Encyclopaedia Britannica, 1951 , xiii, 191. Cabon, *Histoire,* iv, 267. Sannon, iii, 157-68. William Wordsworth, *"To Toussaint L'Ouverture,"* Morning Post (London) 2 February 1803. Emmanuel-Augustin-Dieudonné-Marin-Joseph Las Casas, *Memorial de Sainte-Helène, 1822.*

Li Porté Fusils, Li Porté Boulets:

T.C. Brutus, i, 288-89, 294-95, 304-10. M. J. B. Lemonnier-Delafosse, *Seconde Campaigne de Saint-Domingue* (Paris, 1846), 85-87, 89-90. Dorsainvil, *Manuel,* 155-162. Poyen, *Histoire Militaire,* 417-19, 421-29, 452-56, 458-59. Sannon, iii, 196-99, 203. Madiou, iii, 102. Edward Burt, *Historical Notices of St. Domingo* (Bath, 1844), 37. Castonnet des Fosses, 345-46. Lacroix, ii, 34044. A. P. M. Laujon, *Précis Historique de la Dernière Expedition de Saint-Domingue* (Paris, 1805), 228-30. Logan, *Haiti and Dominican Republic, 94.* Cabon, *Histoire,* iv, 330-31.

Chapter 5 We Must Live Free or Die p.119

Skin of a Blanc for Parchment :

Madiou, iii, 112-19. Dorsainvil, *Manuel,* 163-66. Cabon, *Histoire.* iv, 319-21, 333. T. C. Brutus, i, 333-46.

Massacre of the French :

Madiou iii, 100, 119-20, 126, 128-37, 138-39, 141-44. Bellegarde, *Nation, 87.* T. C. Brutus, i, 347-48; ii, 4. Letter, unknown French emigre from Kingston, 1 June 1804, ArchNat, AF-iv, 1213. Pierre-Etienne Chazotte (ed., Charles Platt), *The Black Rebellion in Haiti* (privately printed, 1927), 72-83, 95-96. Capt John Perkins, RN, to Sir John Duckworth, 30 March 1804, Adm 1/254, PRO. Baskett, 305. Charles Malo, *Histoire de l'Isle de Saint-Domingue* (Paris, 1819), 287-92. Dorsainvil, *Manuel,*169-171 *Tribut de Reconnaissance à Mr. Duncan M'Intosh* (Baltimore, 18o9), 6-7, 10-15.

Dessalines Reigns:

Madiou, iii, 12I-23, 168-74. Saint-Victor Jean-Baptiste, *Les Fondateurs devant l'Histoire* (PauP, undated), 52n. 154n. Burt, 45. Malo, 279, 306-307. Guy-Joseph Bonnet, *Souvenirs Historiques* (Paris, 1864), 137. Bellegarde, *Histoire,* 97, 1O1, 103, 121, 123, 180. T. C. Brutus, ii, 34-38. Lacroix, ii, 254-55. Adolphe Cabon, *L'Histoire Réligieuse d'Haïti* (PauP, 1933), 90-95.

Invasion of Santo Domingo :

Bellegarde, *Histoire*, 100-102. Madiou, iii, 190-206. Welles, *Vineyard, i,* 35, 37-39. Gaspar de Arredondo y Pichardo, *"Memoria de mi Salida de la Isla de Santo Domingo, 1805,"* ms. published in *Clio* (CT), no. 82, 1948. Lemonnier-Delafosse, 126-50. *Nouveau Larousse Illustré* (Paris, 1903), vi, 124. Poyen, *Histoire Militaire.* 489-503. Dorsainvil, *Manuel,* 172.

The Devil Himself Has Burst His Chains

Bellegarde, *Histoire, 99-100,* 102-104, 106-107. Steele. Madiou, iii, 214-16, 225-26, 234-35, 239-40, 246-50, 256, 288, 290-310, 313, 322. Leyburn, 41. Ardouin, vi, 251, 323. T. C. Brutus. ii, 228. Dorsainvil, *Manuel,* 182-83.

Haiti Divided :

Bellegarde, *Histoire, II* I-13. Bonnet, 148. Ardouin, vi, 456. Madiou, iii, 36366, 369-70, 373-74, 379, 400, 411-12. Rouzier, iv, 145-47. Steele. Dorsainvil, *Manuel,* 185-88. Saint-Rémy,Pétion. 333.

Betrayal and Dissension:

J.B. Inginac, *Mémoires* (Kingston, 1843), 23. Dorsainvil, *Manuel, 199,* 202-206. Madiou. iii, 415-18. Bellegarde, *Histoire,* 117-18. Jonathan Brown, *Histon, and Present Condition of St. Domingo* (Philadelphia, 1837), 166-68, 170,176. Paul Verna, *Robert Sutherland, Amigo de Bolivar en Haïti* (Caracas, 1966),12.15-16. Rouzier, i, 164, 361. Bonnet, 167. A. L. Ambroise, "Magloire Ambroise," *RSHHG.* January 1951. Gustave d'Alaux, "L'Empereur Soulouque et Son Empire," *Revue des Deux Mondes*, Paris 1860.

The South Secedes:

Dorsainvil, *Manuel,* 210-212. Brown, ii, 177-78. Capt Sir James Lucas Yeo to Admiralty, Adm 1/263, PRO. Rouzier, i, 66; ii, 205. Cole, 195-98.

Henry by God's Grace :

Bonnet, 143-44. Brown, ii, 181-86. *Almanach Royal*, Royaume d'Haïti, 1811. Burt, 53. Ardouin, vii, 412. Julien Prévost, *Relation des Glorieuses Evénemens qui ont porté leurs Majestes Royales sur le Trône d'Haïti* (Cap Henry, 1811), 157. Welles, *Vineyard.* i, 41-44. Gerard M. Laurent, *Pages d'Histoire d'Haïti* (PauP. 1960), 255ff.

The Kingdom of the North :

Lacroix, ii, 263, 287. *Blackwood's,* IV, 1818. Brown, ii, 203-205. Cole, 211. *Almanach Royal d'Hayti,* 1820. Dorsainvil, *Manuel,* 191-96. Jean Price-Mars. "Henry Christophe," *RSHHG,* January 1934. Mackenzie, ii, 209. Burt, 50. Robin Furneaux, *"The Haiti Connexion,"* Times (London), 18 March 1974.

Papa Bon-Coeur :

Brown, ii, 193-98. Dorsainvil, *Manuel,* 200-201, 212-13, 218. John M. Street, *History and Economic Geography of the Southwest Peninsula of Haiti* (Berkeley, 1960), 181. Laurent, *Pages,* 191-93. Bonnet, 256, 274. François Dalencoeur, *La Fondation de la République d'Haïti par*

Alexandre Pétion (PauP, 1944), 275 ff. Duraciné Vaval, "Pétion: l'Homme et sa Vie," *RSHHG*. July 1932. Apollo Garnier, "Autour de la Mort de Pétion," *RSHHG*, January 1932. Leyburn, 53.

Goman in the Grande-Anse :

Madiou, iii, 383-84, 436-37. Dorsainvil, *Manuel*, 210-211, 221-22. Camille Large, "Goman et l'Insurrection de la Grande-Anse," *RSHHG*, January 1940. Rouzier, iii, 80-81.

Haïti and the Outer World :

Louis E. Elie, *Le Président Boyer et l'Empereur de Russie, Alexandre Ier* (PauP, 1942). Granville to Canning, 13 January 1825, FO 27/329, PRO. Logan, *Diplomatic Relations,* 72, 173, 183, 203-204, 223. *Annals,* 14th Congress, 2d Session, 733. Albert Gallatin, *Writings of Albert Gallatin,* ed., Henry Adams (Philadelphia i879), i, 675. Sir James Lucas Leo to Admiralty, Am 1/263, PRO. *Debates in Congress,* 19th Congress, 1st Session, 330. House Documents, 27th Congress, 3d Session, no. 36, 117. T. C. Brutus, ii, 163-65. Dorsainvil, *Manuel,* 214-16. Ardouin, viii, 180-87. Bellegarde, *Histoire,* 121-22. H. G. Warren, "The Origin of General Mina's Invasion of Mexico," *Southwestern Historical Quarterly,* July 1938. Marion-ainé, *Expédition de Simon Bolivar* (PauP, 1849). François Dalencoeur, *Alexandre Pétion devant l'Humanité* (PauP, 1928), 11, 23. Daniel Florencio O'Leary *Memorias* (Caracas, 1879), xxiv, 283. Dantès Bellegarde, "Pétion et Bolivar," *RSHHG,* October 1941.

They Do Not Know the People I Have to Govern :

Stewart to Thomas Clarkson, 8 December 1820 (letter 46, *Henry Christophe and Thomas Clarkson,* eds., E. L. Griggs and C. H. Prator, Berkeley, 1952). Burt, 60. Brown, ii, 237. *Report, Select Committee on the Extinction of Slavery throughout the British Dominions,* 11 August 1832, 224. Bellegarde, *Histoire,* 127-28. Dorsainvil, *Manuel,* 222-23. William Wilson, "Fragments of Journal," *RSHHG,* October 1951. Schoelcher, ii, 152-55. William Wilson to Clarkson, 5 December 1820 (letter 44, *Christophe and Clarkson*). George Clarke to Clarkson, 4 November 1820 (letter 43, *Christophe and Clarkson*). Cole, 26674.

Chapter 6 Chaos and Contentment p.157

Introduction :

Schoelcher, ii, 156. Cole, 277. Prince Sanders to Clarkson. 2 May 1823 (letter *58, Christophe to Clarkson).* James Franklin, *The Present State of Hayti (*London, 1828), 11. Leyburn, 65.

Conquest of Santo Domingo:

Bellegarde, *Histoire.* 128-31. Jean Price-Mars, "L'Unité Politique de l'Ile d'Haïti." *RSHHG,* October 1937. Welles, Vineyard, *i,* 50-53. Bonnet to Boyer, 27 December 1821, in Bonnet, 3 . Bonnet. 316, 322. Cabon, *Histoire Réligieuse,* 139-41, 156-70. Emilio Rodriguez-Demorizi, *Invasiones Haitiannas de 1801, 1805,1822* (CT. 1955), 305-307.

Relations with France:

Abel-Nicolas Léger, *Histoire Diplomatique d'Haïti* (PauP, 1930), i, 22-25,

30-37,54-63, 90-99, 123-41, 147, 166-71, 173-79, 190-95. Ghislain Gouraige, *L'Indépendance d'Haïti devant la France* (PauP. 1955), 18-19, 26,45-54, 57-62, 86-94, 103-107, 245-50. 252-55, 289, 322-26, 332-35, 343-44. William Wallis Harvey, *Sketches of Hayti* (London, 1827), 3 33. Undated instructions, Minister of Marine to Dauxion-Lavaysse, et al.. in J. B. G. Wallez. *Précis Historique des Négotiations entre la France et Saint-Domingue* (Paris, 1826), App. B, 13-16, 307-312. Dorsainvil,.*Manuel*, 225 -28. Schoelcher, ii, 160-61. Bellegarde. *Histoire*. 131. Pétion to commissioners, to November 1816, in Wallez, 267 ff. Logan, *Diplomatic Relations*, 220. 231-32. *Le Télégraphe*. 17 July 1825. GOH, *Réclamation de la Partie de l'Est d'Haïti par l'Espagne* (PauP, 1830). Ardouin, x, 54, 65, 76-77. W. S. Robertson. *France and Latin-American Independence* (Baltimore, 1939), 447-48, 464-65, 467. Granville to Canning, 25 July 1825, FO 27/331, PRO.

What Disorder, What General Ruin :

Schoelcher, ii, 177, 247-48. 251, 264-65, 298, 332-33, 336-37; i, 113. Mackenzie, i, 82, 113-14; ii, 298. Charles Steedman, RAdm USN, *Memoir and Correspondence 1811-1890* (Cambridge, 1912), 41. Franklin, 268, 306, 337ff. Leyburn, 70-71. 75. Brown, ii, 236, 285. Lepelletier de Saint-Rémy, *Saint-Domingue* (Paris, 1846), ii, 210, 227. Ardouin, x, 5, 71-72, 77; xi, 326ff. Dorsainvil, *Manuel*, 229-33. Rouzier, i, 203, 292; iii, 462-63. Edouard Depestre, *et al.,Discours Parlementaires* (PauP, 1911), 31-33,44-47, 51, 100. Pierre-Eugène de Lespinasse, *Gens d'Autrefois* (reprinted, Paris. 1961), 36-37, 44, 61. Madiou, iv. 68. Log, HMS Scylla. 28 February-18 March 1843, Adm 53/1240, PRO. *Haiti in 1843 (PP. 179-180)*. Price-Mars. *"L'Unité Politique."* Bellegarde, *Histoire*, 139. Bonnet, 376. Price-Mars. preface to Gouraige, vii.

Chapter 7 Darkness Descends p. 175

Rivière-Hérard and the Downfall of the Mulâtres :

Lepelletier de Saint-Rémy, *Saint-Domingue*, ii, 230ff, 245-47, 251-53, 259-Madiou, iv, 11-15, 50n, 57-58, 90, 132, 135-37, 147-48, 152-55, 158-59, 163, 166, 170-71. Dorsainvil, *Manuel*, 235-40. Bellegarde, *Histoire*, 143-45. Welles, *Vineyard*, 58-59, 63-65. J.-N. Léger, 192-93.

Three Old Men :

Dorsainvil, *Manuel*, 243-49. Emmanuel Edouard, *Recueil Général des Lois et Actes du Gouvernement d'Haïti* (Paris, 1888), viii, 404. Bellegarde, *Histoire*, 146-51. Madiou, iv, 277-78, 289, 298, 321-25, 343-50, 385, 393-95, 400-401. A.-N. Léger, i, 243-45, 247-48. D'Alaux, 59n.

Ruin and Schism :

Franklin, 393. Madiou, i, 190; iii, 132-33. Cabon, *Histoire Réligieuse*, 63n, 69, 90-92, 102-103, 105, 121-22, 126-27, 131, 134-35, 139, 145-49, 157, 185-89, 199, 205-12, 225, 236-37, 267-68, 298, 303-305, 308-10. John Candler, *Brief Notices of Hayti* (London, 1842), 72, 97-98, 100, 165.

Saints and Guyons, Rome and Old Dahomey :

Madiou, iv, 361-62. Bellegarde, *Histoire*, 150.D'Alaux, 63ff.

The Tranquillity of the Tomb :

Bellegarde, *Histoire.* 153-55, 57. Justin Bouzon, *Etudes Historiques sur la Présidence de Faustin Soulouque* (Paris, 1894), 12, 100-104, 113-17, 134-36. Dorsainvil, *Manuel,* 252-56, 267. Paul Dhormoys, *Une Visite chez Soulouque* (2d ed, Paris, 1864), 13. D'Alaux, 76, 80, 83-84, 97, 107-109, 116-23, 136-37, 143-47, 151, 172-75, 178-80. Robert M. Walsh, *"My Mission to San Domingo,"* Lippincott's, March 1871, 296.

Soulouque Invades Santo Domingo :

Dorsainvil, *Manuel,* 256-58. Dhormoys, 25, 28-29. A.-N. Léger, i, 249, 253-56, 265-68. Benjamin E. Green to Secretary of State, 27 September 1849, in Manning, *Inter-American Affairs,* vi, 46. Jonathan Elliot to Secretary of State, 24 April 1849, *Inter-American Affairs,* vi, 42. D'Alaux, 190-93, 196. Proclamation, *Moniteur Haïtien,* 5 May 1849. Welles, *Vineyard,* i, 89-91.

A New Emperor and His Court :

Cabon, *Histoire Réligieuse,* 405-408, 422-25. Rouzier, iv, 260-62. Walsh, 303. *Haïti Litteraire et Sociale* (PauP), no. 13, 20 July 1905. Felix Ribeyre, *Cham. sa Vie et son Oeuvre* (Paris, 1884), 11-13. Bellegarde, *Histoire,* 159-60. D'Alaux, 69n, 183-85, 203-204, 208-209. Dorsainvil, *Manuel,* 260-62. *République d'Haïti* (Paris, 1905), 368-69.

If I Were to Beat the Sacred Drums :

D'Alaux, 61, 70-71, 90n, 173, 180, 220. Dhormoys, 36-38. J.-C. Dorsainvil, *Voudou et Névrose* (PauP, 1931), 46. Spenser St. John, *Hayti, or the Black Republic* (London, 1884), 184.

Cimmerian Darkness :

Welles, *Vineyard,* i, 104-105. A. N. Léger, i, 273. Logan, *Haiti and Dominican Republic,* 36. Green to Secretary of State, 19 February 1850 and 15 June 1850, in Manning, vi, 70, 84. Logan. *Diplomatic Relations,* 249-51, 256-57, 273-74. I.-N. Léger, 199. Dorsainvil, *Manuel,* 264-68. D'Alaux, 181, 222n, 249, 250-52. Wyke to Palmerston, 2 5 September 1850, FO II 5/108, PRO, London. Green to Secretary of State, 4 January 1850, with enclosure (Special Agents, vol. 18) NA. Walsh to Secretary of State, 8 April 1851, ibid. Dhormys, 17. Robert Lacombe, *Histoire Monétaire de Saint-Domingue* (Paris, 1958), 64. Bellegarde, *Histoire,* 122. Anténor Firmin, *M. Roosevelt, Président des Etats-Unis et la République d'Haïti.* (Paris,1905) 368-69

The End of Empire:

A.-N. Léger, i. 300-301, 314-1 6. Welles.i, 156-57. D'Alaux, 280-81. Mark B. Bird, *L'Homme Noir* (Edinburgh, 1867), 241. J.-N. Léger, 199, 202. Antoine Michel, *Avènement du Général F. N. Geffrard à la Présidence d'Haïti* (PauP, 1932), xxxviii-x1, 3, 7-8, 11-17, 31, 66, 72, 75, 82, 86, 93. J. M. Ludlow, "Geffrard, President of Haiti," *Good Words* (London, 1862), 524. Byron to Sir H. Stewart. 1 January 1859, Adm 128/43, PRO. Capt R. B. McCrea to MajGen Bell, 1 January 1859, ibid. Byron to Stewart. 24 January 1859, ibid. Commo H. G. Kellett to Stewart, 26 January 1859, ibid. Frédéric Marcelin, *Ducas Hyppolite* (Paris. 1878). 6.

Introduction :

Byron to Stewart. 24 January 1859, Adm 128/43, PRO. St. John, 110, 176.

They Look upon Moderation As Weakness :

Bellegarde. *Histoire*, 165-66, 168. St. John, 15, 108, 110. Dorsainvil, *Manuel*, 272, 277-79, 282. Bird, 267-68, 278, 280-81, 283-86, 291-92. 305-307. F. Marcelin, *Hyppolite*, 72, 118. *Dictionary of American Biography* (NY, 1933). v, 156-57. Emmanuel Lamaute, *Le Vieux Port-au-Prince* (PauP. 1939), 55, 177, 179. Sténio Vincent and L. C. Lhérisson. *La Législation de l'Instruction Publique de la République d'Haïti (1804-1895)* (Paris, 1898), 509. J.-N. Léger, 205. Ludlow, 526. Thomas N. Ussher to Kellett, 4 and 10 September and 13 October 1859, Adm 128/43, PRO.

Goat without Horns :

Dorsainvil, *Manuel*, 282-83. Bellegarde, *Histoire*, 167. Bird, 279. St. John, 197-205,209.

By Schisms Rent Asunder, By Heresies Beset :

Note: This section derives overwhelmingly from Cabon's magisterial *Histoire Réligieuse,* from which specific citation plus a few others are given. Cabon, *Histoire Réligieuse*, 231, 288-89, 291, 294, 319-35, 339, 345-50, 353, 356, 367, 393, 421, 424, 429-30, 440, 445-47. Dhormoys, 36. Dorsainvil, *Manuel, 370-72.* Madiou, iv, 190-95, 227-57.

Geffrard's Diplomacy :

Welles, *Vineyard,* i, 202, 211, 222-23, 243. Dorsainvil, *Manuel,* 276. Duraciné Pouilh, "A la Mémoire de M. Eugène Bourjolly," pamphlet (PauP, 1896). St. John, 103. Lespinasse, 102-106. Logan, *Haiti and Dominican Republic,* 40-42. James D. Richardson, A *Compilation of the .Messages and Papers of the Presidents, 1789-1897* (Washington, 1899), vi, 47. B. F. Whidden to Seward, 6 June 1863 and 22 December 1864, NA (Hayti Despatches). Logan, *Diplomatic Relations,* 305. Seward to H. E. Peck, 20 August 1866, NA (Hayti Instructions).

Sedition, Conspiracy, and Attentat:

Robert L. Rotberg, *Haiti, the Politics of Squalor* (Boston, 1971), 393. Dorsainvil, *Manuel.* 278, 280-84. Marcelin, *Hyppolite,* 51, 67, 77, 80-81, 92, 177-79. Whidden to Seward, 1 October 1862. Auguste Magloire, *Histoire d'Haïti* (PauP, 1909), Pt. 11, vol. ii, 222-23. A. Michel, *Geffrard,* 120. St. John, 105-106, 109, 177, 269. J-N. Léger, 206-207. Firmin. *Roosevelt,* 383. Démesvar Delorme, *Reflexions Diverses sur Mgr. Alexis-Jean-Marie Guilloux* (PauP, 1929), 90.

Salnave's Insurrection :

Dorsainvil, *Manuel,* 284-85. A. Magloire, 11, ii, 232-34. Rouzier, iii, 508; i, 225-26. F. Marcelin, *Hyppolite,* 192-93. Whidden to Seward, 28 August 1865, NA (Hayti Despatches). Peck to Seward, 9 and 14 September 1865, ibid. Adolphe Cabon, *Monseigneur Alexis-Jean-Marie Guilloux* (PauP, 1929), 101.

The Royal Navy Intervenes :

Dorsainvil, *Manuel*, 285. Peck to Seward. 27 September 1865 and 11 December i865, NA (Hayti Despatches). Log, HMS *Bulldog*, Adm 128/50, PRO. Commo Sir F. Leopold McClintock to Adm Sir James Hope, 5 November 1865, with endorsement by CinC, ibid. Precis on the loss of H MS *Bulldog*, Flag Secretary, CinC Jamaica, ibid. Report of Proceedings, HMS *Galatea*, 22 November 1865, ibid. A. Magloire. II, ii, 234. F. Marcelin, *Hyppolite*, *203-204*. *Bulletin de la Révolution*, undated, ibid., 195-202. Logan. *Diplomatic Relations, 320-21.*

His Hour Has Come :

Dorsainvil,*Manuel*, 285-87. F. Marcelin, *Hyppolite*, 207, 231, 233-38. Peck to Seward, 11 September 1865; 26 March, 4 and 20 April, 9 and 14 July, 13 August, 22 October, and 28 December, all 1866; 7 January, 23 February, 11 and 13 March, all 1867, NA (Hayti Despatches). Logan, *Diplomatic Relations, 323.* St. John to FO, 6 June 1866, FO 115/450. PRO. J.-N. Léger, 208-209. Cabon, *Guilloux*, 103, St. John, 108-109, 132, 173. A. Magloire, 11, ii, 262-63, 271-73. Bird, 283, 305, 309, 317-18. *Moniteur Haïtien*, 24 February 1867. *National Cyclopedia of American Biography* (NY. 1904), xii, 115.

Salnave President:

Peck to Seward, 27 March and 6 April 1867, NA(Hayti Despatches). F. Marcelin, *Hyppolite*, 253-59,271, 277-78,284-86. Dorsainvil,*Manuel*, 289-99. Edgar La Selve, *Le Pays des Nègres* (Paris, 1881), 158. Firmin, *Roosevelt*, 388. Ernst Depestre, *Démesvar Delorme* (PauP, 1958), 45-47.

The Cacos Revolt :

Firmin. *Roosevelt*, 388-89. Cabon. *Guilloux*, 122n. Dorsainvil, *Manuel*. 291-92. Rouzier, ii, 40; iii, 270, 282; iv. 237. A. Magloire, II, ii, 300-322, 354-56. François Denis Légitime, "Souvenirs Historiques," *Revue de la Société de Legislation* (PauP), August and November 1907. F. Marcelin, *Hyppolite, 311* . *Moniteur Haïtien*, April 1868.

General Insurrection:

Dorsainvil, *Manuel*, 292-93. St. John, 112. A. Magloire, II, ii, 322-24, 328, 330-31, 341-48. Hollister to Seward, 25 and 27 April and 8 May, all 1868, NA (Hayti Despatches). Cabon, *Guilloux*. 138-39. Légitime, *"Souvenirs."* Firmin, *Roosevelt, 389-90.*

One Long Civil War :

Dorsainvil, *Manuel*, 293-95. Légitime. *"Souvenirs,"* Revue de la Société de *Legisilation* (PauP), November-December 1907; January-May 1908. St. John, 111, 113. Hollister to Seward, 22 September 1868; 10 February 1869, NA (Hayti Despatches). A. Magloire. 11, ii, 334-35, 357-63, 371-73, 382-89, 390424, 425-28, 447-49. G. Vigoreux, "Recits Historique," *Haïti Litteraire et Sociale*, 20 February, 5 June, 20 June. all 1908. *Moniteur Haïtien*, 15 August 1868; 8 May 1869. Logan. *Diplomatic Relations*, 338-42. Bassett to Fish, 20 November and 10 December 1869. NA (Hayti Despatches). F. Marcelin, *Hyppolite*. 318. J.-N. Léger, 214n. Nancy G. Heinl, *"America's First Black Diplomat,"* Foreign Service Journal, August 1973.

Salnave's Downfall:

Dorsainvil. *Manuel*, 295-96. A. Magloire, II, ii, 449-64. Légitime, *"Souvenirs."* *Haïti Litteraire et Sociale,* January 1908. J.-N. Léger, 215. Bassett to Fish, 16 and 17 December 1869; 15 January

1870, NA (Hayti Despatches). St. John, 114- 16, Samuel Hazard, *Santo Domingo Past and Present, with a Glance at Htayti* (NY, 1873). 432-34, 449. Cabon, *Guilloux,* 169. Rouzier, iii, 56. 464. *Moniteur Haïtien,* 18 January 1870.

Chapter 9 Misfortunes without Number 237

Introduction :

Melvil Bloncourt, *Des Richesses Naturelles de la République d'Haïti et sa Situation Economique* (Paris, 1861).

A Mild, Humane, Religious Man :

St. John, 6, 22. Hazard, 436, 452-53. Dorsainvil, *Manuel,* 300, 304-305. C. Texier, Au *Pa ys des Généraux* (Paris, 1891), 258, 260. Firmin, *Roosevelt,* 391-96. Armand Thoby, *Jacques Bonhomme d'Haïti en Sept Tableaux* (PauP, 1901). Depestre, 248. Bassett to Fish, 15 January and 21 March 1870. 27 May 1871; 6 November 1872; 11 March and 6 May 1873, NA (Hayti Despatches). Cabon, *Guilloux,* 176, 228-29. A. Magloire, ii. iii, 1-7. Bellegarde, *Histoire,* 183. Comte de Lemont to Comte de Remusat, to January 1872 (#39), QDO. Rouzier, ii, 25; iii, 443; iv, 190. La Selve, 223-27. *Moniteur Haïtien,* 28 April 1872. Lamaute, 143-45. Michel Fièvre, "Nissage-Saget, 1810-1880." *RSHHG,* July 1933.

Annexation, Intervention, Gunboat Diplomacy :

Dorsainvil,*Manuel,* 303-304. Bellegarde, *Pages,* 179-82. J.-N. Léger, 217-18, Allan Nevins, *Hamilton Fish: Inner History of the Grant Administration* (NY, 1937), 262-78, 588. Bassett to Fish, 17 February 1870 (Enclosure E); 7 and 22 February, 12 April, 3 August, and 8 December, all 1871; 17 January, 21 June, to August, and 23 November, all 1872; 30 January 1873. Bassett to Denis (Foreign Minister), 19 September 1871, NA (Hayti Despatches). Hazard, 437. Fish to Bassett, 31 August 1872, NA (Hayti Instructions). Logan, *Diplomatic Relations,* 347, 353-56. Fish to Mauricio Lopez-Roberts, 28 December 1870, *FornRels US.* 1871, 788. Firmin, *Roosevelt,* 397. Fièvre.

Nissage Stands Down :

Dorsainvil, *Manuel,* 304-308. Bellegarde, *Pages,* 183. J.-N. Léger, 221-22. Bassett to Fish, 17 February 1873; 24 February, 17 April, and 9, 21. 25 May, all 1874, NA (Hayti Despatches). Fièvre.

Tyranny and Its Reward :

Dorsainvil, *Manuel,* 306-308. Doazan (Comte de Lemont) to Decazes, 16 February 1875 (#17), QDO. Bassett to Fish, 16 and 24 June 1874; 26 January, 8 May, 16 July, 21 September, all 1875; 17 February and 27 April 1876, NA (Hayti Despatches). St. John, 118-19, 121-23. Firmin, *Roosevelt.* 398-404. De Vorges to Foreign Minister, 17 April 1876 (#37), QDO. J.-N. Léger, 222-24. Bellegarde, *Histoire,* 185-87. A. Magloire, 11, iii, 12, 18, 32, 195-204, 2 10-1 I, 365-66, 378. Cabon, *Guilloux,* 278. Texier, 259.

Laissez Grainnin :

René Salomon, *Etudes Politiques* (PauP, 1948), 38-43. Cabon, *Guilloux,* 278. J.-N. Léger, 225-29. Texier, 262ff. Bassett to Fish, 27 April, 31 May, 21 June, and 29 July, all 1876; 28 February, 26

830   Written in Blood

March, 23 August, and 3 September, all 1877, NA (Hayti Despatches). Bassett to Evarts, 28 November 1877. Langston to Evarts, 22 December 1877; 18 and 26 March 1878; 8 and 20 February, 15 March, 1 and 19 May, 7 and 30 June, 7, 17, and 18 July, and 6 November, all 1879. De Vorges to Decazes, 15 March 1877 (#7), QDO. J. M. Langston, *From Virginia Plantation to the National Capital* (Hartford, 1894), 38-81. Antoine Michel, *Salomon Jeune et l'Affaire Louis Tanis* (PauP, 1913), 63, 75, 79-84, 91-98, 100-105. 187-90, 218, 222-23. Texier, 261. Firmin, 405, 407, 409. Jean Price-Mars, *Jean-Pierre Boyer-Bazelais et le Drame de Miragoâne* (PauP, 1948), 29. F. Carrie to AmMin, 21 March 1878, FornRels US, 1877, 442. Boisrond-Canal to the People and the Army, 8 July 1878, FornRels US, 1877, 456. Rouzier, iv, 61. Depestre, 289.

A Cheering Sound of Salvation :

Msgr. Alexis-Jean-Marie Guilloux, pastoral letter to Synod, 19 March 1873 (in Cabon, *Guilloux*. 212-13). Bassett to Evarts, 21 July 1877, NA (Hayti Despatches). British and Foreign School Society, Annual Report, May 1817, 34. .*Methodist* (London), XL, 557. Cabon, *Guilloux* 153-60, 163, 166-68, 191-93. *Moniteur Haïtien*, 16 October 1869. R. W. Logan, "Education in Haiti," *Journal* of Negro History, October 1930. 436-18. Langston to Evarts, 24 January 1879.

Salomon at Last :

Dorsainvil, *Manuel*. 313-14, 116-18. Bellegarde, *Histoire*, 191, 193-94. Andre F, Chevallier. *Remembrances* (PauP. 1936), 11. Rodolphe Charmant, *La Vie Incroyable d'Alcius* (PauP. 1946), 77, 88. Cabon, *Guilloux*. 356. Max A. Antoine, *Louis-Etienne Lysius Felicité Salomon Jeune*(PauP, 1968), 53. Langston to Evarts. 22, 24, and 30 October, 6 November, all 1879; 9 April, 8 May, 20 July. and 17 December, all 1880, NA (Hayti Despatches). Edner Brutus. I*nstruction Publique en Haïti. 1492-1945* (PauP, 1948), 264-66, 279. Salomon speech to Ministers. *Moniteur Haïtien* 5 August 1880. *Diffusion Haïtienne, 1804-1954* (PauP, 1954), 129-30. *Moniteur Haïtien*, 7 and 14 October 1880. Langston to Blaine, 18 June 1981. NA (Hayti Despatches). José Rodriguez-Castro. *Cosas de Haiti* (Ponce, 1895), 73ff. St. John, 310. Lamaute, 126. Price-Mars. *Boyer-Bazelais*, 23. Firmin. *Roosevelt*. 443-44. Alfred Jean, *Il y a 70,Ans*, 1883-1943 (PauP, 1944),3.

I Have Been Pushed to Extreme Measures :

Salomon speech, 27 May 1881, in *La Vérité*, 2 June 1883. Langston to Evarts, 9 April and 18 June, both 1880. Langston to Blaine, 4 June, 14 and 15 July, 17 and 28 December, all 1881. Langston to Frelinghuysen, 8 May 1882, NA (Hayti Despatches). Cabon, *Guilloux*. 432-36, 445. Thomas R. Picot, in Catts Pressoir, *Le Protestantisme Haïtien* (PauP, 1945-1946), 292. *Moniteur* Haïtien, 22 April, 6 and 13 May, all 1882. Salomon. Proclamation and Arrêté to People and Army, 11 December 1881. Salomon speech, 10 May 1882, in *L'Oeil* (PauP) 18 May 1882.

The Liberal Insurrection :

Bellegarde, *Histoire*, 193. Charles Desroches, *Matières à Réflexions* (PauP, 1884), 6-12, 52. Price-Mars, *Boyer-Bazelais*, 34-35, 45-46, 53, 68, 92, 121. Langston to Frelinghuysen, 12 and 31 March, 14 and 17 April, 30 May, 11 June, 12 and 25 July, 7 and 8 August, to November, all 1883; 5 January 1884, NA (Hayti Despatches). SecState to Haitian minister, 28 May 1883, NA. Emmanuel Chancy, *Pour l'Histoire* (PauP, 1890), passim. *Moniteur Haïtien*, 3 May 1883. Boyer-Bazelais, Ordre du Jour, 31 May 1883, in Chancy, *Histoire, 43-45*. AmCon Rouzier (Jérémie) to Langston, 9 July 1883. R. Charmant, 95-106. Charles Moravia, *Roses et Camélias* (PauP, 1903), 32. Anténor Firmin, *Une Défense* (Paris, 1892), 124.

Semaine Sanglante :

Jean, 2, 4-5, 8 13, 20 21, 26, 37-38. Langston to Frelinghuysen, 20 November and 17 December 1883; 30 October 1884, NA (Hayti Despatches). C. W. Mosselli, deposition to AmCon, PauP, 30 September 1883; and E. W. Garrido, same, to October 1883, NA (Hayti Despatches). Thomas R. Picot, in Pressoir, 294. Emile Marcelin, *De l'Enfance à la Jeunesse* (PauP, 1934), 32-34. Burdel to Minister of Foreign Affairs, 17 April, 26 September, and 8 October 1883, QDO.

Malheurs sans Nombres :

Circular to all posts, Miragoâne, 27 October 1883, in Chancy, 175. Langston to Frelinghuysen, 20 November and 7 December, both 1883; 18, 19 and 21 January 1884, NA. Cabon, *Guilloux*, 485. R. Charmant, 109-110. Chancy, 186-87, 208-221. Legros to Salomon, 5 and 18 December 1883, in Chancy, 188 and 195. AmCon Vital (Jacmel) to Langston, 3 January 1884, NA. Rouzier, i, 254. Price-Mars, *Boyer-Bazelais*. 13, 120-23.

Inflation, Peculation, Reconstruction :

Paul Deléage, *Haïti en 1886* (Paris, 1887), 66-67, 169-71, 322-28. FornRels US, 1885, passim (reference to Affaire des Mandats and subsequent proceedings). *Times* (London), 6, 9, 17, and 28 September, 4, 8, and 9 November 1887 (Mandats).Cabon, *Histoire Réligieuse*, 490, 544. Dorsainvil, *Manuel*, 316. Belllegarde, *Histoire*, 193-94. Texier, 262-72. Jean, 37.

Salomon and the Great Powers :

Langston to Frelinghuysen, 30 May and 19 November 1883; 1, 17, and 24 December 1884; 23 January 1885, NA. Thompson to Bayard, 13 September 1886; 16 March 1887, NA. Dexter Perkins, *The Monroe Doctrine. 1867-1907* (Baltimore, 1937), 34-37. GOH, Documents Diplomatiques, Affaire Maunder, no. 1 and no. 2 (Paris, 1882). Logan, *Diplomatic Relations,* 372-76, 379-81, 383-86, 388-92, 394-96. Montague, 175-76. Frelinghuysen to Langston, 20 June 1883, 1 February, 21 October 1884; 5 March 1885, NA. Enclosure (Preston's instructions), Langston to Frelinghuysen, 24 December 1884, NA. Thompson to Bayard, 12 July, 13 September 1886; 16 March 1887, NA. Haitian minister to SecState, 11 April 1887, SecState (Bayard) reply, 19 April 1887, NA.

Let Me Take My Soup in Peace:

Thompson to Bayard, 26 September, 17 October, and 28 December 1885; 3 July 1886; 17 March, 18 October 1887; 26 May, 11 June, 16 July, and 18 August 1888, NA. Steele. *Le National*, 9 September 1886. Deleage, 227ff. Anténor Firmin, *Diplomates et Diplomatie* (Cap Haïtien, 1899), 26-27. Dorsainvil, *Manuel, 318. Bellegarde.Histoire*, 194. Texier, 262-72.*La Vérité*, 2 and 9 June 1888. Bayard to Thompson, 16July 1888,NA. AmConGoutier(CapHaïtien)to Thompson, 4 and to August 1888. Salomon to Thompson, it August 1888, enclosed with Thompson to Bayard. 18 August 1888, NA. Ernst Trouillot. *Prospections d'Histoire* (PauP, 1961), 94. Edmond Paul, *Questions Politico-Economiques* (Paris, 1861), 37. "Annual Report of the Bishop of Haiti, 1890" (Appendix to *Annual Report on Foreign Missions of the Protestant Episcopal Church*, 1890). Candelon Rigaud, "Histoire d'Haïti et Histoire de Port-au-Prince," *RSHHG*. October 1934, 36.

Chapter 10 Plots and Revolutions p.283

Introduction :

St. John, x. Flesch to Ribot. 29 June 1891 (no number), QDO. Frédéric Marcelin, *Choses Haïtiennes* (Paris, 1896), 134. François Denis Légitime, *Histoire du Gouvernement du Général Légitime* (Paris, 1891), 26-29, 33, 36, 56-75. Boisrond-Canal to Laforestrie, 14 August 1888, in Légitime, *Histoire, 19n.* Thompson to Bayard, 18 and 25 August and 17 October 1888. NA. Cdr C. M. Chester to SecNav, to September 1888, *FornRels US,* 1888, 922-23. AmCon Goutier (Cap) to Thompson, 9 August 1888, NA. Télémaque to Boisrond-Canal, 17 August 1888, in Légitime, *Histoire,* 28n. Bellegarde, *Histoire, 195-96.* Dorsainvil, *Manuel.* 318-19. Texier, 274-77.

I Will Give Them a Civil War :

Thompson to Bayard, 18 October (no. 216), 29 October, and 18 and 24 December 1888, NA. Arrete. National Assembly, to December 1888, in Senate Executive Document 69 (50th Congress, 2d Session), 222. Montague, 135n, 139-40. FornRels US. 1888, pt. i, 932-1007. RAdm S. B. Luce to SecNav, 29 December 1888, in Senate Document 69, 262-63. Capt F. M. Ramsay to SecNav, 15 November 1888, ibid., 150. *Légitime, Histoire, 150.* Bellegarde, *Histoire,* 196. Hyppolite, Proclamation to the People and the Army, 1 December 1888. Revolutionary Committee of the North to Sesmaisons, Zohrab, et al., 21 November 1888, in FornRels US, 188, pt. 1, 979. Charmant, 123-30. Texier, 277-81.

Légitime Attacks :

Légitime, *Histoire,* 69, 70-73, 100, 111, 116, 119n, 121, 130-33, 138, 141-44, 295. Hesketh Prichard, *Where Black Rules White* (London, 1900), 178-80. R.Charmant, 128. Prophète to Légitime, 2 November 1888, in Légitime, *Histoire,* 97. M. E. Mathon, *Révolutions de 1888-1889* (PauP, 1890), 105-108, 121-23, 160. Légitime to National Assembly, 19 November 1888, in Légitime, *Histoire,* 109ff. Texier, 280, 282. Rouzier, i, 111; ii, 65, 80; iii, 216, 282, iv, 90, 218, 220. Goutier to Rives, to December 1888, NA. RAdm Bancroft Gherardi to SecNav, 6, 12, and 27 March 1889, Naval Records 1775-1910, Area File, NA. Thompson to Blaine, 13 and 16 March, 15 May and 17 June 1889. Welles, *Vineyard,* i, 474. *La Liberté* (Cap Haïtien), 13 April 1889.

Légitime's Downfall :

Rouzier, i, 185; iii, 255; iv, 218, 220, 268. Mathon, *Révolutions,* 115-18, 136-37, 165, 173, 176-86, 243-44. Thompson to Blaine, 14 and 20 May, 27 June, and 8, 17, 23, and 29 August 1889, NA. Gherardi to SecNav, 27 March, 15 May, to and 25 July, 24 August, and 2 September 1889, NA. R. Charmant, 140-42. Dorsainvil, *Manuel,* 320. Texier, 282.

A Prophecy of Peace :

Bellegarde, *Histoire,* 196. Dorsainvil, *Manuel,* 322-23. J.-N. Léger, 243. Thompson to Blaine, 9 and 11 October 1889. Douglass to Blaine, 15, 26, and 31 October and 18 November 1889; 6 January and 13 March 1890, NA. E. Brutus, 296-98. Lamaute, 173. Welles, *Vineyard,* i, 475. F. Marcelin, *Choses, 135-46.* Firmin, *Roosevelt,* 438-39. Georges J. Benjamin, *La Diplomatie d'Anténor Firmin* (Paris, 1906), 62-65.

'Ti Malisse Saves the Môle :

Hollister to Seward, 7 September 1868, NA. Gherardi to SecNav, 27 March and 2 September 1889; 27 January, 26 February, 1 2 March and 13 April (cable) 1891, NA. Philip S. Foner, *Frederick*

Douglass (NY, 1964), 355-59. Benjamin, 85-98. Comte de Sesmaisons to Foreign Minister, 2 June 1889 (#41) QDO. Goutier to Rives (no. 394), 27 December 1889. Montague, 146-61, 176n. Senate Doc 69, 234-38. Logan, *Diplomatic Relations,* 400-405, 425, 434-38, 444, 44850. Thompson to Blaine, 28 May 1889. Preston to Blaine, 22 May 1889, Haïti, Notes, NA. Hannibal Price ("Verax"), *The Haytian Question* (NY, 1891), 14-15, 31-32, 103, 111. Frederick Douglass, " Haiti and the United States, *North American Review,* September-October, 1891. Douglass to Blaine, 31 December 1890; 5, 8, and 29 January, 9 February, 11 March, and 21 and 23 April 1891, NA. Firmin to Douglass and Gherardi, 22 April 1891, in Price, 109-111. E. L. Beach, "Annapolis to Scapa Flow" (unpublished ms., 1919, privately held), 65-66, 68-69, 71. M. E. Flesch to Ribot, 25 January 1891, QDO. Ribot to Flesch, April (no date) 1891 (telegram), QDO. J.-N. Léger, 245-46.

Panama m'ap Tombé :

Jules Auguste, *Quelques Vérités à Propos des Récents Evénements de la République d'Haïti* (Paris, 1891), 15ff. Douglass to Blaine, 27 June 1890; 19 June 1891, NA. Roy Pétion, *En Marge de l'Histoire* (PauP, 1942), 99. Dorsainvil, *Manuel,* 324-27. R. Charmant, 164-66, 168-77. Bellegarde, *Histoire,* 197-98. M. G. de Molinari. A *Panama- La Martinique-Haïti* (Paris, 1887), 275. Trouillot, *Delorme.* 97. Rouzier, ii, 153; iii, 270. E. Mathon, *Frédéric Marcelin* (PauP, 1895), 3-4. Deléage, 389ff. Selden Rodman, *Haiti: The Black Republic* (NY, 1954), 23-24. Flesch to Ribot, 29 May (telegram), 30 May (#78), and 4 June (#79) 1891, QDO. S. Pichon to Berthelot, 12 January 1896, QDO. Marcelin, *Choses,* 131-34.

Drift and Humiliation :

Légitime, *Histoire,* 25. Pichon to Berthelot, 5 April 1896, QDO. Capt N. Sergeant. diary, 19 November 1900, ms. division, LC. Powell to Hay, 1 August 1899, NA. Powell to Sherman, 10, 27 (telegram), 28, and 30 November (telegram), 3, 5, 6 (all telegrams), and 6 December 1897, NA. Smythe to Olney, 28 March 1896, NA. Dorsainvil, *Manuel.* 327-29. J.-N. Léger, 247-50. Bellegarde. *Histoire,* 199-201, 204. Montague, 178-79. Logan, *Diplomatic Relations, 361-62. Revue des Deux Mondes* (Paris), 15 December 1897. Firmin, *Diplomates, 6,* 9, 18. Hogar Nicolas, *L'Occupation Américaine d'Haïti: la Revanche d'Histoire* (Madrid, 1955), 101-106. Frédéric Marcelin, Une *Evolution Nécessaire* (Paris, 1898), 13. Theodore Meyer to Hanatoux, 13 June 1898, QDO.

Simon Sam Abdicates :

Nicolas, 110-111. Montague, 189. "Daily Gleaner" (Kingston), 8 December 1904 and 4 January 1905. "Rotation in Office as it Works in Hayti," unsigned article, *Public Opinion,* 12 January 1905. Powell to Hay, 18 July 1898, 26 April 1900, 17 September 1901, 15 and 23 March, 12 (telegram) and 17 May, and 22 September 1902: 13 and 26 December 1904. Louis Hartmann, *Haïti, les Budgets, Situation Financière* (Paris, 1903), 12-13. Prichard, 43-44, 51. Furniss to Root, 29 August 1907, NA. R. Charmant, 202-203, 214. *Le Nouvelliste, 14* May 1902. T. G. Steward, *The Haitian Revolution* (NY, 1914), 282ff. Farnham to Bryan, 22 January 1914, NA (State Decimal File 838.00/901, 1910-29, Haiti, relations with U.S.).

Firminist Civil War:

Powell to Hay, 15 (telegram), 17, 24, and 30 May, 19, 26 (telegram), 28, and 30 June. 7, 19, and 26 July, 5 (telegram), 9, 11 (telegram), and 15 August 1902, 6 March 1905, NA. Emmanuel Chancy, *Les Evénements de 1902* (PauP, 1905), 50ff, 57-59, 68, 70-74, 87. Benjamin, 140-41, 144 *ff. Le Nouvelliste,* 22 May 1902. J.-N. Léger, 252. Dorsainvil, *Manuel,* 330. R. Charmant, 218-22.

Alcius Charmant. *La Mort de Chicoyé* (Le Havre, 1907), 2-12, 41. Jérémie to Firmin, 11 July 1902, in Firmin, *L'Effort dans le Mal* (reprinted, PauP, 1962), 37.

The Death of Admiral Killick :

Prichard, 102-10. Powell to Hay, 20 and 29 August, 3 (telegram), 6, 9 (telegram), and 13 September 1902, NA. Bellegarde, *Histoire*, 218. J.-N. Léger, 252. Dorsainvil, *Manuel*, 331-32. Steward, 285ff.

Tonton Nord, the Last Leaf :

Powell to Hay, 7 and 17 (telegram) October 1902; 30 March (telegram), to and 25 June, and 2 July 1903; 8 August 1904; 21 February, 2 1 and 29 March, 3 April 1905, NA. Terres to Hay, 22 December 1902, NA. Bellegarde, *Histoire*, 207208, 218. Frédéric Marcelin, *Le Général Nord Alexis* (Paris,1905-1908), i, 9, 18; ii, 32. Frédéric Marcelin, *Bric à Brac* (Paris, 1910), 71, 92, 197. J.-N. Léger, 291n. Joseph Jérémie, *Mémoires* (PauP, 1950), i, 29.

The Centenaire :

Bellegarde, *Histoire*, 207-209. Prichard, 37. Furniss to Root, 24 September 1908, NA. Frédéric Marcelin, *L'Haleine du Centenaire* (Paris, 1901), 13-14. Joseph Jérémie, *Haïti Indépendante* (PauP, 1929). Rosalvo Bobo, quoted in Antoine Bervin, *Louis-Edouard Pouget* (PauP, 1945), 41. Antoine Bervin, *Benito Sylvain* (PauP, 1966), 14-15, 57, 68-71, 144-47, 156-57.

Great Misery Prevails :

Marcelin, *Centenaire*, 63. Terres to Hay, 8 and 21 January 1904, NA. Powell to Hay, 11 May, 8 and 23 June, and to July 1904; 1 February, 17 March, and 29 April 1905, NA. Furniss to Root, 7 March 1906; 29 August, 26 September and 15 October 1907; 1 January 1908, NA. Leslie F. Manigat, "La Substitution de la Préponderance Américaine à la Préponderance Française en Haïti au Debut du XXe Siècle," *Bulletin de la Société d'Histoire Moderne*, October 1966, 8. E. Brutus, 320-21, 334, 340-41. Nancy G. Heinl, "Col. Charles Young," Army, March 1977. Dantès Bellegarde, *Pour une Haïti Heureuse* (PauP, 1928), 189. Anténor Firmin, *Lettres de St. Thomas* (Paris, 1910), 152, 332-39. Léger to Nord Alexis, 4 November 1908, in Marcelin, *Nord Alexis*, i, 13.

Stormy 1908 :

Furniss to Root, 3, 15, and 16 (telegram) January, 1 (dispatch and telegram), 3, and 20 February, 24 March, 15 (telegram) and 18 July, 13 October, 20 November (dispatch and telegram), and 4 December 1908, NA. Marcelin, *Nord Alexis*, iii, 13-19, 21-22, 72, 92, 115-19, 228, 237, 265. R. Charmant, 203, 249ff, 253-57, 259. Bellegarde, *Histoire*, 219-20. Dorsainvil, *Manuel*, 334-35. Sec-State to Furniss (all telegrams), 22 and 31 January, 3 February, 5 and 7 December 1908, NA. Rouzier, iii, 463, 474. Jules Rosemond, *Affaire du 15 Mars* 1908 (PauP, 1910), 3-7. *L'Impartial* (PauP), 17 March 1909. *Daily Telegraph* (Kingston), March 1908. CO, *USS Paducah*, to SecNav, 22 July 1908, NA. CO, USS *Des Moines*, to SecNav, 4 December 1904, NA. Stenio Vincent, *La République* d'Haïti (Brussels, 1910), 277-82. Howard to Grey, 24 January 1909, FO 371/ 3495; Bryce to Grey, 25 January 1908, FO 371/5198, PRO.

Délegué Simon :

Furniss to Root, 20 November and 4, 10, 18, and 21 December 1908, 29 January 1909. Furniss to Bacon, to March 1909. Furniss to Knox, 23 March, 24 July, 8 September, 6 November, and 16 December 1909; 25 March 1910; 2 and 7 March 1911. NA. Bellegarde. *Histoire.* 225. Dorsainvil,*Manuel*, 338-39. Farnham to Bryan. 22 January 1914, NA. 838.00/901. A. LaForest and R. Osson, Le *Général A. Simon dans le Sud* (PauP. 19 10), 263. Jérémie, *Mémoires.* i, 62, 1 00. E.Jore to Pichon, 12 July 1909 (#21), QDO.

Chapter 11 A Public Nuisance p.335

Introduction :

Joseph Justin to the Senate, 1 December 1914 (in *Le Nouvelliste*, s December 1914). Dana G. Munro. *Intervention and Dollar Diplomacy in the Caribbean* (Princeton, 1964), 7, 65ff. Jusserand to Pichon, 10 June 1908 (#235), QDO. Knox to Foreign Relations Committee. 14 May 19 1 i.

Banks and Railroads :

Jérémie, i, 32. Manigat, "Substitution." 6-9, 11. Munro, *Intervention.* 245-55, 126-27. Lucille Atcherson, "History of the Principal Events in the Political Relations of Haiti and the United States" (unpublished monograph, Division of Latin American Affairs, State Department, 1923), 3-6. ONI memo, "The Bank." unsigned, c. 1915, NA, RG-45, WA-7. Hans Schmidt, *The United States Occupations of Haiti, 1915-1934* (New Brunswick, 1971), 33-35, 37-40. Furniss to Knox, 19 March, 30 July, and 2 and 16 September, 1910: 31 March 1911: 2 March 1912: 30 April 1912, NA. Smith to Bryan, 26 January 1914, NA. J. H. Allen, " An Inside View of the Revolution in Haiti," *Current History*, May 1930. Farnham to Bryan, 22 January 1914, NA. J. H. Stabler, Division of Latin American Affairs, to Bryan, 3 May 1934, 838.00/1667. U.S. Senate, *Hearings before the Select Committee on Haiti and Santo Domingo* (67th Congress, 1st and 2d Sessions, 1921-22), i, 105-108, 110-11. Dorsainvil, *Manuel*, 339. Knox to Furniss, 24 September 1910 (telegram), 11 January 1911, NA. Adee to Furniss, 12 October 1910 (telegram), NA. Paul H. Douglas, "The American Occupation of Haiti," *Political Science Quarterly*, June 1927. Paul H. Douglas, "Political History of the Occupation. " *Occupied Haiti*, ed., E. G. Balch (NY, 1927), 18. McAdoo to Lansing, 13 July 1915, NA, 838-77. State Department, Division of Latin American Affairs. memo, "National Railroad of Haiti," unsigned. 10 December 1915, NA, 838-77/047. Joseph Chatelain. *La Banque National* (PauP, 1954), 79-82. Antoine Pierre-Paul, "Les Contrats de Banque et d'Emprunt du Gouvernement d'Antoine Simon," and "Les Contrats de Chemin de Fer et de Figues-Bananes." *RSHHG*, April 1951.

A Great Many Will Die :

R.Charmant, 279-80. Firmin, *L'Effort*, 22-28. Furniss to Knox, 5, 7, and 8 March, 30 April, and 17 September 1910; 17 (telegram), 18, and 20 (dispatch and telegram) February, 9 May (telegram), 20 June (telegram), 13 (telegram), 18, and 25 July, and 2, 3 (telegram), 5, and 12 August 1911, NA. AmCom Livingston (Cap) to Furniss, 27 October 1910, NA. AmCom agent Jérémie (Villedrouin) to Furniss, 26 January 1911, NA. Jérémie, 36-45. J. Bowering to Sir Austen Chamberlain, 6 January 1927, FO 371/A70, PRO. Rouzier, iii, 35758. Atcherson, 19, citing State Department 838.00/1128. J. W. Furniss, *Haiti Who's Who* (with confidential supplement), 28 August 1911, NA. Livingston to Knox, 26 March 1911, NA. Bellegarde, *Histoire*, 225-26. CO, USS *Petrel, to* SecNav, 18 July 1911; CO, *USS Chester*, to SecNav, 27 July 191 I; CO, USS *Des Moines*, to SecNav, 3 August 1911, all NA. Antoine Pierre-Paul, Les *Contre-Vérités d'une Thèse* (PauP, 1963), 29. H. C. Staude to P. W. Henry, 4 August 1911, NA. "Haiti, Relations with U.S., 1910-1929," microfilm roll #3, NA.

The Best Haiti Has Had :

Cable, SecWar to War Dept, 28 July 1911 (paraphrase in Division of Latin American Affairs files, NA). Bellegarde, *Histoire,* 227, 233-34, 236. Atcherson, 8, 10, 12, 20, 47. Dorsainvil, *Manuel,* 339-41. CO, USS *Salem,* to SecNav, 23 August 1911, NA. Furniss to Knox, 6 and 7 August (both telegrams) and 26 August 1911; 25 April, 7 May, 29 July, 8 August (telegrams), and 17 September 1912, NA. Furniss, *Who's Who.* E. Brutus, 347, 364, 371-81. Joseph Pyke to Sir Edward Grey, 26 March and 31 August 1912, FO 371, PRO. H. P. Davis, 145-46. A. Pierre-Paul, 14. Knox speech in *FornRels US, 19* 12, 541-47. Farnham to Bryan, 22 January 1914, NA.

Tancrède Auguste :

Furniss to Knox, 14 August 1911; 8 August (telegram), 28 September and 11 December 1912; 14 January 1913, NA. Furniss to Bryan, 29 April and 2 and 3 May (both telegrams), 1913, NA. Furniss, *Who's Who.* Livingston to Bryan, 10 May 1915. H. H. Johnston, *The Negro in the New World* (London, 1910), 187-88. Memo "The Bank," 3, 5. Pyke to Grey, 31 January 1913, FO 371, PRO. H. P. Davis, 147. Bellegarde, *Histoire, 238.*

The People Never Understood :

Furniss to Bryan, to and 15 May and 17 July 1913, NA. Smith to Bryan, 7 and 24 (telegram) January and 2 February 1914, NA. CO, USS *Nashville,* to SecNav, 7 May 1913, NA. Allen. H. P. Davis, 147-48. R. Charmant, 143-45, 151-53. Pyke to Grey, 13 June 1913, FO 371, PRO. Chatelain, 96-100. Bellegarde, *Histoire,* 239-42. Bellegarde, *Haïti Heureuse,* 250-51. Rouzier, iii, 271; iv, 220. Munro, *Intervention,* 329, 333, 338-39. Lamaute, 147. AmCon agent Vital (Jacmel) to Smith, 12 January 1914, NA. Jules Rosemond, *Davilmar Theodore* (PauP, 1914) unpaginated pamphlet. Stephen Leech to Grey, 21 January (telegram) and 5 and 17 February 1914, FO 371, PRO. *Le Matin* (PauP), 29 January 1914. CO, *HMS Lancaster,* to Admiralty, 5 February 1914, FO 371, PRO.

Prolonged Civil War Likely :

Bellegarde, *Histoire.* 243-44. Smith to Bryan, 4, 5 (telegram), 16, and 21 February and 20 March 1914, NA. Bryan to Smith, 26 February 1914, NA. Livingston to Bryan; 26 March, 26 May, 18 and 22 July, and 19 September 1914, NA. Livingston to Bailly-Blanchard, 29 August and 19 September 1914, NA. Terres to Bryan, 2 May 1914, NA. Hazeltine to Bryan, to June and lo July 1914, NA. Farnham to Bryan, 19 June 1914 (telegram), NA. Bailly-Blanchard to Bryan, 20 July, 21, 23 and 25 October (all telegrams), and to November 1914. Sullivan (AmMin, Dominican Republic) to Bryan, 16 March (telegram) 1914, NA. Leech to Grey, 11, 17, 18, and 21 February, 17 March (dispatch and telegram), 1 April (official dispatch and private letter), and 9 June 1914. CO, HMS *Mutine,* to Leech, 2 February 1914 (in FO 371/348). Edmund Watt to Grey, 23 and 28 June 1914. Foreign Office minute on FO 371/31864. R. M. Kohan to Grey, 7 November 1914 (all foregoing British diplomatic material, FO 371, PRO). Rouzier, v, 85-87. Allen. Furniss, *Who's Who.* Atcherson, 13-14, 24, 50-55, 58. Munro, *Intervention,* 334-41. Memo "The Bank," 7. *CO, USS Washington,* to SecNav, 2 July 1914. CO, USS *Tacoma,* to SecNav, 17 and 24 October 1914. CO, *USS Wheeling,* to SecNav, 3 March 1914.

Un Maître Etranger:

Bailly-Blanchard, 7 and to November, 2, 4, 12 (all telegrams), and 16 December 1914. Bryan to Bailly-Blanchard. 7 December 1914 (telegram). Lansing to Bailly-Blanchard, 4 November 1914.

Bailly-Blanchard to Lansing, 2 December 1914 (telegram). Livingston to Bryan, 19 December 1914 and 27 January 19 1 5. Livingston to Bailly-Blanchard, 20 January 191 5 (all foregoing U.S. diplomatic material, NA). Furniss, *Who's Who*. Atcherson, 60-64, 72-76. Munro, *Intervention, 342-46. Le Nouvelliste,* 5 December 1914. *Moniteur Haïtien,* 26 December 1914. Chatelain, 103-106, 108n. U.S. Senate, *Hearings Before a Select Committee on Haiti and Santo Domingo* (67th Congress, 1 st and 2d Sessions), i, 1 22-23, 287. *FornRels, US,* 1914, 363-70, 373-76. Ménos to Bryan, 22 December 1914, ibid, 371-72. Bryan to Ménos, ibid., 380-81. Lamaute, 243. Bellegarde, *Histoire, 245-46.*

Revolution Is Flourishing :

RAdm W. B. Caperton, USN, to SecNav, "Report of Operations," Caperton Papers, LC. "Activities While inCommand of Cruiser Squadron, U.S. Atlantic Fleet, and Commander-in-Chief, U.S. Pacific Fleet" (unpublished ms.), Caperton Papers, LC. H. P. Davis, 154-56. *Senate Hearings,* i, 286-91, 293-94, 269-99. Capt E. L. Beach, USN, "Admiral Caperton in Haiti" (unpublished ms., 1919, privately held), 1-2, 6. Caperton to SecNav, 12 and 23 February 1915, LC. Kohan to Grey, 1 March 1915, FO 371, PRO.

Action Is Evidently Necessary :

Allen. Munro, *Intervention,* 332, 347, 349-51. Schmidt, 48-49, 56-57, 61-63. Montague, 183n, 205-7. *Senate Hearings,* i, 109. Farnham to Bryan, 11 March 1914. Lansing to Bailly-Blanchard, 29 October 1914 (telegram). BaillyBlanchard to Lansing, 30 October 1914 (telegram). Wilson to Bryan, 13 January 1915 (all foregoing U.S. diplomatic material, NA). U.S. Navy Haiti contingency plans, NA, RG-45, WA-7, boxes 635 and 636. Perl to BethmannHollweg, 27 April 1915, Political Archive, Foreign Ministry, Bonn. Bellegarde, *Histoire,* 249. Fuller to Lansing, 14 June 1915, 838.00/1197. Wilson to Lansing, 2 July 1915, 838.00/1197. Atcherson, 40-45, 76. Lansing to Sen. Medill McCormick, 4 May 1922, in Congressional Record (67th Congress, 2d Session), 1922, LXII, pt. 6, 6485ff.

The Worst Savagery :

R.B. Davis., Jr., Memorandum for SecState, 12 June 1916, NA. Bellegarde, *Histoire.* 246-47, 250. Caperton to SecNav, 12 February 1915, Caperton Papers, LC. Caperton, "Activities While in Command," LC. Kohan to Grey, 31 March 1915, FO 371, PRO. Livingston to Bryan, 1 and to May 1915. Livingston to Langston, 16 and 28 June 1915, NA. C. C. Willard letter to John Shea, 26 June 1915, in State 838.77/119. H. P. Davis, 157-58.

One of the Bloodiest Crimes :

Caperton to SecNav, II July 1915, LC. Beach, "Caperton in Haiti," 10-15, *17-20. Senate Hearings,* i, 301-304. H. P. Davis, 161-66. Heinl conversation with Lucien Chauvet, to September 1959. British Legation synopsis, Haitian Claims Commission Awards, FO 371/A6961, 27 November 1921, PRO. Kohan to Grey, 6 August 1915, FO 371, PRO. R. B. Davis, memo, NA. Stephen Alexis, "In Memoriam," *Le Matin* (PauP), 27 July 1932, also *Le Matin,* 29 July 1915. Pierre Girard, "La Révolution d'Haïti, Juillet, 1915," *Revue Hébdomadaire* (Paris), July 1925. Girard to Delcasse, 31 July 1915 (#45), QDO. George Marvin, "Assassination and Intervention in Haiti," *The World's Work,* February 1916.

The Situation Is Well in Hand :

Log, USS *Washington,* 28 July 1915, NA (RG-24). Kohan to Grey, 6 August and 3 September 1915, FO 371, PRO. Rotberg, 116. Schmidt, 65. R. L. Schreadley, "American Intervention in Haiti," unpublished Ph.D. dissertation, Tufts University, 1969, 95-96. Munro, *Intervention,* 352. Davis to Lansing (telegrams), 27 and 28 July 1915, NA. Lansing to SecNav, MemCon, 28 July 1915, 838.00. SecNav to Caperton, 28 July 1915, no. 15028. ComNavSta Guantanamo to Caperton, 28 July 1915, no. 15128. Atcherson, 81-82. *Senate Hearings,* i, 307-309, 358-59. Beach, "Caperton in Haiti," 21-24. Beach, "Annapolis," 250-55. R. Cuthbertson, PA Surg, USN, to BuMed, August 1915, NA (RG-45). Comdr Cruiser Squadron to SecNav, serial 7216-15 (Report of Operations), 4 August 1915, NA (RG-45). Josephus Daniels to William Allen White, 18 February 1930, Daniels Papers, LC.

Hayti Is a Public Nuisance :

Rotberg, 109. Max Winkler, *Investment of U.S. Capital in Latin America* (Boston, 1928), 275. *Senate Hearings,* i, 63. Adee minute on Goutier to Rives, 17 October 1888, NA.

Chapter 12 Occupation p.395

Introduction :

FornRels US, 1895, i, 588. Bellegarde, *Haïti Heureuse, ii,* 5. Bellegarde, *Histoire.* 247. Lansing to Wilson, 3 August 1915, 830.00/1275B. Lansing to Daniels, 30 July 1915, 838.00/1231a. SecNav to Caperton, 30 July 1915, 18030. Atcherson, 84. Wilson to Lansing, 4 August 1915, 838.00/14i8. Division of Latin American Affairs, MemCon, 29 July 1915, 838.1352. *La Plume* (PauP), 25 August 1915. Montague, 212n. Davis to Lansing (undated, 838.00/90) in Atcherson, 83.

The United States Prefers Dartiguenave :

Caperton to SecNav, 2 August 1915, 838.00/1235. Beach, "*Caperton in Haiti,*" 26-29, 32-36, 39, 42-44, 51, 61-63, 65-73, 84-85. Beach, "*Annapolis,*" 25558, 263-68. R. D. Heinl, Jr., *Soldiers of the Sea* (Annapolis, 1962), 173-75. Caperton, "*Activities While in Command.*" Senate Hearings, i, 312-13, 31517, 320-2 1. R. B. Coffey, "*A Brief History of the Intervention in Haiti,*" U.S. Naval Institute *Proceedings,* August 1922. Roger Gaillard, *Les Cents Jours de Rosalvo Bobo* (PauP, 1975), 229. Livingston to Lansing, 6 and 8 August 1915 (telegrams). R. Bobo, "Open Letter to the President of the U.S.," 22 October 1915, 838.00/1335. B. Danache, *Le Président Dartiguenave et les Americains* (PauP, 1950), 35, 38-40. SecNav to Caperton, 9 August 1915, 838.00/1246a. Atcherson, 87-97. Daniels to White, 18 February 1930, Daniels Papers, LC. Lansing to Davis, to August I915 (telegram), NA. Dartiguenave to Beach, 4 October 1916, Hoover Library, Stanford, Cal. Girard to Delcasse, 13 August I915 (#347), QDO. R. B. Davis, Memorandum. *Paris Herald,* 4 December 1929.

The Only Thing to Do :

Caperton, "Activities While in Command." *Senate Hearings,* i, 65-66, 70, 321, 334-35, 341, 343, 347-48. De la Batie to Briand, 25 October 1916 (#50), QDO. Beach, "Annapolis," 266-68. Beach, "Caperton in Haiti," 79-81. Beach, undated memo, NA, RG-45, WA-7, box 632. Danache, 46-47. Girard to Declasse, 4 September 1915 (#52), QDO. Atcherson, 90-93. Montague, 215, 219-21. Lansing to Wilson, 13 August 1915, in *FornRels US,* Lansing Papers, ii, 526-27. Wilson to Lansing, 13 August 1915, NA. Lansing to Davis, 24 August 1915 (telegram). *FornRels US,* 1915, 436-38. ActSecNav to Caperton, 25 August 1915, NA, RG-45. Lansing to Davis, 29 August 1915 (telegram), 711.38/25a. *Munro, Intervention,* 358, 359n. Benson to Caperton, 25 August 1915;

Source Notes

Caperton to Benson, 31 August 1915, Caperton Papers, LC. Capt Charles Conard (SC) USN, "A Year in Haiti's Customs and Fiscal Service," U.S. Naval Institute *Proceedings*, April 1923. Caperton to Durell, 25 August 1915, Caperton Papers, LC. Ménos to Lansing, 4 and 6 September 1915. *FornRels US*, 1915, 485-86.

No Velvet Glove :

Montague, 221-23. CO Conde to Minister of Marine, 2 September 1915, QDO.Davis to Lansing, 14 and 17 (telegrams) and 21 September 1915, NA. Senate Hearings, i, 38182, 389-92, 394-95. Atcherson, 94-96 (full text of "Interpretive Commentary" is in App. K). SecNav to Caperton, 4 October 1915 (no. 22004) and 13 October (no. 11013) 1915, in Senate Hearings, i, 383 and 385, respectively. Caperton to Benson, 24 September and 26 October 1915, Caperton Papers, LC. Beach, "Caperton in Haiti," 98, too. Beach, "Annapolis," 274-75. FornRels US, 1916, 322-27. "Treaty with Respect to the Finances, Economic Development and Tranquillity of Haiti," U.S. Treaty Series, no. 623. Girard to Delcasse, 13 August 1915, QDO. Georges Sylvain, *Dix Ans de Lutte pour la Liberté* (PauP, 1925), i, 4-6.

They Will Not Disarm :

Livingston to Lansing, 8 August 1915 (telegram), NA. Caperton to SecNav, 7, 2 2, and 26 September (telegrams), 30 October, and 20 November 1915; 8 January 1916 (telegram), NA. Caperton to Benson, 24 September and 21 November 1915, Caperton Papers, LC. Heinl, *Soldiers of the Sea, 174-78. Senate Hearings, i,* 515, 610, 613-17, 677-78, 680. Daniels to Caperton, 20 November 1915, NA. Caperton, "Activities While in Command." Pierre-Paul, *Les Contre-Vérités,* 14-15. Antoine Pierre-Paul, *La Première Protestation Armée contre l'Intervention Americaine de* 1915 (PauP, 1957), 3-5, 7-9, 12-15, 44. De la Batie to Briand, 5 January 1916, 1 June 1916 (#25), and 5 June 1916 (#26), QDO. Girard to Briand, 26 January 1916 (#6), QDO. Waller to Lejeune, 14 February and undated (c. 1 June?) 1916, Lejeune Papers, LC. Simon Lambert to Theogène Degand, 22 May 1916, RG-45, WA-7, NA.

A Confused State of Affairs :

Senate Hearings, i, 512-14, 620. Heinl, *Soldiers of the Sea,* 176-79. Caperton, "Activities while in Command." Munro, *Intervention,* 361, 364, 366-67. Conard. Douglas, "American Occupation." Samuel G. Inman, *Through Santo Domingo and Haiti: A Cruise with the Marines* (NY, 1919), 68. H. P. Davis, 192-93, 195-98. Arthur C. Millspaugh, *Haiti Under American Control, 1915*1930 (Boston, 1930), 64-70. Caperton to Benson, 2 March 1916, Caperton Papers, LC. De la Batie to Briand, 5 June 1916 (#26), QDO.

Dissolution and Dictation :

Senate Hearings, i, 3, 23-26, 415-21, 536-38, 623-26, 695-96, 699-703, 1784. *Moniteur Haïtien,* 5 April 1916. Douglas, "American Occupation." Millspaugh, 72-73, 222-25. Hannibal Price, *Dictionnaire de Législation Administrative Haïtienne* (2d ed., PauP, 1923). J.-C. Dorsainvil, *Quelques Vues Politiques* (PauP, 1934), 15. Bellegarde, *Histoire,* 260-61. Lowell Thomas, *Old Gimlet Eve* (NY, 1932), 212-18. Munro, *Intervention,* 368-71. Welles to Harry Pelham Robbins, 31 March 1927, privately held. Henry L. Stimson and McGeorge Bundy, *On Active Service in Peace and War* (NY, 1948), 184n. De la Batie to Briand, 10 August 1916 (#36) and to Pichon, 21 November 1917 (#39), QDO. Russell to SecNav, 17 June 1918, RG-45, NA. Atcherson, 111-112. Gd'H circular letter (subject: elections), 20 May 1918.

The Occupation Is Not As Popular :

Girard to Briand, 26 January 1916 (#6), QDO. Danache, 45, 50-51, 53-54. E. L. Beach, Jr., *The Wreck of the Memphis* (NY, 1966). Caperton to Benson, 20 July 1916, Caperton Papers, LC. Waller to SecNav, 5 August 1918, NA, 838.00/1405. De la Batie to Briand, 11 December 1916 (#58), QDO. Schmidt, 79-80. *Senate Hearings,* i, 517, 530-31, 645-46. Rouzier, iii, 255. Atcherson, 126-30.

Dartiguenave Balks :

William P. Seabrook, *The Magic Island* (NY, 1929), 115, *138. Senate Hearings,* i. 796-802; ii, 1404-5, 1417, 1420-28, 1442. Dantès Bellegarde, *La Résistance Haïtienne* (Montreal, 1937), 74-84. Raymond Leslie Buell, *The American Occupation of Haiti* (NY, 1929), 353-54. Waller to Lejeune, 20 August 1916, Lejeune Papers, LC. Munro, *Intervention,* 377-84. Schmidt, 110-112. Danache, 78-89. Montague, 229-32. Millspaugh, 77-82. Welles to Hughes, 8 March 1922 (838.00/1417). *Moniteur Haïtien,* 6 and 9 April 1921.

Corvée and Cacos :

Heinl, *Soldiers of the Sea, 234-45. Senate Hearings,* i, 497, 530-33, 557-564, 602-606; ii, 1235-54, 1296-97. *Code Rural d'Haïti,* sec. 3, ch. V, arts. 52-65. Dantès Bellegarde. *Haïti et ses Problemes* (PauP, 1941), 213. Russell to MGC, 17 October 1918, HQMC. J. B. Heim, autopsy report, Charlemagne Péralte, 1 November 1919, HQMC. Charlemagne Péralte to Catlin, undated, 1919, HQMC. "Congolo" to "Maïs Goilté" (pseud.), 27 May, 27 June, 15 and 16 July, and 8 and 11 October 1919, HQMC. Charlemagne Péralte to BrMin, PauP, 7 October 1919, HQMC.

Get Charlemagne :

F.M. Wise, *A Marine Tells It to You* (NY, 1929), 311. Hanneken to Comdt Gd'H, 1 November 1919, HQMC. Meade to multiple addressees (radio message), 29 October 1919, HQMC. Helm, autopsy report, HQMC. Meade to Comdt Gd'H, 1 November 1919. Heinl, *Soldiers of the Sea, 238-40.* Nicolas, 192.

End of Armed Resistance :

Heinl, *Soldiers of the Sea, 241-45,* 630 (note 11). CO, Comillon Subdistrict, to CO, Pétionville, 8 April 1921 ("Description of Principal Bandit Camps"), HQMC. CO, 119 May 1920, HQMC. Methieus Richard, Statement of Interrogation, Hinche, 18 April 1920, HQMC. J. D. Kuser, *Haiti: Its Dawn of Progress after Years in a Night of Revolution (Boston,* 1921), *32ff. Senate Hearings,* ii, 1504, 1660-6 , 1719-20, 1728-31. Russell to MGC, 15 August 1920 ("Report on Activities"), HQMC. Seabrook, 323-31.

Indiscriminate Killings :

A. W. Catlin, sworn statement, 31 December 1919 (in *Senate Hearings, ii,* 1808-10). Hooker to Catlin, 15 February 1919 (in *Senate Hearings,* i, 654).*Senate Hearings* i, 139-43, 239, 425-34, 653-63, 669; ii, 1668, 1753-57. Barnett to Russell, 27 September 1919 (in *Senate Hearings,* ii, 1723). Daniels to White, 18 February 1930. *New York Times,* 21 September and 14 and 15 October 1920. James Weldon Johnson, *Along This Way* (NY, 1923), 355-60. Montague, 23435. Senate Report no. 794 (67th Congress, 2d Session), 26. Minute on FO A8036/4521/20 in FO 371, PRO.

Cacos de Plume :

De la Batie to Ribot, 6 June 1917 (#20), QDO. Russell to CNO, 4 December 1920, NA, RG-80. *Senate Hearings,* i, 32, 44-45, 833; ii, 1306, 1500-1501. Edwards to Chamberlain, 2 April 1927, FO 371/A2394, PRO. Merrell to Kellogg, 18 July 1925 (838.00/2143), also 838.00/2215, undated. *Nation,* 10 July and 4, 11, and 25 September 1920; 25 May 1921. Ernest Gruening, unprinted draft memoirs (1972), 246, 246A, 252-53, 263. *Manchester Guardian,* 11 June 1921. Bellegarde, *Haïti Heureuse,* i, 168-69. *Le Courrier Haïtien* (PauP), 16 April 1921. Russell, "Daily Diary Report," to November 1921 (838.00/1822). "Que Font les Américians en Haïti?" *Les Annales Diplomatiques et Consulaires* (Paris), October 192 1, 1 i. Memorandum, Munro to White, 15 December 1923 (838.00/1999). " Records of Leading Personalities in Hayti, " 17 February 1936, FO 371/A1385/20, PRO. Danache, 58. Bellegarde, *Résistance,* 67n, 69, 71. Division of Latin American Affairs, MemCon, Pierre Hudicourt, 28 November 1924 (838.00/2025). Senate report no. 794, 19. Lamaute, 143-45. Medill McCormick, "Our Failure in Haiti," *Nation,* 1 December 1920. McCormick to Hughes, 14 December 1921 (838.00/1825 1/2).

Russell's Proconsulship :

Hughes to Russell, 11 February and 10 April 1922 (in *FornRels US,* 1922), ii, 461ff. Russell to Hughes, 7 April 1922 (telegram), 838.00/1835, NA. John H. Russell, unpublished "History of Haiti," MarCorps Museum file 4-50. Earl of Cromer, *Modern Egypt* (London, 1908), i, 5. Schmidt, 126. John H. Russell, CO, 1stMarBrig, 15 September 1920, HQMC. Millspaugh, 106-108, 112-13, 135-40, 146-5 1. Rotberg, 127. Bellegarde, *Histoire,* 283. Seabrook, 152. Douglas, "American Occupation," 256-57. Audain, *Choses,* 8. E. D. Watt to Curzon, 26 May 1922, FO 371, PRO. Danache, 153-57. *Le Nouvelliste,* 8 July 1926. H. P. Davis, 248. R. P. G. Edwards to Craigie, 19 February 1929, FO 371/A759, PRO. Edwards to Chamberlain, 24 May 1929, FO 371/A5433, PRO. *Annual Reports of the American High Commissioner at Port-au-Prince* (Washington, D.C., 1922-1929), passim. LtCol Thomas C. Turner to Chief, Bureau of Aeronautics, 19 May 1922 (HQMC General Correspondence, Division of Operations and Training), NA. G. A. Duncan, Cdr USN, *The Public Works of Haiti,* pamphlet (PauP, 1930). Kent C. Melhorn, *The Health of Haiti* (Baltimore, 1930), 10, 17. Buell, 357-60, 361-63. Russell to Cotton, 26 May 1930 (838.00/ 2639 1/2), NA.

Quite Unqualified to Colonize :

Russell to Phillips, 6 September 1922 (838.00/1904), NA. D. C. MacDougal to Russell. confidential memo, 28 February 1924 (enclosure to 838.00/2015), NA. Russell to Kellogg, 31 October 1924 (838.00/2049); 27 April 1925 (838.00/2103); 17 March 1926 (838.00/2208), NA. Merrell to Kellogg, 6 June 1925 (no State Department file number), RG-59, NA. Buell, 371-72, 376, 386. Report of the Financial Adviser-General Receiver, 1923-1924, PP. 82-95. Douglas, "American Occupation," *Political Science Quarterly,* September 1927, 379-86. Winkler. 214-17. New York *World,* 2 May 1922. Schmidt, 179, Gross to Kellogg, 5 May 1927 (838.00/2318), 15 June 1928 (838.00/2334), NA. Cumberland to Munro. 22 April 1929 (838.00/2322), NA. Seabrook, 142, 163. *Le Courrier Haïtien,* 15 July 1925. A. H. Turnage. report of investigation, Port-au-Prince prison, 24 July 1924, enclosure to 838.00/2142), NA. Munro to White, 15 December 1923 (838.00/1999), NA. Shepherd to Eden, 17 February 1936, FO 371/A1385/20, PRO. Edwards to Chamberlain, 16 September 1926, FO 371/ A6367: 19 April 1927, FO 37i/A32I9; 24 May 1929. FO 371/A5433, PRO. *Senate Hearings,* i, 528. Munro, memo. 11 December 1929 ("Military Tribunals in Haiti," 838.00/2). *Cercle Bellevue, 1905-1955* (privately printed, author unknown, PauP. 1955), 44-46. Edwards to Henderson, 19 February and 31 October 1929, FO 371/A759/20 and A7311/759, PRO.

Southerners to Handle Haitians? :

Edwards to Chamberlain. 19 April 1927, FO A3219, PRO. Harry Franck, *Roaming Through the West Indies* (NY. 1920), 118. Douglas, "American Occupation," 368-69. Balch, 133. Leyburn, 103n. Rodman, *Haiti*, 25, Edmund Wilson, *Red, Black, Blond, and Olive* (NY. 1956), 86. Danache, 58, 125-26. Nicolas, 191. Ann Hurst, "Southerners to Handle Haitians?," unpublished term paper, Wellesley College, 4 May 1964, and letter to R. D. Heinl, Jr., 29 June 1964. Compilation of data on American officers, Gd'H, 1 January 1930, BOX 23, File 24, HQMC. Schmidt, 144-45. Waller to Lejeune, 11 June and 1 July 1916, Lejeune Papers, LC. Waller to Butler, 7 July 1916, Haiti Papers, BOX 25, HQMC. Seabrook, 148. Munro, *Intervention,* 361-62, 375.

Children's Crusade :

Logan. "Education in Haiti," 434, 438-40, 444. Joseph Justin, *Les Réformes Necessaires: Questions Haïtiennes d'Actualités* (PauP, 1915), 12. *Exposé Général de la République d'Haïti.* 1892. 85. Russell, Supplement to Daily Diary Report. 1st MarBrig, 4 April 1921, NA. Magowan to Henderson, 12 and 17 December 1929, FO 371/14225/7285 and A11193; 22 September 1930, FO 371/ A6559, PRO. G. J. O'Shea to chief of police, PauP, 6 July 1929, RG-127, NA. *Le Petit Impartial* (PauP), 22 April 1929. Russell to Stimson, 19, 25, 27, and 29 November (838.42/73/74/76/77), 29 November (telegram, 838.42/14); 2 December (838.42/80), and telegrams 2, 3, 4, 6, and 7 December (838.5045/1/3/6/10/12), 1929. "Summary of Strike," unsigned, undated memo, BOX 23, File 24, HQMC. J. H. Russell, "*A Marine Looks Back on Haiti,*" unpublished typescript, Marine Corps Museum, ms. file 4-50. Annual Report to American High Commissioner, 1929, 6-13. L. J. De Bekker, "*The Massacre at Aux Cayes,*" Nation, 19 March 1930. Dean G. Acheson, *Present at the Creation* (NY, 1969), 428. Message of the President to Congress, 7 December 1929 (in *FornRels US,* 1929, iii, 207-208). Herbert Hoover, Statement, 4 February 1930, RG-220, NA.

A Palliative, Not a Remedy :

Caperton to Benson, 21 November 1915, Caperton Papers, LC. *Report of the President's Commission for the Study and Review of Conditions in the Republic of Haiti* (Washington, D.C., 1930), 1-3, 5, 7, 19-21. Cameron W. Forbes, Journal (2d series, III), 1, IO, 14, 16 March 1930, Forbes Papers, LC. Stimson to Hoover, 30 September 1929 (in *FornRels US,* 1929, iii, 205). *Times* (London), 13 December 1929. Russell to Stimson, 26 May 1930 (838.00/2636 1/2). *New York Times* 4 March 1930 and 28 June 1931. *Le Nouvelliste,* 3 March 1930. Helena Hill Weed, "Fresh Hope for Haiti," *Nation,* 19 March 1930. White to Cotton, 11 April 1930 (838.00/2780). Forbes to Hoover, 7 March 1930 (telegram), Rg220, NA. Hoover to Forbes, 8 March 1930 (telegram), RG-220, NA. Cotton to Russell, 29 March 1930 (838.00/2773A). Henry P. Fletcher, "Quo Vadis Haiti?," *Foreign Affairs,* July 1930. Magowan to Henderson, 3, 12, and 17 March 1930, FO 37i/A2216, A2227, A1781, PRO. Lindsay to James G. Macdonald, 15 April 1930; Forbes to Cotton, 17 April 1930, Forbes Papers, LC. British Information Service Analysis, to January 1930, with accompanying FO minute, FO 371/A6I2, PRO.

France, the Church, and the Occupation :

Flesch to Ribot, 14 November 1891 (unnumbered), QDO. *Senate Hearings, i,* 499. De la Batie to Ribot, 6 June 1917 (#20), QDO. Atcherson, 106-109, citing 711.38/47 and 92. Russell to Stimson, 25 November 1929 (838.42/76); 26 March 1930 (838.00/2765); 25 November 1929 (838.42/76); 26 March 1930 (838.00/ 2765). Forbes, 15-17. Magowan to Henderson, 13 March 1930, FO 371/A7140, PRO. Watt to Simon, 28 June 1932, FO 371/A1481, PRO.

Borno Departs :

Source Notes

Magowan to Henderson, 21 March, 3 May, and 5 June 1930, FO 371/A2475/ A2843/A4403, PRO. Dana G. Munro, *The United States and the Caribbean Republics. 1921-1933* (Princeton, 1974), 317. Dana G. Munro, "The American Withdrawal from Haiti," Hispanic-American Review, February 1969. Russell to Stimson, 28 and 30 April 1930 (telegrams), 838.00/2795 and 2798.

Recessional :

Magowan to Henderson, 5 June 1930, 19 November and 12 December 1930, FO 371/A7936, A8097, PRO. Russell to Stimson, 15 September (838.001, Roy/16 for #1738), 23 September (838.00/2887), both 1930. Russell to Kellogg, 14 January 1928 (838.00/2472). Wood (AmCon, Cap) to Stimson, 1 August 1930 (838.00/2868). Grummon to Stimson, 22 May 1930 (838.00/2831). *Haïti-Journal,* 30 July 1942. *Le Nouvelliste,* 30 October 1939. Munro, *Caribbean Republics,* 317-18, 336-37. Munro, "American Withdrawal." Watt to Simon, 5 January 1932, FO 371/A935, PRO. Munro to Stimson, 26 January (838.00/2992), 23 November (telegram, 838.00/3049) 1931; 17 August 1932 (telegram, 838.00/ 3096). Haitianization Executive Agreements (nos. 22 and 46), 5 August 1931 and 7 August 1933. Trouillot, *Prospection,* 110-12. *Le Courrier Haïtien* 5 August 1931 and 6 August 1932. Norman Armour, "Notes re My Recollections of the Visit of Franklin Delano Roosevelt to Haiti, July, 1934," unpublished, undated, privately held. Gerald A. Drew, "FDR Comes to Haiti: 5 July 1934," unpublished, undated, privately held. Vincent to Little, 20 July 1934, in Little Papers, folder #11, HQMC. Armour to Hull, 27 July, 3 August (838.00/3218), 14 August (telegram, 838.00/3229), all 1934. *Le Temps,* 25 August 1934.

Little Better Fitted :

H. L. Stimson. "Memorandum of Conversation with Franklin D. Roosevelt, January 9, 1933, at Hyde Park, N.Y.," Stimson Papers, Yale University Library. Shepherd to Simon, 28 March 1934, FO 371/A2294, PRO. HQMC, confidential memo AO-185-bm, 6 July 1934 (enclosure to 383.246/1, 9 July 1934). MemCon, Edwin C. Wilson to Maj J. C. Fegan, June 1932 (838.00/3084). Leyburn, 107. *Nation,* 3 December 1930.

Chapter 13 Second Independence p.489

Introduction :

Watt to Simon, 22 August 1934, FO 371/A7072, PRO. Armour to Hull, 24 August 1934 (838.00/3251). *Le Nouvelliste,* 21 August 1934. Bellegarde, *Résistance,* 174-75. L. C. Phareaux, *La Vie Contemporaine* (PauP, 1953), 161-63.

Nothing Stands Still :

New York Times, 15 August 1935 ("Haiti Goes Ahead Under Self-Rule"). Démosthènes Pettus Calixte, *The Calvary of a Soldier* (NY, 1939), 30, 41, 84. MemCon, Francis White to W. W. Lancaster, 17 July 1930 (838.00/2852). Munro to Stimson, 24 December 1934 (838.00/3053). Armour to Welles, 7 November 1934, in "Journals," Sumner Welles, unpublished, privately held. Armour to Hull, 27 December 1934; 17 January and 18 March 1935 (838.00/ 3271, 3282, 3291). Gordon to Hull, 27 September 1935; 12 October 1936 (838.00/3318. 3359). Foreign Bondholders Protective Council, Annual Report 1935, passim. Trouillot, *Prospections,* 112. "*New Constitution of Haiti,*" in Pan-American Union Bulletin, LXIX, 1935. H. P. Davis, *Black Democracy,* 1936 ed., 270. Gordon to Hull, 3 February 1936 (State Dept file number illegible in 838.00 series). Shepherd to Eden, 23 June 1935; 11 January, 17 February, and 23 June 1936; 30 November 1937; 9 February 1938, FO 371/A6121, A920, Al 385, A6598, A9065, A990. T. C. Brutus, ii, 21-22. Chapin to

Hull, 7 December 1935 (838.00/3323). Montague, 283-85. De la Rue to Welles, 19 June and 28 October 1935; Welles to de la Rue, 15 June, 1935; Edwin C. Wilson to Welles, 26 November 1937, all in Welles, "Journals." *Encyclopaedia Britannica,* 1951, "Bananas," iii, 18. Mayer to Hull, 30 November 1937 (838.00/3378). Pinkerton to Hull, 19 September 1936 (838.00/3355). Division of Latin American Affairs memorandum, unsigned, 29 March 1937 (838.00/3368). De la Rue to Sparks, 17 September 1940 (no State Dept file number), NA. Bellegarde, *Histoire,* 297-302.

Communists and Griots :

(Note; Except as otherwise documented, information on the Haitian Communist Party has been obtained from reliable sources who have asked not to be identified.) Gordon to Hull, 3 December 1936 (838.00/3361). Rotberg, 159-61. Schmidt, 150-51. François Duvalier (pseud., Abderrahman), *Souvenirs d'Autrefois. 1926-1948* (PauP, 1968), 31, 54-55, 85, 95, 100. G. R. Coulthard, "The French West Indian Background of 'Négritude,' " *Caribbean Quarterly,* December 1961.

Another Grim Chapter :

Shepherd to Eden, 20 May 1936; 16 November and 8 December 1937, FO 371/A4609, A8606, A9261, PRO. De la Rue to Welles, 29 July 1936, in Welles, "Journals." Montague, 288-90. *New York Times,* 21 October 1937. New York *Herald Tribune,* to November 1937. Robert D. Crassweller, *Trujillo: The Life and Times of a Caribbean Dictator* (NY, 1966), 150, 153-59, 244. Albert C. Hicks, *Blood in the Streets* (NY, 1946), v-viii, 104-13. Norweb to Welles, 19 October 1937 (enclosing American legation CT dispatch #16 and telegram #30, both October 1937) and 8 January 1938 in Welles, "Journals." British legation, CT, Annual Report, 1937, FO 371, date and file number unknown. Peterson (BrMin, CT) to Eden, 17 January 1938, FO 371/A1064, PRO. MemCon, F. B. Atwood with Licensiado Ortega Frier, 15 February 1938 (838.00, no file number). Quentin Reynolds, "Murder in the Tropics," *Collier's,* 22 January 1938. De la Rue to Sparks, 17 September 1940. Bellegarde, *Histoire, 302-304.*

The Garde Politicizes :

MemCon, de la Rue to Briggs, 13 December 1937 (838.00/3386). Mayer to Hull, 13 and 23 December 1937 (telegrams); 1 April (838.00/3380, 3389, 3411), 13 June (838.20/11, telegram), 30 June (838.20/13, phone conversation), 8 December, all 1938 (838.105/521); 18 January 1939 (838.20/49). Shepherd to Eden. 15 and 21 December 1937; 4 and it January 1938, FO 371/A9430, A158, A489, A992, PRO. Memo, Scott to Pixley, 13 December 1937 (enclosure to 838.00/ 3384). Calixte, 69-86, 101-10. Bernard Diederich and Al Burt, *Papa Doc,* (NY, 1969),44. Gordon to Hull, 18 February 1937 (838.00/3366). Welles to Norweb, 1 August 1938; Mayer to Welles, 14 December 1937; 27 November 1939, all in Welles, "Journals." Mayer to Briggs, 28 November 1938 (838.20/43). Bellegarde, *Histoire,304.*

Vincent Restores Dictatorship :

Memo, Chapin to Duggan, 21 February 1938 (838.00/3406). Mayer to Hull, 1 November (telegram), 8 and 23 December 1938; 3 February and 22 July 1940 (838.00/3430, 3438, 3441, 3518, 3535). Stenio Vincent, *En Pasant les Jalons* (PauP, 1939), iv, 176-204. J. P. Audain to Duggan, 30 May, 1939 (838.00/3459 1/2). Milo Rigaud, *Contre Vincent* (Paris, 1946). Stanley High, *"Alien Poison,"*Saturday Evening Post, 31 August 1940, 80. Bacon to Finley, 8 January 1940 (838.00/3566). Montague, 288. Bellegarde, *Histoire,* 301, 304-306. U.S. military attach& Haiti report #638, 15 October 1943 (subject: de Catalogne). Sparks to Hull, 20 August 1940 (838.00/3529). H. D. Boyden to Director of Naval Intelligence, 1 and 8 February HQMC. Mayer to Welles, 23 October 1939, in Welles, "Journals," White to Finley, 16 April 1941 (838.00/3618). Sparks to Duggan, 30 September 1940 (838.00/4070). Crassweller, Trujillo, 160-62. De la Rue to Welles, 7 February 1941, Welles, "Journals." Max I., Hudicourt, *Haiti Faces Tomorrow's Peace* (NY, 1945), 11. Memo for Chief, Caribbean Section (subject: Stenio Vincent), 25 June 1943, in G-2 files, box 1774, RG-165, NA.

Another State of the Union :

White to Hull, 9 May 1941 (838.01, Lescot/25); 15 January and 24 February 1942 (838.00/3622, 3627, both telegrams); to September 1943 (838.248/25). Wel(es to Roosevelt, 11 January 1941, in Welles, "Journals . " Alfred Nemours, *Les Presidents Lescot et Trujillo* (PauP, 1942), 19-25. Bellegarde, *Histoire*, 307-11. Crassweller, *Trujillo*, 16o. Armour to Hull, 27 November 1934 (838.00/3271). Shepherd to Eden, 17 February 1936, FO 3 7 1, Al 385, PRO. *Notes Historiques, Armée d'Haïti* (author unknown, PauP, 1954), 43, 45-51. White to Welles, 6 October 1941, in Welles, "Journals." Lescot to Welles, 13 October 1941, ibid. Welles to Msgr. Ready, 27 September and 9 October 1941, ibid. Chatelain, 198-202. "Haiti's War Acts," 2 March 1944 (unsigned memo, WD G-2, RG165, NA). *Le Nouvelliste*, 23 February 1942. Welles to White, 6 April 1942 (telegram, 838.001. Lescot/54A). "Stability Reports," US military attache, PauP, to WD G-2, 23 February 1942-1 April 1944, passim, boxes 1742-43, RG- 165, NA. *Le Matin*, 10 September 1943. US military attache, PauP, 5 June 1942 (subject: Mole St. Nicolas), box 1742, RG-165, NA.

Vive la Liberté, à bas Lescot :

Bellegarde, *Histoire*, 309-310, 313-18. Roosevelt to Welles, 6 September 1943 (838.001, Lescot/87). MemCon, Roosevelt and Lescot, 14 October 1943 (838.001, Lescot/136). State Dept press release #440, 20 October 1943. Secretaire d'Etat de l'Agriculture #168 to L. H. Walker, to June 1941, with enclosure (held by Ex-Im bank). "Shaky *SHADA*," *Fortune*, February 1946. US military attache, PauP, to WD G-2, 26 October and 18 December 1943; 1 April 1944 (subject: *SHADA*), box 1741, RG-165, NA. White to Barber, 22 May 1943 (838.00/10-2644). *Trouillot, Prospections*, 115-18. Hicks, 184-86, 193. Colbert Bonhomme, *Les Lecons et les Origines d'une Révolution Profonde et Pacifique* (PauP, 1946), xiii, 23-24, 27, 29-41. Wilson to Byrnes, 13 January 1946 (838.00/1-1346).

An Example of Professionalism :

Wilson to Byrnes, 22 January, 4 February, 3 May (telegram), 28 May, 29 June (telegram), and 14 and 19 August 1946 (838.00/1-2246, 2-446, 5-2746, 5-2846, 6-2946, 8-1446, 8-1946). Jean-Pierre 0. Gingras, *Duvalier: Caribbean Cyclone* (NY, 1967), 79. Jean-Jacques Doubout and Ulrick Joly, *Notes sur le Developpement du Mouvement Syndical en Haïti* (PauP, 1974), 14-15, 17, 21-22. Bellegarde, *Histoire*, 319-23. Nicolas, 280-84. Miami *Herald*, 2 May 1946. Diederich and Burt, 52-54. MemCon, Wilson to Calixte, 17 August 1946 (in 838 files, no number, NA).

The Noirs Return :

Tittmann to Byrnes, 29 November 1946 (838.00/11-2946). Tittmann to Marshall, 7 and 13 May (838.005-747 and 838.00/11-2947), 14 August (838.00/ 8-1447), and 12 and 13 December (838.00/12-1247, 12-1347), all 1947. PanAmerican Union *Bulletin*, February 1947, 88; October 1947, 58 i. Diederich and Burt, 54-59. M. Rigaud, *Contre Vincent*. Mayer to Hull, 30 November 1937 (838.00/3378). Katherine Dunham, *Island Possessed* (NY, 1969), 44-45. *Time*. 22 November 1948;21 February 1949. *ForRels US*, 1946, xi, 912-31, 947; viii, 728-30. State Dept memo, 19 March 1947 (838.00/3-1947). Memo, Tanner to Tittmann, enclosure with embassy dispatch #500,

28 May 1947. Roger Riou, *Adieu La Tortue* (Paris, 1974), 155-56. Augustin Mathurin, *Assistance Sociale en Haïti, 1804-1972* (PauP, 1972), 231, 234. *New York Times,* 30 December 1946; 28 July 1948. Wilson, *Black, Red,* 87-93. Interview with Edith Efron Bogat, 19 April 1975.

Ici la Renaissance :

Rouzier, ii, 134. Edmund Wilson, "The Marcelins - Novelists of Haiti," N*ation, 15* October 1950. Mercer Cook, "Mountains and Manuscripts," *Americas,* September 1951. Jacques Roumain, *Gouverneurs de la Rosée* (PauP, 1944). Jean Price-Mars, *Ainsi Parla l'Oncle* (Paris, 1928). Jacques C. Antoine, "Litterature from Toussaint Louverture to Jacques Roumain," in Mercer Cook, *An Introduction to Haiti* (Washington, D.C., 1951), 107-11, 116-20. Philippe Thoby-Marcelin and Pierre Marcelin, "Three Haitian Folktales," *Americas,* March 1954. Alfred Verna, "Grande 'Anse, Patrie des Poetes," *Conjonction,* December 1947. Selden Rodman, *The Miracle of Haitian Art* (NY, 1974), 24-26, 36-39, 49-53. Selden Rodman, "A Mural by Wilson Bigaud," *,Magazine of Art,* October 1951. Selden Rodman, "Murals for Haiti," *Art in America,* December 1951. Florence Arquin, "Contemporary Popular Art in Haiti," Pan-American Union *Bulletin,* January 1948. Jason Seley, "A Sculptor in Haiti," *Las Americas,* November 1953. Conversations with the Right Reverend C. Alfred Voegeli, De Witt Peters, Andre Pierre, and Adam Leontus, 1959 to 1963.

Down with Estimé :

Newsweek, 1 and 22 May 1950. Crassweller, *Trujillo,* 236, 242-48. Report by Investigating Committee of the Organ of Consultation, OAS, 13 March 1950, 11-35. *Life,* 28 March 1949. *Parti Communiste d'Haïti,* "Appel au Peuple," 11 March 1947 (enclosure with 838.80/3- 1147). Colbert Bonhomme, *Révolution et Contre-Révolution en Haïti, 1946 à 1957* (PauP, 1957), 21-27, 32-47. Rotberg, *174. Notes Historiques, Armée d'Haïti,* 51-59. Bellegarde, *Histoire, 324-27.* Nicolas, 288-9 i. Lucien Chauvet, *8 Mai 1950,* pamphlet (PauP, 1956). *Time, 24* September, 4 October, 16 November, and 25 December 1949; 5 February and 8, 11, and 12 May 1950; 21 July 1963.

Most Civil of the Military :

Bellegarde, *Histoire,* 328, 266n. Nicolas, 292-98. Colbert Bonhomme, *Révolution et Contre-Révolution, 51,* 54-67, 83-90, 100-121, 123, 197-232. Diederich and Burt, 6o-61, 64-65, 67, 69-75. Rotberg, 178-86. *New York Times,* 28 May, 9 and 16 July, 8 September. and 11 October 1950; 1 January 1951, 7 January and 20 and 27 December 1953; 2, 4, 5, 6, and 11 January and 6 February 1954; 27, 30, and 31 January 1955; 5 January, 23 and 25 May, 11 September, and 7, 8, 9, 11, 13, and 14 December 1956. Newsweek, 23 October 1950. *Time, 15* and 22 February 1954. Maurepas Auguste, *Genèse d'une République Héréditaire* (Paris, 1974), 46-58, 82-92, 97-109, 113-114, 121-22. Joe Alex Morris, "Cruel Beauty of the Caribbean," *Saturday Evening Post.* 17 November 1951. Edith Efron Bogat interview. Paul Corvington, *Bataille de Vertières,* pamphlet (PauP, 1954). Mathurin, 256, 262-63, 265, 267, 269ff, 274-76, 284. M. A. Lubin, letter to the editor, *Negro Historical Bulletin.* January 1955. Ernest Moore, *Haïti* (NY. 1972), 72-84. 247. Washington Post, 27 January 1955. Jacques Val (pseud.), *La Dictature de Duvalier* (Paris, 1972), 17-18, 20-21, 23. Herbert Gold, "Caribbean Caudillo," *Nation.* 5 February 1955. Bernard D. Nossiter, "Haitian Volcano," *Nation,* 26 March 1955. Clément Célestin, *Compilations pour l'Histoire* (PauP, 1958), 1, 26-30. Doubout and July, 26-30. Frederic Sondern, Jr., "Haiti Doesn't Like Dictators," *Reader's Digest.* April 1957.

They Have Gone Mad :

Auguste, 72-81 . 94-95, 109, 116-38, 140-42, 147-50, 156-57, 160, 168-69, 176-80, 184, 232-39, 244-46, 257-64, 268-79, 293-313. Rotberg, 187-90, 19396. Gingras, 90-96. Diederich and Burt, 78-94. *New York Times,* 26 January, 4, 7, and 15 February, 10, 24, and 29 March, 1, 2, 3, 4, 14, and 25 April, 1, 15-21, 23, 24, 26-28 May, 2, 9, 12, 14, 15, 17, and 18 June, 31 August, and 3, 20, 22, and 25 September 1957. Célestin, i, 80-81, 90-93, 95-96, 98-106, 112-43, 167, 226, 301-303, 317-20, 322-25, 331-33, 342, 357-83; ii, 27-30, 35-40, 75-76, 89-92, 233-240, 269; iii, 35-36, 45-51, 146-47, 162. *Le Nouvelliste,* 26 January, 28 February, 1 April, 21 May, and 13 and 19 June 1957. Leslie F. Manigat, *Haiti: Object of International Concern* (Washington, D.C., 1964), 43. *Life, to* June 1957. *Time,* to June 1957. Newsweek, 24 June 1957. Thomas P. Whitney, speech to Overseas Press Club, NY, 13 August 1958. Bonhomme, 303, 307308, 315-43. Val, 23, 25, 27. Duvalier, *Souvenirs d'Autrefois,* 119. Ascencio A.Noel, *Les Responsables des Vêpres du 25 Mai,* pamphlet (PauP, 1957).

Chapter 14 I Am the State p.561

Introduction :

Rotberg, 161-62, 178, 251, 295, 346, 360. *Times* (London), 26 March 1970. Diederich and Burt, 47, 66-67, 70, 77, 279. Castonnet des Fosses, 243. Guillermin, 367-75. Duvalier, *Sovenirs d' Autrefois,* 70. Auguste, 230.

I Have No Enemies :

Celestin, iii, 403-408; iv, 17-30. *New York Times,* 30 September, 1 and 23 October, and 12 and 13 November 1957; 8 and 28 January, 7, 11, and 13 February, 13, 14, and 15 March, 25 April, 1, 3, 5, 6, and 7 May, 30 July, and 1, 2, and 5 August 1958; 28 January, 1 and 2 February, 8 and 14 April, 11, 14, and 22 June, 2 and 3 July, 15, 16, 23, and 25 August, 21 September, and 11 October 1959. Diederich and Burt, 95-105, 107, 112-19, 130, 138-39, 141-43, 146-48. Gingras, 115. Thomas P. Whitney, speech to Overseas Press Club. Trouillot, *Prospections, 353. Life,* 11 August 1958. *New Republic,* 16 March 1964. *Time.* 9 March and 15 June 1959. *New Republic,* 16 March 1964. Val, 36. Proclamation to the People, 5 August 1958, in François Duvalier, *Face au Peuple et à l'Histoire* (PauP, 1961), 116.

Repression Will Be Total :

Rémy Bastien, *Vodun and Politics in Haïti* (Washington, D.C., 1966), 57. Magowan to Henderson, 17 March 1930, FO 371, A3283, PRO. Doubout and Joly, 38, 43-44, 57, 72. Rotberg, 208, 214-15, 220-23, 225-27, 231, 239-40. Diederich and Burt, 156, 158-59, 160-61, 171-74, 176, 184-85. Mathurin, 344. Graham Greene, *The Comedians* (NY, 1967), 156. Manigat, *Haïti, 51-52, 55. New Republic,* 16 March 1964. Heinl to Boucicaut, 20 July 1962, letter, privately held. Nancy G. Heinl, unpublished "Haiti Journal," privately held, passim. Celestin, Hi, 420-61. *New York Times,* 21 and 25 August 1959; 16, 23, 24, 27, 28, and 29 November 1960; 11, 13, 17, 18, and 24 January, 6 February, 9 April, and 1 and to May 1961. *Time,* 31 August 1959; 20 January and 12 May 1961. Cabon, *Histoire Réligieuse,* 91. *Newsweek,* 2 February and 5 December 1960. Val, 67-68, 104-105, 109. François Duvalier, *Mémoires d'un Leader du Tiers Monde* (Paris, 1969), 50-51, 87, 90-91, 94-95, 105, 289, 307, 315-18. John Kohler, "Land of Misfortune," *Saturday Evening Post,* 16 April 1960.

Extraordinarily Resistant:

Curtis to Thurston, 31 May 1963 (no file no.), with enclosure. Rotberg, 209-10, 235-39. New *York Times,* 18, 23, and 24 June, 17 July, 25 August, and 4 September 1960 ; 8 April 1961; 10 August and 26 October 1962. Lester Velie, "The Case of Our Vanishing Dollars in Haiti," *Reader's Digest,* March 1962. Arthur Schlesinger, Jr., A *Thousand Days* (Boston, 1965), 781-82. Duvalier, *Tiers Monde,* 202-206. Robert D. Heinl, Jr., "Papa Doc Angled for JFK's Soul," Washington *Post, 5* July 1964. Robert D. Heinl, Jr., "Haiti," *New Republic. 16* May 1964. Diederich and Burt, 127, 133, 150-51, 167-77, 181-82, 186-89. Rusk to Heinl, 23 September 1975. Interim Report by Select Committee on Intelligence, U.S. Senate, released 20 November 1975,4. Heinl to Boucicaut. Nancy Heinl, "Journal." Report of U.S. Marine Corps Survey Team to Haiti, 18 May-1 June 1958. Robert D. Crassweller, *Caribbean Community* (NY, 1972), 97. *Time,* 2 and 17 February and 17 August 1962. *U.S. News and World Report,* to September 1962. Val, 34. Raymond Sapène, *Proces A: Baby Doc* (Paris, 1973),91-92.

The Terror :

Rotberg, 225-30, 245. Diederich and Burt, 175-76, 189, 194-99, 201, 203-11, 213-17, 221-23, 228, 231ff, 236-37, 240-49, 253-54, 257-63, 288-90, 292-301, 303-306, 310-12, 316. Dom Bonafede, "Haiti Employs U.S. Spies," *New York Herald Tribune,* 4 June 1964. Virginia Prewett, "Duvalier Spies Operate in U.S.," *Washington Daily News,* 4 May 1964. Leland Stowe, "Haiti's Voodoo Tyrant," *Reader's Digest,* November 1963. American embassy, PauP, note #192 to GOH, 1 May 1963. Duvalier, *Tiers Monde,* 106, 122-25, 131-32, 138. Trevor Armbrister, "Any Hope for Haiti?" *Saturday Evening Post, 15* June 1963. Herbert Gold, "Haiti: Hatred Without Hope." *Saturday Evening Post, 24* April 1965. Graham Greene, "Nightmare Republic," *New Republic, 16* November 1963. Hubert Herring, "Dictatorship in Haiti," *Current History,* January 1964. John Bartlow Martin, *Overtaken by Events* (NY, 1966), 394, 416, 422-25, 427, 430-31, 434-40, 444-47. New York *Herald Tribune,* 26 and 27 April 1963. New *York Times,* 14 April and 16 May 1963; 16 July and 24 August *1964. Haïti Observateur* (NY), 2 May 1975, 11-12. *Time,* 3 and 17 May and 26 July 1963; 27 November 1964. *Newsweek,* 27 May and 29 July 1963; 23 November 1964. Washington Star, 22 May 1963. *Le Monde* (Paris), 25 August 1963. Franck Sénat, *Feu Contre Papa Doc* (Paris, 1971), 40-42. *Le Combattant* (NY), 20 October 1967. Sapène, 166.

Thermidor:

New York Times, 7 October 1962; 2 and 30 April, 23 and 29 May, and 16 June 1964; 9 and 15 May and 28 November 1966. Michel Aubourg, "Le Drapeau Dessalinien," *RSHHG.* no. 4 (1958). WashingtonPost, 25 May and 5 July 1964; 27 June 1966. *Time,* 10 April 1964; 27 August 1965; 13 May 1966. Diederich and Burt, 267-69, 277, 281-84, 328-29. Washington *Daily News,* 18 May 1964. Rotberg, 235, 243, 248-49. State Dept press release #152, 8 April 1964. Robert D. Heinl, Jr., "Haiti: Next Mess in the Caribbean?," *Atlantic Monthly,* November 1967. Robert D. Heinl, Jr., "Bailing Out Duvalier," *New Republic.* 14 January 1967. Inter-American Committee on the Alliance for Progress (Subcommittee on Haiti), "Domestic Efforts and Needs for External Financing for Development of Haiti," 5 May 1971, passim. Washington Star, 16 June 1966. Duvalier, *Tiers Monde,* 50-56, 187-91, 211-13, 217-19, 221-87. Sapene, 17881. *Le Combattant, 5* September 1969. *Newsweek,* 27 June 1966. *HispanicAmerican Report,* March-April 1964. *Le Nouveau Monde, 19* September 1965; 9 January 1966. Allen E. Blanchard, interview, 3 November 1975.

The Year Ten, and After :

Bulletin of the International Commission of Jurists (Geneva), August 1963; September 1967. T. E. Weil and F. P. Munson, *Area Handbookfor Haiti* (Washington, D. C., 1972), 127. Diederich and Burt, 168-69, 332ff, 344, 369, 374. *New York Times.* 27 December 1964; 24 November 1966, 5

August 1967; 2 and 3 July 1969; 2 May 1970. Leslie F. Manigat, *Statu Quo en Haïti"* (Paris, 1971), 10-11. "CBS Project Nassau," *Hearings,* House Committee on International and Foreign Commerce (1st and 2d sessions) passim. *Le Combattant,* 16-30 April, 17 May-6 June, 6-13 June, 13-30 June 1969. Graham Greene, letter to *Times* (London), 12 January 1970. Fred Halliday, "New Black Magic," *Ramparts,* January 1973. R. A. Joseph, "An Exile Forecasts Chaos in Haiti," *Wall Street Journal,* 29 December 1970. Ronald Steel, "Haiti," *Atlantic Monthly,* September 1969.

Guinée :

Rotberg, 256n. *New York Times,* 24 May 1970; 23 April 1971. *Wall Street Journal.* 6 July 1970. Virginia Prewett, "When Duvalier Dies," North American Newspaper Alliance, 24 February 1971. Washington Post, 20 and 25 April 1971. *Newsweek,* 26 April 1971. Washington Star, 23 April 1971. Nancy Gordon (pseud.), *"Is Papa Doc's Death a Windfall for Haiti's Many Voodoo Priests?,"* North American Newspaper Alliance, 11 May 1971. *Miami Herald,* 23 April 1971. Mathurin, 397.

Chapter 15 Riding the Tiger p.637
Books and Magazine Articles used as sources for this chapter are listed in the bibliography. Additionally, articles from *Time, Newsweek, Haïti Observateur, Le Petit Samedi Soir, The Wall Street Journal,* the *New York Times,* the *Washington Times,* the *Miami Herald, The Times of London, Haïti Hebdo,* the *Toronto Globe and Mail, Town and Country,* the *Christian Science Monitor, Reuters,* the *Associated Press, Le Figaro, Le Monde,* and the *London Telegraph* provided information used herein.

Chapter 16 Paper and Iron p.705
Books and Magazine Articles used as sources for this chapter are listed in the bibliography. TNH footage for January and February 1986 was provided by Lissa Behrmann. Additionally, articles from *Haïti Observateur, Le Petit Samedi Soir, Time, Newsweek, The Wall Street Journal,* the *New York Times,* the *Washington Times,* the *Miami Herald, The Times of London,* the *Toronto Globe and Mail, Town and Country,* the *Christian Science Monitor, Reuters,* the *Associated Press, Le Figaro, Le Monde,* and the *London Telegraph* provided information used herein.

In breaking with the meticulous methodology of source notes for the first fourteen chapters, I am conscious of doing a disservice to the print journalists who have covered Haiti so superbly in recent years, but beg indulgence as many hundreds of articles clipped over twenty-five years were used. Their papers are mentioned above. Particular thanks therefore to Greg Chamberlain, Douglas Farah, Howard French, Lee Hocksteder, Ray Joseph and Larry Rohter. - M.H.

Voodoo

Introduction :

Times (London), 1 May 1963. Louis Mars, *La Crise de Possession dans le Vaudou* (PauP, 1946), 12-13. Archibald Dalzell, *The History of Dahomey* (London, 1793), intro. M. L. E. Moreau de Saint-Méry, *Description Topographique, Physique, Civile, et Historique de la Partie Française de l'Isle Saint-Domingue* (Philadelphia, 1797), i, 64, 415.

The Cross and the Snake :

Nina-Rodriguez, *L'Animisme Fétichiste des Négres de Bahia* (Bahia,). Alfred Métraux, *Voodoo in Haiti* (NY, 1959), 15. Labat, ii, 141-42. Mars, *La Crise,* 81. Harold Courlander, *The Drum and the Hoe: Life and Lore of the Haitian People* (Berkeley, 1960), 11-12. *New York Times* , 21 May 1957. Louis Maximilien, *Le Vodou Haïtien* (PauP, 1945), 179-81. Hurston, 223. Harold Courlander, *Religion and Politics in Haiti* (Washington, D. C., 1966), 5-6. 1. M. Lewis, *Ecstatic Religion* (Harmondsworth, 1971), 105.

Damballah the Serpent :

James G. Frazer, *The Golden Bough,* abridged ed. (NY, 1958), 620. Price-Mars, *Ainsi Parla l'Oncle,* 118-21. Moreau de Saint-Méry, *Description,* i, 67-68. W. D. Hambly, "Serpent Worship in Africa," *Field Museum of Natural History* (Chicago, 1931). J. Verschueren (pseud.), *La République d'Haïti* (Paris, 1948), iii, 31 . M. E. Descourtilz, *Voyages d'un Naturaliste en Haïti* (Paris, 1933), 115-119. J.-C. Dorsainvil, *Une Explication Philologique du Vodou* (PauP, 1924), 18.

The Voodoo Pantheon :

Verschueren, i, 15-161. Hurston. 139-41, 184. Courlander, *The Drum and the Hoe,* 8, 30, 318-21. Herskovits, 149. Leyburn,145-46. Milo Rigaud, *Le Tradition Voudou et le Voudou Haïtien* (Paris, 1953), 141-47. Louis Mars, *Témoinages I* (Madrid. 1966), 24. Dalzell, 179-82. Maya Deren, *Divine Horsemen: The Living Gods of Haiti* (London, 1953), 62, 137-43, 145. Nina-Rodriguez, 33. Maximilien, 124, 198. Métraux, Voodoo, 28, 92. 128. Odette Mennesson-Rigaud, "Etude sur le Culte des Marrassas en Haïti," pamphlet from *Zaire* (Louvain. June 1952). Odette Mennesson-Rigaud and Lorimer Denis, "Cérémonie en l'Honneur de Marinette," *Bureau d'Ethnologie* (PauP, 1947).

Houngan and Houmfort :

Janheinz Jahn, *Muntu: An Outline of the New African Culture,* transl. by Marjorie Grene (NY, 1961), 54. Bastien, 34. Courlander, *The Drum and the Hoe,* 10-12. Métraux, Voodoo. 62-68. Maximilien. 17-21. Aubin, 14, 43-52.M. Rigaud. 8. 90-92, E. 0. James, *Origins of Sacrifice* (London,1933), 80-85,96-99, 231-33, 274.

Blood Sacrifice :

E. 0. James, 281-283. 269. Price-Mars. *Ainsi Parla l'Oncle,* 156. Verschueren, i. 269, 308; iii. 264-65, 273, 309, 348-49. St. John, 230-31. David Riesman, La *Foule Solitaire* (Paris, 1964), 32. J. A. Skertchley, *Dahomey As It Is* (London, 1874), 186, 261. Jules Faine, *La Philologie Créole* (PauP. 1937), 99. Joseph J. Williams, *Voodoos and Obeahs* (NY, 1932), 43-45. Alexander Murray to Sir Edward Grey. 1 February 1910, FO 371/6508, PRO. J.-N. Léger, 175-79, 35051.

Possession :

James H. Leuba. *The Psychology of Religious Mysticism* (London, 1925), 8-10. Mars, *La* Crise, 191. Métraux, Voodoo, 104-105, 127. Herskovits, 16-18, 88, 91. Michel Leiris. "La Croyance aux Génies Zar en Ethiopie du Nord,"*Journal de Psychologie* (Paris), January-March 1938. Mars, *Témoinages I,* 13. Deren. 26. Aldous Huxley, *The Devils of Loudun* (London, 1952), appendix. Price-Mars. *Ainsi Parla l'Oncle,* 123. Lewis, *Ecstatic Religion,* 47. Lamarque Douyon. "Phénomenologie de la Crise de Possession." *Revue de la Faculté d'Ethnologie,* no. 12, 1967.

A Thin Veil of Secrecy and Discretion:

Stephen Bonsal. *The American Mediterranean* (NY. 1912), 103. Bastien, Vodun *and Politics.* 64. Seabrook, 294-95. Courlander, *The Drum and the Hoe*, 33-34. Métraux. *Voodoo,* 64, 246, 263. Deren. 27-28. Dunham, 60-69. Gordon, "Is Papa Doc's Death a Windfall for Haiti's Voodoo Priests?"

Magic and Spells:

Price-Mars, *Ainsi Parla l'Oncle,* 35. Maximilien, 149-50. Verschueren, i, 300-301. Herskovits, 220. D'Alaux, 63-67. Seabrook, 306-307. Métraux, *Voodoo,* 269-71, 292-300. Albertus Parvus, *Secrets Merveilleux de la Magie Naturelle et Cabalistique du Petit Albert* (Lyons, 1758). Henri d'Almeras, *La FrancMaconnerie et l'Occultisme au XVIII siècle* (Paris, 1904), 11-12. George L. Engels, "Sudden and Rapid Death During Psychological Stress," *Annals of Internal Medicine,* May 1971. M. Rigaud, *La Tradition Voudou,* 164, 249-52. Hurston, 20-21, 191-93. Courlander, *The Drum and the Hoe,* 101. Elsie Clews Parsons, "Spirit Cult in Hayti," *Journal de la Société des Américanistes de Paris.*

stays on board ship 361
Zinglins 189-192, 194, 197-199, 266, 319, 353, 512, 566, 579,
Zombis 784-786

About the Authors

Robert Debs Heinl and Nancy Gordon Heinl, both writers and historians, lived in Haiti from 1959 to 1963. Robert Heinl was Chief of the U.S. Naval Mission to Haiti until declared *persona non grata* by François Duvalier. He fought in World War II and Korea and was the author of eight books as well as numerous magazine articles. He retired from the Marine Corps as a Colonel in 1964 and had a nationally syndicated newspaper column until his death in 1979.

Nancy Gordon Heinl is an independent writer and journalist. She has written extensively on black history and voodoo. Born in London, she came to the United States in 1933. She lives in Washington, D.C.

Michael Heinl (above) went with his parents to Haiti at age nine. There he learned Créole and French, both of which he still speaks. He has returned to Haiti many times over the past twenty years. He received a B.A. from Johns Hopkins and an M.B.A. from U.C.L.A. He is an international business consultant in Washington, D.C.